Contemporary Authors®

NEW REVISION SERIES

ISSN 0275-7176

Contemporary Authors®

A Bio-Bibliographical Guide to
Current Writers in Fiction, General Nonfiction,
Poetry, Journalism, Drama, Motion Pictures,
Television, and Other Fields

NEW REVISION SERIES volume 129

GALE®

Detroit • New York • San Diego • San Francisco • Cleveland • New Haven, Conn. • Waterville, Maine • London • Munich

Contemporary Authors, New Revision Series, Vol. 129

Product Manager
Chris Nasso

Editorial
Katy Balcer, Sara Constantakis, Natalie Fulkerson, Michelle Kazensky, Julie Keppen, Joshua Kondek, Lisa Kumar, Mary Ruby, Lemma Shomali, Susan Strickland, Maikue Vang, Tracey Watson

Permissions
Denise Buckley, Shalice Shah-Caldwell, Emma Hull

Imaging and Multimedia
Randy Bassett, Dean Dauphinais, Leitha Etheridge-Sims, Lezlie Light, Michael Logusz, Dan Newell, Christine O'Bryan, Kelly A. Quin

Composition and Electronic Capture
Kathy Sauer

Manufacturing
Lori Kessler

For more information, contact
Thomson Gale
27500 Drake Rd.
Farmington Hills, MI 48331-3535
Or you can visit our internet site at
http://www.gale.com

LIBRARY OF CONGRESS CATALOG CARD NUMBER 81-640179

ISBN 0-7876-6721-8
ISSN 0275-7176

Printed in the United States of America
10 9 8 7 6 5 4 3 2 1

Contents

Indexing note: All *Contemporary Authors* entries are indexed in the *Contemporary Authors* cumulative index, which is published separately and distributed twice a year.

As always, the most recent Contemporary Authors cumulative index continues to be the user's guide to the location of an individual author's listing.

Preface

Contemporary Authors (*CA*) provides information on approximately 115,000 writers in a wide range of media, including:

- Current writers of fiction, nonfiction, poetry, and drama whose works have been issued by commercial publishers, risk publishers, or university presses (authors whose books have been published only by known vanity or author-subsidized firms are ordinarily not included)

- Prominent print and broadcast journalists, editors, photojournalists, syndicated cartoonists, graphic novelists, screenwriters, television scriptwriters, and other media people

- Notable international authors

- Literary greats of the early twentieth century whose works are popular in today's high school and college curriculums and continue to elicit critical attention

A *CA* listing entails no charge or obligation. Authors are included on the basis of the above criteria and their interest to *CA* users. Sources of potential listees include trade periodicals, publishers' catalogs, librarians, and other users.

How to Get the Most out of *CA*: Use the Index

The key to locating an author's most recent entry is the *CA* cumulative index, which is published separately and distributed twice a year. It provides access to *all* entries in *CA* and *Contemporary Authors New Revision Series* (*CANR*). Always consult the latest index to find an author's most recent entry.

For the convenience of users, the *CA* cumulative index also includes references to all entries in these Thomson Gale literary series: *Authors and Artists for Young Adults, Authors in the News, Bestsellers, Black Literature Criticism, Black Literature Criticism Supplement, Black Writers, Children's Literature Review, Concise Dictionary of American Literary Biography, Concise Dictionary of British Literary Biography, Contemporary Authors Autobiography Series, Contemporary Authors Bibliographical Series, Contemporary Dramatists, Contemporary Literary Criticism, Contemporary Novelists, Contemporary Poets, Contemporary Popular Writers, Contemporary Southern Writers, Contemporary Women Poets, Dictionary of Literary Biography, Dictionary of Literary Biography Documentary Series, Dictionary of Literary Biography Yearbook, DISCovering Authors, DISCovering Authors: British, DISCovering Authors: Canadian, DISCovering Authors: Modules* (including modules for Dramatists, Most-Studied Authors, Multicultural Authors, Novelists, Poets, and Popular/Genre Authors), DISCovering Authors 3.0, *Drama Criticism, Drama for Students, Feminist Writers, Hispanic Literature Criticism, Hispanic Writers, Junior DISCovering Authors, Major Authors and Illustrators for Children and Young Adults, Major 20th-Century Writers, Native North American Literature, Novels for Students, Poetry Criticism, Poetry for Students, Short Stories for Students, Short Story Criticism, Something about the Author, Something about the Author Autobiography Series, St. James Guide to Children's Writers, St. James Guide to Crime & Mystery Writers, St. James Guide to Fantasy Writers, St. James Guide to Horror, Ghost & Gothic Writers, St. James Guide to Science Fiction Writers, St. James Guide to Young Adult Writers, Twentieth-Century Literary Criticism, 20th Century Romance and Historical Writers, World Literature Criticism,* and *Yesterday's Authors of Books for Children.*

A Sample Index Entry:

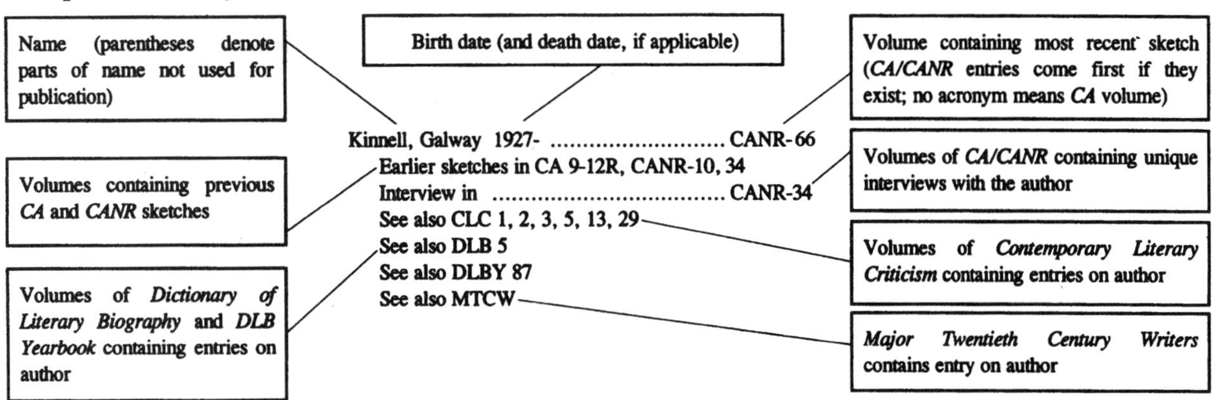

How Are Entries Compiled?

The editors make every effort to secure new information directly from the authors; listees' responses to our questionnaires and query letters provide most of the information featured in *CA.* For deceased writers, or those who fail to reply to requests for data, we consult other reliable biographical sources, such as those indexed in Thomson Gale's *Biography and Genealogy Master Index,* and bibliographical sources, including *National Union Catalog, LC MARC,* and *British National Bibliography.* Further details come from published interviews, feature stories, and book reviews, as well as information supplied by the authors' publishers and agents.

An asterisk (*) at the end of a sketch indicates that the listing has been compiled from secondary sources believed to be reliable but has not been personally verified for this edition by the author sketched.

What Kinds of Information Does An Entry Provide?

Sketches in *CA* contain the following biographical and bibliographical information:

- **Entry heading:** the most complete form of author's name, plus any pseudonyms or name variations used for writing

- **Personal information:** author's date and place of birth, family data, ethnicity, educational background, political and religious affiliations, and hobbies and leisure interests

- **Addresses:** author's home, office, or agent's addresses, plus e-mail and fax numbers, as available

- **Career summary:** name of employer, position, and dates held for each career post; resume of other vocational achievements; military service

- **Membership information:** professional, civic, and other association memberships and any official posts held

- **Awards and honors:** military and civic citations, major prizes and nominations, fellowships, grants, and honorary degrees

- **Writings:** a comprehensive, chronological list of titles, publishers, dates of original publication and revised editions, and production information for plays, television scripts, and screenplays

- **Adaptations:** a list of films, plays, and other media which have been adapted from the author's work

- **Work in progress:** current or planned projects, with dates of completion and/or publication, and expected publisher, when known

- **Sidelights:** a biographical portrait of the author's development; information about the critical reception of the author's works; revealing comments, often by the author, on personal interests, aspirations, motivations, and thoughts on writing

- **Interview:** a one-on-one discussion with authors conducted especially for *CA*, offering insight into authors' thoughts about their craft

- **Autobiographical essay:** an original essay written by noted authors for *CA*, a forum in which writers may present themselves, on their own terms, to their audience

- **Photographs:** portraits and personal photographs of notable authors

- **Biographical and critical sources:** a list of books and periodicals in which additional information on an author's life and/or writings appears

- **Obituary Notices** in *CA* provide date and place of birth as well as death information about authors whose full-length sketches appeared in the series before their deaths. The entries also summarize the authors' careers and writings and list other sources of biographical and death information.

Related Titles in the *CA* Series

Contemporary Authors Autobiography Series complements *CA* original and revised volumes with specially commissioned autobiographical essays by important current authors, illustrated with personal photographs they provide. Common topics include their motivations for writing, the people and experiences that shaped their careers, the rewards they derive from their work, and their impressions of the current literary scene.

Contemporary Authors Bibliographical Series surveys writings by and about important American authors since World War II. Each volume concentrates on a specific genre and features approximately ten writers; entries list works written by and about the author and contain a bibliographical essay discussing the merits and deficiencies of major critical and scholarly studies in detail.

Available in Electronic Formats

GaleNet. *CA* is available on a subscription basis through GaleNet, an online information resource that features an easy-to-use end-user interface, powerful search capabilities, and ease of access through the World-Wide Web. For more information, call 1-800-877-GALE.

Licensing. *CA* is available for licensing. The complete database is provided in a fielded format and is deliverable on such media as disk, CD-ROM, or tape. For more information, contact Thomson Gale's Business Development Group at 1-800-877-GALE, or visit us on our website at www.galegroup.com/bizdev.

Suggestions Are Welcome

The editors welcome comments and suggestions from users on any aspect of the *CA* series. If readers would like to recommend authors for inclusion in future volumes of the series, they are cordially invited to write the Editors at *Contemporary Authors*, Thomson Gale, 27500 Drake Rd., Farmington Hills, MI 48331-3535; or call at 1-248-699-4253; or fax at 1-248-699-8054.

Contemporary Authors Product Advisory Board

The editors of *Contemporary Authors* are dedicated to maintaining a high standard of excellence by publishing comprehensive, accurate, and highly readable entries on a wide array of writers. In addition to the quality of the content, the editors take pride in the graphic design of the series, which is intended to be orderly yet inviting, allowing readers to utilize the pages of *CA* easily and with efficiency. Despite the longevity of the *CA* print series, and the success of its format, we are mindful that the vitality of a literary reference product is dependent on its ability to serve its users over time. As literature, and attitudes about literature, constantly evolve, so do the reference needs of students, teachers, scholars, journalists, researchers, and book club members. To be certain that we continue to keep pace with the expectations of our customers, the editors of *CA* listen carefully to their comments regarding the value, utility, and quality of the series. Librarians, who have firsthand knowledge of the needs of library users, are a valuable resource for us. The *Contemporary Authors* Product Advisory Board, made up of school, public, and academic librarians, is a forum to promote focused feedback about *CA* on a regular basis. The seven-member advisory board includes the following individuals, whom the editors wish to thank for sharing their expertise:

- **Anne M. Christensen,** Librarian II, Phoenix Public Library, Phoenix, Arizona.
- **Barbara C. Chumard,** Reference/Adult Services Librarian, Middletown Thrall Library, Middletown, New York.
- **Eva M. Davis,** Youth Department Manager, Ann Arbor District Library, Ann Arbor, Michigan.
- **Adam Janowski, Jr.,** Library Media Specialist, Naples High School Library Media Center, Naples, Florida.
- **Robert Reginald,** Head of Technical Services and Collection Development, California State University, San Bernadino, California.
- **Stephen Weiner,** Director, Maynard Public Library, Maynard, Massachusetts.

International Advisory Board

Well-represented among the 115,000 author entries published in *Contemporary Authors* are sketches on notable writers from many non-English-speaking countries. The primary criteria for inclusion of such authors has traditionally been the publication of at least one title in English, either as an original work or as a translation. However, the editors of *Contemporary Authors* came to observe that many important international writers were being overlooked due to a strict adherence to our inclusion criteria. In addition, writers who were publishing in languages other than English were not being covered in the traditional sources we used for identifying new listees. Intent on increasing our coverage of international authors, including those who write only in their native language and have not been translated into English, the editors enlisted the aid of a board of advisors, each of whom is an expert on the literature of a particular country or region. Among the countries we focused attention on are Mexico, Puerto Rico, Spain, Italy, France, Germany, Luxembourg, Belgium, the Netherlands, Norway, Sweden, Denmark, Finland, Taiwan, Singapore, Malaysia, Thailand, South Africa, Israel, and Japan, as well as England, Scotland, Wales, Ireland, Australia, and New Zealand. The sixteen-member advisory board includes the following individuals, whom the editors wish to thank for sharing their expertise:

- **Lowell A. Bangerter,** Professor of German, University of Wyoming, Laramie, Wyoming.
- **Nancy E. Berg,** Associate Professor of Hebrew and Comparative Literature, Washington University, St. Louis, Missouri.
- **Frances Devlin-Glass,** Associate Professor, School of Literary and Communication Studies, Deakin University, Burwood, Victoria, Australia.
- **David William Foster,** Regent's Professor of Spanish, Interdisciplinary Humanities, and Women's Studies, Arizona State University, Tempe, Arizona.
- **Hosea Hirata,** Director of the Japanese Program, Associate Professor of Japanese, Tufts University, Medford, Massachusetts.
- **Jack Kolbert,** Professor Emeritus of French Literature, Susquehanna University, Selinsgrove, Pennsylvania.
- **Mark Libin,** Professor, University of Manitoba, Winnipeg, Manitoba, Canada.
- **C. S. Lim,** Professor, University of Malaya, Kuala Lumpur, Malaysia.
- **Eloy E. Merino,** Assistant Professor of Spanish, Northern Illinois University, DeKalb, Illinois.
- **Linda M. Rodríguez Guglielmoni,** Associate Professor, University of Puerto Rico—Mayagüez, Puerto Rico.
- **Sven Hakon Rossel,** Professor and Chair of Scandinavian Studies, University of Vienna, Vienna, Austria.
- **Steven R. Serafin,** Director, Writing Center, Hunter College of the City University of New York, New York City.
- **David Smyth,** Lecturer in Thai, School of Oriental and African Studies, University of London, England.
- **Ismail S. Talib,** Senior Lecturer, Department of English Language and Literature, National University of Singapore, Singapore.
- **Dionisio Viscarri,** Assistant Professor, Ohio State University, Columbus, Ohio.
- **Mark Williams,** Associate Professor, English Department, University of Canterbury, Christchurch, New Zealand.

CA Numbering System and Volume Update Chart

Occasionally questions arise about the *CA* numbering system and which volumes, if any, can be discarded. Despite numbers like "29-32R," "97-100" and "221," the entire *CA* print series consists of only 278 physical volumes with the publication of *CA* Volume 222. The following charts note changes in the numbering system and cover design, and indicate which volumes are essential for the most complete, up-to-date coverage.

***CA* First Revision**

- 1-4R through 41-44R (11 books)
  Cover: Brown with black and gold trim.
  There will be no further First Revision volumes because revised entries are now being handled exclusively through the more efficient *New Revision Series* mentioned below.

***CA* Original Volumes**

- 45-48 through 97-100 (14 books)
  Cover: Brown with black and gold trim.
  101 through 222 (122 books)
  Cover: Blue and black with orange bands.
  The same as previous *CA* original volumes but with a new, simplified numbering system and new cover design.

***CA* Permanent Series**

- *CAP*-1 and *CAP*-2 (2 books)
  Cover: Brown with red and gold trim.
  There will be no further Permanent Series volumes because revised entries are now being handled exclusively through the more efficient *New Revision Series* mentioned below.

***CA* New Revision Series**

- CANR-1 through CANR-129 (129 books)
  Cover: Blue and black with green bands.
  Includes only sketches requiring significant changes; **sketches are taken from any previously published CA, CAP, or CANR volume.**

If You Have:	You May Discard:
CA First Revision Volumes 1-4R through 41-44R and *CA Permanent Series* Volumes 1 and 2	*CA* Original Volumes 1, 2, 3, 4 and Volumes 5-6 through 41-44
CA Original Volumes 45-48 through 97-100 and 101 through 222	**NONE:** These volumes will not be superseded by corresponding revised volumes. Individual entries from these and all other volumes appearing in the left column of this chart may be revised and included in the various volumes of the *New Revision Series*.
CA New Revision Series Volumes *CANR*-1 through *CANR*-129	**NONE:** The *New Revision Series* does not replace any single volume of *CA*. Instead, volumes of *CANR* include entries from many previous *CA* series volumes. All *New Revision Series* volumes must be retained for full coverage.

A Sampling of Authors and Media People Featured in This Volume

Isabel Allende
Allende is the niece of Chilean President Salvador Allende, who was assassinated in a military coup in 1973. That event became a turning point in her life and in her career as a writer. Her highly acclaimed first novel, *The House of the Spirits,* borrows from her own experiences to recount the domestic and political conflicts within three generations of a South American family. Noted for her ability to balance magical realism with political reality and her own feminist touch, Allende has proven her artistry in subsequent novels like *Eva Luna,* which garnered the prestigious American Book Award. Among her recent works is the 2003 memoir *My Invented Country: A Nostalgic Journey through Chile.*

Newt Gingrich
Gingrich rose from Republican congressman from Georgia in 1979 to become Speaker of the House in 1995, on a mission to fight "corruption, bloated government, and a decaying social order," according to *Newsweek* reporter Howard Fineman. Though Gingrich was named *Time* magazine Man of the Year in 1995 and seemed likely to remain in the political forefront, a scandal involving tax violations led to his resignation from the congress in 1999. His book *Lessons Learned the Hard Way: A Personal Report* tells that story. Now active as a lecturer and consultant, Gingrich has also written an alternate-history novel titled *Gettysburg: A Novel of the Civil War,* published in 2003, in which General Robert E. Lee manages to defeat the North at the tide-turning battle.

Marilu Henner
Henner, a star of film, television, and the stage over the last two decades, continues to perform with a vitality that her admirers are eager to emulate. Henner shares the secrets of her personal success in her popular autobiography *By All Means Keep on Moving,* 1994, and the bestseller *Marilu Henner's Total Health Makeover,* 1998. She went on to tackle parenting in *I Refuse to Raise a Brat: Straightforward Advice on Parenting in the Age of Overindulgence,* 1999. Her most recent books include *Healthy Kids: Help Them Eat Smart and Stay Active--for Life!* 2001, and *Healthy Holidays: Total Health Entertaining All Year Round,* 2002.

W. P. Kinsella
Kinsella, a Canadian author of novels and stories, takes pride in being an old- fashioned storyteller. Parlaying his interest in Native American history and his love of baseball, Kinsella has crafted award-winning stories that have brought him international renown. Many of his stories feature a fictional Cree Indian named Silas Ermineskin; and one of his best-known baseball stories, "Shoeless Joe," became the popular film *Field of Dreams.* Kinsella published a new collection of stories in 2000 titled *Japanese Baseball, and Other Stories.* A new edition of his novel *Magic Time* was published in 2001.

Stan Lee
Stan Lee is the cocreator of Marvel Comics' most popular and enduring superheroes—Spider-Man, the Hulk, the X-Men, the mighty Thor, and the Fantastic Four, among others. Frequently credited with having revolutionized the comic-book industry, Lee created characters who appeal not only to adolescents but even to college students. Many of his characters are featured in college courses on popular culture, and Lee himself lectures on college campuses. He is recognized by colleagues and literary critics alike for his significant contributions to the comic-book industry and to the comic book as an art form. In 2002 Lee published his autobiography, *Excelsior! The Amazing Life of Stan Lee.*

David Mamet
Mamet, a highly acclaimed playwright, is noted for the unique language of his work which reflects the character and voice of working-class America. One of Mamet's most successful plays, *Glengarry Glen Ross,* earned the New York Drama Critics' Circle Award for best American play and the Pulitzer Prize in drama. For his screenwriting, Mamet received Academy Award nominations for best adapted screenplay for *The Verdict* and for *Wag the Dog.* Prolific and adept in many genres, Mamet has recently produced the 2001 screenplays *Hannibal* and *Heist* (which he also directed), the 2001 novel *Wilson: A Consideration of the Sources,* and the 2004 play *Dr. Faustus.*

Paule Marshall
Marshall is the Brooklyn-born author of novels and short stories that explore the family relationships and the social

issues that beset black Americans. Critics laud her fiction for its artistry —finely crafted structures, characters that are complex and rich, language that conveys the nuances of the spoken word, especially her skillful rendering of West Indian-Afro-American dialogue. One of Marshall's best-known books is *Praisesong for the Widow,* winner of the American Book Award, that involves a sixty-something widow who has lost touch with her West Indian-Afro-American roots. Her 2000 novel *The Fisher King* is a multigenerational story that portrays the African diaspora from Brooklyn to Paris, set against a jazz background.

Joyce Carol Oates

Oates's prolific output of novels, short stories, criticism, plays, and poetry has earned her a long-standing reputation for consistently interesting work that ranges from stories of upper-class domesticity to horror and psychological crime that reveals a deep understanding of middle America, suburbia, and the temper of the times. She continues to chronicle the American experience in her most recent work, the novels *The Tattooed Girl,* 2003, and *The Falls,* 2004, the short-story collection *I Am No One You Know,* 2004, and her nonfiction collection *The Faith of a Writer: Life, Craft, Art,* 2003.

Acknowledgments

Grateful acknowledgment is made to those publishers, photographers, and artists whose work appear with these authors' essays. Following is a list of the copyright holders who have granted us permission to reproduce material in this volume of *CA*. Every effort has been made to trace copyright, but if omissions have been made, please let us know.

Photographs/Art

Isabel Allende: Allende, photograph. AP/Wide World Photos. Reproduced by permission.

Paul Auster: Auster, photograph. AP/Wide World Photos. Reproduced by permission.

Ellyn Bache: Bache, photograph by Gray Wells. Reproduced by permission of Ellyn Bache.

Alan Baker: Baker, photograph. Reproduced by permission of Alan Baker.

Christophe Bataille: Bataille, photograph. © Sophie Bassouls/Corbis. Reproduced by permission.

Janice Boland: Boland, photograph by James B. Boland. Reproduced by permission of Janice Boland.

Iris Chang: Chang, photograph. AP/Wide World Photos. Reproduced by permission.

Beverly Cleary: Cleary, photograph. Reproduced by permission.

Lucien Clergue: Clergue, photograph by Andanson James. Corbis Sygma. Reproduced by permission.

Pat Conroy: Conroy, photograph. © Jerry Bauer. Reproduced by permission.

Edwidge Danticat: Danticat, photograph by Doug Kanter. AP/Wide World Photos. Reproduced by permission.

Pete Dexter: Dexter, photograph by Walt Zeboski. AP/Wide World Photos. Reproduced by permission.

Marilyn Duckworth: Duckworth, photograph by Jane Ussher. Reproduced by permission of Marilyn Duckworth.

Ed and Barbara Emberley: Emberley, photograph. Reproduced by permission of Barbara Emberley.

Susan Fletcher: Fletcher, photograph by Liz DeMott. Reproduced by permission of Susan Fletcher.

Neil Gaiman: Gaiman, photograph by Kelli Bickman © Kelli Bickman. Reproduced by permission.

Gail Gibbons: Gibbons, photograph. Reproduced by permission.

Newt Gingrich: Gingrich, photograph. AP/Wide World Photos. Reproduced by permission.

Marilyn Hacker: Hacker, photograph by Attar Maher. Corbis Sygma. Reproduced by permission.

Joy Harjo: Harjo, photograph by Abdoo Studios, Inc. Reproduced by permission of the photographer.

Marilu Henner: Henner, photograph. AP/Worldwide Photos. Reproduced by permission.

Susan Hill: Hill, photograph. Courtesy of David R. Godine Publishers. Reproduced by permission.

Linda Hogan: Hogan, photograph by Gary Isaacs. From the jacket of her book *Solar Storms.* NY: Scribner, 1995. © Gary Isaacs. Reproduced by permission of the photographer.

Satomi Ichikawa: Ichiwaka, photograph by Marianne Veron. Reproduced by permission of Satomi Ichikawa.

Tama Janowitz: Janowitz, photograph. AP/Wide World Photos. Reproduced by permission.

Charles Johnson: Johnson, photograph by Mario Suriani. AP/World Wide Photos. Reproduced by permission.

W. P. Kinsella: Kinsella, photograph by Ian Robertson. Reproduced by permission.

William Kotzwinkle: Kotzwinkle, photograph. © Jerry Bauer. Reproduced by permission.

Stan Lee: Lee, photograph. AP/Wide World Photos. Reproduced by permission.

Julius Lester: Lester, photograph. Corbis. Reproduced by permission.

John Marsden: Marsden, 1994, photograph by David Furphy. Reproduced by permission.

Harry Mazer: Mazer, photograph by Ruth Putter. Reproduced by permission.

Norma Foz Mazer: Mazer, photograph by Darkroom on Wheels. Reproduced by permission.

William Meredith: Meredith, photograph. AP/ Wide World Photos. Reproduced by permission.

Joyce Carol Oates: Oates, photograph. AP/Wide World Photos. Reproduced by permission.

Richard Peck: Peck, photograph by Don Gallo. Reproduced by permission of Richard Peck.

David Rabe: Rabe, 1972, photograph. AP/Wide World Photos. Reproduced by permission.

Henry Rollins: Rollins, photograph. AP/Wide World Photos. Reproduced by permission.

J. D. Salinger: Salinger, 1951, photograph. AP/Wide World Photos. Reproduced by permission.

Richard Sanders: Sanders, photograph. Reproduced by permission.

Laura Torres: Torres, photograph. Reproduced by permission of Laura Torres.

Maggie Toy: Toy, photograph. Reproduced by permission.

Elisabeth Vonaburg: Vonarburg, photograph by Robert Laliberte. Reproduced by permission of Elisabeth Vonaburg.

Ruth Wolff: Wolff, photograph by Maron Bloom. Reproduced by permission of Ruth Wolff.

Jacqueline Woodson: Woodson, photograph by Mark Lennihan. AP/Wide World Photos. Reproduced by permission.

Patrica C. Wrede: Wrede, photograph by David Dyer-Bennet. Reproduced by permission.

Cheryl Zach: Zach, photograph by Michelle Grisco. Reproduced by permission of Cheryl Zach.

A

* *Indicates that a listing has been compiled from secondary sources believed to be reliable, but has not been personally verified for this edition by the author sketched.*

ALLENDE, Isabel 1942-

PERSONAL: Surname is pronounced "Ah-*yen*-day"; born August 2, 1942, in Lima, Peru; daughter of Tomas (a Chilean diplomat) and Francisca (Llona Barros) Allende; married Miguel Frias (an engineer), September 8, 1962 (divorced, 1987); married William Gordon (a lawyer), July 17, 1988; children: (first marriage) Paula (deceased), Nicolas; Scott (stepson). *Education:* Educated privately.

ADDRESSES: Home—15 Nightingale Lane, San Rafael, CA 94901. *Agent*—Carmen Balcells, Diagonal 580, Barcelona 21, Spain.

CAREER: United Nations Food and Agricultural Organization, Santiago, Chile, secretary, 1959-65; *Paula* magazine, Santiago, journalist, editor, and advice columnist, 1967-74; *Mampato* magazine, Santiago, journalist, 1969-74; television interviewer for Canal 13/Canal 7 (television station), 1970-75; worked on movie newsreels, 1973-78; *El Nacional,* Caracas, Venezuela, journalist, 1974-75, columnist, 1976-83; Colegio Marroco, Caracas, administrator, 1979-82; writer. Guest teacher at Montclair State College, Montclair, NJ, spring, 1985, and University of Virginia, fall, 1988; Gildersleeve Lecturer, Barnard College, spring, 1988; teacher of creative writing, University of California, Berkeley, spring, 1989.

Isabel Allende

AWARDS, HONORS: Panorama Literario Award (Chile), 1983; Grand Prix d'Evasion (France), 1984; Author of the Year and Book of the Year Awards (Germany), 1984; Point de Mire (Belgium), 1985; Colima Award for Best Novel (Mexico), 1985; Author of the Year Award (Germany), 1986; Quality Paperback Book Club New Voice Award nomination, 1986, for *The House of the Spirits; Los Angeles Times* Book Prize nomination, 1987, for *Of Love and Shadows;* XV Premio Internazionale (Italy), and Mulheres best foreign novel award (Portugal), 1987; *Eva Luna* was named one of *Library Journal*'s Best Books of 1988, awarded an American Book Award, Before Columbus Foundation, 1989, Freedom to Write Pen Club Award, 1991, and XLI Bancarella Literature Award (Italy), and Brandeis University Major Book Collection Award, both 1993.

WRITINGS:

Civilice a su troglodita: Los impertinentes de Isabel Allende (humor), Editorial Lord Cochran (Santiago, Chile), 1974.

La Casa de los espíritus, Plaza y Janés (Barcelona, Spain), 1982, HarperLibros (New York, NY), 1995, translation by Magda Bogin published as *The House of the Spirits,* Knopf (New York, NY), 1985.

La Gorda de porcelana (juvenile; title means "The Fat Porcelain Lady"), Alfaguara (Madrid, Spain), 1984.

De amor y de sombra, Plaza y Janés (Barcelona, Spain), 1984, HarperLibros (New York, NY), 1995, translation by Margaret Sayers Peden published as *Of Love and Shadows,* Knopf (New York, NY), 1987.

Eva Luna, translation by Margaret Sayers Peden published under same title, Knopf (New York, NY), 1988, HarperLibros (New York, NY), 1995.

Cuentos de Eva Luna, Plaza y Janés (Barcelona, Spain), 1990, HarperCollins (New York, NY), 1995, translation by Margaret Sayers Peden published as *The Stories of Eva Luna,* Atheneum (New York, NY), 1991.

El Plan infinito, Editorial Sudamericana (Buenos Aires, Argentina), 1991, translation by Margaret Sayers Peden published as *The Infinite Plan,* HarperCollins (New York, NY), 1993.

Paula (autobiography), Plaza y Janés (Barcelona, Spain), 1994, translation by Margaret Sayers Peden, HarperCollins (New York, NY), 1995.

(With others) *Salidas de madre,* Planeta (Santiago, Chile), 1996.

Afrodita: Recetas, cuentos y otros afrodisiacos, HarperCollins (New York, NY), 1997, translation by Margaret Sayers Peden published as *Aphrodite: A Memoir of the Senses,* HarperFlamingo (New York, NY), 1998.

Hija de la fortuna, Plaza y Janés (Barcelona, Spain), 1999, translation by Margaret Sayers Peden published as *Daughter of Fortune: A Novel,* HarperCollins (New York, NY), 1999.

(And author of foreword) *Conversations with Isabel Allende,* edited by John Rodden, translations from the Spanish by Virginia Invernizzi and from the German and Dutch by John Rodden, University of Texas (Austin, TX), 1999.

Retrato en sepia, Plaza y Janés (Barcelona, Spain), 2000, translation by Margaret Sayers Peden published as *Portrait in Sepia,* HarperCollins (New York, NY), 2001.

La Ciudad de las bestias, Rayo (New York, NY), 2002, translation by Margaret Sayers Peden published as *City of the Beasts* (young adult), HarperCollins (New York, NY), 2002.

Mi país inventado, Areté (Barcelona, Spain), 2003, translation by Margaret Sayers Peden published as *My Invented Country: A Nostalgic Journey through Chile,* HarperCollins (New York, NY), 2003.

El Reino del dragón de oro, Montena Mondadori (Barcelona, Spain), translation by Margaret Sayers Peden published as *Kingdom of the Golden Dragon,* HarperCollins (New York, NY), 2004.

Author of several plays and stories for children. Also contributor to *Los Libros tienen sis propios espíritus: Estudios sobre Isabel Allende,* edited by Marcello Coddou, Universidad Veracruzana, 1986; *Paths of Resistance: The Art and Craft of the Political Novel,* edited by William Zinsser, Houghton Mifflin, 1989; and *El Amor: Grandes escritores latinoamericanos,* Ediciones Instituto Movilizador, 1991.

ADAPTATIONS: The House of the Spirits was filmed in English by Bille August in 1993, starring Meryl Streep, Jeremy Irons, Antonio Banderas, and Vanessa Redgrave.

SIDELIGHTS: When Chilean President Salvador Allende was assassinated in 1973 as part of a military coup against his socialist government, it had a profound effect on his niece, novelist Isabel Allende. "I think I have divided my life [into] before that day and after that day," Allende told *Publishers Weekly* interviewer Amanda Smith. "In that moment, I realized that everything was possible—that violence was a dimension that was always around you." At first, Allende and her family did not believe that a dictatorship could last in Chile; they soon found it too dangerous to remain in the country, however, and fled to Venezuela. Although she had been a noted journalist in Chile, Allende found it difficult to get a job in

Venezuela and did not write for several years; but after receiving word from her grandfather, a nearly one-hundred-year-old man who had remained in Chile, she began to write again in a letter to him. "My grandfather thought people died only when you forgot them," the author explained to Harriet Shapiro in *People.* "I wanted to prove to him that I had forgotten nothing, that his spirit was going to live with us forever." Allende never sent the letter to her grandfather, who soon died, but her memories of her family and her country became the genesis of *The House of the Spirits,* her first novel. "When you lose everything, everything that is dear to you . . . memory becomes more important," Allende commented to *Mother Jones* writer Douglas Foster. With *The House of the Spirits,* the author added, "[I achieved] the recovery of those memories that were being blown by the wind, by the wind of exile."

Following three generations of the Trueba family and their domestic and political conflicts, *The House of the Spirits* "is a novel of peace and reconciliation, in spite of the fact that it tells of bloody, tragic events," claimed *New York Times Book Review* contributor Alexander Coleman. "The author has accomplished this not only by plumbing her memory for the familial and political textures of the continent, but also by turning practically every major Latin American novel on its head," the critic continued. The patriarch of the family, Esteban Trueba, is a strict, conservative man who exploits his workers and allows his uncompromising beliefs to distance him from his wife and children, even in the face of tremendous events.

Allende's grand scope and use of fantastic elements and characters have led many critics to place *The House of the Spirits* in the tradition of the Latin American novel of "magic realism," and they compare it specifically to Nobel-winner Gabriel García Márquez's *One Hundred Years of Solitude.* "Allende has her own distinctive voice, however," noted a *Publishers Weekly* reviewer; "while her prose lacks the incandescent brilliance of the master's, it has a whimsical charm, besides being clearer, more accessible and more explicit about the contemporary situation in South America." In contrast, *Village Voice* contributor Enrique Fernandez believed that "only the dullest reader can fail to be distracted by the shameless cloning from *One Hundred Years of Solitude.* . . . Allende writes like one of the many earnest minor authors that began aping Gabo after his success, except she's better at it than most." "Allende is very much under the influence of Gabriel García Márquez, but she is scarcely an imitator," remarked *Washington Post Book World* critic Jonathan Yardley, concluding that "she is most certainly a novelist in her own right and, for a first novelist, a startlingly skillful, confident one."

While *The House of the Spirits* contains some of the magic realism so characteristic of late-twentieth-century Latin-American fiction, it is counterbalanced by the political realities that Allende recounts. *Times Literary Supplement* reviewer Antony Beevor stated that whereas the early chapters of *The House of the Spirits* seem "to belong firmly in the school of magical realism," a closer reading "suggests that Isabel Allende's tongue is lightly in her cheek. It soon becomes clear that she has taken the genre to flip it over," the critic elaborated. "The metaphorical house, the themes of time and power, the *machista* violence and the unstoppable merry-go-round of history: all of these are reworked and then examined from the other side—from a woman's perspective." Other critics,however, faulted Allende for trying to combine the magical and the political. Richard Eder of the *Los Angeles Times* felt that the author "rarely manages to integrate her magic and her message," while *Nation* contributor Paul West said that the political story is "the book Allende probably wanted to write, and would have had she not felt obliged to toe the line of magical realism." But others maintained that the contrast between the fantastic and political segments is effective, as Harriet Waugh of *Spectator* explained: "[The] magic gradually dies away as a terrible political reality engulfs the people of the country. Ghosts, the gift of foretelling the future and the ability to make the pepper and salt cellars move around the dining-room table cannot survive terror, mass-murder and torture."

Although *The House of the Spirits* includes political approaches similar to other Latin-American works, it also contains "an original feminist argument that suggests [a] women's monopoly on powers that oppose the violent 'paternalism' from which countries like Chile continue to suffer," according to *Chicago Tribune* contributor Bruce Allen. Alberto Manguel likewise considered important Allende's "depiction of woman as a colonial object," as he wrote in the Toronto *Globe and Mail,* a depiction reinforced by Esteban Trueba's cruel treatment of his wife, daughter, and female workers. But despite the concentration on female characters and "the fact that Esteban rapes, pillages, kills and conspires, he never entirely loses the reader's sympathy," commented Waugh. "It is a remarkable achievement to make the old monster lovable not just to his wife, daughter, and granddaughter, and the other women in his life, but also to the reader," Philip Howard contended in the London *Times.* "It is a fair-minded book, that pities and understands people on both sides of the politics." Allen concurred: "The most remarkable feature of this remarkable book is the way in which its strong political sentiments are made to coexist with its extravagant and fascinating narrative. . . . Despite its undeniable debt to *One Hundred Years of Solitude,*" the critic concluded, *The House of the Spirits* "is an original and important work; along with García Márquez's masterpiece, it's one of the best novels of the postwar period, and a major contribution to our understanding of societies riddled by ceaseless conflict and violent change. It is a great achievement, and it cries out to be read."

With *Of Love and Shadows,* which *Detroit Free Press* contributor Anne Janette Johnson called "a frightening, powerful work," Allende "proves her continued capacity for generating excellent fiction. She has talent, sensitivity, and a subject matter that provides both high drama and an urgent political message." The novel begins "matter-of-factly, almost humorously," with the switching of two identically named babies, as Charles R. Larson described it in the *Detroit News.* The story becomes more complex, however, when one of the babies grows up to become the focus of a journalist's investigation; after a reporter and photographer expose the political murder of the girl, they are forced to flee the country. "And so," Larson observed, "Allende begins with vignettes of magical realism, only to pull the rug out from under our feet once we have been hooked by her enchanting tale. What she does, in fact, is turn her story into a thriller." "Love and struggle a la *Casablanca*—it's all there," Gene H. Bell-Villada likewise stated in the *New York Times Book Review.* "Allende skillfully evokes both the terrors of daily life under military rule and the subtler form of resistance in the hidden corners and 'shadows' of her title." But while political action comprises a large part of the story, "above all, this is a love story of two young people sharing the fate of their historical circumstances, meeting the challenge of discovering the truth, and determined to live their life fully, accepting their world of love and shadows," *Christian Science Monitor* reviewer Marjorie Agosin declared. With *Of Love and Shadows* "Allende has mastered the craft of being able to intertwine the turbulent political history of Latin America with the everyday lives of her fictional characters caught up in recognizable, contemporary events."

"Fears that Isabel Allende might be a 'one-book' writer, that her first success . . . would be her only one, ought to be quashed by *Eva Luna,*" asserted Abigail E. Lee in the *Times Literary Supplement.* "The eponymous protagonist and narrator of this, her third novel, has an engaging personality, a motley collection of interesting acquaintances and an interesting angle on political upheavals in the unnamed Latin-American republic in which she lives." Born illegitimate and later orphaned, Eva Luna becomes a scriptwriter and storyteller who becomes involved with a filmmaker—Rolf Carle, an Austrian emigré haunted by his Nazi father—and his subjects, a troop of revolutionary guerrillas. "In *Eva Luna,* Allende moves between the personal and the political, between realism and fantasy, weaving two exotic coming-of-age stories—Eva Luna's and Rolf Carle's—into the turbulent coming of age of her unnamed South American country," Elizabeth Benedict summarized in Chicago's *Tribune Books.* Switching between the stories of the two protagonists, *Eva Luna* is "filled with a multitude of characters and tales," recounted *Washington Post Book World* contributor Alan Ryan. Allende's work is "a remarkable novel," the critic elaborated, "one in which a cascade of stories tumbles out before the reader, stories vivid and passionate and human enough to engage, in their own right, all the reader's attention and sympathy."

Perhaps due to this abundance of stories and characters, John Krich thought that "few of the cast of characters emerge as distinctive or entirely believable," as he commented in the *New York Times Book Review.* "Too often, we find Eva Luna's compatriots revealed through generalized attributions rather than their own actions. . . . Is this magic realism *à la* García Márquez or Hollywood magic *à la* Judith Krantz? We can only marvel at how thin the line becomes between the two, and give Ms. Allende the benefit of the doubt." London *Times* writer Stuart Evans, however, praised Allende's "range of eccentric or idiosyncratic characters who are always credible," and added: "Packed with action, prodigal in invention, vivid in description and metaphor, this cleverly plotted novel is enhanced by its flowing prose and absolute assurance." "*Eva Luna* is a great read that *El Nobel* [García

Márquez] couldn't hope to write," claimed Dan Bellm in the *Voice Literary Supplement,* for the women "get the best political debate scenes, not the men." Lee also saw a serious political side to the novel, noting "an interesting juxtaposition in *Eva Luna* of feminism and revolutionary politics. . . . In all the depictions of women and their relationships with men, though, one feels not a militant or aggressive feminism—rather a sympathetic awareness of the injustices inherent in traditional gender roles." The critic continued, remarking that *Eva Luna* "is an accomplished novel, skillfully blending humour and pathos; its woman's perspective on Latin American is a refreshing one, but it is enjoyable above all for its sensitivity and charm." "Reading this novel is like asking your favorite storyteller to tell you a story and getting a hundred stories instead of one . . . and then an explanation of how the stories were invented . . . and then hearing the storyteller's life as well," concluded Ryan. "Does it have a happy ending? What do you think?"

Daughter of Fortune differs from Allende's previous works in that it moves away from Chile and takes place in the setting of the 1849 California gold rush. The novel also includes a greater cultural mix than her previous works, with British, American, and Chinese characters. The main character, Eliza Somers, who spends several years disguised as a boy, raises questions about the nature of gender and identity, according to Sophia A. McClennan in the *Review of Contemporary Fiction.* Cecilia Novella remarked in *Amerícas* that Allende "provides us with a masterly description of that part of North America that was to become California at the height of the gold rush, painting a vivid picture of boisterous activity, chaos, avarice, unrelieved drudgery, and the broad range of lifestyles, habits and dissolute ways of those drawn there by the gleaming precious metal."

Portrait in Sepia tells the story of Aurora del Valle, who is filled with questions about the mysterious beginnings of her life. When she is five years old, she is sent to live with her grandmother, Paulina, who previously appeared in *Daughter of Fortune.* Paulina, who is wealthy and powerful, provides for her every material need but refuses to answer her questions about the past. Her confusion lingers until adulthood, and perhaps drives her to art: she is a talented photographer. After Paulina dies, she feels more free to explore her own and her family's past, examining her memories as well as those of relatives. At the end of the novel, Allende reveals that one of Aurora's cousins is Clara del Valle, a character from *The House of the Spirits.* Thus, as Teresa R. Arrington noted in *World Literature Today,* "Allende has produced two prequels years after the original novel, thus forming a chronologically out-of-sequence trilogy. The three novels represent a transnational saga that shows us how major historical events across the world can affect the lives of several generations of an extended Chilean family." In *Book,* Beth Kephart observed, "Allende's imagination is a spectacle unto itself—she infects her readers with her own colossal dreams."

In *City of the Beasts* Allende departed from her previous works for adults and wrote a story for young adults. In *Booklist,* she told Hazel Rochman, "The idea of writing for young adults wasn't mine; it was something that my three grandchildren had been asking me to do for a long time." Alexander Cold, the main character in the novel, was modeled after Allende's grandson, Alejandro Frias. Another character, Nadia Santos, was inspired by her two granddaughters, Andrea and Nicole. In the novel, Alexander is sent to stay with his grandmother in the Amazon while his mother receives chemotherapy in Texas. His grandmother is researching a mysterious "beast" that is terrifying everyone in the jungle, and she is part of a group of adventurers that includes a self-centered professor, some photographers, a government doctor, soldiers, local tribespeople, and a guide, Cesar Santos, who brings his daughter, Nadia. Alexander and Nicole must face dangers both physical and supernatural and struggle with both good and evil, but through shamanic techniques taught by the local tribe, they find their own inner strength and emerge transformed. A *Publisher's Weekly* reviewer said of *City of the Beasts,* "Reluctant readers may be intimidated by the thickness of this volume, but the plot moves at a rapid pace, laced with surprises and ironic twists." The reviewer then examined Allende's creation process: "The action and the outcome seem preordained, cleverly crafted to deliver the moral, but many readers will find the author's formula successful with its environmentalist theme, a pinch of the grotesque, and a larger dose of magic."

Allende's 2003 novel *My Invented Country: A Nostalgic Journey through Chile* is a memoir. The book examines Chile and Allende's place in it closely, tracing her relationship to the country and its people since the September 11, 1973, military coup that overthrew

Chile's democracy. She relates stories of her family, historical tales of Chile, and considers how the country has influenced her writing. Allende "paints a fascinating picture of an unusual country," stated Gloria Maxwell in *Library Journal.* "She is unflinchingly honest about detailing Chilean adherence to a class system, the people's fixation with machismo, and their inherent conservatism and clannishness." Allende had a rich source of material at her disposal for the crafting of this book. "Each country has its customs, its manias, its complexes," she writes. "I know the idiosyncrasies of mine like the back of my hand." Another *Library Journal* reviewer, Sheila Kasperek, observed that *My Invented Country* "provides a fuller understanding of her works," and in *Booklist,* Donna Seaman maintained that "Allende's conjuring of her 'invented,' or imaginatively remembered, country is riveting in its frankness and compassion, and her account of why and how she became a writer is profoundly moving."

Allende has shared many memories, both real and fictional, with her readers. She has examined political issues, related stories of her "interesting" childhood, enthralled readers with magical ideas, and shared the beauties of her homeland. The large topical span of Allende's writings makes it difficult to classify the author as a particular type. However, when *San Francisco Chronicle* writer Heather Knight asked Allende how she would like to be remembered after her death, Allende did not mention any of her acclaimed books. Instead, she responded, "I'd like to be remembered by my grandchildren as a grandma who gave them unconditional love, stories, and laughter."

BIOGRAPHICAL AND CRITICAL SOURCES:

BOOKS

Bloom, Harold, editor, *Isabel Allende,* Chelsea House (Philadelphia, PA), 2003.

Coddou, Marcelio, editor, *Los Libros tienen sus propios espíritus: Estudios sobre Isabel Allende,* Universidad Veracruzana (Veracruz, Mexico), 1986.

Contemporary Hispanic Biography, Volume 1, Gale (Detroit, MI), 2003.

Contemporary Literary Criticism, Gale (Detroit, MI), Volume 39, 1986, Volume 57, 1990, Volume 97, 1997.

Feal, Rosemary G., and Yvette E. Miller, editors, *Isabel Allende Today: An Anthology of Essays,* Latin American Literary Review Press (Pittsburgh, PA), 2002.

Hart, Patricia, *Narrative Magic in the Fiction of Isabel Allende,* Fairleigh Dickinson University Press (Teaneck, NJ), 1989.

Levine, Linda Gould, *Isabel Allende,* Twayne Publishers (New York, NY), 2002.

Lindsay, Claire, *Locating Latin American Women Writers: Cristina Peri Rossi, Rosario Ferré, Albalucía, and Isabel Allende,* Peter Lang (New York, NY), 2003.

Postlewate, Marisa Herrera, *How and Why I Write: Redefining Women's Writing and Experience,* Peter Lang (New York, NY), 2004.

Ramblado-Minero, Maria de la Cinta, *Isabal Allende's Writing of the Self: Trespassing the Boundaries of Fiction and Autobiography,* E. Mellen Press (Lewiston, NY), 2003.

Rojas, Sonia Riquelme, and Edna Aguirre Rehbein, editors, *Critical Approaches to Isabel Allende's Novels,* P. Lang (New York, NY), 1991.

Zapata, Celia Correas, *Isabel Allende: Life and Spirits,* translation by Margaret Sayers Peden, Arte Público Press (Houston, TX), 2002.

PERIODICALS

Americas, November-December, 1995, p. 36; September, 1999, Cecilia Novella, review of *Daughter of Fortune,* p. 61; October, 2001, Barbara Mujica, review of *Portrait in Sepia,* p. 63.

Architectural Digest, April, 1995, p. 32.

Atlanta Journal-Constitution, December 2, 2000, Greg Changnon, review of *Portrait in Sepia,* p. C4.

Book, November-December, 2001, Beth Kephart, review of *Portrait in Sepia,* p. 60.

Booklist, February 1, 1998, p. 875; August, 1999, Brad Hooper, review of *Daughter of Fortune,* p. 1984; September 1, 2001, Brad Hooper, review of *Portrait in Sepia,* p. 3; November 15, 2002, Hazel Rochman, review of *City of the Beasts,* p. 590, and interview with Allende, p. 591; April 1, 2003, Donna Seaman, review of *My Invented Country: A Nostalgic Journey through Chile,* p. 1354.

Chicago Tribune, May 19, 1985.

Christian Science Monitor, June 7, 1985; May 27, 1987.

Detroit Free Press, June 7, 1987.

Detroit News, June 14, 1987.
Globe and Mail (Toronto, Ontario, Canada), June 24, 1985; June 27, 1987.
Guardian, November 13, 1999, Alex Clark, review of *Daughter of Fortune,* p. 10; November 30, 2002, Carol Birch, review of *City of the Beasts,* p. 33.
Kirkus Reviews, October 1, 2002, review of *City of the Beasts,* p. 1462; April 1, 2003, review of *My Invented Country,* p. 514.
Library Journal, August, 1999, Barbara Hoffert, review of *Daughter of Fortune,* p. 134; October 15, 2001, Barbara Hoffert, review of *Portrait in Sepia,* p. 105; June 1, 2003, Sheila Kasperek, review of *My Invented Country,* p. 118; October 15, 2003, Gloria Maxwell, review of *My Invented Country,* p. 115.
Los Angeles Times, February 10, 1988.
Los Angeles Times Book Review, June 16, 1985; May 31, 1987.
Mother Jones, December, 1988.
Ms., May-June, 1995, p. 75.
Nation, July 20-27, 1985.
New Leader, November-December, 2001, Philip Graham, review of *Portrait in Sepia,* p. 38.
New Statesman, July 5, 1985.
Newsweek, May 13, 1985.
New York Review of Books, July 18, 1985.
New York Times, May 2, 1985; May 20, 1987; February 4, 1988.
New York Times Book Review, May 12, 1985; July 12, 1987; October 23, 1988; May 21, 1995, p. 11.
People, June 10, 1985; June 1, 1987; June 5, 1995, p. 34; April 20, 1998, p. 47.
Publishers Weekly, March 1, 1985; May 17, 1985; January 19, 1998, p. 360; August 23, 1999, review of *Daughter of Fortune* p. 41; July 16, 2001, review of *Portrait in Sepia,* p. 1142; June 24, 2002, review of *City of the Beasts,* p. 58; April 28, 2003, review of *My Invented Country,* p. 57; June 30, 2003, review of *City of the Beasts.*
Review of Contemporary Fiction, summer, 2000, Sophia A. McClennan, review of *Daughter of Fortune,* p. 184.
St. Louis Post-Dispatch, October 28, 2001, Jan Garden Castro, review of *Portrait in Sepia,* p. G11.
San Francisco Chronicle, October 19, 2001, Heather Knight, review of *City of the Beasts,* p. 1.
Spectator, August 3, 1985.
Sunday Telegraph (London, England), October 14, 2001, Jenny McCartney, review of *Portrait in Sepia,* p. NA.
Time, May 20, 1985.
Times (London, England), July 4, 1985; July 9, 1987; March 22, 1989; March 23, 1989.
Times Literary Supplement, July 5, 1985; July 10, 1987; April 7-13, 1989.
Tribune Books (Chicago, IL), October 9, 1988.
U.S. News and World Report, November 21, 1988.
Village Voice, June 7, 1985.
Voice Literary Supplement, December, 1988.
Wall Street Journal, March 20, 1998.
Washington Post Book World, May 12, 1985; May 24, 1987; October 9, 1988.
World Literature Today, winter, 2002, Teresa R. Arrington, review of *Portrait in Sepia,* p. 115.
World Press Review, April, 1995, p. 47.*

* * *

ANDRE, Alix
See KIMBERLY, Gail

* * *

ANSTRUTHER, Ian 1922-

PERSONAL: Born May 11, 1922, in England; son of Douglas (in business) and Enid (a painter; maiden name, Campbell) Anstruther; married Susan Paten (an architect), November, 1963; children: Sebastian, Toby, Rachel, Harriet, Eleanor. *Ethnicity:* "Scottish-white." *Education:* Attended New College, Oxford.

ADDRESSES: *Home*—Barlavington, Petworth, Sussex, England; fax: 01798 869401. *E-mail*—pardy@anstruther.com.

CAREER: Worked for British Diplomatic Service, London, 1944-49; farmer and writer, 1949—. *Military service:* British Army, Signals Corps, 1939-44; served in European theater; became captain.

MEMBER: Society of Antiquaries of London (fellow).

WRITINGS:

"I Presume": A Study of H. M. Stanley, Geoffrey Bles (London, England), 1956, published as *"Dr. Livingstone, I Presume,"* Dutton (New York, NY), 1957.

The Knight and the Umbrella (Book Society selection), Geoffrey Bles (London, England), 1963.
The Scandal of the Andover Workhouse, Geoffrey Bles (London, England), 1973.
Oscar Browning: A Biography, John Murray (London, England), 1983.
Coventry Patmore's Angel, Haggerston Press (London, England), 1992.
(With Patricia Aske) *The Angel in the House* (collated edition), Haggerston Press (London, England), 1997.
Dean Farrar and "Eric:" A Study of "Eric, or Little by Little" and Its Author, Dean Farrar, together with the Complete Text of the Book, Haggerston Press (London, England), 2002.

SIDELIGHTS: Ian Anstruther once told *CA:* "In 1950 I inherited enough money to be able to retire from the Diplomatic Service. I bought a farm, which I run; at the same time, and every day, I work on my current book. My background is a literary one, the most successful member of the family since the war being the late Jan Struther (who wrote *Mrs. Miniver*). So it was natural for me to take to literature when I had the opportunity, and it was natural for me to live in the country, having been brought up in Scotland, in Argyll, and being of a rather solitary nature."

BIOGRAPHICAL AND CRITICAL SOURCES:

PERIODICALS

Times Literary Supplement, November 25, 1983.*

* * *

AUSTER, Paul 1947-

PERSONAL: Born February 3, 1947, in Newark, NJ; son of Samuel and Queenie (Bogat) Auster; married Lydia Davis (a writer), October 6, 1974 (divorced, 1979); married Siri Hustuedt, June 16, 1981; children: (first marriage) Daniel; (second marriage) Sophie. *Education:* Columbia University, B.A., 1969, M.A., 1970.

ADDRESSES: Agent—c/o Carol Mann Agency, 55 Fifth Avenue, New York, NY 10003-4301.

Paul Auster

CAREER: Poet, novelist, translator, and critic. Worked variously as a merchant seaman, census taker, tutor, telephone operator for Paris bureau of *New York Times,* and caretaker of farmhouse in Provence, France. Teacher in creative writing, Princeton University, 1986-90. Director of short film *Blue in the Face,* Miramax, 1994.

AWARDS, HONORS: Poetry grant, Ingram Merrill Foundation, 1975 and 1982; PEN Translation Center grant, 1977; National Endowment for the Arts fellowship for poetry, 1979, and for creative writing, 1985; Morton Dauwen Zabel Award, American Academy and Institute of Arts and Letters, 1990; PEN/Faulkner Award nomination, 1991, for *The Music of Chance*; Chevalier de l'Ordre des Arts et des Lettres, 1993; Prix Medicis for foreign literature, 1993, for *Leviathan*; Independent Spirit Award, 1996.

WRITINGS:

NOVELS

City of Glass (first part of "New York Trilogy"; also see below), Sun & Moon Press (Los Angeles, CA), 1985.

Ghosts (second part of "New York Trilogy"; also see below), Sun & Moon Press (Los Angeles, CA), 1986.

The Locked Room (third part of "New York Trilogy"; also see below), Sun & Moon Press (Los Angeles, CA), 1987.

In the Country of Last Things, Viking (New York, NY), 1987.

Moon Palace, Viking (New York, NY), 1989.

The Music of Chance, Viking (New York, NY), 1990.

The New York Trilogy (contains *City of Glass, Ghosts,* and *The Locked Room*), Penguin (New York, NY), 1990.

Leviathan, Viking (New York, NY), 1992.

Mr. Vertigo, Viking (New York, NY), 1994.

Timbuktu, Holt (New York, NY), 1999.

(With Sophie Calle) *Double Game,* Violette (London, England), 2000.

The Book of Illusions, Holt (New York, NY), 2002.

Oracle Night, Holt (New York, NY), 2004.

POEMS

Unearth: Poems, 1970-1972, Living Hand (Stanfordville, NY), 1974.

Wall Writing: Poems, 1971-1975, Figures (Berkeley, CA), 1976.

Facing the Music, Station Hill (Barrytown, NY), 1980.

Disappearances: Selected Poems, Overlook Press (Woodstock, NY), 1988.

Collected Poems, Overlook Press (Woodstock, NY), 2004.

Fragments from Cold, Parenthese (Brewster, NY), 1977.

SCREENPLAYS

Smoke and Blue in the Face: Two Screenplays (both produced by Miramax, 1995; also see below), Hyperion/Miramax Books (New York, NY), 1995.

Lulu on the Bridge: A Film (also see below), Holt (New York, NY), 1998.

Three Films: Smoke, Blue in the Face, and Lulu on the Bridge, Picador (New York, NY), 2004.

PLAYS

Eclipse, produced in New York, NY, 1977.

NONFICTION

White Spaces, Station Hill (Barrytown, NY), 1980.

The Invention of Solitude (memoir), SUN (New York, NY), 1982.

The Art of Hunger: Essays, Prefaces, Interviews, Sun & Moon Press (Los Angeles, CA), 1991.

The Red Notebook and Other Writings, Faber (London, England), 1995, published as *The Red Notebook: True Stories,* New Directions (New York, NY), 2002.

Why Write?, Burning Deck (Providence, RI), 1996.

Paul Auster's New York, foreword by Luc Sante, photographs by Frieder Blickle, Holt (New York, NY), 1997.

Hand to Mouth: A Chronicle of Early Failure, Holt (New York, NY), 1997.

The Story of My Typewriter, illustrated by Sam Messer, D.A.P. (New York, NY), 2002.

(Author of introduction) Nathaniel Hawthorne, *Twenty Days with Julian and Little Bunny by Papa,* New York Review Books (New York, NY), 2003.

TRANSLATOR

A Little Anthology of Surrealist Poems, Siamese Banana Press (New York, NY), 1972.

Jacques Dupin, *Fits and Starts: Selected Poems,* Living Hand (Stanfordville, NY), 1974.

(With Lydia Davis) Saul Friedlander and Mahmoud Hussein, *Arabs and Israelis: A Dialogue,* Holmes & Meier (New York, NY), 1975.

Andre de Bouchet, *The Uninhabited: Selected Poems,* Living Hand (Stanfordville, NY), 1976.

(With Lydia Davis) Jean-Paul Sartre, *Life Situations,* Pantheon (New York, NY), 1978.

(With Lydia Davis) Jean Chesneaux, *China: The People's Republic,* Pantheon (New York, NY), 1979.

(With Lydia Davis) Jean Chesneaux and others, *China from the 1911 Revolution to Liberation,* Pantheon (New York, NY), 1979.

Stephane Mallarme, *A Tomb for Anatole,* North Point Press (New York, NY), 1983.

Maurice Blanchot, *Vicious Circles,* Station Hill (Barrytown, NY), 1985.

Philippe Petit, *On the High Wire,* Random House (New York, NY), 1985.

(With Margit Rowell) Joan Miro, *Selected Writings,* G. K. Hall (Boston, MA), 1986.

(With Stephen Romer and David Shapiro) Jacques Dupin, *Jacques Dupin: Selected Poems,* Wake Forest University Press (Winston-Salem, NC), 1992.

(With Lydia Davis and Robert Lamberton) Maurice Blanchot, *The Station Hill Blanchot Reader: Fiction and Literary Essays,* edited by George Quasha, Station Hill/Barrytown (Barrytown, NY), 1999.

EDITOR

Random House Book of Twentieth-Century French Poetry, Random House (New York, NY), 1982.

(And translator) Joseph Joubert, *The Notebooks of Joseph Joubert: A Selection,* North Point Press (Berkeley, CA), 1983.

(With J. Legueil) *Und Jabes: Hommage,* Legueil (Paris, France), 1994.

(With Gerard de Cortanze) *La Solitude du labyrinthe: Essais et entretiens* (title means "The Solitude of the Labyrinth: Essays and Conversations"), Actes Sud (Paris, France), 1997.

(And author of introduction) *I Thought My Father Was God and Other True Stories,* Holt (New York, NY), 2001.

Contributor of articles and translations of poetry to magazines, including *New York Times Book Review, Art News, Poetry, New York Review of Books, Harper's,* and *Saturday Review.*

ADAPTATIONS: The Music of Chance was adapted into the 1993 film of the same title, directed by Philip Haas and starring James Spader and Mandy Patinkin; the film rights to *Mr. Vertigo* were purchased by Miramax, 1994; *City of Glass* was adapted into a comic book by Paul Karasik and David Mazzucchelli, Avon Books, 1993.

SIDELIGHTS: Paul Auster "is one of our most intellectually stimulating fiction writers," observed reviewer Joseph Coates in the *Chicago Tribune,* "but [his] reputation outside a small cult is based on a fuzzy perception that he is some sort of genre writer (mysteries? science fiction?) with cryptic pretensions." The perception of Auster as a genre writer has been due in part to the manner in which he entered the publishing world. For years he labored in relative obscurity as a poet, essayist, and translator of French literature; many of those years he lived in France. Then, in the mid-1980s, he began to attract serious critical attention with his "New York Trilogy," a trio of postmodern detective novels. Appreciation for Auster's mysteries built slowly at first. A grim and intellectually puzzling mystery, *The City of Glass,* the first book in the trilogy, was rejected by seventeen different publishers. Nevertheless, when Sun & Moon Press finally issued the novel in 1985, it attracted far more notice than Auster's earlier work and generated considerable interest in the remaining two projected volumes. Completed in 1987, the trilogy has raised Auster's visibility and marked him as a talent to watch. From critics such as Toronto *Globe and Mail* contributor Margaret Cannon, he began to draw the highest praise: "As a novelist, Paul Auster has gone beyond excellence and given the phrase 'experimental fiction' a good name," Cannon wrote, adding that the novelist "has created bona fide literary works, with all the rigor and intellect demanded of contemporary literature."

Auster's dark vision emerged in the "New York Trilogy"'s first novel, *City of Glass.* On the surface, it appears to exploit the conventions of the detective genre. "The real mystery, however, is one of confused character identity," suggested *New York Times Book Review* contributor Toby Olson, "the descent of a writer into a labyrinth in which fact and fiction become increasingly difficult to separate." The novel opens when Quinn, a pseudonymous detective novelist, receives a phone call intended for a real detective (whose name we will later learn is Paul Auster). Lonely and bored, Quinn takes on Auster's identity and accepts the case. His job is to trail a newly-released mental patient and once-brilliant linguist named Stillman, who had been committed for isolating his son in a locked room for nine years. Now Stillman's son's life is in danger, and so "Auster" is hired.

Critical response to *City of Glass* was highly enthusiastic. "*City of Glass* is about the degeneration of language, the shiftings of identity, the struggle to remain human in a great metropolis, when the city itself is cranking on its own falling-apart mechanical life that completely overrides any and every individual," noted *Los Angeles Times Book Review* critic Carolyn See. She deemed the book "an experimental novel that wanders and digresses and loses its own narrative thread, but with all that . . . thoughtfully and cleverly draws our attention to these questions of self." The way the novel subtly shifts from a standard mystery story to an existential quest for identity also captured Olson's attention in the *New York Times Book Review:* "Each detail, each small revelation must be attended to as significant. And such attention brings ambiguity, confusion, and paranoia. Is it important that Quinn's dead son has the same name as Stillman? What can it mean that 'Quinn' rhymes with 'twin' and 'sin'?" As Canon put it, "This is a novel that's full of intellectual puzzles, not all of them resolved." Despite its challenges, Olson believed that "the book is a pleasure to read, full of suspense and action."

In *Ghosts,* the second volume of the trilogy, Auster continues his investigation of lost identity on a more abstract plane. "A client named White hires a detective named Blue to follow a man named Black," Dennis Drabelle explained in *Washington Post Book World.* "Gradually Blue realizes he's been ruined. All he can do is stare at Black, eternally writing a book in the rented room across the street, and draw a weekly paycheck." Auster's choice of names for his protagonists coupled with his coy and knowing tone throughout the book suggest that he is playing mind games with the reader. The real mystery, he implies, is not within the story but "on some higher level," as Rebecca Goldstein observed, acknowledging that *Ghosts* solves the internal mystery, but leaves the larger questions unanswered. Nonetheless, she judged the work "nearly perfect." Others were less impressed. Margaret Cannon, citing problems with continuity, concluded that *Ghosts* has "as much weight as any middle-of-three work can have. It provides the history and heft for the next book, but it cannot really stand alone as a mystery with a beginning, a middle, and an end."

The trilogy's concluding volume, *The Locked Room,* was widely judged to be the richest and by far the most compelling volume in the trilogy. Less abstract and more accessible, this story features flesh-and-blood characters with whom readers can easily identify. Several reviewers suggested that Auster's use of a first-person narrator enhances the book. "When Auster finally allows himself the luxury of character, what a delicious treat he serves up for the reader!" Carolyn See wrote in the *Los Angeles Times.* Though *The Locked Room* is a mystery like the first two installments, this "story is told in the first person by a genuine character who feels love and pain and envy." Because of the first-person narration "Mr. Auster's philosophical asides now sound heartfelt instead of stentorian and his descents into semiological *Angst* feel genuinely anguished and near," Steven Schiff suggested in the *New York Times Book Review.* He and other critics hypothesized that the nameless narrator represents Auster himself.

The story begins when the narrator is summoned by the wife of an old friend from childhood with whom he has lost touch. Fanshawe, as the friend is called, has disappeared and is presumed dead. A fantastically gifted writer, Fanshawe has left behind some unpublished writings as well as instructions for his friend to see them into print. As time passes, the narrator easily moves into Fanshawe's existence, marrying his wife, publishing his work, and eventually engendering rumors that he is actually Fanshawe or, at least, the man who created the works.

In the same year that *The Locked Room* appeared, Auster published another novel, *In the Country of Last Things.* At first glance, this novel seems a science-fiction tale about a future apocalypse. Anna Blume travels from one continent to a large metropolis on another, where she hopes to find her missing brother. She finds instead a city in chaos filled with ruined buildings, ruined lives, criminals ruling and exploiting the desperate and homeless, "Runners" running themselves to death, and "Leapers" jumping to their deaths from the city's crumbling skyscrapers. Anna relates her search through this hellish environment in a letter to someone left behind on the other continent.

Even though Auster seemed to have shifted from mystery to science fiction in *In the Country of Last Things,* the novel shares stylistic and thematic concerns with the "New York Trilogy." "Once more, as in the three volumes of the 'New York Trilogy,' it's all done with mirrors," commented Katharine Washburn in the *Review of Contemporary Fiction.* "This time, the game is played with, if anything, greater cunning and obliqueness behind the same screen of lucid and uncompromising prose." Washburn also challenged the initial impression that this novel is a typical science-fiction piece. "*In the Country of Last Things* is occupied not with a future dystopia but with a hellish present," she contends. "Its citizens are no more inhabitants of the future than Swift's Houyhnhnms are native to some unmapped mid-Atlantic island. They belong to the here and now, to its ethical, spiritual, and cultural chaos." And, she concluded, "Auster has succeeded with Swiftian guile and ferocity in constructing a world of demolished things which we are forced, immediately and painfully to recognize as our own."

"*The Music of Chance* is an accessible, readable story that can be enjoyed by readers of all levels," Digby Diehl commented in the *Los Angeles Times Book Review.* "It is an exceptional novel about the interplay of freedom and chance which takes you on an engrossing tour of a man's inner life." On its surface, this novel begins as an "odyssey of self-invention," as *New York Times* critic Michiko Kakutani put it, bringing to mind such fictional characters as Mark Twain's Huck Finn, John Updike's Rabbit Angstrom, and Jack Kerouac's Dean Moriarty. Jim Nashe hits the road in search of himself after his wife leaves him and he receives an inheritance from his deceased father. His tour of the country winds down at about the same time as his money runs out. He then meets a young gambler, Pozzi, who entices him into a poker game with two eccentric lottery winners from Pennsylvania. The two lose what they have and fall further into debt. In order to pay off the debt, Nashe and Pozzi are forced to build a stone wall for the eccentrics.

"Writing in brisk, precise prose," commented Kakutani in the *New York Times,*"Mr. Auster lends these events all the suspense and pace of a best-selling thriller." Yet, as the reviewer added, the novel is more than a thriller. Auster "gives Nashe's adventures a brooding philosophical subtext that enables him to explore some of his favorite preoccupations: the roles of randomness and causality, the consequences of solitude, and the limitations of freedom, language and free will in an indifferent world." "The result," found Kakutani, "[is] a chilling little story that's entertaining and provocative, resonant without being overly derivative."

In *The Book of Illusions,* David Zimmer's wife and two sons are killed in a car crash, but the resulting insurance settlement leaves him a very rich man. Driven to a nervous breakdown by grief, Zimmer quits his job as an academic and descends into alcoholism, loneliness, and rage. In an attempt to save himself by finding something to occupy his time, he writes a book about Hector Mann, a silent-movie star who mysteriously disappeared in 1929. As a result, someone claiming to be Mann's wife writes Zimmer, saying that Mann is actually alive. Zimmer is drawn into the lost story of Zimmer's life, which is eerily reminiscent of his own. In the *New Statesman,* Toby Mundy remarked that more than any of Auster's previous works, "this novel is propelled along by synchronicity and chance. Random cataclysms tear through his characters' lives, showing us over and over that the membrane separating madness from sanity and life from death is gossamer-thin and can shred at any moment." In the *Houston Chronicle,* Steven E. Alford remarked, "This is Auster's best book in years," and noted, "Is there an order beneath the seeming randomness of the world that is responsible for the direction of our lives? Auster's 'oeuvre' is a continual meditation on this one question."

I Thought My Father Was God is a compilation of stories Auster solicited from ordinary Americans on National Public Radio. The stories had to be short, and they had to be true. The result, according to a *Publishers Weekly* reviewer, was "worthy of Pulitzer consideration." In the *Guardian,* Ian Sansom observed, "What's remarkable about the stories . . . is how thoroughly accomplished they all are, how much they resemble true works of art; they are not mere effusions or anecdotes." And, he wrote, "It is difficult to think of another book . . . that is so simple and so obvious, so excellent in intention and so elegant in its execution, and which displays such wisdom and such knowledge of human life in all its varieties."

In 2002 Auster published *The Story of My Typewriter,* a collaboration with artist Sam Messer in which Auster's manual Olympia typewriter, which he has used to type his manuscripts since 1974, is featured in pictures with different backdrops: the Brooklyn Bridge, the erect Twin Towers, a shelf of Auster's books, and with the writer himself. A *Publishers Weekly* reviewer called the work an "elegant . . . collaboration" and a "detailed perspective on the old-fashioned machine Auster uses to get the words out of his head."

Like *The Book of Illusions,* Auster's 2004 novel, *Oracle Night,* again features a novelist writing a work that parallels his own life. Sidney Orr decides to return to writing after recovering from an illness that came close to taking his life. He enters a new Brooklyn store and purchases a blue Portuguese notebook, after which he begins to write as he never has before. Orr's book, about a man who walks away from his life after a near-death experience, is also titled *Oracle Night.* Reviewer Troy Patterson pointed out in *Publishers Weekly* that "anyone familiar with Auster's old books . . . can guess that Sidney's fiction will bleed into his reality." Patterson, a fan of Auster's other books, was not as fond of *Oracle Night.* He continued, "His chilling ghostliness, however, has been supplanted by insulting mystic hoo-ha and his smooth plot work replaced by garish leaps and twists." Patterson's opinion, however, is the minority, as *Oracle Night* received several rave reviews. While another *Publishers Weekly* reviewer admitted that "the plot of this bizarrely fascinating novel strains credibility," the reviewer remarked that "Auster's unique genius is to make the absurd coherent," and ultimately called the novel "a darkly suspenseful drama and a moving meditation on chance and loss." In a review for *Booklist,* Donna Seaman wrote of *Oracle Night*: "As one spellbinding and provocative storyline leads into another, characters and readers alike are lured deep into the maze of the psyche until Auster orchestrates a terrifying denouement that burns away all ambiguity, leaving his hero enraptured by the radiance of what matters most: love."

In *Europe Intelligence Wire* Auster told Hadley Freeman that despite the fact that he is viewed as an experimental writer, he has a very traditional view of how narrative should work and how stories should be told: "When I write, the story is always uppermost in my mind, and I feel that everything must be sacrificed to it. All elegant passages, all the curious details, all the so-called beautiful writing—if they are not truly relevant to what I am trying to say, then they have to go." And in *Publishers Weekly,* he told Tim Peters, "I feel that as I get older, time isn't as limitless as it once seemed, so I'm bearing down and writing for the time being. There's a compulsion to keep making stories, to keep sitting at my desk every day writing away at fictitious works." This is fortunate for Auster's fans, especially since, as Seaman wrote, "Auster's approach to storytelling becomes more mystical, more intense, more labyrinthine, and more noir with each novel."

BIOGRAPHICAL AND CRITICAL SOURCES:

BOOKS

Barone, Dennis, editor, *Beyond the Red Notebook: Essays on Paul Auster,* University of Pennsylvania Press (Philadelphia, PA), 1995.

Contemporary Literary Criticism, Volume 47, Gale (Detroit, MI), 1988.

Contemporary Novelists, 7th edition, St. James Press (Detroit, MI), 2001.

Contemporary Theatre, Film, and Television, Volume 23, Gale (Detroit, MI), 1999.

Dictionary of Literary Biography, Volume 227: *American Novelists since World War II,* Gale (Detroit, MI), 2000.

Handler, Nina, *Drawn into the Circle of Its Repetitions: Paul Auster's New York Trilogy,* edited by Dal Salwak, Borgo Press (San Bernardino, CA), 1996.

Holzapfel, Anne M., *The New York Trilogy: Whodunit?: Tracking the Structure of Paul Auster's Anti-Detective Novels,* Lang (New York, NY), 1996.

St. James Guide to Crime and Mystery Writers, 4th edition, St. James Press (Detroit, MI), 1996.

PERIODICALS

Art in America, June 1, 2000, "Books for the Collector's Library," p. 64; July, 2000, Maud Lavin, review of *Double Game,* p. 33.

Atlanta Journal and Constitution, May 24, 1987, p. J6; September 13, 1992, p. N9; October 2, 1994, p. N11.

Atlantic, September, 2002, Brooke Allen, review of *The Book of Illusions,* p. 154.

Book, September, 2000, Allen St. John, review of *I Thought My Father Was God,* p. 11; September 1, 2001, interview with Allen St. John, "To Tell the Truth (sort of)," p. 11; September 1, 2002, "Waking the Dead," p. 74; September-October, 2002, Paul Evans, review of *The Book of Illusions,* p. 74.

Booklist, March 1, 1999, Donna Seaman, review of *Timbuktu,* p. 1102; September 15, 2001, review of *I Thought My Father Was God,* p. 163; June 1, 2002, Donna Seaman, review of *The Book of Illusions,* p. 1644; October 1, 2003, review of *Oracle Night,* p. 275.

Boston Globe, December 13, 1985, p. 79; March 30, 1989, p. 78; October 8, 1990, p. 67; September 13, 1992, p. 106; December 13, 1992, p. B40; July 31, 1994, p. B25; October 1, 2003, Donna Seaman, review of *Oracle Night,* p. 275.

Chicago Tribune, January 28, 1993, sec. 5, p. 3.

Contemporary Literature, Volume 33, 1992, pp. 1-23.

Critique, January 1, 2003, Robert Briggs, "Wrong Numbers: The Endless Fiction of Auster and Deleuze," pp. 213-224.

Daily Telegraph (London, England), October 5, 2002, Justin Cartwright, review of *The Book of Illusions,* p. NA.

Entertainment Weekly, May 28, 1999, review of *Timbuktu,* p. 138; December 14, 2001, "The Week," p. 78; November 28, 2003, Troy Patterson, review of *Oracle Night,* p. 131.

Esquire, August, 1994, p. 123; September, 2002, Adrienne Miller, review of *The Book of Illusions,* p. 78.

Europe Intelligence Wire, October 12, 2002, Nicholas Lezard, review of *True Tales of American Life;* October 26, 2002, Hadley Freeman, profile of Auster.

Globe and Mail (Toronto, Ontario, Canada), March 14, 1987.

Guardian, December 8, 2001, Ian Sansom, review of *I Thought My Father Was God,* p. 10; September 28, 2002, Anthony Quinn, review of *The Book of Illusions,* p. 28; October 12, 2002, Nicholas Lezard, review of *I Thought My Father Was God,* p. 30; October 26, 2002, Hadley Freeman, profile of Auster, p. 20.

Houston Chronicle, December 22, 2002, Steven E. Alford, review of *The Book of Illusions,* p. 21.

Interview, April, 1989, p. 18.

Kirkus Reviews, September 15, 1985, p. 957; June 1, 1986, p. 822; December 15, 1986, p. 1812; January 1, 1987, p. 3; December 15, 1988, p. 1755; August 1, 1990, p. 1020; June 15, 1992, p. 732; July 1, 2002, review of *The Book of Illusions,* p. 896; September 15, 2003, review of *Oracle Night,* pp. 1137-1139.

Kliatt, July 1, 2003, review of *I Thought My Father Was God,* p. 4.

Knight Ridder/Tribune News Service, October 31, 2001, p. K6780.

Library Journal, May 15, 1999, Mirela Roncevic, review of *Timbuktu,* p. 123; October 1, 2000, Debora Miller, review of *Double Game,* p. 86; August, 2001, Mary Pammier Jones, review of *I Thought My Father Was God,* p. 107; August, 2002, Mirela Roncevic, review of *The Book of Illusions,* p. 138; September 1, 2002, "Ten Books for Fall," pp. 48-52; June 1, 2003, Michael Adams, review of *The Book of Illusions,* p. 184.

Los Angeles Times, September 1, 1986; March 2, 1987, p. V4; June 18, 1987, p. V10; March 30, 1989, p. V21; June 27, 1999, Jonathan Levi, review of *Timbuktu.*

Los Angeles Times Book Review, November 17, 1985; October 21, 1990, pp. 2, 8; October 4, 1992, p. 2; July 31, 1994, p. 2.

Maclean's, October 16, 1995, p. 83; May 14, 2001, p. 64.

Mosaic, March, 2000, Eyal Dotan, review of *The Music of Chance,* p. 161.

Nation, November 20, 1982; July 10, 1995, p. 69.

National Review, July 26, 1999, James Gardner, review of *Timbuktu,* p. 57.

New Republic, March 27, 1989, p. 36; June 26, 1995, p. 28.

New Statesman, January 22, 1988, p. 33; March 22, 1991, p. 45; April 8, 1994, p. 37; April 19, 1996, p. 33; June 21, 1999, Toby Mundy, review of *Timbuktu,* p. 49; July 24, 2000, Frances Gilbert, "Real Presence," p. 59; October 14, 2002, Toby Mundy, review of *The Book of Illusions,* p. 50.

Newsweek, September 5, 1994; May 24, 1999, review of *Timbuktu,* p. 74; October 14, 2002, Toby Mindy, "Staring at the Sun," p. 50; November 24, 2003, Susannah Meadows, "Books: What's German for Best Seller?," p. 18.

New Yorker, December 30, 1985; July 18, 1994, p. 25; October 23, 1995, p. 98.

New York Review of Books, August 17, 1989, p. 52; January 17, 1991, p. 31; December 3, 1992, pp. 14, 16.

New York Times, March 7, 1989, p. C19; October 2, 1990, p. C15; September 8, 1992, p. C14; September 1, 2002, D. T. Max, review of *The Book of Illusions,* p. L6.

New York Times Book Review, January 23, 1983; February 27, 1983; January 15, 1984; November 3, 1985; May 25, 1986; June 29, 1986, Rebecca Goldstein, review of *Ghosts,* p. 13; January 4, 1987, p. 14; May 17, 1987, p. 11; March 19, 1989, pp. 8-9; November 4, 1990, p. 15; September 20, 1992, p. 9; August 28, 1994, p. 12; October 2, 1994, p. 32; September 15, 2002, "And Bear in Mind," p. 26; January 5, 2003, Diane Cole, "Masters of the Keyboard," p. 17.

New York Times Magazine, August 30, 1992, p. 41.

Nieman Reports, spring, 2002, Andrew Sussman, review of *I Thought My Father Was God,* p. 81.

Publishers Weekly, March 8, 1999, review of *Timbuktu* p. 45, review of *The Station Hill Blanchot Reader,* p. 58; June 4, 2001, review of *I Thought My Father Was God,* p. 65; January 7, 2002, review of *I Thought My Father Was God,* p. 22; May 27, 2002, review of *The Red Notebook,* p. 34; August 26, 2002, review of *The Book of Illusions,* pp. 42-43, and Tim Peters, interview with Auster, p. 42; October 7, 2002, review of *The Story of My Typewriter,* p. 66; November 10, 2003, review of *Oracle Night,* p. 42.

Review of Contemporary Fiction, spring, 1994, pp. 30-87; fall, 1999, Thomas Hove, review of *Timbuktu,* p. 171; March 22, 2003, Vallerie Ellis, review of *The Red Notebook,* p. 164; June 22, 2003, Thomas Hove, review of *The Book of Illusions,* p. 125.

Rolling Stone, October 5, 1995, p. 77.

San Francisco Chronicle, September 16, 2001, Adair Lara, review of *I Thought My Father Was God,* p. 69; September 16, 2002, James Sullivan, interview with Auster, p. 68.

Smithsonian, October 1, 2001, Donald Dale Jackson, review of *I Thought My Father Was God,* p. 136.

Spectator, October 5, 2002, Miranda France, review of *The Book of Illusions,* p. 43.

Sunday Telegraph (London, England), October 6, 2002, Christopher Taylor, review of *The Book of Illusions.*

Sunday Times (London, England), October 20, 2002, Maggie Gee, review of *The Book of Illusions,* p. 46.

Time, September 5, 1994, p. 76.

Times (London, England), October 2, 2002, Erica Wagner, review of *The Book of Illusions,* p. 17.

Times Literary Supplement, August 30, 1985; October 23, 1992, p. 20.

Tribune Books (Chicago, IL), March 29, 1987, p. 3; March 19, 1989, p. 4; November 4, 1990, p. 5; November 1, 1992, p. 5; September 4, 1994, p. 4.

USA Today, March 17, 1989, p. D4; October 14, 1992, p. D7.

Variety, May 5, 2003, Steven Kotler, "Paul Aster's Judgment Days: Zeus Has Olympus, Odin Had Valhalla, and, for a Short While, the Novelist Had Cannes," pp. S26-S27.

Vogue, August, 1994, p. 158.

Wall Street Journal, September 21, 1990, p. A12; September 15, 1992, p. A14.

Washington Post, October 10, 1990, p. D2.

Washington Post Book World, December 5, 1982; June 15, 1986; March 29, 1987; March 26, 1989, p. 3; September 6, 1992, p. 5; August 28, 1994, p. 3.

World Literature Today, spring, 1995.

ONLINE

Paul Auster's Official Web site, http://www.paulauster.co.uk/ (November 17, 2003).*

B

BACHE, Ellyn 1942-
(E. M. J. Benjamin, Ellen Matthews)

PERSONAL: Surname rhymes with the letter "h"; born January 22, 1942, in Washington, DC; daughter of Herman (a musician) and Clara (Winik) Olefsky; married Terry Bache (a builder), 1969 (deceased); children: Beth, Matt, James, Ben. *Education:* University of North Carolina—Chapel Hill, B.A., 1964; University of Maryland—College Park, M.A., 1967. *Religion:* Jewish.

ADDRESSES: *Agent*—Jonathan Dolger, Jonathan Dolger Agency, 49 East 96th St., Suite 9B, New York, NY 10128.

CAREER: Freelance writer.

MEMBER: Authors Guild, Authors League of America, North Carolina Writers' Network.

AWARDS, HONORS: Willa Cather Fiction Prize, 1992, for *The Value of Kindness.*

WRITINGS:

Ellyn Bache

(Under pseudonym Ellen Matthews) *Culture Clash* (nonfiction), Intercultural Press (Yarmouth, ME), 1982, revised edition, under name Ellyn Bache, 1989.

Safe Passage (novel), Crown (New York, NY), 1988.

Festival in Fire Season (novel), August House (Little Rock, AR), 1992.

The Value of Kindness (short stories), Helicon Nine (Kansas City, MO), 1993.

The Activist's Daughter (novel), Spinster's Ink (Denver, CO), 1997.

(Under pseudonym E. M. J. Benjamin; with husband, Terry Bache) *Takedown* (young adult novel), Banks Channel Books (Wilmington, NC), 1999.

Holiday Miracles: A Christmas/Hanukkah Story (novella), Banks Channel Books (Wilmington, NC), 2001.

Daddy and the Pink Flash (children's picture book), Banks Channel Books (Wilmington, NC), 2002.

(Author of book, with Joyce Cooper and Patricia Ruark) *Writers Bloc* (musical comedy for the stage), first produced in Wilmington, NC, by Thalian Association, 2003.

Contributor of short stories, articles, and reviews to magazines and newspapers, including *McCall's, Seventeen, YM, Good Housekeeping, Shenandoah, New Letters,* and *Washington Post.* Editor of *Antietam Review,* 1983-85; books editor of *Encore,* 1986-89.

ADAPTATIONS: The novel *Safe Passage* was adapted as a film, written by Deena Goldstone, directed by Robert Allan Ackerman, produced by Gale Anne Hurd, and starring Susan Sarandon and Sam Shepard, released by New Line Cinema in 1995.

WORK IN PROGRESS: A novel of women's friendships, set partly in North Carolina and partly in Washington, DC.

SIDELIGHTS: Ellyn Bache once told *CA:* "I started out as a freelance journalist for the *Washington Post* and *Washington Star,* working from home while our children were small. My first book was *Culture Clash,* a journal about sponsoring Vietnamese refugees, but after that I concentrated on fiction. It took six years before my first short story was published in *McCall's*—a great breakthrough for me.

"It's important to me that my novels be 'about' something. *Festival in Fire Season* is on the surface about a wildfire that threatens a southern coastal town during its azalea festival, but it also deals with race relations in the late 1980s. *The Activist's Daughter,* a coming-of-age story about a girl who comes south in 1963 to go to the University of North Carolina, is about the social conditions of that time, for minorities and women and the handicapped."

More recently Bache added: "I wrote my first novel, *Safe Passage,* after our youngest child was in school all day. It's about a family back home waiting to hear the fate of a son/brother who's a Marine in Beirut when the airport there is bombed by terrorists in 1983. It was published in 1988, but sadly became timely again after September 11, 2001. During the 2003 war in Iraq, the 1995 movie version, starring Susan Sarandon and Sam Shepard, was on television almost all night. Yet the book is really a domestic drama about maternal guilt. ('I'm doing something for myself; therefore, I must be neglecting my children, and I'm going to be punished by having something terrible happen to one of them.') I've always thought this accounted for the book being made into a film. The agent and screenwriter and producer were all mothers with busy careers, feeling neglectful of their children. Even Susan Sarandon had the babysitter bring her youngest to the set and insisted she be finished by Easter vacation, so she could take her children skiing.

"*Takedown,* which is one of my favorite books because I wrote it with my late husband, is about a high school wrestler with epilepsy who uses lessons learned from sports to get control of his life. *Holiday Miracles* tries to show the challenges interfaith families face every December. Even my one and only children's picture book, *Daddy and the Pink Flash,* is about how dads help their baby girls learn how brave and smart and capable they are.

"I always want the underlying themes to be serious, but it's important that the work itself be entertaining—funny or suspenseful or gripping in some other way—and not ponderous. When reviewers called *The Activist's Daughter* 'riveting' and *Holiday Miracles* 'deeply moving,' this was very reassuring to me, because it made me feel I was achieving what I was after."

BIOGRAPHICAL AND CRITICAL SOURCES:

PERIODICALS

Belles Lettres: Review of Books by Women, fall, 1988.

New York Times Book Review, January 22, 1989.

Publishers Weekly, September 24, 2001, Jana Riess, review of *Holiday Miracles: A Christmas/Hanukkah Story,* p. 59.

ONLINE

Welcome to Ellyn Bache Home Page, http://www.ellynbache.com/ (February 24, 2004).

* * *

BAKER, Alan 1951-

PERSONAL: Born November 14, 1951, in London, England; son of Bernard Victor (a welder) and Barbara Joan (a tracer; maiden name, Weir) Baker; divorced. *Education:* Attended Croydon Technical College, 1969-71, Hull University, 1971-72, and Croydon Art College, 1972-73; Brighton Art College, B.A. (honours), 1976. *Politics:* Green. *Religion:* Agnostic. *Hobbies and other interests:* Music, waking.

ADDRESSES: Home and office—St. Michaels, Telscombe Village, near Lewes, East Sussex BN7 3HZ, England. *E-mail*—info@alanbakeronline.com.

CAREER: Author and freelance illustrator of children's books. Part-time teacher of illustration at Northbrook College.

AWARDS, HONORS: Whitbread Award and Carnegie Medal commendation, both 1978, both for *The Battle of Bubble and Squeak,* written by Ann Philippa Pearce; Silver Award, Campaign Press Awards, 1990; Gold Award, Creative Circle Awards, 1990; Children's Choice selection, International Reading Association/ Children's Book Council, 1996, for *Gray Rabbit's Odd One Out;* several of Baker's works have been selected for annual "Best Books" commendations.

WRITINGS:

FOR CHILDREN; SELF-ILLUSTRATED

Benjamin and the Box, Lippincott (Philadelphia, PA), 1977.

Benjamin Bounces Back, Lippincott (Philadelphia, PA), 1978.

Benjamin's Dreadful Dream, Lippincott (Philadelphia, PA), 1980.

Alan Baker

Benjamin's Book, Lothrop (New York, NY), 1982.

A Fairyland Alphabet, Deutsch (London, England), 1984.

Benjamin's Portrait, Lothrop (New York, NY), 1986.

One Naughty Boy, Deutsch (London, England), 1989.

Goodnight William, Deutsch (London, England), 1990.

Benjamin's Balloon, Lothrop (New York, NY), 1990.

Two Tiny Mice, Kingfisher (London, England), 1990, Dial (New York, NY), 1991.

Jason's Dragon, BBC Publications (London, England), 1992.

Where's Mouse?, Kingfisher (New York, NY), 1992.

Black and White Rabbit's ABC (also see below), Kingfisher (New York, NY), 1994.

Brown Rabbit's Shape Book (also see below), Kingfisher (New York, NY), 1994.

Gray Rabbit's 1, 2, 3 (also see below), Kingfisher (New York, NY), 1994.

White Rabbit's Colour Book, Kingfisher (London, England), 1994, published as *White Rabbit's Color Book* (also see below), Kingfisher (New York, NY), 1994.

Brown Rabbit's Day, Kingfisher (New York, NY), 1995.

Gray Rabbit's Odd One Out, Kingfisher (New York, NY), 1995.

Little Rabbit's First Word Book, Kingfisher (New York, NY), 1996.

Mouse's Christmas, Copper Beach Books (Brookfield, CT), 1996.

I Thought I Heard: A Book of Nighttime Noises, Aladdin (London, England), Copper Beach Books (Brookfield, CT), 1996.

Little Rabbit's Play and Learn Book (contains *White Rabbit's Color Book, Gray Rabbit's 1, 2, 3, Black and White Rabbit's ABC,* and *Brown Rabbit's Shape Book*), Kingfisher (New York, NY), 1997.

Mouse's Halloween, Copper Beach Books (Brookfield, CT), 1997.

Little Rabbit's Snack Time, Kingfisher (New York, NY), 1998.

Little Rabbit's Bedtime, Kingfisher (New York, NY), 1998.

Little Rabbit's Tell the Time Book, Kingfisher (London, England), published as *Little Rabbit's First Time Book,* Kingfisher (New York, NY), 1999.

Little Rabbit's Picture Word Book, Kingfisher (London, England), 1999.

Look Who Lives in the Ocean, Macdonald (Hove, England), 1998, Bedrick (New York, NY), 1999.

Look Who Lives in the Rain Forest, Macdonald (Hove, England), 1998, Bedrick (New York, NY), 1999.

Look Who Lives in the Arctic, Macdonald (Hove, England), Bedrick (New York, NY), 1999.

Look Who Lives in the Desert, Macdonald (Hove, England), Bedrick (New York, NY), 1999.

Little Rabbit's First Farm Book, Kingfisher (New York, NY), 2001.

ILLUSTRATOR

Ann Philippa Pearce, *The Battle of Bubble and Squeak,* Deutsch (London, England), 1978.

Eleanor Bourne, *Heritage of Flowers,* Hutchinson (London, England), 1980.

Deirdre Headon, *Mythical Beasts,* Hutchinson (London, England), 1981.

Rudyard Kipling, *The Butterfly That Stamped,* Macmillan (London, England), Bedrick (New York, NY), 1982.

Kate Petty, *Snakes,* F. Watts (New York, NY), 1984.

Kate Petty, *Dinosaurs,* F. Watts (New York, NY), 1984.

Kate Petty, *Frogs and Toads,* F. Watts (New York, NY), 1985.

Kate Petty, *Spiders,* F. Watts (New York, NY), 1985.

Michael Rosen, *Hairy Tales and Nursery Crimes,* Deutsch (London, England), 1985.

Gene Kemp, *Mr. Magus Is Waiting for You,* Faber (London, England), 1986.

Robin Lister, reteller, *The Odyssey,* Kingfisher (London, England), 1987, Doubleday (New York, NY), 1988.

Robin Lister, reteller, *The Story of King Arthur,* Kingfisher (London, England), 1988.

Verna Wilkins, *Mike and Lottie,* Tamarind (London, England), 1988, Child's Play (New York, NY), 1993.

Judith Nicholls, *Wordspells,* Faber (London, England), 1988.

Judith Nicholls, *What on Earth?: Poems with a Conservation Theme,* Faber (London, England), 1989.

Jill Bailey, *Gorilla Rescue,* Steck-Vaughn (Austin, TX), 1990.

Jill Bailey, *Mission Rhino,* Steck-Vaughn (Austin, TX), 1990.

Jill Bailey, *Project Panda,* Steck-Vaughn (Austin, TX), 1990.

Jill Bailey, *Save the Tiger,* Steck-Vaughn (Austin, TX), 1990.

Michael Rosen, *Mini Beasties,* Firefly (London, England), 1991, Carolrhoda (Minneapolis, MN), 1992.

Kate Petty, *Stop, Look and Listen, Mr. Toad!,* Barron's (New York, NY), 1991.

Kate Petty, *Mr. Toad to the Rescue,* Barron's (Hauppauge, NY), 1992.

Joni Mitchell, *Both Sides Now,* Scholastic (New York, NY), 1992.

Kate Petty, *Mr. Toad's Narrow Escapes,* Barron's (Hauppauge, NY), 1992.

Gloria Patrick, *A Bug in a Jug and Other Funny Rhymes,* D. C. Heath (Lexington, MA), 1993.

Jill Bennett, *Sorry for the Slug,* Heinemann (London, England), 1994.

Dan Abnett, *Treasure Hunt in the Creepy Mansion,* Salamander (London, England), 1995.

Dan Abnett, *Treasure Hunt in the Lost City,* Salamander (London, England), 1996.

Judy Allen, *Hedgehog in the Garden,* Leopard, 1996.

Fit-a-Shape: Animals; Colors; Opposites; Shapes; Bugs; Patterns; Cloths; Numbers, Running Press (Philadelphia, PA), 1996.

Anita Ganeri, reteller, *Dragons and Monsters,* Macdonald (Hove, England), 1996.

Kate Petty, *Little Rabbit's First Number Book,* Kingfisher (New York, NY), 1998.

Louis De Bernieres, *Red Dog,* Pantheon (New York, NY), 2001.

David Stewart, *Seasons,* F. Watts (New York, NY), 2002.

Dawn Allette, *Caribbean Animals,* Tamarind (London, England), 2004.

Contributor of illustrations to *Creatures Great and Small,* written by Michael Gabb, Lerner (Minneapolis, MN), 1980.

ADAPTATIONS: Benjamin and the Box was featured on the Canadian Broadcasting Corporation (CBC-TV) series *The Friendly Giant,* in March and April of 1980, and on British and Norwegian television.

WORK IN PROGRESS: Three children's books.

SIDELIGHTS: Alan Baker is an English author/illustrator who is best known for his "Rabbits" series of picture books for preschoolers. Baker favors pen-and-ink drawings that depict animals in meticulous detail. At the same time, critics note that his mice, hamsters, and rabbits appeal to youngsters because they have young and beguiling expressions themselves. This is particularly the case in the "Rabbits" series, where bunnies of different hues introduce concepts such as the alphabet, color, shape, and telling time. Another popular Baker work is the "Look Who Lives In" series, in which readers discover interesting animals and plants from various ecosystems. Some commentators contend that Baker's simple texts are merely a vehicle for his extravagant illustrations. Though the visual element often takes precedence in Baker's work, "I like to think of the writing as adding a further dimension to the illustrations," Baker once commented. "The words hold the story line when the idea cannot be illustrated."

In *Benjamin and the Box,* Baker introduces preschoolers to a hapless, nearsighted, persistent little hamster named Benjamin, a character based on a pet from Baker's childhood. In this first book, Benjamin comes upon a box, which he persistently tries to open, using tools, magic spells, and even dynamite. "It was love at first meeting," a reviewer for *Publishers Weekly* declared of *Benjamin and the Box.* In *Benjamin Bounces Back,* the nearsighted Benjamin fails to read the "NO ENTRY" sign on a door, and reluctantly embarks on a series of wild adventures after he pushes through the forbidden entrance. *Benjamin's Dreadful Dream* similarly finds the accident-prone hamster inadvertently touching off a pile of fireworks that blasts him into outer space, when all he really wanted was a midnight snack. "The tenuous story is clearly an excuse for the sparkling illustrations," observed a reviewer for *Junior Bookshelf,* but a *Publishers Weekly* critic maintained that "charmed readers won't forget this larky escapade."

The same brightly colored, realistically detailed illustrations characterize the other stories about Benjamin, including *Benjamin's Book,* in which the hamster accidentally puts a paw print on a clean sheet of paper. In his increasingly frantic attempts to repair the damage, the page gets ever messier, until Benjamin replaces the sheet altogether, but accidentally marks it with another paw print as he leaves. "This is visually appealing, has a quiet humor, and tells a story that's just right in length, scope, and familiarity for the preschool child," noted Zena Sutherland in the *Bulletin of the Center for Children's Books. Benjamin's Portrait* finds the determined hamster attempting a self-portrait after going to a portrait gallery. "Preschoolers will identify with Benjamin's eagerness to try things for himself, as well as his encounters with unexpected troubles," remarked Susan Nemeth McCarthy in *School Library Journal.* Benjamin flies off under the power of a purple balloon in *Benjamin's Balloon,* which *Growing Point*'s Margery Fisher called a "gentle and congenial comedy."

Baker's other recurring animal characters include a number of rabbits featured in some highly regarded concept books that teach very young children about shapes, colors, letters, and numbers. Invariably, critics found that Baker's concept books give a fresh twist to familiar themes. *Black and White Rabbit's ABC* starts with an apple, as many alphabet books do, but then is transformed as a black-and-white rabbit enters the picture and attempts to paint the apple, beginning the reader on "a wry and often very messy journey from A to Z," according to a *Publishers Weekly* reviewer. *Brown Rabbit's Shape Book* features balloons of different shapes, and *White Rabbit's Color Book* is "perhaps the best book of the bunch," according to Ilene Cooper in *Booklist.* In *White Rabbit's Color Book,* a white rabbit falls into a series of paint cans, demonstrating how primary colors mix to become other colors. Throughout each of these concept books, a *Publishers Weekly* critic noted, "sweet-natured humor infuses the clear, precise artwork."

Baker's subsequent "Rabbit" titles are also distinguished by a gently humorous text and striking illustrations combined with a unique slant on a learning concept. In *Brown Rabbit's Day,* a simple story offers the opportunity for color and object identification, counting, and telling time. In *Gray Rabbit's Odd One Out,* preschoolers help Gray Rabbit find his favorite book while learning to sort objects according to a variety of schemes. *Little Rabbit's First Farm Book* takes Rabbit to a farm, where he participates in the chores and meets the resident animals. A *Publishers Weekly* reviewer felt that the title "is perfect for preschoolers."

Baker introduces his readers to animals common to the English forest through which his little heroes travel in *Two Tiny Mice,* another self-illustrated picture book. A *Kirkus Reviews* critic singled out Baker's "expansive, delicately detailed illustrations" for special mention in a review of this work. Introducing animals also forms the basis for Baker's story *Where's Mouse?,* in which Mother Mouse questions one forest animal after another in her search for Baby Mouse. *Where's Mouse?* has accordion-fold pages whose holes give the illusion of three-dimensionality to the illustrations, which *School Library Journal* contributor Christine A. Moesch praised as "delicate and cleverly laid out." Baker employs a similar format in *Mouse's Christmas,* in which Mouse's friends plan a surprise party for him on Christmas Eve.

The "Look Who Lives In" series introduces early readers to the plants and animals in some of the world's more extreme ecosystems. The books offer teasers in which each page shows an animal and hints at the animal on the next page, too. In a *Science Books and Film* review of *Look Who Lives in the Rain Forest,* Michele H. Lee declared that "young children will enjoy guessing the animals' identities" in this "delightful book." A *Kirkus Reviews* critic likewise found *Look Who Lives in the Rain Forest* to be "a good introduction to a habitat" often studied by young students.

Baker's illustrations are acclaimed for their fine detail and for the humor they add to the author's simple tales. According to reviewers, Baker perfected this combination in his popular "Benjamin" series. "Even when one sees only [Benjamin's] feet encased in a snowball, the comic character of the furry creature is unmistakable," remarked Lori A. Janick in *School Library Journal.* Although some critics have found Baker's plots meager, especially when compared to his arresting artwork, reviewers of such concept books as *Gray Rabbit's 1, 2, 3* and *White Rabbit's Color Book* felt that Baker's plots were suitable for holding the attention of his preschool audience. *School Library Journal* contributor Marsha McGrath avowed that Baker's books are "instructional titles that are lots of fun for prereaders."

BIOGRAPHICAL AND CRITICAL SOURCES:

PERIODICALS

Booklist, July, 1994, Ilene Cooper, review of *Black and White Rabbit's ABC, Brown Rabbit's Shape Book,* and *White Rabbit's Color Book,* p. 1952; December 1, 1999, Kathy Broderick, review of *Little Rabbit's First Time Book,* p. 708; November 15, 2001, Ilene Cooper, review of *Little Rabbit's First Farm Book,* p. 580.

Bulletin of the Center for Children's Books, July, 1983, Zena Sutherland, review of *Benjamin's Book,* p. 202.

Growing Point, January, 1978, Margery Fisher, review of *Benjamin and the Box,* p. 3251; November, 1982, Margery Fisher, review of *Benjamin's Book,* p. 3990; March, 1991, Margery Fisher, review of *Benjamin's Balloon,* p. 5486.

Junior Bookshelf, June, 1978, review of *Benjamin and the Box,* p. 133; April, 1979, review of *Benjamin Bounces Back,* p. 91; October, 1980, review of *Benjamin's Dreadful Dream,* p. 232.

Kirkus Reviews, June 15, 1980, review of *Benjamin's Dreadful Dream,* p. 773; May 1, 1991, review of *Two Tiny Mice,* p. 611; December 1, 1992, review of *Where's Mouse?,* p. 1500; June 15, 1999, review of *Look Who Lives in the Rain Forest,* p. 960.

Publishers Weekly, February 27, 1978, review of *Benjamin and the Box;* December 11, 1978, review of *Benjamin Bounces Back,* p. 70; review of *Benjamin's Dreadful Dream,* p. 340; November 23, 1992, review of *Where's Mouse?,* p. 61; March 7, 1994, review of *Gray Rabbit's 1, 2, 3, Black and White Rabbit's ABC, Brown Rabbit's Shape Book,* and *White Rabbit's Color Book,* p. 68;

September 30, 1996, review of *Mouse's Christmas,* p. 90; November 12, 2001, review of *Little Rabbit's First Farm Book,* p. 61.

School Library Journal, May, 1987, Susan Nemeth McCarthy, review of *Benjamin's Portrait,* p. 81; December, 1990, Lori A. Janick, review of *Benjamin's Balloon,* p. 70; February, 1993, Christine A. Moesch, review of *Where's Mouse?,* p. 68; Marsha McGrath, March, 1996, review of *Brown Rabbit's Day* and *Gray Rabbit's Odd One Out,* p. 166; February, 2002, Carolyn Janssen, review of *Little Rabbit's First Farm Book,* p. 96.

Science Books and Film, September, 1999, Michele H. Lee, review of *Look Who Lives in the Rain Forest,* p. 220.

* * *

BATAILLE, Christophe 1971-

PERSONAL: Born October 14, 1971, in Versailles, France; son of Alain and Edith Bataille; married Maguelone Fallot, September 14, 1996. *Ethnicity:* "French." *Religion:* Christian.

ADDRESSES: *Home*—19-21 rue Dumoncel, 75014 Paris, France. *Office*—Éditions Grasset et Fasquelle, 61 rue des Saints-Pères, 75006 Paris, France; fax: 01-42-226-418. *E-mail*—cbataille@edition-grasset.fr.

CAREER: Fiction writer. Éditions Grasset et Fasquelle, Paris, France, member of editorial staff.

AWARDS, HONORS: Winner of the Prix du Premier Roman, 1993, for *Annam,* 1993.

WRITINGS:

Annam (novel), Arlea (Paris, France), 1993, translation by Richard Howard published as *Annam,* New Directions (New York, NY), 1996.

Absinthe (novel), Arlea (Paris, France), 1994, translation by Richard Howard published as *Absinthe,* Northwestern University Press (Evanston, IL), 1999.

Le Maitre des Heures, Arlea (Paris, France), 1997.

Christophe Bataille

Vive l'enfer (fiction), Éditions Grasset at Fasquelle (Paris, France), 1999.

J'envie la Félicité des Bêtes, Éditions Grasset at Fasquelle (Paris, France), 2002.

SIDELIGHTS: Christophe Bataille's first novel, *Annam,* published when he was only twenty-one, received the prestigious French Prix du Premier Roman (first novel prize) in 1993, establishing him as an important writer. In the United States, where it was published three years later in a translation by poet Richard Howard, it also met with literary acclaim.

The novel dramatizes key elements of one of France's earliest official involvements with Vietnam, more than fifty years in advance of its colonization of Saigon. In 1787 the emperor of Vietnam, a boy of seven named Canh, travels to France to beg Louis XVI for help in the form of soldiers and missionaries. The French king denies Canh's request for aid, and before long both Canh and Louis XVI are dead: Canh from pneumonia and Louis guillotined, along with many other members of the French aristocracy, in the bloody French Revolution. Although Canh's plea for help falls on deaf ears within the French court, it has been heard by a retired bishop who is inspired to spread the teachings of Christ among the Vietnamese. Two ships embark to Vietnam in 1789, loaded not only with Dominican missionaries, but with soldiers whose objective it is to aid Prince Regent Nguyen Anh, an expatriate now living in Siam, in his bid to regain leadership of his homeland.

Those missionaries who survive the voyage and the diseases of the jungle fulfill their purpose of claiming souls, while at the same time establishing parishes, constructing dikes, and teaching the French language to the natives. Back in France the revolution takes heads and reconfigures French government, law, and history to the cry of "Liberty, Equality, Fraternity!"—with little attention toward this small Vietnamese mission. France's effort to support Nguyen Anh's return to power (and their support for the missionaries) dwindles and dies. When Nguyen Anh finally comes to power through his own efforts in 1800, he decides to take revenge on the French for betraying their original alliance. He orders that all the French Dominican monks and nuns be put to death. Only one monk and one nun escape murder, protected by the remoteness of the tiny mountain enclave they inhabit with its Vietnamese villagers. Gradually, their distance from the land and church that sent them and from other Christian clergy results in the weakening of their religious vows until they become much like the villagers they had once sought to convert.

The reception of the English translation of Bataille's novel echoed the enthusiasm the book met in its original French version. A *Publishers Weekly* contributor applauded both the writer and the excellent translation. Bataille's *Annam,* the reviewer commented, is "built around short sentences [and] achieves a cumulative lyricism that poignantly captures the unfulfilled promise and tragedy of the period of colonial history it depicts." In a similarly appreciative response, Ray Olson, writing for *Booklist,* noted the novel's "elegant" minimalism and its resultant emotional depth. A contributor to *Kirkus Reviews* described the novel as "skillfully understated" and the translation "beautiful." A number of reviewers pointed out that Bataille published the acclaimed novel at the young age of twenty-one.

BIOGRAPHICAL AND CRITICAL SOURCES:

PERIODICALS

Booklist, September 15, 1996, Ray Olson, review of *Annam,* p. 218.

Chicago Review, spring, 2000, Ihor Junyk, review of *Absinthe,* p. 109.

Kirkus Reviews, August 1, 1996, review of *Annam,* p. 1095.

Publishers Weekly, August 5, 1996, review of *Annam,* p. 432.

* * *

BEISNER, Robert L(ee) 1936-

PERSONAL: Born March 8, 1936, in Lexington, NE; son of E. J. and Charlene (Day) Beisner; married Mary Elizabeth Brinton Stone, June 14, 1959 (divorced, March, 1976); married Valerie French, 1976; children: John, Katharine. *Education:* Attended Hastings College, 1954-56; University of Chicago, M.A., 1960, Ph. D., 1965.

ADDRESSES: Home—3704 35th St. NW, Washington, DC 20016. *Office*—Department of History, American University, Massachusetts and Nebraska Aves. NW, Washington, DC 20016.

CAREER: University of Chicago, Chicago, IL, instructor in social sciences, 1962-63; Colgate University, Hamilton, NY, instructor in history, 1963-65; American University, Washington, DC, assistant professor, 1965-67, associate professor, 1967-71, professor of history, beginning 1971.

MEMBER: American Historical Association, Society of American Historians, Organization of American Historians, Society for Historians of American Foreign Relations, Academy of Political Science, Southern Historical Association, Phi Beta Kappa.

AWARDS, HONORS: Allan Nevins Prize, Society of American Historians, 1966, and John H. Dunning Prize, American Historical Association, 1968, both for thesis, "The Anti-imperialist Impulse: The Mugwumps and the Republicans, 1898-1900"; National Endowment for the Humanities, fellowship, 1968-69, and summer research stipend, 1976.

WRITINGS:

Twelve against Empire: The Anti-imperialists, 1898-1900, McGraw-Hill (New York, NY), 1968, reprinted with new foreword, Imprint (Chicago, IL), 1992, reprinted with new preface, University of Chicago Press (Chicago, IL), 1985.

From the Old Diplomacy to the New, 1865-1900, AHM Publishing (Northbrook, IL), 1975, 2nd edition, Harlan Davidson (Arlington Heights, IL), 1986.

(Editor, with Joan R. Challinor) *Arms at Rest: Peacemaking and Peacekeeping in American History,* Greenwood Press (New York, NY), 1987.

(Editor, with Kurt Hanson) *American Foreign Relations since 1600: A Guide to the Literature,* two volumes, 2nd edition, American Bibliographical Center-Clio Press (Santa Barbara, CA), 2003.

BIOGRAPHICAL AND CRITICAL SOURCES:

PERIODICALS

American Heritage, August, 1968.

Encounter, winter, 1969.

Library Journal, July, 2003, Marcia L. Sprules, review of *American Foreign Relations since 1600: A Guide to the Literature,* p. 71.

New Republic, January 25, 1969.

New York Times Book Review, April 7, 1968.

Washington Post Book World, August 4, 1968.*

* * *

BENJAMIN, E. M. J.
See BACHE, Ellyn

* * *

BINGHAM, Charlotte (Mary Therese) 1942-

PERSONAL: Born June 29, 1942, in Haywards Heath, Sussex, England; daughter of John Michael Ward (seventh baron of Clanmorris and a writer of crime stories) and Madeleine (a writer; maiden name, Ebel) Bingham; married Terence Joseph Brady (an actor and writer), January 15, 1964; children: Candida, Matthew. *Education:* Attended Sorbonne, University of Paris, 1959-60. *Politics:* Liberal. *Religion:* Roman Catholic.

ADDRESSES: Home—Hardway House, Brutow, Somerset, England. *Agent*—A. D. Peters and Co. Ltd., 10 Buckingham St., London WC2N 6BU, England. *E-mail*—charlotte@charlottebingham.com.

CAREER: Playwright, novelist, and writer for television series.

MEMBER: Writers Guild of Great Britain.

AWARDS, HONORS: Best Romantic Novel Award, Romantic Novelists Association, 1996.

WRITINGS:

Coronet among the Weeds (autobiographical; also see below), Random House (New York, NY), 1963.

Lucinda (novel), Heinemann (London, England), 1966.

Coronet among the Grass (autobiographical; also see below), Heinemann (London, England), 1972.

No, Honestly! (contains *Coronet among the Weeds* and *Coronet among the Grass*), Penguin (London, England), 1974.

Belgravia, M. Joseph (London, England), 1983.

Country Life, M. Joseph (London, England), 1985.

To Hear a Nightingale, St. Martin's Press (New York, NY), 1988.

The Business, M. Joseph (London, England), 1989.

Nanny, Doubleday (New York, NY), 1993.

Debutantes, Doubleday (New York, NY), 1995.

The Nightingale Sings, Bantam (New York, NY), 1996.

Kissing Garden, Bantam (New York, NY), 1999.

The Love Knot, Bantam (New York, NY), 2000.

The Blue Note, Doubleday (New York, NY), 2000.

The Season, Bantam (New York, NY), 2001.

Summertime, Doubleday (New York, NY), 2001.

Distant Music, Doubleday (New York, NY), 2002.

The Chestnut Tree, St. Martin's Press (New York, NY), 2003.

The Wind off the Sea, Transworld Publishers (London, England), 2003, Thomas Dunne Books (New York, NY), 2004.

WITH HUSBAND, TERENCE BRADY

Rose's Story (novel), Sphere Books (London, England), 1972, Pocket Books (New York, NY), 1975.
Victoria (novel), W. H. Allen (London, England), 1972.
Victoria and Company (novel), W. H. Allen (London, England), 1974.
Yes, Honestly, Sphere Books (London, England), 1977.

SCRIPTS FOR TELEVISION SERIES; WITH TERENCE BRADY

Take Three Girls, British Broadcasting Corp. (BBC-TV), 1968-71.
(With others) *Upstairs, Downstairs,* LWTV, 1971-73.
No, Honestly!, LWTV, 1974-75.
One of the Family, Thames-TV, 1975.
Yes, Honestly, LWTV, 1975-76.
Plays for Today, BBC-TV, 1977.
Pig in the Middle, LWTV, 1980.
Nanny, BBC-TV, 1981-83.

Also author, with Brady, of television scripts *Away from It All, Thomas and Sarah,* and *The Complete Lack of Charm of the Bourgeoisie.* Creator of program *Oh, Madeline,* ABC-TV, 1983.

Author, with Brady, of plays *One Two Sky's Blue,* 1967, *Making the Party,* 1973, and *Such a Small Word,* 1973, and of radio play *The Victoria Line,* 1971.

Contributor to periodicals, including *Vogue, Harper's, Evening Standard,* and *Catholic Herald.*

WORK IN PROGRESS: A play, "A Dip before Breakfast," with husband, Terence Brady.

SIDELIGHTS: One of Britain's best known and most popular novelists, Charlotte Bingham has sold over three million copies of her books worldwide. In addition to novels such as *The Love Knot* and *The Chestnut Tree,* Bingham has authored fiction with her husband, actor Terence Brady, and has also collaborated with Brady on television scripts and stage plays.

Bingham comes from a literary family. Her father, John Bingham, was the seventh baron of Clanmorris and a writer of crime stories. He was also secretly a high-ranking member of the British intelligence agency MI5, charged with detecting foreign agents at work in England. John Bingham served as the model for John le Carre's fictional character George Smiley, a spymaster who figures into the plots of such best-selling thrillers as *Smiley's People* and *Tinker Tailor Soldier Spy.* although Bingham learned of her father's secret life as a teen, Le Carre did not reveal the secret until 2000. When the books were filmed, actor Alec Guinness played the Smiley character. "When I first watched Smiley I just couldn't believe it. It was like watching my father on screen," Bingham told Ian Starrett in the *News Letter.*

Bingham's literary career began when she was nineteen, and her first published book was her autobiography, *Coronet among the Weeds.* As the author once told *CA:* "I turned to writing at the age of eighteen because of an inability to master the arts of shorthand and typing. The resultant humorous book, *Coronet among the Weeds,* has been described as a book about being a debutante, which I no longer bother to deny, having too much regard for my royalties." *Coronet among the Weeds* proved to be a best-seller. Schofield quoted Bingham explaining: "It was unimaginably thrilling. . . . That whole time had a fairytale quality."

After this first, heady success, Bingham decided to make writing her career. As she told *CA:* "I met and married Terence Brady, who put an end to any treasured thoughts of early retirement by lassoing me into partnership with him." The couple have gone on to collaborate on a number of successes for television. "In the 1970s and 1980s they wrote a string of brilliant TV hits, including *Take Three Girls; Thomas and Sarah; No, Honestly; Upstairs Downstairs* and *Nanny,*" Schofield explained.

BIOGRAPHICAL AND CRITICAL SOURCES:

PERIODICALS

Booklist, January 1, 2003, Neal Wyatt, review of *The Chestnut Tree,* p. 843.
Daily Mail (London, England), March 13, 2001, Lester Middlehurst, "The Spymaster's Daughter, Her Society Scandal and a Tragedy She Will Take to Her Grave," p. 13.

Library Journal, April 15, 1989, Lydia Burruel Johnson, review of *To Hear a Nightingale,* p. 98.

News Letter, March 15, 2001, Ian Starrett, "Charlotte, Her Father, and the Spy Web," p. 18.

New Statesman and Society, July 22, 1988, Sara Maitland, review of *To Hear a Nightingale,* p. 40.

Publishers Weekly, February 17, 1989, review of *To Hear a Nightingale,* p. 66.

ONLINE

Charlotte Bingham Web site, http://www.charlottebingham.com/ (November 6, 2003).*

*   *   *

BOLAND, Janice

PERSONAL: Born in Brooklyn, NY; daughter of Joseph (a photo engraver) and Lena Marchetti (a school teacher) Marino; married James Boland (in corporate finance and real estate), 1960; children: Robert, John. *Education:* Fordham University, B.S.; graduate study at Fordham University; also studied visual arts and graphic communication and design. *Politics:* "Humanitarian." *Religion:* Roman Catholic. *Hobbies and other interests:* Education, herbalism, music, the arts.

ADDRESSES: *Home*—Box 352, Cross River, NY 10518. *Office*—Richard C. Owen Publishers, Inc., Box 585, Katonah, NY 10536.

CAREER: Writer, illustrator, and graphic artist. Richard C. Owen Publishers, Inc., Katonah, NY, director of children's books, 1990—; also worked in editorial, art, and production positions. Former school teacher and adjunct professor of writing and children's book illustration.

MEMBER: Society of Children's Book Writers and Illustrators, National Teachers Association, National Federation of Teachers, Civil Service Employees Association, American Association of University Women.

AWARDS, HONORS: Pick of the List selection, American Booksellers Association, 1993, for *Annabel;* Children's Choice selection, International Reading

Janice Boland

Association/Children's Book Council, 1996-97, for *Annabel Again;* Washington Irving Award, 1998, for *A Dog Named Sam.*

WRITINGS:

Annabel, illustrated by Megan Halsey, Dial (New York, NY), 1993.

Annabel Again, illustrated by Megan Halsey, Dial (New York, NY), 1994.

A Dog Named Sam, illustrated by G. Brian Karas, Dial (New York, NY), 1996.

The Fox, illustrated by Joe Boddy, Richard C. Owen Publishers (Katonah, NY), 1996.

The Strongest Animal, illustrated by Gary Torrisi, Richard C. Owen Publishers (Katonah, NY), 1996.

El Zorro, illustrated by Joe Boddy, Richard C. Owen Publishers (Katonah, NY), 1996.

(And photographer) *The Pond,* Richard C. Owen Publishers (Katonah, NY), 1997.

Zippers, illustrated by Judith Pfeiffer, Richard C. Owen Publishers (Katonah, NY), 1997.

Breakfast with John, illustrated by Joe Veno, Richard C. Owen Publishers (Katonah, NY), 1997.

Sunflowers, illustrated by Joe Veno, Richard C. Owen Publishers (Katonah, NY), 1998.

My Dog Fuzzy, Richard C. Owen Publishers (Katonah, NY), 2001.

So Sleepy, Richard C. Owen Publishers (Katonah, NY), 2001.

Alley Cat, Richard C. Owen Publishers (Katonah, NY), 2002.

Strange Things, Richard C. Owen Publishers (Katonah, NY), in press.

Also author of *Mrs. Murphy's Crows,* Richard C. Owen Publishers (Katonah, NY).

A Dog Named Sam has been translated into Japanese and German; *The Strongest Animal* has been translated into Spanish.

WORK IN PROGRESS: A book about carousels; further tales of Sam the dog's adventures; a picture book about a nonmusical child in a musical family; a book about elephants in New York City; producing a series of fine art etchings; creating oil portraits of horses, dogs, and cats.

SIDELIGHTS: Janice Boland once told *CA*: "Before I could read or write, I was drawing stories. My mother was a schoolteacher and a great advocate of literacy. My father was artistically and musically gifted. Our house was filled with books and drawing material and comic books. I remember understanding the stories in the comic books before I could read, by looking at the pictures. My family loved to tell each other stories about the past and about current happenings and daily home, work, and school experiences. Most of the stories ended in a humorous, dramatic, or memorable way. Every summer my mother, my sister, and I, and our various pets, including a bantam fighting rooster, multiple hamsters, and our big red dog, headed to our country home. There, I explored the outdoors with my dog for company and protection. My mother encouraged my curiosity and fascination with nature and my inclination to encounter it on my own. She fostered in me and my sister a sense of responsibility, independence, inquisitiveness, and wonder.

"My first trade book, *Annabel,* is really a very brief autobiography. When I was writing it I wasn't aware of that, but after it was published I realized how much Mother Pig is like my mother. She expects Annabel to be adventurous and successful in everything she does, and Annabel is. That's the way we were brought up.

"In college I majored in primary education. I took extra literature, art, and design courses and studied with some very inspiring professors. I taught in the New York City public school system and in New York state and Connecticut public and private schools, as well as university-level courses. I continued taking courses in children's literature, writing, communication, design, and the graphic and visual arts. I knew that I really wanted to create children's books from inception to the printed form.

"When my own children were infants their first gifts were books. They loved books. And I now had the perfect excuse to fill our home with children's literature, art, and poetry books.

"My second book, *Annabel Again,* was about an adventure I had as a child. My friend and I discovered an old barn on an abandoned road. It was filled with old spooky stuff and a brass-bound chest. While we were trying to unlock the chest, barn swallows looped and swooped over us. We never did get the chest open—but we knew it was filled with a treasure of gold and jewels.

"My third trade book, *A Dog Named Sam,* is the story of my children's adventures with their yellow Labrador retriever. He was my children's companion and best friend for fifteen years, and did all the silly, endearing things Sam does in my stories.

"In 1990 I began a publishing career, working for Richard C. Owen Publishers, Inc., an educational publishing house. We developed a collection of children's author autobiographies and a collection of good literature books with instructional value for children in kindergarten and first and second grades. It started with a vision that Richard Owen had to create an ever-expanding core reading and writing program of books for beginning and fluent readers and aspiring young writers, books that the children could read with success and enjoyment. With his support and encouragement we created a children's book department of which I am the director. My staff and I work with authors, illustrators, and photographers—ninety-five percent of whom are first timers—to develop the manuscripts and art into benchmark books for children at the emergent, early, and fluent stages of literacy.

"My book *The Strongest Animal,* which is part of our 'Books for Young Learners' collection, was inspired by a friend's visit to the Bronx Zoo while babysitting. *The Fox* is based on a fox who came each morning to see if the pet ducks and chickens my children were raising had forgotten to sleep in their house. *The Pond* is the story of the animals I see throughout the seasons at a little pond two miles from my home. *Breakfast with John* is the story of my little hen, Rose, and her first egg, found by my son John. *Zippers* is the story of what happened to my suitcase in Boston. The book *Sunflowers* grew out of my pleasure in cultivating those fun flowers. All of my additional books are inspired by and based on real-life happenings.

"I work on things simultaneously. I like to write two or three different books at the same time. Each stimulates ideas and enthusiasm for the other. I also love to do research for both my art and my stories. And of course I love to read. Lately, many of my choices for leisure reading have been all kinds of nonfiction such as autobiographies and travel memoirs. The travel books by Dervla Murphy are among my favorites.

"As the director of children's books at Richard C. Owen Publishers, I have opportunities to work with wonderful and gifted authors and artists, such as Denice Fleming, Eve Bunting, Paul Goble, Ruth Heller, James Howe, Jean Van Leeuwen, Jane Yolen, Jonathan London, Patricia Polacco, and Frank Asch, to name just a few. Each one has an impact on my creativity and my commitment to children's literature.

"It is not easy to get published. It takes hard work, dedication, perseverance, and enthusiasm. But what a great feeling it is when you see a child reading and enjoying a book you have created. You feel that you have done something worthwhile.

"My advice to aspiring authors and artists is the same advice I gave my students when I taught courses in writing and illustrating children's literature: 'Visit the children's room at your local library. Read all the books you can. Write every day. Hone your craft. And never give up.'"

Recently Boland described her writing process: "I spend a lot of time observing and thinking. When an idea comes I write it in pencil, making adjustments, changes, additions. Often I write the whole story first in a rough draft, then I put it in the computer and begin revising. Sometimes I revise many times, sometimes very little. Then I put the piece aside and go on to other creative work: art, reading, another manuscript. I return to the piece to refine and revise it. I always read my work aloud; if no one is there to hear, I read aloud to myself. When I believe the work is ready to be seen, I send it out for consideration for publication."

BIOGRAPHICAL AND CRITICAL SOURCES:

PERIODICALS

Booklist, January 15, 1993, p. 918; April 1, 1996, p. 1375.

Kirkus Reviews, February 1, 1996, p. 223.

School Library Journal, March, 1993, pp. 170-171; August, 1995, p. 115; April, 1996, p. 99.

* * *

BRACEWELL, Michael 1958-

PERSONAL: Born August 7, 1958, in London, England; son of George (a civil servant) and Joyce (Crowther) Bracewell. *Education:* University of Nottingham, B.A. (with honors), 1980. *Hobbies and other interests:* London, neoromantic British art, fashion, "postmodernism," music, architecture, food, comedy.

ADDRESSES: *Home*—Sutton, Surrey, England. *Agent*—c/o Author Mail, Jonathan Cape, 20 Vauxhall Bridge Rd., London SW1V 2SA, England.

CAREER: Novelist and author of documentaries and nonfiction. British Council, London, England, former clerk in department of fine arts. Cofounder, *Quick End* (literary magazine).

AWARDS, HONORS: Mail on Sunday/John Llewellyn Rhys Prize shortlist, 1992, for *The Conclave.*

WRITINGS:

NOVELS

The Crypto-Amnesia Club, Carcanet (London, England), 1988.
Divine Concepts of Physical Beauty, Secker & Warburg (London, England), 1989, Knopf (New York, NY), 1990.
The Conclave, Secker & Warburg (London, England), 1992.
Saint Rachel, J. Cape (London, England), 1995.
Perfect Tense, J. Cape (London, England), 2001.

OTHER

England Is Mine: Pop Life in Albion from Wilde to Goldie, Flamingo (London, England), 1998.
The Nineties: When Surface Was Depth, Flamingo (London, England), 2002.
Sam Taylor-Wood, Steidl (Göttingen, Germany), 2002.

Contributor to exhibition catalogs, including *Adam Chodzko,* August Media (London, England), 1999. Author of television documentaries, on Oscar Wilde and Nikolaus Pevsner, for British Broadcasting Corp.(-BBC). Work represented in anthologies, including *The Quick End,* Fourth Estate (London, England), 1988, *The Faber Book of Pop,* Faber (London, England), 1995, and *The Penguin Book of Twentieth-Century Fashion Writing,* Penguin (London, England), 1999. Contributor to periodicals, including *Guardian, Independent on Sunday, Frieze, Agenda, Arena,* and *Excel.*

SIDELIGHTS: Michael Bracewell is a novelist and writer on contemporary art. In both genres, Bracewell has focused on the empty materialism and shallow thinking of contemporary English culture, fashion, and avant-garde trends.

Bracewell's novel *Divine Concepts of Physical Beauty,* for example, features extreme performance artist Kelly O'Kelly, whose dangerous acts could lead to death. Her circle of affluent London friends includes Miles, who is engaged to fashion model Stella, and a homosexual couple whose breakup leads to violent revenge. A contributor to *Publishers Weekly* concluded that Bracewell writes "like a metaphysical poet, with rapier shafts of irony and wit." Bracewell told Richard Marshall in *3 AM* that he considered the book to contain "a kind of high operatic mellow dramatic camp atmosphere."

Bracewell's novel *The Conclave* is an "anatomy of anxiety and strangeness" among the young people in the English middle class, as the author explained to Marshall. "There really were young people at that time thinking in terms of how near am I to somewhere where I can buy a bottle of Perrier water at eleven o'clock at night. I was interested in that state of banality. I was asking where the moral centre of that mind was." Similarly, in the novel *Saint Rachel* Bracewell tells of a depressed young Londoner whose reliance on drugs is told in deadpan, minimalist prose. Chris Savage King, writing in the *New Statesman,* found that Bracewell's prose "unwinds in a slow-motion haze that conveys the joint effect of the drugs and the malaise."

Bracewell deals with many of the same issues raised in his novels in his nonfiction title *The Nineties: When Surface Was Depth,* in which he argues that the English have been overwhelmed by an obsession with celebrity, passing fads, and a kind of infantilism found in the sorts of entertainment successfully marketed to adults. As Bracewell puts it in the book: "The nurturing of our inner child by any means possible achieved a new fashionableness—at the expense, perhaps, of our inner adult." Will Self, reviewing the work for the *New Statesman,* believed that Bracewell presents the nineties "in terms of a series of passing preoccupations." Ian Sansom in the *Guardian* described *The Nineties* as being "made up of odd interviews, think-pieces, and other off-cuts gathered from Bracewell's occasionally brilliant writings for newspapers and magazines, all mixed up together, poured into a mould, and given a book-kind of shape. . . . Enormously tasty, and curiously insubstantial." But according to David Lister in the *Independent,* "Bracewell is amply suited to grapple with the Nineties. His writing bristles with perception and irony—and the decade's one lasting legacy might be irony."

BIOGRAPHICAL AND CRITICAL SOURCES:

PERIODICALS

3AM, September, 2001, Richard Marshall, "An Interview with Michael Bracewell."

Blitz, February, 1988.
Elle, September, 1988.
Face, February, 1988.
Guardian, June 29, 2002, Nicholas Lezard, review of *Perfect Tense;* July 27, 2002, Ian Sansom, review of *The Nineties: When Surface Was Depth.*
Independent, July 18, 2002, David Lister, review of *The Nineties.*
Library Journal, September 15, 2002, Shauna Frischkorn, review of *Sam Taylor-Wood,* p. 60.
Los Angeles Times Book Review, May 15, 1988, p. 6.
New Statesman, January 29, 1988, Boyd Tonkin, review of *The Crypto-Amnesia Club,* p. 30; October 2, 1992, Elizabeth Young, review of *The Conclave,* p. 49; February 3, 1995, Chris Savage King, review of *Saint Rachel,* p. 40; July 15, 2002, Will Self, review of *The Nineties,* p. 48.
New York Times Book Review, July 24, 1988, p. 18.
Publishers Weekly, February 26, 1988, Penny Kaganoff, review of *The Crypto-Amnesia Club,* p. 191; March 23, 1990, Sybil Steinberg, review of *Divine Concepts of Physical Beauty,* p. 63.
Spectator, February 18, 1995, D. J. Taylor, review of *Saint Rachel,* p. 30; June 7, 1997, Jonathan Keates, review of *England Is Mine: Pop Life in Albion from Wilde to Goldie,* p. 44; February 10, 2001, Nicola McAllister, review of *Perfect Tense,* p. 37.
Times Literary Supplement, March 25, 1988, Mark Sanderson, review of *The Crypto-Amnesia Club,* p. 337; June 17, 1988, Eve MacSweeney, review of *The Quick End,* p. 680; October 27, 1989, Jane O'Grady, review of *Divine Concepts of Physical Beauty,* p. 1180.

ONLINE

Contemporary Writers, http://www.contemporarywriters.com/ (November 4, 2003).
Spike, http://www.spikemagazine.com/ (April, 1997), Jason Weaver, review of *England Is Mine.**

* * *

BRUNHOFF, Laurent de 1925-

PERSONAL: Surname is pronounced "*broon*-awf"; born August 30, 1925, in Paris, France; immigrated to the United States, 1985; son of Jean (an author and illustrator) and Cecile (a pianist; maiden name, Sabouraud) de Brunhoff; married second wife Phyllis Rose (an author); children: (first marriage) Anne, Antoine. *Education:* Attended Lycee Pasteur and Academie de la Grande Chaumiere. *Hobbies and other interests:* Gardening, birdwatching, travelling, hiking, watercolor.

ADDRESSES: Home—New York, NY and Key West, FL. *Agent*—c/o Author Mail, Harry N. Abrams, Inc., 100 Fifth Avenue, New York, NY 10011.

CAREER: Author and illustrator of children's books. Began to work seriously at painting about 1945; at the same time he became involved in continuing the "Babar" picture book series his father had originated. *Exhibitions:* Brunhoff's paintings have been displayed at the Galerie Maeght and the Salon de Mai in the 1950s. Original watercolors by Jean and Laurent de Brunhoff have appeared in various museums in the United States, including *Fifty Years of Babar,* 1983-84; *The Art of Babar,* 1990-92; *Babar, Watercolors,* Mary Ryan Gallery, New York, NY, 1987, 1990; National Academy of Design, 1991; *Babar's Museum of Art,* Art Institute of Chicago, 2003; and New York Public Library, 2004.

AWARDS, HONORS: Best Illustrated Books of the Year citation, *New York Times,* 1956, for *Babar's Fair;* Officier des Arts et Lettres, 1984; Walter Award, Parson's School of Design, 1988, for work with educational illustration; Chevalier of the Legion of Honor (France), 1992.

WRITINGS:

SELF-ILLUSTRATED

Serafina the Giraffe, World Publishing (New York, NY), 1961, published in France as *Serafina la Girafe,* Editions du Pont Royal, 1961.
Serafina's Lucky Find, World Publishing (New York, NY), 1962.
Captain Serafina, World Publishing (New York, NY), 1963.
Anatole and His Donkey, translation from French by Richard Howard, Macmillan (New York, NY), 1963.
Bonhomme, translation from French by Richard Howard, Pantheon (New York, NY), 1965.

Gregory and Lady Turtle in the Valley of the Music Trees, translation from French by Richard Howard, Pantheon (New York, NY), 1971, published in France as *Gregory et Dame Tortue,* Ecole Loisirs (Paris, France), 1971.

Bonhomme and the Huge Beast, translation from French by Richard Howard, Pantheon (New York, NY), 1974, published in France as *Bonhomme et la grosse bete qui avait des escailles sur le dos,* Grasset (Paris, France), 1974.

The One Pig with Horns, translation from French by Richard Howard, Pantheon (New York, NY), 1979.

"BABAR" SERIES

Babar et ce coquin d'Arthur, Hachette (Paris, France), 1947, translation by Merle Haas published as *Babar's Cousin: That Rascal Arthur,* Random House (New York, NY), 1948.

Pique-Nique chez Babar, Hachette (Paris, France), 1949, translation by Merle Haas published as *Babar's Picnic,* Random House (New York, NY), 1949.

Babar dans l'ile aux oiseaux, Hachette (Paris, France), 1951, translation by Merle Haas published as *Babar's Visit to Bird Island,* Random House (New York, NY), 1952.

La Fete de Celesteville, Hachette (Paris, France), 1954, translation by Merle Haas published as *Babar's Fair,* Random House (New York, NY), 1954.

Babar et le Professeur Grifaton, Hachette (Paris, France), 1956, translation by Merle Haas published as *Babar and the Professor,* Random House (New York, NY), 1957.

Le Chateau de Babar, Hachette (Paris, France), 1961, translation by Merle Haas published as *Babar's Castle,* Random House (New York, NY), 1962.

Babar's French Lessons, Random House (New York, NY), 1963.

Babar's Spanish Lessons, Spanish text by Roberto Eyzaguirre, Random House (New York, NY), 1965.

Babar Comes to America, translation by M. Jean Craig, Random House (New York, NY), 1965.

Babar fait du ski, Hachette (Paris, France), 1966, translation by Merle Haas published as *Babar Goes Skiing* (also see below), Random House (New York, NY), 1969.

Babar jardinier, Hachette (Paris, France), 1966, translation by Merle Haas published as *Babar the Gardener* (also see below), Random House (New York, NY), 1969.

Babar en promenade, Hachette (Paris, France), 1966, translation by Merle Haas published as *Babar Goes on a Picnic* (also see below), Random House (New York, NY), 1969.

Babar a la mer, Hachette (Paris, France), 1966, translation by Merle Haas published as *Babar at the Seashore* (also see below), Random House (New York, NY), 1969.

Babar Loses His Crown, Random House (New York, NY), 1967, Harry N. Abrams (New York, NY), 2004.

Babar's Games (pop-up book), Random House (New York, NY), 1968.

Babar fait du sport, Hachette (Paris, France), 1969, translation published as *Babar the Athlete* (also see below), Random House (New York, NY), 1971.

Babar campeur, Hachette (Paris, France), 1969, translation published as *Babar the Camper* (also see below), Random House (New York, NY), 1971.

Babar et le docteur, 6th edition, Hachette (Paris, France), 1969, translation published as *Babar and the Doctor* (also see below), Random House (New York, NY), 1971.

Babar artiste peintre, Hachette (Paris, France), 1969, translation published as *Babar the Painter* (also see below), Random House (New York, NY), 1971.

(Reteller) Jean de Brunhoff, *Babar aux sports d'hiver,* 7th edition, Hachette (Paris, France), 1969.

Babar's Moon Trip (pop-up book), Random House (New York, NY), 1969.

Babar's Birthday Surprise (also see below), Random House (New York, NY), 1970, Harry N. Abrams (New York, NY), 2002.

Babar patissier, Hachette (Paris, France), 1970, translation published as *Babar Bakes a Cake* (also see below), Random House (New York, NY), 1974.

Babar musicien, Hachette (Paris, France), 1970, translation published as *Babar's Concert* (also see below), Random House (New York, NY), 1974.

Babar aviateur, Hachette (Paris, France), 1970, translation published as *Babar to the Rescue* (also see below), Random House (New York, NY), 1974.

Babar et l'arbre de Noel, Hachette (Paris, France), 1970, translation published as *Babar's Christmas Tree* (also see below), Random House (New York, NY), 1974.

Babar Visits Another Planet (also see below), translation by Merle Haas, Random House (New York,

NY), 1972, published in France as *Babar sur la planete molle,* Hachette (Paris, France), 1972, reprinted, Harry N. Abrams (New York, NY), 2003.

Meet Babar and His Family (also see below), Random House (New York, NY), 1973, Harry N. Abrams (New York, NY), 2002.

Babar and the Wully-Wully (also see below), Random House (New York, NY), 1975, published in France as *Babar et le Wouly-Wouly,* Hachette (Paris, France), 1975.

Babar Saves the Day, Random House (New York, NY), 1976.

Babar's Mystery (also see below), Random House (New York, NY), 1978, Harry N. Abrams (New York, NY), 2004.

Babar Learns to Cook, Random House (New York, NY), 1978.

Babar the Magician (shape book), Random House (New York, NY), 1980.

About Air (also see below), Random House (New York, NY), 1980.

About Water (also see below), Random House (New York, NY), 1980.

About Earth (also see below), Random House (New York, NY), 1980.

About Fire (also see below), Random House (New York, NY), 1980.

Babar and the Ghost (also see below), Random House (New York, NY), 1981.

(Illustrated with father, Jean de Brunhoff) *Fifty Years of Babar* (exhibition catalogue), introduction by Maurice Sendak, International Exhibitions Foundation (Washington, DC), 1983.

Babar's ABC, Random House (New York, NY), 1983, Harry N. Abrams (New York, NY), 2001.

Babar's Book of Color, Random House (New York, NY), 1984, Harry N. Abrams (New York, NY), 2004.

Babar's Counting Book, Random House (New York, NY), 1986, Harry N. Abrams (New York, NY), 2001.

Babar's Little Girl (also see below), Random House (New York, NY), 1987.

Babar's Little Circus Star, Random House (New York, NY), 1988.

(Illustrator, with Jean de Brunhoff) *The Art of Babar: Drawings and Watercolors by Jean and Laurent de Brunhoff* (catalogue), Art Services International (Alexandria, VA), 1989.

Babar's Busy Year: A Book about Seasons, Random House (New York, NY), 1989.

Babar's Colors and Shapes, Random House (New York, NY), 1989.

Babar's Number Fun, Random House (New York, NY), 1989.

Babar's Paint Box Book, Random House (New York, NY), 1989.

Babar's Busy Week, Random House (New York, NY), 1990.

Isabelle's New Friend, Random House (New York, NY), 1990, reissued as *Babar's Little Girl Makes a Friend,* Harry N. Abrams (New York, NY), 2002.

Hello, Babar!, Random House (New York, NY), 1991.

Babar's Battle, Random House (New York, NY), 1992, Harry N. Abrams (New York, NY), 2002, published in French as *La Victoire de Babar,* Hachette (Paris, France), 1992.

Babar's Bath Book, Random House (New York, NY), 1992.

Babar's Car, Random House (New York, NY), 1992.

Babar's Peekaboo Fair, Random House (New York, NY), 1993.

The Rescue of Babar, Random House (New York, NY), 1993, reprinted as *Babar's Rescue,* Harry N. Abrams (New York, NY), 2004.

Babar's French and English Word Book, Random (New York, NY), 1994.

Babar and the Succotash Bird, Harry N. Abrams (New York), 2000.

Babar's Yoga for Elephants, Harry N. Abrams (New York, NY), 2002.

Babar and the Christmas House, Harry N. Abrams (New York, NY), 2003.

Babar's Museum of Art, Harry N. Abrams (New York, NY), 2003.

Babar Goes to School, Harry N. Abrams (New York, NY), 2003.

Babar and the Gift for Mother, Harry N. Abrams (New York, NY), 2004.

Babar and the Runaway Egg, Harry N. Abrams (New York, NY), 2004.

Portions of the "Babar" series have been translated into eighteen languages.

"BABAR" SERIES; COLLECTIONS

Babar's Trunk (includes *Babar Goes on a Picnic, Babar at the Seashore, Babar the Gardener,* and *Babar Goes Skiing*), Random House (New York, NY), 1969.

Babar's Other Trunk (includes *Babar the Camper, Babar the Athlete, Babar and the Doctor,* and *Babar the Painter*), Random House (New York, NY), 1971.
Babar's Bookmobile (includes *Babar Bakes a Cake, Babar's Concert, Babar to the Rescue,* and *Babar's Christmas Tree*), Random House (New York, NY), 1974.
Babar Box (includes *About Water, About Fire, About Air,* and *About Earth*), Diogenes Verlag (Switzerland), published as *Babar's Little Library,* Random House (New York, NY), 1980.
(With Jean de Brunhoff) *Babar's Anniversary Album: Six Favorite Stories* (includes Jean de Brunhoff's *The Story of Babar, The Travels of Babar,* and *Babar the King,* and Laurent de Brunhoff's *Babar's Birthday Surprise, Babar's Mystery,* and *Babar and the Wully-Wully*), introduction by Maurice Sendak, Random House (New York, NY), 1981, Harry N. Abrams (New York, NY), 2001.
Babar's Family Album: Five Favorite Stories (includes *Meet Babar and His Family, Babar and the Ghost, Babar the Magician, Babar Visits Another Planet,* and *Babar's Little Girl*), Random House (New York, NY), 1991.
Bonjour, Babar!, Random House (New York), 2000.

OTHER

(With Jean de Brunhoff) *Albums roses "Babar,"* Volume VI, Hachette (Paris, France), 1951-53.
(Editor) Jean de Brunhoff, *Les Adventures de Babar* (textbook), Hachette (Paris, France), 1959.
(Illustrator) Auro Roselli, *The Cats of the Eiffel Tower,* Dial (New York, NY), 1967.

ADAPTATIONS: *The Story of Babar* and *Babar Comes to America* were adapted for an animated television film, narrated by Peter Ustinov, by Lee Mendelson/Bill Melendez Productions in 1971. *Babar Comes to America* and *Babar's Birthday Surprise* were reworked for a sound recording, read by Louis Jordan, with music composed and conducted by Don Heckman, Caedmon (New York, NY), 1977. *Babar's Mystery* and *Babar and the Wully-Wully* were issued on disc and cassette, read by the author, by Caedmon (New York, NY). The characters and situations created by Jean and Laurent de Brunhoff were adapted for the animated film *Babar: The Movie,* with voices by Gordon Pinsent and Sarah Polley, by Nelvana, 1989, as well as a television series broadcast in the United States by Home Box Office. Other children's books based on Brunhoff's Babar characters have been produced, including *Babar and the Scary Day* and *Isabelle the Flower Girl,* both written by Ellen Weiss, illustrated by Jean-Claude Gibert, and published by Harry N. Abrams (New York, NY), 2004.

SIDELIGHTS: Perhaps the most famous French import since deep-fried potatoes, Babar the Elephant has charmed young readers around the world since he first appeared in picture books in 1931. "The stories have influenced the imaginations of generations," noted *BookPage*'s Jamie McAlister, "as they turned the colorful pages and learned more about these adventurous and fashionable elephants who walk upright, wear glasses and hats, drive cars, raise children, and exist in their own world with humans as if there were no barriers." Lynne T. Burke, writing in *Reading Today,* noted that "in a world where fame is fleeting, Babar's reputation is legendary; his story never grows old." Created by Jean de Brunhoff with the first title, *The Story of Babar,* the series has been continued by his son, Laurent de Brunhoff, since his father's death in 1937. Laurent de Brunhoff is the author and illustrator of some fifty hardcover and more than a dozen mini books for children. Brunhoff's diligent efforts to craft the pachyderm and its tales in his late father's style have proved successful with children and with some critics, although a few reviewers have asserted that Babar lost part of his distinctiveness and spirit in the transition between father and son. Due to the work of both Brunhoffs, however, Babar has become a classic figure in children's literature and a favorite with readers. The younger Brunhoff is also credited with keeping the situations and activities of Babar contemporary.

Since publishing his first "Babar" story in 1947, the artist has taken Babar on visits to other countries and planets, and has engaged the animal in a number of hobbies, such as camping, cooking, painting, and gardening. Under Brunhoff's guidance, the "Babar" series has expanded to provide readers with an educational experience as the character helps children learn the alphabet, numbers, colors, and other languages. The author has also ventured from Babar's kingdom to create a realm of original animal protagonists in books like *Serafina the Giraffe* and *Bonhomme.* These stories have provided Brunhoff with the opportunity to showcase his own talents for art and storytelling.

Born in 1925, Laurent de Brunhoff showed an early proclivity toward art. This was partly to be expected, for he came from an artistic family: his father, Jean, was a painter and his mother, Cecile, was a musician. As a young child, Laurent, along with his brother Mathieu, were told a miraculous story of a baby elephant who rode on his mother's back and was happy in his jungle home until one day a hunter shot the mother. Thereafter, the baby elephant had to make his own way in the world and soon found himself in the city where he met Old Lady, who liked elephants. Luckily, this lady was wealthy and could provide for the baby elephant. Soon the baby elephant began to learn the ways of man, using money and dressing in posh clothes. The Brunhoff boys so loved the stories their mother was telling them, that they pleaded with their artist father to draw the elephant for them. In an interview with Emma Fisher in *Pied Pipers: Interviews with the Influential Creators of Children's Literature,* Brunhoff further described the beginnings of the amiable pachyderm: "[My father] never had it in mind to write a book for children. He was a painter, and it just happened one day that my mother narrated a story about a little elephant to us, my brother and me. We were five and four. We liked this story of the little elephant and we told my father about it. He simply had the idea of making some drawings for us. Then he became very excited about it and made a whole book, and that was the first one." As Brunhoff told Jennifer M. Brown in a *Publishers Weekly* interview, "He invented the Old Lady, who was not part of the original story my mother told." In fact, the father enjoyed playing with the story so much, that he created a name for the baby, Babar. "My father was an impressionist painter," Brunhoff told Brown. "I think he discovered himself as an artist creating these books."

As it happened, Jean de Brunhoff's brother, Michel, was a publisher and brought out this first tale, *The Story of Babar,* which had already become a family institution. Suddenly, the public, too, was entranced by the goings-on of this friendly elephant, and six more books followed. After being rescued by the Old Lady, Babar returns to his jungle home as king of the elephants and makes his cousin Celeste his queen, setting up home in Celesteville, where the Old Lady comes to live with them. He fathers children, including Flora, Pom, Alexander, and Isabelle, makes the friendship of the monkey Zephir, and of the wise old elephant Cornelius. Then, in 1937, Jean de Brunhoff died of tuberculosis. His son, Laurent, was only twelve. World War II came in 1939, and the young Brunhoff finished his studies in Paris and began painting, setting up a studio in Paris. By the end of the war, he began to think of continuing the "Babar" series, something the publishers had been arguing for since the death of Jean de Brunhoff; however, the mother, Cecile, would not allow it. When her own son broached a story idea to her, though, it was a different matter.

Brunhoff hit on the idea of introducing a cousin, Arthur, into the milieu, and thus was born the second coming of "Babar." As Brunhoff noted to Brown, "I wanted to be as faithful as possible to my father, but I was not the same man." Brunhoff put his own interests into the books: a love of bird-watching sent Babar to a bird island; a new world post-War sent Babar off to a new planet and to the United States. "But deep inside, there is the same philosophy, the same love," Brunhoff further explained to Brown. "That is the world of Babar. There is always a good end."

Brunhoff's first title was *Babar's Cousin: That Rascal Arthur.* Numerous other titles followed: Babar takes up skiing, or goes on a picnic or to the seashore or camping, or visits a doctor. "His stories are just as entertaining," noted Robert Wernick in the *Smithsonian,* "with the same unpredictable but wholly natural turns as his father's. Both mix the farfetched and the familiar, elephant life and human life, with the same easy assurance. Laurent sometimes lets his fancy fly a little freer than his father ever did. His compositions are less symmetrical, often straining to soar off the page." Reviewing the 2001 reissue of Brunhoff's *Babar's ABC* in *Horn Book Guide,* Jennifer M. Brabander found that Babar and company "offer a comforting familiarity." The twenty-six letters of the alphabet make appearances in this title in words from Alexander to Zephir. Reviewing the same title, Janis Campbell noted in the *Detroit Free Press* that the "classic is as fresh and fun as ever." With *Babar's Birthday Surprise,* wife Celeste has the famous Podular make a statue to celebrate Babar in a tale that is a "great joy," according to a reviewer for *Horn Book Guide.*

Babar's popularity on the printed page has made the character a hot merchandizing item for retailers. The pachyderm's image has appeared on an assortment of toys, including stuffed likenesses, as well as T-shirts and a range of other items. Brunhoff's Babar has also been featured on television in a series. A motion picture, *Babar: The Movie,* was released in 1989, based on the characters of the books, not the works themselves. Amid his successes with Babar, Brunhoff has found time to create original stories featuring animal protagonists. These include books such as *Serafina the Giraffe* and *Bonhomme,* two series begun in the 1960s, *Gregory and Lady Turtle in the Valley of the Music Trees,* in 1971, and *The One Pig with Horns,* in 1979. In a review of *Serafina the Giraffe, New York Herald Tribune Book Review* contributor Margaret Sherwood Libby declared, "We are delighted to have him branch out for himself."

Brunhoff came to live in the United States in 1985 and continued to draw his lovable elephant. In *Babar's Little Girl,* baby Isabelle is introduced. Her first big adventure ensues when the family believes she is lost, but in fact the child knows exactly where she is. In *Babar's French and English Word Book,* Brunhoff uses his pachyderm to introduce numerous words in both languages. In *Babar's Battle,* the elephant manages to avert a war with Rataxes, ruler of the rhinoceroses. Though finding the tone a bit "moralistic," a reviewer for *Horn Book Guide* found Babar and his clan as "engaging as ever" in this title. Similarly, another *Horn Book Guide* contributor found *Babar's Little Girl Makes a Friend* a "self-conscious story about interracial friendship." In this tale, Isabelle makes friends with one of the enemy, a rhinoceros.

Isabelle makes another appearance in *The Rescue of Babar.* She is aided by a snake, lion, and monkey in her efforts to free her father from the striped elephants. However, when found in a massive city in the inside of a volcano, Babar at first refuses to go home with Isabelle. Discovering that someone is drugging his watermelon smoothie and clouding his judgment, Isabelle manages to prevail in this story that should be a "favorite with Babar fans," as Janice M. Del Negro wrote in *Booklist.* The return of Babar and Isabelle to Celesteville makes for "a festive close" to this "particularly charming caper," wrote a reviewer for *Publishers Weekly.*

Brunhoff took a vacation from the "Babar" series between 1994 and 2000, returning to his fine arts painting which he had long put on hold. An abstract painter and avid hiker, Brunhoff found plenty to occupy himself. A camping trip into the High Sierras of Yosemite, however, reawakened his desire to work on his favorite elephant. As he told McAlister, "'Suddenly I had an idea for [a] book, and it was very fast, it came very strongly in my mind.'" The book in question was *Babar and the Succotash Bird,* about a beautiful bird that visits Alexander, Babar's son, in the middle of the night. Out hiking the next day, the boy thinks that he meets the same bird again, an animal that makes a call that sounds like "succotash." In fact, this exotic bird is actually a bad sorcerer who captures him. Babar and the family, helped by wise Cornelius, go in search of Alexander, and through the assistance of a good wizard—who was actually the original bird—they are able to rescue him. Despite some reservations about the premise of the tale, Piper L. Nyman, writing in *School Library Journal,* felt that "children will flock to this new adventure." Similarly, a reviewer for *Publishers Weekly* thought that the details of Alexander's escape were "overblown" in this "rather awkwardly paced picture book," but when Brunhoff focuses on Babar and the family, "his work shines." *Booklist*'s Shelley Townsend-Hudson also reported a mixed reception; while finding the "contrived, tacked-on message confusing," Townsend-Hudson also had praise for the "entertaining" illustrations.

With the 2002 *Babar's Yoga for Elephants,* the king of the elephants presents a "lighthearted guide to yoga for pachyderms (and people)," according to a contributor for *Publishers Weekly.* Babar points to cave drawings that prove that even the woolly mammoth practiced yoga. He and Celeste resurrect the practice in Celesteville, and then go on a worldwide tour to spread the word. This introduction is followed by a practical guide to basic yoga movements. The reviewer for *Publishers Weekly* felt that Brunhoff's "signature watercolor renderings" would allow young readers to follow Babar's movements in this "diverting volume." Writing in *Booklist,* Marta Segal Block found the same book a "fun introduction" that is "best used when an adult is nearby."

Brunhoff went on to invent a "whimsical, wry caper," according to a critic for *Publishers Weekly,* in his 2003 *Babar's Museum of Art.* In this tale, Babar and Celeste convert the old Celesteville train station into a museum that will display all the various artworks they have gathered on their many trips abroad. Building the museum is hectic, but opening day finally arrives. Babar and his citizens can enjoy classic works of art from Michelangelo's *The Creation of Adam* to

Botticelli's *Birth of Venus.* Other great artists—thirty in all—are also included. The only difference from the originals is that in Babar's collection, all the human figures in the paintings have been replaced by elephants. The contributor for *Publishers Weekly* praised Brunhoff's "gentle artistic makeovers," further observing that this artwork "skillfully allows young readers an entree to the world of fine art." The same reviewer called the book a "visual treat." More praise came from *Booklist*'s Gillian Engberg, who found the book "as entertaining as it is instructive." Writing in *School Library Journal,* Mary Elam thought readers would discover "entertaining comparisons to classic art collection," while a contributor for *Kirkus Reviews* called the title "another classically plotless but curiously appealing outing."

Brunhoff summed up his feelings about children and his books to Marjorie Fisher in *Who's Who in Children's Books:* "I love children; they are always ready to follow you into a dream. For them there is no border between dream and reality." He added, "If you dream, you escape; but at the same time there are things in my books which are essential in life, even today, and which are not at all an escape—I mean friendship and love, the search for harmony and refusal of violence. And I believe that these traits are common both in my father's books and in my own." Robert Wernick in *Smithsonian* also pointed to Babar's "fundamental nature—imperturbable, gregarious, sweet-tempered. . . . This is a world where misfortune can arrive at any time, but . . . you can always count on a flight of winged elephants . . . to arrive in a blaze of light and rout the dark imps." Brunhoff credits his wife, Phyllis Rose, for her collaboration on the text and stories of his most recent titles.

BIOGRAPHICAL AND CRITICAL SOURCES:

BOOKS

Doyle, Brian, *The Who's Who of Children's Literature,* Schocken Books (New York, NY), 1968.

Fisher, Marjorie, *Who's Who in Children's Books: A Treasury of Familiar Characters of Childhood,* Holt (New York, NY), 1975.

Huerlimann, Bettina, *Three Centuries of Children's Books in Europe,* translated and edited by Brian W. Alderson, Oxford University Press (New York, NY), 1967.

Kingman, Lee, and others, compilers, *Illustrators of Children's Books, 1957-1966,* Horn Book (Boston, MA), 1968.

Kingman, Lee, and others, compilers, *Illustrators of Children's Books, 1967-1976,* Horn Book (Boston, MA), 1978.

Miller, B. M., and others, compilers, *Illustrators of Children's Books, 1946-1956,* Horn Book (Boston, MA), 1958.

Weber, Nicholas Fox, *The Art of Babar,* Abrams (New York, NY), 1989.

Wintle, Justin, and Emma Fisher, *The Pied Pipers: Interviews with the Influential Creators of Children's Literature,* Paddington Press (New York, NY), 1974.

PERIODICALS

Booklist, December 1, 1993, Janice M. Del Negro, review of *The Rescue of Babar,* p. 697; December 1, 2000, Shelley Townsend-Hudson, review of *Babar and the Succotash Bird,* p. 718; October 15, 2002, Marta Segal Block, review of *Babar's Yoga for Elephants,* p. 402; November 1, 2003, Gillian Engberg, review of *Babar's Museum of Art,* pp. 512-513.

Detroit Free Press, May 27, 2001, Janis Campbell, review of *Babar's ABC,* p. 5.

Horn Book, November-December, 1948, Alice M. Jordan, "New Books for Christmas: 'Babar's Cousin,'" p. 452.

Horn Book Guide, spring, 1993, review of *Babar's Car,* p. 12, and review of *Babar's Little Library,* p. 27; spring, 1994, Martha V. Parravano, review of *Babar's Peekaboo Fair,* p. 20, and Patricia Riley, review of *The Rescue of Babar,* p. 31; fall, 1996, Lolly Robinson, review of *Babar's French and English Word Book,* p. 326; spring, 2001, Anne St. John, review of *Babar and the Succotash Bird,* p. 34; spring, 2002, Jennifer M. Brabander, review of *Babar's ABC,* p. 15, and Maeve Visser Knoth, review of *Babar and the Wully-Wully, Babar and the Ghost,* and *Babar's Little Girl,* p. 40; fall, 2002, review of *Babar's Little Girl Makes a Friend,* and *Meet Babar and His Family,* p. 299, and review of *Babar's Battle,* and *Babar's Birthday Surprise,* p. 324.

Kirkus Reviews, September 1, 1948, p. 434; January 15, 1961, p. 53; October 1, 1972, p. 1139; August 15, 2003, review of *Babar's Museum of Art,* p. 1071.

New Society, December 20, 1962, Edmund Leach, "Babar's Civilization Analysed," pp. 16-17.

New York Herald Tribune Book Review, November 14, 1948, p. 6; November 25, 1956, p. 12; November 17, 1957, p. 4; March 5, 1961, Margaret Sherwood Libby, review of *Serafina the Giraffe,* p. 35.

New York Times, November 14, 1948, Alice Fedder, review of *Babar's Cousin: That Rascal Arthur,* November 13, 1949, p. 12; November 2, 1952, p. 24; October 7, 1956, p. 38; November 5, 2001, Geraldine Fabrikant, "After Seventy Years, a Family Sells Its Stake in a Dapper Elephant," p. C5.

Publishers Weekly, November 20, 1961, "Babar: The de Brunhoff Books for Children"; October 28, 1968, "Authors and Editors"; October 11, 1993, review of *The Rescue of Babar,* p. 98; July 17, 2000, review of *Babar and the Succotash Bird,* p. 192, and Jennifer M. Brown, interview with Laurent de Brunhoff, p. 194; March 26, 2001, review of *Babar's ABC,* p. 95; June 10, 2002, "More Babar," p. 62; August 12, 2002, review of *Babar's Yoga for Elephants,* p. 298; September 9, 2002, review of *Babar's Yoga for Elephants,* pp. 60-61; July 21, 2003, review of *Babar's Museum of Art,* p. 193.

Reading Today, December, 2000, Lynne T. Burke, review of *Bonjour, Babar!,* p. 35.

School Library Journal, February, 1984, p. 57; February, 1985, p. 62; September, 1987, p. 162; December, 2000, Piper L. Nyman, review of *Babar and the Succotash Bird,* p. 107; November, 2003, Mary Elam, review of *Babar's Museum of Art,* p. 91.

Smithsonian, July, 1984, Robert Wernick, "A Lovable Elephant That Youngsters Never Forget," pp. 90-96.

Time, December 21, 1970; December, 2000, Piper L. Nyman, review of *Babar and the Succotash Bird,* p. 107; April, 2003, Lisa Gangemi Kropp, review of *Babar's Yoga for Elephants,* pp. 148.

USA Today, December, 2003, "Babar As Inspired by the Masters," pp. 8-9.

ONLINE

BookPage, http://www.bookpage.com/ (September, 2002), Jamie McAlister, "Laurent de Brunhoff Still Reigns over His Royal Legacy."

* * *

BUTTERS, Dorothy Gilman
See GILMAN, Dorothy

* * *

BYRD, Nicole
See ZACH, Cheryl (Byrd)

C

CALLEO, David P(atrick) 1934-

PERSONAL: Born July 19, 1934, in Binghamton, NY; son of Patrick and Gertrude (Crowe) Calleo; married Avis Thayer Bohlen. *Education:* Yale University, B.A. (magna cum laude), 1955, M.A., 1957, Ph.D., 1959.

ADDRESSES: *Home*—626 A St. NE, Washington, DC 20002. *Office*—Department of European Studies, Johns Hopkins School of Advanced International Studies, 1740 Massachusetts Ave. NW, Washington, DC 20036-1984; fax: 202-663-5784. *E-mail*—dcalleo@sais-jhu.edu.

CAREER: Brown University, Providence, RI, instructor in political science, 1959-60; Yale University, New Haven, CT, began as instructor, became assistant professor of political science, 1961-67; U.S. Department of State, consultant to undersecretary for political affairs, 1967-68; Johns Hopkins School of Advanced International Studies, Washington, DC, professor and director of European Studies Program, beginning 1968, Dean Acheson chair, beginning 1988, research associate of Washington Center of Foreign Policy Research, 1968-79, director of the center, 1974-75. Oxford University, research fellow of Nuffield College, 1966-67; senior Fulbright lecturer in Germany, 1975; Yale University, associate fellow, John Edwards College and trustee of Jonathan Edwards Trust. Twentieth Century Fund, project director, 1981-85; Lehrman Institute, vice president and member of board of trustees; Washington Foundation for European Studies, president and trustee. *Military service:* U.S. Army Reserve, 1956-65; became captain.

MEMBER: International Institute for Strategic Studies, Council on Foreign Relations, American Political Science Association, Century Association, Metropolitan Club of Washington, DC, Brook's Club (London).

AWARDS, HONORS: Gladys M. Kammerer Award for best book analyzing American national policy, American Political Science Association, 1973, for *America and the World Political Economy;* Fulbright fellowship, 1982; fellow of North Atlantic Treaty Organization, 1983; fellowships from Rockefeller Foundation, Guggenheim Foundation, and Social Science Research Council.

WRITINGS:

Europe's Future: The Grand Alternatives, Horizon Press (New York, NY), 1965.

Coleridge and the Idea of the Modern State, Yale University Press (New Haven, CT), 1966.

Europe's Future, Hodder & Stoughton (London, England), 1967.

Britain's Future, Horizon Press (New York, NY), 1968.

The Atlantic Fantasy, Johns Hopkins University Press (Baltimore, MD), 1970.

(With Benjamin M. Rowland) *America and the World Political Economy,* Indiana University Press (Bloomington, IN), 1974.

(Editor, with Harold van B. Cleveland, Charles P. Kindleberger, and Lewis E. Lehrman, and contributor) *Money and the Coming World Order,* New York University Press (New York, NY), 1976.

The German Problem Reconsidered: Germany in the World Order, 1870 to the Present, Cambridge University Press (New York, NY), 1978.

The Imperious Economy, Harvard University Press (Cambridge, MA), 1982.

Beyond American Hegemony: The Future of the Western Alliance, Basic Books (New York, NY), 1987.

(Editor, with Claudia Morgenstern) *Recasting Europe's Economies: National Strategies in the 1980s,* University Press of America (Lanham, MD), 1990.

NATO: Reconstruction or Dissolution?, Foreign Policy Institute, Johns Hopkins School of Advanced International Studies (Washington, DC), 1992.

The Bankrupting of America: How the Federal Budget Is Impoverishing the Nation, Morrow (New York, NY), 1992.

(Editor, with Philip Gordon) *From the Atlantic to the Urals: National Perspectives on the New Europe,* Seven Locks (Cabin John, MD), 1992.

Europe and World Order after the Cold War, Old Dominion University (Norfolk, VA), 1996.

(Editor, with Eric R. Staal) *Europe's Franco-German Engine,* Brookings Institution Press (Washington, DC), 1998.

Rethinking Europe's Future, Princeton University Press (Princeton, NJ), 2001, new edition, with afterword by the author, 2003.

Contributor to numerous books, including *Retreat from Empire? The First Nixon Administration,* edited by Robert Osgood, Johns Hopkins University Press (Baltimore, MD), 1973; *The Euro-American System: Economic and Political Relations between North America and Western Europe,* edited by Ernst-Otto Czempiel and Dankwart A. Rustow, Westview (Boulder, CO), 1976; *The End of the Keynesian Era: Essays on the Disintegration of the Keynesian Political Economy,* edited by Robert S. Skidelsky, Holmes & Meier (New York, NY), 1977; *The Future of American Foreign Policy,* edited by Charles W. Kegley, Jr. and Eugene R. Wittkopf, St. Martin's Press (New York, NY), 1992; and *France-Germany, 1983-1993: The Struggle to Cooperate,* edited by Patrick McCarthy, St. Martin's Press (New York, NY), 1993. Contributor to periodicals, including *Social Research, World Policy Journal, Journal of International Affairs, Ethics and International Affairs, Political Science Quarterly, Foreign Affairs,* and *Foreign Policy.*

SIDELIGHTS: David P. Calleo's *The Imperious Economy* "presents a major challenge to conventional economic thinking about the causes of virulent inflation," stated Grant D. Aldonas in the *Los Angeles Times Book Review.* In *The Imperious Economy,* Calleo charges that the devaluation of the American dollar during the past two decades is a result not of deficit spending during the Vietnam War, as is commonly assumed, but rather of older problems that stem from the historic inability of the United States to reconcile domestic and foreign objectives. Calleo "unfolds a subtle analysis of how inflation became embedded in the national fabric," Daniel Yergin wrote in the *Washington Post Book World.* The importance of *The Imperious Economy,* commented Aldonas, is that it "challenges assumptions and forces us to confront the complex interdependence of decisions at home with stature abroad."

Calleo argues in *The Imperious Economy* that chronic monetary inflation began in the United States during the Kennedy era when the government pushed for full employment as a panacea for domestic social unrest while at the same time spending large amounts of capital to maintain its global economic hegemony and military superiority. In order to achieve both full employment and world dominance, Calleo maintains, the United States began a policy of deficit spending in both good times and bad, thus increasing the flow of American currency without any corresponding real growth.

Richard J. Barnett commented in the *New York Times Book Review* that *The Imperious Economy* "is really an essay on the paradoxes of American Power." Calleo's argument is that in its pursuit of greater economic and military power, the United States contradicts its goal of restoring post-World War II Europe and Japan to economic stability and independence and deriving a more equitable world economic balance. "Calleo has long been a student of U.S.-European relations," wrote Aldonas. "He is at his best bringing out essential elements of our alliance and explaining why our security and economic interests sometimes differ. . . . This book is a must for those who hope to join the international economic debate."

BIOGRAPHICAL AND CRITICAL SOURCES:

PERIODICALS

Los Angeles Times Book Review, July 4, 1982, Grant D. Aldonas, review of *The Imperious Economy.*

New York Times Book Review, July 18, 1982, Richard J. Barnett, review of *The Imperious Economy.*

Times Literary Supplement, December 2, 1988.
Washington Post Book World, November 5, 1978; August 29, 1982, Daniel Yergin, review of *The Imperious Economy.**

* * *

CARTLIDGE, Michelle 1950-

PERSONAL: Born October 13, 1950, in London, England; daughter of Haydn Derrick (a director of transportation) and Barbara (a gallery director; maiden name, Feistmann) Cartlidge; married Richard Cook (an artist), June 25, 1982 (divorced, 1994); children: Theo. *Education:* Attended Hornsey College of Art, 1967-68, and Royal College of Art, 1968-70. *Hobbies and other interests:* Travel abroad.

ADDRESSES: *Agent*—Laura Cecil, 17 Alwyne Villas, London N1 2HG, England.

CAREER: Artist, 1970—; writer and illustrator of children's books, 1978—.

MEMBER: Society of Authors.

AWARDS, HONORS: Mother Goose Award, Books for Your Children Booksellers, 1979, for *Pippin and Pod.*

WRITINGS:

MOUSE BOOKS; SELF-ILLUSTRATED

Pippin and Pod, Pantheon (New York, NY), 1978.
A Mouse's Diary, Lothrop, Lee & Shepard (New York, NY), 1981.
Mousework, Heinemann (London, England), 1982.
Welcome to Mouseville, Methuen (New York, NY), 1982.
Baby Mouse, Heinemann (London, England), 1984, Penguin (New York, NY), 1986.
Mouse's Christmas Tree, Penguin (New York, NY), 1985.
Little Mouse Makes a Garden, Walker (New York, NY), 1986.
Little Mouse Makes a Mobile, Walker (New York, NY), 1986.
Little Mouse Makes Cards, Walker (New York, NY), 1986.
Little Mouse Makes Sweets, Walker (New York, NY), 1986.
A House for Lily Mouse, Prentice-Hall (Englewood Cliffs, NJ), 1986.
Mouse House, Dutton (New York, NY), 1990.
Baby Mice, Heinemann (New York, NY), 1991.
Clock Mice, Campbell (London, England), 1991.
Mouse in the House, Dutton (New York, NY), 1991.
Mouse Time, Dutton (New York, NY), 1991.
Mouse's Christmas House: A Story/Activity Book, Andrews & McMeel (Fairway, KS), 1991.
Mouse Theater, Dutton (New York, NY), 1992, published as *Theatre Mice,* Campbell (London, England), 1992.
Baby Mice at Home, Dutton (New York, NY), 1992.
Mouse Letters, Dutton (New York, NY), 1993.
The Mouse Wedding: A Press-out Model Book, Andrew & McMeel (Fairway, KS), 1993.
Mouse Birthday, Dutton (New York, NY), 1994, published as *Birthday Mouse,* Campbell (London, England), 1994.
Mouse's Scrapbook, Dutton (New York, NY), 1995.
Mouse Christmas, Dutton (New York, NY), 1996.
Mouse Magic, Dutton (New York, NY), 1996, published as *Magic Mouse,* Campbell (London, England), 1996.
The Mice of Mousehole: A Movable Picture Book, Walker (New York, NY), 1997.
School Mouse, Campbell (London, England), 1997.
Baby Mouse, Macmillan (New York, NY), 2000.
Mouse Ballet, Simon & Schuster (New York, NY), 2001.
Mouse Fairy Village, Mathew Price, 2001.
Toy Shop, Buster Books, 2003.
Clothes Shop, Buster Books, 2003.
Grocery Shop, Buster Books, 2003.
Café, Buster Books, 2003.

BEAR AND TEDDY BOOKS; SELF-ILLUSTRATED

The Bears' Bazaar: A Story/Craft Book, Lothrop, Lee & Shepard (New York, NY), 1979.
Teddy Trucks, Lothrop, Lee & Shepard (New York, NY), 1981.
Dressing Teddy (cut-out book), Heinemann (London, England), 1983, Penguin (New York, NY), 1986.
Teddy's Holiday, Heinemann (London, England), 1984.

Teddy's Birthday Party, Penguin (New York, NY), 1985.
Bear's Room: No Peeping, Methuen (New York, NY), 1985.
Teddy's Dinner, Simon & Schuster (New York, NY), 1986.
Teddy's Garden, Simon & Schuster (New York, NY), 1986.
Teddy's House, Simon & Schuster (New York, NY), 1986.
Teddy's Toys, Simon & Schuster (New York, NY), 1986.
Teddy's Christmas, Simon & Schuster (New York, NY), 1986.
Hello, Teddy, Heinemann (London, England), 1991.
Bear in the Forest, Dutton (New York, NY), 1991.
Bears on the Go, Dutton (New York, NY), 1992.
Good Night, Teddy, Walker (New York, NY), 1992.
Teddy's Friends, Walker (New York, NY), 1992.
Teddy's Cat, Walker (New York, NY), 1996.

BUNNY BOOKS; SELF-ILLUSTRATED

Playground Bunnies, Walker Books (London, England), 1987.
Seaside Bunnies, Walker Books (London, England), 1987.
Toy Shop Bunnies, Walker Books (London, England), 1987.
Birthday Bunnies, Walker Books (London, England), 1987.
Little Bunny's Picnic, Dutton (New York, NY), 1990.
Bunny's Birthday, Dutton (New York, NY), 1992.

OTHER; SELF-ILLUSTRATED

Little Boxes (cut-out book), Heinemann (London, England), 1983.
Munch and Mixer's Puppet Show: Presenting the Magic Lollipop, Prentice-Hall (Englewood Cliffs, NJ), 1983.
Little Shops, Heinemann (London, England), 1985.
Gerry's Seaside Journey, Heinemann (London, England), 1988.
Rabbit's Party, Heinemann (London, England), 1991.
Duck in the Pond, Dutton (New York, NY), 1991.
Elephant in the Jungle, Dutton (New York, NY), 1991.
Doggy Days, Heinemann (London, England), 1991, Dutton (New York, NY), 1992.
The Cats That Went to the Sea, PictureLions (London, England), 1992.
Fairy Letters, Campbell (London, England), 1993.
Michelle Cartlidge's Book of Words, Dutton (New York, NY), 1994.

OTHER; ILLUSTRATED BY KIM RAYMOND AND RUTH BLAIR

Bella's Birthday Party, Heinemann (London, England), 1994.
Boss Bear's Boat, Heinemann (London, England), 1994.
Gerry Kicks Off, Heinemann (London, England), 1994.
Gerry's Big Move, Heinemann (London, England), 1994.

ILLUSTRATOR

Brian Patten, *Mouse Poems,* Scholastic (New York, NY), 1998.
Brian Patten, *A Year of Mouse Poems,* Scholastic (New York, NY), 2000.

Some of Cartlidge's works have been translated and published in Spanish, Japanese, French, German, Portuguese, Swedish, Dutch, and Welsh.

SIDELIGHTS: When her first book, *Pippin and Pod,* was published in 1978, Michelle Cartlidge was honored with the Mother Goose Award as the "most exciting newcomer to children's book illustration." Since that time, Cartlidge has created a number of children's picture books featuring anthropomorphized mice, bears, and bunnies. Cartlidge's books usually contain few words; they are known for her finely detailed, delicate line drawings and warm pastel watercolors. While some critics have described her characters as static or have reported that it is difficult to tell them apart, many are charmed by the simple plots and cuddly animals Cartlidge portrays.

Cartlidge once told *CA* that she began her career as an artist at an early age. She was just fourteen when she left school to work in a pottery studio. Later, Cartlidge studied pottery at the Hornsey School of Art and then the Royal College of Art. When she was twenty years old, she decided that her pottery "was becoming so fragile that I was the only person who could touch it with safety." Cartlidge began to devote her efforts to drawing. "To support myself, I did odd jobs, waitressing and washing up, but had the opportunity to show publisher and illustrator Jan Pienkowski a selection of cards I'd produced for my family and friends. This resulted in a commission to design a series of cards for Gallery Five."

Cartlidge also wrote that she does her "best to create a world that a child will recognize, the kind of book he or she can step into to mingle with the characters portrayed." Throughout her career, Cartlidge has created picture books which provide activities, see-through windows, or movable parts, so that children "who have enjoyed reading about" her "characters can meet them again in active play." *Little Bunny's Picnic,* for example, has windows on every other page that give children a peek at the next scene. Liza Bliss of *School Library Journal* described this as "a fun gimmick." *Mouse Birthday, Mouse Time, Mouse Theater, Mouse's Scrapbook,* and *Mouse Letters* are movable books; in the latter two books, attached envelopes contain letters and mementos relating to the story. For her younger fans, Cartlidge creates board books with watercolor teddy bears engaged in daily activities, from playing to eating lunch. While these books, which include *Teddy's Friends, Teddy's House, Teddy's Toys, Teddy's Garden,* and *Teddy's Dinner,* do not move, according to *School Library Journal* contributor Linda Wicher in a review of *Teddy's Friends,* they are "easy for young hands to hold."

Cartlidge's first book, *Pippin and Pod,* featuring "dainty line and watercolor" illustrations according to a *Kirkus Reviews* critic, was published in 1978. Set in Cartlidge's childhood neighborhood of Hampstead, London, the book follows the afternoon adventures of two mice. While their mother shops, the brothers wander through a colorfully rendered market, construction site, playground, and park. Then, as a critic for *Publishers Weekly* noted, the "wee mice suddenly realize they're lost and want to go home." The mice finally find their mother and all ends well. Barbara Elleman of *Booklist* complimented Cartlidge's illustrations in the book, stating that the pictures give "a warm feeling to this simply told tale."

The Bears' Bazaar, Cartlidge's next book, presents craft ideas and instructions within a tale about a bear sister and brother. A *Publishers Weekly* reviewer described the book as "a buoyant story with ideas for projects that can involve the whole family." Together with their parents, the bear siblings make a mobile, painted paperweights, paper dolls, gingerbread bears, and mustard men. Although a *Junior Bookshelf* critic voiced some concerns about the presentation of the projects, the reviewer described the overall work as "attractive, with seemingly inexhaustible detail." Writing in *Growing Point,* Margery Fisher called *The Bears' Bazaar* "the most attractive craft-book of last year."

After *The Bears' Bazaar,* Cartlidge continued to produce books about tiny mice or soft-looking bears, all with simple plots or scenes. *A Mouse's Diary* features a mouse girl who writes in her diary about such activities as going to the park, to ballet class, and on a nature walk. A critic for *Growing Point* appreciated how Cartlidge rendered fully detailed scenes with "bright paint and a strong sense of composition." According to a *Publishers Weekly* reviewer, the story "rolls along effortlessly." In *Bear's Room: No Peeping,* Bear is busy working in the house when the mice do their best to spy on him. In "crowded strip pictures," as a *Junior Bookshelf* critic described them, Cartlidge portrayed the large, dressed bear preparing treats, painting a mural in his room, and then taking a bath. At the end of the story, Bear invites the mice into his room for a party, and they take delight in the seesaw he has crafted for them.

Michelle Cartlidge's Book of Words, published in 1994, features a watercolor-rendered mouse family in a number of detailed everyday scenes on double-page spreads. As the mice get dressed, go to school, go grocery shopping, visit the playground and have fun at a birthday party, Cartlidge presents over 300 common words for young children and beginning readers. A *Kirkus Reviews* critic questioned the "conventional picture of mouse family life portrayed" in the book, and noted that the female mice were placed in some stereotypical female roles. Similarly, Patricia Pearl Dole of *School Library Journal* pointed out that the female characters were all in dresses, but observed that chores were "shared by both sexes."

Cartlidge once explained to *CA* how she goes about creating her books. "When planning a book, I like to decide on a location, do lots of sketches, and develop the story from them. The amount of detail I include appeals to children, and Theo, my small son, takes a lively and useful interest in my work. I find him a most useful critic."

BIOGRAPHICAL AND CRITICAL SOURCES:

PERIODICALS

Booklist, October 1, 1978, Barbara Elleman, review of *Pippin and Pod,* pp. 290-291.

Growing Point, May, 1980, Margery Fisher, review of *The Bears' Bazaar: A Story/Craft Book,* p. 3704; November, 1981, review of *A Mouse's Diary,* p. 3960; March, 1983, p. 4046.

Horn Book Guide, fall, 1994, p. 267.

Junior Bookshelf, June, 1980, review of *The Bears' Bazaar,* p. 114; April, 1982; October, 1985, review of *Bear's Room: No Peeping,* p. 211.

Kirkus Reviews, October 1, 1978, review of *Pippin and Pod,* p. 1065; November 15, 1994, review of *Michelle Cartlidge's Book of Words,* p. 1524.

Publishers Weekly, September 25, 1978, review of *Pippin and Pod,* p. 141; March 28, 1980, review of *The Bears' Bazaar,* p. 49; July 16, 1982, review of *A Mouse's Diary,* p. 78; October 28, 1983, p. 70.

School Library Journal, April, 1982, p. 56; August, 1990, Liza Bliss, review of *Little Bunny's Picnic,* p. 126; October, 1992, Linda Wicher, review of *Teddy's Friends,* p. 85; January, 1995, Patricia Pearl Dole, review of *Michelle Cartlidge's Book of Words,* pp. 82-83.

* * *

CEDERING, Siv 1939-
(Siv Cedering Fox)

PERSONAL: Given name rhymes with "Steve"; born February 5, 1939, in Överkalix, Sweden; immigrated to the United States, 1953, naturalized citizen, 1958; daughter of Hilding (a builder) and Elvy (Wikström) Cedering; married David Lawrence Fox, January 19, 1958 (divorced, February, 1982); married Hans Van de Bovenkamp (a sculptor), August 23, 2000; children: (first marriage) Cedering, Lora Fox Gamble, Kell. *Politics:* Democrat.

ADDRESSES: Home—93 Merchant Rd., P.O. Box 89, Sagaponack, NY 11962; fax: 631-537-5751. *E-mail*—siv@hamptons.com.

CAREER: Poet, painter, sculptor, and composer. Has given poetry readings in Japan, Australia, and France, and at universities throughout the United States. University of Massachusetts, visiting lecturer, 1973; Columbia University, visiting writer, 1976; also visiting writer at University of Pittsburgh; conducted workshops in writing, art, and collaborative poetry. American-Scandanavian Foundation, member of publication committee, 1978; consultant. *Exhibitions:* Art work exhibited in about two-dozen group and solo shows, including work at ArtSpace in Amagansett, NY, 1998-2001, Elaine Benson Gallery, 1999-2002, Sculpture Showcase in New Hope, NJ, 2000-01, New Leaf in Berkeley, CA, 2000-02, and prior exhibitions at Nordic Heritage Museum, Adirondack Lakes Center for the Arts, Eastern New Mexico University, and East End Arts Council Gallery; photographs exhibited in New York at Modernage Photography Gallery, 1973.

MEMBER: PEN, Poetry Society of America, Poets and Writers.

AWARDS, HONORS: Poetry prize, Annapolis Fine Arts Festival, 1968; Poetry Society of America, John Masefield Narrative Poetry Award, 1969, and William Marion Reedy Award, 1970, both for "Ceremonial"; Emily Dickinson Award, 1977; photography prize, *Saturday Review,* 1970; Discovery Award, Modernage Photography Gallery, 1973; Borestone Mountain Poetry Award, 1973; fellowships from New York State Council on the Arts, for poetry, 1974-75, and for video, 1975; Pushcart Prizes, fiction category, 1977, for *The Juggler,* and poetry category, 1985; book of the year award, novel category, *Svenska Dagbladet,* 1980, for *Leken i grishuset;* Rhysling Award, best poem on a scientific theme, Science Fiction Poetry Association, 1985; artist's fellow, New York Foundation for the Arts, 1985 and 1992; exhibition prize, East End Arts Council photography show, 1991; grant from Swedish Writers Foundation, 1995-99.

WRITINGS:

UNDER NAME SIV CEDERING FOX

Letters from the Island, Fiddlehead Books (Fredericton, New Brunswick, Canada), 1973.

(Translator into Swedish from the English, Spanish, and Danish) *Det Blommande Trädet* (title means "The Flowering Tree"), Forum (Stockholm, Sweden), 1973.

Cup of Cold Water (poetry and photographs), New Rivers Press (New York, NY), 1973.

Letters from Helge (prose poetry), calligraphy by George Gintole, New Rivers Press (New York, NY), 1974.

(Editor and translator from the Swedish) *Friberg and Palm: Two Swedish Poets,* New Rivers Press (New York, NY), 1974, bilingual edition published as *Two Swedish Poets: Gösta Friberg and Göran Palm,* 1978.

Mother Is (poetry), Stein & Day (New York, NY), 1975.

How to Eat a Fortune Cookie (poetry), illustrated by Sally Soper Bowers, New Rivers Press (New York, NY), 1976.

Joys of Fantasy (nonfiction), photographs by Joseph del Valle, Stein & Day (New York, NY), 1977.

Color Poems: Twenty-three Poetry Broadsides, illustrated by Keith Abbott and others, Calliopea Press (Sausalito, CA), 1978.

The Blue Horse and Other Night Poems (for children), illustrated by Donald Carrick, Seabury (New York, NY), 1978.

UNDER NAME SIV CEDERING

The Juggler (poetry), etchings by Bill Braer, Sagarin Press (Chatham, NY), 1977.

(Editor and translator) *Twenty-seven Swedish Poems,* Calliopea Press (Sausalito, CA), 1978.

Leken i grishuset (novel; title means "The Pighouse Game"), Prisma (Stockholm, Sweden), 1980.

(Translator from the Swedish) Werner Aspenström, *You and I and the World* (poetry), Cross-Cultural Communications (Merrick, NY), 1980.

Oxen (novel; title means "The Ox"), Prisma (Stockholm, Sweden), 1981.

Twelve Pages from the Floating World (poetry), Calliopea Press (Sausalito, CA), 1983.

(And illustrator) *Grisen som ville bli ren* (poetry for children; title means "The Pig Who Wanted to Be Clean"), Rabén & Sjögren (Stockholm, Sweden), 1983.

Letters from the Floating World: Selected and New Poems, University of Pittsburgh Press (Pittsburgh, PA), 1984.

(And illustrator) *Polis, polis, potatisgris* (poetry for children; title means "The Pig and the Stolen Cakes"), Rabén & Sjögren (Stockholm, Sweden), 1985.

(And illustrator) *Grisen som ville bli julskinka* (poetry for children; title means "The Pig and the Christmas Ham"), Rabén & Sjögren (Stockholm, Sweden), 1986.

(And illustrator) *Grisen far till Paris* (poetry for children; title means "The Pig Goes to Paris"), Rabén & Sjögren (Stockholm, Sweden), 1987.

(Translator, with David Swickard) Lars Klinting, *Pearl's Adventure,* R & S Books (New York, NY), 1987.

Mannen i ödebyn (poetry for children; title means "The Man in the Deserted Village"), Rabén & Sjögren (Stockholm, Sweden), 1989.

Letters from an Observatory: New and Selected Poems, 1973-1998, Karma Dog Editions (Sagaponack, NY), 1998.

Composer, lyricist, narrator, and illustrator for several partially animated television programs based on her children's book *Grisen som ville bli ren.* Work included in hundreds of anthologies and textbooks, including *New Voices in American Poetry,* Winthrop, 1973; *Rising Tides: Twentieth-Century American Women,* Pocket Books (New York, NY), 1973; *Best Poems of 1973, Capstan,* 1976; *Uncommon Knowledge: Exploring Diversity through Reading and Writing,* edited by Rose Hawkins and Robert Isaacson, Houghton Mifflin (Boston, MA), 1996; and *Tangled Vines: A Collection of Mother and Daughter Poems,* edited by Lynn Lifshin, Harcourt Brace Jovanovich (New York, NY), 1992. Contributor of poetry, prose, and translations to numerous newspapers and literary magazines, including *Science, Harper's, Shenandoah, Prairie Schooner, Partisan Review, Massachusetts Review, Fiction International, New Republic, Paris Review, Kayak,* and to periodicals in Sweden and Japan; contributor of children's poetry to *Cricket.*

Cedering's English-language poetry has been translated into Swedish and Japanese.

ADAPTATIONS: Cedering's novel *Oxen* was adapted as a film by Sven Nykvist; the film was nominated for an Academy Award for best foreign-language film by the Academy of Motion Picture Arts and Sciences in 1992.

WORK IN PROGRESS: A memoir; poetry for young adults.

BIOGRAPHICAL AND CRITICAL SOURCES:

ONLINE

Warm Welcome from Siv Cedering!, http://www.cedering.com/ (February 27, 2004).

* * *

CHANG, Iris 1968-

PERSONAL: Born March 28, 1968, in Princeton, NJ; daughter of Shau-Jin (a physics professor) and Ying-Ying (a microbiology professor) Chang; married Bretton Lee Douglas (an electrical engineer), August 17, 1991. *Ethnicity:* "Chinese American." *Education:* University of Illinois-Urbana-Champaign, B.S., 1989; Johns Hopkins University, M.S., 1991.

ADDRESSES: *Home*—P.O. Box 641104, San Jose, CA 95164. *Agent*—Susan Rabiner, 240 West 35th St., Suite 500, New York, NY 10001. *E-mail*—irischang@aol.com.

CAREER: Writer. Has worked as a reporter for *Chicago Tribune* and the Associated Press; lecturer on human rights issues and history.

MEMBER: Committee of One Hundred.

AWARDS, HONORS: John D. and Catherine T. MacArthur Foundation Peace and International Cooperation Award; Woman of the Year Award, Organization of Chinese Americans, 1998; honorary doctorates, College of Wooster and California State University—Hayward.

WRITINGS:

Thread of the Silkworm, Basic Books (New York, NY), 1995.

The Rape of Nanking: The Forgotten Holocaust of World War II, Basic Books (New York, NY), 1997.

The Chinese in America: A Narrative History, Viking (New York, NY), 2003.

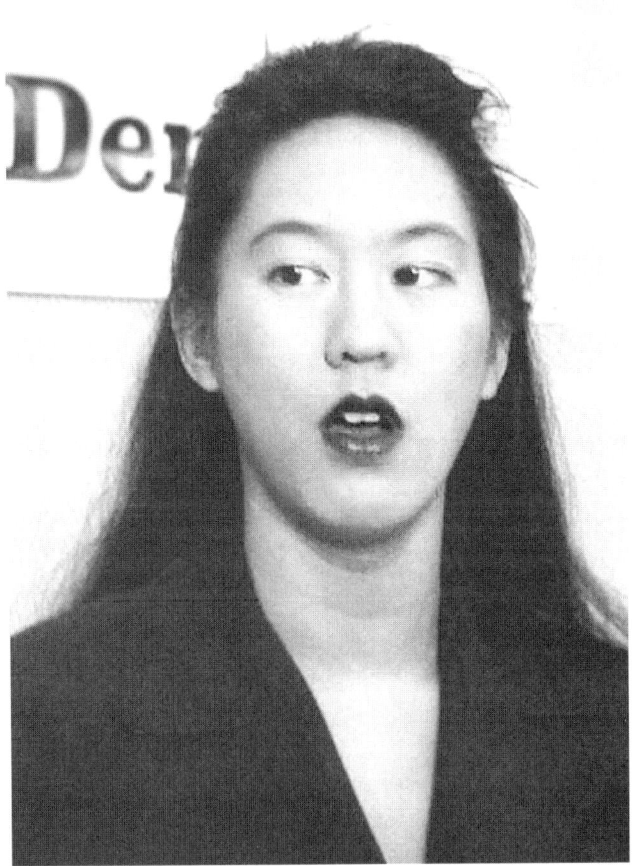

Iris Chang

Contributor to periodicals, including *New York Times*, *Los Angeles Times*, and *Newsweek*. *The Rape of Nanking* has been translated into Chinese and numerous other languages.

ADAPTATIONS: *Thread of the Silkworm* was adapted as an eight-set audiotape, Blackstone Audiobooks, 1998.

WORK IN PROGRESS: Fourth novel in progress.

SIDELIGHTS: Iris Chang, the granddaughter of immigrants who fled China in 1937, is a full-time author and former journalist who has made the issue of human rights, both in China and in the United States, her main focus of research. Her interest in the treatment of the Chinese under the Japanese occupation led to her best-known book, *The Rape of Nanking: The Forgotten Holocaust of World War II.* Chang's grandparents had fled the city shortly before the invasion, narrowly escaping the bloodbath that ensued:

Japanese troops, on order that came down from the Imperial family, tortured and killed more than 300,000 civilians over the course of six to eight weeks. They raped 80,000 women, bayoneted babies, beheaded individuals with swords, skinned people alive, and devised several other extremely cruel ways to murder their victims. Yet this incident remained little known except to those who were personally affected by it. Unlike the Holocaust in Europe, which has been extensively documented and studied and for which Germany has publicly acknowledged guilt, the rape of Nanking was all but forgotten. Chang's book on the subject, however, is perceived by commentators as opening Western eyes to the atrocity.

Chang did extensive research for her project, which was the first full account in English of the Nanking massacre. As a girl, Chang wanted to learn more about the story but could find nothing on the subject in her local library. As a college student with access to better research facilities, she discovered that what little information had been published about Nanking was too scholarly to be readable—these reports, she noted in an interview with Ami Chen Mills on the *MetroActive* Web site, were dry compilations of statistics. The frustration she encountered in her quest for information prompted the young writer to begin work on the story of Nanking herself.

In December, 1994, Chang attended the Global Alliance for Preserving the Truth of the Sino-Japanese War, where she first saw photographs of mutilated bodies in Nanking. "I was walking around in a state of shock," she told Mills. She did research at Yale Divinity School and the National Archives and was allowed to interview survivors in China. Chang had access to much previously unpublished material, including the diaries of foreign missionaries living in China at the time who witnessed the Japanese actions and tried to save Chinese civilians. A particularly interesting discovery was the diary of John Rabe, a German businessman in Nanking who set up an "International Safety Zone" to protect victims. Ironically, Rabe was a Nazi, who wore a swastika armband as he traveled through Nanking trying to help Chinese civilians and who was apparently unaware of the similar actions his native country was taking in Europe against Jews. Rabe became known as "the living Buddha of Nanking," and, because of the interest sparked by Chang's book, his diary has now been published in German, Chinese, and Japanese.

The Rape of Nanking, which was denounced in Japan for allegedly inflating the number of casualties, caused an immediate sensation and became an international best-seller. It was published in the United States at a time of renewed interest in World War II, shortly after the fiftieth anniversary of that conflict. By then the aging survivors of the war were starting to make their stories heard. Korean women came forward to reveal that Japanese soldiers had abused them as involuntary prostitutes. Two novels about Japanese atrocities in China, Paul West's *The Tent of Orange Mist* and R. C. Binstock's *Tree of Heaven,* were published in 1995, and a visual account, Shi Young and James Yin's *Rape of Nanking: An Undeniable History in Photographs,* was also available. Yet Chang's book was the first complete narrative on the subject in English.

Many critics deemed the book well researched and important. In a piece in the *New York Times Book Review,* Orville Schell praised the book highly and provided extensive context for the historical neglect of its subject. A *Publishers Weekly* reviewer called the book a "compelling, agonizing chronicle," and a critic for *Booklist* found it "a literary model of how to speak about the unspeakable." *The Rape of Nanking* was featured by the UPI Network and by *Ashi Shimbun,* a Japanese magazine with a large readership. It was also featured on *The NewsHour with Jim Lehrer* on PBS. The book became a *New York Times* notable book and was cited by the *Bookman Review* syndicate as one of the best books of 1997. *Reader's Digest* featured Chang in a cover story in 1998.

Working on *The Rape of Nanking* was emotionally difficult, admitted Chang, whose family fled China for Taiwan and then emigrated to the United States. "It's really frightening how fast you get used to the atrocities," she commented to Mills about her background reading on the subject. "It's very, very easy to just accept these atrocities and almost see them as banal. It really gave me insight into the true nature of evil and how easily we all can become desensitized." Speaking with David Gergen on PBS, Chang said that she was particularly upset to discover that the Nanking atrocities were committed by ordinary people. "Many of them were model citizens from Japan and when they returned became respectable members of the community," she noted. Extreme concentration of power, she concluded from her research, regardless of race or political affiliation, can create conditions under which seemingly normal human beings could commit crimes against humanity. "So it seems as if almost all people have this potential for evil, which would be unleashed only under certain dangerous social circumstances," she concluded.

Chang made it clear in her interview with Mills that, though her book has prompted comparisons with the Nazi Holocaust, it is "not an attempt to show that one ethnic group's suffering was worse than another's." Chang also noted that, after the United States dropped atom bombs on Japanese civilians in Hiroshima and Nagasaki, the shocked international community viewed Japan as a victim of war rather than an aggressor, which contributed to reluctance to hold Japan accountable for war crimes.

In the interview Chang also considered the issue of China's own reluctance to force Japan to offer significant apologies and reparations, because China so desperately needed Japan as an ally after the war. There is also a "tradition of Chinese political apathy in [the United States]," she commented. "Chinese learned from their ancestors and their parents that politics can be deadly." But she emphasized that, in recent years, activism among Chinese Americans is increasing, in part because the younger generation is beginning to enter fields such as filmmaking or literature, which provide wide-based options for communication. A three-day conference on the Nanking massacre, which Chang helped emcee, was held at Stanford University in 1996—evidence of growing political involvement among second-generation Chinese in Silicon Valley. A trend is also beginning that will require American schoolchildren to learn about the rape of Nanking as part of their history curriculum.

In her writings, Chang has also shown a continuing concern for the treatment of Chinese immigrants here in the United States. Her first book, though it attracted less notice than her work on Nanking, was the well-received *Thread of the Silkworm.* It tells the story of Chinese-American space scientist Hsue Shen Tsien, who was unjustly deported from the United States on trumped-up political charges during the McCarthy era. Chang shows in this book how irrational fears for immigrants and their descendants can be very counterproductive to our country. After being interrogated by the FBI, as Chang explained in an online interview with Robert Birnbaum for *Identity Theory,* Tsien was deported to China "against his will . . . because he was swapped for some American POWs. Here is an example of someone who was just a pawn in this whole chess game of international politics. But the story is so compelling because the intent of the government was to heighten and preserve national security, but the irony is that by deporting him they risked national security. Tsien went back and founded the ballistic missile program in China." A *Choice* reviewer called *Thread the Silkworm* "the most complete account of one of the saddest episodes of the Cold War," and the *Washington Post*'s Daniel Southerland said that Chang "writes compellingly."

Chang's theory about how Chinese immigrants are treated in the United States is that it has a lot to do with economic and political conditions at the time. If times are good, Americans will generally treat people of Chinese descent well. But in other cases, such as during recessions when Americans often saw Chinese immigrants as threats to their jobs, they have met with extreme racism. In her own experience growing up in a liberal university town, Chang did not come up against a great deal of prejudice, and had felt that such racism was something largely in the past. As she told Birnbaum, "I thought racism was soon going to be a relic of the past . . . [until] I saw [anti-Chinese] images explode unto the covers of national magazines in the late '90s."

Curious about the history of the Chinese experience in America, Chang recently researched Chinese immigration over approximately the last 150 years. The result of this research is her third book, *The Chinese in America: A Narrative History.* She explores in these pages the several waves of immigration that have occurred since the mid-nineteenth century, including those who came to America during the Gold Rush years, those who fled Communism in the 1950s, and the recent immigrants of the late-twentieth century who have come to study and find jobs as political tensions between the United States and China eased. *Seattle Times* writer Kimberly B. Marlowe, described the book as "thorough, important and devastating." A *Publishers Weekly* critic admired the way Chang portrayed the "rocky road between identity and assimilation" that Chinese immigrants must endure, concluding that *The Chinese in America* "surpasses even the high level of her best- selling *Rape of Nanking.*" And Brad Hooper, writing in *Booklist,* praised Chang for interspersing personal accounts through her books, "making it a much more human account. . . . This is history at its most dramatic and relevant." *The Chinese in America* was selected by the *San Francisco Chronicle* as one of the best books of 2003, and was nominated for the Bay Area Bookreviewers Association Award.

As in the past, the future of how Chinese Americans are treated in the United States will depend on political and economic developments, according to Chang. For example, as China becomes more technologically advanced, more Chinese engineers may take jobs from Americans, causing tensions to rise. On the other hand, many Americans are adopting more Chinese children into their families, which may foster better understanding between cultures. But whether Chang will write about such issues in the future remains to be seen. "I may attempt a novel," she told Birnbaum. "I think that no matter what you write it requires being honest with oneself and you have to pull yourself out of the whirlwind of daily life to meditate upon what you have experienced. That's a very difficult thing."

BIOGRAPHICAL AND CRITICAL SOURCES:

PERIODICALS

Air & Space-Smithsonian, April, 1996, p. 97.

Atlantic Monthly, April, 1998, review of *The Rape of Nanking: The Forgotten Holocaust of World War II,* pp. 110-116.

Book, May-June, 2003, Eric Wargo, review of *The Chinese in America: A Narrative History,* p. 79.

Booklist, December 1, 1997, p. 606; April 1, 2003, Brad Hooper, review of *The Chinese in America,* p. 1354.

Bulletin of the Atomic Scientist, March-April, 1998, Gretchen Kreuter, review of *The Rape of Nanking,* p. p. 65.

Choice, May 1996, p. 1498.

Christian Science Monitor, May 8, 2003, Terry Hong, "Fu Manchu Doesn't Live Here; The Struggle and Triumph of Chinese-Americans Are an Integral Part of U.S. History," p. 18.

Economist, June 21, 2003, "A Ragged Tale of Riches: Chinese Immigration," p. 76.

Foreign Affairs, May, 1996, p. 139; March-April, 1998, Donald Zagoria, review of *The Rape of Nanking,* p. 163.

Kirkus Reviews, November 1, 1997, p. 1618; March 15, 2003, review of *The Chinese in America,* p. 437.

Library Journal, January, 1998, Steven Lin, review of *The Rape of Nanking,* p. 115; May 15, 1999, Kent Rasmussen, review of *Thread of the Silkworm* (sound recording), p. 144; July, 1999, Kent Rasmussen, review of *The Rape of Nanking,* p. 158; May 1, 2003, Peggy Spitzer Christoff, review of *The Chinese in America,* p. 134.

Los Angeles Times, May 9, 2003, Anthony Day, "The Chinese Immigrant Story, All Part of the American Epic," p. E-26.

Los Angeles Times Book Review, March 24, 1996, p. 10.

National Review, November 10. 1997, p. 57.

Nature, March 14, 1996, p. 117.

New York Times Book Review, December 14, 1997.

Publishers Weekly, October 27, 1997, p. 58; May 5, 2003, review of *The Chinese in America,* p. 216.

Reason, June, 1998, Carl F. Horowitz, review of *The Rape of Nanking,* p. 69; May-June, 2003, review of *The Chinese in America,* p. 216.

San Francisco Chronicle, May 18, 2003, review of *The Chinese in America,* p. M2.

School Library Journal, April, 1998, Judy McAloon, review of *The Rape of Nanking,* p. 160.

Science, April 12, 1996, p. 217.

Science Books & Films, June, 1996, p. 136.

SciTech Book News, March, 1996, p. 55.

Seattle Times, May 18, 2003, Kimberly B. Marlowe, review of *The Chinese in America,* p. K10.

Society, January, 2000, Peter Li, "The Nanking Holocaust Tragedy, Trauma, and Reconciliation," p. 56.

Wall Street Journal, December 29, 1997, p. A9.

Washington Post Book World, January 21, 1996, pp.1-2.

ONLINE

Identity Theory, http://www.identitytheory.com/ (June 2, 2003), Robert Birnbaum, interview with Iris Chang.

Iris Chang Web Site, http://www.irischang.net (February 15, 2004).

MetroActive, http://www.metroactive.com/ (December 12-18, 1996).

Online NewsHour, http://www.pbs.org/newshour/ (February 20, 1998).

CLAPP, Nicholas 1936-

PERSONAL: Born May 1, 1936, in Providence, RI; son of Roger (a lawyer) and Helen Clapp; children: Cristina, Jennifer. *Education:* Brown University, B.A., 1957; University of South Carolina, M.A., 1962. *Hobbies and other interests:* Archaeology, photography, desert and mountain backpacking.

ADDRESSES: Office—1551 South Robertson Blvd., Los Angeles, CA 90035.

CAREER: Documentary film writer, producer, and director; author; lecturer. American Center of Oriental Research, member of board of trustees. *Military service:* Served in U.S. Army.

AWARDS, HONORS: Recipient of more than seventy awards for filmmaking, including several Academy Award nominations from the Motion Picture Academy of Arts and Sciences and Emmy Awards from the Academy of Television Arts and Sciences.

WRITINGS:

The Road to Ubar: Finding the Atlantis of the Sands, Houghton Mifflin (Boston, MA), 1998.

Sheba: Through the Desert in Search of the Legendary Queen, Houghton Mifflin (Boston, MA), 2001.

SIDELIGHTS: Nicholas Clapp is a documentary filmmaker who has also authored books related to his primary career. His 1998 book *The Road to Ubar: Finding the Atlantis of the Sands* resulted from his work on a 1996 *Nova* documentary program for public television titled *Lost City of Arabia.* In *Sheba: Through the Desert in Search of the Legendary Queen,* he tracks the life of the Queen of Sheba, a powerful woman whose activities are recounted in both the Christian bible and the Koran.

While working on a project in southern Arabia for the World Wildlife Fund in the 1980s, Clapp became fascinated with the area. On his return to Los Angeles he began to research the region in hopes of developing another project. A book-shop owner recommended that Clapp read Bertram Thomas's *Arabia Felix,* which includes an account of the fabled ancient city of Ubar. Legends claim that Ubar, once a thriving trade center, descended into wickedness and was destroyed by Allah. Clapp was immediately intrigued, especially when clues from other sources, such as *The Arabian Nights,* suggested that the seemingly fictitious city actually existed. Though he was not trained as an archaeologist, Clapp set out to find Ubar—and succeeded.

Researching the city, conducting the expedition, and writing the resulting book took over a decade. Clapp read extensively about Ubar's history and determined its probable site. He also obtained help from the National Aeronautics and Space Administration, which allowed him to use radar images from the space shuttle to search for traces of the ancient city, beneath the desert sands. Landsat and SPOT—remote sensing satellites—provided images that revealed evidence of tracks through the sand. These tracks were identified as old caravan routes that converged near the Empty Quarter where Ubar was believed to be buried. With a team of experts, including British explorer Sir Ranulph Fiennes, Clapp returned to Arabia to begin excavations.

The Road to Ubar, Clapp's account of his search for the site, recounts the difficulties and triumphs the team faced and its ultimate success in identifying the remains of an ancient city that once was an important link in the frankincense trade. While Clapp argues that the prosperous city was probably destroyed by a distant earthquake between 300 and 500 A.D., he also points out that the growth of Christianity in the region, which diminished demand for frankincense, was also instrumental in the city's decline as a mercantile center.

The Road to Ubar attracted favorable attention, and soon appeared on the *Los Angeles Times* best-seller list. *New York Times Book Review* critic Michiko Kakutani praised it as "a delightfully readable, if often highly speculative, volume that's part travel journal, part Walter Mittyesque daydream and part archeological history." Kakutani pointed out, however, that the chapter in which Clapp uses myth and imagination in an attempt to recreate the life of an Ubar ruler, weakens the book and "fails to fulfill any useful function" in an otherwise "gripping real-life story."

Sheba is based on similar research by Clapp, who traveled through Jerusalem, Arabia, and Ethiopia on the trail of the historic queen, and determines that

Sheba was actually Queen Bilquis, ruler of Saba—modern-day Yemen. Calling the volume "exciting, fast moving, and richly illustrated," *School Library Journal* contributor Christine C. Menefee added that Clapp's "observant eye, pitch-perfect ear, and unfailing sense of humor" will attract readers. While noting the author's tendency toward sensationalism, a *Publishers Weekly* contributor dubbed Clapp "a genial travel companion with a good eye for detail" and praised *Sheba* as a "well-written and informative book that will not disappoint."

BIOGRAPHICAL AND CRITICAL SOURCES:

PERIODICALS

Archaeology, July-August, 1992, p. 6.

Booklist, February 1, 1998; April 15, 2001, Allen Weakland, review of *Sheba: Through the Desert in Search of the Legendary Queen,* p. 1529.

Discover, January, 1993, pp. 56-58.

Kirkus Reviews, January 15, 1998, review of *The Road to Ubar: Finding the Atlantis of the Sands.*

Library Journal, May 15, 2001, Edward K. Werner, review of *Sheba,* p. 140.

Los Angeles Times, May 1, 2001, Michael Harris, review of *Sheba,* p. E3.

New York Times Book Review, February 27, 1998; June 30, 2002, review of *Sheba,* p. 20.

Publishers Weekly, January 19, 1998, review of *The Road to Ubar,* p. 364; April 2, 2001, review of *Sheba,* p. 53.

School Library Journal, December, 2001, Christine C. Menefee, review of *Sheba,* p. 175.

Southern Humanities Review, fall, 2002, Nathan P. Devir, review of *Sheba,* p. 377.

USA Today, May, 1998, p. 80.

Washington Post, July 29, 2001, Paul William Roberts, review of *Sheba,* p. T8.

ONLINE

NASA Observatorium Education Web site, http://www.observe.ivv.nasa.gov/ (September 2, 1998).

New York Times on the Web, http://www.nytimes.com/ (September 2, 1998), Michiko Kakutani, review of *The Road to Ubar.*

Nova Web site, http://web-cr02.pbs.org/ (September 10, 1998), transcript of *Lost City of Arabia.*

CLEARY, Beverly (Atlee Bunn) 1916-

PERSONAL: Born 1916, in McMinnville, OR; daughter of Chester Lloyd and Mable (Atlee) Bunn; married Clarence T. Cleary, October 6, 1940; children: Marianne Elisabeth, Malcolm James (twins). *Education:* University of California—Berkeley, B.A., 1938; University of Washington, Seattle, B.A., 1939. *Hobbies and other interests:* Travel, needlework.

ADDRESSES: Home—CA. *Agent*—c/o Author Mail, William Morrow/HarperCollins, 10 East 53rd St., 7th Floor, New York, NY 10022.

CAREER: Public Library, Yakima, WA, children's librarian, 1939-40; U.S. Army Hospital, Oakland, CA, post librarian, 1942-45; writer for young people, 1950—.

MEMBER: Authors Guild, Authors League of America.

AWARDS, HONORS: Young Readers' Choice Award, Pacific Northwest Library Association, 1957, for *Henry and Ribsy,* 1960, for *Henry and the Paper Route,* 1968, for *The Mouse and the Motorcycle,* 1971, for *Ramona the Pest,* and 1980, for *Ramona and Her Father;* Dorothy Canfield Fisher Memorial Children's Book Award, 1958, for *Fifteen,* 1961, for *Ribsy,* and 1985, for *Dear Mr. Henshaw;* Notable Book citation, American Library Association, 1961, for *Jean and Johnny,* 1966, for *The Mouse and the Motorcycle,* 1978, for *Ramona and Her Father,* and 1984, for *Dear Mr. Henshaw;* South Central Iowa Association of Classroom Teachers' Youth Award, 1968, Hawaii Association of School Librarians/Hawaii Library Association Nene Award, 1971, New England Round Table of Children's Librarians Honor Book Award, 1972, Sue Hefley Award from Louisiana Association of School Librarians, 1972, and Surrey School Book Award from Surrey School District, 1974, all for *The Mouse and the Motorcycle;* Nene Award from Hawaii Association of School Librarians and Hawaii Library Association, 1968, for *Ribsy,* 1969, for *Ramona the Pest,* 1972, for *Runaway Ralph,* and 1980, for *Ramona and Her Father;* William Allen White Award, Kansas Association of School Libraries and Kansas Teachers' Association, 1968, for *The Mouse and the Motorcycle,* and 1975, for *Socks;* Georgia Children's Book Award, College of Education, University of Georgia, 1970, Sequoyah

Beverly Cleary

Children's Book Award, Oklahoma Library Association, 1971, and Massachusetts Children's Book Award nomination, 1977, all for *Ramona the Pest;* New England Round Table of Children's Librarians Honor Book Award, 1972, for *Henry Huggins;* Charlie Mae Simon Award, Arkansas Elementary School Council, 1973, for *Runaway Ralph,* and 1984, for *Ramona Quimby, Age Eight;* Distinguished Alumna Award, University of Washington, 1975; Laura Ingalls Wilder Award, American Library Association (ALA), 1975, for substantial and lasting contributions to children's literature; Golden Archer Award, University of Wisconsin, 1977, for *Socks* and *Ramona the Brave;* Children's Choice Election Award, second place, 1978; *Ramona and Her Father* appeared on *Horn Book*'s honor list, 1978; Mark Twain Award, Missouri Library Association and Missouri Association of School Librarians, 1978, for *Ramona the Brave;* Newbery Honor Book Award from ALA and *Boston Globe-Horn Book* Honor Award, both 1978, both for *Ramona and Her Father;* People Honor Book Award, International Board on Books for Young People, Tennessee Children's Book Award, Tennessee Library Association, Utah Children's Book Award, Children's Library Association of Utah, and Garden State Award, New Jersey Library Association, all 1980, for *Ramona and Her Father;* Regina Medal from Catholic Library Association, 1980, for "continued distinguished contributions to literature"; Land of Enchantment Children's Award and Texas Bluebonnet Award, both 1981, for *Ramona and Her Father;* American Book Award, 1981, for *Ramona and Her Mother; Ramona Quimby, Age Eight* was included on *School Library Journal*'s "Best Books 1981" list; de Grummond Award, University of Mississippi and medallion, University of Southern Mississippi, both 1982, for distinguished contributions to children's literature; *Ralph S. Mouse* was included on *School Library Journal*'s "Best Books 1982" list; Newbery Honor Book Award, ALA and American Book Award nomination, both 1982, for *Ramona Quimby, Age Eight;* Garden State Children's Choice Award, New Jersey Library Association, 1982, for *Ramona and Her Mother,* 1984, for *Ramona Quimby, Age Eight,* and 1985, for *Ralph S. Mouse; Dear Mr. Henshaw* was included on *School Library Journal*'s "Best Books of 1983" list, named *New York Times* Notable Book of 1983, and noted on *Horn Book*'s honor list, 1984; English Award, California Association of Teachers of English, and Golden Kite Award, Society of Children's Book Writers, both 1983, for *Ralph S. Mouse;* Christopher Award, 1983, for *Dear Mr. Henshaw;* Charles Near Simon Award from Arkansas Elementary School Council, Michigan Young Readers Award, and Buckeye Children's Book Award, all 1984, for *Ramona Quimby, Age Eight;* Iowa Children's Choice Award, Iowa Educational Media Association, 1984, for *Ralph S. Mouse;* Newbery Medal, ALA, Commonwealth Silver Medal, Commonwealth Club of California, Dorothy Canfield Fisher Children's Book Award, and *New York Times* notable book citation, all 1984, for *Dear Mr. Henshaw;* U.S. author nominee for Hans Christian Andersen award, 1984; Buckeye Children's Book Award, 1985, for *Ramona and Her Mother; Everychild* honor citation, 1985, for thirty-five year contribution to children's literature; Ludington Award, Educational Paperback Association, 1987; honor book citation, Hawaii Association of School Librarians and the Children and Youth Section of Hawaii Library Association, 1988; honorary doctorate, Cornell College, 1993; National Medal of Arts, 2003. Cleary's books have received more than thirty-five state awards based on the direct votes of her young readers.

WRITINGS:

Henry Huggins, Morrow (New York, NY), 1950, fiftieth anniversary edition, with foreword by Cleary, Harper Collins (New York, NY), 1999.
Ellen Tebbits, Morrow (New York, NY), 1951.
Henry and Beezus, Morrow (New York, NY), 1952.
Otis Spofford, Morrow (New York, NY), 1953.
Henry and Ribsy, Morrow (New York, NY), 1954.
Beezus and Ramona, Morrow (New York, NY), 1955.
Fifteen (teen), Morrow (New York, NY), 1956.
Henry and the Paper Route, Morrow (New York, NY), 1957.
The Luckiest Girl, Morrow (New York, NY), 1958.
Jean and Johnny (teen), Morrow (New York, NY), 1959.
The Real Hole (preschool), Morrow (New York, NY), 1960, revised edition, 1986.
Hullabaloo ABC (preschool), Parnassus (New York, NY), 1960, new edition, with new illustrations, Morrow (New York, NY), 1998.
Two Dog Biscuits (preschool), Morrow (New York, NY), 1961, revised edition, 1986.
Emily's Runaway Imagination, Morrow (New York, NY), 1961.
Henry and the Clubhouse, Morrow (New York, NY), 1962.
Sister of the Bride, Morrow (New York, NY), 1963.
Ribsy, Morrow (New York, NY), 1964.
The Mouse and the Motorcycle, Morrow (New York, NY), 1965.
Mitch and Amy, Morrow, 1967, new edition, illustrated by Bob Marstall, Morrow (New York, NY), 1991.
Ramona the Pest (also see below), Morrow (New York, NY), 1968.
Runaway Ralph, Morrow (New York, NY), 1970.
Socks, Morrow (New York, NY), 1973.
The Sausage at the End of the Nose (play), Children's Book Council, 1974.
Ramona the Brave, Morrow (New York, NY), 1975.
Ramona and Her Father (also see below), Morrow (New York, NY), 1977.
Ramona and Her Mother (also see below), Morrow (New York, NY), 1979.
Ramona Quimby, Age Eight (also see below), Morrow (New York, NY), 1981.
Ralph S. Mouse, Morrow (New York, NY), 1982.
Dear Mr. Henshaw, Morrow (New York, NY), 1983.
Cutting Up with Ramona!, Dell (New York, NY), 1983.
Ramona Forever (also see below), Morrow (New York, NY), 1984.
The Ramona Quimby Diary, Morrow (New York, NY), 1984.
Lucky Chuck, Morrow (New York, NY), 1984.
Beezus and Ramona Diary, Morrow (New York, NY), 1986.
The Growing-Up Feet, Morrow (New York, NY), 1987.
Janet's Thingamajigs, Morrow (New York, NY), 1987.
A Girl from Yamhill: A Memoir, Morrow (New York, NY), 1988.
Meet Ramona Quimby (includes *Ramona and Her Father, Ramona and Her Mother, Ramona Forever, Ramona Quimby, Age Eight,* and *Ramona the Pest*), Dell (New York, NY), 1989.
Muggie Maggie, Morrow (New York, NY), 1990.
Strider, Morrow (New York, NY), 1991.
Petey's Bedtime Story, illustrated by David Small, Morrow (New York, NY), 1993.
My Own Two Feet: A Memoir, Morrow (New York, NY), 1995.
Ramona's World, illustrated by Alan Tiegreen, Morrow (New York, NY), 1999.
Lucky Chuck, illustrated by J. Winslow Higginbottom, HarperCollins (New York, NY), 2002.

Also author of *Ramona and Her Friends* (an omnibus edition), and *Leave It to Beaver* (adapted from television scripts). Contributor to periodicals, including *Woman's Day.*

ADAPTATIONS: Pied Piper produced recordings and filmstrips of *Henry and the Clubhouse,* 1962, and *Ribsy,* 1964. Miller-Brody produced recordings, some with accompanying filmstrips, of *Ramona and Her Father,* 1979, *Beezus and Ramona,* 1980, *Henry Huggins,* 1980, *Henry and Ribsy,* 1980, *Ramona and Her Mother,* 1980, *Ramona the Brave,* 1980, *Ramona Quimby, Age Eight,* 1981, *Henry and Beezus,* 1981, *Ralph S. Mouse,* 1983, and *Dear Mr. Henshaw,* 1984. A six-episode series based on *The Mouse and the Motorcycle, Runaway Mouse,* and *Ralph S. Mouse* was produced by Churchill Films for American Broadcasting Companies, Inc. (ABC-TV); *Ramona,* a ten-part series based on Cleary's character Ramona Quimby, was broadcast on the Public Broadcasting Service (PBS) in 1988; television programs based on the "Henry Huggins" books have appeared in Japan, Sweden, and Denmark. Many of the stories have been adapted for the stage.

SIDELIGHTS: Beverly Cleary's humorous, realistic portraits of American children have rendered her among the most successful writers for young readers. Books were important to Cleary from an early age, for her mother established the first lending library in the small town of McMinnville, Oregon, where Cleary was born. "It was in this dingy room filled with shabby leather-covered chairs and smelling of stale cigar smoke that I made the most magic of discoveries," Cleary recalled in *Top of the News.* "There were books for children!"

Cleary eagerly anticipated attending school and learning to read. Once she became a student, however, she found herself stifled by the rigid teaching methods of that time. "We had no bright beckoning book with such words as 'fun,' 'adventure,' or 'horizon' to tempt us on. . . . Our primer looked grim," she remembered in a *Horn Book* article. "Its olive-green cover with its austere black lettering bore the symbol of a beacon light, presumably to guide us and to warn us of the dangers that lay within. . . . The first grade was soon sorted into three reading groups: Bluebirds, Redbirds, and Blackbirds. I was a Blackbird, the only girl Blackbird among the boy Blackbirds who had to sit in the row by the blackboard. . . . To be a Blackbird was to be disgraced. I wanted to read, but somehow I could not. I wept at home while my puzzled mother tried to drill me on the dreaded word charts."

But under the guidance of her second-grade teacher, Cleary eventually learned "to plod through [the] reader a step or two ahead of disgrace," and she even managed to regain her original enthusiasm for books. She found, however, that the books available to her were ultimately unsatisfactory, for they bore no relation to the life she knew as a middle-class child in Portland, Oregon. Instead of reflecting Cleary's own experiences, the books told of "wealthy English children who had nannies and pony carts or books about poor children whose problems were solved by a long-lost rich relative turning up in the last chapter," she explained in a speech reprinted in *Horn Book.* "I had had enough. . . . I wanted to read funny stories about the sort of children I knew and decided that someday when I grew up I would write them." Cleary has achieved just that, and her books are now common fare in elementary school curricula and individual teachers' lessons plans.

Cleary wrote her funny stories, setting most of her books on or around Klickitat Street, a real street near her childhood home. The children in her books face situations common in real children's lives—finding a stray dog, forgetting to deliver newspapers, the horror of having to kiss in a school play. They misbehave, and they discover that adults are not always fair. In a speech reprinted in *Catholic Library World,* Cleary noted that one of her books, *Otis Spofford,* generated considerable controversy upon publication in 1953, and was even rejected by some libraries, merely because "Otis threw spitballs and did not repent."

Perhaps the most endearing and popular of Cleary's characters is Ramona Quimby, a spunky little girl who would make fairly regular appearances in Cleary's books after Henry Huggins began appearing in the 1950s. But it was not until 1968, with the publication of *Ramona the Pest,* that Ramona had assumed the position of heroine in one of Cleary's publications. Critics, as well as readers, responded enthusiastically to this expansion of Ramona's character, and ensuing works about Ramona would be met with almost unqualified praise. A critic in *Young Readers' Review* commented: "As in all her books about the boys and girls of Klickitat Street, Mrs. Cleary invests [*Ramona the Pest*] with charm, humor, and complete honesty. There are some adults who can remember many incidents from their early childhood; there are few who can remember how they felt about things and why; there are fewer who can communicate these feelings. And fewer still who can retain the humorous aspects. Mrs. Cleary is one of those rare ones. . . . Even boys and girls who dislike stories about children younger than themselves enjoy the incidents in which Ramona makes a pest of herself. . . . Ramona has never been funnier and has never been so sympathetic a character. . . . As usual, this is standard Cleary first-rate entertainment." Polly Goodwin of *Book World* called Ramona "a wonderfully real little girl trying hard to express herself, to understand and be understood in a bewildering world."

The sequel to *Ramona the Pest,* titled *Ramona the Brave,* was equally well received. A reviewer in the *Bulletin of the Center for Children's Books* wrote that it is "diverting [and] written with the ebullient humor and sympathy that distinguish Cleary's stories. Ramona is as convincing a first-grader as a fictional character can be." A *Growing Point* reviewer called it "straight domestic writing at its liveliest and most skillful."

Cleary told *CA* that the books about Ramona reflect a "child's relationship with adults." This is evident in

Ramona and Her Father, in which Mr. Quimby loses his job and begins to smoke too much, prompting Ramona to start a ferocious no-smoking campaign in order to save her father's life. A critic in *Booklist* wrote: "With her uncanny gift for pinpointing the thoughts and feelings of children right down to their own phraseology—while honoring the boundaries of clean, simple writing—the author catches a family situation that puts strain on each of its members, despite their intrinsic strength and invincible humor. . . . [The resulting story is] true, warm-hearted, and funny." A reviewer in *Growing Point* noted that "the humorous tone of these neatly particularized domestic situations is never flippant, and behind it a picture is built up of a stable and sensible American family, in which that wayward individualist Ramona is able to develop in happy security." *Times Literary Supplement* contributor Peter Hunt further praised Cleary for her skill in pulling off "the difficult trick of keeping to a second-grader's viewpoint without being condescending or 'cute.'"

Katherine Paterson analyzed Cleary's brand of humor in a *Washington Post Book World* article. "When I was young there were two kinds of funny—funny ha-ha and funny peculiar," Paterson wrote. "A lot of funny ha-ha things happen in Cleary's books, but her real specialty is another kind of funny, which is a cross between funny ha-ha and funny ahhh. Cleary has the rare gift of being able to reveal us to ourselves while still keeping an arm around our shoulder. We laugh (ha ha) to recognize that funny, peculiar little self we were and are and then laugh (ahhh) with relief that we've been understood at last. . . . Cleary is loved because she can describe simply the complex feelings of a child. But even more, Cleary is able to sketch clearly with a few perfect strokes the inexplicable adult world as seen through a child's eyes."

After publishing *Ramona Forever* in 1984, Cleary allowed fifteen years to pass before she revived the Ramona series with *Ramona's World,* which finds the plucky child in fourth grade. In this tale Ramona gamely endeavors to win a best friend while tolerating the arrival of a baby into her family. During the course of the book, Ramona attempts to vacuum a cat, and while playing in a friend's attic she manages to plunge through the thin ceiling and hang suspended over a dining area. A *Publishers Weekly* critic reported that "most of Ramona's triumphs and traumas are timeless and convincingly portrayed." A *Booklist* reviewer, meanwhile, concluded that "for the most part, this is just what readers have been waiting for: vintage Ramona."

Rosemary Herbert in a 1999 *Boston Herald* article found that Cleary's books were reappearing in the children's sections of bookstores. She asked, "Do you feel as if you've entered a time warp when you browse the children's section of your favorite bookstore? Look around. Here's Ludwig Bemelmans' Madeline. There's Beverly Cleary's Ramona. . . . What brought these plucky girls of the '20s, '30s, '50s and '60s back into print?" Interviewing several publishers provided the answer: "Mindful that parents hold the purse strings, [publishers are] marketing nostalgia to adults rather than books to kids." But in the case of Ramona, Cathryn Mercier, associate director of the Center for the Study of Children's Literature at Simmons College in Boston, assured Herbert, "The release of *Ramona's World*—the first Ramona book to be written by the character's creator in fifteen years—is not clouded in controversy. Like Eloise, Madeline, and Hitty, Ramona remains appealing because she 'exhibits independence of thought and action.'"

The ability to portray the world of adults through a child's perspective is a strength of Cleary's nonfiction as well as her fiction. In her two volumes of autobiographical writing—*A Girl from Yamhill: A Memoir,* which appeared in 1988, and *My Own Two Feet: A Memoir,* which was published in 1995—Cleary "immediately makes one understand why [her] books are perennial favorites," according to Mary M. Burns in *Horn Book.* Recounting Cleary's childhood in Portland, Oregon, during the Great Depression, *A Girl from Yamhill* reveals the real Klickitat Street and shows that the roots of many of the fictional episodes of Ramona Quimby were based on her creator's own life. Praising Cleary's choice of topics—which include the emotional difficulties in moving to a new town, dealing with an overly demonstrative male relative, a less expressive mother whose affection was channelled into molding her children to her own designs, and dealing with the pangs of adolescent first love—Lillian N. Gerhardt wrote in *School Library Journal,* "As with her fiction, readers are likely to want her memoir to go on when they read her last page."

A Girl from Yamhill ends in 1934, as Cleary begins her college education in Southern California. *My Own Two Feet* takes up the story where its predecessor left off, with the future author on a Greyhound bus bound from Oregon to California, ready to begin her life as an independent adult. *My Own Two Feet* "is a Depression story and then a World War II home-front story," explained Perri Klass in the *New York Times Book Review,* "but most remarkably it is a story about craving independence and craving education." From college, where she studied library science, Cleary obtained a job as a children's librarian in Washington. The children she met there would inspire her early attempts at fulfilling her childhood dream of becoming a writer of books for young readers. In between attending college and publishing her first book in 1950, Cleary experienced courtship and marriage, the financial stresses caused by making a living during the Depression years, and an emotional confrontation with a strong-willed, controlling mother. Cleary's "vivid recollections" of the many small events that figured in her journey as a student and young wife "are continued evidence of this author's ability to convince readers," maintained Ruth K. MacDonald in *School Library Journal.* "It's all in the details."

While her autobiographies reveal that many of her books had their basis in her own life, Cleary has also written on topics with which she has not had first-hand experience. Publication of the 1983 volume *Dear Mr. Henshaw,* for example, marked Cleary's response to many letters asking for a book about a child of divorce. In this book, protagonist Leigh Botts's letters to his favorite author reveal his loneliness and confusion following his parents' separation. While Cleary's characteristic humor is still present, *Dear Mr. Henshaw* represents a change in her style and tone, and it is probably the author's most serious work. She remarked in a speech reprinted in *Horn Book:* "When I wrote *Dear Mr. Henshaw,* I did not expect every reader to like Leigh as much as Ramona. Although I am deeply touched that my books have reached two generations of children, popularity has never been my goal. If it had been, I would have written *Ramona Solves the Mystery of the Haunted House and Finds a Baby Brother* or something like *Henry and Beezus Play Doctor,* instead of a book about the feelings of a lonely child of divorce."

Some critics have questioned the role that Cleary's characters (especially Ramona) play in pressuring children to adapt to school homogenization. Linda Benson in *Children's Literature in Education* asked whether "the dominant culture manipulates the character of Ramona, who, if not silenced or entirely subdued by the end of the series, is at least much more civilized according to the norms of the classroom."

But many critics and children alike responded enthusiastically to Cleary's efforts. Natalie Babbitt declared in the *New York Times Book Review:* "Beverly Cleary has written many very good books over the years. This one is the best. It is a first-rate, poignant story. . . . There is so much in it, all presented so simply, that it's hard to find a way to do it justice. Mrs. Cleary knows the voice of children. Dialogue has always been one of the strongest parts of her work. And here, where all is dialogue, that strength can shine alone and be doubly impressive. . . . What a lovely, well-crafted, three-dimensional work this is. And how reassuring . . . to see that a 27th book can be so fresh and strong. Lots of adjectives here; she deserves them all."

Cleary told *CA:* "I doubt if my dear, encouraging high-school English teachers would approve of my writing process today. Fifty years ago, when I began to write, I dutifully tried to outline a story, a task I found so tiresome I quickly abandoned it and simply wrote. I often begin a book in the middle and work out a beginning and an end. This method leads to untidy manuscripts. Revising, however, is the part of writing I enjoy most, and when I can reduce a page to a paragraph, I know my story is headed in the right direction.

"I write in longhand on yellow, lined paper. I write on every third line to leave room for additions. When the manuscript is finished, I fight my enemy, the typewriter, to produce a legible copy for a good typist."

BIOGRAPHICAL AND CRITICAL SOURCES:

BOOKS

Arbuthnot, May Hill, *Children and Books,* 3rd edition, Scott, Foresman, 1964.

Berg, Julie, *Beverly Cleary,* Abdo & Daughters (Edina, MN), 1993.

Books for Children, 1960-65, American Library Association (Chicago, IL), 1966.

Carlsen, R. Robert, *Books and the Teen-Age Reader,* Harper (New York, NY), 1967.

Chambers, Mary, editor, *The Signal Review I: A Selective Guide to Children's Literature,* Thimble Press, 1983.

The Children's Bookshelf, Child Study Association of America, 1965.

Children's Literature Review, Gale (Detroit, MI), Volume 2, 1976, Volume 8, 1985.

Cullinan, Bernice E., and others, *Literature and the Child,* Harcourt (New York, NY), 1981.

Dictionary of Literary Biography, Volume 52: *American Writers for Children since 1960: Fiction,* Gale (Detroit, MI), 1986.

Dreyer, Sharon Spredemann, *The Bookfinder: A Guide to Children's Literature about the Needs and Problems of Youth Aged 2-15,* American Guidance Service, 1977.

Eakin, Mary K., *Good Books for Children: A Selection of Outstanding Children's Books Published, 1950-65,* University of Chicago Press (Chicago, IL), 1966.

Egoff, Sheila A., *Thursday's Child: Trends and Patterns in Contemporary Children's Literature,* American Library Association (Chicago, IL), 1981.

Gannon, Susan R., and Ruth Anne Thompson, editors, *Proceedings of the Thirteenth Annual Conference of the Children's Literature Association,* University of Missouri-Kansas City, May 16-18, 1986, Purdue University Press (West Layfayette, IN), 1988.

Hopkins, Lee Bennett, *More Books by More People,* Citation Press, 1974.

Huck, Charlotte S., and Doris Young Kuhn, *Children's Literature in the Elementary School,* 2nd edition, Holt (New York, NY), 1968.

Kelly, Joanne, *The Beverly Cleary Handbook,* Teacher Ideas Press (Englewood, CO),, 1996.

Larrick, Nancy, *A Teacher's Guide to Children's Books,* Merrill (Cincinnati, OH), 1966.

Pflieger, Pat, *Beverly Cleary,* Twayne (Boston, MA), 1991.

Rees, David, *The Marble in the Water: Essays on Contemporary Writers of Fiction for Children and Young Adults,* Horn Book (Boston, MA), 1980.

Sadker, Myra Pollack, and David Miller Sadker, *Now upon a Time: A Contemporary View of Children's Literature,* Harper (New York, NY), 1977.

Sebesta, Sam Keaton, and William J. Iverson, *Literature for Thursday's Child,* Science Research Associates, 1975.

Sutherland, Zena, and others, *Children and Books,* 6th edition, Scott, Foresman, 1981.

Townsend, John Rowe, *Written for Children: An Outline of English-Language Literature,* Horn Book (Boston, MA), 1981.

PERIODICALS

Atlantic Monthly, December, 1953; December, 1964.

Booklist, September 1, 1953; September 1, 1954; October 1, 1977; May 1, 1979; September 1, 1981; September 1, 1983; September 1, 1984; April 15, 1998, p. 1460; November 15, 1998, p. 598; June 1, 1999.

Book Window, spring, 1981.

Book World, September 8, 1968.

Boston Herald, December 13, 1999, Rosemary Herbert, "The Girls Are Back!," p. 37.

Buffalo News, November 13, 2000, p. D1.

Bulletin of Bibliography, December 1999, p. 219.

Bulletin of the Center for Children's Books, September, 1959; September, 1961; October, 1963; May, 1967; July, 1975; December, 1977; June, 1979; September, 1982; May, 1984; September, 1984.

Catholic Library World, February, 1980; July-August, 1981.

Children's Book Review, spring, 1975.

Children's Literature Association Quarterly, fall, 1998, p. 131.

Children's Literature in Education, June, 1991, p. 97; March, 1999, p. 9.

Christian Science Monitor, September 6, 1951; November 27, 1957; November 15, 1962; October 15, 1979; May 14, 1982; June 6, 1983.

Cincinnati Post, September 25, 2000, p. 1B.

Detroit News, August 10, 1983.

Early Years, August-September, 1982.

Elementary English, November, 1967.

Entertainment Weekly, May 7, 1993, p. 66; August 20, 1993, p. 73.

Five Owls, July-August, 1990, pp. 106-107; September-October, 1991, p. 18; February, 1994, p. 58.

Growing Point, March, 1963; January, 1976; September, 1978; July, 1980; January, 1983; May, 1983.

Horn Book, December, 1951; December, 1959; October, 1962; October, 1963; December, 1964; June, 1969; August, 1970; August, 1975; December, 1977; October, 1982; December, 1982; October, 1983; August, 1984; September, 1984; May-June, 1988, pp. 369-370; November-

December, 1990, p. 738; September-October, 1991, p. 595; May-June, 1995, p. 297; December, 1995, p. 775.
Language Arts, January, 1979.
Library Journal, September 15, 1950; October 15, 1952; September 15, 1957; September 15, 1962.
Lion and the Unicorn: A Critical Journal of Children's Literature, June, 1988, p. 111; December, 1990, p. 58.
Los Angeles Times Book Review, May 22, 1988, p. 11.
New York Herald Tribune Book Review, October 14, 1951; October 12, 1952; September 27, 1953; November 6, 1955; November 18, 1956; November, 1959.
New York Times, December 1, 1999, pp. B2, E2.
New York Times Book Review, September 14, 1952; October 4, 1953; September 26, 1954; September 16, 1956; October 9, 1960; December 26, 1965; October 14, 1979; November 1, 1981; October 23, 1983; November 11, 1984; November 10, 1985; September 9, 1990, p. 17; November 10, 1991, p. 33; November 12, 1995, p. 40; November 21, 1999, p. 28.
Oklahoma Librarian, July, 1971.
Pacific Northwest Library Association Quarterly, April, 1961.
Pacific Sun Literary Quarterly, May 14, 1975.
Parenting, October, 1995, p. 130.
Publishers Weekly, August 4, 1951; August 15, 1953; July 10, 1954; August 13, 1955; September, 1961; April 3, 1967; April 15, 1968; May 14, 1970; March 31, 1975; February 23, 1976; October 1, 1977; July 30, 1979; July 10, 1981; March 2, 1984; July 12, 1993, p. 80; July 17, 1995, p. 138; June 7, 1999, p. 83; November 22, 1999; January 10, 2000, p. 24.
St. Louis Globe-Democrat, February 13, 1984.
Saturday Review, November 17, 1956; October 28, 1961; March 18, 1967; May 9, 1970.
Saturday Review of Literature, November, 1950; November 10, 1951.
School Librarian, June, 1974; June, 1981.
School Library Journal, May, 1988, p. 115; June, 1990, p. 98; February, 1994, p. 78; September, 1995, pp. 222-223; July 1998, p. 71; February 1999, p. 130; August 1999, p. 131; December, 2003, "Beverly Cleary Wins National Medal of Art," p. 25.
Signal, January, 1981.
Southeastern Librarian, fall, 1968.
Times Literary Supplement, July 7, 1978; July 2, 1980; January 13, 1984; November 20, 1984; February, 1985.
Top of the News, December, 1957; April, 1975; winter, 1977.
Tribune Books (Chicago, IL), September 13, 1987.
Washington Post, May 31, 1983; January 10, 1984.
Washington Post Book World, October 9, 1977; July 12, 1981; September 12, 1982; August 14, 1983; September 9, 1984; May 8, 1988; December 10, 1995, p. 20.
Wilson Library Bulletin, October, 1961.
Writers Digest, January, 1983.
Young Readers' Review, November, 1965; February, 1966; May, 1968.

ONLINE

Beverly Cleary Home Page, http://www.beverlycleary.com/ (March 6, 2004).
BookPage, http://www.bookpage.com/ (August, 1999), Miriam Drennen, interview with Cleary.

OTHER

Meet the Newbery Author: Beverly Cleary (filmstrip), Random House/Miller Brody.*

* * *

CLERGUE, Lucien (Georges) 1934-

PERSONAL: Born August 14, 1934, in Arles, France; son of Etienne (an accountant) and Jeanne (a grocer; maiden name, Grangeon) Clergue; married Yolanda Wartel (president of Fondation Vincent van Gogh), January 10, 1963; children: Anne, Olivia. *Ethnicity:* "French." *Education:* University of Provence, doctorate in photography, 1979. *Religion:* Roman Catholic.

ADDRESSES: Home—17 rue Aristide Brand, B.P. 84, 13632 Arles Cedex, France; fax: 33-4-90966081. *Agent*—John Stevenson Gallery, 338 West 23rd St., New York, NY 10011. *E-mail*—lucien.clergue@free.fr.

CAREER: Photographer and author. Rencontres Internationales de la Photographie, Arles, France, founding member, 1970, vice president, 1986; Arles Festival, Arles, artistic director, 1971-75; University of Provence, Marseille, France, instructor, 1976-78; New

Lucien Clergue

School for Social Research, New York, NY, instructor, 1983-84; Arles Festival, artistic director, 1986-88. University of California—Riverside, instructor at Nude Photography Workshop at California Museum of Photography, 1997. Director of films and television specials. *Exhibitions:* Work included in individual shows at galleries, including Kunstgewerbe Museum, Zurich, Switzerland, 1958, 1963; Galerie Montaigne, Paris, France, 1959; Musée des Beaux-Arts, 1962, 1971, 1973; Munchner Stadt Museum, Munich, West Germany (now Germany), 1964; Archives départementales, Grenoble, Switzerland, 1966; Galerie Moderne at Brentano's, New York, NY, 1967; Galerie Madoura, Cannes, France, 1968; Moderna Museet, Stockholm, Sweden, 1969; Art Institute of Chicago, 1970; Ecole des Beaux-Arts, Marseille, France, 1972; Lee Witkin Gallery, New York, NY, 1972, 1979; Jacques Baruch Gallery, Chicago, IL, 1973, 1976; Institute of Contemporary Art, London, England, 1973; Israel Museum, Jerusalem, 1974; Bibliotheque Nationale, Abidjan, Ivory Coast, 1975; French Institute, Copenhagen, Denmark, 1975; Galerie FNAC, Paris, 1976; Church Street Photography Center, Melbourne, Australia, 1978; Shadai Gallery, Tokyo, Japan, 1978; G. Ray Hawkins Gallery, Los Angeles, CA, 1979, 1981; Centre Georges Pompidou, Paris, France, 1980; Editions Gallery, Houston, TX, 1980-81; Parson's School Gallery, New York, NY, 1981; French Institute, Athens, Greece, 1983; George Eastman House, Rochester, NY, 1985; International Center of Photography, New York, NY, 1986; Espace Paul Ricard, Paris, 1996; De Vecchis Gallery, Philadelphia, 1996, 1997; California Museum of Photography, 1997; and John Stevenson Gallery, New York, NY, 2000, 2002. Work included in various group exhibitions, including *Diogenes with a Camera No. Five,* Museum of Modern Art, New York, NY, 1961; *Lucien Clergue-Yasuhiro Ishimoto,* Museum of Modern Art, then various U.S. cities, and *Contemporary Photography,* George Eastman House, Rochester, both 1962; *The Painter and the Photograph,* 1964; *Regards sur la terre des hommes,* Expo Universelle, Montreal, Quebec, Canada; *Man in Sport,* Gallery of Modern Art, New York, NY, and Hemis Fair 68, Houston, TX, all 1967; Musée Cantini, 1968; *Hommages à Pablo Picasso,* Festival d'Avignon, 1973; *The Nude,* Rencontres Internationales de la Photographie, Arles, France, 1975; *Hommage à Jean Cocteau,* London, then British cities, 1977; *Hecho in Latino-America,* Museo de Arte Moderno, Mexico City, Mexico, 1978; *The Nude,* Musée Fabre, 1978; *Photographes de la région Provence-Côte d'Azur,* Ecole des Beaux-Arts, Marseille, 1978; *Ten-Year Anniversary,* Lee Witkin Gallery, New York, NY, 1979; *Looking for Picasso,* International Center of Photography, New York, NY, 1980; *La Camargue vue par deux photographes: Lucien Clergue and Dieter Magnus,* Goethe Institute, Marseille; *Des Clefs des Serrures,* Cannon Gallery, Geneva, Switzerland; *Collection FNAC,* FNAC Gallery, Brussels, Belgium; *Four Generations of French Photographers,* Friends of Photography Gallery, Carmel, CA, 1981; *Hommage à Daniel Sorano,* Maison Jean Vilar, Avignon, France, 1982; *French Photographers,* Fay Gold Gallery, Atlanta, GA, 1983; *On Point Lobos,* Friends of Photography Gallery, Carmel, 1985; *Contemporary Artist,* Clermont-Ferrand, France, 1986; *Man and the Sea,* Art Junction, Nice, France, 1990; and World Press International, Paris, 1997.

MEMBER: Academie d'Arles, Association Nationale Photographes Createurs, Parc Regional Camargue, Societe des Amis Jean Cocteau, Association des Amis de la Fondation St.-John Perse.

AWARDS, HONORS: Prix Louis Lumiere, 1966, for *Drame du taureau;* Academy Award nomination, Academy of Motion Picture Arts and Sciences, 1968, for *Delta de sel;* chevalier, Ordre National du Merite,

1980; Grand Prize from Higashikawa Photography Festival, 1986; award for World Press International show, 1997; chevalier, French Legion of Honor, c. 2003.

WRITINGS:

(Author of foreword and photographer) *Camargue secrete,* P. Belfond (Paris, France), 1976.

Practical Nude Photography, Focal Press (Boston, MA), 1983.

(With Jean Cocteau) *Correspondance,* Actes Sud (Arles, France), 1989.

(With Salvatore Lombardo) *Double fantaisie: Entretien autour d'un doute,* Autres Temps (Marseille, France), 1999.

Contributor to books, including *Langage des sables,* foreword by Roland Barthes, Agep (Marseille, France), 1980. Also contributor to periodicals, including *Le Provencal.*

PHOTOGRAPHER

(With Paul Eluard and Jean Cocteau) *Corps memorable,* Edition Pierre Seghers (Paris, France), 1957.

(With Jean Cocteau and Jean-Marie Magnan) *Poesie der Photographie,* DuMont Schauberg (Cologne, West Germany), 1960.

(With Jean Cocteau and Jean-Marie Magnan) *Toros muertos,* Brussel & Brussel (New York, NY), 1962.

(With Federico García Lorca) *Birth of Aphrodite,* Brussel & Brussel (New York, NY), 1963.

(With Daniel Schmitt) *Le Taureau au Corps,* Editec (Paris, France), 1963.

(With Jean Cocteau) *Le Testament d'Orphee,* Edition du Rocher (Monaco), 1963.

(With Jean Cocteau and others) *Lucien Clergue: A Retrospective Monograph,* Die Arche Verlag (Zurich, Switzerland), 1963.

(With Jean Cocteau) *Numero Uno: A Portrait of Antonio Ordonez in Twenty-four Photographs,* Editec (Paris, France), 1963.

(With Jean Cocteau, M. Gasse, and others) *Lucien Clergue Photographe,* P. Schifferli (Zurich, Switzerland), 1964.

Lucien Clergue: Photographies, 1958-1964, Paradis (Luneville, France), 1964.

(With Jean-Marie Magnan, Robert Marteau, and Paco Tolosa) *El Cordobès,* La Jeune Parque (Paris, France), 1965.

(With Jean-Marie Magnan) *Le Temple tauromacique,* Edition Seghers (Paris, France), 1968.

Nee de la vague, P. Belfond (Paris), 1968, translation published as *Nude of the Sea,* 1980.

(With St.-John Perse) *Genese: 50 photographies sur des themes d'Amers choisis par Saint-John Perse,* P. Belfond (Paris, France), 1973.

(With Michel Tournier) *Lucien Clergue: Mers, plages, sources et torrents, arbres,* Editions Perceval (Paris, France), 1974.

(With Jean-Marie Magnan) *Le Quart d'heure du taureau,* Editions du Chene (Paris, France), 1976.

(With Manitas de Plata) *Musique aux doigts,* R. Laffont (Paris, France), 1976.

La Camargue est au bout des chemins, Agep (Marseille, France), 1978.

(With Christian Baroche) *L'Ecorce indechiffrable,* Editions Rijois (Marseille, France), 1978.

Belle des sables, Agep (Marseille, France), 1979.

(With J. L. Michel) *The Best Nudes,* Haga Shoten (Tokyo, Japan), 1979.

Hommage au paysage comtois, peint par Gustave Courbet et rephotographie par Lucien Clergue (exhibition catalogue), Les Amis de Gustave Courbet (Paris, France), 1979.

Les Saltimbanques, Agep (Marseille, France), 1980.

Eve est noire, Selezioni d'Immagini (Monza, Italy), 1982.

Nude Workshop, Viking (New York, NY), 1982.

Lucien Clergue: Photographs, 1953-1981, 1982.

I Grandi Fotografi: Lucien Clergue, edited by Gianna Rizzoni, Editions Fabbri Milano (Milan, Italy), 1983.

Lucien Clergue, Nippon Geijutsu Shuppansha (Tokyo, Japan), 1983.

Vivre la Provence et la Camargue, Editions Menges (Paris, France), 1983.

(With Jean Dieuzaide) *Variations sur la Croix,* Musee d'Interlinden, 1983.

(With Marianne Fulton) *Eros and Thanatos,* introduction by Michel Tournier, Little, Brown (Boston, MA), 1985.

Passion de femmes: Une lecon de photographie, Editions P. Montel (Paris, France), 1985.

(With Jim Hughes) *Footprints of the Gods: The Point Lobos Saga,* Iris Publications (Boca Raton, FL), 1989.

(With Mauro Corradini and Jean-Marie Magnan) *Dialogo—Vingt deptici inediti di Lucien Clergue, 1980-1990,* Edizioni del Museo (Brescia, Italy), 1991.

(With Jean-Marie Magnan) *Tauromachies,* introduction by Jean Cau, preface by Christian Lacroix, Marval (Paris, France), 1991.
(With Jean Cau and Alain Montcouquiol) *Nimeno II: Torero de France,* Marval (Paris, France), 1992.
(With Jean-Marie Magnan) *Une Faena de Curro Romero,* Marval (Paris, France), 1992.
Picasso, mon ami, Editions Plume (Paris, France), 1993.
(With Françoise Dubost) *Mon paysage: Le paysage prefere des français,* Marval (Paris, France), 1995.
(With C. Baroche and others) *Saint-John Perse: Poete devant la mer,* J & D Editions (Biarritz, France), 1996.
Passion passions, Actes Sud (Arles, France), 1997.
Lucien Clergue: Grands Nus, Umschau/Braus (Heidelberg, Germany), 1999.
David LeHardy Sweet, *Jean Cocteau, Testament of Orpheus,* Viking (New York, NY), 2001.
Arena, Actes Sud (Arles, France), 2001.
El Cordobès, Actes Sud (Arles, France), 2002.

Contributor of photographs to books, including *Saint-John Perse: Bio-bibliografica e poema Amers,* Centro de Arte Moderna, Fundacao Calouste Gulbenkian (Lisbon, Portugal), 1984.

SCREENPLAYS; AND DIRECTOR

La Drame du taureau, Les Films du Jeudi, 1965.
Dans Arles ou sont les Alyscamps, Films de la Pleiade, 1966.
Linares, le jeune torero, Films de la Pleiade, 1966.
Le Phare, Films de la Pleiade, 1966.
Delta de sel, Films de la Pleiade, 1966.
Entrâinement du torero, Films de la Pleiade, 1968.
Mario Prassinos, Films de la Pleiade, 1968.
Flamants Roses de Camargue, Films de la Pleiade, 1969.
Mediterraneenne, Films de la Pleiade, 1969.
Sables, Films de la Pleiade, 1969.
Cap sur Dakar, Arelatys, 1970.
Dressage de chevaux sauvages, Films de la Pleiade, 1970.
La Foret calcinee, Films de la Pleiade, 1970.
Voyage en Camardie, Films de la Pleiade, 1971.

TELEVISION SPECIALS; AND DIRECTOR

Manitas de Plata, Prince de Camargue, Films La Boetie, 1968.
Picasso: Guerre, Amour et Paix, Condor Films/Universal, 1968.
Musimages, Palette/FR3, 1999.

WORK IN PROGRESS: P. H. de Mendoza, for Actes Sud (Arles, France); exhibitions in Munich, Germany, Zurich, Switzerland, and Chicago, IL.

SIDELIGHTS: Lucien Clergue is a prominent photographer who is particularly known for his striking portraits of nudes. He studied basic photography techniques in the late 1940s, while he was still a teenager, and executed his first series of photographs in the mid-1950s. Within a few years Clergue had also befriended (along with Pablo Picasso) the versatile artist Jean Cocteau, a distinguished writer, painter, and filmmaker. Clergue and Cocteau would collaborate on several books, with Clergue supplying the photographs and Cocteau producing the text. Among their books are *Poesie der Photographie, Toros muertos, Numero Uno: A Portrait of Antonio Ordonez in Twenty-four Photographs,* and *Le Testament d'Orphee.* The latter volume derives from photographs made by Clergue while on the set of Cocteau's film of the same title.

In the mid-1960s, even as he remained active as a photographer, Clergue also began working as a filmmaker. He won the Lumiere Prize for his first work, *Drame du Taureau,* which appeared in 1965, and he received an Academy Award nomination for *Delta de sel,* which was released in 1968. Among Clergue's other notable films is *Picasso: Guerre, Amour, et Paix,* a film about the noted twentieth-century Spanish painter and sculptor Pablo Picasso, whom Clergue first met in the early 1950s.

Clergue came to the United States in 1961 and became acquainted with landscape photographer Ansel Adams. A few years later Clergue traveled the country, photographing nudes in urban settings. During the next decade he executed a series of photographs of Death Valley and published *Nude Workshop,* which featured nude photographs from throughout Clergue's career.

Clergue once told *CA:* "I want to create a language of images and this tentative idea was first made concrete with my book *Langage des sables.* The later books, including *Footprints of the Gods: The Point Lobos*

Saga, have the same roots. Meeting with Picasso, Jean Cocteau, and St.-John Perse has been decisive for my career, as they all convinced me to do more and go further. Illustration of their work was more a dialogue than illustration. Photography means writing with light."

BIOGRAPHICAL AND CRITICAL SOURCES:

BOOKS

Contemporary Photographers, St. James Press (Detroit, MI), 1988.

PERIODICALS

American Photographer, January, 1983.
Booklist, February 15, 1986, p. 842.
British Journal of Photography, December 20, 1974.
Camera 35, April, 1978.
Library Journal, May 15, 1986, p. 60.
Los Angeles Times Book Review, October 24, 1982, p. 12; December 22, 1985, p. 4.
Publishers Weekly, September 20, 1985, p. 94.
Saturday Review, December 3, 1966, p. 37.
Zoom, March, 1982.

* * *

COLE, Jennifer
See ZACH, Cheryl (Byrd)

* * *

CONROY, (Donald) Pat(rick) 1945-

PERSONAL: Born October 26, 1945, in Atlanta, GA; son of Donald (a military officer) and Frances Dorothy (Peek) Conroy; married Barbara Bolling, 1969 (divorced, 1977); married Lenore Gurewitz, March 21, 1981; children: (first marriage) Megan; Jessica, Melissa (stepdaughters); (second marriage) Susannah; Gregory, Emily (stepchildren). *Education:* The Citadel, B.A., 1967. *Politics:* Democrat.

Pat Conroy

ADDRESSES: Office—Old New York Book Shop, 1069 Juniper St. NE, Atlanta, GA 30309. *Agent*—IGM Literary, 825 Seventh Ave., Eighth Floor, New York, NY 10019.

CAREER: Novelist. Worked as an elementary schoolteacher in Daufuski, SC, 1969, and as a high school teacher in Beaufort, SC, 1967-69.

MEMBER: Authors Guild, Authors League of America, Writers Guild, PEN.

AWARDS, HONORS: Leadership Development grant, Ford Foundation, 1971; Anisfield-Wolf Award, Cleveland Foundation, 1972, for *The Water Is Wide;* National Endowment for the Arts award, 1974, for achievement in education; Georgia Governor's Award for Arts, 1978; Lillian Smith Award for fiction, Southern Regional Council, 1981; Robert Kennedy Book Award nomination, Robert F. Kennedy Memorial, 1981, for *The Lords of Discipline;* inducted into South Carolina Hall of Fame Academy of Authors, 1988; Academy Award nomination for best screenplay (with Becky Johnson), 1987, for *The Prince of Tides;* Thomas Cooper Society Literary Award, University of South Carolina, 1995; South Carolina Governor's Award in the Humanities for Distinguished Achievement, 1996; Georgia Commission on the Holocaust Humanitarian Award, 1996; Lotos Medal of Merit, 1996, for outstanding literary achievement.

WRITINGS:

The Boo, McClure Press (Verona, VA), 1970.

The Water Is Wide, Houghton Mifflin (Boston, MA), 1972.

The Great Santini, Houghton Mifflin (Boston, MA), 1976.

The Lords of Discipline, Houghton Mifflin (Boston, MA), 1980.

The Prince of Tides, Houghton Mifflin (Boston, MA), 1986.

Beach Music, Nan A. Talese/Doubleday (New York, NY), 1995.

My Losing Season, Nan A. Talese/Doubleday (New York, NY), 2002.

(Adaptor, with Becky Johnson) *The Prince of Tides* (screenplay; based on Conroy's novel), Paramount, 1991.

Author of screenplays, including television movie *Invictus,* 1988, and (with Doug Marlett) film *Ex.*

ADAPTATIONS: The film *Conrack,* based on *The Water Is Wide,* was produced by Twentieth Century-Fox, 1974, and was adapted as a musical by Granville Burgess and produced off-off Broadway, 1987; *The Great Santini* was adapted as a film by Warner Bros., 1979; *The Lords of Discipline* was adapted as a film by Paramount, 1983; Warner Bros. purchased film rights to *My Losing Season.* Several of Conroy's works have been recorded as audiobooks.

SIDELIGHTS: Best-selling novelist Pat Conroy has worked some of his most bitter experiences into stories that present ironic, often jarring, yet humorous views of life and relationships in the contemporary South. Garry Abrams in the *Los Angeles Times* reported that "misfortune has been good to novelist Pat Conroy. It gave him a family of disciplinarians, misfits, eccentrics, liars and loudmouths. It gave him a Southern childhood in which the bizarre competed with the merely strange. It gave him a military school education apparently imported from Sparta by way of Prussia. It gave him a divorce and a breakdown followed by intensive therapy. It gave him everything he needed to write best-sellers, make millions and live in Rome." Brigitte Weeks touched on Conroy's appeal in the *Washington Post:* "With his feet set firmly on his native earth, Conroy is, above all, a storyteller. His tales are full of the exaggeration and wild humor of stories told around a camp fire." A critic for *Publishers Weekly* explained that "Conroy is beloved for big, passionate, compulsively readable novels propelled by the emotional jet fuel of an abusive childhood." According to an essayist for *Contemporary Novelists,* "If a reader has experienced a Conroy novel before, he knows the book will be flawed, he knows the book is 500-plus pages, and he knows the characters are, in many ways, the same ones he knew in the last Conroy novel. But in ways, it's like returning to old friends and familiar places, and the lyricism of the prose is more than most readers can resist."

Critics frequently consider Conroy's novels to be autobiographical. Conroy's father was a Marine Corps pilot from Chicago who believed in strong discipline; his mother was an outwardly yielding Southerner who actually ran the household. "When he [Conroy's father] returned home from work my sister would yell, 'Godzilla's home' and the seven children would melt into whatever house we happened to be living in at the time. He was no match for my mother's byzantine and remarkable powers of intrigue. Neither were her children. It took me thirty years to realize that I had grown up in my mother's house and not my father's," Conroy commented in the *Book-of-the-Month Club News.* Still, critics frequently mention the ambivalent father-son relationships that appear in his novels. Gail Godwin in the *New York Times Book Review* described Conroy's work as having "twin obsessions—oppressive fathers or father figures, and the South. Against both they fight furiously for selfhood and independence, yet they never manage to secede from their seductive entrappers. Some fatal combination of nostalgia and loyalty holds them back; they remain ambivalent sons of their families and their region, alternately railing against, then shamelessly romanticizing, the myths and strictures that imprison them."

Conroy's first work to receive national attention was openly autobiographical. After college graduation he taught English in public high schools, but unsatisfied, he looked for a new challenge. When a desired position in the Peace Corps did not surface, he took a job teaching semiliterate black children on Daufuskie Island, a small, isolated area off the South Carolina coast. But he was not prepared for his new students. They did not know the name of their country, that they lived on the Atlantic Ocean, or that the world was round. On the other hand, Conroy found that his pupils expected him to know how to set a trap, skin a muskrat, and plant okra. He came to enjoy his unusual class, but eventually his unorthodox teaching methods—such as his unwillingness to allow corporal punishment of his students and disregard for the school's administration—cost him his job. As a way of coping with his fury at the dismissal, Conroy wrote *The Water Is Wide,* an account of his experiences. As he told Ted Mahar for the *Oregonian,* "When you get fired like that, you have to do something. I couldn't get a job with the charges the school board leveled against me." The process of writing did more than cool him down however; he also gained a new perspective on his reasons for choosing Daufuskie—Yamacraw Island in the book—and on his own responses to racism. Anatole Broyard described Conroy in the *New York Times Book Review* as "a former redneck and self-proclaimed racist, [who] brought to Yamacraw the supererogatory fervor of the recently converted." In *The Water Is Wide,* Conroy agreed: "At this time of my life a black man could probably have handed me a bucket of cow p——, commanded me to drink it in order that I might rid my soul of the stench of racism, and I would only have asked for a straw. . . . It dawned on me that I came to Yamacraw for a fallacious reason: I needed to be cleansed, born again, resurrected by good works and suffering, purified of the dark cankers that grew like toadstools in my past."

After the successful publication of *The Water Is Wide,* Conroy began writing full time. Although his next book, *The Great Santini,* is a novel, many critics interpreted it as representing the author's adolescence. A writer in the *Virginia Quarterly Review* stated that "the dialogue, anecdotes, and family atmosphere are pure Marine and probably autobiographical." Conroy does draw heavily on his family background in his story of tough Marine Bull Meecham, Bull's long-suffering wife, Lillian, and his eldest son, Ben, who is striving for independence outside his father's control. Robert E. Burkholder wrote in *Critique* that *The Great Santini* "is a curious blend of lurid reality and fantastic comedy. . . . It is primarily a novel of initiation, but central to the concept of Ben's initiation into manhood and to the meaning of the whole novel is the idea that individual myths must be stripped away from Ben and the other major characters before Ben can approach reality with objectivity and maturity." Part of Ben's growing up involves rejecting the image of his father's infallibility. In one scene, Ben finally beats his father at a game of basketball. As the game ends, he tells him: "Do you know, Dad, that not one of us here has ever beaten you in a single game? Not checkers, not dominoes, not softball, nothing."

According to Robert M. Willingham in the *Dictionary of Literary Biography,* after his defeat, "Bull does not outwardly change. He still blusters, curses, flashes toughness and resoluteness, but his family has become more to him than before. When Colonel Meecham's plane crashes and he is killed, one learns that the crash was unavoidable, but Bull's death was not: 'Am commencing starboard turn to avoid populated area. Will attempt to punch out when wings are level. . . .' The priority was to avoid populated areas, 'where people lived and slept, where families slept. Families like my family, wives like my wife, sons like my sons, daughters like my daughters.' He never punched out."

Bull Meecham is modeled on Conroy's father, Colonel Donald Conroy, who "would make John Wayne look like a pansy," as Conroy told Bill McDonald for the South Carolina *State.* Conroy reported that his father initially disliked *The Great Santini,* telling *Chicago Tribune* contributor Peter Gorner: "Dad could only read the book halfway through before throwing it across the room. Then people started telling him he actually was lovable. Now, he signs Christmas cards *The Great Santini,* and goes around talking about childrearing and how we need to have more discipline in the home—a sort of Nazi Dr. Spock." The movie based on the novel helped to change the colonel's attitude. *The Great Santini* starred Robert Duvall, and the Colonel liked the way "his" character came across. In a *Washington Post* interview, Conroy related an incident of one-upmanship that seems borrowed from the book. "He (the Colonel) came to the opening of *The Great Santini* movie here in Washington. I introduced the film to the audience, and in the course of my remarks I pointed out why he had chosen the military as a career. It was, of course, something that occurred to him on the day when he discovered that his body temperature and his IQ were the same number. Then, when it was his turn to talk, all he said was, 'I want to say that my body temperature has always been 160 degrees.' People laughed harder. So you see, I still can't beat him."

Another period of Conroy's life appeared in his next book, *The Lords of Discipline.* According to his father's wishes, Conroy attended the Citadel, South Carolina's venerable military academy. "Quirky, eccentric, and unforgettable" is how Conroy described the academy in the preface to *The Boo,* his first book, which takes a nostalgic look at the Citadel and its commander of cadets during the 1960s. Willingham described the Citadel in another way: "It is also an anachronism of the 1960s with a general disregard for the existence of the outside world." *The Lords of Discipline* paints an even bleaker picture of the institution through the fictionalized Carolina Military Institute. This school, stated Frank Rose in the *Washington Post Book World,* "combines some of the more quaint and murderous aspects of the Citadel, West Point, and Virginia Military Institute."

The Lords of Discipline concerns Will, the narrator, and his three roommates. Will is a senior cadet assigned to watch over the Institute's first black student. The novel's tension lies in the conflict between group loyalty and personal responsibility. Will eventually discovers the Ten, "a secret mafia whose existence has long been rumored but never proven, a silent and malevolent force dedicated . . . to maintain the purity of the Institute—racial purity included," commented Rose. He continued, "What Conroy has achieved is twofold; his book is at once a suspense-ridden duel between conflicting ideals of manhood and a paean to brother love that ends in betrayal and death. Out of the shards of broken friendship a blunted triumph emerges, and it is here, when the duel is won, that the reader finally comprehends the terrible price that any form of manhood can exact."

According to its author, *The Lords of Discipline* describes the love between men. "I wrote it because I wanted to tell about how little women understand about men," he explained in a *Washington Post* article. "The one cultural fact of life about military schools is that they are men living with men. And they love each other. The love between these men is shown only in obscure ways, which have to be learned by them. The four roommates who go through this book are very different from each other, but they have a powerful code. They have ways to prove their love to each other, and they're part of the rites of passage." And contradicting an old myth, Conroy added, "There is no homosexuality under these conditions. If you smile, they'll kill you. You can imagine what would happen to a homosexual."

While *The Lords of Discipline* portrays deep friendships, it also contains a theme common to many of Conroy's books: the coexistence of love and brutality. "This book . . . makes *The Lord of the Flies* sound like *The Sound of Music,*" wrote Christian Williams in the *Washington Post.* A *Chicago Tribune Book World* reviewer warned, "Conroy's chilling depictions of hazing are for strong stomachs only." And George Cohen in a later Chicago *Tribune Books* article described the novel's pull for readers: "It is our attraction to violence—observed from the safest of places—together with our admiration for the rebel who beats the system, and Conroy's imposing ability as a storyteller that make the novel engrossing."

Conroy's *The Prince of Tides* follows Tom Wingo, an unemployed high school English teacher and football coach, on a journey from coastal South Carolina to New York City to help his twin sister, Savannah. Savannah, a well-known poet, is recovering from a nervous breakdown and suicide attempt. In an attempt to help Savannah's psychiatrist understand her patient, Tom relates the Wingo family's bizarre history. Despite the horrors the Wingos have suffered, including several rapes and the death of their brother, a sense of optimism prevails. Judy Bass stated in Chicago's *Tribune Books,* "Conroy has fashioned a brilliant novel that ultimately affirms life, hope and the belief that one's future need not be contaminated by a monstrous past. In addition, Conroy . . . deals with the most prostrating crises in human experience—death of a loved one, parental brutality, injustice, insanity—without lapsing into pedantry or oppressive gloom."

The Prince of Tides attracted critical attention due to its style alone. Some critics felt the novel is overblown: Richard Eder in the *Los Angeles Times Book Review* claimed that "inflation is the order of the day. The characters do too much, feel too much, suffer too much, eat too much, signify too much, and above all, talk too much. And, as with the classical American tomato, quantity is at the expense of quality." Godwin found that while "the ambition, invention and sheer irony in this book are admirable . . . , many readers will be put off by the turgid, high-flown rhetoric that the author must have decided would best match his grandiose designs. And as the bizarre, hyperbolic episodes of Wingo family life mount up, other readers are likely to feel they are being bombarded by whoppers told by an overwrought boy eager to impress or shock." But more critics appreciated what *Detroit News* contributor Ruth Pollack Coughlin called "spectacular, lyrical prose with a bitter sense of humor." The novel is long, admitted Weeks, "monstrously long, yet a pleasure to read, flawed yet stuffed to the endpapers with lyricism, melodrama, anguish and plain old suspense. Given all that, one can brush aside its lapses like troublesome flies."

In his long-awaited *Beach Music,* Conroy continues to mine his personal and family experiences. He weaves into this novel the difficulties of family relationships, the pain of a mother's death, changing friendships, and the personal impact of global events such as the Holocaust, Vietnam, and present-day terrorism. What Conroy creates is a story of family, betrayal, and place. As Don Paul wrote in the *San Francisco Review of Books,* "In *Beach Music* Pat Conroy takes the theme of betrayal and fashions from it a story rambling and uneven and, like the family it portrays, erratic and flawed and magnificent. South Carolina overflows from his pages, sentimental and unforgiving, soft as sleepy pears and hard as turtle shells."

Beach Music is the story of Jack McCall. After his wife commits suicide, McCall leaves South Carolina and takes his young daughter to Italy to escape his memories and his strained relationships with his own and his wife's family. He returns home when his mother becomes ill with leukemia and finds himself caught up in the lives and intrigues of family and close friends. McCall and his friends are forced by current events to revisit the Vietnam era in their small South Carolina community. Some joined the military, some joined the antiwar movement, and some struggled with both. As Paul explained, "Central to the plot is the betrayal of the antiwar movement by a friend who turns out to be an FBI informer." The effects of this act continue to ripple into the novel's present.

The many characters, events, and themes make, in the opinion of *Detroit Free Press* contributor Barbara Holliday, for a long, convoluted book: "Conroy sets out to do too much and loses his focus in this novel. . . . But despite some fine passages, *Beach Music* finally becomes tiring, and that's too bad for one of the country's finer writers." A reviewer offered a more positive evaluation in *Publishers Weekly:* "Conroy has not lost his touch. His storytelling powers have not failed; neither has his fluid, poetic skill with words, nor his vivid imagination. His long-awaited sixth book sings with the familiar Southern cadences, his prose is sweepingly lyrical." And John Berendt, in a *Vanity Fair* profile of Conroy, called *Beach Music* "a novel rich in haunting imagery and seductive, suspenseful storytelling, a worthy successor to *The Prince of Tides.*" Berendt added, "In *Beach Music* . . . Conroy proves once again that he is the master of place, that he can take possession of any locale—Rome, Venice, South Carolina—merely by wrapping his sumptuous prose around it."

Conroy turned to his stint as point guard for the Citadel's basketball team in his memoir *My Losing Season.* The 1966-67 season was a bad one for the team, with an 8-17 record, but Conroy's memory of the time paints it "as an odyssey of hardwood heroics, Olympian fortitude and larger-than-life adversaries, with the occasional temptations of a coed siren," according to Don McLeese in *Book.* Conroy, in fact, argues that losing teaches you more than does winning. "This whole book is a love letter to losing and the lessons it teaches about friendship, courage, honesty and self-appraisal," explained Malcolm Jones in *Newsweek.* A critic for *Kirkus Reviews* admitted that "Conroy can be entertaining and endearingly self-effacing," while Wes Lukowsky in *Booklist* found that "this is a coming-of-age memoir, really, and it is in that context that Conroy's fans will most enjoy it."

Because of the autobiographical nature of Conroy's work, his family often judges his novels more harshly than do reviewers. Although Conroy's mother is the inspiration for shrimper's wife Lila Wingo in *The Prince of Tides,* she died before he finished the novel and never read it. Conroy's sister, who did see the book, was offended. As Conroy told Rick Groen for the Toronto *Globe and Mail,* "Yes, my sister is also a poet in New York who has also had serious breakdowns. We were very close, but she has not spoken to me . . . since the book. I'm saddened, but when you write autobiography, this is one of the consequences. They're allowed to be mad at you. They have the right." This, however, was not the first time a family member reacted negatively to one of Conroy's books. *The Great Santini* infuriated his Chicago relatives: "My grandmother and grandfather told me they never wanted to see me or my children again," Conroy told Sam Staggs for *Publishers Weekly.* Conroy's Southern relatives have also responded to the sex scenes and "immodest" language in his books. Staggs related, "After *The Lords of Discipline* was published, Conroy's Aunt Helen telephoned him and said, 'Pat, I hope someday you'll write a book a Christian can read.' 'How far did you get?' her nephew asked. 'Page four, and I declare, I've never been so embarrassed.'"

Perhaps the most sobering moment for Conroy's autobiographical impulse was when a tragic event from his writing came true. In early manuscripts of *Beach Music* Conroy included a scene where one of the characters, based on his younger brother Tom, commits suicide. Tom Conroy, a paranoid schizophrenic, did commit suicide in August of 1994. Devastated, Conroy removed the scene from *Beach Music.*

Hollywood has given Conroy's novels a warm reception. In addition to the film adaptation of *The Great Santini, The Water Is Wide* was made into *Conrack,* starring Jon Voight, and later became a musical. *The Lords of Discipline* kept the same title as a film featuring David Keith. Conroy himself cowrote the screenplay for *The Prince of Tides,* learning a lesson about Hollywood in the process.

Conroy explained his method of writing to Gorner: "When I'm writing, I have no idea where I'm going. People get married, and I didn't realize they were engaged. People die in these novels and I'm surprised. They take on this little subterranean life of their own. They reveal secrets to me even as I'm doing it. Maybe this is a dangerous way to work, but for me it becomes the pleasure of writing. . . . Critics call me a popular novelist, but writing popular novels isn't what urges me on. If I could write like Faulkner or Thomas Wolfe, I surely would. I'd much rather write like them than like me. Each book has been more ambitious. I'm trying to be more courageous."

An essayist for *Contemporary Southern Writers* concluded: "Conroy's work is distinguished by its focus on characters coping with and attempting to rise above often bitter conflicts within families and relationships and by his loving recreation of Southern settings and culture. . . . Whether the conflicts are more overt and active, as in *The Great Santini,* or slowly revealed and psychological, as in *The Prince of Tides,* Conroy's work is repeatedly peopled with stern and demanding, sometimes abusive father figures and characters attempting to transcend such harshness to establish a more life-embracing identity."

BIOGRAPHICAL AND CRITICAL SOURCES:

BOOKS

Burns, Landon C., *Pat Conroy: A Critical Companion,* Greenwood Press (Westport, CT), 1996.

Contemporary Novelists, 7th edition, St. James Press (Detroit, MI), 2001.

Contemporary Popular Writers, St. James Press (Detroit, MI), 1997.

Contemporary Southern Writers, St. James Press (Detroit, MI) , 1999.

Dictionary of Literary Biography, Volume 6: *American Novelists since World War II, Second Series,* Gale (Detroit, MI), 1980.

PERIODICALS

Atlanta Journal-Constitution, March 27, 1988, p. J1.

Book, November-December, 2002, Don McLeese, review of *My Losing Season,* p. 82.

Booklist, August, 2002, Wes Lukowsky, review of *My Losing Season,* p. 1882.

Book-of-the-Month Club News, December, 1986.

Chicago Tribune, November 25, 1986.

Chicago Tribune Book World, October 19, 1980.

Cincinnati Enquirer, March 25, 1974.

Critique, Volume 21, number 1, 1979.

Detroit Free Press, July 9, 1995, p. 7G.

Detroit News, October 12, 1986; December 20, 1987.

Globe and Mail (Toronto, Ontario, Canada), February 28, 1987; November 28, 1987.

Kirkus Reviews, August 1, 2002, review of *My Losing Season,* p. 1089.

Library Journal, September 1, 2002, James Thorsen, review of *My Losing Season,* p. 184.

Los Angeles Times, February 19, 1983; October 12, 1986; October 19, 1986; December 12, 1986.

Los Angeles Times Book Review, October 19, 1986, p. 3.

Newsweek, October 14, 2002, Malcolm Jones, "Conroy's Literary Slam-Dunk: A Writer Revisits Life As a Jock, and As a Tortured Son," p. 63.
New York Times, January 10, 1987.
New York Times Book Review, July 13, 1972; September 24, 1972; December 7, 1980; October 12, 1986, p. 14.
Oregonian, April 28, 1974.
People, February 2, 1981, p. 67.
Publishers Weekly, May 15, 1972; September 5, 1986; May 8, 1995, p. 286: July 10, 1995, p. 16, July 31, 1995, p. 17; September 30, 2002, Tracy Cochran, "A Winning Career: Pat Conroy Proves That Writing Well Is the Best Revenge," p. 41, and review of *My Losing Season,* p. 60; October 28, 2002, Daisy Maryles, "Conroy's Winning Book," p. 20.
San Francisco Review of Books, July-August, 1995, p. 24.
State (Columbia, South Carolina), March 31, 1974.
Time, October 13, 1986, p. 97; June 26, 1995, p. 77.
Tribune Books (Chicago, IL), September 14, 1986, p. 23; October 19, 1986, p. 3; January 3, 1988, p. 3.
Vanity Fair, July, 1995, p. 108.
Virginia Quarterly Review, autumn, 1976.
Washington Post, October 23, 1980; March 9, 1992, p. B3.
Washington Post Book World, October 19, 1980; October 12, 1986.

ONLINE

Pat Conroy Web site, http://www.patconroy.com (November 6, 2003).*

* * *

COURTNEY, Dayle
See KIMBERLY, Gail

D

DAICHES, David 1912-

PERSONAL: Born September 2, 1912, in Sunderland, England; son of Salis and Flora (Levin) Daiches; married Isobel Janet Mackay, July 28, 1937 (died, 1977); married Hazel Neville, 1978 (died, 1986); children: (first marriage) Alan H., Jennifer R., Elizabeth M. *Education:* University of Edinburgh, M.A. (with first-class honors), 1934; Balliol College, Oxford, M.A., 1937, D.Phil., 1939; Cambridge University, Ph.D., 1939.

ADDRESSES: *Home*—22 Belgrave Crescent, Edinburgh EH4 3AL, Scotland.

CAREER: Balliol College, Oxford, Oxford, England, fellow, 1936-37; University of Chicago, Chicago, IL, assistant professor of English, 1939-43; British Embassy, Washington, DC, second secretary, 1944-46; Cornell University, Ithaca, NY, professor of English, 1946-51, chair of division of literature, 1948-51; Cambridge University, Cambridge, England, university lecturer, 1951-61, fellow of Jesus College, 1957-62; University of Sussex, Brighton, England, professor of English, 1961-77, dean of School of English and American Studies, 1961-67. Visiting professor, University of Indiana, 1956-57; Hill Foundation visiting professor, University of Minnesota, spring, 1966. Fellow, Center for Humanities, Wesleyan University, 1970, and National Humanities Center, North Carolina, 1987. Elliston Lecturer, University of Cincinnati, spring, 1960; Whidden Lecturer, McMaster University, 1964; Ewing Lecturer, University of California at Los Angeles, 1967; Carpenter Memorial Lecturer, Ohio Wesleyan University, 1970; Alexander Lecturer, University of Toronto, 1980; Gifford Lecturer, University of Edinburgh, 1983; lecturer at the Sorbonne. Lecturer on tours in America, Germany, India, Finland, Norway, Italy, Holland, and Denmark.

MEMBER: Royal Society of Literature (fellow), Royal Society of Edinburgh (fellow), Scottish Arts Club.

AWARDS, HONORS: Brotherhood Award, 1957, for *Two Worlds: An Edinburgh Jewish Childhood;* Litt.D., Brown University, 1964; Abe Prize, Tokyo, 1965, for best educational television program; doctor honoris causa, Sorbonne, University of Paris, 1973; D.Litt., University of Edinburgh, 1976, University of Sussex, 1978, University of Stirling, 1980, University of Glasgow, 1987; Saltire Book Award, 1987, for *God and the Poets;* honorary doctorate, Bologna University, 1988; Commander of the Order of the British Empire (CBE).

WRITINGS:

Two Worlds: An Edinburgh Jewish Childhood (autobiography), Harcourt (New York, NY), 1956, reprinted, University of Alabama Press (Tuscaloosa, AL), 1989.

Scotch Whisky: Its Past and Present, Deutsch (London, England), 1969, Macmillan (New York, NY), 1970, 3rd edition, Deutsch, 1978.

A Third World (autobiography), Sussex University Press (Sussex, England), 1971.

A Weekly Scotsman and Other Poems, Black Ace Books (Duns, Scotland), 1994.

CRITICISM

The Place of Meaning in Poetry, Oliver & Boyd (Edinburgh, Scotland), 1935, reprinted, Folcroft Library Editions (Folcroft, PA), 1976.

New Literary Values: Studies in Modern Literature, Oliver & Boyd (Edinburgh, Scotland), 1936, reprinted, Folcroft Library Editions (Folcroft, PA), 1975.

Literature and Society, Gollancz (London, England)), 1938, reprinted, Haskell House (New York, NY), 1970.

The Novel and the Modern World, University of Chicago Press (Chicago, IL), 1939, revised edition, 1960.

Poetry and the Modern World, University of Chicago Press (Chicago, IL), 1940, reprinted, Octagon Books (New York, NY), 1978.

The King James Version of the English Bible: A Study of Its Sources and Development, University of Chicago Press (Chicago, IL), 1941, reprinted, Archon Books (Hamden, CT), 1968.

Virginia Woolf, New Directions (San Francisco, CA), 1942, revised edition, 1963, reprinted, Greenwood Press (Westport, CT), 1979.

Robert Louis Stevenson, New Directions (San Francisco, CA), 1947.

A Study of Literature for Readers and Critics, Cornell University Press (Ithaca, NY), 1948, reprinted, Greenwood Press (Westport, CT), 1972.

Robert Burns, Rinehart (New York, NY), 1950, revised edition, Macmillan (New York, NY), 1966.

Willa Cather: A Critical Introduction, Cornell University Press (Ithaca, NY), 1951, reprinted, Greenwood Press (Westport, CT), 1971.

Stevenson and the Art of Fiction, privately printed (New York, NY), 1951, Darby (Darby, PA), 1980.

Walt Whitman: Man, Poet, Philosopher, Library of Congress (Washington, DC), 1955, reprinted, Folcroft Library Editions (Folcroft, PA), 1974.

Critical Approaches to Literature, Prentice-Hall (Englewood Cliffs, NJ), 1956, 2nd edition, Longman (New York, NY), 1981.

Literary Essays, Oliver & Boyd (Edinburgh, Scotland), 1956, revised edition, 1967, Philosophical Library (New York, NY), 1957.

Milton, Hutchinson (London, England), 1957, revised edition, Norton (New York, NY), 1966.

Two Studies: The Poetry of Dylan Thomas [and] Walt Whitman: Impressionist Prophet, Shenval Press (London, England), 1958, reprinted, Folcroft Library Editions (Folcroft, PA), 1977.

The Present Age in British Literature, Indiana University Press (Bloomington, IN), 1958, published as *The Present Age: After 1920,* Cresset Press (London, England), 1958.

A Critical History of English Literature, two volumes, Ronald Press (New York, NY), 1960, 2nd edition, 1970.

White Man in the Tropics: Two Moral Tales: "Heart of Darkness" by Joseph Conrad [and] "The Beach of Falesa" by Robert Louis Stevenson, Harcourt, Brace (New York, NY), 1962.

George Eliot: Middlemarch, Edward Arnold (London, England), 1962, Barron's (New York, NY), 1963.

D. H. Lawrence, Dolphin Press (Glenrothes, Scotland), 1963, reprinted, Folcroft Library Editions (Folcroft, PA), 1977.

Carlyle and the Victorian Dilemma, Carlyle Society, 1963.

The Paradox of Scottish Culture: The Eighteenth Century Experience, Oxford University Press (New York, NY), 1964.

English Literature, Prentice-Hall (Englewood Cliffs, NJ), 1964.

Myth, Metaphor, and Poetry, Royal Society opf Literature (London, England), 1965.

Time and the Poet, University of Swansea College (Swansea, South Wales), 1965.

More Literary Essays, University of Chicago Press (Chicago, IL), 1968.

The Teaching of Literature in American Universities, Leicester University Press (Leicester, England), 1968.

Some Late Victorian Attitudes, Norton (New York, NY), 1969.

Shakespeare: Julius Caesar, E. Arnold (London, England), 1976.

Robert Fergusson, Scottish Academic Press (Edinburgh, Scotland), 1982.

The New Criticism, Aquila (Portree, Isle of Skye, Scotland), 1982.

Milton: Paradise Lost, E. Arnold (London, England), 1983.

God and the Poets, Clarendon Press (Oxford, England), 1984.

HISTORY AND BIOGRAPHY

Robert Burns and His World, Thames & Hudson (London, England), 1971, Viking (New York, NY), 1972.

Sir Walter Scott and His World, Viking (New York, NY), 1971.

Robert Louis Stevenson and His World, Thames & Hudson (London, England), 1973.

The Last Stuart: The Life and Times of Bonnie Prince Charlie, Putnam (New York, NY), 1973, published as *Charles Edward Stuart: The Life and Times of Bonnie Prince Charlie,* Thames & Hudson (London, England), 1973.

Was: A Pastime from Time Past, Thames & Hudson (London, England), 1975.

James Boswell and His World, Thames & Hudson (London, England), 1975, Scribner (New York, NY), 1976.

Moses: The Man and His Vision, Praeger, (New York, NY), 1975, published as *Moses: Man in the Wilderness,* Weidenfeld & Nicolson (London, England), 1976.

Scotland and the Union, J. Murray (London, England)), 1977.

The Quest for the Historical Moses (booklet), Council of Christians and Jews (London, England), 1977.

Glasgow, Deutsch (London, England), 1977.

Edinburgh, Hamish Hamilton (London, England)), 1978.

The Selected Poems of Robert Burns, Deutsch (London, England), 1979.

(With John Flower) *Literary Landscapes of the British Isles: A Narrative Atlas,* Paddington Press (London, England), 1979.

Literature and Gentility in Scotland, Edinburgh University Press (Edinburgh, Scotland), 1982.

(With Tamas McDonald) *Introducing Robert Burns, His Life and Poetry,* Macdonald Publishers (Edinburgh, Scotland), 1982.

Robert Burns, the Poet, Saltire Society (Edinburgh, Scotland), 1994.

EDITOR

(With William Charvat) *Poems in English, 1530-1940,* Ronald Press (New York, NY), 1950.

A Century of the Essay, British and American, Harcourt (San Diego, CA), 1951.

(With others) *The Norton Anthology of English Literature,* two volumes, Norton (New York, NY), 1962, revised edition, 1974.

The Idea of a New University: An Experiment in Sussex, Deutsch (London, England), 1964, 2nd edition, 1970, MIT Press (Cambridge, MA), 1970.

Emily Brontë, *Wuthering Heights,* Penguin (New York, NY), 1965.

The Penguin Companion to Literature, Volume 1: *Britain and the Commonwealth,* Allen Lane (London, England), 1971, published as *The Penguin Companion to English Literature,* McGraw-Hill (New York, NY), 1971.

(With others) *Literature and Western Civilization,* six volumes, Aldus Books (London, England), 1972-75.

(With Anthony Thorlby) *The Modern World,* (multivolume), Aldus Books (London, England), 1972—.

Andrew Fletcher of Saltoun: Selected Political Writings and Speeches, Scottish Academic Press (Edinburgh, Scotland), 1979.

A Companion to Scottish Culture, E. Arnold (London, England), 1981, Holmes & Meier (New York, NY), 1982, revised edition published as *The New Companion to Scottish Culture,* Polygon (Edinburgh, Scotland), 1993.

Edinburgh: A Traveller's Companion, Constable (London, England), 1986.

(With Peter Jones and Jean Jones) *A Hotbed of Genius: The Scottish Enlightenment, 1730-1790,* University Press (Edinburgh, Scotland), 1986, published as *The Scottish Enlightenment, 1730-1790: A Hotbed of Genius,* Saltire Society (Edinburgh, Scotland), 1996.

A Wee Dram: Drinking Scenes from Scottish Literature, Deutsch (London, England), 1990.

AUTHOR OF INTRODUCTION

George Eliot, *The Mill on the Floss,* Limited Editions Club (New York, NY), 1963.

Robert Burns, *Commonplace Book, 1783-1785,* Centaur Press (Eastergate, England), 1965.

Sir Walter Scott, *Kenilworth,* Limited Editions Club (New York, NY), 1966.

Sir Walter Scott, *The Heart of Midlothian,* Holt, Rinehart & Winston (New York, NY), 1968.

Also author of *Literature and Education in the United States.*

SIDELIGHTS: Robert Alter, a reviewer for *Commentary,* offered this summation of David Daiches as a literary critic: "He commands a very impressive range of English and American literature, with a minutely informed sense of its classical and Continental backgrounds, and he uses all this knowledge gracefully, relevantly, without a trace of pedantry. . . . Virtually everything he writes is sane, lucid, and tactful, and in an age when the language of most literary people is tainted with learned barbarism or stylistic exhibitionism, he writes an eminently civilized prose that seems effortless in its clarity and directness." Daiches himself commented on being a critic in an interview in *Quadrant.* He said, "Some works are better than others and some are great and some have a resonance which stays with you for the rest of your life. Others are good and give pleasure, but don't resonate in the same way. So there's a whole hierarchy of values. And I believe that there is great and there is good and there is not so good and there is bad literature."

Daiches, who has taught in several universities throughout the world, is known for his studies of leading English and Scottish literary figures. Published in 1942, Daiches's *Virginia Woolf* has long been considered an excellent introduction to that author's work. Howard Doughty, writing in *Books,* called it a "competent and intelligent guide" that is "informed with insight into the relation of technical problems to currents of thought and feeling in the writer's time." In a *Canadian Forum* article, Robert Finch commended Daiches for his "brilliance that illuminates more often than it dazzles."

Daiches's 1950 study of Robert Burns has been recognized as one of the best modern books on the subject. A critic for the *Economist* considered *Robert Burns* one of "the most perceptive books about Scottish literature." Writing in *Commonweal,* Virginia Mercier voiced a similar opinion: Daiches "deserves a nobler title than scholar—that of humanist. . . . No critical study has done fuller justice to Burns' work as a song-writer or supplied more information about it." The *New York Herald Tribune Book Review*'s G. F. Whicher believed that the book "is notable for its vigorous grasp of crucial issues and for its success in clearing the air of misapprehensions that have often blurred the understanding of Robert Burns' position and achievement."

Daiches took pride in teaching his students about English and Scottish literature. "I like to think I helped in the rediscovery of Scottish literature," he explained in *Quadrant.* As a professor, he made it a point to effectively communicate the importance of literature. He said, "These things are interesting, poems and novels and plays are interesting, because they illuminate situations in a way that is convincing and moving."

Book World writer Joel Sayre noted that while Daiches's "vocation is English . . . his avocation [is] Pot-Still Highland Malt Scotch Whisky." In *Scotch Whisky: Its Past and Present,* Daiches contends: "The proper drinking of Scotch whisky is more than an indulgence. It is a toast to civilization, a tribute to the continuity of culture, a manifesto of man's determination to use the resources of nature to refresh mind and body and enjoy to the full the senses with which he has been endowed."

Daiches points out that the United States leads the world in Scotch consumption and that approximately ninety-nine percent of all Scotch consumed there is a blended rather than a single malt whisky. He laments that too many Scotch drinkers are unaware that the single malts can be obtained. Sayre related the following anecdote: "When he was a member of the Cornell faculty, Daiches once casually mentioned in a lecture . . . that Mortlach [a single malt] was to be had at Macy's in New York. On his next trip to Manhattan he dropped in at Macy's to stock up his Mortlach supply. 'Sorry, but some damn fool prof up at Ithaca recommended it to his students, and we're all out.'"

BIOGRAPHICAL AND CRITICAL SOURCES:

BOOKS

Oxford Companion to English Literature, revised 5th edition, Oxford University Press (Oxford, England), 1995.

PERIODICALS

Books, September 27, 1942.
Book World, March 8, 1970.
Canadian Forum, November, 1942.
Commentary, May, 1969.
Commonweal, February 23, 1951.
Economist, May 28, 1977.
Newsweek, March 26, 1956.

New York Herald Tribune Book Review, August 26, 1951.
New York Times Book Review, April 12, 1970.
Quadrant, January, 2001, Alan Riach, "A Conversation with David Daiches," p. 72.
Sunday Times (London, England), July 22, 2001, "Burns Expert Hits Out at 'Daft' Plan for International Award," p. 7.
Washington Post, March 30, 1979.
Yale Review, winter, 1970.*

* * *

DANTICAT, Edwidge 1969-

Edwidge Danticat

PERSONAL: Name pronounced "Ed-*weedj* Dan-ti-*kah*"; born January 19, 1969, in Port-au-Prince, Haiti; immigrated to United States, 1981; daughter of André Miracin (a cab driver) and Rose Souvenance (a textile worker) Danticat. *Ethnicity:* "Black." *Education:* Barnard College, B.A. 1990; Brown University, M.F.A., 1993.

ADDRESSES: *Office*—c/o Author Mail, Soho Press, 853 Broadway, No. 1903, New York, NY 10003.

CAREER: Writer, educator, and lecturer, 1994—. New York University, New York, NY, professor, 1996-97; University of Miami, Miami, FL, visiting professor of creative writing, spring, 2000. Also production and research assistant at Clinica Estetico, 1993-94.

MEMBER: Phi Beta Kappa, Alpha Kappa Alpha.

AWARDS, HONORS: *Krik? Krak!* was a finalist for the 1995 National Book Award; named one of twenty "Best of American Novelists" by *Granta,* 1996; Pushcart Prize for short fiction; American Book Award, Before Columbus Foundation, for *The Farming of Bones;* fiction awards from periodicals, including *Caribbean Writer, Seventeen,* and *Essence.*

WRITINGS:

Breath, Eyes, Memory (novel), Soho Press (New York, NY), 1994.
Krik? Krak! (short stories), Soho Press (New York, NY), 1995.
The Farming of Bones (novel), Soho Press (New York, NY), 1998.
(With Jonathan Demme) *Odillon Pierre, Artist of Haiti,* Kaliko Press (Nyack, NY), 1999.
(Editor) *The Beacon Best of 2000: Great Writing by Women and Men of All Colors and Cultures,* Beacon Press (Boston, MA), 2000.
(Editor) *The Butterfly's Way: Voices from the Haitian Dyaspora in the United States,* Soho Press (New York, NY), 2001.
(Translator and author of afterword, with Carrol F. Coates) Jackes Stephen Alexis, *In the Flicker of an Eyelid,* University of Virginia Press (Charlottesville, VA), 2002.
After the Dance: A Walk through Carnival in Haiti, Crown Publishers (New York, NY), 2002.
Behind the Mountains (novel), Orchard Books (New York, NY), 2002.

PLAYS

The Creation of Adam, produced in Providence, RI, 1992.

Dreams Like Me, produced at Brown University New Plays Festival, 1993.

Children of the Sea, produced at Roxbury Community College, 1997.

SIDELIGHTS: Fiction writer Edwidge Danticat conjures the history of her native Haiti in award-winning short stories and novels. She is equally at home describing the immigrant experience—what she calls "dyaspora"—and the reality of life in Haiti today. Danticat's fiction "has been devoted to an unfliching examination of her native culture, both on its own terms and in terms of its intersections with American culture," wrote an essayist in *Contemporary Novelists.* "Danticat's work emphasizes in particular the heroism and endurance of Haitian women as they cope with a patriarchal culture that, in its unswerving devotion to tradition and family, both oppresses and enriches them." Readers will find "massacres, rapes, [and] horrible nightmares in Danticat's fiction," wrote an essayist in the *St. James Guide to Young Adult Writers,* "but above all these are the strength, hope, and joy of her poetic vision."

Danticat's first novel, the loosely autobiographical *Breath, Eyes, Memory,* was a 1998 selection of the Oprah Winfrey Book Club, thus assuring its best-seller status. Other Danticat works have won warm praise as well, with some critics expressing surprise that such assured prose has come from an author so young. *Antioch Review* correspondent Grace A. Epstein praised Danticat for "the real courage . . . in excavating the romance of nationalism, identity, and home." *Time* reporter Christopher John Farley likewise concluded that Danticat's fiction "never turns purple, never spins wildly into the fantastic, always remains focused, with precise disciplined language, and in doing so, it uncovers moments of raw humanness."

Danticat was born in Haiti and lived there the first twelve years of her life. she came to the United States in 1981, joining her parents who had already begun to build a life for themselves in New York City. When she started attending junior high classes in Brooklyn, she had difficulty fitting in with her classmates because of her Haitian accent, clothing, and hairstyle. Danticat recalled for Garry Pierre-Pierre in the *New York Times* that she took refuge from the isolation she felt in writing about her native land. As an adolescent she began work on what would evolve into her first novel, the acclaimed *Breath, Eyes, Memory.* Danticat followed her debut with a collection of short stories, *Krik? Krak!*—a volume which became a finalist for that year's National Book Award. According to Pierre-Pierre, the young author has been heralded as "'the voice' of Haitian-Americans," but Danticat told him, "I think I have been assigned that role, but I don't really see myself as the voice for the Haitian-American experience. There are many. I'm just one."

Danticat's parents wanted her to pursue a career in medicine, and with the goal of becoming a nurse, she attended a specialized high school in New York City. But she abandoned this aim to devote herself to her writing. An earlier version of *Breath, Eyes, Memory* served as her master of fine arts thesis at Brown University, and the finished version was published shortly thereafter. Like Danticat herself, Sophie Caco—the novel's protagonist—spent her first twelve years in Haiti, several in the care of an aunt, before coming wide-eyed to the United States. But there the similarities end. Sophie is the child of a single mother, conceived by rape. Though she rejoins her mother in the United States, it is too late to save the still-traumatized older woman from self-destruction. Yet women's ties to women are celebrated in the novel, and Sophie draws strength from her mother, her aunt, and herself in order to escape her mother's fate.

Breath, Eyes, Memory caused some controversy in the Haitian-American community. Some of Danticat's fellow Haitians did not approve of her writing of the practice of "testing" in the novel. In the story, female virginity is highly prized by Sophie's family, and Sophie's aunt "tests" to see whether Sophie's hymen is intact by inserting her fingers into the girl's vagina. Haitian-American women, some of whom have never heard of or participated in this practice, felt that Danticat's inclusion of it portrayed them as primitive and abusive. American critics, however, widely lauded *Breath, Eyes, Memory.* Joan Philpott in *Ms.* hailed the book as "intensely lyrical." Pierre-Pierre reported that reviewers "have praised Ms. Danticat's vivid sense of place and her images of fear and pain." Jim Gladstone concluded in the *New York Times Book Review* that the novel "achieves an emotional complexity that lifts it out of the realm of the potboiler and into that of poetry." And Bob Shacochis, in his *Washington Post Book World* review, called the work "a novel that rewards a reader again and again with small but exquisite and unforgettable epiphanies." Shacochis added, "You can actually see Danticat grow and mature, come into her own strength as a writer, throughout the course of this quiet, soul-penetrating story about four generations of women trying to hold on to one another in the Haitian diaspora."

Krik? Krak! takes its title from the practice of Haitian storytellers. Danticat told Deborah Gregory of *Essence* that storytelling is a favorite entertainment in Haiti, and a storyteller inquires of his or her audience, "Krik?" to ask if they are ready to listen. The group then replies with an enthusiastic, "Krak!" The tales in this collection include one about a man attempting to flee Haiti in a leaky boat, another about a prostitute who tells her son that the reason she dresses up every night is that she is expecting an angel to descend upon their house, and yet another explores the feelings of a childless housekeeper in a loveless marriage who finds an abandoned baby in the streets. The *New York Times Book Review*'s Robert Houston, citing the fact that some of the stories in *Krik? Krak!* were written while Danticat was still an undergraduate at Barnard College, felt that these pieces were "out of place in a collection presumed to represent polished, mature work." But *Ms.*'s Jordana Hart felt that the tales in *Krik? Krak!* "are textured and deeply personal, as if the twenty-six-year-old Haitian-American author had spilled her own tears over each." Even Houston conceded that readers "weary of stories that deal only with the minutiae of 'relationships' will rejoice that they have found work that is about something, and something that matters."

Danticat's novel *The Farming of Bones* concerns a historical tragedy, the 1937 massacre of Haitian farm workers by soldiers of the Dominican Republic. In the course of less than a week, an estimated twelve to fifteen thousand Haitian workers in the Dominican Republic were slaughtered by the Dominican government or by private citizens in a classic case of "ethnic cleansing." *The Farming of Bones* is narrated by a young Haitian woman, Amabelle Desir, who has grown up in the Dominican Republic after being orphaned. As the nightmare unfolds around her, Amabelle must flee for her life, separated from her lover, Sebastien. In the ensuing decades as she nurses her physical and psychological wounds, Amabelle serves as witness to the suffering of her countrymen and the guilt of her former Dominican employers. The massacre, Danticat told Mallay Charters in *Publishers Weekly,* is "a part of our history, as Haitians, but it's also a part of the history of the world. Writing about it is an act of remembrance."

Dean Peerman wrote in *Christian Century* that "*Breath, Eyes, Memory* was an impressive debut, but *The Farming of Bones* is a richer work, haunting and heartwrenching." In *Nation,* Zia Jaffrey praised Danticat for "blending history and fiction, imparting information, in the manner of nineteenth-century novelists, without seeming to." Jaffrey added: "Danticat's brilliance as a novelist is that she is able to put this event into a credible, human context." Farley also felt that the author was able to endow a horrific episode with a breath of humanity. "Every chapter cuts deep, and you feel it," he stated, continuing on to say that Amabelle's "journey from servitude to slaughter is heartbreaking." In *Américas,* Barbara Mujica concluded that Danticat has written "a gripping novel that exposes an aspect of Dominican-Haitian history rarely represented in Latin American fiction. In spite of the desolation and wretchedness of the people Danticat depicts, *The Farming of Bones* is an inspiring book. It is a hymn to human resilience, faith, and hope in the face of overwhelming adversity." Jaffrey ended her review by concluding that the novel is "a beautifully conceived work, with monumental themes."

Behind the Mountains takes the form of a diary of teenage Haitian Celiane Esperance. Celiane is happy in her home in the mountains of Haiti, but she hasn't seen her father since he left for the United States years before. She had intended to join him in New York, along with her mother and older brother, but visa applications are inexorably slow. After eight years, the visas are granted, and the family reunites in Brooklyn. After an initially joyful reunion, however, the family begins to slowly unravel. A child when her father left Haiti, Celiane is now a young woman with her own mind and will. Her brother, Moy, a nineteen-year-old artist, does not quietly slip back into the role of obedient child. Even more universal concerns, such as the freezing New York winters, difficulties at school, and the need to make a living, chip away at the family's unity. Good intentions go awry in a book showcasing "friction among family members" exacerbated by "the separation and adjustment to a new country," but especially by the inevitable maturation of younger family members and the unwillingness of parents to acknowledge it, wrote Diane S. Morton in *School Library Journal.* Hazel Rochman, writing in *Booklist,* praised the "simple, lyrical writing" Danticat demonstrates in the novel. "Danticat brings her formidable skill as a writer and her own firsthand knowledge of Haiti and immigrating to America to this heartfelt story told in the intimate diary format," wrote Claire Rosser in *Kliatt.*

In addition to her own works, Danticat has also edited the fiction of others, including *The Butterfly's Way: From the Haitian Dyaspora in the United States.* This work is a collection of stories, poems, and essays from Haitian writers living in America and Europe, many of whom are concerned with the feeling of displacement that is perhaps an inevitable consequence of emigration. Denolyn Carroll suggested in *Black Issues Book Review* that the pieces in *The Butterfly's Way* "help paint a vivid picture of what it is like to live in two worlds." Carroll also felt that the work adds "new dimensions of understanding of Haitian emigrant's realities. This compilation is a source of enlightenment for us all." *Booklist* contributor Donna Seaman found the book "a potent and piercing collection" that will help all Americans understand "the frustrations . . . of Haitians who are now outsiders both in Haiti and in their places of refuge."

After the Dance: A Walk through Carnival in Haiti is Danticat's nonfiction account of her first encounter with Carnival, the boisterous, sometimes debauched, sometimes dangerous celebrations that rock Haiti every year. As a child, she did not have the opportunity to attend Carnival. Her family inevitably packed up and left for a remote area in the Haitian mountains each year to escape the celebrations, perpetuating an almost superstitious distrust of the event. At times, though, staying clear has been a good idea. During the regime of Haitian dictator François "Papa Doc" Duvalier, carnival-goers were "subject to beatings and arrest by Duvalier's infamously unregulated militamen," wrote Judith Wynn in the *Boston Herald.* Danticat therefore approaches her first experience of Carnival uneasily. Her trip, however, beginning a week before the actual event, immerses her in the rich culture and history of Haiti, the cultural importance behind Carnival, and the background of the celebration itself. Danticat's "lively narrative" describes a country with a deep history, "influenced by Christianity, voodoo, Europeans, pirates, dictators, past slavery, and an uncertain economy," wrote Linda M. Kaufmann in *Library Journal.* Donna Seaman, writing in *Booklist,* observed that "as in her fiction, Danticat writes about her odyssey with an admirable delicacy and meticulousness," while a *Publishers Weekly* critic noted that the author "offers an enlightening look at the country—and Carnival—through the eyes of one of its finest writers."

"In order to create full-fledged, three-dimensional characters, writers often draw on their encounters, observations, collages of images from the everyday world, both theirs and others," Danticat remarked in a biographical essay in *Comtemporary Novelists.* "We are like actors, filtering through our emotions what life must be like, or must have been like, for those we write about. Truly we imagine these lives, aggrandize, reduce, or embellish, however we often begin our journey with an emotion close to our gut, whether it be anger, curiosity, joy, or fear."

BIOGRAPHICAL AND CRITICAL SOURCES:

BOOKS

Authors and Artists for Young Adults, Volume 29, Gale (Detroit, MI), 1999.

Contemporary Literary Criticism, Volume 94, Gale (Detroit, MI), 1996.

Contemporary Novelists, 7th edition, St. James Press (Detroit, MI), 2001.

St. James Guide to Young Adult Writers, Gale (Detroit, MI), 1999.

Short Stories for Students, Volume 1, Gale (Detroit, MI), 1997.

PERIODICALS

America, November 6, 1999, review of *The Farming of Bones,* p. 10.

Americas, January, 2000, Barbara Mujica, review of *The Farming of Bones,* p. 62; May, 2000, Michele Wucker, profile of Danticat, p. 40.

Antioch Review, winter, 1999, Grace A. Epstein, review of *The Farming of Bones,* p. 106.

Atlanta Journal-Constitution, October 29, 2000, Valerie Boyd, review of *The Beacon Best of 2000: Great Writing by Women and Men of All Colors and Cultures,* p. D3.

Belles Lettres, fall, 1994, Mary Mackay, "Living, Seeing, Remembering," pp. 36, 38; summer, 1995, pp. 12-15.

Black Issues Book Review, January, 1999, review of *The Farming of Bones,* p. 20; May, 2001, Denolyn Carroll, review of *The Butterfly's Way: Voices from the Haitian Dyaspora in the United States,* p. 60.

Bloomsbury Review, September-October, 1994, p. 12.

Booklist, January 1, 1999, review of *The Farming of Bones,* p. 778; March 15, 1999, review of *The Farming of Bones,* p. 1295; June 1, 1999, review of *Breath, Eyes, Memory,* p. 1796; February 15, 2000, Deborah Taylor, review of *Breath, Eyes, Memory,* p. 1096; October 15, 2000, review of *The Beacon Best of 2000,* p. 416; February 15, 2001, Donna Seaman, review of *The Butterfly's Way,* p. 1096; January 1, 2002, review of *The Butterfly's Way,* p. 763; August, 2002, Donna Seaman, review of *After the Dance: A Walk through Carnival in Haiti,* pp. 1895-1896; October 1, 2002, Hazel Rochman, review of *Behind the Mountains,* p. 312.

Boston Globe, Jordana Hart, "Danticat's Stories Pulse with Haitian Heartbeat," p. 70.

Boston Herald, November 17, 2000, Rosemary Herbert, "Writing in the Margins: Author-Editor Edwidge Danticat Celebrates Rich Pageant of Multicultural Stories," p. 43; September 1, 2002, Judith Wynn, review of *After the Dance,* p. 61.

Callaloo, spring, 1996, Renee H. Shea, interview with Danticat, pp. 382-389.

Christian Century, September 22, 1999, Dean Peerman, review of *The Farming of Bones,* p. 885.

Emerge, April, 1995, p. 58.

Entertainment Weekly, September 3, 1999, review of *The Farming of Bones,* p. 63.

Essence, November, 1993, Edwidge Danticat, "My Father Once Chased Rainbows," p. 48; April, 1995, Deborah Gregory, "Edwidge Danticat: Dreaming of Haiti" (interview), p. 56; May, 1996.

Globe and Mail, June 12, 1999, review of *Breath, Eyes, Memory,* p. D4.

Kirkus Reviews, June 1, 2002, review of *After the Dance,* p. 782; September 15, 2002, review of *Behind the Mountains,* p. 1387.

Kliatt, November, 1999, review of *The Farming of Bones,* p. 16; November, 2002, Claire Rosser, review of *Behind the Mountains,* p. 8.

Library Journal, November 1, 2000, Barbara O'Hara, review of *The Butterfly's Way,* p. 80, Ann Burns and Emily Joy, review of *The Butterfly's Way,* p. 103; June 15, 2002, Linda M. Kaufmann, review of *After the Dance,* p. 83.

Ms., March-April, 1994, Joan Philpott, "Two Tales of Haiti," review of *Breath, Eyes, Memory,* pp. 77-78; March-April, 1995, Jordana Hart, review of *Krik? Krak!,* p. 75.

Nation, November 16, 1998, Zia Jaffrey, review of *The Farming of Bones,* p. 62.

Newsday, May 21, 1995, p. A52; March 30, 1995, Richard Eder, "A Haitian Fantasy and Exile," pp. B2, B25.

New York, November 20, 1995, Rebecca Mead, review of *Krik? Krak!,* p. 50.

New York Times, January 26, 1995, Garry Pierre-Pierre, "Haitian Tales, Flatbush Scenes," pp. C1, C8; October 23, 1995, p. B3.

New York Times Book Review, July 10, 1994, Jim Gladstone, review of *Breath, Eyes, Memory,* p. 24; April 23, 1995, Robert Houston, *Krik? Krak!,* p. 22; September 27, 1998, Michael Upchurch, review of *The Farming of Bones,* p. 18; December 5, 1999, review of *The Farming of Bones,* p. 104; December 10, 1999, review of *The Farming of Bones,* p. 36.

New York Times Magazine, June 21, 1998.

O, February, 2002, profile of Danticat, pp. 141-145.

Off Our Backs, March, 1999, review of *Krik? Krak!, The Farming of Bones,* and *Breath, Eyes, Memory,* p. 13.

People, September 28, 1998, review of *The Farming of Bones,* p. 51.

Poets and Writers, January, 1997.

Progressive, January, 1997, p. 39; December, 1998, Matthew Rothschild, review of *The Farming of Bones,* p. 44.

Publishers Weekly, January 24, 1994, pp. 39-40; May 25, 1998; August 17, 1998, Mallay Charters, review of *The Farming of Bones,* p. 42; November 2, 1998, review of *The Farming of Bones,* p. 40; September 11, 2000, review of *The Beacon Best of 2000,* p. 69; December 18, 2000, review of *The Butterfly's Way,* p. 65; May 13, 2002, review of *After the Dance,* pp. 58-59; October 28, 2002, review of *Behind the Mountains,* p. 72.

Quarterly Black Review, June, 1995, Kimberly Hebert, review of *Krik? Krak!,* p. 6.

Reference & User Services Quarterly, spring, 1999, review of *The Farming of Bones,* p. 253.

St. Louis Post-Dispatch, September 21, 1999, Shauna Scott Rhone, review of *The Farming of Bones,* p. D3.

School Library Journal, May, 1995, p. 135; October, 2002, Diane S. Marton, review of *Behind the Mountains,* p. 160.

Time, September 7, 1998, Christopher John Farley, review of *The Farming of Bones,* p. 78.

Times Literary Supplement, April 28, 2000, Helen Hayward, review of *The Farming of Bones,* p. 23.
Times (London, England). March 20, 1999, Rachel Campbell-Johnston, review of *The Farming of Bones,* p. 19.
Village Voice Literary Supplement, July, 1995, p. 11.
Voice of Youth Advocates, December, 1995, p. 299.
Washington Post Book World, April 3, 1994, Bob Shacochis, "Island in the Dark," p. 6; May 14, 1995, Joanne Omang, review of *Krik? Krak!,* p. 4.
World & I, February, 1999, review of *The Farming of Bones,* p. 290.
World Literature Today, spring, 1999, Jacqueline Brice-Finch, "Haiti," p. 373.

ONLINE

Free Williamsburg, http://www.frccwilliamsburg.com/ (February 11, 2003), Alexander Laurence, interview with Danticat.
Voices from the Gaps, http://voices.cla.umn.edu/ (February 11, 2003), "Edwidge Danticat."*

* * *

DAY, Nancy Raines 1951-

PERSONAL: Born October 15, 1951, in Denver, CO; daughter of John Nelson II (an IBM executive) and Cecelia Ann (Ramsey) Raines; married Kenneth Gordon Day (a computer consultant), August 17, 1974; children: Meghan Elaine, Jesse Cort. *Education:* University of Michigan, B.A., 1972; Syracuse University, M.A., 1974. *Politics:* Democrat. *Religion:* Protestant. *Hobbies and other interests:* Swimming, rowing, reading, music.

ADDRESSES: *Agent*—Barbara Kouts, P.O. Box 560, Bellport, NY 11713. *E-mail*—bkouts@aol.com.

CAREER: Business Journals, Inc., Stamford, CT, assistant editor, 1973; New Readers Press, Syracuse, NY, assistant editor, 1973-74; Ziff-Davis Publishing, New York, NY, assistant editor, 1975, associate editor and contributor, 1976-78; freelance writer, 1976—. Volunteer tutor, local elementary and middle schools, 1982—; church school teacher, 1986-2002; teacher, Institute of Children's Literature; teacher and consultant, Soloquest; writer, Krames Communications.

MEMBER: Society of Children's Book Writers and Illustrators, Authors Guild, Media Alliance.

AWARDS, HONORS: Notable Books selection, *New York Times Book Review,* and "Pick of the Lists" selection, American Booksellers Association, both 1995, for *The Lion's Whiskers: An Ethiopian Folktale;* Health Educators Media Award, for *After Your Heart Attack.*

WRITINGS:

Tobacco: Facts for Decisions, New Readers Press (Syracuse, NY), 1978.
Help Yourself to Health, New Readers Press (Syracuse, NY), 1980.
Alcohol and Drug Abuse, Addison-Wesley (New York, NY), 1989.
AIDS and Other Sexually-Transmitted Diseases, Addison-Wesley (New York, NY), 1989.
The Lion's Whiskers: An Ethiopian Folktale, illustrated by Ann Grifalconi, Scholastic (New York, NY), 1995.
A Kitten's Year, illustrated by Anne Mortimer, HarperCollins Publishers (New York, NY), 2000.
Piecing Earth & Sky Together: A Creation Story from the Mien Tribe of Laos, illustrated by Genna Panzarella, Shen's Books (Fremont, CA), 2001.
Double Those Wheels, illustrated by Steve Haskamp, Dutton (New York, NY), 2003.

Contributor of articles to *Americana, U*S* Kids, National Parks and Conservation, Vista USA, Brides, Career Pilot, Medicenter Management, HealthWeek,* and other publications. Author of medical booklets, including *After Your Heart Attack.*

SIDELIGHTS: Nancy Raines Day once told *CA:* "I write for children in hopes of touching them as I was touched by certain books as a child. Observing my own children once again immersed me in what it felt like to be a child, something I'd been busy forgetting as an adult. Among the many books my son and daughter brought me over and over were a few—such as *The Cat in the Hat, The Story about Ping, and Charlotte's Web*—that I could read fifty times and still love. I took it as a challenge to write something lasting like that." Becoming a published author of children's books was somewhat more challenging than Day expected; it took her ten years to get her first book of young people's fiction, *The Lion's Whiskers: An Ethiopian Folktale,* published. Still, Day encourages other aspiring authors. "To others who want to do this important work," she once told *SATA,* "I'd say keep learning all you can and don't give up!"

The Lion's Whiskers is based on a folktale from Ethiopia. When Day discovered this tale, she once recalled, "I was excited to find one about a good stepmother. I believe fairy tales like Cinderella and Hansel and Gretel are important to children trying to reconcile the 'good' and 'bad' aspects of their own mothers. In these times, however, when so many families are trying so hard to 'blend,' I feel such tales give stepmothers an undeservedly bad name. I wanted to give stepparents and stepchildren everywhere a positive story to share."

The Lion's Whiskers follows the story of Fanaye, a woman past childbearing age who longs for a family of her own. When she marries Tesfa and meets his motherless son, Abebe, she is overjoyed. Fanaye tries hard to please the boy, but he wants no part of her. Desperate, Fanaye seeks the wisdom of a shaman—a tribal medicine man. He sends her on a mission to gather three whiskers from a fierce lion for a magic potion that will win her Abebe's love. She collects the whiskers very carefully, by slowly gaining the lion's trust. Once obtained, the whiskers are no longer needed, as Fanaye has also learned how she must likewise gain Abebe's trust and love. "This Ethiopian folktale is full of rich imagery and wisdom: equally compelling are the drama of Fanaye's approach to the lion and the larger message, that distance is sometimes a necessary preface to intimacy," noted a *Publishers Weekly* reviewer. *Booklist* contributor Hazel Rochman also commented favorably on Day's retelling, saying, "The quest is exciting, and the emotions of mother and son are powerful." Susan Dove Lempke, writing in the *Bulletin of the Center for Children's Books,* thought *The Lion's Whiskers* "provides an excellent counterpoint to tales of wicked stepmothers," while *New York Times Book Review* critic Barbara Thompson concluded, "Nancy Raines Day has told a wonderful story, with dignity and warmth. Fanaye changes from a woman who would love any child into one who learns how to love the child she is given, and how to enable him to love her."

Also based on a folktale is *Piecing Earth & Sky Together: A Creation Story from the Mien Tribe of Laos.* Day learned the story from a group of Mien people, noted for their needlework, who were involved in a project in Berkeley, California. In her book, a grandmother tells a tale to her granddaughter while teaching her Mien-style embroidery. The creation story involves a pair of heavenly siblings, one sewing the earth and other the sky. It turns out that the sky, stitched together by Faam Koh, is too small to accommodate the earth created by his sister, Faam Toh, so they must work cooperatively on alterations to make their pieces fit together. Day and her illustrator, Genna Panzarella, have given the story "an intriguing presentation that should reach a wide audience," in the opinion of *Booklist* reviewer GraceAnne A. DeCandido.

While *Piecing Earth & Sky Together* is aimed at grade-school students, some of Day's other books are designed for younger children—preschool age through first grade. These include *A Kitten's Year* and *Double Those Wheels. A Kitten's Year* traces a kitten's development month by month, using simple but evocative language to accompany the vivid artwork by Anne Mortimer, and serving to teach both vocabulary and the months of the year. A *Publishers Weekly* critic noted that Day has produced "supple text," using "cat-like verbs" such as "paws" and "chases." *Booklist* contributor Kathy Broderick described the volume as "like a poem, with more to experience at each reading." *Double Those Wheels* uses a humorous tale-in-rhyme of a monkey delivering pizzas to teach math concepts. He starts out riding a unicycle, then switches to a bicycle, then a car, and so on, doubling the number of wheels on his conveyance each time. "The catchy verse propels the story along," commented a *Publishers Weekly* reviewer, while a *Kirkus Reviews* contributor pronounced the book "a delightful romp."

BIOGRAPHICAL AND CRITICAL SOURCES:

PERIODICALS

Booklist, February 15, 1995, Hazel Rochman, review of *The Lion's Whiskers: An Ethiopian Folktale,* p. 1058; December 15, 1999, Kathy Broderick, review of *A Kitten's Year,* p. 782; April 2, 2002, GraceAnne A. DeCandido, review of *Piecing Earth & Sky Together: A Creation Story from the Mien Tribe of Laos,* p. 1329; October 15, 2003, Kathleen Odean, review of *Double Those Wheels,* p. 417.

Bulletin of the Center for Children's Books, March, 1995, Susan Dove Lempke, review of *The Lion's Whiskers,* p. 232.

Kirkus Reviews, June 15, 2003, review of *Double Those Wheels,* p. 857.

New York Times Book Review, December 3, 1995, Barbara Thompson, review of *The Lion's Whiskers,* p. 72.

Publishers Weekly, March 27, 1995, review of *The Lion's Whiskers,* pp. 85-86; January 17, 2000, review of *A Kitten's Year,* p. 56; May 26, 2003, review of *Double Those Wheels,* p. 68.

School Library Journal, April, 1995, pp. 140-141; August, 2003, Elaine Lesh Morgan, review of *Double Those Wheels,* p. 125.*

* * *

DELTON, Judy 1931-2001

PERSONAL: Born May 6, 1931, in St. Paul, MN; died of a blood infection, December 31, 2001, in St. Paul, MN; daughter of A. F. (a plant engineer) and Alice (a homemaker; maiden name, Walsdorf) Jaschke; married Jeff J. Delton (a school psychologist), June 14, 1958; children: Julie, Jina, Jennifer, Jamie. *Education:* Attended School of Associated Arts, 1950, and College of St. Catherine, 1954-57.

CAREER: Elementary school teacher in parochial schools of St. Paul, MN, 1957-64; freelance writer. Teacher of writing.

MEMBER: Authors Guild, Authors League of America.

AWARDS, HONORS: Book of the Year Award, Child Study Association of America, 1974, for *Two Good Friends,* and 1979, for *Brimhall Turns to Magic* and *On a Picnic;* American Library Association Notable Book Award, 1975, for *Two Good Friendsl;* Outstanding Teacher Award, Metropolitan State University, 1976; Children's Choice, International Reading Association/ Children's Book Council, for *The New Girl at School;* New Jersey Institute of Technology Authors Award, 1980, for *On a Picnic;* North Dakota Children's Choice Award, North Dakota Library Association, 1980, for *My Mom Hates Me in January;* Parents' Choice Award in Literature, Parents' Choice Foundation, 1986, for *Angel's Mother's Boyfriend.*

WRITINGS:

Two Good Friends, Crown (New York, NY), 1974.

Rabbit Finds a Way, Crown (New York, NY), 1975.

Two Is Company, Crown (New York, NY), 1976.

Three Friends Find Spring, Crown (New York, NY), 1977.

Penny-Wise, Fun-Foolish, Crown (New York, NY), 1977.

My Mom Hates Me in January, A. Whitman (Chicago, IL), 1977.

It Happened on Thursday, A. Whitman (Chicago, IL), 1978.

Brimhall Comes to Stay, Lothrop (New York, NY), 1978.

Brimhall Turns to Magic, Lothrop (New York, NY), 1979.

On a Picnic, Doubleday (Garden City, NY), 1979.

The New Girl at School, Dutton (New York, NY), 1979.

Rabbit's New Rug, Parents' Magazine Press (New York, NY), 1979.

The Best Mom in the World, A. Whitman (Chicago, IL), 1979.

Kitty in the Middle, Houghton Mifflin (Boston, MA), 1979.

Kitty in the Summer, Houghton Mifflin (Boston, MA), 1980.

Lee Henry's Best Friend, A. Whitman (Chicago, IL), 1980.

My Mother Lost Her Job Today, A. Whitman (Chicago, IL), 1980.

Groundhog's Day at the Doctor, Parents' Magazine Press (New York, NY), 1981.

I Never Win, Carolrhoda (Minneapolis, MN), 1981.

A Walk on a Snowy Night, Harper (New York, NY), 1982.

I'm Telling You Now, Arthur Ray, Dutton (New York, NY), 1982.

The Goose Who Wrote a Book, Carolrhoda (Minneapolis, MN), 1982.

Only Jody, Houghton Mifflin (Boston, MA), 1982.

A Pet for Duck and Bear, A. Whitman (Chicago, IL), 1982.

Blue Ribbon Friends, Houghton Mifflin (Boston, MA), 1982.

Backyard Angel, Houghton Mifflin (Boston, MA), 1983.

Brimhall Turns Detective, Carolrhoda (Minneapolis, MN), 1983.

Duck Goes Fishing, A. Whitman (Chicago, IL), 1983.

Near Occasion of Sin (novel; young adult), Harcourt (San Diego, CA), 1984.

Kitty in High School, Houghton Mifflin (Boston, MA), 1984.

Bear and Duck on the Run, A. Whitman (Chicago, IL), 1984.

The Twenty-nine Most Common Writing Mistakes and How to Avoid Them (adult), Writers Digest (Cincinnati, OH), 1985.

Angel in Charge, Houghton Mifflin (Boston, MA), 1985.

A Birthday Bike for Brimhall, Houghton Mifflin (Boston, MA), 1985.

I'll Never Love Anything Ever Again, A. Whitman (Chicago, IL), 1985.

The Elephant in Duck's Garden, A. Whitman (Chicago, IL), 1985.

(With Dorothy Tucker) *My Grandma's in a Nursing Home,* A. Whitman (Chicago, IL), 1985.

Rabbit Goes to Night School, A. Whitman (Chicago, IL), 1986.

Angel's Mother's Boyfriend, Houghton Mifflin (Boston, MA), 1986.

Xmas Gift for Brimhall, Houghton Mifflin (Boston, MA), 1986.

The Mystery of the Haunted Cabin, Houghton Mifflin (Boston, MA), 1986.

Angel's Mother's Wedding, Houghton Mifflin (Boston, MA), 1987.

Kitty from the Start, Houghton Mifflin (Boston, MA), 1987.

Blue Skies, French Fries, Dell (New York, NY), 1988.

Camp Ghost-Away, Dell (New York, NY), 1988.

Cookies and Crutches, Dell (New York, NY), 1988.

Grumpy Pumpkins, Dell (New York, NY), 1988.

Hired Help for Rabbit, Macmillan (New York, NY), 1988.

Lucky Dog Days, Dell (New York, NY), 1988.

No Time for Christmas, Carolrhoda (Minneapolis, MN), 1988.

Peanut-Butter Pilgrims, Dell (New York, NY), 1988.

A Pee Wee Christmas, Dell (New York, NY), 1988.

That Mushy Stuff, Dell (New York, NY), 1989.

The Pooped Troop, Dell (New York, NY), 1989.

The Pee Wee Jubilee, Dell (New York, NY), 1989.

Spring Sprouts, Dell (New York, NY), 1989.

Angel's Mother's Baby, Houghton Mifflin (Boston, MA), 1989.

The Bad Bad Bunnies, Dell (New York, NY), 1990.

Rosy Noses, Freezing Toes, Dell (New York, NY), 1990.

Hello Huckleberry Heights, Dell (New York, NY), 1990.

Summer Showdown, Dell (New York, NY), 1990.

Scary, Scary Huckleberry, Dell (New York, NY), 1990.

Merry Merry Huckleberry, Dell (New York, NY), 1990.

Huckleberry Hash, Dell (New York, NY), 1990.

Artificial Grandma, Yearling (New York, NY), 1990.

My Mom Made Me Go to Camp, Delacorte (New York, NY), 1990.

My Mom Made Me Go to School, Delacorte (New York, NY), 1991.

Sonny's Secret, Yearling (New York, NY), 1991.

Sky Babies, Yearling (New York, NY), 1991.

The Perfect Christmas Gift, Macmillan (New York, NY), 1992.

Trash Bash, Yearling (New York, NY), 1992.

Lights, Action, Land-Ho!, Yearling (New York, NY), 1992.

Pee Wees on Parade, Yearling (New York, NY), 1992.

Pee Wees on Skis, Yearling (New York, NY), 1993.

Piles of Pets, Yearling (New York, NY), 1993.

My Mom Made Me Take Piano Lessons, Doubleday (Garden City, NY), 1993.

Fishy Wishes, Dell (New York, NY), 1993.

All Dads on Deck, Bantam Doubleday Dell (New York, NY), 1994.

Greed Groundhogs, Yearling (New York, NY), 1994.

Ship Ahoy!, Hyperion (New York, NY), 1995.

Winning Ticket!, Hyperion (New York, NY), 1995.

Cabin Surprise, Hyperion (New York, NY), 1995.

Ten's a Crowd!, Hyperion (New York, NY), 1995.

Moving Up, Hyperion (New York, NY), 1995.

Next Stop, the White House!, Hyperion (New York, NY), 1995.

Pee Wee's on First, Bantam Doubleday Dell (New York, NY), 1995.

Super Duper Pee Wee!, Yearling (New York, NY), 1995.

Royal Escapade, Hyperion (New York, NY), 1995.

Prize-winning Private Eyes, Hyperion (New York, NY), 1995.

Eggs with Legs, Bantam Doubleday Dell (New York, NY), 1996.

Pee Wee Pool Party, Yearling (New York, NY), 1996.

Halloween Helpers, Yearling (New York, NY), 1997.

Stage Frightened, Yearling (New York, NY), 1997.

Moans and Groans and Dinosaur Bones, Yearling (New York, NY), 1997.

Computer Clues, Yearling (New York, NY), 1998.

Pedal Power, Yearling (New York, NY), 1998.

Planet Pee Wee, Yearling (New York, NY), 1998.

Molly for Mayor, Bantam Doubleday Dell (New York, NY), 1999.
Angel Spreads Her Wings, Houghton Mifflin (Boston, MA), 1999.
Bookworm Buddies, Yearling (New York, NY), 1999.
Send in the Clowns!, Yearling (New York, NY), 1999.
Wild, Wild West, Yearling (New York, NY), 1999.
Winnie the Pooh's Book of Manners, Disney Press (New York, NY), 1999.
Angel Bites the Bullet, Houghton Mifflin (Boston, MA), 2000.
A Big Box of Memories, Dell (New York, NY), 2000.

Author of "Pee Wee Scout" series, "Angel" series, "Kitty" series, and "Condo Kids" series. Contributor of over two hundred essays, articles, poems, and short stories to periodicals, including *Wall Street Journal, Saturday Review, Humpty Dumpty, Publishers Weekly, Marriage, Catholic Digest, Family Digest, Home Life, Today, Women's Circle, Exclusively Yours, Spirit, Cats, Teacher's Lounge, Progressive Women, Capitol, Insight, Today's Christian Mother, Teacher Paper, View, Seasons, Grit, Lutheran Digest, KOA Handbook, Christian Home, Instructor,* and *Highlights for Children.*

ADAPTATIONS: I'm Telling You Now, is available in Braille.

SIDELIGHTS: A prolific writer, Judy Delton published more than a hundred books and over two hundred essays, articles, and short stories during her career. Delton authored several popular children's series including, the "Kitty," "Angel," "Condo Kids," and "Lottery Luck" series. Her forty-book "Pee Wee Scouts" series has sold millions of copies. Delton often used her own life as an inspiration for her books, as she tackled problems that face children and young adults. She once told Kathryn Boardman of the *St. Paul Dispatch:* "I really resent it when people ask me when I am going to write a novel for adults. Children's fiction is a special field. In my opinion it is as important as any other kind of writing. I like to do it and my publishers think I am good at it."

Delton's "Kitty" series follows the life of Kitty, a young, Catholic girl growing up near St. Paul, Minnesota, in the 1940s. The first book of the series, *Kitty in the Middle,* was published in 1979. Like many of Delton's books, it is based on her own experiences as a child. In an interview with *Authors and Artists for Young Adults* (*AAYA*), Delton once said, "In the Seventies, there was a lot of popular interest in tracing people's origins, so I decided to write about growing up Catholic in the forties." The "Kitty" series includes *Kitty in the Middle, Kitty in the Summer,* and *Kitty in High School. Kitty from the Start,* is a prequel to the other books in the series. The book takes Kitty back to third grade, where she worries about choosing between friends and avoiding movies forbidden by the Legion of Decency. Michele Landsberg noted in the *New York Times,* "Thanks to the author Judy Delton's sprightly simplicity, such parochial concerns come across as lively, interesting, and funny."

Delton once commented to *CA*: "Someone once said that an author is fortunate in that he gets to live his life twice, once in the doing and once in the telling. I find that to be true, since I am always reliving my life from some new aspect, often not knowing what is truth and what is illusion." Delton explained that she relived her childhood through the "Kitty" books and that she borrowed from her son's life for the book *Only Jody,* the story of an only boy in a family of four women. She has also looked to her daughter's life for inspiration in her works. "In some way or other, I am always in the book," Delton said.

The first book in Delton's "Angel" series, *Back Yard Angel,* was based partly on her daughter and partly on herself. Delton once noted to *AAYA:* "Angel hates change, just like me. I incorporated my mentality into her. Because my characters are mostly me, emotionally, they usually go through what I do." Angel O'Leary can easily be described as a worrywart. Her outlook on life is a bit pessimistic, to say the least, and she dreams up the worst-case scenario for every situation. The books focus on Angel's changing family life. In *Angel's Mother's Wedding,* which followed *Angel's Mother's Boyfriend,* Mrs. O'Leary announces her upcoming marriage to her boyfriend, Rudy. From there, Angel begins to worry that her mother is not properly preparing for the wedding. As if that's not enough, in *Angel's Mother's Baby,* Angel learns that her mother is pregnant.

The series continues with *Angel Spreads Her Wings* and *Angel Bites the Bullet.* In *Angel Spreads Her Wings,* Angel learns that her family will be flying to Greece to meet her stepfather's parents. This sparks a whole new set of worries for Angel, including flying in an airplane and meeting her new step-grandparents. A *Publishers Weekly* reviewer noted that "Angel slowly discovers that she really doesn't want to be the one whom 'everyone tiptoes around' and who always overreacts, so she makes a stab at embracing change and starts to 'spread her wings.'" The reviewer continued, "Delton's storytelling is natural; her use of dialogue, authentic. It's a lighthearted romp with only a hint of a lesson." In *Angel Bites the Bullet,* Angel must share her bedroom with her mother's friend, Alyce, whose apartment burned down. Angel works with her best friend to better Alyce's situation, and get Alyce out of her hair. Kate McLean, in *School Library Journal,* remarked "The campaign is very funny, especially when laced with Angel's imagined worries about her new family and her desperation to be rid of her houseguest."

Perhaps Delton's most well-known series is the "Pee Wee Scouts," which follows the Pee Wees on their weekly adventures to earn their next merit badge. The books deal with a variety of topics that sometimes teach the reader a lesson. In *Molly for Mayor,* the first book in the "Pee Wee" series, Molly Duff must come up with a creative way to win a mock election against her sly opponent. *Teeny Weeny Zucchinis* follows the Pee Wees as they try to earn their harvest badge. *Booklist* reviewer Lauren Peterson wrote, "Delton's positive portrayal of Jody, a wheelchair-bound boy on whom Molly has a crush, will provide inclusion students with a good role model and promote understanding and awareness among nondisabled readers." Delton's writing, while tuned in to a child's mind, deals with real situations. In *Tricks and Treats,* Molly's dad loses his job, which opens up many questions for Molly. "Many kids will like the way this chapter book combines friendship and scary fun with a fear that's very close to home," noted Hazel Rochman in *Booklist.* The last book in the "Pee Wee Scouts" series is called *A Big Box of Memories.* The Pee Wees must put together a time capsule for the scouts of the future to earn their last badge, but it's hard to decide exactly what to put in the box.

Delton's "Lottery Luck" series focuses on the Green family. In the first book, *Winning Ticket!,* Daisy and Delphie Green convince Aunt Ivy to buy some lottery tickets. The outcome of the book is obvious from the title, but a lesson is learned along the way. A *Publishers Weekly* reviewer noted, "As her buoyant tale draws to a close, the author convincingly interjects a worthy note: when Daisy expresses concern that the windfall will change her family, her parents explain that they will make sure that the truly important things do not change." In *Ten's a Crowd!* Daisy and Delphie are overwhelmed by the number of friends and relatives who show up at their home after they win the lottery. In subsequent books, Daisy, Delphie, and Aunt Ivy have adventures in Washington, DC, and England.

Books in Delton's "Condo Kids" series include *Hello Huckleberry Heights, Huckleberry Hash, Scary, Scary Huckleberry, Merry Merry Huckleberry,* and *Artificial Grandma.* Delton once told *AAYA* that she enjoyed the "Condo Kids" series because it gave her the opportunity to really develop the characters. In *Artificial Grandma,* Delton explores the relationships between children and the elderly.

Delton has authored many other children's books in addition to those in her series. *My Mom Made Me Go to School, My Mom Made Me Go to Camp,* and *My Mom Made Me Take Piano Lessons,* are as much for adults as they are for kids. The books deal with Archie's resistance to his mom's efforts to help him have new, exciting experiences. Archie almost always ends up having a good time once he gives the new activity a chance. The characters of Duck and Bear that appear in some of Delton's books, including *The Perfect Christmas Gift, Two Good Friends,* and *A Pet for Duck and Bear,* are based on Delton and her mother. Delton liked to use animals with human characteristics because it adds to the story. In her book *The Twenty-nine Most Common Writing Mistakes and How to Avoid Them,* Delton explained, "Animals in a fantasy story are not animals and the story is not an animal story." She continued, "Duck is the same kind of perfectionist, the same kind of fanatical housekeeper that my mother was." Bear is more like Delton, "a better cook than housekeeper."

Delton's success as a writer stemmed from her ability to create strong characters, which she attributed to writing "honestly." "To write honestly, you must be inside the characters, know them, and believe in them," she once explained to *AAYA.* "I think kids will generally relate to the characters if they're portrayed honestly."

BIOGRAPHICAL AND CRITICAL SOURCES:

BOOKS

Authors and Artists for Young Adults, Volume 7, Gale (Detroit, MI), 1991.

Continuum Encyclopedia of Children's Literature, Continuum (New York, NY), 2001.

The Twenty-nine Most Common Writing Mistakes and How to Avoid Them, Writers Digest (Cincinnati, OH), 1985.

PERIODICALS

Associated Press, July 2, 1993, Carol Deegan, review of *My Mom Made Me Go to Camp.*

Booklist, October 1, 1992, Ilene Cooper, review of *The Perfect Christmas Gift,* p. 334; June 1, 1994, Kay Weisman, review of *My Mom Made Me Take Piano Lessons,* p. 1836; September 15, 1994, Hazel Rochman, review of *Tricks and Treats,* p. 135; January 1, 1996, Lauren Peterson, review of *Teeny Weeny Zucchinis,* p. 833; May 1, 1999, Lauren Peterson, review of *Angel Spreads Her Wings,* p. 1593; November 1, 2000, Gillian Engberg, review of *Angel Bites the Bullet,* p. 538.

Boston Globe, December 12, 1994, Margaret Hsu, review of *Kitty in the Summer,* p. 13.

Children's Bookwatch, December, 1992, review of *The Perfect Christmas Gift,* p. 2.

Day Care & Early Education, summer, 1994, review of *Two Good Friends,* p. 23, review of *Rabbit Finds a Way,* p. 23.

Horn Book, November-December, 1989, Carolyn K. Jenks, review of *Angel's Mother's Baby,* p. 770; May, 1997, audio book review of *Cookies and Crutches,* p. 357, audio book review of *Camp Ghost-Away,* p. 357; July, 1999, review of *Angel Spreads Her Wings,* p. 463; May-June 2002, "Obituaries," p. 366.

Horn Book Guide, spring, 1992, review of *My Mom Made Me Go to School,* p. 30, review of *I Never Win!,* p. 54, review of *Brimhall Turns Detective,* p. 54; spring 1993, review of *The Perfect Christmas Gift,* p. 27; fall, 1994, review of *My Mom Made Me Take Piano Lessons,* p. 270; fall, 1999, review of *Angel Spreads Her Wings,* p. 290; spring, 2001, review of *Angel Bites the Bullet,* p. 71.

Hudson Star-Observer, June 20, 1974; April, 1977.

Instructor, February, 1993, review of *Angel in Charge,* p. 14.

Kirkus Review, March 1, 1999, review of *Angel Spreads Her Wings,* p. 374.

Library Talk, November, 1992, review of *The Perfect Christmas Gift,* p. 19.

New York Times, April 12, 1987, Michele Landsberg, review of *Kitty from the Start,* p. 48.

Publishers Weekly, January 27, 1992, review of *Hired Help for Rabbit,* p. 98; September 7, 1992, Elizabeth Devereaux, review of *The Perfect Christmas Gift,* p. 68; January 25, 1993, "Federal Court Affirms Pee Wee Scouts' Honor," p. 26; May 15, 1995, review of *Winning Ticket!,* p. 73; October 6, 1997, review of *Pee Wee Scouts,* p. 50; April 12, 1999, review of *Angel Spreads Her Wings,* p. 78.

St. Paul Dispatch, April 2, 1977.

St. Paul Pioneer Press, August 11, 1974; May 31, 1981.

School Library Journal, December, 1984, p. 46; March, 1989, Lori A. Janick, review of *Hired Help for Rabbit,* p. 160; June, 1989, Joyce Gunn-Bradley, review of *Cookies and Crutches,* p. 87, review of *Camp Ghost-Away,* p. 87; October, 1989, Phyllis K. Kennemer, review of *Angel's Mother's Baby,* p. 117; February, 1991, Judith Gloyer, review of *My Mom Made Me Go to Camp,* p. 68; April, 1992, Gale W. Sherman, review of *My Mom Made Me Go to School,* p. 90; October, 1992, review of *The Perfect Christmas Gift,* p. 39; August, 1994, Martha Gordon, review of *My Mom Made Me Take Piano Lessons,* p. 128; January, 1998, DeAnn Tabuchi, review of *Halloween Helpers,* p. 81; February, 1998, Teresa Bateman, audio book review of *Camp Ghost-Away,* p. 72; April, 1999, Susan Helpler, review of *Angel Spreads Her Wings,* p. 133; October, 2000, Kate McLean, review of *Angel Bites the Bullet,* p. 156.

Social Studies, March, 1995, review of *My Grandma's in a Nursing Home,* p. 92.

Writers Digest, June, 1985, p. 39.

ONLINE

BoondocksNet, http://www.boondocksnet.com/ (November 11, 2003), "Judy Delton."

OBITUARIES:

PERIODICALS

Star Tribune (Minneapolis, MN), January 3, 2002, p. 7B.

Washington Post, January 4, 2002, p. B5.*

DEXTER, Pete 1943-

PERSONAL: Born 1943, in Pontiac, MI; married (divorced); married second wife, Dian; children: (second marriage) Casey. *Education:* Received degree from University of South Dakota, 1970. *Hobbies and other interests:* Boxing.

ADDRESSES: *Home*—1170 Markham Way, Sacramento, CA 95818. *Office*—*Sacramento Bee,* 21st and Q Streets, Box 15779, Sacramento, CA 95852. *Agent*—Esther Newberg, International Creative Management, 40 West 57th St., New York, NY 10019.

CAREER: Novelist, journalist, and columnist. *West Palm Beach Post,* Palm Beach, FL, reporter, 1971-72; *Philadelphia Daily News,* Philadelphia, PA, columnist, 1972-84; *Sacramento Bee,* Sacramento, CA, columnist, 1985—; Has also worked as a truck driver, gas station attendant, mail sorter, construction laborer, and salesperson.

AWARDS, HONORS: National Endowment for the Arts grant to write poetry; National Book Award, and National Book Critics Circle Award nomination, both 1988, both for *Paris Trout.*

WRITINGS:

NOVELS

God's Pocket, Random House (New York, NY), 1984.
Deadwood, Random House (New York, NY), 1986.
Paris Trout, Random House (New York, NY), 1988.
Brotherly Love, Random House (New York, NY), 1993.
The Paperboy, Random House (New York, NY), 1995.

SCREENPLAYS

Rush, Metro-Goldwyn-Mayer, 1991.
(With others) *Michael,* New Line Cinema, 1996.

Also author of screenplay *Mulholland Falls.* Contributor to periodicals, including *Esquire, Sports Illustrated,* and *Playboy.*

Pete Dexter

ADAPTATIONS: Dexter's work has been adapted for audiocassette.

WORK IN PROGRESS: Screenplays for *Deadwood* and *Paris Trout;* a novel.

SIDELIGHTS: National Book Award-winning author Pete Dexter is noted for his novels that mix violence with humor, display a sharp ear for dialogue and an eye for local color, and contain well-rounded and often eccentric characters. An outspoken journalist with the *Philadelphia Daily News* for twelve years and with the *Sacramento Bee* since 1985, Dexter turned to writing fiction after nearly being beaten to death by readers who were infuriated by one of his *Daily News* columns. Thus no stranger to brutality, he focuses in his novels on how communities react to violence and murder. Dexter's first book, *God's Pocket,* turns on the death of an abrasive white construction worker in Philadelphia; *Deadwood* relates the assassination of legendary outlaw "Wild Bill" Hickok in a western gold-rush town; *Paris Trout* explores the aftermath of the shooting of an innocent black girl in Georgia; and *The Paperboy* recounts the upcoming execution of an innocent man.

Born in Michigan and raised in Georgia and South Dakota, Dexter graduated from the University of South Dakota in 1970 after attending for eight years (he would quit when the weather got cold). He secured a job as a reporter with the *West Palm Beach Post* but left after two years ("I wasn't the best writer there," he explained in the *New York Times Book Review*). He then worked at a gas station with another former *Post* reporter but quit ("I wasn't even the best writer in the gas station") to join the *Philadelphia Daily News* in 1972. A decade later he was badly beaten in a barroom brawl by baseball-bat and tire-iron-wielding denizens of a Philadelphia neighborhood who were angered by a column he had written about a drug-related murder that happened there. Dexter survived with a broken back and hip and an altered sense of taste from the blows to his head. Forced to give up his favorite pastime, drinking (beer, according to Dexter, now tastes like battery acid), he devoted his spare time to writing. The result was three critically acclaimed novels.

Dexter's first work, *God's Pocket,* begins with what Julius Lester in *New York Times Book Review* called an "auspicious comic opening": "Leon Hubbard died ten minutes into lunch break on the first Monday in May, on the construction site of the new one-story trauma wing at Holy Redeemer Hospital in South Philadelphia. One way or the other, he was going to lose the job." Drug-addict bricklayer Leon prompted his own demise when he threatened a black coworker named Lucien with a straight razor; Lucien consequently bashed Leon in the back of the head with a lead pipe. Glad to be rid of the troublemaker, the other workers and the foreman told the police it was an accidental death. This "random incident," according to Paul Gray in *Time,* turns "into a picaresque romp" when Leon's devoted mother, Jeanie, and her second husband, Mickey, who is constantly trying to prove his devotion to her, believe otherwise. At the grieving mother's request, Mickey must tap his underground connections to find out who killed Leon.

Reviewers of *God's Pocket* commended Dexter for his masterful control of comic situations, fluent prose, and idiomatic dialogue. Gray also appreciated the novel's "impressive ballast of local color," noting that the rough working-class Philadelphia neighborhood called God's Pocket "seems all too real: narrow houses, streets, lives; a place where the Hollywood Bar, the social hub of the area, does 'half its business before noon.'" Some critics, however, criticized *God's Pocket* for being too ambitious. Gray, for instance, complained that Dexter "piles on more complications and coincidences than his novel ought to carry" and added that there are too many characters and subplots. Mickey, for example, in addition to having to please Jeanie by identifying Leon's murderer, must raise six thousand dollars to bury him in a mahogany casket. But because he cannot pay the undertaker for the funeral due to his losing efforts at the racetrack, Mickey is forced to drive Leon's embalmed corpse around in his refrigerated meat truck, which he uses to sell stolen meat for his two-bit mobster boss. For another subplot Dexter created Richard Shellburn, an alcoholic Philadelphia newspaper columnist who is also suspicious of Leon's mysterious demise. Shellburn is later beaten to death by the threatened residents of God's Pocket.

Dexter's second novel, *Deadwood,* focuses on the death of American folk hero James Butler "Wild Bill" Hickok. In the novel, Hickok, his longtime partner "Colorado" Charley Utter, and follower Malcolm Nash escort a wagon train of prostitutes to the Dakota gold rush town of Deadwood in 1876. Hickok, once renowned as the best pistol shot in the West, is now an aging Wild West-show performer who drinks to overcome the pain of syphilis. About a third of the way into *Deadwood* he is shot to death by a hired killer while playing poker in a saloon. "The rest of this hilarious and rousing novel," according to Dennis Drabelle in Chicago's *Tribune Books,* concerns itself with how "the other characters cope with [Hickok's] transformation from living to dead legend."

New York Times Book Review contributor Ron Hansen remarked that after his hero's death Dexter fills the pages of the novel with "some intriguingly extravagant minor characters." Populating Dexter's town of Deadwood are China Doll, a prostitute seeking revenge on Utter for burning the corpse of her brother; her pimp, Al Swearingen, who brutally rapes Nash; "Calamity" Jane Cannery, who claims that she is the widow of Hickok; and trapeze artist Agnes Lake, Hickok's true widow, who befriends Cannery. "All of them become threads in the tapestry of Deadwood," Drabelle noted, "and the town itself becomes the protagonist."

Critics praised *Deadwood* for its local color, shrewd characterization, and deftly handled bawdy situations. "*Deadwood* is unpredictable, hyperbolic and, page after page, uproarious," Hansen attested. It is "a joshing book written in high spirits and a raw appreciation for the past." "The writing is engagingly colloquial without being silly, and well suited to the multiple character points of view," *Village Voice* contributor M. George Stevenson assessed. "And the book *is* very funny and filled with wry observations about the surfaces of frontier life." "With its stylish humor and convincing demonstration of how the fables of the Wild West originated," Drabelle concluded, "*Deadwood* may well be the best Western ever written."

Dexter received the National Book Award and was shortlisted for the National Book Critics Circle Award for his third book, *Paris Trout.* Set in the 1950s in the town of Cotton Point, Georgia, the novel concerns the amoral Paris Trout, a white hardware-store owner and loanshark to the black community who is nonetheless locally respected. When a young black man, Henry Ray Boxer, refuses to make payments on a car he bought from Trout after it was hit by a truck, Trout and a crony barge into the man's home to collect on the loan. Not finding him there, Trout shoots Boxer's mother in the back and kills a fourteen-year old girl who lives with the family.

Reluctantly, the authorities arrest, try, and sentence Trout to three years' hard labor. Convinced of his right to collect on a debt and determined not to do time for what he does not consider a crime, Trout bribes his way out of going to prison. In the aftermath he grows increasingly demented and becomes, in the words of *Los Angeles Times Book Review* contributor Richard Eder, "a primal evil, all will and no humanity." "Before it is over," *Book World* contributor Judith Paterson noted, "[Trout's] unyielding conviction that everything he does is right has thrown the whole town off its moral center and exposed the link between Trout's depravity and the town's silent endorsement of all kinds of inhumanities—including racism, sexism and economic exploitation."

"If *Paris Trout* is about a community hamstrung by its accommodations," Eder continued, "it is also, at every moment, about the individuals caught in the accommodation. Dexter portrays them with marvelous sharpness." An increasingly paranoid Trout sleeps with a sheet of lead under his bed to shield himself from assassination and is convinced that his wife, Hanna, is trying to poison him. Hanna, a stoical schoolteacher who married Trout late in life to escape spinsterhood, is psychologically and sexually brutalized by him throughout their marriage. She consequently has an affair with Trout's gentleman defense lawyer, Harry Seagraves, who represented Trout out of social obligation but abandoned him after the trial. Hanna also hires local attorney Carl Bonner to represent her in divorce proceedings against her husband. "Perfectly offsetting graphic horror and comedy," Dean Faulkner Wells assessed in Chicago's *Tribune Books,* "Dexter brings all these characters together in an explosive conclusion."

"With a touch of the mastery that graces the best fiction about the South," Pete Axthelm observed in his *Newsweek* review of *Paris Trout,* "Dexter has conjured up characters stroked broadly, voices that ring true—and vignettes crafted in miniature in a way that haunts." Numerous critics mentioned similarities between Dexter and various Southern writers, claiming that his dark humor is reminiscent of the works of Flannery O'Connor and that his use of violence is Faulknerian. Dexter is quick to mention, though, that he is not a "Southern" writer (*Paris Trout* is his only book set in the South), but he is grateful for the praise. George Melly in *New Statesman and Society,* in fact, found differences between William Faulkner and Dexter. He noted that although *Paris Trout* is set in Faulkner's South, "it is free of Faulkner's convoluted style. The prose is taut, the feeling for time and place exact."

Dexter also denied the claim of some reviewers that *Paris Trout* symbolizes "racism, class war and inhumanity in the pre-civil-rights-era South," according to Glenn Collins of the *New York Times.* The author told the journalist that the events of *Paris Trout* "could have happened anywhere. The South has no lock on violence. In fact, South Philadelphia is more violent than the South." Deborah Mason in the *New York Times Book Review* commended Dexter for this insight, noting that "at a time when virulent racial incidents can no longer be conveniently fenced off in small Southern towns, Mr. Dexter's great accomplishment is to remind us, with lucidity and stinging frankness, the lengths to which we will go to deny our own racism and to reassure ourselves that we are innocent." Eder agreed. "The monstrousness, even of the decent people, hangs over the entire book," he confessed. "It is one of the elements that make *Paris Trout* a masterpiece, complex and breathtaking."

Dexter's novel *Brotherly Love* begins in an unlikely place—with the death of the two main characters, as reported in a newspaper article. Within the novel's remaining pages, Dexter details how the two men, Peter Flood and his cousin, Michael, grow up in Philadelphia, mature, and end up as targets of separate mob hits. Haunted by the death of his baby sister, which he was unable to prevent, Peter takes morbid thrills in jumping off buildings. He finds some release from the pain of his memories and the pressures of his life in boxing lessons. He becomes a labor racketeer for little other reason than that's what his father did. Peter has little interest in it, except that it's the "family business." Michael becomes a union leader in South Philly. Peter finds himself acting as little more than hired hand for the increasingly vicious Michael. Tired, afraid, and alarmed by Michael's cruelty, Peter finally severs the "now-destructive symbiotic relationship in a deed that caps the series of violent deaths that have gone before," wrote a *Publishers Weekly* reviewer. John Shaw, writing in *Time*, compared *Brotherly Love* with one of Dexter's previous novels, noting that "Though *Brotherly Love* is intentionally a narrower, less spacious novel than *Paris Trout*, its quality is just as high." A *Publishers Weekly* critic commented that the book is "a taut, gripping narrative that memorably examines the dark wellsprings of human behavior." Leah Rozen, writing in *People*, concluded, "All in all, it's an exhilarating novel."

In *The Paperboy*, Dexter draws on his experiences in journalism to tell the story of a pair of reporters exploring what looks like an unjust conviction—and looming execution—in Florida. The sheriff of Moat Country, Florida, Thurmond Call, is an unrepentant racist who "even by Moat county standards, had killed an inappropriate number of Negroes in the line of duty," according to narrator Jack James, recently kicked out of college and a delivery truck driver for his father's newspaper, the *Miami Times*. Spiraling further and further out of control, Sheriff Call stomps to death the drunk and handcuffed Jerome Van Wetter, a member of a poor, inbred family of white swamp-dwelling locals who hunt alligators and shun most contact with anyone outside their clan. Shortly after Jerome's death, Sheriff Call is found in the road near his police cruiser, gutted and dead. Another Van Wetter, Hillary, is arrested, tried, and convicted for the sheriff's murder and is sent to await his own demise on Death Row.

Four years later, investigative reporters Ward James (Jack's brother) and Yardely Acherman discover the case when Charlotte Bess, an aging beauty with a tendency to romance and become engaged to convicted men, comes to them with considerable evidence of Hillary's innocence. The two reporters sense a gross miscarriage of justice. They are sent to investigate by their employer, the *Miami Times*. Ward hires Jack to serve as his and Acherman's chauffeur and assistant—Jack, awed by the famed reporters, gladly agrees, since both journalists lost their drivers licenses over DWI offenses. When the trio arrives in Moat County, however, they discover a town unwilling to talk; even the Van Wetter family, mysterious and more than slightly dangerous, won't help save their kin. With persistence, and Ward's continual confrontations with belligerent sources such as the police, the locals, and the Van Wetters themselves, evidence does emerge, but it is not solid. The stylish Acherman, however, is willing to cut corners and go with what they have—and when Ward is hospitalized after a beating, Acherman simply makes up what's needed to finish the story. Hillary Van Wetter is freed, Ward and Acherman win a Pulitzer for their efforts, but the fabrications of the story are eventually discovered. Paul Gray, writing in *Time*, called *The Paperboy* "hip, hard-boiled, and filled with memorable eccentrics. The reporters' encounters with members of the Van Wetter clan comically—and ominously—juxtapose modern types with people ancient in their cunning and evil." Gilbert Taylor, writing in *Booklist*, observed that Dexter leaves "too many loose ends," but concluded that he "has created vibrant characters who fit snugly in their hot, languid setting." A critic from the *Mystery Guide* Web site remarked that *The Paperboy* is a "wonderful novel, which works in many ways at once: as a study of a family, as a chronicle of a town, and a psychological thriller." The novel has "a special quality seldom seen in fiction—a mesmerizing power of finality," observed Jon Saari in the *Antioch Review*. To reviewer Gene Lyons, writing in *Entertainment Weekly*, "*The Paperboy* is anything but a perfect novel," but he concluded, "It's a wise and fascinating tale well told."

BIOGRAPHICAL AND CRITICAL SOURCES:

BOOKS

Contemporary Literary Criticism, Gale (Detroit, MI), Volume 34, 1985, Volume 55, 1989.

Contemporary Popular Writers, St. James Press (Detroit, MI), 1997.

Modern American Literature, 5th edition, St. James Press (Detroit, MI), 1999.

PERIODICALS

American Journalism Review, April, 1995, review of *The Paperboy,* p. 56.

Antioch Review, summer, 1995, Jon Saari, review of *The Paperboy,* pp. 375-376.

Bestsellers 89, 1989, Issue 2.

Booklist, September 1, 1991, review of *Brotherly Love,* p. 4; September 15, 1991, review of *Brotherly Love,* p. 182; April 15, 1992, Jeanette Larson, review of *Brotherly Love,* p. 1547; November 15, 1994, Gilbert Taylor, review of *The Paperboy,* pp. 555-556; January 1, 1996, review of *Paris Trout,* p. 788; March 15, 1996, review of *The Paperboy,* p. 1272.

Books, March, 1992, review of *Brotherly Love,* p. 21; summer, 1995, review of *The Paperboy,* p. 27.

Bookwatch, December, 1995, review of *The Paperboy* (audio version), p. 3.

Christian Science Monitor, October 28, 1991, Jim Bencivenga, review of *Brotherly Love,* p. 13; February 16, 1995, Catherine Foster, review of *The Paperboy,* p. 12.

Entertainment Weekly, January 27, 1995, Gene Lyons, review of *The Paperboy,* pp. 42-43; January 26, 1996, review of *The Paperboy,* p. 53; May 3, 1996, Ken Tucker, review of *Mulholland Falls,* p. 62.

Gentlemen's Quarterly, February, 1995, Thomas Mallon, review of *The Paperboy,* p. 87.

Guardian, June 20, 1993, review of *Brotherly Love,* p. 28.

Hudson Review, summer, 1992, Dean Flower, review of *Brotherly Love,* pp. 331-332.

Independent, March 27, 1993, Anthony Quinn, "Hellraiser Who Never Met an Adjective He Liked," interview with Pete Dexter, p. 31.

Kirkus Reviews, August 1, 1991, review of *Brotherly Love,* p. 949; November 1, 1994, review of *The Paperboy,* p. 1430.

Kliatt Young Adult Paperback Book Guide, January, 1993, review of *Brotherly Love,* p. 6; March, 1996, review of *The Paperboy,* p. 8.

Law Institute Journal, December, 1996, Christ Hurley, review of *The Paper Boy,* pp. 60-61.

Legal Times, February 20, 1995, Joel Chineson, review of *The Paperboy,* p. 62.

Library Journal, October 1, 1991, Albert E. Wilhelm, review of *Brotherly Love,* pp. 139-140; October 1, 1991, Randy Pitman, review of *Paris Trout,* p. 155; February 15, 1992, Roxanna Herrick, review of *Brotherly Love,* p. 216; January, 1995, David Dodd, review of *The Paperboy,* p. 136.

London Review of Books, October 5, 1995, review of *The Paperboy,* p. 23.

Los Angeles Times, December 1, 1988.

Los Angeles Times Book Review, July 24, 1988; October 6, 1991; January 1, 1995, review of *The Paperboy,* p. 3.

Nation, March 10, 1984.

New Republic, May 27, 1996, Stanley Kauffmann, review of *Mulholland Falls,* pp. 28-29; March 3, 1997, review of *Michael.*

New Statesman, June 30, 1995, Nick Kimberley, review of *The Paperboy,* pp. 38-39; September 6, 1996, Boyd Tonkin, review of *Mulholland Falls,* p. 43.

New Statesman and Society, October 7, 1988, George Melly, review of *Paris Trout,* pp. 38-39.

Newsweek, September 26, 1988, Pete Axthelm, review of *Paris Trout,* p. 74.

New York, September 30, 1991, Rhoda Koenig, review of *Brotherly Love,* p. 75; May 13, 1996, David Denby, review of *Mulholland Falls,* pp. 58-59; September 30, 1991, p. 75.

New York Law Journal, June 8, 1995, Carole Shapiro, review of *The Paperboy,* p. 2.

New York Review of Books, February 16, 1989, Robert Towers, review of *Paris Trout,* pp. 18-19.

New York Times, December 5, 1988; October 4, 1991, Michiko Kakutani, review of *Brotherly Love,* p. C29; January 12, 1995, Christopher Lehmann-Haupt, review of *The Paperboy,* p. C24.

New York Times Book Review, February 19, 1984; April 20, 1986; July 24, 1988, Deborah Mason, review of *Paris Trout,* pp. 7-8; October 13, 1991, Robert Stone, review of *Brotherly Love,* p. 3; April 19, 1992; September 6, 1992, review of *Brotherly Love,* p. 24; April 4, 1993; January 22, 1995, Brent Staples, review of *The Paperboy,* p. 7; January 22, 1995, Barth Healey, "Interview with Pete Dexter," p. 7; June 11, 1995, review of *The Paperboy,* p. 38; December 3, 1995, review of *The Paperboy,* p. 76; January 14, 1996, review of *The Paperboy,* p. 28.

Observer (London, England), June 11, 1995, review of *The Paperboy,* p. 14.

People, October 21, 1991, Leah Rozen, review of *Brotherly Love,* pp. 31-32; January 30, 1995, Dani Shapiro, review of *The Paperboy,* p. 27; May 6, 1996, Ralph Novak, review of *Mulholland Falls,* pp. 18-19.

Publishers Weekly, May 13, 1988, p. 262; August 2, 1991, review of *Brotherly Love,* p. 63; October 4, 1991, Wendy Smith, "Pete Dexter: After His

Roistering Lifestyle, His Career As a Novelist Is a Different Kind of Adventure," pp. 70-71; July 13, 1992, review of *Brotherly Love,* p. 52; November 7, 1994, review of *The Paperboy,* p. 62; February 13, 1995, p. 17.

Quill & Quire, July, 1995, audio review of *The Paperboy,* p. 7.

Rapport, January 1, 1992, review of *Brotherly Love,* p. 20; April, 1992, review of *Brotherly Love,* p. 30; May, 1995, review of *The Paperboy,* p. 22.

Southern Living, March, 1995, review of *The Paperboy,* p. 142.

Spectator, November 18, 1995, review of *The Paperboy,* p. 49.

Sports Illustrated, February 23, 1987.

Time, April 2, 1984; November 4, 1991, John Shaw, review of *Brotherly Love,* p. A4; January 23, 1995, Paul Gray, review of *The Paperboy,* p. 58.

Times Educational Supplement, March 6, 1992, review of *Brotherly Love,* p. 35.

Times Literary Supplement, November 25, 1988, Andrew Rosenheim, review of *Paris Trout,* p. 1306; February 21, 1992, John Sutherland, review of *Brotherly Love,* p. 32; May 19, 1995, Gordon Burn, review of *The Paperboy,* p. 19; December 1, 1995, review of *The Paperboy,* p. 10.

Tribune Books (Chicago, IL), April 6, 1986; August 7, 1988; Dean Faulkner Wells, review of *Paris Trout,* pp. 3, 9; September 6, 1992, review of *Brotherly Love,* p. 2; January 29, 1995, review of *The Paperboy,* p. 6.

Village Voice, June 17, 1986.

Virginia Quarterly Review, summer, 1995, review of *The Paperboy,* p. 95.

Vogue, October, 1991, Mark Marvel, review of *Brotherly Love,* p. 192.

Wall Street Journal, October 7, 1991, Julie Salamon, review of *Brotherly Love,* p. A12.

Washington Post, November 28, 1988.

Washington Post Book World, June 1, 1986; July 10, 1988, Judith Paterson, review of *Paris Trout,* p. 8; November 30, 1988; September 13, 1992, review of *Brotherly Love,* p. 12.

Western American Literature, winter, 1987, Margaret A. Lukens, p. 360.

World & I, March, 1995, review of *The Paperboy,* p. 322.

ONLINE

Mostly Fiction, http://www.mostlyfiction.com/ (December 17, 2002), review of *The Paperboy.*

Mystery Guide, http://www.mysteryguide.com/ (December 17, 2002).*

DOODY, Margaret (Anne) 1939-

PERSONAL: Born September 21, 1939, in St. John, New Brunswick, Canada; daughter of Hubert (an Anglican minister) and Anne (a social worker; maiden name, Cornwall) Doody. *Education:* Dalhousie University, B.A. (with honors), 1960; Lady Margaret Hall, Oxford, B.A. (with first-class honors), 1962, D.Phil., 1968. *Politics:* "Much the same as Dr. Johnson's." *Religion:* Anglican. *Hobbies and other interests:* Detective stories, children's books, theater, travel.

ADDRESSES: *Home*—Princeton, NJ. *Office*—Department of English, McCosh 22, Princeton University, Princeton, NJ 08544.

CAREER: University of Victoria, Victoria, British Columbia, Canada, instructor, 1962-64, assistant professor of English, 1968-69; University of Wales, University College, Swansea, lecturer in English, 1969-76; University of California—Berkeley, visiting associate professor, 1976-77, associate professor of English, 1977-80; Princeton University, Princeton, NJ, professor of English, beginning 1980.

MEMBER: Modern Language Association of America (member of eighteenth-century panel).

AWARDS, HONORS: Guggenheim fellowship, 1978; American Philosophical Society research grant, 1982; Rose Mary Crawshay Prize, British Academy, 1986, for *The Daring Muse: Augustan Poetry Reconsidered.*

WRITINGS:

NONFICTION

A Natural Passion: A Study of the Novels of Samuel Richardson, Clarendon Press (Oxford, England), 1974.

The Daring Muse: Augustan Poetry Reconsidered, Cambridge University Press (New York, NY), 1985.

Frances Burney: The Life in the Works, Rutgers University Press (New Brunswick, NJ), 1988.

(Editor, with Peter Sabor) Frances Burney, *Cecilia,* Oxford University Press (New York, NY), 1988.

(Coeditor) *Samuel Richardson: Tercentenary Essays,* Cambridge University Press (New York, NY), 1989.

(Associate editor) *The Clarissa Project,* AMS Press (New York, NY), 1990-1996.

(Coeditor) Frances Burney, *The Wanderer; or, Female Difficulties,* Oxford University Press (New York, NY), 1991.

(Coeditor) Jane Austen, *Catharine and Other Writings,* Oxford University Press (New York, NY), 1993.

(Editor) Frances Burney, *Evelina; or, The History of a Young Lady's Entrance into the World,* Penguin Books (New York, NY), 1994.

The True Story of the Novel, Rutgers University Press (New Brunswick, NJ), 1996.

(Coeditor) L. M. Montgomery, *The Annotated Anne of Green Gables,* Oxford University Press (New York, NY), 1997.

DETECTIVE NOVELS

Aristotle Detective, Bodley Head (London, England), 1978, Harper (New York, NY), 1980.

The Alchemists, Bodley Head (London, England), 1980.

Aristotle and the Secrets of Life, Century (London, England), 2003.

OTHER

(With Florian Stuber and John Sgueglia) *Clarissa: The Encounter* (one-act play; based on Samuel Richardson's *Clarissa*), first produced in New York, NY, at Circle Repertory Lab Theater, 1983.

(With Florian Stuber) *Clarissa: A Theater Work, Part One,* first produced as three-act play in New York, NY, at Douglas Fairbanks Theater, 1984, produced as two-act play in New York, NY, at West End Theater, 1984.

Contributor to books, including *The State of the Language,* edited by Christopher Ricks and Leonard Michaels, University of California Press (Berkeley, CA), 1980; and *No Alternative: The Prayer Book Controversy,* edited by David Martin and Peter Mullen, Basil Blackwell (Boston, MA), 1981; author of introduction to *Pamela,* by Samuel Richardson, edited by Peter Sabor, Penguin (New York, NY), 1981. Contributor to *Times Literary Supplement.* Advisor to *Studies in English Literature.*

Aristotle Detective has been translated into Italian, French, and German.

SIDELIGHTS: Margaret Doody once told *CA:* "I find that the academic life and the writing of detective stories mesh quite nicely. I look forward to escaping from the eighteenth century from time to time (it seems so very modern to me) and going back to ancient Greece with Aristotle, my Sherlock Holmes. A recent venture into drama has convinced me that I want to stay there. I have several plans for plays. I am very grateful for the chance of working with professional actors under the aegis of Circle Rep Directors' Lab in May, 1983."

BIOGRAPHICAL AND CRITICAL SOURCES:

PERIODICALS

Christian Science Monitor, October 21, 1986.

Times Literary Supplement, November 10, 1978; April 25, 1980; March 14, 1986; June 13, 2003, Roderick Beaton, review of *Aristotle and the Secrets of Life.**

* * *

DOYLE, Charlotte (Lackner) 1937-

PERSONAL: Born June 25, 1937, in Vienna, Austria; immigrated to the United States, 1939; naturalized U.S. citizen; daughter of George (a restaurant worker) and Mary (a poet and homemaker) Lackner; married Jim Doyle (a playwright), 1959. *Education:* Temple University, B.A., 1959; University of Michigan, M.A., 1961, Ph.D., 1965. *Hobbies and other interests:* Camping in national and state parks, traveling to new places, reading, watching public television, playing with the computer.

ADDRESSES: *Office*—Department of Psychology, Sarah Lawrence College, Bronxville, NY 10708-5999. *Agent*—Liza Pulitzer Voges, Kirchoff/Wohlberg, 866 United Nations Plaza, New York, NY 10017. *E-mail*—cdoyle@slc.edu.

CAREER: Sarah Lawrence College, Bronxville, NY, professor of psychology and children's literature.

MEMBER: American Psychological Association (member of executive committee, Division on Psychology and the Arts), Society of Children's Book Writers and Illustrators, American Association for the Advancement of Science.

WRITINGS:

CHILDREN'S BOOKS

Hello Baby, illustrated by Kees de Kiefte, Random House (New York, NY), 1989.
Freddie's Spaghetti, illustrated by Nicholas Reilly, Random House (New York, NY), 1991.
Where's Bunny's Mommy?, illustrated by Rick Brown, Simon & Schuster (New York, NY), 1995.
You Can't Catch Me, illustrated by Roseanne Litziger, HarperCollins (New York, NY), 1997.
Twins!, illustrated by Julia Gorton, Putnam (New York, NY), 2003.
Supermarket, illustrated by Nadine Bernard Westcott, Candlewick Press (Cambridge, MA), in press.

TEXTBOOKS

(With W. J. McKeachie) *Psychology,* Addison-Wesley (Reading, MA), 1966.
(With W. J. McKeachie) *Psychology: The Short Course,* Addison-Wesley (Reading, MA), 1972.
Explorations in Psychology, Brooks/Cole (Monterey, CA), 1987.

Contributor to periodicals, including *Creativity Research Journal.*

SIDELIGHTS: Charlotte Doyle once told *CA:* "I never expected to be writing children's books. I was a college professor, an author of psychology texts and articles, and a researcher into the creative process. Then, one day, I sat down to write a letter to a child, and the letter turned into a children's story. I read it to the children at Sarah Lawrence's Early Childhood Center. The children were so responsive and it was so much fun that I began to hang out there.

"Again and again, being with children has inspired me. I watched some children be loving about having new baby brothers and sisters and others be resentful, and that gave me *Hello Baby.* A child, so happy to be eating spaghetti that it seemed life couldn't get any better, gave me *Freddie's Spaghetti.* Watching very young children happy to be in school, but stopping every once in a while to look around, puzzled, and asking 'Where's Mommy?' inspired *Where's Bunny's Mommy?* Seeing the pleasures of chasing and being chased on the playground led to *You Can't Catch Me.*

"When I write, I try to enter the world of young children, to see the world as a child does. My greatest pleasure is when children recognize the world created by my books as their world, as giving voice to their fears and hopes and joys, and so say to me, 'Read it again.'"

BIOGRAPHICAL AND CRITICAL SOURCES:

PERIODICALS

Booklist, April 1, 1995, p. 1424; February 15, 2003, Kathy Broderick, review of *Twins!,* p. 1073.
New York Times, November 4, 1990.
School Library Journal, June, 1990, p. 98; July, 1995, p. 61; March, 2003, Joy Fleishhacker, review of *Twins!,* p. 191.

* * *

DUCKWORTH, Marilyn (Rose Adcock) 1935-

PERSONAL: Born November 10, 1935, in Auckland, New Zealand; daughter of Cyril John and Irene (Robinson) Adcock; married Harry Duckworth, May 28, 1955 (divorced, 1964); married Ian Macfarlane, October 2, 1964 (divorced, 1972); married Daniel Donovan, December 9, 1974 (died, 1978); married John Batstone, June 8, 1985; children: Helen, Sarah, Anna, Amelia; stepchildren: Michael, Susan, Timothy. *Ethnicity:* "European." *Education:* Attended Victoria University of Wellington, 1953, 1956. *Politics:* "Labour supporter." *Hobbies and other interests:* Playing the violin.

ADDRESSES: *Home*—41 Queen St., Wellington, New Zealand. *Agent*—Tara Wynne, Curtis Brown (Australia) Pty. Ltd., P.O. Box 19, Paddington, New South Wales 2021, Australia.

Marilyn Duckworth

CAREER: Writer. Worked variously in public relations, nursing, factory work, and library work. Guest on media programs.

MEMBER: New Zealand Society of Authors, PEN.

AWARDS, HONORS: Scholarship in Letters, 1961, 1972, 1993; New Zealand Award for Achievement, 1963; Katherine Mansfield fellowship, 1980; New Zealand Book Award for fiction, Queen Elizabeth Arts Council and New Zealand Literary Fund, 1985, for *Disorderly Conduct*; Fulbright visiting writers fellowship, 1986; decorated officer, Order of the British Empire, 1987; Australia-New Zealand Exchange fellowship, 1989; writers fellowship, Victoria University of Wellington, 1990; Hawthornden writers fellowship, Scotland, 1994; Sargeson writers fellowship, 1995; University of Auckland literary fellowship, 1996.

WRITINGS:

NOVELS

A Gap in the Spectrum, Hutchinson (London, England), 1959.

The Matchbox House, Hutchinson (London, England), 1960, Morrow (New York, NY), 1961.

A Barbarous Tongue, Hutchinson (London, England), 1963.

Over the Fence Is Out, Hutchinson (London, England), 1969.

Disorderly Conduct, Hodder & Stoughton (Auckland, New Zealand), 1984.

Married Alive, Hodder & Stoughton (Auckland, New Zealand), 1985.

Rest for the Wicked, Hodder & Stoughton (Auckland, New Zealand), 1986.

Pulling Faces, Hodder & Stoughton (Auckland, New Zealand), 1987.

A Message from Harpo, Hodder & Stoughton (Auckland, New Zealand), 1989.

Unlawful Entry, Random Century (Auckland, New Zealand), 1992.

Seeing Red, Random House (Auckland, New Zealand), 1993.

Leather Wings, Random House (Auckland, New Zealand), 1995.

Studmuffin, Random House (Auckland, New Zealand), 1997.

Swallowing Diamonds, Random House (Auckland, New Zealand), 2003.

OTHER

Other Lover's Children (poetry), Pegasus Press (Christchurch, New Zealand), 1975.

Explosions from the Sun (short stories), Hodder & Stoughton (Auckland, New Zealand), 1989.

Fooling (novella), Hazard Press (Auckland, New Zealand), 1994.

(Editor) *Cherries on a Plate: New Zealand Writers Talk about Their Sisters,* Random House (Auckland, New Zealand), 1996.

Camping on the Faultline: A Memoir, Vintage (Auckland, New Zealand), 2000.

Also author of the plays *Feet First* and *Home to Mother.* Contributor to anthologies including, *New Zealand Short Stories II,* edited by C. K. Stead, Oxford University Press (Oxford, England), 1966; *Best Short Stories 1989,* edited by Giles Gordon and David Hughes, Heinemann (London, England), 1989; *New Zealand Short Stories,* edited by Russell Haley and Susan Davis, Penguin (Auckland, New Zealand), 1989; *Erotic Writing,* edited by Sue McCauley, Penguin (Auckland, New Zealand), 1992; *My Father and Me: New Zealand Women Remember,* edited by Penelope

Hansen, Tandem Press (Auckland, New Zealand), 1992; and *Such Devoted Sisters,* edited by Shena Mackay, Virago (London, England), 1993. Contributor of short stories and articles to periodicals, including *Landfall, New Zealand Listener, Critical Quarterly, Affairs, Education, Metro, Quote Unquote, Svetova Literatura* (Prague, Czechoslovakia), *Oceanic Literature* (China), and *Islands.*

SIDELIGHTS: New Zealander Marilyn Duckworth is a prolific writer of feminist novels, short stories, and verse. Fascinated with the human condition, Duckworth often portrays the tension created when her predominantly female characters attempt to balance their desire for independence with their need for companionship. Duckworth's early novels focus on the interior world of her characters, often in a home setting. In the eighties she began to look outward more, at society and politics, but personal relationships remained central to her work.

Married four times, with children and stepchildren, Duckworth is familiar with the pros and cons of the domestic scene. Wrote Heather Murray of Duckworth's protagonists in *Contemporary Novelists,* "Distinctly unheroic, they stand revealed amid a daily round of chores, pregnancy, children, falling in and out of love, knitting, gardening, and caring for aging parents. They are flawed individuals for whom the reader feels varying amounts of sympathy and . . . considerable irritation." The women who people Duckworth's work reflect the evolution in women's roles and concerns since the 1950s. "As women have been engaged in redefining their status in society, so changing gender roles occupy a prominent and recurring place in Duckworth novels," wrote Murray. *A Barbarous Tongue,* one of Duckworth's early novels, deals with an unwed teenage mother's search for happiness, while *Seeing Red* deals with the potentially destructive nature of family ties. More recently, *Fooling* shows how independence can have a downside.

Disorderly Conduct, which won the New Zealand Book Award, depicts a variety of women on the paths of self-discovery. According to *Contemporary Novelists* essayist Murray, Duckworth is "skilled at creating believable families" and is "particularly good at the intimate conversation of families." While critics outside of New Zealand have had little to say about Duckworth's fiction since her first novel *A Gap in the Spectrum* was widely reviewed in 1959, she has been the recipient of numerous fellowships at home and abroad.

Duckworth once told *CA:* "I might be seen as a feminist writer but when I was first published in 1959, feminism was not a word I knew. I was concerned to write deliberately like a woman, rather than copy the style of male novelists, and to write *for* other women—to tell the truth. In the eighties I became very aware of the uses of humor and irony to make a point. Not wanting to solidify in a rut of social realism, I have moved with my 1997 novel to allegory, which is where I began with my first novel in 1959. *Studmuffin* contains a strong strain of surrealism while retaining a level of stalwart realism and sensitive, irony."

BIOGRAPHICAL AND CRITICAL SOURCES:

BOOKS

Blain, Virginia, Patricia Clements, and Isobel Grundy, *The Feminist Companion to Literature in English: Women Writers from the Middle Ages to the Present,* Yale University Press (New Haven, CT), 1990.

Buck, Claire, editor, *The Bloomsbury Guide to Women's Literature,* Prentice Hall (Englewood Cliffs, NJ), 1992.

Contemporary Novelists, 7th edition, St. James Press (Detroit, MI), 2001.

PERIODICALS

Books and Bookmen, March, 1970, p. 45.

Landfall, May, 1998, Janet Wilson, review of *Studmuffin,* p. 177.

Observer, February 15, 1970, p. 29.

ONLINE

University of Auckland Web Site, http://www.auckland.ac.nz/ (November 6, 1996).

E

EIDELBERG, Paul 1928-

PERSONAL: Born June 21, 1928, in Brooklyn, NY; son of Harry and Sarah (Leimseider) Eidelberg; married Phyllis Leif, December 27, 1947; children: Steven, Sharen, Sarah Elizabeth. *Education:* University of Chicago, M.A., 1957, Ph.D., 1966. *Religion:* Hebrew.

ADDRESSES: *Home*—Shabtai Negbi, Gilo 63/32, Jerusalem, Israel.

CAREER: Sweet Briar College, Sweet Briar, VA, visiting professor of political science, 1966-67; North Carolina State University at Raleigh, assistant professor of politics, 1967-68; Kenyon College, Gambier, OH, associate professor of political science, 1968-70; University of Dallas, Irving, TX, associate professor of political science, 1970-74; Claremont Men's College, Claremont, CA, research professor of political science, 1974-76; Bar-Ilan University, Ramat-Gan, Israel, professor of political science, 1976—; founder, Foundation for Constitutional Democracy; president, Yamin Yisrael political party. Visiting professor of political science, Yeshiva University, New York, NY, 1987-88. Visiting lecturer at colleges and universities, including Kenyon College, 1973, Claremont Men's College, 1975 and 1976, and St. Thomas Aquinas College, 1976. Cofounder, Institute of Statesmanship and Torah-Philosophy, Jerusalem, Israel. *Military service:* U.S. Air Force, 1946-53; became first lieutenant.

MEMBER: American Political Science Association.

AWARDS, HONORS: Earhart Foundation grant, 1974 and 1977; Salvatori Center grant, 1976.

WRITINGS:

The Philosophy of the American Constitution: A Reinterpretation of the Intentions of the Founding Fathers, Free Press (New York, NY), 1968, reprinted, University Press of America (Lanham, MD), 1986.

A Discourse of Statesmanship: The Design and Transformation of the American Polity, University of Illinois Press (Champaign, IL), 1974.

On the Silence of the Declaration of Independence, University of Massachusetts Press (Boston, MA), 1976.

Beyond Detente: Toward an American Foreign Policy, Sherwood Sugden (LaSalle, IL), 1977.

Hamazema shel Sadat, Reshafim (Tel Aviv, Israel), 1978.

Sadat's Strategy, Dawn Publishing (Montreal, Quebec, Canada), 1979.

Jerusalem vs. Athens: In Quest of a General Theory of Existence, University Press of America (Lanham, MD), 1983.

The Case of Israel's Jewish Underground, Dawn (Dollard des Ormeaux, Quebec, Canada), 1985.

Israel's Return and Restoration, [Jerusalem, Israel], 1987.

Beyond the Secular Mind: A Judaic Response to the Problems of Modernity, Greenwood Press (New York, NY), 1989.

(With Will Morrisey) *Our Culture "Left" or "Right": Litterateurs Confront Nihilism,* E. Mellen Press (Lewiston, NY), 1992.

Demophrenia, Prescott Press (Lafayette, LA), 1994.

Judaic Man: Toward a Reconstruction of Western Civilization, Caslon (Middletown, NJ), 1996.

Making Votes Count: They Don't in Isreal!, Ariel Center for Policy Research (Shaarei Tikva, Isreal), 1999.

Jewish Statesmanship Lest Israel Fall, ACPR (Shaarei Tikva, Israel), 2000, University Press of American (Lanham, MD), 2002.

Contributor to periodicals, including *Midstream, International Behavioral Scientist, Congressional Record, The Review of Politics,* and *Journal of Nuclear Medicine.* Contributor of articles to newspapers in various countries, including the United States, Israel, and several European and South American nations.

SIDELIGHTS: Political writer and activist Paul Eidelberg earned his Ph.D. at the University of Chicago, where he studied under the influential scholar Leo Strauss, before relocating to Israel to teach at Bar-Ilan University and eventually enter politics. Eidelberg, an Orthodox Jew who advocates a sound political structure for the State of Israel, is the author of *Jewish Statesmanship Lest Israel Fall.* In that work Eidelberg cites a number of reasons for the tenuous condition of the Jewish state, including heterogeneity—the mixing of races and cultures—"Jews and Arabs," noted reviewer Shmuel Ben-Gad in *Midstream,* "but also amongst Jews who have made aliyah [pilgrimage] from many different countries." Discord between secular and religious Jews and what the author states as "a lack of Jewish statesmanship and Jewish national purpose" also serve to threaten Israel's Jewish identity, according to Ben-Gad's article.

Discussing the country's political system, Eidelberg argues for replacing the parliamentary-based Knesset with one of a U.S.-style democracy. He "recommends a presidential system (with only a Jew eligible to be president) so that a strong, focused policy can be pursued," commented Ben-Gad. "For a similar reason, recommends that the upper house of a bicameral Knesset be largely filled though electoral district elections rather than the current method of proportional representation." Eidelberg also proposes that Jews alone be eligible for membership in the upper house "and would have to be certified as having some prescribed level of Jewish knowledge," as the critic continued. The author's Jews-only policy would also extend to the judiciary.

Is Eidelberg's thinking racist? Bar-Gad felt that the author's arguments are based on his Orthodox interpretations of the Hebrew scriptures; "the book does not intend to be a work of apologetics but rather a creative work based upon the Torah." The reviewer added, "One does not need to be Orthodox to recognize the role religion can play in elevating the national character and strengthening the national will." He said that Eidelberg "writes beautifully" and that a reader need not agree with each of the author's proposals to find value in *Jewish Statesmanship Lest Israel Fall.*

BIOGRAPHICAL AND CRITICAL SOURCES:

PERIODICALS

Canadian Philosophical Review, January, 1990, review of *Beyond the Secular Mind: A Judaic Response to the Problems of Modernity,* p. 11.

Choice, February, 1990, L. E. Newman, review of *Beyond the Secular Mind,* p. 965.

Midstream, September, 2000, Shmuel Ben-Gad, review of *Jewish Statesmanship Lest Israel Fall,* p. 41.

Perspectives on Political Science, winter, 1991, review of *Beyond the Secular Mind,* p. 58.*

* * *

EMBERLEY, Barbara A(nne) 1932-

PERSONAL: Born December 12, 1932, in Chicago, IL; maiden name, Collins; married Edward Randolph Emberley (a writer, artist, and designer), 1955; children: Rebecca Anne, Michael Edward. *Education:* Massachusetts School of Art, B.F.A. *Hobbies and other interests:* Sailing.

ADDRESSES: Home and office—6 Water St., Ipswich, MA 01938; 6 Sanctuary Rd., North Conway, NH 03860-5918.

CAREER: Author, reteller, and illustrator of children's books; also worked as a librarian at Brown University, Providence, RI. Founder, with husband, Ed Emberley, of Bird in the Bush Press.

AWARDS, HONORS: One Wide River to Cross, illustrated by Ed Emberley, received an Art Books for Children citation, Brooklyn Public Library, 1966, and was named a Caldecott Honor Book, American Library

Association (ALA), 1967; *Drummer Hoff,* illustrated by Ed Emberley, won the Caldecott Medal, ALA, and the Lewis Carroll Shelf Award, both 1968.

WRITINGS:

ILLUSTRATED BY HUSBAND, ED EMBERLEY

Night's Nice, Doubleday (Garden City, NY), 1963.
(Reteller) *The Story of Paul Bunyan,* Prentice-Hall (Englewood Cliffs, NJ), 1963, Simon & Schuster (New York, NY), 1994.
(Reteller) *One Wide River to Cross,* Prentice-Hall (Englewood Cliffs, NJ), 1966, Little, Brown (Boston, MA), 1992.
(Reteller) *Drummer Hoff,* Prentice-Hall (Englewood Cliffs, NJ), 1967, published as a board book, Simon & Schuster (New York, NY), 1987.
Simon's Song, Prentice-Hall (Englewood Cliffs, NJ), 1969.

ILLUSTRATOR; WITH HUSBAND, ED EMBERLEY

Seymour Simon, *The BASIC Book,* HarperCollins (New York, NY), 1985.
Seymour Simon, *Bits and Bytes: A Computer Dictionary for Beginners,* HarperCollins (New York, NY), 1985.
Seymour Simon, *How to Talk to Your Computer,* Crowell (New York, NY), 1985.
Seymour Simon, *Meet the Computer,* HarperCollins (New York, NY), 1985.
Franklyn M. Branley, *Flash, Crash, Rumble, and Roll,* HarperCollins (New York, NY), 1985.
Seymour Simon, *Turtle Talk: A Beginner's Book of LOGO,* HarperCollins (New York, NY), 1986.
Franklyn M. Branley, *The Moon Seems to Change,* HarperCollins (New York, NY), 1987.

ADAPTATIONS: Drummer Hoff was adapted for film by Gene Deitch and released by Weston Woods, 1969; it was released as both a sound filmstrip and, later, a video. *The Story of Paul Bunyan* was released as a filmstrip by Educational Enrichment Materials, 1969.

SIDELIGHTS: For sidelights, see sketch on husband, Ed Emberley.

BIOGRAPHICAL AND CRITICAL SOURCES:

BOOKS

Emberley, Ed, *Ed Emberley's Drawing Book of Animals,* Little, Brown (Boston, MA), 1970.
Emberley, Ed, *Go Away, Big Green Monster!,* Little, Brown (Boston, MA), 1992.
Hopkins, Lee Bennett, *Books Are by People: Interviews with 104 Authors and Illustrators of Books for Young People,* Citation Press (New York, NY), 1969.
Hopkins, Lee Bennett, *Pauses: Autobiographical Reflections of 101 Creators of Children's Books,* HarperCollins (New York, NY), 1995.

PERIODICALS

Booklist, October, 1998, Kathleen Squires, review of *Three: An Emberley Family Sketchbook,* p. 96.
Boston Globe, October 19, 1997, Liz Rosenberg, "The New Flexibility of the Board Book," p. P5.
Chicago Sunday Tribune Magazine of Books, May 14, 1961, Joan Beck, review of *The Wing on a Flea: A Book about Shapes,* section 2, p. 2.
Christian Science Monitor, May 7, 1970, Pamela Marsh, review of *Ed Emberley's Drawing Book of Animals,* p. B1.
Horn Book, February, 1964, Virginia Haviland, review of *The Story of Paul Bunyan,* p. 48; August, 1968, Barbara Emberley, "Ed Emberley," pp. 403-406; August, 1968, Ed Emberley, "Caldecott Award Acceptance," pp. 399-402; August, 1978, Ethel L. Heins, review of *Ed Emberley's ABC,* pp. 386-387; March, 1995, review of *The Story of Paul Bunyan,* p. 222.
Instructor, May, 1995, Judy Freeman, review of *Go Away, Big Green Monster!,* p. 78.
Kirkus Reviews, July 15, 1966, review of *One Wide River to Cross,* p. 683; March 15, 2003, review of *Thanks, Mom!*
Library Journal, December 15, 1967, Della Thomas, review of *Drummer Hoff,* p. 602.
New York Times Book Review, May 14, 1961, review of *The Wing on a Flea,* p. 35; January 26, 1964, Barbara Wersba, review of *The Story of Paul Bunyan,* p. 26; October 16, 1966, Barbara Novak O'Doherty, review of *One Wide River to Cross,* p. 38; November 5, 1967, Eve Merriam, review of

Drummer Hoff, p. 71; March 1, 1970, George A. Woods, review of *Ed Emberley's Drawing Book of Animals,* p. 34; July 2, 1978, Selma G. Lanes, review of *Ed Emberley's ABC,* p. 11.

Pittsburgh Post-Gazette Magazine, March 21, 2000, Karen MacPherson, "Artful Books Open Up World of Art to the Young."

Portsmouth Herald, September 30, 2003, Jeanne McCartin, "A Story-Book Existence."

Publishers Weekly, December 26, 1966, review of *One Wide River to Cross,* p. 99; July 25, 1980, "Ed Emberley," pp. 78-79; March 29, 1993, review of *Go Away, Big Green Monster!,* p. 54; March 24, 2003, review of *Thanks, Mom!,* p. 74.

School Library Journal, October, 1963, Eileen Lampert, review of *Night's Nice,* p. 190; March, 1968, Jean Reynolds, "Ed Emberley," pp. 113-114; September, 1978, Gemma DeVinney, review of *Ed Emberley's ABC,* p. 107.

Time, December 21, 1970, Timothy Foote, review of *Ed Emberley's Drawing Book of Animals,* p. 68.

ONLINE

Bulletin of the Center of Children's Books, http://alexia.lis.uiuc.edu/ (August 1, 2002), Jeannette Hulick, "True Blue: Ed Emberley."*

* * *

EMBERLEY, Ed(ward Randolph) 1931-

PERSONAL: Born October 19, 1931, in Malden, MA; son of Wallace Akin (a carpenter and house painter) and Evelyn (a clerk in a clothing store; maiden name, Farrell) Emberley; married Barbara A. Collins (an author and illustrator), 1955; children: Rebecca Anne, Michael Edward. *Education:* Massachusetts School of Art, B.F.A.; also studied at the Rhode Island School of Art (now Rhode Island School of Design). *Religion:* Protestant. *Hobbies and other interests:* Sailing.

ADDRESSES: Home and office—6 Water St., Ipswich, MA 01938; 6 Sanctuary Rd., North Conway, NH 03860-5918.

CAREER: Author and illustrator of children's books; illustrator of textbooks and for periodicals; designer. Also worked as a cartoonist and paste-up artist for a direct-mail advertising firm, Boston, MA. Founder, with wife, Barbara, of Bird in the Bush Press. Designer of children's merchandise for Boston Marathon, 2003. *Military service:* U.S. Army, two years.

AWARDS, HONORS: Notable Book citation, American Library Association (ALA), 1961, for *The Wing on a Flea: A Book about Shapes;* award for best-illustrated book, *New York Times,* 1961, for *The Wing on a Flea,* and 1965, for *Punch and Judy: A Play for Puppets;* Junior Literary Guild selection, 1962, for *The Parade Book,* and 1966, for *Rosebud;* Art Books for Children citation, Brooklyn Public Library, 1966, and Caldecott Honor Book, ALA, 1967, both for *One Wide River to Cross;* New Jersey Authors Award for science, New Jersey Institute of Technology, 1968, for *Ladybug, Ladybug, Fly Away Home;* Caldecott Medal, ALA, and Lewis Carroll Shelf Award, both 1968, both for *Drummer Hoff;* Chandler Book Talk Reward of Merit, 1968; Black-Eyed Susan Book Award (Maryland), 1994-95, for *Go Away, Big Green Monster!*

WRITINGS:

SELF-ILLUSTRATED

The Wing on a Flea: A Book about Shapes, Little, Brown (Boston, MA), 1961, revised edition, 2001.

The Parade Book, Little, Brown (Boston, MA), 1962.

Cock a Doodle Doo: A Book of Sounds, Little, Brown (Boston, MA), 1964.

Punch and Judy: A Play for Puppets, Little, Brown (Boston, MA), 1965.

Rosebud, Little, Brown (Boston, MA), 1966.

Green Says Go, Little, Brown (Boston, MA), 1968.

Klippity Klop, Little, Brown (Boston, MA), 1974.

The Wizard of Op, Little, Brown (Boston, MA), 1975.

A Birthday Wish, Little, Brown (Boston, MA), 1977.

Ed Emberley's ABC, Little, Brown (Boston, MA), 1978.

Ed Emberley's Amazing Look-Through Book, Little, Brown (Boston, MA), 1979.

Ed Emberley's Crazy Mixed-up Face Game, Little, Brown (Boston, MA), 1981.

Six Nature Adventures (contains "The Butterfly," "The Dandelion," "The Chameleon," "The Chicken," "The Frog," and "The Hare"), Little, Brown (Boston, MA), 1982.

Go Away, Big Green Monster!, Little, Brown (Boston, MA), 1992.

Ed and Barbara A. Emberley

Ed Emberley's Three Science Flip Books, Little, Brown (Boston, MA), 1994.

(With Anne Miranda) *Glad Monster, Sad Monster: A Book about Feelings,* Little, Brown (Boston, MA), 1997.

(With Rebecca and Michael Emberley) *Three: An Emberley Family Sketchbook,* Little, Brown (Boston, MA), 1998.

Ed Emberley's Rainbow, Little, Brown (Boston, MA), 2000.

Thanks, Mom!, Little, Brown (Boston, MA), 2003.

ILLUSTRATOR; WRITTEN BY WIFE, BARBARA EMBERLEY

Night's Nice, Doubleday (Garden City, NY), 1963.

(Reteller) *The Story of Paul Bunyan,* Prentice-Hall (Englewood Cliffs, NJ), 1963, Simon & Schuster (New York, NY), 1994.

(Reteller) *One Wide River to Cross,* Prentice-Hall (Englewood Cliffs, NJ), 1966, Little, Brown (Boston, MA), 1992.

(Reteller) *Drummer Hoff,* Prentice-Hall (Englewood Cliffs, NJ), 1967, published as a board book, Simon & Schuster (New York, NY), 1987.

Simon's Song, Prentice-Hall (Englewood Cliffs, NJ), 1969.

ILLUSTRATOR; WITH WIFE, BARBARA EMBERLEY

Seymour Simon, *The BASIC Book,* HarperCollins (New York, NY), 1985.

Seymour Simon, *Bits and Bytes: A Computer Dictionary for Beginners,* HarperCollins (New York, NY), 1985.

Seymour Simon, *How to Talk to Your Computer,* Crowell (New York, NY), 1985.

Seymour Simon, *Meet the Computer,* HarperCollins (New York, NY), 1985.

Franklyn M. Branley, *Flash, Crash, Rumble, and Roll,* HarperCollins (New York, NY), 1985.

Seymour Simon, *Turtle Talk: A Beginner's Book of LOGO,* HarperCollins (New York, NY), 1986.

Franklyn M. Branley, *The Moon Seems to Change,* HarperCollins (New York, NY), 1987.

SELF-ILLUSTRATED; "ED EMBERLEY'S DRAWING BOOK" SERIES

Ed Emberley's Drawing Book of Animals, Little, Brown (Boston, MA), 1970.
Ed Emberley's Drawing Book: Make a World, Little, Brown (Boston, MA), 1972.
Ed Emberley's Drawing Book of Faces, Little, Brown (Boston, MA), 1975.
Ed Emberley's Great Thumbprint Drawing Book, Little, Brown (Boston, MA), 1977.
Ed Emberley's Big Green Drawing Book, Little, Brown (Boston, MA), 1979.
Ed Emberley's Big Orange Drawing Book, Little, Brown (Boston, MA), 1980.
Ed Emberley's Halloween Drawing Book, Little, Brown (Boston, MA), 1980.
Ed Emberley's Big Purple Drawing Book, Little, Brown (Boston, MA), 1981.
Picture Pie: A Circle Drawing Book, Little, Brown (Boston, MA), 1984.
Ed Emberley's Big Red Drawing Book, Little, Brown (Boston, MA), 1987.
Ed Emberley's Christmas Drawing Book, Little, Brown (Boston, MA), 1987.
Ed Emberley's Drawing Box, Little, Brown (Boston, MA), 1988.
Ed Emberley's Second Drawing Box, Little, Brown (Boston, MA), 1990.
Ed Emberley's Thumbprint Drawing Box, Little, Brown (Boston, MA), 1992.
Mosaic: A Step-by-Step Cut and Paste Drawing Book, Little, Brown (Boston, MA), 1995.
Ed Emberley's Picture Pie Two: A Drawing Book and Stencil, Little, Brown (Boston, MA), 1996.
Ed Emberley's Fingerprint Drawing Book, Little, Brown (Boston, MA), 2000.
Ed Emberley's Drawing Book of Weirdos, Little, Brown (Boston, MA), 2002.
Ed Emberley's Drawing Book of Trucks and Trains, Little, Brown (Boston, MA), 2002.
Ed Emberley's Complete Funprint Drawing Book, Little, Brown (Boston, MA), 2002.

SELF-ILLUSTRATED; "ED EMBERLEY'S LITTLE DRAWING BOOK" SERIES

The Ed Emberley Little Drawing Book of Birds, Little, Brown (Boston, MA), 1973.
The Ed Emberley Little Drawing Book of Farms, Little, Brown (Boston, MA), 1973.
The Ed Emberley Little Drawing Book of Trains, Little, Brown (Boston, MA), 1973.
The Ed Emberley Little Drawing Book of Weirdos, Little, Brown (Boston, MA), 1973.
Ed Emberley's Little Drawing Book of Horses, Little, Brown (Boston, MA), 1990.
Ed Emberley's Little Drawing Book of Fish, Little, Brown (Boston, MA), 1990.
Ed Emberley's Little Drawing Book of Trucks, Little, Brown (Boston, MA), 1990.
Ed Emberley's Little Drawing Book of More Weirdos, Little, Brown (Boston, MA), 1990.
Ed Emberley's Little Drawing Book of Sea Creatures, Little, Brown (Boston, MA), 1990.

BOARD BOOKS; "FIRST WORDS" SERIES

Home, Little, Brown (Boston, MA), 1987.
Sounds, Little, Brown (Boston, MA), 1987.
Animals, Little, Brown (Boston, MA), 1987.
Cars, Boats, and Planes, Little, Brown (Boston, MA), 1987.

ILLUSTRATOR

Ruth Bonn Penn, *Mommies Are for Loving,* Putnam (New York, NY), 1962.
Franklyn M. Branley, *The Big Dipper,* Crowell (New York, NY), 1962.
Mary Kay Phelan, *The White House,* Holt (New York, NY), 1962.
Roma Gans, *Birds Eat and Eat and Eat,* Crowell (New York, NY), 1963.
Leslie Waller, *American Inventions,* Holt (New York, NY), 1963.
Richard Schackburg and others, *Yankee Doodle,* Prentice-Hall (New York, NY), 1965.
Letta Schatz, *Rhinoceros? Preposterous!,* Steck-Vaughn (Austin, TX), 1965.
Dorothy Les-Tina, *Flag Day,* Crowell (New York, NY), 1965.
Paul Showers, *Columbus Day,* Crowell (New York, NY), 1965.
M. C. Farquhar, *Colonial Life in America,* Holt (New York, NY), 1965.
Augusta Goldin, *The Bottom of the Sea,* Crowell (New York, NY), 1966.
Agusta Goldin, *Straight Hair, Curly Hair,* Crowell (New York, NY), 1966.

Leslie Waller, *The American West,* Holt (New York, NY), 1966.

Judy Hawes, *Ladybug, Ladybug, Fly Away Home,* Crowell (New York, NY), 1967.

Heywood Broun, *The Fifty-first Dragon,* Prentice-Hall (Englewood Cliffs, NJ), 1968.

Leslie Waller, *Clothing,* Holt (New York, NY), 1969.

Mindel and Harry Sitomer, *What Is Symmetry?,* Crowell (New York, NY), 1970.

Ian Serraillier, *Suppose You Met a Witch,* Little, Brown (Boston, MA), 1973.

John G. Keller, *Krispin's Fair,* Little, Brown (Boston, MA), 1976.

Franklyn M. Branley, *Space City,* Harper (New York, NY), 1991.

Contributor to books, including *Kid-Friendly Web Guide,* by Laura Leininger and others, Monday Morning Books (Palo Alto, CA), 1997; *Kid-Friendly Computer Book,* by Elnora Chambers and others, Monday Morning Books (Palo Alto, CA), 1997; and *Kid-Friendly Start-Ups: Activity Cards for Writing-Geography-Math,* by Elnora Chambers and others, Monday Morning Books (Palo Alto, CA), 1998.. A collection of Ed Emberley's manuscripts and art is included in the de Grummond Children's Literature Collection, University of Southern Mississippi, and the Cooperative Children's Book Center (Madison, WI).

ADAPTATIONS: Drummer Hoff was adapted for film by Gene Deitch and released by Weston Woods, 1969; it was released as both a sound filmstrip and, later, a video. *The Story of Paul Bunyan* was released as a filmstrip by Educational Enrichment Materials, 1969. *Ed Emberley's Three Science Flip Books* was featured on the television program *Reading Rainbow,* PBS Kids. *The Story of Paul Bunyan* was issued in Braille.

SIDELIGHTS: In a career that spans more than forty years, the husband-and-wife team of Ed and Barbara Emberley have become well respected for creating picture books that are noted for their rhythmic texts and vivid art. The pair has taken on the roles of author (Barbara) and artist (Ed) for their collaborations on original works and have acted together to illustrate science books for children by writers Seymour Simon and Franklyn M. Branley. The Emberleys are perhaps best known as the creators of *Drummer Hoff,* a retelling of an old folk song about the build-up to and aftermath of the firing of a cannon by a group of soldiers; *The Story of Paul Bunyan,* a recounting of the legends about the tall-tale hero; and *One Wide River to Cross,* an adaptation of an African-American spiritual about Noah's Ark. Several of the team's works are considered classic examples of juvenile literature and have won prestigious awards; for example, *Drummer Hoff* won the Randolph Caldecott Medal for its illustrations and the Lewis Carroll Shelf Award for its text and pictures, and *One Wide River to Cross* was named a Caldecott Honor Book. The Emberleys have not produced a book that is credited to both of them since 1969. However, Barbara has taken a behind-the-scenes role in helping to produce the works that are written and illustrated by her husband. These titles, which are published under Ed's name, chiefly are activity, concept, picture, and board books. Ed, who has developed a reputation as one of the most prolific and popular authors in the field, has received special attention for his "Drawing Books" series. These best-selling books present step-by-step instructions for creating a variety of subjects, both realistic and fantastic, by using simple geometric shapes. The volumes are credited with introducing young artists to artistic techniques in a particularly understandable and enjoyable manner. Ed also is commended as the creator of *Go Away, Big Green Monster!,* a toy book that uses cut out pictures in a cumulative effect to create and then disembody a scary monster; the book, which is praised for helping children to surmount their fears, often is considered a contemporary classic. Emberley also illustrates books by other authors, and his art has graced works by such writers as Paul Showers, Ian Serraillier, Letta Schatz, and Heywood Broun. In addition, Ed and Barbara's children, Rebecca and Michael Emberley, have worked with their parents on some of their books and have followed in their footsteps to become popular, award-winning author/artists.

As a literary stylist, Barbara employs crisp yet relaxed prose for her texts, which characteristically are drawn from folk songs, folktales, and nursery rhymes. As an illustrator, Ed uses mediums such as pencil, pen and ink, woodcuts, and computer graphics to create his pictures. Emberley often is acknowledged for his originality and skill as both an artist and a designer. His knowledge of production and printing techniques—he and Barbara operate a private printing press and letterpress, Bird in the Bush Press, and publish limited editions of children's books—and strong graphic sensibility are credited with informing the works that he has illustrated. Ed, who tries to vary his technique with every book, characteristically creates energetic, expressive pictures in bold colors, though he also employs more subdued tones. The artist is considered particularly influential, particularly on the children who have learned to appreciate art through his instructional drawing books. Emberley sometimes has been faulted for including difficult elements in his drawing series, for teaching children to copy rather than to draw, and for continuing to produce these works after exhausting his formula; in addition, the quality of his illustrations generally is considered better than that of his texts. However, Emberley is noted as an artist of talent, inventiveness, and expertise and as an author who understands children and what appeals to them. Writing in the *Bulletin of the Center for Children's Books,* Jeannette Hulick commented, "Kids definitely have their own ideas about the kind of books they think are fun and satisfying. Emberley's books are a good example of how sometimes it is perfectly O.K. to give kids what they want." Writing in *School Library Journal,* Jean Reynolds stated, "An Ed Emberley picture book leaves one with a strange feeling of predestination. It is as if to say, 'Why, of course, it had to be done that way because no other way could be right.'" Reynolds concluded, "The deceptive simplicity of the finished book makes the exact basis for its lively appeal difficult to describe. The key seems to lie in that integration of technique, art work, and text that consistently marks an Ed Emberley picture book."

Born in Malden, Massachusetts, Ed Emberley grew up in the nearby town of Cambridge, which also is home to Harvard University; he washed dishes at Harvard for a year to earn money for art school. Emberley's maternal grandfather was a coal miner in Nova Scotia and his paternal grandfather was a sailor in Newfoundland. In his twenties, Emberley's father, Wallace Akin Emberley, left Newfoundland for America and settled in Massachusetts. He and his wife, Evelyn, encouraged Ed, who has said that he always knew that he would become an illustrator, in his early artistic endeavors. In an interview with his wife, Barbara, in *Horn Book,* Emberley stated that this encouragement came "mostly, by lack of discouragement and by having pencils and paper in the house at all times for us to use if we wanted to." Emberley, who liked to read as well as to draw, first began to write stories in kindergarten. Most of his personal library was composed of funny books and old *Life* magazines, although he also liked Beatrix Potter's *The Tale of Peter Rabbit,* Helen Bannerman's *The Story of Little Black Sambo,* and the "Oz" books by L. Frank Baum. As a boy, Emberley looked in vain for a book that would show him how to draw animals. He rectified that situation in 1970 with the publication of the first volume of his art-instruction series, *Ed Emberley's Drawing Book of Animals.* Emberley's dedication read, "For the boy I was, the book I could not find."

Encouraged by his parents and high-school teachers, Emberley went to the Massachusetts School of Art in Boston. Considered one of the best students at the school, he studied painting, illustration, and design as well as printing and production techniques. While at college, Emberley met Barbara Anne Collins, a fellow student who was studying fashion design. Born in Chicago, Illinois, Barbara grew up in Lexington, Massachusetts. After Ed and Barbara received their respective bachelor of fine arts degrees, they married in 1955. Then the Korean War began, and Ed entered the U.S. Army, where he completed a two-year assignment. While in the army, Ed worked as a sign painter and was assigned to a parade division on Governor's Island in New York City. His experience marching in parades later inspired Ed to write and illustrate *The Parade Book,* a nonfiction title for children that was published in 1962. It describes the sights and sounds of parades and features examples from Macy's Thanksgiving Parade in Manhattan, Mardi Gras in New Orleans, and the Tournament of Roses Parade in Pasadena, California, among others. After leaving the army, Ed continued his studies at the Rhode Island School of Art (now the Rhode Island School of Design) in Providence, Rhode Island, where he studied illustration. During this time, Barbara worked as a librarian at Brown University in Providence. After Ed's course of study was completed, the couple moved to Boston, where Ed spent two years working as a paste-up artist and cartoonist for a direct-mail company.

Around the time that their children were born (Rebecca in 1958 and Michael in 1960), the Emberleys agreed that Ed should become a freelance illustrator. He then wrote his first book, *The Wing on a Flea: A Book about Shapes,* which was published in 1961. Described by Lee Bennett Hopkins in *Books Are by People: Interviews with 104 Authors and Illustrators of Books for Young People* as "an imaginative commentary on simple forms such as the triangle of a flea's wing or the beak of a bird," *The Wing on a Flea* uses upbeat rhymes and vigorous drawings in green and blue to demonstrate how to identify circles, rectangles, and triangles in everyday things. Writing in the *New York Times Book Review,* a critic concluded, "Only a real square would deny that here is a wonderful, lively way to learn." In 2001, Ed produced a newly illustrated version of *The Wing on a Flea* that includes full color art; printed on black paper, the book showcases pictures in bright primary colors and shiny accents in gold leaf.

Barbara Emberley's first work, *Night's Nice,* was published in 1963. This picture book soothes young readers and listeners by telling them that night is good for many things, such as sleeping, wishing on a star, and seeing city lights. Ed's illustrations portray the feeling of night by darkening oranges, reds, yellows, and greens while using other, brighter colors. Writing in *School Library Journal,* Eileen Lampert said, "Really effective illustrations illuminate this book." Lampert concluded that *Night's Nice* may lead a reader to "consider the myriad beauties of his world at night." Also in 1962, Ed started to experiment with woodcuts. He sent out a mailer to various publishers of children's books showing a print of Paul Bunyan and Pinocchio along with a note stating that he would like to illustrate the stories of these characters. The publisher Prentice-Hall agreed; in 1963, they published *The Story of Paul Bunyan,* which includes Barbara's text and Ed's illustrations. This collection of anecdotes about the massive lumberjack and his companion Babe the Blue Ox is written in "easy, yarn-spinning prose," according to Barbara Wersba in the *New York Times Book Review,* and is illustrated in bold, detailed woodcuts in brown, blue, green, and white. Noting that the "robust and joyful" pictures "serve the story well," Wersba commented that the "comic exaggerations of the tall tale are beautifully rendered." Virginia Haviland in *Horn Book* called *The Story of Paul Bunyan* a "striking graphic arts achievement." Reviewing the reissued edition in another issue of the same magazine, a critic added that "the straightforward text is a fine introduction" to the tale of the legendary lumberjack.

In 1966, the Emberleys published *One Wide River to Cross,* an adaptation of the African-American spiritual that also serves as a counting book. Barbara describes the gathering of the animals on board the ark, first one by one, then two by two, and leading up to ten by ten; after this, the rains begin. Ed illustrates the book in woodcuts that feature silhouetted figures and pages of varying colors. He includes the animals associated with the ark as well as some figures from folklore, such as the unicorn and the griffin. Writing in the *New York Times Book Review,* Barbara Novak O'Doherty stated that *One Wide River to Cross* is "striking evidence that old themes, properly handled, are inexhaustible wells of inspiration." Alluding to the three books about Noah that had come out that year, a reviewer in *Publishers Weekly* claimed that the Emberleys' version "might well be the one that would have pleased him most of all." A critic in *Kirkus Reviews* suggested, "Buy it in twos, be prepared to have to reread it in tens." *One Wide River to Cross* was the sole runner-up for the Caldecott Medal in 1967.

The Emberleys produced their Caldecott Medal-winning book *Drummer Hoff* in 1967. The rhyming, alliterative text of this work is a retelling of the traditional poem "John Ball Shot Them All," which is about the making of a rifle. Barbara turned this verse into a cumulative rhyme about a group of happy soldiers who build a cannon that makes a loud explosion when their drummer fires it off. Ed's pictures—dynamic, stylized woodcuts that create the effect of thirteen colors through overprinting of red, yellow, and blue—give an antiwar subtext to the story. Both the soldiers and the cannon appear to have been destroyed by the blast; the last picture shows birds, ladybugs, and flowers—used as decorations in the previous pages—taking over the remains of the cannon. Emberley, who based his illustrations on the concept that a woodcut does not have to look like a woodcut, uses his woodcuts as if they were drawings, dropping colors into the open spaces left around the lines. By combining basic colors to create other tones, he was able to produce thirteen varied shades. Reviewers have praised the artist for both the originality of his idea and the success of its execution, and they have commended the reteller for the jaunty flavor of her text. Writing in the *New York Times Book Review,* Eve Merriam called *Drummer Hoff* "a perfect wedding of text and pictures. . . . You don't have to be married to produce this wry, well-bred humor, but in the Emberleys' case, it doesn't hurt." Della Thomas of *Library Journal* stated, "An old folk rhyme is the perfect vehicle for this talented author-artist team." Thomas continued by calling *Drummer Hoff* "one of the liveliest picture books of the year." In 1987, *Drummer Hoff* was issued as a board book to mark its twenty-year anniversary. Liz Rosenberg of the *Boston Globe* commented that the book "continues strong in its board-book incarnation, as full of ferocity and wit as ever. . . . Barbara Emberley's adaptation is a galloping tour de force, and Ed Emberley's pictures a wild combination of the antique and the psychedelic."

In 1970, Ed Emberley produced the first of his "Drawing Book" series, *Ed Emberley's Drawing Book of Animals.* In this work, the artist demonstrates how to draw over fifty animals, from ants to whales, by using geometric shapes, letters, numbers, dots, curlicues, and other symbols. Emberley provides aspiring artists with clear verbal instructions and humorous visual examples. Writing in *Time,* Timothy Foote called *Ed Emberley's Drawing Book of Animals* "that all but unheard-of success, a 'how-to-draw' book that really works." Pamela Marsh of the *Christian Science Monitor* predicted that the book "can turn anyone over eight into an instant artist" and noted that "it makes an encouraging book for those, adults included, who imagine they can't draw for toffee." Writing in the *New York Times Book Review,* George A. Woods said that, after finishing Emberley's book, "I've got a pad full of impressive doodles and drawings and my kids think that I'm a genius!" Since the publication of his first drawing book, Emberley has added more than twenty-five titles to his series. These works, which are divided into "Drawing Books" and "Little Drawing Books," use a format similar to that in *Ed Emberely's Drawing Book of Animals* to center on colors, holidays, faces, birds, animals, motorized vehicles, supernatural characters, and other things that interest children. Emberley also includes works that use fingerprints and thumbprints as their jumping-off points. Throughout his series, the artist gives directions for drawing a wide variety of people, creatures, animals, and objects that reflect both the natural world and that of the imagination. Although these works have been called gimmicky, they generally are considered clever, appealing introductions to art instruction.

Among Emberley's most acclaimed works is *Ed Emberley's ABC,* a title published in 1978. In this book, the artist represents each letter of the alphabet in a double-page spread that contains four panels of pictures that show an animal constructing the individual letter (for example, an ant forms the letter "A" by skywriting in an airplane). Through hand-lettered text and vibrant illustrations, readers are encouraged to find numerous examples of objects that begin with the designated letter. Writing in the *New York Times Book Review,* Selma G. Lanes called it "an eye-dazzler" and "an alphabet not to be missed." Ethel L. Heins in *Horn Book* called *Ed Emberley's ABC* a "substantial and original piece of work. . . . The pages show great ingenuity of conception and design, the color work is strikingly beautiful and subtle, and the whole book . . . constitutes a handsome, unified production." Gemma DeVinney of *School Library Journal* predicted that *Ed Emberley's ABC* "will be snatched up by children eager to peruse its colorful, fun-loving, action-filled pages."

Ed Emberley is the creator of several interactive activity books that engage youngsters by having them do such things as hold pages to the light, turn them sideways, and lift flaps. One of his most popular titles in this genre is *Go Away, Big Green Monster!,* a book published in 1992. In this work, Emberley uses stiff, die-cut pages with peep holes to let children construct and deconstruct the title character. The book starts with a black page and two round yellow eyes that peer from the darkness. Each pages adds a new element, such as a long blue nose, a red mouth, sharp white teeth, and a big green face. Finally, the culmination produces the visage of a frightening monster; however, the text reads, "You Don't Scare Me! So Go Away." Each subsequent page then subtracts each of the scary pieces until the last page is black. The final text reads, "And Don't Come Back! Until I Say So." Writing in *Instructor,* Judy Freeman called *Go Away, Big Green Monster!* "a cleverly designed gem that all ages will adore." A reviewer in *Publishers Weekly* noted that Emberley "makes wonderful use of innovative production techniques in this ingenious offering."

Barbara and Ed Emberley consistently have involved their children, Rebecca and Michael, in their artistic lives. For example, both children helped their mother to make overlays with drawing instructions for their father's books. In an interview with Jeanne McCartin in the *Portsmouth Herald,* Rebecca said, "My father just wanted to hand down every thing he knew to me and my brother. He sure did that. . . . We spent a lot of time together as a family. Creating things was just life. It certainly was not an event. It was just what we did." Rebecca also called her mother a major influence. Barbara taught her daughter how to sew and to design clothing, and Ed taught her to work in silver, copper, and numerous paint mediums. When Rebecca was twelve and Michael ten, they each received sailing dinghy kits from their father. "We sailed [the boats] for years," Rebecca told McCartin. When Rebecca was in high school, her father started training her, taking her into his studio for three house each day during summer vacations. Rebecca recalled to McCartin, "Everything my father learned in college, I learned in high school. He also educated some of my boyfriends those summers. They came around long after they broke up with me." Rebecca and Michael now are both successful author/illustrators of books for children. In 1998, they teamed up with their father to produce *Three: An Emberley Family Sketchbook.* A collection of narratives, drawings, and activities by each artist, the book includes fairy tales, stories, poems, recipes, and autobiographical information. Thematically, the concept of "three" appears throughout; artistically, the book reflects each illustrator's personal style. Ed uses computer-generated art, Rebecca uses woodcuts and paper collages, and Michael uses watercolors and bold ink-and-crayon art. *Booklist* critic Kathleen Squires commented, "The Emberley family delivers a triple dose of fun. . . . Children will be intrigued by this big book of fun." Writing in the *Pittsburgh Post-Gazette Magazine,* Karen MacPherson called *Three: An Emberley Family Sketchbook* "a book that rings with energy" before concluding, "What's best about this book is its message that there are many different ways to be an artist."

Ed Emberley has also received favorable critical attention for his picture book *Thanks, Mom!,* a title published in 2003. The book features Kiko, a little mouse in a circus act. While performing in the center ring, Kiko spies a hunk of cheese and grabs it. He then is chased by a cat, a dog, a tiger, and an elephant—all animals of increasing size—who get their moment in the spotlight. Sailing through the air, Kiko's mother, Koko, frightens the elephant and frees Kiko, who thanks his mom politely and is welcomed warmly in return. At the end of the story, both mother and son enjoy the cheese. Emberley illustrates *Thanks, Mom!* with neon-hued geometric shapes, including stars, stripes, and polka dots, and colorful yellow highlights. A reviewer in *Publishers Weekly* noted, "At once buoyant and understated, Emberley's story. . . slyly delivers lessons in punctuation, pecking order, and manners." Calling *Thanks, Mom!* "a visual lollapalooza," a critic in *Kirkus Reviews* found the work "a classic turning of the tables [that] gives readers both an eyeful and a first taste of allegory."

In his Caldecott Medal acceptance speech, which was reprinted in *Horn Book,* Ed Emberley said, "There is more to illustrating a picture book than knowing how to draw pictures. To an illustrator the picture on the drawing board is merely a means to an end. The end is the printed picture. An illustration could be defined as a picture that can be printed. A good picture is a bad illustration if it cannot be printed well. And, of course, a bad picture is a bad picture no matter how well suited it is to the printing process. I work in many different techniques when preparing illustrations—woodcuts, pencil, pen and ink. But as varied as they are in appearance they have one thing in common—the illustrations are meant to be printed. Although I am primarily an artist and not a printing expert, the necessity to be both dreamer and realist is what fascinates me most about picture-book making." In assessing his career in the field of children's literature, Emberley told Lee Bennett Hopkins in *Pauses: Autobiographical Reflections of 101 Creators of Children's Books,* "Working in the field of children's books is challenging. It is a wonderful field to be involved in. It is one wide river to cross after another, and you never quite feel that you have reached the other side." In an interview in *Publishers Weekly,* Emberley stated, "I love books, even the *feel* of books, not to mention what's inside. And I don't consider myself an illustrator or an author or an instructor. I like to think I am a creator of books. If lightning should strike tomorrow and I could no longer write or draw, I would still find a way of making books my career."

BIOGRAPHICAL AND CRITICAL SOURCES:

BOOKS

Emberley, Ed, *Ed Emberley's Drawing Book of Animals,* Little, Brown (Boston, MA), 1970.

Emberley, Ed, *Go Away, Big Green Monster!,* Little, Brown (Boston, MA), 1992.

Hopkins, Lee Bennett, *Books Are by People: Interviews with 104 Authors and Illustrators of Books for Young People,* Citation Press (New York, NY), 1969.

Hopkins, Lee Bennett, *Pauses: Autobiographical Reflections of 101 Creators of Children's Books,* HarperCollins (New York, NY), 1995.

PERIODICALS

Booklist, October, 1998, Kathleen Squires, review of *Three: An Emberley Family Sketchbook,* p. 96.

Boston Globe, October 19, 1997, Liz Rosenberg, "The New Flexibility of the Board Book," p. P5.

Chicago Sunday Tribune Magazine of Books, May 14, 1961, Joan Beck, review of *The Wing on a Flea: A Book about Shapes,* section 2, p. 2.

Christian Science Monitor, May 7, 1970, Pamela Marsh, review of *Ed Emberley's Drawing Book of Animals,* p. B1.

Horn Book, February, 1964, Virginia Haviland, review of *The Story of Paul Bunyan,* p. 48; August, 1968, Barbara Emberley, "Ed Emberley," pp. 403-406; August, 1968, Ed Emberley, "Caldecott Award Acceptance," pp. 399-402; August, 1978, Ethel L. Heins, review of *Ed Emberley's ABC,* pp. 386-387; March, 1995, review of *The Story of Paul Bunyan,* p. 222.

Instructor, May, 1995, Judy Freeman, review of *Go Away, Big Green Monster!,* p. 78.

Kirkus Reviews, July 15, 1966, review of *One Wide River to Cross,* p. 683; March 15, 2003, review of *Thanks, Mom!*

Library Journal, December 15, 1967, Della Thomas, review of *Drummer Hoff,* p. 602.

New York Times Book Review, May 14, 1961, review of *The Wing on a Flea,* p. 35; January 26, 1964, Barbara Wersba, review of *The Story of Paul Bunyan,* p. 26; October 16, 1966, Barbara Novak O'Doherty, review of *One Wide River to Cross,* p. 38; November 5, 1967, Eve Merriam, review of *Drummer Hoff,* p. 71; March 1, 1970, George A. Woods, review of *Ed Emberley's Drawing Book of Animals,* p. 34; July 2, 1978, Selma G. Lanes, review of *Ed Emberley's ABC,* p. 11.

Pittsburgh Post-Gazette Magazine, March 21, 2000, Karen MacPherson, "Artful Books Open Up World of Art to the Young."

Portsmouth Herald, September 30, 2003, Jeanne McCartin, "A Story-Book Existence."

Publishers Weekly, December 26, 1966, review of *One Wide River to Cross,* p. 99; July 25, 1980, "Ed Emberley," pp. 78-79; March 29, 1993, review of *Go Away, Big Green Monster!,* p. 54; March 24, 2003, review of *Thanks, Mom!,* p. 74.

School Library Journal, October, 1963, Eileen Lampert, review of *Night's Nice,* p. 190; March, 1968, Jean Reynolds, "Ed Emberley," pp. 113-114; September, 1978, Gemma DeVinney, review of *Ed Emberley's ABC,* p. 107.

Time, December 21, 1970, Timothy Foote, review of *Ed Emberley's Drawing Book of Animals,* p. 68.

ONLINE

Bulletin of the Center of Children's Books, http://alexia.lis.uiuc.edu/ (August 1, 2002), Jeannette Hulick, "True Blue: Ed Emberley."*

OTHER

Growing Up Well—Squiggles, Dots, and Lines: A Kid's Video Guide to Drawing and Creating Featuring Illustrator Ed Emberley, Inspired Corp., 2002.

* * *

EPSTEIN, Rachel S. 1941-

PERSONAL: Born September 10, 1941, in Washington, DC; daughter of Herbert (an economist and writer) and Mildred (Fishman) Stein; married Melvin Epstein, December 20, 1964; children: Jonathan, Emily Epstein Landau. *Ethnicity:* "Jewish." *Education:* Wellesley College, B.A., 1963; Pratt Institute, M.L.S., 1967; New York University, M.B.A., 1981. *Politics:* Democrat. *Religion:* Jewish. *Hobbies and other interests:* Music, cooking, walking, bicycling, traveling, reading, studying conversational French.

ADDRESSES: *Agent*—c/o Author Mail, Sterling Publishing Co., Inc., 387 Park Ave. S., New York, NY 10016. *E-mail*—rachel.epstein@worldnet.att.net.

CAREER: J. C. Penney and Co., Inc., New York, NY, training writer, 1981-84; International Council of Shopping Centers, New York, NY, writer, 1984-94; *New York Observer,* New York, NY, shopping columnist, 1989-94; freelance writer, 1994—. United Jewish Appeal (board chair, Brooklyn Women's Campaign, 1996-98; Museum of Jewish Heritage: A Living Memorial to the Holocaust, leader of tours for young people.

MEMBER: Beta Gamma Sigma.

WRITINGS:

(With Nina Liebman) *BizSpeak,* Franklin Watts (Danbury, CT), 1986.

Alternative Investments, Chelsea House (Broomall, PA), 1988.

Careers in the Investment World, Chelsea House (Broomall, PA), 1988.

Investment Banking, Chelsea House (Broomall, PA, 1988.

Investments and the Law, Chelsea House (Broomall, PA, 1988.

Careers in Health Care, introduction by C. Everett Koop, Chelsea House (Broomall, PA, 1989.

Eating Habits and Disorders, introduction by C. Everett Koop, Chelsea House (Broomall, PA, 1990.

Anne Frank, Franklin Watts (Danbury, CT), 1997.

W. K. Kellogg: Generous Genius, Children's Press (Chicago, IL), 2000.

Estee Lauder: Beauty Business Success, Franklin Watts (Danbury, CT), 2000.

(Coauthor) *A Shop of One's Own,* Sterling Publishing (New York, NY), 2002.

BizSpeak has been translated into Vietnamese.

SIDELIGHTS: The writings of Rachel S. Epstein span a wide variety of subjects that reflect her educational background in business as well as her cultural heritage. Epstein's business books for young adults provide their audiences with useful information about vocations in business. *Careers in the Investment World* does not merely give a description of the career, but describes a typical workday and the advantages and disadvantages of the job. A *Booklist* reviewer praised Epstein's "objective and uncomplicated" presentation of facts that "otherwise might become jargon-laden and dry." *Investment Banking* utilizes case studies of successful companies such as Apple Computers and introduces readers to concepts such as takeovers, mergers, and acquisitions.

Epstein shifted gears from business to medicine with *Careers in Health Care.* This book explores the many opportunities available in the medical field, looking at careers as widely varied as surgical specialists, dentists, school nurses, allied health professionals, and biomedical engineers. Particularly useful to students is the information on the type and length of training needed for each profession. Also included are sections on major health issues such as AIDS, high medical costs, and health maintenance organizations. A reviewer for *Appraisal: Science Books for Young People* said Epstein covers medical careers "thoroughly yet succinctly," describing the book as "an excellent introductory work for children considering a career in the health care field." Former surgeon general C. Everett Koop provided the introduction for this and Epstein's next book, *Eating Habits and Disorders.* Along with tracing the history of eating disorders, Epstein examines the symptoms of anorexia nervosa and bulimia, outlining information on the help and treatment of victims.

Epstein then turned to an event in her own cultural history with *Anne Frank,* her look at the famous Holocaust diarist. The biography focuses on the Frank family's years in hiding and includes reminiscences of the people who helped the Franks survive as long as they did. Other details include black-and-white photographs of the family and quotations from Anne's historic diary. The book "should motivate students to read the diary and other books about World War II," according to *School Library Journal* reviewer Susan Pine. In a *Booklist* review, Ellen Mandel called the story an "honest, yet age-appropriate account."

Epstein once commented: "I feel most proud of the book about Anne Frank. . . . I have spent many years doing volunteer work to raise money for poor young women in Israel and also for other Jewish people in need around the world. It was wonderful to put my professional and volunteer worlds together in a book which, if it helps just one person have some understanding of the Holocaust and, perhaps, helps another person become more understanding of people who are different from him or her, will have achieved something. I have also greatly enjoyed speaking to school children about Anne Frank. I have been surprised by how much they know about her already and how sensitive they are to the issue of prejudice."

She added: "Writing for me is a little like playing with a big puzzle where there is no one right answer and there is an infinite number of pieces; for every thought there are many words, and many combinations of words that can be used, and for every group of ideas there is more than one order in which they can be expressed. The fun is in finding the combinations which tell the story most clearly and pleasantly. By pleasantly, I mean the combinations that sound the best. As I write I am saying everything to myself, so the way the words sound is extremely important to me."

BIOGRAPHICAL AND CRITICAL SOURCES:

PERIODICALS

Appraisal: Science Books for Young People, winter, 1990, review of *Careers in Health Care,* pp. 24-25.

Booklist, March 1, 1988, review of *Careers in the Investment World,* pp. 1128, 1332; June 1, 1989, pp. 1716-1717; December 1, 1997, Ellen Mandel, review of *Anne Frank,* pp. 617-618.

School Library Journal, August, 1989, p. 156; August, 1990, p. 168; November, 1997, Susan Pine, review of *Anne Frank,* p. 126.

* * *

ERLINE, N. T.
See RAGEN, Naomi

F

FEIFFER, Jules (Ralph) 1929-

PERSONAL: Born January 26, 1929, in Bronx, New York; son of David (held a variety of positions, including dental technician and sales representative) and Rhoda (a fashion designer; maiden name, Davis) Feiffer; married Judith Sheftel (a film production executive), September 17, 1961 (divorced); married Jennifer Allen (a journalist); children: (first marriage) Kate; (second marriage) Halley, Julie. *Education:* Attended Art Students League, New York, NY, 1946, and Pratt Institute, 1947-48 and 1949-51.

ADDRESSES: *Home*—325 West End Ave., New York, NY 10023. *Office*—c/o Universal Press Syndicate, 4900 Main St., Kansas City, MO 64112.

CAREER: Assistant to cartoonist Will Eisner, 1946-51, and ghostwriter for Eisner's comic book *The Spirit,* 1949-51; author of syndicated cartoon strip, *Clifford,* 1949-51; held a variety of positions in the art field, 1953-56, including producer of slide films, writer for Columbia Broadcasting System's *Terry Toons,* and designer of booklets for an art firm; author of cartoon strip (originally titled *Sick, Sick, Sick,* later changed to *Feiffer*), published in *Village Voice,* 1956-97, published weekly in London *Observer,* 1958-66, and 1972-82, and regularly in *Playboy,* beginning 1959, *New Yorker,* beginning 1993, and *New Statesman & Society,* beginning 1994; syndicated cartoonist, beginning 1959, including syndication by Universal Press Syndicate, Kansas City, MO. Yale University, faculty member at Yale Drama School, 1973-74. Columbia University, senior fellow in National Arts Journalism Program, 1997-98. *Military service:* U.S. Army, Signal Corps, 1951-53; worked in cartoon animation unit.

MEMBER: PEN, American Academy of Arts and Letters (member of board of directors), Authors League of America, Authors Guild (life member), Dramatists Guild (member of council), Writers Guild of America East.

AWARDS, HONORS: Special George Polk Memorial Award, Department of Journalism, Long Island University, 1962; named most promising playwright of 1966-67 season by New York drama critics; London Theater Critics Award, 1967, and Obie Award from *Village Voice,* 1969, both for *Little Murders;* Outer Circle Critics Award, 1969, for *Little Murders,* and 1970, for *The White House Murder Case;* Antoinette Perry Award nomination, best play, 1976, for *Knock Knock;* Pulitzer Prize for editorial cartooning, 1986.

WRITINGS:

CARTOON COLLECTIONS

Sick, Sick, Sick, McGraw-Hill (New York, NY), 1958, published with introduction by Kenneth Tynan, Collins (New York, NY), 1959.

Passionella, and Other Stories (also see below), McGraw-Hill (New York, NY), 1959.

Boy, Girl, Boy, Girl, Random House (New York, NY), 1961.

Feiffer's Album, Random House (New York, NY), 1963.

The Penguin Feiffer, Penguin (New York, NY), 1966.

Feiffer's Marriage Manual, Random House (New York, NY), 1967.

Feiffer on Civil Rights, Anti-Defamation League of B'nai B'rith (New York, NY), 1967.

Pictures at a Prosecution: Drawings and Text from the Chicago Conspiracy Trial, Grove Press (New York, NY), 1971.

Feiffer on Nixon: The Cartoon Presidency, Random House (New York, NY), 1974.

(With Israel Horovitz) *VD Blues,* Avon (New York, NY), 1974.

Tantrum: A Novel in Cartoons, Knopf (New York, NY), 1979.

Popeye: The Movie Novel (based on the screenplay by Feiffer), edited by Richard J. Anobile, Avon (New York, NY), 1980.

Jules Feiffer's America: From Eisenhower to Reagan, edited by Steve Heller, Knopf (New York, NY), 1982.

(Coauthor) *Outer Space Spirit, 1952,* Kitchen Sink Press (Princeton, WI), 1983.

Marriage Is an Invasion of Privacy and Other Dangerous Views, Andrews & McMeel (Fairway, KS), 1984.

Feiffer's Children, Andrews & McMeel (Fairway, KS), 1986.

Ronald Reagan in Movie America: A Jules Feiffer Production, Andrews & McMeel (Fairway, KS), 1988.

The Complete Color Terry and the Pirates, Remco, 1990.

PUBLISHED PLAYS

The Explainers (satirical review; produced in Chicago, IL, at Playwright's Cabaret Theater, 1961), McGraw-Hill (New York, NY), 1960.

Crawling Arnold (one act; first produced in Spoleto, Italy, at Festival of Two Worlds, 1961; first produced in United States in Cambridge, MA, at Poets' Theater, 1961), Dramatists Play Service (New York, NY), 1963.

Hold Me! (first produced off-Broadway at American Place Theater, 1977), Random House (New York, NY), 1963.

The Unexpurgated Memoirs of Bernard Mergendeiler (one-act; first produced in Los Angeles, CA, at Mark Taper Forum, 1967), Random House (New York, NY), 1965.

Little Murders (two-act comedy; first produced on Broadway at Broadhurst Theater, 1967; first American play produced on the West End, London, England, by Royal Shakespeare Company at Aldwych Theater, 1967; also see below), Random House (New York, NY), 1968, reprinted, Penguin (New York, NY), 1983.

(With others) *Dick and Jane* (one act; produced in New York, NY, at Eden Theater as part of *Oh! Calcutta!,* devised by Kenneth Tynan, 1969; also see below), published in *Oh! Calcutta!,* edited by Kenneth Tynan, Grove (New York, NY), 1969.

Feiffer's People: Sketches and Observations (produced as *Feiffer's People* in Edinburgh, Scotland, at International Festival of Music and Drama, 1968), Dramatists Play Service (New York, NY), 1969.

The White House Murder Case: A Play in Two Acts [and] Dick and Jane: A One-Act Play (*The White House Murder Case* first produced off-Broadway at Circle in the Square Downtown, 1970), Grove (New York, NY), 1970.

Knock Knock (first produced in New York, NY, at Circle Repertory Theater, 1976), Hill & Wang (New York, NY), 1976.

Elliot Loves (first produced on Broadway, 1989), Grove (New York, NY), 1989.

Anthony Rose, Dramatists Play Service (New York, NY), 1990.

UNPUBLISHED PLAYS

The World of Jules Feiffer, produced in New Jersey at Hunterdon Hills Playhouse, 1962.

God Bless, first produced in New Haven, CT, at Yale University, 1968; produced on the West End by Royal Shakespeare Company at Aldwych Theater, 1968.

Munro (adapted by Feiffer from story in *Passionella, and Other Stories*), first produced in Brooklyn, NY, at Prospect Park, 1971.

(With others) *Watergate Classics,* first produced in New Haven, CT, at Yale University, 1973.

Grownups, first produced in Cambridge, MA, at Loeb Drama Center, 1981; produced on Broadway at Lyceum Theater, December, 1981.

A Think Piece, first produced in New York, NY, at Circle Repertory Theater, 1982.

Carnal Knowledge (revised version of play of same title originally written c. 1970; also see below), first produced in Houston, TX, at Stages Repertory Theater, 1988.

Also author of *Interview* and *You Should Have Caught Me at the White House,* both c. 1962.

SCREENPLAYS

Munro (animated cartoon; adapted by Feiffer from story in *Passionella, and Other Stories*), Rembrandt Films, 1961.

Carnal Knowledge (adapted from Feiffer's unpublished, unproduced play of same title written c. 1970), Avco Embassy, 1971.

Little Murders (adapted by author from play of same title), Twentieth Century-Fox, 1971.

Popeye, Paramount/Walt Disney Productions, 1980.

Also author of the unproduced screenplays, *Little Brucie, Bernard and Huey,* and *I Want to Go Home.*

FOR CHILDREN

The Man in the Ceiling, HarperCollins (New York, NY), 1993.

A Barrel of Laughs, a Vale of Tears, HarperCollins (New York, NY), 1995.

Meanwhile, Harpercrest (New York, NY), 1997.

(With Daniel M. Pinkwater) *Five Novels: The Boy from Mars, Slaves of Spiegel, The Snarkout Boys, The Avocado of Death, The Last Gur,* Farrar, Straus & Giroux (New York, NY), 1997.

I Lost My Bear, William Morrow (New York, NY), 1998.

Bark: George, HarperCollins Juvenile Books (New York, NY), 1999.

OTHER

(Illustrator) Robert Mines, *My Mind Went All to Pieces,* Dial (New York, NY), 1959.

(Illustrator) Norton Juster, *The Phantom Tollbooth,* Random House (New York, NY), 1961.

Harry, the Rat with Women (novel), McGraw-Hill (New York, NY), 1963.

(Editor and annotator) *The Great Comic Book Heroes,* Dial (New York, NY), 1965, published with new illustrations and without original comic-book stories), Fantagraphics (Stamford, CT), 2003.

Silverlips (television play), Public Broadcasting Service, 1972.

(With Herb Gardner, Peter Stone, and Neil Simon) *Happy Endings* (television play), American Broadcasting Companies, 1975.

Akroyd (novel), Simon & Schuster (New York, NY), 1977.

(Author of introduction) Rick Marshall, editor, *The Complete E. C. Segar Popeye,* Fantagraphics (Stamford, CT), 1984.

Feiffer: The Collected Works, Volume 1: *Clifford,* Fantagraphics (Stamford, CT), 1989.

Feiffer: The Collected Works, Volume 2: *Munro,* Fantagraphics (Stamford, CT), 1989.

Feiffer: The Collected Works, Volume 3: *Sick, Sick, Sick,* Fantagraphics (Stamford, CT), 1991.

Feiffer: The Collected Works: Passionella, Fantagraphics (Stamford, CT), 1993.

(With Ted Rall) *Revenge of the Latchkey Kids: An Illustrated Guide to Surviving the '90s and Beyond,* Workman Publishing Company, 1998 (New York, NY).

(Illustrator) Florence Parry Heide, *Some Things Are Scary,* Candlewick Press (Cambridge, MA), 2000.

ADAPTATIONS: *The Feiffer Film,* based on Feiffer's cartoons, was released in 1965; *Harry, the Rat with Women* was made into a play and produced in Detroit, MI, at Detroit Institute of Arts, 1966; *Passionella, and Other Stories* was adapted by Jerry Bock and Sheldon Harnick into "Passionella," a one-act musical produced on Broadway as part of *The Apple Tree,* 1967; *Jules Feiffer's America: From Eisenhower to Reagan* was adapted by Russell Vandenbroucke into a play titled *Feiffer's America; What Are We Saying?,* a parody on Feiffer's cartoons, was produced in Rome, Italy.

SIDELIGHTS: On learning that *Hudson Review* contributor John Simon described Jules Feiffer's play *Little Murders* as "bloody-minded," and made reference to its "grotesque horror" and "hideous reality," those who only know Feiffer as a cartoonist and not as a playwright might be more than a little surprised. Such brutal words are unexpected when used to characterize the work of a cartoonist—whom we might imagine would only want to make us laugh.

Feiffer revealed the origins of his somewhat black humor in a *Washington Post* interview with Henry Allen: "Back then [in the 1950s], comedy was still working in a tradition that came out of World War I. . . . Comedy was mired in insults and gags. It was Bob Hope and Bing Cosby, Burns and Allen, Ozzie and Harriet. There was no such thing as comedy about relationships, nothing about the newly urban and collegiate Americans. What I was interested in was using humor as a reflection of one's own confusion, ambivalence and dilemma, dealing with sexual life as one knew it to be." His cartoons presented a mixture of social commentary and political satire previously reserved for the editorial page of the newspaper.

From the beginning of his career Feiffer avoided the silliness expected of a nonpolitical cartoonist. His characters include people who are odd enough to be humorous but who at the same time can elicit a painful, empathetic response from his readers: Passionella, who achieves movie stardom because she has the world's largest breasts; Bernard Mergeneiler, known for his romantic failures; and an inventor who creates a "Lonely Machine" that makes light conversation and delivers sympathetic remarks whenever necessary.

Feiffer's concerns as a cartoonist have followed him to the stage, but some critics have faulted Feiffer's plays for being too dependent on his cartoons for inspiration. In the *Village Voice* Carll Tucker, for example, commented: "Feiffer's genius as a cartoonist is for dramatic moments—establishing and comically concluding a situation in eight still frames. His characters have personality only for the purpose of making a point: They do not have, as breathing dramatic characters must, the freedom to develop, to grow away from their status as idea-bearers."

Other critics voiced their approval for what they have seen as the influence of Feiffer's cartoons in his work for the theater. In Alan Rich's *New York* magazine review of Feiffer's play, *Knock Knock,* for example, the critic noted: "What gives [the play] its humor—and a great deal of it is screamingly funny—is the incredible accuracy of [Feiffer's] language, and his use of it to paint the urban neurosis in exact colors. This we know from his cartoons, and we learn it anew from this endearing, congenial theater piece." Other commentators on New York's theatrical scene, such as *Dictionary of Literary Biography* contributor Thomas Edward Ruddick, have been able to separate Feiffer's dramatic work from his other creative efforts. "Feiffer's plays show considerable complexity of plot, character, and idea, and command attention," Ruddick noted, "not dependent upon Feiffer's other achievements. His plays, independently, constitute a noteworthy body of work."

Those who enjoyed Feiffer for his adults-only satire may have been surprised to see the cartoonist venture into the children's book market in the 1990s. For his part, Feiffer is the father to essentially three generations of girls; in 1993, when *The Man in the Ceiling* was published, he had thirty-one-year-old Kate, eleven-year-old Halley (to whom that book is dedicated) and fifteen-month-old Julie. "I'm glad they're girls," the author told *Publishers Weekly* writer John F. Baker. "Boys are terribly active and geared toward just the sort of sports I was never any good at."

Feiffer's attraction to the youth market arose "from a combination of his fond recollections of reading to Halley as a small child . . . and an illustrator friend's interest in doing a book," according to Baker. In *The Man in the Ceiling,* Feiffer writes and illustrates the tale of Jimmy, a little boy who dreams of being a cartoonist. His aptitude for drawing underscores the fact that the boy is "not much good at anything else, including such boyish but unFeiffer-like pastimes as sports," Baker continued.

"Yes, I did cartoons as a kid, just like Jimmy," Feiffer admitted in the *Publishers Weekly* piece. "And I rediscovered some of them while I was working on [the book]. But those drawings of Jimmy's were the toughest part; I had to get the tone just right—they mustn't be too satirical—and it terrified me for a long time. I left them right to the end."

Feiffer's caution was rewarded by the favorable reviews that greeted *The Man in the Ceiling.* Jonathan Fast, in fact, singled out Jimmy's artwork, noting in his *New York Times Book Review* piece, "the adventures of Mini-Man, Bullethead and The Man in the Ceiling, Jimmy's *magnum opus,* are reprinted in glorious pencil and run as long as six pages." Evidently Feiffer's efforts also reached a younger audience: Nine-year-old reviewer Erin Smith told the *San Francisco Review of Books* that the work "has great pictures. The story is just as funny. The best pictures are the comics that Jimmy drew."

In 1995 Feiffer released his second children's book, *A Barrel of Laughs, a Vale of Tears.* The volume is comprised of fairy tales with a slightly acerbic air meant to appeal to children and parents alike. Featuring King Whatchamacallit, who speaks in spoonerisms: "My son, when you're around, no till gets soiled—er, no soil gets tilled; no noo gets shailed—that is, no shoe gets nailed." Another urbane character, J. Wellington Wizard, amused children's author Daniel

M. Pinkwater. "Written with conviction, not to say innocence, Mr. Feiffer's ebullient story renders the reader capable of maximum suspension of disbelief—and what would be corny is touching instead," Pinkwater declared in the *New York Times Book Review.*

As Feiffer revealed to Baker, the best part of being a children's author is the honest response from his young readers: "It's much more direct even than in the theater, so much more heartening. You create something out of love and devotion, and when you get it back, you can't believe it."

BIOGRAPHICAL AND CRITICAL SOURCES:

BOOKS

Anobile, Richard J., *Popeye: The Movie Novel,* Avon (New York, NY), 1980.

Cohen, Sarah Blacher, editor, *From Hester Street to Hollywood: The Jewish-American Stage and Screen,* Indiana University Press (Bloomington, IN), 1983.

Contemporary Dramatists, 4th edition, St. James Press (Detroit, MI), 1988.

Contemporary Literary Criticism, Gale (Detroit, MI), Volume 2, 1974, Volume 8, 1978, Volume 64, 1991.

Corliss, Richard, *Talking Pictures: Screenwriters in the American Cinema,* Overlook Press (New York, NY), 1974.

Dictionary of Literary Biography, Gale (Detroit, MI), Volume 7: *Twentieth-Century American Dramatists,* 1981, Volume 44: *American Screenwriters, Second Series,* 1986.

PERIODICALS

American Cinematographer, January, 1971, p. 37.

American Film, December, 1980; July-August, 1987, p. 36.

Chicago, April, 1988, p. 32.

Chicago Tribune, June 29, 1979; November 2, 1982.

Commonweal, December 1, 1989, p. 676; August 10, 1990, p. 455.

Harper's, September, 1961, pp. 58-62.

Hudson Review, summer, 1967, John Simon, review of *Little Murders.*

Library Journal, July, 2003, pp. 69-70.

Los Angeles Times, November 13, 1988.

Newsweek, June 18, 1990, p. 58.

New York, February 2, 1976, Alan Rich, review of *Knock Knock;* May 16, 1976; December 21, 1981, pp. 81-82; May 25, 1987, p. 108; November 26, 1990, p. 33; December 3, 1990, p. 148.

New Yorker, May 18, 1987, p. 87; November 2, 1992, p. 55.

New York Times, January 21, 1977; December 15, 1981; May 7, 1987.

New York Times Book Review, December 19, 1982, p. 8; November 14, 1993, Jonathan Fast, review of *The Man in the Ceiling,* p. 57; December 31, 1995, Daniel M. Pinkwater, review of *A Barrel of Laughs, a Vale of Tears,* p. 12.

Publishers Weekly, October 25, 1993, John F. Baker, review of *The Man in the Ceiling,* p. 62; November 20, 1995.

San Francisco Review of Books, April-May, 1994, Erin Smith, review of *The Man in the Ceiling.*

School Library Journal, February, 1994, p. 102.

Time, June 18, 1990, p. 85.

Village Voice, February 2, 1976, article by Carll Tucker.

Washington Post, August 17, 1979, interview by Henry Allen.*

* * *

FERGUSON, Alane 1957-

PERSONAL: Born February 8, 1957, in Cumberland, MD; daughter of Edward (an aerospace engineer) and Gloria (a children's author; maiden name, Flister) Skurzynski; married Ronald Ferguson (a sales and marketing professional), October 11, 1980; children: Kristin Ann, Daniel Edward, Katherine Alane. *Education:* Attended Westminster College and University of Utah. *Politics:* "Environmentalist." *Religion:* Lutheran.

ADDRESSES: Home—1460 Conifer Trail, Elizabeth, CO 80107. *E-mail*—aferguson@sprynet.com.

CAREER: Author of children's books.

AWARDS, HONORS: Edgar Allan Poe Award, Mystery Writers of America, 1990, Belgium Children's Choice Award, and International Reading Association's Young

Adult Choice citation, all for *Show Me the Evidence;* Children's Crown Classic citation, for *Cricket and the Crackerbox Kid;* New York Public Library Books for the Teen Age designation, and American Library Association Recommended Book for the Reluctant Young-Adult Reader, both for *Overkill;* Edgar Allan Poe Award nomination, 1992, for *Overkill,* and 1998, for *Wolf Stalker.*

WRITINGS:

That New Pet!, illustrated by Catherine Stock, Lothrop (New York, NY), 1987.

Show Me the Evidence (for teens), Bradbury (New York, NY), 1989.

Cricket and the Crackerbox Kid, Bradbury (New York, NY), 1990.

The Practical Joke War, Bradbury (New York, NY), 1991.

Overkill (for teens), Bradbury (New York, NY), 1992.

Stardust, Bradbury (New York, NY), 1993.

Poison, Bradbury (New York, NY), 1994.

A Tumbleweed Christmas, Bradbury (New York, NY), 1995.

Secrets, Macmillan (New York, NY), 1995.

(With Ellen Conford and Lee Wardlaw) *See You in September,* Flare, 1995.

"MYSTERY SOLVERS" SERIES; WITH MOTHER, GLORIA SKURZYNSKI; FOR YOUNG ADULTS

Mystery of the Spooky Shadow, Troll Publications (Matewah, NJ), 1996.

Mystery of the Fire in the Sky, Troll Publications (Matewah, NJ), 1997.

Mystery of the Haunted Silver Mine, Troll Publications (Matewah, NJ), 1997.

Mystery of the Vanishing Creatures, Troll Publications (Matewah, NJ), 1997.

"NATIONAL PARK" MYSTERY SERIES; WITH GLORIA SKURZYNSKI; FOR YOUNG ADULTS

Wolf Stalker, National Geographic Society (Washington, DC), 1997.

Rage of Fire, National Geographic Society (Washington, DC), 1998.

Cliff Hanger, National Geographic Society (Washington, DC), 1999.

Deadly Waters, National Geographic Society (Washington, DC), 1999.

Ghost Horses, National Geographic Society (Washington, DC), 2000.

The Hunted, National Geographic Society (Washington, DC), 2000.

Over the Edge, National Geographic Society (Washington, DC), 2001.

Valley of Death, National Geographic Society (Washington, DC), 2001.

Running Scared, National Geographic Society (Washington, DC), 2002.

Out of the Deep, National Geographic Society (Washington, DC), 2002.

Escape from Fear, National Geographic Society (Washington, DC), 2002.

Buried Alive, National Geographic Society (Washington, DC), 2003.

SIDELIGHTS: Alane Ferguson has written a number of books for young adults and children. Many of her books deal with multicultural issues and present young people solving mysteries. With her mother, Gloria Skurzynski, Ferguson has authored the popular "National Park" mystery series, all of which are set in America's national parks and involve the Landon family. The first novel in the series, *Wolf Stalker,* was nominated for the Mystery Writers Association's Edgar Allan Poe Award.

Ferguson once explained to *CA* how she came to write her first book: "All through my childhood I talked nonstop to my parents, my four sisters, and to my dolls. I always loved communicating but never wanted to commit my thoughts to the page. To me, ideas were fluid and needed to be unfettered by pen and paper. That conviction dogged me throughout my adolescence and well into adulthood. But when my oldest daughter was less than thrilled at the announcement of the upcoming birth of my second child, I decided to comfort her on paper. *That New Pet!,* a picture book, was born right along with my son. And so was my desire to write."

That New Pet! tells the story of the disruptions that can occur when a new baby comes into a family's life. This unusual family, however, is made up of Joanne and Teddy, parents of the copper-haired infant, and

Crackers the parrot, Bones the dog, and Siam the cat. The three animals, at first disturbed and jealous of the "new pet," finally to come to love and accept the new family member. Writing for *Horn Book,* Ethel R. Twichell noted that the book is suffused with "good nature and good humor." Reviewing *That New Pet!* for *Publishers Weekly,* Diane Roback stated, "Ferguson's first book contains the warm ring of truth."

Ferguson turned to writing novels for young teens with her next work, *Show Me the Evidence.* In this work "the story is convincing, the emotions intense, and the suspense exceptionally well maintained," according to Roger Sutton, writing for the *Bulletin of the Center for Children's Books.* Janaan, a teenage girl from a strict, old-world Arab family, is understandably shaken when her baby brother dies of Sudden Infant Death Syndrome (SIDS). Within six months, two other babies with whom Janaan has had contact also die, and she finds herself accused of murder. Janaan and her best friend, Lauren, must unravel the mystery and prove Janaan's innocence.

One of the subthemes of *Show Me the Evidence,* the joys and strains of growing friendships, also surfaces in Ferguson's *Cricket and the Crackerbox Kid.* Written for middle-grade readers, it is the story of Cricket Winslow, an only child with no friends who gets caught up in a snobby, well-to-do clique. However, she soon meets Dominic, a "crackerbox kid" from the wrong side of town. The two become best friends until they discover that Treasure, the beloved dog Cricket rescued from the pound, is really Dominic's recently lost pet. A trial and a jury of fellow fifth graders must then decide the true owner of the dog. When the trial is over, no one is able to answer Cricket's question, "Is legally right the same thing as just plain right?" Carolyn K. Jenks stated in a *Horn Book* review that the two main characters, who "interact in friendship, anger, and sorrow—are honest and believable, as is their love for one beautiful springer spaniel."

A more lighthearted look at friendship is included in Ferguson's tale of sibling rivalry, *The Practical Joke War,* when middle child Taffy discovers that her "friend" Susan is really interested in Taffy's brother, Russell. The main plot of the book revolves around Taffy, Russell, and their younger brother, Eddy, who engage in an all-out war of pranks and practical jokes, complete with shifting alliances, shaving cream, and precariously perched buckets of water. Reviewer Todd Morning praised the book in *School Library Journal,* stating that it "accurately portrays the rough-and-tumble of family life."

Ferguson returns to murder mystery in *Overkill,* another novel for young teens. High school senior Lacey Brighton, dealing with her parents' divorce and a rocky relationship with her older sister, seeks out a therapist to help her understand the violent nightmares she has been having. In one of these dreams, Lacey stabs her best friend, Celeste, with whom she recently argued. When Celeste is found dead, Lacey reveals her dream to the police and is subsequently arrested for the crime. Released on bail arranged by her lawyer-sister, Lacey learns about the criminal justice system and finds out some painful truths about the loyalty of friends during times of crisis. According to Patricia Gosda, writing for *Voice of Youth Advocates,* "the tension builds until the identity of the killer is revealed in a neat, satisfying conclusion."

Providing the tension in Ferguson's 1993 book, *Stardust,* is the more mundane crisis of eleven-year-old Haley Loring who, for the past several years, has portrayed Samantha Love on a popular television sitcom. Grown out of the part, Haley and her family move to a small town where she tries to fit in with the rest of the sixth graders, but finds herself relying on Samantha's tough-talking persona to help her get along. In the end, however, Haley realizes she can "dare to be herself, and find real friends," as summarized by Susan W. Hunter in a review for *School Library Journal.*

Ferguson has coauthored a number of young-adult mystery novels with her mother, Skurzynski. The pair collaborated on the "Mystery Solvers" series before launching the "National Park" mystery series for the National Geographic Society. In each novel for the latter series, the setting is one of America's national parks and the mystery revolves around the Landon family, a veterinarian mother, a photographer father, and the two siblings Jack and Ashley Landon. In the process of solving a mystery, Jack and Ashley also learn something about nature and the importance of preserving its beauties.

The first novel in the series, *Wolf Stalker,* is set in Yellowstone Park, where park officials have recently reintroduced wolves. When a nearby rancher's dog is killed and the wolves are suspected, someone begins hunting the creatures. But Jack and Ashley track down the real culprit and, by doing so, save the wolves. Elizabeth Drennan of *Booklist* praised *Wolf Stalker* as a "fast-paced novel filled with nature facts and great descriptions of natural phenomena." In *Cliff Hanger* the Landons visit Mesa Verde Park with their foster daughter, Lucky. A threatening cougar in the area, combined with Lucky's mysterious doings, lead to what Ilene Cooper in *Booklist* described as "a spine-chilling conclusion." *The Hunted* finds the Landons in Glacier National Park, where they track down poachers preying on bear cubs and assist a Mexican boy, an illegal alien who is living in the rugged wilderness. Janet Gillen in *School Library Journal* called *The Hunted* "an exciting adventure." *Ghost Horses* finds the Landons in Zion National Park with their two new foster children, both members of the Shoshone Indian tribe. A flash flood, the mysterious deaths of mustang horses, and personal conflicts between the children create what Ann Cook in *School Library Journal* called "an exciting and (don't tell anybody) educational read."

Ferguson once commented: "A good bit of the energy I once flung around in spoken words is now committed to paper. As I travel to schools across the country, I see many students whose own communication stops exactly where mine used to: in talking to friends. I try to convert them. If there is a satisfaction beyond my own storytelling, it is the opportunity to stoke the writing fire in others. The pure fun of creating characters and worlds is catching, and the rewards are permanent.

"My home is always filled with my children and their friends. So many come so often that they're almost family, and I've given them a name—my 'almosters.' This large and varied group of kids will talk about what worries them, what excites them, and what makes them laugh, and why. I pay attention to what they're saying and take their concerns seriously. Often I try to help them with their problems, but mostly, just listening is enough. Though I would never betray the secrets of these young people, they make me aware of the kinds of difficulties—and joys—that fill their world, and these things I *can* write about. As I hear them articulate their thoughts and dreams, new characters for future stories come to life in my imagination. The characters in my books are based on a combination of the child in me, my own children, and the almosters who share my days (and my refrigerator!).

"It's a joy to receive letters from children who've felt as if they've met Cricket in *Cricket and the Crackerbox Kid,* or have laughed at the jokes in *The Practical Joke War,* or were scared by the twists and turns of my mystery novels. When they connect back to me, I feel as though I'm spinning stories for an ever-widening circle of friends. What a marvelous reward for setting my thoughts onto paper!"

BIOGRAPHICAL AND CRITICAL SOURCES:

PERIODICALS

Booklist, January 1, 1993, p. 801; March 15, 1993, p. 1345; December 15, 1997, Elizabeth Drennan, review of *Wolf Stalker,* p. 698; June 1, 1998, Lauren Peterson, review of *Rage of Fire,* p. 1769; April 15, 1999, Ilene Cooper, review of *Cliff Hanger,* p. 1532; June 1, 2000, Anne O'Malley, review of *The Hunted,* p. 1898; December 15, 2000, Denise Wilms, review of *Ghost Horses,* p. 821.

Book Report, November-December, 1997, Mary Hofmann, review of *Secrets,* p. 34.

Bulletin of the Center for Children's Books, April, 1989, Roger Sutton, review of *Show Me the Evidence,* p. 193.

Horn Book, December, 1986, Ethel R. Twichell, review of *That New Pet!,* p. 732; July-August, 1990, Carolyn K. Jenks, review of *Cricket and the Crackerbox Kid,* p. 453.

Kirkus Reviews, April 15, 1993, p. 527.

Locus, May, 1994, p. 48.

New Advocate, spring, 1994, p. 820.

New York Times Book Review, January 18, 1987, p. 28.

Publishers Weekly, December 12, 1986, Diane Roback, review of *That New Pet!,* p. 51; November 21, 1994, review of *Poison,* p. 78; May 12, 1997, review of *Secrets,* p. 76.

School Library Journal, March, 1987, p. 143; June, 1991, Todd Morning, review of *The Practical Joke War,* p. 102; June, 1993, Susan W. Hunter, review of *Stardust,* p. 105; January, 1995, Lisa Dennis, review of *Poison,* p. 137; March, 1996, Susan W. Hunter, review of *See You in September,* p. 218; October, 1996, Jane Marino, review of *Tumbleweed Christmas,* p. 35; July, 1997, Nancy Schimmel, review of *Secrets,* p. 93; January, 1998, Marlene Gawron, review of *Wolf Stalker,* p. 114; July, 1998, Janet Gillen, review of *Rage of Fire,*

p. 99; May, 1999, Jana R. Fine, review of *Cliff Hanger,* p. 130; October, 1999, Linda L. Plevak, review of *Deadly Waters,* p. 158; August, 2000, Janet Gillen, review of *The Hunted,* p. 190; November, 2000, Ann Cook, review of *Ghost Horses,* p. 162.

Voice of Youth Advocates, April, 1993, Patricia Gosda, review of *Overkill,* p. 24.

ONLINE

Bring Utah Authors and Illustrators to Your School, http://www.rickwalton.com/utahauth/ (November 5, 2003), "Alane Ferguson."

Children's Literature Comprehensive Database, http://www.childrenslit.com/ (March 20, 2003), Donna Freedman, "Nothing Will Engage You Like a Murder: Young-Adult Mystery Author Alane Ferguson."*

* * *

FINE, Carla 1946-

PERSONAL: Born May 29, 1946, in New York, NY; daughter of Benjamin (a writer and educator) and Lillian (a professor of literature; maiden name, Chafetz) Fine; married Harry Reiss (a physician), September 3, 1968 (died, 1989). *Education:* New York University, B.A., 1968; Columbia University, M.S. (with honors), 1969.

ADDRESSES: *Home and office*—477 West 22nd St., New York, NY 10011. *Agent*—Wendy Lipkind Agency, 225 East 57th St., New York, NY 10022.

CAREER: *Colony Reporter* (weekly newspaper), Guadalajara, Mexico, assistant editor, 1969-73; writer, 1973—. Lecturer on the role of contemporary women in America to groups throughout the United States and South America, 1981—.

MEMBER: Authors Guild.

WRITINGS:

Barron's Guide to Foreign Medical Schools, Barron's (Woodbury, NY), 1979.

Married to Medicine: An Intimate Portrait of Doctors' Wives, Atheneum (New York, NY), 1981.

No Time to Say Goodbye: Surviving the Suicide of a Loved One, Doubleday (New York, NY), 1997.

Strong, Smart, and Bold: Empowering Girls for Life, Cliff Street Books (New York, NY), 2001.

Contributor of articles to periodicals, including *Cosmopolitan, Omni,* and *Woman's Day.*

SIDELIGHTS: Carla Fine interviewed more than one hundred physicians' spouses and combined that information with scientific data to write *Married to Medicine: An Intimate Portrait of Doctors' Wives.* In a review for the *Washington Post Book World,* Carol Eron called the book a "thoughtful and thorough work" with "much specific information . . . that will interest anyone who is closely related to, or contemplating becoming closely related to, a physician, as well as future doctors themselves."

In 1989, Fine's physician husband committed suicide. Faced with a range of emotions from anger and despair to shame and confusion, Fine sought help from books but could not find any that spoke to her particular situation. She wrote *No Time to Say Goodbye: Surviving the Suicide of a Loved One* in an attempt to reach out to other spouses and close family members who were living in the aftermath of a relative's suicide. *Booklist* correspondent Brian McCombie called *No Time to Say Goodbye* "a compassionate guide for dealing with the guilt, anger, and confusion." The reviewer concluded that the book is "sensitive and curative." John Langone in the *New York Times* likewise praised the title, deeming it "helpful" and noting that it "does much to lighten the anguish that suicide and contemplating it spawn."

Strong, Smart, and Bold: Empowering Girls for Life is based on the programs offered by Girls Inc., an advocacy group for girls aged six through eighteen. Fine's book outlines the principles behind Girls Inc. and offers practical advice on enhancing self-esteem, recognizing gender stereotypes, and finding meaningful lifelong interests. Kay Brodie in *Library Journal* felt that the "very readable" work "fills a niche in the market of parenting books."

Fine told *CA:* "My father, Benjamin Fine, is the author of more than twenty-eight books, and the sound of the typewriter has always been a source of comfort and inspiration for me. The written word, both in fiction and nonfiction, gives me a sense of purpose and identity.

"Mothers still advise their daughters to 'marry a nice doctor who will take care of you.' Marriage to a physician provides instant status, economic stability, and association with the most respected profession in the United States. Yet, for most women married to physicians, it means constantly disrupted plans, unpredictable hours, and a vast amount of time spent alone. In a society where being married, having children, and acquiring material wealth are often equated with the happy ending of the female American marital dream, the essential need for a woman to establish her own identity apart from her husband's accomplishments is often overlooked.

"The ironies involved in the discrepancies between appearance and reality in the lives of doctors' wives—and other women who are also married to highly successful professional men—are important to examine and explore. The majority of women married to physicians don't want to be known as 'Mrs. Doctor' any more."

BIOGRAPHICAL AND CRITICAL SOURCES:

PERIODICALS

Booklist, December 1, 1996, Brian McCombie, review of *No Time to Say Goodbye: Surviving the Suicide of a Loved One,* p. 624.

Critic, August, 1981.

Library Journal, March 1, 2001, Kay Brodie, review of *Strong, Smart, and Bold: Empowering Girls for Life,* p. 122.

New York Times, November 19, 2002, John Langone, "Two Perspectives on Suicide," p. F7.

Publishers Weekly, November 4, 1996, review of *No Time to Say Goodbye,* p. 56.

Washington Post Book World, April 5, 1981.

ONLINE

Carla Fine Home Page, http://www.carlafine.com (September 26, 2003).*

* * *

FLETCHER, Susan (Clemens) 1951-

Susan Fletcher

PERSONAL: Born May 28, 1951, in Pasadena, CA; daughter of Leland Phipps (a chemical engineer; in sales) and Reba Gail (a teacher; maiden name, Montgomery) Clemens; married Jerry Fletcher (a marketing consultant), June 4, 1977; children: Kelly. *Education:* University of California—Santa Barbara, B.A. (with highest honors), 1973; University of Michigan, M.A., 1974.

ADDRESSES: *Home and office*—32475 Armitage Rd., Wilsonville, OR 97070; fax: 503-694-5177. *Agent*—Emilie Jacobson, Curtis Brown Ltd., 10 Astor Pl., New York, NY 10003. *E-mail*—susanfletcher@centurytel.net.

CAREER: Campbell-Mithun (advertising agency), Minneapolis, MN, and Denver, CO, media buyer, 1974-77, advertising copywriter, 1977-79; Portland Community College, Portland, OR, lecturer, 1988-90; writer, 1990—. Vermont College, teacher of writing for children.

MEMBER: Society of Children's Book Writers and Illustrators, Authors Guild, Authors League of America, Phi Beta Kappa.

AWARDS, HONORS: Mary Jane Carr Young Readers Award, Oregon Institute of Literary Arts, 1990, for *Dragon's Milk;* "young adults' choice selections,"

International Reading Association, 1991, for *Dragon's Milk,* and c. 1993, for *Flight of the Dragon Kyn;* American Library Association, citations among "best books for young adults," c. 1993, for *Flight of the Dragon Kyn,* and c. 1998, for *Shadow Spinner,* and citation among "notable books for older readers," c. 1998, for *Shadow Spinner;* citation among "notable children's trade books in the field of social studies," Children's Book Council, blue ribbon, *Bulletin of the Center for Children's Books,* and "best book" designation, *School Library Journal,* all c. 1998, for *Shadow Spinner.*

WRITINGS:

NOVELS FOR CHILDREN

The Haunting Possibility (mystery), Crosswinds, 1988.
Dragon's Milk (fantasy), Atheneum (New York, NY), 1989.
The Stuttgart Nanny Mafia, Atheneum (New York, NY), 1991.
Flight of the Dragon Kyn ("prequel" to *Dragon's Milk*), Atheneum (New York, NY), 1993.
Sign of the Dove (sequel to *Dragon's Milk*), Atheneum (New York, NY), 1996.
Shadow Spinner, Atheneum (New York, NY), 1998.
Walk across the Sea, Atheneum Books for Young Readers (New York, NY), 2001.

Contributor to periodicals, including *Ms., Woman's Day, Family Circle, Mademoiselle,* and *New Advocate.*

SIDELIGHTS: Susan Fletcher is the author of children's novels, including the fantasy novel trilogy containing *Dragon's Milk,* its "prequel," *Flight of the Dragon, Kyn,* and its sequel, *Sign of the Dove. Dragon's Milk,* whose imagined setting was derived from pictures of Wales, specifically revolves around a babysitting adventure. Kaeldra, the protagonist, is an adopted child whose green eyes identify her as a descendent of the dragon-sayers, humans who are able to communicate with dragons telepathically. When her younger sister becomes ill and can only be healed by dragon's milk, Kaeldra must search for a dragon. She finds one and agrees to babysit for its three offspring, called draclings, in exchange for the milk. The mother goes out to find food, planning to return in a short while; unfortunately, she is killed, leaving Kaeldra to protect the draclings from men who want to destroy them. Critics found *Dragon's Milk* entertaining and imaginative. Focusing on the novel's blend of action, suspense, magic, and romance, they also noted Fletcher's clever and convincing portrayal of the draclings.

In the *Something about the Author Autobiography Series* (*SAAS*), Fletcher remembered the genesis of *Dragon's Milk,* her second novel for children. "While I was sending out *The Haunting Possibility,* an idea began to tease at the edges of my mind. . . . [The local librarian] had directed me to some really fine fantasy novels for children, and I began to be drawn to that genre. I envisioned a book consisting of ten or twelve feminist fairy tales. [Although a life-long fan of fairy tales,] I began to be troubled by their messages for girls. It seemed to me that the typical fairy-tale heroine . . . would sit around being beautiful, singing nicely, and being kind to birds and animals until her boyfriend—The Prince—came along and solved all her problems for her. . . . So I decided to write a story about a girl who had the courage to solve her own problems. I thought back to my childhood and tried to remember what I ever did that required courage.

Fletcher drew on her own experiences as a babysitter in crafting *Dragon's Milk.* The author recalled how hard it was to babysit for four unruly little boys, commenting in *SAAS:* "Now, that took courage. Or stupidity—I'm not sure which. So I envisioned a short fairy tale in which a spunky, fairy-tale girl would baby-sit something fairy-taleish, like . . . dragons!" The tale was initially imagined as a short story, however that changed after she first told the story to her then-young daughter. "She was enthralled—and her enthusiasm infected me," Fletcher stated in *SAAS,* "I decided that I wanted to spend more time with this story—that I would make it into a novel. Little did I suspect that it eventually would turn into a trilogy and take up nearly a decade of my life."

Fletcher detailed in *SAAS* how some other personal experiences are manifested in her writing. As an early teenager, after years of caring for her pet bird, she gave it away and it died shortly thereafter. "[Although Brecky was old], I am convinced . . . that she died of a broken heart. . . . I wonder if this is why birds play such a big part in my books. There are so many birds—doves and falcons in my dragon books, pigeons in my book about *Shadow Spinner*. Maybe this is my way of atoning for what I did to Brecky. Or maybe it simply reflects the affection I felt for all my birds." Another of her pets, Nimbus the cat, has also been influential. "While I wrote *Dragon's Milk,* Nimbus sat on my lap, purring and kneading my legs with her claws. It's no coincidence that the draclings thrum and knead Kaeldra's legs with their talons."

Other intimate details of Fletcher's life have surfaced in her stories. Although now of average height, as a child she grew faster than her peers. She reported in *SAAS* that "the main characters in my first two novels are tall and gawky, because that's how I still think of myself." Fletcher's daughter, Kelly, is intertwined throughout her writing. As she noted in *SAAS:* "Kelly has influenced my writing in many ways over the years. Bits of her life sometimes make their way into my books. After reading parts of *The Stuttgart Nanny Mafia,* Kelly protested, 'Mom, You plagiarized my life!'" At age thirty-nine, Fletcher was diagnosed with cancer. In her *SAAS* essay, she wrote: "I've never written directly about my year of fighting cancer, and I find it hard to do so even now. But the experience has infiltrated my work. Once during the time when I was writing *Sign of the Dove,* I heard a Jewish couple speak about the people who helped the German Jews during the Holocaust. . . . Suddenly, I realized that the book I was writing was about rescuers—people who help those who are in trouble, at risk to themselves and with no expectation of gain. On some level, it was about the people who helped *me.* And so the book is dedicated to them—my rescuers."

Fletcher's research, revisions, and writing colleagues are all important and cherished parts of her writing process. Research, as she described in *SAAS,* provides her "the grounding to be able to build up a believable world." Her research is based within a library as well as outside of it. "For *Flight of the Dragon Kyn,*" she noted in *SAAS,* "I joined a zoo program and worked with birds of prey, cleaning the mutes and castings from their cages, cutting up baby chickens and mice for them to eat." She further revealed in *SAAS:* "I play for awhile—with my research and stray ideas—before I begin [writing]. . . . Then when I do start writing I allow myself to write really badly at first if I need to. . . . I know it will get better when I write the next draft. I *do* re-write—compulsively. . . . I wish I could get it right in the first or second draft but I just can't. So I rewrite . . . until the words *sound* right." As for her writing colleagues, which she considers "dear friends," Fletcher commented in *SAAS:* "The nurturing and concrete help I've received from these friends has fed my growth as a writer. Ellen Howard, for instance, connected me with my editor and christened my baby dragons 'draclings.' But there's something even more—an energy, a synergy. At our meetings, ideas are kicked up like dust on a country road. And I love listening to my friends' stories! They show me what is possible, and the excitement I feel about their work spurs me to better my own."

More recently, Fletcher told *CA* about her inspiration for writing *Shadow Spinner.* "One day, as I was reading the book review section of our local newspaper, I found a review of a book written by a woman who had grown up in a Middle Eastern harem. She was about my age, and something about this just intrigued me. It wasn't the idea of women in harems. It was the idea of children growing up there. What must that be like?

"I read everything I could get my hands on about children and Middle Eastern harems. I remember going to bookstores and libraries, just *hungry.* While I was on this obsessive reading binge, I bumped into Shahrazad.

"Of course, I knew about Shahrazad. But somehow I hadn't thought about her for a long time. What an amazing character! She saved her life, and the lives of all the young women in the city where she lived, not by any physical feats she performed, not even by her death-defying nightly storytelling act, but by the virtue of the life-affirming nature of storytelling itself. This led me to a meditation on what are good stories? Why are they valuable? How can they save our lives, in more than the physical sense?"

Fletcher continued: "There were several seeds of inspiration for *Walk across the Sea.* First, for some reason, I was haunted by lighthouses. For years before I began to write the book—a decade at least—I had been fascinated with them. I honestly can't explain why. The smell of the kerosene, the heat of the beacon as it passes, the raging storms, the inevitable suggestion of ghosts, the romantic image of a guiding light in the dark—I don't know what it was. For ten years, while I was writing other things, I explored the lighthouses up and down the Oregon and Washington coasts at every opportunity. One day, when I went to visit my parents in Brookings, Oregon, they arranged an outing just south of the Oregon border to the lighthouse in Crescent City, California.

"As soon as I saw it, I knew it was *the one.* It looked just like a house, a cute little house, only with a tower rising up out of it. Children had actually lived there, actually helped tend the light. Also, it was on a tidal island. During low tide, you could walk out to it; during high tide, it was surrounded by water. There was something about that place that drew me, something I couldn't quite get hold of. Eleanor Cameron has said that fantasy novels have a sense of 'the compelling power of place.' So, of course, do historical novels. Part of what was drawing me about this particular place was a characteristic concern of fantasy writer: borders, thresholds, the permeable membrane between seen and unseen worlds, in this case the above-water world and the undersea world.

"Second, when I was researching the history of the lighthouse, I caught sight of a little index card on the wall of the historical museum in Crescent City. On that card was typed, with a faded ribbon, the bare outline of the events of the expulsion of the Chinese from Crescent City in 1886—taken from their homes; loaded into carts; put on a boat and shipped to San Francisco. I was shocked. Given what I knew about the history of racism in this country, I probably shouldn't have been. But I was—shocked also that I had never heard about it. It seemed to me that, if I didn't know about this, probably a lot of other people might not, either. It seemed to me that we all *ought* to know about it—that, like the interning of the Japanese Americans during World War II, this chapter in our history should be laid out onto the air.

"Finally, I wanted to revisit and explore the intense and lonely experience I had when I began to question my religious faith. It would have helped me at the time to have company, to know that other young people might be having the same questions and doubts."

BIOGRAPHICAL AND CRITICAL SOURCES:

BOOKS

Something about the Author Autobiography Series, Volume 25, Gale (Detroit, MI), 1998.

PERIODICALS

Booklist, January 15, 1994, Deborah Abbott, review of *Flight of the Dragon Kyn,* p. 931; May 1, 1996, Sally Estes, review of *Sign of the Dove,* p. 1506; June 1, 1998, Hazel Rochman, review of *Shadow Spinner,* p. 1746; November 1, 2001, Hazel Rochman, review of *Walk across the Sea,* p. 476.

Book Report, March-April, 1990, Sylvia Feicht, review of *Dragon's Milk,* p. 31; March-April, 1994, Sylvia Feicht, review of *Flight of the Dragon Kyn,* p. 34; January-February, 1997, Sylvia Feicht, review of *Sign of the Dove,* p. 34; January-February, 1999, Vickie Hoff, review of *Shadow Spinner,* p. 60.

Horn Book, January-February, 1990, Ann A. Flowers, review of *Dragon's Milk,* p. 69; January-February, 1994, Ann A. Flowers, review of *Flight of the Dragon Kyn,* p. 73; September-October, 1996, Ann A. Flowers, review of *Sign of the Dove,* p. 595; July-August, 1998, Mary M. Burns, review of *Shadow Spinner,* p. 488.

Kirkus Reviews, October 15, 2001, review of *Walk across the Sea,* p. 1482.

Kliatt, July, 2003, Claire Rosser, review of *Walk across the Sea,* p. 20.

Magazine of Fantasy and Science Fiction, May, 1993, Orson Scott Card, review of *Dragon's Milk,* p. 39.

Publishers Weekly, August 16, 1991, review of *The Stuttgart Nanny Mafia,* p. 58; November 5, 2001, review of *Walk across the Sea,* p. 69.

School Library Journal, April, 1988, Kathy Fritts, review of *The Haunting Possibility,* p. 119; November, 1989, Susan M. Harding, review of *Dragon's Milk,* p. 106; October, 1991, Judie Porter, review of *The Stuttgart Nanny Mafia,* p. 122; November, 1993, Margaret A. Chang, review of *Flight of the Dragon Kyn,* p. 108; May, 1996, Lisa Dennis, review of *Sign of the Dove,* p. 112; June, 1998, Patricia A. Dollisch, review of *Shadow Spinner,* p. 145; November, 2001, William McLoughlin, review of *Walk across the Sea,* p. 154.

* * *

FLORMAN, Samuel C(harles) 1925-

PERSONAL: Born January 19, 1925, in New York, NY; son of Arthur M. and Hannah (Weingarten) Florman; married Judith Hadas (a teacher), August 19, 1951; children: David, Jonathan. *Education:* Dartmouth College, B.S., 1944, C.E., 1973; Columbia University, M.A. , 1947.

ADDRESSES: Home—55 Central Park W, New York, NY 10023. *Office*—Kreisler Borg Florman, 97 Montgomery St., Scarsdale, NY 10583. *E-mail*—scf@aol.com.

CAREER: Associated with Hegeman Harris Co. in Venezuela, 1948, Thompson-Starrett Co., New York, NY, 1949-53, and Joseph P. Blitz, Inc., New York, NY, 1953-55; Kreisler Borg Florman Construction Co., Scarsdale, NY, principal, 1955—; writer. Hospital for Joint Disease, New York, NY, trustee, 1976; New York Hall of Science, trustee, 1996; Thayer School of Engineering, Dartmouth College, Hanover, NH, Board of Overseers. *Military service:* U.S. Navy, 1944-46.

MEMBER: American Society of Civil Engineers (fellow), American Society for Engineering Education, National Society of Professional Engineers, National Academy of Engineering, New York Academy of Sciences.

AWARDS, HONORS: Stevens Award, Stevens Institute of Technology, 1976, for articles and books dealing with the relationship of technology to the general culture; Ralph Coats Roe Medal, American Society of Mechanical Engineers, 1982; Robert Fletcher award, Thayer School of Engineering, 1983.

WRITINGS:

Engineering and the Liberal Arts, McGraw-Hill (New York, NY), 1968.

The Existential Pleasures of Engineering, St. Martin's Press (New York, NY), 1976.

Blaming Technology: The Irrational Search for Scapegoats, St. Martin's Press (New York, NY), 1981.

The Civilized Engineer, St. Martin's Press (New York, NY), 1987.

The Introspective Engineer, St. Martin's Press (New York, NY), 1996.

The Aftermath: A Novel of Survival, St. Martin's Press (New York, NY), 2001.

Contributing editor of *Harper's* magazine. Contributor of over one hundred articles to professional journals and popular magazines.

SIDELIGHTS: Samuel Florman is a writer as well as a practicing engineer and vice president of Kreisler Borg Florman Construction Company in Scarsdale, New York. As a writer he is best known for his popularization of the engineering profession in such books as *The Existential Pleasures of Engineering,* and *The Civilized Engineer.*

Florman is not only an optimistic supporter for technology; he also firmly believes that engineers should be well educated in the humanities as well. In an interview with *IEEE Technology & Science Magazine,* Florman told Terri Bookman, "I think that engineers have been short-changed by their advisors and by their own inhibitions and by their prospective employers. And then, sometimes, they wake up and they're forty and they regret they didn't take humanities courses, or when they're in their thirties, they're thinking of leadership participation in society and wish they had taken more of certain types of courses. When they get older, they think about the meaning of life, they wish even more that they had taken these courses."

The main themes of Florman's books are engineering and the humanities, society's perceptions of engineers and engineering, the relationship between engineering and nature, ethical issues for engineers, and the changing attitudes toward technology.

Florman addressed the public's fears of technology in his 1981 book *Blaming Technology: The Irrational Search for Scapegoats.* Florman told Bookman, "Well, in the 1960s, young people, in particular, were rebelling against a lot of things, and technology, seeming to be a part of what the 'establishment' was, came in for its share of blame."

The Introspective Engineer asked rhetorical questions about the absence of engineers from popular culture and why engineers, who have clearly revolutionized our lives, are never heroes of novels. Florman remedied the situation in 2001 with the publication of his first novel, *The Aftermath: A Novel of Survival.* In this end-of-civilization scenario, a comet has hit Earth and the only survivors are in small communities in South Africa and Madagascar and a group of engineers on a seminar cruise in the Indian Ocean.

Since almost everything is destroyed, the Africans and the engineers get together and build a new civilization from the Stone Age up. Jackie Cassada wrote in

Library Journal, "The author of several paeans to the science of engineering (*The Introspective Engineer*), first novelist Florman puts his talent as a raconteur to good use in a tale reminiscent of the expository fiction of sf's early writers."

BIOGRAPHICAL AND CRITICAL SOURCES:

PERIODICALS

Booklist, March 1, 1996, Gilbert Taylor, review of *The Introspective Engineer,* p. 1113.

Changing Times, April, 1983, review of *Blaming Technology: The Irrational Search for Scapegoats,* p. 81.

Chemical & Engineering News, July 19, 1982, William Spindel, review of *Blaming Technology,* p. 45.

Commentary, June, 1982, Jeffrey Marsh, review of *Blaming Technology,* p. 67.

Commonweal, December 18, 1987, Carl Mitcham, review of *The Civilized Engineer,* p. 758.

Fortune, February 22, 1982, Harry Schwartz, review of *Blaming Technology,* p. 161.

Isis, December, 1998, John M. Staudenmaier, review of *The Civilized Engineer,* p. 717.

Issues in Science and Technology, fall, 1990, Joseph Bordogna, Paul E. Torgersen, John A. Alic, Richard B. Gold, Don Weinert, comments on Samuel C. Florman's article "Producing Engineers for the 'Real World', " in *Issues in Science and Technology,* spring, 1990 (letter to the editor), p. 20.

Kirkus Reviews, July 15, 1981, review of *Blaming Technology,* p. 916; March 1, 1996, review of *The Introspective Engineer,* p. 1113; October 1, 2001, review of *The Aftermath: A Novel of Survival,* p. 1381.

Library Journal, October 1, 1981, Daniel La Rossa, review of *Blaming Technology,* p. 1911; March 1, 1982, review of *Blaming Technology,* p. 51; June 1, 1987, R. E. Bilstein, review of *The Civilized Engineer,* p. 123; March 1, 1998, Ellis Mount, Barbara A. List, review of *The Civilized Engineer,* p. 33; December, 2001, Jackie Cassada, review of *The Aftermath,* p. 181.

New Scientist, April 27, 1996, Cliff Friend, review of *The Introspective Engineer,* p. 48.

New York Times, December 5, 1982, review of *Blaming Technology,* p. 56; January 9, 1983, review of *Blaming Technology,* p. 39.

New York Times Book Review, December 20, 1981, Lynn White, Jr., review of *Blaming Technology,* p. 5; February 9, 1997, review of *The Introspective Engineer,* p. 32; April 28, 2002, Gerald Jonas, review of *The Aftermath,* p. 20.

Public Works, September, 1982, review of *Blaming Technology,* p. 27.

Publishers Weekly, July 24, 1981, Genevieve Stuttaford, review of *Blaming Technology,* p. 140; February 13, 1987, review of *The Civilized Engineer,* p. 83; November 12, 2001, review of *The Aftermath,* p. 41.

Reason, December, 1996, review of *The Existential Pleasures of Engineering,* p. 42.

Science Books and Films, spring, 1982, review of *Blaming Technology,* p. 203; spring, 1987, review of *The Civilized Engineer,* p. 37.

Science News, March 30, 2002, review of *The Aftermath,* p. 207.

SciTech Book News, May, 1987, review of *The Civilized Engineer,* p. 30; November, 1996, review of *The Introspective Engineer,* p. 81.

Technology and Culture, January, 1989, Elting Morison, review of *The Civilized Engineer,* p. 138; October, 1997, Sarah K. A. Pfatteicher, review of *The Existential Pleasures of Engineering,* p. 1022.

ONLINE

Al Teich's Technology and the Future Toolkit Web site, http://www.alteich.com/ (May 1, 2002), articles and an interview with Samuel Florman.*

* * *

FORNI, P(ier) M(assimo) 1951-

PERSONAL: Born October 16, 1951, in Bologna, Italy. *Education:* Attended Universita degli Studi, Venice, 1970-71; Universita degli Studi, Pavia, laurea in Lettere e Filosofia (cum laude), 1974; graduate study at Universita Cattolica del Sacro Cuore, 1974-77; University of California, Los Angeles, Ph.D., 1981.

ADDRESSES: Home—707 Howard Rd., Baltimore, MD 21208. *Office*—219 Gilman Hall, Johns Hopkins University, Baltimore, MD 21218; fax: 410-516-8403. *E-mail*—choosingcivility@jhu.edu.

CAREER: Educator, editor, and author. Istituto Gonzaga, Milan, Italy, instructor, 1976-78; University of California, Los Angeles, research assistant at Center for Medieval and Renaissance Studies, 1980-81, lecturer in Italian, 1981-82; University of Pittsburgh, Pittsburgh, PA, assistant professor of Italian, 1983-85; Johns Hopkins University, Baltimore, MD, assistant professor, 1985-90, associate professor, 1990-95, professor of Italian literature, 1995, cofounder and codirector, Johns Hopkins Civility Project, 1997, and codirector of symposium "Reassessing Civility: Forms and Values at the End of the Century," 1998. Visiting professor at University of Virginia, 1985, University of California, Davis, 1992, University of Pennsylvania, 1993, and Universita degli Studi, Venice, 1994. Gives readings from his works.

MEMBER: Associazione Internazionale per gli Studi di Lingua e Letteratura Italiana, American Association of Teachers of Italian, American Association for Italian Studies, American Boccaccio Association.

AWARDS, HONORS: Almo Collegio Borromeo competition winner, 1971, alumni fellow, 1981; Lerici prize, 1986, for *Il Legame musaico;* grant from National Endowment for the Humanities, 1987; Smarties Book Prize, 1990, and Selezione Bancarellino prize, 1992, both for *La Collina degli agrifogli;* fellow at Villa i Tatti, Harvard University Center for Italian Renaissance Studies, 1993-94; Kenan grant, 1994; Lila Wallace/*Readers Digest* grant, 1994; *Adventures in Speech* named *Choice* Outstanding Book of 1996; School of Continuing Studies and Johns Hopkins University Alumni Association Excellence in Teaching Award, 1998; Certificate of Appreciation, Cecil County, MD, Health Department, 1998.

WRITINGS:

(Editor with Giorgio Cavallini) Fredi Chiappelli, *Il Legame musaico: Saggi di letteratura italiana,* Storia e Letteratura (Rome, Italy), 1984.

(Editor) Giovanni Boccaccio, *Ninfale Fiesolano,* Mursia (Milan, Italy), 1991.

(Translator from the English) P. Fisk, *La Collina degli agrifogli* (translation of *Midnight Blue*), Dragno (Milan, Italy), 1991.

Forme complesse nel Decameron, Olschki (Florence, Italy), 1992.

(Coeditor) *Forma e parola: Studi in memoria di Fredi Chiappelli,* Bulzoni (Rome, Italy), 1992.

(Editor) *I fioretti di San Francesco,* Garzanti (Milan, Italy), 1993.

(Editor, with Renzo Bragantini) *Lessico critico Decameroniano,* Bollati Boringhieri (Turin, Italy), 1993.

Adventures in Speech: Rhetoric and Narration in Boccaccio's "Decameron," University of Pennsylvania Press (Philadelphia, PA), 1996.

Hotel pace dei monti (poems), Greco & Greco (Milan, Italy), 1996.

Choosing Civility: The Twenty-five Rules of Considerate Conduct, St. Martin's Press (New York, NY), 2002.

Contributor of articles, poems, and reviews to periodicals in Italian and English, including *Italian Quarterly* and *Thought.* Member of editorial board, *Carte Italiane,* 1980-81, *MLN (Modern Language Notes),* 1985—, and *Romance Quarterly,* 1993—.

SIDELIGHTS: P. M. Forni has written extensively about fourteenth-century writer Giovanni Boccaccio. Forni once told *CA:* "In the field of literary criticism, I have pursued my interests in the workings of the creative process, focusing on Giovanni Boccaccio (1313-1375). In particular, I have studied the ways in which authors belonging to different centuries of Italian literature have utilized their sources. Among the modern poets and novelists on whose work I have published are Giovanni Pascoli, Carlo Emilio Gadda, Giacomo Noventa, and Luciano Erba."

In *Adventures in Speech: Rhetoric and Narration in Boccaccio's "Decameron,"* Forni examines how Boccaccio adapted some earlier traditional stories in his book and how he created original stories from familiar Italian word play. In one story, for example, the mother superior of a convent is awoken suddenly in the middle of the night. She accidently puts her lover's trousers on her head, mistaking them in the darkness for her headdress, and thus reveals her indiscretion to all the other nuns. The plot of the story is derived from an old Italian proverb, "to go around with one's trousers on one's head," meaning to always get things wrong. Victoria Kirkham, reviewing the title for *Renaissance Quarterly,* found that "Forni's project yokes classical rhetoric and contemporary literary theory—esthetic domains in which he is equally at ease—to argue notions that are as profound in their insightfulness as they are elegant in their simplicity."

In 1997 Forni cofounded Johns Hopkins University's Civility Project, a means of acquainting university students with the rules of polite behavior in a society where such niceties have long been disregarded. In addition to teaching students, the project also reached out to Baltimore high school students and to inmates in the Maryland penal system. As Forni explained to Stephen Goode in *Insight on the News:* "I would say that civility is a transcending of the self. When you're being polite and you're exercising good manners, you are transcending yourself. You go beyond yourself, and you show an active concern for the well-being of others. That's civility by any standards!" In 1998 Forni codirected "Reassessing Civility: Forms and Values at the End of the Century," an international symposium.

As an outgrowth of the Civility Project, Forni penned *Choosing Civility: The Twenty-five Rules of Considerate Conduct,* a book designed to "help readers rediscover time-honored practices that are often overlooked in our fast-paced and stressful lives," as a writer for the *Headlines@Hopkins* Web site noted. Commenting on his interest in the subject of social niceties, Forni explained: "In recent years I have approached the notions of civility, manners, and politeness. In my current work, I study those notions from historical, anthropological, psychological, and sociological points of view."

BIOGRAPHICAL AND CRITICAL SOURCES:

PERIODICALS

Insight on the News, December 29, 1997, Stephen Goode, "Johns Hopkins' Professor Forni Explores the Rules of Respect," p. 31.

Renaissance Quarterly, summer, 1998, Victoria Kirkham, review of *Adventures in Speech: Rhetoric and Narration in Boccaccio's "Decameron,"* p. 613.

ONLINE

Department of Romance Languages and Literatures, Johns Hopkins University, http://webapps.jhu.edu/romancelanguages/ (November 6, 2003), "P. M. Forni."

Dr. Forni's Civility Web site, http://www.jhu.edu/civility/ (November 6, 2003).

Headlines@Hopkins, http://www.jhu.edu/news_info/ (November 6, 2003).*

* * *

FOX, Siv Cedering
See CEDERING, Siv

* * *

FRIEDMAN, Lawrence M(eir) 1930-

PERSONAL: Born April 2, 1930, in Chicago, IL; son of I. M. and Ethel (Shapiro) Friedman; married Leah Feigenbaum, March 27, 1955; children: Jane, Amy. *Education:* University of Chicago, A.B., 1948, J.D. 1951, ML.L., 1953. *Religion:* Jewish. *Hobbies and other interests:* Music, literature, history, Bible studies.

ADDRESSES: Home—724 Frenchman's Rd., Palo Alto, CA 94305-1005. *Office*—School of Law, Stanford University, Nathan Abbott Way, Stanford, CA 94305-9991. *E-mail*—lmf@leland.stanford.edu.

CAREER: D'Ancona, Pflaum, Wyatt & Riskind (law firm), Chicago, IL, associate, 1955-57; St. Louis University, Law School, St. Louis, MO, 1957-61, began as assistant professor, became associate professor; University of Wisconsin, Madison, Law School, 1961-68, began as associate professor, became professor of law; Stanford University, Stanford, CA, professor of law, 1968-76, Marion Rice Kirkwood Professor of Law, 1976—. David Stouffer Memorial Lecturer, Rutgers University Law School, 1969; fellow, Center for Advanced Study in the Behavioral Sciences, 1973-74; Sibley lecturer, University of Georgia Law School, 1976; Wayne Morse lecturer, University of Oregon, 1985; fellow, Institute for Advanced Study, Berlin, Germany, 1985; Childress memorial lecturer, St. Louis University, 1987. *Military service:* U.S. Army, 1953-54; became sergeant.

MEMBER: American Academy of Arts and Sciences, Law and Society Association (president, 1979-81), American Society for Legal History (vice president, 1987-89; president, 1990—).

AWARDS, HONORS: Scribes Award, 1974, for *A History of the American Law;* Triennial award from the Order of Coif, 1976; Willard Hurst prize, 1982. LL.D. from University of Puget Sound, 1977, City University of New York, 1989, University of Lund (Sweden), 1993, John Marshall Law School, 1995, and University Macerata (Italy), 1998.

WRITINGS:

Contract Law in America, University of Wisconsin Press (Madison, WI), 1965.

Government and Slum Housing: A Century of Frustration, Rand McNally (New York, NY), 1968.

(With Stewart Macaulay) *Law and the Behavioral Sciences,* Bobbs-Merrill (Indianapolis, IN), 1969, 2nd edition, 1977.

A History of American Law, Simon & Schuster, 1973, 2nd edition, 1985.

The Legal System: A Social Science Perspective, Russell Sage Foundation (New York, NY), 1975.

Law and Society: An Introduction, Prentice-Hall (Englewood Cliffs, NJ), 1978.

(With Robert V. Percival) *The Roots of Justice: Crime and Punishment in Alameda County, California, 1870-1910,* University of North Carolina Press (Chapel Hill, NC), 1981.

(With Curt D. Furberg and David L. DeMets) *Fundamentals of Clinical Trials,* J. Wright/PSG Inc. (Boston, MA), 1982.

American Law, Norton (New York, NY), 1984.

Total Justice: What Americans Want from the Legal System and Why, Russell Sage Foundation (New York, NY), 1985.

Your Time Will Come: The Law of Age Discrimination and Mandatory Retirement, Russell Sage Foundation (New York, NY), 1985.

(Editor, with Harry N. Scheiber) *American Law and the Constitutional Order: Historical Perspectives,* Harvard University Press (Cambridge, MA), 1988.

The Republic of Choice: Law, Authority, and Culture, Harvard University Press (Cambridge, MA) 1990.

Crime and Punishment in American History, Basic Books (New York, NY), 1993.

(Editor, with Stewart Macaulay and John Stookey) *Law and Society: Readings on the Social Study of Law,* Norton (New York, NY), 1995.

(Editor, with Harry N. Scheiber) *Legal Culture and the Legal Profession,* Westview Press (Boulder, CO), 1996.

The Crime Conundrum: Essays on Criminal Justice, Westview Press (Boulder, CO), 1997.

The Horizontal Society, Yale University Press (New Haven, CT), 1999.

American Law in the 20th Century, Yale University Press (New Haven, CT), 2002.

Law in America: A Short History, Modern Library (New York, NY), 2002.

(Editor, with Rogelio Perez-Perdomo) *Legal Culture in the Age of Globalization: Latin America and Latin Europe,* Stanford University Press (Stanford, CA), 2003.

SIDELIGHTS: Noted Stanford law professor Lawrence M. Friedman has written and edited scholarly works on the laws and legal system of the United States. Two works in particular, *American Law* and *A History of American Law,* have earned praise for their depth, attention to detail, and coherency.

In his 1984 work *American Law,* Friedman analyzes the social forces that have shaped and are shaped by legal doctrine. The text spans the roots of American law through contemporary concerns with First Amendment rights and the problems of racial relations and equality, as dealt with under such landmark mandates as the 1954 *Brown vs. Board of Education* Supreme Court decision outlawing segregation in public schools, the Civil Rights Act of 1964, and the Voting Rights Act of 1965. Regarding *American Law, New York Times* reviewer Francis A. Allen stated that Friedman "achieves the considerable feat of raising interesting points in the discussions of almost every topic he addresses" and has the "admirable capacity of bringing together knowledge and insights gleaned from scores, perhaps hundreds," of sources, "integrating the information into a generally coherent whole." Allen concluded that the author "has proved himself a perceptive and knowledgeable guide." *Los Angeles Times Book Review* contributor Merton Kamins wrote, "The organization is logical and clearheaded. The prose is lucid, clean, laced with wit and arresting images. Simplifying but never simple-minded, this is a remarkable book."

Friedman has also written a legal reference book, the widely-acclaimed *A History of the American Law.* This overview assesses the highly complex subject of multijurisdictional American law, including sociological and anthropological subtexts, an area of special concern and expertise for the author. *New York Times Book Review* contributor Calvin A. Woodward stated that the 1985 version is both richer and more balanced than the earlier volume because of Friedman's decision to place "slightly more emphasis on noneconomic factors. Crime (and criminology and penology) and family law are given rather more, certainly more sensitive, attention than earlier." Summarizing Friedman's book, Woodward wrote, "Every law student must be in his debt, and every historian may find in his example the model for his own future work. The very least we can say is that he has provided us with the best single, coherent history of American law that now exists." Woodward concluded, "It will surely provide the introduction to the history of American law taught and learned in universities and law schools throughout this country for many years to come."

In 2002 Friedman published his sequel to *A History of the American Law, American Law in the Twentieth Century.* In this work Friedman examines three stages in the development of American law over the last century: the old order of legal formalism, the New Deal era, and the post-Reagan years. Stephen K. Shaw's review for *Library Journal* noted, "This substantial work covers both legal and historical developments and convincingly situates U.S. law in its broader social context." In *Law in America: A Short History,* Professor Friedman provides a "concise and lucid overview of the development of the law as it parallels the track of American social, economic, political, and cultural history," noted *Library Journal* contributor Philip Y. Blue. A *Kirkus Reviews* writer observed that in order to answer the question of why law is so central to American society, Friedman "sketches the relationship between the development of our society and the concomitant growth of American law from colonial times to the present."

BIOGRAPHICAL AND CRITICAL SOURCES:

PERIODICALS

Annals of the American Academy of Political and Social Science, Rhode E. Howard-Hassmann, review of *The Horizontal Society,* p. 228.

Booklist, May 15, 2002, Vernon Ford, review of *American Law in the 20th Century,* p. 1489.

Choice, October, 1999, M. Klatte, review of *The Horizontal Society,* p. 414.

Contemporary Sociology, July, 1994, John R. Stutton, review of *Crime and Punishment in American History,*, p. 574.

Criminal Law Bulletin, May-June 1994, review of *Crime and Punishment in American History,* p. 293; July-August, 1994, Alan H. Mass, review of *Crime and Punishment in American History,* p. 397.

Ethics, January, 1987, p. 505.

Harvard Law Review, May, 1994, review of *Crime and Punishment in American History,* p. 1813.

Journal of American History, December, 1983, p. 688; December, 1986, p. 724.

Journal of Interdisciplinary History, summer, 1995, Roger Lane, review of *Crime and Punishment in American History,* p. 149.

Kirkus Reviews, May 1, 2002, review of *Law in America: A Short History,* p. 635.

Legal Times, Robert J. Cottrol, February 14, 1994, review of *Crime and Punishment in American History,* p. 58.

Library Journal March 1, 1999, Ellen Gilbert, review of *The Horizontal Society,* p. 102; April 15, 2002, Philip Y. Blue, review of *Law in America,* p. 106; May 15, 2002, Stephen K. Shaw, review of *American Law in the 20th Century,* p. 112.

Los Angeles Times Book Review, January 6, 1985, p. 9; March 23, 1986, p. 14.

New York Times Book Review, December 2, 1984, Francis A. Allen, review of *American Law,* p. 73; January 19, 1986, p. 32; February 16, 1986, p. 31; May 23, 1999, Todd Gitlin, review of *The Horizontal Society.*

Perspectives on Political Science, spring, 1998, Roger Handberg, review of *The Crime Conundrum: Essays on Criminal Justice,* p. 124; winter, 2000, Joseph C. Bertolini, review of *The Horizontal Society,* p. 58.

Political Science Quarterly, winter, 1991, p. 746.

Publishers Weekly, March 8, 1999, review of *The Horizontal Society,* p. 56.

Reviews in American History, William J. Stuntz, review of *Crime and Punishment in American History,* p. 153.

Trial, April, 1994, review of *Crime and Punishment in American History,* p. 72.

Tribune Books (Chicago, IL), October 4, 1987, p. 23.*

G

GAIMAN, Neil (Richard) 1960-

PERSONAL: Born November 10, 1960, in Portchester, England; son of David Bernard (a company director) and Sheila (a pharmacist; maiden name, Goldman) Gaiman; married Mary Therese McGrath, March 14, 1985; children: Michael Richard, Holly Miranda, Madeleine Rose Elvira. *Politics:* "Wooly." *Religion:* Jewish. *Hobbies and other interests:* "Finding more bookshelf space."

ADDRESSES: *Agent*—Merilee Heifetz, Writer's House, 21 West 26th St., New York, NY 10010.

CAREER: Freelance journalist, 1983-87; full-time writer, 1987—.

MEMBER: Comic Book Legal Defense Fund (board of directors), International Museum of Cartoon Art (advisory board), Science Fiction Foundation (committee member), Society of Strip Illustrators (chair, 1988-90), British Fantasy Society.

AWARDS, HONORS: Mekon Award, Society of Strip Illustrators, and Eagle Award for best graphic novel, both 1988, both for *Violent Cases;* Eagle Award for best writer of American comics, 1990; Harvey Award for best writer, 1990 and 1991; Will Eisner Comic Industry Award for best writer of the year and best graphic album (reprint), 1991; World Fantasy Award for best short story, 1991, for "A Midsummer Night's Dream"; Will Eisner Comic Industry Award for best writer of the year, 1992; Harvey Award for best

Neil Gaiman

continuing series, 1992; Will Eisner Comic Industry Award for best writer of the year and best graphic album (new), 1993; Gem Award, Diamond Distributors, for expanding the marketplace for comic books, 1993; Will Eisner Comic Industry Award for best writer of the year, 1994; Guild Award, International Horror Critics, and World Fantasy Award nomination, both 1994, both for *Angels and Visitations: A Miscellany* and short story "Troll Bridge;" GLAAD Award for best comic of the year, 1996, for *Death: The Time of Your Life;* Eagle Award for best comic, 1996; Lucca

Best Writer Prize, 1997; *Newsweek* list of best children's books, 1997, for *The Day I Swapped My Dad for Two Goldfish;* Defender of Liberty Award, Comic Book Legal Defense Fund, 1997; MacMillan Silver Pen Award, 1999, for *Smoke and Mirrors: Short Fictions and Illusions;* Hugo Award nomination, 1999, for *Sandman: The Dream Hunters;* Mythopoeic Award for best novel for adults, 1999, for *Stardust: Being a Romance within the Realms of Faerie;* Nebula Award nomination, 1999, for screenplay for the film *Princess Mononoke;* Hugo Award for best science fiction/fantasy novel, Bram Stoker Award for best novel, Horror Writers Association, and British Science Fiction Association (BSFA) Award nomination, all 2002, all for *American Gods;* BSFA Award for best short fiction, Elizabeth Burr/Worzalla Award, Bram Stoker Award, Horror Writers Association, Hugo Award nomination, and Prix Tam Tam Award, all 2003, all for *Coraline.* Gaiman has received international awards from Austria, Brazil, Canada, Finland, France, Germany, Italy, and Spain. His script *Signal to Noise* received a SONY Radio Award.

WRITINGS:

GRAPHIC NOVELS AND COMIC BOOKS

Violent Cases, illustrated by Dave McKean, Titan (London, England), 1987, Tundra (Northampton, MA), 1991, Dark Horse Comics (Milwaukie, OR), 2003.

Black Orchid (originally published in magazine form in 1989), illustrated by Dave McKean, D.C. Comics (New York, NY), 1991.

Miracleman, Book 4: The Golden Age, illustrated by Mark Buckingham, Eclipse (Forestville, CA), 1992.

Signal to Noise, illustrated by Dave McKean, Dark Horse Comics (Milwaukie, OR), 1992.

The Books of Magic (originally published in magazine form, four volumes), illustrated by John Bolton and others, D.C. Comics (New York, NY), 1993.

The Tragical Comedy, or Comical Tragedy, of Mr. Punch, illustrated by Dave McKean, VG Graphics (London, England), 1994, Vertigo/D.C. Comics (New York, NY), 1995, also published as *Mr. Punch.*

(Author of text, with Alice Cooper) *The Compleat Alice Cooper: Incorporating the Three Acts of Alice Cooper's The Last Temptation,* illustrated by Michael Zulli, Marvel Comics (New York, NY), 1995, published as *The Last Temptation,* Dark Horse Comics (Milwaukie, OR), 2000.

Angela, illustrated by Greg Capullo and Mark Pennington, Image (Anaheim, CA), 1995, published as *Spawn: Angela's Hunt,* Image (Anaheim, CA), 2000.

Stardust: Being a Romance within the Realms of Faerie, illustrated by Charles Vess, D.C. Comics (New York, NY), 1997-98, text published as *Stardust,* Spike (New York, NY), 1999.

(Author of text, with Matt Wagner) *Neil Gaiman's Midnight Days,* D.C. Comics (New York, NY), 1999.

Green Lantern/Superman: Legend of the Green Flame, D.C. Comics (New York, NY), 2000.

Harlequin Valentine, illustrated by John Bolton, Dark Horse Comics (Milwaukie, OR), 2001.

Murder Mysteries (based on play of the same title, also see below), illustrated by P. Craig Russel, Dark Horse Comics (Milwaukie, OR), 2002.

"SANDMAN" SERIES

Sandman: The Doll's House (originally published in magazine form), illustrated by Mike Dringenberg and Malcolm Jones III, D.C. Comics (New York, NY), 1990.

Sandman: Preludes and Nocturnes (originally published as *Sandman,* Volumes 1-8), illustrated by Sam Keith, Mike Dringenberg, and Malcolm Jones III, D.C. Comics (New York, NY), 1991.

Sandman: Dream Country (originally published as *Sandman,* Volumes 17-20; includes "A Midsummer's Night's Dream"), illustrated by Kelley Jones, Charles Vess, Colleen Doran, and Malcolm Jones III, D.C. Comics (New York, NY), 1991.

Sandman: Season of Mists (originally published as *Sandman,* Volumes 21-28), illustrated by Kelley Jones, Malcolm Jones III, Mike Dringenberg, and others, D.C. Comics (New York, NY), 1992.

Sandman: A Game of You (originally published as *Sandman,* Volumes 32-37), illustrated by Shawn McManus and others, D.C. Comics (New York, NY), 1993.

Sandman: Fables and Reflections (originally published as *Sandman,* Volumes 29-31, 38-40, 50), illustrated by Bryan Talbot, D.C. Comics (New York, NY), 1994.

Death: The High Cost of Living (originally published in magazine form, three volumes), illustrated by Dave McKean, Mark Buckingham, and others, D.C. Comics (New York, NY), 1994.

Sandman: Brief Lives (originally published as *Sandman,* Volumes 41-49), illustrated by Jill Thompson, Dick Giordano, and Vince Locke, D.C. Comics (New York, NY), 1994.

Sandman: World's End (originally published as *Sandman,* Volumes 51-56), illustrated by Dave McKean, Mark Buckingham, Dick Giordano, and others, D.C. Comics (New York, NY), 1994.

(Author of text, with Matt Wagner) *Sandman: Midnight Theatre,* illustrated by Teddy Kristiansen, D.C. Comics (New York, NY), 1995.

(Editor, with Edward E. Kramer) *The Sandman: Book of Dreams,* HarperPrism (New York, NY), 1996.

Sandman: The Kindly Ones (originally published as *Sandman,* Volumes 57-69), illustrated by Marc Hempel, Richard Case, and others, D.C. Comics (New York, NY), 1996.

Death: The Time of Your Life, illustrated by Mark Buckingham and others, D.C. Comics (New York, NY), 1997.

(Author of commentary and contributor) *Dustcovers: The Collected Sandman Covers, 1989-1997,* illustrated by Dave McKean, Vertigo/D.C. Comics (New York, NY), 1997, published as *The Collected Sandman Covers, 1989-1997,* Watson-Guptill (New York, NY), 1997.

Sandman: The Wake, illustrated by Michael Zulli, Charles Vess, and others, D.C. Comics (New York, NY), 1997.

(Reteller) *Sandman: The Dream Hunters,* illustrated by Yoshitaka Amano, D.C. Comics (New York, NY), 1999.

The Quotable Sandman: Memorable Lines from the Acclaimed Series, D.C. Comics (New York, NY), 2000.

The Sandman: Endless Nights, illustrated by P. Craig Russell, Milo Manara, and others, D.C. Comics (New York, NY), 2003.

OTHER FICTION

(With Terry Pratchett) *Good Omens: The Nice and Accurate Prophecies of Agnes Nutter, Witch* (novel), Gollancz (London, England), 1990, revised edition, Workman (New York, NY), 1990.

(With Mary Gentle) *Villains!* (short stories), edited by Mary Gentle and Roz Kaveney, ROC (London, England), 1992.

(With Mary Gentle and Roz Kaveney) *The Weerde: Book One* (short stories), ROC (London, England), 1992.

(With Mary Gentle and Roz Kaveney) *The Weerde: Book Two: The Book of the Ancients* (short stories), ROC (London, England), 1992.

Angels and Visitations: A Miscellany (short stories), illustrated by Steve Bissette and others, DreamHaven Books and Art (Minneapolis, MN), 1993.

Neverwhere (novel), BBC Books (London, England), 1996, Avon (New York, NY), 1997.

Smoke and Mirrors: Short Fictions and Illusions (short stories), Avon (New York, NY), 1998.

American Gods (novel), William Morrow (New York, NY), 2001.

(Reteller) *Snow Glass Apples,* illustrated by George Walker, Biting Dog Press (Duluth, GA), 2003.

SCREENPLAYS

(With Lenny Henry) *Neverwhere,* BBC2 (London, England), 1996.

Signal to Noise, BBC Radio 3 (London, England), 1996.

Day of the Dead: An Annotated Babylon 5 Script (originally aired as the episode "Day of the Dead" for the series *Babylon 5,* Turner Broadcasting System, 1998), DreamHaven (Minneapolis, MN), 1998.

Princess Mononoke (motion picture; English translation of the Japanese screenplay by Hayao Miyazak), Miramax (New York, NY), 1999.

FOR CHILDREN

The Day I Swapped My Dad for Two Goldfish (picture book), illustrated by Dave McKean, Borealis/White Wolf (Clarkson, GA), 1997, HarperCollins (New York, NY), 2004.

Coraline (fantasy), illustrated by Dave McKean, Bloomsbury (London, England), HarperCollins (New York, NY), 2002.

The Wolves in the Walls (picture book), illustrated by Dave McKean, HarperCollins (New York, NY), 2003.

OTHER

Duran Duran: The First Four Years of the Fab Five (biography), Proteus (New York, NY), 1984.

Don't Panic: The Official Hitch-Hiker's Guide to the Galaxy Companion, Titan (London, England), Pocket Books (New York, NY), 1988, revised edition with additional material by David K. Dickson published as *Don't Panic: Douglas Adams and the Hitchhiker's Guide to the Galaxy,* Titan (London, England), 1993.

Warning: Contains Language (readings; compact disc), music by Dave McKean and the Flash Girls, DreamHaven (Minneapolis, MN), 1995.

(Co-illustrator) *The Dreaming: Beyond the Shores of Night,* D.C. Comics (New York, NY), 1997.

(Co-illustrator) *The Dreaming: Through the Gates of Horn and Ivory,* D.C. Comics (New York, NY), 1998.

Neil Gaiman: Live at the Aladdin (videotape), Comic Book Legal Defense Fund (Northampton, MA), 2001.

(With Gene Wolfe) *A Walking Tour of the Shambles* (nonfiction), American Fantasy Press (Woodstock, IL), 2001.

Murder Mysteries (play), illustrated by George Walker, Biting Dog Press (Duluth, GA), 2001.

Adventures in the Dream Trade (nonfiction and fiction), edited by Tony Lewis and Priscilla Olson, NESFA Press (Framingham, MA), 2002.

EDITOR

(With Kim Newman) *Ghastly beyond Belief,* Arrow (London, England), 1985.

(With Stephen Jones) *Now We Are Sick: A Sampler,* privately published, 1986, published as *Now We Are Sick: An Anthology of Nasty Verse,* DreamHaven (Minneapolis, MN), 1991.

(With Alex Stewart) *Temps,* ROC (London, England), 1991.

(With Alex Stewart) *Euro Temps,* ROC (London, England), 1992.

Also author of the comic book *Outrageous Tales from the Old Testament.* Creator of characters for comic books, including Lady Justice; Wheel of Worlds; Mr. Hero, Newmatic Man; Teknophage; and Lucifer. Coeditor of *The Utterly Comic Relief Comic,* a comic book that raised money for the UK Comic Relief Charity in 1991. Contributor to *The Sandman Companion,* D.C. Comics (New York, NY), 1999, and has contributed prefaces and introductions to several books. Gaiman's works, including the short story "Troll Bridge," have been represented in numerous anthologies. Contributor to newspapers and magazines, including *Knave, Punch, Observer, Sunday Times* (London, England) and *Time Out.* Gaiman's books have been translated into other languages, including Bulgarian, Danish, Dutch, Finnish, French, German, Greek, Hungarian, Italian, Japanese, Norwegian, Spanish, and Swedish. He has written scripts for the films *Avalon, Beowulf, The Confessions of William Henry Ireland, The Fermata, Modesty Blaise,* and others.

ADAPTATIONS: The Books of Magic was adapted into novel form by Carla Jablonski and others into several individual volumes, including *The Invitation, The Blindings,* and *The Children's Crusade,* issued by HarperCollins (New York, NY). *Neverwhere* was released on audio cassette by HighBridge (Minneapolis, MN), 1997; *American Gods* was released on cassette by Harper (New York, NY), 2001; *Coraline* was released as an audio book read by the author, Harper (New York, NY), 2002; *Two Plays for Voices* (*Snow Glass Apples* and *Murder Mysteries*) was released as an audio book and on audio CD, Harper (New York, NY), 2003. Several of Gaiman's works have been optioned for film, including *Sandman,* by Warner Bros.; *The Books of Magic,* by Warner Bros.; *Death: The High Cost of Living,* by Warner Bros.; *Good Omens,* by Renaissance Films; *Neverwhere,* by Jim Henson Productions; *Chivalry,* by Miramax; *Stardust,* by Miramax and Dimension Films; and *Coraline,* by Pandemonium Films. *Signal to Noise* was made into a stage play by NOWtheater (Chicago, IL).

WORK IN PROGRESS: 1602, a serialized story for Marvel Comics; *The Graveyard Book,* for HarperCollins (New York, NY); *Mirror Mask,* a film directed by Dave McKean for Jim Henson Productions and Columbia Tristar; a script for *A Short Film about John Bolton;* a television series based on *The Day I Swapped My Dad for Two Goldfish,* for Sunbow; an album of original songs for the record label Dancing Ferret Discs.

SIDELIGHTS: An English author of comic books, graphic novels (text and pictures in a comic-book format published in book form), prose novels, children's books, short fiction, nonfiction, and screenplays, Neil Gaiman is a best-selling writer who is considered perhaps the most accomplished and influential figure in modern comics as well as one of the most gifted of contemporary fantasists. Characteristically drawing from mythology, history, literature, and popular culture to create his works, Gaiman blends the everyday, the fantastic, the frightening, and the humorous to present his stories, which reveal the mysteries that lie just outside of reality as well as the insights that come from experiencing these mysteries. He refers to the plots and characters of classical literature and myth—most notably fairy tales, horror stories, science fiction, and traditional romances—while adding fresh, modern dimensions. In fact, Gaiman is credited with developing a new mythology with his works, which address themes such as what it means to be human; the importance of the relationship between humanity and art; humanity's desire for dreams and for attaining what they show; and the passage from childish ways of thinking to more mature understanding. Although most of the author's works are not addressed to children, Gaiman often features child and young adult characters in his books, and young people are among Gaiman's greatest and most loyal fans. The author has become extremely popular, developing a huge cult-like following as well as a celebrity status. The author perhaps is best known as the creator of the comic-book and graphic-novel series about the Sandman. This character, which is based loosely on a crime-fighting superhero that first appeared in D.C. Comics in the 1930s and 40s, is the protagonist of an epic series of dark fantasies that spanned eight years and ran for seventy-five monthly issues. Gaiman introduces the Sandman as an immortal being who rules the Dreaming, a surreal world to which humans go when they fall asleep. As the series progresses, the Sandman discovers that he is involved with the fate of human beings on an intimate basis and that his life is tied intrinsically to this relationship. The "Sandman" series has sold millions of copies in both comic book and graphic novel formats and has inspired companion literature and a variety of related merchandise.

As a writer for children, Gaiman has been the subject of controversy for creating *Coraline,* a fantasy for middle-graders about a young girl who enters a bizarre alternate world that eerily mimics her own. Compared to Lewis Carroll's nineteenth-century fantasy *Alice's Adventures in Wonderland* for its imaginative depiction of a surreal adventure, *Coraline* has been questioned as an appropriate story for children because it may be too frightening for its intended audience. Gaiman also is the creator of two picture books for children, *The Day I Swapped My Dad for Two Goldfish,* a comic-book-style fantasy about a boy who trades his dad for two attractive goldfish, and *The Wolves in the Walls,* which features a brave girl who faces the wolves that have taken over her house. The author's adult novel *American Gods,* the tale of a young drifter who becomes involved with what appears to be a magical war, was a critical and popular success that helped to bring Gaiman to a mainstream audience. Among his many works, Gaiman has written a biography of the English pop/rock group Duran Duran; a comic book with shock-rocker Alice Cooper that the latter turned into an album; a satiric fantasy about the end of the world with English novelist Terry Pratchett; comic books about Todd MacFarlane's popular character Spawn; and scripts for film, television, and radio, both original scripts and adaptations of his own works. Gaiman wrote the English-language script for the well-received Japanese anime film *Princess Mononoke;* the script of the episode "Day of the Dead" for the television series *Babylon 5;* and both a television script and a novel called *Neverwhere* that describes how an office worker rescues a young woman who is bleeding from a switchblade wound and is transported with her to London Below, a mysterious and dangerous world underneath the streets of England's largest city. Throughout his career, Gaiman has worked with a number of talented artists in the fields of comic books and fantasy, including John Bolton, Michael Zulli, Yoshitaka Amaro, Charles Vess, and longtime collaborator Dave McKean.

As a prose stylist, Gaiman is known for writing clearly and strongly, using memorable characters and striking images to build his dreamlike worlds. Although his books and screenplays can range from somber to creepy to horrifying, Gaiman is commended for underscoring them with optimism and sensitivity and for balancing their darkness with humor and wit. Reviewers have praised Gaiman for setting new standards for comic books as literature and for helping to bring increased popularity to both them and graphic novels. In addition, observers have claimed that several of the author's works transcend the genres in which they are written and explore deeper issues than those usually addressed in these works. Although Gaiman occasionally has been accused of being ponderous and self-indulgent, he generally is considered a phenomenon, a brilliant writer and storyteller whose works reflect his inventiveness, originality, and wisdom. Writing in *St. James Guide to Horror, Ghost, and Gothic Writers,* Peter Crowther noted that when Gaiman "is on form (which is most of the time), he is without peer. . . . His blending of poetic prose, marvelous inventions, and artistic vision has assured him of his place in the vanguard of modern-day dark fantasists." Keith R. A. DeCandido of *Library Journal* called Gaiman "arguably the most literate writer working in mainstream comics." Referring to Gaiman's graphic novels, Frank McConnell of *Commonweal* stated that the author "may just be the most gifted and important storyteller in English" and called him "our best and most bound-to-be-remembered writer of fantasy."

Born in Portchester, England, Gaiman was brought up in an upper-middle-class home. His father, David, was the director of a company, while his mother, Sheila, worked as a pharmacist. As a boy, Gaiman was "a completely omnivorous and cheerfully undiscerning reader," as he told Pamela Shelton in an interview for *Authors and Artists for Young Adults (AAYA).* In an interview with Ray Olson of *Booklist,* Gaiman recalled that he first read *Alice in Wonderland* "when I was five, maybe, and always kept it around as default reading between the ages of five and twelve, and occasionally picked up and reread since. There are things Lewis Carroll did in *Alice* that are etched onto my circuitry." Gaiman was a voracious reader of comic books until the age of sixteen, when he felt that he outgrew the genre as it existed at the time. At his grammar school, Ardingly College, Gaiman would get "very grumpy . . . when they'd tell us that we couldn't read comics, because 'if you read comics you will not read OTHER THINGS.'" He asked himself, "Why are comics going to stop me reading?" Gaiman proved that his teachers were misguided in their theory: he read the entire children's library in Portchester in two or three years and then started on the adult library. He told Shelton, "I don't think I ever got to 'Z' but I got up to about 'L'."

When he was about fourteen, Gaiman began his secondary education at Whitgift School. When he was fifteen, Gaiman and his fellow students took a series of vocational tests that were followed by interviews with career advisors. Gaiman told Shelton that these advisors "would look at our tests and say, 'Well, maybe you'd be interested in accountancy,' or whatever. When I went for my interview, the guy said, 'What do you want to do?' and I said, 'Well, I'd really like to write American comics.' And it was obvious that this was the first time he'd ever heard that. He just sort of stared at me for a bit and then said, 'Well, how do you go about doing that, then?' I said, 'I have no idea—you're the career advisor. Advise.' And he looked like I'd slapped him in the face with a wet herring; he sort of stared at me and there was this pause and I went on for a while and then he said, 'Have you ever thought about accountancy?'" Undeterred, Gaiman kept on writing. He also was interested in music. At sixteen, Gaiman played in a punk band that was about to be signed by a record company. Gaiman brought in an attorney who, after reading the contract being offered to the band, discovered that the deal would exploit them; consequently, Gaiman refused to sign the contract. By 1977, he felt that he was ready to become a professional writer. That same year, Gaiman left Whitgift School.

After receiving some rejections for short stories that he had written, Gaiman decided to become a freelance journalist so that he could learn about the world of publishing from the inside. He wrote informational articles for British men's magazines with titles like *Knave.* Gaiman told Shelton that being a journalist "was terrific in giving me an idea of how the world worked. I was the kind of journalist who would go out and do interviews with people and then write them up for magazines. I learned economy and I learned about dialogue." In 1983, he discovered the work of English comic-strip writer Alan Moore, whose *Swamp Thing* became a special favorite. Gaiman told Shelton, "Moore's work convinced me that you really could do work in comics that had the same amount of intelligence, the same amount of passion, the same amount of quality that you could put in any other medium." In 1984, Gaiman produced his first book, *Duran Duran: The First Four Years of the Fab Five.* Once he had established his credibility as a writer, Gaiman was able to sell the short stories that he had done earlier in his career. In 1985, Gaiman married Mary Therese McGrath, with whom he has three children: Michael, Holly, and Madeleine (Maddy). At around this time, Gaiman decided that he was ready to concentrate on fiction. In addition, the comics industry was experiencing a new influx of talent, which inspired Gaiman to consider becoming a contributor to that medium.

In 1986, Gaiman met art student Dave McKean, and the two decided to collaborate. Their first work together was the comic book *Violent Cases.* Serialized initially in *Escape,* a British comic that showcased new strips, *Violent Cases* was published in book form in 1987. The story recounts the memories of an adult narrator—pictured by McKean as a dark-haired young man who bears a striking resemblance to Gaiman—who recalls his memories of hearing about notorious Chicago gangland leader Al Capone from an elderly osteopath who was the mobster's chiropractor. As a boy of four, the narrator had his arm broken accidentally by his father. In the office of the osteopath, the boy was transfixed by lurid stories about Chicago of the 1920s but, in the evenings, he had nightmares in which his own world and that of Capone's would intersect. As the story begins, the adult narrator is trying to make sense of the experience. According to Joe Sanders of the *Dictionary of Literary Biography,* the narrator "discover[s] that grownups are as prone to uncertainty, emotional outbursts, and naïve rationalization as children. The boy is delighted, the grownup narrator perplexed, to see how 'facts' change to fit an interpreter's needs." Writing in London's *Sunday Times,* Nicolette Jones called *Violent Cases* "inspired and ingenious," while Cindy Lynn Speer, writing in an essay on the author's Web site, dubbed it "a brilliant tale of childhood and memory."

At around the same time that *Violent Cases* was published in book form, Gaiman produced the comic book *Outrageous Tales from the Old Testament,* which is credited with giving him almost instant notoriety in the comic-book community. Gaiman teamed with McKean again to do a limited-run comic series, *Black Orchid,* the first of the author's works to be released by D.C. Comics, the publisher of the original "Superman" and "Batman" series. A three-part comic book, "Black Orchid" features an essentially nonviolent female heroine who fights villains that she hardly can remember. Gaiman then was offered his choice of inactive D.C. characters to rework from the Golden Age of Comics (the 1930s and 1940s). He chose the Sandman. Originally, the character was millionaire Wesley Dodds who hunted criminals by night wearing a fedora, cape, and gas mask. Dodds would zap the crooks with his gas gun and leave them sleeping until the police got to them. When Gaiman began the series in 1988, he changed the whole scope of the character. The Sandman, who is also called Dream, Morpheus, Oneiros, Lord Shaper, Master of Story, and God of Sleep, became a thin, enigmatic figure with a pale face, dark eyes, and a shock of black hair. The Sandman is one of the Endless, immortals in charge of individual realms of the human psyche. The Sandman's brothers and sisters in the Endless are (in birth order) Destiny, Death, Destruction, the twins Desire and Despair, and Delirium (formerly Delight); Dream (the Sandman) falls between Death and Destruction.

In the "Sandman" book *Preludes and Nocturnes,* Gaiman introduces the title character, the ageless lord of dreams, who has just returned home after being captured by a coven of wizards and held in an asylum for the criminally insane for seventy-two years. Dream finds that his home is in ruins, that his powers are diminished, and that his three tools—a helmet, a pouch of sand, and a ruby stone—have been stolen. He finds his missing helpers and the young girl who has become addicted to the sand from his pouch; he also visits Hell to find the demon who stole his helmet and battles an evil doctor who has unleashed the power of dreams on the unsuspecting people of Earth. Dream comes to realize that his captivity has affected him: he has become humanized, and he understands that he eventually will have to die. In *The Doll's House,* Dream travels across the United States searching for the Arcana, the stray dreams and nightmares of the twentieth century that have taken on human form; the story is interwoven with a subplot about a young woman, Rose Walker, who has lost her little brother. In *Dream Country,* Gaiman features Calliope, a muse and the mother of Dream's son, Orpheus; the story also brings in a real character, actor/playwright William Shakespeare. In *Season of Mists,* Dream meets Lucifer, who has left his position as ruler of Hell and has left the choice of his successor to Dream.

A Game of You features Barbara (nicknamed Barbie), a character who had appeared in *The Doll's House.* Barbie is drawn back into the dream realm that she ruled as a child in order to save it from the evil Cuckoo, who plans to destroy it. *Fables and Reflections* is a collection of stories featuring the characters from the series and includes Gaiman's retelling of the Greek myth of Orpheus. In *Brief Lives,* Dream and Delirium embark on a quest to find their little brother Destruction, who exiled himself to Earth three hundred years before. *World's End* includes a collection of tales told by a group of travelers who are waiting out a storm in an inn. *The Kindly Ones* brings the series to its conclusion as Hippolyta (Lyta) Hall takes revenge upon Dream for the disappearance of her son. Lyta, who has been driven mad by anger and grief, asks the help of the title characters, mythological beings also known as the Furies. The Kindly Ones take out Lyta's revenge on Dream, who succumbs to their attack. The tale comes full cycle, and Dream's destiny is joined with that of humans in death. In the final chapter of the series, *The Wake,* a funeral is held for Dream; however, as Gaiman notes thematically, dreams really never die, and Dream's role in the Endless is taken on in a new incarnation. The Sandman also appears in a more peripheral role in *The Dream Hunters,* a retelling of the Japanese folktale "The Fox, the Monk, and the Mikado of All Night's Dreaming."

Next to the Sandman, Death, Dream's older sister, is the most frequently featured and popular character in the series. Death is charged with shepherding humans who are about to die through their transitions. Once a century, she must come to Earth as a sixteen-year-old girl in order to remind herself what mortality feels like. In contrast to Dream, who characteristically is isolated, brooding, and serious, Death, who is depicted as a spike-haired young woman who dresses like a punk rocker or Goth girl, has a more open and kindly nature. Death is featured in two books of her own, *Death: The High Cost of Living* and *Death: The Time of Your Life.* In the first story, she helps Sexton, a teen who is contemplating suicide, rediscover the joys in being alive as they journey through New York City and, in the second, she helps Foxglove, a newly successful musician, to reveal her true sexual orientation as her companion Hazel prepares to die. Death and the rest of the Endless are also featured in *The Sandman: Endless Nights,* in which Gaiman devotes an individual story to each of the seven siblings.

Writing in *Commonweal* about the "Sandman" series, Frank McConnell stated, "*Sandman* is not just one of the best pieces of fiction being done these days; . . . it emerges as *the* best piece of fiction being done these days." McConnell stated that what Gaiman has done with the series "is to establish the fact that a comic book can be a work of high and very serious art—a story that other storytellers, in whatever medium they work, will have to take into account as an exploration of what stories can do and what stories are for." The critic concluded, "I know of nothing quite like it, and I don't expect there will be anything like it for some time. . . . Read the damn thing; it's important." Peter Crowder of the *St. James Guide to Horror, Ghost, and Gothic Writers* noted that, with the "Sandman" series of comic books, Gaiman "has truly revolutionized the power of the medium." Crowder called the various volumes of collected stories "almost uniformly excellent, and any one of them would make a good starting point for those readers who, while well-versed in the field of Gothic prose literature, have yet to discover the rare but powerful joy inherent in a great comic book." In 1996, D.C. Comics surprised the fans of "Sandman" by announcing the cancellation of the series while it was still the company's best-seller; however, D.C. had made this arrangement with Gaiman at the beginning of the series. "Sandman" has sold more than seven million copies; individual copies of the stories also have sold in the millions or in the hundreds of thousands. "A Midsummer's Night's Dream," a story from *Dream Country,* won the World Fantasy Award for the best short story of 1991. This was the first time that a comic book had won an award that was not related to its own medium, and the event caused an uproar among some fantasy devotees. The "Sandman" stories have inspired related volumes, such as a book of quotations from the series, and merchandise such as action figures, stuffed toys, trading cards, jewelry, and watches.

In 1994, Gaiman told Ken Tucker of *Entertainment Weekly,* "Superhero comics are the most perfectly evolved art form for preadolescent male power fantasies, and I don't see that as a bad thing. I want to reach other sorts of people, too." In 1995, he told Pamela Shelton, "If you're too young for *Sandman,* you will be bored silly by it. It's filled with long bits with people having conversations." Speaking to Nick Hasted of the *Guardian* in 1999, Gaiman said, "Right now, as things stand, *Sandman* is my serious work. . . . It is one giant, overarching story, and I'm proud of it. Compared to *Sandman,* all the prose work so far is trivia." In 2003, Gaiman wrote an introduction to *The Sandman: King of Dreams,* a collection of text and art from the series with commentary by Alisa Kwitney. He commented, "If I have a concern over *The Sandman,* the 2,000-page story I was able to tell between 1988 and 1996, it is that the things that have come after it, the toys (whether plastic and articulated or soft and cuddly), the posters, the clothes, the calendars and candles, the companion volume, and even the slim book of quotations, along with the various spin-offs and such—will try people's patience and goodwill, and that a book like this will be perceived, not unreasonably, as something that's being used to flog the greasy patch in the driveway where once, long ago, a dead horse used to lie. The ten volumes of *The Sandman* are what they are, and that's the end of it."

Throughout his career, Gaiman has included young people as main characters in his works. For example, *The Books of Magic,* a collection of four comics published in 1993, predates J. K. Rowling's "Harry Potter" series by featuring a thirteen-year-old boy, Tim

Hunter, who is told that he has the capabilities to be the greatest wizard in the world. Tim, a boy from urban London who wears oversized glasses, is taken by the Trenchcoat Brigade—sorcerers with names like The Mysterious Phantom Stranger, the Incorrigible Hellblazer, and the Enigmatic Dr. Occult—on a tour of the universe to learn its magical history. Tim travels to Hell, to the land of Faerie, and to America, among other places, each of them showing him a different aspect of the world of magic. He also searches for his girlfriend, Molly, who has been abducted into the fantasy realms; after he finds her, the two of them face a series of dangers as they struggle to return to their own world. At the end of the story, Tim must make a decision to embrace or reject his talents as a wizard. *The Books of Magic* also includes cameos by the Sandman and his sister Death. Writing in *Locus,* Carolyn Cushman said, "It's a fascinating look at magic, its benefits and burdens, all dramatically illustrated [by John Bolton, Scott Hampton, Charles Vess, and Paul Johnson], and with a healthy helping of humor." Speaking of the format of *The Books of Magic,* Michael Swanwick of *Book World* noted, "The graphic novel has come of age. This series is worth any number of movies."

In 1994, Gaiman produced *The Tragical Comedy, or Comical Tragedy, of Mr. Punch* (also published as *Mr. Punch*), a work that he considers one of his best. In this graphic novel, which is illustrated by Dave McKean, a young boy is sent to stay with his grandparent by the seaside while his mother gives birth to his baby sister. While on his visit, the boy encounters a mysterious puppeteer and watches a Punch and Judy show, a sometimes violent form of puppet-theater entertainment. Through a series of strange experiences, he ends up rejecting Mr. Punch's promise that everyone in the world is free to do whatever they want. Sanders of the *Dictionary of Literary Biography* called *Mr. Punch* "perhaps Gaiman and McKean's most impressive collaboration," while Crowder called it "an impressive work, rich not only in freshness and originality but also in compassion, Gaiman's hallmark. . . . The collective impact is literally breathtaking." Writing in *Commonweal,* Frank McConnell noted, "This stunning comic book-graphic novel—whatever—is easily the most haunting, inescapable story I have read in years."

In 1996, Gaiman and McKean produced their first work for children, the picture book *The Day I Swapped My Dad for Two Goldfish.* In this tale, a little boy trades his father for two of his neighbor's goldfish while his little sister stares, horrified. When their mother finds out what has happened, she is furious. She makes the children go and get back their father who, unfortunately, has already been traded for an electric guitar. While on their quest to find him, the siblings decide that their father is a very good daddy after all. The children finally retrieve their father, who has been reading a newspaper all during his adventure. At home, their mother makes the children promise not to swap their dad any more. Writing in *Bloomsbury Review,* Anji Keating called *The Day I Swapped My Dad for Two Goldfish* "a fabulously funny tale" and dubbed the protagonists' journey to fetch their father "delightful." Malcolm Jones of *Newsweek* predicted that Gaiman and McKean "may shock a few grandparents . . . but in fact the most shocking thing they've done in this droll story is to take the illegible look of cutting-edge magazines like *Raygun* and somehow make it readable."

In 2003, Gaiman and McKean produced a second picture book, *The Wolves in the Walls.* In this work, young Lucy hears wolves living in the walls of the old house where she and her family live; of course, no one believes her. When the wolves emerge to take over the house, Lucy and her family flee. However, Lucy wants her house back, and she also wants the beloved pig-puppet that she left behind. She talks her family into going back into the house, where they move into the walls that had been vacated by the wolves. Lucy and her family frighten the usurpers, who are wearing their clothes and eating their food. The wolves scatter, and everything seems to go back to normal until Lucy hears another noise in the walls; this time, it sounds like elephants. In her *Booklist* review of *The Wolves in the Walls,* Francisca Goldsmith found the book "visually and emotionally sophisticated, accessible, and inspired by both literary and popular themes and imagery." Writing in *School Library Journal,* Marian Creamer commented that "Gaiman and McKean deftly pair text and illustration to convey a strange, vivid story," and predicted, "Children will delight in the 'scary, creepy tone.'"

Gaiman's first story for middle-graders, *Coraline,* outlines how the title character, a young girl who feels that she is being ignored by her preoccupied parents, enters a terrifying, malevolent alternate reality to save them after they are kidnapped. The story begins when Coraline and her parents move into their new house, which is divided into apartments. Left to her own devices, bored Coraline explores the house and finds a door in the empty flat next door that leads to a world that is a twisted version of her own. There, she meets two odd-looking individuals who call themselves her "other mother" and "other father." The Other Mother, a woman who looks like Coraline's except for her black-button eyes and stiletto fingernails, wants Coraline to stay with her and her husband. Tempted by good food and interesting toys, Coraline considers the offer. However, when the girl returns home, she finds that her parents have disappeared. Coraline discovers that they are trapped in the other world, and she sets out to save them. The Other Mother, who turns out to be a soul-sucking harpy, enters into a deadly game of hide-and-seek with Coraline, who discovers new qualities of bravery and resolve within herself. Before returning home, Coraline saves herself, her parents, and some ghost children who are trapped in the grotesque world.

After its publication, *Coraline* became a subject of dispute. Some adult observers saw it as a book that would give nightmares to children. However, other observers have noted that the children of their acquaintance who read the book consider it an exciting rather than overly frightening work. A reviewer in *Publishers Weekly* noted that Gaiman and illustrator McKean "spin an electrifyingly creepy tale likely to haunt young readers for many moons. . . . Gaiman twines his tale with a menacing tone and crisp prose fraught with memorable imagery . . . , yet keeps the narrative just this side of terrifying." Writing in *School Library Journal,* Bruce Anne Shook commented, "The story is odd, strange, even slightly bizarre, but kids will hang on every word. . . . This is just right for all those requests for a scary book." Stephanie Zvirin of *Booklist* added that Gaiman offers "a chilling and empowering view of children, to be sure, but young readers are likely to miss such subtleties as the clever allusions to classic horror movies and the references to the original dark tales of the Brothers Grimm." A critic in *Kirkus Reviews* found *Coraline* "not for the faint-hearted—who are mostly adults anyway—but for stouthearted kids who love a brush with the sinister, *Coraline* is spot on." *Coraline* has won several major fantasy awards and has become an international bestseller.

In his interview with Pamela Shelton, Gaiman said, "What I enjoy most is when people say to me, 'When I was sixteen I didn't know what I was going to do with my life and then I read *Sandman* and now I'm at university studying mythology' or whatever. I think it's wonderful when you've opened a door to people and showed them things that would never have *known* they would have been interested in." Gaiman finds it satisfying to introduce his readers to mythology. He told Shelton, "You gain a cultural understanding to the last 2,500 to 3,000 years, which, if you lack it, there's an awful lot of stuff that you will simply never quite understand." He noted that, in *Sandman,* even readers unfamiliar with the Norse god Loki or the three-headed spirit of Irish mythology "sort of half-know; there's a gentle and sort of delightful familiarity with these tales. It feels right. And I think that's probably the most important thing. Giving people this stuff, pointing out that it can be interesting, but also pointing out what mythologies do know. And how they affect us." In an interview with Nick Hasted in the *Guardian,* Gaiman stated, "What I'm fighting now is the tendency to put novelists in a box, to make them write the same book over and over again. I want to shed skins. I want to keep awake. I definitely have a feeling that if I'm not going forward, if I'm not learning something, then I'm dead."

BIOGRAPHICAL AND CRITICAL SOURCES:

BOOKS

Authors and Artists for Young Adults, Gale (Detroit, MI), Volume 19 (author interview with Pamela Shelton), 1996, Volume 42, 2002.

Dictionary of Literary Biography, Volume 261: *British Fantasy and Science Fiction Writers since 1960,* Gale (Detroit, MI), 2002.

Kwitney, Alisa, *The Sandman: King of Dreams,* introduction by Neil Gaiman, Chronicle Books (San Francisco, CA), 2003.

St. James Guide to Horror, Ghost, and Gothic Writers, St. James Press (Detroit, MI), 1998.

PERIODICALS

Bloomsbury Review, July-August, 1997, Anji Keating, review of *The Day I Swapped My Dad for Two Goldfish,* p. 21.

Booklist, August, 2002, Ray Olson, "The *Booklist* Interview: Neil Gaiman," p. 19, and Stephanie Zvirin, review of *Coraline,* p. 1948; August, 2003, Francisca Goldsmith, review of *The Wolves in the Walls,* p. 1989.

Book World, April 7, 2002, Michael Swanwick, "Reel Worlds," p. 3.

Commonweal, December 2, 1994, Frank McConnell, review of *Mister Punch,* p. 27; October 20, 1995, Frank McConnell, review of *Sandman,* p. 21; June 19, 1998, Frank McConnell, review of *Neverwhere,* p. 21

Entertainment Weekly, June 24, 1994, Ken Tucker, review of *Sandman,* pp. 228-229.

Guardian (London, England), July 14, 1999, Nick Hasted, "The Illustrated Man," p. 12.

Kirkus Reviews, June 15, 2002, review of *Coraline,* p. 88.

Library Journal, September 15, 1990, Keith R. A. DeCandido, review of *The Golden Age,* p. 104.

Locus, April, 1993, Carolyn Cushman, review of *The Books of Magic,* p. 29.

Newsweek, December 1, 1997, Malcolm Jones, review of *The Day I Swapped My Dad for Two Goldfish,* p. 77.

Publishers Weekly, June 24, 2002, review of *Coraline,* p. 57.

School Library Journal, August, 2002, Bruce Anne Shook, review of *Coraline,* p. 184; September, 2003, Marian Creamer, review of *The Wolves in the Walls,* p. 178.

Sunday Times (London, England), July 15, 1990, Nicolette Jones, review of *Violent Cases.*

ONLINE

Neil Gaiman Home Page, http://www.neilgaiman.com/ (May, 2002), Cindy Lynn Speer, "An Essay on Neil Gaiman and Comics."*

* * *

GALLISON, Kate

See GALLISON, Kathleen

* * *

GALLISON, Kathleen 1939-
(Kate Gallison)

PERSONAL: Born November 14, 1939, in Philadelphia, PA; daughter of Herbert E. (a salesman and freelance writer) and Georgena (Hill) Gallison; married Samuel Graff, November 11, 1961 (divorced, March, 1975); married Harold E. Dunn (a reference librarian), June 2, 1982; children: (first marriage) Leonard P., Charles W.; (second marriage) John Thomas. *Education:* Attended Douglass College, Rutgers University, 1957-60; Thomas A. Edison College (now State College), B.A., 1979. *Religion:* Episcopalian.

ADDRESSES: Agent—c/o Author Mail, Delacorte Press, 1745 Broadway, New York, NY 10019. *E-mail*—webmaster@kategallison.com.

CAREER: Writer. *Washington Post,* Washington, DC, library clerk, 1960-61; American Telephone & Telegraph Co. (AT&T), accounting clerk, 1961-62; homemaker, amateur actress, cartoonist, puppeteer, and part-time sales clerk, 1961-73; sales clerk, 1973-74; clerk-bookkeeper for New Jersey Division of Youth and Family Services, 1974-79; New Jersey Department of the Treasury, Trenton, computer programmer-analyst, 1979-84; Applied Data Research, Princeton, NJ, technical writer, beginning 1984.

MEMBER: Mystery Writers of America, Authors Guild, Authors League of America.

WRITINGS:

MYSTERY NOVELS; UNDER NAME KATE GALLISON

Unbalanced Accounts, Little, Brown (Boston, MA), 1986.

The Death Tape, Little, Brown (Boston, MA), 1987.

The Jersey Monkey: A Nick Magaracz Mystery, St. Martin's Press (New York, NY), 1992.

Bury the Bishop, Dell (New York, NY), 1995.

Devil's Workshop, Dell (New York, NY), 1996.

Unholy Angels, Dell (New York, NY), 1996.

Hasty Retreat: A Mother Lavinia Grey Mystery, Delacorte (New York, NY), 1997.

Grave Misgivings: A Mother Lavinia Grey Mystery, Delacorte (New York, NY), 1998.

Also author of historical novel *Bucko.* Contributor to books, including *More Murder, They Wrote,* edited by Elizabeth Foxwell and Martin H. Greenberg, Boulevard Books, 1999; and *Murder Most Catholic,* edited by Ralph McInerny, 2002. Also contributor of short stories to periodicals, including *Ellery Queen Mystery Magazine.*

SIDELIGHTS: Kathleen Gallison is the author of often satiric mystery novels featuring either the hapless gumshoe Nick Magaracz (in her first three titles), or Mother Lavinia Grey (in her next five). In her first mystery novel, *Unbalanced Accounts,* the author introduces Magaracz, "a very poor man's Sam Spade," according to *New York Times* reviewer John Gross. Set in Trenton, New Jersey, the tale centers on several hundred missing checks that Magaracz must recover. A *Washington Post Book World* critic reported, "There are some funny moments and lots of bright banter. But these are only flashes in a mystery that often strains painfully to be wildly comic and witty." Although also critical of the story's plot and angle, Ashok Chandrasekhar asserted in the *New York Times Book Review* that "Gallison's writing shows promise," commending the author's dialogue and the characterization of Magaracz. In Gross's opinion, *Unbalanced Accounts* is "a well-above-average debut." Other reviewers, however, were more enthusiastic, appreciating the dark humor and the author's spoofing of such writers as Raymond Chandler and Lew Archer. Gallison does this by setting her story in decidedly unglamorous Trenton, where the crooks, and even the hero, are often stupid and incompetent, forced to endure uninspiring jobs in order to slog through their insipid lives; the style, too, makes fun of the tough-talking, hard-boiled narratives that come from the mouths of heroes like Sam Spade. The result, attested Connie Fletcher in *Booklist,* is a "superb black comedy."

About her debut novel, Gallison once told *CA:* "*Unbalanced Accounts* takes place in Trenton because I know Trenton; I was there for eighteen years, longer than I've lived anywhere. Trenton is a collection of communities, each with its own ways and values, where all the old-timers know all the other old-timers' complete history and antecedents, and nobody lives anything down. In the novel I took a look at the state government—right now probably the largest community in town—with sidelong glances at New Jersey life in general. I was enormously amused to note that only the reviewers from Mississippi and Texas seemed to notice how wicked and degenerate some of the characters were. On the East Coast, for instance, everybody knows somebody like Freddie Gruver, the no-account womanizing druggie, so he doesn't seem especially remarkable."

Gallison followed *Unbalanced Accounts* with two more Magaracz mysteries: *The Death Tape* and *The Jersey Monkey.* In the former, Magaracz takes a job with New Jersey's department of Tax Enforcement for the rather quotidian reason that the position offers dental benefits that will cover his daughter's braces. Investigating what he thinks is a case of mere tax fraud at the department, Magaracz accidentally uncovers a group of antitax, antigovernment survivalists who have faked their deaths, withdrawn all their money from their bank accounts, and now plan to blow up government buildings. The members of the group, who call themselves the Posse Comitatus, are not all that bright, however, when it comes to explosives; at one point in the story several of them accidentally get themselves killed when one of their detonators is stolen and set off by a junkie. In *The Jersey Monkey* Magaracz finds himself investigating murders at a pharmaceutical company where a new AIDS drug has been developed. The company is going through tough merger negotiations when two employees are poisoned. Suspects include a chemist who used to be a stripper, an unscrupulous veterinarian in charge of the lab monkeys that are being subjected to testing, and a greedy executive. Noting one particularly funny moment when Magaracz has to interrogate a monkey using sign language, a *Publishers Weekly* reviewer called *The Jersey Monkey* a "lighthearted romp."

After writing three books featuring Magaracz, Gallison abandoned the character and created Mother Lavinia Grey (Mother Vinnie), an Episcopalian pastor who, like the author's first sleuth, lives in New Jersey. Considered less blatantly satirical than her first novels, these books combine murder mysteries with inside views of Church bureaucracy and politics, flavored with humorous portrayals of the quirky Mother Vinnie's parishioners of St. Bede's. In her debut, Mother Vinnie turns amateur sleuth at a diocesan convention when one of the attending bishops is murdered. Later installments include *Unholy Angels,* in which Mother Vinnie is faced with the problem of finding out who murdered two of Fishersville, New Jersey's most prominent citizens, and *Hasty Retreat,* where she tries to escape her hectic duties at a monastery only to become entangled in another mystery in which a monk is killed.

More recently, Gallison completed the Mother Vinnie mystery *Grave Misgivings.* The plot in this tale is set off when a man's search for his father's remains at a Fishersville cemetery leads him to Mother Vinnie. After she does some investigating, strange secrets start to reveal themselves about a flood and other goings on in the town back in 1955. Although a *Publishers Weekly* reviewer complained that in the climax of the novel Mother Vinnie "stupidly lets herself be put in mortal danger," the critic nevertheless praised *Grave Misgivings* as an "amusing story that features a distinctive and usually appealing heroine."

Gallison once told *CA:* "When I was very young, I wanted to be a cartoonist, but I couldn't draw very well. Then I wanted to write a series of detective novels, and now I'm going to do it. Trenton provides an interesting setting, and I try to depict real Trenton people in blood-and-thunder situations. What emerges can be pretty funny.

"I began writing stories in kindergarten, as soon as I learned to read and make letters. I wrote a science fiction novel called *Master Mechanic*—that is, I printed it, I couldn't do cursive—in a brown saddle-stitched composition book. The book got lost in one of our moves; my father was transferred every four years or so. There were other stories over the years but *Master Mechanic* was the only full-length book. It was about a mad scientist who made human beings out of salt.

"In fifth grade I discovered the work of an author (I don't remember his name) who wrote screamingly funny short stories for *American Legion Magazine*. I began to model my style on this guy, with some success, writing funny short stories and reading them in class. In high school I came upon P. G. Wodehouse and aped him for a while. I did a three-act English drawing-room comedy in tenth grade. Nobody would produce it. I read mystery stories; I read Manning Coles. I thought of myself as a secret English person and used English spellings. In the end I was unable to keep from aping Wodehouse.

"I went to college. At Douglass everyone wrote very serious things, so I tried to do that too. The literary magazine rejected my efforts. I started a cartoon strip in the college paper, and one of the serious girls wrote a long-faced poem about it, which was published in the literary magazine. After I left school I wrote very little—short pieces for newspapers sometimes. Erma Bombeck did it better.

"About the time my first marriage was breaking up I wrote a semiautobiographical novel of the Mad Housewife genre, the sort of thing we all do when divorcing. It was good therapy but unpublishable; when it was finished I was happy to notice that my style had improved. P. G. Wodehouse was gone."

BIOGRAPHICAL AND CRITICAL SOURCES:

PERIODICALS

Booklist, March 15, 1986, Connie Fletcher, review of *Unbalanced Accounts.*

Chicago Sun-Times, March 15, 1986, Henry Kisor, review of *The Death Tape.*

Ellery Queen Mystery Magazine, mid-December, 1986, Allen J. Hubin, review of *Unbalanced Accounts.*

Globe and Mail (Toronto, Ontario, Canada), April 26, 1986.

Library Journal, July, 1997, Rex E. Klett, review of *Hasty Retreat,* p. 130.

Los Angeles Times Book World, July 6, 1986.

New York Times, April 4, 1986.

New York Times Book Review, April 13, 1986.

Publishers Weekly, February 28, 1986, review of *Unbalanced Accounts;* May 29, 1987, review of *The Death Tape;* January 13, 1992, review of *The Jersey Monkey,* p. 49; July 22, 1996, review of *Unholy Angels,* p. 235; May 19, 1997, review of *Hasty Retreat,* p. 69; August 10, 1998, review of *Grave Misgivings,* p. 373.

Washington Post Book World, May 18, 1986.

ONLINE

Kate Gallison Web site, http://www.kategallison.com (November 12, 2003).*

* * *

GIBBONS, Gail (Gretchen) 1944-

PERSONAL: Born August 1, 1944, in Oak Park, IL; daughter of Harry George (a tool and die designer) and Grace (Johnson) Ortmann; married Glenn Gibbons, June 25, 1966 (died, May 20, 1972); married Kent Ancliffe (a builder), March 23, 1976; children: (stepchildren) Rebecca, Eric. *Education:* University of Illinois, B.F.A., 1967. *Politics:* Democrat. *Hobbies and other interests:* Reading, art work.

Gail Gibbons

ADDRESSES: Home and office—Corinth, VT 05039. *Agent*—c/o Author Mail, Holiday House, 424 Madison Ave., New York, NY 10017.

CAREER: WCIA-Television, Champaign, IL, artist, 1967-69; Bob Howe Agency, Chicago, IL, staff artist, 1969-70; WNBC-Television, House of Animation, New York, NY, staff artist, 1970-76; writer, 1976—; United Press International, New York, NY, freelance artist, 1977—.

AWARDS, HONORS: New York City Art Director Club award, 1979, for *The Missing Maple Syrup Sap Mystery;* American Institute of Graphic Arts award, 1979, for *Clocks and How They Go;* National Science Teachers Association (NSTA)/Children's Book Council award, 1980, for *Locks and Keys,* and 1982, for *Tool Book;* certificate of appreciation from U.S. Postmaster General, 1982, for *The Post Office Book: Mail and How It Moves;* American Library Association notable book award, 1983, for *Cars and How They Go,* and 1985, for *The Milk Makers; Washington Post*/Children's Book Guild Award, 1987, for contribution to nonfiction children's literature; National Council of Social Studies Notable Children's Trade Book in the Field of Social Studies, 1983, 1987, 1989, 1990, and 1992; NSTA Outstanding Science Trade Books for Children, 1983, 1987, 1991, 1998; International Reading Association Children's Choice Award, 1989 and 1995; American Bookseller Pick of the Lists, 1992.

WRITINGS:

SELF-ILLUSTRATED; FOR CHILDREN

Willy and His Wheel Wagon, Prentice-Hall (Englewood Cliffs, NJ), 1975.

Salvador and Mister Sam: A Guide to Parakeet Care, Prentice-Hall (Englewood Cliffs, NJ), 1976.

Things to Make and Do for Halloween, F. Watts (New York, NY), 1976.

Things to Make and Do for Columbus Day, F. Watts (New York, NY), 1977.

Things to Make and Do for Your Birthday, F. Watts (New York, NY), 1978.

The Missing Maple Syrup Sap Mystery; or, How Maple Syrup Is Made (fiction), Warne (New York, NY), 1979.

Clocks and How They Go, Crowell (New York, NY), 1979.

Locks and Keys, Crowell (New York, NY), 1980.

The Too Great Bread Bake Book, Warne (New York, NY), 1980.

Trucks, Crowell (New York, NY), 1981.

The Magnificent Morris Mouse Clubhouse (fiction), F. Watts (New York, NY), 1981.

Tool Book, Holiday House (New York, NY), 1982.

The Post Office Book: Mail and How It Moves, Crowell (New York, NY), 1982.

Christmas Time, Holiday House (New York, NY), 1982.

Boat Book, Holiday House (New York, NY), 1983.

Paper, Paper, Everywhere, Harcourt (New York, NY), 1983, reprinted, 1997.

Thanksgiving Day, Holiday House (New York, NY), 1983.

New Road!, Crowell (New York, NY), 1983.

Sun Up, Sun Down, Harcourt (New York, NY), 1983.

Tunnels, Holiday House (New York, NY), 1984.

Department Store, Crowell (New York, NY), 1984.

Fire! Fire!, Crowell (New York, NY), 1984.

Halloween, Holiday House (New York, NY), 1984.

The Seasons of Arnold's Apple Tree, Harcourt (New York, NY), 1984.

Playgrounds, Holiday House (New York, NY), 1985.

Lights! Camera! Action!: How a Movie Is Made, Crowell (New York, NY), 1985.
Fill It Up!: All about Service Stations, Crowell (New York, NY), 1985.
Check It Out: The Book about Libraries, Harcourt (New York, NY), 1985.
The Milk Makers, Macmillan (New York, NY), 1985.
Happy Birthday!, Holiday House (New York, NY), 1986.
From Path to Highway: The Story of the Boston Post Road, Crowell (New York, NY), 1986.
Flying, Holiday House (New York, NY), 1986.
Up Goes the Skyscraper!, Four Winds Press (New York, NY), 1986.
Valentine's Day, Holiday House (New York, NY), 1986.
Dinosaurs, Holiday House (New York, NY), 1987.
Deadline!: From News to Newspaper, Crowell (New York, NY), 1987.
Trains, Holiday House (New York, NY), 1987.
Weather Forecasting, Four Winds Press (New York, NY), 1987.
Zoo, Crowell (New York, NY), 1987.
The Pottery Place, Harcourt (New York, NY), 1987.
Sunken Treasure, Crowell (New York, NY), 1988.
Prehistoric Animals, Holiday House (New York, NY), 1988.
Farming, Holiday House (New York, NY), 1988.
Dinosaurs, Dragonflies, and Diamonds: All about Natural History Museums, Four Winds Press (New York, NY), 1988.
Marge's Diner, Crowell (New York, NY), 1989.
Monarch Butterfly, Holiday House (New York, NY), 1989.
Easter, Holiday House (New York, NY), 1989.
Catch the Wind!: All about Kites, Little, Brown (Boston, MA), 1989.
Beacons of Light: Lighthouses, Morrow (New York, NY), 1990.
How a House Is Built, Holiday House (New York, NY), 1990.
Weather Words and What They Mean, Holiday House (New York, NY), 1990.
Surrounded by Sea: Life on a New England Fishing Island, Little, Brown (Boston, MA), 1991.
From Seed to Plant, Holiday House (New York, NY), 1991.
Whales, Holiday House (New York, NY), 1991.
The Puffins Are Back!, HarperCollins (New York, NY), 1991.
Recycle!: A Handbook for Kids, Little, Brown (Boston, MA), 1992.
The Great St. Lawrence Seaway, Morrow (New York, NY), 1992.
Sharks, Holiday House (New York, NY), 1992.
Say Woof!: The Day of a Country Veterinarian, Macmillan (New York, NY), 1992.
Stargazers, Holiday House (New York, NY), 1992.
Puff—Flash—Bang!: A Book about Signals, Morrow (New York, NY), 1993.
Pirates: Robbers of the High Seas, Little, Brown (Boston, MA), 1993.
Frogs, Holiday House (New York, NY), 1993.
The Planets, Holiday House (New York, NY), 1993.
Spiders, Holiday House (New York, NY), 1993.
Caves and Caverns, Harcourt (New York, NY), 1993.
Christmas on an Island, Morrow (New York, NY), 1994.
Wolves, Holiday House (New York, NY), 1994.
St. Patrick's Day, Holiday House (New York, NY), 1994.
Nature's Green Umbrella: Tropical Rain Forests, Morrow (New York, NY), 1994.
Emergency!, Holiday House (New York, NY), 1994.
Country Fair, Little, Brown (Boston, MA), 1994.
Bicycle Book, Holiday House (New York, NY), 1994.
Knights in Shining Armor, Little, Brown (Boston, MA), 1995.
The Reasons for Seasons, Holiday House (New York, NY), 1995.
Sea Turtles, Holiday House (New York, NY), 1995.
Planet Earth, Inside Out, Morrow (New York, NY), 1995.
Dogs, Holiday House (New York, NY), 1996.
Deserts, Holiday House (New York, NY), 1996.
Cats, Holiday House (New York, NY), 1996.
Music Maker, Simon & Schuster (New York, NY), 1996.
Gulls . . . Gulls . . . Gulls, Holiday House (New York, NY), 1997.
The Honey Makers, Morrow (New York, NY), 1997.
Click!: A Book about Cameras and Taking Pictures, Little, Brown (Boston, MA), 1997.
The Moon Book, Holiday House (New York, NY), 1997.
Marshes and Swamps, Holiday House (New York, NY), 1998.
Soaring with the Wind: The Bald Eagle, Morrow (New York, NY), 1998.
Yippee-Yay!: A Book about Cowboys and Cowgirls, Little, Brown (Boston, MA), 1998.
Penguins!, Holiday House (New York, NY), 1998.
The Art Box, Holiday House (New York, NY), 1998.
Bats, Holiday House (New York, NY), 1999.

Santa Who?, Morrow (New York, NY), 1999.
Pigs, Holiday House (New York, NY), 1999.
Exploring the Deep, Dark Sea, Little, Brown (Boston, MA), 1999.
The Pumpkin Book, Holiday House (New York, NY), 1999.
Behold—the Dragons!, Morrow (New York, NY), 1999.
Apples, Holiday House (New York, NY), 2000.
My Basketball Book, HarperCollins (New York, NY), 2000.
My Football Book, HarperCollins (New York, NY), 2000.
Rabbits, Rabbits, and More Rabbits!, Holiday House (New York, NY), 2000.
My Soccer Book, HarperCollins (New York, NY), 2000.
My Baseball Book, HarperCollins (New York, NY), 2000.
Behold . . . the Unicorns!, HarperCollins (New York, NY), 2001.
Ducks!, Holiday House (New York, NY), 2001.
Christmas Is . . ., Holiday House (New York, NY), 2001.
Tell Me, Tree . . . : All about Trees for Kids, Little Brown (Boston, MA), 2002.
Polar Bears, Holiday House (New York, NY), 2002.
The Berry Book, Holiday House (New York, NY), 2002.
Giant Pandas, Holiday House (New York, NY), 2002.
Halloween Is . . ., Holiday House (New York, NY), 2002.
Chicks and Chickens, Holiday House (New York, NY), 2003.
Mummies, Pyramids, and Pharaohs: A Book about Ancient Egypt, Little, Brown (Boston, MA), 2003.
Quilting Bee, HarperCollins (New York, NY), 2003.
Grizzly Bears, Holiday House (New York, NY), 2003.
Horses!, Holiday House (New York, NY), 2003.

ILLUSTRATOR

Jane Yolen, *Rounds about Rounds*, F. Watts (New York, NY), 1977.
Judith Enderle, *Good Junk*, Dandelion Press (New York, NY), 1979.
Catharine Chase, *Hot and Cold*, Dandelion Press (New York, NY), 1979.
Catharine Chase, *The Mouse in My House*, Dandelion Press (New York, NY), 1979.
Catharine Chase, *My Balloon*, Dandelion Press (New York, NY), 1979.
Catharine Chase, *Pete, the Wet Pet*, Dandelion Press (New York, NY), 1979.
Catharine Chase, *The Mouse at the Show*, Dandelion Press (New York, NY), 1980.
Joanna Cole, *Cars and How They Go*, Crowell (New York, NY), 1983.

WORK IN PROGRESS: The Quilting Bee, for HarperCollins (New York, NY); *Mummies, Pyramids, and Pharaohs*, for Little, Brown (Boston, MA); *Thanksgiving Is . . .*, for Holiday House (New York, NY).

SIDELIGHTS: Gail Gibbons is a prolific author of nonfiction books for children. Her self-illustrated titles have informed an entire generation about the mysterious workings of mechanical items from clocks to trucks, the organization behind the bustle at post offices, department stores, and fire houses, and the science behind everything from weather forecasting to building a skyscraper. Her books on the natural world have ranged widely through animals both familiar and exotic, plants, the planets, dinosaurs, and the seasons. As Jennifer Crichton once remarked in *Publishers Weekly*, Gibbons "writes and illustrates books that demystify life's everyday workings for readers in the five-to-nine age range." In 1987, when Gibbons won the *Washington Post*/Children's Book Guild Award for nonfiction, the judges noted: "The enormous breadth of subjects that Gail Gibbons has brought to life is astonishing." They further commented that Gibbons's works "are free-flowing fountains of information."

Born in Oak Park, Illinois, in 1944, Gibbons showed artistic talents at an early age and was encouraged by her parents to draw, write, and paint. "I consider myself quite fortunate because I never had to debate with myself as to what I wanted to do with my life," the author recalled in *Something about the Author Autobiography Series (SAAS)*. After earning an undergraduate degree in art from the University of Illinois, she found work as a graphic artist for television, first in Chicago and then in New York City. Her credits for WNBC-TV include the *Today Show* and *Saturday Night Live*, As Gibbons once told *CA:* "I became interested in writing children's books when in college—one of my instructors was involved in illustrating children's books. I did a children's show, *Take a Giant Step*, for National Broadcasting Corp. for two years, doing all the artwork; this made me more interested in writing and drawing for children." Her first husband's untimely death provided further impetus to move from television to print.

A background in television graphics helped Gibbons to create a distinctive illustration style that fits her nonfiction subject matter perfectly. "The bright colors I use come from my television background," Gibbons explained in a *Booklist* interview. "A television image is only on the screen for about ten seconds, so it has to be very readable and simple." Clear images and contrasting colors are a hallmark of Gibbons's work, and as Martha Rosen observed in *School Library Journal,* "The colorful, cartoon-like illustrations reinforce the message of the text."

Gibbons gravitated to nonfiction for several reasons. First, a market existed for books that explain facts to very young children. Second, choosing nonfiction allows the author to research many subjects that fascinate her, and that research includes travel to exotic locales and interviews with scientists and naturalists. Third, Gibbons feels strongly that nonfiction is important for children, that it nurtures their curiosity and helps them to make sense of the world. As a reviewer in *Horn Book* put it, when children begin to explore a topic, they usually want to familiarize themselves with the subject "by getting a grip on facts and basic jargon; Gibbons provides such a service."

Although they range widely in the subjects they treat, many of Gibbons's books follow a similar format. The topic at hand is clearly explained with bold graphic illustrations, and pages at the end of the book expand upon some of the more difficult concepts or offer suggestions, recipes, and vocabulary terms. In her series of sports books, *My Baseball Book, My Football Book, My Soccer Book* and *My Basketball Book,* she explains how the rules work for each game, the equipment used, the scoring, and the playing field, with brief glossaries at the end of each title. Susan Dove Lempke in her *Booklist* review noted: "These books make the sports understandable."

In her *SAAS* essay, Gibbons wrote: "Nonfiction requires a tremendous amount of research. . . . I usually am working on a number of books all at the same time. I might be illustrating one, researching another, and working on the writing of another. . . . Whenever I am speaking to children, teachers, and librarians, I always stress how much I feel that nonfiction is important. I am constantly impressed in seeing what is happening in schools and libraries around the country. There is a sincere excitement about good literature coming from these places. I like to encourage others to write, hoping that it will be as exciting and rewarding to them as it has been to me."

BIOGRAPHICAL AND CRITICAL SOURCES:

BOOKS

Authors of Books for Young People, Scarecrow Press (Metuchen, NJ), 1990.

Children's Books and Their Creators, Houghton Mifflin (Boston, MA), 1995.

Children's Literature Review, Volume 8, Gale (Detroit, MI), 1985.

St. James Guide to Children's Writers, 5th edition, St. James Press (Detroit, MI), 1999.

Something about the Author Autobiography Series, Volume 12, Gale (Detroit, MI), 1991, pp. 71-82.

PERIODICALS

Booklist, November 1, 1979, Barbara Elleman, review of *Clocks and How They Go,* p. 448; December 1, 1994, Stephanie Zvirin, "The *Booklist* Interview: Gail Gibbons," pp. 676-677; December 1, 1995, Carolyn Phelan, review of *Bicycle Book,* p. 630; March 15, 1997, Kay Weisman, review of *The Honey Makers,* p. 1245; May 1, 2000, Susan Dove Lempke, review of *My Baseball Book,* p. 1672; August, 2000, Gillian Engberg, review of *Apples,* p. 2144; September 15, 2001, Gillian Engberg, review of *Polar Bears,* p. 225; March 1, 2002, Carolyn Phelan, review of *The Berry Book,* p. 1137.

Chicago Tribune Book World, December 12, 1982.

Children's Book Review Service, spring, 1984, Barbara S. Worth, review of *Department Store,* p. 122.

Horn Book, December, 1979, Ann A. Flowers, review of *Clocks and How They Go,* p. 676; December, 1980, Karen Jameyson, review of *Locks and Keys,* p. 653; July-August, 1985, Elizabeth S. Watson, review of *The Milk Makers,* pp. 463-464; November-December, 1987, Nancy Vasilakis, review of *The Pottery Place,* pp. 758-759; January, 2000, review of *Bats,* p. 97; July-August, 2002, Danielle J. Ford, review of *Tell Me, Tree: All about Trees for Kids,* p. 484.

New York Times Book Review, November 18, 1979; September 26, 1982, George A. Woods, review of *The Post Office Book: Mail and How It Moves,* p. 31.

Publishers Weekly, February 18, 1983, review of *Paper, Paper, Everywhere,* p. 129; July 27, 1984, Jennifer Crichton, "Picture Books That Explain," pp. 88-89.

School Library Journal, December, 1984, Harriet Otto, review of *The Seasons of Arnold's Apple Tree,* p. 70; April, 1985, Eldon Younce, review of *The Milk Makers,* p. 78; June-July, 1987, Martha Rosen, review of *Deadline!: From News to Newspaper,* p. 82; September, 1989, Mary Lou Budd, review of *Marge's Diner,* p. 226; March, 1998, John Sigwald, review of *Yippee-Yay!: A Book about Cowboys and Cowgirls,* p. 195; September, 2000, Louise L. Sherman, review of *Apples,* p. 216; September, 2001, Edith Ching, review of *Polar Bears,* p. 214; December, 2001, Teri Markson, review of *Behold . . . the Unicorns!,* p. 121; March, 2002, Anne Chapman Callaghan, review of *The Berry Book,* p. 214.

ONLINE

Gail Gibbons Web site, http://www.gailgibbons.com/ (January 21, 2003).

* * *

GILMAN, Dorothy 1923-
(Dorothy Gilman Butters)

PERSONAL: Born June 25, 1923, in New Brunswick, NJ; daughter of James Bruce (a minister) and Essa (Starkweather) Gilman; married Edgar A. Butters, Jr. (a teacher), September 15, 1945 (divorced, 1965); children: Christopher and Jonathan. *Education:* Attended Pennsylvania Academy of Fine Arts, 1940-45, University of Pennsylvania and Art Students' League, 1963-64. *Politics:* Democrat. *Religion:* Unitarian Universalist.

ADDRESSES: *Home*—Westport, CT. *Agent*—Howard Morhaim Literary Agency, 175 Fifth Ave., New York, NY 10010-7703.

CAREER: Samuel Fleischer Art Memorial, Philadelphia, PA, instructor in drawing in adult evening school, two years; switchboard operator, New Jersey Bell Telephone Co., one year; Cherry Lawn School, Darien, CT, instructor in creative writing, 1969-70.

MEMBER: Authors Guild.

AWARDS, HONORS: Catholic Book Award for *A Nun in the Closet.*

WRITINGS:

FOR YOUNG ADULTS, EXCEPT AS NOTED; UNDER NAME DOROTHY GILMAN BUTTERS

Enchanted Caravan, illustrations by Janet Smalley, Macrae Smith (Philadelphia, PA), 1949, published as *Caravan,* Doubleday (New York, NY), 1992.

Carnival Gypsy, Macrae Smith (Philadelphia, PA), 1950.

Ragamuffin Alley, Macrae Smith (Philadelphia, PA), 1951.

The Calico Year, Macrae Smith (Philadelphia, PA), 1953.

Four-Party Line, Macrae Smith (Philadelphia, PA), 1954.

Papa Dolphin's Table (for children), Knopf (New York, NY), 1955.

Girl in Buckskin (Junior Literary Guild selection), Macrae Smith (Philadelphia, PA), 1956.

Heartbreak Street (Junior Literary Guild selection), Macrae Smith (Philadelphia, PA), 1958.

Witch's Silver (Junior Literary Guild selection), Macrae Smith (Philadelphia, PA), 1959.

Masquerade, Macrae Smith (Philadelphia, PA), 1961, published as *Heart's Design,* Berkley (New York, NY), 1963.

Ten Leagues to Boston Town (Junior Literary Guild selection), Macrae Smith (Philadelphia, PA), 1962.

The Bells of Freedom (Weekly Reader Book Club selection), illustrations by Carol Wilde, Macrae Smith (Philadelphia, PA), 1963, reprinted, Peter Smith, 1984.

(Under name Dorothy Gilman) *The Maze in the Heart of the Castle,* Doubleday (New York, NY), 1983.

ADULT NOVELS

The Unexpected Mrs. Pollifax, Doubleday (New York, NY), 1966, reprinted, Fawcett (New York, NY), 1985, published as *Mrs. Pollifax, Spy,* Tandem (London, England), 1971.

Uncertain Voyage, Doubleday (New York, NY), 1967, reprinted, Fawcett (New York, NY), 1989.
The Amazing Mrs. Pollifax, Doubleday (New York, NY), 1970, Fawcett (New York, NY), 1986.
The Elusive Mrs. Pollifax, Doubleday (New York, NY), 1971, reprinted, Gale (Detroit, MI), 1993.
A Palm for Mrs. Pollifax, Doubleday (New York, NY), 1973.
A Nun in the Closet, Doubleday (New York, NY), 1975, published as *A Nun in the Cupboard,* R. Hale (London, England), 1976.
The Clairvoyant Countess, Doubleday (New York, NY), 1975.
Mrs. Pollifax on Safari, Doubleday (New York, NY), 1977.
The Tightrope Walker, Doubleday (New York, NY), 1979, reprinted, Curley (South Yarmouth, MA), 1992..
Mrs. Pollifax on the China Station, Doubleday (New York, NY), 1983.
Mrs. Pollifax and the Hong Kong Buddha, Doubleday (New York, NY), 1985.
Mrs. Pollifax and the Golden Triangle, Doubleday (New York, NY), 1988.
Incident at Badamya (Literary Guild alternate selection), Doubleday (New York, NY), 1989.
Mrs. Pollifax and the Whirling Dervish, Doubleday (New York, NY), 1990.
Mrs. Pollifax and the Second Thief, Doubleday (New York, NY), 1993.
Mrs. Pollifax Pursued, Wheeler (Hingham, MA), 1995.
Mrs. Pollifax and the Lion Killer, Fawcett Columbine (New York, NY), 1996.
Mrs. Pollifax, Innocent Tourist, Random House (New York, NY), 1997.
Thale's Folly, Ballantine Books (New York, NY), 1999.
Mrs. Pollifax Unveiled, Ballentine Books (New York, NY), 2000.
Kaleidoscope: A Countess Karitska Novel, Ballantine Books (New York, NY), 2002.

OTHER

(Contributor) *On Creative Writing,* edited by Paul Engle, Dutton (New York, NY), 1964.
A New Kind of Country (nonfiction), Doubleday (New York, NY), 1978.

Contributor to *Good Housekeeping, Jack and Jill, Redbook, Ladies' Home Journal, Cosmopolitan, Writer,* and other magazines; contributor of short stories, under name Dorothy Gilman Butters, to *Redbook.*

ADAPTATIONS: The Unexpected Mrs. Pollifax was filmed by United Artists in 1970 as "Mrs. Pollifax—Spy," starring Rosalind Russell. *Mrs. Pollifax, Innocent Tourist* was recorded as an audiobook, as was *Mrs. Pollifax Unveiled* by Brillance Audio, 2000.

SIDELIGHTS: Dorothy Gilman began her career as a novelist by writing books for children during the 1950s. Of her young-adult titles written under her married name, Dorothy Gillman Butters, the first, *The Enchanted Caravan,* was republished as *Caravan* a half-century after its debut. During the mid-1960s Gilman began writing mystery novels under her maiden name. Among her sleuths is the sixty-year-old Mrs. Pollifax, an unlikely but sympathetic detective who stars in more than a dozen titles written over a thirty-year period, and the psychically endowed Madame Karitska of *The Clairvoyant Countess* and *Kaleidoscope.*

A writer of popular suspense novels, Gilman "creates appealing characters whose 'ordinary' lives are changed by their encounters with danger," explained Mary Helen Becker in *Twentieth-Century Crime and Mystery Writers.* "Naive and innocent to begin with, apparently handicapped by age, poverty, or emotional problems, they pit their courage, perseverance, and resourcefulness (fortified by inner strength discovered in time of need), against the organized powers of evil." Gilman's most popular creation is Mrs. Emily Pollifax, a bored and lonely New Jersey widow in her sixties who applies to the CIA for a job and is chosen for special assignments. Looking more like a tourist than a spy, "Mrs. Pollifax is (at least, on the surface) the archetypal little old lady," wrote *New York Times Book Review* contributor Allen J. Hubin. Likewise, *New York Times* reviewer Thomas Lask called Mrs. Pollifax "the picture of the innocent abroad." *Under the Covers* reviewer Harriet Klausner likened Mrs. Pollifax to sleuth Jessica Fletcher of the popular *Murder She Wrote* television series. She praised Gilman's 2000 offering, *Mrs. Pollifax Unveiled,* for its "fresh" characters and smoothly flowing narrative. While remarking that the subgenre of "cozy spy thriller" is a rarity at the turn of the millennium, *Library Journal*'s I. Pour-El noted that sales of Gilman's titles are good, which is a likely result of the "slick and charming" quality of her books, to quote Rex E. Klett, also of *Library Journal.*

The Pollifax novels chronicle their intrepid heroine's adventures in exotic locales, where her kindly and sympathetic nature often leads her to involve herself with a variety of unusual people. As Becker explained, "Warmhearted and open minded, Mrs. Pollifax is without prejudice and is always sympathetic to those in trouble." This sympathy for strangers, however, frequently involves her in adventures unforeseen by her CIA employers. But the resourceful Pollifax always extracts herself from real trouble. "Disarmingly self-mocking, whenever she is in a tight spot, Mrs. Pollifax imagines what would happen in the movies and acts accordingly, all the while regretting her own clichés," Becker stated.

Lask, however, considered the spy as sometimes too inactive: "Mrs. Pollifax is like an obstacle around whom the rough waters churn and boil. Things happen to her rather than the other way around, and her chancy approach to events [is] so open-eyed that it's a wonder she survives at all." Commenting on *Mrs. Pollifax and the Golden Triangle,* Elaine S. Povich of the *Chicago Tribune* noted a similar failing: "The book keeps readers wondering what is coming next, but it fails to portray Emily Pollifax as much more than a victim of events she cannot control." Other reviewers, however, willingly accept the elderly lady as an alternative to the James Bond stereotype. Hubin concluded: "Mrs. Pollifax is an enchantress—long may she terrorize spydom!"

Whatever the novels' supposed shortcomings, they have long been popular, as evidenced by their continual reprinting. In 1992 *The Amazing Mrs. Pollifax* saw its twenty-third printing. Yet in 2000 Gilman took a vacation from Mrs. Pollifax, revisiting instead Madame Karitska of her 1975 novel *The Clairvoyant Countess.* In *Kaleidoscope,* a "tantalizing sequel" to quote a *Publishers Weekly* reviewer, Madame Karitska uses her psychic powers to solve a string of mysteries brought to her by clients and by serendipity. Several critics found the work flawed but enjoyable, including a *Kirkus Reviews* contributor, who dubbed the heroine likeable but described the work as a collection of "uneven" short stories that vary from "the sentimental to the melodramatic." Writing in *Booklist,* GraceAnne A DeCandido remarked that the characters are not fully developed and dubbed the work overall a "light read with some heavy underpinnings" because of its subplot about terrorist activity. Despite any shortcomings, this "well-written, episodic adventure . . . will appeal to many," predicted *Library Journal*'s Rex E. Klett.

BIOGRAPHICAL AND CRITICAL SOURCES:

BOOKS

Twentieth-Century Crime and Mystery Writers, 3rd edition, St. James Press (Detroit, MI), 1991.

PERIODICALS

Booklist, January 1, 2000, GraceAnne A. DeCandido, review of *Mrs. Pollifax Unveiled,* p. 883; December 1, 2001, GraceAnne A. DeCandido, review of *Kaleidoscope: A Countess Karitska Novel,* p. 632.

Chicago Tribune, February 25, 1988.

Kirkus Reviews, January 15, 1999, review of *Thale's Folly,* p. 107; December 1, 1999, review of *Mrs. Pollifax Unveiled,* p. 1851; November 1, 2001, review of *Kaleidoscope,* p. 1518.

Kliatt Young Adult Paperback Book Guide, January, 1999, review of *Mrs. Pollifax, Innocent Tourist* (audio version), pp. 46+.

Library Journal, February 1, 2000, Rex E. Klett, review of *Mrs. Pollifax Unveiled,* p. 121; February 1, 2001, I. Pour-El, review of *Mrs. Pollifax Unveiled* (audio version), p. 144; December, 2001, Rex E. Klett, review of *Kaleidoscope,* p. 178.

Mystery Reader, March 12, 2002, review of *Kaleidoscope.*

New York Times, January 1, 1972.

New York Times Book Review, March 20, 1966; October 15, 1967; March 8, 1970.

Publishers Weekly, January 24, 2000, review of *Mrs. Pollifax Unveiled,* p. 295; December 24, 2001, review of *Kaleidoscope,* p. 45.

Times Literary Supplement, February 23, 1967.

ONLINE

Dorothy Gilman Home Page, http://www.geocities.com/jmkowalchuk/ (May 29, 2004).

Stop, You're Killing Me! (murder mystery site), http://www.stopyourekillingme.com/Dorothy-Gilman.html/ (November 9, 2003).

Under the Covers, http://www.silcon.com/ (May 8, 2003), Harriet Klausner, review of *Mrs. Pollifax Unveiled,* and review of *Thale's Folly.**

GINGRICH, Newt(on Leroy) 1943-

PERSONAL: Born June 17, 1943, in Harrisburg, PA; son of Robert Bruce and Kathleen (Daugherty) Gingrich; married Jacqueline Battley, 1962 (divorced); married Marianne Ginther, 1981 (divorced, 2000); married Callista Bisek, August 18, 2000; children: Linda Kathleen, Jacqueline Sue. *Education:* Emory University, B.A., 1965; Tulane University, M.A., 1968, Ph.D., 1971. *Religion:* Baptist.

ADDRESSES: *Home*—Virginia. *Office*—The Gingrich Group, LLC, 1301 K St. NW, Suite 800 W, Washington, DC 20005.

CAREER: West Georgia College, Carrollton, professor of history and environmental studies, 1970-78; U.S. House of Representatives, Washington, DC, representative from Sixth District of Georgia and member of Administrative Committee and Public Works and Transportation Committee, 1979-89, House Republican Whip, 1989, Speaker of the House, 1995-99; The Gingrich Group (communications and consulting firm), Washington, DC, and Atlanta, GA, currently chief executive officer. Cofounder, Congressional Military Reform Caucus; founder, Center for Health Transformation. Reinhardt College, Waleska, GA, adjunct professor, 1994-95; distinguished visiting scholar and professor, National Defense University; Hoover Institution, Stanford University, Palo Alto, CA, distinguished visiting fellow. Member, U.S. Commission on National Security/21st Century, the Hart/Rudman Commission, beginning 1999; board member, Juvenile Diabetes Foundation; member, Defense Policy Board; American Enterprise Institute, Washington, DC, senior fellow; member, Congressional Clearinghouse on the Future; member of Terrorism Task Force, Council on Foreign Relations; honorary chair, Nano-Business Alliance; advisory board member, Museum of the Rockies. Has also worked as a news and political analyst for Fox News Channel.

MEMBER: American Academy of Arts and Letters, World Future Society, Conservative Opportunity Society (cofounder), Sierra Club, Georgia Conservancy, Kiwanis Club.

AWARDS, HONORS: *Time* magazine Man of the Year, 1995; Georgia Citizen of the Year, March of Dimes, 1995; Legislative Conservationist of the Year, Georgia

Newt Gingrich

Wildlife Federation, 1998; Science Pioneer award, Science Coalition, 2001, for outstanding contributions to educating the public about science.

WRITINGS:

(Author of preface) Alfred Balitzer, *A Nation of Associations,* American Society of Association Executives and American Medical Political Action Committee, 1981.

(With Marianne Gingrich and David Drake) *Window of Opportunity: A Blueprint for the Future,* Tor (New York, NY), 1984.

(Author of foreword) Teresa Donovan, Marcella Donovan, and Joseph Piccione, *Voluntary School Prayer: Judicial Dilemma, Proposed Solutions,* Free Congress Research and Education Foundation, 1984.

(Author of foreword) David Dean, editor, *Low Intensity Conflict and Modern Technology,* Air University Press (Washington, DC), 1986.

(Author of introduction) Perry Smith and others, *Creating Strategic Vision,* National Defense University Press (Washington, DC), 1987.

(Author of foreword) Gordon Jones and John Marini, editors, *Imperial Congress,* Pharos Books (Jupiter, FL), 1988.

Contract with America: The Bold Plan to Change the Nation, Times Books (New York, NY), 1994.

Quotations from Speaker Newt: The Little Red, White, and Blue Book of the Republican Revolution, Workman (New York, NY), 1995.

(With Bill Tucker) *To Renew America,* HarperCollins (New York, NY), 1995.

Restoring the Dream: The Bold New Plan by House Republicans, Times Books (New York, NY), 1995.

(With William R. Forstchen) *1945* (novel), Baen Publishing Enterprises (New York, NY), 1995.

Newt Gingrich's Renewing American Civilization (sound recording), Audio Renaissance Tapes, 1997.

Lessons Learned the Hard Way: A Personal Report, HarperCollins (New York, NY), 1998.

(With William Forstchen) *Gettysburg: A Novel of the Civil War,* St. Martin's Press (New York, NY), 2003.

(With Dana Pavey and Anne Woodbury) *Saving Lives & Saving Money,* Alexis de Tocqueville Institution, 2003.

Contributor to books, including *Liberal Cliches/Conservative Solutions,* edited by Phil Crane, Green Hill (Ottawa, IL), 1984; *Nuclear Arms: Ethics, Strategy, Politics,* edited by Jim Woolsey, ICS Press (San Francisco, CA), 1984; and *House of Ill Repute,* edited by Dan Renberg, Princeton University Press (Princeton, NJ), 1987. Member of editorial board, *Biosecurity and Bioterrorism.*

SIDELIGHTS: Whatever one's political viewpoint, politician, writer, and orator Newt Gingrich may go down in history as a symbol of the state of America during the 1990s. Beginning his political career as a Republican congressman from Georgia in a hotly Democratic House of Representatives, Gingrich parlayed both the power of his party and his personal fortitude over the next sixteen years, becoming Speaker of the House in 1995. Working under the shadow of the popular administration of Democratic president Bill Clinton, Gingrich proposed to do battle with the political status quo. His mission, according to *Newsweek* reporter Howard Fineman, has been clear from the beginning of his career: to fight "corruption, bloated government and a decaying social order." To Gingrich, Fineman explained, "politics really is a matter of life or death, of good or evil, of domination or loss. He has spent a career trying to prove that politics is as tough as war, as important to freedom."

Gingrich was born into the transient world occupied by many military families. As the stepson of a career officer in the U.S. military, young Newt attended five schools over an eight-year period during his childhood, and lived in three states and two countries in the process. In 1956 the thirteen-year-old Gingrich and his family witnessed the Hungarian Uprising while stationed in that area of the Eastern European shatterzone. The family lived under the constant threat of violence during their stay there. A visit to the battlefield at Verdun the following spring further impressed the young student of the importance of history, and of political power. "All that summer I kept thinking to myself, 'This is crazy,'" Gingrich revealed to Fineman. "'People really do bad things to each other.'" The realization that politics was the vehicle for such evil, and that political power in the hands of those dedicated to "right" could make a positive difference for society, would remain his guiding principle, fueling his interest in military history and setting his later course in U.S. politics.

While making his views clear to members of his Georgia constituency during his early tenure as congressman, Gingrich enlightened U.S. readers as to his vision for a "very different, more optimistic, decentralized, growth-oriented, safer American future" in *Window of Opportunity: A Blueprint for the Future,* published in 1985 by science-fiction publisher Tor Books and promoted through funding by various special interest groups. Written while Gingrich was a member of the executive committee of the Clearinghouse of the Future and was actively involved in the formation of the Congressional Space Caucus, *Window of Opportunity* presents ways in which U.S. social and political ills can be solved by technology. Addressing such diverse issues as social security, space exploration, and traditional values, the volume also contains the conservative back-slapping and antiwelfare-state rhetoric that have since become characteristic of its author. The book was hailed as "offering a hopeful political and social strategy to realize the American dream" by fellow congressman Jack Kemp in the *American Spectator.*

The year 1995 found Gingrich an almost ubiquitous presence in the media—from the cover of *Time,* where he was pronounced 1995's Man of the Year, to CNN, C-SPAN, and the nightly news, Gingrich's leadership of the Republican freshman congress in its efforts to balance the federal budget received constant coverage. Gingrich's visibility on television was matched by his appearance on bookstore shelves, smiling from the dust jacket of his second book, titled *To Renew America,* written with Bill Tucker.

A manifesto of Gingrich's beliefs, the book is divided into five parts: "Visions and Strategies," "The Six Challenges," "The Contract with America," "The Ongoing Revolution," and the forward-looking "A New Beginning: The America We Will Create." While praising Gingrich for addressing the issue of spending reforms with regard to both the Senate and the House of Representatives, Kevin Philips noted that, like *Window of Opportunity, To Renew America* "is stuffed with Pollyannaish views of how technology will uplift politics, culture and public policy." Reviewing the work in the *Washington Post Book World,* Philips also stated that while Gingrich "has his strong points as a historian . . . he didn't get tenure in his years [teaching] at West Georgia College, and his book is sure to inspire a competition among snickering history professors to scalp the speaker in professional journals." Michael Lind made a similar observation in the *New York Times Book Review,* calling Gingrich's philosophical underpinnings "the antiseptic high-tech future familiar to those of us who grew up between the 1939 World's Fair and the Apollo missions," and questioning the speaker's use of "*Reader's Digest* and *The Saturday Evening Post* from around 1955" as a realistic baseline from which to judge the failure of modern society.

The fictional work *1945,* also published in 1995, takes another futuristic look at contemporary society, this time from a viewpoint created through an alternate history of World War II. In the novel, Nazi leader Adolf Hitler is severely injured in a plane crash in late 1941, the day before the actual Japanese bombing of Pearl Harbor, leaving others to orchestrate the war. Under the leadership of Nazis such as Albert Speer, war is never declared on the United States, nor is Russia invaded. Instead, Germany focuses on the conquest of Western Europe, while the United States is left to quickly defeat Japan. By 1943 most of Europe is in the hands of the Germans. The States, with no threat of a Communist menace, take arms development—including the atomic bomb—at a more leisurely pace, leaving themselves open to German attack. While noting that the scenario is a credible one, *New York Times Book Review* contributor Donald E. Westlake criticized the lack of setting and character development, noting, "There isn't a scene in the book in which the characters aren't in uniform." He went on to add, "There is no discernible theme and scant literary ambition" in the book, "though some of the descriptions of military equipment have a certain poetry about them." In the *Times Literary Supplement,* however, Tom Shippey observed that Gingrich and coauthor William R. Fortschen skillfully employ the conventions of the alternative-history genre. The point of such novels, according to Shippey, is not just to show what went wrong about a particular event but to "create a sense of the fragility of the real world we too often accept as inevitable." In this, the reviewer felt, the authors succeeded very well.

Although some reviewers felt that Gingrich's forte might not be fiction, his accomplishments as a politician loom large. "A tough operator, a master of the workings of modern representative politics, a man of ideas and a subversively high level of culture" was how David Frum characterized Gingrich in a review of *To Renew America* in the *Times Literary Supplement.* Unlike other U.S. politicians, Frum observed, "he is not a man to confuse feeling with doing. Which is why," the critic noted, "unlike the soon to be forgotten Bill Clinton, Newt Gingrich . . . is poised to dominate American politics for a decade."

Frum's prediction, however, did not pan out. Gingrich barely won reelection in 1995 and was soon plagued by federal investigators who suspected him of tax violations. Of the seventy-five charges filed against him, he was exonerated of all but one, which he admitted to. The result was a $300,000 fine, and the scandal resulted in Gingrich being attacked by many members of his own party. The Republicans became divided, but with no clear leader among their ranks to replace Gingrich, the speaker retained his position in the House. Although he was reelected again in 1998, Gingrich had lost his taste for politics and in 1999 he resigned (some say he was pressured to do so) not only as Speaker of the House but as a congressman. He describes some of his travails in Congress in his 1998 book, *Lessons Learned the Hard Way: A Personal Report.* Gingrich subsequently became a political commentator for Fox News, and he founded his own communications and consulting firm, The Gingrich Group.

Now active as a teacher at the National Defense University, a lecturer, consultant, and advisor, Gingrich has continued to write. In the spirit of his earlier novel, *1945,* Gingrich cowrote another alternate-history novel with William Forstchen titled *Gettysburg: A Novel of the Civil War.* Published in 2003, the story draws a "what if" scenario in which General Robert E. Lee takes direct charge of the Confederacy's troops at Gettysburg, outflanks the Union's General Meade, and manages to defeat the North at the historic, tide-turning battle. *Gettysburg* garnered more positive reviews than *1945,* even though a *Publishers Weekly* critic noticed the authors' "certain bias" for the characters on the side of the Confederacy. The reviewer declared the novel a "well-executed" story that will prove to be a "veritable feast" for buffs of historical fiction and Civil War history. A *Library Journal* contributor similarly noted that *Gettysburg* "will appeal to Civil War aficionados." Harry Levins, writing for the *Knight Ridder/Tribune News Service* described the book as "interesting" and "well crafted."

Among his many other pursuits and interests, Gingrich has been heavily involved in the currently hot topic of health care, and he serves on the board of the Juvenile Diabetes Foundation. Consistent with his attitude in *Window of Opportunity,* in his other 2003 book, *Saving Lives & Saving Money,* the former speaker believes that technology can go a long way toward resolving the current health crisis in America. The book, which was written with Dana Pavey and Anne Woodbury, also maintains that part of the solution lies in preventive care, innovation, and a focus on the individual. Content not to be holding political office any longer, in a 2002 *Time* magazine interview with Douglas Waller, Gingrich revealed his continuing optimism in the opportunities technological advances may bring humanity. "If you look at science, technology and entrepreneurship," he insisted, "the twenty-first century ought to be a century of more choices, greater quality and lower cost. I'm trying to take this very simple model and teach companies how to apply it and governments how to change to encourage it."

BIOGRAPHICAL AND CRITICAL SOURCES:

BOOKS

Andersen, Alfred F., *Challenging Newt Gingrich: Chapter by Chapter,* Tom Paine Institute (Eugene, OR), 1996.

Bentley, P. F., *Newt: Inside the Revolution,* Collins (San Francisco, CA), 1995.

Drew, Elizabeth, *Showdown: The Struggle between the Gingrich Congress and the Clinton White House,* Simon & Schuster (New York, NY), 1996.

Maraniss, David, *"Tell Newt to Shut Up!": Prizewinning Washington Post Journalists Reveal How Reality Gagged the Gingrich Revolution,* Simon & Schuster (New York, NY), 1996.

Steely, Mel, *The Gentleman from Georgia: The Biography of Newt Gingrich,* Mercer University Press (Macon, GA), 2000.

Warner, Judith, *Newt Gingrich: Speaker to America,* Signet (New York, NY), 1995.

Wilson, John K., *Newt Gingrich: Capitol Crimes and Misdemeanors,* Common Courage (Monroe, ME), 1996.

PERIODICALS

American Spectator, December 1984.

Business Week, June 12, 1995, p. 34; May 20, 1996, p. 32.

Commonweal, October 6, 1995, p. 26.

Economist, July 8, 1995, p. 83; April 5, 1997, "In Defence of Newt," p. 25.

Fortune, March 31, 1997, David Shribman, "Newt Gingrich's Balancing Act," p. 42.

Gentlemen's Quarterly, January, 1996, p. 120.

Harper's, September, 1995, p. 5.

Insight on the News, January 30, 1995, p. 13; July 17, 1995, p. 8; December 2, 1996, Rick Kozak, "Speaker's Long Night Ends in Historic Victory," p. 12; August 25, 1997, David Wagner, "Who Is Newt?," p. 14.

Knight Ridder/Tribune News Service, July 9, 2003, Harry Levins, review of *Gettysburg: A Novel of the Civil War,* p. K0075.

Ladies Home Journal, November, 1995, p. 144.

Library Journal, June 15, 2003, "Rewriting the Civil War," p. 1000.

Maclean's, January 27, 1997, "Newt Gingrich Gets Fined $300,000," p. 31.

Meet the Press, June 17, 1990, p. 1; December 1, 1991, p. 1.

Nation, August 14, 1995, p. 174.

National Review, October 9, 1995, p. 62; October 23, 1995, p. 62; January 27, 1997, William F. Buckley, Jr., "What Next for Newt?," p. 62.

New Criterion, December, 1998, James Bowman, "The Gingrich Story," p. 64.

New Republic, January 23, 1995, p. 6; August 14, 1995, p. 34; May 6, 1996, David Grann, "The New Newt," p. 10; December 16, 1996, Hanna Rosin, "Newest Newt," p. 12.

New Statesman, November 13, 1998, Andrew Stephen, "Dinosaur Man Slips into Oblivion," p. 30.

Newsweek, January 9, 1995, pp. 28-34; December 11, 1995, Michael Isikoff and Weston Kosova, "The Trouble with Newt: An Ethics Probe May Be Closing In on the Speaker," p. 40; December 18, 1995, Michael Isikoff and Weston Kosova, "Why Newt's in Trouble," p. 36; July 24, 2000, "Newt's New Cyberworld: The Fallen Speaker Starts Over Again in Silicon Valley," p. 36.

New York Review of Books, August 10, 1995, p. 7.

New York Times Book Review, July 9, 1995, p. 10; July 23, 1995, p. 3.

People, August 30, 1999, "Talk of the Town: After Filing for Divorce from Wife, Marianne, Ex-Speaker Newt Gingrich Goes Public with a Not-So-Secret Romance," p. 65; November 29, 1999, "Combat Zone: The Opening Round of Gingrich v. Gingrich Signals the Start of a Long, Bitter Conflict," p. 217.

Publishers Weekly, July 29, 2002, "Newt's New Look at Gettysburg," p. 14; May 12, 2003, review of *Gettysburg,* p. 44.

Rolling Stone, December 29, 1994, p. 164.

Saturday Review, November, 1984.

Time, December 25, 1995, pp. 4, 48, 84; February 12, 1996, "When the Newt Falls," p. 20; November 18, 1996, Karen Tumulty, "The Man with the Plastic Bucket," p. 56; January 30, 1997, Karen Tumulty, "Julius Speaker: Uh-Oh, Newt Gingrich Is in Trouble Again, and Guess Which 'Friend' Has That Lean and Hungry Look?," p. 33; April 20, 1998, James Carney, "Newt's Secret Plan: To Stay Right Where He Is," p. 28; November 16, 1998, "Fall of the House of Newt," p. 38; November 22, 1999, "Newt: The Health Nut: In This Chapter of His Life, the Former Speaker Has Become Obsessed—with His Fitness and Yours," p. 47; April 15, 2002, Douglas Waller, "10 Questions for Newt Gingrich," p. 17.

Times Literary Supplement, September 22, 1995, p. 7; December 8, 1995, Tom Shippey, "Secret-Weapon School," p. 21.

U.S. News & World Report, April 10, 1995, p. 26; November 10, 1997, Douglas Stanglin, "Newt on Track for a Comeback: Gingrich Hitches His Political Star to Trade Agreement," p. 23; November 16, 1998, "The Speaker's Silence," p. 27; February 7, 2000, Lynn Rosellini, "Starting Over: The New Newt Gingrich," p. 20.

Vanity Fair, September, 1995, p. 147.

Village Voice, November 27, 1984.

Voice of Youth Advocates, April 1985, p. 62.

Washingtonian, July, 1995, p. 37.

Washington Monthly, September, 1995, p. 44.

Washington Post Book World, July 23, 1995, pp. 1, 14.

ONLINE

Gingrich Group, http://www.gingrichgroup.com/ (February 24, 2004).*

*   *   *

GIRARD, Joe 1928-

PERSONAL: Born Joseph Girardi, November 1, 1928, in Detroit, MI; son of Antony (an automobile assembly worker) and Grace (Stabile) Girardi; married June Krantz, June 2, 1951; children: Joe, Grace. *Politics:* Independent. *Religion:* Roman Catholic.

ADDRESSES: *Office*—P.O. Box 358, Eastpointe, MI 48021.

CAREER: Entrepreneur and author. Building contractor in Detroit, MI, 1949-63; Merollis Chevrolet, East Detroit, MI, new car and truck salesman, 1963-78; professional motivational speaker, 1978—. *Military service:* U.S. Army, 1947.

AWARDS, HONORS: Golden Plate Award, American Academy of Achievement, 1975; named Super Salesman of the Century by *Forbes* magazine, 1977; made *Guinness Book of World Records* twelve times for achieving top annual vehicle sales in the world; named to Automotive Hall of Fame, 2001.

WRITINGS:

(With Stanley H. Brown) *How to Sell Anything to Anybody,* Simon & Schuster (New York, NY), 1977.

(With Robert Casemore) *How to Sell Yourself,* introduction by Norman Vincent Peale, Simon & Schuster (New York, NY), 1980.

(With Robert L. Shook) *How to Close Every Sale,* Warner Books (New York, NY), 1989.

(With Robert Casemore) *Mastering Your Way to the Top: Secrets for Success from the World's Greatest Salesman and America's Leading Business People,* Warner Books (New York, NY), 1995.

Also author of sales technique film series and sales-training program.

ADAPTATIONS: Girard's books have been adapted as audiobooks and videocassettes.

SIDELIGHTS: In 1966 investigators from the *Guinness Book of World Records* undertook an eight-month study to officially determine if Joe Girard, salesman at Merollis Chevrolet of East Detroit, Michigan, was indeed the world's greatest salesperson. After consulting sales figures from corporations around the world, checking retail sales generated by salespeople involved with big-ticket items such as automobiles, boats, or houses, *Guinness* declared Girard the "world's greatest" at the job of selling. His record-breaking total of 1,425 cars and trucks sold retail in 1973 alone has never been equaled. So impressive was Girard's career record for vehicle sales—13,001 total—that he was the first salesman ever named to the Automotive Hall of Fame. Girard has also become a best-selling author and motivational speaker who imparts his success tips to corporate groups and individuals who want to excel.

Born and raised in Detroit, Girard first began working in construction as a home builder. He moved into new-car sales in 1963 and within three years had established himself as a top salesman. For twelve consecutive years he sold more cars on a one-on-one basis than any other person in the world. During his peak years he mailed an estimated 13,000 greeting cards per month to customers and hired his own staff out of pocket to prep vehicles and help recruit new buyers.

By 1977, according to a *Forbes* report, Girard was "spending only sixty percent of his working time selling cars." The rest of his time was devoted to promoting training programs aimed at helping others achieve greater levels of success in their lives. In an effort to reach an even wider audience, Girard soon published his first book, *How to Sell Anything to Anybody.* After the book's publication, he left his sales position in order to devote his full attention to telling others about his book and about his ideas on selling.

In *How to Sell Anything to Anybody,* as a *Business Week* reviewer noted, Girard develops two separate but interrelated stories. "The first is a series of thoughtful suggestions on the art of selling," explained the reviewer. "The second, more engaging story, is that of Joe Girard."

Girard's selling tips include the ways salespeople can organize their time and business, how they can appear honest and down-to-earth to their clients, and, most important in the Girard credo, how they can develop a positive mental attitude. Other Girard hints include having distinctive business cards printed, sending former customers birthday and holiday greetings, and getting the customer to feel "obliged" to the salesperson. One way Girard used to carry out this last hint was to keep several different brands of cigarettes in his desk. When he saw a customer patting his pockets looking for a cigarette, Girard would offer his client a smoke and let him keep the entire pack. Sometimes, he would even offer "the shirt off his back" to satisfy a customer and used to keep a spare shirt in his office just in case someone took him up on his offer.

A major portion of *How to Sell Anything to Anybody* is devoted to the story of Girard's life, a story that, according to Vicky Billington in the *Detroit News,* "has a definite rags-to-riches theme." Girard gives a capsulized autobiography in the introduction of the book and also explains why he decided to become an author. He says: "For the first thirty-five years of my life I was the world's biggest loser. I got thrown out of about forty different jobs. I lasted only ninety-seven days in the U.S. Army. I couldn't even make it as a crook. . . . How I got from there to here is what this book is about."

In his second book, *How to Sell Yourself,* the super salesman details what a *Publishers Weekly* reviewer called Girard's "strategy of personal salesmanship." According to Girard, the first step in selling ourselves to others is selling ourselves to ourselves. Girard reveals how individuals can take stock of their strengths and weaknesses and take charge of their lives. Norman Vincent Peale—author of the best-selling self-help book *The Power of Positive Thinking*—contributed the introduction to *How to Sell Yourself,* calling the book "one of the best books in [the motivational] field. In my opinion, it will become a classic in the success literature of our time. . . . Girard can help you. I know, for he has helped me."

In 2001 Girard was elected to the Automotive Hall of Fame, located in Dearborn, Michigan. The honor placed him alongside such automotive pioneers as Henry Ford, Charles Kettering, and Harvey Firestone. As David Rouse observed in a *Booklist* review of *Mastering Your Way to the Top: Secrets from the World's Greatest Salesman and America's Leading Business People,* Girard has achieved success because he is able to communicate so well with other people. The critic concluded of Girard: "He makes it all sound so easy and straightforward."

BIOGRAPHICAL AND CRITICAL SOURCES:

BOOKS

Girard, Joe, *How to Sell Anything to Anybody,* Simon & Schuster (New York, NY), 1978.

Girard, Joe, *How to Sell Yourself,* Simon & Schuster (New York, NY), 1980.

PERIODICALS

Adcrafter, November 4, 1977.

Automotive News, March 12, 2001, "Automotive Hall of Fame Honors Five," p. 14.

Booklist, March 15, 1995, David Rouse, review of *Mastering Your Way to the Top: Secrets for Success from the World's Greatest Salesman and America's Leading Business People,* p. 1293.

Business Week, May 1, 1978.

Detroit News, January 19, 1978; August 7, 2001, Maureen McDonald, "World-Record Salesman Earns Spot in Automotive Hall of Fame," p. 2.

Forbes, November 1, 1977.

Newsweek, July 2, 1973.

Publishers Weekly, December 10, 1979; August 14, 1981; January 16, 1995, review of *Mastering Your Way to the Top,* p. 450.

West Coast Review of Books, March, 1978.

ONLINE

Joe Girard Web site, http://www.joegirard.com (November 8, 2003).*

* * *

GIRLING, Richard 1945-

PERSONAL: Born November 14, 1945, in Hitchin, England; son of William George (a sales manager) and Betty (a civil servant; maiden name, Pontin) Girling; married Rosemary King, September 20, 1969; children: Thomas. *Education:* Attended Hitchin Boys' Grammar School in Hertfordshire, England. *Religion:* "Skeptic."

ADDRESSES: *Home*—Crouches, Newnham, near Baldock, Hertfordshire, England. *Office*—*Sunday Times,* 200 Grays Inn Rd., London WC1, England. *Agent*—Curtis Brown Ltd., 1 Craven Hill, London W2 3EP, England.

CAREER: *Sunday Times,* London, England, sub-editor of magazine, 1970-73, editor of letters page, 1973-75, editor of "Scene" page, beginning 1975, currently investigative reporter. Fellow Commoner of Corpus Christi College, Cambridge, 1981. Member of board of management of Watch Trust for Environmental Education.

AWARDS, HONORS: British Press Award, "specialist writer of the year," 2002.

WRITINGS:

Ielfstan's Place (novel), Heinemann (London, England), 1981, published as *The Forest on the Hill,* Viking (New York, NY), 1982.

Sprigg's War (novel), Heinemann (London, England), 1984.

(Editor) *The Sunday Times Travel Book,* David & Charles (Newton Abbot, England), 1985.

(Editor) *The New Sunday Times Travel Book,* David & Charles (Newton Abbot, England), 1986.

(Editor) *The Sunday Times Travel Book Three,* David & Charles (Newton Abbot, England), 1987.

(Editor) *The Sunday Times Lifeplan,* Collins (London, England), 1987.

(Editor) *The Making of the English Garden,* Macmillan (London, England), 1988.

(Editor) *The Best of Sunday Times Travel,* David & Charles (Newton Abbot, England), 1988.

(Editor, with Shona Crawford Poole) *Sunday Times Cook's Companion,* Ebury, 1993.

(Author of text) *Hidden Depths: From Autostereogram to Hypervision,* Studio Editions (London, England), 1994.

The View from the Top: A Panoramic Guide to Finding Britain's Most Beautiful Vistas, photographs by Paul Barker, Little, Brown (Boston, MA), 1997.

Contributor to *The Sunday Times Bedside Book,* edited by George Darby, Deutsch (London, England), 1978; and *The Sunday Times Book of the Countryside,* edited by Philip Clarke, Brian Jackman, and Derrik Mercer, Macdonald (London, England), 1980. Contributor to magazines and newspapers.

SIDELIGHTS: Richard Girling is a former editor of the "Scene" page in the *Sunday Times,* a leisure and environment section, responsible for covering conservation, ecology, architecture, travel, gardening, motoring, and property. Girling still works for the section, now as an investigative reporter on environmental issues. His 2001 feature stories on hoof-and-mouth disease and abuses in the salmon industry helped him to win the 2002 "specialist writer of the year" citation from the British Press Awards. Girling is also noted for editing travel books, and is the author of *The View from the Top: A Panoramic Guide to Finding Britain's Most Beautiful Vistas,* a book that explores fifteen of the best vistas in the British Isles and offers maps and directions to the sites.

Girling once commented: "The documentary style of my historical fiction grows out of a fascination with 'the spirit of place,' which is also the concern of conservation, and out of a determination not to fall into the traditionally florid, falsely romantic mold of historical novel writing.

"*The Forest on the Hill* is the history of an English rural community, from its first stirrings in 15,000 B.C. to the end of the Great War, told not as a single connective narrative but as a series of short stories or vignettes, each designed to be a reflection of an age. There is a conscious emphasis on historical correctness—some of it necessarily brutal—for it is my ambition that the reader should lay down the book and say, 'That is what it must have been like'; *not,* 'I wish I had been there.'

"Out of a true understanding of the past grows an appreciation of the present, from which in turn emerges one of the founding principles of conservation: That none of it should have been in vain."

BIOGRAPHICAL AND CRITICAL SOURCES:

PERIODICALS

Library Journal, June 15, 1982.

Sunday Times, March 24, 2002, "*Sunday Times* Wins Top Press Award," p. 2.*

* * *

GRACE, Sherrill E(lizabeth) 1944-

PERSONAL: Born August 18, 1944, in Ormstown, Quebec, Canada; daughter of Alfred and Elizabeth (Cribbs) Perley. *Education:* University of Western Ontario, B.A., 1965; McGill University, M.A., 1970, Ph. D., 1974.

ADDRESSES: *Office*—Department of English, University of British Columbia, Vancouver, British Columbia V6T 1W5, Canada.

CAREER: McGill University, Montreal, Quebec, Canada, lecturer, 1974-75, assistant professor of English, 1975-77; University of British Columbia, Vancouver, assistant professor, 1977-81, associate professor of English, beginning 1981.

MEMBER: Association of Canadian University Teachers of English, Association of Canadian Studies, Canadian Comparative Literature Association, Association of Canadian and Quebec Literature, Canadian Association for American Studies, Modern Language Association of America.

AWARDS, HONORS: Grants from Canada Council, 1977, and Social Sciences and Humanities Research Council of Canada, 1978-79, 1981-83; grant from Canadian Federation for the Humanities, 1983, for publication of *The Voyage That Never Ends: Malcolm Lowry's Fiction.*

WRITINGS:

Violent Duality: A Study of Margaret Atwood, Véhicule Press, 1980.

The Voyage That Never Ends: Malcolm Lowry's Fiction, University of British Columbia Press (Vancouver, British Columbia, Canada), 1982.

(Editor, with Lorraine Weir) *Margaret Atwood: Language, Text, and System,* University of British Columbia Press (Vancouver, British Columbia, Canada), 1983.

(Editor) *Sursum Corda! The Collected Letters of Malcolm Lowry,* University of Toronto Press (Toronto, Ontario, Canada), 1995.

Canada and the Idea of North, McGill-Queen's University Press (Kingston, Ontario, Canada), 2002.

Contributor to books, including *The Art of Malcolm Lowry,* edited by Anne Smith, Vision Press (London, Ontario, Canada), 1978; and *The Art of Margaret Atwood,* edited by Cathy Davidson and Arnold Davidson, House of Anansi Press (Toronto, Ontario, Canada), 1981; author of introduction, *The Circle Game,* by Margaret Atwood, House of Anansi Press (Toronto, Ontario, Canada), 1978. Contributor to literature and Canadian studies journals.

SIDELIGHTS: Sherrill E. Grace once told *CA:* "The title *The Voyage That Never Ends* is Lowry's own title for the sequence of interrelated novels that he was working on when he died. I used it because I discuss his incomplete enterprise and his manuscripts. Furthermore, the title summarizes most aptly his approach to art and his philosophy. My work on expressionism, in fact, began with expressionism in Lowry and over the past few years has become quite a passion with me. I am examining expressionism in literature, painting, and film (the old German silent expressionist films are superb!), and have also been working on Eugene O'Neill's early plays: *The Emperor Jones, The Hairy Ape, All God's Chillun, The Great God Brown,* et cetera."

BIOGRAPHICAL AND CRITICAL SOURCES:

PERIODICALS

Books in Canada, March, 2003, Eric Miller, review of *Canada and the Idea of North,* pp. 29-30.*

* * *

GRAHAM, Don B(allew) 1940-

PERSONAL: Born January 30, 1940, in Lucas, TX; son of Willie (a merchant) and Myrtle Joyce (a clerk; maiden name, Ballew) Graham; married Lois Volpone (divorced); married Betsy Anne Berry (a writer), June 14, 1991. *Education:* North Texas State University, B.A., 1962, M.A. (summa cum laude), 1964; University of Texas, Ph.D., 1971. *Hobbies and other interests:* Travel, writing.

ADDRESSES: Home—8704 Mariscal Canyon Dr., Austin, TX 78759-7154. *Office*—Department of English, University of Texas, Parlin Hall, Rm. 108, 1 University Station B5000, Austin, TX 78712-1164. *E-mail*—dgbb@mail.utexas.edu.

CAREER: Southwest Texas State University, San Marcos, instructor in English, 1965-69; University of Pennsylvania, Philadelphia, assistant professor of English, 1971-76; University of Texas at Austin, professor, 1976-85, J. Frank Dobie Regents Professor of American and English literature, 1985—. Texas Institute of Letters, former president.

MEMBER: Modern Language Association, Texas Institute of Letters.

AWARDS, HONORS: Austin Writers League award for best nonfiction book, 1998; Spurs Teaching Award, 2001.

WRITINGS:

The Fiction of Frank Norris: The Aesthetic Context, University of Missouri Press (Columbia, MO), 1978.

(Editor, with William T. Pilkington) *Western Movies,* University of New Mexico Press (Albuquerque, NM), 1979.

(Editor) *Critical Essays on Frank Norris,* G. K. Hall (Boston, MA), 1980.

Cowboys and Cadillacs: How Hollywood Looks at Texas, Texas Monthly (Austin, TX), 1983.

(Editor, with James W. Lee and William T. Pilkington) *The Texas Literary Tradition: Fiction, Folklore, History,* College of Liberal Arts, University of Texas Press (College Station, TX), 1983.

Texas: A Literary Portrait (criticism), Corona (San Antonio, TX), 1985.

(Editor) *South by Southwest: Twenty-four Stories from Modern Texas,* University of Texas Press (College Station, TX), 1986.

No Name on the Bullet: A Biography of Audie Murphy, Viking (New York, NY), 1989.

Giant Country: Essays on Texas, TCU Press (Ft. Worth, TX), 1998.

Kings of Texas: The 150-Year Saga of an American Ranching Empire, Wiley (Hoboken, NJ), 2003.

(Editor) *Lone Star Literature: From the Red River to the Rio Grande,* W. W. Norton (New York, NY), 2004.

Contributor and writer-at-large for *Texas Monthly.*

WORK IN PROGRESS: Dick and Jane in France, a travel book.

SIDELIGHTS: Don B. Graham, a professor of English, has written a number of books relating to the people and literature of his native Texas. One book that has gained particular critical notice is his *No Name on the Bullet: A Biography of Audie Murphy.* Murphy, a Texas native who died in a 1971 plane crash, was a World War II army hero, the most highly decorated soldier in American history, who later became a B-movie actor. He wrote a book about his experiences called *To Hell and Back,* which was made into a movie in which he also starred. His private life, however, included two divorces, gambling debts, and psychological ailments that are now recognized as the symptoms of posttraumatic stress from the war. Graham, according to critics, writes about Murphy with sympathy and skill in what Leah Rozen described in *People* as a "first-rate biography. Graham does justice to Murphy's war heroics," the reviewer maintained. The author also reveals how Murphy's years after the war "were an increasingly sad 'postscript to battle.'"

Graham has written on many other Texas themes, including its literature, its lifestyle, and how it is portrayed in Hollywood films. His *Kings of Texas: The 150-Year Saga of an American Ranching Empire,* for example, is a six-generation saga about the family who established Texas's largest ranch, covering hundreds of thousands of acres. The story ends as, like so many other ranches in Texas, the land is taken over by a corporate entity. *Library Journal* contributor Charlie Cowling called the book "an easy-to-read popular narrative . . . [that is] highly recommended for Southwestern libraries." Graham has also edited an anthology of Texas authors, *Lone Star Literature: From the Red River to the Rio Grande,* a collection that Pam Kingsbury described in *Library Journal* as "by turns, humorous, grandiose, larger than life, and touching." In addition, Graham, a movie aficionado, has focused on Hollywood's perception of Texas and Texans in his 1983 book, *Cowboys and Cadillacs: How Hollywood Looks at Texas.*

BIOGRAPHICAL AND CRITICAL SOURCES:

PERIODICALS

American History Illustrated, January-February, 1991, review of *No Name on the Bullet: A Biography of Audie Murphy,* p. 8.

Journal of Broadcasting & Electronic Media, winter, 1985, Douglas Gomery, review of *Cowboys and Cadillacs: How Hollywood Looks at Texas,* pp. 101-103.

Library Journal, May 15, 1989, John Smothers, review of *No Name on the Bullet,* p. 74; March 1, 2003, Charlie Cowling, review of *Kings of Texas: The 150-Year Saga of an American Ranching Empire,* p. 103; September 1, 2003, Pam Kingsbury, review of *Lone Star Literature: From the Red River to the Rio Grande,* p. 166.

New York, July 31, 1989, Rhoda Koenig, review of *No Name on the Bullet,* p. 64.

New York Times Book Review, September 10, 1989, Gib Johnson, review of *No Name on the Bullet,* p. 27.

People, September 25, 1989, Leah Rozen, review of *No Name on the Bullet,* p. 29.

Publishers Weekly, May 9, 1986, John Mutter, review of *South by Southwest: Twenty-four Stories from Modern Texas,* p. 251; June 2, 1989, review of *No Name on the Bullet,* p. 76.

ONLINE

Don B. Graham Web site, http://www.en.utexas.edu/faculty/dgraham/ (November 24, 2003).*

* * *

GRAVER, Elizabeth 1964-

PERSONAL: Born July 2, 1964, in Los Angeles, CA; daughter of Lawrence (a professor of English) and Suzanne (a professor of English; maiden name, Levy) Graver; married James Russell Pingeon; children: Sylvie, Chloe. *Education:* Wesleyan University, Middletown, CT, B.A., 1986; Washington University, St. Louis, MO, M.F.A., 1990; doctoral study at Cornell University, 1990-92.

ADDRESSES: Home—47 Old Sudbury Rd., Lincoln, MA 01773. *Office*—Department of English, Boston College, Chestnut Hill, MA 02467-3806. *Agent*—Richard Parks, R. Parks Agency, 138 East 16th St., Suite 5B, New York, NY 10003. *E-mail*—graver@bc.edu.

CAREER: Freelance journalist, 1984-87; Washington University, St. Louis, MO, instructor in creative writing, 1989; Cornell University, Ithaca, NY, instructor in creative writing, 1991-92; Boston College, Chestnut Hill, MA, visiting assistant professor, 1993-95, assistant professor, 1995-99, associate professor of English, 1999—, coordinator of Creative Nonfiction Program, 1999—, director of Creative Writing Concentration, 1999-2000, founder and director of "Fiction Days" reading series, 1995—. Emerson College, member of adjunct graduate faculty, 1992; Wesleyan University, Middletown, CT, visiting writer, 1993; PEN Prison Writing Project, writing mentor, 2002—. "Share Our Strength" (annual reading series), organizer, 1993-95; Somerville Gardens Oral History Project, chronicler, 1995; gives readings from her works; teacher of community writing workshops.

MEMBER: PEN American Center, Associated Writing Programs, Phi Beta Kappa.

AWARDS, HONORS: Fellow, Bread Loaf Writers' Conference, 1986; Fulbright grant for Neuilly-sur-Seine, France, 1987-88; competition winner, Massachusetts Writers' Exchange Program, 1991, for the short story "Around the World"; Drue Heinz Literature Prize, University of Pittsburgh Press, 1991, for *Have You Seen Me?;* fellow of National Endowment for the Arts, 1992; grant from Barbara Deming Memorial Fund, 1992; fellow at MacDowell Artists' Colony, 1994, 1998, and at Blue Mountain Center Artists' Colony, 1996; shared first-place award, American Fiction Contest, 1996, for "Islands without Names"; selection as "best book of the year" by both *Chicago Tribune* and *Glamour,* 1997, for *Unravelling;* named among Notable Books of the Year and Notable Paperbacks, both *New York Times Book Review,* 1997, for *Unravelling,* and 1999, for *The Honey Thief;* Guggenheim fellow, 1997; Cohen Award, *Ploughshares,* 2001, for the short story "The Mourning Door."

WRITINGS:

Have You Seen Me? (short stories), University of Pittsburgh Press (Pittsburgh, PA), 1991.
Unravelling (novel), Hyperion (New York, NY), 1997.
The Honey Thief (novel), Hyperion (New York, NY), 1999.
Awake (novel), Holt (New York, NY), 2004.

Work represented in anthologies, including *Street Songs I: New Voices in Fiction,* Longstreet Press (Atlanta, GA), 1990; *Best American Short Stories,* Houghton Mifflin (Boston, MA), 1991; *Sacred Ground: Writings about Home,* edited by Barbara Bonner, Milkweed Editions (Minneapolis, MN), 1996; *An Intricate Weave: Women Write about Girls and Girlhood,* edited by Marlene Miller, Iris Editions (Laguna Beach, CA), 1997; and *Passing the Word: Writers on Their Mentors,* edited by Jeffrey Skinner and Lee Martin, Sarabande Books (Louisville, KY), 2001. Contributor of articles, short stories, poetry, and reviews to periodicals, including *Ploughshares, River Styx, Tikkun, Shenandoah, Antaeus, Southern Review, Southwest Review, Seventeen, Story,* and *Prism International.*

The novel *The Honey Thief* was been published in German, Hebrew, and Chinese.

ADAPTATIONS: One of Graver's short stories, "The Boy Who Fell Forty Feet," was performed in Chicago, IL, at Organic Theater and also broadcast on the

Chicago-area public radio program, *Stage Readings,* both 1993. Another piece, "Surtsey" was performed as a reading in New York, NY, at Symphony Space, and broadcast on National Public Radio, both 2001.

SIDELIGHTS: With two English professors for parents, it might seem inevitable that Elizabeth Graver would take an interest in literature from an early age. In an interview for *Contemporary Literary Criticism,* she noted the influence of works by Charlotte Brontë, George Eliot, Toni Morrison, and others; but her own personal experience, she said, had little effect on her work. She has sought instead to write from the points of view of others, to experience vicariously worlds other than her own. "I guess my primary aim as an author," she said, "is to never repeat myself, but rather to push the boundaries of my work and my imagination each time I write something—to take risks and be as fluid as possible, so that each new story suggests new things to me, rather than being yet another turn around the same circle."

The stories in her award-winning first book *Have You Seen Me?* often center around bewildered, alienated children who use fantasy to make sense of a troubled world. Hence Willa in the title story, its name taken from the question which often appears on milk cartons along with a photograph of a missing child, postulates an alternative reality for those vanished boys and girls: "To call those children missing, Willa knew, only meant that they were missing for somebody, even though maybe they were found for someone else. Just because they were not at home did not mean they were wandering the earth alone. There were too many of them, just look at all those cartons . . . soon there were masses of them, whole underground networks. When she went to the supermarket with her mother she spotted them sometimes, kids poking holes in the bags of chocolate in the candy aisle or thumbing through a comic book—kids in matted gray parkas that once were white. They had large pupils and pale skin from living inside the earth." In Willa's imagination, the term "underground" takes on a literal meaning, signifying a world of caves that house the lost children.

Problems of communication abound in these stories: the protagonist of "The Counting Game" simply refuses to speak; the narrator in "Music for Four Doors" finds in her autistic neighbor's dreamlike world a mirror of her own; and a young girl in "The Experimental Forest" finds that an older man mistakes her desire for intimacy as an offer of sex. Fortunately he declines the apparent advance, but she fails to make her true needs known: "I wanted to tell him that all I needed was a little something, a tiny bit of change to poke a pinhole through my summer so that I could see through it—a small hole so that some air could reach through the heat and clear things out." Quoting this sentence, Dean Flower in the *Hudson Review* observed, "Graver's stories are full of such eloquent moments as this, and it's only her first book."

Graver followed *Have You Seen Me?* six years later with a novel, *Unravelling.* The title itself is a pun of sorts: the protagonist, Aimee Slater, has worked in the yarn mills of nineteenth-century Lowell, Massachusetts. At fifteen she goes to work against her mother's wishes, and quickly finds herself on her back atop a bolt of cloth, the mill's mechanic atop her. Pregnant with twins from this dalliance, Aimee returns to her mother, who forces her to give up the children. Afterward Aimee removes herself to a shack on the edge of her New Hampshire town, where she lives alone for years, not merely ashamed but embittered as well. In time she finds solace in the company of another outcast, "the village cripple," Amos, who becomes her lover; but her anger at her mother remains unresolved until Aimee—now thirty-eight and well aware that the older woman does not have long to live—crosses her woods to her family's home.

A reviewer in *Publishers Weekly,* while noting that "the narrative strains too obviously for poignant moments" in places, nonetheless concluded that "its depiction of the dissonance between what Aimee's heart tells her and what her world expects of her is genuinely haunting." John Gregory Brown of Chicago's *Tribune Books* likewise pointed out "a few moments when the novel falters—Aimee's obsession with an incident of childhood sexual exploration with her consumptive brother, for instance, introduces an element to the story and to Aimee's character that isn't quite convincing"; but, he concluded, the book as a whole is "an absolutely affecting portrait of adolescence."

Graver's research of her subject matter won her praise from several critics, including Brown, who called her description of factory life "utterly convincing." He quoted this passage, taken from Aimee's first day at the mill: "Threads hanging like a steady sheet of rain before my face, to be coaxed through the tiniest of holes. My task sounded as if it came out of the stories my mother used to tell me, of princesses locked up in towers and told to make golden cloaks out of piles of flax. But the place—the place was worlds apart from the still, stone rooms of those old tales." *Unravelling,* wrote Benjamin DeMott in the *New York Times Book Review,* "creates a home-on-the-margins beyond cant—a kind of exiles' utopia, intensely imagined, right-valued, memorable." Grace Anne De Candido of *Booklist* concluded that "Graver's mastery of emotional resonance carries the reader along."

Recently, Graver told *CA*: "*The Honey Thief* is a contemporary novel about a mother-daughter relationship and the way the past defines—and deforms—the present. The summer that eleven-year-old Eva is picked up on her fourth shoplifting charge, her mother, Miriam, decides that the only solution is to move from Manhattan to a quiet town in upstate New York. There, she tells Eva, they can have a 'normal' life. But what Miriam doesn't tell her daughter, or anyone else, is that Eva's stealing scares her for a different reason, one related to a past she has been trying to ignore. As tensions mount between mother and daughter, it is, oddly enough, Eva's secret friendship with Burl—a reclusive beekeeper who lives down the road—that ultimately helps the two find their way back to each other.

"*Awake* tells the story of a mother who seeks freedom for her young son and rediscovers her own need for it in the process. It began as a story about a family with a child who has a rare disease that means he can't be exposed to sunlight. Quickly, though, it became something else, in that process of transformation that makes writing so astonishing for me. The novel is, at heart, an examination of a woman's identity as—given sudden breathing room—she looks around at her life and finds that she has lost track of essential pieces of herself. What, exactly, are safety and freedom? And at what cost—to one's self and to the people in one's life—should they be protected and pursued?"

BIOGRAPHICAL AND CRITICAL SOURCES:

BOOKS

Contemporary Literary Criticism, Volume 70, Gale (Detroit, MI), 1992.

PERIODICALS

Booklist, July, 1997, Grace Anne De Candido, review of *Unravelling,* p. 1796.

Book Report, March, 1992, p. 331.

Boston Review, October, 1991.

Hudson Review, summer, 1992, Dean Flower, review of *Have You Seen Me?,* p. 337.

Kirkus Reviews, January 15, 2004, review of *Awake,* p. 53.

Library Journal, February 1, 2004, Beth E. Andersen, review of *Awake,* p. 122.

Los Angeles Times Book Review, February 21, 1993, p. 11.

New York Times Book Review, August 17, 1997, Benjamin DeMott, review of *Unravelling,* p. 7.

Publishers Weekly, June 23, 1997, review of *Unravelling,* p. 69.

Tribune Books (Chicago, IL), September 7, 1997, John Gregory Brown, review of *Unravelling,* p. 4.

H

HACKER, Marilyn 1942-

PERSONAL: Born November 27, 1942, in New York, NY; daughter of Albert Abraham (a management consultant) and Hilda (a teacher; maiden name, Rosengarten) Hacker; married Samuel R. Delany (a writer), August 22, 1961 (divorced, 1980); partner of Karyn London, 1986-1999; children: Iva Alyxander Hacker-Delany. *Ethnicity:* "Secular Jewish-European Diaspora." *Education:* New York University, B.A., 1964. *Politics:* "Progressive, feminist, socialist."

ADDRESSES: *Home*—New York, NY, and Paris, France. *Office*—230 West 105 St., Apt. 13C, New York, NY 10025. *Agent*—Frances Collin, P.O. Box 33, Wayne, PA 19087-0033. *E-mail*—110165.74@ compuserve.com.

CAREER: Poet, editor. Has worked variously as a teacher, mail sorter, and editor. Antiquarian bookseller in London, England, 1971-76. George Washington University, Washington, DC, Jenny McKean Moore Chair in Writing, 1974; Columbia University, New York, NY, American Studies Institute, adjunct professor in creative writing, 1979-81; Hofstra University, professor of creative writing, 1997-99; City College of New York, director of creative writing M.A. program, 1999—, professor of French, graduate center, 2003—. Writer in residence, State University of New York, Albany, 1988, and Columbia University, 1988; University of Cincinnati, Cincinnati, OH, George Elliston poet-in-residence, 1988; American University, Washington, DC, distinguished writer-in-residence,

Marilyn Hacker

1989; visiting professor of creative writing, State University of New York, Binghamton, 1990, University of Utah, Salt Lake City, 1995, and Barnard College, New York, NY, 1995; Brandeis University, Waltham,

MA, Fannie Hurst Visiting Professor of Poetry, 1996; Washington University, St. Louis, MO, Fannie Hurst Writer-in-Residence, 1997.

MEMBER: PEN, Poetry Society of America, Authors Guild, Authors League of America, Feminist Writers Guild.

AWARDS, HONORS: Lamont Poetry Selection, Academy of American Poets, 1973, for *Presentation Piece;* New York YWHA Poetry Center Discovery award, 1973, for "new" poets; National Endowment for the Arts grants, 1974, 1985, 1995; National Book Award in Poetry, 1975, for *Presentation Piece;* New York State Foundation for the Arts Creative Artists Public Service grant, 1979-80; Guggenheim Foundation fellowship, 1980-81; Coordinating Council of Little Magazines' editor's fellowship, 1984; Ingram Merrill Foundation fellowship, 1984; Robert F. Winner Memorial Award, 1987, for "Letter from Goose Creek: April," and 1989, for "Two Cities"; Lambda Literary Award in Poetry, 1991, for *Going Back to the River;* John Masefield Memorial Award from Poetry Society of America and B. F. Conners Award from *Paris Review,* both 1994, both for "Cancer Winter"; Reader's Choice Award, *Prairie Schooner,* 1995; Lambda Literary Award in Poetry and Lenore Marshall Poetry Prize, Academy of American Poets, both 1995, both for *Winter Numbers;* Poet's Prize, 1996, for *Selected Poems;* Strousse awards, *Prairie Schooner,* 1998, 1999; Crossing Boundaries award, *International Quarterly,* 1999, for translation; New York Foundation for the Arts grant, 1999-2000; John Frederick Nims Memorial Prize, *Poetry,* 2001, for translations in the October-November, 2000, French issue; Fulbright Senior Research fellowship, translation and creative writing, 2001; Audre Lorde Award for Lesbian Poetry, and Smart Family Foundation Award, both 2001; Willis Barnstone Poetry Translation Prize, University of Evansville, 2003, for translation of sequence by Marie Etienne, National Book Critics Circle Award nomination, 2004, for *She Says.*

WRITINGS:

POETRY

The Terrible Children, privately printed, 1967.

(With Thomas M. Disch and Charles Platt) *Highway Sandwiches,* privately printed, 1970.

Presentation Piece, Viking (New York, NY), 1974.

Separations, Knopf (New York, NY), 1976.

Taking Notice, Knopf (New York, NY), 1980.

Assumptions, Knopf (New York, NY), 1985.

Love, Death, and the Changing of the Seasons, Arbor House (New York, NY), 1986, reprinted, W. W. Norton (New York, NY), 1995.

Going Back to the River, Random House (New York, NY), 1990.

The Hang-Glider's Daughter: Selected Poems, Onlywomen Press (London, England), 1990.

Selected Poems, 1965-1990, W. W. Norton (New York, NY), 1994.

Winter Numbers, W. W. Norton (New York, NY), 1994.

First Cities: Collected Early Poems, 1960-1979, W. W. Norton (New York, NY), 2003.

Desesperanto: Poems, 1999-2002, W. W. Norton (New York, NY), 2003.

OTHER

(Editor, with Samuel R. Delany) *Quark I-IV,* four volumes, Paperback Library (New York, NY), 1970-71.

The Poetry and Voice of Marilyn Hacker (sound recording), Caedmon, 1976.

Treasury of American Jewish Poets Reading Their Poems (sound recording), edited by Paul Kresh, Spoken Arts Recordings, 1979.

Marilyn Hacker (sound recording), University of Missouri, New Letters, 1979.

(Editor) *Woman Poet: The East,* Women in Literature (Reno, NV), 1982.

Five Poems of Marilyn Hacker: Soprano and Chamber Ensemble (printed music), C. F. Peters (New York, NY), 1989.

Hub of Ambiguity: For Soprano and Eight Players, 1984 (printed music), Donemus, 1992.

(Translator) Claire Malroux, *Edge,* Wake Forest University Press (Wake Forest, NC), 1996.

Squares and Courtyards, W. W. Norton (New York, NY), 2000.

(Translator) Claire Malroux, *A Long-Gone Sun,* Sheep Meadow Press (New York, NY), 2000.

(Translator) Vénus Khoury-Ghata, *Here There Was Once a Country,* Oberlin College Press (Oberlin, OH), 2001.

(Translator) Vénus Khoury-Ghata, *She Says,* Graywolf Press (St. Paul, MN), 2003.

(Translator) Claire Malroux, *Birds and Bison,* Sheep Meadow Press (New York, NY), 2004.

Contributor to periodicals, including *Nation, Paris Review, Poetry, PN Review,* (U.K.), *Poetry London,* (U.K.), and *Women's Review of Books.* Editor, *City,* 1967-70, *Quark* (speculative fiction quarterly), 1969-70, *Little Magazine,* 1977-80, *Thirteenth Moon,* 1982-86, and *Kenyon Review,* 1990-94. Editor of special issue of *Ploughshares,* winter, 1989-90, and spring, 1996. Coeditor of issue on contemporary French poetry, *Poetry,* November, 2000.

WORK IN PROGRESS: Another book; translations of Hédi Kaddom and Guy Goffette.

SIDELIGHTS: In her award-winning first book, *Presentation Piece,* poet Marilyn Hacker defined the dimensions of a poetic universe that she would continue to explore in her later work. Verse forms included in the book are sonnets, sestinas, villanelles, blank verse, and heroic couplets. Hacker largely stays within these formal boundaries in her subsequent books. Within these traditional poetic forms, Hacker couches the urgency of love, desire and alienation in brash, up-to-the minute language, writing from her perspective as a feminist, a lesbian, a cancer sufferer, and a member of the extended family of women. Judith Barrington, writing in *Women's Review of Books,* identified Hacker as a "radical formalist" to describe that juxtaposition of the traditional and the vernacular.

Carol S. Oles has interpreted Hacker's formalism as a political device. "When she writes in forms associated with the primarily male poets canonized by literary history," Oles observed in a *Nation* article, "it is as if she were slipping, in broad daylight, into a well-guarded preserve. She uses the decorous sonnet, sestina and villanelle to contain a vernacular, often racy speech." Hacker herself might not agree with that analysis, as she commented in an interview with Karla Hammond in *Frontiers:* "The language that we use was as much created and invented by women as by men." According to Felicia Mitchell in the *Dictionary of Literary Biography,* Hacker "has insisted and shown that the traditional poetic forms are as much women's as they are men's—even if men were acclaimed and published more frequently in the past."

A native of New York City, Hacker attended New York University in the early 1960s, earning her B.A. in 1964. In 1961 she married writer Samuel R. Delany; despite Delany's homosexuality, the couple remained married for thirteen years, during which time they had a daughter. In the 1970s, Hacker spent much of her time living in London and working as a book dealer. She returned to the United States in 1976 but has divided her time since then between the United States and France, editing literary periodicals such as *Ploughshares* and the *Kenyon Review,* and teaching at a number of colleges and universities. Openly lesbian since the late 1970s, Hacker has created a poetry that is "feminist in its themes as it reveals how the personal is political," noted Mitchell.

Mitchell suggested that Hacker's first three books, *Presentation Piece,* which won the National Book Award, *Separations,* and *Taking Notice,* can be viewed as a trilogy. While all three are concerned with "a modern woman's psyche, played against the context of city streets and personal memories," the third collection, published in 1980, shows signs of increasing "self-awareness." The poems "grew richer and less arcane. Her tone softened, even hinted at joy." According to Mitchell, reviews of *Taking Notice* suggested that "the breadth of Hacker's vision was increasing as her experiences gave her more depth of emotion, and that her blend of formal structure and informal speech seemed less contrived and more natural." The poems in *Taking Notice* "betray their imprisonment in the material present," Mary Kinzie stated in the *American Poetry Review.* "There is here no beauty that makes the heart yearn, no broad consciousness guiding the verses, and no spiritual truth. There are only things." She concluded that the collection "is work that practically dares us to find a fault with its skill, and I find little to mitigate my judgment that the gauge is thrown by poems in which failed irony, dull lists, turgid diction, and a superficial formalism are artlessly exaggerated." While criticizing those poems in the collection that stray from the sonnet form, a *Washington Post Book World* reviewer remarked that "at her best no one handles the colloquial sublime . . . better than Marilyn Hacker. She is a master of progressive pentameter, of measuring, interrupting and holding the line, and of letting it go on, of letting it pile into sentences and juxtapositions."

Several critics characterized Hacker's 1985 collection, *Assumptions,* as a personally revealing and compassionate work. Here the poet's concerns revolve around relationships among women: as mother and daughter, as friends, as lovers, and as mythic figures which inform women's consciousness. In the book's first section, Hacker's relationship with her own mother is explored, precipitated by the poet's efforts to explain herself to her own daughter, Iva. Hacker had written about her mother and her daughter in earlier collections, but as Oles noted, in *Assumptions* acceptance, and finally forgiveness, have occurred. It is that autobiographical note of Hacker's verse that J. D. McClatchy praised in *New York Times Book Review:* "how relationships evolve, how love changes from passion to friendship, how we watch ourselves come clear or obscured in the eyes of others—these problems are traced in a remarkable series of epistolary poems to her ex-lovers and portraits of her family." In *Women's Review of Books,* contributor Kathleen Aguero wrote, "Hacker's voice manages to be intimate and intellectual at the same time. The forms she uses so expertly lend her just enough distance to be personal and self-conscious about craft, about language as a repository of meaning, without being self-indulgent."

Oles pointed out that the title *Assumptions* can be read as a reference to Catholicism, and that the collected verses contain similar references to "communicants," "sin," and "salvation." Oles concluded that Hacker is advocating "the creation of a new faith for unbelievers in the old." Along these lines, the book's final section, "The Snow Queen," uses the characters of Hans Christian Andersen to create a new feminist mythology. Hacker gives new life to Andersen's characters as portraits of women's possibilities, whose ultimate quest is to define themselves. The Snow Queen, a powerfully evil figure in Andersen's tale, is here redefined as one of the admirable "bad old ladies" who takes charge of her own life and is rewarded when her "daughters slog across the icecap to get drunk" with them. These literary figures are in the end part of the extended family of women—mothers and daughters—to whom Hacker feels a debt and a connection.

Hacker's next book, *Love, Death and the Changing of the Seasons,* is an extended narrative, comprised mainly of sonnets, that describes the arc of a love affair between a poet living in New York and France and a younger woman. Kathleen West described it in *Prairie Schooner* as "the unfolding of a grand passion that is in no way lessened by its entanglement with twentieth-century angst and American self-deprecatory humor." The characters meet in a poetry class taught by the older woman, Hack. Their relationship develops against a backdrop of what West called "New York freneticism, trans-Atlantic travel, and the energy of love." Hacker mainly uses Petrarchan sonnets to tell the story, peppering it with English and French slang, strong erotic language, the details of everyday life, a wide-ranging set of friends, and literary allusions—especially to Shakespeare, whose sonnets to a younger lover are an obvious reference point. As West pointed out, Hacker can combine Penelope, Persephone, French phrases, and the Shirelles into a single poem. Marilyn French, in a review in the *Nation,* summed up the book as "deeply satisfying. It allows the reader, in the concentrated and vivid way only poetry provides, to be immersed in the texture of one woman's actuality. . . . Unlike any other love poems I know, Hacker's sequence provides a context that offers a tacit explanation of how one can go on when the heart is shattered."

In 1990's *Going Back to the River,* Hacker again published a collection of formally constructed poems grouped into sections and based on personal themes. Elizabeth Alexander wrote in the *Voice Literary Supplement* that the collection addresses "themes that have long absorbed Marilyn Hacker: geographies, languages, the marking of her own places across various landscapes, and the creation of rituals." Alexander felt that the book falls short of Hacker's earlier work, that the autobiographical focus that had previously provided such a rich source of material, fails in this collection. "Hacker fans . . . will want to read this volume to see what she's thinking about and eating. . . . But only a few of the poems show what she's capable of." One poem that Alexander did praise, however, is the final poem, "Against Silence," addressed to Hacker's former mother-in-law, Margaret Delany. Delany had been an early hero of Hacker's, as a woman who earned her own living, "unduped and civilized." As a victim of stroke, the elderly Delany is less and less able to speak, leaving the poet "mourning your lost words . . . at a loss / for words to name what my loss of you is."

Judith Barrington, reviewing *Going Back* for *Women's Review of Books,* found Hacker's "brilliant" form to be an integral aspect of the poetry's meaning. She quoted, as an example, the poem "Cultural Exchange," in which a Hispanic woman muses on the contradictions she sees in the behavior of her employers: North Americans who think that women are "all one class" yet who still employ a domestic. The sestina form, noted Barrington, is "perfect for conveying the nature of cross-cultural exchanges, with their moments of connection and their odd near-misses."

Some reviewers have commented that Hacker's adherence to formal structure has resulted in poems that are nothing more than technical exercises. Ben Howard found in *Poetry* that the more formal poems of *Presentation Piece* "fall victim to artifice," while finding the poems in freer forms to be "more convincing." However, as Hacker has continued to develop her distinctive combination of traditional forms and radical themes, many reviewers have appreciated her accomplishments. By the time *Going Back to the River* was published, Hacker was so well known for her adherence to traditional forms that Alexander could refer to her "familiar technical dexterity." Alexander went on to note that while the poet uses "tightly rhymed and metered structures such as sestinas and villanelles, she nonetheless brings a colloquial ease and grace to the forms. She builds her rhythm on the rhyme itself, which forges connections between unlike quantities, and she uses her language to make those unlikely companions jibe."

Hacker has also been praised for her use of language. "Over and again one encounters images of the body, especially the tongue; of salt upon the tongue; of the sea, cliffs, a beach; of lovers awakening," Howard noted of *Presentation Piece*. "And it becomes apparent that the poet is attempting to formulate, in these and related images, a language of instinct and feeling—of a woman's bodily awareness—and to express the body's longings, including its 'inadmissible longings' as they are shaped and repressed in personal relationships." In *Contemporary Women Poets*, contributor Jane Augustine described the poet's language as "hard-edged," "darkly jewel-encrusted, redolent of a devastated inner world of difficult loving, tangled sexuality, and convoluted relationships. Semiprecious gems—onyx, amethyst, alexandrite—express the hardness, mystery, and richness of experience," Augustine noted of Hacker's early work in particular.

Selected Poems, 1965-1990 is a collection of poems from five previous books (all except *Love, Death, and the Changing of the Seasons*). In addition to highlighting Hacker's formal skill, "this retrospective collection documents the extent to which she has consistently articulated the complexities of contemporary culture, as a feminist, as a lesbian, and simply as a politically aware human being," noted *Lambda Book Report* contributor Sue Russell. Observing that Hacker's signature style is traceable from her earliest works, a *Publishers Weekly* reviewer praised the collection "for its great heart and its embrace of the female condition." *Library Journal* reviewer Steve R. Ellis commented on Hacker's unique ability in "negotiating the boundary of the feminist and lesbian canon while generating a buzz around [her] early work." And Lawrence Joseph declared in the *Voice Literary Supplement:* "Part of Hacker's genius is her use of traditional forms, or variations on them, as an integral level of expression." Writing in the *New York Times Book Review,* David Kirby stated, "There are no ticktock rhymes in her work; her use of enjambment, slant rhyme and metrical variation produces a line so lissome and fluid that, once engaged, the reader glides on as swiftly as a child in a water slide."

Published at the same time as *Selected Poems* and the winner of the Lenore Marshall Poetry Prize, 1994's *Winter Numbers* "represents a darker vision than one is accustomed to from Hacker," according to Russell. Russell found "the same clear image of women's bodies, together or alone, this time augmented by a starkly vivid physical consciousness of aging and disease in the self or others." *Women's Review of Books* contributor Adrian Oktenberg noted that Hacker's typical scenes and characters in this collection are now "almost always tinged with a deeper sense of brevity, mutability and loss; and the sense of a future, both individual and collective, is now very much in doubt." Joseph remarked, "Hacker's voices are more mellifluously startling and alive than ever" as "the central motifs of her poetry . . . revolve around, simultaneously, the destruction of one's own body and that of the body politic." "As a Jew who lives part-time in Paris, her 'chosen diaspora,' Hacker writes hauntingly of the Holocaust. As a lesbian who lives part-time in America, Hacker writes with tremendous force about bigotry, AIDS, and breast cancer," explained Matthew Rothschild in the *Progressive.* The critic concluded, "It is the specter of death that lends this work its unforgettable power." "Although I am hesitant to equate 'darker' with 'deeper,' or even 'better,' as if the experience of human suffering in itself entitled one to added respect," remarked Russell, "I can say without hesitation that *Winter Numbers* is a stunning achievement bound to be quoted widely, and, one hopes, read by a broadening audience." Kirby declared, "Once again Ms. Hacker's supple formalism gives backbone to ideas and images that might overwhelm a lesser poet, and once again one sees how good this poet is, so good that anyone else trying to do what she does would only look foolish." "Dark as her subject is,

Hacker's poems illuminate," commented a reviewer for *Publishers Weekly.* Oktenberg added, "The news in *Winter Numbers* is that one remains oneself in illness, and perhaps becomes more so."

As Hacker has entered middle age, her poems have more and more reflected a somber mood as well as a frustration for international events in a world dominated by American foreign policies. Her 2000 collection, *Squares and Courtyards,* is divided into two sections: "Scars on Paper" and "Paragraphs from a Daybook." "The first operates primarily within the realm of interiority and includes forty-one poems in quatrain, sonnet, haiku, alexandrine, and (of course) Sapphic forms," as Veronica Mitchell described it in her *Gay and Lesbian Review Worldwide* assessment. "'Paragraphs from a Daybook' is loosely an extended sonnet sequence that examines territory mined by the poet's life as an activist, socialist, daughter, mother, lover, and now, a single-breasted Amazon." The collection addresses a number of issues, including the death of loved ones, AIDS, her own breast cancer, anti-Semitism, family, friendship, nature, and life on the streets of New York City and Paris. While many of the poems here are grim in subject, *Booklist* critic Ray Olson observed that Hacker is simultaneously "too engaged in living to indulge grief" even when relating her daughter's pain over the death of her friend in a car accident. Yet death is a repeated theme through these verses, and a corollary is the poet's insistence that "language as a force . . . does not necessarily survive or tell the whole story," as Beatrix Gates explained it in the *Lambda Book Report.* Redemption is discovered, nevertheless, through "Hacker's devotion to words, friends, food, and nature," according to Matthew Rothschild in the *Progressive.* Although at times the poems in *Squares and Courtyards* contain too much "heavy-handed imagery," stated one *Publishers Weekly* reviewer, when the poet "drops her formal guard" she displays an effective "emotional pitch and range." Olson concluded that the verses in this collection are "poised, intelligently lively, honorably serious." And Gates, who especially praised Hacker's scenes of city life in New York and Paris as "poignant," felt that the poet "lets the junctures of the world teach us and echoes the lesson in ferocious, plain precision."

After republishing some of her early work in *First Cities: Collected Early Poems, 1960-1979,* Hacker next put out a collection of original verses in *Desesperanto: Poems, 1999-2002.* The title, as several critics noted, is formed from a combination of the words "despair" and "Esperanto," the artificially created international language, and it reflects Hacker's view of the world as she straddles the Atlantic Ocean, with one foot in Paris and the other in New York City. As Hacker continues to struggle with the issues of pain, life as a lesbian, the illness of loved ones, and the death of others, her personal experiences of sadness are paralleled by anger over world events dictated by America's actions. A contributor to *Publishers Weekly* described the book as a combination of "lucid . . . autobiography, outspoken progressive politics and a casual mastery of elaborate forms." The poet's sense of loneliness is combined with "sensory precision and an abiding sense of history," wrote *Booklist* contributor Donna Seaman, noting that Hacker paints "vibrant collages of city life" that comprise a "magnificent" collection.

Maxine Kumin noted in a *Nation* article that in Hacker's poems "love and grief come together . . . infused with passion and wit and rendered in intricately woven formal patterns that stun the ear with their vernacular grace." Summarizing Hacker's work in *Feminist Writers,* contributor Renee Curry noted that "Much of Hacker's life work has been to frame the nameless inside the names, to work on providing forms for the formless." Hacker's significance to modern poetry, Curry added, "is synonymous with her persistent contribution of her own life experiences and her own life's wisdom to the feminist lesbian canon."

BIOGRAPHICAL AND CRITICAL SOURCES:

BOOKS

Contemporary Literary Criticism, Gale (Detroit, MI), Volume 5, 1976, Volume 9, 1978, Volume 23, 1983, Volume 72, 1992, Volume 91, 1996.

Contemporary Women Poets, St. James Press (Detroit, MI), 1997.

Dictionary of Literary Biography, Volume 120: *American Poets since World War II, Third Series,* Gale (Detroit, MI), 1992.

Feminist Writers, St. James Press (Detroit, MI), 1996.

Parini, Jay, editor, *Contemporary Poetry,* Oxford University Press (New York, NY), 2004.

PERIODICALS

Advocate, September 20, 1994, John Weir, "Marilyn Hacker," p. 51.

American Book Review, May-June, 2002, Elaine Equi, reviews of *Here There Was Once a Country* and *A Long-Gone Sun,* p. 16.

American Poetry Review, July, 1981, pp. 13-14; May-June, 1996, pp. 23-27.

AWP Chronicle, March-April, 1996.

Belles Lettres, spring, 1991, p. 52; winter, 1996, pp. 34-35.

Bloomsbury Review, March, 1996, p. 23.

Booklist, January 1, 2000, Ray Olson, review of *Squares and Courtyards,* p. 864; April 1, 2003, Donna Seaman, review of *Desesperanto: Poems, 1999-2002,* p. 1368.

Choice, September, 1976, p. 822.

Frontiers, fall, 1981, pp. 22-27.

Gay and Lesbian Review Worldwide, July, 2001, Veronica Mitchell, "Private Spaces Made Public," p. 41.

Hudson Review, summer, 1995, p. 339.

Kliatt, fall, 1985, p. 29.

Lambda Book Report, November, 1994, p. 27; April, 2000, Beatrix Gates, "Death, Be Not Proud," p. 17.

Library Journal, August, 1980, Suzanne Juhasz, review of *Taking Notice,* p. 1639; February 1, 1985, Suzanne Juhasz, review of *Assumptions,* p. 100; October 15, 1986, Fred Muratori, review of *Love, Death, and the Changing Seasons,* p. 99; April 15, 1990, Kathleen Norris, review of *Going Back to the River,* p. 96; September 15, 1994, p. 73; April 1, 1997, p. 95; August, 2003, Ellen Kaufman, review of *Desesperanto,* p. 89.

Los Angeles Times Book Review, December 28, 1980, p.7; June 30, 1985, p. 4; October 19, 1986, p. 8; September 2, 1990, p. 9.

Ms., April, 1975; March, 1981, p. 78.

Nation, September 18, 1976, p. 250; April 27, 1985; November 1, 1986; December 27, 1986, Maria Margaronis, review of *Love, Death, and the Changing Seasons,* p. 738; January 21, 1991, Beatrix Gates, review of *Going Back to the River,* p. 64; November 7, 1994, p. 548; December 26, 1994, p. 813; December 18, 1995, p. 800.

New Republic, September 7, 1974, p. 24.

New Statesman, August 21, 1987, Margaret Mulvihill, review of *Love, Death, and the Changing Seasons,* p. 23.

New Yorker, November 21, 1994, p. 133.

New York Times, November 22, 1995, p. B4.

New York Times Book Review, January 12, 1975, p. 2; August 8, 1976, pp. 12, 16; October 12, 1980, Charles Molesworth, review of *Taking Notice,* p. 37; May 26, 1985; June 21, 1987, p. 13; March 12, 1995; December 3, 1995, p. 80.

Poetry, April, 1975, p. 44; February, 1977, p. 285; July, 1981, p. 231; December, 1985, Sandra M. Gilbert, review of *Assumptions,* p. 167; July, 1991, Stephen Yenser, review of *Going Back to the River,* p. 221.

Poetry London, autumn, 2003, D. M. Black, review of *Desesperanto.*

Prairie Schooner, winter, 1987; fall, 1992, pp. 129-31.

Progressive, January, 1995, pp. 43-44; January, 2001, Matthew Rothschild, review of *Squares and Courtyards,* p. 42.

Publishers Weekly, August 8, 1980, review of *Taking Notice,* p. 70; January 4, 1985, review of *Assumptions,* p. 65; September 12, 1986, John Mutter, review of *Love, Death, and the Changing Seasons,* p. 90; March 2, 1990, Penny Kaganoff, review of *Going Back to the River,* p. 77; August 29, 1994, p. 67; September 26, 1994, p. 58; December 6, 1999, review of *Squares and Courtyards,* p. 72; January 22, 2001, review of *A Long-Gone Sun,* p. 321; May 19, 2003, review of *Desesperanto,* p. 67.

Times Literary Supplement, October 29, 1976, p. 1348; July 10, 1987, p. 748; December 1, 1995, p. 10.

Tribune Books, May 26, 1974; January 11, 1981, p. 3.

Voice Literary Supplement, April, 1990, pp. 6-7; February, 1995, p. 25.

Wall Street Journal, November 11, 1986, Raymond Sokolov, review of *Love, Death, and the Changing Seasons,* p. 34.

Washington Post Book World, November 2, 1980, p. 11; February 1, 1987, p. 6.

Women's Review of Books, September, 1985, p. 13; July, 1990, p. 28; April, 1995, pp. 10-11; July, 2001, Sandra Gilbert, "The Past Recaptured," pp. 26-27; November, 2003, Carolyne Wright, review of *She Says* and *Here There Was Once a Country,* pp. 16-17.

World Literature Today, spring, 2001, Bruce King, review of *A Long-Gone Sun,* p. 359; winter, 2002, Maryann De Julio, review of *Here There Was Once a Country,* p. 180.*

* * *

HAMILTON, Alastair 1941-

PERSONAL: Born May 20, 1941, in Barnet, London, England; son of Hamish (a publisher) and Yvonne (maiden name, Vicino; present surname, Pallavicino) Hamilton; married Cecilia Mucchi, May 18, 1968.

Education: King's College, Cambridge, B.A., 1962, M.A., 1967, Ph.D., 1982. *Hobbies and other interests:* "Visiting Islamic movements."

ADDRESSES: Home—Willemshof 4, 2312 MX Leiden, Netherlands. *Office*—Opleiding Engels, University of Leiden, P.O. Box 9515, 2300 RA Leiden, Netherlands. *E-mail*—a.hamilton@let.leidenuniv.nl.

CAREER: University of Urbino, Urbino, Italy, professor of English, 1977-88; University of Amsterdam, Amsterdam, Netherlands, professor of radical reformation history, 1987-2001; University of Leiden, Louise Thijssen-Schouten Professor of the History of Ideas, 1986—.

WRITINGS:

The Appeal of Fascism: A Study of Intellectuals and Fascism, 1919-1945, Anthony Blond (London, England), 1970.

The Family of Love, James Clarke (Cambridge, England), 1981.

William Bedwell, the Arabist, 1563-1632, E. J. Brill (Leiden, Netherlands), 1985.

Heresy and Mysticism in Sixteenth-Century Spain: The Alumbrados, University of Toronto Press (Toronto, Ontario, Canada), 1992.

Europe and the Arab World: Five Centuries of Books by European Scholars and Travellers from the Libraries of the Arcadian Group, Oxford University Press (New York, NY), 1994.

(Editor, with Sjouke Voolstra and Piet Visser) *From Martyr to Muppy (Mennonite Urban Professionals): A Historical Introduction to Cultural Assimilation Processes of a Religious Minority in the Netherlands, the Mennonites,* Amsterdam University Press (Amsterdam, Netherlands), 1994.

The Apocryphal Apocalypse: The Reception of the Second Book of Esdras (4 Ezra) from the Renaissance to the Enlightenment, Oxford University Press (New York, NY), 1999.

(Editor, with Alexander H. de Groot and Maurits H. van den Boogert) *Friends and Rivals in the East: Studies in Anglo-Dutch Relations in the Levant from the Seventeenth to the Early Nineteenth Century,* Brill (Boston, MA), 2000.

Arab Culture and Ottoman Magnificence in Antwerp's Golden Age, Oxford University Press (New York, NY), 2001.

SIDELIGHTS: "It is high praise for a scholarly author that he can take a complex and arcane subject and make it appear neither," wrote Andrew Pettegree in the *Journal of Ecclesiastical History.* Pettegree was referring to author Alastair Hamilton, and Hamilton's book *The Apocryphal Apocalypse: The Reception of the Second Book of Esdras (4 Ezra) from the Renaissance to the Enlightenment.* In this work the author, a former professor of "radical reformation history" in the Netherlands, examines 2 Esdras, which was reputedly written by Ezra the Scribe who was among the "minor Prophets" of the Old Testament. The text, according to *Utopian Studies* contributor Derk Visser, "is a short apocalypse that was probably written at the end of the first century CE. It is thus approximately contemporaneous with the canonical Book of Revelation."

The 2 Esdras' end-of-the-world scenario was quoted freely in its time, but was less well-remembered than the Book of Revelation. All that changed in the later centuries, however. Hamilton shows, said Visser, "the apparent popularity of 2 Esdras after the Middle Ages. It was quoted by authors on the margins of the established Churches, whether Catholic, Calvinist or Lutheran; by authors of such visionary movements as Paracelsians and Rosicrucians as well as by English millenarians of the seventeenth and eighteenth centuries." In assessing the influence of 2 Esdras, Hamilton "shows a mischievous pleasure in the darker side of Renaissance scholarship," Pettegree commented. "He is also sensitive . . . to the connections between biblical prophetic scholarship and the contemporary relationship with the eastern world."

The eastern world was indeed a subject of Hamilton's *Arab Culture and Ottoman Magnificence in Antwerp's Golden Age,* published in 2001. In the sixteenth century, scholar Gorophis Becanus argued, "that not only was language divine in origin, but that its original form was Dutch," as Robert Irwin noted in the *Times Literary Supplement.* This was an example of the thinking during Antwerp's intellectual golden age; the same Renaissance era saw the rise of artist Albrecht Durer in Germany and the publication of Thomas More's *Utopia* in England.

But as Europe prospered, was the influence of the mideastern cultures being acknowledged? "In the sixteenth and seventeenth centuries it was rare indeed for scholars to study Arabic in order to understand

Islam or the Arabs better," wrote Irwin. "Rather, Arabic was mostly studied for the light its grammar and vocabulary shed on other related Semitic tongues." Hamilton sheds light on some of the leading Arabists of the Dutch Renaissance, including Benito Arias Montano and what Irwin called, "the greatest Arabist of the sixteenth century," Guillaume Postel. But Antwerp was shut off from international contact with the invasion of the Spanish in 1585. And as Hamilton wrote in *Arab Culture and Ottoman Magnificence,* after that, "with the deaths of the greatest Arabists of the seventeenth century . . . the interest in Arabic grammar and lexicography, which had been growing ever since the days of Postel, appears to have come to a halt. It would only resume properly in the nineteenth century."

BIOGRAPHICAL AND CRITICAL SOURCES:

PERIODICALS

American Historical Review, February, 1994, Sara Nalle, review of *Heresy and Mysticism in Sixteenth-Century Spain: The Alumbrados,* p. 252.

Book Collector, autumn, 1995, review of *Europe and the Arab World: Five Centuries of Books by European Scholars and Travelers from the Libraries of the Arcadian Group,* p. 410.

Catholic Biblical Quarterly, October, 2001, David Bryan, review of *The Apocryphal Apocalypse: The Reception of the Second Book of Esdras (4 Ezra) from the Renaissance to the Enlightenment,* p. 720.

English Historical Review, February, 1996, J. R. L. Highfield, review of *Heresy and Mysticism in Sixteenth-Century Spain,* p. 169.

Journal of Ecclesiastical History, October, 2001, Andrew Pettegree, review of *The Apocryphal Apocalypse,* p. 260.

Journal of Modern History, March, 1995, Lu Ann Homza, review of *Heresy and Mysticism in Sixteenth-Century Spain,* p. 198.

Journal of Theological Studies, April, 1995, R. W. Truman, review of *Heresy and Mysticism in Sixteenth-Century Spain,* p. 392; April, 2001, A. Frederic Klijn, review of *The Apocryphal Apocalypse,* p. 194.

New Statesman & Society, May 27, 1994, Laurence O'Toole, "Literature and Evil," p. 37.

Renaissance and Reformation, spring, 1995, review of *Heresy and Mysticism in Sixteenth-Century Spain,* p. 80.

Renaissance Quarterly, autumn, 1994, Allyson Poska, review of *Heresy and Mysticism in Sixteenth-Century Spain,* p. 691.

Sixteenth-Century Journal, winter, 2001, Robin Barnes, review of *The Apocryphal Apocalypse,* p. 1156.

Theological Studies, September, 1994, Mary Giles, review of *Heresy and Mysticism in Sixteenth-Century Spain,* p. 587.

Times Literary Supplement, June 24, 1994, Robert Irwin, review of *Europe and the Arab World,* p. 32; April 21, 2000, Anthony Grafton, review of *The Apocryphal Apocalypse,* p. 5; June 28, 2002, Robert Irwin, "Arabian Antwerp," p. 6.

Utopian Studies, spring, 2000, Derk Visser, review of *The Apocryphal Apocalypse,* p. 260.

* * *

HARJO, Joy 1951-

PERSONAL: Born May 9, 1951, in Tulsa, OK; daughter of Allen W. and Wynema (Baker) Foster; children: Phil, Rainy Dawn. *Education:* University of New Mexico, B.A., 1976; University of Iowa, M.F.A., 1978; attended Anthropology Film Center, Santa Fe, 1982. *Hobbies and other interests:* Performing on the saxophone with band Joy Harjo and Poetic Justice.

ADDRESSES: Home—1140-D, Alewa Dr., Honolulu, HI 96817. *E-mail*—katcvpoet@aol.com.

CAREER: Institute of American Indian Arts, Santa Fe, NM, instructor, 1978-79, 1983-84; Arizona State University, Tempe, lecturer in creative writing and poetry, 1980-81; University of Colorado, Boulder, assistant professor, 1985-88; University of Arizona, Tucson, associate professor, 1988-90; University of New Mexico, Albuquerque, professor, 1991-97. Visiting professor of creative writing at the University of Montana, 1985, at University of Hawaii at Manoa, 2003. Writer and consultant for Native American Public Broadcasting Consortium, National Indian Youth Council, and National Endowment for the Arts, all 1980-83. Member of steering committee of En'owkin Centre International School of Writing. Writer-in-residence at schools, including Navajo Community College, 1978; University of Alaska Prison Project, 1981; and Institute of Alaska Native Arts,

Joy Harjo

1984. Recordings with band, Joy Harjo and Poetic Justice, include *Furious Light,* 1986, *The Woman Who Fell from the Sky,* 1994, and *Letter from the End of the Twentieth Century,* 1997.

MEMBER: PEN (member of advisory board), PEN New Mexico (member of advisory board).

AWARDS, HONORS: Academy of American Poetry Award and University of New Mexico first-place poetry award, both 1976; National Endowment for the Arts fellow, 1978; named one of the Outstanding Young Women in America, 1978, 1984; first place in poetry, Santa Fe Festival for the Arts, 1980; Arizona Commission on the Arts Creative Writing fellow, 1989; American Indian Distinguished Achievement Award, 1990; Josephine Miles Award for excellence in literature, PEN Oakland, William Carlos Williams award, Poetry Society of America, and American Book Award, Before Columbus Foundation, all 1991, for *In Mad Love and War;* Wittner Bynner Poetry fellowship, 1994; Lifetime Achievement award, Native Writers' Circle of the Americas, 1995; Oklahoma Book Arts award, 1995, for *The Woman Who Fell from the Sky;* Delmore Schwartz Memorial award, and Mountains and Plains Booksellers' award, both 1995, both for *In Mad Love and War;* Bravo Award, Albuquerque Arts Alliance, 1996; New Mexico Governor's Award for excellence in the arts, 1997; Lila Wallace/*Reader's Digest* Fund Writers' Award, 1998; National Council on the Arts, presidential appointment, 1998; 1998 Outstanding Musical Achievement Award presented by The First Americans in the Arts Council; Honorary doctorate, St. Mary-in-the-Woods College, 1998; Charlotte Zolotow Award, Highly Commended Book, 2001, and Wordcraft Circle of Native Writers and Storytellers Writer of the Year Award, both for *The Good Luck Cat;*Arrell Gibson Award for Lifetime Achievement, Oklahoma Center for the Book, 2003; Oklahoma Book Award, 2003, for *How We Became Human.*

WRITINGS:

POETRY

The Last Song (chapbook; also see below), Puerto Del Sol Press (Las Cruces, NM), 1975.

What Moon Drove Me to This? (contains *The Last Song*), I. Reed Books (New York, NY), 1980.

She Had Some Horses, Thunder's Mouth Press (New York, NY), 1983.

Secrets from the Center of the World, illustrated by Steven Strom, University of Arizona Press (Tucson, AZ), 1989.

In Mad Love and War, Wesleyan University Press (Middletown, CT), 1990.

The Woman Who Fell from the Sky, Norton (New York, NY), 1994.

A Map to the Next World: Poetry and Tales, Norton (New York, NY), 2000.

How We Became Human: New and Selected Poems, 1975-2001, Norton (New York, NY), 2002.

OTHER

(Editor with Gloria Bird) *Reinventing the Enemy's Language: North American Native Women's Writing,* Norton (New York, NY), 1997.

The Good Luck Cat (children's fiction), illustrated by Paul Lee, Harcourt (San Diego, CA), 2000.

Also author of the film script *Origin of Apache Crown Dance,* Silver Cloud Video, 1985; coauthor of the film script *The Beginning,* Native American Broadcasting Consortium; author of television plays, including *We Are One, Uhonho,* 1984, *Maiden of Deception Pass,* 1985, *I Am Different from My Brother,* 1986, and *The Runaway,* 1986. Contributor to numerous anthologies and to several literary journals, including *Conditions, Beloit Poetry Journal, River Styx, Tyuoyi,* and *Y'Bird.*

WORK IN PROGRESS: A collection of personal essays.

SIDELIGHTS: Strongly influenced by her Muskogee Creek heritage, feminist and social concerns, and her background in the arts, Joy Harjo frequently incorporates Native American myths, symbols, and values into her writing. Her poetry additionally emphasizes the Southwest landscape and the need for remembrance and transcendence. She once commented, "I feel strongly that I have a responsibility to all the sources that I am: to all past and future ancestors, to my home country, to all places that I touch down on and that are myself, to all voices, all women, all of my tribe, all people, all earth, and beyond that to all beginnings and endings. In a strange kind of sense [writing] frees me to believe in myself, to be able to speak, to have voice, because I have to; it is my survival." In answer to a question from Pam Kingsbury for the *Southern Scribe,* Harjo remarked, "I am most often defined by others as: Native American, feminist, western, southwestern, primarily. I define myself as a human writer, poet and musician, a Muskoke writer (etc.)—and I'm most definitely of the west, southwest, Oklahoma and now my path includes LA and Honolulu . . . it throws the definition, skews it. It would be easier to be seen, I believe, if I fit into an easy category, as in for instance: The New York School, the Black Mountain School, the Beats—or even as in more recently, the slam poets. But I don't."

Harjo's work is largely autobiographical, informed by her love of the natural world and her preoccupation with survival and the limitations of language. Her first volume of poetry was published in 1975 as a nine-poem chapbook titled *The Last Song.* These early compositions, mainly set in Oklahoma and New Mexico, reveal Harjo's remarkable power and insight, especially as evident in the title poem, "The Last Song," and in "3 AM." Harjo wrote in "3 AM" about an exasperating airport experience: "the attendant doesn't know / that third mesa / is a part of the center / of the world / and who are we just two indians / at three in the morning trying to find our way back home." Commenting on "3 AM" in *World Literature Today,* John Scarry wrote that the poem "is a work filled with ghosts from the Native American past, figures seen operating in an alien culture that is itself a victim of fragmentation. . . . Here the Albuquerque airport is both modern America's technology and moral nature—and both clearly have failed. Together they cannot get these Indians to their destination, a failure that stretches from our earliest history to the sleek desks of our most up-to-date airline offices."

What Moon Drove Me to This?, Harjo's first full-length volume of poetry, appeared four years later and includes the entire contents of *The Last Song.* "With this collection," C. Renee Field wrote in the *Dictionary of Literary Biography,* "Harjo continued to refine her ability to find and voice the deep spiritual truths underneath everyday experiences, especially for the Native American." In an interview with Laura Coltelli in *Winged Words: American Indian Writers Speak,* Harjo shares the creative process behind her poetry: "I begin with the seed of an emotion, a place, and then move from there. . . . I no longer see the poem as an ending point, perhaps more the end of a journey, an often long journey that can begin years earlier, say with the blur of the memory of the sun on someone's cheek, a certain smell, an ache, and will culminate years later in a poem, sifted through a point, a lake in my heart through which language must come."

The search for freedom and self-actualization considered central to Harjo's work, is particularly noted in her third book of poetry, *She Had Some Horses,* in which she frequently incorporates prayer-chants and animal imagery. For example, in "The Black Room," a poem about childhood rape, Harjo repeats the mantric line "She thought she woke up." In the title poem, "She Had Some Horses," one of Harjo's most highly regarded and anthologized poems, she describes the "horses" within a woman who struggles to reconcile contradictory personal feelings and experiences to achieve a sense of oneness. The poem concludes: "She had some horses she loved. / She had some horses she hated. / These were the same horse." As Field observed, "The horses are spirits, neither male nor female, and, through them, clear truths can be articulated." As Scarry noted, "Harjo is clearly a highly political and feminist Native American, but she is even more the poet of myth and the subconscious; her images and landscapes owe as much to the vast stretches of our hidden mind as they do to her native Southwest."

Nature is central to Harjo's works, as evident in her 1989 prose poetry collection *Secrets from the Center of the World.* Each poem in this volume is accompanied by a color photograph of the Southwest landscape, which, as Margaret Randall noted in *Women's Review of Books,* works to "create an evocative little gem, intensely personal, hauntingly universal." Offering praise for the volume in the *Village Voice,* Dan Bellm wrote, "*Secrets* is a rather unlikely experiment that turned into a satisfying and beautiful book. . . . As Harjo notes, the pictures 'emphasize the "not-separate" that is within and that moves harmoniously upon the landscape.'" According to Randall, "There is no alteration in these photographs, nor do the poems lack a word or possess one too many. Language and visual image are perfectly tuned and balanced, producing an experience in which neither illustrates the other but each needs its counterpart." Bellm similarly added, "The book's best poems enhance this play of scale and perspective, suggesting in very few words the relationship between a human life and millennial history."

Her best-known volume, the multiaward-winning *In Mad Love and War,* is more overtly concerned with politics, tradition, remembrance, and the transformational aspects of poetry. In the first section, which relates various acts of violence, including the murder of an Indian leader as well as others' attempts to deny Harjo her heritage, Harjo explores the difficulties many Native Americans face in modern American society: "we have too many stories to carry on our backs like houses, we have struggled too long to let the monsters steal our sleep, sleep, go to sleep. But I never woke up. Dogs have been nipping at my heels since I learned to walk. I was taught to not dance for a rotten supper on the plates of my enemies. My mother taught me well." The second half of the book frequently emphasizes personal relationships and change.

"Harjo's range of emotion and imagery in this volume is truly remarkable," wrote Scarry. "She achieves intimacy and power in ways that send a reader to every part of the poetic spectrum for comparisons and for some frame of reference." In the poem "Autobiography," a mother describes to her daughter how God created humans to inhabit the earth. In another, "Javelina," Harjo invokes the strong voice of "one born of a blood who wrestled the whites for freedom, and I have since lived dangerously in a diminished system." Leslie Ullman noted in the *Kenyon Review,* "Like a magician, Harjo draws power from overwhelming circumstance and emotion by submitting to them, celebrating them, letting her voice and vision move in harmony with the ultimate laws of paradox and continual change." Commenting on "Javelina," Ullman added that Harjo's "stance is not so much that of a representative of a culture as it is the more generative one of a storyteller whose stories resurrect memory, myth, and private struggles that have been overlooked, and who thus restores vitality to the culture at large." Praising the volume in the *Prairie Schooner,* Kathleen West wrote, "*In Mad Love and War* has the power of beauty and prophecy and all the hope of love poised at its passionate beginning. It allows us to enter the place 'we haven't imagined' and allows us to imagine what we will do when we are there."

In 1994, Harjo followed *In Mad Love and War* with *The Woman Who Fell from the Sky,* another book of prose poetry. The title is based on an Iroquois myth about the descent of a female creator. As Frank Allen noted in *Library Journal,* Harjo is concerned with the vying forces of creation and destruction in contemporary society, embodied in such symbolism as wolves and northern lights contrasted with alcoholism and the Vietnam War. *Booklist* reviewer Pat Monaghan praised the poems as "stunning, mature, wholehearted, musical," and the collection together as a "brilliant, unforgettable book."

A Map to the Next World: Poetry and Tales includes a long introduction and much commentary with the poems. As a *Publishers Weekly* reviewer described, "A facing-page dialogue between poetry and prose, the absorbing long poem 'Returning from the Enemy,' attempts to reconcile memories of the poet's absent father with memories of her own children, of ancestors and of 'each trigger of grass:' 'We want to know if it's possible to separate and come back together, as the river licking the dock merges with the sea a few blocks away. / Long-legged birds negotiate the shore for food. / I am not as graceful as these souls.'"

How We Became Human: New and Selected Poems, 1975-2001, in the words of a *Publishers Weekly* reviewer, "show the remarkable progression of a writer determined to reconnect with her past and make sense of her present, drawing together the brutalities of contemporary reservation life with the beauty and sensibility of Native American culture and mythology." Including poems from every previous collection, *How We Became Human*, according to Pam Kingsbury of the *Library Journal*, "explores the role of the artist in society, the quest for love, the links among the arts, what constitutes family, and what it means to be human. Using the chant/myth/storytelling forms of her ancestors, she draws the reader into the awareness that 'one people is related to another.'" The same *Publishers Weekly* critic remarked that Harjo "contends that poetry is not only a way to save the sanity of those who have been oppressed to the point of madness, but that it is a tool to rebuild communities and, ultimately, change the world: 'All acts of kindness are lights in the war for justice.' Alive with compassion, pain and love, this book is unquestionably an act of kindness." Harjo is currently writing a book of stories that is half-memoir, half-fiction and working on a book project with Laguna Pueblo photographer Lee Marmon.

Harjo has also branched out into children's fiction with *The Good Luck Cat. School Library Journal* reviewer Joy Fleischhacker recommended the story of a cat that has outlived eight of its nine lives: "Harjo's text presents some striking images while still maintaining a believably childlike tone. The realistic acrylic paintings beautifully convey both action scenes (Woogie falling from a tree) and quiet moments (the hopeful girl placing her missing pet's bowl and toys on the back step). Lee has a knack for capturing the cat's agility and suppleness. Details woven into the story and pictures provide a glimpse of the protagonist's Native American heritage." A *Publishers Weekly* reviewer observed, "Harjo combines a childlike voice with a command of detail and imagery ('When I pet her she purrs as if she has a drum near her heart')."

In addition to her fictional works, Harjo has done much to popularize other Native American women writers. An interview with Laura Coltelli, published as *Spiral of Memory: Interviews: Joy Harjo,* appeared in 1997 and offers additional insight into the writer's background, art, and views on poetry. And in *Reinventing the Enemy's Language: North American Native Women's Writing,* Harjo presents a collection of stories that act to spur readers to social and political activism. The works, from such authors as Louise Erdrich and diarist Mary Brave Bird, present a new genre, according to *Progressive* contributor Mark Anthony Rolo, but rather than faddish, it is "a new sphere of storytelling, part of a larger hidden culture. These writers immunize us against the plague of marginalization. Their growing acceptance is a shift away from the Western literary canon. Perhaps this is the kind of politics Harjo and Bird should lobby for in the second volume of North American native women's writings."

Consistently praised for the depth and thematic concerns in her writings, Harjo has emerged as a major figure in contemporary American poetry. Sometimes, for taking a position on numerous political, social, economic, and humanitarian issues, she has received criticism for being overly "politically correct." But, as Field noted, "She does not tell her reader how to feel but simply tells the truth she sees. Harjo's poetry is not so much about 'correctness' as it is about continuance and survival." While Harjo's work is often set in the Southwest, emphasizes the plight of the individual, and reflects Creek values, myths, and beliefs, her oeuvre has universal relevance. Bellm asserted: "Harjo's work draws from the river of Native tradition, but it also swims freely in the currents of Anglo-American verse—feminist poetry of personal/political resistance, deep-image poetry of the unconscious, 'new-narrative' explorations of story and rhythm in prose-poem form." According to Field, "To read the poetry of Joy Harjo is to hear the voice of the earth, to see the landscape of time and timelessness, and, most important, to get a glimpse of people who struggle to understand, to know themselves, and to survive."

Paula Gunn Allen in *The Sacred Hoop* stated that Harjo's "thrust, in her work . . . is toward reconciliation of the polarities into an order that is harmonious, balanced, and whole." Harjo "articulates her certain understanding of the spherical unity of the universe, its essential 'spiritness,' . . . in her poetry" and, quoting her: "I have this image. It's not a generator, it's not a power plant. But it's like they have these different points in between. So it's a place, it's a poem, like a globular, like a circle with center points all over. And poems are like that. They have circuits."

Commenting on her writing as a means of survival, Harjo told Coltelli, "I don't believe I would be alive today if it hadn't been for writing. There were times when I was conscious of holding onto a pen and letting the words flow, painful and from the gut, to keep from letting go of it all. Now, this was when I was much younger, and full of self-hatred. Writing helped me give voice to turn around a terrible silence that was killing me. And on a larger level, if we, as Indian people, Indian women, keep silent, then we will disappear, at least in this level of reality." Field noted, "As Harjo has continued to refine her craft, her poems have become visions, answers to age-old questions, keys to understanding the complex nature of twentieth-century American life, and guides to the past and the future."

Harjo told *CA:* "I agree with Gide that most of what is created is beyond us, is from that source of utter creation, the Creator, or God. We are technicians here on Earth, but also co-creators. I'm still amazed. And I still say, after writing poetry for all this time, and now music, that ultimately humans have a small hand in it. We serve it. We have to put ourselves in the way of it, and get out of the way of ourselves. And we have to hone our craft so that the form in which we hold our poems, our songs in attracts the best.

"My particular road is not about taking established forms and developing them. I admire a finely constructed sonnet but I do not wish to work in that Euro-classical form. I honor that direction, but I am working to find my own place and one who is multicultural, multiracial. I am influenced by Muscogean forms, European and African forms, as well as others that have deeply moved me, say for instance, Navajo. When I began writing poetry as a painting major at the University of New Mexico, I was learning Navajo language. It influenced me deeply because intimate to the language were the shapes of the landscape, the history. I became aware of layers of meaning marked by sandhills, by the gestures of the earth.

"African-American influences in poetry and music have been critical to my development as a writer and musician. This is not something new. There is history and a relationship between Africans and Muscogean peoples begun in the southeastern U.S. We've influenced each other, yet this influence is rarely talked about. I can hear the African influence in our stomp dance music, and can hear Muscogean influence in jazz, the blues, and rock. It's all there.

"I have also taken up saxophone and perform professionally with my band. I am asked often about how music has informed my poetry, changed it. It's difficult to say exactly, except to acknowledge that of course it has all along. The first poetry I heard and recognized as pure poetry was the improvised line of a trumpet player on a jazz tune on the radio when I was four years old. That was it. I've been trying to get it right ever since. Sometimes I hear the origin of that line when I'm at the stomp grounds. One of these days I'll be able to sing it, write it." Harjo's interest in music has taken the form of combining poetry and song, poetry and saxophone, and she tours with her band, Poetic Justice.

BIOGRAPHICAL AND CRITICAL SOURCES:

BOOKS

Balassi, William, John F. Crawford, and Annie O. Eysturoy, editors, *This Is about Vision: Interviews with Southwestern Writers,* University of New Mexico Press (Albuquerque, NM), 1990.

Brogan, Jacqueline Vaught, and Cordelia Chavez Candelaria, editors, *Women Poets of the Americas: Toward a Pan-American Gathering,* University of Notre Dame Press (Notre Dame, IN), 1999.

Bruchac, Joseph, editor, *Survival This Way: Interviews with American Indian Poets,* University of Arizona Press (Tucson, AZ), 1987.

Bryan, Sharon, ed., *Where We Stand: Women Poets on Literary Tradition,* Norton (New York, NY), 1993.

Buelens, Gert, and Ernst Rudin, editors, *Deferring a Dream: Literary Sub-Versions of the American Columbiad,* Birkhauser (Boston, MA), 1994.

Coltelli, Laura, editor, *Winged Words: American Indian Writers Speak,* University of Nebraska Press (Lincoln, NE), 1990.

Coltelli, Laura, editor, *Native American Literatures.* SEU (Pisa, Italy), 1994.

Coltelli, Laura, editor, *The Spiral of Memory: Interviews: Joy Harjo,* University of Michigan Press (Ann Arbor, MI), 1996.

Contemporary Literary Criticism, Volume 83, Gale (Detroit, MI), 1994.

Contemporary Women Poets, St. James Press (Detroit, MI), 1997.

Dictionary of Literary Biography, Gale (Detroit, MI), Volume 120: *American Poets since World War II,* 1992, Volume 175: *Native American Writers of the United States,* 1997.

Gunn Allen, Paula, *The Sacred Hoop: Recovering the Feminine in American Indian Traditions,* Beacon Press (Boston, MA), 1986.

Harjo, Joy, *She Had Some Horses,* Thunder's Mouth Press (New York, NY), 1983.

Harjo, Joy, *In Mad Love and War,* Wesleyan University Press, 1990.

Hinton, Laura, and Cynthia Hogue, editors, *We Who Love to Be Astonished: Experimental Women's Writing and Performance Poetics,* University of Alabama Press (Tuscaloosa, AL), 2002.

Hobson, Geary, editor, *The Remembered Earth: An Anthology of Contemporary Native American Literature,* Red Earth, 1979.

Keller, Lynn, and Cristanne Miller, editors, *Feminist Measures: Soundings in Poetry and Theory,* University of Michigan Press (Ann Arbor, MI), 1994.

Norwood, Vera, and Janice Monk, editors, *The Desert Is No Lady: Southwestern Landscapes in Women's Writing and Art,* Yale University Press (New Haven, CT), 1987.

Pettit, Rhonda, *Joy Harjo,* Boise State University (Boise, ID), 1998.

Swann, Brian, and Arnold Krupat, editors, *I Tell You Now: Autobiographical Essays by Native American Writers,* University of Nebraska Press (Lincoln, NE), 1987.

PERIODICALS

Albuquerque Journal, February 7, 1997 p. E13; May 11, 1997, p. C9; September 15, 2002, p. F8.

Albuquerque Tribune, February 7, 1997, p. B4; January 21, 1998, p. C6.

American Book Review, April-May, 1991, pp. 10-11.

American Indian Quarterly, spring, 1983, p. 27; spring, 1991, p. 273; fall, 1992, p. 533; winter, 1995, p. 1; spring, 2000, p. 200.

American Studies International, June, 1997, p. 88.

Belles Lettres, summer, 1991, pp. 7-8; summer, 1994, p. 46.

Bloomsbury Review, March-April, 1996; November-December, 1997, p. 18.

Booklist, November 15, 1994, p. 573; June 1, 1997, p. 1649; February 1, 2000, p. 1005.

Boston Herald, April 10, 2003, p. 067.

Buffalo News (Buffalo, NY), October 4, 1998, p. G6.

Current Biography, August, 2001, p. 50.

ELF: Eclectic Literary Forum, fall, 1995, p. 44.

Guardian (London, England), October 18, 2003, p. 7.

Kenyon Review, spring, 1991, pp. 179-83; summer, 1993, pp. 57-66.

Legacy: A Journal of American Women Writers, 2002, p. 106.

Library Journal, October 15, 1994, p. 72; November 15, 1994, p. 70; June 1, 1997, p. 100; June 15, 2002, p. 70.

Los Angeles Times, February 10, 1989, section 5, pp. 1, 14-16.

MELUS, spring, 1989-90; fall, 1993, p. 41; summer, 1994, p. 35.

Ms., July-August, 1991; September-October, 1991, p. 73.

Native American Literatures: Forum, 1989, p. 185.

North Dakota Quarterly, spring, 1985, pp. 220-234.

Oregonian (Portland, OR), October 19, 1998.

Poetry, August, 1996, pp. 281-302.

Poets and Writers Magazine, 1993, p. 23.

Prairie Schooner, summer, 1992, pp. 128-132.

Progressive, December, 1997, p. 42.

PSA News: Newsletter of the Poetry Society of America, winter, 1993, p. 17.

Publishers Weekly, November 28, 1994, p. 54; November 28, 1994, p. 54; April 21, 1997, p. 57; January 10, 2000, p. 58; May 22, 2000, p. 92; June 17, 2002, p. 58.

Religion and Literature, spring, 1994, p. 57; summer, 2001, p. 59.

Rochester Democrat and Chronicle (Rochester, NY), March 29, 2000, p. 1c.

San Francisco Chronicle, September 7, 1997, p. 2.

School Library Journal, April, 2000, p. 106.

Small Press Review, March, 1983, p. 8.

Studies in American Indian Literatures: The Journal of the Association for the Study of American Indian Literatures, spring, 1994, p. 24; spring, 1995, p. 45.

Village Voice, April 2, 1991, p. 78.

Washington Post, August 20, 2000, p. X12.

Western American Literature, summer, 2000, p. 131.

Whole Earth Review, summer, 1995, p. 43; summer, 1998, p. 99.

wicazo sa review: A Journal of Native American Studies, 2000 p. 27.

Women's Review of Books, July, 1990, pp. 17-18.

World Literature Today, winter, 1991, pp. 167-168; spring, 1992, pp. 286-291.

ONLINE

PAL: Perspectives in American Literature—A Research and Reference Guide, http://www.csustan.edu/english/reuben/pal/chap10/harjo.html/ (March 10, 2004).

Poetry Magazine, http://www.poetrymagazine.com/ (March 3, 2003).

Southern Scribe, http://www.southernscribe.com/ (March 3, 2003), interview with Harjo.

OTHER

The Power of the Word (video), with Bill Moyers, PBS Video (Alexandria, VA), 1989.*

* * *

HARRIS, Jana 1947-

PERSONAL: Born September 21, 1947, in San Francisco, CA; daughter of Richard H. (a meat packer) and Cicely Ann (Herman) Harris; married Mark Allen Bothwell (a biochemist), August 19, 1977. *Education:* University of Oregon—Eugene, B.S. (with honors), 1969; San Francisco State University, M.A., 1972.

ADDRESSES: *Office*—32814 120 St. SE, Sultan, WA 98294. *Agent*—Charlotte Sheedy Literary Agency, 145 West 86th St., New York, NY 10024. *E-mail*—jnh@u.washington.edu.

CAREER: San Francisco State University, San Francisco, CA, instructor in poetry in the schools, 1972-78; Modesto Junior College, Modesto, CA, instructor in creative writing, 1975-78; City University of New York, New York, NY, instructor in creative writing, 1980—; Manhattan Theatre Club, New York, NY, acting director for writers-in-performance series, 1980-86; University of Washington, Seattle, instructor, 1986—. Founder and editor, *Switched-on Gutenberg* (Internet poetry journal). Co-coordinator of women-in-poetry program for Intersection, Inc., 1972-73; coordinator for Cody's Books "Poetry Reading" series, 1975-78; poet-in-residence for Alameda County Neighborhood Arts Program, 1977-78. Coproducer of "Planet on the Table," a literary program broadcast on KPFA-Radio, 1975-78, and "The Unheard of Hour," a literary interview program broadcast on KSAN-Radio, 1977. Educational mathematics consultant for Project SEED, Inc., at Lawrence Hall of Science at the University of California—Berkeley, 1970-76. Appeared movie *Festival of the Bards,* 1978.

MEMBER: Poets and Writers, Associated Writing Programs, Feminist Writers' Guild, Poets and Writers of New Jersey, Pi Mu Epsilon.

AWARDS, HONORS: Berkeley Civic Arts Commission grant, 1974; New Jersey State Council on the Arts poetry fellowship, 1981; *Manhattan As a Second Language* and *Oh How Can I Keep on Singing? Voices of Pioneer Women* both received Pulitzer Prize nominations; *Alaska* was a Book-of-the-Month Club selection, English-Speaking Union selection, and Books-across-the-Sea Program selection.

WRITINGS:

POETRY

This House That Rocks with Every Truck on the Road, Jungle Garden (Fairfax, CA), 1976.

Pin Money, Jungle Garden (Fairfax, CA), 1977.

The Clackamas, The Smith, 1980.

Who's That Pushy Bitch?, Jungle Garden (Fairfax, CA), 1981.

Manhattan As a Second Language, Harper (New York, NY), 1982.

The Sourlands, Ontario Review Press (Princeton, NJ), 1989.

Oh How Can I Keep on Singing? Voices of Pioneer Women, Ontario Review Press (Princeton, NJ), 1993.

The Dust of Everyday Life: An Epic Poem of the Pacific Northwest, Sasquatch Books (Seattle, WA), 1997.

We Never Speak of It: Idaho-Wyoming Poems, 1889-90, Ontario Review Press (Princeton, NJ), 2003.

FICTION

Alaska (novel), Harper (New York, NY), 1980.

The Pearl of Ruby City (mystery novel), St. Martin's Press (New York, NY), 1998.

Also author of *Running Scared: Early Poems,* Spring Valley. Contributor to books, including *This Is Women's Work,* edited by Susan Efros, Panjandrum, 1974; *Anthology of the First Annual Women's Poetry Festival of San Francisco,* edited by Noni Noward, New World Press, 1977; *City of Buds and Flowers: A*

Poet's Eye View of Berkeley, edited by John Oliver Simon, Aldebaran Review, 1977; *Nineteen Plus One: An Anthology of San Francisco Poetry,* edited by A. D. Winans, Second Coming Press, 1978; *Calafia: The California Poetry,* edited by Ishmael Reed, Yardbird Publishing, 1979; *Networks: An Anthology of Women Poets,* edited by Carol Simone, Vortex, 1979; and *Anthology of the City College of New York Poetry Festival,* edited by Barry Wallenstein, City College of the City University of New York, 1979. Contributor of numerous poems, essays, short stories, and articles to periodicals, including *Nation, Poetry Flash, Ms., Fiction West, Berkeley Poetry Review,* and *New Women's Times Feminist Review*. Associate editor and cofounder, *Poetry Flash,* 1972-78; guest editor, *Libera,* 1973; coeditor, *Feminist Writer's Guild National Newsletter,* 1978.

ADAPTATIONS: *Oh How Can I Keep on Singing? Voices of Pioneer Women* is being adapted for television.

WORK IN PROGRESS: A sequel to *The Pearl of Ruby City;* a contemporary thriller novel; more poetry.

SIDELIGHTS: Poet and fiction writer Jana Harris has spent much of her life in rugged areas of Alaska and Oregon, where she developed a fascination for the stories of pioneer life in the western United States. In the past, she has worked on an Alaskan fishing boat, and she currently owns a farm in the Cascade Mountains. Coming to know the elderly residents of such towns as Sitka, Alaska, where she interviewed people in their eighties and older, Harris wanted to tell their stories. As she told Cathy Sova in a *Mystery Reader* interview, for example, she wrote her mystery novel, *The Pearl of Ruby City,* "because I live on a farm [and] I was interested in reading about a time when agrarian life was the norm, not an anomaly. In the beginning, what I was looking for was common ground. I've been formulating this theory, when America exited the family farm, following World War II, our nation lost its way and hasn't quite found it again."

In her first novel, *Alaska,* which is based on a collection of first-person interviews Harris obtained from longtime Alaska residents while she hitchhiked through the state in 1971, the author reproduced a history of Alaska from 1867 to the present, told from the perspective of succeeding generations of its women characters. *Best Sellers* critic Lucille Crane pronounced the novel "a fine study of a little-known subject and uniquely organized to tell a wonderful story." As with *Alaska,* Harris's poems also often take the form of narratives from the perspective of pioneer women. Her *Oh How Can I Keep on Singing? Voices of Pioneer Women* is based, as she told Sova, on "the real life reminiscences of women who lived near the silver mining camp of Ruby in the Okanogan Valley in central Washington state." This evolved into a collection of poetic monologues told in the voices of young and old pioneers. Although a *Publishers Weekly* critic found the poetry "technically uninspiring and the voices . . . not adequately differentiated," the reviewer still considered their stories to be "moving." *Booklist* reviewer Pat Monaghan praised the book for its "marvelous details" and "dramatic individual stories of women's lives on the frontier."

Oh How Can I Keep on Singing? evolved into Harris's second novel, *The Pearl of Ruby City,* which focuses on the life of a laundress living in the same locale as the characters in the earlier poetry collection. Pearl Ryan is a young woman of twenty-one who has fled a troubled past in New York City and settled in a small Washington town. Here, she saves money to go to medical school by working as a laundress and helping out the local doctor. When the town's mayor is murdered, Pearl is worried that investigations into the crime might reveal her past, and so she becomes an amateur sleuth to find the true criminal and protect her privacy. Some reviewers of this mystery novel enjoyed the colorful cast of characters and period details, while others felt they muddled the storyline. A *Publishers Weekly* critic observed that "too much period detail and too many characters" result in a plot that "never develops." On the other hand, *Library Journal* writer Rex E. Klett called *The Pearl of Ruby City* a "lively first novel," while Budd Arthur, commenting in *Booklist,* appreciated the "unmistakable lyricism" of the writing, which he attributed to Harris's background as a poet.

Harris has also published another collection of narrative poems, *We Never Speak of It: Idaho-Wyoming Poems, 1889-90.* This book again tells the story of life in America over a century ago, mostly from the viewpoint of women characters.

Harris once told *CA:* "I write to document my own reality. I sit at a desk eight to twelve hours a day writing. Because writing is often an isolating experience and an arduous task, I have several desks in different cities: Ringoes, New Jersey; New York City; and Berkeley, California. I find that changing my surroundings often changes the light on my subjects. When the area around one desk gets too dirty, I move to another desk, hoping that someone will clean up in my absence. I have never been afflicted with writer's block; I think that writer's block is a male affliction. I have never not been able to write. I have, however, been afraid; afraid that everything I write will be bad, afraid that I'll keep writing the same boring story or poem over and over, and afraid that some critic will call my characters trite."

BIOGRAPHICAL AND CRITICAL SOURCES:

PERIODICALS

Best Sellers, January, 1981, Lucille Crane, review of *Alaska.*

Booklist, October 15, 1977; October 15, 1993, Pat Monaghan, review of *Oh How Can I Keep on Singing? Voices of Pioneer Women,* p. 413; September 1, 1998, Budd Arthur, review of *The Pearl of Ruby City,* p. 70; March 1, 2003, Ray Olson, review of *We Never Speak of It: Idaho-Wyoming Poems, 1889-90,* p. 1141.

Library Journal, January 15, 1982, review of *Manhattan As a Second Language,* p. 181; December 1, 1982, Bill Katz, review of *Quilt,* p. 2240; October 1, 1993, Frank Allen, review of *Oh How Can I Keep on Singing?,* p. 98; October 1, 1998, Rex E. Klett, review of *The Pearl of Ruby City,* p. 138.

Ms., July, 1981, Mary Thom, review of *Alaska,* p. 26; September, 1982, Jane Bosveld, review of *Manhattan As a Second Language,* p. 94.

New York Times, November 16, 1980, Michael Malone, review of *Alaska,* p. 24.

People, November 29, 1993, Sara Nelson, review of *Oh How Can I Keep on Singing?,* p. 33.

Publishers Weekly, September 26, 1980, Barbara A. Bannon, review of *Alaska,* p. 116; December 18, 1981, Sally A. Lodge, review of *Manhattan As a Second Language,* p. 69; October 11, 1993, review of *Oh How Can I Keep on Singing?,* p. 82; August 10, 1998, review of *The Pearl of Ruby City,* p. 372.

ONLINE

Mystery Reader, http://www.themysteryreader.com/nf-harris.html/ (January 6, 1999), Cathy Sova, "New Faces 8—Jana Harris."*

HENNER, Marilu 1952-

PERSONAL: Born April 6, 1952, in Chicago, IL; daughter of Joe (a car dealer), and Loretta (a dance instructor) Henner; married Frederic Forrest (an actor), September 28, 1980 (divorced, 1982); married Rob Lieberman (a television film producer and director), 1990; children: (second marriage) Nicholas Morgan, Joseph Marlin. *Education:* Attended University of Chicago.

ADDRESSES: *Agent*—International Creative Management, 8942 Wilshire Blvd., Beverly Hills, CA 90211.

CAREER: Television, film, and stage actress and author. Principal television appearances include *Taxi,* 1978-83, *Evening Shade,* 1990, and *Marilu,* 1994. Film roles include *Between the Lines,* 1977, *Bloodbrothers,* 1978, *Dream House,* 1981, *Hammett,* 1983, *The Man Who Loved Women,* 1983, *Johnny Dangerously,* 1984, *Mister Roberts,* 1984, *Cannonball Run II,* 1984, *Rustlers' Rhapsody,* 1985, *Stark,* 1985, *Perfect,* 1985, *Grown Ups,* 1985, *Love with a Perfect Stranger,* 1986, *Grand Larceny,* 1987, *Lady Killers,* 1988, *L.A. Story,* 1991, *Andy Kaufman: I'm from Hollywood,* 1992, *Noises Off,* 1992, *Chains of Gold,* 1992, *Batman: Mask of the Phantasm,* 1993, *Chasers,* 1994, *Fight for Justice: The Nancy Conn Story,* 1995, *For the Children: The Irvine Fertility Scandal,* 1996, *My Son Is Innocent,* 1996, *Titanic,* 1996, *Batman and Mr. Freeze: Sub Zero,* 1998, *The Titanic Chronicles,* 1999, *Man on the Moon,* 1999, *A Tail of Two Bunnies,* 2000, *Lost in the Pershing Point Hotel,* 2000, *Rocket's Red Glare,* 2000, and *Enemies of Laughter,* 2000. Actress in plays, including *Grease,* 1973, *Over Here,* 1974, *Social Security,* 1987, *Chicago,* 1997, *Annie Get Your Gun,* 2000, and *The Tale of the Allergist's Wife,* 2002.

AWARDS, HONORS: Five Golden Globe nominations for best actress in a comedy series, for *Taxi.*

WRITINGS:

(With Jim Jerome) *By All Means Keep on Moving,* Pocket Books (New York, NY), 1994.

(With Laura Morton) *Marilu Henner's Total Health Makeover: Ten Steps to Your B.E.S.T. Body: Balance, Energy, Stamina, Toxin-Free,* ReganBooks (New York, NY), 1998.

Marilu Henner

(With Morton) *The Thirty-Day Total Health Makeover,* ReganBooks (New York, NY), 1999.

(With Ruth Velikovsky Sharon) *I Refuse to Raise a Brat: Straightforward Advice on Parenting in the Age of Overindulgence,* ReganBooks (New York, NY), 1999.

(With Lorin Henner) *Healthy Life Kitchen,* ReganBooks (New York, NY), 2000.

(With Lorin Henner) *Healthy Kids: Help Them Eat Smart and Stay Active—for Life!,* ReganBooks (New York, NY), 2001.

Healthy Holidays: Total Health Entertaining All Year Round, ReganBooks (New York, NY), 2002.

SIDELIGHTS: Perhaps best known for her role as Elaine Nardo in the hit comedy series *Taxi,* which ran from 1978 to 1983, Marilu Henner has had a successful acting career in a wide variety of media; these include film, television situation comedies and dramas, stage musicals, and her own talk show, *Marilu.* It is difficult to find a review of Henner's acting that does not note her energy and likability, qualities she also manifests in her line of books on health and parenting. *Good Housekeeping* contributor Joanna Powell noted: "Since the publication of her first best-selling book, *Total Health Makeover,* . . . Henner's credentials as actress, dancer, and perennial talk-show guest have been eclipsed by her success as a bankable self-help author." Indeed, Henner continues to perform on stage and in films with a vitality that surpasses her considerable vigor during the 1980s, creating a market for her suggestions on how to stay fit and healthy.

Henner seemed destined for acting from an early age; most notably, at age eighteen she played Marty in a local production of *Grease,* and two years later she left college to tour with the show's national company. Henner's life was eventually marked by sadness when her father died suddenly at the age of fifty-two of a heart attack at a Christmas party. Her mother became ill eight years later with devastating arthritis that damaged her spinal cord and led to circulatory problems. The actress went home to help nurse Loretta Henner during the last four months of her life. Her mother died in May, 1978, at the age of fifty-eight, two weeks before Henner was cast in her career-making role in *Taxi.*

Henner's autobiography, *By All Means Keep on Moving,* is notable for the energy of Henner's voice as well as for her candor about her many sexual liaisons with costars over the years. Part of the story of Henner's childhood is the romance she observed between her parents, whom she recalled in an interview for *Redbook.* She said they were "romantic, lusty, hot for each other. When Dad came home, we would run to wherever my mother was because he would throw her down into a dance-dip position. My mother used to complain that he treated her more like a hundred-dollar hooker than a wife. They were wild." Her autobiography makes clear that Henner inherited her parents' "lust for life."

Most reviews of Henner's autobiography were positive. A critic in *Publishers Weekly* called the book an "upbeat story of a dynamic woman who keeps on moving no matter what." A *Kirkus* reviewer remarked on the frank sexuality of the book, quoting a "prose pheromone" from the book's introduction: "I have never apologized for my sexuality. . . . I'm a big fan of sex." Henner, the reviewer continued, "presents herself as Horatio Alger with legs."

As she approached her mid-forties—characteristically a difficult age for Hollywood actresses—Henner continued to be busy with stage and film projects while raising two young sons. More than one reporter noted that she appeared to be more trim at midlife than she was in her twenties, and the actress has capitalized upon this fact and has authored a series of books on how to promote a healthy lifestyle while working and caring for children. Among these best- sellers are *Marilu Henner's Total Health Makeover: Ten Steps to Your B.E.S.T. Body, Healthy Life Kitchen,* and *I Refuse to Raise a Brat: Straightforward Advice on Parenting in an Age of Overindulgence.*

Marilu Henner's Total Health Makeover and its companion, *The Thirty-Day Total Health Makeover,* are fitness books based on Henner's own diet, exercise, and health philosophy. She eats an all-natural vegetable diet and avoids dairy, red meat, and refined sugar. Although she engages in formal exercise classes, she is infamous for her suggestion that busy women can lose weight by dancing alone in the house for a mere twenty minutes three or four times per week. Her parenting advice is contained in *I Refuse to Raise a Brat,* written with psychologist Ruth Velikovsky Sharon. "At first glance, some of Henner's nutritional advice may seem a little left of center, though never quite outrageously unbelievable," noted *Atlanta Journal-Constitution* contributor Lillian Lee Kim. "But obviously it has worked for her."

Prior to her work in television and film, Henner began her acting career in stage shows, and she has returned to the stage in such roles as Annie Oakley in the touring company of *Annie Get Your Gun,* Roxie Hart in the Broadway version of *Chicago,* and the frankly sexual Lee in the Broadway hit *The Tale of the Allergist's Wife.* As Everett Evans observed in the *Houston Chronicle,* "There's a palpable excitement around Marilu Henner" as she moves into a new phase of her acting career. The actress told the *New York Post* that she is motivated by a simple philosophy: "You have one body your entire life, so you better take care of it well."

BIOGRAPHICAL AND CRITICAL SOURCES:

BOOKS

Zannos, Susan, *Female Stars of Nutrition and Weight Control: Featuring Profiles of Suzanne Sommers, Oprah Winfrey, Nadia Comaneci, and Marilu Henner,* Mitchell Lane (Bear, DE), 2001.

PERIODICALS

Atlanta Journal-Constitution, August 17, 1998, Lillian Lee Kim, "Health Watch: Henner Shares Secrets of Youthful Look," p. B3.

Back Stage West, November 30, 2000, Les Spindle, review of *Annie Get Your Gun,* p. 16.

Entertainment Weekly, October 14, 1994, p. 45.

Good Housekeeping, June, 1999, Joanna Powell, "Marilu Henner," p. 29.

Houston Chronicle, December 21, 2000, Everett Evans, "Hello Marilu," p. 1.

Kirkus Reviews, August 15, 1994, p. 1116.

Newsweek, September 3, 1990, pp. 70-71.

New Yorker, February 11, 1991, p. 74.

New York Post, June 18, 2002, "From Fads and Flab to Fab: Marilu's Tops after Giving up Yo-Yo Ways," p. 38; June 23, 2002, "Bedded Bliss: Marilu Henner Delights in Her Many Affairs," p. 50.

People, September 19, 1994, pp. 187-191.

Publishers Weekly, September 19, 1994, p. 62; September 20, 1999, "Parenting Issues," p. 83.

Redbook, April, 1993, pp. 32-34.

San Francisco Chronicle, May 30, 1997, Liz Smith, "Henner's Stepping off to *Chicago,*" p. D11.

Variety, November 11, 1996, p. 34.

ONLINE

Marilu Henner Web site, http://www.marilu.com/ (November 13, 2003).*

* * *

HILL, Susan (Elizabeth) 1942-

PERSONAL: Born February 5, 1942, in Scarborough, England; daughter of R. H. and Doris Hill; married Stanley W. Wells (a Shakespearean scholar), April 23, 1975; children: Jessica, Imogen (deceased), Clemency. *Education:* King's College, London, B.A. (with honors), 1963. *Religion:* Anglican. *Hobbies and other interests:* Walking in the English countryside, friends, reading, broadcasting.

ADDRESSES: *Home*—Midsummer Cottage, Church Lane, Beckley, Oxford OX3 9UT, England. *Agent*—Vivien Green, Sheil Land, 43 Doughty St., London WC1N 2LF, England. *E-mail*—susan@susan-hill.com.

Susan Hill

CAREER: Novelist, playwright, and critic, 1960—. *Coventry Evening Telegraph,* Coventry, England, literary critic, 1963-68; *Daily Telegraph,* London, England, monthly columnist, 1977—. Fellow of King's College, London, 1978. Presenter, *Bookshelf,* Radio 4, 1986-87.

AWARDS, HONORS: Somerset Maugham Award, 1971, for *I'm the King of the Castle;* Whitbread Literary Award for fiction, 1972, for *The Bird of Night;* John Llewelyn Rhys Memorial Prize, 1972, for *The Albatross;* Royal Society of Literature fellow, 1972.

WRITINGS:

NOVELS

The Enclosure, Hutchinson (London, England), 1961.

Do Me a Favour, Hutchinson (London, England), 1963.

Gentleman and Ladies, Hamish Hamilton (London, England), 1968, Walker (New York, NY), 1969.

A Change for the Better, Hamish Hamilton (London, England), 1969, Penguin (New York, NY), 1980.

I'm the King of the Castle, Viking (New York, NY), 1970.

Strange Meeting, Hamish Hamilton (London, England), 1971, Saturday Review Press (New York, NY), 1972.

The Bird of Night, Saturday Review Press (New York, NY), 1972.

In the Springtime of the Year, Saturday Review Press (New York, NY), 1974.

The Woman in Black: A Ghost Story, Hamish Hamilton (London, England), 1983, David Godine (Boston, MA), 1986.

Air and Angels (romance), Mandarin (London, England), 1991.

The Mist in the Mirror: A Ghost Story, Sinclair-Stevenson (London, England), 1992.

Mrs. de Winter, Morrow (New York, NY), 1993.

The Service of Clouds, Chatto & Windus (London, England), 1997, Vintage (New York, NY), 1999.

JUVENILE

The Ramshackle Company (play), produced in London, England, 1981.

One Night at a Time, illustrated by Vanessa Julian-Ottie, Hamish Hamilton (London, England), 1984.

Through the Kitchen Window, illustrated by Angela Barrett, Hamish Hamilton (London, England), 1984, Stemmer House (Owings Mills, MD), 1986.

Go Away, Bad Dreams!, illustrated by Vanessa Julian-Ottie, Random House (New York, NY), 1985.

Can It Be True?: A Christmas Story, illustrated by Angela Barrett, Viking (New York, NY), 1988.

Mother's Magic, illustrated by Alan Marks, David & Charles (Newton Abbot, Devon, England), 1988.

Suzy's Shoes, illustrated by Priscilla Lamont, Puffin (New York, NY), 1989.

Stories from Codling Village, illustrated by C. Crossland, Julia MacRae (New York, NY), 1990.

I Won't Go There Again, illustrated by Jim Bispham, Julia MacRae (New York, NY), 1990.

Septimus Honeydew, illustrated by Carol Thompson, Julia MacRae (New York, NY), 1990.

(Editor) *The Walker Book of Ghost Stories,* illustrated by Angela Barrett, Walker (New York, NY), 1990, published as *The Random House Book of Ghost Stories,* Random House (New York, NY), 1991.

The Glass Angels, illustrated by Valerie Littlewood, Candlewick Press (Cambridge, MA), 1992.

A Very Special Birthday, Walker (New York, NY), 1992.

King of Kings, illustrated by John Lawrence, Candlewick Press (Cambridge, MA), 1993.

Beware, Beware, illustrated by Angela Barrett, Candlewick Press (Cambridge, MA), 1993.

White Christmas, Candlewick Press (Cambridge, MA), 1994.

The Christmas Collection, Candlewick Press (Cambridge, MA), 1994.

(Editor and author of introduction) *The Spirit of Britain: An Illustrated Guide to Literary Britain,* Hodder Headline (London, England), 1994.

(Coauthor) *Diana: The Secret Years,* Ballantine (New York, NY), 1998.

Simba's A-Z, Disney Press (New York, NY), 1998.

Backyard Bedtime, illustrated by Barry Root, HarperCollins (New York, NY), 2001.

Stuart Hides Out, illustrated by Lydia Halverson, HarperCollins (New York, NY), 2001.

Stuart Sets Sail, illustrated by Lydia Halverson, HarperCollins (New York, NY), 2001.

*Stuart at the Fun House,*illustrated by Lydia Halverson, HarperCollins (New York, NY), 2001.

Stuart at the Library, illustrated by Lydia Halverson, HarperCollins (New York, NY), 2001.

Ruby Bakes a Cake, illustrated by Margie Moore, HarperCollins (New York, NY), 2004.

Also author of *I've Forgotten Edward,* 1990, and *Pirate Poll,* 1991.

RADIO PLAYS

Miss Lavender Is Dead, British Broadcasting Corp. (-BBC Radio), 1970.

Taking Leave, BBC Radio, 1971.

The End of the Summer, BBC Radio, 1971.

Lizard in the Grass, BBC Radio, 1971.

The Cold Country, BBC Radio, 1972.

Winter Elegy, BBC Radio, 1973.

Consider the Lilies, BBC Radio, 1973.

A Window on the World, BBC Radio, 1974.

Strip Jack Naked, BBC Radio, 1974.

Mr Proudham and Mr Sleight, BBC Radio, 1974.

The Cold Country and Other Plays for Radio (includes *The Cold Country, The End of Summer, Lizard in the Grass, Consider the Lilies,* and *Strip Jack Naked*), BBC Publications (London, England), 1975.

On the Face of It, BBC Radio, 1975, published in *Act 1,* edited by David Self and Ray Speakman, Hutchinson (London), 1979.

The Summer of the Giant Sunflower, BBC Radio, 1977.

The Sound That Time Makes, BBC Radio, 1980.

Here Comes the Bride, BBC Radio, 1980.

Chances, BBC Radio, 1981, stage adaptation produced in London, 1983.

Out in the Cold, BBC Radio, 1982.

Autumn, BBC Radio, 1985.

Winter, BBC Radio, 1985.

OTHER

The Albatross (short stories), Hamish Hamilton, 1971, published as *The Albatross and Other Stories,* Saturday Review Press (New York, NY), 1975.

The Custodian (short stories), Covent Garden Press (London, England), 1972.

A Bit of Singing and Dancing (short stories), Hamish Hamilton (London, England), 1973.

The Elephant Man, Cambridge University Press (New York, NY), 1975.

(Editor and author of introduction) Thomas Hardy, *The Distracted Preacher and Other Tales,* Penguin (London, England), 1980.

(Editor, with Isabel Quigly) *New Stories V,* Hutchinson (London, England), 1980.

Improving Interpersonal Competence, Kendall/Hunt Publishing, 1982.

(Translator, with Jonathan Tittler) Adalberto Ortiz, *Juyungo: The First Black Ecuadorian Novel,* Three Continents, 1982.

The Magic Apple Tree: A Country Year, Hamish Hamilton (London, England), 1982, Holt (New York, NY), 1983.

(Editor) *Ghost Stories,* Hamish Hamilton (London, England), 1983.

(Editor) *People: Essays and Poems,* Chatto & Windus (London, England), 1983.

The Lighting of the Lamps, David & Charles, 1986.

Books Alive!: Using Literature in the Classroom, Heinemann (London, England), 1986.

Shakespeare Country, photographs by Rod Talbot, Penguin (London, England), 1987.

(Editor, with Joelie Hancock) *Literature-Based Reading Programs at Work,* Heinemann Educational (London, England), 1988.

Through the Garden Gate, David & Charles (London, England), 1988.

Lanterns across the Snow, Crown (New York, NY), 1988.

The Spirit of the Cotswolds, photographs by Nick Meers, M. Joseph (London, England), 1988, Viking (New York, NY), 1990.

Family (autobiography), Viking (New York, NY), 1989.

(With Tim Hill) *The Collaborative Classroom: A Guide to Co-operative Learning,* Heinemann (London, England), 1990.

(Editor) *The Parchment Moon: An Anthology of Modern Women's Short Stories,* M. Joseph (London, England), 1990, published as *The Penguin Book of Modern Women's Short Stories,* Penguin (New York, NY), 1991.

(Author of introduction) F. M. Mayor, *The Rector's Daughter,* Penguin (London, England), 1992.

Crown Devon: The History of S. Fielding and Co., Jazz (Stratford-upon-Avon, England), 1993.

(Editor) *Contemporary Women's Short Stories,* M. Joseph (London, England), 1995.

(With Rory Stuart) *Reflections from a Garden,* illustrated by Ian Stephens, Pavilion (London, England), 1995.

Listening to the Orchestra, and Other Stories, Long Barn Books (Ebrington, England), 1997.

(Editor, with Sophia Topley) Deborah Vivien Freeman-Mitford Cavendish, *Counting My Chickens, and Other Home Thoughts,* introduction by Tom Stoppard, Long Barn Books (Ebrington, England), 2001, Farrar, Straus (New York, NY), 2002.

The Boy Who Taught the Beekeeper to Read (stories), Chatto & Windus (London, England), 2003.

Also author of *Last Summer's Child* (television play; based on her story "The Badness within Him," 1980. Contributor to *Winter's Tales 20,* edited by A. D. Maclean, Macmillan (London, England), 1974, St. Martin's (New York, NY), 1975, and *Penguin New Short Stories.*

A collection of Hill's manuscripts is housed at Eton College Library.

ADAPTATIONS: *Gentleman and Ladies* was adapted as a radio play in 1970; *The Woman in Black: A Ghost Story* was adapted for the stage in 1989 by Stephen Mallatratt.

WORK IN PROGRESS: Two crime novels, *The Various Haunts of Men* and *The Pure in Heart.*

SIDELIGHTS: Susan Hill, declared Gale Harris in *Belles Lettres,* "has been called one of the outstanding novelists of our times." She is "a precociously talented writer," the reviewer continued, who "published her first novel in 1960 when she was eighteen and wrote nine more by the age of thirty-two." Hill's work spans many genres, ranging from the adult novels *Strange Meeting* and *In the Springtime of the Year* to the children's stories *Septimus Honeydew* and *The Glass Angels,* from the Gothic mystery *The Woman in Black: A Ghost Story* to the autobiographical *Family.* In all her works Hill "has shown a painful awareness of the dark abysses of the spirit—fear, grief, loneliness, and loss," remarked Margaret Willy in *Contemporary Novelists.* Despite a period of sixteen years after her marriage in 1975 during which she wrote no adult novels, Hill has maintained a productive writing schedule, creating books on gardening and the English countryside, children's books, and book reviews. She has also written many successful radio plays for the British Broadcasting Corporation.

Ann Gibaldi Campbell wrote in the *Dictionary of Literary Biography* that Hill's career was shaped by the reading she did to fill the solitude she experienced as the only child of older parents, as well as by other events in her life. Hill's children's books often explore themes of self-growth. In *I Won't Go There Again* she addresses the problem of a young child who does not want to go to school, while in *Suzy's Shoes* the heroine requires a visit with the queen before she understands when it is appropriate for shoes to be off, and when they should stay on. *Septimus Honeydew* illustrates another type of family crisis as a small boy, terrified by night fears, seeks the solace of his parents' bed every evening. In her 1993 children's book, *Beware, Beware,* Hill again explores the themes of fear and the tension between childhood desires and parental limits. As a *Publishers Weekly* reviewer observed, "The lure of the world beyond the window proves irresistible for the pinafored heroine of this beautifully paced picture book." And, continued the reviewer, "Hill's choice of language is meticulous, her work so carefully crafted as to magnify the import of each word, its resonance and its associations."

The author's own life, and especially the life of one of her children, is the subject of *Family.* The autobiography tells of Hill's premature second daughter, Imogen, and the infant's struggle to stay alive. Imogen was born only twenty-five weeks into Hill's pregnancy and lived for only five weeks afterwards. But during those five weeks she put up a fierce struggle for life. According to Dulcie Leimbach in the *New York Times Book Review,* Hill's detailing of this event will encourage women with problem pregnancies. Leimbach summarized: "Most especially, this book offers a telescopic look at one very young and courageous life."

Hill's writings often present characters who love each other with a spiritual, rather than physical, passion and, through that love, learn to love themselves. Many of Hill's novels are about people who live lifestyles outside the mainstream—"solitary, secretive people," Harris noted, "who are awakened through intimacy with another person into a deeper understanding of life." *Strange Meeting,* for instance, is about two soldiers in World War I. Soldier John Hilliard, wounded by shrapnel, is returning to the trenches when he meets David Barton, a soldier whose blithe spirit has not yet been broken by the war. Hilliard's regard for Barton deepens into love—a love that survives Barton's eventual disillusionment, cynicism, and emotional withdrawal. *In the Springtime of the Year* tells of Ruth, a newly widowed woman who has to adjust not only to her new isolation, but also to the hostility of her husband's family, who resent her self-sufficiency and seeming lack of emotion. Ruth comes to understand her feelings about her husband's death and learns that love is, in fact, sometimes stronger than death. "As Ruth learns to endure the long, dark tunnel of grief," Harris found, "she gains hope that she will emerge 'more herself, remade, whole.'"

Hill portrays her characters' development through carefully chosen language. She places them in isolated spots, emphasizing their situations with a strong sense of atmosphere. For example, as Jonathan Raban stated in *London* magazine, the tone of Hill's *A Change for the Better* "is rooted in its dialogue: Miss Hill has created a stylized, yet brilliantly accurate grammar and vocabulary for her distressed gentlefolk—an entirely authentic idiom to be spoken by the living dead as they inhabit their shabby-genteel wasteland. Their language is rigid, archaic, and metrical, a mixture of drab proverbs, oratorical flourishes borrowed from popular romance, and catch phrases from the more sober varieties of adman's English." Raban concluded by noting that Hill has "a fine sense of pace and timing and a delicious eye for incongruous detail."

Other critics have also noted Hill's ability to create atmosphere and mood. *Books and Bookmen* contributor J. A. Cuddon remarked that in the title story of the story collection *The Albatross* "atmosphere and environment are evoked with great skill and feeling and the characters are presented and developed with a kind of austere compassion." Cuddon continued: "The language is spare, the dialogue terse and the tone beautifully adjusted to the severe vision. . . . The narrative, the events, are simple enough, but long after one has read these stories one is left with a curious, hard-edged almost physical sensation; a feeling of chill and desolation. But not depression. Miss Hill's art brings an elation of its own."

Some critics disagree about Hill's success in presenting her ideas in her stories. In a review of *Strange Meeting* in *Books and Bookmen,* Diane Leclercq wrote: "Coming hard on the heels of Susan Hill's very considerable achievements in her most recent work, one expects great things from [this book] . . . In many respects one gets them: the hard-edged prose, the painstaking detail, some aspects of the portrayal of Hilliard, and many of the minor characters. But the . . . radical weakness is, perhaps, a failure to realize any of the attitudes that people must have had in the situation at the Western Front." Yet, Margaret Willy believed that Hill understands both characters and situation. Despite the fact that the story at the heart of *Strange Meeting* is a story of men at war and not part of Hill's personal experience, Willy maintained that Hill offers a "convincing depiction of life from a male viewpoint" and "depicts with power, and at times almost intolerable poignancy, the doomed friendship of two young officers drawn together by their mutual daily contact with destruction and imminent death." Willy added, "There is also an irresistible attraction between opposite temperaments and family backgrounds: the reserved, introspective Hilliard finding inhibition magically thawed in the warmth of his companion Barton's easy, outgoing generosity."

New Republic reviewer Michele Murray believed that some of Hill's works have been misjudged. Murray wrote: "*The Bird of the Night* lacks all those elements that automatically stamp a new novel as 'profound' or 'important,' and worth noticing. What it has instead are qualities rarely found in contemporary fiction and apparently not much valued, which is a pity." "It is a thoroughly 'created piece of work,'" Murray declared, "a novel wrought of language carefully designed to tell a story drawn, not from the surface of the author's life or fragments of her autobiography, but from the heart of the imagination. . . . The careful shaping of material to make its effect with the utmost economy, adhered to and practiced by such modern masters as Gide, Woolf, Colette, and Pavese, seems to have fallen into abeyance, and it is good to see it once again employed with such great skill."

Murray called *In the Springtime of the Year* "another triumph by an artist who, in her quiet, steady way, is fast becoming one of the outstanding novelists of our time." She went on to say that Hill "has already demonstrated her mastery of character-drawing and fictional technique in her earlier novels, but *In the Springtime of the Year,* with its deliberate stripping away of almost all the elements of conventional fiction, represents a remarkable advance in what is turning out to be a considerable *oeuvre* for such a young writer." Margaret Atwood commented in the *New York Times Book Review* that, despite "lapses into simple-mindedness, *In the Springtime of the Year* justifies itself by the intensity of those things it does well: moments of genuine feeling, moments of vision. It is less a novel than the portrait of an emotion, and as this it is poignant and convincing."

Hill's skill in generating atmosphere is reflected in perhaps her best-known book, *The Woman in Black: A Ghost Story.* In keeping with the tradition of the horror story, *The Woman in Black* "could almost pass for a Victorian ghost novel," remarked E. F. Bleiler in the *Washington Post Book World.* The essayist for *Contemporary Novelists* called *The Woman in Black* "an atmospherically charged ghost story . . . related in a formal, rather stately past idiom, although carefully unlocated in any particular time. Full of Jamesian echoes and undercurrents, it traces with chilling compulsiveness the progress of a mysterious and sinister haunting." In the novel, lawyer Arthur Kipps travels to northern England to settle the estate of client Mrs. Drablow. At the deceased woman's remote gothic estate, he beings to witness ghostly visitations by a pale woman in old-fashioned dress, and the house begins to reveal secrets from the Drablow family past.

Donna Cox in *Intertexts* found that Hill successfully invigorated some trappings of the Victorian novel: "*The Woman in Black* is a tip-tilted text where the darkness of maternal rage and murderous horror at the centre of subject formation is depicted. The missing or dead mother of so many popular Victorian texts haunts these pages—she has become an avenging presence. The mechanics of maternal attachment, encountering the loss of the infant as object, loops back into infantile anger which is boundless and transgressive. The mother's loving gaze becomes the instrument of death."

Times Literary Supplement contributor Patricia Craig found that "the fullest flavour is extracted from every ingredient that goes into *The Woman in Black.*" An essayist for the *St. James Guide to Horror, Ghost, and Gothic Writers* believed that "*The Woman in Black* does manage to be truly menacing in places, due to Hill's fine atmospheric descriptions." Bleiler's only objections to the story were its initially slow plot development and the somewhat "confusing, perhaps even unnecessary" circumstances of the main character's situation. But the story as a whole, Bleiler concluded, "is certainly memorable, one of the strongest stories of supernatural horror that I have read in many years."

Equally evocative settings and atmosphere characterize *The Mist in the Mirror,* Hill's 1992 return to gothic fiction. It tells the story of James Monmouth, orphaned as a boy and raised in British colonial Africa. Monmouth discovers the writings of the English traveler Conrad Vane. After the death of his guardian, Monmouth sets out to retrace Vane's travels and, after twenty years' travel, to uncover the secrets of Vane's personal past. In the process, according to *Times Literary Supplement* reviewer Toby Fitton, Monmouth finds "resonances of his own lost childhood—a tantalizing response deep within him whose significance he cannot quite grasp. He soon finds his way to a remote ancestral property in Yorkshire, where the echoes of his childhood continue but are crowded out by evil immanences that eventually involve him in an ordeal of the soul. He manages to extricate himself and to allay the evil haunting him." The atmosphere, according to Ruth Pavey in the London *Observer,* is pure Victorian London: "the lamplight, leather armchairs, crackling fire, anchovy paste . . . the murky November night, empty streets, footsteps, chiming clocks." Pavey concluded by calling the book "a faultlessly stylish ghost story."

Despite her long and varied career with its numerous well-respected books, Hill may have received the most attention from general readers for her 1993 novel *Mrs. de Winter.* The novel is Hill's sequel to the 1938 best-seller *Rebecca* by Daphne du Maurier. With the approval of du Maurier's family, Hill finished the story du Maurier began, taking up the voice of the book's nameless narrator, Maxim de Winter's second wife, ten years after the end of *Rebecca.* The destruction of Manderley, de Winter's family estate, has not fully exorcised the ghost of the murdered Rebecca, his first wife. And when "the de Winters, having restlessly knocked around Europe for years, are drawn home following the death of Maxim's sister," explained Lisa Schwarzbaum in *Entertainment Weekly,* there is more tragedy ahead. Some reviewers found Hill's picture of the de Winter's lives a satisfying conclusion to plot threads du Maurier left hanging. "Far from wrapping things up nicely," stated *New Statesman* contributor Kathryn Hughes, du Maurier's "resolution is morally—and novelistically—untenable. Hill's task is to work out the moral plot of *Rebecca* to its final conclusion. Not until Maxim de Winter has paid for the murder of his first wife with his own life can the ghost of Rebecca be laid to rest." Other reviewers were not convinced. *New Yorker* reviewer Sally Beauman called *Mrs. de Winter* a "superficial . . . pastiche." "In all fairness," wrote novelist Rachel Billington in the *New York Times Book Review,* "Ms. Hill has found a psychologically appropriate and dramatic end to her sequel, but that is not enough."

From *Strange Meeting* to *Mrs. de Winter,* Hill displays an understanding of the transforming effect of disaster. Her protagonists, wrote Harris, "are able to transcend experiences that might be considered brutal, sorrowful, or sordid because they have been allowed a glimpse of another truth beneath the surface of things. Revelations of this nature have been called the gift of angels. This gift is waiting for readers who explore the works of Susan Hill."

BIOGRAPHICAL AND CRITICAL SOURCES:

BOOKS

Allen, Walter, *The Short Story in English,* Oxford University Press (New York, NY), 1981.

Contemporary Literary Criticism, Volume 4, Gale (Detroit, MI), 1973.

Contemporary Novelists, 6th edition, St. James Press (Detroit, MI), 1996.

Dictionary of Literary Biography, Volume 139: *British Short-Fiction Writers, 1945-1980,* Gale (Detroit, MI), 1994.

Hogg, James, editor, *English Language and Literature: Positions and Dispositions,* University of Salzburg Press (Salzburg, Austria), 1990.

Jefferson, Douglas, and Graham Martin, editors, *The Uses of Fiction,* Open University Press, 1982.

Lukianowicz, Anna, *At Odds with the Rest of the World: Characters in Susan Hill's Early Fiction,* Giardini (Pisa, Italy), 1994.

St. James Guide to Horror, Ghost, and Gothic Writers, St. James Press (Detroit, MI), 1998.

Sambrook, Hana, *Susan Hill: I'm the King of the Castle,* Longman (London, England), 1992.

Staley, Thomas F., editor, *Twentieth-Century Women Novelists,* Barnes & Noble (Totowa, NJ), 1982.

PERIODICALS

Back Stage West, August 23, 2001, Holly Hildebrand, "Hearts and Darkness," p. 6.

Belles Lettres, spring, 1993, pp. 11-12.

Best Sellers, October 1, 1970.

Booklist, December 1, 1991, p. 698; October 15, 1994, p. 426.

Books and Bookmen, April, 1971; January, 1972; June, 1974.

Bookseller, October 23, 1971; February 21, 2003, Nicolette Jones, "A Chouchou of an Author," p. 33.

English Review, February, 2003, Alan Jones, "Who Is Haunted by What in *The Woman in Black?,*" p. 10.

Entertainment Weekly, October 22, 1993, p. 67.

Horn Book, January-February, 1994, p. 64.

Horticulture, November, 1996, Jane Barker Wright, review of *Reflections from a Garden,* p. 57.

Intertexts, spring, 2000, Donna Cox, "'I Have No Story to Tell!': Maternal Rage in Susan Hill's *The Woman in Black,*" p. 74.

Junior Bookshelf, February, 1991, p. 24.

Listener, October 8, 1970.

London, November, 1969.

New Republic, February 16, 1974; May 18, 1974.

New Statesman, January 31, 1969; January 25, 1974; November 26, 1993, pp. 44-45.

New Yorker, November 8, 1993, pp. 127-38.

New York Times Book Review, March 30, 1969; May 27, 1973; May 18, 1974; January 21, 1990, p. 21; November 7, 1993, p. 23.

Observer (London, England), November 1, 1992, p. 62.

Publishers Weekly, September 6, 1993, p. 94; July 2, 2001, review of *Backyard Bedtime,* p. 78.

School Library Journal, May, 1991, p. 57; February, 1994, p. 6.

Spectator, October 24, 1992, p. 34; October 9, 1993, p. 39; October 26, 1996, Charlotte Moore, review of *Listening to the Orchestra and Other Stories,* p. 46; July 12, 2003, Francis King, review of *The Boy Who Taught the Beekeeper to Read,* p. 40.

Sunday Times (London, England), March 24, 1991, p. C6.

Sunday Times Magazine, November 23, 1986, p. A114.

Times Literary Supplement, October 14, 1983; October 30, 1992, p. 21; October 15, 1993, p. 19.

Variety, June 18, 2001, Charles Isherwood, review of *The Woman in Black,* p. 26.

Washington Post, May 19, 1974.

Washington Post Book World, August 24, 1986; December 4, 1994.

ONLINE

Susan Hill Web site, http://www.susan-hill.com/ (November 6, 2003).*

* * *

HOGAN, Linda 1947-

Linda Hogan

PERSONAL: Born July 16, 1947, in Denver, CO; daughter of Charles and Cleona (Bower) Henderson; married Pat Hogan (divorced); children: Sandra Dawn Protector, Tanya Thunder Horse. *Ethnicity:* "Tribal affiliation is Chickasaw." *Education:* University of Colorado at Boulder, M.A., 1978. *Hobbies and other interests:* Gardening and Native Science.

ADDRESSES: Home—P. O. Box 141, Idledale, CO 80453. *Office*—CB 226, English Department, University of Colorado, Boulder, CO 80309.

CAREER: Has worked variously as a nurse's aide, dental assistant, waitress, homemaker, secretary, administrator, teacher's aide, library clerk, freelance writer, and researcher; poet-in-schools for states of Colorado and Oklahoma, 1980-84; workshop facilitator in creative writing and creativity, 1981-84; Colorado College, Colorado Springs, assistant professor in TRIBES program, 1982-84; University of Minnesota—Twin Cities, Minneapolis, associate professor of American and of American Indian studies, 1984-89; University of Colorado, Boulder, professor of English, 1989—.

MEMBER: Writers Guild, Authors Guild, PEN, American Academy of Poets.

AWARDS, HONORS: Five Civilized Tribes Playwriting Award, 1980, for *A Piece of Moon;* short fiction award, *Stand Magazine,* 1983; Western States Book Award honorable mention, 1984; fellow, Colorado Independent Writers, 1984, 1985; National Endowment for the Arts grant, 1986; American Book Award, Before Columbus Foundation, 1986, for *Seeing Through the Sun;* Guggenheim fellowship, 1990; Colorado Book Award, 1993, for *The Book of Medicines;* Lannan Foundation Award, 1994; finalist for a Pulitzer Prize for *Mean Spirit,* and for a National Book Critics Circle Award for *The Book of Medicines;*

Lifetime Achievement Award from the Native Writers' Circle of the Americas, 1998.

WRITINGS:

POETRY

Calling Myself Home, Greenfield Review Press (Greenfield, NY), 1979.

Daughters, I Love You, Loretto Heights Women's Research Center (Denver, CO), 1981.

Eclipse, American Indian Studies Center, University of California (Los Angeles, CA), 1983.

Seeing through the Sun, University of Massachusetts Press (Amherst, MA), 1985.

Savings, Coffee House Press (Minneapolis, MN), 1988.

The Book of Medicines, Coffee House Press (Minneapolis, MN), 1993.

OTHER

A Piece of Moon (three-act play), produced in Stillwater, OK, 1981.

That Horse (short fiction), Pueblo of Acoma Press, 1985.

(Editor, with Carol Buechal and Judith McDaniel) *The Stories We Hold Secret,* Greenfield Review Press (Greenfield, NY), 1986.

Mean Spirit (novel), Atheneum (New York, NY), 1990.

Red Clay: Poems and Stories, Greenfield Review Press (Greenfield, NY), 1991.

Dwellings: A Spiritual History of the Living World (essays), Norton (New York, NY), 1995.

Solar Storms (novel), Scribner (New York, NY), 1995.

(Editor, with Brenda Peterson and Deena Metzger) *Between Species: Women and Animals,* Ballantine (New York, NY), 1997.

Power (novel), Norton (New York, NY), 1998.

(Coeditor) *Intimate Nature: The Bond between Women and Animals,* Fawcett Columbine (New York, NY), 1998.

(Coeditor) *The Sweet Breathing of Plants: Women Writing on the Green World,* North Point Press, 2001.

The Woman Who Watches Over the World: A Native Memoir, Norton (New York, NY), 2001.

(With Brenda Peterson) *Sightings: The Gray Whale's Mysterious Journey,* National Geographic Society (Washington, DC), 2001.

(Editor, with Brenda Peterson) *Face To Face: Women Writers on Faith Mysticism, and Awakening,* North Point Press (New York, NY), 2004.

Contributor to *I Tell You Now,* edited by Brian Swann, University of Nebraska Press (Lincoln, NE), 1987. Author of screenplays *Mean Spirit* and *Aunt Moon,* both 1986, and of the television documentary *Everything Has a Spirit.* Guest editor of *Frontiers,* 1982.

SIDELIGHTS: Linda Hogan, a member of the Chickasaw tribe, draws on her Native American heritage in both fiction and verse. Noted for novels, short stories, and poems that are characterized by a combination of a strong female perspective, a deep theological insight, and a sensitivity to the natural world that has been called uniquely Native American, Hogan has been honored with numerous awards. Her 1994 novel, *Mean Spirit,* was a finalist for both the Pulitzer Prize and the National Book award. Of her poetry in particular, essayist Laurel Smith wrote in *Contemporary Women Poets* that Hogan "combines lyrical and political elements . . . that prompt us to reconsider the ways we know our world and ourselves."

Hogan's first novel, *Mean Spirit,* depicts murder in a community of Osage Indians living in Oklahoma during the oil boom of the early-1920s. The discovery of oil has enriched the Osage, but it has also attracted the attention of unscrupulous white oil barons. The murder of Grace Blanket, owner of a large plot of oil-rich land—committed in front of both her daughter, Nora, and Nora's friend, Rena Graycloud—proves to be the first link in a chain of events designed to deprive the Osage of their territory. The escalating violence and bloodshed bring federal police officer Stace Red Hawk from Washington to Oklahoma to investigate, but to solve the mystery he first has to overcome government corruption and cultural prejudice.

In *Mean Spirit,* commented Sybil Steinberg in *Publishers Weekly,* Hogan "mines a rich vein of Indian customs and rituals, and approaches her characters with reverence, bringing them to life with quick, spare phrases." Joseph A. Cincotti, reviewing the novel for the *New York Times Book Review,* stated that Hogan "has an eye for detail, and the Native American rituals and customs" depicted in the book are skillfully observed. Cincotti declared, however, that the author fails "to enlist much affection" for the plight of the characters she depicts. *School Library Journal* contributor Lynda Voyles called *Mean Spirit* "thought-provoking and unsettling," and added that it should prove to be "a valuable supplement to social studies classes."

In her 1995 novel *Solar Storms,* Hogan recounts the dislocation and suffering of Native Americans through the spiritual journey of Angel Jensen, a seventeen-year-old Native American girl with unexplained facial scars that symbolize the fragmentation and enduring affliction of her people. Angel leaves a foster home in Oklahoma to revisit her birthplace in a town near the border lakes of Minnesota. There she encounters her great-grandmother, Agnes Iron, her great-great-grandmother, Dora Rouge, and a Chickasaw friend named Bush, who help Angel reconstruct her lost ancestral origins and early life. Together the women embark on a canoe voyage to join a protest against the construction of a hydroelectric power plant that threatens to destroy tribal lands. Despite its setting in the 1970s, the lesson of Hogan's work is an allegory representing the destruction by more powerful foreign cultures of the lands belonging to indigenous peoples around the globe. Reviewing the novel in the *New York Times Book Review,* Maggie Garb noted that Hogan's "sensuous descriptions of the sights, smells and sounds of the natural world are tempered by heart-wrenching depictions of rural poverty," while in the *Los Angeles Times Book Review* contributor Susan Heeger described *Solar Storms* as "stunning," a book through which it is learned that true humanity depends on connections "to family, friends, nature, the whole of life—rather than lording it over the rest of creation."

Although Hogan published her first novel in 1990, she has been writing poetry since the 1970s. Her first collection, 1979's *Calling Myself Home,* was cited by Smith as "introduc[ing] ideas of identity and community that continue to be compelling elements in all her writing." Including works about the quest for one's origins, Hogan weaves together strong characters with images of the landscape that sustains them, and includes several works about members of her own family. The poet also deals with birth and metamorphosis in such poems as "Celebration: Birth of a Colt" and "The River Calls Them," about tadpoles' transition into frogs.

In *Eclipse,* published in 1983, Hogan retains the perspective established in *Calling Myself Home* and based in her Chickasaw heritage and her faith in female strength. Containing poems confronting such areas of concern as nuclear armaments and advancing the causes of Native Americans that were previously published in *Daughters, I Love You, Eclipse* also includes poems that attempt to reconnect readers with the natural world, honoring each of the four winds, the sky father, and the mother earth. "Hogan crafts phrases of common speech and weaves the lines in natural idioms," noted Kenneth Lincoln in the book's foreword. "The verses carry the muted voices of talk before sleep, quieting the world, awaiting the peace of home. . . . Her poems offer a careful voicing of common things not yet understood, necessary to survival."

With her 1993 poetry collection *The Book of Medicines* Hogan invokes the therapeutic power of rhyme to treat the psychic damage inflicted by human conquest over nature and other people. Drawing on Native American folklore, ritual, and female spirituality, Hogan's incantations address profound manifestations of illness, grief, and the failure of science in the modern world. In one poem, "The Alchemists," she contrasts ancient attempts to transmute lead into gold with a contemporary physician's effort to heal the sick. Robyn Selman described Hogan's work as "ecopoetry" in her essay in the *Voice Literary Supplement,* particularly as the poems in this volume "take as their subject the very elements of life—fire, air, earth, and water—set into motion with bears, fishes, and humans." Carl L. Bankston noted in the *Bloomsbury Review,* "Hogan's fine sense of rhythm weaves through images of nature and of humankind's uneasy place in nature. These are dreamlike images that draw on Native American legends of the time before time when the First People were at once animals and people." As Robert L. Berner concluded in *World Literature Today, "The Book of Medicines* is a significant step, indeed a giant stride, in the development of a major American poet."

Hogan's *Dwellings: A Spiritual History of the Living World* is a collection of seventeen essays that explore the interconnectedness of nature, religion, and myth. Alternating between storyteller and poet, Hogan relates the universality of minor occurrences in daily life, especially as reflected in the essential relationship between humans and various creatures, including bats, wolves, and birds of prey at a rehabilitation center for wildlife. Heidi E. Erdrich observed in the *Women's Review of Books,* "Hogan's sense of mystery impels these essays, whose topics range from Hiroshima to the space probe Voyager to humor in captive primates."

The title of the collection alludes to its central theme, that of home and shared existence. According to Liz Caile in the *Bloomsbury Review,* "By honoring all creatures, we grow stronger and more content—that is the message of this book."

Hogan once told *CA:* "My writing comes from and goes back to the community, both the human and the global community. I am interested in the deepest questions, those of spirit, of shelter, of growth and movement toward peace and liberation, inner and outer. My main interest at the moment is in wildlife rehabilitation and studying the relationship between humans and other species, and trying to create world survival skills out of what I learn from this."

BIOGRAPHICAL AND CRITICAL SOURCES:

BOOKS

American Indian Biographies, Salem Press (Pasadena, CA), 1999.
American Women Writers, St. James Press (Detroit, MI), 2000.
Beacham's Guide to Literature for Young Adults, Volume 12, Gale (Detroit, MI), 2001.
Contemporary Literary Criticism, Volume 73, Gale (Detroit, MI), 1993.
Contemporary Women Poets, St. James Press (Detroit, MI), 1997.
Cotelli, Laura, *Winged Words: American Indian Writers Speak,* University of Nebraska Press (Lincoln, NE), 1990.
Dictionary of Literary Biography, Volume 175: *Native American Writers of the United States,* Gale (Detroit, MI), 1997.
Directory of American Poets and Fiction Writiers, Poets and Writers (New York, NY), 1998.
Eclipse, American Indian Studies Center, University of California (Los Angeles, CA), 1983.
Native North American Literature, Gale (Detroit, MI), 1994.
Notable Native Americans, Gale (Detroit, MI), 1995.
This Is about Vision: Interviews with Southwestern Writers, University of New Mexico Press (Albuquerque, NM), 1990.
Twentieth-Century Western Writers, 2nd edition, Gale (Detroit, MI), 1992.
Writers Directory, 16th edition, Gale (Detroit, MI), 2001.

PERIODICALS

Bloomsbury Review, November-December, 1993; September-October, 1995.
Booklist, January 1, 1999, p. 781; February 1, 2001, p. 1031; May 15, 2001, p. 1723; January 1, 2002, p. 756, 763.
Choice, June, 1986, p. 1508; April, 1989, p. 1328.
E, January-February, 2002, p. 60.
English Journal, March, 1994, p. 100.
Explorations in Sights and Sounds, summer, 1985.
Journal of Ethnic Studies, spring, 1988, pp. 107-117.
Kirkus Reviews, June 15, 1995, p. 835; August 15, 1995, p. 1132.
Kliatt, November, 1999, p. 43.
Library Journal, February 1, 2001, p. 101; June 1, 2001, p. 174.
Los Angeles Times, November 4, 1990, p. B3.
Los Angeles Times Book Review, July 30, 1995, p. 6; January 21, 1996, p. 2.
Ms., March-April, 1994, p. 70; November-December, 1995, p. 91.
New York Times Book Review, February 24, 1991, p. 28; November 26, 1995, p. 19.
Off Our Backs, December, 1999, p. 10.
Publishers Weekly, August 3, 1990, pp. 63-64; June 26, 1995, p. 101; August 28, 1995, p. 104; January 1, 2001, p. 81; May 21, 2001, p. 92.
School Library Journal, April, 1991, pp. 153-154.
Studies in American Indian Literature, spring, 1994, pp. 83-98; fall (special Hogan issue), 1994.
Voice Literary Supplement, November, 1993, p. 8.
Washington Post, December 6, 1990, p. D3.
Women's Review of Books, February, 1996, p. 11.
World Literature Today, spring, 1994, pp. 407-408.

ONLINE

Voices from the Gaps, http://voices.cla.umn.edu/ (June 26, 1999), Hogan biography and criticism of her works.*

* * *

HOOPER, Patricia 1941-

PERSONAL: Born May 4, 1941, in Saginaw, MI; daughter of John (a pilot and furniture store owner) and Edythe (maiden name, Sharpe) Hooper; married John Everhardus (an attorney), June 22, 1963;

children: John, Katherine. *Education:* University of Michigan, B.A., 1963, M.A., 1964.

ADDRESSES: Home—616 Yarmouth Rd., Bloomfield Township, MI 48301.

CAREER: Writer.

MEMBER: Poetry Society of America, Detroit Women Writers.

AWARDS, HONORS: Five Hopwood Awards, University of Michigan; Norma Farber First Book Award, Poetry Society of America, 1984, for *Other Lives;* Bernice W. Ames Award; Writer's Community Residency Award, National Writer's Voice, 1997.

WRITINGS:

Other Lives: Poems, Elizabeth Street Press (New York, NY), 1984.

A Bundle of Beasts (juvenile), illustrated by Mark Steele, Houghton Mifflin (Boston, MA), 1987.

The Flowering Trees, State Street Press (Brockport, NY), 1995.

How the Sky's Housekeeper Wore Her Scarves (juvenile; alternate selection of Children's Book-of-the-Month Club), illustrated by Susan L. Roth, Little, Brown (Boston, MA), 1995.

At the Corner of the Eye (poetry), Michigan State University Press (East Lansing, MI), 1997.

A Stormy Ride on Noah's Ark (juvenile), illustrated by Lynn Munsinger, Putnam (New York, NY), 2001.

Where Do You Sleep, Little One? (juvenile), illustrated by John Winch, Holiday House (New York, NY), 2001.

Work represented in anthologies. Contributor to magazines, including *American Scholar, Poetry, American Poetry Review,* and *Atlantic Monthly.*

SIDELIGHTS: Patricia Hooper is a poet as well as a children's author noted for her inventiveness. Betsy Hearne of the *Bulletin of the Center for Children's Books* noted the "exceptionally ingenious wordplay" that marks the twenty-five poems contained in *A Bundle of Beasts,* Hooper's first book for children. In this work, the author begins with the archaic names for groups of animals; thus, "A *Skein* of Wildfowl" is made by a "fast-knitting Grandma"; while a "*Cast* of Hawks" holds a "play for its prey," explained Cynthia Dobrez in *School Library Journal.* "Musically, the verse sings with the kind of lilting, spontaneous rhythms that [Shel] Silverstein and Jack Prelutsky manage so easily," commented Hearne, "and the tone is humorous as well." The book closes with information on Hooper's sources and suggested readings for adventurous students to find more, making this an ideal book for older children in a language arts program as well as the picture-book crowd, according to reviewers.

Reviews of Hooper's second book for children, *How the Sky's Housekeeper Wore Her Scarves,* were mixed. The imaginative flair of Hooper's premise, which Lauralyn Persson dubbed "an original *pourquoi* tale" in *School Library Journal,* was often praised. In this work, the author invents a housekeeper in the sky, who polishes the sun, dusts the moon, and does other similar chores while wearing a different colored scarf for each task. But when the rains come she stops her work, until the sun asks her back. She drapes the objects in the heavens with her scarves so that she may find her way home in the rain, and when the sun comes out to share the sky with the rain, a rainbow is created. Several critics considered Susan L. Roth's collage illustrations to have merit. "Unfortunately," commented a *Publishers Weekly* critic, "Hooper's plot is belabored and convoluted, arcing off in untidy and overlong tangents." While not all reviewers of *How the Sky's Housekeeper Wore Her Scarves* agreed, a reviewer for *Kirkus Reviews* remarked that "Hooper imbues her tale of origins with a sense of timelessness; her gods are fascinating if on the demanding side." More than one observer felt that the text was overshadowed by what *Booklist* contributor Julie Walton termed "Roth's almost hyperactive collages." "Nonetheless," Walton concluded, "the book remains a solid choice for its bold artistry and imaginative storytelling."

Where Do You Sleep, Little One? considers the resting places of creatures, from insects to large animals. It ends with a final scene that depicts the animals standing watch at the Nativity, although it is not so identified. A *Publishers Weekly* contributor described Hooper's rhymes as "simple but evocative."

Hooper focuses on the voyage itself in *A Stormy Ride on Noah's Ark.* The meek and mild animals are afraid to sleep for fear their meat-eating traveling companions might make a meal of them. But the carnivores are frightened by the storm that brings all the animals together with the realization that they must contribute to each other's safety and comfort. A wren sings, a mouse tells a story, and a spider spins a "web of sleep" to ease the fears of the mightiest of beasts. *Booklist*'s Shelle Rosenfeld noted that the story is a universal one, "about the importance of developing trust, overcoming differences, and cooperating for the common good." A *Horn Book* critic concluded, "This (ultimately) peaceful bedtime story is a lighthearted yet respectful companion to traditional retellings of the biblical tale."

BIOGRAPHICAL AND CRITICAL SOURCES:

PERIODICALS

Booklist, August, 1987, p. 1748; March 15, 1995, Julie Walton, review of *How the Sky's Housekeeper Wore Her Scarves,* p. 1334; September 1, 2001, Marta Segal, review of *Where Do You Sleep, Little One?,* p. 115; October 1, 2001, Shelle Rosenfeld, review of *A Stormy Ride on Noah's Ark,* p. 337.

Bulletin of the Center for Children's Books, July-August, 1987, Betsy Hearne, review of *A Bundle of Beasts,* p. 210.

Horn Book, November-December, 2001, review of *A Stormy Ride on Noah's Ark,* p. 736.

Kirkus Reviews, July 15, 1987, p. 1070; April 15, 1995, review of *How the Sky's Housekeeper Wore Her Scarves,* p. 558; September 15, 2001, review of *A Stormy Ride on Noah's Ark,* p. 1359.

Publishers Weekly, October 5, 1984, p. 79; May 8, 1995, review of *How the Sky's Housekeeper Wore Her Scarves,* p. 295; August 27, 2001, review of *Where Do You Sleep, Little One?,* p. 83.

School Library Journal, January, 1988, Cynthia Dobrez, review of *A Bundle of Beasts,* p. 73; June, 1995, Lauralyn Persson, review of *How the Sky's Housekeeper Wore Her Scarves,* p. 87; December, 2001, Kathy Piehl, review of *A Stormy Ride on Noah's Ark,* p. 104.

* * *

HUBBARD, Dolan 1949-

PERSONAL: Born February 20, 1949, in Wingate Township, NC; son of Olin (a farmer, cook, textile worker, and furniture worker) and Elizabeth (a homemaker, domestic worker, and seamstress; maiden name, Kendall) Hubbard; married Jennie Ruth Hampton, July 15, 1973; children: Aisha Katherine Elizabeth, Desmond Jelani. *Ethnicity:* "Black American." *Education:* Catawba College, B.A., 1971; University of Denver, M.A., 1974; University of Illinois—Urbana-Champaign, Ph.D., 1986; University of North Carolina—Chapel Hill, postdoctoral study, 1986-88. *Religion:* African Methodist Episcopal Zion. *Hobbies and other interests:* Reading, travel, antique furniture, gardening, old movies, sports.

ADDRESSES: *Home*—2413 Hartfell Rd., Timonium, MD 21093-2514. *Office*—Department of English and Language Arts, Morgan State University, 1700 East Cold Spring Lane, Baltimore, MD 21251; fax: 443-885-8225. *E-mail*—dhubbard@morgan.edu.

CAREER: High school teacher in Frederick County, MD, teacher, 1971-72; manager of a men's store in Salisbury, SC, 1972-73; high school teacher in Middletown, MD, 1974-76; Catawba College, Salisbury, minority counselor and admissions counselor, 1976-77; Winston-Salem State University, Winston-Salem, NC, instructor, 1977-82; University of Cincinnati, Cincinnati, OH, assistant professor, 1988-89; University of Tennessee, Knoxville, assistant professor, 1989-94; University of Georgia, Athens, associate professor of English and African-American studies, 1994-98; Morgan State University, Baltimore, MD, professor of English and chair of Department of English and Language Arts, 1998—. George Mason University, Du Bois Lecturer, 2002; guest speaker at other institutions, including University of Paris, State University of New York—Albany, Franklin Pierce College, University of Alabama, Emmanuel College, Franklin Springs, GA, and Missouri Southern State College; guest on media programs. Coproducer of a two-part documentary history of the College Language Association titled *Black Scholars in America,* 2000; Baltimore Afro-American Essay Contest (for eighth-graders), judge, 2000. Catawba College, member of board of trustees, 1994—. Big Brothers/Big Sisters of Winston-Salem, volunteer, 1980-82.

MEMBER: Modern Language Association of America (chair of Division on Black American Literature and Culture, 1996), American Literature Association, Association of Governing Boards of Colleges and Universities, College Language Association (president, 1994-96), National Council of Teachers of English,

Association of Departments of English (member of executive committee, 2002-04), MELUS, Richard Wright Circle, Langston Hughes Society (president, 2000-04), Zora Neale Hurston Society, Middle Atlantic Writers Association, South Atlantic Modern Language Association (president of administrative committee, 2002), South Atlantic Association of Departments of English, Black Caucus of the National Council of Teachers of English and Conference on College Composition and Communication.

AWARDS, HONORS: National Endowment for the Humanities, fellowship, 1985, grant, 1991; Carolina minority postdoctoral scholar, 1986-88; *The Sermon and the African-American Literary Imagination* was selected by *Choice* as an "outstanding academic book" for 1995.

WRITINGS:

The Sermon and the African-American Literary Imagination, University of Missouri Press (Columbia, MO), 1994.

(Editor) *Recovered Writers/Recovered Texts: Race, Class, and Gender in Black Women's Literature,* University of Tennessee Press (Knoxville, TN), 1997.

(Editor, with others) *The Collected Works of Langston Hughes,* Volume 4: *The Novels: "Not without Laughter" and "Tambourines to Glory,"* University of Missouri Press (Columbia, MO), 2001.

(Editor and author of introduction) *The Souls of Black Folk: One Hundred Years Later,* University of Missouri Press (Columbia, MO), 2003.

(Editor, with Ethel Young Minor) *The Library of Black America Collection of Black Sermons,* Lawrence Hill Books (Chicago, IL), 2004.

Contributor to books, including *American Short Story Writers: A Collection of Critical Essays,* edited by Julie Brown, Garland Publishing (New York, NY), 1994; *Critical Essays on Zora Neale Hurston,* edited by Gloria L. Cronin, G. K. Hall (New York, NY), 1998; *Du Bois and Race: Essays in Celebration of the Centennial Publication of "The Souls of Black Folk,"* edited by Chester J. Fontenot, Jr., Mercer University Press (Macon, GA), 2001; and *Critical Methods of the Black United States, 1868-1982,* edited by Barbara Christian and R. Baxter Miller, Modern Language Association of America (New York, NY). Member of editorial board of the series "The Collected Works of Langston Hughes," University of Missouri Press (Columbia, MO). Contributor of articles and reviews to academic journals, including *CLA Journal, Black Issues in Higher Education, Obsidian II, Centennial Review, Black American Literature Forum,* and *Franklin Pierce Studies in Literature.* Editor, *Langston Hughes Review,* 1994-98; member of editorial board, *Texas Studies in Literature and Language,* 1996-2002; advisory editor, *African American Review,* 1993—.

SIDELIGHTS: Dolan Hubbard once told *CA:* "I was inspired to write by my teachers at Granite Quarry (North Carolina) Colored Elementary School, from 1957 to 1963. In a rigidly segregated America, these teachers challenged us to be our best and told us that we could achieve anything that we wanted. Rosebud Aggrey, my fourth-grade teacher, from a distinguished Ghanian-American family, always gave her best students extra work and also had us serve as tutors for the slower students. She humanized the learning experience for me.

"When I write, I write to tell the untold stories of these faceless American heroes. By this, I mean that my criticism situates blacks in the American experience as actors and not as reactors. Stylistically, I want my writing to sing, for I feel that criticism need not be dull or dry. For me, criticism is a narrative, and I try to illuminate the drama involved in the critical moment."

BIOGRAPHICAL AND CRITICAL SOURCES:

PERIODICALS

Choice, February, 1996, Rebecca Bartlet Fischer, "*Choice* Interviews Dolan Hubbard," pp. 901-903.

New York Times, July 31, 2001, Jo Thomas, "Returning All the Works of Langston Hughes to Print."

I

ICHIKAWA, Satomi 1949-

PERSONAL: Born January 15, 1949, in Gifu, Japan; moved to Paris, France, 1971; daughter of Harumi (a teacher) and Nobuko Ichikawa. *Education:* Attended college in Japan. *Hobbies and other interests:* Collecting dolls (used), piano, dance.

ADDRESSES: *Home*—Paris, France. *Agent*—c/o Author Mail, Philomel Books, 375 Hudson St., New York, NY 10014.

CAREER: Author and illustrator of books for children, 1974—. *Exhibitions:* Gallery Printemps Ginza, Japan, 1984.

AWARDS, HONORS: Special mention for Prix "Critici in Erba," Bologna Children's Book Fair, 1978, for *Suzette et Nicolas au marché;* Kodansha Prize (Japan), 1978, for illustrations in *Sun through Small Leaves: Poems of Spring;* Sankei Prize (Japan), 1981, for illustrations in *Keep Running, Allen!;* Notable Book selection, American Library Association, for *Dance, Tanya.*

WRITINGS:

SELF-ILLUSTRATED

A Child's Book of Seasons (poetry), Heinemann (London, England), 1975, Parents' Magazine Press (New York, NY), 1976.

Satomi Ichikawa

Friends, Heinemann (London, England), 1976, Parents' Magazine Press (New York, NY), 1977.

Suzette et Nicolas dans leur jardin, Gautier-Languereau (Paris, France), 1976, translation by Denise Sheldon published as *Suzanne and Nicholas in the Garden,* F. Watts (New York, NY), 1977.

Suzette et Nicolas au marché, Gautier-Languereau (Paris, France), 1977, translation by Denise Sheldon published as *Suzanne and Nicholas at the Market,* F. Watts (New York, NY), 1977, adaptation by Robina Beckles Wilson published as *Sophie and Nicky Go to Market,* Heinemann (London, England), 1984.

Let's Play, Philomel (New York, NY), 1981.

Children through Four Seasons, Kaisei-sha (Tokyo, Japan), 1981.

Angels Descending from the Sky, Kaisei-sha (Tokyo, Japan), 1983.

Children in Paris (two volumes), Kaisei-sha (Japan), 1984.

Furui oshiro no otomodachi, Kaisei-sha (Tokyo, Japan), 1984, translation published as *Nora's Castle,* Philomel (New York, NY), 1986.

Beloved Dolls, Kaisei-sha (Tokyo, Japan), 1985.

Nora's Stars, translation from the Japanese, Philomel (New York, NY), 1989.

Nora's Duck, translation from the Japanese, Philomel (New York, NY), 1991.

Nora's Roses, translation from the Japanese, Philomel (New York, NY), 1993.

(With Patricia Lee Gauch) *Fickle Barbara,* Philomel (New York, NY), 1993.

Nora's Surprise, translation from the Japanese, Philomel (New York, NY), 1994.

Please Come to Tea!, Heinemann (London, England), 1994.

Isabela's Ribbons, Philomel (New York, NY), 1995.

La Robe de Nöel, L'École des loisirs (Paris, France), 1999, translation published as *What the Little Fir Tree Wore to the Christmas Party,* Philomel (New York, NY), 2001.

The First Bear in Africa!, Philomel (New York, NY), 2001.

My Pig Amarillo: A Tale from Guatemala, Philomel (New York, NY), 2003.

La-La Rose, Philomel (New York, NY), 2003.

ILLUSTRATOR

Elaine Moss, compiler, *From Morn to Midnight* (poetry), Crowell (New York, NY), 1977.

Clyde R. Bulla, *Keep Running, Allen!,* Crowell (New York, NY), 1978.

Marie-France Mangin, *Suzette et Nicolas et l'horloge des quatre saisons,* Gautier-Languereau (Paris, France), 1978, translation published as *Suzanne and Nicholas and the Four Seasons,* F. Watts (New York, NY), 1978, translation by Joan Chevalier published as *Suzette and Nicholas and the Seasons Clock,* Philomel (New York, NY), 1982, adaptation by Robina Beckles Wilson published as *Sophie and Nicky and the Four Seasons,* Heinemann (London, England), c. 1985.

Cynthia Mitchell, *Playtime* (poetry), Heinemann (London, England), 1978, Collins (New York, NY), 1979.

Cynthia Mitchell, compiler, *Under the Cherry Tree* (poetry), Collins (New York, NY), 1979.

Michelle Lochak and Marie-France Mangin, *Suzette et Nicolas et le cirque des enfants,* Gautier-Languereau (Paris, France), 1979, translation by Joan Chevalier published as *Suzanne and Nicholas and the Sunijudi Circus,* Philomel (New York, NY), 1980.

Marcelle Vérité, *Suzette et Nicolas aiment les animaux,* Gautier-Languereau (Paris, France), 1980.

Marcelle Vérité, *Suzette et Nicolas au Zoo,* Gautier-Languereau (Paris, France), 1980.

Robina Beckles Wilson, *Sun through Small Leaves: Poems of Spring,* Collins (New York, NY), 1980.

Marcelle Vérité, *Shiki no kodomotachi,* Kaisei-sha (Tokyo, Japan), 1981.

Martine Jaureguiberry, *La Joyeuse semaine de Suzette et Nicolas,* Gautier-Languereau (Paris, France), 1981, translation by Joan Chevalier published as *The Wonderful Rainy Week: A Book of Indoor Games,* Philomel (New York, NY), 1983.

Resie Pouyanne, *Suzette et Nicolas: L'Annee en fetes,* Gautier-Languereau (Paris, France), 1982.

Robina Beckles Wilson, *Merry Christmas! Children at Christmastime around the World,* Philomel (New York, NY), 1983.

Resie Pouyanne, *Suzette et Nicolas font le tour du monde,* Gautier-Languereau (Paris, France), 1984.

Cynthia Mitchell, editor, *Here a Little Child I Stand: Poems of Prayer and Praise for Children,* Putnam (New York, NY), 1985.

Marie-France Mangin, *Sophie bout de chou,* Gautier-Languereau (Paris, France), 1987.

Elizabeth Laird, *Happy Birthday!: A Book of Birthday Celebrations,* Philomel (New York, NY), 1988.

Sylvia Clouzeau, *Butterfingers,* translation from the French by Didi Charney, Aladdin Books (New York, NY), 1988.

Marie-France Mangin, *Sophie and Simon,* Macmillan (New York, NY), 1988.

Patricia Lee Gauch, *Dance, Tanya* (also see below), Philomel (New York, NY), 1989.

Elizabeth Laird, *Rosy's Garden: A Child's Keepsake of Flowers,* Philomel (New York, NY), 1990.

Patricia Lee Gauch, *Bravo, Tanya,* Philomel (New York, NY), 1992.

Patricia Lee Gauch, *Fickle Barbara,* Philomel (New York, NY), 1993.

Patricia Lee Gauch, *Tanya and Emily in a Dance for Two* (also see below), Philomel (New York, NY), 1994.

Patricia Lee Gauch, *Tanya Steps Out,* Philomel (New York, NY), 1996.

Patricia Lee Gauch, *Tanya and the Magic Wardrobe,* Philomel (New York, NY), 1997.

Eiko Kadono, *Grandpa's Soup,* Eerdmans (Grand Rapids, MI), 1999.

Janet Taylor Lisle, *The Lost Flower Children,* Puffin (New York, NY), 1999.

Patricia Lee Gauch, *Presenting Tanya, the Ugly Duckling* (also see below), Philomel (New York, NY), 2000.

Maryann K. Cusimano, *You Are My I Love You,* Philomel (New York, NY), 2001.

Patricia Lee Gauch, *Tanya and the Red Shoes,* Philomel (New York, NY), 2002.

Patricia Lee Gauch, *The Tanya Treasury* (contains *Dance, Tanya; Tanya and Emily in a Dance for Two;* and *Presenting Tanya, the Ugly Duckling,* Philomel (New York, NY), 2002.

SIDELIGHTS: Japanese-born Satomi Ichikawa lives in Paris, France, where she creates books and illustrations for children. Ichikawa's life has not lacked adventure or daring. She taught herself to draw after being inspired by a famous French illustrator and then submitted her work to an English publisher without benefit of agent or network contacts. More than thirty years after deciding to illustrate books, she is still kept busy on her own stories and those of others, including the popular "Tanya" series about a budding young ballerina. *School Library Journal* correspondent Jacqueline Elsner called Ichikawa's illustrations "masterful," adding that each figure the artist draws, "whether animal, toy, or person, is full of life, humor, and expression in every gesture."

Unlike many prominent illustrators, Ichikawa had not been drawing for years before submitting her work to publishers. She had not thought, as a child, that she would be interested in illustrating children's books. "I had no idea what I wanted to become," she once told *CA.* "I took a general course of study for women in college. Girls in Japan were usually expected to work for a few years after college and then get married."

Although she was unsure of her career goals, Ichikawa was sure that she wanted to experience life beyond the small town in which she grew up. Some Italian friends she had met in Japan persuaded her to visit them in Italy, and from there she took a trip to France. When she explored Paris, as she recalled, "I felt at home right away. . . . Japan is beautiful, all of my family is there, but I grew up in the countryside where people are more conservative and where traditions tend to be restrictive." In Paris, Ichikawa "discovered true freedom of spirit." She decided to live permanently in Paris, and while working as an *au pair* (a live-in governess) to support herself, she began to study French.

It was at that time that Ichikawa encountered the work of illustrator Maurice Boutet de Monvel, who died in 1913. Moved by his gentle watercolors, she began to search for his books in second-hand book shops. "I didn't know whether Boutet de Monvel was alive or dead," she told Herbert R. Lottman in *Publishers Weekly.* "But I fell in love with his work and wanted to try something of my own. In Paris you are nothing if you don't work."

Inspired by Boutet de Monvel's example, Ichikawa began to draw. "Since I had never drawn before, I started by observing real life in the gardens and in the playgrounds of Paris," she once related to *CA.* While she viewed the reality she was drawing with the images of Boutet de Monvel in mind, Ichikawa gradually began to develop her own style. "Although I am Japanese," she explained, "my drawings are more European, because my awakening happened here. While I lived in Japan, I never paid much attention to its special beauty, so that it is difficult for me to draw Japanese children and scenes." What has transpired for the well-traveled artist is a bibliography that celebrates multiculturalism. She has written and illustrated books set in Guatemala, Africa, Japan, France, and England, and some of her work—especially that featuring animals—is quite simply universal.

As Lottman noted in *Publishers Weekly,* "Ichikawa's initial attempts to have her work published were filled with as much verve . . . as the rest of her life." During a vacation in England, Ichikawa walked into a London bookstore and copied the names and addresses of children's book editors from the books on the shelf. She then visited the editor with the closest address, Heinemann. After perusing the thirty drawings Ichikawa had brought with her, the editor decided to publish her illustrations and the ideas behind them as

A Child's Book of Seasons. In a review for *Horn Book,* Ethel L. Heins described the illustrations as "charming, beautifully composed." Ichikawa's career as an illustrator had begun.

Since the publication of that first work, Ichikawa has seen her own books and books that she has illustrated published in various languages in England, France, the United States, and Japan. Especially notable among these books is the "Suzanne and Nicholas" series. In the first, *Suzanne and Nicholas in the Garden,* originally published as *Suzette et Nicolas dans leur jardin,* the children enjoy a summer day in the garden. When Nicholas informs Suzanne that another world exists outside the garden, Suzanne decides that the garden is big enough, "for the moment." As Gayle Celizic wrote in *School Library Journal,* the book conveys a "sense of peace and contentment."

Suzanne and Nicholas continue their adventures in *Suzanne and Nicholas at the Market,* originally published as *Suzette et Nicolas au marché,* and *Suzette and Nicholas and the Seasons Clock,* written by Marie-France Mangin and first appearing in France as *Suzette et Nicolas et l'horloge des quatre saisons. Junior Bookshelf* critic Berna Clark found the illustrations in *Suzanne and Nicholas at the Market* to be "very charming." Similarly, *School Library Journal* correspondent Jane F. Cullinane commended *Suzette and Nicholas and the Seasons Clock* for its "delightful pastel illustrations."

Also prominent in Ichikawa's work is the series of "Nora" books that she conceived and wrote herself. The inspiration for the creation of the first of these came from Ichikawa's summer stay in a friend's castle. As she once recalled for *CA,* "There was no electricity, and every night I went to my room with a candle—going up and down stairs and walking along endless hallways. I stayed there for a month and a half and had no intention of working. But I was so inspired that I wrote the story of a little girl visiting this castle and in every room she discovers a presence—a king, an old piano—reminders of another life." Ichikawa especially enjoyed the creation of *Nora's Castle,* the first book which she developed "from beginning to end—a very satisfying experience," she said, adding, "I have come to see that this is the best way to work."

The "Nora" books have been generally well received. *Nora's Stars,* in which Nora's toys come alive at night and help her gather the stars from the sky, was described as "charming" and "cozy" by Jane Yolen in the *Los Angeles Times Book Review.* Sally R. Dow, writing for *School Library Journal,* noted favorably the "whimsical mood of this quiet bedtime fantasy." In *Nora's Duck,* Nora finds a wounded duckling and takes it to Doctor John, who provides care and a home for other stricken animals on his farm. Doctor John lovingly tends to the duckling, and Nora takes it back to its pond to be reunited with its mother. Ann A. Flowers wrote in *Horn Book* that the "quiet delicacy" of Ichikawa's illustrations "mirrors the compassion and trust of the story." A reviewer for *Kirkus Reviews* commented that Ichikawa's "sweet, precise style is perfect for this idyll," and Jody McCoy related in *School Library Journal* that the book is an "excellent choice to encourage discussion of the humane treatment of animals."

In *Nora's Roses,* Nora is home with a bad cold. She passes the time by watching passersby enjoy her blooming rose bush. When a hungry cow robs the bush of all but one last bloom, Nora preserves the only rose left by drawing a picture of it. Carolyn Phelan of *Booklist* observed that Ichikawa's technique "captures . . . the beauty of a rose in bloom, and the determination of a young child." A critic for *Quill & Quire* also praised Ichikawa, proclaiming that her "illustrative technique is a delight." In her *School Library Journal* review, Lori A. Janick commented: "The story has a gentle sweetness enhanced by exquisite watercolor illustrations."

Ichikawa once told *CA* that the books *Dance, Tanya; Bravo, Tanya;* and *Tanya and Emily in a Dance for Two,* the first three installments in the "Tanya" series, are very important in her life. "This is the first time that my love for dance and my drawing have joined," she said. "Thanks to P. L. Gauch, who wrote these stories of Tanya especially for me!" When readers first meet Tanya in *Dance, Tanya,* she is a preschooler who loves to dance and who envies her older sister, who gets to go to dancing school and be in recitals. After attending her sister's recital, Tanya beguiles her family by dancing her own version of *Swan Lake.* Her reward comes soon after: her own leotard and dancing slippers, and lessons at her sister's school. Denise Wilms said of *Dance, Tanya* in *Booklist,* "Gauch's sweet story gains strength from Ichikawa's soft watercolor paintings."

Tanya's adventures continue in further books, including *Bravo, Tanya; Tanya and the Red Shoes; Tanya and Emily in a Dance for Two; Presenting Tanya, the Ugly Duckling;* and *Tanya Steps Out.* All of these stories communicate not only a love of classical ballet, but also the frustrations and challenges of learning to perform a demanding art. In *Tanya and the Red Shoes,* for instance, Tanya gets the pointe shoes she has longed for—and the blisters, calluses, and clumsiness that goes with them. *Tanya and Emily in a Dance for Two* describes the budding friendship between Tanya and Emily, the best dancer in the class. The girls find inspiration from each other when Tanya teaches Emily to dance like the animals at the zoo, and Emily helps Tanya to perfect her *cabriolet. Bravo, Tanya* was commended by a *Kirkus Reviews* contributor, who wrote that "Ichikawa captures the joy and energy of the dance in her sensitive paintings." In her *Horn Book* review of *Tanya and Emily in a Dance for Two,* Hanna B. Zeiger noted that Tanya's escapades provide "a delight for the dancer hidden in all of us."

Ichikawa has set some of her picture books in locations far removed from her home in Paris. *Isabela's Ribbons* features a Puerto Rican youngster in her verdant tropical milieu. Isabel loves ribbons and hide-and-seek, but no other children want to play with her. However, when her fantasies begin to run away with her, she finally makes new friends. A *Publishers Weekly* critic wrote: "Gaily patterned watercolors packed with playful details make this book a joy to behold."

The animals of the African savanna work together with a young boy to help reunite a teddy bear with its owner in *The First Bear in Africa!* Meto is fascinated when a family of tourists visits his village with a teddy bear as he has never seen a bear before. When the toy gets left behind, Meto runs across the savanna after the family, pausing only to show the strange beast to the lion, hippo, giraffe, and elephant that he meets on the way. A *Publishers Weekly* reviewer deemed the book "a light, appealing caper," while *School Library Journal* contributor Alicia Eames called it "a sweet and idealized tale of universal fellowship."

Ichikawa spins another universal tale through an exotic location in *My Pig Amarillo: A Tale from Guatemala.* Pablito is delighted when he is given a pet pig, and soon pig and boy have become fast friends. When Amarillo the pig disappears without a trace, Pablito searches endlessly and weeps into his pillow when Amarillo fails to return. It falls to Pablito's grandfather to school the boy on coping with grief and loss. Claiming the work is "sure to become a classic," a *Kirkus Reviews* critic called the volume "a masterpiece of picture-book making." *Booklist*'s Ilene Cooper commented favorably on the way Ichikawa "wraps the story in universal emotions: love, longing, grief, hope."

Although Ichikawa is writing more of her own books, she still finds time to illustrate some titles by other authors. *You Are My I Love You,* written by Maryann K. Cusimano, explores the love between a mother and child teddy bear as they share a day together. A *Publishers Weekly* reviewer noted that the text and illustrations work together, "instantly communicating all that the reader needs to know about the wonders of loving and being loved." In *Grandpa's Soup,* written by Eiko Kadono, a grieving widower learns to communicate with the world again by trying over and over to re-create his wife's meatball soup. The story made its debut in Japan, but according to Marta Segal in *Booklist,* its "gentle lessons on coping with grief are applicable to any culture."

Ichikawa works very hard at her craft, often turning out as many as three books a year. According to Michael Patrick Hearn in a *Horn Book* article, Boutet de Monvel's work "is kept alive" through Ichikawa's art, as her illustrations continue to delight children around the world. Several decades after her departure from Japan, she continues to live in Paris. Because, as she once commented, an "artist must feel complete freedom in order to create," her work is enriched by her life in the city. Ichikawa once asserted, "Coming to Paris was a rebirth for me." Her paintings that capture the exuberance, imagination, and joy of childhood have found fans all over the world.

BIOGRAPHICAL AND CRITICAL SOURCES:

BOOKS

Children's Literature Review, Volume 62, Gale (Detroit, MI), 2000.

Ichikawa, Satomi, *Suzanne and Nicholas in the Garden,* F. Watts (New York, NY), 1977.

PERIODICALS

Booklist, September 1, 1989, Denise Wilms, review of *Dance, Tanya,* pp. 70-71; March 15, 1993, Carolyn Phelan, review of *Nora's Roses,* p. 1360; December

1, 1999, Marta Segal, review of *Grandpa's Soup,* p. 712; September 1, 2001, GraceAnne A. DeCandido, review of *What the Little Fir Tree Wore to the Christmas Party,* p. 120; April 1, 2003, Ilene Cooper, review of *My Pig Amarillo: A Tale from Guatemala,* p. 1396.

Five Owls, September-October, 1994, review of *Nora's Surprise,* p. 12.

Horn Book, June, 1976, Ethel L. Heins, review of *A Child's Book of Seasons,* pp. 280-281; April, 1979, Michael Patrick Hearn, "Satomi Ichikawa," p. 180; March, 1992, Ann A. Flowers, review of *Nora's Duck,* p. 191; November-December, 1994, Hanna B. Zeiger, review of *Tanya and Emily in a Dance for Two,* p. 718; May, 1999, review of *The Lost Flower Children,* p. 333.

Junior Bookshelf, April, 1978, Berna Clark, review of *Suzanne and Nicholas at the Market,* p. 89.

Kirkus Reviews, May 1, 1989, review of *Nora's Stars,* p. 693; November 1, 1991, review of *Nora's Duck,* p. 1404; April 1, 1992, review of *Bravo, Tanya,* p. 464; May 1, 2003, review of *My Pig Amarillo,* p. 678.

Los Angeles Times Book Review, June 4, 1989, Jane Yolen, review of *Nora's Stars,* p. 11.

Publishers Weekly, June 7, 1993, Herbert R. Lottman, "In the Studio with Satomi Ichikawa," p. 19; August 21, 1995, review of *Isabela's Ribbons,* p. 65; April 12, 1999, review of *The Lost Flower Children,* p. 75; November 8, 1999, review of *Grandpa's Soup,* p. 66; March 12, 2001, review of *The First Bear in Africa!,* p. 90; April 9, 2001, review of *You Are My I Love You,* p. 73; May 12, 2003, review of *My Pig Amarillo,* p. 66.

Quill & Quire, April, 1993, Joanne Schott, review of *Nora's Roses,* p. 36.

School Library Journal, April, 1983, Jane F. Cullinane, review of *Suzette and Nicholas and the Seasons Clock,* p. 104; March, 1987, Gayle Celizic, review of *Suzette and Nicholas in the Garden,* p. 146; July, 1989, Sally R. Dow, review of *Nora's Stars,* pp. 66-67; November, 1991, Jody McCoy, review of *Nora's Duck,* p. 1404; June, 1993, Lori A. Janick, review of *Nora's Roses,* pp. 77-78; May, 1994, Jacqueline Elsner, review of *Nora's Surprise,* p. 96; September, 1994, Cheri Estes, review of *Tanya and Emily in a Dance for Two,* p. 184; June, 1999, Susan Pine, review of *Presenting Tanya, the Ugly Duckling,* pp. 95-96; June, 2001, Alicia Eames, review of *The First Bear in Africa!,* p. 118; October, 2001, review of *What the Little Fir Tree Wore to the Christmas Party,* p. 66; May, 2003, Marge Loch-Wouters, review of *My Pig Amarillo,* p. 122.*

ISAACS, Ronald (Howard) 1947-

PERSONAL: Born September 10, 1947, in Toronto, Ontario, Canada; U.S. citizen; son of David (in sales) and Gertrude (a homemaker) Isaacs; married, June 20, 1971; wife's name Leora W.; children: Keren, Zachary. *Ethnicity:* "Jewish." *Education:* Jewish Theological Seminary of America, B.H.L., 1969, M.A., 1971, Rabbi, 1974; Columbia University, B.A., 1969, M.A., 1971, Ed.D., 1979. *Hobbies and other interests:* Sports memorabilia, music.

ADDRESSES: *Office*—Temple Sholom, 594 North Bridge St., Bridgewater, NJ 08807; fax: 908-707-9055. *E-mail*—isaccsrl@optonline.net.

CAREER: Voices Four (Hebrew liturgical folk-rock ensemble, cofounder and performer, 1969-73; Greenburgh Hebrew Center, Dobbs Ferry, NY, principal and youth director, 1973-75; Temple Sholom, Bridgewater, NJ, rabbi, 1975—, and codirector of Temple Sholom Hebrew High School. Rutgers University, visiting lecturer, 1976-82; Jewish Theological Seminary of America, adjunct lecturer, 2002. United Synagogue of Conservative Judaism, Kadima rabbi for Northern New Jersey Region, 1982-92; Coalition for the Advancement of Jewish Education, board member, 1992-94; Northern New Jersey Rabbinical Assembly, vice president, 1995-96; Rabbinical Assembly of America, chair of publications committee, 2001. Lovin' Company (Hebrew liturgical folk-rock ensemble), founder and performer, 1980-82; WCTC-Radio, host of *Jewish American Hour,* 1990-94; recorded the albums *Arbaah Kolote: The Voices Four,* released by Monitor Recordings in 1969, and *Our Rock and Our Redeemer,* Monitor Recordings, 1971. Camp Ramah in the Poconos, head of music and coordinator of Ramah Family Camp and Shabbat Plus Adult Learning Program, summers, 1988-2001. United Way of Somerset Valley, board member, 1990-93; Human Relations Council of Bridgewater, board member, 1999—; Bridgewater Police Department, member of Committee of Chaplains, 2001—.

MEMBER: Faith in Action (board member, 1999—).

AWARDS, HONORS: D.H.L., Jewish Theological Seminary of America, 2001.

WRITINGS:

(With wife, Leora Isaacs) *Jewish Expressions: My Holiday Activity Book,* Ktav Publishing House (Jersey City, NJ), 1986.

The Jewish Instructional Games Book, New York Board of Jewish Education (New York, NY), 1986.

Shabbat Delight: A Celebration in Stories, Songs, and Games, Ktav Publishing House (Jersey City, NJ), 1987.

(With Leora Isaacs) *Reflections: A Jewish Grandparents' Gift of Memories,* Jason Aronson (Northvale, NJ), 1987.

The Jewish Family Game Book for the Sabbath and Festivals, Ktav Publishing House (Jersey City, NJ), 1989.

The Bride and Groom Handbook, Behrman House (West Orange, NJ), 1990.

(With Leora Isaacs) *Gleanings: Four Shavuot Scripts,* Leeron Publishers (Bridgewater, NJ), 1990.

(With Leora Isaacs) *Loving Companions: Our Jewish Wedding Album,* Jason Aronson (Northvale, NJ), 1991.

(With Kerry M. Olitzky) *The Jewish Mourner's Handbook,* Ktav Publishing House (Jersey City, NJ), 1992.

Rites of Passage: Guide to the Jewish Life Cycle, Ktav Publishing House (Jersey City, NJ), 1992.

(With Kerry M. Olitzky) *The Discovery Haggada,* Ktav Publishing House (Jersey City, NJ), 1992.

(With D. Pressman) *Shma Kolaynu: A High Holy Day Youth Machzor,* Ktav Publishing House (Jersey City, NJ), 1992.

(With Kerry M. Olitzky) *A Glossary of Jewish Life,* Jason Aronson (Northvale, NJ), 1992.

(With Kerry M. Olitzky) *The How-to Handbook for Jewish Living,* Ktav Publishing House (Jersey City, NJ), Volume 1, 1993, Volume 2, 1996.

Becoming Jewish: A Handbook for Conversion, Ktav Publishing House (Jersey City, NJ), 1993.

(With S. Arlen and R. Wagner) *Chain of Life: A Curricular Guide,* Coalition for the Advancement of Jewish Education (New York, NY), 1993.

The Jewish Information Source Book: A Dictionary and Almanac, Jason Aronson (Jersey City, NJ), 1993.

(With Leora Isaacs) *Jewish Family Matters: A Leader's Guide,* United Synagogue of Conservative Judaism (New York, NY), 1994.

(With D. Pressman) *Siddur Shir Chadash for Youth and Family,* Ktav Publishing House (Jersey City, NJ), 1994.

(With Kerry M. Olitzky) *Doing Mitzvot: Mitzvah Projects for Bar/Bat Mitzvah,* Ktav Publishing House (Jersey City, NJ), 1994.

(With Kerry M. Olitzky) *Sacred Celebrations: A Jewish Holiday Handbook,* Jason Aronson (Northvale, NJ), 1994.

(With Kerry M. Olitzky) *Critical Documents of Jewish History: A Sourcebook,* Jason Aronson (Northvale, NJ), 1995.

Lively Student Prayer Services: A Handbook of Teaching Strategies, Ktav Publishing House (Jersey City, NJ), 1995.

(With Kerry M. Olitzky) *Sacred Moments: Tales of the Jewish Life Cycle,* Jason Aronson (Northvale, NJ), 1995.

Derech Eretz: Pathways to an Ethical Life, United Synagogue Department of Youth (New York, NY), 1995.

Critical Jewish Issues: A Book for Teenagers, Ktav Publishing House (Jersey City, NJ), 1996.

The Jewish Book of Numbers, Jason Aronson (Northvale, NJ), 1996.

Words for the Soul: Jewish Wisdom for Life's Journey, Jason Aronson (Jersey City, NJ), 1996.

Mitzvot: A Sourcebook for the 613 Commandments, Jason Aronson (Northvale, NJ), 1996.

Madrich LeGabbai: A Gabbai's How-to Manual, Ktav Publishing House (Jersey City, NJ), 1996.

Close Encounters: Jewish Views of God, Jason Aronson (Northvale, NJ), 1996.

Sacred Seasons: A Sourcebook for the Jewish Holidays, Jason Aronson (Northvale, NJ), 1997.

Every Person's Guide to Jewish Prayer, Jason Aronson (Northvale, NJ), 1997.

Sidra Reflections: Guide to Sidrot and Haftarot, Ktav Publishing House (Jersey City, NJ), 1997, leader's guide, 1998.

(With Kerry M. Olitzky) *Rediscovering Judaism: Bar and Bat Mitzvah for Adults; A Course of Study,* Ktav Publishing House (Jersey City, NJ), 1997.

Jewish Bible Almanac, Jason Aronson (Northvale, NJ), 1997.

Miracles: A Jewish Perspective, Jason Aronson (Northvale, NJ), 1997.

Jewish Music: Its History, People, and Song, Jason Aronson (Northvale, NJ), 1997.

Divination, Magic, and Healing: The Book of Jewish Folklore, Jason Aronson (Northvale, NJ), 1998.

Ascending Jacob's Ladder: Jewish Views of Angels, Demons, and Evil Spirits, Jason Aronson (Northvale, NJ), 1998.

The Jewish Book of Etiquette, Jason Aronson (Northvale, NJ), 1998.

Judaism, Medicine, and Healing, Jason Aronson (Northvale, NJ), 1998.

(Editor) *The Jewish Sourcebook on the Environment and Ecology,* Jason Aronson (Northvale, NJ), 1998.

Messengers of God: A Jewish Prophets Who's Who, Jason Aronson (Northvale, NJ), 1998.

Every Person's Guide to Shabbat, Jason Aronson (Northvale, NJ), 1998.

Every Person's Guide to Shavuot, Jason Aronson (Northvale, NJ), 1998.

Every Person's Guide to Death and Dying in the Jewish Tradition, Jason Aronson (Northvale, NJ), 1999.

Exploring Jewish Ethics and Values, Ktav Publishing House (Jersey City, NJ), 1999.

Every Person's Guide to Jewish Philosophy and Philosophers, Jason Aronson (Northvale, NJ), 1999.

(With Kerry M. Olitzky) *I Believe: The Thirteen Principles of Faith: A Confirmation Textbook,* Ktav Publishing House (Jersey City, NJ), 1999.

Reaching for Sinai: How-to Handbook for Celebrating a Meaningful Bar/Bat Mitzvah, Ktav Publishing House (Jersey City, NJ), 1999.

Every Person's Guide to the High Holy Days, Jason Aronson (Northvale, NJ), 1999.

The Tabernacle, the Temple, and Its Royalty, Jason Aronson (Northvale, NJ), 1999.

Every Person's Guide to Holiness: The Jewish Perspective, Jason Aronson (Northvale, NJ), 1999.

Every Person's Guide to Jewish Blessings, Jason Aronson (Northvale, NJ), 1999.

Beginnings: Raising a Jewish Child, United Synagogue of Conservative Judaism (New York, NY), 2000.

The Bible: Where Do You Find It, and What Does it Say?, Jason Aronson (Northvale, NJ), 2000.

Every Person's Guide to Jewish Law, Jason Aronson (Northvale, NJ), 2000.

Animals in Jewish Thought and Tradition, Jason Aronson (Northvale, NJ), 2000.

Every Person's Guide to Jewish Sexuality, Jason Aronson (Northvale, NJ), 2000.

Every Person's Guide to the Book of Proverbs and Ecclesiastes: Biblical Wisdom for the Twenty-first Century, Jason Aronson (Northvale, NJ), 2000.

Every Person's Guide to Sukkot, Shemini Atzeret, and Simchat Torah, Jason Aronson (Northvale, NJ), 2000.

Every Person's Guide to Purim, Jason Aronson (Northvale, NJ), 2000.

Every Person's Guide to Hanukkah, Jason Aronson (Northvale, NJ), 2000.

Every Person's Guide to Passover, Jason Aronson (Northvale, NJ), 2000.

The Talmud: What Does it Say and Where Can You Find It?, Jason Aronson (Northvale, NJ), 2000.

Every Person's Guide to What's Kosher and What's Not, Jason Aronson (Northvale, NJ), 2000.

Ask the Rabbi: The Book of Answers to Jewish Kids' Questions, Jason Aronson (Northvale, NJ), 2000.

Every Person's Guide to Aggadah, Jason Aronson (Northvale, NJ), 2000.

Building the Faith: A Book of Inclusion for Dual-Faith Families, Federation of Jewish Men's Clubs (New York, NY), 2001.

Understanding the Hebrew Prophets, Ktav Publishing House (Jersey City, NJ), 2001.

Defending the Faith: Trials and Great Debates in Jewish History, Ktav Publishing House (Jersey City, NJ), 2001.

Entering the Biblical Text: Exploring Jewish Values in the Torah, Ktav Publishing House (Jersey City, NJ), 2000.

Can You Believe It: Amazing Jewish Facts and Curiosities, Jason Aronson (Northvale, NJ), 2001.

Ethics for Everyday Living: Jewish Wisdom for the Twenty-first Century, Jason Aronson (Northvale, NJ), 2001.

Every Person's Guide to the Book of Psalms, Jason Aronson (Northvale, NJ), 2001.

Exploring the Jewish Prophets, Ktav Publishing House (Jersey City, NJ), 2001.

(With Kerry M. Olitzky) *The Third "How-to" Handbook for Jewish Living,* Ktav Publishing House (Jersey City, NJ), 2002.

Let My People Go: An Instant Lesson on World Slavery, Torah Aura (Los Angeles, CA), 2002.

Legends of Biblical Heroes: A Sourcebook, Jason Aronson (Northvale, NJ), 2002.

A Taste of Text: An Introduction to the Talmud and Midrash, UAHC Press (New York, NY), 2003.

Ask the Rabbi: The Who, What, When, Where, Why, and How of Being Jewish, Jossey-Bass (San Francisco, CA), 2003.

Life's Little Book of Big Jewish Advice, Ktav Publishing House (Jersey City, NJ), 2004.

Gates of Heaven: A Handbook for Unveilings and Visiting the Cemetery, Ktav Publishing House (Jersey City, NJ), 2004.

Essential Judaism in a Nutshell, Ktav Publishing House (Jersey City, NJ), 2004.

Author of sourcebooks for Kadima Encampments, 1982-92. Creator of *The Pocket Size Ungame: Spiritual Version,* released by Ungame Co., 1983. Contributor to periodicals, including *Kol Kadima, United Synagogue Jewish Living Now, Pedagogic Reporter, Jewish Education,* and *Impact.* Member of editorial board, *Shofar.*

SIDELIGHTS: Ronald Isaacs once told *CA:* "I write as I prepare to teach my courses for our own Hebrew high school and adult education programs. I try to write for a couple of hours each day and generally choose a topic which I have always enjoyed teaching or reading about, but which I would like to research further."

BIOGRAPHICAL AND CRITICAL SOURCES:

PERIODICALS

Booklist, October 15, 2003, Ilene Cooper, review of *Ask the Rabbi: The Who, What, Where, Why, and How of Being Jewish,* p. 402.

Library Journal, January 1, 2001, Graham Christian, review of *Every Person's Guide to Purim,* p. 117.

Publishers Weekly, August 25, 2003, review of *Ask the Rabbi,* p. 57.

J

JANOWITZ, Tama 1957-

PERSONAL: Born April 12, 1957, in San Francisco, CA; daughter of Julian Frederick (a psychiatrist) and Phyllis (a poet and professor; maiden name, Winer) Janowitz; married Tim Hunt (curator of the Andy Warhol Foundation), 1992; children: Willow (adopted daughter). *Education:* Barnard College, B.A., 1977; Hollins College, M.A., 1979; postgraduate studies at Yale University School of Drama, 1980-81; Columbia University, M.F.A., 1985.

ADDRESSES: *Agent*—Amanda Urban, International Creative Management, 40 West 57th St., New York, NY 10019.

CAREER: Model with Vidal Sassoon (international hair salon) in London, England, and New York, NY, 1975-77; Kenyon and Eckhardt, Boston, MA, assistant art director, 1977-78; Fine Arts Work Center, Provincetown, MA, writer-in-residence, 1981-82; freelance journalist, 1985—. Appeared in film *Slaves of New York,* 1989; and in the first MTV "literary" video, *A Cannibal in Manhattan,* 1987. Member of board of directors, Barnard College Arts and Literature Committee, 1974-75.

Tama Janowitz

MEMBER: Poets and Writers, Writers' Community (fellow, 1976), Associated Writing Program.

AWARDS, HONORS: Breadloaf Writers' Conference, 1975; Elizabeth Janeway Fiction Prize, 1976 and 1977; Amy Loveman Prize for poetry, 1977; Hollins College fellowship, 1978; National Endowment for the Arts grants, 1982 and 1986; Coordinating Council of Literary Magazines/General Electric Foundation award, 1984; Ludwig Vogelstein Foundation award, 1985; Alfred Hodder Fellow in the Humanities, Princeton University, 1986-87.

WRITINGS:

NOVELS

American Dad, Putnam (New York, NY), 1981.

A Cannibal in Manhattan, Crown (New York, NY), 1987.

The Male Cross-Dresser Support Group, Crown (New York, NY), 1992.

By the Shores of Gitchee Gumee, Crown (New York, NY), 1996.

A Certain Age, Doubleday (New York, NY), 1999.

Peyton Amberg, St. Martin's Press (New York, NY), 2003.

OTHER

Slaves of New York, Crown (New York, NY), 1986, Tri-Star, 1989.

Hear That? (children's fiction), SeaStar Books (New York, NY), 2001.

Area Code 212: New York Days, New York Nights (reminiscences), Bloomsbury (New York, NY), 2002.

Contributor to *Wanting a Child: Twenty-two Writers on Their Difficult but Mostly Successful Quests for Parenthood in a High-Tech Age*, edited by Jill Bialosky and Helen Schulman, Farrar, Straus & Giroux (New York, NY), 1999; and *Wonderful Town: New York Stories from "The New Yorker,"* edited by David Remnick, Random House (New York, NY), 2000. Contributor of short stories to magazines and periodicals, including *Paris Review, Mississippi Review,* and *Pawn Review.* Restaurant reviewer, *New York Press.* Contributor of articles to magazines, including *Rolling Stone* and *Mademoiselle.*

ADAPTATIONS: Slaves of New York was made into a movie starring Bernadette Peters and directed by Ismail Merchant and James Ivory, 1989.

SIDELIGHTS: Since the publication of her first novel, *American Dad,* at age twenty-three, author Tama Janowitz has captured media headlines, as much for her flamboyant and engaging personality and notoriety as friend to the late Andy Warhol as for her postmodernist fiction. A witty and sensitive observer of New York City's inner life, she has sometimes been taken to task—along with fellow novelists Bret Easton Ellis and Jay McInerney—for, as Terrence Rafferty commented in the *New Yorker,* "believing that the goal of their [literary] elders' activity was their celebrity . . . rather than their vision." Thomas De Pietro described the Janowitz "vision" in the *Hudson Review:* "Her rock-and-roll sensibility is new-wave and, although her characters prefer groups like Teenage Jesus and The Circle Jerks, she herself comes off like a literary Cyndi Lauper, a connoisseur of kitsch capable of being assimilated into the mainstream." Though often in interviews Janowitz offers a Marilyn Monroe-ish cluelessness, her incisive if indigestible observations on the dark underbelly of U.S. culture belie the pose.

Earl Przepasniak, the protagonist and narrator of Janowitz's debut novel, *American Dad,* is eleven years old when his parents divorce. Earl's father, a psychiatrist, is an amiable, self-absorbed, pot-smoking philanderer whose unrepressed behavior upsets and embarrasses the family. His mother, a poet, is killed halfway through the novel during a fight with her ex-husband over alimony payments. Earl's father is convicted of involuntary manslaughter—Earl testifies against him at the trial—and sentenced to ten-to-fifteen years in prison. With his mother dead and his father in jail, Earl decides to travel abroad and goes to London, where he pursues women and indulges in various other misadventures. Upon his return from Europe, Earl is, as several reviewers of *American Dad* observed, predictably wiser, and his enhanced sense of self leads to improved relations with his father.

Although Arnold Klein of the *Soho News* found *American Dad* "episodic and trivial," he noted that it has the "considerable virtue of being funny." Klein also appreciated Janowitz's depiction of Earl's psychiatrist father, which he called "an uncannily acute portrayal of a distinct social type." Garrett Epps stated in the *New Republic,* "There is not a false note in the presentation of this engaging villain." David Quammen, writing for the *New York Times Book Review,* lamented the untimely death of Earl's mother, whom he believed to be the novel's most well-drawn and endearing character. Echoing the reaction of several other reviewers, Quammen praised the novelist for her "fine comedic inventiveness, especially as applied in light dabs to character." According to Epps, Janowitz also has "a sharp eye for the things of this world . . . and her sensuous writing enlivens the book." Reviewers generally agreed that the first half of *American Dad* is the stronger half, and the novel flounders, according to some, after Earl embarks on what one reviewer termed a European rite-of-passage trip. "Earl's adventures are mostly filler," wrote Epps, "[and they mar] what is otherwise one of the most impressive first novels I've read in a long time."

Slaves of New York, Janowitz's follow-up to *American Dad,* is a collection of twenty-two interconnected short stories—many of which originally appeared in the *New Yorker.* The stories center on Eleanor, a shy young jeweler who is financially bound to her boyfriend Stash—a self-proclaimed artist—because he has enough money to pay the rent. *Slaves* takes readers into the behind-the-scenes lives of Manhattan's bohemian elite: painters who adopt blood and ground-up bones as an artistic medium, pimps who contemplate the categorical imperative of philosopher Immanuel Kant, and a host of "couples" whose relationships are dictated by the lack of affordable housing in the Big Apple. "Janowitz writes about people who are not terribly nice," noted Victoria Radin in *New Statesman,* "with an underlying hopefulness that they'll get nicer; and she shows how little control they have over themselves or their lives without pitying or inflating them." While agreeing that *Slaves* is "resoundingly successful as a comedic look" at city dwellers, a reviewer for the *Los Angeles Times Book Review* also found that "pleasantly distracted by Janowitz's solid sense of humor, we don't notice that her characters' spiritual quest is largely for show." Indeed, the main criticism of *Slaves of New York* is that Janowitz's characters possess no depth: *Village Voice* reviewer Carol Ashnew termed them "permanent transients in a dress-up and play-act milieu full of style without the slightest pretense of substance." Despite (or because of?) the mixed critical response, Janowitz was asked to write the screenplay for a film version of *Slaves of New York,* which starred Bernadette Peters and was released in 1989.

After the popular success of *Slaves of New York,* its publisher, Crown, released a work of Janowitz juvenilia in an attempt to continue her momentum on the best-seller lists. A novel of the absurd and heavily indebted to the literature of the past, *A Cannibal in Manhattan* "begins as a travesty of *Robinson Crusoe,*" according to *Newsweek*'s David Lehman, and "borrows liberally from Evelyn Waugh's *Black Mischief,* broadly imitat[ing] the satire of *Candide.*" Unlike its predecessors, *A Cannibal in Manhattan* fared poorly with critics, who, as Rafferty noted in the *New Yorker,* had been fast becoming inured to the "death of the novel. . . . In more idealistic times, . . . the publication of . . . *A Cannibal in Manhattan* . . . might have been the occasion of panic in the streets of Morningside Heights, or for hastily convened symposia in *Partisan Review.*" Taking place in the heart of the Big Apple, Janowitz's satire finds noble cannibal savage Mgungu Yabba Mgungu (even the unlikeliness of such a name coming from the South Pacific comments on the cosseted ignorance of the characters) plucked from his South Sea island home—where he had been living with three wives and assorted children and pigs—and transplanted to New York City by a society heiress playing part-time Peace Corps volunteer. Believing himself to have been selected to become her spouse, Mgungu attempts to fit in with his fiance's high-society friends, where, according to *Times Literary Supplement* reviewer Peter Reading, his activities serve "to accentuate the real absurdity, viciousness and debasement of the sophisticated civilization into which he is deposited." At the close of a dinner party after the couple's wedding, some so-called friends finally reveal to Mgungu that all his new bride really wanted was the recipe for a native hallucinogen and that it doesn't really matter now because his new wife has been freshly offered by underworld pals and served up as the main course at dinner. Some critics considered the cynical humor that redeemed *Slaves* to be unsuccessful in Janowitz's second novel. "Given the book's grisly central metaphor, the tone is shockingly light," observed Rafferty. "If we're really living in a country—or, at least, a city—of cannibals, shouldn't we be a little disturbed?"

Janowitz's same satiric voice "is instantly recognizable," Robert Plunket noted in a review of her next novel, *The Male Cross-Dresser Support Group* for the *New York Times Book Review.* Janowitz is, he stated, "precise, fearless, with the intuitive rhythm of someone who was born funny. . . . Most of all, it's great fun to see a first-rate comic mind tackle the important issues of the day—sexual identity, family values, the shocking behavior of rich WASP's with enormous trust funds." In this 1992 effort, readers are introduced to Pamela Trowel, a woman who lives a meaningless existence in a Manhattan apartment and supports herself with a mindless job selling advertising space for a low-budget hunting magazine until she encounters meaning in the form of a nine-year-old boy called Abdhul. She and the homeless waif become attached to each other and, after Pamela gets fired from her job, they decide to escape from New York rather than be separated by a city bureaucracy seemingly intent upon destroying supportive relationships between children and caring adults. The problem of sexual identity implied by the novel's title comes into play after Abdhul becomes lost; Pamela must adopt the identity of the popular "Paul" in order to discover his whereabouts. "In this postfeminist era, when women still suffer from a lack of status and a lot of disillusionment, . . . Pamela is a kind of comic urban Everywoman," explained Susan Heeger in the *Los Angeles Times Book Review.* "But she's loyal and courageous," Heeger added, "and it's heartening to watch her find her way in the wilderness, despite all those who want to trample her." The author commented on the plight of her protagonist in the *Boston Globe,* telling interviewer Matthew Gilbert: "God knows the men don't come off well in this book, but the women are even worse. I mean women are so rotten to each other, particularly in New York. They're so competitive and back-stabbing and desperate."

In Janowitz's next novel, *By the Shores of Gitchee Gumee,* she broke away from her customary New York setting to write about life with the Slivenowiczes, a wacky, dysfunctional family living in a trailer on the outskirts of a tacky resort town in upstate New York. Their story involves the explosion of their home and their subsequent wanderings to Florida and Los Angeles. *Booklist* reviewer Donna Seaman approved of the "nimble, satisfyingly nasty, and wholly unexpected humor in [Janowitz's] newest novel." The book features Evangeline Slivenowicz, mother of five children by five different fathers. Her eldest daughter, Maud, functions as the story's narrator, one described by Seaman as "outrageously mercenary and amusingly foul-mouthed." The reviewer found the book audacious: "Who, in their wildest literary dreams, would ever have imagined the city cynic Janowitz parodying that most sentimental and overrated of American poets, Henry Wadsworth Longfellow?"

Not all critics shared Seaman's enthusiasm for *Gitchee Gumee,* however. Margot Mifflin in *Entertainment Weekly* found little appeal in the Slivenowiczes or their adventures, stating, "Janowitz seems to believe that a harebrained story starring irretrievably stupid characters constitutes parody. . . . Even judged by the sitcom standards it aspires to, *Gitchee Gumee* is pretty thin stuff." A *Publishers Weekly* reviewer was also unsatisfied with the book, calling it "painfully precious" and finding "equally awkward" the author's "arbitrary footnotes and haphazard allusions to, and quotations from, early American poetry. The dialogue and incidents dart rapid-fire at the reader as in a screwball comedy—but the screws here are loose, and what aims to be funny comes off as merely frantic."

Janowitz returned to her usual New York setting in her 1999 offering, *A Certain Age,* which the publishing world was already enthusiastically passing around in photocopy form before it appeared in public. The city's social climbers and their cocktail-party circuit are reexamined by the author, this time with the focus on an unmarried woman in her thirties and her ruthless quest for a wealthy, well-connected husband. Mark Lindquist of the *Seattle Times* highly recommended the new novel: "A few times a decade, at most, the right author mines the right territory at the right time, and that's what has happened here—*A Certain Age* is a brilliant Zeitgeist novel, smart and funny and fearless. A classic comeback." Lindquist remarked that "Janowitz has an empathy for her characters that distinguishes [the novel] from other postmodern fare." *Entertainment Weekly* reviewer A. J. Jacobs called *A Certain Age* "an homage to Edith Wharton's *House of Mirth,*" but found that it fell far short of Wharton's work. The protagonist, Bridget Jones, is "one of the least likable characters in modern fiction history," stated Jacobs, making it hard to take 317 pages of reading about her. Elizabeth Gleick also found the book unappealing, noting in *Time:* "A hateful heroine and a catalog of her conspicuous consuming do not an amusing read make." A *People* reviewer was more pleased with the book, approving of its "knowing wink at a decaying demimonde." While allowing that "Janowitz's premise wears thin," the writer asserted that "her story amuses to the end." Emily Symon in the *Buffalo News* observed, "There's a great tradition of female writers who focus their powers of observation and description on the genteel brutality of upper class life; *A Certain Age* is simply the latest installment in a long-running serial," adding "Florence, seemingly absent the day they passed out heart and moral fiber, is a classic antihero—a semitragic end seems inevitable for her, though her story is told cleverly enough that it's possible to root for Florence in a wan, curious, halfhearted way" and finally, Janowitz is "still funny, which makes *A Certain Age* bearable in light of what it so surgically exposes about human female nature." Julie Lewis in a *Weekend Australian* interview noted, "A woman's status among the elite of New York is still based on who she [is] married to," and quoted Janowitz:"'I blame women for that. I blame women for sneering at other women when they are not paired off with somebody.'" Lewis added, "This feminism-free, super-wealthy class, [Janowitz] feels, is taking over her town. 'New York used to be the sort of city you could come to and still find a cheap apartment, get a job as a waitress, work in a coffee shop, pay the rent, go out at night and do performance art or paint. Now it's a city just for the very, very rich.'" It also seems that by the time she published *A Certain Age,* Janowitz's own life had veered away from that of her heroines'. The same year, she contributed to a book about the challenges of adopting children. She had met and married an Englishman who came to appraise Andy Warhol's possessions after his death, they had adopted a Chinese baby, and Janowitz had begun writing comic restaurant reviews and (very sensible) parenting advice for magazines. She published the children's book *Hear That?* in 2001.

Janowitz's next novel, *Peyton Amberg,* both touched and impressed London *Guardian*'s Fay Weldon, who commented: "Madame Bovary, in the guise of Peyton Amberg, runs amok in Manhattan and is destroyed: that's the gist of this wonderful novel. It's not nice, mind you, not out of some well-behaved creative writing course the other side of the Atlantic, just glitteringly, angrily, ferociously accurate about the realities of the world." Weldon continued, "Janowitz allows her heroine no mercy, as the girl with the mad, abusive mother, 'hideous hippie hair sprouting from her head in various colours, like some terrible mutant dandelion', descends from the fantasy of happiness to the depths of degradation. . . . It is one of the funniest books I have read, and the bleakest." Peyton Amberg comes from a downwardly mobile Boston family, has married boringly, and become a travel agent, which gives her the room to have endless increasingly awful affairs in exotic places. The *New York Times*'s Mary Elizabeth Williams found that "Janowitz's harsh view of modern sex and her smooth way around the ugliest of encounters can make for vivid reading. She writes with brazen realism, but replaces Flaubert's poetic brutality with crude shocks." In the *Financial Times,* Lilian Pizzichinni commented, "as Janowitz herself has aged, so has her female lead and the result is a bleakness as compelling as was her youthful promise." "What is interesting here is that Janowitz has ditched the glamour to give us the dirt." Pizzichinni continued, "In a series of harrowing episodes Janowitz makes clear that Peyton's schizophrenic mother and absentee father contributed to her inability to connect, feel love or be possessed of a sense of worth. But Janowitz leavens the despair with a captivating ironic detachment: 'There were only another fifty years to get through before (Barry) died,' Peyton figures on her honeymoon. Meanwhile, she seeks out casual sex and new sensations to avoid the drudgery of married life."

Like her protagonist Earl in *American Dad,* Janowitz is the product of a broken marriage between a psychiatrist and a poet; critics noted that she interjects in the fictional lives of the characters she creates the ability to seek unusual ways of dealing with permissive parents or unstructured lifestyles. Several critics also noted parallels between Janowitz and Eleanor, the heroine of *Slaves of New York.* "Her story isn't as much mine as eighty of my girlfriends," Janowitz responded to Gini Sikes in an interview for *Mademoiselle.* "Just because I write that stuff doesn't mean it has anything to do with me." However, she also admitted to *CA* that an autobiographical element does run through her work. "I write about myself by pretending to be others," Janowitz once explained. "In my first novel I am a young boy trying to win his father's approval; in my second I am an elderly 'primitive' cannibal visiting 'civilized' New York City for the first time; and in [*Slaves of New York*] I am a young painter who is burdened with the weight of all of history, and is preoccupied with death and immortality."

In commenting on the "writing life," Janowitz has described the act of rising from bed as a daily struggle. "But generally the need to go to the bathroom and the desire for Wheat Chex forces me to get up," she quipped to *CA*. "Then there is the floor to be swept, and the thought that perchance on this day some mail will come. . . . This is not to say that I despise life. On the contrary, life is an overwhelming experience for me, so much so that getting out of bed becomes an Everest of Olympian proportions for me to climb. The glory of eating Wheat Chex is quite beyond belief. And then if I can actually drag myself to the typewriter and get some words down on paper, what joy I experience!

"For me, writing is overwhelmingly difficult, yet not so difficult, it seems, as actually having to go out and get a job. . . . Some people, sadly, are not meant to work, but I have learned this about myself at an early age. Certain people (though whom I cannot say) might feel that as a writer I should be working in order to collect experience; but it was Flannery O'Connor who said that each person has had enough experiences by the age of twenty to write for the rest of his or her life. Or something to that effect."

BIOGRAPHICAL AND CRITICAL SOURCES:

PERIODICALS

Baltimore News-American, May 24, 1981.

Baltimore Sun, June 7, 1981.

BELL: Belgian Essays on Language and Literature, 2002, p. 93.

Booklist, June 1, 1996, p. 1630; May 1, 1999, p. 1558.

Boston Globe, September 9, 1992, p. 69.

Boston Phoenix, May 12, 1981.

Buffalo News (Buffalo, NY), December 19, 1999, p. E6.

Childhood Education, fall, 2001, p. 50.

Daily Mail (London, England), August 29, 2003, p. 56.

Daily Telegraph (London, England), July 27, 2002; August 23, 2003.

Entertainment Weekly, September 13, 1996, p. 125; July 30, 1999, p. 64.

Evening Standard (London, England), July 15, 2002, p. 47.

Financial Times, July 20, 2002, p. 4; August 16, 2003, p. 33.

Fresno Bee (Fresno, CA), September 19, 1999, p. E3, interview with Janowitz.

Guardian (London, England), May 20, 2000, p. 11; September 6, 2003, p. 28.

Herald (Glasgow, Scotland), May 11, 2000, p. 22.

Horizon, June, 1981.

Houston Chronicle, April 4, 1981.

Hudson Review, autumn, 1986, p. 489.

Independent (London, England), July 17, 1999, p. 9; May 13, 2000, p. 11; May 27, 2000, p. 6; August 30, 2003, p. 25.

Independent on Sunday (London, England), October 27, 1996, p. 25; July 26, 1998, p. 27; July 3, 1999, p. 15; July 4, 1999, p. 5; July 18, 1999, p. 9; May 14, 2000, p. 48; September 7, 2003, p. 19.

Interview, August, 1981.

Irish Times (Dublin, Ireland), October 4, 2003, p. 61.

Kirkus Reviews, June 15, 1996.

Library Journal, July, 1996, p. 160; May 15, 1999, p. 126.

Listener, February 19, 1987, p. 36.

London Review of Books, February 5, 1987, pp. 12-13.

Los Angeles Times Book Review, April 26, 1987, p. 14; October 18, 1987, p. 10; September 13, 1992, p. 1; October 18, 1987, p. 10.

Mademoiselle, April, 1989, pp. 102, 104, 276.

Newark Star-Ledger, April 26, 1981.

New Republic, June 6, 1981; February 1, 1988, pp.29-34.

New Statesman, February 27, 1987; March 4, 1988, p. 26.

Newsweek, September 7, 1987, p. 72.

New York Daily News, May 21, 1981.

New Yorker, October 26, 1987, pp. 142-146.

New York Times, October 19, 2003, p. ST11; October 26, 2003, p. 24.

New York Times Book Review, May 17, 1981; October 4, 1987, p. 12; August 20, 1992, p. 3; October 20, 1996, p. 13; August 8, 1999, p. 9; October 26, 2003, p. 24.

Observer (London, England), September 14, 2003, p. 6, interview with Janowitz.

Opera News, November, 1996, p. 26.

People, September 9, 1996, p. 38; July 19, 1999, p. 43.

Pittsburgh Press, July 20, 1981.

Publishers Weekly, June 17, 1996, p. 44; May 31, 1999, p. 62; April 16, 2001, p. 65; November 18, 2002, p. 14; September 1, 2003, p. 61; October 20, 2003, p. 51.

Rocky Mountain News (Denver, CO), August 15, 1999, p. 1E.

School Library Journal, June, 2001, p. 120.

Scotsman (Edinburgh, Scotland), July 29, 2000, p. 2, interview with Janowitz.

Seattle Times, August 5, 1999, p. G16.

Soho News, April 15, 1981.

Spectator, November 14, 1992, p. 39.

Springfield Republican, August 30, 1981.

Sunday Telegraph (Surrey Hills, Australia), November 24, 2002, p. T16.

Sunday Times (London, England), August 31, 2003, p. 52.

Tampa Tribune, August 8, 1999, p. 5.

Time, October 19, 1987, pp. 77-79; September 7, 1992, p. 69; August 2, 1999, p. 96.

Times (London, England), September 12, 2001, p. 17; June 29, 2002, p. 18; August 20, 2003, p. 9.

Times Literary Supplement, March 4-10, 1988, p. 245; July 2, 1999, p. 21.

Village Voice, August 5, 1986.

Wall Street Journal, July 22, 1986, p. 28; October 19, 1992, p. A12; July 30, 1999, p. W11.

Washington Post Book World, August 30, 1992, p. 2; October 20, 1996, p. 6.
Washington Times. August 29, 1999, p. 6.
Weekend Australian (Sydney, New South Wales, Australia), August 7, 1999, p. R10.
West Coast Review of Books, July, 1981.

ONLINE

Bold Type, http://www.randomhouse.com/boldtype/ (August 1999), Janowitz biography.
BookReporter, http://www.bookreporter.com/ (March 11, 2004), Joni Rendon, review of *Peyton Amberg.*
CityPaper, http://citypaper.net/ (July 22-29, 1999), Kristin Keith, review of *A Certain Age.*
EyeWeekly, http://www.eye.net/ (March 31, 1994), Elizabeth Mitchell, "Seeking That Tama-Friendly Audience."
Guardian Unlimited, http://books.guardian.co.uk/ (September 6, 2003), review of *Peyton Amberg.*
NewYork Metro, http://www.newyorkmetro.com/ (August 9, 1999), Vanessa Grigoriadis, review of *A Certain Age.**

* * *

JOHNSON, Charles (Richard) 1948-

Charles Johnson

PERSONAL: Born April 23, 1948, in Evanston, IL; son of Benjamin Lee and Ruby Elizabeth (Jackson) Johnson; married Joan New (an elementary school teacher), June, 1970; children: Malik, Elizabeth. *Education:* Southern Illinois University, B.A., 1971, M.A., 1973; postgraduate work at State University of New York at Stony Brook, 1973-76. *Religion:* Buddhist

ADDRESSES: *Office*—Department of English, University of Washington, Seattle, WA 98105.

CAREER: Writer, cartoonist, and educator. *Chicago Tribune,* Chicago, IL, cartoonist and reporter, 1969-70; *St. Louis Proud,* St. Louis, MO, member of art staff, 1971-72; University of Washington, Seattle, assistant professor, 1976-79, associate professor, 1979-82, professor of English (Pollock Professor for Excellence in English, the University's first endowed chair in writing), 1982—. Director of Associated Writing Programs Awards Series in Short Fiction, 1979-81, member of board of directors, 1983—.

AWARDS, HONORS: Named journalism alumnus of the year by Southern Illinois University, 1981; Governors Award for Literature from State of Washington, 1983, for *Oxherding Tale;* Callaloo Creative Writing Award, 1983, for short story "Popper's Disease"; citation in *Pushcart Prize*'s Outstanding Writers section, 1984, for story "China"; Prix Jeunesse Award for the screenplay *Booker,* 1985; National Book Award, 1990, for *Middle Passage*; MacArthur Foundation Fellow, 1998; Honorary Ph.D., State University of New York at Stony Brook, 1999; Pacific Northwest Writers Association Achievement Award, 2001.

WRITINGS:

NOVELS

Faith and the Good Thing, Viking (New York, NY), 1974, reprinted, Simon & Schuster (New York, NY), 2001.
Oxherding Tale, Indiana University Press (Bloomington, IN), 1982.

Middle Passage, Macmillan (New York, NY), 1990.
Dreamer, Scribner (New York, NY), 1998.

CARTOON COLLECTIONS

Black Humor (self-illustrated), Johnson Publishing, 1970.
Half-Past Nation Time (self-illustrated), Aware Press, 1972.

Contributor of cartoons to periodicals, including *Ebony, Chicago Tribune, Jet, Black World,* and *Players.*

TELEVISION SCRIPTS

Charlie's Pad (fifty-two-part series on cartooning), PBS, 1970-1980.
Charlie Smith and the Fritter Tree, PBS "Visions" series, 1978.
(With John Alman) *Booker,* PBS, 1983.

Contributor of scripts to numerous television series, including *Up and Coming,* PBS, 1981, and *Y.E.S., Inc.,* PBS, 1983.

OTHER

The Sorcerer's Apprentice (short stories), Atheneum (New York, NY), 1986.
Being and Race: Black Writing since 1970, Indiana University Press (Bloomington, IN), 1988.
Pieces of Eight, Discovery Press (Los Angeles, CA), 1989.
(Author of foreword) *Rites of Passage: Stories about Growing up by Black Writers from around the World,* Hyperion (New York, NY), 1993.
(Author of introduction) *On Writers and Writing,* Addison-Wesley (Reading, MA), 1994.
(Coeditor) *Black Men Speaking,* Indiana University Press (Bloomington, IN), 1997.
(Author of foreword) *Northwest Passages,* Bruce Barcott, Sasquatch Press (Seattle, WA), 1997.
(Coauthor) *Africans in America: America's Journey through Slavery,* Harcourt Brace (San Diego, CA), 1998.
(Coauthor) *I Call Myself an Artist: Writings by and about Charles Johnson,* Indiana University Press (Bloomington, IN), 1999.
(Author of foreword)*A Treasury of North American Folktales,* Norton (New York, NY), 1999.
(Editor, with Yuval Taylor) *I Was Born a Slave: An Anthology of Classic Slave Narratives,* Volume 1: *1772-1849,* Payback (Edinburgh, Scotland), 1999.
(With Jean Toomer and Rudolph P. Byrd) *Essentials,* LPC Group (Chicago, IL), 2001.
(Coauthor) *King: The Photobiography of Martin Luther King, Jr.,* Viking (New York, NY), 2000.
(Editor, with Max Rodriguez and Carol Taylor) *Sacred Fire: The QBR 100 Essential Black Books,* John Wiley (New York, NY), 2000.
Soulcatcher and Other Stories, Harcourt (San Diego, CA), 2001.
(Author of introduction) *Uncle Tom's Cabin,* (150th Anniversary Edition), Oxford University Press (New York, NY), 2002.
(Author of foreword) Fredrik Stromberg, *Black Images in the Comics: A Visual History,* Fantagraphics Books 2003.
Turning the Wheel: Essays on Buddhism and Writing, Scribner (New York, NY), 2003.

Contributor to *Thor's Hammer: Essays on John Gardner,* edited by Jeff Henderson, Arkansas Philological Association, 1986. Work represented in anthologies, including *Best American Short Stories, 1982,* edited by John Gardner and Shannon Ravenel, Houghton Mifflin (Boston, MA), 1982. Contributor of short stories and essays to periodicals, including *Mother Jones, Callaloo, Choice, Indiana Review, Nimrod, Intro 10, Obsidian,* and *North American Review.* Fiction editor of *Seattle Review,* 1978—.

A special collection of Johnson's papers is held at the University of Delaware Library.

ADAPTATIONS: Middle Passage, Africans in America, and *Dreamer* have been adapted for audio cassette; John Singleton/Warner Bros. bought the film rights for *Middle Passage* in 1997.

SIDELIGHTS: "Charles Johnson has enriched contemporary American fiction as few young writers can," observed *Village Voice* critic Stanley Crouch, adding that "it is difficult to imagine that such a talented artist will forever miss the big time." A graduate of Southern

Illinois University, Johnson studied with the late author John Gardner, under whose guidance he wrote *Faith and the Good Thing*. Though Johnson had written six "apprentice" novels (the second of which became *Middle Passage*) prior to his association with Gardner, *Faith* was the first to be accepted for publication. Johnson once commented that he shares "Gardner's concern with 'moral fiction'" and believes in the "necessity of young (and old) writers working toward becoming technicians of language and literary form."

Faith and the Good Thing met with an enthusiastic response from critics such as Garrett Epps of *Washington Post Book World,* who judged it "a brilliant first novel" and commended its author as "one of this country's most interesting and inventive younger writers." Roger Sale, writing in the *Sewanee Review,* had similar praise. He commented: "Johnson, it is clear, is a writer, and if he works too hard at it at times, or if he seems a little too pleased with it at other times, he is twenty-six, and with prose and confidence like his, he can do anything."

The book is a complex, often humorous, folktale account of Faith Cross, a Southern black girl traveling to Chicago in search of life's "Good Thing," which she has learned of from her dying mother. In her quest, noted *Time*'s John Skrow, Faith "seeks guidance from a swamp witch, a withered and warty old necromancer with one green and one yellow eye," who "spouts philosophy as if she were Hegel." Skrow deemed the work a "wry comment on the tension felt by a black intellectual," and Annie Gottleib of the *New York Times Book Review* called *Faith and the Good Thing* a "strange and often wonderful hybrid—an ebullient philosophical novel in the form of a folktale-cum-black-girl's odyssey." She noted that the novel's "magic falls flat" on occasion, "when the mix . . . is too thick with academic in-jokes and erudite references," but she added that "fortunately, such moments are overwhelmed by the poetry and wisdom of the book." In conclusion, Gottleib found the novel "flawed yet still fabulous."

Johnson once described his second novel, *Oxherding Tale,* as "a modern, comic, philosophical slave narrative—a kind of dramatization of the famous 'Ten Oxherding Pictures' of Zen artist Kakuan-Shien," which represent the progressive search of a young herdsman for his rebellious ox, a symbol for his self. The author added that the novel's style "blends the eighteenth-century English novel with the Eastern parable."

Like his first novel, Johnson's *Oxherding Tale* received widespread critical acclaim. It details the coming of age of Andrew Hawkins, a young slave in the pre-Civil War South. Andrew is conceived when, after much drinking, plantation owner Jonathan Polkinghorne convinces his black servant, George Hawkins, to swap wives with him for the evening. Unaware that the man sharing her bed is not her husband, Anna Polkinghorne makes love with George and consequently becomes pregnant with Andrew. After the child is born Anna rejects him as a constant reminder of her humiliation, and he is taken in by George's wife, Mattie. Though he is raised in slave quarters, Andrew receives many privileges, including an education from an eccentric tutor who teaches him about Eastern mysticism, socialism, and the philosophies of Plato, Schopenhauer, and Hegel. In an interview with Rob Trucks of *TriQuarterly*, Johnson pointed out that *Oxherding Tale*, which he said was very special for him, "threw a lot of people because they didn't know what to do with this book. They didn't understand it. People seem to think ideologically, very often, about Black art, and they have presuppositions in their mind, and all kinds of sociological clichés." He wrote the nonfiction work *Being and Race* to try and bridge this kind of gap in understanding.

Writing in *Literature, Fiction, and the Arts Review,* Florella Orowan called Andrew "a man with no social place, caught between the slave world and free white society but, like the hapless hero Tom Jones, he gains from his ambiguous existence the timeless advantage of the Outsider's omniscience and chimerism: he can assume whatever identity is appropriate to the situation." *Oxherding Tale* accompanies its hero on a series of adventures that include an exotic sexual initiation, an encounter with the pleasures of opium, escape from the plantation, "passing" as white, and eluding a telepathic bounty hunter called the Soulcatcher. As Michael S. Weaver observed in *Gargoyle,* Andrew "lives his way to freedom through a succession of sudden enlightenments. . . . Each experience is another layer of insight into human nature" that has "a touch of Johnson's ripe capacity for laughter." The book's climax, noted Crouch, is "remarkable for its brutality and humble tenderness; Andrew must dive into the briar patch of his identity and risk destruction in order to express his humanity."

Weaver admitted that "at times *Oxherding Tale* reads like a philosophical tract, and may have been more adequately billed as Thus Spake Andrew Hawkins."

But he concluded that the novel "is nonetheless an entertaining display of Johnson's working knowledge of the opportunities for wisdom afforded by the interplay between West and East, Black and White, man and woman, feeling and knowing—all of them seeming contradictions." According to Crouch, the novel is successful "because Johnson skillfully avoids melodramatic platitudes while creating suspense and comedy, pathos and nostalgia. In the process, he invents a fresh set of variations on questions about race, sex, and freedom."

In the short-story collection *The Sorcerer's Apprentice,* Johnson continues to examine spiritual, mystical, and philosophical matters through the essentially realistic filter of historical African-American experience. Magic, however, particularly African voodoo practices, plays an essential role in most of the stories, lending these tales an element of the fantastic "without," as Michael Ventura noted in the *New York Times Book Review,* "getting lost in fantasy." Johnson's overriding concern in this volume is with transcending the self, examining the importance of, and terror involved in, surrendering to nonrational forces. For example, in the title story, an older former slave in South Carolina—the Sorcerer—tries unsuccessfully to pass his abilities on to a young man born in freedom. He laments the fact that the youth has become too American, too rational, to accept African magic. Johnson writes that "magic did not reside in ratiocination, education, or will. Skill was of no service. . . . God or creation, or the universe—it had several names—had to *seize* you, *use* you, as the Sorcerer said, because it needed a womb, shake you down, speak through you until the pain pearled into a beautiful spell that snapped the world back together." Ventura concluded that "Mr. Johnson's spell of a book comes on with the authority of a classic."

In 1990, Johnson's literary stature was officially recognized when he won the National Book Award for his novel *Middle Passage.* Set in 1830, the story concerns the newly freed slave Rutherford Calhoun, an ardent womanizer, an admitted liar, and a thief who runs from New Orleans ahead of bill collectors and away from an ill-fated romance. He stows away on a ship, the Republic, that is setting out on a round-trip voyage to Africa where it will fill its hold with slaves. As the novel progresses, the ship's captain is revealed to be a kind of mad genius, the crew is shown to be comprised of a variety of unsavory sea-going types, and the slaves who are eventually transported are—like the Sorcerer in *The Sorcerer's Apprentice*—members of the (fictional) Allmuseri tribe of wizards. *Middle Passage,* like much of Johnson's fiction, relates the many aspects of the African-American experience through a fantastically tinted literary realism. Writing in *African American Review,* Daniel M. Scott III concluded of *Middle Passage:* "As Johnson sings the world, he searches experience and perception for the roots of reality and the doorways to transformation. Writing, understood as a mode of thought, *is* the middle passage, between what has been and what will be, between the word and the world." In answer to Trucks's question, "What do you think the protagonists of your first three novels—Faith Cross (*Faith and the Good Thing*), Andrew Hawkins (*Oxherding Tale*), and Rutherford Calhoun (*Middle Passage*)—have in common?" Johnson replied, "All those characters are seekers, questers (and adventurers). Fredrick T. Griffiths, the critic, rightly calls them 'phenomenological pilgrims.' He's so right—my characters are adventurers of ideas, truth-seekers (and thus have the philosophical impulse, even when they're not trained philosophers), and hunger for wisdom."

It is not to be wondered at, then, that Johnson's next novel, the *Dreamer*, is set during Dr. Martin Luther King's 1966 Chicago campaign. Johnson, who has been a teacher for almost half his life, says that he enjoys doing research for his novels, relating to Trucks that "when I wrote *Oxherding Tale,* I speed-read every book on slavery in the State University of New York at Stony Brook's library, just because I wanted to immerse myself in that, in all the slave narratives. I spent six years just reading stuff on the sea, reading literature on the sea for *Middle Passage,* everything from Appolonius to *Voyage of Argo* forward to Conrad. All of Melville I looked at again, nautical dictionaries. Everything about the sea, because I didn't know that stuff." So, of course, "Dreamer embodies a great deal of history and biography." Johnson continued, "All of '92 I just was reading King. I was going off to do promotion for *Middle Passage,* lectures and stuff, and I would take the King books with me, so it was all going on continuously. I was accumulating. . . . sort of gathering things . . . on the Civil Rights movement. Letting all of that stuff come together until I was ready to write, and the first thing I was ready to write was the Prologue."

Calling the novel a "gospel," Johnson said of King, "He really was a philosopher. In the past, you know, I might have a problem I'm writing about and I'd ask, What would Kant have to say about this or What would Hegel say?, but now it's pretty easy for me to say, What would King say about this? I have a sense now," a statement that solves the question John Seymour of the *Nation* asked: "How does Johnson do it? How does he handle, with insight and sympathy, the Reverend Doctor's torment over the value of the risks he takes for the Movement's sake? Or the cost in time missed with his wife and children?"

Dreamer focuses on the last few months of King's life. As Seymour described, "It is the summer of 1966. More to the point, it is one of those long, hot summers that leave a trail of smoldering ashes, shattered nerves and broken lives in cities throughout the decade. A sad but dauntless Martin Luther King, Jr. is marooned in Chicago, struggling to forge strategy for social transcendence as all around him sirens roar, windows explode, contradictions surface, hope dies." In the midst of the violence, a man who looks so like him as to be a double is brought to his room and offers to stand in for him in dangerous situations. King tells his friends to take to a safe house Chaym Smith and teach him about the Movement. The complicated relationship in which more than physical appearances elide between the two men proceeds through the book, without satisfying the reader with neatly tied-up ends.

Seymour commented that Johnson grabs hold of situations where he can explore "the various ways one can be. Not just be black or white or even American. Just be." "In engaging King's ghost," Seymour continued, "Johnson sets himself up for more ferocious versions of the tut-tuts he caught in some quarters for his antic spins on slave narratives. He raises the stakes in Dreamer not only by presuming to enter the mind and heart of a martyred icon but by imposing a Prince-and-the-Pauper thriller motif to explore what it meant—still means—to lead, to follow, to seek a path to freedom."

Continuing his search for like answers, *The Soulcatcher and Other Stories* was published in 2001. Judy Lightfoot in the *Seattle Times* described it as a peaceful work, despite the fact that it is about experiences under slavery: "Johnson's tales vary widely in technique. Characters are black and white, male and female, old and young, mute and eloquent, enslaved and elite; and the genres include dramatic monologues, personal letters, diary entries, and traditional omniscient storytelling. Yet something gently draws this diversity into harmony. It might be called a spirit of good will—a curious phrase, perhaps, for a book about slavery. But although Johnson faces history's horrors squarely, and his characters have righteously indignant moments, his book transcends indignation and blame."

Aside from the fiction, Johnson has coedited and coauthored several works, including *Black Men Speaking,* a volume of voices from all walks of life, *Africans in America: America's Journey through Slavery, I Call Myself an Artist: Writings by and about Charles Johnson,* and *King: The Photobiography of Martin Luther King, Jr.* James R. Kuhlman in *Library Journal* described Johnson's 2003 book, *Turning the Wheel: Essays on Buddhism and Writing,* as "an uncommon and useful overview of black American involvement in Buddhism." Although *Seattle Times* reviewer Kari Wergeland experienced the essays as scattered over a wider terrain and somewhat heavyhanded and uneven, she did conclude, "However, Johnson is a true renaissance man. His judicious knowledge of philosophy, history, literature, science, and other disciplines shines through all of his essays. He is a compassionate critic, and his pieces on novels such as Harriet Beecher Stowe's *Uncle Tom's Cabin,* Ralph Ellison's *Invisible Man* (a masterpiece which should get more attention in our universities), and Sinclair Lewis's *Kingsblood Royal* offer plenty of grist for the mill."

Johnson told *CA:* "As a writer I am committed to the development of what one might call a genuinely systematic philosophical black American literature, a body of work that explores classical problems and metaphysical questions against the background of black American life. Specifically, my philosophical style is phenomenology, the discipline of Edmund Husserl, but I also have a deep personal interest in the entire continuum of Asian philosophy from the Vedas to Zen, and this perspective inevitably colors my fiction to some degree.

"I have been a martial artist since the age nineteen and a practicing Buddhist since about 1980. So one might also say that in fiction I attempt to interface Eastern and Western philosophical traditions, always with the hope that some new perception of experience—especially 'black experience'—will emerge from these meditations."

BIOGRAPHICAL AND CRITICAL SOURCES:

BOOKS

Byrd, Rudolph P., editor, *I Call Myself an Artist: Writings by and about Charles Johnson,* Indiana University Press (Bloomington, IN), 1999.

Clark, Keith, editor, *Contemporary Black Men's Fiction and Drama,* University of Illinois Press (Urbana, IL), 2001.

Collier, Gordon, and Frank Schulze-Engler, editors, *Crabtracks: Progress and Process in Teaching the New Literatures in English,* Rodopi (Amsterdam, Netherlands), 2002.

Contemporary Authors Autobiography Series, Volume 18, Gale (Detroit, MI), 1994.

Contemporary Literary Criticism, Gale (Detroit, MI), Volume 7, 1977, Volume 51, 1988, Volume 65, 1991.

Cope, Kevin L., and Anna Battigelli, editors, *1650-1850: Ideas, Aesthetics, and Inquiries in the Early Modern Era,* AMS (New York, NY), 2003.

Dictionary of Literary Biography, Volume 33: *Afro-American Fiction Writers after 1955,* Gale (Detroit, MI), 1984.

Fabre, Genevieve, editor, *Parcours identitaires,* Presses de la Sorbonne Nouvelle (Paris, France), 1993.

Gates, Henry Louis, Jr., and Carl Pedersen, editors, *Black Imagination and "The Middle Passage,"* Oxford University Press (Oxford, England), 1999.

Hakutani, Yoshinobu, and Robert Butler, editors, *The City in African-American Literature,* Fairleigh Dickinson University Press (Madison, NJ), 1995.

Karrer, Wolfgang, and Barbara Puschmann-Nalenz, editors, *The African-American Short Story, 1970-1990,* Wissenschaftlicher (Trier, Germany), 1993.

Little, Jonathan, *Charles Johnson's Spiritual Imagination,* University of Missouri Press (Columbia, MO), 1997.

Nash, William R., *Charles Johnson's Fiction,* University of Illinois Press (Urbana, IL), 2002.

Rushdy, Ashraf H. A., *Neo-Slave Narratives: Studies in the Social Logic of a Literary Form,* Oxford University Press (New York, NY), 1999.

Stovall, Linny, editor, *Sex, Family, Tribe,* Blue Heron (Hillsboro, OR), 1992.

Travis, Molly Abel, *Reading Cultures: The Construction of Readers in the Twentieth Century,* Southern Illinois University Press (Carbondale, IL), 1998.

PERIODICALS

African-American Review, fall, 1992, p. 373; spring, 1995, p. 109; winter, 1995, pp. 631, 645, 657; winter, 1996, special issue; fall, 1999, pp. 401, 417; spring, 2003, p. 105.

American Quarterly, September, 1997, p. 531.

American Review, winter, 1996, p. 527.

Arizona Quarterly: A Journal of American Literature, Culture, and Theory, summer, 1994, p. 73.

Black American Literature, winter, 1991, p. 689.

Black Issues Book Review, January, 2001, p. 43.

Black Issues in Higher Education, October 30, 1997, p. 28.

Booklist, March 15, 1993, p. 1364; July, 1997, p. 1782; September 1, 1998, p. 3; January 1, 1999, p. 900; June 1, 1999, p. 1857; November 1, 2000, p. 499; March 1, 2001, p. 1226.

Brick, spring, 2002, p. 133.

Callaloo, October, 1978; fall, 1999, p. 1028; spring, 2003, p. 504.

Christian Science Monitor, October 15, 1998, p. B7.

Chronicle of Higher Education, January 16, 1991, p. A3.

College English, November, 1997, p. 753.

College Language Association Journal, June, 1978; September, 1986, p. 1.

Commonweal, December 2, 1994.

Comparatist: Journal of the Southern Comparative Literature Association, May, 2002, p. 121.

Contemporary Literature, summer, 1993, p. 159; spring, 2001, p. 160.

CR: The New Centennial Review, winter, 2001, p. 67.

Current Biography, September, 1991, p. 26.

Ebony, June, 2001, p. 23.

Essence, April, 1991, p. 36; January, 2001, p. 64.

Financial Times, September 26, 1998, p. 8.

Forbes, March 16, 1992, p. S26.

Gargoyle, June, 1978.

Grand Rapids Press (Grand Rapids, MI), November 4, 2003, p. B1.

Hemingway Review, 1999, p. 114.

Houston Chronicle (Houston, TX), June 7, 1998, p. 22.

Independent (London, England), October 10, 1998, p. 14.

Independent on Sunday (London, England), October 25, 1998, p. 11; May 2, 1999, p. 13; July 11, 1999, p. 12.

Jet, December 17, 1990, p. 28; November 29, 1999, p. 20.

Journal of African-American and African Arts and Letters, summer, 1997, p. 531.

Kentucky Philological Review, 1991, p. 27.

Kliatt, March, 1995.

Library Journal, May 1, 1990, p. 112; October 1, 1991, p. 159; July 1997, p. 109; April 1, 1998, p. 122; September 15, 1998, pp. 90, 128; November 1, 2000, p. 100; January 1, 2001, p. 130; April 15, 2001, p. 134; June 1, 2003, p. 120.
Literature, Fiction, and the Arts Review, June 30, 1983; January 22, 1995.
Los Angeles Times Book Review, June 24, 1990.
Massachusetts Review: A Quarterly of Literature, the Arts and Public Affairs, summer, 2001, p. 253.
Narrative, October, 1994, p. 179.
Nation, September 13, 1986, p. 226; April 27 1998, p. 27.
New England Review, spring, 1998, p. 49.
New Republic, December 24, 1990, p. 26.
New Yorker, December 20, 1982.
New York Review of Books, January 17, 1991, p. 3.
New York Times, November 28, 1990, pp. B1, C13; November 29, 1990, p. C22; January 2, 1991, pp. B1, C9; April 5, 1998; April 8, 1998, pp. B9, E11; July 1, 1990; June 15, 2003, p. 14.
New York Times Book Review, January 12, 1975; January 9, 1983; February 5, 1986; March 30, 1986, p. 7; July 1, 1990, p. 8; April 5, 1998, p. 14; October 18, 1998, p. 28; June 15, 2003, p. 14.
Olympian (Olympia, WA), June 10, 2001, p. D2.
People, January 14, 1991, p. 73; December 11, 2000, p. 55.
Popular Photography, April, 2001, p. 74.
Postscript: Publication of the Philological Association of the Carolinas, 1994, p. 1.
Publishers Weekly, April 6, 1990, p. 103; December 14, 1990, p. 14; April 12, 1991, p. 24; February 28, 1994, p. 65; January 13, 1997, p. 24; February 23, 1998, p. 50; September 21, 1998, p. 62.
Representations, spring, 1997, p. 24.
San Francisco Chronicle, April 19, 1998, p. 1.
School Library Journal, October, 1988, p. 176; August, 1994, p. 105; June, 1999, p. 80; April 2001, p. 173.
Seattle Post-Intelligencer (Seattle, WA), May 30, 2003, p. 25.
Seattle Times, March 29, 1998, p. M1; April 5, 1998, p. M2; 25 March, 2001, p. E12; June 22, 2003, p. K14.
Sewanee Review, January, 1975.
Shakespeare Survey: An Annual Survey of Shakespeare Studies and Production, 1998, p. 45.
Soundings: An Interdisciplinary Journal, winter, 1997, p. 607.
Studies in American Fiction, autumn, 1991, p. 141; spring, 1997, p. 81.
Sycamore: A Journal of American Culture, spring, 1997, p. 19.
Time, January 6, 1975.
Times Literary Supplement (London, England), January 6, 1984.
TriQuarterly, winter-summer, 2000, p. 537.
U.S. News & World Report, December 10, 1990, p. 21.
Village Voice, July 19, 1984.
Washington Post Book World, December 15, 1982; February 16, 1986; December 4, 1990, p. D1; December 13, 1990, p. A23; 24 August, 1997; April 11, 1998, p. B1; November 8, 1998, p. 1.

ONLINE

African-American Literature Book Club, http://aalbc.com/ (March 12, 2004), "Charles Johnson."
Columns, University of Washington Alumni Magazine, http://www.washington.edu/ (June, 1999), "Charles Johnson."
University of Washington Showcase, http://www.washington.edu/ (March 12, 2004), "Charles Johnson: National Book Award Winner."*

* * *

JOHNSON, Sandy

PERSONAL: Female.

ADDRESSES: *Home*—508 Union Ave., Knoxville, TN 37902.

CAREER: Writer.

WRITINGS:

The CUPPI (novel), Delacorte Press (New York, NY), 1979.
Walk a Winter Beach, Delacorte Press (New York, NY), 1982.
Against the Law (nonfiction), Bantam (New York, NY), 1986.
(Compiler and author of introductions and notes) *The Book of Elders: The Life Stories of Great American Indians,* photographs by Dan Budnick, HarperSanFrancisco (San Francisco, CA), 1994.

The Book of Tibetan Elders: Life Stories and Spiritual Wisdom from the Great Spiritual Masters of Tibet, Riverhead Books (New York, NY), 1996.

The Brazilian Healer with the Kitchen Knife and Other Stories of Mystics, Shamans, and Miracle-Makers, Rodale Press (Emmaus, PA), 2003.

SIDELIGHTS: Sandy Johnson is a novelist and nonfiction author whose works include a fictionalized account of an actual police investigation, a nonfiction account of a prison escape, and two researches into spiritual wisdom. Her debut novel, *The CUPPI,* draws its title from an acronym used by the New York City Police Department for Circumstances Undetermined Pending Police Investigation. The novel centers on the mysterious death of a twelve-year-old runaway who had inadvertently become involved with a child pornography and prostitution ring.

Noting that *The CUPPI* is based on a real case investigated by the New York police, a reviewer in *Publishers Weekly* praised the novel as "a solid, gripping and utterly realistic first novel" and added that the issues raised by the subject would serve to raise reader awareness of big-city problems. Newgate Callendar in the *New York Times Book Review* called the book "competent though conventional" and concluded that "what saves the book is the close look it takes at an unsavory side of life." Reviewer Marion Hanscom in *Library Journal* judged the story "interesting and frightening."

A sensational true story also provided the basis of *Against the Law.* In this work Johnson traces the events surrounding a prison escape in which a female attorney helped her convicted client flee from jail in Tennessee in March, 1983, and then lived with him in Florida until the pair were apprehended by federal agents in August of that year.

Representing a shift in subject matter and genre, *The Book of Elders: The Life Stories of Great American Indians* combines transcripts of conversations with Native American elders, with introductory and connective material by Johnson, and photographs by Dan Budnick. Roger Welsch in *Western Historical Quarterly* called the work "a sort of impressionistic approach to native American spiritualism" and judged its effect "powerful." A follow-up volume, *The Book of Tibetan Elders: Life Stories and Spiritual Wisdom from the Great Spiritual Masters of Tibet,* presents interviews with Tibetan elders who have been living in exile since the Chinese invasion in 1959.

BIOGRAPHICAL AND CRITICAL SOURCES:

PERIODICALS

Library Journal, October 1, 1979, Marion Hanscom, review of *The CUPPI,* pp. 2118-2119; June 15, 2003, Mary E. Jones, review of *The Brazilian Healer with the Kitchen Knife and Other Stories of Mystics, Shamans, and Miracle-Makers,* p. 78.

New York Times Book Review, October 21, 1979, Newgate Callendar, review of *The CUPPI,* p. 28.

Publishers Weekly, July 2, 1979, review of *The CUPPI;* pp. 95-96; June 27, 1986, p. 83.

Western Historical Quarterly, summer 1995, Roger Welsch, review of *The Book of Elders: The Life Stories of Great American Indians,* pp. 233-234.*

K

KANIUT, Larry (LeRoy) 1942-

PERSONAL: Born January 9, 1942, in Deer Park, WA; son of Lawrence (a truck driver) and Vivian Lenore (a homemaker; maiden name, Kralman) Kaniut; married Pamela Diane Timmons (a homemaker), August 28, 1964; children: Ginger Diane, Jill Rose, Benjamin Chane. *Education:* Attended Warner Pacific College, 1960-62, and Portland State College (now University), 1962-63; Linfield College, B.A., 1965, M.Ed., 1966. *Religion:* Protestant.

ADDRESSES: *Office*—2600 Huffman Rd., Anchorage, AK 99516. *E-mail*—Larry@Kaniut.com.

CAREER: A. J. Dimond High School, Anchorage, AK, English teacher and athletic coach, beginning 1966. Summer employee of Alaska Department of Fish and Game; worked as house-builder and commercial fisherman.

WRITINGS:

NONFICTION

Alaska Bear Tales, Alaska Northwest Publishing (Anchorage, AK), 1983, reprinted, 2003.

More Alaska Bear Tales, Alaska Northwest Books (Anchorage, AK), 1989.

Cheating Death: Amazing Survival Stories from Alaska, Epicenter Press (Fairbanks, AK), 1994.

Some Bears Kill: True Life Tales of Terror, Safari Press (Long Beach, CA), 1997.

Danger Stalks the Land: Alaskan Tales of Death and Survival, St. Martin's Press (New York, NY), 1999.

(Author of preface) Evan Swenson, *One Last Cast: From Alaska Outdoors Radio Magazine,* Publication Consultants (Anchorage, AK), 2000.

Bear Tales for the Ages: From Alaska and Beyond, Paper Talk (Anchorage, AK), 2001.

Contributor of stories to *Outdoor Life, Outdoor America, Anchorage Times,* and *Alaska.*

WORK IN PROGRESS: *Alaska's Fun Bears.*

SIDELIGHTS: Larry Kaniut has written several best-selling books on exciting, real-life adventures in the wilds of Alaska. Telling the stories of people who survived bear attacks, plane crashes, avalanches, and mountain-climbing accidents, Kaniut's books have proven popular with those readers who enjoy the outdoors.

In *Cheating Death: Amazing Survival Stories from Alaska,* Kaniut gathers eighteen stories of individuals who faced death in the Alaskan wilderness, including one person who survived a small-plane crash in the mountains. Norman Goldman, in an online review for *Boots 'n' All,* found that Kaniut's book "is written in a style that provides the reader with vivid pictures of the actual near-death happenings." *Danger Stalks the Land: Alaskan Tales of Death and Survival* presents tales drawn not only from contemporary sources but from older accounts as well. One story concerns Billy Mitchell, later known for his Army court martial, who fell through the ice while dogsledding in Alaska. Another story deals with a fisherman who became mired in tidal mudflats; despite rescue efforts, including the use of a helicopter, the man eventually drowned when the tide moved back in and covered him. Writing in *School Library Journal,* Judy McAloon called Kaniut "a good storyteller" whose book offers "harrowing true-life, people-against-the-elements tales."

Kaniut once told *CA:* "Beginning with my personal conversion to Christianity in 1957, my life turned around. I began to view life as worth living to its fullest and to center my decisions on the question, 'What would Jesus do?' Because of my desire to serve God by following the teachings of his son, Jesus Christ, many doors have opened.

"My wife, Pam, and I share the belief that God is a personal god whose love for man prompted him to send Jesus to redeem man, who had made a mess of things since Adam and Eve's time. This belief has allowed us to pray for God's will in our lives. As a direct answer to prayer we moved to Alaska to teach English in 1966, and we will remain until we feel God leading us to leave.

"As a result of teaching literature of the North, I wished to edit a book of Alaskan adventures, and in 1969 began to contact publishers, asking if they would be interested in such a book. In 1973 I approached Alaska Northwest Publishing Company with this query, which other publishers had rejected. Alaska Northwest responded likewise but felt that I 'had a feel for' their work and asked me to do a bear book. I told them that I wasn't qualified but would give it a shot. As *Alaska Bear Tales* developed, I wanted to educate and entertain the reader, hopefully with advice on practical solutions in the case of a bear run-in. As a compilation, most of the book summarizes experiences of those encountering bears. Some of my views and values are also reflected (i.e., treat bears with respect, be prepared, don't give up, give God his due credit).

"My desire to write teen novels is to encourage them to fulfill their potential—to be themselves to the fullest, not someone else. I also wish to speak to parents, encouraging them to love their kids, to hug them and say 'I love you.' I want kids to know that they 'count,' one and all, and that they are unique. I also want kids to know that the acceptance and security that they seek will come only through the commitment of their souls to the one who created them, and that through Jesus the Christ they can fulfill their potential."

BIOGRAPHICAL AND CRITICAL SOURCES:

PERIODICALS

American West, January-February, 1984, review of *Alaska Bear Tales,* p. 54.

Publishers Weekly, November 18, 1983, "Alaska Publisher Has Winner in Bear Book," p. 55.

School Library Journal, June, 2000, Judy McAloon, review of *Danger Stalks the Land: Alaskan Tales of Death and Survival,* p. 176.

ONLINE

Boots 'n' All, http://www.bootsnall.com/ (July, 2002), Norman Goldman, review of *Cheating Death: Amazing Survival Stories from Alaska.*

Larry Kaniut Web site, http://www.kaniut.com/ (November 13, 2003).*

* * *

KIMBERLY, Gail
(Alix Andre, Dayle Courtney)

PERSONAL: Born in New York, NY; daughter of Wilbert R. (an architect) and Evelyn (a real estate agent; maiden name, Cox) Kimberly; married Antonius J. Van Achthoven, February 8, 1951 (divorced, 1973); married Kellin Francis (in chemical sales), November 14, 1980; children: (first marriage) Leslie Achthoven Cordova, Eric, Michelle Achthoven Bergstrom, Judi Achthoven Palmer. *Education:* Attended Pasadena City College.

ADDRESSES: *Agent*—Kirby McCauley Ltd., 310 East 46th St., New York, NY 10017. *E-mail*—GKfrancis@aol.com.

CAREER: Columbia Broadcasting System, Los Angeles, CA, secretary, 1957-60; Brown Brothers Adjusters, Pasadena, CA, secretary, 1963-67; University of

California, College of Medicine, Orange, secretary, 1967-69; Milliman & Robertson (actuarial consultants), Pasadena, secretary, 1971-74; writer, beginning 1974.

MEMBER: Science Fiction Writers of America, Society of Children's Books Authors and Illustrators, California Writers Club.

WRITINGS:

Flyer (science-fiction novel), Popular Library (New York, NY), 1972.
Dracula Began (horror novel), Pyramid Publications (New York, NY), 1973.
Star Jewel (juvenile science fiction), Scholastic (New York, NY), 1975.
Goodbye Is Just the Beginning (romance fiction), Zebra Books (New York, NY), 1978.
Pavan for a Dead Marriage (novel), Zebra Books (New York, NY), 1979.
Secret at the Abbey (mystery fiction), Harlequin (Buffalo, NY), 1980.
Child of Faerie (juvenile fantasy fiction), Scholastic (New York, NY), 1993.

Work represented in anthologies, including *The Other Side of Tomorrow,* Random House (New York, NY), 1973; *The Far Side of Time,* Dodd, Mead (New York, NY) 1974; and *Dystopian Visions,* Prentice-Hall (Englewood Cliffs, NJ), 1975. Contributor of stories to adult and juvenile magazines in the United States and England, including *Galaxy, Alfred Hitchcock's Mystery Magazine,* and *Gothic Stories.* Some writings appear under the pseudonyms Alix Andre and Dayle Courtney.

WORK IN PROGRESS: Kitling, science fiction; *Birthmark,* an occult romance.

SIDELIGHTS: Gail Kimberly once told *CA*: "I started writing when I was seven years old, turning out poetry and fantastic tales with wild abandon. My parents thought they were great, but nobody else seemed interested in my writing until high school.

"When my two children were small, I wrote during their nap time, one to two hours every afternoon. When they were in school, I usually held down full-time jobs and wrote evenings and weekends. After I had sold several science-fiction short stories to one editor, he requested that I write a novel for him. His request came at the same time as my separation from my husband, and although I had six months to write the novel, I found my personal life interfering so much with my writing time that I had to ask for an extension. He gave me three weeks. *Flyer* was written in those three weeks, and while it was subsequently published, I'd hate to try doing that again.

"Since I was raised in Canada, many of my stories have a Canadian background. I've traveled across Canada and the United States, and made a camping tour of Europe that lasted six months. I lived for a year in Hawaii, on the island of Oahu, and wrote a science-fiction novel there, set in the Hawaii of the future.

"I've written both juvenile and adult stories, and my favorite genre, to read and write, is science fiction/fantasy, although I love mysteries, occult stories, and adventure yarns."

BIOGRAPHICAL AND CRITICAL SOURCES:

PERIODICALS

Pasadena Star-News, June 25, 1975.

* * *

KINSELLA, W(illiam) P(atrick) 1935-

PERSONAL: Born May 25, 1935, in Edmonton, Alberta, Canada; son of John Matthew (a contractor) and Olive Mary (a printer; maiden name, Elliot) Kinsella; married Myrna Salls, December 28, 1957 (divorced, 1963); married Mildred Irene Clay, September 10, 1965 (divorced, 1978); married Ann Ilene Knight (a writer), December 30, 1978 (divorced, 1997); married Barbara L. Turner, March 2, 1999; children: (first marriage) Shannon, Lyndsey, Erin. *Education:* University of Victoria, B.A., 1974; University of Iowa, M.F.A., 1978. *Religion:* Atheist.

ADDRESSES: Home—15325 19-A Ave., White Rock, British Columbia V4A 8S4, Canada; Box 2162, Blaine, WA 98230-2162. *Office*—P.O. Box 3067, Sumas, WA

W. P. Kinsella

98295-3067; and 9442 Nowell, Chilliwack, British Columbia V2P 4X7, Canada. *Agent*—Nancy Colbert, 55 Avenue Rd., Toronto, Ontario M5R 3L2, Canada.

CAREER: Government of Alberta, Edmonton, Canada, clerk, 1954-56; Retail Credit Co., Edmonton, Alberta, Canada, manager, 1956-61; City of Edmonton, Alberta, Canada, account executive, 1961-67; Caesar's Italian Village (restaurant), Victoria, British Columbia, Canada, owner, 1967-72; student and taxicab driver in Victoria, 1974-76; University of Iowa, Iowa City, instructor, 1976-78; University of Calgary, Calgary, Alberta, Canada, assistant professor of English and creative writing, 1978-83; author, 1983—.

MEMBER: American Amateur Press Association, Society of American Baseball Researchers, American Atheists, Enoch Emery Society.

AWARDS, HONORS: Award from Canadian Fiction, 1976, for story "Illianna Comes Home"; honorable mention in *Best American Short Stories 1980,* for "Fiona the First"; Houghton Mifflin Literary fellowship, 1982, Books in Canada First Novel Award, 1983, and Canadian Authors Association prize, 1983, all for *Shoeless Joe*; Writers Guild of Alberta O'Hagan novel medal, 1984, for *The Moccasin Telegraph*; Alberta Achievement Award for Excellence in Literature; Stephen Leacock Medal for Humor, 1987, for *The Fencepost Chronicles*; Author of the Year Award, Canadian Booksellers Association, 1987; Laurentian University, Ontario, Canada, D.Litt., 1990; University of Victoria, D.Litt, 1991; decorated, Order of Canada, 1994.

WRITINGS:

Dance Me Outside (stories), Oberon Press (Ottawa, Ontario, Canada), 1977, published as *Dance Me Outside: More Tales from the Ermineskin Reserve,* David Godine (Boston, MA), 1986.

Scars: Stories, Oberon Press (Ottawa, Ontario, Canada), 1978.

Shoeless Joe Jackson Comes to Iowa (stories), Oberon Press (Ottawa, Ontario, Canada), 1980, Southern Methodist University Press (Dallas, TX), 1993.

Born Indian, Oberon Press (Ottawa, Ontario, Canada), 1981.

Shoeless Joe (novel; based on title story in *Joe Jackson Comes to Iowa*), Houghton Mifflin (Boston, MA), 1982.

The Ballad of the Public Trustee (chapbook), Standard Editions (Vancouver, British Columbia, Canada), 1982.

The Moccasin Telegraph (stories), Penguin Canada (Toronto, Ontario, Canada), 1983, published as *The Moccasin Telegraph and Other Indian Tales,* David Godine (Boston, MA), 1984, published as *The Moccasin Telegraph and Other Stories,* Penguin Books (New York, NY), 1985.

The Thrill of the Grass (chapbook), Standard Editions (Vancouver, British Columbia, Canada), 1984, new edition with additional stories, Penguin Books (New York, NY), 1984.

The Alligator Report (stories), Coffee House Press (Minneapolis, MN), 1985.

The Iowa Baseball Confederacy (novel), Houghton Mifflin (Boston, MA), 1986.

Five Stories (stories), illustrations by Carel Moiseiwitsch, Tanks (Vancouver, British Columbia, Canada), 1986.

The Fencepost Chronicles (stories), Totem Press (Don Mills, Ontario, Canada), 1986, Houghton Mifflin (Boston, MA), 1987.

Red Wolf, Red Wolf (stories), Collins (Toronto, Ontario, Canada), 1987.

The Further Adventures of Slugger McBatt: Baseball Stories by W. P. Kinsella, Collins (Toronto, Ontario, Canada), 1987, Houghton Mifflin (Boston, MA), 1988, reprinted as *Go the Distance,* Southern Methodist University Press (Dallas, Texas), 1995.

(With wife, Ann Knight) *The Rainbow Warehouse* (poetry), Pottersfield Press (East Lawrencetown, Nova Scotia, Canada), 1989.

Two Spirits Soar: The Art of Allen Sapp: The Inspiration of Allan Godor (art book), Stoddart (Toronto, Ontario, Canada), 1990.

The Miss Hobbema Pageant, HarperCollins (Toronto, Ontario, Canada), 1990.

The First and Last Annual Six Towns Area Old Timers' Baseball Game, wood engravings by Gaylord Schanilec, Coffee House Press (Minneapolis, MN), 1991.

Box Socials (novel), HarperCollins (Toronto, Ontario, Canada), 1992, Ballantine (New York, NY), 1993.

(With Furman Bisher and Dave Perkins) *A Series for the World: Baseball's First International Fall Classic,* Woodford Press (San Francisco, CA), 1992.

The Dixon Cornbelt League, and Other Baseball Stories, HarperCollins (Toronto, Ontario, Canada), 1993, HarperCollins (New York, NY), 1995.

Even at This Distance, Pottersfield Press (East Lawrencetown, Nova Scotia, Canada), 1994.

Brother Frank's Gospel Hour (stories), HarperCollins (Toronto, Ontario, Canada), 1994, Southern Methodist University Press (Dallas, TX), 1996.

(Author of introduction) Peter Williams, *When the Giants Were Giants: Bill Terry and the Golden Age of New York Baseball* (stories), Algonquin Books of Chapel Hill (Chapel Hill, NC), 1994.

The Winter Helen Dropped By (novel), HarperCollins (Toronto, Ontario, Canada), 1995.

If Wishes Were Horses, HarperCollins (Toronto, Ontario, Canada), 1996.

Magic Time, Doubleday Canada (Toronto, Ontario, Canada), 1998, Voyageur Press (Stillwater, MN), 2001.

The Silas Stories, HarperCollins (Toronto, Ontario, Canada), 1998.

The Secret of the Northern Lights, Thistledown Press (Saskatoon, Saskatchewan, Canada), 1998.

Japanese Baseball, and Other Stories, Thistledown Press (Saskatoon, Saskatchewan, Canada), 2000.

(Editor, contributor, and author of introduction) *Baseball Fantastic: Stories,* Quarry Press (Kingston, Ontario, Canada), 2000.

Contributor to *Ergo!: The Bumbershoot Literary Magazine,* edited by Judith Roche, Bumbershoot, 1991, and to numerous anthologies. Also author of foreword to *Hummers, Knucklers, and Slow Curves: Contemporary Baseball Poems,* edited by Don Johnson, University of Illinois Press (Champaign, IL), 1991.

ADAPTATIONS: *Shoeless Joe* was adapted and produced as the motion picture *Field of Dreams,* released in 1989 by Universal; *Shoeless Joe* was also optioned for musical-stage adaptation by Dreamfields Ltd.; *Dance Me Outside* was produced as a motion picture by Norman Jewison in 1995; *The Iowa Baseball Confederacy* was adapted for sound recording by New Letters, 1986; "Lieberman in Love" in *Red Wolf, Red Wolf* was adapted and produced as a short film by Christine Lahti for Chanticleer Films; *The Dixon Cornbelt League* was optioned for motion picture by Sony/TriStar.

SIDELIGHTS: Canadian author W. P. Kinsella has won an international readership with his imaginative fiction. Some of Kinsella's short stories follow the daily escapades of characters living on a Cree Indian reservation, while some of his longer works, including *Shoeless Joe* and *The Iowa Baseball Confederacy,* mix magic and the mundane in epic baseball encounters. A determined writer who published his first story collection at the age of forty-two, Kinsella has won numerous awards, and his books have been adapted into successful films, such as *Field of Dreams.*

A Cree Indian named Silas Ermineskin brought Kinsella his first literary recognition, beginning in 1974. Ermineskin was the most prominent member of a large cast of characters Kinsella created in a series of stories based on a government reservation for the Cree people. Kinsella portrayed this life in nearly one hundred stories, collected in *Dance Me Outside, Scars, Born Indian,* and *The Moccasin Telegraph.* Both Canadian and U.S. critics expressed admiration for what Kinsella accomplished in these tales. *Prairie Schooner* contributor Frances W. Kaye noted, "W. P. Kinsella is not an Indian, a fact that would not be extraordinary were it not for the stories Kinsella writes about . . . a Cree World. Kinsella's Indians are counterculture figures in the sense that their lives counter the predominant culture of North America, but there is none of the worshipfully inaccurate portrayal of 'the Indians' that has appeared from Fenimore Cooper through Gary Snyder." In *Wascana Review,* George Woodcock likewise cited Kinsella for an approach that "restores proportion and brings an artistic authenticity to the portrayal of contemporary Indian life which we have encountered rarely in recent years." Anthony Brennan offered a similar assessment in *Fiddlehead,* writing that *Dance Me Outside* "is all the more refreshing because it quite consciously eschews ersatz heroics and any kind of nostalgic, mythopoeic reflections on a technicolor golden age."

In 1980 Kinsella published *Shoeless Joe Jackson Comes to Iowa,* a collection of short pieces set in Iowa, urban Canada, and San Francisco. The title story also was selected to appear in an anthology titled *Aurora: New Canadian Writing 1979.* An editor at Houghton Mifflin saw Kinsella's contribution to *Aurora* and contacted the author about expanding the story into a novel. "It was something that hadn't occurred to me at all," Kinsella recalled in *Publishers Weekly.* "I told [the editor], 'I've never written anything longer than 25 pages, but if you want to work with me, I'll try it.'" Much to Kinsella's surprise, the editor agreed. Kinsella set to work expanding "Shoeless Joe Jackson Comes to Iowa," but he decided instead to leave the story intact as the first chapter and build on the plot with a variety of other material. "I enjoyed doing it very much," he said. "They were such wonderful characters I'd created, and I liked being audacious in another way. I put in no sex, no violence, no obscenity, none of that stuff that sells. I wanted to write a book for imaginative readers, an affirmative statement about life."

Shoeless Joe, a novel-length baseball fable set on an Iowa farm, won Kinsella the Houghton Mifflin Literary fellowship in 1982. The story follows a character named Ray Kinsella in his attempts to summon the spirits of the tarnished 1919 Chicago White Sox by building a ballpark in his cornfield. Among the ghostly players lured to Kinsella's perfectly mowed grass is Shoeless Joe Jackson, the White Sox star player who fell in scandal when it was revealed that his team threw the World Series. As the story progresses, the same mysterious loudspeaker voice that suggested construction of the ballpark says, "Ease his pain," and Ray Kinsella sets off to kidnap author J. D. Salinger for a visit to Fenway Park. The novel blends baseball lore with legend and historical figures with fictional characters. "I've mixed in so much, I'm not sure what's real and what's not," Kinsella told *Publishers Weekly,* "but as long as you can convince people you know what you're talking about, it doesn't matter. If you're convincing, they'll believe it."

Kinsella cemented his reputation as a writer of literary merit with *Shoeless Joe.* According to *Los Angeles Times* critic Alan Cheuse, the work "stands as fictional homage to our national pastime, with resonances so American that the book may be grounds for abolishing our northern border." *Detroit News* writer Ben Brown explained, "What we have here is a gentle, unselfconscious fantasy balanced perilously in the air above an Iowa cornfield. It's a balancing act sustained by the absolutely fearless, sentimentality-risking honesty of the author. And it doesn't hurt a bit that he's a master of the language. . . . This is an utterly beautiful piece of work." *Christian Science Monitor* contributor Maggie Lewis stated, "The descriptions of landscape are poetic, and the baseball details will warm fans' hearts and not get in the way of mere fantasy lovers. This book would make great reading on a summer vacation. In fact, this book *is* a summer vacation." But *Washington Post* critic Jonathan Yardley wrote, *Shoeless Joe* "is a book of quite unbelievable self-indulgence, a rambling exercise the only discernible point of which seems to be to demonstrate, ad infinitum and ad nauseam, what a wonderful fellow is its narrator/author."

Kinsella continued to express his fascination with baseball in his 1986 novel, *The Iowa Baseball Confederacy.* Jonathan Webb described the work in *Quill & Quire*: "*The Iowa Baseball Confederacy* contains bigger magic, larger and more spectacular effects, than anything attempted in *Shoeless Joe.* Kinsella is striving for grander meaning: the reconciliation of immovable forces—love and darker emotions—on conflicting courses." Time travel and a ballgame that lasts in excess of 2,600 innings are two of the supernatural events in the story; characters as diverse as Teddy Roosevelt and Leonardo da Vinci make cameo appearances. Chicago *Tribune Books* contributor Gerald Nemanic wrote: "Freighted with mythical machinery, *The Iowa Baseball Confederacy* requires the leavening of some sprightly prose. Kinsella is equal to it. His love for baseball is evident in the lyrical descriptions of the game."

Toronto *Globe and Mail* reviewer William French suggested that Kinsella lifts baseball to a higher plane in his novels. The author, French noted, is "attracted as much to the metaphysical aspects as the physical, intrigued by how baseball transcends time and place and runs like a subterranean stream of consciousness through the past century or so of American history. . . . His baseball novels are animated by a lighthearted wit and bubbling imagination, a respect for mystery and magic." "To be obsessed with baseball is to be touched by grace in Kinsella's universe," wrote Webb, "and a state of grace gives access to magic." Webb felt that in *The Iowa Baseball Confederacy,* Kinsella fails to persuade the reader to go along with his magic. French likewise stated: "In the end [of the novel], Kinsella's various themes don't quite connect. But it hardly matters; we're able to admire the audacity of Kinsella's vision and the sheen of his prose without worrying too much about his ultimate meaning." *Los Angeles Times Book Review* contributor Roger Kahn called *The Iowa Baseball Confederacy* "fun and lyric and poignant."

Although baseball surfaces as a theme in Kinsella's 1991 novel, *Box Socials,* the work primarily revolves around the young narrator, Jamie O'Day, and the quirky characters who live in and around 1940s Fark—a small town near Edmonton, Alberta, Canada. Filled with "crackpots bizarre enough to put [American humorist] Garrison Keillor to shame," commented Joyce R. Slater in Chicago *Tribune Books, Box Socials* features such individuals as Little Wasyl Podolanchuk, one of the only Ukrainian dwarfs in the province; teenaged Truckbox Al McClintock, who once batted against Hall of Fame pitcher Bob Feller; and bachelor Earl J. Rasmussen, who lives in the hills with 600 sheep and delights in belting out "Casey at the Bat" at whim. Reviewers noted that *Box Socials* is essentially a coming-of-age tale about the curious and wide-eyed Jamie, who learns about sex by listening in on the women who gab with his mother, and who attends his first box social and bids on poor, downtrodden Bertha Sigurdson's lunch, even though Velvet Bozniak paid him to bid on hers. "The 'little box social' turns out to be a humdinger," Fannie Flagg stated in the *New York Times Book Review,* "if you've never been to a box social, go to this one. Along with a lot of laughs, we are given a touching and sensitive portrayal of the love, sometimes happy, sometimes heartbreaking, between young men and young women, and experience the pangs of first love through Jamie's eyes." Other reviewers praised Kinsella's leisurely narrative style. Patrick Goldstein in the *Los Angeles Times Book Review* remarked that *Box Socials* is "a delightful comic ramble, written in a quirky, digressive style that reads like a cross between [American avant-garde writer] Gertrude Stein and [American cartoonist] Al Capp." "If long-winded, seemingly pointless stories make you anxious," pointed out Slater, "Kinsella's not your man. If you're patient enough to stay for the payoff, if you're an admirer of the perfect wry phrase buried in verbiage, he will give you more than your money's worth."

Kinsella once again mixed magic and baseball in his 1993 work, *The Dixon Cornbelt League and Other Baseball Stories.* In this collection of nine stories, Kinsella uses mysticism and conflict to explore human nature. Supernatural events permeate many of the tales: "The Baseball Wolf" shows what happens when a shortstop transforms into a wolf in order to revive his fading career; in "The Fadeaway," even death cannot stop pitcher Christy Mathewson from relaying pitching tips to the Cleveland Indians through a dugout phone. Stephen Smith of *Quill & Quire* noticed the lack of "baseball activity" in *The Dixon Cornbelt League* and instructed the reader to "choose your own baseball imagery" when judging the stories. The story "Eggs" takes on a more realistic and serious topic. "Eggs" is an account of a pitcher's premature retirement due to the loss of his ability to throw a fastball. The pitcher's aspiration to return to baseball is unsupported by his wife and his unhappiness grows. *Publishers Weekly* critic Sybil S. Steinberg appreciated Kinsella's stories because they "read like lightning" and present "fascinating scenarios," yet she felt Kinsella does not fully satisfy his readers, does not offer enough substance or depth in the characters and their stories. Drew Limsky expressed a similar viewpoint in the *Washington Post Book World,* writing that "although Kinsella's voice is frequently winning even after he's run out of ideas, some of the entries are so slight they barely qualify as stories; they seem to belong to some lesser genre—tales or anecdotes, perhaps."

Kinsella has also produced short fiction on a variety of themes. *The Alligator Report,* published in 1985, contains stories that pay homage to surrealist Richard Brautigan, one of Kinsella's favorite authors. In a *Village Voice* review, Jodi Daynard wrote, "Kinsella's new stories replace humor with wit, regional dialect with high prose. . . . He uses surrealism most effectively to highlight the delicate balance between solitude and alienation, not to achieve a comic effect. . . . These are images that resonate—not comic ones, alas, but stirring, not woolly-wild, but urban gothic." *New York Times Book Review* contributor Harry Marten noted that in *The Alligator Report* Kinsella continued "to define a world in which magic and reality combine to make us laugh and think about the perceptions we take for granted."

In his 1994 book of short stories, *Brother Frank's Gospel Hour,* Kinsella revisits the inhabitants of Hobbema, Alberta. Two familiar inhabitants include Silas Ermineskin, a Cree writer, and his comical partner Frank Fencepost. The humorous pair return in the short story "Bull," a lighthearted rendering of an artificial insemination case in the Alberta Supreme Court. The other stories in *Brother Frank* cover a range of topics. "Rain Birds" looks at the results of corporate farming on nature; the reality of child abuse is explored in "Dream Catcher"; a boy ascertains the parallels between the sexes in "Ice Man"; and in "Brother Frank's Gospel Hour" comedy turns a staid gospel show upside down. Critical reaction to *Brother Frank* was predominantly positive. Scott Anderson of *Quill & Quire* credited Kinsella for his "understanding of human foibles" and his revelry in "the inventiveness of the human spirit in adversity."

Kinsella took a break from writing about America's favorite pastime in his 1995 novel, *The Winter Helen Dropped By.* Set in a small town in Alberta, Canada, Kinsella's four-part novel depicts one year during the Great Depression through the eyes of eleven-year-old Jamie O'Day, the narrator of *Box Socials.* "Every story is about sex or death, or sometimes both," begins O'Day as he takes readers through a steady succession of marriages, funerals, pregnancies, and the like. In the novel's first section, an Indian woman arrives at the O'Day's farmhouse in the middle of a blizzard. Another section finds a local widow in the midst of wedding preparations while small-town gossip threatens to muffle the celebration. And Jamie views his parents through childish eyes in "Rosemary's Winter," which Paul J. Robichaud praised in his *Quill & Quire* review as "the strongest section of the novel." Heavy with child, Jamie's mother has to get to town, but the creek has flooded. Her dreamer husband's solution to the dilemma is to construct a sailboat, which in his creative vision he sees as a "wheelless windwagon." While noting that Kinsella sometimes affects a too-down-home air, Robichaud added that *The Winter Helen Dropped By* "affords the reader a glimpse into a world that no longer exists, and provides considerable laughter and feeling while doing so."

Kinsella's literary alter ego, Ray Kinsella, and Gideon Clarke, a character from *The Iowa Baseball Confederacy,* both return in the novel *If Wishes Were Horses,* published in 1996. Their role in this book is to listen to the strange tale of Joe McCoy, a washed-up pitcher who is on the run from the FBI after committing some crimes, including kidnapping. Joe believes that his wrongdoings have been prompted by unseen forces controlling him, and that he has another life more real than the one he has been living through. *Maclean's* reviewer Brian Bethune remarked: "In Kinsella's hands McCoy's colliding lives and ever more hallucinatory situation propel an absorbing story of longing and regret, in which the hero can taste and smell experiences that never happened. It is also very funny."

Kinsella suffered personal troubles in the late 1990s. He became embroiled in a legal case with Evelyn Lau, a writer and former romantic companion of Kinsella's, over a tell-all article she wrote and published detailing their relationship. While engaged in this case, in 1997 Kinsella was struck by a car and suffered the loss of his senses of smell and taste. He also claimed that, although doctors failed to prove a medical reason, injuries suffered in the accident had deprived him of his ability to write creatively. He did publish *Magic Time* in 1998, a novel he had begun six years earlier but never finished to his satisfaction. 'It's far from my best work, but if anybody wants to publish anything. . . . It's like playing baseball: if you get an at-bat, you take what you can,' Kinsella told Stephen Smith in *Saturday Night.* A *Publishers Weekly* reviewer called it "a warmhearted, homespun novel by the award-winning author." The plot takes in the trials and tribulations of a student athlete who ends up in what may be a beautifully disguised prison, and the book "satisfies with its endearing characters and baseball lore," concluded the reviewer.

BIOGRAPHICAL AND CRITICAL SOURCES:

BOOKS

Contemporary Authors Autobiography Series, Volume 7, Gale (Detroit, MI), 1988.

Contemporary Literary Criticism, Gale (Detroit, MI), Volume 27, 1984, Volume 43, 1987.

Contemporary Novelists, St. James Press (Detroit, MI), 2001.

Contemporary Popular Writers, St. James Press (Detroit, MI), 1997.
St. James Guide to Fantasy Writers, St. James Press (Detroit, MI), 1996.

PERIODICALS

*Booklist,*January 15, 1995, Dennis Dodge, review of *The Dixon Cornbelt League and Other Baseball Stories,* p. 895; March 15, 1995, Ted Hipple, review of the sound recording of *The Iowa Baseball Confederacy,* p. 1343.
Books in Canada, October, 1981; February, 1984; November, 1984; October, 1993, pp. 41-42; September, 1994, pp. 38-39; October, 1995, pp. 45-46.
Canadian Literature, summer, 1982; autumn, 1995, pp. 149-50.
Christian Science Monitor, July 9, 1982.
Detroit Free Press, May 4, 1986.
Detroit News, May 2, 1982; May 16, 1982.
Explicator, spring, 1995, Clarence Jenkins, "Kinsella's *Shoeless Joe,*" p. 179.
Fiddlehead, fall, 1977; spring, 1981.
Globe and Mail (Toronto, Ontario, Canada), November 17, 1984; April 27, 1985; April 12, 1986.
Library Journal, February 1, 1982; November 1, 1990, p. 125; March 1, 1993, p. 85.
Los Angeles Times, August 26, 1982.
Los Angeles Times Book Review, May 23, 1982; July 6, 1986; March 29, 1992, p. 6.
Maclean's, May 11, 1981; April 19, 1982; July 23, 1984; May 1, 1989, p. 66; November 11, 1991, Victor Dwyer, review of *Box Socials,* p. 90; July 12, 1993, pp. 60-61; December 16, 1996, Brian Bethune, review of *If Wishes Were Horses,* p. 69; March 16, 1998, "From Love Story to Lawsuit," p. 12.
National Review, October 24, 1986, Mike Shannon, review of *The Iowa Baseball Confederacy,* p. 60.
Newsweek, August 23, 1982.
New York Review of Books, November 5, 192, pp. 41-45.
New York Times Book Review, July 25, 1982; September 2, 1984; January 5, 1986; April 20, 1986; May 19, 1991, p. 36; March 1, 1992, p. 29; July 12, 1992, p. 33; December 19, 1993, p. 14.
Prairie Schooner, spring, 1979.
Publishers Weekly, April 16, 1982; October 19, 1990, Penny Kaganoff, review of *Red Wolf, Red Wolf,* p. 53; March 2, 1992, review of *Box Socials,* p. 48; September 27, 1993, review of *Shoeless Joe Jackson Comes to Iowa,* p. 58; December 5, 1994, review of *The Dixon Cornbelt League,* pp. 65-66; February 13, 1995, p. 18; October 29, 2001, review of *Magic Time,* p. 36.
Quill & Quire, June, 1982; September, 1984; April, 1986; December, 1991, p. 17; June, 1993, p. 27; July, 1994, p. 94; September, 1995, p. 68.
Saturday Night, August, 1986, pp. 45-47; September, 1999, Stephen Smith, "A Loss for Words," p. 14.
Seattle Times, May 6, 1999, "*Shoeless Joe* Author Files B.C. Suit," p. B2.
Tribune Books (Chicago, IL), April 25, 1982; March 30, 1986; May 3, 1992, p. 6.
Village Voice, December 4, 1984; April 1, 1986.
Wascana Review, fall, 1976.
Washington Post, March 31, 1982.
Washington Post Book World, March 30, 1995, p. 4.*

* * *

KOTZWINKLE, William 1938-

PERSONAL: Born November 22, 1938, in Scranton, PA; son of William John (a printer) and Madolyn (a housewife; maiden name, Murphy) Kotzwinkle; married Elizabeth Gundy (a writer), 1970. *Education:* Attended Rider College and Pennsylvania State University. *Hobbies and other interests:* Folk guitar.

ADDRESSES: *Agent*—c/o Author Mail, Frog, 1435-A Fourth St., Berkeley, CA 94710.

CAREER: Writer. Worked as a short-order cook and an editor in the mid-1960s.

AWARDS, HONORS: National Magazine Awards for fiction, 1972, 1975; O. Henry Prize, 1975; World Fantasy Award for best novel, 1977, for *Doctor Rat;* North Dakota Children's Choice Award, 1983, and Buckeye Award, 1984, both for *E.T., the Extra-Terrestrial: A Novel;* Bread Loaf Writers Conference Scholarship.

WRITINGS:

Elephant Bangs Train (short stories), Pantheon (New York, NY), 1971.
Hermes 3000, Pantheon (New York, NY), 1972.

William Kotzwinkle

The Fan Man, Avon (New York, NY), 1974.

Night-Book, Avon (New York, NY), 1974.

Swimmer in the Secret Sea, Avon (New York, NY), 1975, reprinted, Chronicle Books (San Francisco, CA), 1994.

Doctor Rat, Knopf (New York, NY), 1976.

Fata Morgana, Knopf (New York, NY), 1977.

Herr Nightingale and the Satin Woman, illustrated by Joe Servello, Knopf (New York, NY), 1978.

Jack in the Box, Putnam (New York, NY), 1980, published as *Book of Love,* Houghton Mifflin (Boston, MA), 1982.

Christmas at Fontaine's, illustrated by Joe Servello, Putnam (New York, NY), 1982.

Queen of Swords, illustrated by Joe Servello, Putnam (New York, NY), 1983.

Seduction in Berlin (poetry), illustrated by Joe Servello, Putnam (New York, NY), 1985.

Jewel of the Moon (short stories), Putnam (New York, NY), 1985.

The Exile, Dutton (New York, NY), 1987.

The Midnight Examiner, Houghton Mifflin (Boston, MA), 1989.

Hot Jazz Trio, illustrated by Joe Servello, Houghton Mifflin (Boston, MA), 1989.

The Game of Thirty, Houghton Mifflin (Boston, MA), 1994.

The Bear Went over the Mountain, Doubleday (New York, NY), 1996.

FOR CHILDREN

The Fireman, illustrated by Joe Servello, Pantheon (New York, NY), 1969.

The Ship That Came Down the Gutter, illustrated by Joe Servello, Pantheon, 1970.

Elephant Boy: A Story of the Stone Age, illustrated by Joe Servello, Farrar, Straus & Giroux (New York, NY), 1970.

The Day the Gang Got Rich, illustrated by Joe Servello, Viking (New York, NY), 1970.

The Oldest Man and Other Timeless Stories, illustrated by Joe Servello, Pantheon (New York, NY), 1971.

The Return of Crazy Horse, illustrated by Joe Servello, Farrar, Straus & Giroux (New York, NY), 1971.

The Supreme, Superb, Exalted, and Delightful, One and Only Magic Building, illustrated by Joe Servello, Farrar, Straus & Giroux (New York, NY), 1973.

Up the Alley with Jack and Joe, illustrated by Joe Servello, Macmillan (New York, NY), 1974.

The Leopard's Tooth, illustrated by Joe Servello, Houghton Mifflin (Boston, MA), 1976.

The Ants Who Took Away Time, illustrated by Joe Servello, Doubleday (Garden City, NY), 1978.

Dream of Dark Harbor, illustrated by Joe Servello, Doubleday (Garden City, NY), 1979.

The Nap Master, illustrated by Joe Servello, Harcourt (New York, NY), 1979.

E.T., the Extra-Terrestrial: A Novel (novelization of screenplay by Melissa Mathison), Putnam (New York, NY), 1982.

Superman III (novelization of screenplay by David and Leslie Newman), Warner Books (New York, NY), 1983.

Great World Circus, illustrated by Joe Servello, Putnam (New York, NY), 1983.

Trouble in Bugland: A Collection of Inspector Mantis Mysteries, illustrated by Joe Servello, David R. Godine (Boston, MA), 1983.

E.T., the Book of the Green Planet: A New Novel (based on a story by Steven Spielberg), Putnam (New York, NY), 1985.

The World Is Big and I'm So Small, illustrated by Joe Servello, Crown (New York, NY), 1986.

Hearts of Wood and Other Timeless Tales, David R. Godine (Boston, MA), 1986.

The Million Dollar Bear, illustrated by David Catrow, Knopf (New York, NY), 1995.

Tales from the Empty Notebook, illustrated by Joe Servello, Marlowe (New York, NY), 1996.

(With Glenn Murray) *Walter, the Farting Dog,* illustrated by Audrey Colman, Frog (Berkeley, CA), 2001.

(With Glenn Murray) *Walter, the Farting Dog: Trouble at the Yard Sale,* illustrated by Audrey Colman, Frog (Berkeley, CA), 2004.

Also author of screenplays, including *Nightmare on Elm Street Four: The Dream Master* and *Dreaming of Babylon.* Author of screen adaptations of *Book of Love, The Exile,* and *Christmas at Fontaine's.* Contributor of short stories to books and periodicals, including *Great Esquire Fiction, Redbook's Famous Fiction,* and *O. Henry Prize Stories,* 1975. Contributor to magazines and newspapers, including *New York Times* and *Mademoiselle.*

ADAPTATIONS: *Jack in the Box* was filmed as *Book of Love* in 1992; Jim Henson Productions has optioned *The Bear Went over the Mountain.*

WORK IN PROGRESS: More "Walter, the Farting Dog" titles with Glenn Murray and Audrey Colman.

SIDELIGHTS: William Kotzwinkle is a versatile writer who has penned books for all sorts of reading tastes. His fertile imagination has produced science fiction, children's stories, mysteries, and satire. Perhaps the easiest way to characterize his work is to say that it does not fit into any particular category. Even in the realm of writing novelizations of popular movies, Kotzwinkle has excelled. His *E.T., the Extra-Terrestrial: A Novel,* based on the film by the same name, offers a completely different point of view and a great deal more detail than the film contains. Though better known for his adult novels, Kotzwinkle has written numerous books for children and young adults and has done so throughout his career. In an interview with *Publishers Weekly* correspondent Walter Gelles, the author said: "I always think I'll never do another [children's book], but something in me keeps bubbling up, the inner child who wants us to reexperience the world in a spontaneous way."

Kotzwinkle was born in 1938 in Scranton, Pennsylvania, a mid-sized city near the New York border. He was the only child and enjoyed a warm relationship with his father, a printer, and his stay-at-home mother. A *Dictionary of Literary Biography* contributor observed: "In describing the beginnings of his awareness of himself as a writer, Kotzwinkle recalls his father on a hike pointing to the Lackawanna Valley as if presenting the richness of the world to him and his mother taking him to a wading pool where a tadpole in his hand seemed, he said, like an 'exquisite jewel.'" Certainly the young Kotzwinkle was taken by the beauty of nature, but he did not gravitate to serious writing until he became a student at Pennsylvania State University. There he began writing poetry and honing his narrative skills in drama and playwrighting seminars.

In 1957, Kotzwinkle dropped out of Penn State and went to live in New York City, where he embraced the bohemian lifestyle so popular then among younger writers. He supported himself by working as a short-order cook, a department store Santa Claus, a promotions writer for Prentice-Hall, and a reporter for a tabloid, among other odd jobs. An old school friend, Joe Servello, helped Kotzwinkle to sell his first book in 1969. That book, *The Fireman,* is based on one of Kotzwinkle's fondest childhood memories—the day his grandfather, a fireman, allowed him to sit behind the wheel of the fire truck. "After such excitement, no ordinary profession could hold me," Kotzwinkle is quoted as saying in *Dictionary of Literary Biography.* Kotzwinkle added that he thought the book was successful because it was the first piece of work in which he was able to reconnect with one of the peak moments of his childhood.

Kotzwinkle established himself in the 1970s as a prolific author who never seemed to repeat himself. Some of his best-known adult books were published during this time, including *The Fan Man,* a lyrical meditation on the Greenwich Village art scene of the 1960s. His 1976 book *Doctor Rat* was one of the first to denounce scientific experimentation on animals. An eco-fable, *Doctor Rat* introduces readers to the title character, an educated rat who undertakes experiments on other animals. A movement of free animals of all species attempts to break into the lab and uncage the imprisoned animals. In his *Harper's* review of the book, Robert Stone called Kotzwinkle an author who is "not afraid to take the kind of risks that are necessary for the production of a serious novel."

It was also during the early part of his career that Kotzwinkle wrote *Jack in the Box,* perhaps his most autobiographical work. Set in a coal mining region of Pennsylvania, *Jack in the Box* explores the slow maturation process of one Jack Twiller, who is bewildered by much of what he sees around him and is just as uncomfortable within his own mind. "The novel is an audacious attempt to join the ends of the spectrum of YA literature, the fading wonder of the child's world with the bleakness of a looming adult life stretching onward through decades of boredom," observed a contributor to the *St. James Guide to Young Adult Writers.* "Kotzwinkle's narration of Twiller's maturation, full of screw-ups and failed schemes, is an illuminating account of how small gains in self-awareness and a deepening understanding of the world can lead to a construction of the self that can withstand the inevitable further screw-ups and failures of existence."

Film director Steven Spielberg became acquainted with Kotzwinkle's work by reading *The Fan Man.* While preparing the movie *E.T.,* Spielberg invited Kotzwinkle to Hollywood and asked him to write the film's novelization. Novels based on movies are generally done quickly and without much attention to style or substance, but Kotzwinkle was quite taken by the character of the empathetic extra-terrestrial. His adaptation of Melissa Mathison's screenplay was written from E.T.'s point of view, stressing the evolution of love and humanity on the character's home planet. Kotzwinkle is quoted in the *Dictionary of Literary Biography* as saying that E.T. "is definitely not human. . . . [He has] a quality of humanity *that is yet to come,* and it has to do with love."

E.T., the Extra-Terrestrial made the best-seller lists and has sold more than three million copies. The contributor to the *Dictionary of Literary Biography* observed: "The public accepted it as a separate work of art. In a sense, it is the culmination of Kotzwinkle's previous writing for younger readers; he presents E.T. as a manifestation of humanity's undeveloped cosmic consciousness that finds its expression in imagination and fantasy but which can be objectified because it is so much a part of common human desire." The critic added: "Kotzwinkle uses E.T. to present the positive side of his environmental concerns through a figure whose strength and appeal comes from his symbiotic bond with every sentient organism in the universe. . . . Kotzwinkle is emphasizing his belief that environment is life and that proper care and concern for the planet is essential for the survival of every form of life, as well as a source of nourishment for the soul."

In his *Publishers Weekly* interview with Gelles, Kotzwinkle said that his book version of *E.T.* communicates, to adults as well as children, "a powerful archetype that is dawning for humanity, the little helper from the stars. UFO visitations represent the alien within us. The alien is a missing link for us, a missing piece of our awareness."

Together, Spielberg and Kotzwinkle plotted another E.T. story that was published as *E.T., the Book of the Green Planet: A New Novel.* In this book, E.T. has returned to his home planet but longs to go back to Earth—"the green planet"—to visit Elliott and help him through adolescence. According to Jill Grossman, who assessed the book in the *New York Times Book Review,* Kotzwinkle's "strong suit here is his imagination and playfulness with language." The *Dictionary of Literary Biography* essayist wrote of the novel: "Even more than *Doctor Rat,* it is a revealing allegory relating human nature to aspects of biodiversity."

It is no coincidence that Kotzwinkle feels so strongly about environmental concerns. Since the early 1970s, he has avoided big cities, preferring to live in rural seaside Maine with his writer wife. He rarely does book tours, does not keep a Web site, and does not court celebrity the way some authors do. In a rare *People* magazine interview, he told Brenda Eady: "I want children to think the guy who wrote *E.T.* is weird."

Kotzwinkle has a low opinion of much of children's literature, as he explained to Gelles: "When Robert Louis Stevenson wrote *Treasure Island* there was no such thing as 'children's books.' But once they became a separate category, it unleashed a river of trash. So much of this writing is condescending, permeated with an austere sense of looking down at the child." Critics rarely note these tendencies in Kotzwinkle's work. Some of his adult novels could easily be understood by younger readers, and some of his children's books provide diversion for adults. *Trouble in Bugland: A Collection of Inspector Mantis Mysteries,* for instance, borrows from Sherlock Holmes for a series of stories featuring a praying mantis detective who solves crimes in the insect world. While the insects in the stories speak and act somewhat like people, each different species behaves according to its characteristics in the natural world. It is no surprise, then, that Inspector Mantis is calm and calculating, able to detect other insects' weaknesses.

"Initially, Mantis and Hopper resemble the anthropomorphic equivalents of animated cartoons, cute creatures with human attributes," observed an essayist in *St. James Guide to Young Adult Writers.* "As the tales progress, the characters, especially Mantis, assume an allegorical ambiguity closer to the complexity of human nature than the single-trait dominance required by children's books. The struggle to overcome evil and seek justice has an essential appeal to any reader not consumed by cynicism, while the satisfaction inherent in seeing a riddle revealed is an important element of a story for young adults discovering the increasingly ambiguous nature of almost everything." In her *New York Times Book Review* assessment of *Trouble in Bugland,* Ann Cameron concluded that readers of all ages would "appreciate the book's sly mock seriousness and flights of rhetoric and imagination."

The author is also at home with more conventional picture books for the youngest readers. In *The Million Dollar Bear,* a valuable teddy bear—the first ever made, in fact—is languishing in the locked safe of a stingy business tycoon. Eventually the bear escapes and finds its way into a home with children—and a grandfather who proclaims it worthless and allows them to play with it as freely as they wish. Writing in the *Washington Post Book World,* Michael Dirda concluded: "All in all, this is a very good picture book. . . . If you find the moral a tad sappy, well, you'll just have to grin and bear it."

Walter the dog has quite another problem in *Walter, the Farting Dog.* His gas attacks have landed him in the pound, and the family that has just adopted him discovers that they, too, cannot stand the stink. Just in time to save himself, however, Walter foils a burglary at his new home with his secret weapon: flatulence. A *Publishers Weekly* reviewer declared that Walter's antics "should have children rolling in the aisles during read-aloud." *Booklist*'s Ilene Cooper likewise felt that children would find the book "hysterical."

The success of *Walter, the Farting Dog* has only verified what Kotzwinkle wants his audience to think: that he is weird, unpredictable, and very much in touch with what makes children laugh—and think. Though he is uncertain of what books may lie in his future, Kotzwinkle told *People* interviewer Eady, "I know I'll end up a little old guy telling stories on a mountain somewhere."

BIOGRAPHICAL AND CRITICAL SOURCES:

BOOKS

Beacham's Popular Fiction Update, Beacham Publishing (Washington, DC), 1991, pp. 693-704.

Children's Literature Review, Volume 6, Gale (Detroit, MI), 1994, pp. 180-185.

Contemporary Literary Criticism, Gale (Detroit, MI), Volume 5, 1976, Volume 14, 1980, Volume 35, 1985.

Contemporary Novelists, 7th edition, St. James Press (Detroit, MI), 2001.

Dictionary of Literary Biography, Volume 173: *American Novelists since World War II, Fifth Series,* Gale (Detroit, MI), 1996, pp. 98-107.

St. James Guide to Fantasy Writers, St. James Press (Detroit, MI), 1996.

St. James Guide to Young Adult Writers, 2nd edition, St. James Press (Detroit, MI), 1999.

Twentieth-Century Science-Fiction Writers, 3rd edition, St. James Press (Detroit, MI), 1991.

PERIODICALS

Atlantic, May, 1974; June, 1976; July, 1977.

Booklist, February 15, 2002, Ilene Cooper, review of *Walter, the Farting Dog,* p. 1020.

Chicago Tribune, May 5, 1989.

College Literature, spring, 2000, Robert E. Kohn, "The Ambivalence in Kotzwinkle's Beat and Bardo Ties," p. 103.

Harper's, June, 1976, Robert Stone, review of *Doctor Rat.*

Listener, July 22, 1976.

Los Angeles Times Book Review, January 22, 1984, p. 8; June 14, 1987, p. 10; April 30, 1989; November 19, 1989, p. 8; September 11, 1994, Susan Salter Reynolds, review of *Swimmer in the Secret Sea,* p. 6.

Nation, November 4, 1996, Dan Wakefield, review of *The Bear Went over the Mountain,* p. 31.

New Republic, March 2, 1974.

Newsweek, May 31, 1982, p. 63.

New Yorker, March 25, 1974; July 25, 1977.

New York Times, April 9, 1971, Thomas Lask, "Of Elephants and Air Strikes," p. 29.

New York Times Book Review, January 10, 1974; November 2, 1975; May 30, 1976, Richard P. Brickner, review of *Doctor Rat,* p. 8; May 1, 1977; November 9, 1980; July 11, 1982, pp. 31-32; January 1, 1984, Ann Cameron, review of *Trouble in Bugland: A Collection of Inspector Mantis Mysteries,* p. 23; May 5, 1985, Jill Grossman, review of *E.T., the Book of the Green Planet: A New Novel,* p. 24; January 4, 1987, p. 33; May 10, 1987, pp. 1, 38; May 14, 1989, p. 27; February 25, 1990, p. 13.

Observer, January 8, 1978.

People, April 22, 1985, Ralph Novak, review of *E.T., the Book of the Green Planet,* p. 26; May 27, 1985, Brenda Eady, "From Any Angle, E.T.'s Biographer William Kotzwinkle Is Not an Alien to Success."

Publishers Weekly, November 10, 1989, Walter Gelles, "William Kotzwinkle," pp. 46-47; October 16, 1995, review of *The Million-Dollar Bear,* p. 60; October 8, 2001, review of *Walter, the Farting Dog,* p. 63.

San Francisco Review of Books, spring, 1985, R. E. Nowicki, "An Interview with William Kotzwinkle," pp. 7-8.

Saturday Review, May 29, 1976; April 30, 1977.

School Library Journal, February, 1984, p. 74; January, 1996, Patricia Pearl Dole, review of *The Million-Dollar Bear,* p. 86.

Times Literary Supplement, January 7, 1983, p. 13.

Village Voice, September 15, 1975; June 28, 1976, Anne Larsen, "Did Doctor Rat Sell Out?," p. 45; August 24, 1982, Ariel Dorfman, "Norteamericanos, Call Home," pp. 39-40; August 8, 1989, p. 49.

Washington Post Book World, October 1, 1995, Michael Dirda, review of *The Million-Dollar Bear,* p. 6.

Writer's Digest, July, 1992, Michael Schumacher, "The Inner Worlds of William Kotzwinkle," p. 34.*

L

LANDES, David S(aul) 1924-

PERSONAL: Born April 29, 1924, in New York, NY; son of Harry and Sylvia (Silberman) Landes; married Sonia Tarnopol (an educator), March 19, 1944; children: Jane Landes Foster, Richard Allen, Alison Landes Fiekowsky. *Education:* City College (now of the City University of New York), A.B., 1942; Harvard University, A.M., 1943, Ph.D., 1953. *Religion:* Jewish. *Hobbies and other interests:* Playing squash.

ADDRESSES: *Agent*—Sandra Dijkstra Literary Agency, 1155 Camino del Mar, Del Mar, CA 92104-2605.

CAREER: Columbia University, New York, NY, assistant professor, 1952-55, associate professor of economics, 1955-58; University of California—Berkeley, professor of history and economics, 1958-64; Harvard University, Cambridge, MA, professor of history, 1964-72, Leroy B. Williams Professor of History and Political Science, 1972-75, Robert Walton Goelet Professor of French History, 1975-80, Coolidge Professor of History and professor of economics, beginning 1980, now professor emeritus, director of Center for Middle Eastern Studies, 1966-68. Center for Advanced Study in the Behavioral Sciences, Palo Alto, CA, fellow, 1957-58; Churchill College, Cambridge, fellow, 1966-69. Cambridge University, Ellen McArthur Lecturer, 1964; University of Paris, associate professor at Sorbonne, 1972-73; visiting professor, University of Zurich, 1978, Eidgenössische Hochschule, Zurich, 1978, and École des Hautes Études en Sciences Sociales, Paris, 1982. National Academy of Sciences, member, also chair of National Academy of Sciences/Social Science Research Council history panel, 1966-70; Council for Research on Economic History, chair, 1963-66. *Military service:* U.S. Army, Signal Corps, 1943-46; became first lieutenant.

MEMBER: American Academy of Arts and Sciences (fellow), American Historical Association, American Philosophical Society (fellow), Economic History Association (president, 1976-77; member of board of trustees), Society for French Historical Studies, British Academy (fellow), Royal Historical Society, Economic History Society (England), Societe d'Histoire Moderne, Gesellschaft für Sozial-und Wirtschaftgeschichte, Koninklijke Academie van Belgie (Belgium), Accadémia dei Lincei (Rome, Italy).

AWARDS, HONORS: D.H.C., University of Lille, 1973, University of Ancona, 1990, Eidgenössische Technische Hochschule, 1993, and Bard College, 1999; honorary doctorates from University of Geneva, 1990, and University of Neuchatel, 1991; Social Science Research Council grant for France, 1960-61; Rockefeller Foundation fellow, 1960-61; National Book Critics Circle Award nomination, 1983, for *Revolution in Time: Clocks and the Making of the Modern World;* first laureate, Prix Européen du Livre d'Economie, 2000, for *The Wealth and Poverty of Nations: Why Some Are So Rich and Some So Poor;* named honorary professor, Ecole des Hautes Etudes Commerciales, 2000.

WRITINGS:

Bankers and Pashas: International Finance and Economic Imperialism in Egypt, Harvard University Press (Cambridge, MA), 1958.

(Editor) *The Rise of Capitalism,* Macmillan (New York, NY), 1966.

The Unbound Prometheus: Technological Change and Industrial Development in Western Europe from 1750 to the Present, Cambridge University Press (New York, NY), 1969.

(Editor, with Charles Tilly) *History As Social Science,* Prentice-Hall (Englewood Cliffs, NJ), 1971.

(Coauthor) *Estudios sobre al naciemiento y desarrollo del capitalismo,* Spanish translation from the English by Jorge Fabra Utray, Ayuso, 2nd edition, 1972.

(Editor) *Western Europe: The Trials of Partnership,* Lexington Books (Lexington, MA), 1977.

Revolution in Time: Clocks and the Making of the Modern World, Harvard University Press (Cambridge, MA), 1983.

(Editor, with Patrice Higonnet and Henry Rosovsky) *Favorites of Fortune: Technology, Growth, and Economic Development since the Industrial Revolution,* Harvard University Press (Cambridge, MA), 1991.

La Favola del cavallo morto; ovvero, La Rivoluzione industriale revisitate, Donzelli Editore (Rome, Italy), 1994.

The Wealth and Poverty of Nations: Why Some Are So Rich and Some So Poor, W. W. Norton (New York, NY), 1998.

Also author of *A che servono i padroni: Le alternative storiche dell'industrializzazione,* Bollati Boringhieri (Turin, Italy). Contributor to books, including *Culture Matters: How Values Shape Human Progress,* edited by Lawrence E. Harrison and Samuel P. Huntington, Basic Books (New York, NY), 2000; and *The British Industrial Revolution: An Economic Perspective,* 2nd edition, edited by Joel Mokyr, Westview (Boulder, CO). Contributor to history journals. Associate editor, *Journal of Economic History,* 1954-60.

WORK IN PROGRESS: Dynasties: The Advantages and Disadvantages of Close Familiarity in Business.

SIDELIGHTS: David S. Landes's *The Unbound Prometheus: Technological Change and Industrial Development in Western Europe from 1750 to the Present* is "an indispensable reference guide . . . [which] offers a great deal more . . . [than] its deft synthesis of monographic and learned journal material, its resumes of the technical aspects of invention and industrial organization, and its marshaling of intelligently selected statistical data," wrote Theodore Roszak in the *Nation.* Landes, a former professor of economics and history at Harvard University, discusses in his book "a wide range of most important interpretive emphases on and insights into modern economic thought and scholarship," according to Roszak, while "the more technical features of industrialization are treated with admirable breadth . . . and the context of social and political history is never lost from sight." Roszak concluded that *The Unbound Prometheus* "fully deserves the place it is bound to hold for the next generation or more as a standard comparative study of industrial development in [Western Europe]."

Landes's later book, *Revolution in Time: Clocks and the Making of the Modern World,* reflects a similar comprehensiveness as the author examines the evolution of clocks and clock-making from a cultural, technological, and economic perspective, while discussing the impact that the discipline of timekeeping has had on civilization over the centuries. As Landes traces the cultural origins, technological advancements, and economic development of the clock, the focus of the book, noted E. J. Hobsbawm in the *New York Review of Books,* emerges as "the peculiar and revolutionary sense of time [the clock] made possible, established, and reflected [which] proved to be essential to modern capitalism, the first and still dominant form of industrial society." "The main subject," Hobsbawm continued, ". . . is the revolution in the world's capacity to produce . . . [and] the clock happens to be a superb way into this subject and its problems." In his introduction to the book, Landes describes *Revolution in Time* as "a first attempt at a general history of time measurement and its contribution, for better or worse, to what we call modern civilization."

In the first section of the book, which, as Philip Morrison pointed out in *Scientific American,* offers the author's discussion "of the enigmatic origins of the clock . . . in late medieval Europe," Landes suggests a connection between timekeeping, Christianity, and commerce in the West. Norman Stone in the London *Times* explained that "the regularity of time had already been much more evident in the medieval West than elsewhere, if only because monastic communities had to perform their prayers punctually . . . [and] as in other matters in the Middle Ages, there was a mysterious relationship of religion and commerce, which did not occur in other parts of the world." "The West," observed David Cannadine in the *London Review of Books,* "needed pervasive, public time: with the clock as with everything else, necessity was the mother of invention." As Landes unravels the beginnings of man's interest in regulating time, "this emerging punctuality," as Robert Coles in the *New Yorker* called it, "gets . . . an analysis worthy of its complex sources . . . in a splendidly erudite yet accessible series of chapters."

After discussing the cultural origins of regulating time and the emergence of the first timekeeping devices, Landes directs his attention to the scientific and technological history of clocks. Morrison describes this account as "the story of the 500 years of evolution from the heavy turret clocks to the chronometer and watches cheap and fine." The most notable developments in this history, as Coles relates, were "the emergence of the spring-driven clock (in the beginning of the fifteenth century) and the watch (toward the end of the century) [which] marked the onset of a new individualism." Cannadine found that "Landes's account of coiled springs, pendulums, minute and second hands, and jewelled bearings makes fascinating reading, and is peppered with a rich array of crackpot ideas, unscrupulous plagiarists, disputes about priority, unhonoured genius and the like." And, added the reviewer, the book demonstrates its author's "ability to write of technology, machinery and gadgetry with authority, enthusiasm and finesse." "[*Revolution in Time*] is a notable addition to the literature of science and technology," wrote Tracy Kidder in the *New York Times Book Review.*

In the final and largest section of the book, Landes traces the economic history of clocks and the clock industry, covering a time period of seven hundred years, from the invention of the clock to the modern "quartz revolution." Morrison called this "a major contribution to economic history for the general reader, graceful and full of wit, fresh and scrupulously documented." In Hobsbawm's opinion, the clock provides a model for studying economic development; he wrote, "the clock gave rise to an industry whose history encapsulates that of modern industrial development as a whole, including its shifts from one country to another." "Clocks are thus instruments for measuring not only time but history," Hobsbawm concluded. In following these shifts, "Landes has done a superb job in describing the development of the industry in Britain, France, the United States, Switzerland, and Japan," wrote John Kenneth Galbraith in the *New Republic.*

Cannadine found modern parallels to the stages of the clock industry presented by Landes, noting that the "account of British decline [in the clock industry] has a dismal and contemporary ring to it: high costs, conservative styling, obsolescent techniques, entrepreneurial complacency and resistance by labour to innovation." These developments foreshadow "The Quartz Revolution," the book's closing in which, according to Derek Howse in the *Washington Post,* "we see the beginnings of the decline of the mechanical timekeeper." While Cannadine detected a "sombre note" in "the demise of the clock as the supreme means of measuring time," there is also a sense of "success" at the end of the book "which finishes with the triumph of time: public and uniform, universal and irresistible."

A number of critics were impressed with Landes's achievements in *Revolution in Time.* Galbraith praised the book for its "meticulous" accounting of the "mechanical achievement and economic development" of the clock industry, and added that the book "is at its most fascinating when it takes leave of these matters to explore the whole range of religious, social, cultural, commercial, and industrial questions that derive from, or are associated with, the measurement of time." Hobsbawm called this study an "important contribution to the history of the rise and fortunes of capitalism, as well as to the comparative dynamics of societies." "Indeed," he continued, "anyone interested in the development, conflicts, and interactions of classes—nobility, bourgeoisie, craftsmen, proletariat—in European history might do well to start here." Howse believed that *Revolution in Time* will be of value to a wide audience, noting that "for the layman, the author has a particular talent for making technical matters seem simple [and] for the scholar, the references are impeccable and give evidence of deep study of the subject." "[Landes] has treated complex and difficult matters in a style that any educated person can appreciate, without the slightest hint of esotericism, professional display, or condescension," commented Hobsbawm. "Without a doubt," Howse concluded, "this book will become a standard work on the history of timekeeping—and it's fun to read."

BIOGRAPHICAL AND CRITICAL SOURCES:

PERIODICALS

London Review of Books, July 19, 1984, David Cannadine, review of *Revolution in Time: Clocks and the Making of the Modern World.*

Nation, November 24, 1969, Theodore Roszak, review of *The Unbound Prometheus: Technological Change and Industrial Development in Western Europe from 1750 to the Present.*

New Republic, October 10, 1983, John Kenneth Galbraith, review of *Revolution in Time.*

Newsweek, October 31, 1983.

New Yorker, September 24, 1984, Robert Coles, review of *Revolution in Time.*

New York Review of Books, December 8, 1983, E. J. Hobsbawm, review of *Revolution in Time.*

New York Times Book Review, October 23, 1983, Tracy Kidder, review of *Revolution in Time.*

Scientific American, April, 1984, Philip Morrison, review of *Revolution in Time.*

Times (London, England), August 9, 1984, Norman Stone, review of *Revolution in Time.*

Times Literary Supplement, April 6, 1984.

Washington Post, December 12, 1983, Derek Howse, review of *Revolution in Time.*

* * *

LANDY, Marcia 1931-

PERSONAL: Born June 24, 1931, in Cleveland, OH; daughter of Isidore and Goldie (Baratz) Kanevsky. *Ethnicity:* "Caucasian." *Education:* Ohio University, A.B., 1953; University of Rochester, M.A., 1961, Ph. D., 1962.

ADDRESSES: Home—2307 Pittock St., Pittsburgh, PA 15217. *Office*—Department of English, 526 AH, University of Pittsburgh, Pittsburgh, PA 15260; fax: 412-624-6639. *E-mail*—mlandyt@pitt.edu.

CAREER: University of Pittsburgh, Pittsburgh, PA, began as assistant professor, became professor of English and film studies, 1967—, distinguished service professor, 1998.

MEMBER: Modern Language Association of America, Society for Cinema Studies, AAIS.

WRITINGS:

Fascism in Film, Princeton University Press (Princeton, NJ), 1986.

British Genres, Princeton University Press (Princeton, NJ), 1991.

Imitations of Life, Wayne State University Press (Detroit, MI), 1991.

Queen Christina, British Film Institute (London, England), 1996.

Cinematic Uses of the Past, University of Minnesota Press (Minneapolis, MN), 1997.

The Folklore of Consensus, State University of New York Press (Albany, NY), 1998.

Italian Film, Cambridge University Press (New York, NY), 2000.

(Editor and author of introduction) *The Historical Film: History and Memory in Media,* Rutgers University Press (New Brunswick, NJ), 2001.

Also author of *Film, Politics, and Gramsci,* University of Minnesota Press (Minneapolis, MN).

BIOGRAPHICAL AND CRITICAL SOURCES:

PERIODICALS

Choice, September, 2000, S. Vander Closter, review of *Italian Film,* p. 136.

Film Quarterly, fall, 2001, John David Rhodes, review of *Italian Film,* p. 64.

Public Historian, winter, 2002, Thomas Cripps, review of *The Historical Film: History and Memory in Media,* p. 103.

Publishers Weekly, June 5, 2000, review of *Italian Film,* p. 86.

Quarterly Review of Film and Video, April, 2002, Philip Mosley, review of *The Historical Film,* p. 187.

* * *

LaPIERRE, Laurier L. 1929-

PERSONAL: Born November 21, 1929, in Lac Megantic, Quebec, Canada; son of Lionel and Aldora (Bilodeau) LaPierre; married Paula Armstrong, May 28, 1960 (divorced); children: Dominic, Thomas. *Education:* University of Toronto, B.A., 1955, M.A., 1957,

Ph.D., 1962; University of Prince Edward Island, LL. D., 1970. *Politics:* "No one knows!" *Religion:* "A distant Roman Catholic." *Hobbies and other interests:* "I cook to survive and I garden because I am."

ADDRESSES: Home—285 Fairmond Ave., Ottawa, Ontario K1Y 1Y4, Canada. *Agent*—Westwood Creative Artists, 94 Harbord St., Toronto, Ontario M5S 1G6, Canada. *E-mail*—laurier.lapierre@sympatico.ca.

CAREER: Educator and author. University of Regina, Regina, Saskatchewan, Canada, Bell Professor of Journalism; University of Western Ontario, London, Ontario, Canada, lecturer, 1960-62; McGill University, Toronto, Ontario, Canada, lecturer, 1963-64, became associate professor of history, beginning 1965, became director of French-Canadian studies program; Telefilm Canada, chair, until 2000; Canadian Senate, Ottawa, Ontario, senator, 2000—. *La Saberdache Quebeçoise* (collection), director. Host of radio and television programs, including *This Hour Has Seven Days* and *LaPierre;* moderator of the Radio-Quebec television series *En se racontant l'histoire d'ici;* Station CKVU, Vancouver, British Columbia, Canada, commentator and programmer. Former director of the Spicer Commission and moderator of Citizen's Forum.

AWARDS, HONORS: Named officer, Order of Canada, 1994.

WRITINGS:

(Editor) *Four o'Clock Lectures: French-Canadian Thinkers of the Nineteenth and Twentieth Centuries,* McGill University Press (Montreal, Quebec, Canada), 1966.

Genesis of a Nation: British North America, 1776-1867 (radio script), International Service, Canadian Broadcasting Corp. (Toronto, Ontario, Canada), 1966.

The Apprenticeship: Canada from Confederation to the Eve of the First World War (radio script), International Service, Canadian Broadcasting Corp. (Toronto, Ontario, Canada), 1967.

(Editor) *Québec: Hier et aujourd'hui,* Macmillan (Toronto, Ontario, Canada), 1967.

(Editor) *Essays on the Left: Essays in Honor of T. C. Douglas,* McClelland & Stewart (Toronto, Ontario, Canada), 1971.

(Editor) *If You Love This Country: Facts and Feelings on Free Trade,* McClelland & Stewart (Toronto, Ontario, Canada), 1987.

1759: The Battle for Canada, McClelland & Stewart (Toronto, Ontario, Canada), 1990.

Canada, My Canada: What Happened?, McClelland & Stewart (Toronto, Ontario, Canada), 1992.

Sir Wilfrid Laurier and the Romance of Canada, Stoddart (Toronto, Ontario, Canada), 1996.

Québec: A Tale of Love, Penguin Books Canada (Toronto, Ontario, Canada), 2001.

WORK IN PROGRESS: Vancouver: A Tale of a City; The Spinning Wheel: The War of the Iroquois from the Founding of Quebec to the American Revolution.

SIDELIGHTS: Canadian historian, writer, educator, and broadcaster Laurier L. LaPierre once stated that the reason he wrote and was concerned about history was that his fellow Canadians refused "to share common history" and that he wanted them to feel it with more emotion, rather than see it in strictly political terms. Although a history professor at Canadian institutions such as McGill University, LaPierre has found time to devote to his side projects, which include radio and television programs and numerous historical and politically oriented books. In his works, such as a biography about his namesake and former Canadian Prime Minister Sir Wilfrid Laurier, the recurring theme has been that there is a need for a truer Canadian nationalism. Many critics have commented that LaPierre's entertaining narrative has set his works apart from many books of history, which, while deserving merit, tend to bore the reader.

In 1987 LaPierre edited a book titled *If You Love This Country: Facts and Feelings on Free Trade,* which includes essays by more than forty prominent Canadians, all of whom opposed the free-trade pact with the United States being negotiated at the time. People such as Margaret Atwood, Frank Stronach, David Suzuki, and Peter Newman list various reasons why free trade would be problematic for their country, and describe how economic, social, cultural, and political issues would be impacted if such a deal were struck. "Canada is not just a blot on the map. It is a country. It is a land. It is the sum total of our willingness to live in Canada and to be of it in order to build a society which is just and sane and capable of making a distinct contribution to the peaceful evolution of mankind,"

LaPierre wrote in the introduction. Many reviewers who read the book were impressed with its broad scope. In *Books in Canada* George Grant wrote, "Taken all in all, this is a powerful statement of what a turning point the free-trade deal will be in Canadian life." *Quill & Quire* contributor Allan Gould, who expressed a fear of American expansionism himself, wrote that *If You Love This Country* "managed to capture [Canadians'] most profoundly felt fears of being eaten alive by gun-toting, money-grubbing, porno-and-violence-ridden vandals from the south." However, David Frum of *Saturday Night* believed that some of the criticism exaggerated the threats posed by free trade. *If You Love This Country,* he wrote, "preserves forever the tone and mood of the country's protectionist intellectuals. Some of that tone and mood is, frankly, a little nutty." Feeling that some of the essays were not of an objective voice, Frum went on to note, "Despite its . . . promises of facts as well as feelings, *If You Love This Country* tells us very little of what is known to be true about the free-trade deal with the United States, and considerably too much of what is known positively to be not true."

In *1759: The Battle for Canada,* LaPierre writes about the most significant event in Canada's history—the British defeat of the French at Quebec during the French and Indian War—and incorporated modern television news techniques into his approach. He wrote from the perspective of a journalist who was at the scene of the events, interviewing historical characters and personalities as they were in the process of making history. Peter C. Newman, reviewing the book for *Maclean's,* wrote that the climactic battle and surrounding events are "made understandable at last." He noted that LaPierre's method is "an exciting new way of recounting history." However, in *Quill & Quire,* W. J. Eccles expressed concern with LaPierre's lack of source citation. Eccles wrote that without such citation, "the unwary reader has no way of knowing what is based on sound evidence and what is a flight of fancy." "In short," Eccles wrote, "this book is not history, but fiction."

When LaPierre was the director of the Spicer Commission, he moderated the Citizen's Forum, which enabled him to travel throughout Canada and meet many of the citizens who attended the events and voiced their opinions about national issues. LaPierre became disenchanted with the general negativity and ignorance he found along the way. As a result, he wrote *Canada, My Canada: What Happened?* In the book, LaPierre covers the breadth of pivotal events and the different peoples who have shaped and forged Canada into the country it is today. Covering a span of 10,000 years, he includes the arrival of the First Nations (Indians), Europeans, and all that have come after. Reviewing the book for *Canadian Materials,* Louise Dick commended it as an "intensely personal interpretation of Canadian history." She stated that *Canada, My Canada* was "not a formal history but a personal statement." *Quill & Quire* reviewer Carol Goar wrote that "LaPierre's style is expansive, colorful, flamboyant," adding, "LaPierre is too much of a storyteller to be a pure historian. The result is a thoroughly engaging book."

In the biography *Sir Wilfrid Laurier and the Romance of Canada,* LaPierre argues that Laurier, Canada's prime minister from 1896 to 1911, is much more than just the face on the Canadian five-dollar bill. "For his life to have any value in our day, I must, as much as possible, rediscover him in the intimacy of his soul," LaPierre writes in the introduction. In the picture which LaPierre paints, Laurier was the instrumental figure who was responsible for convincing the people that they could see themselves as Canadians rather than as British subjects. A self-confessed admirer of Laurier, LaPierre believes the statesman ranks with Sir John A. Macdonald, considered the father of Canadian Confederacy. John Bemrose of *Maclean's* felt LaPierre captured the essence of Canadian pride which the critic felt was lacking in these modern days. Within the pages of *Siir Wilfrid Laurier and the Romance of Canada,* Bemrose wrote, "is a sense of the land, as much ideal as reality, that many Canadians would love to recapture in these cynical times." Although Bemrose noted that LaPierre "has not discovered anything startlingly new about his hero," he thought it gave a "fresh view" of Laurier. In *Canadian Forum,* Kevin Burns noted that one of the book's strengths was its incorporation of some of Laurier's speeches, but believed that LaPierre could have gone a bit further to connect with today's reader. However, he felt that, overall, the book was engaging and that "LaPierre's Laurier emerges as a complicated, energizing force, an uncommon hero." In *Quill & Quire* Bob Rae commented, "LaPierre is a shrewd as well as a passionate observer."

LaPierre once told *CA:* "I have to write for it is divine! But I hate reviews. I find often that some of my reviewers have reviewed the book they wanted to write or have written! Too bad!

"I write to tell the people of my country that Canada is worth loving and cherishing; that it is an experience in human living; and that it is a prototype of the political ensembles of the twenty-first century. The twentieth century indeed belonged to Canada—the twenty-first will see us at the center of human life on the planet. We have to be prepared.

"Vive le Canada!"

BIOGRAPHICAL AND CRITICAL SOURCES:

BOOKS

LaPierre, Laurier L., *1759: The Battle for Canada,* McClelland & Stewart (Toronto, Ontario, Canada), 1990.

LaPierre, Laurier L., editor, *If You Love this Country: Facts and Feelings on Free Trade,* McClelland & Stewart (Toronto, Ontario, Canada), 1987.

PERIODICALS

Beaver: Exploring Canada's History, April-May, 1997, p. 38.

Books in Canada, January-February, 1988, George Grant, review of *If You Love This Country,* pp. 18-19; March, 1991, p. 49; February, 1993, p. 28.

Canadian Forum, September, 1995, p. 40; April, 1997, Kevin Burns, review of *Sir Wilfrid Laurier and the Romance of Canada,* pp. 46-47.

Canadian Materials, May, 1988, p. 105; January, 1993, Louise Dick, review of *Canada, My Canada: What Happened?,* p. 32.

Catholic Insight, May, 2002, "Marriage under Attack," p. 29.

Choice, April, 1967, p. 216.

Maclean's, November 26, 1990, Peter C. Newman, review of *1759: The Battle for Canada,* p. 52; February 11, 1991, p. 50; May 20, 1991, p. 52; January 13, 1997, John Bemrose, review of *Sir Wilfred Laurier and the Romance of Canada,* p. 65; October 1, 2001, Allan Fotheringham, "The Senate's New Boy," p. 88.

Queen's Quarterly, winter, 1988, p. 881.

Quill & Quire, February, 1988, Allan Gould, review of *If You Love This Country,* pp. 24-25; November, 1990, W. J. Eccles, review of *1759,* p. 24; October, 1992, Carol Goar, review of *Canada, My Canada,* p. 25; November, 1996, Bob Rae, review of *Sir Wilfrid Laurier and the Romance of Canada,* p. 34.

Saturday Night, April, 1988, David Frum, review of *If You Love This Country,* pp. 61-63.

* * *

LAYTON, Irving (Peter) 1912-

PERSONAL: Original surname, Lazarovitch; name legally changed; born March 12, 1912, in Neamtz, Romania; immigrated to Canada, 1913; son of Moses and Keine (a grocery store operator; maiden name, Moscovitch) Lazarovitch; married Faye Lynch, September 13, 1938 (marriage ended); married Frances Sutherland, September 13, 1946 (marriage ended); married Aviva Cantor (a writer of children's stories), September 13, 1961 (marriage ended); married Harriet Bernstein (a publicist; divorced, March 19, 1984); married Anna Pottier, November 8, 1984; children: (second marriage) Max Rubin, Naomi Parker; (third marriage) David Herschel; (fourth marriage) Samantha Clara. *Education:* McDonald College, B.S., 1939; McGill University, M.A., 1946.

ADDRESSES: Home—6879 Monkland Ave., Montreal, Quebec H4B 1J5, Canada. *Agent*—Lucinda Vardey Agency, 297 Seaton St., Toronto M5A 2T6, Canada.

CAREER: Jewish Public Library, Montreal, Quebec, Canada, lecturer, 1943-58; high school teacher in Montreal, 1945-60; Sir George Williams University (now Sir George Williams Campus of Concordia University), Montreal, lecturer, 1949-65, poet in residence, 1965-69; University of Guelph, Guelph, Ontario, Canada, poet in residence, 1969-70; York University, Toronto, Ontario, Canada, professor of English literature, 1970-78; poet. University of Ottawa, poet in residence, 1978; Concordia University, Montreal, poet in residence at Sir George Williams Campus, 1978, adjunct professor, 1988, writer in residence, 1989; University of Toronto, writer in residence, 1981. *Military service:* Canadian Army, Artillery, 1942-43; became lieutenant.

MEMBER: PEN, Canadian Civil Liberties Union, Istituto Pertini (Florence, Italy; honorary member).

AWARDS, HONORS: Canada Foundation fellow, 1957; Governor-General's Award, 1959, for *A Red Carpet for the Sun;* Canada Council, awards, 1959 and 1960, Special Arts Award, 1963 and 1968, senior arts fellowship and travel grant, 1973 and 1979, long term arts award, 1979-81; President's Medal, University of Western Ontario, 1961, for poem "Keine Lazarovitch 1870-1959"; Prix Litteraire de Quebec, 1963, for *Balls for a One-Armed Juggler;* Centennial Medal, 1967; D.C.L., Bishops University, 1970, and Concordia University, 1976; member of Order of Canada, 1976; Life Achievement Award, *Encyclopedia Brittanica,* 1978; nominated for Nobel Prize by Italy and South Korea, 1982, again by Italy, 1983.

WRITINGS:

POETRY, EXCEPT AS INDICATED

Here and Now, First Statement (Montreal, Quebec, Canada), 1945.

Now Is the Place (poetry and short stories), First Statement (Montreal, Quebec, Canada), 1948.

The Black Huntsmen, privately printed, 1951.

Love the Conqueror Worm, Contact (Toronto, Ontario, Canada), 1951.

(With Louis Dudek and Raymond Souster) *Cerberus,* Contact (Toronto, Ontario, Canada), 1952.

In the Midst of My Fever, Divers (Palma de Mallorca, Spain), 1954.

The Long Peashooter, Laocoon (Boulder, CO), 1954.

The Cold Green Element, Contact (Toronto, Ontario, Canada), 1955, Italian translation from the English published as *Il Freddo verde elemente,* Editore Einaudi (Turin, Italy), 1974.

The Blue Propeller, Contact (Toronto, Ontario, Canada), 1955.

The Bull Calf, Contact (Toronto, Ontario, Canada), 1956.

Music on a Kazoo, Contact (Toronto, Ontario, Canada), 1956.

The Improved Binoculars, introduction by William Carlos Williams, J. Williams (Highlands, NC), 1956.

A Laughter in the Mind, J. Williams (Highland, NC), 1958.

A Red Carpet for the Sun, McClelland & Stewart (Toronto, Ontario, Canada), 1959.

The Swinging Flesh (poetry and short stories), McClelland & Stewart (Toronto, Ontario, Canada), 1961.

Balls for a One-Armed Juggler, McClelland & Stewart (Toronto, Ontario, Canada), 1963.

The Laughing Rooster, McClelland & Stewart (Toronto, Ontario, Canada), 1964.

Collected Poems, McClelland & Stewart (Toronto, Ontario, Canada), 1965.

Periods of the Moon, McClelland & Stewart (Toronto, Ontario, Canada), 1967.

The Shattered Plinths, McClelland & Stewart (Toronto, Ontario, Canada), 1968.

Selected Poems, McClelland & Stewart (Toronto, Ontario, Canada), 1969.

The Whole Bloody Bird: Obs, Aphs, and Pomes, McClelland & Stewart (Toronto, Ontario, Canada), 1969.

Nail Polish, McClelland & Stewart (Toronto, Ontario, Canada), 1971.

The Collected Poems of Irving Layton, McClelland & Stewart (Toronto, Ontario, Canada), 1971.

Lovers and Lesser Men, McClelland & Stewart (Toronto, Ontario, Canada), 1973.

The Pole-Vaulter, McClelland & Stewart (Toronto, Ontario, Canada), 1974.

Seventy-five Greek Poems, McClelland & Stewart (Toronto, Ontario, Canada), 1974.

The Darkening Fire: Selected Poems, 1945-1968, McClelland & Stewart (Toronto, Ontario, Canada), 1975.

The Unwavering Eye: Selected Poems, 1969-1975, McClelland & Stewart (Toronto, Ontario, Canada), 1975.

For My Brother Jesus, McClelland & Stewart (Toronto, Ontario, Canada), 1976.

The Covenant, McClelland & Stewart (Toronto, Ontario, Canada), 1977.

The Collected Poems of Irving Layton, McClelland & Stewart (Toronto, Ontario, Canada), 1977.

The Uncollected Poems of Irving Layton, 1936-1959, Mosaic Press (Oakville, Ontario, Canada), 1977.

The Selected Poems of Irving Layton, New Directions Publishing (New York, NY), 1977.

The Tightrope Dancer, McClelland & Stewart (Toronto, Ontario, Canada), 1978.

(With Carlo Mattioli) *Irving Layton, Carlo Mattioli,* Edizioni (Milan, Italy), 1978.

The Love Poems of Irving Layton, (deluxe edition), McClelland & Stewart (Toronto, Ontario, Canada), 1979, regular edition, 1980.

Droppings from Heaven, McClelland & Stewart (Toronto, Ontario, Canada), 1979.

For My Neighbors in Hell, Mosaic Press (Oakville, Ontario, Canada), 1980.

Europe and Other Bad News, McClelland & Stewart (Toronto, Ontario, Canada), 1981.

In un'eta di ghiaccio (bilingual; title means "In an Ice Age"), 1981.

A Wild Peculiar Joy, McClelland & Stewart (Toronto, Ontario, Canada), 1982.

Shadows on the Ground (portfolio), Valley Editions (Oakville, Ontario, Canada), 1982.

The Gucci Bag, Mosaic Press (Oakville, Ontario, Canada), 1983.

The Love Poems of Irving Layton, with Reverence and Delight, Valley Editions (Oakville, Ontario, Canada), 1984, reprinted, 2003.

A Spider Danced a Cosy Jig, Stoddart (Toronto, Ontario, Canada), 1984.

(With Salvatore Fiume) *A Tall Man Executes a Jig* (portfolio), 1985.

Selected Poems, [Seoul, South Korea], 1985.

Where Burning Sappho Loved, [Athens, Greece], 1985.

Dance with Desire: Love Poems, McClelland & Stewart (Toronto, Ontario, Canada), 1986, revised edition published as *Dance with Desire: Selected Love Poems,* Porcupine's Quill (Erin, Ontario, Canada), 1993, bilingual Italian-English edition published as *Danza di desiderio,* Editore Piovan (Albano, Italy), 1993.

Final Reckoning: Poems, 1982-1986, Valley Editions (Oakville, Ontario, Canada), 1987.

Fortunate Exile, McClelland & Stewart (Toronto, Ontario, Canada), 1987.

A Wild Peculiar Joy: Selected Poems, 1945-1989, McClelland & Stewart (Toronto, Ontario, Canada), 1989.

Tutto sommato poesie, 1945-1988 (bilingual Italian-English edition), 1989.

Fornalutx: Selected Poems, 1928-1990, McGill-Queen's University Press (Kingston, Ontario, Canada), 1992.

Il Cacciatore sconcertato (bilingual Italian-English edition), Longo (Ravenna, Italy), 1993.

NONFICTION

Engagements: The Prose of Irving Layton, edited by Seymour Mayne, McClelland & Stewart (Toronto, Ontario, Canada), 1972.

Taking Sides (prose), McClelland & Stewart (Toronto, Ontario, Canada), 1977.

(With Dorothy Rath) *An Unlikely Affair: The Irving Layton-Dorothy Rath Correspondence,* Valley Editions (Oakville, Ontario, Canada), 1980.

(With David O'Rourke) *Waiting for the Messiah: A Memoir,* McClelland & Stewart (Toronto, Ontario, Canada), 1985.

Wild Gooseberries: Selected Letters of Irving Layton, 1939-89, edited by Francis Mansbridge, Macmillan (New York, NY), 1989.

(With Robert Creeley) *Irving Layton & Robert Creeley: The Complete Correspondence,* University of Toronto Press (Toronto, Ontario, Canada), 1990.

EDITOR

(With Louis Dudek) *Canadian Poems, 1850-1952,* Contact (Toronto, Ontario, Canada), 1952, 2nd edition, 1953.

Pan-ic: A Selection of Contemporary Canadian Poems, Alan Brilliant, 1958.

(And author of introduction) *Poems for Twenty-seven Cents,* [Montreal, Quebec, Canada], 1961.

Love Where the Nights Are Long: Canadian Love Poems, McClelland & Stewart (Toronto, Ontario, Canada), 1962.

Anvil: A Selection of Workshop Poems, [Montreal, Quebec, Canada], 1966.

(And author of introduction) *Anvil Blood: A Selection of Workshop Poems,* [Toronto, Ontario, Canada], 1973.

Shark Tank, [Toronto, Ontario, Canada], 1977.

Rawprint, Workshop, Concordia University (Montreal, Quebec, Canada), 1989.

Poetry represented in numerous anthologies, including, *Book of Canadian Poetry,* edited by A. J. M. Smith, Gage (Toronto, Ontario, Canada), 1948; *Oxford Book of Canadian Verse,* edited by A. J. M. Smith, Oxford University Press (New York, NY), 1960; *How Do I Love Thee: Sixty Poets of Canada (and Quebec) Select and Introduce Their Favourite Poems from Their Own Work,* edited by John Robert Colombo, M. G. Hurtig (Edmonton, Alberta, Canada), 1970; and *Irving Layton/Aligi Sassu Portfolio,* 1978. Author of introduction, *Poems to Colour: A Selection of Workshop Poems,* York University (Downsview, Ontario, Canada), 1970. Contributor of poetry to various periodicals, including *Poetry, Canadian Forum,* and *Sail.*

Fiction represented in anthologies, including *Book of Canadian Stories,* edited by D. Pacey, Ryerson (Toronto, Ontario, Canada), 1950; and *Canadian Short*

Stories, edited by R. Weaver and H. James, Oxford University Press (New York, NY), 1952. Contributor of short stories to periodicals.

Cofounder and editor, *First Statement* and *Northern Review,* between 1941 and 1943; associate editor, *Contact,* 1952-54; past associate editor, *Black Mountain Review,* and several other magazines.

Layton's writings have been translated into more than ten languages, including Italian and Spanish. His papers are housed at the library of Concordia University, Montreal, Quebec, Canada.

ADAPTATIONS: Layton's poetry has been released on several audio recordings.

SIDELIGHTS: A controversial and outspoken literary figure, Irving Layton is known for writing energetic, passionate, and often angry verse. In an attempt to "disturb the accumulated complacencies of people," Layton confronts what he views as sources of evil in the twentieth century, suggesting that these "malignant forces" have contributed to moral and cultural decay in the modern world. A prolific writer, Layton has published nearly fifty volumes of poetry in as many years, with verse ranging, as noted Canadian critic George Woodcock wrote in his book *Odysseus Ever Returning: Essays on Canadian Writers and Writing,* "from the atrocious to the excellent."

Layton was born in Romania to Jewish parents and immigrated to Canada with his family at age one. His father Moses was a religious man whom Layton has described as "a visionary, a scholar"; his mother, Keine, supported the family by running a small grocery store. In 1939 Layton received a bachelor's degree from McDonald College, and in 1946 he earned a master's degree in economics and political science from McGill University. While living in Montreal in the early 1940s, Layton, along with Louis Dudek and John Sutherland, began editing *First Statement;* some of his earliest poems were published in this literary journal which highlighted the work of young Canadian writers and emphasized the social and political aspects of Canadian life. Layton published his first volume of poetry, *Here and Now,* in 1945. His earliest volumes met with minimal success, but in the 1950s, according to Ira Bruce Nadel in the *Dictionary of Literary Biography,* "Layton discovered a voice that could unite his skeptical vision and energetic, provocative language." *A Red Carpet for the Sun,* which included some of his best-known poems from previous volumes, proved to be his first major success, earning him popular praise as well as the Governor-General's Award for Poetry in 1959. At this time he became what Tom Marshall called in *Harsh and Lovely Land* an "unusual phenomenon—a genuinely popular poet." Layton went on to write several more collections of verse over the next thirty years, maintaining a consistent thematic approach as well as exhibiting a forthright and contentious public personality.

Many critics have discussed Layton as a romantic poet in the tradition of William Blake and Walt Whitman; he explores elemental passions, exalts the individual—particularly the poet—and examines the relationship between the physical and the spiritual. In his works he rails against social injustice, identifying keenly with the helpless and innocent; as a result many of his poems feature images of trapped and wounded animals. Constituting a significant portion of his oeuvre, his love lyrics—sensual, erotic, and explicitly sexual—are intended to shock a Puritanical society, and their effectiveness is due in part to the juxtaposition of images of love and beauty with those of violence and death. Thus, in his poetry of liberation, Layton challenges what he views as the unhealthy gentility and complacency of Canadian society. A number of Layton's poems deal with his approach to religion. Layton's view of organized religion as a source of evil and corruption dating from ancient times to the present day has aroused controversy among his readers. Particularly controversial are some of the poems in *For My Brother Jesus* in which he suggests that, "by publicizing a stereotype of the Jew for nearly two thousand years," Christendom "prepared the soil on which the death camps and the crematoria could spring-up and flourish." Layton explores the horrors of the Holocaust in a number of works, including "For Anne Frank" and "The Final Solution." Commentators noted that, beginning with *Balls for a One-Armed Juggler,* Layton became increasingly concerned with addressing what he has described as "the exceptionally heinous nature of twentieth-century evil," citing the Holocaust as a primary example. He offers poetry as a means of salvation, however, and asserts that the poet has an obligation to address social ills in an attempt to counteract corruption, greed, and complacency.

A number of critics have commented on Layton's poetic mission. Several commentators, however, praised Layton's vitality, power, and range. While many critics acknowledge Layton's role in broadening Canadian literary standards to include sexually explicit imagery, his erotic love poetry—and his views on women in general—have aroused considerable indignation. Some scholars asserted that his love poems do not, as Layton has asserted, celebrate sexual love. Many of Layton's love poems are collected in *Dance with Desire,* published in 1986 and in a revised edition in 1993.

Layton once told *CA:* "One of my sisters thought I should be a plumber or an electrician; another saw in me the ability to become a peddler; my third and oldest sister was sure I was devious and slippery enough to make a fine lawyer or politician. My mother, presiding over these three witches, pointed to the fly-spotted ceiling, indicating God by that gesture, and said, 'He will be what the Almighty wants him to be.'

"My devout mother turned out to be right. From earliest childhood I longed to match sounds with sense; and when I was older, to make music out of words. Everywhere I went, mystery dogged my steps. The skinny dead rat in the lane, the fire that broke out in our house on Sabbath eve, the energy that went with cruelty and the power that went with hate. The empty sky had no answers for my queries and the stars at night only winked and said nothing.

"I wrote my first poem for a teacher who was astonishingly beautiful. For weeks I mentally drooled over the white cleavage she had carelessly exposed to a precocious eleven-year-old. So there it was: the two grand mysteries of sexuality and death. I write because I'm driven to say something about them, to celebrate what my limited brain cannot comprehend. To rejoice in my more arrogant moods to think the Creator Himself doesn't comprehend His handiwork. I write because the only solace He has in His immense and eternal solitude are the poems and stories that tell Him—like all creators, He too is hungry for praise—how exciting and beautiful, how majestic and terrible are His works and to give Him an honest, up-to-date report on His most baffling creation, Man. I know whenever I put in a good word for the strange biped He made, God's despair is lessened. Ultimately, I write because I am less cruel than He is."

BIOGRAPHICAL AND CRITICAL SOURCES:

BOOKS

Bennet, Joy, and James Polson, *Irving Layton: A Bibliography, 1934-1977,* Concordia University Libraries (Montreal, Quebec, Canada), 1979.

Burgess, G. C. Ian, *Irving Layton's Poetry: A Catalogue and Chronology,* McGill University (Montreal, Quebec, Canada), 1974.

Cameron, Elspeth, *Irving Layton: A Portrait,* Stoddart (Toronto, Ontario, Canada), 1985.

Contemporary Literary Criticism, Gale (Detroit, MI), Volume 2, 1974, Volume 15, 1980.

Dictionary of Literary Biography, Volume 88: *Canadian Writers, 1920-1959, Second Series,* Gale (Detroit, MI), 1989.

Dudek, Louis, *Selected Essays and Criticism,* Tecumseh Press (Ottawa, Ontario, Canada), 1978.

Francis, Wynne, *Irving Layton and His Works,* ECW Press (Toronto, Ontario, Canada), 1984.

Layton, Irving, *For My Brother Jesus,* McClelland & Stewart (Toronto, Ontario, Canada), 1976.

Layton, Irving and David O'Rourke, *Waiting for the Messiah: A Memoir,* McClelland & Stewart (Toronto, Ontario, Canada), 1985.

Mandel, Eli, *Irving Layton,* Forum House Publishing (Toronto, Ontario, Canada), 1969, revised edition published as *The Poetry of Layton,* 1981.

Marshall, Tom, *Harsh and Lovely Land,* University of British Columbia Press (Vancouver, British Columbia, Canada), 1979.

Mayne, Seymour, editor, *Irving Layton: The Poet and His Critics,* McGraw Hill/Ryerson Press (Toronto, Ontario, Canada), 1978.

Meyer, Bruce, and Brian O'Riordan, *In Their Words: Interviews with Fourteen Canadian Writers,* House of Anansi Press (Toronto, Ontario, Canada), 1984.

Rizzardi, Alfredo, editor, *Italian Critics on Irving Layton,* Editore Piovan (Albano, Italy), 1988.

Woodcock, George, *Odysseus Ever Returning: Essays on Canadian Writers and Writing,* McClelland & Stewart (Toronto, Ontario, Canada), 1970, pp. 76-92.

PERIODICALS

Books in Canada, April, 1993, p. 54; March, 2003, Chris Jennings, review of *The Love Poems of Irving Layton, with Reverence and Delight,* pp. 39-40.

Canadian Forum, June, 1969; February-March, 1989, p. 28.

Canadian Literature, autumn, 1962, pp. 21-34; spring, 1972, pp. 102-104; autumn, 1972, pp. 70-83; winter, 1973, pp. 12-13, 18; winter, 1980, pp. 52-65; autumn, 1992, p. 138; autumn, 1993, p. 150.

Fiddlehead, spring, 1967; summer, 1967.
Maclean's, November 19, 1990, p. 45.
Mosaic, January, 1968, pp. 103-111.
New Republic, July 2, 1977.
New York Times Book Review, October 9, 1977.
Queen's Quarterly, winter, 1955-1956, pp. 587-591.
Quill & Quire, July, 1993, p. 46.
Record (Sherbrooke, Quebec, Canada), November 2, 1984.
Saturday Night, April, 1988, p. 59; March, 1996, p. 32.
Village Voice, March 31, 1966.
Waves, winter, 1987, pp. 4-13.*

OTHER

Poet: Irving Layton Observed (video cassette), directed by Donald Winkler, National Film Board of Canada, 1986.
A Tall Man Executes a Jig (video cassette; documentary on Layton), directed by Donald Winkler, National Film Board of Canada, 1986.

* * *

Stan Lee

LEE, Stan 1922-

PERSONAL: Born Stanley Martin Lieber, December 28, 1922, in New York, NY; name legally changed; son of Jack (a dress cutter) and Celia (Solomon) Lieber; married Joan Clayton Boocock, December 5, 1947; children: Joan C., Jan (deceased). *Education:* Attended high school in New York, NY.

ADDRESSES: *Home*—Los Angeles, CA. *Office*—Marvel Enterprises, 10 East 40th St., New York, NY 10016.

CAREER: Comic-book writer, editor, publishing executive, and film and television producer. Timely Comics (then Atlas Comics; now Marvel Comics), New York, NY, editorial assistant and copywriter, 1939-42, editor, 1942-72, publisher and editorial director, 1972—; associated with Marvel Productions, Los Angeles, CA. Adjunct professor of popular culture at Bowling Green State University; gives lectures on college campuses. Film appearances include as a hot dog vendor in *X-Men,* Twentieth Century-Fox, 2000; as a bystander in Times Square in *Spider-Man,* Columbia, 2002; as himself in *Mallrats,* Gramercy, 1995; and in shorts and cameo appearances. Narrator and voice-over actor for animated series based on Marvel Comics, including *Spider-Man and His Amazing Friends,* NBC, 1981; *The Incredible Hulk,* NBC, 1982; *The Fantastic Four,* syndicated, 1994; *Iron Man,* syndicated, 1994; and *Spider-Man,* Fox, 1994. Film and television producer; executive producer on films such as *Captain America,* Columbia, 1991; *Blade,* New Line Cinema, 1998; *X-Men,* 2000; and *Spider-Man,* 2002. Executive producer of television series, including *Biker Mice from Mars,* syndicated, 1993; *Silver Surfer,* Fox, 1998; *The Avengers,* Fox, 1999; and *X-Men: Evolution,* WB, 2000. His character Stripperella debuted in an animated feature, 2003. *Military service:* U.S. Army, 1942-45; became sergeant.

MEMBER: American Federation of Television and Radio Artists, National Academy of Television Arts and Sciences, National Cartoonists Society, Academy of Comic Book Arts (founder and president), Friars Club.

AWARDS, HONORS: Six Alley awards, 1963-68; award from Society for Comic Art Research and

Preservation, 1968; Eureka Award, *Il Targa* (Milan, Italy), 1970, for world's best comic writing; annual award from Popular Culture Association, 1974; publisher of the year award from Periodical and Book Association of America, 1978; award from Academy of Comic Book Arts; honorary degree from Bowling Green State University.

WRITINGS:

(With John Buscema) *How to Draw Comics the Marvel Way,* Simon & Schuster (New York, NY), 1978.

Dunn's Conundrum (novel), Harper & Row (New York, NY), 1985.

The GOD Project (novel), Grove & Weidenfeld (New York, NY), 1990.

(With George Mair) *Excelsior! The Amazing Life of Stan Lee* (autobiography), Simon & Schuster (New York, NY), 2002.

COMIC BOOKS AND GRAPHIC NOVELS

The Mighty Thor, illustrated by Jack Kirby, Lancer Books (New York, NY), 1966.

Spider-Man Collector's Album, illustrated by Steve Ditko, Lancer Books (New York, NY), 1966.

Origins of Marvel Comics, Simon & Schuster (New York, NY), 1974.

Son of Origins of Marvel Comics, Simon & Schuster (New York, NY), 1975.

Bring on the Bad Guys: Origins of Marvel Villains, Simon & Schuster (New York, NY), 1976.

The Superhero Women, Simon & Schuster (New York, NY), 1977.

The Best of Spidey Super Stories, Simon & Schuster (New York, NY), 1978.

(With John Buscema) *How to Draw Comics the Marvel Way,* Simon & Schuster (New York, NY), 1978.

The Incredible Hulk, Simon & Schuster (New York, NY), 1978.

The Silver Surfer, illustrated by Jack Kirby, Simon & Schuster (New York, NY), 1978.

Marvel's Greatest Superhero Battles, Simon & Schuster (New York, NY), 1978.

Doctor Strange, Simon & Schuster (New York, NY), 1979.

The Fantastic Four, Simon & Schuster (New York, NY), 1979.

Captain America, Simon & Schuster (New York, NY), 1979.

Stan Lee Presents the Best of the Worst, Harper (New York, NY), 1979.

Complete Adventures of Spider-Man, Simon & Schuster (New York, NY), 1979.

(Presenter) *The Uncanny X-Men,* Marvel Comics (New York, NY), 1984.

The Best of Spider-Man, Ballantine Books (New York, NY), 1986.

Marvel Masterworks Presents Amazing Spider-Man (originally published as *The Amazing Spider-Man,* numbers 1-10), illustrated by Steve Ditko, Marvel Comics (New York, NY), 1987.

Marvel Masterworks Presents The X-Men (originally published as *The Uncanny X-Men* numbers 1-10), illustrated by Jack Kirby, Marvel Comics (New York, NY), 1987.

Monster Masterworks, Marvel Entertainment Group (New York, NY), 1989.

Silver Surfer: Judgment Day, illustrated by John Buscema, Marvel Comics (New York, NY), 1988.

The Enslavers ("Silver Surfer" graphic novel) Marvel Comics (New York, NY), 1990.

Marvel Masterworks Presents the Silver Surfer, illustrated by John Buscema, Marvel Comics (New York, NY), 1991.

Marvel Masterworks Presents Thor, illustrated by Jack Kirby, Marvel Comics (New York, NY), 1991.

Marvel Masterworks Presents Daredevil (originally published as *Dardevil, the Man without Fear,* numbers 1-10), illustrated by Wally Wood, Marvel Comics (New York, NY), 1991.

Marvel Masterworks Presents Doctor Strange (originally published as *Strange Tales,* numbers 110-111, 114-141), illustrated by Steve Ditko, Marvel Comics (New York, NY), 1992.

Marvel Masterworks Presents Iron Man (originally published as *Tales of Suspense,* numbers 39-50), illustrated by Don Heck, Marvel Comics (New York, NY), 1992.

Captain America, the Movie!, Marvel Comics (New York, NY), 1992.

The First Startling Saga of the Silver Surfer: The Coming of Galactus!, illustrated by Jack Kirby and Joe Sinnott, Marvel Comics (New York, NY), 1992.

Just Imagine Stan Lee Creating the DC Universe (includes *Just Imagine Stan Lee's Batman,* illustrated by Joe Kubert, *Just Imagine Stan Lee's Wonder Woman,* illustrated by Jim Lee, *Just*

Imagine Stan Lee's Superman, illustrated by John Buscema, *Just Imagine Stan Lee's Green Lantern,* illustrated by Dave Gibbons, *Just Imagine Stan Lee's Aquaman,* illustrated by Scott McDaniel, (with Michael Uslan) *Just Imagine Stan Lee's JLA,* illustrated by Jerry Ordway, and *Just Imagine Stan Lee's The Flash,* illustrated by Kevin Maguire), DC Comics (New York, NY), 2002.

EDITOR

The Ultimate Spider-Man, Byron Preiss Multimedia (New York, NY) 1994.
The Ultimate Silver Surfer, Byron Preiss Multimedia (New York, NY) 1995.
The Ultimate Super-Villains, Byron Preiss Multimedia (New York, NY) 1996.
The Ultimate X-Men, Byron Preiss Multimedia (New York, NY) 1996.
(With Kurt Busiek) *Untold Tales of Spider-Man,* Byron Preiss Multimedia (New York, NY) 1997.
(With Peter David) *The Ultimate Hulk,* Byron Preiss Multimedia (New York, NY) 1998.
X-Men Legends, illustrated by Mike Zeck, Berkley Books (New York, NY), 2000.

Author of syndicated comic strips, including *My Friend Irma,* 1952, *Mrs. Lyons' Cubs,* 1957-58, *Willie Lumpkin,* 1960, *The Incredible Hulk,* and *Spider-Man.* Also editor of television scripts.

ADAPTATIONS: Included among the many media adaptations of Stan Lee's work are *The Incredible Hulk,* a television series broadcast by Columbia Broadcasting System (CBS-TV), and a number of television specials featuring Spider-Man, Doctor Strange, and Captain America, broadcast by CBS-TV. Major motion pictures involving Lee's creations and cocreations include *X-Men, Spider-Man, Daredevil,* and *Hulk.*

SIDELIGHTS: Stan Lee is the cocreator of many of Marvel Comic's most popular superheroes, including Spider-Man, the Hulk, Daredevil, the X-Men, Iron Man, and the Fantastic Four. "Lee's metamorphosis from bespectacled kid in the Bronx to living symbol of a billion-dollar entertainment empire is every bit as impressive as any superhero origin story," wrote L. D. Meagher on the *CNN* Web site. As a youth, Lee was an avid reader, deeply immersed in the world of books and words. He was strongly influenced by swashbuckling actor Errol Flynn, as well as literary heroes such as Tom Swift, the Hardy Boys, and boy detective Poppy Ott. These characters kept Lee immersed in prose fiction and the fantasies spun out with the written word. Fueled by the desire to be a great novelist, Lee began writing early in life, winning the *New York Herald Tribune* essay contest three times in a row while in his early teens. At age seventeen, Lee—then known as Stanley Lieber—accepted a job with Timely Comics, owned by cousin-in-law Martin Goodman. Lee started with menial office chores and some proofreading for the company's line of comics. Within a year, however, Lee was doing some writing for Timely—his first published writing in comics was, ironically, a two-page text piece that appeared in *Captain America,* Number 3. He signed the piece "Stan Lee," reserving his real name for use on the serious works of literature he expected to write once he finished his stint in comics. "Circumstances conspired against him," stated a writer in *St. James Encyclopedia of Popular Culture.*

In the early 1940s, Lee found himself writing whatever material that Timely Comics' chief employees, editor/writer Joe Simon and artist/writer Jack Kirby, didn't have time for, according to an essayist in *Authors and Artists for Young Adults.* When Simon and Kirby left to work for rival DC Comics and begin forging stellar reputations for themselves in comics, both singly and as a team, Lee inherited their entire workload. At age twenty, Lee became the editor and main writer of a major comic-book publisher. Over the next two decades, Lee wrote prolifically, almost superheroically, in a wide range of genres, from westerns to romances, horror to science fiction, and perhaps most significantly, superheroes and costumed adventurers.

By the late 1950s and early 1960s, comics were in a protracted slump, near death and barely limping onward. The industry had suffered a tremendous blow in the 1950s with accusations by psychologist Frederic Wertham that comics were responsible for, among other things, juvenile delinquency. Wertham's views, codified in the book *Seduction of the Innocent,* were taken seriously, and senate hearings were held on the matter. Combined with difficulties with distributors, the once-robust comics industry seemed doomed. Publishers were trying different ways to revive interest in their books. Superheroes, minor figures compared to the popular horror and science fiction comics of the 1950s, were again getting some play in the comics' pages. In 1960, Atlas (formerly Timely) publisher Goodman noticed the success of the "Justice League of America," or "JLA," a team book published by rival DC. Goodman suggested to Lee that he create a superhero team along the lines of the JLA. Lee, by then "tired of following trends and cranking out hack work," took a gamble on his wife's advice, remarked the writer in *St. James Encyclopedia of Popular Culture.* Lee's wife advised him to write the book however he wanted; at best, Goodman would like it, and at worst, he'd fire Lee, which would allow Lee to leave the industry as he'd been planning. In response, Lee created *The Fantastic Four,* which appeared in 1961 and became the keystone of what would eventually be known as The Marvel Universe and a publishing epoch called The Marvel Age of Comics.

Other titles quickly followed the successful *Fantastic Four.* In collaboration with artist Jack Kirby, Lee was cocreator of characters such as the Incredible Hulk, the X-Men, and the Mighty Thor. In 1962, Lee and artist Steve Ditko created the Amazing Spider-Man. Appearing in *Amazing Fantasy,* Number 15, the final issue of a comic featuring predominantly science fiction and twist-ending fantasy stories, Spider-Man was well received and remained consistently popular from the feature's inception. Lee and Kirby began fleshing out The Fantastic Four, a team of four superheroes who argued, sulked, and fought among themselves more like a family than a group of colleagues—indeed, Sue Storm (the Invisible Girl) and Johnny Storm (the Human Torch) were siblings; Reed Richards (Mr. Fantastic) would eventually wed Sue; and Ben Grimm (the Thing) was a close friend of Reed's. "In collaboration with Jack Kirby, Lee made 'The Fantastic Four' grander, wackier, and at the same time, more human than anything the competition was producing," wrote the *St. James Encyclopedia of Popular Culture* essayist. "Most of the grandeur came from the imagination and pencil of Jack Kirby, but the humanity and sense of fun came from the dialogue and captions written by Stan Lee." Throughout the 1960s, Marvel's characters evolved and took on a greater sophistication as The Marvel Age of Comics unfolded. "The Marvel Age brought its own sensibility and vernacular expressed by characters who developed through their adventures instead of merely bouncing over tall buildings in a single bound from one escapade to the next," wrote Frank Houston on the *Salon.com* Web site.

Frequently credited with having revolutionized the comic-book industry, Lee created characters who appeal not only to the traditional adolescent comic-book audience, but also to college students. In *Quest,* Lee offered this explanation of the broad appeal of his work: "For the younger reader, there were colorful costumes, action, excitement, fantasy, and bigger-than-life adventures. For the newly proselytized older reader, we offered unexpectedly sophisticated plots and subplots, a college-level vocabulary, satire, science fiction, and as many philosophical and sociological concepts as we could devise."

Among the "sociological concepts" or social problems that Spider-Man comics have dealt with over the years are drug abuse, pollution, and racial injustice. "From 1967 to 1973, Spider-Man addressed himself to every important issue confronting American Society," wrote Salvatore Mondello in his essay on Spider-Man for the *Journal of Popular Culture.* "Once contemporary issues were discussed, 'The Amazing Spider-Man' became a subtle persuader, fashioning and reflecting public and popular attitudes under the rubric of entertainment." It was during this period that Spider-Man's popularity on college campuses blossomed. "In an era demanding relevance," Mondello noted, "few magazines were more typical or current than Lee's comic book."

Critics provide several explanations for the popular appeal of Lee's comic-book characters. One oft-cited explanation is that each of Lee's heroes, in addition to having a variety of superpowers, has flaws—human failings with which readers can identify. Peter Parker, a postgraduate science student whose encounter with a radioactive spider left him with spider-like superpowers, is one example. As Spider-Man, Parker uses his web-spinning powers to fight such villains as the Cyclone, Doctor Octopus, the Kingpin, and the Lizard. An impressive superhero, Parker is nonetheless a pitiable character who suffers from financial worries, dandruff, and an overprotective aunt. "Sure, he's a superhero," Lee admitted in *Quest.* "Sure, he's a regular one-man army. Sure, he's practically indestructible. But you're a lot better off. You seem to handle life's little vicissitudes far better than he can. Even though he's a living legend, you can feel superior to him. Now, how can you help but love a guy like that?" Though comics have long been considered part of the children's demographic, Lee avoided focusing on any particular age group. "When I was at Marvel, in all honesty, I tried to write stories that would interest me," Lee said in an interview for *Brandweek.* "I'd say, what would I like to read? Then I'd try to write them clearly enough so that a youngster could enjoy and appreciate and understand the story, and I tried to write them intelligently enough so that an older person would enjoy it, too." Lee's work helped spark the revolution in thinking that comic books were not simply a children's entertainment medium, a renaissance that persists today with the increasingly popular form of graphic novels and consistent adult interest in traditional-form comic books.

The audience for Lee's comic books eventually grew to include college students and professors. Several colleges now offer courses on popular culture that feature many of Lee's characters, and Lee himself discusses his creations in lectures on college campuses. He is recognized by colleagues and literary critics alike for his significant contributions to the comic-book industry and to the comic book as an art form. According to Jeanette Kahn, publisher of *Superman* comic books, among others, at DC Comics, Lee is "the living superhero for the American comic industry."

With collaborator George Mair, Lee presented an autobiographical account of his life and industry history in *Excelsior! The Amazing Life of Stan Lee.* The book's title is based on one of the many catchphrases Lee used in his bombastic work for Marvel Comics. He would often conclude text pieces or his "Stan's Soapbox" editorial feature with the word "Excelsior!" as a combination of signature statement, rousing cheer, and exhortation to his readers to bigger and better things—though few probably knew that Lee had adopted the word because it sounded noble and dignified, and that excelsior was actually a type of packing material. In the book, Lee traces his career from the early days of comics in the 1940s to his height as the living embodiment of Marvel Comics. The Stan Lee persona is evident throughout the book, observed Stephen Weiner in *Library Journal.* The narrative "tone is warm, straight-talking, and simultaneously confident and insecure—the same traits with which Lee imbued his superheroes."

A detailed critical biography of Lee appeared in 2003. *Stan Lee and the Rise and Fall of the American Comic Book,* by Jordan Raphael and Tom Spurgeon, provides a detailed examination of Lee's development as a writer, his role in the creation of Marvel comics and in the comic-book renaissance of the early 1960s, and his place in the inexorable decline of the industry throughout the 1990s. Both Raphael and Spurgeon are well-steeped in the history and current state of the comic industry as both fans and serious journalists in the comics field, and their work is "an earnest, well-researched portrait of Marvel's mostly beloved living icon," wrote Richard Pachter on the *Miami Herald* Web site. Along with the positive side of Lee's long tenure in the industry, the authors also dissect the darker elements, including assertions that Lee has long accepted more credit for the creation of the early Marvel characters than he was due, at the expense of artist collaborators such as Jack Kirby and Steve Ditko. Raphael and Spurgeon "give Lee his due for shepherding Marvel Comics to the apex of the industry," Meagher wrote on the *CNN* Web site. "They also deflate some of the claims Lee, his fans, and his company have made about the role he played in giving birth to some of Marvel's iconic characters." Still, "the authors make an unimpeachable case for [Lee's] accomplishments as an editor, packager, production manager, and promoter," Pachter remarked, roles that "may have had more significance than the actual comics" in the company's growth as it outstripped rival publishers such as DC Comics.

Lee continues to be active in the print and video entertainment industry. In 2001, Lee formed his own production company, POW! Entertainment, which has secured deals with a number of companies for both children's entertainment features and programs for older viewers. POW! (at first glance a tribute to stereotypical comic-book sound effects, but which Lee says stands for Purveyors of Wonder) focuses on movies, television shows, and animation, according to an interview with Lee on the *GameNow* Web site. Lee was signed by video game producer Activision in late 2003 to work on games based on Marvel Comics characters. In July, 2003, Lee's character Stripperella debuted in an animated feature on TNN, later to be known as SpikeTV. With the tagline "Stripper by night, superhero by later night," the show follows the adventures of Erotica Jones, a stripper turned do-gooder who combats crime with fighting moves direct from the brass pole and with clever gadgets concealed in skimpy clothing and cosmetic cases. The show courts the adult male audience sought by SpikeTV with its double entendres, ribald storylines, and abundant animation of the female form. Although the character may be considered a bit of a departure from Lee's usual wholesome super characters, it is a parody rather than a straightforward drama, "a funny spoof of superheroes," wrote Shawn McKenzie on the *Entertain Your Brain!* Web site. Heavy with "pop-culture references, celebrity voices, and music-video pyrotechnics," the show provides a look at what might happen if Stan Lee "went to work for MTV," wrote Hal Erickson on the MSN Web site.

Lee's post-Marvel undertakings have not all been successful. An experiment in creating online comics ended in failure for Lee when one of his partners in Stan Lee Media was hit with criminal charges and the company failed. Bankruptcy proceedings at Marvel Comics resulted in contract difficulties for Lee—he had been under perpetual contract with the company he helped build, but Marvel's financial problems let Lee out of his exclusive deal. Eventually, Lee also sued over compensation from some of the highly successful Marvel-based films that have appeared since *Blade* and *X-Men* blazed onto the screen. But these setbacks came to be little more than the type of temporary defeat that Lee consistently used to create drama for his characters. He continues to write, produce, and create in the field that he has embraced for more than six decades.

Lee's quirky, soul-searching superheroes have entertained generations of avid readers, sparked nascent imaginations, increased vocabularies and reading abilities, and inspired philosophical contemplation of deceptively simple concepts such as "with great power comes great responsibility." In comics, "Lee's career is basically 'a meditation on the potential of the most damaged individuals to transcend the self-destructive society in which they operate,'" wrote the essayist in *Authors and Artists for Young Adults.* "For this new generation of superheroes, the super power itself is one element of their angst. In creating such a cast of unwilling heroes, Lee and company also revamped the idea of what constitutes heroism in America."

BIOGRAPHICAL AND CRITICAL SOURCES:

BOOKS

Authors and Artists for Young Adults, Volume 49, Gale (Detroit, MI), 2003.

Berger, Arthur Asa, *The Comic-Stripped American,* Walker (New York, NY), 1973.

Contemporary Literary Criticism, Volume 17, Gale (Detroit, MI), 1981.

Harvey, Robert C., *The Art of the Comic Book,* University Press of Mississippi (Jackson, MS), 1996.

Jones, Gerard, and Will Jacobs, *The Great Comic Book Heroes,* Prima Publishing (Rocklin, CA), 1997.

Kraft, David Anthony, *Captain America: The Secret Story of Marvel's Star-Spangled Super Hero,* Children's Press (Chicago, IL), 1981.

Kraft, David Anthony, *The Fantastic Four: The Secret Story of Marvel's Cosmic Quartet,* Children's Press (Chicago, IL), 1981.

Kraft, David Anthony, *The Incredible Hulk: The Secret Story of Marvel's Gamma-Powered Goliath,* Children's Press (Chicago, IL), 1981.

Lee, Stan, and George Mair *Excelsior! The Amazing Life of Stan Lee* (autobiography), Simon & Schuster (New York, NY), 2002.

Raphael, Jordan, and Tom Spurgeon, *Stan Lee and the Rise and Fall of the American Comic Book,* Chicago Review Press (Chicago, IL), 2003.

St. James Encyclopedia of Popular Culture, St. James Press (Detroit, MI), 2000.

PERIODICALS

AdWeek, May 1, 2000, Steve Pond, "Marvel Comics' Master Creates New Heroes for the Web," p. 30.

Best Sellers, March, 1985, review of *Dunn's Conundrum,* p. 454.

Booklist, February 1, 1990, review of *Marvel Masterworks Presents Amazing Spider-Man,* p. 1080; November 1, 1995, Carl Hays, review of *The Ultimate Silver Surfer,* p. 458; November 1, 1995, review of *The Ultimate Silver Surfer,* p. 461.

Books & Bookmen, review of *Dunn's Conundrum,* p. 30.

Bookwatch, January, 1996, review of *The Ultimate Silver Surfer,* p. 1.

Brandweek, May 1, 2002, Steve Pond, interview with Stan Lee.

Comic Book Marketplace, July, 1993, Bob Brodsky, "Maestro of the Marvel Mythos," pp. 28-54.

Entertainment Weekly, May 24, 2002, Marc Bernardin, review of *Excelsior! The Amazing Life of Stan Lee,* p. 90.

Independent (London, England), June 27, 2002, "How I Got Here: Stan Lee, Creator of Spider-Man," p. 15; July 1, 2002, Charles Shaar, "The Monday Book: The Amazing Life of Mr. Marvel by His Biggest Fan," p. 12.

Industry Standard, March 19, 2001, Laura Rich, "The Trials of a Comic-Book Hero," p. 45.

Interview, October, 1991, Henry Cabot Beck, "The Amazing Stan Lee," pp. 110-111.

Journal of Popular Culture, summer, 1976; fall, 1994, "Cultural and Mythical Aspects of a Superhero: *The Silver Surfer,* 1969-1970," pp. 203-213.

Kirkus Reviews, October 15, 1984, review of *Dunn's Conundrum,* p. 977; November 15, 1989, review of *The GOD Project,* p. 148; October 15, 1994, review of *The Ultimate Spider-Man,* p. 1366.

Library Journal, December, 1984, review of *Dunn's Conundrum,* p. 2298; January, 1990, review of *The GOD Project,* p. 148; December, 1994, review of *The Ultimate Spider-Man,* p. 139; October 15, 1995, review of *The Ultimate Silver Surfer,* p. 91; May 15, 2002, Stephen Weiner, review of *Excelsior!,* p. 93.

Listener, July 18, 1935, review of *Dunn's Conundrum,* p. 29.

Locus, January, 1995, review of *The Ultimate Spider-Man,* p. 50.

New Republic, July 19, 1975.

New Statesman, April 19, 1985, review of *Dunn's Conundrum,* p. 109.

New York Times, December 31, 1979; October 21, 1999, Frank Houston, "Creator of Fantastic Four Is Ready to Spin More Tales On-Line," p. D8; May 3, 2002, Peter M. Nichols, "How Spidey Was Hatched," p. E3.

New York Times Book Review, September 5, 1976; November 18, 1979; April 7, 1985, review of *Dunn's Conundrum,* p. 90; January 14, 1990, review of *The GOD Project,* p. 23.

Observer (London, England), April 14, 1985, review of *Dunn's Conundrum,* p. 23.

People, January 29, 1979.

Publishers Weekly, January 4, 1985, review of *Dunn's Conundrum,* p. 60; November 8, 1985, review of *Dunn's Conundrum,* p. 59; November 24, 1989, review of *The GOD Project,* p. 59; October 11, 1993, review of *How to Draw Comics the Marvel Way,* p. 56; October 11, 1993, review of the "Marvel Masterworks" series, p. 56; October 22, 2001, review of *The Alien Factor,* p. 54.

Quest, July-August, 1977.

Rolling Stone, September 16, 1971.

San Francisco Review of Books, March, 1995, review of *The Best of the World's Worst,* p. 36.

School Library Journal, May, 1996, Karen Sokoll, review of *The Ultimate Spider-Man,* p. 148; May, 2002, James O. Cahill, review of *The Alien Factor,* pp. 179-180.

Science Fiction Chronicle, June, 1995, review of *The Ultimate Spider-Man,* p. 38; May, 1996, review of *The Ultimate Silver Surfer,* p. 61; April, 2002, review of *Five Decades of the X-Men,* p. 50.

Tampa Tribune, March 8, 2002, "Caught Up Again by Hero Spider-Man," p. 1.

Time, February 5, 1979; February 14, 2000, "Look Up on the Net! It's . . . Cyber Comics: Stan Lee Takes *The 7th Portal* and Backstreet Boys On-Line," p. 76.

Tribune Books (Chicago, IL), February 18, 1990, review of *The GOD Project,* p. 7.

USA Today, January 4, 1985, review of *Dunn's Conundrum,* p. 3D.

Variety, September 17, 1986, Tom Bierbaum, "Stan Lee's Imperfect Heroes Lifted Marvel to Top of Heap," pp. 81-82.

Video Business, April 22, 2002, Lawrence Lerman, "Along Came a Spider-Man," p. 24.

Village Voice, December 23, 1974; December 15, 1975; December 13, 1976.

Voice of Youth Advocates, June, 1985, review of *Dunn's Conundrum,* p. 132; October, 1995, review of *The Ultimate Spider-Man,* p. 207; April, 1997, review of *The Ultimate X-Men,* p. 48.

Wall Street Journal, August 23, 1999, Colleen DeBaise, "Spider-Man Creator Takes Comics to the Web," p. B6F.

Washington Post, February 4, 1992, Richard Harrington, "Stan Lee: Caught in Spidey's Web," p. D1.

World & I, review of *The Silver Surfer,* p. 435.

ONLINE

Animation World Web site, http://www.awn.com/ (July, 1997), Michael Goodman, "Stan Lee: Comic Guru."

CNN Web site, http://www.cnn.com/ (May 4, 2002), "Stan Lee: 'Insectman' Just Didn't Sound Right," interview with Stan Lee; (October 8, 2003), L. D. Meagher, "New Biography Offers Context for Marvel Comics King," review of *Stan Lee and the Rise and Fall of the American Comic Book.*

Entertain Your Brain! Web site, http://www.entertainyourbrain.com/ (July 4, 2003), review of *Stripperella.*

GameNow Web site, http://www.gamenowmag.com/ (October 1, 2003), "Call Me Stan," interview with Stan Lee.

Green Man Review On-Line, http://www.greenmanreview.com/ (November 7, 2003), Michael M. Jones, review of *Stan Lee and the Rise and Fall of the American Comic Book.*

IGN FilmForce Web site, http://www.filmforce.igm.com/ (June 26, 2000), Kenneth Plume, "Interview with Stan Lee," April 20, 2002, Kenneth Plume, "Nuff Said—An Interview with Stan Lee."

Lambiek, http://www.lambiek.net/ (November 7, 2003), biography of Stan Lee.

L.A. Weekly On-Line, http://www.laweekly.com/ (January 4-10, 2002), Jonathan Vankin, "The Neurotic Superhero: Stan Lee and His Human Marvels."

Miami Herald On-Line http://www.miamiherald.com/ (September 1, 2003), Richard Pachter, "Comic-Book Industry Comes to Life in Authors' Hands," review of *Stan Lee and the Rise and Fall of the American Comic Book.*

MSN, http://entertainment.msn.com/ (November 7, 2003), review of *Stripperella.*

Onion A.V. Club, http://www.theonionavclub.com/ (June 20, 2001), Tasha Robinson, "Stan Lee."

Salon.com, http://www.salon.com/ (August 17, 1999), Frank Houston, "Brilliant Careers: Stan Lee."

Spiderman Insider Web site, http://www.spidermaninsider.com/ (November 7, 2003), biography of Stan Lee.

Stan Lee and the Rise and Fall of the American Comic Book Web site, http://www.stanleebook.com/ (November 7, 2003).*

* * *

LEHMAN, Ernest Paul 1915-

PERSONAL: Born 1915, in New York, NY; son of Paul (co-owner of women's clothing shops) and Gertrude (co-owner of women's clothing shops) Lehman; married, 1942; wife's name Jacqueline (died, 1994); married; second wife's name Laurene; children: Roger, Alan; (second marriage) Jonathan Maxwell. *Education:* City University of New York, B.A.

ADDRESSES: *Office*—c/o Writers Guild of America, 7000 West Third St., Los Angeles, CA 90048-4329.

CAREER: Screenplay writer, film producer, and author. Has also worked as a radio comedy writer, Broadway press agent, freelance short-story writer, and as copy editor for a Wall Street financial magazine.

Ernest Paul Lehman

MEMBER: Writers Guild of America West (member of council, 1965-69, president, 1983-85), Screenwriters Guild (member of executive board).

AWARDS, HONORS: All for best screenplay: Writers Guild nomination, 1954, for *The Executive Suite;* Writers Guild award, and Academy Award, Academy of Motion Picture Arts and Sciences, both 1954, both for *Sabrina;* Writers Guild Award, 1956, for *The King and I;* Writers Guild nomination and Academy Award nomination, both 1959, both for *North by Northwest;* Writers Guild award and Academy Award nomination, both 1961, both for *West Side Story;* Writers Guild award, 1965, for *The Sound of Music;* Writers Guild award and Academy Award nomination, both 1966, both for *Who's Afraid of Virginia Woolf?*; honorary Academy Award, 2001, for body of work.

WRITINGS:

SCREENPLAYS

(Author of screen story, with Geza Harcseg) *The Inside Story,* Republic, 1948, re-released as *The Big Gamble,* Republic, 1954.

Executive Suite (adapted from the novel by Cameron Hawley), Metro-Goldwyn-Mayer, 1954.

(With Billy Wilder and Samuel Taylor) *Sabrina* (adapted from the play *Sabrina Fair,* by Taylor), Twentieth Century-Fox, 1954.

The King and I (adapted from the play by Richard Rodgers and Oscar Hammerstein), Twentieth Century-Fox, 1956.

Somebody up There Likes Me (adapted from the autobiography by Rocky Graziano with Rowland Barber), Metro-Goldwyn-Mayer, 1956.

(With Clifford Odets) *Sweet Smell of Success* (adapted from Lehman's novella *Tell Me about It Tomorrow*), United Artists, 1957.

North by Northwest (Metro-Goldwyn-Mayer, 1959), Viking (New York, NY), 1972.

From the Terrace (adapted from the novel by John O'Hara), Twentieth Century-Fox, 1960.

West Side Story (adapted from the play by Arthur Laurents), United Artists, 1961.

The Prize (adapted from the novel by Irving Wallace), Metro-Goldwyn-Mayer, 1963.

The Sound of Music (adapted from the play by Howard Lindsay and Russell Crouse), Twentieth Century-Fox, 1965.

Who's Afraid of Virginia Woolf? (adapted from the play by Edward Albee), Warner Bros., 1966.

Hello Dolly (adapted from the play *The Matchmaker* by Thorton Wilder), Twentieth Century-Fox, 1969.

(And director) *Portnoy's Complaint* (adapted from the novel by Philip Roth), Warner Bros., 1972.

Family Plot (adapted from the novel *The Rainbird Pattern* by Victor Canning), Universal, 1976.

(With Kenneth Ross and Ivan Moffat) *Black Sunday* (adapted from the novel by Thomas Harris), Paramount, 1977.

FICTION

The Comedian and Other Stories, New American Library (New York, NY), 1957.

Sweet Smell of Success and Other Stories, New American Library (New York, NY), 1957.

The French Atlantic Affair (novel), Atheneum (New York, NY), 1977.

Farewell Performance (novel), McGraw-Hill (New York, NY), 1983.

FICTION

Screening Sickness and Other Tales of Tinsel Town (collected articles), Putnam (New York, NY), 1982.

Contributor of articles and short stories to numerous publications, including *Esquire, Redbook, Collier's, Harper's, Liberty, Town and Country, Cosmopolitan,* and *American Mercury.* Columnist, *American Film.*

ADAPTATIONS: Lehman's story "The Comedian" was filmed as part of CBS-TV's *Playhouse 90* in 1957; *The French Atlantic Affair* was produced as a television miniseries in 1979.

SIDELIGHTS: One of the most successful screenwriters of the 1960s and 1970s, Ernest Paul Lehman crafted film scripts in an array of genres from comedy-musical to *noir* thriller during a career spanning four decades. His versatility led to work on projects as diverse as *The Sound of Music* and *Who's Afraid of Virginia Woolf?,* and he is best known for his work on the Alfred Hitchcock-directed movies *North by Northwest* and *Family Plot.* In the *Dictionary of Literary Biography,* Nick Roddick called Lehman "a champion of the well-crafted, what-happens-next screenplay" and a film writer who has achieved "critical and commercial successes." Lehman has been nominated several times for for Academy Awards in the category of Best Screenplay.

Lehman grew up on Long Island and drifted into creative writing while a student at the College of the City of New York. His first published work, a profile of bandleader Ted Lewis, appeared in 1939; for the following thirteen years his work appeared in such magazines as *Collier's, Esquire, Liberty, Redbook, American Mercury,* and *Cosmopolitan.* As a young college graduate in Manhattan he held several editorial positions, including a copy-writing job for a publicity agency that provided the background for his story and screenplay *Sweet Smell of Success.* Lehman also sold pieces to magazines. After his short story *The Comedian* appeared in *Collier's* in 1953, Paramount Studios brought him to Hollywood to work on a screenplay adaptation. That project was ultimately canceled, but Lehman received other screenwriting assignments and settled permanently in California.

Lehman's scripts defy easy categorization. Some, like *Executive Suite* and *Sweet Smell of Success,* serve as exposés of the business world. Others, such as *Sabrina* and *Somebody up There Likes Me,* offer uplifting stories of underdogs who achieve beyond their dreams. Still others—most notably *Who's Afraid of Virginia Woolf?* and *Portnoy's Complaint*— are adaptations of gripping works of literature that explore serious and complicated themes. It was the 1959 Hitchcock thriller *North by Northwest,* however, that elevated Lehman into screenwriting's top echelon. The original story involves a New York advertising executive (played in the film by Cary Grant) who is abducted in a case of mistaken identity. The character escapes his kidnappers but almost loses his life in the process as he must outwit and outrun the tenacious and imaginative criminals. Roddick declared *North by Northwest* Lehman's "finest work, a model of screenplay construction as well as a fine piece of dramatic writing."

In addition to his dramas, Lehman adapted quite a number of musicals for the screen. Most went on to be huge commercial successes, from the 1956 film *The King and I,* starring Yul Brynner—which won four of the eight Academy Awards for which it was nominated—to the immensely popular *The Sound of Music,* which won an Academy Award for best picture in 1964. The author scored another hit with his *West Side Story,* which Roddick characterized as "a great deal more than a simple adaptation. . . . [The changes give] bite to the movie, balancing the tendency for it to become an overly sentimental love story with a downbeat setting."

In some respects Lehman's career reached an apex in the mid-1960s, when he was acclaimed for his work on *Who's Afraid of Virginia Woolf?, West Side Story,* and *The Sound of Music.* Thereafter, his productions of *Hello, Dolly!* and *Portnoy's Complaint* drew negative reviews and did little business at the box office. His last screenplay, *Black Sunday,* proved successful as an action-thriller based on a terrorist plot to bomb the Super Bowl. *Black Sunday* was released in 1977; since that time Lehman has turned his attention to other challenges.

One of those challenges has been fiction, including the suspense-filled novel *The French Atlantic Affair.* Lehman's screenwriting experience is reflected in this work: Metro-Goldwyn-Mayer bought the movie rights before the book was even released, and it was eventually made into a television miniseries. A synopsis of the plot reveals its adaptability to the screen. The story follows two unemployed aerospace engineers and their partners in crime—seventy-four married couples—as they attempt to "shipjack" a France-bound ocean liner and demand thirty-five million dollars in ransom. While the three thousand other passengers are unaware of the scheme, the conspirators promise authorities they'll bomb the ship within forty-eight hours if their demands aren't met. When an irate wife complains to the ship's captain about her husband's smuggled ham radio, the ship's crew is able to renew its communication with land. Eventually, the plot spans the Atlantic as the presidents of France and the United States, the French police, the U.S. Navy, French and American media personalities, and an American think tank work to avoid the looming disaster.

Lehman's second novel, *Farewell Performance,* appeared in 1982, and was followed by a collection of Lehman's columns from *American Film,* titled *Screening Sickness and Other Tales of Tinsel Town.* From 1983 to 1985 Lehman served as president of the Writers Guild of America, West. In 1986 he wrote the screenplay for a film titled *I Am Zorba,* but the project was abandoned before the film was made. In 1987, 1988, and 1990, Lehman wrote and coordinated the 59th, 60th, and 62nd Academy Awards shows on ABC-TV.

Lehman continued to write in the 1990s, producing a satirical article in the *Los Angeles* magazine, and adapting Noel Coward's *Hay Fever* for film, but the film was never made. He also worked on an original screenplay, *Dancing in the Dark,* and an autobiography, both not yet published.

Lehman's collected papers are archived at the Harry Ransom Humanities Research Center at the University of Texas at Austin. The collection includes business and personal correspondence, early short stories and articles, outlines and successive drafts of screenplays, typescripts, proofs, technical drawings, publicity materials, and newspaper articles by and about Lehman.

BIOGRAPHICAL AND CRITICAL SOURCES:

BOOKS

Contemporary Theatre, Film, and Television, Volume 22, Gale (Detroit, MI), 1999.

Corliss, Richard, *Talking Pictures: Screenwriters in the American Cinema, 1927-1973,* Overlook Press (Woodstock, NY), 1974, pp. 188-195.

Dictionary of Literary Biography, Volume 44: *American Screenwriters, Second Series,* Gale (Detroit, MI), 1986, pp. 157-165.

Ernest Lehman: An American Film Institute Seminar on His Work, Microfilming Corporation of America (Glen Rock, NJ), 1977.

Taylor, John Russell, *Hitch: The Life and Times of Alfred Hitchcock,* Pantheon (New York, NY), 1978, published as *Hitch: The Life and Work of Alfred Hitchcock,* Faber (London, England), 1978.

PERIODICALS

American Film, October, 1976, pp. 33-48.
Christian Science Monitor, September 23, 1977.
Cleveland Plain Dealer, August 7, 1977.
Cosmopolitan, July, 1975, pp. 168-171, 182.
Denver Post, September 18, 1977.
Houston Chronicle, August 8, 1977.
Kirkus Reviews, June 1, 1977.
Newsweek, April 4, 1977.
New York Times, October 30, 1983.
New York Times Book Review, September 4, 1977.
Philadelphia Sunday Bulletin, November 13, 1977.
Saturday Review, April 30, 1977.
Sight and Sound, winter, 1967-1968, pp. 26-27.
Times (London, England), December 30, 1969.

ONLINE

Academy of Motion Picture Arts and Sciences, http://www.oscars.org/ (May 28, 2003), "73rd Annual Academy Awards, Honorary Award."

Curtain Up, http://www.curtainup.com/ (May 28, 2003), Elyse Sommer, review of *Sweet Smell of Success.*

Ernest Lehman Collection, http://hrc.utexas.edu/ (May 28, 2003).

MSN Entertainment, http://entertainment.msn.com/ (May 28, 2003), "Ernest Lehman."

Overlook Press, http://www.overlookpress.com/ (May 28, 2003), "Fiction, *The Sweet Smell of Success.*"

Writers Guild of America, http://www.wga.org/ (May 28, 2003), articles about the author.

* * *

LESTER, Julius (Bernard) 1939-

Julius Lester

PERSONAL: Born January 27, 1939, in St. Louis, MO; son of W. D. (a minister) and Julia (Smith) Lester; married Joan Steinau (a researcher), 1962 (divorced, 1970); married Alida Carolyn Fechner, March 21, 1979; children: (first marriage) Jody Simone, Malcolm Coltrane; (second marriage) Elena Milad (stepdaughter), David Julius. *Education:* Fisk University, B.A., 1960.

ADDRESSES: Office—University of Massachusetts, Judaic Studies, Herter Hall, Amherst, MA 01003. *E-mail*—jbles@concentric.net.

CAREER: Newport Folk Festival, Newport, RI, director, 1966-68; New School for Social Research, New York, NY, lecturer, 1968-70; WBAI-FM, New York, NY, producer and host of live radio show *The Great Proletarian Cultural Revolution,* 1968-75; University of Massachusetts, Amherst, professor of Afro-American studies, 1971-88, professor of Near Eastern and Judaic studies, 1982—, acting director and associate director of Institute for Advanced Studies in Humanities, 1982-84; Vanderbilt University, Nashville, TN, writer-in-residence, 1985. Professional musician and singer. Host of live television show *Free Time,* WNET-TV, 1971-73. Lester's photographs of the 1960s civil rights movement have been exhibited at the Smithsonian Institution and are on permanent display at Howard University.

AWARDS, HONORS: Newbery Honor Book citation, 1969, and Lewis Carroll Shelf Award, 1970, both for *To Be a Slave;* Lewis Carroll Shelf Award, 1972, and National Book Award finalist, 1973, both for *The Long Journey Home: Stories from Black History;* Lewis Carroll Shelf Award, 1973, for *The Knee-High Man and other Tales;* honorable mention, Coretta Scott King Award, 1983, for *This Strange New Feeling,* and 1988, for *Tales of Uncle Remus: The Adventures of Brer Rabbit;* University of Massachusetts Distinguished Teacher's Award, 1983-84, and Faculty Fellowship Award, 1985; National Professor of the Year Silver Medal Award, 1985, and Massachusetts State Professor of the Year and Gold Medal Award for National Professor of the Year, both 1986, all from Council for Advancement and Support of Education; chosen distinguished faculty lecturer, 1986-87.

WRITINGS:

(With Pete Seeger) *The Twelve-String Guitar As Played by Leadbelly,* Oak (New York, NY), 1965.

Look Out Whitey! Black Power's Gon' Get Your Mama!, Dial (New York, NY), 1968.

To Be a Slave, Dial (New York, NY), 1969; thirtieth anniversary edition, illustrated by Tom Feelings, Dial (New York, NY), 1998.

Black Folktales, Baron (New York, NY), 1969.

Search for the New Land: History As Subjective Experience, Dial (New York, NY), 1969.

Revolutionary Notes, Baron (New York, NY), 1969.

(Editor) *The Seventh Son: The Thoughts and Writings of W. E. B. Du Bois,* two volumes, Random House (New York, NY), 1971.

(Compiler, with Rae Pace Alexander) *Young and Black in America,* Random House (New York, NY), 1971.

The Long Journey Home: Stories from Black History, Dial (New York, NY), 1972, reprinted, Puffin Books (New York, NY), 1998.

The Knee-High Man and Other Tales, Dial (New York, NY), 1972.

Two Love Stories, Dial (New York, NY), 1972.

(Editor) Stanley Couch, *Ain't No Ambulances for No Nigguhs Tonight* (poems), Baron (New York, NY), 1972.

Who I Am (poems), Dial (New York, NY), 1974.

All Is Well: An Autobiography, Morrow (New York, NY), 1976.

This Strange New Feeling, Dial (New York, NY), 1982.

Do Lord Remember Me (novel), Holt (Orlando, FL), 1984, reprinted, Arcade (New York, NY), 1998.

The Tales of Uncle Remus: The Adventures of Brer Rabbit, Dial (New York, NY), 1987.

More Tales of Uncle Remus: The Further Adventures of Brer Rabbit, His Friends, Enemies, and Others, Dial (New York, NY), 1988.

Lovesong: Becoming a Jew (autobiography), Holt (Orlando, FL), 1988.

How Many Spots Does a Leopard Have? and Other Tales, illustrated by David Shannon, Scholastic (New York, NY), 1989.

Falling Pieces of the Broken Sky (essays), Arcade (New York, NY), 1990.

Further Tales of Uncle Remus: The Misadventures of Brer Rabbit, Brer Fox, Brer Wolf, the Doodang, and Other Creatures, illustrated by Jerry Pinkney, Dial (New York, NY), 1990.

The Last Tales of Uncle Remus, illustrated by Jerry Pinkney, Dial (New York, NY), 1994.

And All Our Wounds Forgiven (adult novel), Arcade (New York, NY), 1994.

John Henry, illustrated by Jerry Pinkney, Dial (New York, NY), 1994.

The Man Who Knew Too Much: A Moral Tale from the Baile of Zambia, illustrated by Leonard Jenkins, Clarion (New York, NY), 1994.

Othello: A Retelling, Scholastic (New York, NY), 1995.

Sam and the Tigers: A New Telling of Little Black Sambo, illustrated by Jerry Pinkney, Dial Books (New York, NY), 1996.

How Butterflies Came to Be, Scholastic (New York, NY), 1997.

Shining, illustrated by Terea Shaffer, Silver Whistle (San Diego, CA), 1997.

Black Cowboy, Wild Horses: A True Story, illustrated by Jerry Pinkney, Dial Books (New York, NY), 1998.

From Slave Ship to Freedom Road, illustrated by Rod Brown, Dial (New York, NY), 1998.

When the Beginning Began: Stories about God, the Creatures, and Us, illustrated by Emily Lisker, Silver Whistle (San Diego, CA), 1999.

What a Truly Cool World, illustrated by Joe Cepeda, Scholastic (New York, NY), 1999.

Uncle Remus: The Complete Tales (reprint in one volume of works originally published separately 1987-1994), illustrated by Jerry Pinkney, Phyllis Fogelman Books (New York, NY), 1999.

Albidaro and the Mischievous Dream, illustrated by Jerry Pinkney, Phyllis Fogelman Books (New York, NY), 2000.

The Blues Singers: Ten Who Rocked the World, illustrated by Lisa Cohen, Jump at the Sun/Hyperion (New York, NY), 2001.

When Dad Killed Mom, Silver Whistle (San Diego, CA), 2001.

Ackamarackus: Julius Lester's Sumptuously Silly Fantastically Funny Fables, illustrated by Emilie Chollat, Scholastic (New York, NY), 2001.

Why Heaven Is Far Away, illustrated by Joe Cepeda, Scholastic (New York, NY), 2002.

Pharaoh's Daughter: A Novel of Ancient Egypt, Silver Whistle (San Diego, CA), 2000.

Let's Talk about Race, illustrated by Karen Barbour, HarperCollins (New York, NY), 2004.

Contributor of essays and reviews to numerous magazines and newspapers, including *New York Times Book Review, New York Times, Nation, Katallagete, Democracy, National Review, New Republic, Reform Judaism, Commonweal,* and *Village Voice.* Associate editor, *Sing Out,* 1964-70; contributing editor, *Broadside of New York,* 1964-70. Lester's books have been translated into seven languages.

SIDELIGHTS: Julius Lester is "foremost among . . . black writers who produce their work from a position of historical strength," wrote critic John A. Williams in the *New York Times Book Review.* Drawing on old documents and folktales, Lester fashions stories that proclaim the heritage of black Americans and "attempt to recreate the social life of the past," noted Eric Foner and Naomi Lewis in the *New York Review of Books.* Lester's tales are more than simple reportage. Their purpose, as the reviewers pointed out, is "not merely to impart historical information, but to teach moral and political lessons." Because he feels that the history of minority groups has been largely ignored, Lester intends to furnish his young readers with what he calls "a usable past" and with what the Foner and Lewis called "a sense of history which will help shape their lives and politics."

Lester has distinguished himself as a civil-rights activist, musician, photographer, radio and talk-show host, professor, poet, novelist, folklorist, and talented writer for children and young adults. His characters fall into two categories: those drawn from Afro-American folklore and those drawn from black or Judaic history. The former are imaginary creatures, or sometimes animals, such as *The Knee-High Man's* Mr. Bear and Mr. Rabbit; the latter are real people, "ordinary men and women who might appear only in . . . a neglected manuscript at the Library of Congress," according to William Loren Katz in the *Washington Post Book World.* Critics find that Lester uses both types of characters to reveal the black individual's struggle against slavery.

Black Folktales, Lester's first collection of folk stories, features larger-than-life heroes—including a cigar-smoking black God—shrewd animals, and cunning human beings. While some of the characters are taken from African legends and others from American slave tales, they all demonstrate that "black resistance to white oppression is as old as the confrontation between the two groups," said Williams. Most reviewers applaud Lester's view of African-American folklore and praise his storytelling skills, but a few object to what they perceive as the antiwhite tone of the book. Zena Sutherland, writing in the *Bulletin of the Center for Children's Books,* called *Black Folktales* "a vehicle for hostility. . . . There is no story that concerns white people in which they are not pictured as venal or stupid or both."

Lester also deals with white oppression in his second collection of folktales, *The Knee-High Man and Other Tales.* Although these six animal stories are funny, *New York Times Book Review* critic Ethel Richards suggested that "powerfully important lessons ride the humor. In 'The Farmer and the Snake,' the lesson is that kindness will not change the nature of a thing—in this case, the nature of a poisonous snake to bite." A *Junior Bookshelf* reviewer pointed out that this story—as well as others in the book—reflects the relationship between owner and slave. While pursuing the same theme, Lester moves into the realm of nonfiction with *The Long Journey Home: Stories from Black History,* a documentary collection of slave narratives, and *To Be a Slave,* a collection of six stories based on historical fact. Both books showcase ordinary people in adverse circumstances and provide the reader with a look at what Lester calls "history from the bottom up." *Black Like Me* author John Howard Griffin, writing in the *New York Times Book Review,* commended Lester's approach, saying that the stories "help destroy the delusion that black men did not suffer as another man would in similar circumstances," and Eric Foner and Naomi Lewis applauded the fact that "Lester does not feel it is necessary to make every black man and woman a super-hero." *New York Times Book Review* contributor Rosalind K. Goddard recommended Lester's writing as both lesson and entertainment writing, "These stories point the way for young blacks to find their roots, so important to the realization of their identities, as well as offer a stimulating and informative experience for all."

In *Lovesong: Becoming a Jew,* Lester presents the autobiographical story of his conversion to the Jewish faith. Beginning with his southern childhood as the son of a Methodist minister, following his years of atheism and civil rights activity, and ending with his exploration of many faiths, *Lovesong* concludes with Lester's embrace of Judaism in 1983. Discussing the book in a *Partisan Review* article, David Lehman remarked that the author relates his experiences with "conviction and passion."

With *How Many Spots Does a Leopard Have?* Lester drew from folktales of both the African and Jewish traditions to write new stories in a modern language. "Although I am of African and Jewish ancestry," Lester writes in his introduction to the collection, "I am also an American. . . . I have fitted the story to my mouth and tongue." Assessing the collection in the *Los Angeles Times Book Review,* Sonja Bolle called the stories "so lively they positively dance."

Lester's books often retell traditional folk tales, turning familiar stories on end while presenting them in a contemporary setting with morals intact and appropriate for today's youth. His "Uncle Remus" series has taken the "almost impenetrable phonetic transcription of the dialect" of Harris's telling and made it, according to Mary M. Burns of *Horn Book,* "more accessible through Lester's translations into Standard English. Moreover, the tales no longer suffer from the stereotyped image of Uncle Remus, which confirmed black inferiority."

In *Othello: A Retelling,* Lester tackles Shakespeare in a "re-imagining" that retains the questions about perceptions, race, and the nature of love and friendship central to the bard's original play, while modernizing the characters and adding psychological depth to make the story more appealing to today's youth.

Sam and the Tiger is a "hip and hilarious retelling" of the Little Black Sambo story, according to a *Publishers Weekly* reviewer. *John Henry* is a retelling of the popular American legend with a focus on Henry's African-American heritage. In *Black Cowboy, Wild Horses,* Lester evokes the legendary stature of real cowboy Bob Lemmons and the majesty of the Wild West.

Lester's first adult novel, *And All Our Wounds Forgiven,* is a powerful, disturbing, and controversial revisitation of the civil rights movement. Wilfred D. Samuels writing for the *African American Review,* called this fiction an attempt by Lester to "demythologize" civil rights leader Dr. Martin Luther King, Jr.

In Lester's *Shining* a young girl named Shining, growing up in a tribal society, is rejected by the women of the tribe for her refusal to speak and sing. However, after conveying a message through a "wordless song of forgiveness" that she has absorbed their culture, "Shining goes on to become designated successor to The One, a regal deity charged with guarding all souls living and dead," according to a critic for *Kirkus Reviews.* Shining's song shows her people "that she has been listening to them all along, hearing their joys, sorrows, and fears," continued the reviewer. Lester offers a preface at the beginning of *Shining* stating that through the book, he was able to, according to the *Kirkus* reviewer, "explore his own relationship with music and listening."

Lester created a funky and playfully outlandish view of Heaven in *What a Truly Cool World.* Presenting a mythical view of the afterlife in contemporary terms, Lester describes a God who walks around in slippers, has a wife named Irene, and a secretary named Bruce. Lester published a delightful sequel, *Why Heaven Is Far Away,* in which the people of earth are being overwhelmed by snakes.

When the Beginning Began is a fusion of Lester's mixed heritage, blending the irreverence of the African-American storytelling tradition he admired and learned from his father and the imaginative inquiry of Judaism's midrashim, stories that extend and interpret bible stories. Ilene Cooper of *Booklist* called this "a reverent, wise, witty, and wonderfully entertaining book, handsomely produced."

From Slave Ship to Freedom Road is a vividly illustrated historical narration of the reality of slavery. *Pharaoh's Daughter* is a historically rich retelling of Moses—Lester-style. *Albidaro and the Mischievous Dream* is the story of what happens in a world where teddy bears in dreams tell children they can do anything they want.

Ackamarackus: Julius Lester's Sumptuously Silly Fantastically Funny Fables has been well received by the critics, generating numerous positive reviews. Wendy Lukehart of the *School Library Journal* described *Ackamarackus* as a "riotous collection" of six tales, each "featuring irrepressible animals, laugh-out-loud descriptions, alliterative language, turns of phrase that dance off the tongue, and two pithy morals brimming with wisdom and wit."

Lester continued to prove his versatility and dexterity as an writer in *When Dad Killed Mom,* a psychological mystery for young adults. A reviewer for *Publishers Weekly* described this book as "subtly and credibly done," a mystery that explores the murder and the complex feelings of the two child protagonists as they deal with the death of their mother at their father's hand. "In the end, they are learning to make new lives for themselves and to somehow live with their losses, though their lives have been forever altered," wrote Paula Rohrlick in *Kliatt.* Rohrlick continued, Lester "succeeds in creating some suspense," and though it's "not a cheerful read," Lester weaves "an engrossing story."

The Blues Singers brings Lester back to his musician roots with the creation of this picture book in tribute to the blues and ten great performers of this rich music. The book unfolds through historically rich profiles of jazz greats such as Bessie Smith, Muddy Waters, and B. B. King told in anecdotal style through a fictional grandfather storytelling for his granddaughter.

Lester once talked about goals as a writer and his belief that his main purpose as a writer is to educate. Lending credence to this position is the fact that much of his work has been either historical sketches or historically based fiction, all with his unique twist, often offering an insider view of the African-American experience. It is in his work for children and young adults that this author best demonstrates his purpose. "What children need are not role models," Lester told an audience of the New England Library Association in a speech reprinted in *Horn Book,* "but heroes and heroines. A hero is one who is larger than life. Because he or she is superhuman, we are inspired to expand the boundaries of what we had thought was possible. We are inspired to attempt the impossible, and in the attempt, we become more wholly human. . . . The task of the hero and heroine belongs to us all. That task is to live with such exuberance that what it is to be human will be expanded until the asphyxiating concepts of race and gender will be rendered meaningless, and then we will be able to see the rainbow around the shoulders of each and every one of us, the rainbow that has been there all the while."

BIOGRAPHICAL AND CRITICAL SOURCES:

BOOKS

Authors and Artists for Young Adults, Volume 12, Gale (Detroit, MI), 1994.

Chevalier, Tracy., *Twentieth-Century Children's Writers,* 3rd edition, St. James Press (Chicago, IL), 1989.

Children's Literature Review, Gale (Detroit, MI), Volume 2, 1976, Volume 41, 1997.

Contemporary Black Biography, Volume 9, Gale (Detroit, MI), 1995.

Krim, Seymour, *You and Me,* Holt, 1972.

Page, James A., and Jae Min Roh, compilers, *Selected Black American, African, and Caribbean Authors,* Libraries Unlimited (Littleton, CO), 1985.

St. James Guide to Young Adult Writers, 2nd edition, St. James Press (Detroit, MI), 1999.

Schomburg Center Guide to Black Literature, Gale (Detroit, MI), 1996.

Silvey, Anita, editor, *Children's Books and Their Creators,* Houghton Mifflin (Boston, MA), 1995.

Spradling, Mary Mace, *In Black and White,* 3rd edition, Gale (Detroit, MI), 1980.

PERIODICALS

African American Review, spring, 1998, Nikola-Lisa, review of *John Henry: Then and Now,* p. 51; spring, 1997, Wilfred D. Samuels, review of *And All Our Wounds Forgiven,* p. 176.

American Visions, December, 1998, review of *Black Cowboy, Wild Horses,* p. 35.

Black Issues Book Review, May, 2001, review of *Pharaoh's Daughter,* p. 82; September, 2001, Khafre Abif, review of *The Blues Singers: Ten Who Rocked the World,* p. 76.

Bloomsbury Review, March, 1995, review of *The Man Who Knew Too Much,* p. 27.

Booklist, February 15, 1994, review of *The Last Tales of Uncle Remus,* p. 1081; June 1, 1994, review of *John Henry,* p. 1809; January 15, 1995, review of *The Last Tales of Uncle Remus,* p. 861; October 14, 1994, Hazel Rochman, review of *The Man Who Knew Too Much,* p. 4342; February 15, 1995, review of *John Henry,* p. 1069, 1094; February 15, 1995, Ilene Cooper, review of *Othello: A Retelling,* p. 1074; April 1, 1995, review of *John Henry,* p. 1411; November 1, 1995, audio book review of *To Be a Slave,* p. 494; March 15 1996, review of *Othello,* p. 1282; March 15, 1996, review of *Othello,* p. 1294; June 1, 1996, review of *Sam and the Tigers,* p. 1722; June 1, 1996, review of *The Tales of Uncle Remus,* p. 1727; January 1997, review of *Sam and the Tigers,* p. 768; April 1, 1997, review of *Sam and the Tigers,* p. 1296; February 15 1998, review of *From Slave Ship to Freedom Road,* p. 1009; May 1, 1998, Michael Cart, review of *Black Cowboy, Wild Horses,* p. 1522; January 1, 1999, review of *From Slave Ship to Freedom Road,* p. 783; February 15, 1999, review of *From Slave Ship to Freedom Road,* p. 1068; February 15, 1999, Ilene Cooper, review of *What a Truly Cool World,* p. 1076; March 15, 1999, review of *From Slave Ship to Freedom Road,* p. 1297; March 15, 1999, audio book review of *John Henry,* p. 1319; April 15, 1999, Shelley Townsend-Hudson, review of *When the Beginning Began: Stories about God, the Creatures, and Us,* p. 1529; October 1, 1999, Ilene Cooper, review of *When the Beginning Began,* p. 372; April 1, 2000, Ilene Cooper, review of *Pharaoh's Daughter,* p. 1474; July, 2000, Hazel Rochman, review of *From Slave Ship to Freedom Road,* p. 2025; September 15, 2000, Hazel Rochman, review of *Albidaro and the Mischievous Dream,* p. 246; February, 2001, Grace Anne A. DeCandido, review of *Ackamarackus: Julius Lester's Sumptuously Silly Fantastically Funny Fables,* p. 1056; May 14, 2001, review of *When Dad Killed Mom,* p. 83; June 1, 2001, Stephanie Zvirin, review of *The Blues Singers,* p. 1870; February 15, 2002, Patricia Austin, audio book review of *To Be a Slave,* p. 1038; September 15, 2003, Paul Shackman, audio book review of *Further Tales of Uncle Remus,* p. 253.

Book Report, February 15, 2001, review of *Othello,* p. 38; September 1, 2001, review of *The Blues Singers,* p. 77; October 1, 2002, John Green, review of *Why Heaven Is Far Away,* p. 345

Book Talker, September, 1990, Pamela A. Todd, review of *How Many Spots Does a Leopard Have?,* p. 5.

Book World, September 3, 1972, William Loren Katz, review of *Long Journey Home,* p. 9.

Bulletin of the Center for Children's Books, April, 1969, Zena Sutherland, review of *To Be a Slave,* pp. 129-130; February, 1970, Zena Sutherland, review of *Black Folktales,* p. 101; October, 1994, Elizabeth Bush, review of *John Henry,* p. 54; November, 1994, review of *The Man Who Knew Too Much,* p. 92; March, 1995, review of *Othello,* p. 241; July, 1996, review of *Sam and the Tigers,* p. 378; February, 1998, review of *From Slave Ship to Freedom Road,* p. 212; May, 1998, review of *Black Cowboy, Wild Horses,* p. 327; February, 1999, review of *What a Truly Cool World,* p. 207; April, 1999, review of *When the Beginning Began,* p. 285; March, 2001, review of *Ackamarackus,* p. 268; May, 2001, review of *The Blues Singers,* p. 342; May, 2001, review of *When Dad Killed Mom,* p. 342.

Catholic Library World, March, 1997, review of *John Henry,* p. 14.

Children's Book and Play Review, May, 2001, review of *Albidaro and the Mischievous Dream,* p. 13.

Children's Book Review Service, December, 1994, review of *John Henry,* p. 43; February, 1995, review of *The Man Who Knew Too Much,* p. 76; November, 1996, review of *Sam and the Tigers,* p. 26; May, 1998, review of *From Slave Ship to Freedom Road,* p. 119.

Children's Bookwatch, February, 1995, review of *The Man Who Knew Too Much,* p. 5; June, 2001, review of *Ackamarackus,* p. 4.

Christian Century, July 20, 1988, Douglas Stone, review of *Lovesong,* p. 682.

Dissent, winter, 1989, p. 116.

Early Childhood Education Journal, spring, 1997, review of *Sam and the Tigers,* p. 176; fall, 1997, review of *John Henry,* p. 48.

Emergency Librarian, September, 1995, review of *Othello,* p. 58; September, 1996, review of *Othello.*

English Journal, January, 1996, review of *Othello,* p. 89.

Entertainment Weekly, January 28, 1994, review of *The Last Tales of Uncle Remus,* p. 70.

Essence, August, 1989, p. 98; July, 1991, p. 100.

Horn Book, October, 1972, review of *The Knee-High Man and Other Tales,* p. 463; June, 1975, review of *Who I Am,* p. 198; August, 1982, review of *This Strange New Feeling,* pp. 414-415; July-August, 1987, Mary M. Burns, review of *The Tales of Uncle Remus,* pp. 477-478; September-October, 1988, Mary M. Burns, review of *More Tales of Uncle Remus,* pp. 639-40; January-February, 1990, review of *How Many Spots Does a Leopard Have?,* p. 79; July-August, 1990, Elizabeth S. Watson, review of *Further Tales of Uncle Remus,* p. 478; May, 1994, review of *The Last Tales of Uncle Remus,* p. 341; November-December, 1994, Ann A. Flowers, review of *John Henry,* p. 739; fall, 1994, review of *The Last Tales of Uncle Remus,* p. 342; January, 1996, audio book review of *To Be A Slave,* p. 105; September, 1996, review of *Sam and the Tigers,* p. 536; July-August, 1998, Lauren Adams, review of *Black Cowboy, Wild Horses,* p. 477; March, 1999, Margaret A. Bush, review of *What a Truly Cool World,* p. 196; July, 1999, review of *When the Beginning Began,* p. 476; January, 2000, review of *Uncle Remus: The Complete Tales,* p. 61; July, 2000, review of *Pharaoh's Daughter,* p. 460; May 1, 2001, Deborah Z. Porter, review of *When Dad Killed Mom,* p. 330; November-December, 2002, Joanna Rudge Long, review of *Why Heaven Is Far Away,* p. 735.

Hungry Mind Review, summer, 1995, review of *Othello,* p. 41; spring, 1998, review of *From Slave Ship to Freedom Road,* p. 45.

Instructor, November, 1995, review of *The Last Tales of Uncle Remus,* p. 51; May, 1998, review of *Sam and the Tigers,* p. 62.

Interracial Books for Children Bulletin, 1975, Barbara Walker, review of *Who I Am,* p. 18;

Journal of Adolescent and Adult Literacy, October, 1997, review of *Sam and the Tigers,* p. 161;

Journal of Reading, May, 1995, review of *Othello,* p. 687.

Junior Bookshelf, February, 1975.

Kirkus Reviews, January 1, 1994, review of *The Last Tales of Uncle Remus,* p. 70; May 1, 1994, review of *And All Our Wounds Forgiven,* p. 581; October 15, 1994, review of *John Henry,* p. 1410; October 15, 1994, review of *The Man Who Knew Too Much,* p. 410; March 15, 1995, review of *Othello,* p. 386; August 1, 1996, review of *Sam and the Tigers,* p. 1154; November 15, 1997, review of *From Slave Ship to Freedom Road,* p. 1709; May 1, 1998, review of *Black Cowboy, Wild Horses,* p. 661; December 15, 1998, review of *What a Truly Cool World,* p. 1799; April 15, 1999, review of *When the Beginning Began,* p. 631; April 1, 2001, review of *The Blues Singers,* p. 499; April 1, 2001, review of *When Dad Killed Mom,* p. 500; October 1, 2003, review of *Shining,* p. 1226.

Kliatt, May, 1998, review of *Othello,* p. 14; May 1, 2001, review of *When Dad Killed Mom,* p. 12; July, 2003, Paula Rohrlick, review of *When Dad Killed Mom,* p. 24.

Language Arts, October, 1995, review of *John Henry,* p. 437.

Learning, November, 1996, review of *Sam and the Tigers,* p. 29.

Library Journal, January 1, 1975, Deborah H. Williams, review of *Who I Am,* p. 54.

Library Talk, November, 1994, review of *John Henry,* p. 23; May, 1995, review of *The Man Who Knew Too Much,* p. 52; September, 1995, review of *John Henry,* p. 43.

Los Angeles Times Book Review, January 31, 1988; January 27, 1991, p. 8; January 22, 1995, review of *John Henry,* p. 8; December 8, 1996, review of *Sam and the Tigers,* p. 19; March 25, 2001, review of *Ackamarackus,* p. 6; July 8, 2001, review of *The Blues Singers,* p. 12; December 2, 2001, review of *The Blues Singers,* p. 15; December 2, 2001, review of *Ackamarackus,* p. 16.

Magpies, March, 1997, review of *Sam and the Tigers,* p. 27.

Nation, June 22, 1970.

New Advocate, summer, 1990, p. 206; summer, 1995, review of *John Henry,* p. 209.

New Yorker, November 18, 1996, review of *Sam and the Tigers,* p. 98.

New York Review of Books, April 20, 1972, Eric Foner and Naomi Lewis, review of *Long Journey Home,* pp. 41-42.

New York Times, December 7, 1998, review of *Black Cowboy, Wild Horses,* p. E7; August 12, 2001, Peter Keepnews, review of *The Blues Singers,* p. 24; December 22, 2002, Sandy MacDonald, review of *Why Heaven Is Far Away,* p. 18.

New York Times Book Review, November 3, 1968, John Howard Griffin, review of *To Be a Slave,* p. 7; November 9, 1969, John A. Williams, review of *Black Folktales,* p. 10; October 11, 1972, Anatole Broyard, review of *Two Love Stories,* p. 41; July 23, 1972, Rosalind K. Goddard, review of *Long Journey Home,* p. 8; February 4, 1973, Ethel Richards, review of *The Knee-High Man and Other Tales,* p. 8; September 5, 1982; February 17, 1985;

February 9, 1986, review of *To Be a Slave,* p. 32; May 17, 1987, p. 32; January 31, 1988, Joel Oppenheimer, review of *The Soul That Wanders,* p. 12; January 14, 1990, review of *How Many Spots Does a Leopard Have?,* p. 17; August 12, 1990, p. 29; August 7, 1994, review of *And All Our Wounds Forgiven,* p. 14; June 19, 1994, review of *The Last Tales of Uncle Remus,* p. 28; November 13, 1994, Jack Zipes, review of *John Henry,* p. 30; April 23, 1995, review of *Othello,* p. 27; November 10, 1996, review of *Sam and the Tigers,* p. 34; August 12, 2001, review of *The Blues Singers,* p. 24.

Parents, December, 1994, review of *John Henry,* p. 24.

Parents Choice, 1994, review of *John Henry,* p. 18; September, 1995, review of *Othello,* p. 14.

Partisan Review, Volume 57, number 2, 1990, pp. 321-325.

Plays, October, 1998, review of *Black Cowboy, Wild Horses,* p. 64.

Publishers Weekly, October 20, 1969, review of *Black Folktales,* p. 60; January 19, 1970, review of *To Be a Slave,* p. 83; June 5, 1972, review of *Long Journey Home,* p. 140; August 7, 1972, review of *The Knee-High Man and Other Tales,* p. 50; August 28, 1972, review of *Two Love Stories,* p. 259; March 20, 1987, Mary M. Burns, review of *The Tales of Uncle Remus,* p. 80; February 12, 1988, Barry List, "PW Interviews: Julius Lester," pp. 67-68; October 27, 1989, review of *How Many Spots Does a Leopard Have?,* p. 68; September 14, 1990, review of *Falling Pieces of the Broken Sky,* p. 115; May 2, 1994, review of *And All Our Wounds Forgiven,* p. 282; July 18, 1994, review of *To Be a Slave,* p. 31; September 4, 1994, review of *John Henry,* p. 108; November 7, 1994, review of *The Man Who Knew Too Much,* p. 241; March 20, 1995, review of *Othello,* p. 62; August 5, 1996, review of *Sam and the Tigers,* p. 441; December 1, 1997, review of *From Slave Ship to Freedom Road,* p. 54; April 6, 1998, review of *Black Cowboy, Wild Horses,* p. 78; November 23, 1998, review of *To Be a Slave,* p. 69; January 4, 1999, review of *What a Truly Cool World,* p. 89; February 1, 1999, review of *The Tales of Uncle Remus,* p. 87; March 22, 1999, review of *When the Beginning Began,* p. 89; November 8, 1999, review of *Uncle Remus: The Complete Tales,* p. 70; December 13 1999, review of *From Slave Ship to Freedom Road,* p. 85; October, 2000, review of *Albidaro and the Mischievous Dream,* p. 81; February 12, 2001, Sally Lodge, "Working at His Creative Peak," p. 180; March 5, 2001, review of *Ackamarackus,* p. 79; May 14, 2001, review of *The Blues Singers,* p. 81; May 14, 2001, review of *When Dad Killed Mom,* p. 83; June 30, 2003, review of *When Dad Killed Mom,* p. 82.

Quill & Quire, December, 1989, Susan Perren, review of *How Many Spots Does a Leopard Have?,* p. 24.

Reading Teacher, February, 1994, review of *Long Journey Home,* p. 410; November, 1995, review of *John Henry,* p. 238; December, 1995, review of *John Henry,* p. 329; March, 1999, review of *From Slave Ship to Freedom Road,* p. 628; April, 1999, review of *Black Cowboy, Wild Horses,* p. 761; November, 1999, review of *Black Cowboy, Wild Horses,* p. 250; November, 1999, review of *From Slave Ship to Freedom Road,* p. 254; May, 2001, review of *Sam and the Tigers,* p. 812; October, 2001, review of *Pharaoh's Daughter,* p. 186.

School Librarian, May, 1988, Irene Babsky, review of *The Tales of Uncle Remus,* p. 72.

School Library Journal, May, 1969, Evelyn Geller, "Julius Lester: Newbery Runner-Up"; September 1976, Kathryn Robinson, review of *All Is Well,* p. 146; April, 1982, Hazel Rochman, review of *This Strange New Feeling,* p. 83; April, 1987, Kay McPherson, review of *The Last Tales of Uncle Remus,* p. 99; June-July, 1988, Kay McPherson, review of *More Tales of Uncle Remus,* p. 92; November, 1989, Kay McPherson, review of *How Many Spots Does the Leopard Have?,* p. 99; May, 1990, Kay McPherson, review of *Further Tales of Uncle Remus,* p. 99; January, 1994, review of *The Last Tales of Uncle Remus,* p. 124; November, 1994, review of *John Henry,* p. 98; December, 1994, review of *The Man Who Knew Too Much,* p. 124; April 1995, Margaret Cole, review of *Othello,* p. 154; August, 1996, review of *Sam and the Tigers,* p. 126; December, 1996, review of *Sam and the Tigers,* p. 30; February 1998, review of *From Slave Ship to Freedom Road,* p. 119; November, 1997, review of *Sam and the Tigers,* p. 41; June, 1998, review of *Black Cowboy, Wild Horses,* p. 113; August, 1998, review of *Black Cowboy, Wild Horses,* p. 43; April, 1999, review of *What a Truly Cool World,* p. 102; May, 1999, review of *When the Beginning Began,* p. 139; June, 2000, Barbara Scotto, review of *Pharaoh's Daughter,* p. 148; November, 2000, Julie Cummins, review of *Albidaro and the Mischievous Dream,* p. 126; March, 2001, Wendy Lukehart, review of *Ackamarackus,* p. 214; May, 2001, Francisca Goldsmith, review of *When Dad Killed Mom,*

p. 155; June, 2001, review of *The Blues Singers,* p. 138; December, 2001, review of *The Blues Singers,* p. 47.

Social Education, April, 1995, review of *John Henry,* p. 216; April, 1995, review of *The Last Tales of Uncle Remus,* p. 216; April, 1997, review of *Sam and the Tigers,* p. 5; May, 1999, review of *Black Cowboy, Wild Horses,* p. 8; May, 1999, review of *From Slave Ship to Freedom Road,* p. 7; October, 2002, Miriam Lang Budin, review of *Why Heaven Is Far Away,* p. 118; October, 2002, Bonnie Bolton, audio book review of *The Tales of Uncle Remus: The Adventures of Brer Rabbit,* p. 87.

Time, September 9, 1996, review of *Sam and the Tigers,* p. 72.

Times Literary Supplement, April 3, 1987.

Tribune Books (Chicago, IL), February 26, 1989, p. 8; February 11, 1990, p. 6; November 13, 1994, review of *John Henry,* p. 6; April 29, 2001, review of *Ackamarackus,* p. 8; July 1, 2001, review of *When Dad Killed Mom,* p. 2.

Village Voice, September 17, 1996, review of *Sam and the Tigers,* p. 49.

Voice of Youth Advocates, June, 1995, review of *Othello,* p. 96; April, 1998, review of *This Strange New Feeling,* p. 43; February, 1999, review of *From Slave Ship to Freedom Road,* p. 412; June, 1999, Kathleen Beck, review of *When the Beginning Began,* p. 134; February, 2001, review of *Pharaoh's Daughter,* p. 399; August, 2001, review of *The Blues Singers,* p. 225; October, 2001, review of *Voice of Youth Advocates,* p. 280.

Washington Post, March 12, 1985.

Washington Post Book World, September 3, 1972; February 14, 1988; December 4, 1994, review of *John Henry,* p. 21; February 11 1996, review of *And All Our Wounds Forgiven,* p. 12; June 7, 1998, review of *Black Cowboy, Wild Horses,* p. 8.

ONLINE

Children's Literature, http://www.childrenslit.com/ (November 22, 2003), "Julius Lester."

Houghton Mifflin Education Place, http://www.eduplace.com/kids/hmr/ (November 22, 2003), "Julius Lester."

KidsReads, http://www.kidsreads.com/ (November 22, 2003), Shannon Maughan, review of *Ackamarackus.*

Once upon a Lap, http://wildes.home.mindspring.com/OUAL/int/ (November 22, 2003), reprint of interview with Lester.

Rutgers University, http://scils.rutgers.edu/ (March 28, 1999), "Julius Lester."*

LIVINGSTON, Jane S(helton) 1944-

PERSONAL: Born February 12, 1944, in Upland, CA; daughter of Leonard and Frances (Dundas) Shelton. *Education:* Pomona College, B.A., 1965; Harvard University, M.A., 1966.

ADDRESSES: *Agent*—c/o Author Mail, Chronicle Books, 85 Second St., Sixth Floor, San Francisco, CA 94105.

CAREER: Los Angeles County Museum of Art, Los Angeles, CA, curator of modern art, 1967-75; Corcoran Gallery of Art, Washington, DC, associate director and chief curator, 1975-89. Member of museum advisory panel of National Endowment for the Arts, 1976-79.

MEMBER: International Council of Museums, Association of American Museums, College Art Association of America, Artists Space (New York, NY; trustee), American Art Alliance.

AWARDS, HONORS: Decorated with Order of the Crown Belgium.

WRITINGS:

(With Maurice Tuckman) *Art and Technology,* Viking (New York, NY), 1970.

Ed McGowin's True Stories, Corcoran Gallery of Art (Washington, DC), 1975.

M. Alvarez Bravo, David R. Godine (Boston, MA), 1976.

Black Folk Art in America, 1930-1980, University Press of Mississippi (Jackson, MS), 1982.

Wisconsin Biennial, 1982, Madison Art Center (Madison, WI), 1982.

Ad Reinhardt, Seventeen Works, Corcoran Gallery of Art (Washington, DC), 1984.

(Author of essay) Frances Fralin, editor, *The Indelible Image: Photographs of War, 1846 to the Present,* Abbeville Press (New York, NY), 1985.

(With Alan Fern and Michael Evans) *People and Power: Portraits from the Federal Village,* Abrams (New York, NY), 1985.

(With Robert Frank and others) *Charles Pratt: Photographs,* Aperture (Millerton, NY), 1985.

(With Rosalind E. Krauss) *L'Amour fou: Photography and Surrealism,* with an essay by Dawn Ades, Abbeville Press (New York, NY), 1985.
(With John Ashbery and others) *Kitaj Paintings, Drawings, Pastels,* Thames & Hudson (New York, NY), 1986.
(With Samuel Beckett and others) *Arikha,* Thames & Hudson (New York, NY), 1986.
(With John Beardsley) *Hispanic Art in the United States: Thirty Contemporary Painters and Sculptors,* Abbeville Press (New York, NY), 1987.
(With Frances Fralin and Declan Haun) *Odyssey: The Art of Photography at National Geographic,* Thomasson-Grant (Charlottesville, VA), 1988.
Lee Miller, Photographer, Thames & Hudson (New York, NY), 1989.
Thomas Chimes: The Hermes Cycle, Locks Art Publications (Philadelphia, PA), 1992.
The New York School: Photographs, 1936-1963, Stewart, Tabori & Chang (New York, NY), 1992.
(Adapter) Pierre Borhan, editor, *Andre Kertesz: His Life and Work,* Little Brown (Boston, MA), 1994.
(Author of essay) Mary Shanahan, editor, *Evidence, 1944-1994* (Richard Avedon exhibit), Random House (New York, NY), 1994.
Oyvind Fahlstrom: die Installationen (exhibition catalog), Cantz (Ostfildern, Germany), 1995.
(Editor, with Dena Andre and Philip Brookman) *Hospice: A Photographic Inquiry,* photographs by Jim Goldberg, Little, Brown (Boston, MA), 1996.
Visions of Victory: A Century of Sports Photography, Pindar Press (New York, NY), 1996.
(Author of essay) Eleanor Lanahan, editor, *Zelda, an Illustrated Life: The Private World of Zelda Fitzgerald,* Abrams (New York, NY), 1996.
The Art of Richard Diebenkorn, University of California Press (Berkeley, CA), 1997.
Strange but True: The Arizona Photographs of Allen Dutton, Corcoran Gallery of Art (Washington, DC), 2001.
(With others) *The Quilts of Gee's Bend: Masterpieces from a Lost Place,* Tinwood Books (Atlanta, GA), 2002.
(With others) *Gee's Bend: The Women and Their Quilts,* Tinwood Books (Atlanta, GA), 2002.
The Paintings of Joan Mitchell, University of California Press (Berkeley, CA), 2002.
Richard Diebenkorn: Figurative Works on Paper, Chronicle Books (San Francisco, CA), 2003.

Author of exhibition catalogs. Corresponding editor of *Art in America,* 1970—.

SIDELIGHTS: Curator, art expert, and author Jane S. Livingston is a writer of major books and exhibition catalogs on art and photography. In addition to her own books, Livingston has edited and contributed to the work of other writers and has adapted volumes considered key to the art world. Among her earliest published works is *Black Folk Art in America, 1930-1980,* a catalog published in conjunction with an exhibition of African-American folk art that traveled across the United States in 1982 and 1983. Livingston's catalog features biographies and artwork for twenty African-American folk artists, including photographs, illustrations, and descriptions of their art.

In her next major effort, Livingston combined her interests in art and photography. Along with Rosalind Krauss and Dawn Ades, she studied the role photography played in the Surrealism movement, publishing her conclusions in a catalog for a traveling exhibition titled, *L'Amour fou: Photography and Surrealism.* "In this rich picture book," a reviewer for *Publishers Weekly* said, the authors "examine the very extensive role of photography (an unlikely medium on the face of it) in the surrealist movement. . . . A scholarly tour de force."

Moving away from photography temporarily, Livingston next turned her attention to realism. In *Arikha,* Livingston remarked that the work of this Israeli artist is "like the power of experienced life itself, in which subject matter is rarely, until later, the issue." *Hispanic Art in the United States: Thirty Contemporary Painters and Sculptors* was also created to accentuate a traveling exhibition. This book includes essays, photographs, illustrations, and biographical sketches of thirty Hispanic artists.

In her first major offering as a solo writer, *Lee Miller: A Photographer Rediscovered,* Livingston "interweaves an informative, well-written text with full-page reproductions of [Miller's] photographs," noted Steven Hupp of the *Library Journal.* Fashion model, photographer, mother, and war correspondent Lee Miller's remarkable talent is presented in this "rich selection of her finest photographs," said Hupp, "one that will ensure Lee Miller's place among the great photographers of the twentieth century."

Livingston has continued to produce volume after volume of acclaimed and well-received books and catalogs, including *Evidence, 1944-1994,* which the publisher described as the "definitive account of the life and work of Richard Avedon." *The New York School: Photographs, 1936-1963* displays the collective photographs of a loosely defined group of photographers who lived and worked in New York City during the 1930s, 40s, and 50s. *Indelible Image: Photographs of War, 1946 to the Present* is a collection of 135 select images of war. *Odyssey: The Art of Photography at National Geographic* is a retrospective of National Geographic's outstanding photojournalism over the past century.

Showing the dramatic range encompassed by Livingston's work, her next photographic collection represents a topic controversial in its artistic value. *Hospice: A Photographic Inquiry* was created as a result of a joint sponsorship between the Corcoran Gallery of Art and the National Hospice Foundation. The book was then edited by Livingston. Essays and biographical portfolios interspersed throughout the collected photographs make for an impressive book.

Strange but True: The Arizona Photographs of Allen Dutton is a companion volume for Dutton's first solo exhibition at a major museum, an immense project comprising thousands of images taken over almost two decades. In two separate volumes, Livingston presents the masterful and stunning folk creations of the women of Gee's Bend, Alabama. *The Quilts of Gee's Bend: Masterpieces from a Lost Place* and its sister volume *Gee's Bend: The Women and Their Quilts* illustrate in print the visual exhibition that toured the United States.

The Paintings of Joan Mitchell is another exhibition catalog published to accompany a traveling exhibition of the artist's work. Mitchell, considered a foremost abstract expressionist in American art, expresses dislike for the public's propensity to pigeonhole her as either an artist or as a woman. "Using Mitchell's journals and correspondence, Livingston follows the evolution of Mitchell's painting and discusses her technique, which showed more concern with color than with the integrity of the medium," commented Sandra Rothenberg in a review for the *Library Journal.*

Livingston has taken part in two books featuring American painter Richard Diebenkorn, who has been most often associated with California. Diebenkorn has been known for his characteristic style, modernist, bright palette, and thick brushwork. He shocked the art world when he abruptly shifted to representational art, but his eventual return to the abstract is seen in a series of paintings titled *Ocean Park.* The first book which involved Livingston is titled *The Art of Richard Diebenkorn,* a catalog accompanying a traveling exhibit of his work. It is characterized as "a comprehensive catalog . . . intended to enhance understanding of his devotion to modernism and the influences upon his accomplishments," said Joan Levin of the *Library Journal.*

BIOGRAPHICAL AND CRITICAL SOURCES:

PERIODICALS

American Reference Books Annual, 1983, review of *Black Folk Art in America, 1930-1980,* p. 386.

Art in America, November, 1989, Brian Wallis, "Can a Crippled Corcoran Survive?," p. 41.

Bloomsbury Review, March, 1993, review of *The New York School: Photographs, 1936-1963,* p. 92; July, 1998, review of *The Art of Richard Diebenkorn,* p. 4.

Booklist, November 15, 1988, review of *Odyssey: The Art of Photography at National Geographic,* p. 529; September 1, 1989, review of *Lee Miller, Photographer,* p. 23; February 1, 1993, review of *The New York School,* p. 964; December 18, 1993, review of *Black Folk Art in America, 1930-1980,* p. 1042; November 1, 1997, Donna Seaman, review of *The Art of Richard Diebenkorn,* p. 445; September 1, 2002, Donna Seaman, review of *The Paintings of Joan Mitchell,* p. 38.

Bookman's Weekly, October 31, 1988, review of *Odyssey,* p. 1678; March 22, 1993, review of *The New York School,* p. 1220.

Bookwatch, February, 1993, review of *The New York School,* p. 4.

Burlington, December, 1997, review of *The Art of Richard Diebenkorn,* p. 900.

Business Week, December 12, 1988, review of *Odyssey,* p. 133.

Choice, March, 1989, review of *Odyssey,* p. 1145; March, 1993, review of *The New York School,* p. 1136.

Christian Science Monitor, December 18, 1992, review of *The New York School,* p. 11.

Entertainment Weekly, January 29, 1993, review of *The New York School,* p. 53.

Hungry Mind Review, November, 1989, review of *Lee Miller, Photographer,* p. 9; winter, 1997, review of *The Art of Richard Diebenkorn,* p. 14.

Kliatt Young Adult Paperback Book Guide, September, 1989, review of *Black Folk Art in America, 1930-1980,* p. 51.

Library Journal, November 15, 1985, review of *The Indelible Image,* p. 89; December, 1988, review of *Odyssey,* p. 100; January, 1989, review of *Odyssey,* p. 44; September 1, 1989, review of *Lee Miller, Photographer,* p. 188; October, 1989, review of *Black Folk Art in America, 1930-1980,* p. 23; December 6, 1992, review of *The New York School,* p. 41; January, 1998, Joan Levin, review of *The Art of Richard Diebenkorn,* p. 95; September 15, 2002, Sandra Rothenberg, review of *The Paintings of Joan Mitchell,* p. 58; October 15, 2003, Ellen Bates, review of *Richard Diebenkorn: Figurative Works on Paper,* p. 65.

Maclean's, December 12, 1988, review of *Odyssey,* p. 61.

New Republic, February 3, 1986, Richard Howard, review of *L'Amour fou: Photography and Surrealism,* p. 33; June 13, 1994, Jed Perl, review of *Richard Avedon: Evidence, 1944-1994,* p. 33.

New Statesman, July 22, 1994, review of *Odyssey,* p. 43.

New York, December 14, 1992, review of *The New York School,* p. 92.

New York Times, March 21, 1982, review of *Black Folk Art in America, 1930-1980,* p. 31; December 8, 1985, Andy Grundberg, review of *L'Amour fou,* p. 24; September 14, 1989, Barbara Gamarekian, "Curator of Mapplethorpe Resigns Posts at Corcoran," p. B3.

New York Times Book Review, July 30, 1989, review of *Lee Miller, Photographer,* p. 17; December 6, 1992, review of *The New York School,* p. 20; December 8, 2002, Christopher Benfey, "Art," review of *The Paintings of Joan Mitchell,* p. 20.

Petersen's Photographic, March, 1989, review of *Odyssey,* p. 78.

PSA Journal, July, 1988, Daniel H. deCournoyer, review of *L'Amour fou,* p. 10.

Publishers Weekly, 1985, review of *The Indelible Image,* p. 412; April 18, 1994, review of *Evidence, 1944-1994,* p. 52; May 6, 1996, review of *Zelda, an Illustrated Life: The Private World of Zelda Fitzgerald,* p. 63.

Reference and Research Book News, December, 1991, review of *The New York School,* p. 38.

School Library Journal, October, 1996, Barbara Hawkins, review of *Zelda,* p. 166.

Times Literary Supplement, March 19, 1993, review of *The New York School,* p. 9.

Tribune Books (Chicago, IL), December 4, 1988, review of *Odyssey,* p. 5; December 6, 1992, review of *The New York School,* p. 3.

Utne Reader, July, 1991, review of *Lee Miller, Photographer,* p. 132.

Village Voice Literary Supplement, November, 1992, review of *The New York School,* p. 21.

Washington Post, December 14, 1992, Jo Ann Lewis, "Portrait of a Curator: Life after the Corcoran" (interview), p. B1.

West Coast Review of Books, 1989, review of *Odyssey,* p. 59.

Women's Review of Books, October, 1989, review of *Lee Miller, Photographer,* p. 7.

ONLINE

University of California Press, http://www.ucpress.edu/ (November 22, 2003), "Jane Livingston."*

* * *

LYNCH, Thomas 1948-

PERSONAL: Born October 16, 1948, in Detroit, MI; married; wife's name Mary Tata; children: Heather, Tom, Michael, Sean. *Ethnicity:* "American." *Education:* Wayne State University, certification in mortuary science.

ADDRESSES: *Office*—Lynch and Sons, 404 East Liberty, Milford, MI 48381. *Agent*—Richard McDonough. *E-mail*—thoslynch@aol.com.

CAREER: Writer. Lynch and Sons (funeral home), Milford, MI, funeral director.

AWARDS, HONORS: American Book Award, 1998, and nomination for National Book Award, both for *The Undertaking: Life Studies from the Dismal Trade.*

WRITINGS:

Skating with Heather Grace (poetry), Knopf (New York, NY), 1986.

Grimalkin and Other Poems, J. Cape (London, England), 1994.

The Undertaking: Life Studies from the Dismal Trade (essays), W. W. Norton (New York, NY), 1997.
Still Life in Milford (poetry), W. W. Norton (New York, NY), 1998.
Bodies in Motion and at Rest: On Metaphor and Mortality (essays), W. W. Norton (New York, NY), 2000.

WORK IN PROGRESS: Godhelpus: We Irish and Americans, essays; *Late Fictions,* short stories; *Walking Papers,* poetry.

SIDELIGHTS: Essayist, poet, and funeral director Thomas Lynch has written three critically acclaimed volumes of poetry and two award-winning volumes of essays. By using his own daily routine as poetic fodder, Lynch has transformed the mundane task of preparing the dead into a life-affirming event. His lyrical, elegaic poems describe the dead citizens of Milford, Michigan, his own family relationships, and scenes and myths from his Irish Catholic upbringing.

Skating with Heather Grace, Lynch's first collection, contains forty-two poems that feature scenes from his everyday life, and his wife, dog, children, and work all make appearances. Some of the poems are set in Michigan, while others use Ireland or Italy as a backdrop. The title poem is a "tender meditation" about Lynch's daughter, according to a *Publishers Weekly* critic. *Library Journal* reviewer Rosaly DeMaios Roffman found that the poems "unpretentiously rehearse the dreams of the dying as they celebrate the everchanging relationships of the living." Lynch, according to Roffman, crafts poems that weave symbolism and mythology into the human experience. Of particular merit are the poems about Argyle, the mythical Sin-Eater who tends to the souls of the dead, Roffman suggested.

Lynch's second volume, *Grimalkin and Other Poems,* likewise contains elements of the poet's professional and personal life mixed with his ruminations about Irish culture and history. One can hear echoes of the Catholic liturgy, the church choir, and the "voices of lament in his ancestral County Clare, and all of the sacred mysteries for him were translated early into women's flesh," according to *Agenda* critic Alan Wall. In a "strong" and "elegiac" poetic voice, according to Wall, Lynch buries the dead and other things, such as a marriage, old loves, and the sexual ghosts of his childhood, with equal panache.

The Undertaking: Life Studies from the Dismal Trade is a collection of twelve essays that reflect the author's "eloquent, meditative observations on the place of death in small-town life," according to a critic in *Kirkus Reviews.* Lynch's poetic vision is indelibly colored by his undertaking business, and what he sees often contrasts with what lies on the surface. While his wife admires the architectural styles of buildings they encounter on an evening stroll, he sees a couple, wonderful dancers both, dead from asphyxiation in the garage. From the embalming of his own father to the opening of the newly refurbished bridge to the Milford cemetery, Lynch writes about death "with dignity and passion," according to a *Publishers Weekly* reviewer, resulting in "a superb collection of essays." *Observer* reviewer Matthew Sweeney admired the "balance and clarity" of Lynch's writing, which occupies different emotional registers, "moving from the humorous to the tender to the stern." Dispelling the myths about people in his trade, Lynch wrote, "I am no more attracted to the dead than the dentist is to your bad gums, the doctor to your rotten innards, or the accountant to your sloppy expense records." His profession has provided Lynch not only with a living, but with a unique vantage point from which to observe the entire cycle of life.

Bodies in Motion and at Rest: On Metaphor and Mortality is a collection of essays described by *New York Times Book Review* contributor Sherie Posesorski as an "engaging hybrid of memoir, meditation, and comic monologue. . . . Lynch approaches his subjects with a beautifully executed balance of irreverence with reverence, gallows humor with emotional delicacy, and no-nonsense immanence with lyrical transcendence." Lynch writes of his Roman Catholic childhood, his family, being a father, and the relationship between "mortuary and literary arts."

Barbara Brown Taylor wrote in *Christian Century* that "hailed as 'a cross between Garrison Keillor and William Butler Yeats,' Lynch is living proof of his thesis that familiarity with the facts of death improves one's capacity for the wonders of life. . . . The essays in this book contain wrenching accounts of his and his son's battles with addiction as well as luminous tales of love between husband, wife, parent, and child." Taylor said readers "may expect a poet's eye for image and a poet's ear for language, as well as a poet's ability to hold open the door to meaning without shoving anyone through."

BIOGRAPHICAL AND CRITICAL SOURCES:

BOOKS

Lynch, Thomas, *The Undertaking: Life Studies from the Dismal Trade,* W. W. Norton (New York, NY), 1997.

PERIODICALS

Agenda, autumn, 1994, Alan Wall, review of *Grimalkin and Other Poems,* p. 241.

American Book Collector, July, 1982, p. 57.

Bomb, summer, 2000, Glenn Moomau, review of *Bodies in Motion and at Rest: On Metaphor and Mortality,* p. 21.

Booklist, March 15, 1988, p. 1226; August, 1998, Donna Seaman, review of *Still Life in Milford,* p. 1954; June 1, 2000, Donna Seaman, review of *Bodies in Motion and at Rest,* p. 1803.

Christian Century, November 18, 1998, review of *The Undertaking,* p. 1119; November 22, 2000, Barbara Brown Taylor, review of *Bodies in Motion and at Rest,* p. 1216.

Commonweal, September 11, 1987, p. 507; June 19, 1998, Frank McConnell, review of *The Undertaking,* p. 20.

Georgia Review, summer, 1987, p. 507; fall, 2002, Sanford Pinsker, review of *Bodies in Motion and at Rest,* pp. 854-862.

Hudson Review, autumn, 1987, p. 508; summer, 1999, Thomas M. Disch, review of *Still Life in Milford,* p. 315.

Inc., July, 1998, review of *The Undertaking,* p. 11.

Insight on the News, July 17, 2000, Stephen Goode, "Lynch Writes from Unique Background," p. 36.

Kiplinger's Personal Finance, February, 2002, Kristin Davis, "Six Feet Under: Thomas Lynch Has Buried 6,000 of His Neighbors; He Talks about the Business of Death," p. 78.

Kirkus Reviews, May 1, 1997, review of *The Undertaking,* p. 699.

Knight Ridder/Tribune News Service, June 21, 2000, Marta Salij, "Thomas Lynch: Poet in Motion," p. K2676.

Library Journal, March 1, 1987, Rosaly DeMaios Roffman, review of *Skating with Heather Grace,* p. 79; September 15, 1998, Barbara Hoffert, review of *Still Life in Milford,* p. 83.

Nation, June 9, 1997, p. 28.

New York Review of Books, September 24, 1998, A. Alvarez, review of *The Undertaking,* p. 24.

New York Times, July 23, 1997, p. C14; May 31, 2000, Richard Bernstein, review of *Bodies in Motion and at Rest,* p. E8; June 8, 2000, Dinitia Smith, "Matters of Life and Death: A Prizewinning Writer Holds onto His Day Job as a Funeral Director," p. E1.

New York Times Book Review, October 4, 1987, p. 24; September 24, 2000, Sherie Posesorski, review of *Bodies in Motion and at Rest,* p. 23.

Observer, October 9, 1994, p. 24; October 23, 1994, p. 17; November 20, 1994, pp. 2, 5; April 6, 1997, Matthew Sweeney, review of *The Undertaking,* p. 17.

Poetry, May, 1988, p. 104; December, 1998, John Taylor, review of *Still Life in Milford,* p. 184.

Publishers Weekly, December 26, 1986, review of *Skating with Heather Grace,* p. 54; May 5, 1997, review of *The Undertaking,* p. 184; June 29, 1998, review of *Still Life in Milford,* p. 53.

Quadrant, March, 1998, Iain Bamforth, review of *The Undertaking,* p. 81.

Spectator, July 15, 2000, Harry Mount, review of *Bodies in Motion and at Rest,* p. 34.

Times Educational Supplement, December 23, 1994, p. 19.

Times Literary Supplement, September 25, 1998, David Wheatley, review of *Still Life in Milford,* p. 24; July 14, 2000, David Wheatley, review of *Bodies in Motion and at Rest,* p. 27.

U.S. Catholic, November, 2002, "What Makes a Good Funeral? The Editors Interview Thomas Lynch," p. 12.

Virginia Quarterly Review, summer, 1987, p. 100.

Washington Post Book World, May 3, 1987, p. 8.

M

MACGOYE, Marjorie (King) Oludhe 1928-

PERSONAL: Born 1928, in Southampton, England; immigrated to Kenya, 1954; naturalized Kenyan citizen, 1964; married D. G. W. Oludhe Macgoye (a clinic official; died, 1990); children: four. *Ethnicity:* "Caucasian." *Education:* University of London, B.A. and M.A.

ADDRESSES: *Home*—P.O. Box 70344, Nairobi 00400, Kenya.

CAREER: Poet and novelist. Worked as a missionary bookseller.

AWARDS, HONORS: Sinclair Prize of Fiction, 1986, for *Coming to Birth;* Arts and Africa Poetry Award, British Broadcasting Corp.

WRITINGS:

FICTION

Growing Up at Lina School (young adult), East African Publishing House (Nairobi, Kenya), 1971, reprinted, Heinemann (Nairobi, Kenya), 1988.

Murder in Majengo, (in "New Fiction from Africa" series), Oxford University Press (Nairobi, Kenya), 1972.

Coming to Birth, Heinemann (Nairobi, Kenya), 1986, Feminist Press (New York, NY), 2000.

The Present Moment, Heinemann (Nairobi, Kenya), 1987, Feminist Press (New York, NY), 2000.

Street Life (novella), Heinemann (Nairobi, Kenya), 1987.

Victoria and Murder in Majengo, Macmillan (London, England), 1993.

Homing In, East African Educational Publishers (Nairobi, Kenya), 1994.

Chira, East African Educational Publishers (Nairobi, Kenya), 1997.

The Black Hand Gang (juvenile), East African Educational Publishers (Nairobi, Kenya), 1997.

OTHER

Song of Nyarloka and Other Poems, Oxford University Press (New York, NY), 1977.

(Editor) Charles Hayes, *Stima: An Informal History of the EAP&L,* East African Power and Lighting Co. (Nairobi, Kenya), 1983.

The Story of Kenya: A Nation in the Making, Oxford University Press (Nairobi, Kenya), 1986.

Moral Issues in Kenya, Uzima Press (Nairobi, Kenya), 1996.

Make It Sing and Other Poems, East African Educational Publishers (Nairobi, Kenya), 1998.

Contributor to anthologies; contributor of short stories to magazines.

SIDELIGHTS: Marjorie Oludhe Macgoye, a Kenyan poet and novelist, was born and educated in England before moving to Kenya in 1954 as a missionary bookseller. According to her entry in *The Feminist*

Companion to Literature in English, she has said, "I am so much enmeshed in my Luo family and community I am not afraid of writing from within it either." In 1964, immediately following independence, she became a Kenyan citizen.

Macgoye began to publish her writing after immigrating to Kenya, beginning with several stories in magazines. Macgoye's success grew as she moved to book-length fiction, and her novels and poetry began getting published in the early 1970s. Macgoye has won several awards for her work, and her fiction is frequently anthologized. She has additionally produced a variety of other works, including *Growing Up at Lina School,* a novel for young adults; *Murder in Majengo,* a thriller; and various nonfiction work.

Macgoye's award-winning novel, *Coming to Birth,* follows the life of a Kenyan woman between 1956 and 1978, paralleling her personal development with Kenya's struggle for independence. Protagonist Paulina Were leaves her village at age sixteen to live in Nairobi with her new husband. It is an unhappy marriage and after two miscarriages she returns to village life, but not before having gained a new strength and independence from life in the city. She supports herself by teaching needlework to village women and eventually has a child by another man. After her child is killed, she returns to Nairobi, where she encounters her estranged husband. Their new life together holds the promise of the child they could not have earlier.

In the *London Review of Books,* Graham Hough noted that although the novel is not "feminist," it provides "a striking statement of the cause feminists have at heart." Adewale Maja-Pearce, writing in the *Times Literary Supplement,* praised the language of the novel, but suggested that Macgoye "tries to do too much—when she attempts to make [Paulina and her husband's] story carry the burden of postcolonial politics."

Macgoye's subsequent novel, *The Present Moment,* examines the lives of seven elderly women spending their remaining years in an old people's home in Nairobi. The women, who come from diverse tribal backgrounds, pass the time sharing stories of their youth, from old lovers, to political turmoil, to the deaths of their children. Nicholas Spice, writing in the *London Review of Books,* complimented Macgoye's ability to present the wretched lives of these women, a "true underclass," without directly attributing blame. She does the same with the effects of colonial rule, allowing the injustices to become "self-evident."

In her *New Statesman* review, Nancee Oku Bright described *The Present Moment* as "an intelligent novel with complex and ultimately vibrant characters" but asserted that "the dialogue often seems stilted and overwritten and the text so saturated with detail that we become confused." Jo-Ann Goodwin, writing in the *Times Literary Supplement,* also believed that the reader could become confused because of the "overcrowded" text. Goodwin went on to praise Macgoye's use of language, however, saying that "Macgoye has created an idiom representative of the country, alien and yet intimate, to describe an existence which is both disturbing and fascinating."

J. Roger Kurtz reviewed Macgoye's novel *Homing In* for *World Literature Today,* remarking that it "is clearly a Kenyan novel, intended for an audience familiar with recent Kenyan history." It is the story of elderly widow Ellen Smith and her caretaker, Martha Kimani. Kurtz described it as being "about finding identity and a sense of belonging, whether it is for a former English schoolteacher like Ellen in a former colony, or for the children of Kenyans like Martha in a British setting."

Kurtz noted that *Chira* "is not the first Kenyan novel to feature characters with AIDS, but it is the first to treat the disease in a serious and extended manner." The title, a Luo term for any wasting disease, noted Kurtz, is also a metaphor for "contemporary Kenyan society, in which hidden truths, obligations, and networks of responsibility—the unspoken realities of life whose evocation and exploration are a Macgoye trademark—constitute the unseen social viruses that occasionally break the surface."

Make It Sing and Other Poems is a five-part collection, the second of which consists of Macgoye's most important poem, "Song of Nyarloka," first published in 1977. The other sections are titled "Poet's Poetry," "Crossing Over," "Songs of Freedom," and "Public Events." Approximately half of the poems appear here for the first time, and "as always in Macgoye's writing," noted Kurtz, "there are references to Kenyan national events and personalities, and as always, Macgoye relies heavily on metaphors, images, and myth from the Luo experience. These elements, undergirded by a modernist esthetic and socialist Christian commitment, are Macgoye hallmarks. In all her writing there is a sense of history as a tragedy, as a landscape in which ordinary people struggle to overcome difficult limitations. But at the end, there is also always some new birth waiting to happen."

Macgoye once told *CA:* "I have been flattered to have my work compared to that of Chester Himes. Unfortunately, the implication is sometimes that the subjects are far-out, an underclass. But these lives are central in their own context, carrying political weight and consciousness, enmeshed in society, not uniformly wretched. It is the academic and disengaged writer who is in the extreme position. And the story is usually not what they tell one another but what they refrain from telling."

More recently, Macgoye told *CA*: "I am a witness to my Christian faith before I am a writer. This does not mean writing about 'religious' subjects but trying to understand and empathize with those around me and helping the reader to do the same. Since elaborate conversation and rhetoric are the principal arts of East Africa, the verbal medium is appropriate."

BIOGRAPHICAL AND CRITICAL SOURCES:

BOOKS

Blain, Virginia and others, *The Feminist Companion to Literature in English,* Yale University Press (New Haven, CT), 1990, p. 690.

Buck, Claire, editor, *The Bloomsbury Guide to Women's Literature,* Prentice-Hall General Reference (Upper Saddle River, NJ), 1992, pp. 768-769.

Kibera, Valerie, *Motherlands: Black Women's Writing from Africa, the Caribbean, and South Asia,* Women's Press (London, England), 1991.

Kurtz, J. R., *Urban Obsessions, Urban Fears: The Post-colonial Kenyan Novel,* African World Press (Trenton, NJ), 1998.

PERIODICALS

Black Issues Book Review, March, 2001, Denolyn Caroll, review of *Coming to Birth,* p. 55.

Books, June, 1987, p. 31.

British Book News, May, 1987, p. 299; June, 1987, p. 368.

London Review of Books, July 3, 1986, Graham Hough, review of *Coming to Birth,* p. 22; July 9, 1987, Nicholas Spice, review of *The Present Moment,* p. 14.

New Statesman, June 13, 1986, p. 27-29; September 4, 1987, Nancee Oku Bright, review of *The Present Moment,* p. 30.

Observer, June 8, 1986, p. 25; July 12, 1987, p. 23.

Research in African Literatures, summer, 2002, J. R. Kurtz, "Crossing Over: Identity and Change in Marjorie Oludhe Macgoye's 'Song of Nyarloka,'" pp. 100-118.

Times Literary Supplement, September 5, 1986, Adewale Maja-Pearce, review of *Coming to Birth,* p. 977; August 28, 1987, Jo Ann Goodwin, review of *The Present Moment,* p. 929.

World Literature Today, autumn, 1995, J. Roger Kurtz, review of *Homing In,* p. 853; autumn, 1997, J. Roger Kurtz, review of *Chira,* p. 852; autumn, 1999, J. Roger Kurtz, review of *Make It Sing and Other Poems,* p. 797.

* * *

MacGREGOR, John M. 1941-

PERSONAL: Born March 14, 1941, in Montreal, Quebec, Canada; son of Charles Edward (a welder) and Florence Grace (a church secretary; maiden name, Eaman) MacGregor. *Education:* McGill University, B.A. (with honors), 1966; Princeton University, M.A., 1969, Ph.D., 1978.

ADDRESSES: Home—4845 17th St., San Francisco, CA 94117.

CAREER: Ontario College of Art, Toronto, Ontario, Canada, professor of psychology of art, 1971-85; writer. Art historian, independent scholar, art exhibit organizer, and psychotherapist; lecturer at numerous universities, art institutions, and associations in the United States, Canada, England, and Switzerland; visiting scholar at the School of Psychiatry of the Menninger Foundation, 1969-70, and with Anna Freud at the Hampstead Clinic, 1975-76.

AWARDS, HONORS: Canada Council research fellow, 1975; Pro Helvetia fellow, 1987; Ernst Kris Award, American Society of Psychopathology of Expression, 1990.

WRITINGS:

The Discovery of the Art of the Insane, Princeton University Press (Princeton, NJ), 1989.

Metamorphosis: The Fiber Art of Judith Scott: The Outsider Artist and the Experience of Down's Syndrome, Creative Growth Art Center (Oakland, CA), 1999.

Also author of catalog essays, including *L'Art Brut: Images of an Alter World,* and *Outsiders and Insiders: Parallel Visions in Modern Art.* Contributor of essays and articles to numerous periodicals.

SIDELIGHTS: In addition to his formal education in art history, John M. MacGregor has researched and trained in the fields of psychiatry, psychoanalysis, psychology, and the psychopathology of art. He utilizes this interdisciplinary approach in his first publication, *The Discovery of the Art of the Insane.* The book presents a historical study of the discovery and ensuing validation of the artwork of insane individuals. Such works were originally regarded as meaningless scribbles and only received attention from the patients' psychiatrists. But by the second half of the twentieth century, these creations were deemed to have therapeutic as well as legitimate artistic value. MacGregor shares this viewpoint. Although his book focuses mainly on actual psychotics and their works of art, MacGregor also addresses the underlying issue of the social acknowledgment of mentally imbalanced people. In a review of *The Discovery of the Art of the Insane* in the *Times Literary Supplement,* Liam Hudson declared, "This beautifully produced book chronicles one of the more remarkable transformations of our time: the movement of mad thought and mad art from the very edge of our collective vision to a point close to its center."

MacGregor offers several reasons why the existence and works of insane artists have been legitimatized over the years. One factor was the advent of romanticism, the literary, artistic, and philosophical movement that began in the eighteenth century and was characterized by emphasis on the imagination and emotions. Seemingly ruled by these traits, psychotics became the subject of odd fascination. Later, Austrian psychoanalyst Sigmund Freud's theories led to the belief that the unconscious mind could be the source of artistic inspiration and creativity, and that mentally deranged people could more easily access this part of the mental system. More recently, the artwork of the insane has shown similarities to various genres in modern art, especially *art brut* ("raw art"); surrealism, a movement characterized by the combination of apparently incongruent images; and expressionism, which focuses on the artist's emotional responses to objects rather than the objects themselves. In his review of *The Discovery of the Art of the Insane* in the *New York Times Book Review,* Michael Vincent Miller stated, "Some Expressionist and Surrealist painters deliberately imitated the works of schizophrenics, who, they proclaimed, were the superior masters."

Miller questioned the difference between sane and insane inspiration in art. He commented, "If there is a border between them, we have not yet been very successful in mapping it." Hudson suggested that sane and insane artists "tap the same unconscious reservoirs of psychic energy, and differ, not in principle, but in the terms on which access to this reservoir is achieved." This debate—brought to the fore in MacGregor's book *The Discovery of the Art of the Insane*—provides an example of how insane art has been legitimatized. As Miller proclaimed, "Two centuries of romanticism and modernism have left us a peculiar legacy: sanity seems to have little place in modern art."

BIOGRAPHICAL AND CRITICAL SOURCES:

PERIODICALS

New York Times Book Review, December 17, 1990.

Times Literary Supplement, March 22, 1990.*

* * *

MAMET, David (Alan) 1947-

PERSONAL: Surname is pronounced "*Mam*-et"; born November 30, 1947, in Chicago IL; son of Bernard Morris (an attorney) and Lenore June (a teacher; maiden name, Silver) Mamet; married Lindsay Crouse (an actress), December 21, 1977 (divorced); married Rebecca Pidgeon (an actress), 1991; children: Willa, Zosia, Clara. *Education:* Attended Neighborhood

Playhouse School of the Theater, 1968-69; Goddard College, B.A., 1969. *Politics:* "The last refuge of the unimaginative." *Religion:* "The second-to-last."

ADDRESSES: *Agent*—Howard Rosenstone, Rosenstone/Wender, 3 East 48th St., New York, NY 10017.

CAREER: Playwright, screenwriter, director, and producer. Marlboro College, special lecturer in drama, 1970. St. Nicholas Theater Company, Chicago, IL, founder, 1973, artistic director, 1973-76, member of board of directors, beginning 1973; Goodman Theater, Chicago, associate artistic director, 1978-79. Goddard College, artist-in-residence in drama, 1971-73; Illinois Arts Council, faculty member, 1974; University of Chicago, visiting lecturer in drama, 1975-76 and 1979; Yale University, School of Drama, teaching fellow, 1976-77; New York University, guest lecturer, 1981; Columbia University, associate professor of film, 1988. Producer of motion pictures, including *Lip Service,* 1988, *Hoffa,* 1992, and *A Life in the Theater,* 1993. Actor in motion pictures, including *Black Widow,* 1986, and *The Water Engine,* 1992. Directed *Ricky Jay: On the Stem,* 2002, and "Ricky Jay and His 52 Assistants." Has also worked in a canning plant, a truck factory, at a real estate agency, and as a window washer, office cleaner, and taxi driver. Atlantic Theater Company, chairman of the board.

MEMBER: Dramatists Guild, Writers Guild of America, Actors Equity Association, PEN, United Steelworkers of America, Randolph A. Hollister Association.

AWARDS, HONORS: Joseph Jefferson Award, 1975, for *Sexual Perversity in Chicago,* and 1976, for *American Buffalo;* Obie Awards, *Village Voice,* for best new American play, 1976, for *Sexual Perversity in Chicago* and *American Buffalo,* for best American play, 1983, for *Edmond,* and for best play, 1995, for *The Cryptogram;* Children's Theater grant, New York State Council on the Arts, 1976; Rockefeller grant, 1976; Columbia Broadcasting System fellowship in creative writing, 1976; New York Drama Critics' Circle Award for best American play, 1977, for *American Buffalo,* and 1984, for *Glengarry Glen Ross;* Outer Critics Circle Award, 1978, for contributions to the American theater; Academy Award nomination for best adapted screenplay, Academy of Motion Picture Arts and Sciences, 1983, for *The Verdict,* and 1997, for *Wag the Dog;* Society for West End Theatre Award, 1983; Pulitzer Prize for drama, Joseph Dintenfass Award, Elizabeth Hull-Warriner Award, Dramatists Guild, Antoinette Perry ("Tony") Award nomination, American Theater Wing, for best play, all 1984, all for *Glengarry Glen Ross;* Tony Award nomination for best reproduction of a play, 1984, for *American Buffalo;* Tony Award for best play, 1988, for *Speed-the-Plow;* American Academy and Institute of Arts and Letters Award for Literature, 1986; Golden Globe Award nomination for best screenplay, 1988, for *House of Games;* Writers Guild Award nomination for best screenplay based on material from another medium, 1988, for *The Untouchables.*

WRITINGS:

PLAYS

Lakeboat (one-act; produced in Marlboro, VT, 1970; revised version produced in Milwaukee, WI, 1980), Grove (New York, NY), 1981.

Duck Variations (one-act; produced in Plainfield, VT, 1972; produced Off-Off-Broadway, 1975), published in *Sexual Perversity in Chicago and Duck Variations: Two Plays,* Grove (New York, NY), 1978.

Sexual Perversity in Chicago (one-act; produced in Chicago, 1974; produced Off-Off-Broadway, 1975), published in *Sexual Perversity in Chicago and Duck Variations: Two Plays,* Grove (New York, NY), 1978.

Squirrels (one-act), produced in Chicago, 1974.

The Poet and the Rent: A Play for Kids from Seven to 8:15 (produced in Chicago, 1974), published in *Three Children's Plays,* Grove Press (New York, NY), 1986.

American Buffalo (two-act; produced in Chicago, 1975; produced on Broadway, 1977), Grove (New York, NY), 1977.

Reunion (one-act; produced with *Sexual Perversity in Chicago,* Louisville, KY, 1976; produced Off-Broadway with *Dark Pony* and *The Sanctity of Marriage,* 1979), published in *Reunion and Dark Pony: Two Plays,* Grove (New York, NY), 1979, also published in *Reunion, Dark Pony, and The Sanctity of Marriage: Three Plays,* Samuel French (New York, NY), 1982.

Dark Pony (one-act; produced with *Reunion,* New Haven, CT, 1977; produced Off-Broadway with *Reunion* and *The Sanctity of Marriage,* 1979), published in *Reunion and Dark Pony: Two Plays,* Grove (New York, NY), 1979, also published in *Reunion, Dark Pony, and The Sanctity of Marriage: Three Plays,* Samuel French (New York, NY), 1982.

All Men Are Whores (produced in New Haven, 1977), published in *Short Plays and Monologues,* Dramatists Play Service (New York, NY), 1981.

A Life in the Theatre (one-act; produced in Chicago, 1977; produced Off-Broadway, 1977), Grove (New York, NY), 1978.

The Revenge of the Space Pandas; or, Binky Rudich and the Two-Speed Clock (produced in Queens, NY, 1977), Sergel (Chicago, IL), 1978.

(And director) *The Woods* (two-act; produced in Chicago, 1977; produced Off-Broadway, 1979), Grove (New York, NY), 1979.

The Water Engine: An American Fable (two-act; produced as a radio play on the program *Earplay,* Minnesota Public Radio, 1977; stage adaptation produced in Chicago, 1977; produced Off-Broadway, 1977), published in *The Water Engine: An American Fable and Mr. Happiness: Two Plays,* Grove (New York, NY), 1978.

Mr. Happiness (produced with *The Water Engine,* on Broadway, 1978), published in *The Water Engine: An American Fable and Mr. Happiness: Two Plays,* Grove (New York, NY), 1978.

Lone Canoe; or, The Explorer (musical), music and lyrics by Alaric Jans, produced in Chicago, 1979.

The Sanctity of Marriage (one-act; produced Off-Broadway with *Reunion* and *Dark Pony,* 1979), published in *Reunion, Dark Pony, and The Sanctity of Marriage: Three Plays,* Samuel French (New York, NY), 1982.

Shoeshine (one-act; produced Off-Off-Broadway, 1979), in *Short Plays and Monologues,* Dramatists Play Service (New York, NY), 1981.

Short Plays and Monologues, Dramatists Play Service (New York, NY), 1981.

A Sermon (one-act), produced Off-Off-Broadway, 1981.

Donny March, produced 1981.

Litko (produced in New York, NY, 1984), published in *Short Plays and Monologues,* Dramatists Play Service (New York, NY), 1981.

Edmond (produced in Chicago, 1982; produced Off-Broadway, 1982), Grove (New York, NY), 1983.

The Disappearance of the Jews (one-act), produced in Chicago, 1983.

The Dog, produced 1983.

Film Crew, produced 1983.

4 A.M., produced 1983.

Glengarry Glen Ross (two-act; produced on London's West End, 1983; produced on Broadway, 1984), Grove (New York, NY), 1984.

Five Unrelated Pieces (contains *Two Conversations, Two Scenes,* and *Yes, but So What;* produced Off-Off-Broadway, 1983), published in *A Collection of Dramatic Sketches and Monologues,* Samuel French (New York, NY), 1985.

Vermont Sketches (contains *Pint's a Pound the World Around, Deer Dogs, Conversations with the Spirit World,* and *Dowsing;* produced in New York, NY, 1984), published in *A Collection of Dramatic Sketches and Monologues,* Samuel French (New York, NY), 1985.

The Shawl [and] *Prairie du Chien* (one-act plays; produced at Lincoln Center, New York, NY, 1985), Grove (New York, NY), 1985.

A Collection of Dramatic Sketches and Monologues, Samuel French (New York, NY), 1985.

Vint (one-act; based on Anton Chekov's short story; produced in New York, NY, with six other one-act plays based on Chekov's short works, under the collective title *Orchards,* 1985), published in *Orchards,* Grove (New York, NY), 1986.

(Adaptor) Anton Chekov, *The Cherry Orchard* (produced at Goodman Theatre, 1985), Grove (New York, NY), 1987.

Three Children's Plays (contains *The Poet and the Rent: A Play for Kids from Seven to 8:15, The Revenge of the Space Pandas; or, Binky Rudich and the Two-Speed Clock,* and *The Frog Prince*), Grove (New York, NY), 1986.

The Woods, Lakeboat, Edmond, Grove (New York, NY), 1987.

Speed-the-Plow (produced on Broadway, 1988), Grove (New York, NY), 1988.

Where Were You When It Went Down?, produced in New York, NY, 1988.

(Adaptor and editor) Anton Chekov, *Uncle Vanya,* Grove (New York, NY), 1989.

Goldberg Street (short plays and monologues), Grove (New York, NY), 1989.

Bobby Gould in Hell, produced with *The Devil and Billy Markham* by Shel Silverstein, New York, NY, 1989.

Five Television Plays: A Waitress in Yellowstone; Bradford; The Museum of Science and Industry

Story; A Wasted Weekend; We Will Take You There, Grove (New York, NY), 1990.

Oleanna (also see below; produced 1991), Pantheon (New York, NY), 1992, Dramatists Play Service (New York, NY), 1993.

(Adaptor) Anton Chekov, *The Three Sisters: A Play,* Samuel French (New York, NY), 1992.

A Life with No Joy in It, and Other Plays and Pieces (contains *Almost Done, Monologue, Two Enthusiasts, Sunday Afternoon, The Joke Code, A Scene, Fish, A Perfect Mermaid, Dodge, L.A. Sketches, A Life with No Joy in It, Joseph Dintenfass,* and *No One Will Be Immune*), Dramatists Play Service (New York, NY), 1994.

Plays—One (collection; includes *Duck Variations, Sexual Perversity in Chicago, Squirrels, American Buffalo, The Water Engine,* and *Mr. Happiness*), Methuen (London, England), 1994.

(And director) *The Cryptogram* (also see below; produced in London, 1994; produced Off-Broadway, 1995), Dramatists Play Service (New York, NY), 1995, Vintage (New York, NY), 1995.

The Old Neighborhood: Three Plays (also see below; includes *The Disappearance of the Jews, Jolly,* and *Deeny*), Vintage (New York, NY), 1998.

Boston Marriage (produced at the American Repertory Theater in Cambridge, MA, 1999, produced at Joseph Papp Public Theater, 2002), Vintage (New York, NY), 2002.

David Mamet Plays: 4 (includes *The Cryptogram, Oleanna,* and *The Old Neighborhood*), Methuen (London, England), 2002.

(Director) *Ricky Jay: On the Stem,* produced at the Second Stage Theatre, New York, NY, 2002.

Dr. Faustus: A Play, Vintage (New York, NY), 2004.

SCREENPLAYS

The Postman Always Rings Twice (adaptation of the novel by James M. Cain), Paramount, 1981.

The Verdict (adaptation of the novel by Barry Reed), Columbia, 1982.

(And director) *House of Games* (based on a story by Mamet; produced by Orion Pictures, 1987), Grove (New York, NY), 1987.

The Untouchables (based on the television series), Paramount, 1987.

(With Shel Silverstein; and director) *Things Change* (produced by Columbia Pictures, 1988), Grove (New York, NY), 1988.

We're No Angels (adaptation of the 1955 film of the same name; produced by Paramount, 1989), Grove (New York, NY), 1990.

(And director) *Homicide* (produced by Columbia, 1991), Grove (New York, NY), 1992.

Glengary Glen Ross (based on Mamet's play of the same title), New Line Cinema, 1992.

The Water Engine (teleplay; based on Mamet's play of the same title), Amblin Television, 1992.

Hoffa, Twentieth Century-Fox, 1992.

Texan (film short), Chanticleer Films, 1994.

(And director) *Oleanna* (based on Mamet's play of the same title), Samuel Goldwyn, 1994.

Vanya on 42nd Street (adapted from the play *Uncle Vanya* by Anton Chekhov), Film Four International, 1994.

American Buffalo (based on Mamet's play of the same title), Samuel Goldwyn, 1996.

(And director) *The Spanish Prisoner,* Sweetland Films, 1997, published in *The Spanish Prisoner and The Winslow Boy: Two screenplays,* Vintage (New York, NY), 2002.

The Edge, Twentieth Century-Fox, 1997.

Wag the Dog (based on the novel *American Hero* by Larry Beinhart), New Line Cinema, 1997.

Lansky, HBO, 1998.

(And director) *State and Maine,* Fine Line Pictures, 2000.

Lakeboat, Oregon Trail Films, 2000.

Whistle, Geisler-Roberdeau, 2000.

Dr. Jekyll and Mr. Hyde (based on the novel by Robert Louis Stevenson), 2000.

(With Steven Zaillian) *Hannibal* (based on the novel by Thomas Harris), Metro-Goldwyn-Mayer, 2001.

(And director) *Heist,* Morgan Creek Productions, 2001.

NOVELS

The Village, Little, Brown (New York, NY), 1994.

The Old Religion: A Novel (historical fiction), Free Press (New York, NY), 1997.

Bar Mitzvah, Little, Brown (New York, NY), 1999.

The Chinaman, Overlook Press (Woodstock, NY), 1999.

Henrietta, Houghton Mifflin (New York, NY), 1999.

Jafsie and John Henry, Free Press (New York, NY), 1999.

Wilson: A Consideration of the Sources, Overlook Press (Woodstock, NY), 2001.

NONFICTION, EXCEPT AS NOTED

Writing in Restaurants (essays, speeches, and articles), Penguin (New York, NY), 1987.
Some Freaks (essays), Viking (New York, NY), 1989.
(With Donald Sultan and Ricky Jay) *Donald Sultan: Playing Cards,* edited by Edit deAk, Kyoto Shoin (Kyoto, Japan), 1989.
The Hero Pony: Poems, Grove Weidenfeld (New York, NY), 1990.
On Directing Film, Viking (New York, NY), 1992.
The Cabin: Reminiscence and Diversions, Random House (New York, NY), 1992.
A Whore's Profession: Notes and Essays (includes *Writing in Restaurants, Some Freaks, On Directing Film,* and *The Cabin*), Faber (New York, NY), 1994.
Make-Believe Town: Essays and Remembrances, Little, Brown (Boston, MA), 1996.
True and False: Heresy and Common Sense for the Actor (essays), Pantheon (New York, NY), 1997.
Three Uses of the Knife: On the Nature and Purpose of Drama (part of the "Columbia Lectures on American Culture" series), Columbia University Press (New York, NY), 1998.
On Acting, Viking (New York, NY), 1999.
David Mamet in Conversation, edited by Leslie Kane, University of Michigan Press (Ann Arbor, MI), 2001.
(Author of foreword) Jimmy Kennedy, Maya Kennedy, and Marialisa Calta, *River Run Cookbook: Southern Comfort from Vermont,* HarperCollins (New York, NY), 2001.
South of the Northeast Kingdom, National Geographic Society (Washington, DC), 2002.
(With Lawrence Kushner) *Five Cities of Refuge: Weekly Reflections on Genesis, Exodus, Leviticus, Numbers, and Deuteronomy,* Schocken Books (New York, NY), 2003.

FOR CHILDREN

Warm and Cold (picture book), illustrations by Donald Sultan, Solo Press (New York, NY), 1984.
(With wife, Lindsay Crouse) *The Owl,* Kipling Press (New York, NY), 1987.
Passover (picture book), illustrated by Michael McCurdy, St. Martin's Press (New York, NY), 1995.
The Duck and the Goat (picture book), illustrated by Maya Kennedy, St. Martin's Press (New York, NY), 1996.

Also author of *No One Will Be Immune and Other Plays and Pieces;* the play *Oh Hell;* the teleplay *A Life in the Theater,* based on Mamet's play of the same title; and episodes of the TV series *Hill Street Blues,* NBC, 1987, and *L.A. Law,* NBC. Contributor to *Donald Sultan: in the Still-Life Tradition,* with Steven Henry Madoff, 1999. Contributing editor, *Oui,* 1975-76.

ADAPTATIONS: The film *About Last Night. . . ,* released by Tri-Star Pictures in 1986, was based on Mamet's *Sexual Perversity in Chicago.*

SIDELIGHTS: David Mamet has acquired a great deal of critical recognition for his plays, each one a microcosmic view of the American experience. "He's that rarity, a pure writer," noted Jack Kroll in *Newsweek,* "and the synthesis he appears to be making, with echoes from voices as diverse as Beckett, Pinter, and Hemingway, is unique and exciting." Since 1976, Mamet's plays have been widely produced in regional theaters and in New York City. One of Mamet's most successful plays, *Glengarry Glen Ross,* earned the New York Drama Critics' Circle Award for best American play and the Pulitzer Prize in drama, both in 1984. Critics have also praised Mamet's screenwriting; he received Academy Award nominations for best adapted screenplay for *The Verdict* in 1983, and for *Wag the Dog* in 1997.

Mamet "has carved out a career as one of America's most creative . . . playwrights," observed Mel Gussow in the *New York Times,* "with a particular affinity for working-class characters." These characters and their language give Mamet's work its distinct flavor. Mamet is, according to Kroll, "that rare bird, an American playwright who's a language playwright." "Playwriting is simply showing how words influence actions and vice versa," Mamet explained to *People* contributor Linda Witt. "All my plays attempt to bring out the poetry in the plain, everyday language people use. That's the only way to put art back into the theater." Mamet has been accused of eavesdropping, simply recording the insignificant conversations of which everyone is aware; yet, many reviewers recognize the playwright's artistic intent. Jean M. White commented in the *Washington Post* that "Mamet has an ear for vernacular speech and uses cliche with telling effect." Furthermore, added Kroll, "Mamet is the first playwright to create a formal and moral shape out of the undeleted expletives of our foul-mouthed time."

In his personal and creative life, Mamet has resisted the lure of Broadway, its establishment, and its formulas for success. He was born and raised in Chicago—his father was a labor lawyer. His parents divorced while Mamet and his sisters were young. The Windy City serves not only as inspiration for much of his work, but it has also provided an accepting audience for Mamet's brand of drama, especially in the early days of his career, when he worked nights as a busboy at The Second City and spent his days with the theater crowd and writing his plays. "Regional theaters are where the life is," he told Robin Reeves in *Us.*"They're the only new force in American theater since the 30s." Yet, despite Mamet's seeming indifference to Broadway and the fact that the language and subject matter of his plays make them of questionable commercial value, several of his plays have been featured on Broadway.

The first of Mamet's plays to be commercially produced were *Sexual Perversity in Chicago* and *Duck Variations. Sexual Perversity* portrays the failed love affair between a young man and woman, each trying to leave behind a relationship with a homosexual roommate. The dialogue between the lovers and their same-sex roommates reveals how each gender can brutally characterize the other. Yet, "the play itself is not another aspect of the so-called battle of the sexes," observed C. Gerald Fraser in the *New York Times.* "It concerns the confusion and emptiness of human relationships on a purely physical level." *New Yorker* reviewer Edith Oliver maintained that "the piece is written with grace," and found it "one of the saddest comedies I can remember." In *Duck Variations,* two old Jewish men sit on a bench in Chicago looking out on Lake Michigan. Their observation of the nearby ducks leads them into discussions of several topics. "There is a marvelous ring of truth in the meandering, speculative talk of these old men," maintained Oliver, "the comic, obsessive talk of men who spend most of their time alone, nurturing and indulging their preposterous notions." In the conversation of these men, wrote T. E. Kalem in *Time,* Mamet "displays the Pinter trait of wearing word masks to shield feelings and of defying communication in the act of communicating." *Duck Variations* reveals, according to Oliver, that Mamet is an "original writer, who cherishes words and, on the evidence at hand, cherishes character even more." "What emerges is a vivid sense of [the old men's] friendship, the fear of solitude, the inexorable toll of expiring lives," concluded Kalem.

Mamet emerged as a nationally acclaimed playwright with his 1975 two-act *American Buffalo.* "America has few comedies in its repertory as ironic or as audacious as *American Buffalo,*" proclaimed John Lahr in the *Nation.* Set in a junk shop, the play features the shop's owner, an employee, and a friend engaged in plotting a theft; they hope to steal the coin collection of a customer who, earlier in the week, had bought an old nickel at the shop. When the employee fails to tail the mark to his home, the plot falls into disarray. Although little takes place, Oliver commented in the *New Yorker,* "What makes [the play] fascinating are its characters and the sudden spurts of feeling and shifts of mood—the mounting tension under the seemingly aimless surface, which gives the play its momentum."

American Buffalo confirmed Mamet's standing as a language playwright. Reviewing the play in the *Nation,* Lahr observed, "Mamet's use of the sludge in American language is completely original. He hears panic and poetry in the convoluted syntax of his beleaguered characters." As Frank Rich of the *New York Times* remarked, "Working with the tiniest imaginable vocabulary . . . Mamet creates a subterranean world with its own nonliterate comic beat, life-and-death struggles, pathos and even affection."

In this play, critics also saw Mamet's vision of America, "a restless, rootless, insecure society which has no faith in the peace it seeks or the pleasure it finds," interpreted Lahr. "*American Buffalo* superbly evokes this anxious and impoverished world." Its characters, though seemingly insignificant, reflect the inhabitants of this world and their way of life. "In these bumbling and inarticulate meatheads," believed Lahr, "Mamet has found a metaphor for the spiritual failure of entrepreneurial capitalism."

Since its first Chicago production in 1975, *American Buffalo* has been produced in several regional theaters and has had three New York productions. In Mamet's management of the elements of this play, *New York Times* reviewer Benedict Nightingale highlighted the key to its success: "Its idiom is precise enough to evoke a city, a class, a subculture; it is imprecise enough to allow variation of mood and feeling from production to production." Nightingale added in another article, "*Buffalo* is as accomplished as anything written for the American stage over . . . the last twenty years."

In 1979 Mamet was given his first opportunity to write a screenplay. As he told Don Shewey in the *New York*

Times, working on the screenplay for the 1981 film version of James M. Cain's novel *The Postman Always Rings Twice* was a learning experience. Director Bob Rafelson "taught me that the purpose of a screenplay is to tell the story so the audience wants to know what happens next," Mamet maintained, "and to tell it in pictures." He elaborated, "I always thought I had a talent for dialogue and not for plot, but it's a skill that can be learned. Writing for the movies is teaching me not to be so scared about plots." Mamet's screenplay for *The Postman Always Rings Twice* has received mixed reviews. Its critics often point, as Gene Siskel did in the *Chicago Tribune,* to Mamet's "ill-conceived editing of the book's original ending." Yet, except for the ending, suggested Vincent Canby in the *New York Times,* "Mr. Mamet's screenplay is far more faithful to the novel than was the screenplay for Tay Garnett's 1946 version." Thus, Robert Hatch noted in the *Nation,*"Mamet and Rafelson recapture the prevailing insanity of the Depression, when steadiness of gaze was paying no bills and double or nothing was the game in vogue."

In the 1982 film *The Verdict,* screenwriter Mamet and director Sydney Lumet "have dealt powerfully and unsentimentally with the shadowy state that ideas like good and evil find themselves in today," observed Jack Kroll in *Newsweek.* The film stars Paul Newman as a washed-up lawyer caught in a personal, legal, and moral battle. "Mamet's terse screenplay for *The Verdict* is . . . full of surprises," contended Janet Maslin in the *New York Times;* "Mamet has supplied twists and obstacles of all sorts." "Except for a few lapses of logic and some melodramatic moments in the courtroom," proclaimed a *People* reviewer, "[this] script from Barry Reed's novel is unusually incisive." Kroll detailed the screenplay's strong points, calling it "strong on character, on sharp and edgy dialogue, on the detective-story suspense of a potent narrative." In a *New Republic* article, Stanley Kauffmann concluded, "It comes through when it absolutely must deliver: Newman's summation to the jury. This speech is terse and pungent: the powerful have the power to convert all the rest of us into victims and that condition probably cannot be changed, but must it always prevail?"

After writing *The Verdict* Mamet began working on his next play, *Glengarry Glen Ross.* Mamet's Pulitzer Prize-winning play is "so precise in its realism that it transcends itself," observed Robert Brustein in the *New Republic,*"and takes on reverberant ethical meanings. It is biting, . . . showing life stripped of all idealistic pretenses and liberal pieties." The play is set in and around a Chicago real estate office whose agents are embroiled in a competition to sell the most parcels in the Florida developments Glengarry Highlands and Glen Ross Farms. "Craftily constructed, so that there is laughter, as well as rage, in its dialogue, the play has a payoff in each scene and a cleverly plotted mystery that kicks in with a surprise hook at its ending," wrote Richard Christiansen in the *Chicago Tribune.*

As in Mamet's earlier plays, the characters and their language are very important to *Glengarry Glen Ross.* In the *Nation,* Stephen Harvey commented on Mamet's ability to create characters who take on a life of their own within the framework of the play: In *Glengarry,* "he adjusts his angle of vision to suit the contours of his characters, rather than using them to illustrate an idea." Mamet told Kastor of the *Washington Post,*"I think that people are generally more happy with a mystery than with an explanation. So the less that you say about a character the more interesting he becomes." Mamet uses language in a similar manner. Harvey noted, "The pungency of Glengarry's language comes from economy: if these characters have fifty-word vocabularies, Mamet makes sure that every monosyllable counts." And as Kroll remarked, "His antiphonal exchanges, which dwindle to single words or even fragments of words and then explode into a crossfire of scatological buckshot, make him the Aristophanes of the inarticulate." Mamet is, according to *New York Times* reviewer Benedict Nightingale, "the bard of modern-day barbarism, the laureate of the four-letter word." In the *New York Times Magazine,* Richard Eder remarked, "From the beginning, Mr. Mamet's most notable and noticeable quality was his extraordinary use of speech. He concentrated not upon cultivated expression but upon that apparent wasteland of middle American speech. It was the language of the secretary, the salesman, the file clerk, the telephone lineman, the small-time crook, the semiliterate college kid. It was grotesquely realistic."

For the real estate agents in *Glengarry Glen Ross,* the bottom line is sales. And, as Robert Brustein noted, "Without a single tendentious line, without any polemical intention, without a trace of pity or sentiment, Mamet has launched an assault on the American way of making a living." Nightingale called the play "as scathing a study of unscrupulous dealing as the

American theater has ever produced." The Pulitzer Prize awarded to Mamet for *Glengarry Glen Ross* not only helped increase its critical standing, but it also helped to make the play a commercial success. However, unlike his real estate agents, Mamet is driven by more than money. He told Kastor, "In our interaction in our daily lives we tell stories to each other, we gossip, we complain to each other, we exhort. These are means of defining what our life is. The theater is a way of doing it continually, of sharing that experience, and it's absolutely essential."

The Cryptogram, Mamet's 1994 play, "dramatizes a child's emotional abuse in a way that no other American play has ever attempted: from the child's point of view," according to *New Yorker* critic John Lahr. The playwright draws on his personal experiences of violent outbreaks, mistrust, and betrayal that he encountered in his own family, but the play blurs such autobiographical elements between its author's fictions. Taking place in Chicago over the span of a single month during the late 1950s, the play's main character, ten-year-old John, is trying to make sense of the double message dispensed by his parents and family friends: lies and unkept promises are commonplace, yet he is expected to trust those who deceive him. "People may or may not say what they mean," Mamet explained to Lahr, "but they *always* say something designed to get what they want." Characteristically, language plays an important role in *The Cryptogram:* as its author noted, "The language of love is . . . fairly limited. 'You're beautiful,' 'I need you,' 'I love you,' 'I want you.' Love expresses itself, so it doesn't need a lot of words. On the other hand, aggression has an unlimited vocabulary."

While Mamet's direction of *The Cryptogram* received the traditional mixed reviews from critics due to his fractured language, *New York Times* reviewer Vincent Canby found much to praise. Calling the play "a horror story that also appears to be one of Mr. Mamet's most personal plays," Canby noted, "It's not about the sort of physical abuse we see in television docudramas, but about the high cost of the emotional games played in what are otherwise considered to be fairly well-adjusted families." *The Cryptogram* received the Obie Award from the *Village Voice* for best play in 1995.

In 1994, on the heels of *The Cryptogram,* Mamet published his first novel, *The Village.* Taking place in a small, once-thriving town in New England, the novel reveals the emotional complexity of the lives of its characters. From Dick, the hardware-store owner fighting to stay in business, Manis, a local prostitute, and especially Henry, an "outsider" retired and escaping a failed marriage who wants to recapture the macho lifestyle of a century ago, Mamet captures "the flat, dark underside of the flapjack of small town life that Thorton Wilder's 'Our Town' served as the fluffy, arcing top to," according to *Tribune Books* reviewer Ross Field. While reviewers noted that the novel's characters and central idea are well conceived, the novel's dialogue caused some critics to water down their enthusiasm for the book. James McManus contended in the *New York Times Book Review* that, "because of the novel's design and mechanical problems, the potency of [some] scenes tends not to accumulate. For a playwright of such muscular succinctness, Mr. Mamet has a narrative prose that turns out to be weirdly precious." However, in his review for the *Washington Post Book World,* Douglas Glover praised *The Village.* "Mamet's novel explores a community with its own laws, language, codes, habits and sense of honor," noted Glover. "It does so with a deft reverence for the real—Mamet's eye for detail and his ear for the rhythms of vernacular speech are incomparable—coupled with a certain difficulty of approach, an avant-garde edge."

In addition to plays and screenplays, Mamet has published several collections of essays, including *Writing in Restaurants, Some Freaks, On Directing Film, The Cabin,* and *Make-Believe Town,* the first four volumes later collected as *A Whore's Profession: Notes and Essays.* These revealing collections are packed with Mamet's fascinating thoughts, opinions, recollections, musings, and reports on a variety of topics such as friendship, religion, politics, morals, society, and of course, the American theater. "The thirty pieces collected in David Mamet's first book of essays contain everything from random thoughts to firmly held convictions," stated Richard Christiansen in his review of *Writing in Restaurants* for Chicago's *Tribune Books,* "but they all exhibit the author's singular insights and moral bearing." Christiansen pointed out that "many of the essays have to do with drama, naturally, but whether he is talking to a group of critics or to fellow workers in the theater, Mamet is always urging his audience to go beyond craft and into a proud, dignified, loving commitment to their art and to the people with whom they work."

The Cabin, published in 1992, contains twenty essays that reflect their author's macho concerns—guns, cigars, beautiful women—as well as his life as a writer. The work's structure was characterized by *Los Angeles Times Book Review* critic Charles Solomon as "a succession of scenes illuminated by an erratic strobe light: A single moment appears in harsh focus, then vanishes." We follow the author from his tumultuous childhood in "The Rake" to a description of his New Hampshire haven where he does his writing in the title essay. The two dozen essays in *Make-Believe Town* recall Mamet's love of the theater and his respect for his Jewish heritage and introduce those "appalled" by the language of his stage plays to "Mamet the thoughtful learner, teacher, the friend, the literary critic, the hunger-nature writer, the culture, press and film critic, the political commentator, the moralist and, most delightfully, the memoirist," according to *Tribune Books* critic John D. Callaway.

With his play *Boston Marriage,* Mamet departed from his more well-known use of tough male characters to portray an elegant pair of Victorian lesbians. In this comedy of manners, Anna has become the mistress of a wealthy married man in order to supplement her income, and Claire has fallen in love with a younger woman. When that young woman wonders how Anna has acquired her mother's heirloom necklace, both affairs are endangered, leading the two women to concoct a complicated scheme to get themselves out of trouble. As a reviewer remarked in *Curtain Up,* this play, rather than being a radical departure for Mamet, "is in fact just another example of his versatility."

In 2001, Mamet took on two major projects. The first was a new novel, *Wilson: A Consideration of Sources,* which examines the impact of the Internet on society. Set far in the future, *Wilson* introduces a society dependent who has placed all information in books and paper archives on the Internet, destroying the original sources. When the Internet crashes, the only remaining source of information is the hard drive of Mrs. Wilson's computer. Mamet's book is composed in skewed sections as disorderly as the world he creates in it, much to the dismay of some critics. Frank J. Baldaro wrote in *American Theatre* that *Wilson* is "an incomprehensible work that spills over with names but is devoid of characters." Baldaro disliked the novel's structure, calling it a "collage of faked bits and fragments" which "teems with incidents and anecdotes, but lacks either plot or sense—it's ultimately a literary stunt that dares to ridicule the jargon and bombast of scholarly writing, but is itself monumentally unfunny, apocalyptically cryptic and impossible to decode." A reviewer for *Publishers Weekly,* however, liked the ridicule in Mamet's work. The reviewer called the work "an imitation of a scholarly work—or at least the sort of scholarly work that might be undertaken in the 24th century," concluding, "Mamet's *jeu d'esprit* will certainly surprise those who imagine the author of *American Buffalo* operates only in the backstreets idiom of his plays." Joseph Dewey of the *Review of Contemporary Fiction* appreciated Mamet's take on the future in *Wilson*: "Mamet targets with luscious savvy and deadpan irony the limitless pretense of academics, hungry for tenure, to suture history . . . to talk their way into reasonable order."

Mamet also penned a script for the film sequel to *Silence of the Lambs, Hannibal.* In the script, Hannibal has escaped prison and is hiding out in Florence, Italy, as a museum curator. FBI detective Clarice Starling (played in the second movie by Julianne Moore) is reassigned to his case and proceeds to track him down. While the sequel to the original thriller was anxiously awaited by audiences, some were disappointed at the movie's lack of horror, blood, and guts. "Hannibal is more shocking, and amusing, than disturbing," wrote Brian D. Johnson in *Maclean's.* Johnson also stated that "despite some exquisite moments, *Hannibal* feels overwrought." Todd McCarthy praised the first movie, remarking in *Variety* that "the public will . . . exhibit a ravenous appetite for the continuing saga of one of contemporary literature and cinema's most fascinating villains." McCarthy admitted that the sequel was "ultimately more shallow and crass at its heart than its predecessor," but concluded that "*Hannibal* is nevertheless tantalizing, engrossing, and occasionally startling."

Writing for the *Times Literary Supplement,* Andrew Hislop declared that "Mamet has been rightly acclaimed as a great dialogist and a dramatist who most effectively expresses the rhythms of modern urban America (though the poetic rather than mimetic qualities of his dialogue are often underestimated). The best writing in [*Writing in Restaurants*] comes when he muses on the details of America—and his own life." Hislop continued, "Running through the book is the idea that the purpose of theatre is truth but that the decadence of American society, television and the materialism of Broadway are undermining not just the economic basis but the disciplines and dedication necessary for true theatre."

BIOGRAPHICAL AND CRITICAL SOURCES:

BOOKS

Bigsby, C. W. E., *David Mamet,* Methuen (London, England), 1985.

Bock, Hedwig, and Albert Wertheim, editors, *Essays on Contemporary American Drama,* Max Hueber (Munich, Germany), 1981, pp. 207-223.

Brewer, Gay, *David Mamet and Film: Illusion/ Disillusion in a Wounded Land,* McFarland (Jefferson, NC), 1993.

Carroll, Dennis, *David Mamet,* St. Martin's Press (New York, NY), 1987.

Contemporary Dramatists, 6th edition, St. James Press (Detroit, MI), 1999.

Contemporary Literary Criticism, Gale (Detroit, MI), Volume 9, 1978, pp. 360-361; Volume 15, 1980, pp. 355-358; Volume 34, 1985, pp. 217-224; Volume 46, 1988, pp. 245-256; Volume 91, 1996, pp. 143-155.

Contemporary Theatre, Film, and Television, Volume 27, Gale (Detroit, MI, 2000.

Dean, Anne, *David Mamet: Language As Dramatic Action,* Fairleigh Dickinson University Press (Teaneck, NJ), 1990.

Drama Criticism, Volume 4, Gale (Detroit, MI), 1994.

Kane, Leslie, *David Mamet's Glengarry Glen Ross: Text and Performance,* Garland (New York, NY), 1996.

Kane, Leslie, editor, *David Mamet: A Casebook,* Garland (New York, NY), 1991.

Kane, Leslie, *Weasels and Wisemen: Education, Ethics, and Ethnicity in David Mamet,* St. Martin's Press (New York, NY), 1999.

King, Kimball, *Ten Modern American Playwrights,* Garland (New York, NY), 1982.

St. James Encyclopedia of Popular Culture, St. James Press (Detroit, MI), 2000.

PERIODICALS

America, May 15, 1993, p. 16; September 23, 1995, p. 26; June 5, 1999, Richard A. Blacke, "Boy Overboard," p. 14.

American Theatre, December 1, 1999, p. 9; November, 2002, Frank J. Baldaro, review of *Wilson: A Consideration of the Sources,* p. 80; November 1, 2002, Frank J. Baldaro, review of *Wilson,* pp. 80-81; November 1, 2002, Randy Gener, "Speed the Plot: Six Playwrights Parlay Their Dramatic Themes into New Fiction," pp. 75-76; January 1, 2003, Jonathan Kalb, "Stardust Melancholy," pp. 42-49.

Back Stage, November 22, 2002, Julius Novick, review of *Boston Marriage,* p. 48.

Booklist, December 1, 1992; June 1, 1994.

Broadcasting & Cable, September 25, 2000, "CBS Teams with Mamet, Morrie Author," p. 28; September 30, 2002, "Pariah Television," p. 18.

Chicago, January, 1990, p. 65.

Chicago Tribune, January 18, 1987, p. 7; October 11, 1987; May 4, 1988; February 19, 1989; December 10, 1989.

Christian Century, September 13, 2000, James M. Wall, "Probing the Depths," p. 932.

Commonweal, December 4, 1992, p. 15.

Daily News, March 26, 1984.

Daily Variety, November 21, 2002, review of *Boston Marriage,* p. 2.

Entertainment Weekly, August 21, 1992, pp. 50-51; June 9, 1995, p. 68; July 9, 1999, review of *Lansky,* p. 82; January 12, 2001, "What to Watch," p. 61; November 16, 2001, Lisa Schwarzbaum, review of *Heist,* p. 144; December 7, 2001, "Cybertalk," p. 108; November 29, 2002, Doug Brod, review of *Glengarry Glen Ross*; December 13, 2002, Lawrence Frascella, review of *Boston Marriage,* p. 92.

Financial Times, December 5, 2001, Alastair Macaulay, review of *Boston Marriage,* p. 18; May 17, 2002, Lisa Schwarzbaum, review of *Ricky: Jay on the Stem,* p. 71.

Gentlemen's Quarterly, October, 1994, p. 110.

Georgia Review, fall, 1983, pp. 601-611.

Harper's, May, 1978, pp. 79-80, 83-87.

Hollywood Reporter, September 5, 2001, Michael Rechtshaffen, review of *Heist,* p. 2.

Insight on the News, January 9, 1995, p. 26; January 1, 2001, Rex Roberts, "Cinema Verite," p. 27.

Interview, December 1, 2000, Guy Flatley, review of *State and Maine,* p. 58.

Kirkus Reviews, April 15, 1996, p. 580.

Library Journal, January, 1991, p. 106; June 1, 1996, p. 106; March 15, 2001, Barry X. Miller, review of *State and Maine,* p. 87.

London Review of Books, July 7, 1994, p. 7.

Los Angeles Times, November 27, 1979; June 25, 1984; July 7, 1987; October 11, 1987.

Los Angeles Times Book Review, December 13, 1992, p. 3; March 6, 1994, p. 8; June 30, 1996, p. 10; July 28, 1996, p. 11.

Maclean's, December 25, 2000, Brian D. Johnson, "Holiday Escapades: Tales of Self-Absorbed Man Enjoying Mid-life Epiphanies Dominate This Season's Fare," p. 148; February 19, 2001, Brian D. Johnson, "Haute-Cannibal Cuisine," p. 48; November 12, 2001, Brian D. Johnson, "A Knack for Noir," p. 53.

Modern Drama, September, 1991, Jack V. Barbara, review of *American Buffalo,* pp. 271-72, 275.

Nation, May 19, 1979, pp. 581-582; April 14, 1981; October 10, 1981; April 28, 1984, pp. 522-523; June 27, 1987, pp. 900-902; December 30, 2002, David Kaufman, review of *Boston Marriage,* p. 35.

National Review, January 18, 1993, p. 28; May 31, 1999, John Simon, "Film: Pidgeon Feathers," p. 70; March 5, 2001, John Simon, "Ominous Appetites"; February 5, 2001, John Simon, "Lost and Found."

New Leader, April 16, 1984, pp. 20-21; December 14, 1992, p. 26.

New Republic, July 12, 1982, Robert Brustein, review of *Edmond,* pp. 23-24; February 10, 1986, pp. 25-26, 28; October 29, 1990, pp. 32-37; April 24, 1995, p. 46; May 24, 1999, p. 32; January 29, 2001, p. 28; April 30, 2001, p. 30.

New Statesman & Society, September 30, 1983, pp. 33, 36; July 2, 1993, p. 34; June 2, 2003, Sheridan Morley, "Norwegian Wood: Sheridan Morley on a Damp Ibsen, an Early Mamet, and Shakespeare out of His Time," p. 46.

Newsweek, February 28, 1977, p. 79; March 23, 1981; November 8, 1982; December 6, 1982; April 9, 1984, p. 109; October 19, 1987; November 9, 1992, p. 65.

New York, December 20, 1982, pp. 62, 64; June 8, 1987, pp. 68-69; March 9, 1992, p. 77; November 9, 1992, p. 72; November 30, 1992, p. 129; August 2, 1993, p. 50; October 11, 1993, p. 79; February 21, 1994, p. 52; February 12, 2001, David Ansen, "Knock, Knock. Who's There?," p. 56; November 19, 2001, Devin Gordon, review of *Heist,* p. 69.

New Yorker, November 10, 1975, Edith Oliver, review of *Sexual Perversity in Chicago,* pp. 135-136; October 31, 1977, pp. 115-116; January 16, 1978; October 29, 1979, p. 81; June 15, 1981; November 7, 1983; June 29, 1987, pp. 70-72; November 16, 1992, pp. 121-126; August 1, 1994, p. 70; April 10, 1995, pp. 33-34.

New York Post, December 24, 1985; March 26, 1984.

New York Times, July 5, 1976; March 18, 1979; April 26, 1979; May 26, 1979; June 3, 1979; October 19, 1979; March 20, 1981; May 29, 1981; June 5, 1981; February 17, 1982; May 17, 1982; June 17, 1982; October 24, 1982; October 28, 1982, p. C20; December 8, 1982; May 13, 1983; October 9, 1983, pp. 6, 19; November 6, 1983; March 26, 1984, p. C17; March 28, 1984; April 1, 1984; April 18, 1984; April 24, 1984; September 30, 1984; February 9, 1986; April 23, 1986; January 1, 1987; March 15, 1987; June 3, 1987; October 11, 1987; May 4, 1988; December 4, 1989; April 14, 1995, p. C3.

New York Times Book Review, December 17, 1989; January 17, 1993, p. 24; November 20, 1994, p. 24; April 9, 1995, p. 20; July 14, 1996, p. 17.

New York Times Magazine, March 12, 1978, Richard Eder, profile of Mamet, pp. 40, 42, 45, 47.

People, November 12, 1979; December 20, 1982; May 4, 1987.

Playboy, September, 1994, p. 78; April, 1995, p. 51.

Premiere, January, 1990, p. 108.

Publishers Weekly, November 16, 1992, p. 55; July 4, 1994, p. 52; April 8, 1996, p. 46; September 24, 2001, review of *Wilson,* p. 67; August 4, 2003, "Five Cities of Refuge: Weekly Reflections on Genesis, Exodus, Leviticus, Numbers, and Deuteronomy," p. 75.

Review of Contemporary Fiction, June 22, 2002, Joseph Dewey, review of *Wilson,* p. 224.

Sarasota Herald Tribune, August 10, 2001, Philip Booth, review of *Lakeboat,* p. 14.

Saturday Review, April 2, 1977, p. 37.

Smithsonian, June 1, 2001, Kathleen Burke, review of *River Run Cookbook: Southern Comfort from Vermont,* p. 124.

Time, July 12, 1976; April 9, 1984, p. 105; December 25, 1989, pp. 87-90; August 24, 1992, p. 69; November 2, 1992, p. 69; October 18, 1993, p. 109; August 29, 1994, p. 71; May 17, 1999, Richard Corliss, "The Winslow Boy," p. 90; December 25, 2000, Joel Stein, "David Mamet," p. 164; January 15, 2001, Richard Corliss, review of *State and Maine,* p. 138; January 29, 2001, Jess Cagle, "The Bite Stuff," p. 60; November 19, 2001, Richard Schickel, review of *Heist,* p. 143.

Times Literary Supplement, January 29, 1988; July 15, 1994, Jim McCue, review of *A Whore's Profession: Notes and Essays,* p. 21; February 16, 1996, p. 23.

Tribune Books (Chicago, IL), January 18, 1987; December 13, 1992, p. 7; May 5, 1996, p. 3.

Us, January 10, 1978.

Variety, February 24, 1992, p. 257; May 11, 1992, p. 127; August 24, 1992, p. 65; April 5, 1993, p. 185; February 7, 1994, p. 60; June 21, 1999, Markland Taylor, review of *Boston Marriage,* p. 88; August 16, 1999, Michael Fleming, "Mamet Moves into Comedy with *Maine,*" p. 13; November 1, 1999, Charles Isherwood, review of *The Water Engine* and *Mr. Happiness,* p. 99; January 17, 2000, Robert Hofler, review of *Sexual Perversity in Chicago* and *The Duck Variations,* p. 140; February 14, 2000, Matt Wolf, review of *American Buffalo,* p. 49; March 6, 2000, Robert L. Daniels, review of *Glengarry Glen Ross,* p. 50; March 20, 2000, Charles Isherwood, review of *American Buffalo,* p. 36; April 17, 2000, Emanuel Levy, review of *Lakeboat,* p. 28; September 4, 2000, Eddie Cockrell, review of *State and Maine,* p. 19; February 5, 2001, Todd McCarthy, review of *Hannibal,* p. 37; April 16, 2001, Matt Wolf, review of *Boston Marriage,* p. 39; September 10, 2001, David Rooney, review of *Heist,* p. 62; January 7, 2002, Chris Jones, review of *Glengarry Glen Ross,* p. 53; May 13, 2002, Charles Isherwood, review of *Ricky Jay,* p. 32; May 26, 2003, Matt Wolf, review of *Sexual Perversity in Chicago,* p. 42; August 4, 2003, Matt Wolf, review of *Edmond,* p. 30.

Village Voice, July 5, 1976, Ross Wetzsteon, profile of Mamet, pp. 101, 103-04; May 7, 1979, Eileen Blumenthal, review of *The Woods,* p. 103.

Washington Post, May 4, 1988.

World Literature Today, summer, 1982, p. 518.

ONLINE

CurtainUp, http://www.curtainup.com/ (May 28, 2003), review of *Boston Marriage* and *Ricky Jay.*

David Mamet Review (newsletter of the David Mamet Society), http://mamet.eserver.org/ (November 20, 2003).

FilmMakers, http://www.filmmakers.com/ (November 20, 2003), "David Alan Mamet: Filmography and Credits."

Salon.com, http://www.salon.com/ (May 28, 2003), interview with Mamet.

Smithsonian Online, http://www.smithsonianmag.si.edu/ (November 20, 2003), "Book Reviews: *River Run Cookbook.*"

Sony Pictures Web site, http://www.sonypictures.com/ (November 20, 2003), "Ricky Jay."*

MANDEL, Brett H. 1969-

PERSONAL: Born May 10, 1969, in Philadelphia, PA; son of Stephan (a manufacturer's representative) and Sharyn (a secretary; maiden name, Weissman; present surname, Dershovitz) Mandel; married Laura Weinbaum. *Ethnicity:* "White." *Education:* Hamilton College, B.A. (magna cum laude), 1991; University of Pennsylvania, M.B.A., 1993. *Politics:* Democrat. *Religion:* Jewish. *Hobbies and other interests:* Sports, politics.

ADDRESSES: Home—2303 Lombard St., Philadelphia, PA 19146. *Office*—Office of the City Controller, 12th Floor MSB, 1401 Arch St., Philadelphia, PA 19102; fax: 215-686-3832. *E-mail*—brett@libertynet.org.

CAREER: Philadelphia Independent Charter Commission, Philadelphia, PA, assistant policy director, 1992-94; Pennsylvania Economy League, Philadelphia, policy analyst and project manager, 1994-96; City of Philadelphia, began as assistant city controller, became director of financial and policy analysis, 1996—. Professional baseball player with Ogden Raptors, Ogden UT, 1994; also player with Philadelphia Comets baseball team and Delaware Valley Men's Hockey League; guest on media programs. Greater Philadelphia Regional Review Advisory Board, member; City Center Residents' Association, board member; Friends of Fitler Square, member; Big Brothers/Big Sisters, member.

MEMBER: National Writers Union, Phi Beta Kappa.

AWARDS, HONORS: Special Project Award, National Association of Local Government Auditors, 1999, for *Philadelphia: A New Urban Direction.*

WRITINGS:

Minor Players, Major Dreams, University of Nebraska Press (Lincoln, NE), 1997.

(With Kevin J. Babyak, Jonathan A. Saidel, and David A. Volpe) *Philadelphia: A New Urban Direction,* Saint Joseph's University Press (Philadelphia, PA), 1999.

Is This Heaven? The Magic of the Field of Dreams, Rowman & Littlefield (Lanham, MD), 2002.

Contributor to periodicals, including *Public Integrity.*

SIDELIGHTS: Brett H. Mandel once told *CA:* "The idea that launched whatever writing career I have came to me as an inspiration to mix my love of baseball and desire to do more than play in a Sunday League with my need to find a job since my then-current job was ending. I came up with the idea to convince a minor league team to sign me to a player's contract for a season, so I could write a book on the minor league experience and tell the inside story of the young men who were chasing their dreams in the minor leagues. After ten months of phone calls and hard work, I was able to convince the Ogden Raptors of the Pioneer Rookie League to accept the idea and let me on board for their inaugural season. I really enjoyed the freedom to express my thoughts in a book format and hope I was able to convey everything I experienced to readers.

"My experience writing my first book and writing about minor-league baseball probably does not describe the usual writing process. I typed away on a laptop computer while enduring fifteen-hour road trips on the team bus. One happy side effect was that the other players allowed me to spread across two seats so I could have enough elbow room. When not typing on the bus, I typed away in front of a television tuned into *Headline News.* I found that it was just enough distraction to give me a break whenever I wanted to look up, but enough repetition that I could tune it out when I needed to work. I was pretty much manic about the need to put something on paper (or on disk, I guess) and religiously typed for at least two hours each day for the seventy-seven days of the season. At the end of the season, I had over 400 pages of single-spaced text that I spent three months crafting into a story—again, with *Headline News* as background. Try it. Not only does it provide neutral background noise, but you'll never be more up on current events."

* * *

MARDON, Austin Albert 1962-

PERSONAL: Born June 25, 1962, in Edmonton, Alberta, Canada; son of Ernest George (a professor of English and a writer) and May Gertrude (a teacher; maiden name, Knowler) Mardon; married Stephanie Ngar Ling Liu, August 24, 1996 (divorced, 2001). *Ethnicity:* "British." *Education:* University of Grenoble, certificate in French language, 1979; University of Lethbridge, B.A., 1985; attended University of Calgary and University of Alberta; South Dakota State University, M.Sc., 1988; Texas A&M University, M.Ed., 1990; attended University of North Dakota, 1990, and Newman College, 2001. *Politics:* Progressive Conservative. *Religion:* Roman Catholic. *Hobbies and other interests:* Reading, walking, computer simulations.

ADDRESSES: Home—10324 119th St., Suite 16, Edmonton, Alberta T5K 1Z6, Canada. *Office*—P.O. Box 1223, Main Post Office, Edmonton, Alberta T5J 2M4, Canada. *E-mail*—mardon@freenet.edmonton.ab.ca.

CAREER: Antarctic Institute of Canada, president, 1985—, member of board of directors, 1991—, researcher, 1992—. Greenwich University, adjunct faculty member, 2000—. U.S. Antarctic Research Program, member of National Aeronautics and Space Administration/National Science Foundation meteorite recovery expedition in Antarctica, 1986-87; historical researcher on Alberta culture and multiculturalism, 1989-91; consultant to Stargate Research Laboratory and Consumer Network. Prosper Place Clubhouse of Edmonton, chair, 1993-99; Regional Mental Health Advisory Committee, member of board of directors, 1999—, chair of Capital region, 2000-01; Unsung Heroes Support Group for Schizophrenics, cochair. Edmonton Public Library Board, trustee, 2001—. *Military service:* Canadian Primary Army Reserves, Artillery, 1981, 1984-85; served in Antarctica; received Duke of Edinburgh Medal and U.S. Congressional Antarctic Service Medal.

MEMBER: American Polar Society (life member), Committee on Space Research, Russian Academy of Arts and Science, Schizophrenia Society of Alberta (member of board of directors of Edmonton chapter, 1999—, and provincial chapter, 2000—), Sigma Pi Sigma, Gamma Theta Upsilon, Explorers Club (international fellow).

AWARDS, HONORS: Canadian Governor-General's Caring Award, 1998; Canadian Mental Health Association, Nadine Stirling Award, 1999, President's Award, 2002; honorary Ph.D., Greenwich University, 2000; Flag of Hope Award, Schizophrenia Society of Canada, 2001; Golden Jubilee Medal, Queen Elizabeth II, 2002; Distinguished Alumnus Award, University of Lethbridge, 2002.

WRITINGS:

A Conspectus of the Contribution of Herodotus to the Development of Geographical Thought, 1990.

(Translator, with father, Ernest G. Mardon) Donald Munro, *A Description of the Western Isles of Scotland,* RTAJ Fry Press (Edmonton, Alberta, Canada), 1990.

(With Ernest G. Mardon) *Alberta Ethnic Mormon Politicians,* RTAJ Fry Press (Edmonton, Alberta, Canada), 1990.

(With Ernest G. Mardon) *The Alberta Judiciary Dictionary,* RTAJ Fry Press (Edmonton, Alberta, Canada), 1990.

International Law and Space Rescue Systems, 1991.

Kensington Stone and Other Essays, 1991.

A Transient in Whirl, 1991.

(Coauthor) *Alberta Ethnic German Politicians,* 1991.

(Coauthor) *When Kitty Met the Ghost,* 1991.

(With Ernest G. Mardon) *Alberta Mormon Politicians,* Fisher House Press, 1991.

(Coauthor) *The Girl Who Could Walk through Walls,* 1991.

(With Ernest G. Mardon) *The Men of the Dawn: Alberta Politicians from the North West Territories of the District of Alberta and Candidates for the First Alberta General Election, 1882-1905,* RTAJ Fry Press (Edmonton, Alberta, Canada), 1991.

(With Ernest G. Mardon and John Williams) *Down and Out and on the Run in Moscow,* Shoe String Press (Edmonton, Alberta, Canada), 1992.

(With Ernest G. Mardon) *Alberta General Election Returns and Subsequent Byelections, 1882-1992,* Documentary Heritage Society of Alberta, 1993.

(With Ernest G. Mardon) *Edmonton Political Biographical Dictionary, 1882-1990: A Work in Progress,* Shoe String Press (Edmonton, Alberta, Canada), 1993.

(With Ernest G. Mardon) *Biographical Dictionary of Alberta Politicians,* Shoe String Press (Edmonton, Alberta, Canada), 1993.

(Coauthor) *Alberta Executive Council, 1905-1990,* 1994.

(With Ernest G. Mardon) *Community Names of Alberta,* Shoe String Press (Edmonton, Alberta, Canada), 1995, expanded 2nd edition, edited by Larry Erdos, Golden Meteorite Press (Edmonton, Alberta, Canada), 1998.

(With M. F. Korn) *Alone against the Revolution,* Golden Meteorite Press (Edmonton, Alberta, Canada), 1997.

(Coauthor) *Many Christian Saints for Children,* Golden Meteorite Press (Edmonton, Alberta, Canada), 1997.

(Coauthor) *Early Catholic Saints,* Golden Meteorite Press (Edmonton, Alberta, Canada), 1997.

(Coauthor) *Later Christian Saints,* Golden Meteorite Press (Edmonton, Alberta, Canada), 1997.

(Editor) M. F. Korn, *Stygian Relics of the Lachrymose,* Golden Meteorite Press (Edmonton, Alberta, Canada), 1998.

(Editor) M. F. Korn, *The Spectral Carnival Show and Other Stories,* Golden Meteorite Press (Edmonton, Alberta, Canada), 1998.

(Coauthor) *Childhood Memories and Legends of Christmas Past,* Golden Meteorite Press (Edmonton, Alberta, Canada), 1998.

(Photographer) Joanna Wong, *Songs of My Heart: A Chinese Woman's Story,* Golden Meteorite Press (Edmonton, Alberta, Canada), 1999.

(Coauthor) *United Farmers of Alberta,* 1999.

(Editor) *A Wake of Evil,* 1999.

Political Networks in Alberta, 1905-1992, Golden Meteorite Press (Edmonton, Alberta, Canada), 2001.

(With Ernest G. Mardon) *Alberta Anglican Politicians: Historical and Biographical Profiles,* Anglican Parish of Christ Church (Edmonton, Alberta, Canada), 2001.

(With Ernest G. Mardon) *The Liberals in Power in Alberta, 1905-1921,* privately printed (Edmonton, Alberta, Canada), 2001.

(With Ernest G. Mardon) *Alberta Catholic Politicians,* Golden Meteorite Press (Edmonton, Alberta, Canada), 2001.

(With Ernest G. Mardon) *What Is in a Name? The History of Alberta Federal Riding Names,* privately printed (Lethbridge, Alberta, Canada), 2002.

Contributor of more than 100 articles to periodicals, including *Science, Spaceflight, Explorers Club Journal, Polar Times,* and *Meteor News.*

WORK IN PROGRESS: A book on the author's expedition to Antarctica; research for a political history of Alberta.

SIDELIGHTS: Austin Albert Mardon once told *CA:* "I am a seventh-generation North American on the paternal side. My ancestors arrived in the New England colonies as Ulster Scots in 1732. My great-grandfather Andrew Dickey (1829-1911), an iron manufacturer from Albany, New York, crossed the Great Plains and the mountains as a young man to work in the California gold fields in 1849.

"As a child, I did not have good health. For several winters I accompanied my mother and sister to Hawaii. I became a good swimmer and was for the first time with Americans who still fascinate me to this day. High school did not change me. I received only one award; that was at a science fair. I had proposed towing icebergs down from Greenland through the Hudson's Bay to James Bay, and then pumping the clean water over to the major cities of the Great Lakes to supply them with fresh water.

"When I was a late teenager, I returned to the glen in the north of Scotland to stay with my grandmother in the manor where my father was raised. I still recall looking across the stormy waters of the Pentland Firth to the Orkney island where my paternal grandmother's ancestor came from 400 years earlier. I was deeply moved. The pace of life was different. While being a proverbial geek and nerd in Canadian schools, I was accepted, even playing sports such as rugby, when I was in Scotland.

"When I was seventeen, my sister Mary and I were sent for the summer to attend the University of Grenoble. Years before, my paternal grandparents had first met, then fallen in love and married while they were students at Grenoble. That summer changed me from a boy to a man. I shared ideas with fellow international students and became fully aware of different ideas and ways of life.

"I then attended the University of Lethbridge. While on campus, I served in the Canadian Primary Reserves, taking my basic training at the Canadian Armed Forces Base at Dundurn, Saskatchewan. I graduated in 1985 with a major in cultural geography. I first had the idea of using aerial photography to directly detect surficial lying meteorites while in my last term at Lethbridge.

"I became a graduate student at the South Dakota State University in Brookings. I found the move from the Coulee country of southern Alberta was no great cultural shock. I was still on the Great Plains. My later move to Texas was not so successful, as it was a different physical and social environment.

"In 1986 I was invited to become a member of the 1986-1987 Antarctic meteorite expedition of the National Aeronautics and Space Administration and National Science Foundation. I joined the six-man expedition in Christchurch, New Zealand. We flew to McMurdo Sound Base, then into the interior in the vicinity of Beardmore Glacier, with our equipment, supplies, snowmobiles, sledges, and tents. On three occasions, additional food was dropped by parachute. We were on the edge of the vast Antarctic polar plateau, 170 miles from the South Pole station, the locale in the Lewis Cliff ice tongue where hundreds of meteorites were found by the team. There were intense katabatic winds, which we called Chinook winds in southern Alberta, similar to the winds that exposed the ice-concentrated meteorite placer fields.

"In January, 1987, our team was picked up by a ski-equipped plane and taken, first to McMurdo, and then on to New Zealand. I suffered environmental exposure during my sojourn on the polar plateau and received the U.S. Congressional Antarctic Service Medal. On my return to Alberta, I gave a series of lectures on Antarctica at the University of Calgary and the University of Lethbridge. I was then interviewed to be a member of the Canadian/Soviet Arctic traverse from northern Siberia to Ellesmere Island in the Canadian Arctic. I failed to get on that expedition.

"I was, however, a member of a failed meteorite recovery expedition in the Canadian Arctic near Resolute, Northwest Territories. I wrote a paper on my conversation with locals on what the Inuit thought of meteorites: a vast garden of rocks. In the eyes of the Inuit, a meteorite is a sacred religious object. Before the whites arrived, meteoritic iron and nickel were the only metals that the Inuit had. In the legends in the west, there is some reference to 'star' swords likely made out of meteorite iron and nickel.

"In the late 1980s I was accepted to join an Argentinian Antarctic expedition, but my membership was canceled at the last moment because of a fire at an Argentinian base in the Antarctic. I also unsuccessfully attended the Space Studies Program at the University of North Dakota. All the while I thought of one of the things that Bill Cassidy, the head of the U.S. Antarctic Meteorite Recovery Program, had told me in the middle of a blizzard on the edge of the Antarctic polar plateau: he was getting a doctorate in real life.

"In my articles, my most important contribution was a series on the *Anglo Saxon Chronicle.* This is a unique running commentary on all sorts of events in England, written during the medieval period. The surviving four manuscripts, a product of Benedictine monks, are a yearly diary that state the most important events of the year. Unique for the time, it was written in the vernacular. Entries include important religious, political, social, and astronomical events. With the assistance of my father, a medieval scholar, I found eleven cometary events in the *Chronicle* that were not referred to in any astronomical literature. These were the only European references for several hundred years, and were not found elsewhere in the literature. I also wrote about the two meteor showers recorded in the *Chronicle.*

"My darkest moment was a one-week trip to Moscow, where I was one of the 'last casualties' of the cold war. I went from beyond the edge of the world to the heart of darkness that was known as the end of the Soviet Empire. My articles and books came in spite of what happened before and after Moscow."

BIOGRAPHICAL AND CRITICAL SOURCES:

PERIODICALS

Edmonton Journal, January 5, 1992.

* * *

MARSDEN, John 1950-

PERSONAL: Born September 27, 1950, in Melbourne, Victoria, Australia; son of Eustace Cullen Hudson (a banker) and Jeanne Lawler (a homemaker; maiden name, Ray) Marsden. *Ethnicity:* "Anglo-Australian." *Education:* Mitchell College, diploma in teaching, 1978; University of New England, B.A., 1981. *Hobbies and other interests:* Conservation.

ADDRESSES: Home—R.M.B. 1250, Romsey, Victoria 3434, Australia. *Agent*—Jill Grinberg, Anderson Grinberg Literary Management, 266 West 23rd St., New York, NY 10011.

John Marsden

CAREER: Geelong Grammar School, Geelong, Victoria, Australia, English teacher, 1982-90; writer, 1991—; primary school teacher, c. 1995. Worked at various jobs, including truck driver, hospital worker, and delivery person, c. 1968-77.

AWARDS, HONORS: Children's Book of the Year Award, Children's Book Council of Australia (CBCA), 1988, Premier's Award (Victoria, Australia), 1988, Young Adult Book Award (New South Wales, Australia), 1988, Alan Marshall Award, 1988, Christopher Award, 1989, KOALA (Kids Own Australian Literature Awards), 1989, Notable Book, American Library Association, 1989, and COOL Award (Canberra's Own Outstanding List), 1995, all for *So Much to Tell You . . .;* Writers' Fellowship, Australia Council, 1993; Australian Multicultural Children's Book Award, 1994, YABBA (Young Australians Best Book Award), 1995, WAYRBA (West Australian Young Readers' Books Award), 1995, KOALA Award, 1995, COOL Award, 1996 and 2001, BILBY Award (Books I Love Best Yearly), 1998, CYBER Award (Children's Yearly Best Ever Reads), 2000, and New South Wales Talking Book Award, all for *Tomorrow, When the War Began;* Grand Jury Prize for Australia's favorite young person's novel, 1996, for *Letters from the Inside;* New South Wales Talking Book Award, and CYBER Award, both for *The Dead of Night;* Book of the Year Award, Australian Booksellers Association, 1998, and WAYRBA Award, 1999, both for *Burning for Revenge;* WAYRBA Award, 1998, COOL Award, 1999, and Buxtehude Bulle (Germany), 2000, all for *The Third Day, the Frost;* KOALA Award, 1999, for *Cool School: You Make It Happen;* Children's Book of the Year Award, CBCA, 1999, for *The Rabbits;* COOL Award, and WAYRBA Award, both 2000, both for *The Night Is for Hunting.*

WRITINGS:

FOR YOUNG ADULTS

So Much to Tell You . . . , Walter McVitty (Glebe, Australia), 1988, Little, Brown (Boston, MA), 1989, stage adaptation by the author published as *So Much to Tell You: The Play,* Walter McVitty (Montville, Australia), 1994.

The Journey, Pan (Sydney, Australia), 1988.

The Great Gatenby, Pan (Sydney, Australia), 1989.

Staying Alive in Year Five, Piper (Sydney, Australia), 1989.

Out of Time, Pan (Sydney, Australia), 1990.

Letters from the Inside, Pan Macmillan (Sydney, Australia), 1991, Houghton Mifflin (Boston, MA), 1994.

Take My Word for It: Lisa's Journal, Pan Macmillan (Sydney, Australia), 1992.

Looking for Trouble, Pan Macmillan (Sydney, Australia), 1993.

Cool School: You Make It Happen, Pan Macmillan (Sydney, Australia), 1995.

Checkers, Pan Macmillan (Sydney, Australia), 1996, Houghton Mifflin (Boston, MA), 1998.

Creep Street: You Make It Happen, Macmillan (Sydney, Australia), 1996.

Dear Miffy, Pan Macmillan (Sydney, Australia), 1997.

Winter, Pan Macmillan (Sydney, Australia), 2000, Scholastic (New York, NY), 2002.

Millie, Pan Macmillan (Sydney, Australia), 2002.

"TOMORROW, WHEN THE WAR BEGAN" SERIES

Tomorrow, When the War Began, Pan Macmillan (Sydney, Australia), 1993, Houghton Mifflin (Boston, MA), 1995.

The Dead of Night, Pan Macmillan (Sydney, Australia), 1994, Houghton Mifflin (Boston, MA), 1997.

The Third Day, the Frost, Pan Macmillan (Sydney, Australia), 1995, published as *A Killing Frost,* Houghton Mifflin (Boston, MA), 1998.

Darkness, Be My Friend, Pan Macmillan (Sydney, Australia), 1996, Houghton Mifflin (Boston, MA), 1999.

Burning for Revenge, Pan Macmillan (Sydney, Australia), 1997, Houghton Mifflin (Boston, MA), 2000.

The Night Is for Hunting, Pan Macmillan (Sydney, Australia), 1998, Houghton Mifflin (Boston, MA), 2001.

The Other Side of Dawn, Pan Macmillan (Sydney, Australia), 1999, Houghton Mifflin (Boston, MA), 2002.

While I Live: The Ellie Linton Chronicles, Pan Macmillan (Sydney, Australia), 2003.

NONFICTION, EXCEPT AS NOTED

Everything I Know about Writing (nonfiction), Macmillan (Sydney, Australia), 1993.

(Editor) *This I Believe: Over 100 Eminent Australians Explore Life's Big Questions* (essays), Random House (Milsons Point, Australia), 1996.

(Editor) *For Weddings and a Funeral* (poetry), Pan Macmillan (Sydney, Australia), 1996.

Secret Men's Business: Manhood: The Big Gig (nonfiction), Pan Macmillan (Sydney, Australia), 1998.

Marsden on Marsden: The Stories behind John Marsden's Bestselling Books, Pan Macmillan (Sydney, Australia), 2000.

The Head Book, Pan Macmillan (Sydney, Australia), 2001.

The Boy You Brought Home: A Single Mother's Guide to Raising Sons, Pan Macmillan (Sydney, Australia), 2002.

A Day in the Life of Me, Lothian Books (Port Melbourne, Australia), 2002.

PICTURE BOOKS

Prayer for the Twenty-first Century, Lothian (Port Melbourne, Australia), 1997, Star Bright Books (New York, NY), 1998, also published as *Message for the Twenty-first Century,* Ticktock (Tonbridge, England), 1999.

Norton's Hut, illustrated by Peter Gouldthorpe, Lothian Books (Port Melbourne, Australia), 1998, Star Bright Books (New York, NY), 1999.

The Rabbits, illustrated by Shaun Tan, Lothian Books (Port Melbourne, Australia), 1998.

Contributor to *Goodnight & Thanks for the Teeth: A Fairies' Tale,* Pan Macmillan (Sydney, Australia), 1999.

ADAPTATIONS: The Journey was adapted into an opera of the same name and published by the Australian Music Centre (Grosvenor Place, Australia), 1999.

SIDELIGHTS: John Marsden is one of the most popular writers for teens in Australia and the author of the critically acclaimed "Tomorrow, When the War Began" series. The reasons for Marsden's international fame are twofold, claim critics. First, he is known for not talking down to his audience, fully aware that for many teenagers, life is bleak, challenging, and dangerous. Second, he is applauded for his ability to craft exciting adventure stories in which the young protagonists are called to adult action—with all its moral and ethical implications. This is particularly the case in the "Tomorrow, When the War Began" series, in which a group of teens engage in a guerilla war against a vastly superior force that has occupied Australia. Noting that Marsden's titles "have consistently met with overwhelming critical and commercial success," *Horn Book* reviewer Karen Jameyson concluded: "Marsden has always touted the importance of writing honestly, of not shielding the young from topics that some might see as too depressing or shocking. And this frankness and honesty have clearly struck a chord with young adults."

Marsden debunked some of the myths of his native Australia in an essay he wrote for the *Something about the Author Autobiography Series* (*SAAS*). "Growing up in Australia wasn't a matter of kangaroos, surfboards, and the wild outback," he said. "Not for me, anyway. My childhood was spent in the quiet country towns in the green southern states of Victoria and Tasmania. It was peaceful, secure, and often very boring." Marsden's father managed a bank, a responsibility he held for forty-eight years. This had a marked yet contrary effect on the young Marsden. He related: "Perhaps one of the things I've done in my adult life is to react against that kind of commitment. At the latest count, I've had thirty-two different jobs."

Growing up in small Australian towns during the 1950s gave Marsden experiences that were quite different from children in urban America during the same era. In Marsden's village, ice was still delivered to people for their iceboxes, cooking was mainly done on stoves powered by fuel, and no one he knew owned a television set. "I first saw television when I was ten years old. In our small Tasmanian town, an electrical shop brought in a TV and put it in their window for the wedding of Princess Margaret. On the great day, the whole town gathered in front of the shop and the set was switched on. All we saw was 'snow'—grey and white static, with a few figures vaguely visible through the murk," Marsden wrote in *SAAS.*

Marsden was too infatuated with literature to care if his family had a television. "I read and read and read," he commented. "When I ran out of books for boys I read the girls' books. . . . Some days, I'd borrow three titles (the maximum allowed) from the town library, read them, and get them back to the library by five o'clock, in time to exchange them for three more before the library shut. I'd become a speed reader without really trying!" Marsden also found another pastime that was to help him with his later writing. "My favourite game was to draw a town layout on the driveway with chalk and use little model cars to bring the town to life. Perhaps that's how I first became used to creating and living in imaginary worlds," he recalled in *SAAS.*

Marsden became such a lover of books that by the time he was in grade three, he had memorized *The Children of Cherry Tree Farm.* His teacher would use him when she wanted to take a break. "She'd have me stand up in front of the class and recite the next chapter to the other kids . . . from memory. She'd go off to the staff room and leave me there. I loved it! Maybe that's where I got my first taste of the power of storytelling."

That school year was also a difficult one for Marsden. His teacher would fly into rages and yell at the children. She believed in corporal punishment and would cane the children for the slightest disobedience. Each Friday, the teacher would give the class a ten-question quiz; if a student failed to answer at least seven questions correctly, he was beaten. "Recently, I met up with a girl who'd been in that class with me," Marsden related. "As she talked about those Friday tests, she started to tremble with the memories. At the age of forty-four, she was still haunted by her grade-three days." When Marsden was promoted to the next grade, he was rewarded in two ways. His teacher was much more nurturing, and she saw in him the seeds of a writer, letting him edit the school paper. "This was my first taste of publication," he told *SAAS.* "It was a heady experience. Seeing my name in print, having people—even adults—reacting to and commenting on what I'd written was powerful stuff."

At the age of ten, Marsden moved with his family to Sydney. Having mainly grown up in country towns, he was fascinated by the switch from rural to urban life. "I thought Sydney was huge and exotic, and wildly exciting," Marsden commented. "I spent my first week collecting bus tickets, to the amusement of the staff in the hotel where we stayed. Riding on the escalators was as good as Disneyland."

Marsden's parents enrolled him at King's School, a prestigious private school that was run like a military establishment. There was very little Marsden liked about the place, from the stuffy uniforms to the military drills they were required to perform. He also felt out of touch with happenings in the world. "The rest of the Western world was embarking on a decade of drugs, free love, and the Beatles, but at King's, boys continued to salute their teachers, drill with rifles for hours every week, and stand to attention when speaking to prefects." Marsden spent his time in somewhat subversive activities. He wrote short books with plots that were stolen from famous mystery novels, distributed his underground newspaper about new rock bands, and read books under his desk during class.

At the time, Marsden found that there was very little literature written for adolescents. He read adult literature but was quite taken aback by his first experience with J. D. Salinger's *Catcher in the Rye,* a classic coming-of-age story that was—and still is—controversial. The book "had me gasping for breath," Marsden commented in *SAAS.* "I'd never dreamt you were allowed to write like that. . . . For the first time I was reading a genuine, contemporary teenage voice. If I've had any success at capturing teenage voices on paper, it's because of what I learnt at the age of fifteen from J. D. Salinger."

School had very little settling influence on Marsden. He continued being a rebel despite the conservative atmosphere. "I began to question everything: religion, education, law, parenting. All the institutions and customs that I'd been taught to accept unquestioningly," he related to *SAAS.* It is of little surprise that when Marsden graduated from King's he had not received any military awards or promotions. He did, however, win some academic prizes, including one for a 40,000-word essay on poets of World War I.

After graduating, Marsden enrolled at the University of Sydney but soon lost interest in his studies and dropped out. He then tried his hand at many exotic jobs. He told *SAAS* that some of his employment included "collecting blood, looking after a mortuary at nights, working in a side-show, being a night clerk in the casualty department of Sydney Hospital, and guarding Australia's oldest house from vandals." Marsden's interest in these occupations, however, generally waned rather quickly. "Once I mastered a job, I got bored with it and started restlessly looking for the next challenge. Maybe that was a reaction to the boredom of my early life and the tedium of most of my years in schools."

Marsden continued to write and submitted a novel to a publisher that was rejected. He drifted from job to job, yet somehow succeeded in finishing the first year of a law school course. However, he slipped into a deep depression and ended up in a psychiatric institution, where he met a fourteen-year-old girl who would not speak to anyone. Marsden wondered about this, and on the girl's last day at the institution, he got to talk to her. The girl's plight became the inspiration for Marsden's novel *So Much to Tell You. . . .*

At the age of twenty-seven, bored with his latest promotion to a desk job at a delivery company, Marsden saw a newspaper advertisement about teaching classes and decided to apply. "I'd always had a vague idea that I might enjoy teaching, but then I'd had the same vague ideas about other jobs and they hadn't worked out. . . . From the very first day, however, I knew I'd found my vocation." Marsden soon had a position teaching at Geelong Grammar School, a very famous Australian school. After several years of teaching, he was encouraged to resume writing.

Marsden told *SAAS* that during a school holiday "I sat down and started to write. I made two decisions that turned out to be critical. One was to use the diary format, the other was to aim it at teenage readers.

These two decisions seemed to free me to write more fluently than before. I worked in an intensity of emotion, a state that I often slip into when writing." On the very last day of his vacation, Marsden finished the book. He sent it off to a variety of publishers but received only negative responses. Luckily, a chance meeting with a bookseller helped Marsden get the manuscript into the right hands.

So Much to Tell You . . . focuses on a mute girl who is sent to a special boarding school rather than a psychiatric hospital. The girl has been physically scarred in an accident. Readers get to know her through her diary entries, where her secrets are gradually revealed: her father scarred her with acid that was meant to injure her mother. One of the girl's teachers is able to break into her silent world, and at the end of the novel, there is the hope that she will begin coming out of her isolation. The book caught on quickly and soon became an Australian best- seller. "A good proportion of the first print run was bought by my students, who were smart enough to know how to improve their grades in English," Marsden joked.

Many reviewers offered favorable comments about *So Much to Tell You. . . .* Jo Goodman, writing in *Magpies,* declared that the book was "a riveting first novel which grips the reader from the start," adding: "I found the observation and the characters authentic, the suspense gripping, and the slow and subtle revelation of the truth both painful and illuminating." *School Library Journal* contributor Libby K. White asserted: "Marsden is a master storyteller." I. V. Hansen, commenting in *Children's Literature in Education,* claimed that the novel offers "a moving story, tragic, simple, generous, tender. It is the kind of novel that seems to come from nowhere, yet we know it has been with us all the time."

In *The Journey,* Marsden builds a fable around adolescent coming-of-age rituals. In this tale, a society sends its adolescents on a journey of self-discovery; the youths return with seven stories of experience and enlightenment. The local council then judges whether the stories are sufficient to allow the youths to pass into adulthood. Margot Nelmes commented in *Reading Time* that "this is a rare book, fortifying to the spirit, gripping, and worthy of reading more than once."

Marsden turned to lighter works with the publication of *The Great Gatenby* and *Staying Alive in Year Five. The Great Gatenby* is about the popular but reckless Erle Gatenby, who causes trouble wherever he goes. *Staying Alive in Year Five* offers one boy's perspective on his class's experience with an unusual teacher named Mr. Merlin. *Reading Time* reviewer Halina Nowicka termed *Staying Alive* "a really good, humorous story."

Marsden's *Letters from the Inside* and *Dear Miffy* have evoked controversy. *Letters from the Inside* centers around two girls, Mandy and Tracy, who have become pen pals. After a few exchanges of letters, Tracy reveals that she is actually serving time in a maximum security prison. Mandy admits that her brother is quite violent, and the end of the novel alludes to the fact that Mandy might have been attacked by him. In *Reading Time,* Ashley Freeman called *Letters from the Inside* a "compelling story, which totally involves the reader." Other critics were alarmed by the manner in which Marsden presented the subject of domestic violence. Elizabeth Gleick contended in the *New York Times Book Review* that the book "might be faulted for one reason and one reason alone: it offers not the palest glimmer of hope."

Dear Miffy, which features a jacket notice warning that its contents "may offend some readers," has engendered a similar reaction. In this novel, institutionalized teenager Tony, who comes from a broken home and a working-class environment, writes to his girlfriend, Miffy, a beautiful girl from a wealthy and very troubled family. Tony's letters, which are never mailed, recount their relationship from its turbulent beginnings through its tragic conclusion. *Dear Miffy* is filled with violence, sex, and profanity set against a backdrop of corruption, injustice, and dysfunctional families. Discussing the controversy surrounding the work in *Horn Book,* Jameyson wrote: "In inevitable parallel with the U.S. discussion about *The Chocolate War,* [critics] point out that the shades of gray in this book are so dark as to be unrealistic. Surely no life can be so dismal; surely no group of characters can be so totally lacking in redeeming features; surely no slice of life can be so void of . . . hope." Other commentators have rallied to Marsden's support, however, commending his forthright treatment of difficult subjects and his capacity to endow his protagonists with an authentic teenage voice.

Marsden's best known work, the "Tomorrow, When the War Began" series, has made him an international writer of renown. The multivolume series begins with a simple premise. A small group of Australian teens returns from a camping trip in the bush to discover that, in their absence, Australia has been invaded and occupied by an enemy force. The politics behind the war is kept deliberately vague as the teens themselves decide to do what they can to help push the invaders from Australian soil. The plot thickens quickly because this is not fantasy or science fiction; it is a plausible, realistic adventure saga in which the young heroes face life-threatening situations and respond to them in very human ways. Marsden told *SAAS* that the series was born from one of his own childhood fantasies, "of a world without adults, a world in which the adults had magically disappeared and the kids were left to run the place."

The first book in the series, *Tomorrow, When the War Began,* introduces the narrator, Ellie Linton, and the mixed-gender group of friends who will join her to fight the war. Returning from a camping trip in a canyon they have nicknamed "Hell," Ellie and her friends discover that everyone in their town has been captured, and they must fend for themselves. Quickly, the group organizes to resist the invaders, blowing up a lawn mower to kill one soldier. Theirs is not the mindless violence of a video game, however. Each character reacts to the trauma of war and displacement differently, and Ellie is only one of the teens who struggles with the ethics of killing on one hand and the grip of mortal fear on the other. *Horn Book* contributor Maeve Visser Knoth described *Tomorrow, When the War Began* as "a riveting adventure through which Marsden explores the capacity for evil and the necessity of working together to oppose it."

Subsequent volumes in the series have generated a high level of excitement among the author's fans. Marsden has said that he wanted all of his "Tomorrow, When the War Began" books to have the same level of style and execution that the first one had. Judging by the reaction of some reviewers, he has succeeded in that goal. *The Dead of Night* and *The Third Day, the Frost* further the story of the teenagers as the war in their country continues. Reviewing *The Dead of Night* for *Voice of Youth Advocates,* Alice F. Stern commented: "If you hope for a plot with any closure, you will not find it here. What you will find is a strong adventure story, a little romance, and an excellent psychological study." *Horn Book* reviewer Jennifer M. Brabander praised *The Dead of Night* as "riveting," citing favorably the depth of Marsden's characters and adding: "Thoughtful explorations of the nature of fear, bravery, and violence—natural conversations during wartime—add depth and balance to the edge-of-the-seat action and intense first-person narration."

By the time *Burning for Revenge* appeared, Marsden was a celebrity with a shelf full of Australian awards, most of them voted upon by his teenaged readers. *Burning for Revenge* lifted him into another category altogether. This novel, in which Ellie, Fi, Kevin, Homer, and Lee launch an attack on an airfield and try to civilize a gang of feral children, won the prestigious Book of the Year Award from the Australian Booksellers Association. What made this award particularly special was that Marsden's work was judged not against other young adult novels, but against adult fiction—and he won. He is the first children's author ever to win that particular citation. In her *School Library Journal* review of *Burning for Revenge,* Susie Paige noted that the characters "are so believable that readers forget that the story is fiction." Calling Marsden "a master at creating tension and excitement," *Booklist* critic Frances Bradburn declared *Burning for Revenge* "riveting."

"Tomorrow, When the War Began" found its conclusion in the seventh novel, *The Other Side of Dawn,* in which Ellie and her surviving friends finally find reunion with their loved ones after a final, climactic battle. A *Kirkus Reviews* critic predicted that the many fans of the series worldwide "will be sorry to reach their final chapter in such an outstanding story of friendship, courage, and survival." Fortunately, those legions of readers need not part with Ellie entirely—Marsden has commenced a new, postwar series also featuring the courageous narrator.

Marsden has written numerous other titles in tandem with his series. *The Rabbits* and *Norton's Hut* are picture books, but their intended audience is not necessarily children. *Norton's Hut* is a ghost story about a group of hikers caught out by a blizzard and the strange, silent fellow who shares his home with them during the storm. *The Rabbits* is an allegory of the European conquest of Australia, using the metaphor of the destructive rabbit population that has been such a plague to the continent. "This book is a title to jolt readers," Jameyson said in her *Horn Book* review of *The Rabbits.* "There is no doubt as to the writer's intentions: to sober, sadden, and provoke."

Marsden's novels *Checkers* and *Winter* each feature female protagonists at odds with the adults around them. The heroine of *Checkers* tells her tale from a mental hospital to which she has been sent after a nervous breakdown. Bit by bit, the character reveals the events that led to a family crisis, brought on by her father's unethical business practices. *Booklist* critic Shelle Rosenfeld called *Checkers* a "fascinating, intricately woven novel" notable for its "strong psychological exploration." In *Voice of Youth Advocates,* Gloria Grover also characterized *Checkers* as "an emotionally compelling story."

The protagonist in *Winter* is strong and determined—and she needs to be. Sixteen-year-old Winter returns alone to her estate, Warriewood, to find it neglected and ransacked by those who were paid to care for it. She sets about restoring the home, in the process becoming a detective to discover the real truth behind her parents' deaths when she was four. Winter is hardly a pushover. She takes charge of her life and does not let an adult conspiracy keep her from finding out what she needs to know. In *School Library Journal,* Miranda Doyle concluded that youthful readers would "especially enjoy the ferocity with which Winter stands up to the adults who try to take advantage of her." A *Kirkus Reviews* critic found Winter to be "an appealingly gutsy narrator who keeps the story moving."

"I imagine I'll always be writing, all my life, because there is something within me that needs to tell stories," Marsden related to *SAAS.* "The other passion of my life is the preservation of life. The older I get, the more disturbed I get by the wanton destruction of other creatures by humans. . . . I hope I continue to improve in my treatment of my fellow creatures, be they animal or vegetable."

Marsden makes no apologies for the sensitive issues he covers in his fiction, or the fact that his stories are not always happily resolved. He told *Horn Book* contributor Jameyson, "I keep reminding myself I'm not writing for babies. These are people who in any other culture or any other time would be treated as full adults."

BIOGRAPHICAL AND CRITICAL SOURCES:

BOOKS

Authors and Artists for Young Adults, Volume 20, Gale (Detroit, MI), 1997.

Children's Literature Review, Volume 34, Gale (Detroit, MI), 1995.

St. James Guide to Young Adult Writers, 2nd edition, St. James Press (Detroit, MI), 1999.

Something about the Author Autobiography Series, Volume 22, Gale (Detroit, MI), 1996, pp. 169-185.

Twentieth-Century Young Adult Writers, St. James Press (Detroit, MI), 1994.

PERIODICALS

Booklist, May 15, 1998, Frances Bradburn, review of *A Killing Frost,* p. 1617; October 15, 1998, Shelle Rosenfeld, review of *Checkers,* p. 412; June 1, 1999, Roger Leslie, review of *Darkness, Be My Friend,* p. 1814; October 1, 2000, Frances Bradburn, review of *Burning for Revenge,* p. 332.

Children's Literature in Education, September, 1989, I. V. Hansen, "In Context: Some Recent Australian Writing for Adolescents," pp. 151-163.

Horn Book, July-August, 1995, Maeve Visser Knoth, review of *Tomorrow, When the War Began,* p. 467; September-October, 1997, Karen Jameyson, "Contents May Offend Some Readers," pp. 549-552, and Jennifer M. Brabander, review of *The Dead of Night,* pp. 575-576; May, 1999, Karen Jameyson, "Brush Strokes with History," p. 364; November-December, 2002, Jennifer M. Brabander, review of *The Other Side of Dawn,* p. 762.

Kirkus Reviews, August 15, 2001, review of *The Night Is for Hunting,* p. 1216; July 1, 2002, review of *Winter,* p. 958; August 15, 2002, review of *The Other Side of Dawn,* p. 1229.

Magpies, March, 1988, Jo Goodman, review of *So Much to Tell You . . . ,* p. 30.

New York Times Book Review, November 13, 1994, Elizabeth Gleick, review of *Letters from the Inside,* p. 29.

Publishers Weekly, May 25, 1998, review of *Prayer for the Twenty-first Century,* p. 88; September 7, 1998, review of *Checkers,* p. 96; August 26, 2002, Elizabeth Devereaux, "Bestseller Down Under," p. 70.

Reading Time, Volume 33, number 2, Margot Nelmes, review of *The Journey,* p. 28; Volume 33, number 4, Halina Nowicka, review of *Staying Alive in Year Five,* p. 24; Volume 35, number 4, 1991, Ashley Freeman, review of *Letters from the Inside,* p. 32.

School Library Journal, May, 1989, Libby K. White, review of *So Much to Tell You . . . ,* p. 127;

October, 2000, Susie Paige, review of *Burning for Revenge,* p. 166; August, 2002, Miranda Doyle, review of *Winter,* p. 194.

Voice of Youth Advocates, February, 1998, Alice F. Stern, review of *The Dead of Night,* p. 387; December, 1998, Gloria Grover, review of *Checkers,* p. 356.

ONLINE

John Marsden Home Page, http://www.johnmarsden.com/ (December 20, 2003).

* * *

MARSHALL, Paule 1929-

PERSONAL: Born Valenza Pauline Burke, April 9, 1929, in Brooklyn, NY; daughter of Samuel and Ada (Clement) Burke; married Kenneth E. Marshall, 1950 (divorced, 1963); married Nourry Menard, July 30, 1970; children (first marriage): Evan. *Education:* Brooklyn College (now of the City University of New York), B.A. (cum laude), 1953; attended Hunter College (now of the City University of New York), 1955.

ADDRESSES: Home—407 Central Park W, New York, NY 10025. *Office*—Feminist Press, c/o Gerrie Nuccio, P.O. Box 334, Old Westbury, NY 11568; 19 University Pl., 214, New York, NY 10003; fax: 212-995-4019.

CAREER: Freelance writer and educator. New York University, currently professor of English, distinguished chair in creative writing. Worked as librarian in New York Public Libraries; *Our World* magazine, New York City, staff writer, 1953-56; lecturer on creative writing at Yale University, 1970—; Helen Gould Sheppard Professor in Literature and Culture, New York University, 1997—; lecturer on black literature at colleges and universities including Oxford University, Columbia University, Michigan State University, Lake Forrest College, and Cornell University. Teacher of creative writing at universities such as Columbia University, University of Iowa, and University of California, Berkeley.

MEMBER: PEN American Center, Authors Guild, Authors League of America, Langston Hughes Society, Zora Neale Hurston Society, W. E. B. Du Bois Society, Modern Language Association, Phi Beta Kappa.

AWARDS, HONORS: Guggenheim fellowship, 1960; Rosenthal Award, National Institute of Arts and Letters, 1962, for *Soul Clap Hands and Sing;* Ford Foundation grant, 1964-65; National Endowment for the Arts grant, 1967-68 and 1977; Creative Artists Public Service fellowship, 1974; American Book Award, Before Columbus Foundation, 1984, for *Praisesong for the Widow; Los Angeles Times* Book Award nomination, 1992, for *Daughters;* MacArthur Foundation fellowship, 1992; Black Caucus of the American Library Association Literary Award, 2001, for *The Fisher King;* Dos Passos Prize for Literature.

WRITINGS:

Brown Girl, Brownstones (novel), Random House, 1959, with an afterword by Mary Helen Washington, Feminist Press (Old Westbury, NY), 1981.

Soul Clap Hands and Sing (short stories; includes "British Guiana"), Atheneum (New York, NY), 1961.

The Chosen Place, the Timeless People, Harcourt (New York, NY), 1969.

Praisesong for the Widow (novel), Putnam (New York, NY), 1983.

Reena, and Other Stories (includes novella *Merle,* and short stories "The Valley Between," "Brooklyn," "Barbados," and "To Da-duh, in Memoriam"), with commentary by the author, Feminist Press (Old Westbury, NY), 1983, reprinted as *Merle: A Novella and Other Stories,* Virago Press, 1985.

Daughters (novel), Atheneum (New York, NY), 1991.

Language Is the Only Homeland: Bajan Poets Abroad (nonfiction), [Bridgetown, Barbados], 1995.

The Fisher King, Scribner (New York, NY), 2000.

Contributor of short stories to periodicals and to anthologies such as *Afro-American Writing 2,* edited by Richard Long and Eugenia Collier, New York University Press (New York, NY), 1972.

SIDELIGHTS: "My work asks that you become involved, that you think," writer Paule Marshall once commented in the *Los Angeles Times.* "On the other hand, . . . I'm first trying to tell a story, because I'm always about telling a good story." In her works, "history and community, shapers of the past and the present, are vital subtexts in the lives of Marshall's characters," wrote Joyce Pettis in the *Dictionary of*

Literary Biography. "Just as important," Pettis continued, "Marshall explores the notion of cultural continuity through identification with African heritage and culture as a means of healing the psychic fragmentation that has resulted from colonization and segregation. Her fiction is noted for its artistry—for finely crafted structures, fluid narrative, for language that conveys the nuances of the spoken word, and for characters that are especially complex and rich."

Marshall received her first training in storytelling from her mother, a native of Barbados, and her mother's West Indian friends, all of whom gathered for daily talks in Marshall's home after a hard day of "scrubbing floor." Marshall pays tribute to these "poets in the kitchen" in a *New York Times Book Review* essay where she describes the women's gatherings as a form of inexpensive therapy and an outlet for their enormous creative energy. She writes: "They taught me my first lessons in the narrative art. They trained my ear. They set a standard of excellence. This is why the best of my work must be attributed to them; it stands as testimony to the rich legacy of language and culture they so freely passed on to me in the wordshop of the kitchen."

The standard of excellence set by these women has served Marshall well in her career as a writer. Her novels and stories have been lauded for their skillful rendering of West Indian-Afro-American dialogue and colorful Barbadian expressions. *Dictionary of Literary Biography* contributor Barbara T. Christian believes that Marshall's works "form a unique contribution to Afro-American literature because they capture in a lyrical, powerful language a culturally distinct and expansive world." This pursuit of excellence makes writing a time-consuming effort, according to Marshall. "One of the reasons it takes me such a long time to get a book done," she explained in the *Los Angeles Times,* "is that I'm not only struggling with my sense of reality, but I'm also struggling to find the style, the language, the tone that is in keeping with the material. It's in the process of writing that things get illuminated."

Marshall indicates, however, that her first novel, *Brown Girl, Brownstones,* was written at a faster pace. "I was so caught up in the need to get down on paper before it was lost the whole sense of a special kind of community, what I call Bajan (Barbadian) Brooklyn, because even as a child I sensed there was something special and powerful about it," she stated in the *Los Angeles Times.* When the novel was published in 1959 it was deemed an impressive literary debut, but because of the novel's frank depiction of a young black girl's search for identity and increasing sexual awareness, *Brown Girl, Brownstones* was largely ignored by readers. The novel was reprinted in 1981, and is now considered a classic in the female bildungsroman genre, along with Zora Neale Hurston's *Their Eyes Were Watching God* and Gwendolyn Brooks's *Maud Martha.*

The story has autobiographical overtones, for it concerns a young black Brooklyn girl, Selina, the daughter of Barbadian immigrants Silla and Deighton. Silla, her ambitious mother, desires most of all to save enough money to purchase the family's rented brownstone. Her father, Deighton, on the other hand, is a charming spendthrift who'd like nothing better than to return to his homeland. When Deighton unexpectedly inherits some island land, he makes plans to return there and build a home. Silla meanwhile schemes to sell his inheritance and fulfill her own dream.

Selina is deeply affected by this material conflict, but "emerges from it self-assured, in spite of her scars," wrote Susan McHenry in *Ms.* Selina eventually leaves Brooklyn to attend college. Later, realizing her need to become acquainted with her parents' homeland, she resolves to go to Barbados. McHenry observed: "*Brown Girl, Brownstones* is meticulously crafted and peopled with an array of characters, and the writing combines authority with grace. . . . Marshall . . . should be more widely read and celebrated." Carol Field commented in the *New York Herald Tribune Book Review:* "[*Brown Girl, Brownstones*] is an unforgettable novel written with pride and anger, with rebellion and tears. Rich in content and in cadences of the King's and 'Bajan' English, it is the work of a highly gifted writer."

Marshall's most widely reviewed work to date is *Praisesong for the Widow,* winner of the American Book Award. The novel is thematically similar to *Brown Girl, Brownstones* in that it also involves a black woman's search for identity. This book, though, concerns an affluent widow in her sixties, Avatara (Avey) Johnson, who has lost touch with her West Indian-Afro-American roots. In the process of struggling to make their way in the white-dominated world,

Avey and her husband, Jerome (Jay), lost all of the qualities that made them unique. Novelist Anne Tyler remarked in the *New York Times Book Review,* "Secure in her middle-class life, her civil service job, her house full of crystal and silver, Avey has become sealed away from her true self."

While on her annual luxury cruise through the West Indies, however, Avey has several disturbing dreams about her father's great aunt, whom she visited every summer on a South Carolina island. She remembers the spot on the island where the Ibo slaves, upon landing in America, supposedly took one look around at their new life and walked across the water back to Africa. Avey decides to try to escape the uneasiness by flying back to the security of her home. While in her hotel on Grenada awaiting the next flight to New York, Avey reminisces about the early years of her and Jay's marriage, when they used to dance to jazz records in their living room, and on Sundays listen to gospel music and recite poetry. Gradually, though, in their drive for success they lost "the little private rituals and pleasures, the playfulness and wit of those early years, the host of feelings and passions that had defined them in a special way back then, and the music which had been their nourishment," writes Marshall in the novel.

In the morning, Avey becomes acquainted with a shopkeeper who urges her to accompany him and the other islanders on their annual excursion to Carriacou, the island of their ancestors. Still confused from the past day's events, she agrees. During the island celebration, Avey undergoes a spiritual rebirth and resolves to keep in close contact with the island and its people and to tell others about her experience.

Reviewers question if Avey's resolution is truly enough to compensate for all that she and Jay have lost, if "the changes she envisions in the flush of conversion are commensurate with the awesome message of the resisting Ibos," to use *Voice Literary Supplement* reviewer Carol Ascher's words. "Her search for roots seems in a way the modern, acceptable equivalent of the straightened hair and white ways she is renouncing," wrote *Times Literary Supplement* contributor Mary Kathleen Benet, who added: "On the other hand there is not much else she can do, just as there was not much else Jerome Johnson could do. Paule Marshall respects herself enough as a writer to keep from overplaying her hand; her strength is that she raises questions that have no answers."

Los Angeles Times Book Review contributor Sharon Dirlam offered this view: "[Avey] has learned to stay her anger and to swallow her grief, making her day of reckoning all the more poignant. She has already missed the chance to apply what she belatedly learns, except for the most important lesson: What matters is today and tomorrow, and, oh yes, yesterday-life, at age thirty, age sixty, the lesson is to live." Jonathan Yardley concluded in the *Washington Post Book World:* "*Praisesong for the Widow* . . . is a work of quiet passion—a book all the more powerful precisely because it is so quiet. It is also a work of exceptional wisdom, maturity and generosity, one in which the palpable humanity of its characters transcends any considerations of race or sex; that Avey Johnson is black and a woman is certainly important, but Paule Marshall understands that what really counts is the universality of her predicament."

Reena, and Other Stories, although a collection of short stories, contains the title story, "Reena" and the novella *Merle,* adapted from the novel *The Chosen Place, the Timeless People.* The title is based on a protagonist of the novel. "Reena" is frequently anthologized, particularly in collections of writings by African-American women writers. In her introductory comments to a reissued version of *Black-Eyed Susans/ Midnight Birds: Stories by and about Black Women,* Mary Helen Washington refers to its theme of cultural identity and the role of the African-American female. Dr. Washington's commentary and analysis bolster Paule Marshall's accompanying sketch for "Reena." "Reena" is autobiographical and is a continuation of *Brown Girl, Brownstones.* Marshall describes Reena as like herself "from a West Indian-American background who had attended the free New York City colleges during the forties and fifties. The theme would be our efforts to realize whatever talents we had and to be our own persons in the face of the triple-headed hydra of racism, sexism, and class bias we confronted each day."

Daughters, Marshall's 1991 novel, has been widely acclaimed. According to the author, the novel explores significant personal themes. "Ursa is a young urban woman trying to come to terms with the two worlds that shaped her. . . . Her mother is American, her father West Indian. [I] wanted to write something that was symbolic of the two wings of the black diaspora in this part of the world." Defining the role of the female—upwardly mobile, well-educated—in the black diaspora is the cog around which *Daughters* turns. In the *New York Times Book Review,* Susan Fromberg Schaeffer saw that the key for Ursa is in what she learns from those most important in her life. Ursa learns that "to be human one must be of use. To be of use, men and women must work together—and that the relationship between the sexes is far more complicated than Ursa has ever imagined." Working together involves a struggle—sometimes erupting in conflict between men and women. Ursa discovers by novel's end that she must not evade struggle/conflict toward a common goal. She learns to stop allowing love for another to becloud her judgment, as in the case of ignoring the corruption that her father, Primus, confused with success. Ursa learns that she is "hobbled by love of her father . . . and so complete is his possession of her that she needs to 'abort' him." Ursa must break free to define herself, continue to be "useful," continue to love all humans, yet not be bogged down by that love and get off course. "Marshall shows us how . . . women can—and perhaps should—find themselves becoming men's consciences."

Marshall's novel, *The Fisher King,* published in 2000, is a multigenerational story that serves as a "wonderful rendering of the African diaspora (from Brooklyn to Paris) in its many complexities," observed Adele S. Newson-Horst in *World Literature Today.* "Set against the backdrop of a triangular relationship, *The Fisher King* at once celebrates and delineates the nuances of diaspora interactions—a reality perhaps best captured by the musical form of jazz," Newson-Horst observed. In the 1940s, widow Ulene Payne struggles to make a living, but makes whatever sacrifices are necessary to provide classical piano lessons for her talented son, Everett (also known as Sonny-Rett). Her neighbor, Florence McCullum, lives in elegance and has little trouble providing for her daughter, Cherisse, who is blessed with a wonderful singing voice and has great promise as a singer. But Sonny-Rett soon discovers that classical piano is not to his liking, and begins to play in jazz clubs, where his reputation is made and strengthened. Cherisse, too, abandons her formal singing career and accompanies Sonny to his gigs, along with her best friend, Hattie Carmichael. Soon, Sonny-Rett and Cherisse are married, and Hattie becomes manager of their business affairs. Rather than embracing their children's success in the jazz field (which was then considered a scandalous form of music), Ulene and Florence are mortified and bitterly disappointed that Sonny-Rett and Cherisse did not follow the path provided to them. To escape their parents' resentment—as well as deepening racism throughout America—Cherisse, Sonny-Rett, and Hattie move to Paris and sever ties with family and friends in the United States. Each family blames the other for the problem, and a generations-long feud begins to smolder.

At the novel's opening, it is forty years since the trio left for Europe. Sonny-Rett and Cherisse are dead, and Hattie is the parent, friend, and guardian of their grandson, who is also called Sonny. When Sonny-Rett's brother, Edgar, a successful developer, seeks to inaugurate his neighborhood music hall with a concert honoring the memory and music of his brother, he finds Hattie and Sonny in Paris and flies them in for the event. Hattie chafes at returning, but goes for Sonny's sake. Florence and Ulene find a common interest in great-grandson Sonny, who tries in his own way to reunite the fractured families. "Jazz gives the novel its pulse, but finally this is a family drama, and Marshall beautifully evokes the myriad ways that families are torn asunder when love and power intermingle," commented Bill Ott in *Booklist.* A *Publishers Weekly* reviewer observed that "Marshall writes with verve, clarity, and humor, capturing the cadences of black speech while deftly portraying the complexity of family relationships and the social issues that beset black Americans." Similarly, Maxine E. Thompson, writing on the *BookReporter* Web site, noted that "the writing itself is subtle and quiet but exciting. Marshall has an ear for dialect, and her plots are well thought out." *New York Times* reviewer Lori Leibovich remarked that the "prose is full of expert dialogue, mellifluous rhythms, and sharply drawn portraits of Sonny-Rett's loved ones." Newson-Horst called *The Fisher King* "a national treasure as much as the musical form it employs to tell the story of the diaspora."

BIOGRAPHICAL AND CRITICAL SOURCES:

BOOKS

Black Literature Criticism, Gale (Detroit, MI), 1992.

Bruck, Peter, and Wolfgang Karrer, editors, *The Afro-American Novel since 1960,* B. R. Gruener, 1982.

Christian, Barbara, *Black Women Novelists,* Greenwood Press, 1980.

Contemporary Novelists, 7th edition, St. James Press (Detroit, MI), 2001.

Coser, Stelamaris, *Bridging the Americas: The Literature of Paule Marshall, Toni Morrison, and Gayl Jones,* Temple University Press, 1995.

DeLamotte, Eugenia G., *Places of Silence, Journeys of Freedom: The Fiction of Paule Marshall,* University of Pennsylvania Press (Philadelphia, PA), 1998.

Denniston, Dorothy Haner, *The Fiction of Paule Marshall: Reconstructions of History, Culture, and Gender,* University of Tennessee Press, 1995.

Dictionary of Literary Biography, Gale (Detroit, MI), Volume 157: *Twentieth-Century Caribbean and Black African Writers, Third Series,* 1995, Volume 227: *American Novelists since World War II, Sixth Series,* 2000.

Evans, Mari, editor, *Black Women Writers, 1950-1980,* Anchor Press, 1984.

Hathaway, Heather, *Caribbean Waves: Relocating Claude McKay and Paule Marshall,* Indiana University Press (Bloomington, IN), 1999.

Herdeck, Donald E., editor, *Caribbean Writers,* Volume 1: *Anglophone Literature from the Caribbean,* Three Continents Press, 1979.

Hine, Darlene Clark, editor, *Black Women in America,* Carlson Publishing (Brooklyn, NY), 1993.

Magill, Frank N., editor, *Great Women Writers,* Holt (New York, NY), 1994.

Mainiero, Lina, editor, *American Women Writers,* Frederick Ungar Publishing (New York, NY), 1979-1982.

Melchior, Bernhard, *"Re/Visioning" the Self away from Home: Autobiographical and Cross-cultural Dimensions in the Works of Paule Marshall,* P. Lang (New York, NY), 1998.

Morgan, Janice T., and Colette T. Hall and Carol L. Snyder, editors, *Redefining Autobiography in Twentieth-Century Women's Fiction: An Essay Collection,* Garland, 1991, pp. 135-147.

Pettis, Joyce Owens, *Toward Wholeness in Paule Marshall's Fiction,* University Press of Virginia, 1996.

Shaw, Harry B., editor, *Perspectives of Black Popular Culture,* Popular Press, 1990, pp. 93-100.

Smith, Valerie, Lea Baechler, and A. Walton Litz, editors, *African American Writers,* Scribner (New York, NY), 1991.

Sorkin, Adam J., editor, *Politics and the Muse: Studies in the Politics of Recent American Literature,* Popular Press, 1989, pp. 179-205.

Spradling, Mary Mace, editor, *In Black and White,* Gale (Detroit, MI), 1980.

Wall, Cheryl A., editor, *Changing Our Own Words: Essays on Criticism, Theory, and Writing by Black Women,* Rutgers University Press, 1989, pp. 196-211.

Washington, Mary Helen, editor, *Black-Eyed Susans/Midnight Birds: Stories by and about Black Women,* Anchor Press (New York, NY), 1989.

PERIODICALS

Black American Literature Forum, winter, 1986; spring-summer, 1987.

Booklist, July, 2000, Bill Ott, review of *The Fisher King,* p. 2008; November 1, 2001, Nancy Spillman, review of *The Fisher King,* p. 513.

Callaloo, spring-summer, 1983; winter, 1987, pp. 79-90; winter, 1997, pp. 127-141; winter, 1999, review of *Praisesong for the Widow,* p. 208.

Chicago Tribune Book World, May 15, 1983.

Christian Science Monitor, January 22, 1970; March 23, 1984.

CLA Journal, March, 1961; September, 1972.

College Language Association Journal, September, 1995, pp. 49-61.

Critical Arts, Volume 9, number 1, 1995, pp. 21-29.

Critical Quarterly, summer, 1971.

Essence, May, 1980.

Freedomways, 1970.

Journal of American Culture, winter, 1989, pp. 53-58.

Journal of Black Studies, December, 1970.

Journal of Caribbean Studies, winter, 1989-spring, 1990, pp. 189-199.

London Review of Books, March 7, 1985.

Los Angeles Times, May 18, 1983.

Los Angeles Times Book Review, February 27, 1983.

MELUS, fall, 1995, pp. 99-120.

Ms., November, 1981.

Nation, April 2, 1983.

Negro American Literature Forum, fall, 1975.

Negro Digest, January, 1970.

New Letters, autumn, 1973.

New Yorker, September 19, 1959.

New York Herald Tribune Book Review, August 16, 1959.

New York Review of Books, April 28, 1983.

New York Times, November 8, 1969; February 1, 1983; November 26, 2000, Lori Leibovich, "Books in Brief: Fiction; Sounds Good, Feels Bad," review of *The Fisher King,* p. 21.

New York Times Book Review, November 30, 1969; January 9, 1983; February 20, 1983.
Novel, winter, 1974.
Obsidian II, winter, 1990, pp. 1-21.
Publishers Weekly, January 20, 1984, pp. 90-91; August 7, 2000, review of *The Fisher King,* p. 71.
Religion and Literature, spring, 1995, pp. 49-61.
Saturday Review, September 16, 1961.
Southern Review, winter, 1992, pp. 1-20.
Times Literary Supplement, September 16, 1983; April 5, 1985.
Village Voice, October 8, 1970; March 22, 1983; May 15, 1984.
Voice Literary Supplement, April, 1982.
Washington Post, February 17, 1984.
Washington Post Book World, January 30, 1983.
World Literature Today, summer-autumn, 2001, Adele S. Newson-Horst, review of *The Fisher King,* p. 148.
World Literature Written in English, autumn, 1985, pp. 285-298.

ONLINE

Bella Stander Home Page, http://www.bellastander.com/ (February/March, 2001), interview with Marshall.
BookReporter, http://www.bookreporter.com/ (May 28, 2003), Maxine E. Thompson, review of *The Fisher King.*
Caribbean Hall of Fame Web site, http://www.sie.edu/~carib/ (May 29, 2003), "Paule Marshall."
Emory University Web site, http://www.emory.edu/ (May 28, 2003), "Paule Marshall."
New York University Web site, http://www.nyu.edu/ (May 29, 2003).
Voices from the Gaps, http://voices.cla.umn.edu/ (May 28, 2003), "Paule Marshall."
Writer Online, http://www.writermag.com/ (September, 2002), "Established Writers Share Their Writing Practices."*

* * *

MATTHEWS, Ellen
See BACHE, Ellyn

* * *

MATUTE (AUSEJO), Ana María 1925(?)-

PERSONAL: Born July 26, 1925 (some sources say 1926), in Barcelona, Spain; daughter of Facundo and Maria (Ausejo) Matute; married, 1952 (divorced 1963); children: Juan-Pablo. *Education:* Attended Damas Negras French Nuns College.

ADDRESSES: *Home*—Provenza 84, Dcha A-3 deg., Barcelona 29, Spain.

CAREER: Writer. Visiting professor at Indiana University, Bloomington, 1965-66, and at University of Oklahoma, Norman, 1969. Writer-in-residence at University of Virginia, Charlottesville, 1978-79.

MEMBER: Hispanic Society of America, American Association of Teachers of Spanish and Portuguese (honorary fellow), Sigma Delta Pi (Hispanic chapter).

AWARDS, HONORS: Premio Nadal, runner up, 1947, for *Los abel,* and winner, 1960, for *Primera memoria;* Caé Gijon prize, 1952, for *Fiesta al noroeste;* Planeta prize, 1954, for *Pequeño teatro;* critics prize and Premio Nacional de Literature, 1958, and Premio Miguel Cervantes, 1959, both for *Los Hijos muertos;* Lazarillo prize, 1965, for *El Polizón del "Ulises";* Fastenrath Prize, 1969, for *Los Soldados lloran de noche.*

WRITINGS:

Los Abel (title means "The Abels") Destino (Barcelona, Spain), 1948, reprinted, 1981.
Fiesta al noroeste, La Ronda [and] *Los Niños buenos* (titles mean "Festival of the Northwest," "The Round," [and] "The Good Children"), A. Aguado (Madrid, Spain), 1953.
Fiesta al noroeste, (title means "Festival of the Northwest"), 1953, translation by Phoebe Ann Porter published as *Celebration in the Northwest,* University of Nebraska Press (Lincoln, NE), 1997.
Pequeño teatro (title means "Little Theater"), Planeta (Barcelona, Spain), 1954.
En esta tierra (title means "On This Land"), Exito (Barcelona, Spain), 1955.
Los Cuentos, vagabundos (title means "The Stories, Vagabonds"), Ediciones G.P. , 1956.

Los Niños tontos (title means "The Foolish Children"), Arion (Madrid, Spain), 1956, reprinted, Media Vaca (Valencia, Spain), 2000.

El País de la pizarra (title means "The Country of the Blackboard"), Molino (Barcelona, Spain), 1957.

El Tiempo (title means "The Time"), Mateu, 1957, reprinted, Destino (Barcelona, Spain), 1981.

Los Hijos muertos, Planeta (Barcelona, Spain, 1958, translation by Joan MacLean published as *The Lost Children,* Macmillan (New York, NY), 1965.

Los Mercaderes (title means "The Merchants"), Destino (Barcelona, Spain), 1959.

Paulina, el mundo y las estrellas (title means "Pauline, the World and the Stars"), Garbo (Barcelona, Spain), 1960.

El Saltamontes verde [y] *El Aprendiz* (titles mean "The Green Grasshopper" [and] "The Apprentice"), Lumen (Barcelona, Spain), 1960.

Primera memoria, Destino (Barcelona, Spain), 1960, translation by Elaine Kerrigan published as *School of the Sun,* Pantheon (New York, NY), 1963, reprinted, Columbia University Press (New York, NY), 1989, translation by James Holman Mason published as *Awakening,* Hutchinson (London, England), 1963.

Tres y un sueño (title means "Three and a Dream"), Destino (Barcelona, Spain), 1961, reprinted, 1993.

A la mitad del camino (title means "In the Middle of the Road"), Rocas (Barcelona, Spain), 1961.

Historias de la artámila, Destino (Barcelona, Spain), 1961, reprinted, 1997, also published as *Doce historias de la artámila,* Harcourt (New York, NY), 1965.

El Arrepentido (title means "The Repentant One"), Rocas (Barcelona, Spain), 1961.

Libro de juegos para los niños de los otros (title means "Book of Games for the Children of Others"), Lumen (Barcelona, Spain), 1961.

Caballito loco [and] *Carnivalito* (titles mean "Crazy Little Horse" [and] "Little Carnival"), Lumen (Barcelona, Spain), 1962.

El Río (title means "The River"), Argos (Barcelona, Spain), 1963.

Los Soldados lloran de noche (title means "The Soldiers Weep at Night"), Destino, 1964, translation by Robert Nugent and Maria Jose de la Camara published as *Soldiers Cry by Night,* Latin American Literary Review Press (Pittsburgh, PA), 1995.

El Polizón del "Ulises" (title means "The Draft of 'Ulysses'"), Lumen (Barcelona, Spain), 1965.

Algunos muchachos (title means "Some Children"), Destino (Barcelona, Spain), 1968, reprinted, 1982, translation by Michael Scott Doyle published as *The Heliotrope Wall and Other Stories,* Columbia University Press (New York, NY), 1989.

La Trampa, Destino (Barcelona, Spain), 1969, translation published as *The Trap,* Latin American Literary Review Press (Pittsburgh, PA), 1996.

La Torre vigía (title means "The Watch Tower"), Lumen (Barcelona, Spain), 1971, reprinted, Plaza & Janés (Barcelona, Spain), 1994.

Olvidado rey Gudú (title means "Forgotten King Gudu"), Lumen (Barcelona, Spain), 1980, 3rd edition, Espasa (Madrid, Spain), 1996.

Diablo vuelve a casa (title means "Devil, Come Back Home"), Destino (Barcelona, Spain), 1980.

Sólo un pié descalzo Lumen (Barcelona, Spain), 1983.

La Virgen de Antioquía y otros relatos, Mondadori (Madrid, Spain), 1990.

De ninguna parte y otros relatos, Fundacion de los Ferrocarriles Españoles, 1993.

*Luciérnagas,*2nd second edition, Destino (Barcelona, Spain), 1993.

El Verdadero final de la bella durmiente, Lumen (Barcelona, Spain), 1995.

Casa de juegos prohibidos: Textos inocentes, Espasa (Madrid, Spain), 1997.

Ana María Matute: La Voz del silencio, interviews conducted by Marie-Lise Gazarian-Gautier, Espasa (Madrid, Spain), 1997.

Fireflies, translation from the Spanish by Glafyra Ennis, P. Lang (New York, NY), 1998.

(Contributor) *El Corazón tardío,* Planeta (Barcelona, Spain), 1998.

Cuentos del mar, Sociedad Estatal (Lisboa, Spain), 1998.

Aranmanoth, Espasa (Madrid, Spain), 2000.

En el tren, Irreverences (Madrid, Spain), 2001.

Cuentos de infancia, Ediciones Martinez Roca (Barcelona, Spain), 2002.

Also author of *La Pequeña vida* (title means "The Little Life"), Tecnos.

SIDELIGHTS: Ana María Matute is considered by many critics to be one of Spain's most important fiction writers. From her first significant success, *The Lost Children,* to more recent publications such as *Soldiers Cry by Night, En el tren,* and *Cuentos de infancia,* themes of war and the rites of passage continue to dominate. The elements of myth, fantasy, fairy tale, and the supernatural transform typical tales into the unique magic only Matute creates.

Matute was ten years old when the Spanish Civil War broke out; it disrupted her education and became a potent, permanent force in her life. As a child, she has said, she confronted the fact that the world is filled with much that is terrifying.

By the time she published her first story, Matute was using writing as a vehicle for expressing anger toward a cruel, unjust world. The civil war became a recurring theme in her work, sometimes merely as a backdrop (as in *Pequeño teatro*), but more often as her central concern. Nevertheless, unlike many postwar Spanish writers, Matute is not a political partisan: she conveys what Desmond MacNamara called "unpolitical Spanish pessimism," focusing not on party machinations but on the angst of her people, particularly the children.

Indeed, Matute "sees the world through the eyes of childhood [with a] quality of mystery, of magic, of fairy tale, combined in a unique mixture with the harsh and bitter realities of life," wrote George Wythe in *Books Abroad.* Her children are introverted victims of an adult world whose cruelty they cannot understand; and they suffer the existential pains of alienation and despair one usually thinks of as reserved for adults.

Matute creates her hostile world by means of an imaginative, personal style characterized, J. Wesley Childers has noted, "by simile, metaphor, oxymoron, and the use of natural phenomena to reflect human frustrations." To Rafael Bosch of *Books Abroad,* her language is "direct and wonderfully simple without ceasing to be tremendously creative and poetic."

In *A la mitad del camino* ("In the Middle of the Road"), Matute presents a collection of essays that contains some of the clearest, nonfictionalized statements of her attitudes toward life. *Los Abel* is her first novel, a psychological study and chronicle of personal growth in the midst of the disintegration of a family, Cain and Abel style. *Fiesta al Noreste* is a prize-winning short novel providing excellent examples of Matute's style and narrative skills. In *The Lost Children* (*Los Hijos muertos*), Matute begins an ambitious work chronicling generations of a family torn by civil war. A prize-winning trilogy collectively titled *Los Mercanderes* uses myth to reinforce unchanging behavior and returns to the themes of Cain and Abel and the innocence of youth.

Matute's manuscripts are housed at the Mugar Library of Boston University, which has organized the Ana María Matute Collection. Editions of her books continue to be reprinted and have appeared in many languages, including Italian, French, German, Russian, Portuguese, Swedish, Polish, Japanese, Hebrew, Lithuanian, Bulgarian, and Esperanto.

BIOGRAPHICAL AND CRITICAL SOURCES:

BOOKS

Bede, Jean-Albert, and William B. Edgerton, general editors, *Columbia Dictionary of Modern European Literature,* 2nd edition, revised and updated, Columbia University Press (New York, NY), 1980.

Contemporary Literary Criticism, Volume 11, Gale (Detroit, MI), 1979.

Contemporary Women Writers of Spain, Twayne (New York NY), 1998.

Diaz, Janet, *Ana María Matute,* Twayne (New York NY), 1971.

Gazarian-Gautier, Marie-Lise, *Interviews with Spanish Writers,* Dalkey Archive Press (Elmwood Park, IL), 1991.

Jones, Margaret E. W., *The Literary World of Ana María Matute,* University Press of Kentucky (Lexington, KY), 1970.

Miller, Beth, editor, *Women in Hispanic Literature: Icons and Fallen Idols,* University of California Press (Berkeley, CA), 1983.

Perez, Janet, *Contemporary Women Writers of Spain,* Twayne (New York NY), 1988.

Robinson, Lillian S., compiler and editor, *Modern Women Writers,* Continuum (New York, NY).

Schneider, Marshall J., and Irwin Stern, editors, *Modern Spanish and Portuguese Literatures,* Continuum (New York, NY), 1988.

Schwartz, Ronald, *Spain's New Wave Novelists,* Scarecrow (Metuchen, NJ), 1976.

Ulyatt, Philomena, *Allegory, Myth, and Fable in the Work of Ana María Matute* (dissertation), University of Newcastle upon Tyne, 1977.

Vinson, James and Daniel Kirkpatrick, editors, *Contemporary Foreign Language Writers,* St. Martins Press (New York NY), 1984.

Zipes, Jack, editor, *The Oxford Companion to Fairy Tales,* Oxford University Press (New York, NY), 2000.

PERIODICALS

Books Abroad, summer, 1962, Rafael Bosch, review of *Historias de la artámila,* p. 303; winter, 1966, George Wythe, pp. 19-20; winter, 1970; summer, 1972.

Christian Science Monitor, May 20, 1965, Elizabeth Janeway, review of *The Lost Children,* p. 7.

Dalhousie Review, spring, 1990, Marian G. R. Coope, review of *Heliotrope and Other Stories,* p. 131.

Hispania, March, 1998, review of *Olvidado rey Gudú,* p. 121; March, 2001, review of *Aranmanoth,* p. 82.

Journal of Spanish Studies, winter, 1976, Elizabeth Ordonez, review of *The Trap,* pp. 180-81, 187-89.

Library Journal, February 15, 1995, Jack Shreve, review of *Soldiers Cry by Night,* p. 182.

Modern Language Journal, November, 1966, December, 1971.

New Leader, July 5, 1965, Richard Howard, review, pp. 19-20.

New Statesman, October 27, 1967.

New York Times, April 21, 1963, Mildred Adams, review, p. 4; April 27, 1997, William Ferguson, review of *Celebration in the Northwest,* p. 25.

New York Times Book Review, May 14, 1989, Richard Burgin, review of *Heliotrope and Other Stories,* p. 22.

Publishers Weekly, January 27, 1989, Sybil Steinberg, review of *Heliotrope and Other Stories,* p. 451; December 5, 1994, review of *Soldiers Cry by Night,* p. 70; September 16, 1996, review of *The Trap,* p. 38.

Revista de Estudios Hispanicos, May, 1980, J. Townsend Shelby, review, p. 6.

Times Literary Supplement, December 28, 1967; October 8, 1971; August 4, 1989, Abigail E. Lee, review of *Heliotrope and Other Stories,* p. 858.

Translation Review Supplement, July, 1998, review of *Celebration in the Northwest,* p. 23; July, 1999, review of *Fireflies,* p. 24.

World and I, February, 1998, Marie-Lise Gazarian-Gautier, review of *Celebration in the Northwest,* p. 274.

ONLINE

Florida International University Web site, http://www.fiu.edu/ (November 22, 2003), Women Faculty Book Club, review of *The Trap.*

New York Times Web site, http://www.nytimes.com/ (November 22, 2003) William Ferguson, review of *Celebration in the Northwest.**

* * *

MAZER, Harry 1925-

PERSONAL: Born May 31, 1925, in New York, NY; son of Sam (a dressmaker) and Rose (a dressmaker; maiden name, Lazeunick) Mazer; married Norma Fox (a novelist), February 12, 1950; children: Anne, Joseph, Susan, Gina. *Education:* Union College, B.A., 1948; Syracuse University, M.A., 1960.

ADDRESSES: Home and office—Brown Gulf Rd., Jamesville, NY 13078. *Agent*—Marilyn Marlow, Curtis Brown Ltd., Ten Astor Pl., New York, NY 10003.

CAREER: Railroad brake man and switchtender for New York Central, 1950-55; New York Construction, Syracuse, NY, sheet metal worker, 1957-59; Central Square School, Central Square, NY, teacher of English, 1959-60; Aerofin Corp., Syracuse, welder, 1960-63; full-time writer, 1963—. *Military service:* U.S. Army Air Forces, 1943-45; became sergeant; received Purple Heart and Air Medal.

MEMBER: Authors Guild, Authors League of America, Society of Children's Book Writers, American Civil Liberties Union.

AWARDS, HONORS: Kirkus Reviews Choice list, 1974, for *The Dollar Man;* Children's Choice list, International Reading Association, 1977, for *The Solid Gold Kid;* Best Books for Young Adults list, American Library Association (ALA), 1977 (with Norma Fox Mazer), for *The Solid Gold Kid,* 1978, for *The War on Villa Street,* 1979, for *The Last Mission,* 1981, for *I Love You, Stupid!,* 1986, for *When the Phone Rang,* and 1987, for *The Girl of His Dreams;* Dorothy Can-

Harry Mazer

field Fisher Children's Book Award nomination, 1979, for *The War on Villa Street; New York Times* Best Books of the Year list, 1979, and ALA Best of the Best Books list, 1970-83, both for *The Last Mission;* New York Public Library Books for the Teen Age list, 1980, for *The Last Mission,* 1986, for *Hey Kid! Does She Love Me?,* 1988, for *The Girl of His Dreams,* and 1989, for *Heartbeat; Booklist* Contemporary Classics list, 1984, and German "Preis der Lesseratten," both for *Snowbound;* Arizona Young Readers Award nomination, 1985, for *The Island Keeper;* Iowa Teen Award Master List, 1988, for *When the Phone Rang;* Books for Reluctant Readers, ALA, 1988, for *The Girl of His Dreams,* and 1989, for *City Light;* West Australian Young Reader's Book Award, Australian Library and Information Association, 1989, for *When the Phone Rang;* Quick Picks for Reluctant Young Adult Readers, ALA, 1998, for *Twelve Shots: Outstanding Stories about Guns;* Best Books, *School Library Journal,* 1998, and Fanfare list, *Horn Book,* 1999, both for *The Wild Kid.*

WRITINGS:

YOUNG ADULT NOVELS

Guy Lenny, Delacorte (New York, NY), 1971, reprinted, Avon (New York, NY), 1988.

Snow Bound, Delacorte (New York, NY), 1973.

The Dollar Man, Delacorte (New York, NY), 1974.

(With wife, Norma Fox Mazer) *The Solid Gold Kid,* Delacorte (New York, NY), 1977.

The War on Villa Street, Delacorte (New York, NY), 1978.

The Last Mission, Delacorte (New York, NY), 1979.

The Island Keeper: A Tale of Courage and Survival, Delacorte (New York, NY), 1981.

I Love You, Stupid!, Crowell Junior Books (New York, NY), 1981.

When the Phone Rang, Scholastic (New York, NY), 1985.

Hey Kid! Does She Love Me?, Crowell Junior Books (New York, NY), 1985.

Cave under the City, Crowell Junior Books (New York, NY), 1986.

The Girl of His Dreams, Crowell Junior Books (New York, NY), 1987.

City Lights, Scholastic (New York, NY), 1988.

(With Norma Fox Mazer) *Heartbeat,* Bantam (New York, NY), 1989.

Someone's Mother Is Missing, Delacorte (New York, NY), 1990.

(With Norma Fox Mazer) *Bright Days, Stupid Nights,* Bantam (New York, NY), 1992.

Who Is Eddie Leonard?, Delacorte (New York, NY), 1993.

The Dog in the Freezer: Three Novellas, Simon & Schuster (New York, NY), 1997.

The Wild Kid, Simon & Schuster (New York, NY), 1998.

A Boy at War: A Novel of Pearl Harbor, Simon & Schuster (New York, NY), 2001.

OTHER

(Editor) *Twelve Shots: Outstanding Short Stories about Guns,* Delacorte (New York, NY), 1997.

Also contributor to *Speaking for Ourselves: Autobiographical Sketches by Notable Authors of Books for Young Adults,* Volume 1, compiled and edited by Donald R. Gallo, National Council of Teachers of English (Urbana, IL), 1990.

ADAPTATIONS: Snow Bound was filmed as an *NBC After School Special* in 1978.

SIDELIGHTS: "Harry Mazer writes about young people caught in the midst of moral crises, often of their own making," asserted Kenneth L. Donelson in *Voice of Youth Advocates.* "Searching for a way out, they discover themselves, or rather they learn that the first step in extricating themselves from their physical and moral dilemmas is self-discovery. Intensely moral as Mazer's books are," the critic continued, "they present young people thinking and talking and acting believably," a characteristic which accounts for Mazer's popularity. In *The Girl of His Dreams,* for example, Mazer relates the romance of two ordinary young adults with "a credibility apart from its fairy-tale ending," commented Marianne Gingher in the *Los Angeles Times,* a credibility due to the "dimensional characters." Although "contrivances abound," the critic believed that "the happy ending feels earned. Harry Mazer writes deftly about the nature of adolescent yearning, both from a boy's and girl's perspective." And *Snow Bound,* the tale of two mismatched teens who are caught unprepared in a New York blizzard and must cooperate to survive, has a similar appeal. *New York Times Book Review* contributor Cathleen Burns Elmer noted that "occasionally a plot turn seems contrived," but she admitted that the book has a "capacity to enthrall [that] lies in the *mature* reader's willingness to suspend disbelief. *Snow Bound* is a crackling tale; Mazer tells it with vigor and authority."

The Dollar Man presents another "average" youth in uncommon circumstances; Marcus Rosenbloom is overweight, prone to daydreaming, and obsessed with finding out the identity of his father, about whom his single mother refuses to speak. "The idea is not novel, or even presented with extraordinary subtlety or style," observed Tobi Tobias in the *New York Times Book Review,* "but there is such charged energy in Mazer's work and Marcus is such an authentic person that you care, very much, what happens." "Not incidentally," a *Kirkus Reviewer* writer remarked, "this is an outstandingly empathetic and realistic study of . . . a food addict and, moreover, a sensitive interior view—undistorted by the self-discounting sarcasm that has become a narrative cliche—of the kind of kid who is usually shoved into the background . . . but who in this case deserves the front and center attention Mazer accords him." The result, concluded the critic, is "a rare combination—uncompromising yet ever so easy to connect with."

Mazer brings his life experience to the keyboard when he writes. According to one biographer, "The halls and the stairs were Mazer's playground, and he grew up between two worlds—the park and the street—both of which he would later use in his novels."

The Last Mission, based in part on Mazer's experiences in World War II, "represents an amazing leap in writing, far surpassing anything [the author] had written before," claimed Donelson. Fifteen-year-old Jack Raab is Jewish and so desperate to fight against Hitler that he borrows his older brother's identification to enlist in the Army Air Forces. Jack is trained as a gunner, and he and his fellow crew members fly out of England on over twenty missions before being hit by enemy fire; Jack bails out and is the only one to survive—but he ends up a German prisoner of war. While war stories form a much-explored genre, Paxton Davis felt *The Last Mission* stands out; as he detailed in the *New York Times Book Review,* the force of Mazer's novel "lies less with details of Air Force training and service . . . than with the emotional substance upon which the experience depends. For Jack Raab is no mere author's pawn," the critic explained. "The reader feels his shock and grief at losing his friends, suffers with him the doubts and apprehensions that being a Jewish prisoner inevitably raise, and especially, experiences with him the bewildering mixture of relief and repugnance that comes with returning to civilian life."

A *Kirkus Reviews* writer, however, believed that "despite Mazer's evident and convincing first-hand acquaintance with the material," the novel is a "reduction of a genre that is best met at full strength." Donelson, on the other hand, asserted that *The Last Mission* "conveys better than any other young adult novel, and better than most adult novels, the feeling of war and the desolation it leaves behind. . . . This book is a remarkable achievement, both for its theme and its portrait of a young man who searches and acts and finds the search futile and the actions incoherent." As Davis concluded, "Mazer is a prize-winning writer for young people. No wonder."

In *Someone's Mother's Missing,* Mazer tells the story of Lisa Allen, a young girl whose world falls apart when her father passes away. Her mother cannot cope with the void and the mountain of bills he left behind, so she leaves Lisa. A *Publishers Weekly* reviewer criticized this book and felt that its "overly brief and choppy chapters omit many details and preclude examination of the characters' motives or the impact the events have on their lives." Mazer tells the tale of another troubled teen in *Who Is Eddie Leonard?* Eddie, a teenage boy, shows up at the home of a family whose son has been missing for years. He claims to be their son, but they never quite trust him or believe his assertions. The father eventually locates the boy's birth certificate, proving that he is not their son. A *Publishers Weekly* reviewer observed, "Mazer does a better job with internal monologue than with dialogue," but added that "the character does work" in spite of this flaw. The same reviewer felt that Eddie is "a metaphor for the alienation that many teenagers feel" and that readers may "appreciate the unsentimental treatment of the main character, who is far from perfect and far from innocent."

Mazer's disturbance about the accessibility of guns among today's youth led to the compilation of *Twelve Shots: Outstanding Short Stories about Guns.* Mazer invited young people to write stories about the way guns are present in people's lives. "The result is a varied, involving collection with stories by familiar writers such as Walter Dean Meters, Chris Lynch, Rita Williams-Garcia, and Richard Peck," observed Helen Rosenberg in *Booklist.* Rosenberg also noted, "Some stories are serious and subtly antigun, others are hilarious."

A twelve-year-old boy with Down's syndrome narrates *The Wild Kid.* When Sammy gets lost in the woods, he is kidnapped by Kevin, a juvenile delinquent. Kitty Flynn in *Horn Book* described the book as both "harrowing and touching." She added that "Mazer manages to portray both the victim and the victimizer as sympathetic." Kevin finally makes an anonymous call to the police and then disappears back into the woods. *Booklist*'s John Peters remarked, "Kevin's sudden disappearance makes a stimulating loose end that may, paradoxically, strengthen readers' responses to this survival-story-with-a-difference."

Mazer once told *CA:*"I felt—I've always felt—that I write and even speak with difficulty. I think I am a writer not because this was something I did well—an inborn talent—but for the opposite reason, because I did it so poorly. I was like the child suffering from polio who determines to become a runner.

"Everything I've done as a writer I've done despite the feeling that I have no natural talent. I've never felt articulate or fluent, rarely felt that flow of language. When I think of the origins of these feelings, I wonder if this may be physical, some form of dyslexia. My mother, despite strenuous efforts, never learned to read or write with fluency and my brother seemed to have the same problem in school."

The author added: "When I started writing I had no idea I would find myself writing for young readers. My agent suggested I do something in this area, and I discovered that I liked writing about this time of life. Adolescence for me was so intense, so filled with joy, pain, expectations, hope, despair, energy, that though those years are far behind me they remain real to me, and have a vividness and clarity that events much closer to me in time do not have. To my surprise I discovered a thirteen-year-old voice inside me.

"In writing for the young you can't allow yourself the diversions, the long descriptions, philosophical ruminations, endless dialogues of other fictions. You have to rivet the interest of your reader rapidly. I don't expect my reader to be any more patient than I am.

"A greater danger, though, is to oversimplify, to write down, to fudge on emotion, and development, and the realistic working out of the story. Good children's fiction is finally no different than good adult fiction. It needs fully shaped characters, conflict, and development. It has form, a beginning, middle and end.

"I'm interested in character, in those parts of people that are hidden, misunderstood, areas of deprivation, longing, separation and isolation. I write out of the memory of those feelings in myself. When I feel the conflict in the character, the disparate feelings, then I begin to feel the truth of the character, the inner tension, the opposing emotions, that inform the book as well."

For an earlier published interview, see entry in *Contemporary Authors,* Volume 97-100.

BIOGRAPHICAL AND CRITICAL SOURCES:

BOOKS

Butler, Francelia, editor, *Children's Literature Review,* Volume 4, Temple University Press (Philadelphia, PA), 1975, p. 206.

Children's Literature Review, Volume 16, Gale (Detroit, MI), 1989.

Lystad, Mary, *Twentieth-Century Young Adult Writers,* St. James Press (Detroit, MI), 1994.

Nilsen, Alleen Pace, and Kenneth L. Donelson, *Literature for Today's Young Adults,* Scott, Foresman (Glenview, IL), 1985.

Reed, Arthea J. S., *Presenting Harry Mazer,* Twayne (New York, NY), 1996.

Something about the Author Autobiography Series, Volume 11, Gale (Detroit, MI), 1991.

PERIODICALS

Booklist, January 15, 1992, review of *I Love You, Stupid!,* p. 933; November 15, 1991, review of *Someone's Mother Is Missing,* p. 74; June 15, 1992, Stephanie Zvirin, review of *Bright Days, Stupid Nights,* p. 1826; October 1, 1992, review of *Cave under the City,* p. 341; November 15, 1993, Chris Sherman, review of *Who Is Eddie Leonard?,* p. 614; March 15, 1994, review of *Who Is Eddie Leonard?,* p. 1358; April 15, 1994, audio book review of *The Last Mission,* p. 1548; March 15, 1997, Ilene Cooper, review of *The Dog in the Freezer: Three Novellas,* p. 1236; August, 1997, Helen Rosenberg, review of *Twelve Shots: Outstanding Short Stories about Guns,* p. 1899; August, 1998, John Peters, review of *The Wild Kid,* p. 2007; April 1, 2001, Carolyn Phelan, review of *A Boy at War: A Novel of Pearl Harbor,* p. 1481.

Book Report, November-December, 1989, Mary I. Purucker, review of *Heartbeat,* p. 45; March-April, 1991, Catherine M. Andronik, review of *Someone's Mother Is Missing,* p. 45; January-February, 1993, Rebecca A. T. Neuhedel, review of *Bright Days, Stupid Nights,* p. 48; May-June, 1994, Theresa Snow, review of *Who Is Eddie Leonard?,* p. 45; September-October, 1997, Mary R. Oran, review of *The Dog in the Freezer,* p. 44; September-October, 1997, Judith M. Garner, review of *Presenting Harry Mazer,* p. 65.

Books for Keeps, November, 1992, review of *Someone's Mother Is Missing,* p. 25.

Bulletin of the Center for Children's Books, October, 1997, Elizabeth Bush, review of *Twelve Shots,* p. 61; March 15, 1998, review of *Twelve Shots,* p. 1226; November, 1998, review of *The Wild Kid,* p. 108.

Catholic Library World, September, 1999, review of *Twelve Shots,* p. 29.

Children's Book Review Service, November, 1997, review of *Twelve Shots,* p. 36; September, 1998, review of *The Wild Kid,* p. 11.

Children's Bookwatch, March, 1991, p. 3; March, 1994, review of *Who Is Eddie Leonard?,* p. 3.

Emergency Librarian, May, 1997, review of *The Last Mission,* p. 10; November, 1997, review of *The Dog in the Freezer,* p. 51; January, 1998, review of *Twelve Shots,* p. 50.

English Journal, May, 1980, Alleen Pace Nilsen, review of *The Last Mission,* p. 93; November, 1980, G. Robert Carlsen, review of *The Last Mission,* p. 88; April, 1982, Dick Abrahamson, review of *I Love You, Stupid!,* p. 81; February, 1994, review of *Who Is Eddie Leonard?,* p. 81; December 1996, John W. Conner and Kathleen M. Tessmer, review of *When the Phone Rang,* p. 60; February, 1988, Judith M. Beckman and Elizabeth A. Belden, review of *The Girl of His Dreams,* p. 85; November, 1992, Tom Romano, "Authors' Insights: Turning Teenagers into Readers and Writers," p. 96; February, 1997, "Mazers Share Life, Writing with ALAN Breakfast Audience," p. 100.

Horn Book, February, 1980, Paul Heins, review of *The Last Mission,* p. 63; June, 1981, Ann A. Flowers, review of *The Island Keeper,* p. 311; February, 1982, Karen M. Klockner, review of *I Love You, Stupid!,* p. 53; March-April, 1987, Hanna B. Zeiger, review of *Cave under the City,* p. 211; March-April, 1988, Margaret A. Bush, review of *The Girl of his Dreams,* p. 209; July-August, 1988, Nancy Vasilakis, review of *City Lights,* p. 502; September-October, 1998, Kitty Flynn, review of *The Wild Kid,* p. 611; September-October, 1989, Nancy Vasilakis, review of *Heartbeat,* p. 630.

Horn Book Guide, spring, 1994, review of *Who Is Eddie Leonard?,* p. 88; spring, 1998, review of *The Dog in the Freezer,* p. 77; spring, 1998, review of *Twelve Shots,* p. 158; spring, 1999, review of *The Wild Kid,* p. 71; fall 2001, review of *A Boy at War* p. 324.

Journal of Adolescent and Adult Literacy, May, 1997, review of *When the Phone Rang,* p. 669; December, 1997, review of *Twelve Shots,* p. 321.

Junior Bookshelf, February, 1992, review of *Someone's Mother Is Missing,* p. 39.

Kirkus Reviews, August 15, 1974; January 1, 1980; May 15, 1985; September 15, 1985; December 1, 1993, review of *Who Is Eddie Leonard?,* p. 1526; March 15, 1997, review of *The Dog in the Freezer,*

p. 466; July 1, 1997, review of *Twelve Shots,* p. 1033; July 15, 1998, review of *The Wild Kid,* p.1038; April 15, 2001, review of *A Boy at War,* p. 589.

Kliatt, November, 1992, audio book review of *The Last Mission,* p. 58; July, 1995, review of *Who Is Eddie Leonard?,* p. 9; November, 1998, review of *Twelve Shots,* p. 22; April 1, 2001, review of *A Boy at War,* p. 12.

Los Angeles Times, March 12, 1988, Marianne Gingher, "A Boy Who Runs Meets a Girl Anxious to Catch Up"; June 10, 2001, review of *A Boy at War* p. 16.

New Statesman and Society, February 23, 1990, John Yandell, review of *The Girl of his Dreams,* p. 35.

New York Times, March 15, 1981, review of *The Last Mission,* p. 35; September 13, 1981, Feenie Ziner, review of *The Island Keeper,* p. 50; November 15, 1981, Paxton Davis, review of *I Love You, Stupid!,* p. 69; July 18, 1982, review of *The Island Keeper,* p. 27.

New York Times Book Review, August 12, 1973, Cathleen Burns Elmer, review of *Snow Bound,* p. 8; August 12, 1973, review of *A Boy at War,* p. 24; November 17, 1974; December 2, 1979, Paxton Davis, review of *The Last Mission,* p. 41; March 15, 1981, review of *The Last Mission,* p. 86; September 13, 1981, Feenie Ziner, review of *The Island Keeper,* p. 50; November 15, 1981, Paxton Davis, review of *I Love You, Stupid!,* p. 69; July 18, 1982, review of *The Island Keeper,* p. 27; June 1, 1997, review of *The Dog in the Freezer,* p. 36.

Publishers Weekly, May 31, 1985, review of *Hey Kid! Does She Love Me?* p. 57; November 1, 1985, review of *When the Phone Rang,* p. 65; December 12, 1986, Diane Roback, review of *Cave under the City,* p. 56; August 14, 1987, Diane Roback, review of *The Girl of His Dreams,* p. 232; March 18, 1988, Kimberly Olson Fakih and Diane Roback, review of *City Lights,* p. 89; May 19, 1989, Kimberly Olson Fakih and Diane Roback review of *Heartbeat,* p. 86; August 10, 1990, Diane Roback, Richard Donahue, review of *Someone's Mother Is Missing,* p. 446; June 22, 1992, review of *Bright Days, Stupid Nights,* p. 63; November 8, 1993, review of *Who Is Eddie Leonard?,* p. 79; July, 1995, review of *Who Is Eddie Leonard?,* p. 9; February 10, 1997, review of *The Dog in the Freezer,* p. 84; August 17, 1998, review of *The Wild Kid,* p. 73; May 7, 2001, review of *A Boy at War,* p. 247.

School Librarian, November, 1991, review of *Someone's Mother Is Missing,* p. 153.

School Library Journal, December, 1978, Robert Unsworth, review of *The War on Villa Street,* p. 62; April, 1981, Lorraine Douglas, review of *The Island Keeper,* p. 142; October, 1981, Kay Webb O'Connell, review of *I Love You, Stupid!,* p. 152; August, 1983, review of *I Love You, Stupid!,* p. 485; November, 1985, Cynthia K. Leibold, review of *When the Phone Rang,* p. 100; December, 1986, Christine Behrmann, review of *Cave under the City,* pp. 105-106; January, 1988, Libby K. White, review of *The Girl of his Dreams,* p. 86; May, 1988, Robert E. Unsworth, review of *City Lights,* p. 110; October, 1988, Carol A. Edwards, review of *The Wild Kid,* p. 140; June, 1989, Trish Ebbatson, review of *Heartbeat,* p. 124; September, 1980; September, 1990, Kathryn Harris, review of *Someone's Mother Is Missing,* p. 255; April, 1992, Carolyn Noah, review of *Cave under the City,* p. 42; July, 1992, Cindy Darling Codell, review of *Bright Days, Stupid Nights,* p. 90; July, 1997, Darcy Schild, review of *The Dog in the Freezer,* p. 96; November, 1993, Lucinda Snyder Whitehurst, review of *Who Is Eddie Leonard?,* p. 125; September, 1997, Tom S. Hurlburt, review of *Twelve Shots,* p. 221; December, 1998, review of *The Wild Kid,* p. 26; May, 2001, William McLoughlin, review of *A Boy at War,* p. 156.

Voice of Youth Advocates, February, 1983, Kenneth L. Donelson, "Searchers and Doers: Heroes in Five Harry Mazer Novels," pp. 19-21; October, 1984; February, 1991, review of *Someone's Mother Is Missing,* p. 354; February, 1992, review of *Someone's Mother Is Missing,* p. 408; December, 1993, review of *City Lights,* p. 278; April, 1994, Ruth E. Dishnow, review of *Who Is Eddie Leonard?,* p. 29; June, 1994, review of *Who Is Eddie Leonard?,* p. 72; August, 1997, review of *Twelve Shots,* p. 190; April, 1998, review of *Twelve Shots,* p. 40; February, 1999, review of *The Wild Kid,* p. 437; June, 2001, review of *A Boy at War* p. 124; February, 2002, review of *A Boy at War,* p. 409.

Washington Post Book World, July 10, 1977.

Wilson Library Bulletin, March, 1985, Patty Campbell, review of *Hey Kid! Does She Love Me?,* p. 485; February, 1986, Patty Campbell, review of *When the Phone Rang,* p. 46; November, 1986, Patty Campbell, review of *Cave under the City,* p. 50; October, 1988, Cathi MacRae, review of *City Lights,* p. 80; September, 1989, Jeff Blair, review of *Heartbeat,* p. S8; May, 1991, review of *Someone's Mother Is Missing,* p. 65.

ONLINE

National Book Foundation Web site, http://www.nationalbook.org/ (November 8, 2003), "Family Literacy Author Residencies 2001."

Rebeccas Reads, http://www.rebeccasreads.com/ (November 8, 2003), Sandi von Pier, review of *A Boy at War.*

Writers Block Online, http://www.writersblock.ca/ (November 8, 2003), Dianna Bocco, "Real Characters—Real Life: An Interview with Harry Mazer."*

* * *

MAZER, Norma Fox 1931-

PERSONAL: Born May 15, 1931, in New York, NY; daughter of Michael and Jean (Garlen) Fox; married Harry Mazer (a novelist), February 12, 1950; children: Anne, Joseph, Susan, Gina. *Education:* Attended Antioch College and Syracuse University. *Politics:* "I believe in people—despise institutions while accepting their necessity."

ADDRESSES: Home and office—115 Fourth Ave., New York, NY 10003; fax: 315-682-1839. *E-mail*—norfox@aol.com.

CAREER: Writer, 1964—.

AWARDS, HONORS: National Book Award nomination, 1973, for *A Figure of Speech;* Lewis Carroll Shelf Award, University of Wisconsin, 1975, for *Saturday the Twelfth of October,* 1976, for *Dear Bill, Remember Me? and Other Stories;* American Library Association (ALA) Notable Book citation, 1976, for *Dear Bill, Remember Me? and Other Stories,* and 1988, for *After the Rain;* Christopher Award, 1976, for *Dear Bill, Remember Me? and Other Stories; New York Times* Outstanding Books of the Year list, 1976, for *Dear Bill, Remember Me? and Other Stories,* 1984, for *Downtown; School Library Journal* Best Books of the Year list, 1976, for *Dear Bill, Remember Me? and Other Stories,* 1997, for *When She Was Good,* 1979, for *Up in Seth's Room,* 1988, for *After the Rain;* ALA Best Books for Young Adults list, 1976, for *Dear Bill, Remember Me? and Other Stories,* 1977, (with Harry Mazer) for *The Solid Gold Kid,* 1979, for *Up in Seth's*

Norma Fox Mazer

Room, 1983, for *Someone to Love,* 1984, for *Downtown,* 1988, for *After the Rain,* 1989, for *Silver,* 1993, for *Out of Control,* 1998, for *When She Was Good;* Children's Book Council/International Reading Association Children's Choice, 1978, for *The Solid Gold Kid,* 1986, for *A, My Name Is Ami,* 1989, for *Heartbeat;* ALA Best of the Best Books list, 1970-83, for *Up in Seth's Room;* Austrian Children's Books list of honor, 1982, for *Mrs. Fish, Ape, and Me, the Dump Queen;* Edgar Award, Mystery Writers of America, 1982, for *Taking Terri Mueller;* German Children's Literature prize, 1982, for *Mrs. Fish, Ape, and Me, the Dump Queen;* New York Public Library Books for the Teenage List, 1984, for *Downtown,* 1989, for *Silver,* 1990, for *Heartbeat* and for *Waltzing on Water,* 1991, for *Babyface,* 1994, for *Out of Control,* and, 1995, for *Missing Pieces;* California Young Readers Medal, 1985, for *Taking Terri Mueller;* Iowa Teen Award, 1985-86, for *When We First Met,* 1989, for *Silver;* Association of Booksellers for Children Choice, Canadian Children's Books Council Choice, *Horn Book* Fanfare Book, Newbery Honor Book, all 1988, all for *After the Rain;* ALA One Hundred Best of the Best Books, 1968-1993, for *Silver* and for *The Solid Gold Kid;* German Literature Prize, 1989, for *Heartbeat;* American Booksellers Pick of the Lists, 1990, for *Babyface,*

1992, for *Bright Days, Stupid Nights,* 1993, for *Out of Control,* 1994, for *Missing Pieces;* International Reading Association Teacher's Choice, for *Babyface, Bright Days, Stupid Nights, Out of Control, and Missing Pieces;* Editor's Choice, *Booklist,* 1997, for *When She was Good.*

WRITINGS:

YOUNG ADULT FICTION

I, Trissy, Delacorte (New York, NY), 1971, reprinted, Dell (New York, NY), 1986.
A Figure of Speech, Delacorte (New York, NY), 1973.
Saturday the Twelfth of October, Delacorte (New York, NY), 1975.
Dear Bill, Remember Me? and Other Stories, Delacorte (New York, NY), 1976.
(With husband, Harry Mazer) *The Solid Gold Kid,* Delacorte (New York, NY), 1977.
Up in Seth's Room, Delacorte (New York, NY), 1979.
Mrs. Fish, Ape, and Me, the Dump Queen, Dutton (New York, NY), 1980.
Taking Terri Mueller, Avon/Morrow (New York, NY), 1981.
Summer Girls, Love Boys, and Other Short Stories, Delacorte (New York, NY), 1982.
When We First Met, Four Winds (New York, NY), 1982.
Downtown, Avon/Morrow (New York, NY), 1983.
Someone to Love, Delacorte (New York, NY), 1983.
Supergirl (screenplay novelization), Warner Books (New York, NY), 1984.
A, My Name Is Ami, Scholastic (New York, NY), 1986.
Three Sisters, Scholastic (New York, NY), 1986.
After the Rain, Morrow (New York, NY), 1987.
B, My Name Is Bunny, Scholastic (New York, NY), 1987.
Silver, Morrow (New York, NY), 1988.
(With Harry Mazer) *Heartbeat,* Bantam (New York, NY), 1989.
Babyface, Morrow (New York, NY), 1990.
C, My Name Is Cal, Scholastic (New York, NY), 1990.
D, My Name Is Danita, Scholastic (New York, NY), 1991.
E, My Name Is Emily, Scholastic (New York, NY), 1991.
(With Harry Mazer) *Bright Days, Stupid Nights,* Morrow (New York, NY), 1992.
Out of Control, Morrow (New York, NY), 1993.
Missing Pieces, Morrow (New York, NY), 1995.
When She Was Good, Arthur A. Levine Books (New York, NY), 1997.
Crazy Fish, Morrow (New York, NY), 1998.
Good Night, Maman, Harcourt Brace (San Diego, CA), 1999.
Girlhearts, HarperCollins (New York, NY), 2001.

OTHER

(With Axel Daimler) *When We First Met* (novel), Learning Corporation of America, 1984.
(Editor, with Margery Lewis) *Waltzing on Water: Poetry by Women,* Dell (New York, NY), 1989.
(Editor, with Jacqueline Woodson) *Just a Writer's Thing: A Collection of Prose and Poetry from the National Book Foundation's 1995 Summer Writing Camp,* National Book Foundation (New York, NY), 1996.
(With Nathan Aaseng, Myra C. Livingston, and others) *Courage: How We Face Challenges,* Troll Communications (Mahwah, NJ), 1997.

Also contributor to *Sixteen . . . Short Stories by Outstanding Writers for Young Adults,* edited by Donald R. Gallo, Delacorte (New York, NY), 1984; *Short Takes,* by Elizabeth Segal, Lothrop (New York, NY), 1986; *Visions: Nineteen Short Stories by Outstanding Writers for Young Adults,* edited by Donald R. Gallo, Delacorte (New York, NY), 1987; "Ice-Cream Syndrome (aka Promoting Good Reading Habits)," In *Authors' Insights: Turning Teenagers into Readers and Writers,* edited by Donald R. Gallo, Boynton/Cook (Portsmouth, NH), 1992; *Leaving Home: Stories,* edited by Hazel Rochman and Darlene Z. McCampbell, HarperCollins (New York, NY), 1997; *Stay True: Short Stories about Strong Girls,* edited by M. Singer, 1998; *Places I Never Meant to Be: Original Short Stories by Censored Writers,* edited by Judy Blume, Simon & Schuster (New York, NY), 1999; *Hot Flashes: Women Writers on the Change of Life,* edited by Lynne Taetzsch; *Ultimate Sports,* edited by Donald R. Gallo; and *Night Terrors,* edited by L. Duncan.

Also contributor of stories, articles, and essays to magazines, including *Jack and Jill, Ingenue, Calling All Girls, Child Life, Boys and Girls, Redbook, English Journal, Voice of Youth Advocates, Signal, Top of the News,* and *ALAN Review.*

ADAPTATIONS: Mazer's novels recorded on audio cassette and released by Listening Library include *Taking Terri Mueller,*1986, *Dear Bill, Remember Me? and Other Stories,*1987, and *After the Rain,*1988. The novel *When We First Met* was filmed for television by Home Box Office, 1984.

WORK IN PROGRESS: Several novels; a short story.

SIDELIGHTS: "It's not hard to see why Norma Fox Mazer has found a place among the most popular writers for young adults these days," observed Suzanne Freeman in the *Washington Post Book World.* "At her best, Mazer can cut right to the bone of teenage troubles and then show us how the wounds will heal. She can set down the everyday scenes of her characters' lives in images that are scalpel sharp," the critic continued, adding that "what's apparent throughout all of this is that Mazer has taken great care to get to know the world she writes about. She delves into the very heart of it with a sure and practiced hand." *New York Times Book Review* contributor Barbara Wersba described Mazer as "a dazzling writer" who "brings to her work a literacy that would be admirable in any type of fiction." For example, in *A Figure of Speech,* Mazer's story of an elderly man neglected by all of his family except his granddaughter, "the fine definition of all characters, the plausibility of the situations and the variety of insights into motivation make [the novel] almost too good to be true," Tom Heffernan asserted in *Children's Literature: Annual of the Modern Language Association Seminar on Children's Literature and the Children's Literature Association.* "There is no point at which it passes into an area of depiction or explanation that would exceed the experience of a young adolescent. But there is also no point at which the psychological perceptiveness and narrative control would disappoint an adult reader."

Born the middle daughter of three, Mazer grew up in Glens Falls, New York. Mazer noted in a *Teen Reads* interview that she taught herself to read when she was four or five and "read voraciously from then on. The love of reading and stories perhaps led to my want to be a writer."

Mazer has been especially acclaimed for her young adult novels. She has written a number of award-winning and highly acclaimed books for young adults, some with her husband, critically acclaimed author Henry Mazer. Her characters are not always likable, but they are believable young people on the verge of adulthood struggling with issues of importance.

Mazer's short-story collections also have a broad appeal, as reviewers have commented about *Summer Girls, Love Boys and Other Short Stories.* Bruce Bennett, for instance, noted in the *Nation* that the collection "is accessible to teenagers as well as adults. Most of the characters are young people," the critic elaborated, "but Mazer writes about them with an affectionate irony that older readers will appreciate." Because Mazer "has the skill to reveal the human qualities in both ordinary and extraordinary situations as young people mature," stated *New York Times Book Review* contributor Ruth I. Gordon, ". . . it would be a shame to limit their reading to young people, since they can show an adult reader much about the sometimes painful rite of adolescent passage into adulthood." Strengthening the effect of Mazer's collections is that they are "written specifically as a book, a fact which gives the stories an unusual unity and connectedness," related Bennett. "Clearly, Mazer appreciates the short-story form, with its narrow focus and spotlit moments," commented a *Kirkus Reviews* writer about *Dear, Bill, Remember Me? and Other Stories,* "where others might do up the same material as diluted novels."

While she has earned praise for her forays into the short-story form, it is Mazer's novels that have brought her the most recognition, both with critics and readers. *Taking Terri Mueller,* for example, earned Mazer an Edgar Award from the Mystery Writers of America although she had not intended it as a mystery. The book follows Terri Mueller and her father as they wander from town to town, never staying in one place for more than a year. Although Terri is happy with her father, she is old enough to wonder why he will never talk about her mother, who supposedly died ten years ago. An overheard discussion leads her to discover that she had been kidnaped by her father after a bitter custody battle. "The unfolding and the solution of the mystery [of the truth about Terri's mother] are effectively worked," remarked a *Horn Book* reviewer; "filled with tension and with strong characterization, the book makes compelling reading." Freeman similarly observed that despite the potential for simplifying Terri's conflict, "Mazer does not take the easy way out in this book. There are no good guys or bad guys. There are no easy answers." The critic concluded, "We believe in just about everything Terri does, because Mazer's writing makes us willing to believe. She wins us completely with this finely wrought and moving book."

In her Newbery Honor Book, *After the Rain,* Mazer returns to the subject of a elderly man dying; but in this instance, grandfather Izzy rebuffs his loving family, and granddaughter Rachel must exert herself to build a relationship with him. As it becomes clear to her that Izzy is dying and needs companionship, Rachel decides to regularly spend her free time with him. "It's surprising that she should make such a decision," claimed *Washington Post Book World* contributor Cynthia Samuels, "but once the reader accepts her choice and begins to join her on her daily visits with the crotchety old man, the story becomes both moving and wise." The result, continued the critic, is a book that "deals with death and loss in an original and sensitive way." Carolyn Meyer, however, felt that there is a lack of tension in the story: "you never really worry that Rachel won't do the right thing," she wrote in the *Los Angeles Times Book Review.* In contrast, a *Kirkus Reviews* critic suggested that "what distinguishes this book, making it linger in the heart, are the realistic portrayals of the tensions, guilt, and sudden, painfully moving moments involved in Rachel's and Izzy's situations." As a *Horn Book* reviewer concluded, Izzy's "harsh, rough personality [is] so realistic and recognizable that we feel we have known him and can understand the sorrow that overcomes Rachel. [*After the Rain* is] a powerful book, dealing with death and dying and the strength of family affection."

With the publication of *Good Night, Maman,* Mazer ventures into historical young adult fiction. The novel centers around twelve-year-old Karin, who must struggle to find freedom and begin a new life without her beloved mother. The Nazis have sent Karin's father to a prison in Poland and Karin, her brother, and her mother are in hiding in an attic. When they are told they must leave, the children head south. Karin and her brother eventually board a ship headed to America, but they must leave their ill-stricken mother behind. "This moving World War II story is neither highly dramatic nor politically charged. It is the very personal and immediate experience of a young girl grappling with the loss of her old life and a new life that changes daily," explained Lauren Adams in *Horn Book.* A *Publishers Weekly* reviewer concluded, "The strength of this novel lies in its intimate recognition of the way adolescents think and feel." Mazer explained in a *Teen-Reads* interview that writing historical fiction is difficult because you have to fit a fictional character into an actual event. "I had to write this novel over completely four times, and this was because I was working out how to balance fiction and history," she remarked. To prepare to write the book, Mazer said, "I read a fair number of books, most of them memoirs of people who had lived through the Holocaust. What struck me was that despite the numbing universality of that murderous time, each person's story, each survivor's story, was unique, distinct. . . . my intention in writing this book was not to write history, but to write the unique history of an individual, albeit a fictional one."

Like *Good Night, Maman,* Mazer's novel *Girlhearts* deals with a young girl's loss of her mother. Sarabeth Silver must deal with the loss of her mother, the only parent and family member she knows. Because she has no one else to turn to, Sarabeth must eventually track down her long-lost extended family members, who had turned their back on her mother when she became pregnant at sixteen. "With a pitch-perfect intensity, Mazer captures the fractured sense of loss, of self, of time, that comes with a death in the family," explained GraceAnn A. DeCandido in *Booklist.* Writing in *School Library Journal,* Susie Paige noted, "The theme of death and renewal is not a new one, but Mazer's characters deal with the process in a realistic, heartrending manner."

Mazer once told *CA:*"I seem to deal in the ordinary, the everyday, the real. I should like in my writing to give meaning and emotion to ordinary moments. In my books and stories I want people to eat chocolate pudding, break a dish, yawn, look in a store window, wear socks with holes in them. . . ."

BIOGRAPHICAL AND CRITICAL SOURCES:

BOOKS

Authors and Artists for Young Adults, Gale (Detroit, MI), Volume 5, 1990, Volume 36, 2000.

Butler, Francelia, editor, *Children's Literature: Annual of the Modern Language Association Seminar on Children's Literature and the Children's Literature Association,* Volume 4, Temple University Press (Philadelphia, PA), 1975.

Children's Literature Review, Volume 23, Gale (Detroit, MI), 1991.

Contemporary Literary Criticism, Volume 26, Gale (Detroit, MI), 1983.

Holtze, Sally Holmes, *Presenting Norma Fox Mazer,* Twayne (New York, NY), 1987.

Reed, Arthea J., *Norma Fox Mazer: A Writer's World,* Scarecrow Press (Lanham, MD), 2000.

St. James Guide to Young Adult Writers, 2nd edition, St. James Press (Detroit, MI), 1999.

Twentieth-Century Children's Writers, 3rd edition, St. James Press (Detroit, MI), 1989.

PERIODICALS

Booklist, June 1-15, 1993, review of *Out of Control,* p. 1804; April 1, 1995, Merri Monks, review of *Missing Pieces,* p. 1388; September, 1997, Stephanie Zvirin, review of *When She Was Good,* p. 118; January 1, 1998, Bill Ott, "Editors' Choice '97," p. 725; April 15, 1998, Stephanie Zvirin, "What Grandparents Teach," p. 1445; August, 1999, Hazel Rochman, review of *Good Night, Maman,* p. 2053; November 15, 1999, Stephanie Zvirin review of *When She Was Good,* p. 613; June, 2000, Stephanie Zvirin, review of *When She Was Good,* p. 1875; July, 2001, GraceAnne A. DeCandido, review of *Girlhearts,* p. 2000.

Book Report, January-February, 1998, Marilyn Heath, review of *When She Was Good,* p. 35; November, 1999, Sherry York, "Child Sexual Abuse: A Bibliography of Young Adult Fiction," p. 30; November-December, 2001, Catherine M. Andronik, review of *Girlhearts,* p. 61.

Bulletin of the Center for Children's Books, October, 1997, Deborah Stevenson, review of *When She Was Good,* p. 61; December, 1999, review of *Good Night, Maman,* p. 53; April, 2001, review of *Girlhearts,* p. 310.

Children's Book and Play Review, March, 2002, review of *Girlhearts,* p. 12.

Emergency Librarian, January, 1998, review of *When She Was Good,* p. 50.

Horn Book, April, 1983, review of *Taking Terri Mueller,* p. 172-173; September, 1987; November 1999, Lauren Adams, review of *Good Night, Maman,* p. 743.

Journal of Adolescent and Adult Literacy, November, 2001, "Young Adults' Choices for 2001: A Project of the International Reading Association," p. 191.

Kirkus Reviews, October 1, 1976, review of *Dear Bill, Remember Me?,* pp. 1101-1012; May 1, 1987, review of *After the Rain,* p. 723; October 15, 1999, review of *Good Night, Maman,* p. 1647; April 1, 2001, review of *Girlhearts,* p. 502.

Kliatt, September, 1999, review of *Good Night, Maman,* p. 10; May, 2001, review of *Good Night, Maman,* p. 21; July, 2001, review of *Girlhearts,* p. 12.

Los Angeles Times, September 12, 1987.

Los Angeles Times Book Review, July 5, 1987.

Nation, March 12, 1983.

New York Times Book Review, March 17, 1974, Jill Paton Walsh, review of *A Figure of Speech,* p. 8; October 19, 1975; January 20, 1980; March 13, 1983, Ruth I. Gordon, review of *Summer Girls, Love Boys, and Other Stories,* p. 29; November 25, 1984; June 17, 2001, Emily-Greta Tabourin, review of *Girlhearts,* p. 25.

*Publishers Weekly,*July 27, 1990, review of *Babyface,* p. 235; November 8, 1991, review of *E, My Name Is Emily,* p. 64; June, 22, 1992, review of *Bright Days, Stupid Nights,* p. 63; April 5, 1993, review of *Out of Control,* p. 79; July 21, 1997, review of *When She Was Good,* p. 202; June 12 1995, review of *Missing Pieces,* p. 62; November 8, 1999, review of *Good Night, Maman,* p. 69; April 23, 2001, review of *Girlhearts,* p. 21; April 23 2001, review of *Good Night, Maman,* p. 248.

School Library Journal, September, 1980; March, 1991, Judith Porter, review of *C, My Name Is Cal,* p. 193; March, 1991, Connie Tyrrell Burns, review of *D, My Name Is Danita,* p. 193; November, 1991, Susan Oliver, review of *E, My Name Is Emily,* p. 120; July, 1992, Cindy Darling Codell, review of *Bright Days, Stupid Nights,* p. 90; January, 1998, review of *When She Was Good,* p. 43; December, 1999, Amy Lilien-Harper, review of *Good Night, Maman,* p. 137; May, 2001, Susie Paige, review of *Girlhearts,* p. 156.

Teacher Librarian, December, 2001, Rosemary Chance, review of *Young Women Speak Out,* p. 23.

Tribune Books (Chicago, IL), June 17 2001, review of *Gladhearts,* p. 4.

Voice of Youth Advocates, August, 1993, review of *Out of Control,* p. 154; April, 1998, review of *When She Was Good,* p. 38; August, 2001, review of *Girlhearts,* p. 204.

Washington Post Book World, July 10, 1977; April 10, 1983, Suzanne Freeman, "The Truth about the Teens," p. 10; October 14, 1984; March 9, 1986; May 10, 1987, Cynthia Samuels, review of *After the Rain,* p. 19.

ONLINE

TeenReads, http://www.teenreads.com/ (November 4, 2003), "Author Profile: Norma Fox Mazer Interview."*

* * *

McGARRY, Jean 1952-

PERSONAL: Born June 18, 1952, in Providence, RI; daughter of Frank and Deborah (Sklover) McGarry. *Education:* Harvard University, A.B., 1970; Johns Hopkins University, M.A., 1983.

ADDRESSES: Home—100 West University Parkway, Baltimore, MD 21210. *Office*—The Writing Seminars, Johns Hopkins University, Baltimore, MD 21210. *Agent*—Helen Brann, 157 West 57th St., New York, NY 10019.

CAREER: Johns Hopkins University, Baltimore, MD, lecturer in English, 1983-85; University of Missouri—Columbia, assistant professor of English, 1985-86; George Washington University, Washington, DC, associate professor of English, 1986-87; Johns Hopkins University, Baltimore, affiliated with writing seminars, 1988—.

AWARDS, HONORS: Short Fiction Prize from *Southern Review,* 1985, for *Airs of Providence;* Pushcart Prize, 1987, for "World with a Hard K"; grants from National Endowment for the Arts, 1987.

WRITINGS:

Airs of Providence (short stories), Johns Hopkins University Press (Baltimore, MD), 1985.

The Very Rich Hours (novel), Johns Hopkins University Press (Baltimore, MD), 1987.

The Courage of Girls, Rutgers University Press (New Brunswick, NJ), 1992.

Jean McGarry Reading from Her Fiction (sound recording), Raft, 1993.

Home at Last, Johns Hopkins University Press (Baltimore, MD), 1994.

Gallagher's Travels, Johns Hopkins University Press (Baltimore, MD), 1997.

Dream Date (short stories), Johns Hopkins University Press (Baltimore, MD), 2002.

Contributor to periodicals, including *New Yorker* and *Yale Review.*

SIDELIGHTS: Jean McGarry, a fiction writer and instructor, splits her publications between novels and story collections. In the former category is *The Courage of Girls,* in which McGarry creates "a lively novel" centered on "so quiet a character" as Loretta Costello St. Cyr, according to a *Publishers Weekly* reviewer. Loretta, married to an academic, is a resident of New York City; the woman's depression following a miscarriage compels her to leave her husband and live with an aunt and uncle who acted as Loretta's parents after her own died when she was nine. The *Publishers Weekly* contributor lauded McGarry's "deftly drawn characters" who "give this poignant novel its vibrancy." The title character of McGarry's 1997 novel *Gallagher's Travels* is Caff Gallagher, a newly minted college journalist, who joins the staff of the Wampanoag, Rhode Island, *Times,* penning pieces for the Women's Page. But her ambition moves the young woman to big-city Michigan, where she must struggle again in the soft features while chasing the big stories. A *Publishers Weekly* reviewer pointed to "pithy but uninspired prose" in this novel, though *Library Journal* critic Mary Margaret Benson had a more positive reaction, calling McGarry's writing "often gritty and terse but also ironically humorous."

The Rhode Island setting of *Gallagher's Travels* is also spotlighted in *Home at Last,* a book of short stories. Indeed, the author refers to specific locals in the Providence and Pawtucket environs in relating "incisive portraits of men and women, boys and girls; riveting details that surround the characters, their crises, and their environments," in the view Thomas Gullason, reviewing the book for *Studies in Short Fiction.* Gullason found a story titled "The Raft" as "one of the best . . . both haunting and touching in its depiction of his father's suicide on ten-year-old Jimmy McGinnis." McGarry's 2002 collection, *Dream Date,* includes such tales as "Among the Philistines," in which an arrogant professor gets his just desserts during a disastrous dinner party. In "Body and Soul," an extramarital affair takes a poignant turn when a man discovers his paramour has cancer. The book showcases the author's ability to "[observe] life from both male and female viewpoints with asexual agility," according to *Booklist*'s Carol Haggas. A *Kirkus Reviews* writer likewise felt that "McGarry is equally comfortable in the voices of men and women," and decided that "it's hard to find a weak link" in *Dream Date.*

BIOGRAPHICAL AND CRITICAL SOURCES:

PERIODICALS

American Book Review, November, 1987, review of *The Very Rich Hours,* p. 16.
Belles Lettres, fall, 1988, review of *The Very Rich Hours,* p. 11.
Best Sellers, March, 1986, review of *Airs of Providence,* p. 444.
Booklist, May 15, 1987, review of *The Very Rich Hours,* p. 1409; April 15, 1992, review of *The Courage of Girls,* p. 1503; May 1, 2002, Carol Haggas, review of *Dream Date,* p. 1509.
Georgia Review, winter, 1994, review of *Home at Last,* p. 800.
Kirkus Reviews, April 15, 1987, review of *The Very Rich Hours,* p. 584; March 1, 1992, review of *The Courage of Girls,* p. 275; June 15, 1997, review of *Gallagher's Travels,* p. 900; May 1, 2002, review of *Dream Date,* p. 604.
Library Journal, August, 1977, Mary Margaret Benson, review of *Gallagher's Travels,* p. 132; April 1, 1992, review of *The Courage of Girls,* p. 148; May 1, 1994, review of *Home at Last,* p. 140; February 15, 1998, review of *Gallagher's Travels,* p. 196.
New Yorker, November 9, 1987, review of *The Very Rich Hours,* p. 155.
New York Times Book Review, October 11, 1987, review of *The Very Rich Hours,* p. 56; June 28, 1992, review of *The Courage of Girls,* p. 18.
North American Review, March, 1986, review of *Airs of Providence,* p. 69.
Publishers Weekly, May 8, 1987, review of *The Very Rich Hours,* p. 61; March 2, 1992, review of *The Courage of Girls,* p. 50; March 28, 1994, review of *Home at Last,* p. 92; July 7, 1997, review of *Gallagher's Travels,* p. 51; June 24, 2002, review of *Dream Date.*
Studies in Short Fiction, summer, 1986, review of *Airs of Providence,* p. 331; winter, 1988, review of *The Very Rich Hours,* p. 83; summer, 1996, Thomas Gullason, review of *Home at Last,* p. 435.
Times Literary Supplement, May 29, 1992, review of *The Courage of Girls,* p. 21.
Village Voice Literary Supplement, May, 1992, review of *The Courage of Girls,* p. 7.
Women's Review of Books, July, 1992, review of *The Very Rich Hours, Airs of Providence,* and *The Courage of Girls,* p. 328.*

* * *

McGIMPSEY, David 1962-

PERSONAL: Born January 28, 1962, in Montreal, Quebec, Canada; son of John A. (a welder) and Mary McGimpsey; married Carol Dennison (a sales representative), 1994. *Ethnicity:* "Scots-Irish." *Education:* Concordia University, B.A., 1988, M.A. 1990; Dalhousie University, Ph.D., 1997. *Religion:* Protestant. *Hobbies and other interests:* Music, travel, sport.

ADDRESSES: Home—215-1575 Summerhill Ave., Montreal, Quebec H3H 1CS, Canada. *Agent*—c/o Author Mail, ECW Press, 2120 Queen St. E, Suite 200, Toronto, Ontario M4E 1E2, Canada. *E-mail*—cmcgimpsey@sympatico.ca.

CAREER: Poet, fiction writer, journalist, and popular culture critic.

MEMBER: Association of Canadian University Teachers of English, Modern Language Association of America, Sports Literature Association, Quebec Writers' Federation, Writers' Federation of Nova Scotia.

AWARDS, HONORS: Clare Fooshee Memorial Award, 1993; Lyle Olsen Graduate Award for Sport Literature.

WRITINGS:

Lardcake (poetry), ECW Press (Toronto, Ontario, Canada), 1996.
Dogboy (poetry), ECW Press (Toronto, Ontario, Canada), 1998.
Imagining Baseball: America's Pastime and Popular Culture, Indiana University Press (Bloomington, IN), 2000.
Hamburger Valley, California (poetry), ECW Press (Toronto, Ontario, Canada), 2001.

Television critic for a newspaper.

SIDELIGHTS: David McGimpsey once told *CA:*"I never planned it, but since my first published poems 'the batmann sonnets,' I have been turning a lifelong interest in American popular culture towards poetry. I like to believe I have come by this interest honestly, rather than with a preconceived notion of how my work will 'challenge' existing prejudices. Like many children of the seventies, I grew up watching television and now, as a poet, I am putting this 'education' into the context of real North American life. My work is not a simple celebration or critique of popular forms. Rather, I hope that by looking into both the well-known and the trivial to come to a fuller account of the joys and terrors in my own heart. The poets who most influenced me were the confessional poets (Plath in particular) and I continue to be attracted by poetry of strong personal voice.

"Whatever the general allusivity of my poetry, I still write poems that have nothing to do with TV or popular culture. However, because of the parodic matrix of most of my material, I find my tone moves quickly from the somber towards humor. If there is one thing that I am most pleased about in the reception of my work, it would be that so many have shared my sense of humor and have laughed at my poetry. I have worked as a television critic for a newspaper, but it is in poetry, where I feel that my experience with TV is most thoroughly expressed—perhaps this is due to poetry's place as the least commercially viable form of entertainment."

BIOGRAPHICAL AND CRITICAL SOURCES:

PERIODICALS

Books in Canada, March, 2003, Robert Moore, review of *Hamburger Valley, California.**

* * *

MEREDITH, William (Morris) 1919-

PERSONAL: Born January 9, 1919, in New York, New York; son of William Morris and Nelley Atkin (Keyser) Meredith. *Education:* Princeton University, A.B. (magna cum laude), 1940. *Politics:* Democrat.

William Meredith

ADDRESSES: *Office*—337 Kitemaug Road, Uncasville, CT 06382.

CAREER: *New York Times,* New York, NY, 1940-41, began as copy boy, became reporter; Princeton University, Princeton, New Jersey, instructor in English and Woodrow Wilson fellow in writing, 1946-50; University of Hawaii, Honolulu, associate professor of English, 1950-51; Connecticut College, New London, associate professor, 1955-65, professor of English, 1965-83, professor emeritus. Middlebury College, Middlebury, VT, instructor at Bread Loaf School of English, 1958-62. Member of Connecticut Commission on the Arts, 1963-65; director of the humanities, Upward Bound Program, 1964-68; poetry consultant, Library of Congress, 1978-80. *Military service:* U.S. Army Air Forces, 1941-42; U.S. Navy, Naval Aviation, 1942-46; served in Pacific Theater; became lieutenant. U.S. Naval Reserve, active duty in Korean War as naval aviator, 1952-54; became lieutenant commander; received two Air Medals.

MEMBER: National Institute of Arts and Letters, Academy of American Poets (chancellor), American Choral Society (second vice president).

AWARDS, HONORS: Yale Series of Younger Poets Award for *Love Letter from an Impossible Land,* 1943; Harriet Monroe Memorial Prize, 1944, and Oscar Blumenthal Prize, 1953, for poems published in *Poetry;* Woodrow Wilson fellowship, Princeton University, 1946-47; Rockefeller grant, 1948, 1968; *Hudson Review* fellow, 1956; National Institute of Arts and Letters grant in literature, 1958; Ford Foundation fellowship for drama, 1959-60; Loines Prize from National Institute of Arts and Letters, 1966; Borestone Mountain Poetry Award for *The Wreck of the "Thresher,"* 1964; Van Wyck Brooks Award, 1971; honorary Doctorate of Humane Letters, Carnegie Mellon University, 1972; Connecticut College Medal, University of Connecticut, 1983, 1996; National Endowment for the Arts grant, 1972, fellow, 1984; Guggenheim fellow, 1975-76; International Vaptsarov Prize for Literature, Bulgaria, 1979; Carl Sandburg Award, from the International Platform Association, 1979; Honorary Doctorate of Literature, Keene State College, 1988; *Los Angeles Times* Prize, 1987; Pulitzer Prize for poetry, 1988, for *Partial Accounts: New and Selected Poems;* Academy of American Poets fellowship, 1990; Honorary Bulgarian Citizenship, Presidential Decree, for efforts to make Bulgarian literature accessible in the United States, 1996; National Book Award for Poetry for *Effort at Speech: New and Selected Poems,* 1997; Honorary Doctorate, American University of Bulgaria, 1998.

WRITINGS:

POETRY

Love Letter from an Impossible Land, Yale University Press (New Haven, CT), 1944.

Ships and Other Figures, Princeton University Press (Princeton, NJ), 1948.

The Open Sea and Other Poems, Knopf (New York, NY), 1958.

The Wreck of the "Thresher" and Other Poems, Knopf (New York, NY), 1964.

Winter Verse, privately printed, 1964.

Year-End Accounts, privately printed, 1965.

Two Pages from a Colorado Journal, privately printed, 1967.

Earth Walk: New and Selected Poems, Knopf (New York, NY), 1970.

Hazard, the Painter, Knopf (New York, NY), 1975.

The Cheer, Knopf (New York, NY), 1980.

Partial Accounts: New and Selected Poems, Knopf (New York, NY), 1987.

Effort at Speech: New and Selected Poems, TriQuarterly Books/Northwestern University Press (Evanston, IL), 1997.

OTHER

(Librettist) *The Bottle Imp* (opera, music by Peter Whiton; adaptation of the story by Robert Louis Stevenson), first produced in Wilton, Connecticut, 1958.

(Editor) *Shelley: Poems,* Dell (New York, NY), 1962.

(Translator) Guillaume Apollinaire, *Alcools: Poems, 1898-1913,* Doubleday (New York, NY), 1964.

(Editor) *University and College Poetry Prizes, 1960-1966, in Memory of Mrs. Fanny Fay Wood,* Academy of American Poets (New York, NY), 1966.

(Editor, with Mackie L. Jarrell) *Eighteenth-Century Minor Poets,* Dell (New York, NY), 1968.

Selected Poems, 1977 (recording), Watershed, 1977.

Reasons for Poetry and the Reason for Criticism (lectures), Library of Congress (Washington, DC), 1982.

(Editor) Denise Levertov and others, translators, *Poets of Bulgaria,* Unicorn Press (Greensboro, NC), 1985.

The Poet and the Poem, Library of Congress (Washington, DC), 1990.

Poems Are Hard to Read, University of Michigan Press, 1991.

(Editor, with Richard Harteis) *Window on the Black Sea: Bulgarian Poetry in Translation,* Carnegie Mellon University Press (Pittsburgh, PA), 1992.

Contributor to magazines. Opera critic, *Hudson Review,* 1955-56.

William Meredith's poems have been recorded for the Archive of Recorded Poetry and Literature, 1994, 1995.

Meredith's collected manuscripts are housed at Middlebury College in Vermont.

SIDELIGHTS: William Meredith writes a formal, disciplined poetry concerned with the proper balance between the natural and civilized worlds. His poems, Matthew Flamm commented in the *Village Voice*, are "polished and direct, formal and natural, in equal measure," while his poetic voice is that "of someone who has been thinking for years about his place in the world, with no illusions of importance." A *Publishers Weekly* critic explained that Meredith's poems are "exercises in discipline and craft—objective in the choice and handling of theme, clear and simple in style and restrained in tone. He is a master in the use of meter, rhyme and stanzaic structure. . . . The perfectly achieved formal aspects of Meredith's poetry mark him as a writer whose bedrock values transcend time and place." In 1985, Meredith received a Pulitzer Prize for his collection *Partial Accounts: New and Selected Poems,* and in 1997 he received the National Book Award for Poetry for *Effort at Speech: New and Selected Poems.*

Meredith first began writing poetry in college. After graduating in 1940, he worked for a year as a reporter with the *New York Times* before joining the army. In 1942 he transferred to the U.S. Navy to become a pilot, serving on aircraft carriers in the Pacific Theater for the duration of World War II. In 1952, he re-enlisted to fly missions in the Korean War as well. Following his military service Meredith pursued an academic career, teaching English at Connecticut College from 1955 to 1983. A severe stroke in 1983 forced an early retirement from teaching and months of rehabilitation to regain his speech.

Meredith has always written a personal poetry rendered in traditional poetic forms, using these forms as frameworks for individual expression. Like fellow New Englander Robert Frost, to whom he is often compared, Meredith writes unadorned, formal verse. As Moul explained, the poet believes that "immediacy of image and idea, spoken in the poet's own voice, are and should be the poet's object." A critic for the *Antioch Review* described Meredith's poems as "beautifully worked, distinct objects, the language at once exciting and unobtrusive—what keeps them together is a tone wistful and ironic, which gives them the air of events as inevitable to the reader as to the poet." James Dickey, writing in his *Babel to Byzantium,* noted a "certain in-group variety of bookish snobbery that is probably Meredith's one outstanding weakness as a writer," but nonetheless found that "at his best he is a charming poet, cultivated, calm, quietly original, expansive and reflective, moving over wide areas slowly, lightly, mildly and often very memorably."

Over the years, Meredith's production of poetry has been modest in size. Writing in *Corgi Modern Poets in Focus 2,* the poet commented: "Chiefly I think my poverty of output stems from the conviction that an unnecessary poem is an offense to the art." But Moul disagreed: "Meredith's 'poverty of output' is instead a rare thing among poets, a discriminating taste."

Meredith's first collection of poems, *Love Letter from an Impossible Land,* was chosen by Archibald MacLeish for publication in the Yale Series of Younger Poets in 1944. Half the poems in the collection were written while Meredith was still in college, and many of these were derivative of other poets' work. But critics felt that the poems based on Meredith's war experiences as a pilot displayed emotional honesty. A *Christian Century* reviewer explained that the "poems born out of the war are true, and often eloquent and revealing." Ruth Lechlitner in *Poetry* found, "When William Meredith leaves the book-shelves and becomes the flyer, he becomes also a poet in his own right."

In 1948 Meredith's second collection of poems was published. *Ships and Other Figures* again draws upon Meredith's time in the Navy for subject matter. Milton Crane, writing in the *New York Times,* described the poems as "cool, intellectual, and self-contained. . . . [Meredith's] detachment bespeaks no incapacity for more overt emotional expression, but a deliberate decision to set down his observations and conclusions as clearly and succinctly as possible." Writing in the *Saturday Review of Literature,* G. P. Meyer noted, "That a poet today can still write with affection of people and things and communicate that feeling to others, is something to celebrate."

Open Sea and Other Poems appeared in 1958, displaying a poetry more adventurous than previously suspected of Meredith. As Richard Howard stated in his *Alone with America: Essays on the Art of Poetry in the United States since 1950,* with *Open Sea and Other Poems,* Meredith "insisted on play, on a response to selfhood as pleasure, on the morality of virtuosity." At the same time, Howard admitted that for Meredith, "all art, poetic or otherwise, is an act of self-defense against the world changing its meaning from moment to moment, against the difference, against things becoming *other,* against their loss of identity. For him, poetry is a way of asserting that things are what they are—the insight of self-reference—and that when they mean something else, order as well as delight is endangered."

Meredith published *The Wreck of the "Thresher" and Other Poems,* in 1964, a book whose title poem is an elegy to an American submarine lost at sea in 1963. Despite the shift in tone, Meredith's handling of the tragic theme was met with critical applause. According to Fred Bornhauser in the *Virginia Quarterly Review* "the elegance is compounded of compassion, intelligence, and linguistic precision," while S. F. Morse in the *New York Times Book Review* stated that "*The Wreck of the 'Thresher'* is an accomplishment of a very high order. . . . The title poem may well come to stand as a model of the elegy in our time." Keith Moul in the *Dictionary of Literary Biography* found that "the consensus is that Meredith attains a consistently high level of performance" in *The Wreck of the "Thresher."*

Gathering poems from the previous twenty-five years, *Earth Walk* reveals the range of Meredith's early work. Victory Howes in the *Christian Science Monitor* called Meredith "a poet of hairline precisions, minute discriminations, and subtle observings. . . . How quickly the strangeness, the wonder, would pass from things were it not for poets like William Meredith." *Earth Walk,* according to Moul, is "a just selection that as much emphasizes [Meredith's] variety as his quirks. Much of his best writing is here."

With *Partial Accounts: New and Selected Poems,* Meredith gathered poems from throughout his long writing career to give an overview of his poetic achievement. Publication of the book provided an opportunity for critics to assess Meredith's contribution to the genre. Among those critics is Linda Gregerson in *Poetry.* She observed that *Partial Accounts* documents Meredith's serious use of formal poetic structures. Meredith, Gregerson wrote, "is a poet who asks us seriously to consider the rhymed quatrain as a unit of perceptual pacing, the villanelle as the ambivalent and ritual simulation of fate, the sestina as a scaffolding for directed rumination, the sonnet as an instrument for testing the prodigious or the ineffable against the longing-for-shapeliness we know as 'argument.'" She concluded, "Touched as they are by goodness, rich in craft and thoughtfulness, the poems collected here should find themselves well-treated by their readers." Edward Hirsch, in his evaluation of *Partial Accounts* for the *New York Times Book Review,* saw Meredith as a poet who has "emphasized the need for a civilizing intelligence and humane values. In one sense, all of his work constitutes a desire to recognize and then move beyond catastrophe and despair—whether personal, social or historical. Book by book, he has evolved into a poet by sly wit and quiet skill, working out a thoughtful esthetic of orderliness."

During the years in which he worked as a consultant in poetry for the Library of Congress, Meredith became acquainted with Bulgarian poets, an alliance that eventually resulted in the publication of his *Poets of Bulgaria,* a work that includes some of his own translations. A subsequent collection *Window on the Black Sea: Bulgarian Poetry in Translation,* featured translations by twenty-seven American poets.

Meredith received the National Book Award for Poetry for *Effort at Speech: New and Selected Poems,* a compilation of both new and previously published poems. Writing in *Poetry* Christian Wiman believed that, despite his many awards, Meredith has chiefly resigned himself to minor status. "It is for this reason that I prefer the poems in which Meredith isn't talking about poetry," Wiman explained, "or at least isn't going about it with a good deal of humor." Wiman concluded that, "At his best, Meredith is a poet of suburban decency" who is "emotionally ingenious, cautiously sage, intelligent, diffident," and "clever." A *Publishers Weekly* reviewer lauded *Effort at Speech,* describing it as "a medic's kit for the tired at heart." The same reviewer noted that the earlier poems in the book "are as subtle as aspirin" and are "so easily digestible in their precise meter and perfectly tuned end-rhyme, their power goes virtually unnoticed until the reader lifts his eyes from the page to find himself moved."

Publishers Weekly reviewer John F. Baker noted that Meredith had difficulty speaking after receiving the National Book Award for Poetry because of a stroke suffered years earlier. "He admitted later to reporters that he had been 'utterly surprised' to win and that though his health had much improved, he was still unable to 'visualize' new poems."

BIOGRAPHICAL AND CRITICAL SOURCES:

BOOKS

Dickey, James, *Babel to Byzantium,* Farrar, Straus (New York, NY), 1968, pp. 197-198.
Dictionary of Literary Biography, Gale (Detroit, MI) Volume 5, 1980, pp. 46-53.
Encyclopedia of American Literature, Continuum (New York, NY), 1999.
Howard, Richard, *Alone with America: Essays on the Art of Poetry in the United States since 1950,* Atheneum (New York, NY), 1971, revised edition, 1980.
Robson, Jeremy, *Corgi Modern Poets in Focus 2,* Transworld Publishers, 1971, pp. 117-125.
Rotella, Guy, *Three Contemporary Poets of New England,* Twayne (New York, NY), 1983.

PERIODICALS

American Scholar, autumn, 1965.
Antioch Review, spring, 1970.
Atlantic, February, 1981, review of *The Cheer,* p. 94.
Christian Century, April 19, 1944.
Christian Science Monitor, October 15, 1970.
Commonweal, January 24, 1958; December 4, 1981, Josephine Jacobsen, review of *The Cheer,* p. 692.
Georgia Review, spring, 1976.
Hollins Critic, February, 1979.
Hudson Review, autumn, 1970; autumn, 1975; spring, 1981.
Kenyon Review, summer, 1988.
Los Angeles Times Book Review, November 30, 1980.
Nation, June 15, 1970.
New Republic, June 14, 1975.
New York Review of Books, June 15, 1972.
New York Times Book Review, September 27, 1964; September 21, 1975; March 22, 1981, Paul Breslin, review of *The Cheer,* p. 86; July 31, 1988, Edward Hirsch, review of *Partial Accounts: New and Selected Poems,* p. 20.
Parnassus, spring-summer, 1976; fall, 1981.
Partisan Review, winter, 1971-72.
Plum Review, fall-winter, 1992.
Poetry, July, 1944; November, 1948; September, 1958; February, 1966; July, 1971; January, 1976; December, 1981, Robert B. Shaw, review of *The Cheer,* p. 173; February, 1988, Linda Gregerson, review of *Partial Accounts,* p. 423; August, 1998, Christian Wiman, review of *Effort at Speech: New and Selected Poems,* p. 281.
Publishers Weekly, April 10, 1987, John Mutter, review of *Partial Accounts,* p. 90; May 26, 1997, review of *Effort at Speech,* p. 80; November 24, 1997, John F. Baker, "National Book Awards Surprise," p. 48.
Saturday Review, August 8, 1970.
Saturday Review of Literature, April 29, 1944; May 15, 1948; March 22, 1958.
Sewanee Review, winter, 1972; winter, 1973.
Shenandoah, winter, 1971.
Southwest Review, 1992, Neva Harrington, "The Language of the Tribe."
Village Voice, August 18, 1987.
Virginia Quarterly Review, summer, 1975; summer, 1981; autumn, 1987.
Washington Post, October 11, 1978.
World Literature Today, spring, 1989.
Yale Review, December, 1944; June, 1958; winter, 1971.

ONLINE

William Meredith Home Page, http://www.conncoll.edu/meredith/ (June 3, 2004).*

* * *

MILLER, Russell 1938-

PERSONAL: Born June 17, 1938, in Ilford, Essex, England; son of Albert Edward (a clerk) and Queenie Alice (Russel) Miller; married Stephenie Lesley Gardner, June 8, 1963 (divorced); married Renate Marie Charlotte Kohler (a journalist), September 21, 1977; children: (first marriage) Tamsin Lesley, Sasha Kate; (second marriage) Barnaby Charles Edward, Charlotte Alice.

ADDRESSES: *Home*—Brighton, England. *Agent*—Sterling Lord Literistic, 65 Bleecker St., New York, NY 10012-2420.

CAREER: East London News Agency, London, England, apprentice reporter, 1955-57; *Ilford Recorder,* Ilford, Essex, England, reporter, 1957-58, chief reporter and news editor, 1960-62; reporter for *Daily Sketch and Sunday Dispatch,* 1962-65; freelance writer for *Sunday Times,* 1972-98; freelance writer for *Night and Day,* 1998-2002; writer. *Military service:* British Army, 1958-60; served with British Army of the Rhine (BAOR) in Germany; became acting captain.

MEMBER: Groucho Club (London).

AWARDS, HONORS: Magazine Writer of the Year award, 1984 and 1992, for articles appearing in *Sunday Times Magazine;* British Press award commendations, 1987 and 1988; *Colour* magazine Writer of the Year, 1989.

WRITINGS:

(With Roger Boar) *The Incredible Music Machine,* edited by Jacques Lowe, Quartet/Visual Arts (London, England), 1983.

Bunny: The Real Story of "Playboy," Michael Joseph, 1984, Holt (New York, NY), 1985.

The House of Getty, Michael Joseph, 1985, Holt (New York, NY), 1986.

Bare-Faced Messiah: The True Story of L. Ron Hubbard, Holt (New York, NY), 1988.

Nothing Less Than Victory: The Oral History of D-Day W. Morrow (New York, NY), 1993.

Magnum: Fifty Years at the Front Line of History, Grove Press (New York, NY), 1997.

Behind the Lines: The Oral History of Special Operations in World War II, St. Martin's Press (New York, NY), 2002.

WITH THE EDITORS OF TIME-LIFE BOOKS

The Resistance, Time-Life Books, 1979, reprinted, 1998.

The East Indiamen, Time-Life Books, 1981.

The Commandos, Time-Life Books, 1982, reprinted, 1998.

The Soviet Air Force at War, Time-Life Books, 1983.

Continents in Collision, Time-Life Books, 1983.

ADAPTATIONS: The movie *Lorenzo's Oil* starring Nick Nolte and Susan Sarandon, was based off one of Miller's features in *Sunday Times Magazine.*

WORK IN PROGRESS: A biography of a double agent in World War II.

SIDELIGHTS: British journalist Russell Miller has written books about three well-known Americans and their respective business empires: Hugh Hefner, founder of *Playboy* magazine; J. Paul Getty, oil magnate; and L. Ron Hubbard, founder of the Church of Scientology. Critics generally praised these books as lively, informative biographies.

In *Bunny: The Real Story of "Playboy,"* Miller chronicles Hefner's unique place in American culture. After growing up in the Midwest and working as a cartoonist in Chicago, Hefner decided to start a magazine that catered to adult males. He compiled the first issue of *Playboy*—which featured nude photos of Marilyn Monroe—on his dining room table. Very soon the magazine was a huge success and Hefner became a celebrity, attracting attention for his lavish, free-wheeling lifestyle—two magnificent mansions and a steady stream of beautiful women. The magazine's popularity continued to rise in the 1960s and 1970s but declined in the 1980s, due in part to increased competition. Heavily burdened by Hefner's expensive habits, the *Playboy* empire has lost much of its luster entering the 1990s. But under the leadership of Hefner's daughter, Christie, the magazine managed to avoid collapse.

Reviewers commended Miller for writing an entertaining portrait of Hefner and his empire. "This is no peep-and-wink production, but a solidly reported piece of cultural journalism," noted *Washington Post Book World* critic Jonathan Yardley. "*Bunny* is thorough, incisive, unsparing and deliciously funny." *Times Literary Supplement* contributor Craig Brown agreed, calling the book "witty and meticulous."

Miller's next book, *The House of Getty,* is a study of oil executive J. Paul Getty. Miller reveals Getty as a mean-spirited, greedy workaholic who neglected his family while becoming one of the world's richest men. Reviews of the book were mixed, with several critics lamenting the book's lack of comprehensive detail. *New York Times Book Review* contributor Jane O'Reilly, for instance, commented that Miller "seems to rely too heavily on the kind of information found in celebrity clip files, and he makes some startling omissions and mistakes." *Washington Post* reviewer L. J.

Davis, who also expressed reservations about the book, nevertheless lauded the author's "powers of anecdote" and called *The House of Getty* "moderately interesting."

In *Bare-Faced Messiah,* Miller explores the life of L. Ron Hubbard, who founded the religion known as Scientology. Basing the religion on so-called "dianetic" theory, which proves the existence of a soul-like entity that maintains itself through reincarnation, Hubbard claimed that Scientology could "free the world from war and endow disciples with superhuman abilities," noted Charles Platt in the *Washington Post.* Hubbard gained many followers and amassed a fortune before his death in 1986. Platt termed the book "impressively thorough" in its treatment of Hubbard and Scientology.

Miller undertakes an oral history of one of World War II's more famous military operations in *Nothing Less Than Victory: The Oral History of D-Day.* Calling on dozens of interviews with witnesses and participants in D-Day—as well as documentary sources such as diaries, letters, news reports, and official documents—Miller presents a book that shows "what it was like on both sides to be young and at war in 1944," wrote Brian Bond in the *English Historical Review.* "Miller has succeeded very well in his stated aim of drawing out the participants' feelings, as distinct from more impersonal, factual recollections of what it was like," Bond observed. First-hand accounts from commanders such as Bradley, Eisenhower, and Montgomery mix with in-the-mud and on-the-beach stories from soldiers who carried the massive D-Day assault forward on their backs. Miller relates the fears of combat novices, the frustrations of commanders awaiting delayed orders, and the compassionate actions of civilians and medical personnel facing the result of the devastating fighting. Miller also gives a voice to German soldiers, which results in the other side having a "greater voice than in other recent D-Day histories," a *Publishers Weekly* critic wrote. Though Bond noted that Miller doesn't believe the book is strictly a military history since he accepted and reported material on faith as it was given to him, the book is still considered "a superb oral history," wrote the *Publishers Weekly* critic.

Tending once again to his journalistic roots, Miller examines the history of the Magnum photographic agency in his 1998 *Magnum: Fifty Years at the Front Line of History.* A pioneering cooperative agency, Magnum has throughout its history been loosely organized, even anarchic at times, noted Gretchen Garner in *Booklist.* However, its photographers consistently produce high-quality work. The agency is also known for its groundbreaking role in retaining copyrights for photographers. Despite persistent financial stress brought on by its structure, the agency persists, "part dysfunctional family, part brilliant brotherhood of talent," Garner remarked. In the book, "Miller affords a rich feast of personalities, adventure, world conflicts, and the issues of journalistic ethics," Garner wrote. Miller offers detailed information on the role of photography in politics since World War II, and "has written an engaging narrative, full of vivid characters saying memorable things," observed the *Publishers Weekly* critic.

Another military history by Miller appeared in 2002. In *Behind the Lines: The Oral History of Special Operations in World War II,* Miller again goes directly to the most reliable sources for his history: WW II survivors of both the British Special Operations Executives and the U.S. Office of Strategic Services (later the Central Intelligence Agency). Miller knits together the interviews with other documentary sources such as letters and reports. The special operations forces worked to disable the enemy from within their own territory. Volunteer operatives "fomented industrial and military sabotage, labor agitation, disinformation, attacks against leaders like Hitler and Heydrich, boycotts, and riots," remarked a *Kirkus Review* critic. Others were specially trained in operations involving cryptography, hand-to-hand combat, document forgery, and radio telegraphy. Miller provides first-hand stories of fear of capture, brutal treatment in captivity, botched missions, and uncooperative elements. A *Kirkus Reviews* critic called *Behind the Lines* a "first-of-a-kind compilation," and Mark Ellis, writing in *Library Journal,* noted that it is "an enjoyable and fascinating read" of interest to generalists and military specialists alike.

While Miller's works address significant subjects and events—especially to those who lived them—the author holds a modest opinion of his own writing. Miller once told *CA:* "I have a faint hope that one day it will be possible to produce a piece of writing that might be something more than mere ephemera."

BIOGRAPHICAL AND CRITICAL SOURCES:

PERIODICALS

Booklist, May 1, 1998, Gretchen Garner, review of *Magnum: Fifty Years at the Front Line of History,*

p. 1479; November 1, 2002, Gilbert Taylor, review of *Behind the Lines: The Oral History of Special Operations in World War II,* p. 453.
Books, spring, 1999, review of *Magnum,* p. 21.
English Historical Review, June, 2001, Brian Bond, review of *Nothing Less Than Victory: The Oral History of D-Day,* p. 762.
Entertainment Weekly, June 19, 1998, review of *Magnum,* p. 68.
Kirkus Reviews, October 15, 2002, review of *Behind the Lines,* p. 1519.
Library Journal, October 15, 2002, Mark Ellis, review of *Behind the Lines,* p. 84.
Mademoiselle, September, 1985.
New Republic, October 14, 1985, Joseph Nocera, review of *Bunny: The Real Story of "Playboy,"* pp. 36-40.
New York Times Book Review, September 8, 1985; March 30, 1986.
Observer, September 30, 1984.
Publishers Weekly, May 23, 1994, review of *Nothing Less Than Victory,* p. 75; March 23, 1998, review of *Magnum,* p. 85.
Tikkun, September 1, 2000, p. 68.
Time, March 17, 1986.
Times Literary Supplement, March 8, 1985; January 17, 1986.
Washington Post, March 14, 1986; June 28, 1988.
Washington Post Book World, August 18, 1985.

* * *

MOODY, Bill 1941-

PERSONAL: Born September 27, 1941, in Webb City, MO; son of Hugh and Helen (Shaw) Moody; children: Sarah. *Ethnicity:* "Caucasian." *Education:* University of Nevada, Las Vegas, M.A., 1987.

ADDRESSES: Home—Sonoma County, CA. *Agent*—Philip Spitzer, 50 Talmage Farm Lane, East Hampton, NY 11937.

CAREER: Jazz drummer, 1963—; freelance writer, 1968—; disc jockey and radio programmer, 1989-97. Former English instructor at University of Nevada, Las Vegas; Sonoma State University, Rohnert Park, CA, creative writing instructor. *Military service:* United States Air Force, 1959-62.

MEMBER: Mystery Writers of America, International Crime Writers Association.

WRITINGS:

The Jazz Exiles: American Musicians Abroad (nonfiction), foreword by Stanley Dance, University of Nevada Press (Reno, NV), 1993.

NOVELS

Solo Hand, Walker (New York, NY), 1994.
Death of a Tenor Man, Walker (New York, NY), 1995.
The Sound of the Trumpet, Walker (New York, NY), 1997.
Bird Lives!, Walker (New York, NY), 1999.
Looking for Chet Baker, Walker (New York, NY), 2002.

ADAPTATIONS: Death of a Tenor Man has been optioned for a film and is under development with Steve Jones.

SIDELIGHTS: Starting out with a single premise, jazz drummer and writer Bill Moody continually asks himself "the 'what if' and 'why' questions as I'm writing," as he explained to Jesse Hamlin in the *San Francisco Chronicle.* "It's a discovery process as you go," Moody further noted. This jazz-like composition practice is utilized in Moody's mystery novels, which draw on his own background as a jazz musician. His detective character Evan Horne is a jazz pianist whose cases involve the world of nightclubs, recording studios, and crooked agents. "I'm always fascinated by stuff that hasn't been figured out," he told Hamlin.

Moody explained in an article for *Writer's Digest* that he first thought of a "jazz detective" in 1968 while playing in a jazz band in Czechoslovakia. When the Soviet Army invaded the country during his stay there, Moody wrote about the turmoil for several music magazines. He also began speculating about a jazz musician spy character. "A jazz musician spy hadn't been done," he remembered in *Writer's Digest,* "nor had Prague during that hectic period figured prominently in an espionage novel. I knew both character and place. I figured it a sure winner." Unfortunately, Moody's espionage novel could not find a publisher.

But one editor suggested he try a mystery instead. Moody gave it a try: "I put the spy novels aside and created a jazz musician turned amateur sleuth caught up in the backstabbing record business."

In *Solo Hand* Moody introduced jazz pianist Evan Horne. As the novel opens, Horne is in Los Angeles recovering from an automobile accident that has injured his right hand—the hand he needs most for piano solos. He becomes involved in a mystery when someone tries to blackmail singer Lonnie Cole, whom Evan has accompanied. Cole has just done a duet album with a famous country singer, and the mail brings a package of photographs of him and the country artist caught in embarrassing circumstances at a party, along with a request that Horne deliver a million-dollar extortion fee. In order to convince Cole that he is not involved in the plot himself, Horne undertakes the investigation, intent on discovering who is behind the blackmail attempt. In the process, Horne winds up knocked unconscious in a marina but triumphs despite his novice status as a sleuth. A *Publishers Weekly* reviewer praised *Solo Hand* as "entertaining" and further noted that "Moody's portrayals of the backstabbing music industry and a royalties scam ring true."

Moody puts his knowledge of jazz history to use when Evan Horne reappears in *Death of a Tenor Man.* This time Horne is in Las Vegas assuaging boredom by assisting with a friend's research into the death of real-life jazz tenor saxophonist Wardell Gray in 1955—a death officially attributed to a drug overdose. He is also playing unobtrusive piano at a shopping mall in the gambler's paradise, trying to get his injured hand back into shape for more demanding performances. While helping look up the facts on Gray's demise, Horne is threatened with bodily harm by organized criminal henchmen if he does not give up his inquiry, but this only piques him to peer more closely at the available information. On the trail of answers, Horne also discovers much about the racial tension in Las Vegas's past—Gray's body was found in the desert outside the city the day after he wielded his saxophone at the brand-new Moulin Rouge, which was the first Las Vegas casino and hotel open to both whites and African Americans. Moody ornaments *Death of a Tenor Man* with other real jazz stories and musicians besides the late Wardell Gray, according to another *Publishers Weekly* critic, who went on to assert that the author "exhibits perfect pitch when writing lovingly about music. . . . These pages sing." Marilyn Stasio, writing in the *New York Times Book Review,* also applauded Moody's efforts in *Death of a Tenor Man.* She called Evan Horne an "immensely likable hero" and declared that in this "sad, bluesy story" many other characters "have life and soul." Bill Ott in *Booklist* concluded that "the Vegas setting is nicely realized, and the use of the real-life Gray case proves fascinating, especially to jazz fans."

The Sound of the Trumpet finds Horne helping a friend with some studio tapes that may have been recorded by 1950s jazz trumpet legend Clifford Brown. While trying to verify whether they are Brown's recordings, Horne lands in the middle of a murder investigation when the owner of the disputed tapes dies. "Moody uses his musical knowledge to introduce a gallery of colorful figures . . . and delivers a distinctively pleasurable, if not especially compelling, mystery," according to a reviewer for *Publishers Weekly.* Rex E. Klett in *Library Journal* called the novel "well written, plausible, and down to earth," while Ott, writing in *Booklist,* called the novel "a must for jazz fans, who will appreciate Moody's grasp of the music."

Speaking to Michael Bourne in *Down Beat,* Moody speculated as to just when Evan Horne's injured hand may allow him to return full-time to a career as a jazz pianist and leave the amateur detective work behind. "I let him play a little in *Death of a Tenor Man* and *The Sound of the Trumpet,*" Moody commented to Bourne, "and his hand is getting better. He's eager to get on with his career in music, of course, but in the next book he'll have a much more compelling reason to get involved in the story. In the last two books, he's been helping his friend Ace with what appears to be some simple research and gets caught up. But, sometimes, that's the way things happen. You start to do something that you think will be easy and uncomplicated, and before you know it, you're way in over your head."

In Horne's fourth outing, *Bird Lives!,* he does battle with a serial killer who is busily killing smooth-jazz saxophonists and leaving behind bird feathers on their corpses as a morbid sort of clue for jazz aficionados. With *Looking for Chet Baker,* fifth in the series, Moody deals with the real-life mystery surrounding the death of the great jazz trumpeter Chet Baker, who was found dead on the sidewalk outside the Amsterdam hotel where he was staying; however, it was never determined whether he had fallen, jumped, or was pushed out of the window to his death. In the book, Horne has now recovered enough from the hand injury to try and get his career back online with a gig in Amsterdam. His old friend, Ace Buffington, a professor of English, contacts him in hopes of getting Horne's help with research on a book about Baker. Though Horne turns his friend down, he is soon very much involved, as he has been lodged into the same hotel in Amsterdam where Baker died, and also the same, it now appears, from which Buffington has also suddenly gone missing. All the professor's research materials have been left behind, and now Horne grows concerned. Tracing the whereabouts of his missing friend, he also must follow Baker in his last days, hoping both trails will lead to Buffington.

Moody's tale of mystery and historical reconstruction won positive critical attention. Katy Munger, writing in the *Washington Post Book World,* found it to be a "wonderful variation on a familiar theme." Munger further felt that Moody's inside knowledge of jazz and the life of traveling jazz musicians help to create descriptions that "resonate with a passion that makes this book sing." Dick Lochte, writing in the *Los Angeles Times,* also thought that Moody's book "hits all the right notes" and ventured that the book has the "potential for turning mystery lovers into jazz fans. And vice versa." For *Booklist*'s Ott, *Looking for Chet Baker* is the "best in a steadily improving series," and Klett, writing in *Library Journal,* found the book "intricately described, carefully paced, and gently suspenseful." Peter Cannon, reviewing the novel in *Publishers Weekly,* had further praise, commenting that Moody "does a wonderful job of re-creating [Chet Baker] and his times." Julius Lester, writing in the *Los Angeles Times,* commended Moody's "wonderful mystery series" in total, singling out *Looking for Chet Baker* for its "fluid" writing, "tight" plot, and the "wealth of interesting minor characters." And similarly, Gene Santoro, in the *New York Times Book Review,* praised Moody as a "fluent writer with a good ear for dialogue, a deft and ingratiating descriptive touch, a talent for characterization, and a genuine feel for the jazz world."

Shortly after publication of this fifth novel in the series, Moody's publishers, Walker, announced that it would be ceasing publication of its mystery line. Moody's next Evan Horne mystery will need to find a new home. But for the author, accustomed to the ever-changing venues of a jazz musician, such dislocations are par for the course. Moody once told CA: "Perseverance and believing in your work are probably the two most important factors in getting published. Don't give up one publisher too soon."

BIOGRAPHICAL AND CRITICAL SOURCES:

PERIODICALS

Booklist, October 15, 1995, Bill Ott, review of *Death of a Tenor Man,* p. 388; February 15, 1997, Bill Ott, *The Sound of the Trumpet,* p. 1007; February 15, 2002, Bill Ott, review of *Looking for Chet Baker,* pp. 995-996.

Down Beat, June, 1997, Michael Bourne, review of *The Sound of the Trumpet,* p. 14.

Kirkus Reviews, January 1, 2002, review of *Looking for Chet Baker,* p. 20.

Library Journal, January, 1997, Rex E. Klett, review of *The Sound of the Trumpet,* p. 152; February 1, 2002, Rex E. Klett, review of *Looking for Chet Baker,* p. 135.

Los Angeles Times, March 27, 2002, Dick Lochte, review of *Looking for Chet Baker,* p. E2; May 10, 2002, Don Heckman, review of *Looking for Chet Baker,* p. F21; May 12, 2002, Julius Lester, review of *Looking for Chet Baker,* p. R6.

New York Times Book Review, January 7, 1996, Marilyn Stasio, review of *Death of a Tenor Man,* p. 24; April 7, 2002, Gene Santoro, review of *Looking for Chet Baker,* p. 29.

Publishers Weekly, December 20, 1993, review of *Solo Hand,* p. 53; October 23, 1995, review of *Death of a Tenor Man,* pp. 60-61; December 16, 1996, review of *The Sound of the Trumpet,* p. 45; January 7, 2002, Peter Cannon, review of *Looking for Chet Baker,* p. 49.

San Francisco Chronicle, March 16, 2002, Jesse Hamlin, "Moody's Clues: Jazz Drummer Delves into the Mysteries of the Music World in His Novels," p. D1.

Washington Post Book World, March 31, 2002, Katy Munger, review of *Looking for Chet Baker,* p. 13.

Writer's Digest, February, 1996, p. 6.

ONLINE

All about Jazz, http://www.allaboutjazz.com/ (October 30, 2003), "Bill Moody."

Bill Moody Mystery and Jazz, http://www.billmoodyjazz.com/ (October 30, 2003).

OTHER

All Things Considered (Public Broadcasting Service radio program), March 15, 2002, Liana Hansen, interview with Bill Moody.

N

NASH, Ralph (Lee) 1925-

PERSONAL: Born February 22, 1925, in Sullivan, IN; son of Cecil E. and Flossie F. (Raines) Nash; married Berta Struman (a scholar of Renaissance bibliography), December 17, 1949; children: Thomas, Richard. *Ethnicity:* "Caucasian." *Education:* Duke University, A.B., 1945, M.A., 1946; Harvard University, Ph.D., 1951. *Politics:* Democrat.

ADDRESSES: Home—Huntington Woods, MI. *Agent*—c/o Author Mail, Wayne State University Press, 4809 Woodward Ave., Detroit, MI 48201-1309.

CAREER: University of Louisville, Louisville, KY, instructor in English, 1948-50; Washington University, St. Louis, MO, assistant professor of English, 1950-54; Wayne State University, Detroit, MI, instructor, 1955-58, assistant professor, 1958-61, associate professor, 1961-65, professor of Renaissance literature, 1965-88, assistant chair, 1965-68, chair, Department of English, 1968-71.

MEMBER: Modern Language Association of America, American Association of Teachers of Italian, Renaissance Society of America, North Central Renaissance Society.

WRITINGS:

(Translator) Jacopo Sannazaro, *Arcadia and Piscatorial Eclogues,* Wayne State University Press (Detroit, MI), 1966.

(Translator) T. Tasso, *Jerusalem Delivered,* Wayne State University Press (Detroit, MI), 1986.

(Translator and author of commentary) *The Major Latin Poems of Jacopo Sannazaro,* Wayne State University Press (Detroit, MI), 1996.

Contributor to books, including *Studies in Honor of John Wilcox,* Wayne State University Press (Detroit, MI), 1958. Contributor of articles, poetry, and reviews to scholarly journals. Poetry editor, *Perspective,* 1950s.

WORK IN PROGRESS: A verse translation of *Seven Odes of Horace;* verse translations of the late plays of Sophocles, *Philoctetes* and *Oedipus Coloneus.*

SIDELIGHTS: Ralph Nash told *CA:* "I have always been primarily interested in writing poetry and secondarily interested in discussing poems. I stopped publishing poems, partly because of my wife's twenty-five-year illness resulting from brain surgery, partly because I didn't want to publish poems to further what we call 'a career.'

"I have come to realize that my poems have been consistently concerned with the puzzling and conflicting problems arising from the human race's origins as a herd animal that became, through the development of a remarkable brain, the top predator in the world, threatening to destroy the world as we have known it. One who reads the works I have chosen to translate will probably see that the same thread runs through those poems. I used to call this 'political versus pastoral,' but it's not a dichotomy—it's deep within us all."

Nash reads Italian, French, German, Spanish, Latin, and Greek.

NASR, Seyyed Hossein 1933-

PERSONAL: Surname is pronounced as one syllable, the last two letters slurred; born April 7, 1933, in Tehran, Persia (now Iran); son of Valiallah (an educator) and Ashraf (Kia) Nasr; married Soussan Danechvary, November 21, 1958; children: one son, one daughter. *Education:* Massachusetts Institute of Technology, B.S., 1954; Harvard University, Ph.D., 1958. *Religion:* Muslim. *Hobbies and other interests:* Traditional and sacred art.

ADDRESSES: Office—Department of Religion, Temple University, Philadelphia, PA 19122.

CAREER: University of Tehran, Tehran, Iran, assistant professor of history of science and philosophy, 1958-63, professor, 1963-79; dean of letters, 1968-72, vice chancellor, 1970-71; Harvard University, visiting professor, 1962, 1965; American University of Beirut, Aga Khan Professor of Islamic Studies, 1964-65; Aryamehr University, Tehran, chancellor, 1972-75; Princeton University, visiting professor, 1975; University of Utah, Salt Lake City, visiting professor, 1979; Temple University, Philadelphia, PA, professor of Islamic studies, 1979-84; Gifford Lecturer, University of Edinburgh, 1981; George Washington University, Washington, DC, professor of Islamic studies, 1984—; Cornell University, Ithaca, NY, A. D. White professor-at-large, 1991—. Chair of governing board, Regional Cooperation for Development Institute (Iran, Pakistan, Turkey).

MEMBER: International Congress of Orientalists, Congress of Iranologists, Congress of Mediaeval Philosophy, International Institute of Philosophy, Imperial Iranian Academy of Philosophy (director, 1974-79), Sigma Xi, Harvard/M.I.T. Association of Tehran (president), Temenos Academy.

AWARDS, HONORS: Royal Book Award of Iran, for *Nazar-i mutafakkiran-i islami dar barih-i tabiat;* honorary doctorate, Uppsala University, 1977.

WRITINGS:

(Editor and author of introduction and notes) Sadr al-Din Shirazi, *Risalah-i se asl* (title means "The Three Principles"), University of Tehran Press (Tehran, Iran), 1961.

Hirmis wa niwishtihay-i hirmisi (title means "Hermes and Hermetic Writings in the Islamic World"), University of Tehran Press (Tehran, Iran), 1961.

Nazar-i mutafakkiran-i islami dar barih-i tabiat (title means "Concepts of Nature in Islamic Thought during the Fourth Century"), University of Tehran Press (Tehran, Iran), 1962.

Three Muslim Sages: Avicenna, Suhrawardi, ibn Arabi, Harvard University Press (Cambridge, MA), 1964.

An Introduction to Islamic Cosmological Doctrines: Conceptions of Nature and Methods Used for Its Study by the Ikhwan al-Safa, al-Biruni, and ibn Sina, Belknap Press (Cambridge, MA), 1964.

(With H. Corbin) *Histoire de la philosophie islamique,* Gallimard (Paris, France), 1964.

Ideals and Realities of Islam, Allen & Unwin (Boston, MA), 1966.

Islamic Studies: Essays on Law and Society, the Science, and Philosophy and Sufism, Librairie du Liban (Kesrouwan, Lebanon), 1967.

Encounter of Man and Nature, Allen & Unwin (Boston, MA), 1968.

Science and Civilization in Islam, Harvard University Press (Cambridge, MA), 1968.

Ma'arif-i islami dar jahan-i mu'asir (title means *The Islamic Intellectual Heritage in the Contemporary World*), Shirkat-i jihi (Tehran, Iran), 1970, 2nd edition, 1974.

(Editor) *Historical Atlas of Iran,* University of Tehran Press (Tehran, Iran), 1971.

Sufi Essays, Allen & Unwin (Boston, MA), 1972.

(Editor, with M. Mohaghegh, and author of introduction) Abu Rayhan Biruni and Ibn Sina, *Al-As'ilah wa'l-ajwibah* (title means "Questions and Answers"), High Council of Culture and the Arts (Tehran, Iran), 1973.

Al-Biruni: An Annotated Bibliography, High Council of Culture and the Arts (Tehran, Iran), 1973.

Jalal al-Din Rumi: Supreme Persian Poet and Sage, High Council of Culture and the Arts (Tehran, Iran), 1974.

(Translator and editor) Allamah Tabatabai, *Shi'ite Islam,* State University of New York Press (Albany, NY), 1975.

(With R. Beny) *Persia, Bridge of Turquoise,* McClelland & Stewart (Toronto, Ontario, Canada), 1975.

(With W. Chittick) *An Annotated Bibliography of Islamic Science,* Volume I, Imperial Iranian Academy of Philosophy (Tehran, Iran), 1975.

Islam and the Plight of Modern Man, Longman (Upper Saddle River, NJ), 1976.

Islamic Science: An Illustrated Study, World of Islam Festival Trust (London, England), 1976.

Western Science and Asian Culture, Indian Council for Cultural Relations (New Delhi, India), 1976.

(Editor) *Melanges offerts à Henry Corbin,* (Tehran, Iran), 1977.

Islamic Life and Thought, Allen & Unwin (Boston, MA), 1981.

(Editor) *The Essential Writings of Frithjof Schuon,* Amity House (Amity, NY), 1986.

(With Jaroslav Pelikan and Joseph Kitagawa) *Comparative Work Ethics: Judeo-Christian, Islamic, and Eastern,* Library of Congress (Washington, DC), 1985.

Islamic Art and Spirituality, State University of New York Press (Albany, NY), 1987.

(Editor) *Islamic Spirituality: Foundations,* Crossroad (New York, NY), 1987.

(Editor and annotator) *Shiism: Doctrines, Thought, and Spirituality,* State University of New York Press (Albany, NY), 1988.

Expectation of the Millennium: Shi'ism in History, State University of New York Press (Albany, NY), 1989.

Knowledge and the Sacred, State University of New York Press (Albany, NY), 1989.

Traditional Islam in the Modern World, K. Paul International (New York, NY), 1990.

(Editor) *Islamic Spirituality: Manifestations,* Crossroad (New York, NY), 1991.

(Editor) *Religion of the Heart: Essays Presented to Frithjof Schuon on His Eightieth Birthday,* Foundation for Traditional Studies (Washington, DC), 1991.

An Introduction to Islamic Cosmological Doctrines, State University of New York Press (Albany, NY), 1993.

Islamic Art and Spirituality, Mizan, 1993.

The Need for a Sacred Science, State University of New York Press (Albany, NY), 1993.

A Young Muslim's Guide to the Modern World, Library of Islam (Des Plaines, IL), 1993.

Muhammad, Man of God, KAZI Publications (Chicago, IL), 1995.

(Editor, with Oliver Leaman) *History of Islamic Philosophy* Routledge (New York, NY), 1996.

The Islamic Intellectual Tradition in Persia, Curzon Press (Richmond, Surrey, England), 1996.

Religion and the Order of Nature, Oxford University Press (New York, NY), 1996.

Sadr al-Din Shirazi and His Transcendent Theosophy: Background, Life and Works, Institute for Humanities and Cultural Studies (Tehran, Iran), 1997.

Man and Nature: The Spiritual Crisis in Modern Man, ABC International Group (Chicago, IL), 1997.

Islamic-Christian Dialogue: Problems and Obstacles to Be Pondered and Overcome, Georgetown University (Washington, DC), 1998.

The Spiritual and Religious Dimensions of the Environmental Crisis, Temenos Academy (London, England), 1999.

(Coeditor) *An Anthology of Philosophy in Persia,* Oxford University Press (New York, NY), 1999.

A Journey through Persian History and Culture, Iqbal Academy Pakistan (Lahore, Pakistan), 2000.

The Heart of Islam: Enduring Values for Humanity, HarperSanFrancisco (San Francisco, CA), 2002.

Islam: Religion, History, and Civilization, HarperSanFrancisco (San Francisco, CA), 2003.

Contributor of numerous articles in French, English, Persian, and Arabic to professional journals.

SIDELIGHTS: Prolific author and professor Seyyed Hossein Nasr is an Islamic scholar of prodigious output and deep dedication to the study of Islam. A *Publishers Weekly* reviewer called him "probably America's leading Islamicist" in a review of *Islam: Religion, History, and Civilization,* while another *Publishers Weekly* writer referred to Nasr as "a living legend in Islamic studies" in a review of *The Heart of Islam: Enduring Values for Humanity.* A career scholar and researcher, "Nasr is a leading expert on Islam, having made extraordinary contributions to the study of science, philosophy, mysticism, and Shiism over several decades," wrote Leonard T. Librande in the *Journal of Ecumenical Studies.*

Nasr was born on April 7, 1933, in Tehran, Iran, "into a family of distinguished scholars and physicians," wrote a biographer on the *Seyyed Hossein Nasr Foundation* Web site. "His father, Seyyed Valiallah, a man of great learning and piety, was a physician to the Iranian royal family, as was his father before him," the biographer wrote. Nasr received the usual Persian primary school education, and studied additional subjects such as Islam and the French language at home. "However, for Nasr, it was the long hours of discussion with his father, mostly on philosophical and theological issues, complemented by both reading and reaction to the discourses carried on by those who came to his father's house, that constituted an essential aspect of his early education and which in many ways set the pattern and tone of his intellectual development," the *Nasr Foundation* biographer observed.

When he was twelve years old, Nasr came to the United States and continued his education. He earned a scholarship to the Massachusetts Institute of Technology (MIT) and was "the first Iranian student to be admitted as an undergraduate at MIT," the *Nasr Foundation* biographer wrote. He embarked on a study of physics, motivated by the "desire to gain knowledge of the nature of things, at least at the level of physical reality." An intellectual and spiritual crisis in his second year led him to realize that physics would not answer the many metaphysical questions he had about the world. He sought answers in courses in the humanities, philosophy, the history of science, and related subjects. Though Nasr continued in the physics program and graduated with honors, "his heart was no longer with physics," wrote the *Nasr Foundation* biographer.

Nasr earned a master's degree in geology and geophysics from Harvard in 1956, and later a Ph.D. in the history of science and learning from the same institution at the age of twenty-five. He completed his first book, *Science and Civilization in Islam,* while studying at Harvard, and it was published by Harvard University Press in 1968. Harvard also published his doctoral dissertation in 1964. After earning his Ph.D., Nasr declined an assistant professor position at Harvard and returned to Iran, where he accepted a position as associate professor of philosophy and the history of science in the Faculty of Letters at Tehran University.

Nasr continued his academic career in Iran for many years. He created the Imperial Iranian Academy of Philosophy under the appointment of the Queen of Iran in 1973, attracting top-flight philosophers and scholars from around the world. He was visiting lecturer and professor at several American universities from the 1960s to the 1980s, including the University of Chicago, where he delivered the Rockefeller Lectures in 1966; the American University of Beirut, where he spent a year as the first Aga Khan Professor of Islamic Studies from 1964 to 1965; Princeton University and the University of Utah, where he conducted short seminars; the University of Edinburgh, where he delivered the Gifford Lectures; and the University of Toronto, where he delivered the Wiegand Lectures on the philosophy of religion. All the while, Nasr continued to write, producing books such as *Knowledge and the Sacred* which he called "a gift from Heaven," wrote the *Nasr Foundation* biographer. "He was able to write the texts of the lectures [that comprise the book] with great facility and speed and within a period of less than three months, they were completed. Nasr says it was as though he was writing from a text he had previously memorized."

Though Nasr is an exile from Iran, having left his homeland in 1979 during the Islamic Revolution, he remains one of the world's top-flight Islamic scholars. He "leads an extremely active intellectual life with a very busy schedule of teaching at the university and lecturing at many institutions in America and around the world, writing scholarly works, being involved in several intellectual projects simultaneously, and meeting individuals who are interested in traditional thought," noted the *Nasr Foundation* biographer. "At the same time, he leads a very intense spiritual life spent in prayer, meditation, and contemplation and also providing spiritual counsel for those who seek his advice and guidance."

Nasr's many works have consistently garnered high praise from critics and reviewers. In *Religion and the Order of Nature,* Nasr "shows how Western thought moved away from the idea that nature was sacred, and came to see it as something to be used and exploited by humans," wrote Margaret Barker in the *Ecologist.* This view has expanded around the world and has led to global-scale destruction of the environment by humans unrestrained by any ideas of the sacredness of nature that religion would provide. Barker called *Religion and the Order of Nature* "a magnificent book, pleading for a return to metaphysics, the knowledge of what is behind and beyond nature." William French, writing in the *Journal of Religion,* described it as a "superb study," while Patti H. Clayton in the *Quarterly Review of Biology* called it a "difficult but rewarding read." Barker concluded that the book is a "fascinating and rewarding volume."

In *The Heart of Islam: Enduring Values for Humanity,* a book specially commissioned by HarperCollins in the aftermath of the September 11, 2001, attacks, Nasr presents a detailed discussion of what Islam is, and is not, and how it reconciles with the world's view of Islam since the late summer of 2001. "Nasr does not sidestep the issues that non-Muslims have on their minds, but he addresses them within the context of the vitality and vision of Islam more generally," wrote Steve Young in *Library Journal.* In the book, Nasr "elucidates Islamic attitudes toward God, revelation, tradition, law, prayer, fasting, afterlife, and human responsibility with clarity and conviction," wrote James Carroll in the *New York Times.* "His vision of the complexities of Islamic history and the diversity of Islamic practice around the globe is particularly important as antidote to the crude stereotyping to which Muslims have long been subjected." Although a *Publishers Weekly* critic thought the book lacked a focus and "guiding thesis," Carroll concluded, "Members of the 'general Western public' will put this book down with a fuller grasp of why Islam has shaped the religious impulse of so many and why it still does. For that reason alone, *The Heart of Islam* should find a wide readership."

Similarly, *Islam: Religion, History, and Civilization* was called "a good, up-to-date introduction to Islamic faith and history" by John Green, writing in *Booklist.* "Nasr presents the religion of more than a billion people today without prejudice or preference," wrote a *Publishers Weekly* critic, concluding that the book "manages to be sweeping in scope yet accessible in style." Green deemed the book "a deep, thoughtful, sympathetic introduction" to Islam's longstanding and deeply varied history. A *Kirkus Reviews* critic concluded that *Islam: Religion, History, and Civilization* is "a useful resource for readers seeking an introduction to Islamic thought and its major schools."

Nasr is competent in French and German in addition to Persian, Arabic, and English; he has some knowledge of Italian and the classical languages.

BIOGRAPHICAL AND CRITICAL SOURCES:

PERIODICALS

Booklist, June 15, 1991, review of *Ideals and Realities of Islam,* p. 1939; January 1, 2003, John Green, review of *Islam: Religion, History, and Civilization,* p. 812.

Choice, July, 1987, review of *Islamic Art and Spirituality,* p. 1684; July, 1987, review of *Traditional Islam in the Modern World,* p. 1711; December, 1987, review of *Islamic Spirituality: Foundations,* p. 638; May, 1991, review of *Islamic Spirituality: Manifestations,* p. 1506; February, 1994, review of *An Introduction to Islamic Cosmological Doctrines,* p. 949; October, 1996, review of *History of Islamic Philosophy,* p. 293.

Christian Century, August 21, 1991, review of *Islamic Spirituality: Manifestations,* p. 775.

Commonweal, January 28, 1983, review of *Knowledge and the Sacred,* p. 59; February 25, 1983, review of *Knowledge and the Sacred,* p. 117; July 17, 1988, review of *Islamic Spirituality: Foundations,* p. 380.

Ecologist, January, 2000, Margaret Barker, review of *Religion and the Order of Nature,* p. 46.

International Philosophical Quarterly, March, 1996, review of *An Introduction to Islamic Cosmological Doctrines,* p. 123.

Isis, September, 1994, review of *An Introduction to Islamic Cosmological Doctrines,* p. 504; December, 1994, review of *The Need for Sacred Science,* p. 681.

Journal of Ecumenical Studies, summer, 1998, Leonard T. Librande, review of *Religion and the Order of Nature,* p. 515.

Journal of Religion, October, 1989, review of *Islamic Spirituality: Foundations,* p. 589; April, 1991, review of *Expectation of the Millennium,* p. 298; April, 1992, review of *Knowledge and the Sacred,* p. 284; October, 1999, William French, review of *Religion and the Order of Nature,* p. 689.

Kirkus Reviews, November 15, 2002, review of *Islam: Religion, History, and Civilization,* p. 1680.

Library Journal, October 1, 1998, review of *A Young Muslim's Guide to the Modern World,* p. 61; October 1, 1998, review of *Shiism: Doctrines, Thought, and Spirituality,* p. 62; October 1, 2002, Steve Young, review of *The Heart of Islam: Enduring Values for Humanity,* p. 102.

Middle East Journal, winter, 1988, review of *Traditional Islam in the Modern World,* p. 130; winter, 1988, review of *Islamic Art and Spirituality,* p. 141; autumn, 1988, review of *Islamic Spirituality: Foundations,* p. 692; autumn, 1989, review of *Shiism,* p. 709; summer, 1990, review of *Knowledge and the Sacred,* p. 539; winter, 1991, review of *Expectation of the Millennium,* p. 160; spring, 1992, review of *Islamic Spirituality: Foundations,* p. 343; autumn, 1992, review of *Islamic Spirituality: Manifestations,* p. 713; autumn, 2002, Charles E. Butterworth, review of *An Anthology of Philosophy in Persia,* pp. 735-736.

New York Times, September 8, 2002, James Carroll, "Articles of Faith," review of *The Heart of Islam,* section 7, p. 13.

Parabola, May, 1987, review of *Islamic Art and Spirituality,* p. 98; November, 1987, review of *Islamic Spirituality: Foundations,* p. 102; February, 1995, review of *The Need for Sacred Science,* p. 99; May, 1997, review of *Religion and the Order of Nature,* p. 122; August, 1998, review of *Religion and the Order of Nature,* p. 102.

Philosophy East and West, July, 2003, J. E. Tiles, "The Lives and Minds of Traditions," p. 403.

Philosophy in Review, February, 1997, review of *History of Islamic Philosophy,* p. 58.

PR Newswire, April 27, 2003, "PNCHonors Five Giants in the Arts, Science, and Public Service."

Publishers Weekly, February 1, 1991, review of *Islamic Spirituality: Manifestations* and review of *Islamic Spirituality: Foundations,* p. 61; August 12, 2002, review of *The Heart of Islam,* pp. 295-296; December 23, 2002, review of *Islam,* p. 64.

Quarterly Review of Biology, Patti H. Clayton, review of *Religion and the Order of Nature,* p. 453.

Reference & Research Book News, April, 1991, review of *Traditional Islam in the Modern World,* p. 1; September, 1993, review of *An Introduction to Islamic Cosmological Doctrines,* p. 1; November, 1993, review of *The Need for a Sacred Science,* p. 3; November, 1996, review of *History of Islamic Philosophy,* p. 1.

Religious Studies Review, April, 1984, review of *Knowledge and the Sacred,* p. 153; October, 1984, review of *Knowledge and the Sacred,* p. 348; July, 1988, review of *Islamic Spirituality: Foundations,* p. 267; April, 1992, review of *Islamic Spirituality: Manifestations,* p. 159; October, 1998, review of *Religion and the Order of Nature,* p. 400.

Review for Religious, May, 1991, review of *Islamic Spirituality: Manifestations,* p. 474.

Times Literary Supplement, March 5, 1982.

University Press Book News, September, 1989, review of *Knowledge and the Sacred,* p. 5; April, 1992, review of *Knowledge and the Sacred,* p. 284.

ONLINE

Seyyed Hossein Nasr Foundation Web site, http://www.nasr.org/ (November 21, 2003), biography of Nasr.

Spirituality & Health Web site, http://www.spiritualityhealth.com/ (November 21, 2003), Frederick and Mary Ann Brussat, review of *The Heart of Islam.**

O

OATES, Joyce Carol 1938-
(Rosamond Smith, a pseudonym)

PERSONAL: Born June 16, 1938, in Lockport, NY; daughter of Frederic James (a tool and die designer) and Caroline (Bush) Oates; married Raymond Joseph Smith, January 23, 1961. *Education:* Syracuse University, B.A., 1960; University of Wisconsin, M.A., 1961.

ADDRESSES: *Office*—Council of the Humanities, 223 185 Nassau St., Princeton University, Princeton, NJ 08544. *Agent*—John Hawkins, 71 West 23rd St., New York, NY 10010; (for plays) Peter Franklin, c/o William Morris Agency, 1350 Avenue of the Americas, New York, NY 10019. *E-mail*—jcsmith@princeton.edu.

CAREER: Writer. University of Detroit, Detroit, MI, instructor, 1961-65, assistant professor, 1965-67; University of Windsor, Windsor, Ontario, Canada, member of English department faculty, 1967-78; Princeton University, Princeton, NJ, writer-in-residence, 1978-81, professor, 1987—, currently Roger S. Berlind Distinguished Professor in the Humanities.

MEMBER: PEN, American Academy of Arts and Letters, Phi Beta Kappa.

AWARDS, HONORS: *Mademoiselle* college fiction award, 1959, for "In the Old World"; National Endowment for the Arts grants, 1966, 1968; Guggenheim fellowship, 1967; O. Henry Award, 1967, for "In the Region of Ice," 1973, for "The Dead," and 1983, for

Joyce Carol Oates

"My Warszawa"; Rosenthal Award, National Institute of Arts and Letters, 1968, for *A Garden of Earthly Delights;* National Book Award nomination, 1968, for *A Garden of Earthly Delights,* and 1969, for *Expensive People;* National Book Award for fiction, 1970, for *them;* O. Henry Special Award for Continuing Achievement, 1970 and 1986; Lotos Club Award of Merit,

1975; Pushcart Prize, 1976; *Unholy Loves* selected by the American Library Association as a notable book of 1979; *Bellefleur* nominated for a *Los Angeles Times* Book Prize in fiction, 1980; St. Louis Literary Award, 1988; Rhea Award for the short story, Dungannon Foundation, 1990; Alan Swallow Award for fiction, 1990; co-winner, Heidemann Award for one-act plays, 1990; Bobst Award for Lifetime Achievement in Fiction, 1990; National Book Award nomination, 1990, for *Because It Is Bitter, and Because It Is My Heart;* National Book Critics Circle Award nomination, and Pulitzer Prize finalist, both 1993, both for *Black Water;* Bram Stoker Lifetime Achievement Award for horror fiction, 1994; best new play nomination, American Theatre Critics Association, 1994, for *The Perfectionist;* Pulitzer Prize finalist, 1995, for *What I Lived For;* Bram Stoker Award for Horror, Horror Writers of America, and Fisk Fiction Prize, both 1996, both for *Zombie;* O. Henry Prize Story, 2001, for "The Girl with the Blackened Eye"; National Book Award and Pulitzer Prize finalist, both 2001, both for *Blonde;* Best American Mystery Stories designation, 2002, for "High School Sweetheart"; Peggy V. Helmerich Distinguished Author Award, Tulsa Library Trust, 2002; Common Wealth Literature Award of Distinguished Service, PNC Financial Services Group, 2003.

WRITINGS:

NOVELS

With Shuddering Fall, Vanguard Press (New York, NY), 1964.

A Garden of Earthly Delights, Vanguard Press (New York, NY), 1967, revised edition, Random House (New York, NY), 2003.

Expensive People, Vanguard Press (New York, NY), 1967.

them, Vanguard Press (New York, NY), 1969, reprinted with introduction by Greg Johnson and afterword by the author, Modern Library (New York, NY), 2000.

Wonderland, Vanguard Press (New York, NY), 1971, revised, Ontario Review Press (New York, NY), 1992.

Do with Me What You Will, Vanguard Press (New York, NY), 1973.

The Assassins: A Book of Hours, Vanguard Press (New York, NY), 1975.

Triumph of the Spider Monkey: The First-Person Confession of the Maniac Bobby Gotteson As Told to Joyce Carol Oates (novella; also see below), Black Sparrow Press (Santa Barbara, CA), 1976.

Childwold, Vanguard Press (New York, NY), 1976.

Son of the Morning, Vanguard Press (New York, NY), 1978.

Unholy Loves, Vanguard Press (New York, NY), 1979.

Cybele, Black Sparrow Press (Santa Barbara, CA), 1979.

Bellefleur, Dutton (New York, NY), 1980.

Angel of Light, Dutton (New York, NY), 1981.

A Bloodsmoor Romance, Dutton (New York, NY), 1982.

Mysteries of Winterthurn, Dutton (New York, NY), 1984.

Solstice, Dutton (New York, NY), 1985, revised edition, Ontario Review Press (Princeton, NJ), 2000.

Marya: A Life, Dutton (New York, NY), 1986.

You Must Remember This, Dutton (New York, NY), 1987.

American Appetites, Dutton (New York, NY), 1989.

Because It Is Bitter, and Because It Is My Heart, Dutton (New York, NY), 1990.

I Lock My Door upon Myself, Ecco Press (New York, NY), 1990, revised edition, Ontario Review Press (Princeton, NJ), 2002.

The Rise of Life on Earth, New Directions (New York, NY), 1991.

Black Water, Dutton (New York, NY), 1992.

Foxfire: Confessions of a Girl Gang, Dutton (New York, NY), 1993.

What I Lived For, Dutton (New York, NY), 1994.

Zombie, Dutton (New York, NY), 1995.

Tenderness, Ontario Review Press (New York, NY), 1996.

We Were the Mulvaneys, Dutton (New York, NY), 1996.

First Love: A Gothic Tale, Ecco Press (New York, NY), 1996.

Man Crazy, Dutton (New York, NY), 1997.

My Heart Laid Bare, Dutton (New York, NY), 1998.

Broke Heart Blues: A Novel, Dutton (New York, NY), 1999.

Blonde: A Novel, HarperCollins (New York, NY), 2000.

Middle Age: A Romance, Ecco Press (New York, NY), 2001.

Beasts, Carroll & Graf (New York, NY), 2002.

I'll Take You There: A Novel, Ecco (New York, NY), 2002.

The Tattooed Girl: A Novel, Ecco (New York, NY), 2003.

Rape: A Love Story (novella), Carroll & Graf (New York, NY), 2003.

The Falls: A Novel, Ecco (New York, NY), 2004.

NOVELS; UNDER PSEUDONYM ROSAMOND SMITH

Lives of the Twins, Simon & Schuster (New York, NY), 1988.

Soul/Mate, Dutton (New York, NY), 1989.

Nemesis, Dutton (New York, NY), 1990.

Snake Eyes, Simon & Schuster (New York, NY), 1992.

You Can't Catch Me, Dutton (New York, NY), 1995.

Double Delight, Dutton (New York, NY), 1997.

Starr Bright Will Be with You Soon, Dutton (New York, NY), 1999.

The Barrens, Carroll & Graf (New York, NY), 2001.

SHORT STORIES

By the North Gate, Vanguard Press (New York, NY), 1963.

Upon the Sweeping Flood and Other Stories, Vanguard Press (New York, NY), 1966.

The Wheel of Love and Other Stories, Vanguard Press (New York, NY), 1970.

Marriages and Infidelities, Vanguard Press (New York, NY), 1972.

The Goddess and Other Women, Vanguard Press (New York, NY), 1974.

Where Are You Going, Where Have You Been?: Stories of Young America, Fawcett (New York, NY), 1974, published as *Where Are You Going, Where Have You Been?: Selected Early Stories,* Ontario Review Press (Princeton, NJ), 1993, expanded edition, edited and with an introduction by Elaine Showalter, Rutgers University Press (New Brunswick, NJ), 1994.

The Hungry Ghosts: Seven Allusive Comedies, Black Sparrow Press (Santa Barbara, CA), 1974.

The Poisoned Kiss and Other Stories from the Portuguese, Vanguard Press (New York, NY), 1975.

The Seduction and Other Stories, Black Sparrow Press (Santa Barbara, CA), 1975.

Crossing the Border: Fifteen Tales, Vanguard Press (New York, NY), 1976.

Night Side: Eighteen Tales, Vanguard Press (New York, NY), 1977.

All the Good People I've Left Behind, Black Sparrow Press (Santa Barbara, CA), 1978.

The Lamb of Abyssalia, Pomegranate (Cambridge, MA), 1980.

A Sentimental Education, Dutton (New York, NY), 1981.

Last Days, Dutton (New York, NY), 1984.

Wild Nights (limited edition), Croissant (Athens, OH), 1985.

Raven's Wing, Dutton (New York, NY), 1986.

The Assignation, Ecco Press (New York, NY), 1988.

Where Is Here?, Ecco Press (New York, NY), 1992.

Heat: And Other Stories, Plume (New York, NY), 1992.

Where Are You Going, Where Have You Been?: Selected Early Stories, Ontario Review Press (New York, NY), 1993.

Haunted: Tales of the Grotesque, Dutton (New York, NY), 1994.

Will You Always Love Me? and Other Stories, Dutton (New York, NY), 1995.

The Collector of Hearts: New Tales of the Grotesque, Dutton (New York, NY), 1999.

Faithless: Tales of Transgression, Ecco Press (New York, NY), 2001.

I Am No One You Know: Stories, Ecco Press (New York, NY), 2004.

POETRY

Women in Love and Other Poems, Albondacani Press (New York, NY), 1968.

Anonymous Sins and Other Poems (also see below), Louisiana State University Press (Baton Rouge, LA), 1969.

Love and Its Derangements: Poems (also see below), Louisiana State University Press (Baton Rouge, LA), 1970.

Angel Fire (also see below), Louisiana State University Press (Baton Rouge, LA), 1973.

Dreaming America (limited edition), Aloe Editions, 1973.

Love and Its Derangements and Other Poems (includes *Anonymous Sins and Other Poems, Love and Its Derangements,* and *Angel Fire*), Fawcett (New York, NY), 1974.

The Fabulous Beasts, Louisiana State University Press (Baton Rouge, LA), 1975.

Season of Peril, Black Sparrow Press (Santa Barbara, CA), 1977.

Women Whose Lives Are Food, Men Whose Lives Are Money: Poems, illustrated by Elizabeth Hansell, Louisiana State University Press (Baton Rouge, LA), 1978.

The Stepfather (limited edition), Lord John Press (Northridge, CA), 1978.

Celestial Timepiece (limited edition), Pressworks (Dallas, TX), 1981.

Invisible Woman: New and Selected Poems, 1970-1972, Ontario Review Press (New York, NY), 1982.

The Luxury of Sin (limited edition), Lord John Press (Northridge, CA), 1983.

The Time Traveler, Dutton (New York, NY), 1989.

Tenderness: Poems, Ontario Review Press (New York, NY), 1996.

NONFICTION

The Edge of Impossibility: Tragic Forms in Literature, Vanguard Press (New York, NY), 1972.

The Hostile Sun: The Poetry of D. H. Lawrence, Black Sparrow Press (Santa Barbara, CA), 1973.

New Heaven, New Earth: The Visionary Experience in Literature, Vanguard Press (New York, NY), 1974.

Contraries: Essays, Oxford University Press (Oxford, England), 1981.

The Profane Art: Essays and Reviews, Dutton (New York, NY), 1983.

On Boxing, Doubleday (New York, NY), 1987, expanded edition, Ecco Press (New York, NY), 1994.

(With Eileen T. Bender) *Artist in Residence,* Indiana University Press (Bloomington, IN), 1987.

(Woman) Writer: Occasions and Opportunities, Dutton (New York, NY), 1988.

Conversations with Joyce Carol Oates, edited by Lee Milazzo, University Press of Mississippi (Jackson, MS), 1989.

Where I've Been, and Where I'm Going: Essays, Reviews, and Prose, Plume (New York, NY), 1999.

The Faith of a Writer: Life, Craft, Art, Ecco Press (New York, NY), 2003.

FOR YOUNG ADULTS

Big Mouth & Ugly Girl, HarperTempest (New York, NY), 2002.

Small Avalanches and Other Stories, HarperTempest (New York, NY), 2003.

Freaky Green Eyes, HarperTempest (New York, NY), 2003.

FOR CHILDREN

Come Meet Muffin!, illustrated by Mark Graham, Ecco Press (New York, NY), 1998.

Where Is Little Reynard? (picture book), illustrated by Mark Graham, HarperCollins (New York, NY), 2003.

PLAYS

The Sweet Enemy, produced Off-Broadway, 1965.

Sunday Dinner, produced Off-Broadway, 1970.

Ontological Proof of My Existence (produced Off-Off-Broadway, 1972), published in *Partisan Review,* Volume 37, 1970.

Miracle Play, Black Sparrow Press (Santa Barbara, CA), 1974.

Three Plays, Ontario Review Press (New York, NY), 1980.

Presque Isle, produced in New York City at Theater of the Open Eye, 1984.

Triumph of the Spider Monkey, produced at the Los Angeles Theatre Center, 1985.

American Holiday, produced at the Los Angeles Theatre Academy, 1990.

In Darkest America: Two Plays, Samuel French (New York, NY), 1991.

I Stand before You Naked (produced in New York City at the American Place Theatre; also see below), Samuel French (New York, NY), 1991.

How Do You Like Your Meat? (also see below), produced in New Haven, CT, 1991.

Twelve Plays (contains *Tone Cluster, The Eclipse, How Do You Like Your Meat?, The Ballad of Love Canal, Under/ground, Greensleeves, The Key, Friday Night, Black* [also see below], *I Stand before You Naked, The Secret Mirror* [also see below], and *American Holiday*), Plume (New York, NY), 1991.

Black, produced at the Williamstown Summer Festival, 1992.

Gulf War, produced by the Ensemble Studio Theatre, 1992.

The Secret Mirror, produced in Philadelphia at the Annenberg Theatre, 1992.

The Rehearsal, produced by the Ensemble Studio Theatre, 1993.

The Perfectionist (also see below; produced in Princeton, NJ, 1993), published in *The Perfectionist and Other Plays,* Ecco Press (New York, NY), 1995.

The Truth-Teller, Circle Rep Play-in-Progress, 1993.
The Perfectionist and Other Plays, Ecco Press (New York, NY), 1995.
HERE SHE IS!, produced in Philadelphia, 1995.
New Plays, Ontario Review Press (New York, NY), 1998.

EDITOR OR COMPILER

Scenes from American Life: Contemporary Short Fiction, Random House (New York, NY), 1973.
(With Shannon Ravenel) *Best American Short Stories of 1979,* Houghton Mifflin (Boston, MA), 1979.
Night Walks, Ontario Review Press (New York, NY), 1982.
First-Person Singular: Writers on Their Craft, Ontario Review Press (New York, NY), 1983.
(With Boyd Litzinger) *Story: Fictions Past and Present* (textbook), Heath (Lexington, MA), 1985.
(With Daniel Halpern) *Reading the Fights: The Best Writing about the Most Controversial of Sports,* Holt (New York, NY), 1988.
The Best American Essays, Ticknor & Fields (New York, NY), 1991.
(With Daniel Halpern) *The Sophisticated Cat: A Gathering of Stories, Poems, and Miscellaneous Writings about Cats,* Dutton (New York, NY), 1992.
The Oxford Book of American Short Stories, Oxford University Press (New York, NY), 1992.
George Bellows: American Artist, Ecco Press (New York, NY), 1995.
The Essential Dickinson, Ecco Press (New York, NY), 1996.
American Gothic Tales, Plume (New York, NY), 1996.
Story: The Art and the Craft of Narrative Fiction, Norton (New York, NY), 1997.
The Best of H. P. Lovecraft, Ecco Press (New York, NY), 1997.
(With R. V. Cassill) *The Norton Anthology of Contemporary Fiction,* Norton (New York, NY), 1997.
(Also author of introduction) *Telling Stories: An Anthology for Writers,* Norton (New York, NY), 1997.
(With Janet Berliner) *Snapshots: Twentieth-Century Mother-Daughter Fiction,* David R. Godine (Boston, MA), 2000.
The Best American Essays of the Century, Houghton (Boston, MA), 2000.
The Best New American Voices 2003, Harvest (San Diego, CA), 2002.

Also author of foreword, *Saving Graces: Images of Women in European Cemeteries,* by David Robinson, Norton (New York, NY), 1995. Contributor of fiction, poetry, and nonfiction to periodicals, including *New York Times Book Review, New York Times Magazine, New York Review of Books, New Yorker, Harper's, Times Literary Supplement, Michigan Quarterly Review, Mademoiselle, Vogue, Hudson Review, Paris Review, Grand Street, Atlantic Monthly, Poetry,* and *Esquire.* Editor, with husband, Raymond Smith, of *Ontario Review.*

Most of Oates's manuscripts, including her ongoing journal, are housed in Special Collections, Syracuse University Library.

ADAPTATIONS: Oates's short story "In the Region of Ice" was made into an Academy Award-winning short feature in the 1970s; "Daisy" was adapted for the stage by Victoria Rue and produced Off-Off-Broadway at the Cubiculo, February, 1980; the story "Where Are You Going, Where Have You Been?" was adapted for the screen as *SmoothTalk,* directed by Joyce Chopra and produced by Martin Rosen, Spectrafilm, 1981; the story "Norman and the Killer" was made into a short feature; an opera based on *Black Water* was developed by the American Music Festival Theatre, Philadelphia, with composer John Duffy, 1996; *Foxfire* was adapted as a motion picture, 1996; *Getting to Know You,* a film based on Oates's 1992 short-story collection *Heat,* was released, 2000; *We Were the Mulvaneys* was adapted as a teleplay for the Lifetime network, 2002. Some of Oates's works have been adapted for sound recordings, including the play *Black* by L.A. Theatre Works, "The Woman Who Laughed," by L.A. Theatre Works, 1994, *American Appetites,* by L.A. Theatre Works, 2000, *The Best American Essays of the Century,* 2001, *Middle Age: A Romance, Blonde,* and *Big Mouth & Ugly Girl.*

WORK IN PROGRESS: Sexy, for HarperTempest (New York, NY), 2005.

SIDELIGHTS: For over four decades, Joyce Carol Oates has produced a large body of work consisting of novels, short stories, criticism, plays, and poetry. Few living writers are as prolific as Oates, whose productivity is the cause of much commentary in the world of letters. Not a year has gone by since the mid-1960s in which she has not published at least one book; occasionally as many as three have been released in a single year. Her contributions to the field of poetry alone would be considered a significant output. "Any assessment of Oates's accomplishments should admit that the sheer quantity and range of her writing is impressive," observed a *Contemporary Novelists* essayist. The essayist added: "Oates is a writer who embarks on ambitious projects; her imagination is protean; her energies and curiosity seemingly boundless; and throughout all her writing, the reader detects her sharp intelligence, spirit of inquiry, and her zeal to tell a story."

A prodigious output means nothing if readers do not buy the books. Oates has established a reputation for consistently interesting work, ranging in genre from stories of upper-class domesticity to horror and psychological crime, but everywhere she reveals "an uncanny knack for understanding middle America, suburbia, and the temper of the times," to quote the *Contemporary Novelists* critic. Violence and victimization often feature in Oates's stories and novels, but existential questions of self-discovery abound as well. In an era of postmodernism and deconstruction, she writes in a classic mode of real people in extreme situations. As one *Publishers Weekly* reviewer put it, "Reading an Oates novel is like becoming a peeping tom, staring without guilt into the bright living rooms and dark hearts of America."

In *Book* Oates said, "I am a chronicler of the American experience. We have been historically a nation prone to violence, and it would be unreal to ignore this fact. What intrigues me is the response to violence: its aftermath in the private lives of women and children in particular." Susan Tekulve in *Book* felt that, like nineteenth-century writer Edgar Allan Poe, "Oates merges Gothic conventions with modern social and political concerns, creating stories that feel at once antique and new. But she also shares Poe's love of dark humor and a good hoax." *New York Times Book Review* correspondent Claire Dederer found the author's novels "hypnotically propulsive, written in the key of *What the Hell Is Going to Happen Next?* Oates pairs big ideas with small details in an ideal fictional balancing act, but the nice thing is that you don't really notice. You're too busy rushing on to the next page."

Oates has not limited herself to any particular genre or even to one literary style. She is equally at ease creating realistic short stories—for which she won an O. Henry Special Award for Continuing Achievement—or parodistic epics, such as the popular Gothic novels *Bellefleur, A Bloodsmoor Romance,* and *Mysteries of Winterthurn,* all published in the 1980s. She attracts readers because of her ability to spin suspenseful tales and to infuse the ordinary with terror. As Oates stated in a *Chicago Tribune Book World* discussion of her themes, "I am concerned with only one thing: the moral and social conditions of my generation." Henry Louis Gates, Jr. wrote in the *Nation* that "a future archeologist equipped with only her *oeuvre* could easily piece together the whole of postwar America."

Born into a working-class family, Oates grew up in rural Erie County, New York, spending a great deal of time at her grandparents' farm. She attended a one-room school as a child and developed a love for reading and writing at an early age. By fifteen, she had completed her first novel and submitted it for publication, only to discover that those who read it found it too depressing for younger readers. Oates graduated from Syracuse University in 1960 and earned her master's degree the following year from the University of Wisconsin. It was at Wisconsin that she met and married her husband, Raymond Joseph Smith, with whom she has edited the *Ontario Review.* The newlyweds moved to Detroit, where Oates taught at the University of Detroit between 1961 and 1967. After one of her stories was anthologized in the *Best American Short Stories,* she decided to devote herself to creative writing.

Urban issues are a major theme in Oates's writing, such as her 1969 novel *them,* which earned a National Book Award in 1970. However, her early work also reveals her preoccupation with fictitious Eden County, New York, a setting based on her childhood recollections. Betty De Ramus is quoted in the *Encyclopedia of World Biography* as saying: "Her days in Detroit did more for Joyce Carol Oates than bring her together with new people—it gave her a tradition to write from, the so-called American Gothic tradition of exaggerated horror and gloom and mysterious and violent incidents."

The novel *them* chronicles three decades, beginning in 1937, in the life of the Wendall family. The novel "is partly made up of 'composite' characters and events, clearly influenced by the disturbances of the long hot summer of 1967," Oates acknowledged. Although regarded as a self-contained work, *them* can also be considered the concluding volume in a trilogy that explores different subgroups of U.S. society. The trilogy includes *A Garden of Earthly Delights,* about the migrant poor, and *Expensive People,* about the suburban rich. The goal of all three novels, as Oates explained in the *Saturday Review,* is to present a cross-section of "unusually sensitive—but hopefully representative—young men and women, who confront the puzzle of American life in different ways and come to different ends."

A story of inescapable life cycles, *them* begins with sixteen-year-old Loretta Botsford Wendall preparing for a Saturday night date. "Anything might happen," she muses innocently, unaware of the impending tragedy. After inviting her date to bed with her, Loretta is awakened by the sound of an explosion. Still half asleep, she realizes that her boyfriend has been shot in the head by her brother. Screaming, she flees the house and runs into the street where she encounters an old acquaintance who is a policeman. Forced to become his wife in return for his help, Loretta embarks on a future of degradation and poverty. The early chapters trace Loretta's flight from her past, her move to Detroit, and her erratic relationships with her husband and other men. The rest of the book focuses on two of Loretta's children, Jules and Maureen, and their struggle to escape a second generation of violence and poverty.

New York Times reviewer John Leonard wrote, "*them,* as literature, is a reimagining, a reinventing of the urban American experience of the last thirty years, a complex and powerful novel that begins with James T. Farrell and ends in a gothic dream; of the 'fire that burns and does its duty.'" Leonard added: "*them* is really about all the private selves, accidents and casualties that add up to a public violence." *Christian Science Monitor* contributor Joanne Leedom also noted the symbolic importance that violence assumes and links it to the characters' search for freedom: "The characters live, love, and almost die in an effort to find freedom and to break out of their patterns. They balance on a precipice and peer over its edge. Though they fear they may fall, they either cannot or will not back away, for it is in the imminence of danger that they find life force. The quest in *them* is for rebirth; the means is violence; the end is merely a realignment of patterns."

Throughout the 1970s, Oates continued her exploration of American people and institutions, combining social analysis with vivid psychological portrayals: *Wonderland* probes the pitfalls of the modern medical community; *Do with Me What You Will* focuses upon the legal profession; *The Assassins: A Book of Hours* attacks the political corruption of Washington, D.C.; *Son of the Morning* traces the rise and fall of a religious zealot who thinks he's Christ; and *Unholy Loves* examines shallowness and hypocrisy within the academic community. In these and all her fiction, the frustrations and imbalance of individuals become emblematic of U.S. society as a whole.

Oates's short stories of this period exhibit similar themes, and many critics judged her stories to be her finest work. "Her style, technique, and subject matter achieve their strongest effects in this concentrated form, for the extended dialogue, minute detail, and violent action which irritate the reader after hundreds of pages are wonderfully appropriate in short fiction," *Dictionary of Literary Biography* contributor Michael Joslin observed. "Her short stories present the same violence, perversion, and mental derangement as her novels, and are set in similar locations: the rural community of Eden County, the chaotic city of Detroit, and the sprawling malls and developments of modern suburbia."

One of Oates's most popular and representative short stories is "Where Are You Going, Where Have You Been?" Frequently anthologized, the story first appeared in 1966 and is considered by many to be a masterpiece of the short form. It relates the sexual awakening of a teenage girl by a mysterious older man through circumstances that assume strange and menacing proportions; it is a study in the peril that lurks beneath the surface of everyday life.

The protagonist, fifteen-year-old Connie, is a typical teenager who argues with her mother over curfews and hair spray, dreams about romantic love with handsome boys, and regards her older, unmarried sister as a casualty. One Sunday afternoon Connie is left home alone. The afternoon begins ordinarily enough with Connie lying in the sun. "At this point," noted Greg Johnson in *Understanding Joyce Carol Oates,* "the story moves from realism into an allegorical dream-vision. Recalling a recent sexual experience as 'sweet, gentle, the way it was in movies and promised in songs,' Connie opens her eyes and 'hardly knew where she was.' Shaking her head 'as if to get awake,' she feels troubled by the sudden unreality of her surroundings, unaware—though the reader is aware—that she has entered a new and fearsome world."

Shortly afterward, a strange man about thirty years old appears in a battered gold convertible. His name is Arnold Friend. Excited by the prospect but also cautious, Connie dawdles about accepting his invitation to take a ride. Friend becomes more insistent until, suddenly, it becomes clear that Friend has no ordinary ride in mind. He makes no attempt to follow Connie as she flees into the house, but he also makes it clear that the flimsy screen door between them is no obstacle. As Mary Allen explains in *The Necessary Blankness: Women in Major American Fiction of the Sixties,* "his promise not to come in the house after her is more disturbing than a blunt demand might be, for we know he will enter when he is ready."

Oates explores another genre with her Gothic novels *Bellefleur, A Bloodsmoor Romance,* and *Mysteries of Winterthurn.* These novels are an homage to old-fashioned Gothics and were written with "great intelligence and wit," according to Jay Parini. Oates told Parini that she considers the novels "parodistic" because "they're not exactly parodies, because they take the forms they imitate quite seriously." The novels feature many of the stock elements of conventional Gothics, including ghosts, haunted mansions, and mysterious deaths. But the plots are also tied to actual events. "I set out originally to create an elaborate, baroque, barbarous metaphor for the unfathomable mysteries of the human imagination, but soon became involved in very literal events," Oates explained in the *New York Times Book Review.* Her incorporation of real history into imaginary lives lends these tales a depth that is absent from many Gothic novels. Though fanciful in form, they are serious in purpose and examine such sensitive issues as crimes against women, children, and the poor, as well as the role of family history in shaping destiny. For these reasons, Johnson believed that "the gothic elements throughout her fiction, like her use of mystical frameworks, serve the larger function of expanding the thematic scope and suggestiveness of her narratives."

Bellefleur is a five-part novel that encompasses thousands of years and explores what it means to be an American. It is the saga of the Bellefleurs, a rich and rapacious family with a "curse," who settle in the Adirondack Mountains. Interwoven with the family's tale are real people from the nineteenth century, including abolitionist John Brown and Abraham Lincoln, the latter who in the novel fakes his own assassination in order to escape the pressures of public life. In his *New York Times Book Review* assessment of the book, John Gardner wrote that its plot defies easy summarization: "It's too complex—an awesome construction, in itself a work of genius," and summarized it as "a story of the world's changeableness, of time and eternity, space and soul, pride and physicality versus love." *Los Angeles Times Book Review* contributor Stuart Schoffman called the Bellefleurs' story "an allegory for America: America the vain, the venal, the violent." Wrote *New York Times* critic Leonard: "On one level, *Bellefleur* is Gothic pulp fiction, cleverly consuming itself. . . . On another level, *Bellefleur* is fairy tale and myth, distraught literature. . . . America is serious enough for pulp and myth, Miss Oates seems to be saying, because in our greed we never understood that the Civil War really was a struggle for the possession of our soul." Oates herself has acknowledged that the book was partially conceived as a critique of "the American dream," and critics generally agreed that this dimension enhances the story, transforming the Gothic parody into serious art. Among the most generous assessments was Gardner's; he called *Bellefleur* "a symbolic summation of all this novelist has been doing for twenty-some years, a magnificent piece of daring, a tour de force of imagination and intellect."

In 1990 Oates returned to familiar themes of race and violence in *Because It Is Bitter, and Because It Is My Heart.* The story tells of a bond shared between Jinx Fairchild, a black sixteen-year-old living in the small industrial town of Hammond, New York, and Iris Courtney, a fourteen-year-old white girl who seeks help from Jinx when a town bully begins harassing her. During a scuffle, Jinx inadvertently kills the boy, and the story follows Jinx and Iris as their lives are guided by the consequences of this event. Encompassing the years 1956 to 1963, the book explores the issues of racial segregation and downward mobility as the two characters struggle to overcome their past by escaping from the confines of their hometown. "Iris and Jinx are linked by a powerful bond of secrecy, guilt and, ultimately, a kind of fateful love, which makes for a . . . compelling . . . story about the tragedy of American racism," wrote Howard Frank Mosher in the *Washington Post Book World.*

In *American Appetites,* Oates also explores life among the upper-middle class and finds it just as turbulent and destructive beneath the surface as the overtly violent lives of her poorer, urban characters. Ian and Glynnis McCullough live the illusion of a satisfying life in a sprawling suburban house made of glass, surrounded by a full social life and Glynnis's gourmet cooking. When Glynnis discovers her husband's cancelled check to a young woman they once befriended, however, the cracks in their carefully constructed lifestyle are revealed, leading to a fatal incident. *American Appetites* is a departure for Oates in that it is told in large part as a courtroom drama, but critics seem not as impressed by Oates's attempt at conveying the pretentiousness of this group of people as with her grittier tales of poverty and racism. Hermione Lee, writing in the London *Observer,* felt that the theme of Greek tragedy and its "enquiry into the human soul's control over its destiny . . . ought to be interesting, but it feels too ponderous, too insistent." Likewise, Robert Towers in the *New York Times Book Review* praised Oates's "cast of varied characters whom she makes interesting, . . . places them in scrupulously observed settings, and involves them in a complex action that is expertly sustained," but somehow they produce an effect opposite of the one intended. "We're lulled into a dreamy observation of the often dire events and passions that it records," Towers concluded. Bruce Bawer in a *Washington Post Book World* review found the device of conveying ideas "through intrusive remarks by the narrator and *dramatis personae*" ineffective and "contrived." However, Bawer suggested that although *American Appetites* conveys "no sense of tragedy . . . or of the importance of individual moral responsibility," it does "capture something of the small quiet terror of daily existence, the ever-present sense of the possibility of chaos."

Oates reconstructs a familiar scenario in her award-winning *Black Water,* a 1992 account of a tragic encounter between a powerful U.S. senator and a young woman he meets at a party. While driving to a motel, the drunken senator steers the car off a bridge into the dark water of an East Coast river, and although he is able to escape, he leaves the young woman to drown. The events parallel those of Senator Edward Kennedy's fatal plunge at Chappaquiddick in 1969 that left a young campaign worker dead, but Oates updates the story and sets it twenty years later. Told from the point of view of the drowning woman, the story "portrays an individual fate, born out of the protagonist's character and driven forward by the force of events," according to Richard Bausch in the *New York Times Book Review.* Bausch called Oates's effort "taut, powerfully imagined and beautifully written . . . it continues to haunt us." A tale that explores the sexual power inherent in politics, *Black Water* is not only concerned with the historical event it recalls but also with the sexual-political power dynamics that erupted over Clarence Thomas's nomination for Supreme Court Justice in the early 1990s. It is a fusion of "the instincts of political and erotic conquest," wrote Richard Eder in the *Los Angeles Times Book Review.*

Oates's 1993 novel *Foxfire: Confessions of a Girl Gang* recounts in retrospect the destructive sisterhood of a group of teenage girls in the 1950s. The story is pieced together from former Foxfire gang member Maddy Wirtz's memories and journal and once again takes place in the industrial New York town of Hammond. The gang, led by the very charismatic and very angry Legs Sadovsky, chooses their enemy—men—the force that Legs perceives as responsible for the degradation and ruin of their mothers and friends. The girls celebrate their bond to one another by branding each others' shoulders with tattoos. But as they lash out with sex and violence against teachers and father figures, they "become demons themselves—violent and conniving and exuberant in their victories over the opposite sex," wrote *Los Angeles Times Book Review* contributor Cynthia Kadohata. Although Oates acknowledged to *New York Times Book Review* critic Lynn Karpen that *Foxfire* is her most overtly feminist book, she wanted to show that though "the bond of sisterhood can be very deep and emotionally gratifying," it is a fleeting, fragile bond.

In portraying the destructive escapades of these 1950s teenagers, Oates is "articulating the fantasies of a whole generation," remarked *Times Literary Supplement* contributor Lorna Sage, "putting words to what they didn't quite do." Likening the book to a myth, Oates told Karpen that *Foxfire* "is supposed to be a kind of dialectic between romance and realism." Provoking fights, car chases, and acts of vandalism, the Foxfire gang leaves their mark on the gray town—antics that get Legs sent to reform school, "where she learns that women are sometimes the enemy, too," noted Kadohata. *New York Times Book Review* critic John Crowley likened the novel to a Romantic myth whose hero is more compelling than most of the teen-angst figures of the 1950s. Legs, Crowley noted, is "wholly convincing, racing for her tragic consummation impelled by a finer sensibility and a more thoughtful daring than is usually granted to the tragic male outlaws we love and need."

Sexual violence invades another upstate New York family in Oates's *We Were the Mulvaneys,* published in 1996. In sharp contrast to the isolated, emotionally impoverished family introduced in *First Love,* the Mulvaneys are well-known, high-profile members of their community: Michael Mulvaney is a successful roofing contractor and his wife, Corinne, dabbles at an antiques business. As told by Judd, the youngest of the three promising Mulvaney sons, the family comes unraveled after seventeen-year-old Marianne is raped by a fellow high school student. Ashamed of his daughter's "fall from grace," proud and patriarchal Michael banishes her to the home of a relative, an action that drives him to the drunken state that results in the loss of home and job. Meanwhile, other family members succumb to their individual demons. The saga of a family's downfall is uplifted by more positive changes a decade later, which come as a relief to readers who identify with the Mulvaneys as compelling representatives of the contemporary American middle class.

Although, as with much of her fiction, Oates has denied any autobiographical basis for *We Were the Mulvaneys* other than a familiarity with the northern New York setting and once owning a cat answering to the description of the title family's household pet, the creative process involved in creating the novel is almost as evocative as personal experience. "Writing a long novel is very emotionally involving," Oates told Thomas J. Brady in the *Philadelphia Inquirer.* "I'm just emotionally stunned for a long time after writing one." *We Were the Mulvaneys,* which at 454 pages in length qualifies as "long," took many months of note-taking, followed by ten months of writing, according to its author. After being chosen by Oprah Winfrey as one of her book club editions, the novel became the first of Oates's works to top the *New York Times* best-seller list.

Throughout her prolific writing career Oates has distributed her vast creative and emotional energies between several projects at once, simultaneously producing novels, stories, verse, and essays, among other writings. In her 1995 horror novel, *Zombie,* she seductively draws readers into the mind of a serial killer on the order of Jeffrey Dahmer. While straying from fact far enough to avoid the more heinous aspects of Dahmer-like acts, Oates plugs readers directly into the reality of her fictitious protagonist, Quentin P., who "exists in a haze of fantasies blurred by drugs and alcohol and by his inherent mental condition of violent and frenzied desires, thoughts and obsessions," according to *New York Times Book Review* critic Steven Marcus. Through the twisted experimentation on young men (involving, among other things, an ice pick) that Quentin hopes will enable him to create a zombie-like companion who will remain loyal to him forever, Oates "is certain to shock and surely to offend many readers," warned *Tribune Books* critic James Idema, "but there could be no gentler way to tell the story she obviously was compelled to tell."

Within her nonfiction writing, Oates's foray into sports philosophy resulted in the book-length essay *On Boxing,* which led to at least one television appearance as a commentator for the sport. She also submitted a mystery novel to a publisher under a pseudonym and had the thrill of having it accepted before word leaked out that it was Oates's creation. Inspired by her husband's name, in 1988 Oates published the novel *Lives of the Twins* under the name Rosamond Smith. "I wanted a fresh reading; I wanted to escape from my own identity," Linda Wolfe quoted Oates as saying in the *New York Times Book Review.* She would use the Smith pseudonym again for several more mystery novels, including *Soul/Mate,* a story about a lovesick psycho-killer, *Nemesis,* another mystery concerning aberrational academics, and *Snake Eyes,* a tale of a tattooed psychopathic artist.

Oates's 1997 novel *Man Crazy* is a reverse image of *Zombie;* it tells the first-person story of a "pathological serial victim," Ingrid Boone, who through a rag-tag childhood, a promiscuous and drugged-out adolescence, and a stint with a satanic motorcycle cult, has her personal identity nearly destroyed. *New York Review of Books* critic A. O. Scott commented that Oates "continually seeks out those places in our social, familial and personal lives where love and cruelty intersect. . . . Oates is clearly interested in exploring the boundary between a world where cruelty lurks below the surface of daily life and one in which daily life consists of overt and constant brutality."

Published in 2000, one of Oates's most successful novels to date is *Blonde,* a fictional re-working of the life of Marilyn Monroe. Oates told a writer at *Publishers Weekly* that, while she was not intent upon producing another historical document on the tragic star, she did want to show "what she was like from the inside." According to some critics, Oates was successful in her endeavor. *Booklist* contributor Donna Seaman commented that the author "liberates the real woman behind the mythological creature called Marilyn Monroe." A *Publishers Weekly* reviewer found the novel "dramatic, provocative and unsettlingly suggestive," adding that Oates "creates a striking and poignant portrait of the mythic star and the society that made and failed her." In *World Literature Today,* Rita D. Jacobs concluded that *Blonde* "makes the reader feel extraordinarily empathetic toward the character Marilyn Monroe and her longing for acceptance and a home of her own."

Oates's first published works were short stories, and she has continued to pen them throughout her career. Her collections of short fiction alone amount to more work than many writers finish in a lifetime. A *Publishers Weekly* reviewer remarked that with her short works Oates has "established herself as the nation's literary Weegee, prowling the mean streets of the American mind and returning with gloriously lurid takes on our midnight obsessions." Whether in macabre horror stories such as those in *The Collector of Hearts: New Tales of the Grotesque* or in realistic works such as those found in *Faithless: Tales of Transgression,* Oates offers "a map of the mind's dark places," wrote *New York Times Book Review* contributor Margot Livesey. *Orlando Sentinel* correspondent Mary Ann Horne stated that in *Faithless,* Oates "does what she does best . . . delving into the dark areas of ordinary consciousness, bringing back startling images from the undercurrent of modern fears and secrets."

Oates uses secrets as a diving board for her exploration of a small town's psyche in *Middle Age: A Romance,* published in 2001. The book opens with the drowning death of sculptor Adam Brandt as he tries to rescue a child. His death becomes a catalyst for the residents of Salthill-on-Hudson, New York. Adam's former lovers begin to investigate his life, dissatisfied husbands become inspired to finally leave, and singles find their soul mates. In *Booklist,* Carol Haggas approved of the title: "Few caught in the throes of middle age would categorize it as 'romantic,' yet what makes Oates's characters romantic is how well they fare on their journeys of personal reinvention and whether they, and the reader, enjoy the trip." While the book received some criticism for lack of a linear plot, *New York Times* critic Claire Dederer viewed that as a strength of Oates's writing. "Naked of a compelling plot, in a strange sense Oates's remarkable ability is clearer than ever. We have time to notice the careful construction of theme, the attention to a cohesive philosophy, the resonant repetition of detail." More than one reviewer noted that the ending of *Middle Age* proves more redemptive than most of Oates's previous fictions. As Beth Kephart summarized in *Book,* "There is light, a lot of it, at the end of this long book." A *Publishers Weekly* contributor concluded it is "reminiscent of her powerful *Black Water,* but equipped with a happy ending, Oates's latest once more confirms her mastery of the form." *St. Louis Post-Dispatch* reviewer Lee Ann Sandweiss likewise noted that *Middle Age* is "Oates's most compassionate and life-affirming work to date. . . . This novel establishes, beyond any doubt, that Joyce Carol Oates is not only [one of] America's most prolific writers but also one of our most gifted."

From the introspection of middle age, Oates moved to the self-discovery of early adulthood in *I'll Take You There.* Called her most autobiographical novel to date, the book deals with an unnamed protagonist as she comes of age at Syracuse University in the early 1960s. Like Oates, "Anellia" (as she calls herself) is raised on a farm in western New York state and is the first in her family to go to college. Anellia cloaks herself in guilt and low self-esteem, bequeathed to her by her brothers and father. They blame her for her mother's death from cancer developed shortly after Anellia was born. Desperate for a mother figure and female companionship, the poor Anellia joins a snobby, bigoted sorority where she seems to be singled out for torment because of her finances and lack of grooming. She feels special pain from the antagonistic relationship she has with the sorority's British housemother, Mrs. Thayer. She uncovers Mrs. Thayer's excessive drinking and both of them are forced to leave the house, humiliated.

Still desperate for love and affection, she starts an affair with African-American philosophy graduate student Vernon Matheius. Vernon is intent on ignoring the civil rights struggles of the times, believing that philosophy is his personal salvation. Their relationship is categorized by discord and Anellia also snoops through his life and uncovers the fact that he has a wife and children he is denying. As Anellia deals with the fallout from her discovery and her separation from Vernon, she receives word that her father, who she thought dead, is dying in Utah. She travels west to be with him at his bedside, hoping to gain a sense of familial kinship. In a twist of irony, she is not allowed to look directly at her father, but steals a glimpse of him through a mirror, which kills him from distress when he sees her.

Critics and fans described *I'll Take You There* as a hallmark of Oates's consistent excellence in style, form, and theme. *Los Angeles Times Book Review* critic Stanley Crouch praised Oates's "masterful strength of the form, the improvisational attitude toward sentence structure and the foreshadowing, as well as the deft use of motifs." Even perceived weaknesses by some critics are regarded by others as quintessential Oatesian mechanics. In Rachel Collins's review for *Library Journal,* she questioned the heavy use of characterization and psychological backgrounding that takes place in about the first 100 pages. A *Publisher's Weekly* reviewer reflected that "Oates's fans will be pleased by the usual care with which she goes about constructing the psychology of Anellia and Vernon." Collins went on to call the book "a bit formulaic," noting that the romance between Anellia and Vernon lacks "the intense sexual energy present in Oates's other works." *Booklist* contributor Donna Seaman wrote that the scenes with Anellia and Vernon are "intense and increasingly psychotic" and Oates's "eroticism verges on the macabre and the masochistic." Vicky Hutchings in the *New Statesman* concluded the book is neither "depressing nor dull, but full of edgy writing as well as mordant wit."

Published in 2003, *The Tattooed Girl* is the story of thirty-nine-year-old writer Joshua Seigl, who has been diagnosed with a debilitating nerve condition. In need of an assistant, he interviews and rejects a number of graduate students, and impulsively hires the vacuous Alma Busch. While it seems like an act of charity, Seigl is increasingly patronizing to Alma, thinking that he has "rescued" her. Alma is described as dim-witted and slow, suffering from a lack of self-esteem and scarred by past sexual trauma, which resulted in the crude tattoo on her face. Seigl, of course, is unaware of Alma's anti-Semitism, which is born of her disfigurement and fueled by her sadistic waiter boyfriend, Dmitri Meatte. As Seigl's health deteriorates, Alma gains psychological strength to sabotage Seigl's health, finances, and mental well-being and eventually hatches a plan to take his life.

While a *Kirkus Reviews* contributor called *The Tattooed Girl* "better-than-average Oates," some reviewers found the characterization of Seigl, Alma, and Dmitri inconsistent. *New York Times* writer Michiko Kakutani said, "The novel gets off to a subtle and interesting start. . . . Oates's keen eye for psychological detail seems to be fully engaged in these pages." Yet she argued that "the attention to emotional detail evinced in the novel's opening pages—in which she limned Seigl's fears of mortality and his anxieties about his family and work—evaporates by the middle of the book, replaced by horror-movie plots and cartoony characters." In the *New York Times Book Review* Sophie Harrison noted that Alma, Seigl, and Dmitri's actions "contradict their given characters, and the irony doesn't always feel intentional." The *Kirkus Reviews* contributor observed that "Oates is onto something with the bruised, malleable figure of Alma," but the secondary figures of Dmitri and Seigl's hypomaniac sister Jet "have nothing like its principal's realness." Even so, Oates continued to receive praise for her style, including a review in *Booklist* which described *The Tattooed Girl* as a "mesmerizing, disturbing tale" told with "her usual cadenced grace."

Also published in 2003 was Oates's second book for young adult readers, *Small Avalanches and Other Stories,* in which she reprises some of her previously published short stories for adults as well as new material. The twelve stories all deal with young people taking risks and dealing with their consequences. As with her adult fiction, Oates maintains her dark tone. *School Library Journal* reviewer Allison Follos observed, "The stories have a slow, deliberate, and unsettling current." James Neal Webb on the *BookPage* Web site echoed that "Oates's trademark is her ability to tap, uncontrived, into the danger that's implicit in everyday life."

In addition to her fiction and poetry, Oates lays claim to a large body of critical essays, ranging in subject matter from literature and politics to sports and quality of life. Although she has said that she does not write quickly, she also has admitted to a driving discipline that keeps her at her desk for long hours. In an era of computers, she continues to write her first drafts in longhand and then to type them on conventional typewriters. She told *Writer:* "Writing to me is very instinctive and natural. It has something to do with my desire to memorialize what I know of the world. The act of writing is a kind of description of an inward or spiritual reality that is otherwise inaccessible. I love transcribing this; there's a kind of passion to it."

BIOGRAPHICAL AND CRITICAL SOURCES:

BOOKS

Allen, Mary, *The Necessary Blankness: Women in Major American Fiction of the Sixties,* University of Illinois Press (Champaign, IL), 1974.

Authors and Artists for Young Adults, Gale (Detroit, MI), Volume 15, 1987, Volume 52, 2003.

Beacham's Guide to Literature for Young Adults, Volume 11, Gale (Detroit, MI).

Bender, Eileen, *Joyce Carol Oates,* Indiana University Press (Bloomington, IN), 1987.

Bloom, Harold, editor, *Modern Critical Views: Joyce Carol Oates,* Chelsea House (New York, NY), 1987.

Concise Dictionary of American Literary Biography: Broadening Views, 1968-1988, Gale (Detroit, MI), 1989.

Contemporary Literary Criticism, Gale (Detroit, MI), Volume 1, 1973, Volume 2, 1974, Volume 3, 1975, Volume 6, 1976, Volume 9, 1978, Volume 11, 1979, Volume 15, 1980, Volume 19, 1981, Volume 33, 1985, Volume 52, 1989, Volume 108, 1998.

Contemporary Novelists, St. James Press (Detroit, MI), 2001.

Contemporary Poets, St. James Press (Detroit, MI), 1996.

Contemporary Popular Writers, St. James Press (Detroit, MI), 1997.

Daly, Brenda O., *Lavish Self-Divisions: The Novels of Joyce Carol Oates,* University Press of Mississippi (Jackson, MS), 1996.

Dictionary of Literary Biography, Gale (Detroit, MI), Volume 2: *American Novelists since World War II,* 1978, Volume 5: *American Poets since World War II,* 1980, Volume 130, *American Short Story Writers since World War II,* 1993.

Dictionary of Literary Biography Yearbook: 1981, Gale (Detroit, MI), 1982.

Encyclopedia of World Biography, 2nd edition, Gale (Detroit, MI), 1998.

Encyclopedia of World Literature in the Twentieth Century, St. James Press (Detroit, MI), 1999.

Feminist Writers, St. James Press (Detroit, MI), 1996.

Johnson, Greg, *Understanding Joyce Carol Oates,* University of South Carolina Press (Columbia, SC), 1987.

Johnson, Greg, *Joyce Carol Oates: A Study of the Short Fiction,* Twayne (Boston, MA), 1994.

Johnson, Greg, *Invisible Writer: A Biography of Joyce Carol Oates,* Dutton (New York, NY), 1998.

Mayer, Sigrid, and Martha Hanscom, *The Reception of Joyce Carol Oates's and Gabriele Wohlmann's Short Fiction,* Camden House (Columbia, SC), 1998.

Modern American Literature, 5th edition, St. James Press (Detroit, MI), 1997.

Reference Guide to American Literature, 4th edition, St. James Press (Detroit, MI), 1999.

Reference Guide to Short Fiction, 2nd edition, St. James Press (Detroit, MI), 1999.

St. James Guide to Horror, Ghost, and Gothic Writers, St. James Press (Detroit, MI), 1998.

Short Story Criticism, Volume 6, Gale (Detroit, MI), 1990.

Twentieth-Century Culture: American Culture after World War II, Gale (Detroit, MI), 1994.

Twentieth-Century Romance and Historical Writers, 2nd edition, St. James Press (Detroit, MI), 1990.

Wagner, Linda W., editor, *Joyce Carol Oates: The Critical Reception,* G. K. Hall (Boston, MA), 1979.

Waller, G. F., *Dreaming America: Obsession and Transcendence in the Fiction of Joyce Carol Oates,* Louisiana State University Press (Baton Rouge, LA), 1979.

Watanabe, Nancy Ann, *Love Eclipsed: Joyce Carol Oates's Faustian Moral Vision,* University Press of America (Lanham, MD), 1997.

PERIODICALS

America, March 16, 1996, p. 18; November 17, 2003, Richard Fusco, review of *A Garden of Earthly Delights,* p. 19.

American Literature, September, 1997, p. 642.

Atlanta Journal-Constitution, December 16, 2001, Michael Upchurch, "*Middle Age* Full of Lingering Expectations," p. C5.

Atlantic Monthly, October, 1969; December, 1973; September, 1997, p. 118.

Book, March, 2001, Susan Tekulve, review of *Faithless: Tales of Transgression,* p. 70; May, 2001, Kristin Kloberdanz, "Joyce Carol Oates," p. 42; November-December, 2001, Beth Kephart, review of *Middle Age: A Romance,* p. 65.

Booklist, April 15, 1998, Brad Hooper, review of *My Heart Laid Bare,* p. 1357; July, 1999, Donna Seaman, review of *Where I've Been, and Where I'm*

Going: Essays, Reviews, and Prose, p. 1917; January 1, 2000, Donna Seaman, review of *Blonde,* p. 835; February 1, 2001, Donna Seaman, review of *Faithless,* p. 1020; July, 2001, Carol Haggas, review of *Middle Age,* p. 1952; October 1, 2001, Donna Seaman, review of *Beasts,* p. 300; August, 2002, Donna Seaman, review of *I'll Take You There,* p.1886; March 1, 2003, Joanne Wilkenson, review of *The Tattooed Girl,* p.1108

Chicago Tribune Book World, September 30, 1979; July 27, 1980; January 11, 1981; August 16, 1981; February 26, 1984; August 12, 1984; January 13, 1985; February 23, 1986.

Choice, March, 1997, p. 1160.

Christian Century, January 13, 2004, p. 7.

Christian Science Monitor, October 30, 1969.

Detroit News, January 15, 1964; May 21, 1972; November 13, 1977; July 27, 1980; October 11, 1981; October 17, 19982; March 11, 1984; February 3, 1985.

Entertainment Weekly, June 20, 2003, review of *The Tattooed Girl,* p. 78; January 9, 2004, Gillian Flynn, review of *Rape: A Love Story,* p. 83.

Globe and Mail (Toronto, Ontario, Canada), February 11, 1984; April 25, 1987.

Kirkus Reviews, December 15, 2002, review of *I'll Take You There,* p.1855; April 1, 2003, review of *The Tattooed Girl,* p. 501.

Library Journal, August 1996, p. 113; August, 1999, Nancy Patterson Shires, review of *Where I've Been, and Where I'm Going,* p. 89; August, 2000, Mary Jones, review of *The Best American Essays of the Century,* p. 102; April 1, 2001, Caroline Mann, review of *The Barrens,* p. 133; July, 2001, Rebecca Bollen, review of *Faithless,* p. 74; August, 2001, Josh Cohen, review of *Middle Age,* p. 164; September 15, 2001, Rochelle Ratner, review of *We Were the Mulvaneys,* p. 130; October 1, 2001, review of *Beasts,* p. 143; September 15, 2002, Rachel Collins, review of *I'll Take You There,* p. 93.

Los Angeles Times, April 2, 1981; February 18, 1986; October 13, 1986; November 7, 1986; August 7, 1987; January 31, 1988; July 21, 1988; December 9, 1988; April 16, 1990l April 15, 2003, Josh Cohen, review of *The Tattooed Girl,* p. 126; October 1, 2003, Marianne Orme, review of *The Faith of a Writer: Life, Craft, Art,* p. 75; January, 2004, Josh Cohen, review of *Rape,* p. 159; February 1, 2004, Joshua Cohen, review of *I Am No One You Know,* p. 126; March 1, 2004, Rochelle Ratner, review of *The Tattooed Girl,* p. 126.

Los Angeles Times Book Review, August 12, 1980; September 19, 1982; January 8, 1984; September 30, 1984; January 6, 1985; March 1, 1987; August 16, 1987; January 15, 1989; May 10, 1992; August 22, 1993; October 22, 1995, p. 6; January 26, 2003, Stanley Crouch, "Picking Up Where Faulkner Left Off," p.3.

Nation, July 2, 1990, pp. 27-29.

New Leader, January-February, 2002, Brooke Allen, review of *Beasts,* p. 28.

Newsmakers, Issue 4, 2000.

New Statesman, January 27, 2003, Vicky Hutchings, review of *I'll Take You There,* p.55; January 19, 2004, Helena Echlin, review of *The Tattooed Girl,* p. 55.

Newsweek, September 29, 1969; March 23, 1970; August 17, 1981; September 20, 1982; February 6, 1984; January 21, 1985; March 24, 1986; March 9, 1987; August 17, 1987; April 10, 2000, David Gates, "Goodbye, Norma Jeane," p. 76.

New Yorker, December 6, 1969; October 15, 1973; October 5, 1981; September 27, 1982; February 27, 1984.

New York Review of Books, December 17, 1964; January 2, 1969; October 21, 1971; January 24, 1974; October 21, 1982; August 16, 1990; December 21, 1995, p. 32; September 15, 1996, p. 11; September 21, 1997, p. 10.

New York Times, September 5, 1967; December 7, 1968; October 1, 1969; October 16, 1971; June 12, 1972; October 15, 1973; July 20, 1980; August 6, 1981; September 18, 1982; February 10, 1984; January 10, 1985; February 20, 1986; February 10, 1987; March 2, 1987; March 4, 1987; August 10, 1987; April 23, 1988; December 21, 1988; March 30, 1990; August 29, 2003, Michiko Kakutani, "Child of Hell Is Plague on His House."

New York Times Book Review, November 10, 1963; October 25, 1964; September 10, 1967; November 3, 1968; September 28, 1969; October 25, 1970; October 24, 1971; July 9, 1972; April 1, 1973; October 14, 1973; August 31, 1975; November 26, 1978; April 29, 1979; July 15, 1979; October 7, 1979; July 20, 1980; January 4, 1981; March 29, 1981; August 16, 1981; July 11, 1982; September 5, 1982; February 12, 1984; August 5, 1984; January 20, 1985; August 11, 1985; March 2, 1986; October 5, 1986; March 15, 1987; August 16, 1987; January 3, 1988; October 2, 1988; January 1, 1989; January 15, 1989; June 4, 1989, p. 16; May 10, 1992; August 15, 1993; February 13, 1994, p. 34; October 16, 1994, p. 7; October 8,

1995, p. 13; March 10, 1996, p. 7; March 7, 1999, Margot Livesey, "Jellyfish for Dinner Again?," p. 29; September 16, 2001, Claire Dederer, "AARP Recruits," p. 7; January 6, 2002, Amy Benfer, review of *Beasts,* p. 16; May 19, 2002, Lois Metzger, review of *Big Mouth & Ugly Girl,* p. 32; July 13, 2003, Sophie Harrison, "Now I Have Saved Her," p.15.

New York Times Magazine, July 27, 1980; January 3, 1988.

Observer (London, England), August 27, 1989.

Orlando Sentinel, June 27, 2001, Mary Ann Horne, review of *Faithless.*

Philadelphia Inquirer, January 26, 1997.

PR Newswire, April 27, 2003, "PNC Honors Five Giants in the Arts, Science and Public Service," p. PHSA00127042003.

Publishers Weekly, June 24, 1996, p. 44; August 5, 1996, p. 430; April 20, 1998, review of *My Heart Laid Bare,* p. 45; May 17, 1999, review of *Broke Heart Blues,* p. 55; June 28, 1999, review of *Where I've Been, and Where I'm Going,* p. 68; February 14, 2000, review of *Blonde,* p. 171, "PW Talks with Joyce Carol Oates," p. 172; June 5, 2000, review of *Blonde,* p. 61; January 29, 2001, review of *Faithless,* p. 65; March 26, 2001, review of *The Barrens,* p. 60; August 13, 2001, review of *Middle Age,* p. 284; October 22, 2001, review of *Beasts,* p. 43; April 22, 2002, review of *Big Mouth & Ugly Girl,* p. 71; August 26, 2002, Rachel Collins, review of *I'll Take you There,* p. 93; September 30, 2002, review of *Best New American Voices 2003,* p. 51; February 10, 2003, review of *Small Avalanches and Other Stories,* p. 189; April 21, 2003, review of *The Tattooed Girl,* p. 36; September 15, 2003, Kate Pavao, "PW Talks with Joyce Carol Oates," p. 65, and review of *Freaky Green Eyes,* p. 66; November 24, 2003, review of *Rape,* p. 41; February 2, 2004, review of *I Am No One You Know,* p. 57.

St. Louis Post-Dispatch, September 9, 2001, Lee Ann Sandweiss, "Oates's Latest Is Absorbing, Life-Affirming," p. H10.

Saturday Review, October 26, 1963; November 28, 1964; August 5, 1967; October 26, 1968; November 22, 1969; October 24, 1970; June 10, 1972; November 4, 1972; August, 1981; March-April, 1985.

School Library Journal, July, 2003, Allison Follos, review of *Small Avalanches and Other Stories,* p. 134.

Time, January 3, 1964; November 1, 1968; October 26, 1970; August 25, 1980; August 17,1981; October 4, 1982; February 23, 1987; August 31, 1987; January 9, 1989; April 17, 2000, Paul Gray, "The Anatomy of an Icon," p. 82.

Times Literary Supplement, June 4, 1970; January 11, 1974; September 12, 1980; March 20, 1981; January 29, 1982; January 28, 1983; July 20, 1984; March 22, 1985; October 18, 1985; January 16, 1987; December 18, 1987; February 14, 1988; September 15, 1989; August 13, 1993, p. 19.

Tribune Books (Chicago, IL), March 1, 1987; July 19, 1987; April 18, 1988; December 18, 1988; April 15, 1990; March 10, 1996; November 5, 1996, pp. 3, 5.

Washington Post Book World, February 22, 1981; August 16, 1981; September 30, 1984; January 6, 1985; February 23, 1986; November 30, 1986; March 8, 1987; January 8, 1989; April 8, 1990.

World Literature Today, autumn, 1996, pp. 959-960; winter, 2001, Rita D. Jacobs, review of *Blonde,* p. 115; summer, 2003, James Knudson, review of *Faithless,* p. 92.

Writer, October, 2001, "Joyce Carol Oates," p. 66; January, 2004, Chuck Leddy, review of *The Faith of a Writer,* p. 45.

Writer's Digest, February, 2001, Katie Struckel, "Find Identity with Joyce Carol Oates," p. 22.

ONLINE

BookPage, http://www.bookpage.com/ (September 1, 2003), James Neal Webb, review of *Small Avalanches and Other Stories.**

* * *

O'CONNELL, Jack 1959-

PERSONAL: Born December 25, 1959, in Worcester, MA; son of James W. (in business) and Eileen C. (a registered nurse; maiden name, Hackett) O'Connell; married Nancy Murphy (a school psychologist), July 8, 1982. *Education:* College of the Holy Cross, B.A., 1981.

ADDRESSES: Home—91 Longfellow Rd., Worcester, MA 01602. *Office*—554 Pleasant St., Worcester, MA 01602. *Agent*—Nat Sobel, Sobel Weber Associates Inc., 146 East Nineteenth St., New York, NY 10003.

CAREER: Jim O'Connell Insurance Agency, Worcester, MA, beginning 1981; writer.

AWARDS, HONORS: Mysterious Discovery Award, Warner Books/Mysterious Press, 1991.

WRITINGS:

Box Nine (novel), Warner Books/Mysterious Press (New York, NY), 1992.
Wireless, Mysterious Press (New York, NY), 1993.
The Skin Palace, Mysterious Press (New York, NY), 1996.
Word Made Flesh, Harper Flamingo (New York, NY), 1999.

Contributor of short stories to periodicals, including *New England Review.*

SIDELIGHTS: Jack O'Connell writes genre-bending, literate noir thrillers set in the fictitious Massachusetts city of Quinsigamond. Often suffused with dream imagery and subtle nods to postmodernism, O'Connell's stories nonetheless exhibit the conventional techniques of the thriller: unexpected plot twists, obsession with the seedy and unspeakable, and heroes who must examine themselves in order to solve crimes or save their skins. "I take characters who I genuinely care about and I put them in a pressure cooker."

O'Connell won the Mysterious Discovery Award for his first novel, *Box Nine,* the story of a female detective who seeks the purveyors of a drug that causes murderous rages. His second book, *Wireless,* explores the world of radio "jammers" who target controversial talk show hosts for death. A *Publishers Weekly* reviewer noted that the book is peopled by "the weirdest collection of dysfunctional oddballs this side of TV's *Twin Peaks.*" In *The Skin Palace,* an experimental photographer and a filmmaker with ties to the mob chart a path to each other through a labyrinth of pornographers, evangelists, and feral children. "This dense, illusory novel will propel readers into a dreamlike state," observed *Booklist* reviewer Wes Lukowsky. The reviewer also found the work "intensely" compelling.

Word Made Flesh had its advent as one of O'Connell's simplest narratives, but over the course of its production the author brought many literary influences to bear upon plot and sensibility. "This dense allegorical novel rigorously moves through an unfamiliar, labyrinthine dystopia, but eventually the puzzle pieces fall into place," maintained a *Publishers Weekly* reviewer. The story, once again set in Quinsigamond, revolves around a sadistic book collector and a hapless ex-detective who collide during the course of a murder investigation. *Booklist* correspondent Thomas Gaughan called *Word Made Flesh* "a wildly original novel" enhanced by O'Connell's "gracefully orotund narrative style."

In the *Worcester Phoenix,* Laura Kiritsy described O'Connell's Quinsigamond as "a city filled with shady dealings that take place in the dark shadows of decrepit factory buildings, all-night diners, and seedy nightclubs. Corruption, madness, and murder are not merely the ills of urban living, they are lifestyle choices. Inhabited by exiles, misfits, crooks, and the criminally insane, Quinsigamond is brewing with people who have some sordid tale that they're (sometimes literally) dying to tell, and it seems that words just aren't sufficient to get the point across." O'Connell does not deny that his fictional city has been influenced by his lifelong residence in Worcester, Massachusetts, but he is quick to add that all of his work is filtered through a fertile imagination. "I don't plug the nuts and bolts of my city into my book," he explained in an interview with *Crime Time.* "Instead, I let my imagination warp the city, enlarge it. I pillage its DNA and radiate it until it glows neon." Elsewhere in the same interview he said: "I see my books as transcriptions of what I call the dreamlife. Books are visions, even when they're banal visions. They come into the world by way of an obsessive process wherein compulsive individuals spend inordinate amounts of time in self-imposed solitary confinement, hearing voices and transcribing those voices."

BIOGRAPHICAL AND CRITICAL SOURCES:

PERIODICALS

Booklist, January 1, 1996, Wes Lukowsky, review of *The Skin Palace,* p. 797; April 15, 1999, Thomas Gaughan, review of *Word Made Flesh,* p. 1483.
Magazine of Fantasy and Science Fiction, April, 2000, James Sallis, review of *Word Made Flesh,* p. 36.
New York Times Book Review, February 2, 1992, Marilyn Stasio, review of *Box Nine,* p. 19; January 7, 1996, Marilyn Stasio, review of *The Skin Palace,* p. 24.

Publishers Weekly, November 15, 1991, review of *Box Nine,* p. 66; September 20, 1993, review of *Wireless,* p. 64; October 30, 1995, review of *The Skin Palace,* p. 47; May 3, 1999, review of *Word Made Flesh,* p. 67.

ONLINE

Crime Time, http://www.crimetime.co.uk/interviews/jackoconnell.html/ (April 11, 2003), interview with author.

Worcester Phoenix, http://www.worcesterphoenix.com/ (August 27, 1999), Laura Kiritsy, "Grime Story: Descending into Quinsigamond in Jack O'Connell's *Word Made Flesh* Is One Scary Taxi Ride."*

* * *

OLSON, Keith W(aldemar) 1931-

PERSONAL: Born August 4, 1931, in Poughkeepsie, NY; son of Ernest Waldemar and Elin (Rehnstrom) Olson; married Marilyn Wittschen, September 10, 1955; children: Paula, Judy. *Ethnicity:* "Caucasian." *Education:* State University of New York, Albany, B.A., 1957, M.A., 1959; University of Wisconsin, Ph. D., 1964. *Politics:* "Registered independent but with rare exception vote Democratic." *Religion:* Unitarian Universalist. *Hobbies and other interests:* Swedish culture, camping.

ADDRESSES: *Home*—10746 Kinloch Rd., Silver Springs, MD 20903. *Office*—Department of History, University of Maryland, College Park, MD 20746. *E-mail*—ko6@umail.umd.edu.

CAREER: Syracuse University, Syracuse, NY, taught in department of history, 1963-66; University of Maryland, College Park, 1966—, became professor of history. Appearances on radio and television regarding presidential history in the twentieth century. *Military service:* U.S. Army, Finance Corps, 1952-54.

MEMBER: American Historical Association, Organization of American Historians, American-Scandinavian Foundation, State Historical Society of Wisconsin, Swedish-American Historical Society, Center for the Study of the Presidency, Society of Historians of American Foreign Relations, Finnish Historical Society (honorary member).

AWARDS, HONORS: Runner-up, Frederick Jackson Turner Prize, Organization of American Historians, for *The G.I. Bill, the Veterans, and the Colleges*; Fulbright fellow, 1986-87, 1993-94; twice recipient of outstanding teaching awards, Panhellenic Association. Honorary doctorate, University of Tampere, Finland, 2000.

WRITINGS:

The G.I. Bill, the Veterans, and the Colleges, University Press of Kentucky (Lexington, KY), 1974.

Biography of a Progressive, Franklin K. Lane, 1864-1921, Greenwood Press (Westport, CT), 1979.

Watergate: The Presidential Scandal That Shook America, University Press of Kansas (Lawrence, KS), 2003.

Contributor to books, including *Encyclopedia Americana, Oxford Companion to United States History,* the *Eleanor Roosevelt Encyclopedia, American National Biography, American-Historic Sites, Encyclopedia USA, Encyclopedia of World War I,* the *Harry S. Truman Encyclopedia,* the *Historical Dictionary of the Progressive Era, Government Agencies, Great Lives from History: American Series, The Human Tradition in America since 1945, In Search of a Continent: A North American Studies Odyssey, After Consensus, The Road to War, Charting an Independent Course: Finland's Place in the Cold War and in U.S. Foreign Policy,* and *The Encyclopedia of American Political History.* Contributor to periodicals, including *American Quarterly, Historian, Wisconsin Magazine of History, Wilson Quarterly, Mid-America, Educational Record,* and *Progressive.* Contributor of book reviews for *Washington Star,* 1966-70.

WORK IN PROGRESS: Research on Dwight D. Eisenhower and civil rights.

SIDELIGHTS: A professor of twentieth-century U.S. history at the University of Maryland, Keith W. Olson is the author of several well-received works of history. In his 1974 title *The G.I. Bill, the Veterans, and the*

Colleges, he details the educational benefits accruing to veterans as a result of the G.I. Bill, and the impact such a state-sponsored educational program had on colleges and universities around the country. Olson examines Progressivism in politics in his 1979 title *Biography of a Progressive, Franklin K. Lane, 1864-1921.*

In his 2003 title *Watergate: The Presidential Scandal That Shook America,* he commemorates the thirtieth anniversary of that landmark affair with an "elegant, succinct account," according to a contributor for *Publishers Weekly.* Watergate, a name often invoked to describe presidential wrong-doings of any sort, began as a rather tawdry 1972 break-in of the Democratic National Committee headquarters in Washington's Watergate building in hopes of finding incriminating material on White House critics and to plant listening devices. Caught in the act, these self-described "plumbers" turned out to be in the employ of President Richard Nixon's White House. The ensuing investigation and scandal rocked the nation and ultimately led to Nixon leaving office in disgrace. The cast of characters in the national drama was large, including the ex-CIA operatives acting as the break-in artists; the energetic young journalists on the *Washington Post,* Bob Woodward and Carl Bernstein, and their "Deep Throat" secret source; the stubborn Judge John J. Sirica, who vowed to get to the bottom of the case; the White House staffers; and of course President Nixon himself and the tapes he made of all Oval Office conversations. According to the same *Publishers Weekly* writer, Olson manages to deal with all these details in an "excellent, compact narrative."

John W. Dean, himself a participant in the affair as White House counsel, wrote in a Chicago *Tribune Books* review that Olson's book is "particularly timely" in light of the comparisons between Nixon's use of national security as an excuse to withhold evidence and similar concerns of President George W. Bush. According to Dean, "There has never been a better time to recall the lessons of Watergate, lest history repeat itself." Dean further noted that Olson's account is "different" than those supplied by several hundred other writers on the subject in that it provides a "concise and readable overview of the entire mess." For Dean, Olson also managed to make "highly complex and convoluted information accessible, not to mention interesting." Karl Helicher, writing in *Library Journal,* also thought Olson's book was an "excellent investigation" and one that would appeal to both "newcomers to Watergate and those who vividly remember it."

For David M. Oshinsky, however, writing in the *New York Times,* Olson's account "catches little of this drama." Olson's book is, according to Oshinsky, a "dry piece of work, faithful to the subject without truly extending its reach." Oshinsky also complained that Olson left out "the most important variable: Nixon himself." Yet Robert J. Spitzer, reviewing *Watergate* in *Perspectives on Political Science,* felt that Olson added "plenty" of new information on the scandal. According to Spitzer, one of Olson's aims in the book was to demonstrate that—contrary to some opinions—Nixon was not driven from office by the so-called liberal press but by a bipartisan effort in Congress. For Spitzer, *Watergate* is a "brilliant synthesis . . . of a history that all presidency students need to know."

Olson told *CA:* "Looking back, three factors may account for my interest in history and in writing. I grew up in Hyde Park, New York, the home of President Franklin D. Roosevelt. In public school and as an undergraduate I was blessed with teachers and professors of a high quality. My family life and culture reflected a Swedish father and a mother with most of her relatives still in Sweden. This combination of family life, Hyde Park, and marvelous teachers stimulated an early interest in history.

"Writing requires solitude and that reflects one characteristic of my personality. One of my leisure activities is running and when possible cross-country skiing. Both sports involve an element of solitude.

"I hope that my books will have a long shelf life; that students and scholars will consult the books in the future because they rest on thorough research. Clear writing, judicious analysis, and convincing conclusions."

BIOGRAPHICAL AND CRITICAL SOURCES:

PERIODICALS

Library Journal, March 15, 2003, Karl Helicher, review of *Watergate: The Presidential Scandal That Shook America,* p. 98.

New York Times, July 10, 2003, David M. Oshinsky, review of *Watergate,* p. E9.
Perspectives on Political Science, summer, 2003, Robert J. Spitzer, review of *Watergate,* p. 166.
Publishers Weekly, March 10, 2003, review of *Watergate,* pp. 62- 63.
Tribune Books (Chicago, IL), May 11, 2003, John W. Dean, review of *Watergate,* p. 1.

ONLINE

University of Maryland Web site, http://www.history.umd.edu/ (October 29, 2003), "Keith W. Olson."

* * *

OWENS, Carole (Ehrlich) 1942-

PERSONAL: Born December 7, 1942, in Minneapolis, MN; daughter of Jerome D. (a psychologist) and Amy Ann (an education specialist; maiden name, Scott) Schein; children: Todd Frederick, Joseph Eric. *Education:* University of Maryland—College Park, B.A., 1970; Catholic University of America, M.A., 1977; Yeshiva University, Ph.D., 1987.

ADDRESSES: Home and office—P.O. Box 1207, Stockbridge, MA 01262.

CAREER: Youth leader and advocate for Montgomery County Recreation Department, 1970-72; Family Service, Rockville, MD, counselor and supervisor of preadjudication diversion program of Crisis Home Program, 1972-74; Karma House (residential drug treatment center), Rockville, administrator, 1974-75; Jewish Social Service Agency, Rockville, program development director, 1975-77; United Jewish Appeal Federation of Montgomery County, Bethesda, MD, program development director, 1977-79; licensed clinician in private practice. Catholic University of America, instructor; Cooper-Hewitt Museum, lecturer; teacher in adult education programs. Narrator and consultant for television programs, including *Chronicles,* Public Broadcasting Service; *America's Castles,* Arts and Entertainment; *City Confidential,* Arts and Entertainment; *Wealth and Power,* Home and Garden Television.

MEMBER: International Society for Political Psychology, American Association of Marriage and Family Therapists (clinical member), New York Academy of Sciences.

WRITINGS:

The Berkshire Cottages: A Vanishing Era, Cottage Press (Stockbridge, MA), 1984.
Bellefontaine: Historical Narrative, Canyon Ranch (Lenox, MA), 1989.
Who Killed Carrie Knox?, Berkshire Web (Pittsfield, MA), 1992.
The Lost Days of Agatha Christie (mystery), Cottage Press (Stockbridge, MA) 1995.

Contributor to education journals and popular magazines, including *Parade, Ladies' Home Journal, Boston Globe, Victoria, Country Inns,* and *New England Travel and Life.*

SIDELIGHTS: Carole Owens once told *CA:* "My writing is concerned alternately with the problems of today and the lifestyles of yesterday. I was prompted to write *The Berkshire Cottages: A Vanishing Era* because of my interest in the 'romantic' Victorian era and its serious effect on all of us today. I believe that instead of being removed from our twentieth century, the Victorian era, indeed, 'invented' it. How is that true? During the Gilded Age in America, scientific thought eclipsed romantic thought and has since dominated American higher education, dictated research methods, and has thereby defined 'truth.' Secondly, mass production and mass consumption patterns 'invented' by our Victorian ancestors have formed and enhanced our daily life-style, affected our economic aspirations, and caused most of the modern problems of pollution and energy and resource shortages.

"My approach to *Berkshire Cottages* might have been from an architectural, economic, or historical perspective, but in fact it was from the perspective of a social historian. It is people—how they thought, lived, treated one another, and dreamed—that interest me as a family therapist and as a writer. The doors of the Berkshire Cottages were the portals into the lives of our ancestors."

P

PARK, Paul (Claiborne) 1954-

PERSONAL: Born October 1, 1954, in Williamstown, MA; son of David Allen (a physicist, professor, and writer) and Clara (a professor and writer; maiden name, Claiborne) Park; married Deborah Brothers, 1994; two children: Miranda, Lucius Lionel. *Education:* Hampshire College, A.B., 1975. *Politics:* "Left." *Religion:* Episcopalian.

ADDRESSES: *Home*—Box 10, Petersburg, New York 12138. *Agent*—Adele Leone, 26 Nantucket Place, Scarsdale, NY 10583.

CAREER: Author and instructor. Smith Greenland Advertising, New York, NY, copywriter and production assistant, 1977-78; Town Squash, Inc., New York, NY, manager, 1979-85; Potala Asian Imports, Pittsfield, MA, 1986-90. Visiting instructor in creative writing, Writers' Center, Bethesda, MD, 1988, Johns Hopkins University, Baltimore, MD, 1988-94, Williams College, Williamstown, MA, 1989, 1991, 1994, 1996. Also worked as a construction worker, political aide, and doorman, New York, NY, 1975-77. Works part-time for eZiba.com, an online retailer.

WRITINGS:

"STARBRIDGE CHRONICLES" SERIES

Soldiers of Paradise (also see below), Arbor House (New York, NY), 1987.

Sugar Rain (also see below), Morrow (New York, NY), 1989.

The Cult of Loving Kindness, Morrow (New York, NY), 1991.

The Sugar Festival (omnibus; includes *Soldiers of Paradise* and *Sugar Rain*), Guild America Books (New York, NY), 1989.

OTHER NOVELS

Coelestis, HarperCollins (London, England), 1993, republished as *Celestis,* Tor (New York, NY), 1995.

The Gospel of Corax, Soho Press (New York, NY), 1996.

Three Marys, Cosmos Books (Canton, OH), 2003.

SIDELIGHTS: Paul Park has been deemed "one of the finest authors on the 'humanist' wing of American science fiction," explained *Infinity Plus* reviewer Nick Gevers. Critics have praised Park's novels for using strange and grotesque material to reveal human warmth.

Park's "Starbridge" trilogy is set on a planet on which the cycle of the seasons takes 80,000 days, much longer than the human lifespan. Most of the action takes place in Charn, a city-state ruled by a totalitarian society set on organizing for survival during a half-century of winter. This society is savage and contrasts sharply with a heretical cult of antinomials, reminiscent of twentieth-century hippies. Writing in *Twentieth-Century Science-Fiction Writers,* reviewer E. R. Bishop praised Park's depiction of Charn "with its toppling buildings and mud streets, its derelict harbour where the hulks of warships lie tilted in the ooze, its slums, taverns, brothels, palaces, prisons, all clear and detailed in the light of other suns." The same reviewer noted that through Park's "matter-of-fact approach, we learn through what seems chance references that the carnivorous 'horses' have beaks, claws, horns, and wings; that gasoline is used as an explosive and gunpowder as a motor fuel, that the spring 'sugar rain' is laced with hydrocarbons, à la Velikowsky, so that Charn city burns every year, while the foresighted protect their valuables in asbestos bags." The reviewer explained, "This meticulously prepared background supports Park's grander flights; the terrible and pathetic fate of the antinomials; the fall of theocracy; Charity Starbridge's wanderings in the labyrinth under Charn; Thanakar Starbridge's passage through the monstrous prison Mountain of Redemption, with its million tormented inmates."

In an interview with *ElectricStory,* Park discussed the creation of his "Starbridge" trilogy. "I worked a lot of stupid jobs after college, and taught squash for many years in Manhattan. I quit in 1983 to write a novel. With a notebook and a couple of shirts, I flew to New Delhi telling myself I couldn't come back until I had completed a manuscript," he explained. *Soldiers in Paradise,* Park's first novel and the first in the "Starbridge Chronicles," was written while Park traversed Sri Lanka, Nepal, Rajasthan, Burma, Thailand, Indonesia, and other parts of Asia over the course of two years.

A *Publishers Weekly* reviewer observed that Park's novel *Celestis* "seems planted on firmer ground" than his trilogy, but added, "the oddly disengaging revolution through which the author's new characters wander tends to skew the fine-edged balance he is apparently trying to maintain between futility and passion." *Celestis* features Katherine Styreme, an alien whose man-made medication has given her human qualities. When Katherine is kidnapped by terrorists, she is deprived of her medication and her alien characteristics return. The same *Publishers Weekly* reviewer concluded, "Park produces some beautiful writing here as well as some compelling insight into the nature of 'the world outside our small blinkered range,'" but felt Park's "repeated emphasis on how sexual bonding promotes a false sense of communication detracts from an otherwise impressive treatise on the nature of mind, matter, and reality."

Park reinterprets the life of Christ in his controversial *Gospel of Corax* featuring Corax, a slave with amazing abilities who runs away after his master's death. Along his travels from Palestine to the Himalayas, Corax rescues "Jeshua of Nazareth," a still-unknown Jesus, from a Jewish jail after he's been accused of treason. *Booklist* reviewer Steve Shroeder remarked, "If it made the right people angry, this book could move a sizable Christian audience to the kind of passion that Satanic verses inspired among the Muslims." Shroeder later clarified that the book "is not a 'gospel' in the technical sense" but is simply historical fiction. A *Publisher's Weekly* reviewer described the book as "a dark narrative, full of brutality and misery—so much, in fact, that at times the gruesomeness borders on the cartoonish." The same reviewer went on the say, "What's more likely to rub some readers raw" is the "novel's claim of Eastern influence of Jesus' teaching . . . and its implied favoring of Buddhism over biblical religion."

Park explores life after Jesus' death in *Three Marys,* which tells the story of the "three Marys": Mary of Magdala, Jesus' mother Mary, and Mary of Bethany. In an *Infinity Plus* interview, Park remarked that while he is proud of the novel, he sees its commercial difficulties. He described the book as a "retelling of the stories of the Gospels and the Book of Acts from the points of view of some of the women that surround Jesus, and to understand and appreciate how I have changed the stories in a thousand minute ways, some quite specific knowledge is essential." Gevers noted that Park's "powerful, densely written narratives of religious and existential crisis on worlds at once exotic and familiar have won him comparisons with Gene Wolfe and Brian Aldiss at their finest."

BIOGRAPHICAL AND CRITICAL SOURCES:

BOOKS

Twentieth-Century Science-Fiction Writers, 3rd edition, St. James Press (Chicago, IL), 1991, pp. 615-616.

PERIODICALS

Analog Science Fiction and Fact, October, 1995, review of *Celestis,* p. 162.

Atlantic Monthly, July, 1996, review of *The Gospel of Corax,* p. 109.

Booklist, July, 1996, Steve Schroeder, review of *The Gospel of Corax,* pp. 1804-1806; October 1, 1998, Ray Olsen, review of *The Gospel of Corax,* p. 293.

Book World, September, 1991, review of *The Cult of Loving Kindness,* p. 8; October 13, 1996, review of *The Gospel of Corax,* p. 4.

Kirkus Reviews, June 1, 1991, review of *The Cult of Loving Kindness,* p. 700; April 15, 1995, review of *Celestis,* p. 515; April 1, 1996, review of *The Gospel of Corax,* p. 478.

Library Journal, August, 1996, review of *The Gospel of Corax,* p. 113.

Locus, February, 1990, review of *Soldiers of Paradise,* p. 54; November, 1990, review of *Sugar Rain,* p. 60; June, 1991, review of *The Cult of Loving Kindness,* p. 15; August, 1991, review of *The Cult of Loving Kindness,* p. 51; September, 1993, review of *Coelestis,* p. 15; February, 1994, review of *Coelestis,* p. 36.

New York Times Book Review, October 7, 1990, review of *Sugar Rain,* p. 38; October 27, 1991, review of *The Cult of Loving Kindness,* p. 30; November 22, 1992, review of *The Cult of Loving Kindness,* p. 40; July, 9, 1995, review of *Celestis,* p. 18; July 14, 1996, review of *The Gospel of Corax,* p. 15; May 4, 1997, review of *Celestis,* p. 32.

Publishers Weekly, June 14, 1991, review of *The Cult of Loving Kindness,* p. 48; May 15, 1995, review of *Celestis,* pp. 59-61; April 8, 1996, review of *The Gospel of Corax,* p. 53; July 28, 1997, review of *The Gospel of Corax,* p. 72.

Science Fiction Chronicle, March, 1994, review of *Coelestis,* p. 32; February, 1994, review of *Coelestis,* p. 28.

Utne Reader, November, 1996, review of *The Gospel of Corax,* p. 88.

Virginia Quarterly Review, winter, 1997, review of *The Gospel of Corax,* p. 22.

Washington Post Book World, October 25, 1987.

ONLINE

ElectricStory, http://www.electricstory.com/ (November 22, 2002), interview with Paul Park.

Infinity Plus Web site, http://www.infinityplus.co.uk/ (October 2000), Nick Gevers, "Shadowy Figures, Infinitely Debatable."*

PEARS, Iain (George) 1955-

PERSONAL: Born August 8, 1955, in Coventry, England; son of George Derrick (an industrialist) and Betty Mitchell (a magistrate; maiden name, Proudfoot) Pears; married Ruth Harris (an academic), January 7, 1985. *Education:* Wadham College, Oxford, B.A., 1977, M.A., 1979; Wolfson College, Oxford, D.Phil., 1982; postdoctoral study at Yale University, 1987-88.

ADDRESSES: *Home*—c/o 69 Kenilworth Rd., Coventry CV4 7AF, England. *Agent*—Curtis Brown Ltd., 162-168 Regent St., London W1R 5TA, England.

CAREER: Writer. Reuters News Agency, correspondent, Rome, Italy, 1983-84, corporate and banking correspondent, London, England, 1984-87.

AWARDS, HONORS: Getty fellow, 1987-88.

WRITINGS:

NOVELS

An Instance of the Fingerpost, Riverhead Books (New York, NY), 1998.

The Immaculate Deception, Scribner (New York, NY), 2000.

The Dream of Scipio, Riverhead Books (New York, NY), 2002.

"JONATHAN ARGYLL" MYSTERY SERIES

The Raphael Affair, Gollancz (London, England), 1990, Harcourt (New York, NY), 1992.

The Titian Committee, Gollancz (London, England), 1992, Harcourt (New York, NY), 1993.

The Bernini Bust, Gollancz (London, England), 1992, Harcourt (New York, NY), 1994.

The Last Judgement, Gollancz (London, England), 1994, Scribner (New York, NY), 1996.

Giotto's Hand, Gollancz (London, England), 1995, Scribner (New York, NY), 1997.

Death and Restoration, Gollancz (London, England), 1996, Scribner (New York, NY), 1998.

NONFICTION

The Discovery of Painting: The Growth of Interest in the Arts in England, Yale University Press (New Haven, CT), 1988.

Contributor to art and financial journals.

SIDELIGHTS: British art dealer Jonathan Argyll is often caught up in investigations of art fraud, theft, and murder in Iain Pears's mystery novels. Working with his lover, Flavia de Stefano of the Italian National Art Theft Squad, Argyll tracks down art thieves and killers in Rome. According to a critic for *Publishers Weekly,* Pears "writes with a Beerbohm-like wit." In addition to his mysteries featuring Argyll and Flavia, Pears has also published an historical mystery, *An Instance of the Fingerpost,* set in the England of the 1660s.

In *The Titian Committee,* Argyll and Flavia track down the killer of an American art historian, a British art collector, and a French art philosopher. The plot revolves around possible art fraud involving Titian paintings. "The real work of art here," wrote Marilyn Stasio in the *New York Times Book Review,* "is the plot, a piece of structural engineering any artist would envy."

In *The Bernini Bust* Argyll tries to sell some artwork to the Moresby Museum in Los Angeles, but when the museum's benefactor is killed and a marble bust goes missing, Argyll finds himself calling upon Flavia for assistance. "With sharply etched characters and art world lore," noted the critic for *Publishers Weekly,*"Pears's latest tale is a lark in grand British style."

In *The Last Judgement,* Argyll agrees to act as delivery man for a Parisian painting bought by a Rome collector. But the collector is found murdered, someone tries to steal the painting from Argyll, and the authorities demand that the painting—possibly stolen—be returned. The story, according to the *Publishers Weekly* reviewer, "delivers its plot twists at a rapid clip." Emily Melton in *Booklist* called *The Last Judgement* "a sophisticated, adventurous, and gripping story that is sure to hold wide appeal."

An Instance of the Fingerpost is set in England of the 1660s and uses the murder of an Oxford fellow as the starting point for a "sprawling tale of politics and passion, science and sex, religion and revenge," as Bill Ott wrote in *Booklist.* Four characters provide contradictory accounts of the murder, all of the narrators being "variously self-deluded, self-protective, and so unreliable that from the novel's first sentence on, anything you read may be a lie," according to Mark H. Harris in *Entertainment Weekly.*"When the denouement comes," Richard Bernstein wrote in the *New York Times,* "it is with a new and final twist, one whose quality of surprise is the final proof of this talented author's almost infinite capacity to replace one understanding of things with another." Pears "masterfully mixes human drama, history lesson, and intellectual puzzle in this challenging but thoroughly compelling novel," Ott concluded.

Argyll returns in *The Immaculate Deception,* published in 2000. Newly married to Flavia de Stefano, now acting head of the art theft department of the Italian police force, Argyll and his new bride contemplate impending parenthood while Flavia worries about whether she will permanently succeed her retiring boss, General Taddeo Bottando, as the head of the art theft division. When a priceless piece of art is stolen while on loan to the Italian government, Argyll accompanies his new bride on a mission to retrieve the painting. Matters are complicated by orders from Prime Minister Sabauda that Flavia cannot use any public monies to pay any ransoms for the painting. As she investigates, she uncovers an old case of murder and political corruption that promises to further complicate her attempts to recover the painting. In the meantime, Argyll discovers clues that appear to link Bottando to the missing artwork. When persons connected to the painting and investigation begin dying, Argyll and Flavia face difficult decisions and moral dilemmas.

"Pears offers a glimpse of the painstaking process of authenticating ancient works of art," commented *Library Journal* critic Caroline Mann. Reviewer Bill Ott, writing in *Booklist,* observed that "Pears masterfully incorporates the missing painting's history into the fabric of the story. Best of all, though, is his wonderful grasp of the moral ambiguity at the heart of Italian life." Although a *Publishers Weekly* reviewer did not find *The Immaculate Deception* to be a "scintillating mystery," the reviewer did remark that Pears "nicely portrays the Italian art world" in the book.

The year 2002 saw the appearance of *The Dream of Scipio,* a complex and detailed historical novel spanning fifteen centuries in Provence, Italy. "The story unfolds in three time frames, in each of which a man and a woman are in love, civilization itself is crumbling, and Jews become the scapegoats for larger cultural anxieties," remarked a *Publishers Weekly* reviewer. In fifth-century Rome, wealthy Roman nobleman Manlius Hippomanes sacrifices his pagan beliefs to become a Christian bishop in order to raise an army to protect Provence from invading hordes of barbarians. Manlius writes *The Dream of Scipio,* a neo-Platonic allegory used to record the wisdom of his teacher and platonic mentor, Sophia. Manlius's strategy ultimately fails, but the manuscript of *The Dream of Scipio* survives.

In the fourteenth century, Olivier de Noyen rediscovers the manuscript. Olivier, a poet and scholar, lives in Florence during the time of the Black Death, and spends much of his time in fear of the devastating disease. Olivier falls in love with a Jewish servant girl he sees in the marketplace. But when Olivier's patron, the zealous and determined Cardinal Ceccani, places blame for the plague on the Jews, Olivier places his safety—even his life—at risk for the sake of his love.

While the Nazis devastate twentieth-century Europe, classical scholar and historian Julien Barneuve studies the poetry of Olivier de Noyen and becomes interested in the *Dream of Scipio* manuscript. When France falls to the Nazis and the Holocaust staggers forward into horrific reality, however, Julien finds himself in the unwilling position of censor and propagandist, who must struggle to protect his own love, a Jewish painter. "As Pears juggles these stories and themes in extremely complex but immensely satisfying three-part harmony, we come to see how actions both abominable and compassionate spring from the same idea," wrote Bill Ott in *Booklist.*

"Each of the three men is ennobled, and victimized, by his love for a woman chosen to be sacrificed for a 'greater good,'" wrote a *Kirkus Reviews* critic. "And each endures a separation illustrating the Platonic concept that virtue is wholeness, evil the violent sundering of an ideal unity of harmonized parts." Charles observed that "Pears handles these relationships like everything in this novel—with extraordinary delicacy, capturing the full tragedy and beauty of thwarted affection."

David McAllister, writing in the *Times Literary Supplement,* called *The Dream of Scipio* "a beautifully constructed novel, and Pears jumps effortless between the three narratives, as the choice that faces each character is made clear and the 'Dream' of the philosophy is put to the test. The novel builds to a bloody, tense, and highly topical denouement, in which political expedience demands the persecution of a minority, and individual resistance seems futile, selfish, and naive." Barbara Hoffert, reviewing the book in *Library Journal,* noted that "the plotting is a marvel, and the text moves smoothly among the three eras," while *BookPage* reviewer Mark Tarallo remarked that "Pears skillfully reveals the commonalities and linkages between the protagonists." Critic Susan Tekulve, in *Book,* opined that the author's "weighty themes take precedence over plot and character development, and the narrative lacks dramatic tension." Still, most critics enjoyed the heft and complexity of Pears's book. John Crowley, writing in *New York Times,* commented that "Pears's story is like one of those symmetrical, seemingly patent but teasingly complex knots that decorate ancient Celtic manuscripts. Three interwoven stories twine in and out of one another, revealing similarities, creating patterns and connections."

Pears avoids the clichés of mystery writing and continues to enthrall readers with his carefully constructed and seamless plots that have even the best detectives perplexed until their conclusions. With so many continued successes, it is hard to imagine where Pears will take Jonathan Argyll next. Wherever author and character find their next mystery, readers are sure to be equally entertained.

BIOGRAPHICAL AND CRITICAL SOURCES:

PERIODICALS

American Libraries, January, 1999, review of *An Instance of the Fingerpost,* p. 104.

Book, July-August, 2002, Susan Tekulve, review of *The Dream of Scipio,* p. 82.

Booklist, April 1, 1996, Emily Melton, review of *The Last Judgement,* p. 1347; June 1, 1997, Bill Ott, review of *Giotto's Hand,* pp. 1667-1668; December 1, 1997, Bill Ott, review of *An Instance of the Fingerpost,* p. 587; August 1, 1998, Bill Ott, review of *Death and Restoration,* pp. 1976-1977;

January 1, 1999, review of *An Instance of the Fingerpost,* p. 779; September 1, 2000, Bill Ott, review of *The Immaculate Deception;* May 1, 2002, Bill Ott, review of *The Dream of Scipio,* p. 6; January 1, 2003, review of *The Dream of Scipio,* p. 793; September 15, 2003, Candace Smith, review of *The Dream of Scipio,* p. 252.

Christian Century, November 18, 1998, review of *An Instance of the Fingerpost,* p. 1119.

Discover, February 1, 1999, Michael M. Abrams, review of *An Instance of the Fingerpost,* p. 95.

Drood Review of Mystery, January, 2001, review of *The Bernini Bust,* p. 22.

Entertainment Weekly, March 20, 1998, p. 84; March 23, 1998, Mark H. Harris, review of *An Instance of the Fingerpost,* p. 84; March 5, 1999, review of *An Instance of the Fingerpost,* p. 59.

Kirkus Reviews, May 1, 2002, review of *The Dream of Scipio,* p. 606.

Kliatt, September 1, 2003, Nola Theiss, review of *The Dream of Scipio,* p. 20.

Library Journal, January 1, 1998, Susan Gene Clifford, review of *An Instance of the Fingerpost,* pp. 143-144; October 1, 1998, Kristen L. Smith, sound recording review of *An Instance of the Fingerpost,* p. 149; November 1, 2000, Caroline Mann, review of *The Immaculate Deception,* p. 142; May 15, 2002, Barbara Hoffert, review of *The Dream of Scipio,* p.127.

Los Angeles Times Book Review, March 25, 2001, review of *The Immaculate Deception,* p. 9.

Maclean's, June 22, 1998, Barbara Wickens, "Foul Play for Fair Days," p. 54; July 15, 2002, Brian Bethune, "Evil Men Do," p. 60.

Newsweek, April 17, 1998, Malcolm Jones, Jr., review of *An Instance of the Fingerpost,* p. 75.

New York Times, April 3, 1998; June 23, 2002, John Crowley, "Unsolicited Manuscript," review of *The Dream of Scipio,* section 7, p. 26.

New York Times Book Review, October 24, 1993; September 18, 1994; March 22, 1998; March 7, 1999, review of *An Instance of the Fingerpost,* p. 28.

People, March 23, 1998, David Lehman, review of *An Instance of the Fingerpost,* p. 37; July 22, 2002, Laura Italiano, review of *The Dream of Scipio,* p. 35.

Publishers Weekly, August 3, 1992, review of *The Raphael Affair,* p. 63; August 2, 1993, review of *The Titian Committee,* p. 64; June 27, 1994, review of *The Bernini Bust,* p. 58; January 29, 1996, review of *The Last Judgement,* p. 87; June 9, 1997, review of *Giotto's Hand,* p. 42; December 1, 1997, review of *An Instance of the Fingerpost,* p. 43; August 3, 1998, review of *Death and Restoration,* p. 77; September 25, 2000, review of *The Immaculate Deception,* p. 92; May 27, 2002, review of *The Dream of Scipio,* p. 35.

Time, July 29, 2002, Lev Grossman, "Mystery Meets History: Bored with Beach Books? Want Something Fancier Than Clancy? Try These Sophisticated Euro-thrillers," p. 62.

Times Literary Supplement, May 24, 2002, David McAllister, "The Bubble of Civility," review of *The Dream of Scipio,* p. 23.

Washington Post Book World, June 17, 2001, review of *An Instance of the Fingerpost,* p. 4; December 2, 2001, review of *The Immaculate Deception,* p. 7.

ONLINE

BookPage, http://www.bookpage.com/ (November 20, 2003), Mark Tarallo, review of *The Dream of Scipio.*

Pittsburgh Post-Gazette Online, http://www.post-gazette.com/ (November 17, 2002), Len Barcousky, review of *The Dream of Scipio.**

* * *

PECK, Richard (Wayne) 1934-

PERSONAL: Born April 5, 1934, in Decatur, IL, USA; son of Wayne Morris (a merchant) and Virginia (a dietician; maiden name, Gray) Peck. *Education:* Attended University of Exeter, 1955-56; DePauw University, B.A., 1956; Southern Illinois University, M.A., 1959; further graduate study at Washington University, 1960-61. *Politics:* Republican. *Religion:* Methodist.

ADDRESSES: Home—155 East 72nd St., New York, NY 10021. *Office*—c/o Delacorte Press, 1 Dag Hammarskjold Plaza, New York, NY 10017. *Agent*—Sheldon Fogelman, 155 East 72nd St., New York, NY 10021.

CAREER: Southern Illinois University at Carbondale, instructor in English, 1958-60; Glenbrook North High School, Northbrook, IL, teacher of English, 1961-63;

Richard Peck

Scott, Foresman Co., Chicago, IL, textbook editor, 1963-65; Hunter College of the City University of New York and Hunter College High School, New York, NY, instructor in English and education, 1965-71; writer, 1971—. Assistant director of the Council for Basic Education, Washington, DC, 1969-70; English-Speaking Union fellow, Jesus College, Oxford University, England, 1973; lecturer. *Military service:*U.S. Army, 1956-58; served in Stuttgart, Germany.

MEMBER: Authors Guild, Authors League of America, Delta Chi.

AWARDS, HONORS: Child Study Association of America's Children's Book of the Year citations, 1970, for *Sounds and Silences,* 1971, for *Mindscapes,* and 1986, for *Blossom Culp and the Sleep of Death;* Writing Award, National Council for the Advancement of Education, 1971; Edgar Allan Poe Award runner-up, Mystery Writers of America, 1974, for *Dreamland Lake;* Best Books of the Year citations, American Library Association (ALA), 1974, for *Representing Super Doll,* 1976, for *Are You in the House Alone?,* and 1977, for *Ghosts I Have Been;* ALA Notable Book citations, 1975, for *The Ghost Belonged to Me,* and 1985, for *Remembering the Good Times;* Friends of American Writers Award (older category), 1976, for *The Ghost Belonged to Me;* Edgar Allan Poe Award for best juvenile mystery novel, 1976, and Author's Award, New Jersey Institute of Technology, 1978, both for *Are You in the House Alone?; School Library Journal*'s Best Books of the Year citations, 1976, for *Are You in the House Alone?,* 1977, for *Ghosts I Have Been,* and 1985, for *Remembering the Good Times; New York Times* Outstanding Book of the Year citation, 1977, for *Ghosts I Have Been;* Illinois Writer of the Year citation, Illinois Association of Teachers of English, 1977; *School Library Journal*'s Best of the Best 1966-1978 citations, for *Dreamland Lake,* and *Father Figure.* New York Public Library Books for the Teen Age citations, 1980, for *Pictures That Storm inside My Head,* 1981, for *Ghosts I Have Been,* and 1982, for *Are You in the House Alone?* and *Close Enough to Touch;* ALA Best Books for Young Adults citations, 1981, for *Close Enough to Touch,* 1985, for *Remembering the Good Times,* and 1987, for *Princess Ashley; School Library Journal*'s Best Books for Young Adults citations, 1981, for *Close Enough to Touch,* 1983, for *This Family of Women,* and 1985, for *Remembering the Good Times;* ALA's Young Adult Services Division's Best of the Best Books 1970-1983 citations, for *Are You in the House Alone?* and *Ghosts I Have Been;* ALA's Margaret Edwards Young Adult Author Achievement Award, 1990; Newberry Honor designation and National Book Award finalist designation for *A Long Way from Chicago,* 1999; National Humanities Medal for lifetime achievement, 2001; Newbery Medal, 2001, for *A Year down Yonder;* nominated for the National Book Award for young people's literature, 2003, for *The River Between Us;* Scott O'Dell Award for Historical Fiction, 2004, for *The River between Us.*

WRITINGS:

YOUNG ADULT NOVELS, EXCEPT AS NOTED

Don't Look and It Won't Hurt, Holt (New York, NY), 1972.

Dreamland Lake, Holt (New York, NY), 1973, reprinted, Puffin Books (New York, NY), 2000.

Through a Brief Darkness, Viking (New York, NY), 1973.

Representing Super Doll, Viking (New York, NY), 1974.

The Ghost Belonged to Me, Viking (New York, NY), 1975.

Are You in the House Alone? (with teacher's guide), Viking (New York, NY), 1976, reprinted, Puffin Books (New York, NY), 2000.

Ghosts I Have Been (sequel to *The Ghost Belonged to Me*), Viking (New York, NY), 1977.

Monster Night at Grandma's House (for juveniles), illustrations by Don Freeman, Viking (New York, NY), 1977, revision illustrated by Don Freeman, Dial Books for Young Readers (New York, NY), 2003.

Father Figure, Viking (New York, NY), 1978.

Secrets of the Shopping Mall, Delacorte (New York, NY), 1979.

Close Enough to Touch, Delacorte (New York, NY), 1981.

The Dreadful Future of Blossom Culp (sequel to *Ghosts I Have Been*), Delacorte (New York, NY), 1983, reprinted, Puffin Books (New York, NY), 2001.

Remembering the Good Times, Delacorte (New York, NY), 1985.

Blossom Culp and the Sleep of Death, Delacorte (New York, NY), 1986.

Princess Ashley, Delacorte (New York, NY), 1987.

Those Summer Girls I Never Met, Delacorte (New York, NY), 1988.

Unfinished Portrait of Jessica, Delacorte (New York, NY), 1991.

Bel-Air Bambi and the Mall Rats, Delacorte Press (New York, NY), 1993.

The Last Safe Place on Earth, Delacorte Press (New York, NY), 1995.

Lost in Cyberspace, Dial Books for Young Readers (New York, NY), 1995.

The Great Interactive Dream Machine: Another Adventure in Cyberspace, Dial Books (New York, NY), 1996.

A Long Way from Chicago: A Novel in Stories, Dial Books (New York, NY), 1998.

Strays Like us, Dial Books (New York, NY), 1998.

A Year down Yonder, Dial Books (New York, NY), 2000.

Fair Weather, Dial Books (New York, NY), 2001.

The River Between Us, Dial/Penguin (New York, NY), 2003.

ADULT NOVELS

Amanda/Miranda Viking (New York, NY), 1980.

New York Time, Delacorte (New York, NY), 1981.

This Family of Women Delacorte (New York, NY), 1983.

Voices after Midnight, Dell (New York, NY), 1990.

London Holiday, Viking (New York, NY), 1998.

The Teacher's Funeral: A Comedy in Three Parts, Dial (New York, NY), 2004.

EDITOR

(With Ned E. Hoopes) *Edge of Awareness: Twenty-five Contemporary Essays,* Dell (New York, NY), 1966.

Sounds and Silences: Poetry for Now, Delacorte (New York, NY), 1970.

Mindscapes: Poems for the Real World, Delacorte (New York, NY), 1971.

Leap into Reality: Essays for Now, Dell (New York, NY), 1972.

Urban Studies: A Research Paper Casebook, Random House (New York, NY), 1973.

Transitions: A Literary Paper Casebook, Random House (New York, NY), 1974.

Pictures That Storm inside My Head (poetry anthology), Avon (New York, NY), 1976.

OTHER

(With Norman Strasma) *Old Town, A Complete Guide: Strolling, Shopping, Supping, Sipping,* 2nd edition, [Chicago, IL], 1965.

(With Mortimer Smith and George Weber) *A Consumer's Guide to Educational Innovations,* Council for Basic Education (Washington, DC), 1972.

(With Stephen N. Judy) *The Creative Word 2,* (Peck was not associated with other volumes), Random House (New York, NY), 1974.

Write a Tale of Terror, Book Lures, 1987.

Anonymously Yours (autobiography), Silver Burdette, 1991.

Love and Death at the Mall: Teaching and Writing for the Literate Young, Delacorte Press (New York, NY), 1994.

Invitations to the World: Teaching and Writing for Young, Dial (New York, NY), 2002.

Contributor to books, including *Literature for Today's Young Adults,* edited by Kenneth L. Donelson and Alleen Pace Nilsen, Scott, Foresman (Glenview, IL),

1980, *Sixteen: Short Stories by Outstanding Young Adult Writers,* edited by Donald R. Gallo, Delacorte (New York, NY), 1984, and *Visions: Nineteen Short Stories by Outstanding Writers for Young Adults,* edited by Donald R. Gallo, Delacorte (New York, NY), 1987. Author of column on the architecture of historic neighborhoods for the *New York Times.* Contributor of poetry to several anthologies. Contributor of poems to *Saturday Review* and *Chicago Tribune Magazine.* Contributor of articles to periodicals, including *American Libraries, PTA Magazine* and *Parents' Magazine.* Some of Peck's works have been translated into other languages.

ADAPTATIONS: Audio cassette versions of Peck's books include *The Ghost Belonged to Me,* Live Oak Media, 1976, *Don't Look and It Won't Hurt* (filmstrip with cassette), Random House, and *Remembering the Good Times* (cassette), Listening Library, 1987. Television movies based on his books include *Are You in the House Alone?,* CBS, 1977, *Child of Glass* (based on *The Ghost Belonged to Me*), Walt Disney Productions, 1979, and *Father Figure,* Time-Life Productions, 1980. Cineville Production Company bought the film rights for *Don't Look and It Won't Hurt* in 1991.

SIDELIGHTS: Richard Peck's books on such traumatic subjects as suicide, unwanted pregnancy, death of a loved one, and rape have won critical acclaim for their realism and emotional power. Peck has written numerous popular books for young adults, books that assist these readers to develop their self-confidence. He has also written adult novels that show his commitment to eliminating sexual stereotypes. Peck told Roger Sutton in a *School Library Journal* interview that when writing for younger readers, he tries to visualize his audience: "As I'm typing I'm trying to look out over the typewriter and see faces. I don't certainly want to 'write for myself' because I'm trying to write across a generation gap." When writing for any age group, Peck told Jean F. Mercier in *Publishers Weekly,* he tries to "give readers leading characters they can look up to and reasons to believe that problems can be solved." The consistently high quality of Peck's work has been recognized with numerous awards.

Peck became familiar with contemporary adolescent problems while teaching high school. He liked his students, but after several years became discouraged and quit, once telling *CA* that teaching "had begun to turn into something that looked weirdly like psychiatric social work." Peck decided instead to write books for teenagers that featured the problems he had seen. "Ironically, it was my students who taught me to be a writer, though I had been hired to teach *them,*" he said in a speech published in *Arkansas Libraries.* "They taught me that a novel must entertain first before it can be anything else. I learned that there is no such thing as a 'grade reading level'; a young person's 'reading level' and attention span will rise and fall according to his degree of interest. I learned that if you do not have a happy ending for the young, you had better do some fast talking." He observed that young adults are most concerned with winning approval from their peers and seeking reassurance from their reading material. It is with these needs in mind that Peck writes about the passage from childhood to adulthood. He believes that in a young adult novel, "the reader meets a worthy young character who takes one step nearer maturity, and he or she takes that step independently."

Peck's first novel, *Don't Look and It Won't Hurt,* concerned the consequences of a teenage pregnancy. Knowing that teens don't identify with protagonists they view as losers, he told the story of alienation and healing from the viewpoint of the young mother's younger sister. This fifteen-year old manages to keep her beleaguered family together, "parenting" her parents in a role reversal that appeals to readers of this age group. She is also instrumental in the sister's recovery after it is decided she will give the baby up for adoption. The novel received much critical praise and became a long-lasting popular success.

Peck's controversial novel about a teenage girl who is raped, *Are You in the House Alone?,* won the Edgar Allan Poe Award in 1976. *Bulletin of the Center for Children's Books* writer Zena Sutherland was impressed by the novel's scope: "Peck sees clearly both society's problem and the victim's: the range of attitudes, the awful indignity, the ramifications of fear and shame." Peck explained in his speech, "I did not write the novel to tell the young about rape. They already know what that is." He said he wrote it to warn the young that criminals are regrettably sometimes treated with more respect than victims even though victims of crime live in the shadow of that experience for the rest of their lives. *New York Times Book Review* critic Alix Nelson thought that Peck "ought to be congratulated for connecting with, and raising the consciousness of, his target audience . . . on a subject most people shun."

Close Enough to Touch, a love story written in response to a young man's request that Peck should write a book about dating, is related by its young male narrator. In his speech Peck said: "It might please some boys to be given this voice. It might surprise some girls that boys have emotions too. Mother never told them. Mothers are still telling daughters that boys only want one thing. How wrong they are. Boys want a great deal." When the boy's first love dies, he suddenly has to cope with the fact that just as no one had prepared him for intimacy with the opposite sex, no one has prepared him to face grief. "There is no sexual content in this book," Peck explained. "This is a novel about the emotions, not the senses."

In 1980, Peck published *Amanda/Miranda,* a novel written for adult readers. It is a romantic story set on the oceanliner *Titanic,* which sank in the Atlantic on its maiden voyage in 1912. Peck explained to Mercier that he didn't want this romance to reflect stereotypical sex roles, despite the fact that "in period novels, women are usually the prizes for men of ingenuity." Instead, Peck made the heroine "the ingenious one in adversity, winner of the male prize, for a change." *Amanda/Miranda* was a bestseller and has been translated into nine languages.

"Peck is adept at sketching a character in a few lines," commented a contributor to *St. James Guide to Young Adult Writers.* Even secondary characters seem fully realized, particularly those characters of parents who are struggling with the difficult job of child-rearing. Peck also "writes sensitively about the emotions of boys and their relationships, especially those between father and son." Commenting on *Father Figure,* in which Jim Atwater's mother commits suicide, the essayist wrote that "Jim is left fending off feelings of guilt, and describes his pent-up emotions and subsequent events in a glib tone, as if from a long distance." When left in the care of an elderly grandmother, Jim takes charge of his younger brother, Byron; when it is finally arranged that Jim and Byron will go to live with their father, Jim's resentment of the man, who had left the family eight years earlier, causes anger and jealousy over the relationship that develops between Byron and their father.

In his "Blossom Culp" books, Peck mixed humor and the supernatural. Set in the years 1913 and 1914, they feature spirited young Blossom Culp, who makes her own rules for life and has psychic powers. In such books as *The Ghost Belonged to Me* and *Ghosts I Have Been,* Blossom is revealed as a strong and resourceful young heroine. Through the use of time-travel plot devices, readers are introduced to Ancient Egypt and the women's suffrage movement in *Blossom Culp and the Sleep of Death.* The ghost characters in the Culp books are "distinct and memorable," wrote the contributor in the St. James Guide to Young Adult Writers. Past and future are also blended with ease in Peck's science-fiction-influenced novels *Lost in Cyberspace* and *The Great Interactive Dream Machine.*

Peck came up with an unusual character named Grandma Dowdel in *A Long Way from Chicago,* a collection of "seven thoroughly entertaining stories," wrote *Horn Book* reviewer Kitty Flynn. Living in a small town in Illinois during the Depression, this grandmother continually surprises readers and her visiting grandchildren with antics such as throwing cherry bombs and stealing the sheriff's boat. The collection showcases the author's skill with dialogue and drama, according to Flynn. "Told with verve, economy, and assurance, each tale is a small masterpiece of storytelling, subtly building on the ones that precede it. Taken as a whole, the novel reveals a strong sense of place, a depth of characterization, and a rich sense of humor." *A Long Way from Chicago* was named a Newbery Honor book, and Peck created a sequel, *A Year down Yonder,* in 2000. Grandma's influence on others is again portrayed with "wit, gentleness, and outrageous farce," affirmed Hazel Rochman in *Booklist.*

Rural Illinois was again the setting for *Fair Weather,* a humorous, exciting story that takes place at the 1893 Chicago World's Fair. Flynn, in another *Horn Book* review, wrote that the fair itself can be seen as a character, as the major characters are changed by their contact with it. The central character, Rosie, along with an older sister and a younger brother, are invited to leave their farm home to see the fair, while staying with a widowed aunt in the city. Peck "makes the exposition come alive as much for his twenty-first-century readers as for his richly imagined characters," wrote Flynn. The author's humor and skillful use of cameo appearances by famous historical personages is alluded to by Kit Vaughan in her *School Library Journal* review, which calls *Fair Weather* "marvelously funny." "Peck's unforgettable characters, cunning dialogue and fast-paced action will keep readers of all ages in stitches as he captures a colorful chapter in American history," concluded a *Publishers Weekly* writer.

In *The River between Us,* Peck explores some of the consequences of the Civil War, particularly for those women who were of mixed race. Light-skinned women often had a higher social status under the slavery system than those with darker skin, but they knew this advantage would be lost if the South did not win the war. Many of those who could pass for white or Spanish fled to begin new lives in Mexico or the free states. In the story, which is framed as a remembrance within the larger story, two mysterious women get off a steamboat in southern Illinois. One of the new arrivals appears to be rich, stylish, and very worldly; the other, of darker complexion, is thought by some to be her slave. When they announce that it is too dangerous for them to continue traveling, they are taken in by a local woman. "Peck's spare writing has never been more eloquent than in this powerful mystery in which personal secrets drive the plot and reveal the history," wrote *Booklist* contributor Hazel Rochman. *Horn Book* reviewer Peter D. Sieruta described this as a "powerful novel" with a "stunning conclusion."

Peck's characters are generally known for their independence and individuality. He feels that these qualities are especially important for characters in teenage fiction, writing in *Literature for Today's Young Adults* that we need to "indicate to the young that all of life need not be as cruelly conformist and conservative as adolescence." He concluded that the future of young adult fiction is in "books that invite the young to think for themselves instead of for each other."

Peck strongly believes that American attitudes about public education have resulted in a system that has put young people at a disadvantage, instead of equipping them for survival in the real world. Addressing other writers in his speech, he said, "Our readers of the 1980's are citizens of the moment not only because they are very young, but because they are no longer taught much history or foreign language or geography or cartography or scripture, which combines history, geography, poetry, and faith. You and I, we people of the word, spend our lives hollering across the famous generation gap, hoping to hear an answering echo." Survivors of the ravaged educational system and permissive parenting are few, he observed. Children raised in permissive homes tend not to look up to others because they view parents and teachers as their servants, Peck told Sutton. They tend to look down on others while viewing themselves as heroes. "There is not anywhere you can go from a permissive home. The rest of the world has rules," he said in his speech. His concerns about lack of strong moral values and the rise of consumer culture are expressed somewhat humorously in books such as *Secrets of the Shopping Mall* and *Bel-Air Bambi and the Mall Rats.*

He concluded that, fortunately, "There is another America, of course, beyond this somber landscape. An America revealed chiefly in books—by novels: of the past, on this year's list, of novels yet to be written. This America is one of self-reliance and coming from behind; of characters who learn to accept the consequences of their actions; of happy endings worked for and almost achieved; of being young in an old world and finding your way in it; of a nation of people hasty and forgetful but full still of hope; of limitless distances and new beginnings and starting over; of dreams like mountaintops, and rivers that run to the sea. We owe our young this record of our dreams, and if you and I do not put that record into their hands, who will?"

When asked what he hopes to accomplish in his books for young adults, Peck told Sutton, "I don't know what books can do, except one point is that I wish every kid knew that fiction can be truer than fact, that it isn't a frivolous pastime unless your reading taste is for the frivolous. I wish they knew that being literate is a way of being successful in any field. I wish they all wanted to pit their own experience against the experiences they see in books. And I wish they had to do a little more of that in order to pass the class in school. But in books you reach an awful lot of promising kids who write back good literate letters and give you hope. So that's the hope I have."

BIOGRAPHICAL AND CRITICAL SOURCES:

BOOKS

Children's Literature Review, Volume 15, Gale (Detroit, MI), 1988, pp. 146-166.

Contemporary Literary Criticism, Volume 21, Gale (Detroit, MI), 1982.

Donelson, Kenneth L. and Alleen Pace Nilsen, editors, *Literature for Today's Young Adults,* Scott, Foresman (Glenview, IL), 1980.

St. James Guide to Young Adult Writers, 2nd edition, St. James Press (Detroit, MI), 1999.

Something about the Author Autobiography Series, Volume 2, Gale (Detroit, MI), 1986, pp. 175-186.

Twentieth Century Children's Writers, St. Martin's Press (New York, NY), 1989.

Twentieth-Century Young Adult Writers, first edition, St. James Press (Detroit, MI), 1994.

Writers for Young Adults, Scribner (New York, NY), 1997.

PERIODICALS

American Libraries, April, 1973.

Arkansas Libraries, December, 1981, pp. 13-16.

Book, Kathleen Odean, review of *A Year down Yonder,* p. 83.

Booklist, September 1, 1998, Hazel Rochman, review of *A Long Way from Chicago,* p. 113; March 15, 1999, reviews of *A Long Way from Chicago* and *Strays Like Us,* p. 1301; November 15, 1999, Frances Bradburn, review of *Amanda/Miranda,* p. 615; April 15, 2000, Jeannette Larson, review of *A Long Way from Chicago* (audio version), p. 1561; October 15, 2000, Hazel Rochman, review of *A Year down Yonder,* p. 436; December 1, 2000, Stephanie Zvirin, review of *A Year down Yonder,* p. 693; April 1, 2001, Stephanie Zvirin, review of *A Year down Yonder,* p. 1486; September 1, 2001, Carolyn Phelan, review of *Fair Weather,* p. 110, Jean Hatfield, review of *A Year down Yonder,* p. 128; January 1, 2002, review of *Fair Weather,* p. 767; April 1, 2003, Brian Wilson, review of *Fair Weather* (audio version), p. 1412; September 15, 2003, review of *The River between Us,* p. 239.

Bulletin of the Center for Children's Books, March, 1977.

Christian Science Monitor, January 25, 2001, review of *A Year down Yonder,* p. 21.

English Journal, February, 1976, pp. 97-99; November, 2001, James Blasingame, Jr., review of *A Year down Yonder,* p. 117.

Fresno Bee (Fresno, CA), October 8, 2002, Nzong Xiong, "Newbery Medal Winner to Speak at Fresno State," p. E1.

Horn Book, November, 1998, review of *A Long Way from Chicago,* p. 738; January, 2000, review of *Amanda/Miranda,* p. 82; May, 2000, Kristi Beavin, review of *A Long Way from Chicago* (audio version), p. 342; November, 2000, Kitty Flynn, review of *A Year down Yonder,* p. 761; November-December, 2001, Kitty Flynn, review of *Fair Weather,* p. 757; May-June, 2003, Kristi Elle Jemtegaard, review of *Fair Weather* (audio version), p. 377; September-October, 2003, Peter D. Sieruta, review of *The River between Us,* p. 616.

Los Angeles Times, April 3, 1981.

Midwest Living, March-April, 2002, Jennifer Wilson, review of *Fair Weather,* p. 28.

New York Times Book Review, June 27, 1971; November 12, 1972, pp. 8, 10; July 27, 1975, p. 8; November 14, 1976, p. 29; December 2, 1979; August 16, 1998, Kimberly B. Marlowe, review of *London Holiday,* p. 17; March 11, 2001, Jim Gladstone, review of *A Year down Yonder,* p. 27; November 18, 2001, Ilene Cooper, review of *Fair Weather,* p. 45.

Plain Dealer (Cleveland, OH), July 6, 1999, Karen Sandstrom, "Richard Peck's Appeal More than Kids Stuff," p. 1E.

Psychology Today, September, 1975, pp. 11, 75.

Publishers Weekly, March 14, 1980; December 19, 1994, p. 55; March 6, 1995, p. 71; September 4, 1995, p. 70; September 2, 1996, p. 131; July 6, 1998, review of *A Long Way from Chicago,* p. 61; September 25, 2000, review of *A Year down Yonder,* p. 118; July 23, 2001, review of *Fair Weather,* p. 77; July 14, 2003, review of *The River between Us,* p. 77; July 21, 2003, Jennifer M. Brown, interview with Richard Peck, p. 169; November 10, 2003, review of *The River between Us,* p. 38; January 19, 2004, "Richard Peck Wins O'Dell Prize," p. 26.

St. Louis Post-Dispatch, August 29, 1999, Barbara Hertenstein, review of *London Holiday,* p. T5.

School Library Journal, May, 1986, pp. 37-39; June, 1990, pp. 36-40 (interview); May, 1992, p. 147; December, 1993, p. 27; October, 1994, p. 49; April, 1995, p. 154; September, 1995, p. 202; September, 1996, p. 206; August, 1998, Molly Connally, review of *London Holiday,* p. 197; September, 2000, Gerry Larson, review of *A Year down Yonder,* p. 236; April, 2001, Barbara Wysocki, review of *A Year down Yonder,* p. 92; September, 2001, Kit Vaughan, review of *Fair Weather,* p. 231; June, 2002, "Richard Peck Wins National Humanities Medal," p. 16; April, 2003, Jo-Ann Carhart, review of *Fair Weather* (audio version), p. 87; September, 2003, Connie Tyrrell Burns, review of *The River between Us,* p. 218; November, 2003, Carol Fazioli, review of *Anonymously Yours,* p. 83.

Times Literary Supplement, August 21, 1981.

Top of the News, winter, 1978, pp. 173-177; spring, 1987, pp. 297-301.
Washington Post Book World, November 10, 1974, p. 8; May 1, 1983.
Writing!, November-December, 2001, Catherine Gourley, interview with Richard Peck, p. 26.
Young Adult Cooperative Book Review, February, 1977.

ONLINE

BookPage Web site, http://www.bookpage.com/ (October, 2003), Linda Castellitto, interview with Richard Peck.*

* * *

PIZZEY, Erin 1939-

PERSONAL: Born February 19, 1939, in Tsingtao, China; married (separated); children: Leo, Amos. *Ethnicity:* "Irish." *Education:* Educated in convent schools. *Religion:* "I believe in God in all his aspects."

ADDRESSES: *Home*—Flat 5, 29 Lebanon Park, Twickenham, Middlesex TW1 3DH, England. *E-mail*—pizzey@pizzeyl.freeserve.co.uk.

CAREER: Writer. Chiswick Women's Aid, London, England, founder and chair; established several other shelters for abused women and children.

AWARDS, HONORS: Italian Peace Prize, 1978; Nancy Astor Award for journalism, 1983, 1985; made honorary citizen of St. Giovanni D'Asso, Italy, 1992; St. Valentino Palm d'Oro, 1994.

WRITINGS:

NOVELS

The Watershed, Hamish Hamilton (London, England), 1983.
In the Shadow of the Castle, Hamish Hamilton (London, England), 1984.
First Lady, Collins (New York, NY), 1986.
The Consul General's Daughter, Collins (New York, NY), 1987.
The Snow Leopard of Shanghai, Collins (London, England), 1989.
Other Lovers, HarperCollins (New York, NY), 1989.
Swimming with Dolphins, HarperCollins (New York, NY), 1990.
Morningstar, HarperCollins (New York, NY), 1992.
For the Love of a Stranger, HarperCollins (New York, NY), 1993.
Kisses, HarperCollins (New York, NY), 1995.
The Wicked World of Women, HarperCollins (New York, NY), 1996.

OTHER

Scream Quietly or the Neighbours Will Hear, Penguin (New York, NY), 1974, adapted by the author as a television play of the sme title, 1974.
Infernal Child: A Memoir, Gollancz (London, England), 1978.
The Slut's Cook Book, illustrated by Anny White, Macdonald (London, England), 1981.
(With Jeff Shapiro) *Prone to Violence,* Hamlyn (London, England), 1982.
Erin Pizzey Collects, Hamlyn (London, England), 1983.
That Awful Woman (television play), 1989.
Sanctuary (television play), 1989.
Requiem (screenplay), 1990.
Shadows (screenplay), 1993.
The Emotional Terrorist and the Violence-Prone, Commoners' Publishing (Ottawa, Ontario, Canada), 1998.

Contributor to magazines.

WORK IN PROGRESS: Two novels, *The Fame Game* and *The City of Secrets;* a television drama series for British Broadcasting Corp.

SIDELIGHTS: Erin Pizzey is an activist who writes both nonfiction works about women's social problems, especially domestic violence, and romance novels that defy the conventions of their genre. "You might find it strange that a leading feminist . . . should also be known as a successful writer of romantic/blockbuster novels," noted P. Campbell in *Twentieth-Century Romance and Historical Writers.* "However, Erin

Pizzey's books are not formula romances." Her characters are average, believable people who deal with tragedies and often emerge stronger than before.

"I write to tell the truth, however unpalatable, of women's lives," Pizzey commented in *Romance and Historical Writers.* Pizzey has recounted the real-life stories of abused women and children, and her work on their behalf, in *Scream Quietly or the Neighbours Will Hear, Infernal Child: A Memoir,* and *Prone to Violence.* Pizzey was a founder of Chiswick Women's Aid in London in 1971; it was the world's first shelter for battered women. *Scream Quietly or the Neighbours Will Hear* covers the beginnings of this organization. A *Publishers Weekly* reviewer pronounced the book "direct and lucid," as well as a "badly needed expose" on domestic violence. *America* commentator G. M. Anderson found the work "a pioneering book, and in terms of its impact one of the most important." Anderson described Pizzey's writing style as "informed with a determined individuality that [is] balanced by clarity and conciseness, and even by humor." *Infernal Child* provides both an update on Chiswick Women's Aid and insight into the experiences that shaped Pizzey's world view. Her father abused her mother, not physically, but emotionally; Pizzey believes that her commitment to helping victimized women had its roots in her observation of her father's behavior and in her eventual forgiveness of him. *Books and Bookmen* contributor Frank Longford deemed *Infernal Child* "a remarkable piece of autobiography," although he thought Pizzey's compassion for her father a bit excessive. Longford lauded Pizzey's generous spirit, but drew the line at "thanking God (which is what it comes to) for her father's maltreatment of his family as described." The account of Pizzey's cause-related work continues in *Prone to Violence,* written with fellow activist Jeff Shapiro. "The book should be read for its journalistic reporting of actual incidents; the psychologising of the authors is not of very much interest," remarked H. J. Eysenck in *Books and Bookmen.* Eysenck praised Pizzey's hands-on approach to treating social ills, though, finding it preferable to government solutions—which the reviewer characterized as bureaucratic and wasteful.

An abusive relationship is the subject of one of Pizzey's novels, *In the Shadow of the Castle.* The book's heroine, Bonnie, marries an older, wealthy man, Angus McPherson, who brutalizes her both emotionally and physically. Like many of the men in Pizzey's novels, he masks his true nature, concealing his cruelty with a charming demeanor. Bonnie endures his abuse for several years, but finally decides to leave him; unfortunately, he pursues her. "Bonnie's life as a battered wife is realistically and frighteningly portrayed," observed Campbell. Pizzey's other novels display a feminist bent as well. These include *First Lady,* a multigenerational family saga featuring several strong women characters, and *The Snow Leopard of Shanghai,* which chronicles a remarkable woman's life in mid-twentieth-century China.

Campbell described Pizzey as "an important voice in contemporary fiction" and praised her for exploring difficult topics with honesty and wit. "Everything from child abuse to homosexuality is treated seriously in Pizzey's novels, and her ability to create interesting characters in fascinating settings makes her a popular author," Campbell concluded. Pizzey once commented to *CA:* "I am concerned about the need to understand human relationships. I work mostly with violent relationships and the needs of the women, children, and men which have to be met. All my writing reflects this search and helps me think ahead to how we can see the family in the future."

Recently Pizzey added: "I am in the early stages of pioneering a new drama series with the British Broadcasting Corporation. For a non-artist, the transition from the verbal to the visible is fascinating and difficult. My work with victims of domestic violence continues, and much of my writing is influenced by the cases that come to me. I am also researching my new novel, *The City of Secrets.* It is set in Siena, Italy, which is indeed the most secretive city in the world. I travel all over the world, speaking about domestic violence and my writing. This gives me an opportunity to talk to people and to recognize how universal is the need to tell stories and for all of us to know and to experience love."

BIOGRAPHICAL AND CRITICAL SOURCES:

BOOKS

Pizzey, Erin, *Infernal Child: A Memoir,* Gollancz (London, England), 1978.

Twentieth-Century Romance and Historical Writers, St. James Press (Detroit, MI), 1994.

PERIODICALS

America, February 18, 1978, G. M. Anderson, review of *Scream Quietly or the Neighbours Will Hear,* p. 126.

Books and Bookmen, January, 1979, Frank Longford, review of *Infernal Child: A Memoir,* pp. 31-32; December, 1982, H. J. Eysenck, review of *Prone to Violence,* p. 38.

Publishers Weekly, October 3, 1977, review of *Scream Quietly or the Neighbours Will Hear,* p. 87.

Times Literary Supplement, November 15, 1974, p. 1290.

* * *

POLLITT, Michael G(erald) 1967-

PERSONAL: Born October 23, 1967, in Belfast, Northern Ireland; son of David (a bank manager) and Olive (Harpur) Pollitt; married Yvonne Abbott, 2000. *Education:* Sidney Sussex College, Cambridge, B.A. (with honors), 1989; Brasenose College, Oxford, M.Phil., 1991, D.Phil., 1994. *Religion:* Christian.

ADDRESSES: Office—Judge Institute of Management, Cambridge University, Trimpington St., Cambridge CB2 1AG, England; fax 44-1223-339701. *E-mail*—m.pollitt@jims.cam.ac.uk.

CAREER: Oxford University, Oxford, England, lecturer at Trinity College, Brasenose College, Worcester College, and Balliol College, 1991-94; Cambridge University, Cambridge, England, lecturer in applied industrial organization, 1994-99, lecturer in business economics, 1999-2001, senior lecturer, 2001—, fellow and director of studies in economics at Sidney Sussex College, 1994—, dean of discipline, 1997-2000. European School of Management, visiting lecturer, 1994-95; London Business School, visiting lecturer, 1996; speaker at Queen's University, Belfast, and Reitaku University, 1996, University of Surrey, 1997, and University of Dundee, 1998. Consultant to World Bank.

MEMBER: European Business Ethics Network, Royal Economic Society, Productivity Analysis and Research Network, Association of Christian Economists.

AWARDS, HONORS: Economic and Social Research Council grants, 1994-95, 1997—; CMI grant, 2001—.

WRITINGS:

Ownership and Performance in Electric Utilities: The International Evidence on Privatization and Efficiency, Oxford University Press (Oxford, England), 1995.

(Editor, with Ian W. Jones, and contributor) *The Role of Business Ethics in Economic Performance,* St. Martin's Press (New York, NY), 1998.

(With Lars Bergman and others) *A European Market for Electricity,* Centre for Economic Policy Analysis (London, England), 1999.

(Editor, with Sanford V. Berg and Masatsugu Tsuji) *Private Initiatives in Infrastructure: Priorities, Incentives, and Performance,* Edward Elgar (Northampton, MA), 2002.

(Editor, with Ian W. Jones) *Understanding How Issues in Business Ethics Develop,* Palgrave-Macmillan (New York, NY), 2002.

Contributor of articles and reviews to periodicals, including *Fiscal Studies, Oxford Economic Papers, Journal of Energy Literature, Oxford Energy Forum, Journal of the Association of Christian Economists, International Journal of Strategic Management,* and *Journal of Industrial Economics.*

WORK IN PROGRESS: Research on productivity analysis and measurement with special reference to the measurement of electricity, and on the impact of multinationals on social capital.

BIOGRAPHICAL AND CRITICAL SOURCES:

ONLINE

Cambridge-MIT Institute Electricity Project, http://www.econ.cam.ac.uk/electricity/people/pollitt/ (April 4, 2004).

* * *

PROULX, Monique 1952-

PERSONAL: Born January 17, 1952, in Quebec City, Quebec, Canada; daughter of Gustave Proulx and France de la Chevrotiere. *Ethnicity:* "Quebecoise." *Education:* Laval University, baccalaureate.

ADDRESSES: Home—4563 rue Hutchison, Montreal, Quebec H2V 4A1, Canada.

CAREER: Writer.

MEMBER: Societe des auteurs et compositeurs dramatique (SACD; French Society of Dramatique Authors and Composers), SACDEC, Union des ecrivaines et ecrivains quebecois (UNEQ; Union of Quebec Writers), Artistes pour la paix (Artists for Peace).

AWARDS, HONORS: Adrienne-Choquette Prize and *Journal de Montréal* Grand Prize, both 1984, both for *Sans coeur et sans reproche;* Quebec/Paris Prize, Desjardins Best Novel of the Year Prize, and Booksellers Grand Prize, all 1994, for *Homme invisible à la fenêtre;* Best Canadian Movie Award, Critique Award and Best Movie Award, and Salamandre d'or, best screenplay, all 1994, for *Le Sexe des étoiles;* Cristal Globe, best film and best screenplay, both 1998, for *Le Coeur au poing.*

WRITINGS:

FICTION

Sans coeur et sans reproche (short stories), Québec/Amérique (Montreal, Quebec, Canada), 1983.

Le Sexe des étoiles (novel), Québec/Amérique (Montreal, Quebec, Canada), 1987, translation by Matt Cohen published as *Sex of the Stars,* Douglas & McIntyre (Vancouver, British Columbia, Canada), 1996.

Homme invisible à la fenêtre (novel), Boréal (Montreal, Quebec, Canada), 1993, translation by Matt Cohen published as *Invisible Man at the Window,* Douglas & McIntyre (Vancouver, British Columbia, Canada), 1994.

Les Aurores montréales (short stories), Boréal (Montreal, Quebec, Canada), 1996, translation by Matt Cohen published as *Aurora Montrealis,* Douglas & McIntyre (Vancouver, British Columbia, Canada), 1997.

Le Coeur est un muscle involontaire (novel), Boréal (Montreal, Quebec, Canada), 2002, translation by David Homel and Fred A. Reed published as *The Heart Is an Involuntary Muscle,* Douglas & McIntyre (Vancouver, British Columbia, Canada), 2003.

SCREENPLAYS

Gaspard et fils, Vision-4, 1988.

A la vie a l'amour, ACPAV, 1989.

Le Futile et l'essentiel, TVOntarion, 1991.

Le Sexe des étoiles, Productions du Regard, 1993.

Le Coeur au poing, Cite/Amerique, 1998.

Le Grand Serpent du monde, Office national du film du Canada, 1999.

Souvenirs intimes (adapted from the novel *Homme invisible à la fenêtre*), Productions du Regard, 1999.

WORK IN PROGRESS: An original screenplay.

SIDELIGHTS: Monique Proulx writes films and has published award-winning novels and short stories. *Le Sexe des étoiles* centers around a brilliant male microbiologist who undergoes a transsexual transformation. The book details Marie-Pierre's impact on those around him, who include a novelist, a talk-show researcher, and Marie-Pierre's own astronomy-obsessed daughter, Camille, whom she fathered while a male. Elaine Kalman Naves, writing in *Quill & Quire,* found "noteworthy" Proulx's comfort with science "and how organically she incorporates Camille's fascination with the stars into her text. This passion for astronomy adds a touch of the metaphysical to the exploration of sexual 'otherness.'"

The setting of *Homme invisible à la fenêtre* is Montreal's literary Plateau district where Max, a paraplegic expressionist painter, lives and works in an abandoned building and interacts with the few people who are part of his life. Marguerite Andersen wrote in the *Canadian Book Review Annual* that the novel "is undoubtedly a masterpiece—intellectually stimulating, emotionally frightening, and masterfully translated" as *Invisible Man at the Window.* The characters include Gerald, a sculptor; Maggie, an actress; an art historian and her son; and Max's mother. Lady, Max's lover of twenty years before, moves into a loft facing his and begins watching him and phoning him nightly. Max's mother moves into the apartment next to his, but Max avoids involvement with both women, wanting only to be an observer, rather than a participant in life. Instead, he paints them and the other characters on canvas. Eileen Manion wrote in *Books in Canada* that Max "views others with 'the voracity of an eye that sees . . . without prejudice,' but on himself he turns a punishing irony to avoid the self-pity . . . he fears would destroy his will to live." Manion said Proulx maintains the suspense "almost to the end. . . . I read it with the intense commitment and absorption of a whodunit." Manion called *Homme invisible à la fenêtre* a "stunning novel about love . . . about the artistic process and its connection with the artist's inner life." *Homme invisible à la fenêtre* "is a treasure of Quebec literature: a beautiful, intelligent, joyful horror, much like life itself," wrote Kathleen Hickey in *Quill & Quire.*

Proulx's second volume of short stories, *Les Aurores montréales,* is a portrait of referendum and post-referendum Montreal. Declared by critics to cut across every kind of boundary—linguistic, political, racial, sexual, and ethnic—this sequence of twenty-seven stories has been said to unveil a complex and multi-faceted city. *Les Aurores montréales* shot to the top of the best-seller lists and was thought by critics to confirm Monique Proulx's position as one of the outstanding Quebec fiction writers of her generation. Maureen Garvie in *Quill & Quire* stated, "A superb translation by Matt Cohen now allows anglophones to step through the looking glass to marvel. . . . Finishing the book, the reader is convinced Monique Proulx is yet another reason why Canada would be infinitely poorer without Quebec."

BIOGRAPHICAL AND CRITICAL SOURCES:

PERIODICALS

Books in Canada, February, 1995, Eileen Manion, review of *Homme invisible à la fenêtre,* pp. 29-30.

Canadian Book Review Annual, 1995, Marguerite Andersen, review of *Homme invisible à la fenêtre,* p. 182; 1996, p. 173.

Canadian Literature, autumn, 1989, p. 265.

Essays on Canadian Writing, spring, 2002, Michael Eberle-Sinatra, review of the film *Le Sexe des étoiles.*

Montreal Gazette, March 13, 1998.

Quebec Studies, spring-summer, 2001, Denise Rochat, "Corps derobe: Handicap et condition postmoderne dans *Homme invisible à la fenêtre* de Monique Proulx," pp. 113-127.

Quill & Quire, September, 1994, Kathleen Hickey, review of *Homme invisible à la fenêtre,* p. 58; May, 1996, Elaine Kalman Naves, review of *Le Sexe des étoiles* p. 25; December, 1997, Maureen Garvie, review of *Les Aurores montréales,* p. 24.

R

RABE, David (William) 1940-

PERSONAL: Born March 10, 1940, in Dubuque, IA; son of William (a meatpacker) and Ruth (a department store worker; maiden name, McCormick) Rabe; married Elizabeth Pan (a laboratory technician), 1969 (marriage ended); married Jill Clayburgh (an actress), March, 1979; children: (first marriage) Jason; (second marriage) Michael, Lily. *Education:* Loras College, B.A., 1962; Villanova University, M.A., 1968.

ADDRESSES: *Office*—Grove/Atlantic Monthly Press, 841 Broadway, New York, NY 10003. *Agent*—United Talent Agency, 9560 Wilshire Blvd., 5th Floor, Beverly Hills, CA 90212.

CAREER: Playwright. Worked various jobs, 1963-65; *New Haven Register,* New Haven, CT, feature writer, 1969-70; Villanova University, Villanova, PA, assistant professor, 1970-72, consultant, beginning 1972. *Military service:* U.S. Army, 1965-67; served in Vietnam.

MEMBER: Philadelphia Rugby Club.

AWARDS, HONORS: Rockefeller grant, 1967; Associated Press Award, 1970, for series of articles written on Daytop addict rehabilitation program; Obie Award for distinguished playwriting from *Village Voice,* Drama Desk Award, and Drama Guild Award, all 1971, all for *The Basic Training of Pavlo Hummel;* Elizabeth Hull-Kate Warriner Award from Dramatists Guild, 1971, *Variety* poll award, 1971, Outer Circle Award, 1972, and Antoinette Perry (Tony) Award for best play

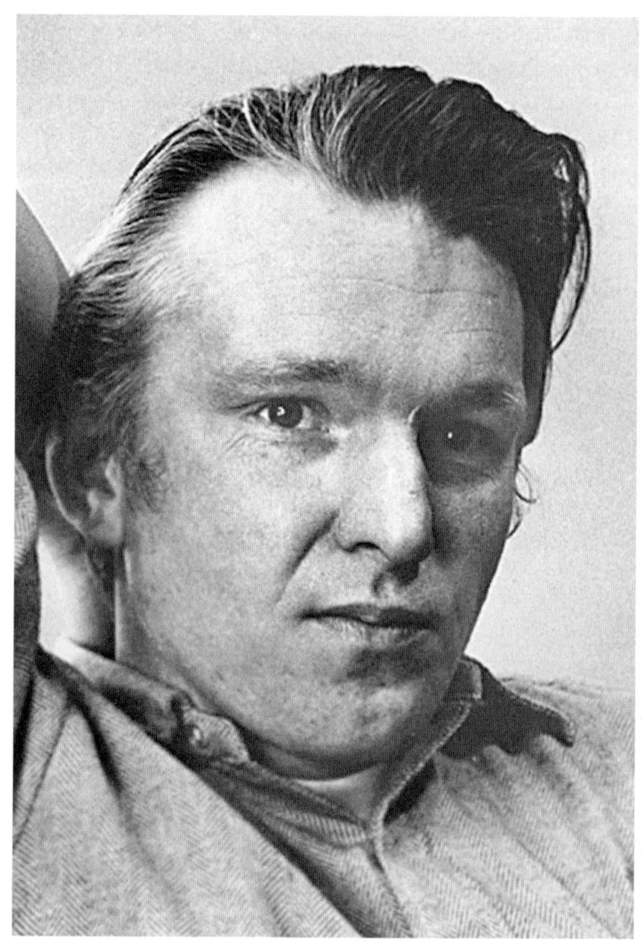

David Rabe

of 1971-72 season on Broadway, 1972, all for *Sticks and Bones;* New York Drama Critics Circle citation, 1972; Antoinette Perry Award Nominations for best play, 1974, for *Boom Boom Boom* and 1985, for *Hurlyburly;* Antoinette Perry Award Nominations for best play, New York Drama Critics Circle Award for best American play, 1976, for *Streamers;* National Institute and American Academy Award in Literature, 1976; Guggenheim fellowship, 1976.

WRITINGS:

PLAYS

Chameleon, produced at Loras College, Dubuque, IA, 1959.

Two Plays by David Rabe (contains *Sticks and Bones;* also see below; two-act, produced in New York at Anspacher Theatre, November 7, 1971, produced on Broadway at John Golden Theatre, August 1, 1972; and *The Basic Training of Pavlo Hummel;* also see below; first produced in New York at Newman Stage of The Public Theatre, May 20, 1971), Viking (New York, NY), 1973, published as *The Basic Training of Pavlo Hummel and Sticks and Bones: Two Plays,* Penguin (New York, NY), 1978.

The Orphan (also see below), produced in New York at Anspacher Theatre, April 18, 1973, revised version published as *The Orphan: A Play in Two Acts,* Samuel French (New York, NY), 1975.

In the Boom Boom Room (also see below; three-act; produced on Broadway at Vivian Beaumont Theatre, November 8, 1973), Knopf (New York, NY), 1975, revised edition with a note by the author (produced in New York, 1986), Grove Press (New York, NY), 1986.

Burning, produced in New York, 1974.

Streamers (also see below; produced in New Haven, CT, at Long Wharf Theater, 1976; produced on Broadway at Mitzi Newhouse Theater, 1976), Knopf (New York, NY), 1977.

Goose and Tomtom (produced in New York, 1982), Grove Press (New York, NY), 1986.

Hurlyburly (also see below; three-act; produced in New York, 1984); Grove Press (New York, NY), 1985, revised edition (produced in Los Angeles, 1988), Grove Weidenfeld (New York, NY), 1990.

Sticks and Bones: A Play in Two Acts, Samuel French (New York, NY), 1972, revised edition, 1987.

Those the River Keeps, (produced in Princeton, NJ, 1991), Grove Weidenfeld (New York, NY), 1991, published as *Those the River Keeps: A Drama in Two Acts,* Samuel French (New York, NY), 1994, published with *Hurlyburly* as *Those the River Keeps and Hurlyburly: Two Plays,* Grove Press (New York, NY), 1995.

The Vietnam Plays, Volume 1: *The Basic Training of Pavlo Hummel* [and] *Sticks and Bones,* Volume 2: *Streamers* [and] *The Orphan,* Grove Press (New York, NY), 1993.

A Question of Mercy: Based upon the Journal by Richard Selzer, (produced off-Broadway, 1997), Dramatists Play Service (New York, NY), 1998.

The Dog Problem, produced by the Atlantic Theater Company, New York, NY, 2001.

Also author of *The Crossing* (one-act).

SCREENPLAYS, EXCEPT AS NOTED

I'm Dancing as Fast as I Can, Paramount, 1982.

Streamers (adapted from his play), United Artists, 1983.

Casualties of War, Columbia, 1989.

(With Dennis McIntyre) *State of Grace,* Orion, 1990.

(With Robert Towne and David Rayfiel) *The Firm* (screenplay), Paramount, 1993.

Recital of the Dog (novel), Grove Press (New York, NY), 1993.

The Crossing Guard (novelization of the screenplay by Sean Penn), Hyperion Press (Westport, CT), 1995.

Hurlyburly (adapted from his play), Fine Line Features, 1998.

In the Boom Boom Room (adapted from his play), 1999.

A collection of Rabe's manuscripts is housed at the Mugar Memorial Library, Boston University.

SIDELIGHTS: David Rabe tackles difficult issues such as war, drug abuse, and misogyny in plays filled with lyrical language, profanities, black humor, and alienated characters. Works such as *Sticks and Bones, In the Boom Boom Room,* and *Hurlyburly* portray the playwright's dark view of American life, played out "within a series of metaphoric arenas—living rooms, military barracks, disco bars—where his characters collide violently against each other, but where, primarily, they struggle with their own society-fostered delusions," wrote Mark W. Estrin in *Contemporary Dramatists.* Rabe's most acclaimed works usually feature intense confrontation. He has proven his willingness to experiment with various theatrical formats, and according to *Dictionary of Literary Biography* writer James A. Patterson, "He blends humor and fear expertly and shows no tendency toward sentimentality."

Rabe was born to a middle-class family in Iowa. During high school, he was involved in sports and band, and he also began writing poetry and short stories. He was offered a football scholarship to Loras College in Dubuque, but majored in English instead, and became involved with the campus theater company. His first play, *Chameleon,* was performed on the campus in 1959. He also contributed to the campus literary magazine, winning several prizes for poetry and short stories. After earning his bachelor's degree in 1962, he went to Villanova University to work on a master's degree in theater, but he dropped out of the program (he later completed it) and was drafted into the army in 1965.

Rabe's army training and deployment to Vietnam were at first viewed by him as little more than an adventure. He did not take part in combat, but worked as a support person for a military hospital unit. At one point he tried to get a transfer to a combat unit, until the true horror of the killing struck him. He also discovered that he was unable to write while there, even though he felt he should. The experience itself was too horrible to amplify it by writing about it.

When Rabe was discharged after two years of duty, he came home to begin a very productive writing period. Drafts of four plays and one novel were all completed within one year. He returned to Villanova to finish his master's degree on a fellowship, and the university became a favored spot for him to try out new works. In 1969 Rabe married Elizabeth Pan, and soon after they moved to New Haven, Connecticut, where he worked at a newspaper, writing theater reviews and articles on subjects such as conscientious objectors and drug rehabilitation programs.

Rabe set about trying to get his drama professionally produced, sending copies of *The Basic Training of Pavlo Hummel* to several directors and theater agencies, including Joseph Papp at the Public Theater, a multi-stage venue in New York. Papp was enthusiastic about the play and arranged for its production. It was an immediate hit, and ran for 363 performances, winning Rabe several prestigious awards. Critical response was also generally positive. When *Sticks and Bones* joined *Pavlo Hummel* on one of the Public's stages in 1971, Rabe became the only playwright, other than Shakespeare, to have two plays performed concurrently at that theater. *Pavlo Hummel* is told in both realistic and surrealistic flashbacks. The play opens with the death of the title character, killed by a grenade thrown by a fellow soldier. Flashbacks relate his army life up until that point. *Sticks and Bones* and another play from that era, *Streamers,* also deal with the war and its effects. While the plays seemed to many to carry a strong anti-war sentiment, Rabe has consistently objected that he sought only to portray the reality of war, not to make any kind of political statement.

Rabe's thrust on the American family in *Sticks and Bones* is made apparent by the names of his main characters: Ozzie, Harriet, David, and Rick, the names of the family in the long-running, wholesome television series *Ozzie and Harriet.* In contrast to the security provided by Harriet's fudge, Ozzie's possessions, and Rick's guitar, David, when he speaks, reminds his family of the atrocities of Vietnam or his love for a "yellow girl." Henry Hewes gave this interpretation of the play's end: "Since David is unchangeable, the family must get rid of him and the memories he brought from the war. They do this by strangling the personification of the Vietnamese girl, who has been silently appearing throughout the play, and by helping David to kill himself. But the suggestion at the end of the play is that David will not entirely die, and that America will never quite exorcise the ghosts of Vietnam."

Variety described *Sticks and Bones* as "wordy and repetitious," suffering from the inarticulateness of its hero. Despite these reservations, the reviewer praised the "shattering impact" of Rabe's play—"a work of passion by a gifted writer." Clive Barnes cited "this interestingly flawed play" as being "far less confident in its style and texture" than *Pavlo Hummel,* stating Rabe's inexperience must "take the rap" for "the occasionally ponderous symbolism." Nonetheless, continued Barnes, *Sticks and Bones*"has a moral force that neither flinches nor sermonizes. This is surely all too unusual in our theater."

In *The Orphan,* Rabe reworked the myth of Oresteia, examining issues of fate and destiny. The characters of Agamemnon, Clytemnestra, and Orestes are juxtaposed with modern characters who testify about their experiences in Vietnam and with the Manson family. It is, wrote Carla J. McDonough in *Dictionary of Literary Biography,* "a rather jolting mix of contemporary and classical characters, dress, speech, and events." More experimental, as well as less controlled and sophisticated than his earlier plays, *The Orphan* was also less successful, closing after only fifty-three performances. Rabe's next play, *In the Boom Boom Room,* was not an immediate hit, but has become one of the most enduring works in his oeuvre. The story revolves around Chrissy, a young woman who wants to be a serious dancer, but who goes from dancing in a nightclub to a topless bar during the course of the play. Memories of physical and sexual abuse well up in her, and conditions in the club are metaphors for the meanness of life. Chrissy's relationships are destructive and unsuccessful. McDonough commented that "ultimately it seems to have no strong focus other than the message that without love, a person's life is hellacious." This was Rabe's first play to feature a female character. *Commonweal* reviewer Gerald Weales explained that "although much of *In the Boom Boom Room* is overextended and overexplained, at his best Rabe has an oblique style which is attractive because it suggests more than it defines, because it opens the audience to possibility."

Rabe returned to the backdrop of war and again found award-winning acclaim with *Streamers* in 1976. The barracks room set in a Virginia army camp functioned as a microcosm for the racial, sexual, and social tension in American society. Richie, a homosexual, Roger, an African American, and Billy, a professed homophobe, manage to adjust to each other's personalities, only to be stirred up by Carlyle, a new recruit whose anger affects them all. Weales found that in *Streamers* (the "most realistic of the Rabe plays") "it is obvious that Billy's interfering impulses, his failure to understand Richie or Carlyle, the violence hidden in his angry innocence provide a workable analogy for the American presence in Southeast Asia." And yet, he continued, "Rabe clearly does not intend that his play should have a narrowly political reference." It is, the reviewer felt, a play about a "world . . . in which, eventually, everyone's parachute refuses to open."

Rabe's next play, *Goose and Tomtom,* has ranked as one of his least successful works. The title characters are a pair of paranoid jewel thieves, living under the thrall of Lorraine, a streetwalker with plans to rule the world. Early in the play, Lorraine sticks pins into the arms of Goose and Tomtom to see which one is tougher. Both are so afraid of her that they never remove the pins, which become a running gag. *New York Times* reviewer Mel Gussow characterized *Goose and Tomtom* as a "vaudeville turn;" writing in the same newspaper, Wilborn Hampton termed the play "peculiar and slight." Gussow did give Rabe credit for trying something new, acknowledging that "one has to honor the attempt of a talented artist to break out of his mode," but he considered it "necessary to acknowledge the fact that 'Goose and Tomtom' lacks a light touch" and concluded that it "could be considered a long-delayed exploding cigar, a slow burn followed by a single anticlimactic pop."

Hampton felt *Goose and Tomtom* had more serious flaws than simply not being funny enough. In his view, the play "works much too hard at trying to be shocking and violent. As a result, any dark humor is dissipated in its predictability." Warning that "throughout the play there is a lot of whacking and torture," he further noted, "what is missing in all this mayhem is any kind of focus," concluding, "the whole exercise, whether viewed as a comedic analysis of the decline of Western society or just as a spoof . . . is pointless."

New York contributor John Simon went so far as to say, "After *Goose and Tomtom,* I feared not just for David Rabe's talent, but even for his sanity." But he announced that Rabe redeemed himself with his next drama, the highly-praised *Hurlyburly. Hurlyburly* is set in Hollywood, and its chief characters are all men involved in the film industry. The action, such as it is, involves their drinking, drug abuse, loveless sex, and shallow philosophizing. Their talk goes on so incessantly that Rabe included lines such as "blah-blah-blah" and "rapateeta" to symbolize its meaninglessness. Although there is a great deal of humor in the play, it is really concerned with the breakdown of morals in modern society, as epitomized in Southern California. "The picture of Hollywood is bleak," observed Clive Barnes in the *New York Post.* "Zombie denizens seem preoccupied. . .'with pharmaceutical experiments testing the parameters of the American dream.'" Barnes summed up: "Rabe has written a strange, bitterly funny, self-indulgent, important play. . . . I was entertained, horrified, intrigued, and disturbed by *Hurlyburly.*"

Robert Brustein analyzed the play's theme in depth in the *New Republic.* "What the play is about, I believe, is how the disintegration of American values has created a sense of anomie and a pronounced loss of purpose. Rabe's metaphor for this is cocaine." He further noted that *Hurlyburly* showed some marked stylistic changes from the playwright's earlier work—changes that in his opinion lifted Rabe's work to a new level. "Like [Eugene] O'Neill, who achieved greatness only when he adopted an unadorned Ibsenian realism, Rabe's style is now informed by the implicit *verismo* of David Mamet rather than the tendentious exhortations of Arthur Miller. . . . Besides displaying a dazzling new technique—not just a flawless command of dialogue, but an improved understanding of the nuances of human conflict—he has documented a chronicle of post-Vietnam War American life as pieced together from the shards of our shattered beliefs. Probing the social-metaphysical secrets revealed to only the most visionary playwrights, he has correctly seen that the plague of cocaine, which has infected virtually the entire entertainment industry, is less a disease than a symptom of a much larger malaise that is infecting virtually the entire country, thus giving us insights into our fall from grace, if not into our capacity for redemption."

Not all critics were as wholehearted in their praise of *Hurlyburly,* however. *New York Times* reviewer Frank Rich wrote that the first half of the play "offers some of Mr. Rabe's most inventive and disturbing writing," but he added that "it crash lands at midpoint." "Mr. Rabe remains a dynamic chronicler of the brutal games that eternally adolescent American men can play," Rich went on. "When his buddies aren't assaulting one another, they're on search-and-destroy missions against the No. 1 enemy—the women they invariably refer to as 'broads,' 'ghouls,' 'bitches' or worse." Rich remarked that the play fails when it attempts to show its characters' softer sides. "The ensuing revelations aren't terribly revealing," he wrote, "and the tributes to the tough guys' previously hidden vulnerability are banal. . . . This is a paltry, amorphous payoff to the strong buildup."

Other reviewers, such as *Newsweek*'s Jack Kroll, had no reservations about calling *Hurlyburly* a virtual masterpiece. Kroll called it "a powerful permanent contribution to American drama" and "a challenging work. Starting out as a tough, funny play about some Hollywood wise guys, it swerves, darts and drives deep into a darkness shot through with the emergency lights of anxiety and despair. . . . The climax, with its casual, nutty, almost comedic violence, has a frightening inevitability. Rabe's vision of the wasteland may not be impeccably structured, but it has a savage sincerity and a crackling theatrical vitality. . . . This deeply felt play deserves as wide an audience as possible." Rabe later adapted the play as a successful motion picture.

One of *Hurlyburly*'s characters, the self-destructive, emotional, would-be actor Phil, became the center of Rabe's next play, *Those the River Keeps.* This drama shows Phil in the years before the events of *Hurlyburly.* Having cut his ties with the East Coast mafia, Phil runs to California to realize his dream of acting, but he cannot escape the guilt he feels over his past crimes. When an old mobster associate shows up and urges Phil to join him on a hit mission, Phil is unable to turn him away. Rabe explained the major themes and metaphor of the title to Francis X. Clines of the *New York Times:*"Are there wounds in the past so strong that they'll pull you back no matter what you do? How do they seep into you unconsciously in indirect ways where you think you're doing one thing but really doing something else? What's the cut-off point where you can't get out?" *Those the River Keeps* was less well received than its predecessor. *Christian Science Monitor* contributor April Austin noted that "Phil's constant harping on the fact that life is essentially meaningless gets tiresome. . . . Rabe needs to trim chunks of the dialogue, or risk turning off the audience he has wooed into Phil's corner." *Variety* critic Jeremy Gerard wrote, "Yet it's also true that, like David Mamet (his stylistic opposite), Rabe hears poetry in the stuttering attempts of ordinary people trying to connect." Austin allowed, however, that the play "is powered by funny and pugnacious one-liners. It's mostly the put-down kind of humor, but it's a welcome break from Phil's self-absorption. . . . It's an interesting, if not thoroughly engrossing, piece of theater."

Rabe drew on the experience of his Vietnam plays when he wrote the screenplay for the film *Casualties of War.* The film, which *Rolling Stone* critic Peter Travers called "flawed but overwhelming," is based on a 1969 nonfiction article about a squad of American soldiers who were court-martialed for kidnapping, gang-raping, and then murdering a Vietnamese girl. The one member of the squad who did not participate in the rape and murder was a new arrival, Sven Ericksson, who later testified against the others. "The piece, published soon after in book form under the title *Casualties of War,*" Travers continued, "was both grim truth and a devastating metaphor for American imperialism." Some critics, however, felt that the film did not live up to the potential of either the director or the screenwriter. "In [Rabe's] screenplay all the characters seem familiar, not from life but from previous films or plays or novels," stated *New Republic* film reviewer Stanley Kauffman; "all of them are pushed around like charade figures to symbolize Quality A in conflict with Quality B. Following the story is less like watching a drama unfold than like watching a recipe being filled, a cup of bitterness, a spoonful of lust, a dash of remorse, etc." "Rabe champions the real Ericksson's point of view, which insists upon moral responsibility but which contradicts the film's social determinism," explained Gavin Smith in *Film Comment.* "A troubled discrepancy lies at this intersection of psychosocial behaviorism and humanist moralism that prevents the film from fully articulating a coherent point of view."

Rabe also was the coauthor of the screenplay adaptation of John Grisham's novel *The Firm. New York* movie critic David Denby described the film version of the story as "exciting, well acted, and smartly written, but I find myself in the bizarre position of asking for a trashier approach." Denby believed that the film, by trying to insert a sense of morality in Grisham's amoral novel, succeeded only in making *The Firm* feel "priggish and self-deluded." "The movie tries to produce real emotions and even, God help us, a few real people," Denby explained. "The way [director Sydney] Pollack and company have adapted the material, it no longer makes sense. The movie retains Grisham's pop structure but denies the audience a pop payoff." "Sometimes you can't fight the power of pop; you just have to go with it," he concluded. "Instead, Pollack and his crew have turned a terrific piece of escapist fiction into an earnest seminar on the dangers of greed."

Rabe is also the author of two novels: *Recital of the Dog,* an original story, and *The Crossing Guard,* a novelization of the screenplay of the movie by Sean Penn. *Los Angeles Times Book Review* contributor Erika Taylor called the latter book "interesting to read," and concluded that "by the end of 'The Crossing Guard,' Rabe fully inhabits his sad, emotionally complex novel." *New York Times Book Review* critic Randall Short, while acknowledging Rabe's status as "one of America's most distinguished playwrights [and] the possessor of a passionate moral imagination," felt that Rabe is out of his element in writing fiction rather than plays. He called the former book "uncomfortably reminiscent of a world-class pianist trying to impress his admirers by playing the violin." "It isn't that Mr. Rabe has difficulty with the form of the novel," *New York Times* contributor Michiko Kakutani wrote. "It's that he has abandoned the galvanic language and dark, sympathetic humor that made his finest plays so powerful and affecting."

More favorably reviewed was Rabe's *A Question of Mercy,* a dramatic adaptation of a 1991 *New York Times Magazine* essay by Richard Selzer. The subject was whether or not a doctor should help a terminally ill patient commit suicide. In Rabe's play, Dr. Chapman is called upon by Thomas, a man whose lover, Anthony, is dying of AIDS. Chapman narrates the play and ponders aloud the questions he confronts as he deals with the two men. *Back Stage Web site* reviewer Victor Gluck stated that the play is "riveting, not depressing, because it is about active choices and their consequences. It makes the viewer examine euthanasia in a whole new light." *New York Times* writer Ben Brantley noted that the writing demonstrates "elegance, discipline, restraint, not traits habitually associated with the author." McDonough observed, "The play explores the moral and emotional dilemmas without preaching, a trap that Rabe has fallen into in the past." Robert L. Daniels described the worth of *A Question of Mercy,* writing in *Variety:* "With unsettling candor and disturbing insight, the play arouses pity and understanding of a troubling subject."

BIOGRAPHICAL AND CRITICAL SOURCES:

BOOKS

Beidler, Philip D., *American Literature and the Experience of Vietnam,* University of Georgia Press (Athens, GA), 1982, pp. 85-136, 137-192.

Contemporary Dramatists, 6th edition, St. James Press (Detroit, MI), 1999.

Contemporary Literary Criticism, Gale (Detroit, MI), Volume 4, 1975; Volume 8, 1978; Volume 33, 1985.

Dictionary of Literary Biography, Gale (Detroit, MI), Volume 7: *Twentieth-Century American Dramatists,* 1981, Volume 228: *Twentieth-Century American Dramatists, second series,* Gale (Detroit, MI), 2000.

Hughes, Catharine, *Plays, Politics and Polemics,* Drama Book Specialists (New York, NY), 1973.

Kolin, Philip C., *David Rabe: A Stage History and a Primary and Secondary Bibliography,* Garland Publishing (New York, NY), 1988.

Simon, John, *Uneasy Stages: A Chronicle of the New York Theater, 1963-73,* Random House (New York, NY), 1975.

Zinman, Toby Silverman, *David Rabe: A Casebook,* Garland Publishing (New York, NY), 1991.

PERIODICALS

After Dark, August, 1972.

America, May 15, 1976.

American Theatre, July-August, 1997, Stephanie Coen, interview with David Rabe, p. 22.

Atlantic, December, 1976.

Austin American-Statesman (Austin, TX), January 15, 1999, review of *Hurlyburly,* p. E3.

Back Stage, March 7, 1997, David Sheward, review of *A Question of Mercy,* p. 52; July 6, 2001, Julius Novick, review of *The Dog Problem,* p. 40; July 27, 2001, Victor Gluck, review of *A Question of Mercy,* p. 31; February 15, 2002, Jeannette Toomer, review of *In the Boom Boom Room,* p. 54.

Back Stage West, December 4, 1997, Kerry Reid, review of *Hurlyburly,* p. 22; February 11, 1999, Madeleine Shaner, review of *Streamers,* p. 15; May 20, 1999, David-Edward Hughes, review of *A Question of Mercy,* p. 21; July 20, 2000, Brad Schreiber, review of *Question of Mercy,* p. 30.

Boston Globe, July 18, 1990, p. 66; May 11, 1993, p. 29.

Chicago Tribune, August 1, 1985, section 5, p. 7; February 24, 1987, section 5, p. 5; March 7, 1991, section 1, p. 28; February 7, 1993, section 14, p. 6.

Christian Science Monitor, May 17, 1993, p. 12; February 8, 1994, p. 12.

Commentary, July, 1976.

Commonweal, December 14, 1973; May 21, 1976.

Critical Quarterly, spring, 1982, pp. 73-82.

Cue, December 4, 1971; December 3, 1973.

Entertainment Weekly, December 8, 1995, p. 63; January 8, 1999, review of *Hurlyburly,* p. 44.

Film Comment, July-August, 1989, p. 49.

Interview, March, 1993, p. 84.

Library Journal, September 1, 1995, p. 209.

Los Angeles, January, 1989, p. 190; January, 1993, p. 125.

Los Angeles Times, February 6, 1985, section 6, p. 7; January 27, 1988, section 6, p. 6; November 17, 1988, section 6, p. 1; December 8, 1988, section 6, p. 1; December 11, 1988, p. C53; April 6, 1995, p. F10; September 20, 1995, p. F5.

Los Angeles Times Book Review, April 4, 1993, p. 7; December 10, 1995.

Nation, November 26, 1973; December 3, 1973; May 8, 1976; May 14, 1977.

National Review, August 9, 1993, p. 63.

New Republic, May 26, 1973; December 1, 1973; June 12, 1976; August 6, 1984, pp. 27-29; October 2, 1989, p. 26.

Newsday, March 2, 1972.

Newsweek, December 20, 1971; February 23, 1976; July 2, 1984, pp. 65, 67.

New York, September 17, 1973; July 16, 1984, pp. 42-45; July 12, 1993, p. 53; March 10, 1997, John Simon, review of *A Question of Mercy,* p. 52.

New Yorker, May 29, 1971; March 11, 1972; May 3, 1976; May 2, 1977; August 21, 1989, p. 76; February 7, 1993, pp. 32-34; February 7, 1994, p. 32; March 24, 1997, John Lahr, review of *A Question of Mercy,* p. 86.

New York Post, March 11, 1972; June 22, 1984.

New York Sunday News, April 1, 1973.

New York Theatre Critics' Reviews, June 25, 1984, p. 235.

New York Times, May 30, 1971; November 3, 1971; November 8, 1971; December 12, 1971; April 19, 1973; April 29, 1973; November 9, 1973; May 8, 1977; May 8, 1982, p. 17; June 22, 1984, p. C3; February 12, 1993, p. C31; January 30, 1994, section 2, p. 5; February 1, 1994, p. C13; April 19, 1995, p. C13; February 26, 1997, Ben Brantley, review of *A Question of Mercy.*

New York Times Book Review, February 7, 1993, p. 21.

Publishers Weekly, November 16, 1992, p. 46; August 21, 1995, p. 48.

Rapport, 6, 1994, p. 26.

Rocky Mountain News (Denver, CO), January 26, 2001, Lisa Bornstein, review of *A Question of Mercy,* p. D16.

Rolling Stone, September 7, 1989, p. 31.

Sarasota Herald Tribune (Sarasota, FL), March 5, 1999, Amanda Schurr, review of *Hurlyburly,* p. 20.

Saturday Review, November 27, 1971; April 17, 1976.

Seattle Post-Intelligencer, December 25, 1998, Paula Nechak, review of *Hurlyburly,* p. 21.

Seattle Times, December 25, 1998, Misha Berson, review of *Hurlyburly,* p. I6; May 6, 1999, Misha Berson, review of *A Question of Mercy,* p. G28; May 13, 1999, Michael Upchurch, review of *A Question of Mercy,* p. C1.
Tampa Tribune (Tampa, FL), March 12, 1999, review of *Hurlyburly,* p. 5.
Time, May 3, 1975; May 9, 1977; August 21, 1989, p. 54; January 18, 1999, Richard Schickel, review of *Hurlyburly,* p. 86.
Tribune Books (Chicago, IL), January 3, 1993, p. 6; February 7, 1993, p. 6.
Variety, March 8, 1972; February 7, 1994, p. 60; March 3, 1997, Robert L. Daniels, review of *A Question of Mercy,* p. 78; February 21, 2000, Markland Taylor, review of *The Dog Problem,* p. 49; June 11, 2001, Robert Hofler, review of *The Dog Problem,* p. 25.
Village Voice, November 15, 1973.
Washington Post, July 9, 1990, p. B2; July 20, 1990, p. WW14.
Washington Times, December 28, 1998, Gary Arnold, review of *Hurlyburly,* p. 11.
Weekend Australian, March 13, 1999, David Stratton, review of *Hurlyburly,* p. R20.
Winston-Salem Journal (Winston-Salem, NC), June 25, 1999, Mark Burger, review of *Hurlyburly,* p. E4.
World Literature Today, spring, 1994, p. 371.*

* * *

RAGEN, Naomi 1949-
(N. T. Erline)

PERSONAL: Born July 10, 1949, in Brooklyn, NY; daughter of Louis (a cab driver) and Ada (a secretary; maiden name, Fogel) Terlinsky; married Alex Ragen (a systems analyst), November 24, 1969; children: Bracha, Asher, Rachel, Akiva. *Education:* Brooklyn College of the City University of New York, B.A. (cum laude), 1971; Hebrew University of Jerusalem, M.A., 1975. *Religion:* Orthodox Jewish.

ADDRESSES: Home—c/o P.O. Box 23004, Ramot, Jerusalem, Israel. *Agent*—Lisa Bankoff, International Creative Management, 40 West 57th St., New York, NY 10019. *E-mail*—naomi@naomiragen.com.

CAREER: Israel Environmental Protection Service, Jerusalem, publications editor, 1975-79; freelance writer, 1979-81; University of Santa Clara, Santa Clara, CA, director of development communications, 1981-82; San Jose Hospital Foundation, San Jose, CA, development coordinator, 1982-84; fiction writer, 1984—.

MEMBER: International PEN, Authors Guild, Authors League of America.

WRITINGS:

NOVELS

Jephte's Daughter, Warner Books (New York, NY), 1989.
Sotah, Crown (New York, NY), 1992.
The Sacrifice of Tamar, Crown (New York, NY), 1994.
The Ghost of Hannah Mendes, Simon & Schuster (New York, NY), 1998.
Chains around the Grass, Toby Press (Jerusalem, Israel), 2002.

OTHER

(Editor, under pseudonym N. T. Erline) Baruch Halpui Epstein, *My Uncle the Netziv,* Targum Press (Southfield, MI), 1988.
(Editor, under pseudonym N. T. Erline) Baruch Halpui Epstein, *Recollections: The Torah Temimah Recalls the Golden Age of European Jewry,* translation by Moshe Dombe, Targum Press (Southfield, MI), 1989.
Minyan Nashim (play; title means "A Quorum of Women"), produced in Tel Aviv, Israel, at Habimah, 2002.

Columnist, *Jerusalem Post,* 1998-2001. Contributor to periodicals, including *Hadassah, Environmental Management,* and *Features from Jerusalem.*

SIDELIGHTS: Naomi Ragen's novels explore individual struggles within ultra-Orthodox Jews' faith and traditions. Ragen once told *CA:* "My writing is deeply reflective of the philosophy, idioms, and values of the Old Testament, the Talmud, and related sources. D. H. Lawrence was a model, as well as E. M. Forster, Irwin

Shaw, and Leo Tolstoy, who was also a deeply religious writer. Good and evil, their definition and interaction, interest me.

"My first novel, *Jephte's Daughter,* deals with the modern-day world of Chassidic Jews in Jerusalem. It is the coming-of-age story of a young Chassidic woman who struggles to reconcile deeply felt religious teachings with her own desire for freedom and growth. My character's education is very similar to my own Orthodox upbringing. The main difficulty was to demonstrate convincingly that religion can enrich as well as suffocate, depending on its interpretation. Though I was aiming for a mass readership, I didn't want to achieve popularity by embracing the easy, cliche road of having her abandon religion and embrace modern secularism. It was vital to me that my character find her freedom without abandoning her religious beliefs—to show that the two are not mutually exclusive.

"I wanted the reader to identify with her love for her religion, to feel compassion for her suffering despite the foreignness of her lifestyle. I wanted the reader to step into her shoes, to understand her reasoning, to see the world through her eyes. I tried to achieve this through vivid, accurate detail."

Jephte's Daughter tells the story of Batsheva, a young woman from a prosperous Orthodox Jewish family in Los Angeles, when she is transplanted to Jerusalem following a marriage arranged by her father to a Talmudic scholar who turns out to be abusive. She must escape with her son to seek a new life. "Despite eloquent writing and vivid characters," wrote a *Publishers Weekly* critic, the story "falters under convenient plot machinations that compromise the full development of its religious and emotional themes." *New York Times Book Review* contributor Katrina Blickle noted that while the portrayal of Batsheva is "sympathetic and realistic," the novel fails to overcome "repetitive, breathless prose . . . ridiculous plot . . . and sophomoric theologizing." In contrast, a *Kirkus Reviews* assessment described *Jephte's Daughter* as an "emotionally potent book" that is "written with welcome, no-nonsense clarity, and resolutely surely sure of its subject matter."

Ragen's second novel, *Sotah,* "continues her exploration of orthodox Jewish life in [a] story of a woman accused of adultery," commented a *Kirkus Reviews* contributor. The woman, Dina, lives among the ultra-Orthodox Jewish community in Jerusalem; as a result of the accusations, she leaves for New York. "This readable, but at times simplistic novel. . . [is] a stronger work of fiction than *Jephte's Daughter,*" determined a *Publishers Weekly* critic, who praised *Sotah*'s ability to hold "the reader's attention throughout." According to *Rapport* reviewer John R. Carroll, *Sotah* "is rich . . . rich in history, rich in characterizations, rich in details and rich in [religious] tradition. . . . [outlining] for the non-Jew a world that may seem foreign and distant, but remains very very real." Carroll wrote: "One does not have to be Jewish to appreciate Dina's story." According to Ragen, this is the ultimate compliment.

Ragen once explained to *CA* her goal in writing: "Bruno Bettelheim wrote in *Surviving the Holocaust* that 'this ability of our imagination to suffer with and for our fellow human beings is the best, possibly the only protection against another catastrophe such as the one Hitler's Third Reich brought about.' A novel that reaches out to readers and draws them into an alien culture, a new environment, allowing them to exercise and extend their compassion toward fictional characters is a humanizing experience. If my work has achieved that even once with even one reader, I'd consider it a success."

The Sacrifice of Tamar, Ragen's third novel, once again expounds on her belief that, as a *Kirkus Reviews* contributor reported, "fulfillment can be found outside the rigid boundaries of community but within the teachings of the commandments." In this story Tamar, a married Orthodox Jewish woman, is raped by a black man and subsequently becomes pregnant. Unsure if the rapist or her husband the father—her child was born with white skin—Tamar discloses the attack only to two close woman friends but is plagued by her secret for decades. "Despite an awkward, self-conscious opening, this rewarding novel gradually endears itself to the patient reader," remarked Glen Gerhart in *Rapport.* Gerhart called the novel "a satisfyingly poignant story. . . . a chronicle of the moral and spiritual quest we all must make," but noted that at times Ragen's extensive discussion of religious and cultural customs interferes with her storytelling. A *Publishers Weekly* critic also found this aspect of the book tedious and complained that the novel presented few new revelations about the "insular and provincial world that she has chosen to portray." This reviewer concluded that Ragen's "plots are becoming hackneyed" despite her being "an able storyteller" and her facility for dialogue. *Kirkus Reviews* summed up *The Sacrifice of Tamar* by calling it "cliche-ridden and predictable, but also strangely affecting."

BIOGRAPHICAL AND CRITICAL SOURCES:

PERIODICALS

Kirkus Reviews, November 1, 1988, review of *Jephte's Daughter,* p. 1559; August 1, 1992, review of *Sotah,* p. 943; August 15, 1994, review of *The Sacrifice of Tamar,* pp. 1080-1081.

New York Times Book Review, April 2, 1989, Katrina Blickle, review of *Jephte's Daughter,* p. 28; March 5, 1995, p. 14.

Publishers Weekly, October 28, 1988, review of *Jephte's Daughter,* p. 63; August 31, 1992, review of *Sotah,* p. 64; September 12, 1994, review of *The Sacrifice of Tamar,* p. 81.

Rapport, March, 1993, John R. Carroll, review of *Sotah,* p. 27; May, 1995, Glen Gerhart, review of *The Sacrifice of Tamar,* p. 21.

Times (London, England), July 17, 1989.

ONLINE

Naomi Ragen Home Page, http://www.naomiragen.com/ (April 5, 2004).

* * *

RIKER, Leigh 1941-

PERSONAL: Born May 24, 1941, in Akron, OH; daughter of Robert Andrew (an auditor) and Mona (a secretary; maiden name, Perry) Bartley; married Donald K. Riker (a scientist), October 30, 1965; children: Scott, Hal. *Education:* Kent State University, B.A., 1963. *Hobbies and other interests:* Travel, history of the Middle Ages, movies, gardening, playing the piano, long walks, reading, horseback riding.

ADDRESSES: Home and office—683 Deer Run Trail, Lebanon, OH 45036. *Agent*—Curtis Brown Ltd., 10 Astor Place, New York, NY 10003. *E-mail*—LeighRiker@aol.com.

CAREER: John Wiley & Sons (publisher), New York, NY, secretary to the executive editor in textbook division, 1964-66; University of Kansas, Lawrence, secretary in economics department, 1966-68; American Association for the Advancement of Science, New York, NY, administrative assistant, 1968-70; self-employed typist and manuscript editor, 1970-76; freelance writer, 1976—; Writer's Digest School, editorial associate, 1991. Also taught creative writing at Writer's Digest School. Full-time writer. Has served as a judge for the RITA Awards, the Women's Fiction Writers Association's Great Beginnings, the Northwest Houston RWA Lone Star Writing Competition, the Wyoming Writers Adult Fiction contest, and the Connecticut RWA Now and Then writing contests.

MEMBER: Authors Guild, Romance Writers of America (Ohio Valley chapter), Published Authors Network (former cochair, Career Planning Subcommittee), Novelists, Inc.

WRITINGS:

Heartsong, Popular Library (New York, NY), 1985.

Acts of Passion, Popular Library (New York, NY), 1985.

Morning Rain, Harper (New York, NY), 1991.

Unforgettable, Harper (New York, NY), 1993.

Tears of Jade, Harper (New York, NY), 1993.

Just One of Those Things, Harper (New York, NY), 1994.

Oh, Susannah, Harper (New York, NY), 1995.

Danny Boy, Harper (New York, NY), 1995.

Lady Killer (e-book), StarPublications.com, 2000.

Strapless, Red Dress Ink (Don Mills, Ontario, Canada), 2002.

Contributor of short stories to *Woman's World,* under name Leigh Bartley, and of articles to writers' magazines.

WORK IN PROGRESS: Double Take, a romance for Intrigue; a project for Red Dress Ink.

SIDELIGHTS: Leigh Riker has crafted romance novels featuring endearing heroines who grapple with tragedy. Her characterization, real-life conflict, and crisp writing have earned her a loyal following and much critical acclaim.

Riker's novel *Acts of Passion* introduced heroine Gillian Shephard, an actress aspiring for a part in a Broadway play. Gillian is granted her dream, but only to have it fall through, along with her romantic relationship. Gillian is left to pick up the pieces of her life alone. Gillian is like many of Riker's heroines in that readers can relate to her struggles and failures—a reason why so many devour her books. Riker's heroine Erin Brodey Sinclair is an unhappily married woman struggling to keep her marriage together in *Danny Boy.* Erin's husband, Danny, contests with problems beyond the marriage, as his brother, Ken, pines away for Erin and resents Danny for neglecting the woman whom Ken truly loves. Writing for the *Romantic Times Book Club* reviewer Jill M. Smith observed, "Riker delivers a powerful and deeply moving exploration of a troubled marriage and a family on the brink of destruction." Smith then explained how this book differs from similar books on the market: "Ms. Riker expertly reveals the soul of this family, where there are no villains, just fallible, but caring, human beings."

Riker's novel *Strapless* may be the most well-received of all her novels. Darcie Baxter is a New York woman approaching thirty who yearns for success in her career and satisfaction in her current romantic relationship. Darcie is not a jet-setter, however. She lives in an apartment with her grandmother and works at Wunderthings Lingerie International, a company seeking to open an Australian branch and in search of someone to lead the operation. Darcie longs to be a travelling executive and is thrilled to receive the promotion. In Australia, she meets and has an affair with sheep rancher Dylan Rafferty. But when Darcie's two weeks Down Under are over, she discovers that Dylan is serious about her and wants a wife and family. With Darcie's career on the rise, she finds herself with some serious and unexpected decisions to make, pondering the modern woman's quandary of how to balance career and family—if Darcie decides that a family is what she wants. *All Readers* reviewer Harriet Klausner termed *Strapless* "an engaging contemporary romance that adds the flavor of Sydney to the mix." Klausner maintained that "the story line [of *Strapless*] is fun," and "readers will relish Leigh Riker's wild Down Under ride." In a review for *Booklist,* Kristine Huntley suggested a similar opinion of the book, calling it a "snappy, satisfying summer read."

"Before I started writing *Strapless,* I had wanted a fresh challenge," Riker told reviewer Lori A. May in an interview published in *Heartstrings* online. Commenting on her move toward mainstream fiction, Riker reported, "*Strapless* provided that [challenge] and I love taking this new direction for my work. But I think my voice has always been mainstream." When asked by interviewer May about the problems of taking a new direction with *Strapless,* Riker confessed that "writing *Strapless* just wasn't that difficult. In fact, it was a joy. For the first few weeks, my fingers just flew at the computer, a good sign, and that's rare, believe me. This book was a gift." Riker related to May details of the wonderful feedback she has gotten from readers, some with questions about writing themselves. To those who are inspired to write, Riker has this advice to offer: "If you have the dream to write, don't let anyone stop you." Riker once told *CA:* "I can remember having the urge to write from the age of eight. During grammar school I wrote what amounted to a teen soap opera. Had I practiced regularly from then on, I would have been published far sooner than I was." Riker concluded her interview with May by relating a message to her loyal readers: "You are the other end of the communication that runs between reader and writer, and a direct line to the heart."

BIOGRAPHICAL AND CRITICAL SOURCES:

PERIODICALS

Booklist, August, 2002, Kristine Huntley, review of *Strapless.*

ONLINE

All Readers, http://www.allreaders.com/ (January 23, 2004), Harriet Klausner, review of *Strapless.*

Eclectics, http://www.eclectics.com/ (January 23, 2004), "Leigh Riker."

Heartstrings, http://romanticfiction.com/ (January 23, 2004), Lori A. May, "An Interview with Leigh Riker."

Love Romances, http://www.loveromances.com/ (January 23, 2004), review of *Strapless.*

Red Dress Ink, http://www.reddressink.com/ (January 23, 3004), "Authors: Leigh Riker."

Romantic Times Book Club, http://www.romantictimes.com/ (January 23, 2004), "Author Information: Leigh Riker."*

ROBB, J. D.
See ROBERTS, Nora

* * *

ROBERTS, Nora 1950-
(J. D. Robb)

PERSONAL: Born October 10, 1950, in Washington, DC; daughter of Bernard Edward (a company president) and Eleanor (a company vice president; maiden name, Harris) Robertson; married Ronald Aufdem-Brinke, August 17, 1968 (divorced, January, 1985); married Bruce Wilder (a carpenter), July 6, 1985; children: (first marriage) Daniel, Jason. *Education:* Attended public schools in Silver Spring, MD. *Politics:* Democrat. *Religion:* Roman Catholic.

ADDRESSES: *Home*—Keedysville, MD. *Agent*—Amy Berkower, Writers House, Inc., 21 West 26th St., New York, NY 10010. *E-mail*—write2nora@msn.com.

CAREER: Novelist, 1979—. Wheeler & Korpeck, Silver Spring, MD, legal secretary, 1968-70; The Hecht Co., Silver Spring, clerk, 1970-72; R. & R. Lighting, Silver Spring, secretary, 1972-75.

MEMBER: Romance Writers of America, Washington Romance Writers.

AWARDS, HONORS: Golden Medallion, Romance Writers of America, 1982, for *The Heart's Victory,* 1983, for *This Magic Moment* and *Untamed,* 1984, for *Opposites Attract* and *A Matter of Choice,* and 1986, for *One Summer;* named best contemporary author by *Romantic Times,* 1984; Reviewer's Choice Award, *Romantic Times,* 1984, for *Reflections,* 1985, for *Partners,* and 1986, for *One Summer;* MacGregor series named best series by *Romantic Times,* 1985; Silver Certificate, *Affaire du Coeur,* 1985, for the MacGregor series; Waldenbooks Award, 1985, for *One Man's Art,* 1986, for *A Will and a Way,* 1988, for *The Last Honest Woman,* 1993, for *Gabriel's Angel* and for *For the Love of Lilah;* Maggie Award, Georgia Romance Writers of America, 1985, for *Partners;* first author inducted into Romance Writers of America Hall of Fame, 1986; RITA Award, Romance Writers of America, 1990, for *Public Secrets,* 1991, for *Night Shift,* and 1992, for *Divine Evil;* B. Dalton Award for *Public Secrets, A Man for Amanda,* and *Suzannah's Surrender.*

WRITINGS:

ROMANCE NOVELS

Blithe Images, Silhouette (New York, NY), 1982.
Song of the West, Silhouette (New York, NY), 1982.
Search for Love, Silhouette (New York, NY), 1982.
Island of Flowers, Silhouette (New York, NY), 1982.
The Heart's Victory, Silhouette (New York, NY), 1982.
From This Day, Silhouette (New York, NY), 1983.
Her Mother's Keeper, Silhouette (New York, NY), 1983.
Once More with Feeling, Silhouette (New York, NY), 1983.
Untamed, Silhouette (New York, NY), 1983.
Reflections, Silhouette (New York, NY), 1983.
Dance of Dreams, Silhouette (New York, NY), 1983, reprinted, Hall (Thorndike, ME), 2000.
Tonight and Always, Silhouette (New York, NY), 1983, reprinted, 1990.
This Magic Moment, Silhouette (New York, NY), 1983.
Endings and Beginnings, Silhouette (New York, NY), 1984.
Storm Warning, Silhouette (New York, NY), 1984.
Sullivan's Woman, Silhouette (New York, NY), 1984.
Rules of the Game, Silhouette (New York, NY), 1984.
Less of a Stranger, Silhouette (New York, NY), 1984.
A Matter of Choice, Silhouette (New York, NY), 1984.
The Law Is a Lady, Silhouette (New York, NY), 1984.
First Impressions, Silhouette (New York, NY), 1984.
Opposites Attract, Silhouette (New York, NY), 1984.
Promise Me Tomorrow, Silhouette (New York, NY), 1984.
Partners, Silhouette (New York, NY), 1985.
The Right Path, Silhouette (New York, NY), 1985.
Boundary Lines, Silhouette (New York, NY), 1985.
Dual Image, Silhouette (New York, NY), 1985.
Night Moves, Harlequin (Toronto, Canada), 1985.
Summer Desserts, Silhouette (New York, NY), 1985.
Lessons Learned, Silhouette (New York, NY), 1986.
The Art of Deception, Silhouette (New York, NY), 1986.
One Summer, Silhouette (New York, NY), 1986.
Second Nature, Silhouette (New York, NY), 1986.

Treasures Lost, Treasures Found, Silhouette (New York, NY), 1986.
Risky Business, Silhouette (New York, NY), 1986.
A Will and a Way, Silhouette (New York, NY), 1986.
Home for Christmas, Silhouette (New York, NY), 1986.
Mind over Matter, Silhouette (New York, NY), 1987.
Temptation, Silhouette (New York, NY), 1987.
Hot Ice, Bantam (New York, NY), 1987, reprinted, 2002.
Sacred Sins, Bantam (New York, NY), 1987.
Brazen Virtue, Bantam (New York, NY), 1988.
Local Hero, Silhouette (New York, NY), 1988.
The Name of the Game, Silhouette (New York, NY), 1988.
Rebellion, Harlequin (Toronto, Canada), 1988.
Sweet Revenge, Bantam (New York, NY), 1989.
Loving Jack, Silhouette (New York, NY), 1989.
Best Laid Plans, Silhouette (New York, NY), 1989.
Lawless, Harlequin (Toronto, Canada), 1989.
Gabriel's Angel, Harlequin (Toronto, Canada), 1989.
The Welcoming, Silhouette (New York, NY), 1989.
Public Secrets, Bantam (New York, NY), 1990.
Genuine Lies, Bantam (New York, NY), 1991.
With This Ring, Harlequin (Toronto, Canada), 1991.
Carnal Innocence, Bantam (New York, NY), 1992.
Unfinished Business, Harlequin (Toronto, Canada), 1992.
The Welcoming, Chivers North America (Hampton, NH), 1992.
Honest Illusions, Putnam (New York, NY), 1992.
Divine Evil, Bantam (New York, NY), 1992.
Second Nature, Harlequin (Toronto, Canada), 1993.
Private Scandals, Putnam (New York, NY), 1993.
Boundary Lines, Harlequin (Toronto, Canada), 1994.
Hidden Riches, Putnam (New York, NY), 1994.
(With others) *Birds, Bees and Babies: The Best Mistake,* Silhouette (New York, NY), 1994.
Silhouette Christmas: All I Want for Christmas, Silhouette (New York, NY), 1994.
True Betrayals, Putnam (New York, NY), 1995.
Montana Sky, Putnam (New York, NY), 1996.
From the Heart, Thorndike Press (Thorndike, ME), 1997.
Sanctuary, Putnam (New York, NY), 1997.
The Reef, Putnam (New York, NY), 1998.
Homeport, Putnam (New York, NY), 1998.
Genuine Lies, Bantam (New York, NY), 1998.
River's End, Putnam (New York, NY), 1999.
Irish Rebel, Silhouette (New York, NY), 2000.
Carolina Moon, Berkley (New York, NY), 2001.
The Villa, Putnam (New York, NY), 2001.
Midnight Bayou, Putnam (New York, NY), 2001.
Three Fates, Putnam (New York, NY), 2002.
Chesapeake Blue, Putnam (New York, NY), 2002.
A Little Magic, Berkley (New York, NY), 2002.
Cordina's Crown Jewel, Silhouette (New York, NY), 2002.
Cordina's Royal Family, Silhouette (New York, NY), 2002.
Birthright, Putnam (New York, NY), 2003.
Engaging the Enemy, Silhouette (New York, NY), 2003.

"MACGREGOR" SERIES

Playing the Odds, Silhouette (New York, NY), 1985.
Tempting Fate, Silhouette (New York, NY), 1985.
All the Possibilities, Silhouette (New York, NY), 1985.
One Man's Art, Silhouette (New York, NY), 1985.
For Now, Forever, Silhouette (New York, NY), 1987.
Rebellion, Harlequin (Toronto, Canada), 1988.
In from the Cold, Harlequin (Toronto, Canada), 1990.
The MacGregor Brides, Silhouette (New York, NY), 1997.
The Winning Hand, Silhouette (New York, NY), 1998.
The MacGregor Grooms, Silhouette (New York, NY), 1998.
The MacGregors: Serena-Caine, Silhouette (New York, NY), 1998.
The MacGregors: Daniel-Ian, Harlequin (Toronto, Canada), 1999.
The MacGregors: Alan-Grant, Silhouette (New York, NY), 1999.
The Perfect Neighbor, Harlequin (Toronto, Canada), 1999.

"IRISH" SERIES

Irish Thoroughbred, Silhouette (New York, NY), 1981.
Irish Rose, Silhouette (New York, NY), 1988.
Irish Rebel, Silhouette (New York, NY), 2000.

"CORDINA" SERIES

Affaire Royale, Silhouette (New York, NY), 1986.
Command Performance, Silhouette (New York, NY), 1987.
The Playboy Prince, Silhouette (New York, NY), 1987.

"O'HURLEY" SERIES

The Last Honest Woman, Silhouette (New York, NY), 1988.
Dance to the Piper, Silhouette (New York, NY), 1988.
Skin Deep, Silhouette (New York, NY), 1988.
Without a Trace, Silhouette (New York, NY), 1991.

"THOSE WILD UKRAINIANS" SERIES

Taming Natasha, Silhouette (New York, NY), 1990.
Luring a Lady, Silhouette (New York, NY), 1991.
Falling for Rachel, Silhouette (New York, NY), 1993.
Convincing Alex, Silhouette (New York, NY), 1994.
Waiting for Nick, Silhouette (New York, NY), 1997.
Considering Kate, Silhouette (New York, NY), 2001.

"NIGHT" SERIES

Night Shift, Silhouette (New York, NY), 1991.
Night Shadow, Silhouette (New York, NY), 1991.
Nightshade, Silhouette (New York, NY), 1993.
Night Smoke, Silhouette (New York, NY), 1994.
*Night Shield,*Silhouette (New York, NY), 2000.

"CALHOUN WOMEN" SERIES

Courting Catherine, Silhouette (New York, NY), 1991.
A Man for Amanda, Silhouette (New York, NY), 1991.
For the Love of Lilah, Silhouette (New York, NY), 1991.
Suzannah's Surrender, Silhouette (New York, NY), 1991.
Megan's Mate, Silhouette (New York, NY), 1996.

"HORNBLOWER" SERIES

Time Was, Silhouette (New York, NY), 1993.
Times Change, Silhouette (New York, NY), 1993.

"BORN IN . . ." SERIES

Born in Fire, Jove (New York, NY), 1994.
Born in Ice, Jove (New York, NY), 1995.
Born in Shame, Jove (New York, NY), 1996.

"MACKADE" SERIES

The Return of Rafe MacKade, Silhouette (New York, NY), 1995.
The Pride of Jared MacKade, Silhouette (New York, NY), 1995.
The Heart of Devin MacKade, Silhouette (New York, NY), 1996.
The Fall of Shane MacKade, Silhouette (New York, NY), 1996.

"STAR" SERIES

Hidden Star, Silhouette (New York, NY), 1997.
Captive Star, Silhouette (New York, NY), 1997.
Secret Star, Silhouette (New York, NY), 1998.

"DONOVAN LEGACY" SERIES

Captivated, Silhouette (New York, NY), 1992.
Entranced, Silhouette (New York, NY), 1992.
Charmed, Silhouette (New York, NY), 1992.
Enchanted, Silhouette (New York, NY), 1999.
Donovan Legacy, Harlequin (Toronto, Canada), 1999.

"QUINN BROTHERS" TRILOGY AND SEQUEL

Sea Swept, Thorndike Press (Thorndike, ME), 1998.
Rising Tides, Jove (New York, NY), 1998.
Inner Harbor, Thorndike Press (Thorndike, ME), 1999.

"DREAM" TRILOGY

Holding the Dream, Thorndike Press (Thorndike, ME), 1997.
Daring to Dream, Thorndike Press (Thorndike, ME), 1997.
Finding the Dream, Thorndike Press (Thorndike, ME), 1997.
Three Complete Novels by Nora Roberts (includes *Daring to Dream, Holding the Dream,* and *Finding the Dream*), Putnam (New York, NY), 1999.

"THREE SISTERS ISLAND" TRILOGY

Dance upon the Air, Jove (New York, NY), 2001.
Heaven and Earth, Jove (New York, NY), 2001.
Face the Fire, Jove (New York, NY), 2002.

"IRELAND" TRILOGY

Jewels of the Sun, Jove (New York, NY), 1999.
Tears of the Moon, Jove (New York, NY), 2000.
Heart of the Sea, Jove (New York, NY), 2000.

"ONCE UPON A . . ." SERIES; WITH OTHERS

Once upon a Castle, Jove (New York, NY), 1998.
Once upon a Star, Jove (New York, NY), 1999.
Once upon a Rose, Jove (New York, NY), 2001.
Once upon a Kiss, Berkley (New York, NY), 2002.
Once upon a Midnight, Jove (New York, NY), 2003.

"KEY" SERIES

Key of Light, Jove (New York, NY), 2003.
Key of Knowledge, Jove (New York, NY), 2003.
Key of Valor, Jove (New York, NY), 2004.

UNDER PSEUDONYM J. D. ROBB; EXCEPT AS NOTED

(With Susan Plunkett, Dee Holmes, and Claire Cross) *Silent Night,* Putnam (New York, NY), 1998.
(As J. D. Robb and Nora Roberts) *Remember When,* Putnam (New York, NY), 2003.

"IN DEATH" SERIES; UNDER PSEUDONYM J. D. ROBB

Naked in Death, Berkley (New York, NY), 1995.
Glory in Death, Berkley (New York, NY), 1995.
Rapture in Death, Berkley (New York, NY), 1996.
Ceremony in Death, Berkley (New York, NY), 1997.
Vengeance in Death, Berkley (New York, NY), 1997.
Holiday in Death, Berkley (New York, NY), 1998.
Immortal in Death, Berkley (New York, NY), 1998.
Midnight in Death: Anthology, Berkley (New York, NY), 1998.
Loyalty in Death, Berkley (New York, NY), 1999.
Conspiracy in Death, Berkley (New York, NY), 1999.
Witness in Death, Berkley (New York, NY), 2000.
Judgment in Death, Berkley (New York, NY), 2000.
Betrayal in Death, Berkley (New York, NY), 2001.
Seduction in Death, Berkley (New York, NY), 2001.
(With Laurell K. Hamilton, Susan Krinard, and Maggie Shayne) *Out of this World,* Jove (New York, NY), 2001.
Reunion in Death, Berkley (New York, NY), 2002.
Purity in Death, Berkley (New York, NY), 2002.
Portrait in Death, Berkley (New York, NY), 2003.
Imitation in Death, Berkley (New York, NY), 2003.
Divided in Death, Berkley (New York, NY), 2004.
Visions in Death, Putnam (New York, NY), 2004.

SIDELIGHTS: With over 150 books to her credit, and frequently publishing more than half a dozen titles per year, Nora Roberts has established herself convincingly not only as a prolific author but an award-winning author of romance novels. According to Barbara E. Kemp in *Twentieth-Century Romance and Historical Writers,* Roberts's prodigious output has done little to diminish its quality. "Roberts's well deserved reputation and following," Kemp observed, "are based on her skill as a writer." She went on to add that readers have learned that they can depend upon Roberts to "provide an interesting, often adventure-filled plot, colorful, well-researched settings, well-defined, believable characters, and a satisfying love story." According to Roberts's Web site, in 2001 an average of thirty-four Nora Roberts novels were sold every minute.

In addition to the ever-present element of romance, Roberts's novels often blend elements from other genres, including those of mystery, science fiction, and fantasy. In *Sacred Sins* the heroine, psychiatrist Tess Court, comes to the aid of homicide detectives who are tracking down a serial killer. *Time Was* and *Time Changes* detail the exploits and love affairs of time-traveling brothers from the twenty-third century. The supernatural, including witches and psychic healers, features prominently in Roberts's "Donovan Legacy" series, which revolves around three cousins who possess extrasensory powers. The "Donovan Legacy" books can also be numbered among Roberts's popular family-series novels. Other series that center on the exploits of particular families include "Those Wild Ukrainians," the award-winning "MacGregor" novels, and the "Cordina" series, which deals with the royal family of an imaginary Mediterranean country that bears more than a passing resemblance to Monaco. Kemp credited the success of Roberts's family series with the fact that she "develops [the families] . . . with such skill that there is a real sense of belonging and continuity, much as there is in a real family."

Roberts likes to publish connecting books in paperback so as readers finish one book in a series, they can reach for the next.

Like a number of other established romance writers, Roberts has begun to broaden the base of her readership by branching out into mainstream novels. About Roberts's first mainstream novel, *Honest Illusions,* Joyce Slater noted in Chicago's *Tribune Books* that the author "has a warm feel for her characters and an eye for the evocative detail." A reviewer in *Authors and Artists for Young Adults* considered Roberts's *Montana Sky* "her real breakthrough to mainstream." In the novel, Jack Mercy leaves his Montana Ranch to his three daughters, half-sisters who don't know one another at all. Jack requires that the women live together for a year, or the ranch will be sold. The women must learn to live with one another, while dealing with a series of crimes on the ranch.

Roberts has authored a number of books under the pseudonym J. D. Robb. Her "In Death" series, set more than fifty years in the future, focuses on New York City police lieutenant Eve Dallas. Like many of Roberts's characters, Eve Dallas is a strong, determined and intelligent woman, something that appeals to Roberts's female readers. Making her debut in *Naked in Death,* the character of Dallas continues to solve crimes in the subsequent novels. "Intensely female yet unfeminine in any traditional sense, Dallas has a complex edge that transcends genre stereotypes," wrote a *Publishers Weekly* reviewer about *Portrait in Death.*

Roberts published *Remember When* using both her own name and her pseudonym, J. D. Robb. The novel is broken into two parts, tied together by a diamond heist. Laine Tavish, the daughter of an infamous thief, owns an antique store. As the novel progresses, she becomes the target of a killer out to recover her father's share of the take. She also falls in love with Max Gannon, an insurance investigator in search of the missing diamonds. Fast-forward fifty years into the future, when Laine's granddaughter, Samantha, writes a book about the still missing diamonds. When another murder occurs, Lt. Eve Dallas is on scene to investigate. A *Publishers Weekly* reviewer noted, "A true master of her craft, Roberts has penned an exceptional tale that burns with all the brilliance and fire of a finely cut diamond." *Booklist* reviewer John Charles concluded, *Remember When* "is another addictive blend of scintillating prose and sharply etched characters that will dazzle and delight her devoted readers."

Roberts's success as an author may be credited to the fact that she spends eight hours per day writing. Roberts's name has consistently remained on the *New York Times* Best-sellers List. A *Publishers Weekly* reviewer summarized Roberts's abilities as a writer, calling her "a storyteller of immeasurable diversity and talent." *Library Journal*'s Michael Rogers remarked, "Roberts is always a crowd pleaser." Debbie Ann Weiner's review of *The Villa* on *BookReporter* noted Roberts's "remarkable ability to write one engrossing best-seller after another."

"Relationships are Roberts's stock in trade," noted Jeanny V. House in a review of *River's End* published on *BookReporter,* "not just the romances, which Roberts presents with skill and passion, but also the relationships between family and friends." Roberts once told *CA:* "I write relationship books, most often about ongoing romantic involvements. Writing stories about people and their emotions is my primary motivation. Entertainment is always the primary focus."

BIOGRAPHICAL AND CRITICAL SOURCES:

BOOKS

Authors and Artists for Young Adults, Volume 35, Gale (Detroit, MI), 2000.

Little, Denise, and Laura Hayden, editors, *The Official Nora Roberts Companion,* introduction by Roberts, Berkley (New York, NY), 2002.

Twentieth-Century Romance and Historical Writers, 3rd edition, St. James Press (Detroit, MI), 1994.

PERIODICALS

Booklist, July, 1992, review of *Honest Illusions,* p. 1920; January 1, 1997, review of *Sanctuary,* p. 780; May 15, 1994, p. 1665; March 15, 1998, p. 1203; September 15, 1998, p. 707; January 1, 1999, Melanie Duncan, review of *River's End,* p. 793; November 15, 1999, Patty Engelmann, review of *Jewels of the Sun,* p. 608; September

15, 2000, Nina Davis, review of *Pride of Jared MacKade,* p. 225, and Donna Seaman, review of *Jewels of the Sun,* p. 226; December 1, 2000, review of *Tears of the Moon,* p. 743, and review of *Sacred Sins,* p. 743; April 15, 2001, review of *Dance upon the Air,* p. 1508; July, 2001, review of *Out of this World,* p. 1991; August, 2001, Whitney Scott, review of *The Villa,* p. 2143; September 1, 2001, review of *Midnight Bayou,* p. 4; September 15, 2001, review of *Considering Kate,* p. 212; October 1, 2001, review of *Once upon a Rose,* p. 304; December 15, 2001, audio book review of *Brazen Virtue,* p. 745; March 1, 2002, review of *Reunion in Death,* p. 1098; May 15, 2002, Diana Tixier Herald, review of *Face the Fire,* p. 1582; August, 2003, John Charles, review of *Remember When,* p. 1927.

BookPage, June, 2001, review of *Dance upon the Air,* p. 24; October, 2001, review of *Once upon a Rose,* p. 30; April, 2002, review of *Three Fates,* p. 8.

Bookseller, June 20, 2003, "So Good They Named Her Twice: Having Had Considerable Success with Romance Veteran Nora Roberts, Piatkus Is Now Relaunching the Writer's Alter Ego, J. D. Robb," p. 28.

Bookwatch, February, 1999, audio book review of *Inner Harbor,* p. 10.

Detroit Free Press, August 5, 2001, review of *Dance upon the Air,* p. 4E.

Drood Review of Mystery, January, 2001, review of *Carolina Moon,* p. 22.,

Kirkus Reviews, January 1, 1999, review of *River's End,* p. 15; February 1, 2001, review of *The Villa,* p. 129; September 1, 2001, review of *Midnight Bayou,* p. 1241; January 1, 2003, review of *Birthright,* p. 21; July 15, 2003, review of *Remember When,* p. 933.

Kliatt, January, 1999, audio book review of *Sanctuary,* p. 47; July, 1999, audio book review of *A Man for Amanda,* p. 44.

Library Journal, June 15, 1992, p. 103; June 1, 1994, review of *Hidden Riches,* p. 162; August, 1995, review of *Born in Ice,* p. 64; February 1, 1996, p. 139; November 1, 1998, p. 138; February 1, 1999, Jodie L. Israel, review of *River's End,* p. 123, and review of *The Reef,* p. 137; February 15, 1999, Michael Rogers, review of *Holding the Dream,* p. 189; April 15, 1999, audio book review of *Inner Harbor,* p. 164; June 1, 1999, audio book review of *River's End,* p. 206; February 15, 2000, Margaret Ann Hanes, review of *Carolina Moon,* p. 198; March 1, 2000, Jodi L. Israel, review of *Jewels of the Sun,* p. 142; February 15, 2001, review of *The Villa,* p. 155; March 1, 2001, audio book review of *Glory in Death,* p. 152; May 15, 2001, Kristin Ramsdell, review of *Dance upon the Air,* p. 107; June 15, 2001, Barbara Perkins, review of *The Villa,* p. 122; January, 2002, review of *Dance upon the Air,* p. 51; February 15, 2002, review of *Three Fates,* p. 131; March 15, 2002, review of *Betrayal in Death,* p. 126; August, 2002, Shelley Mosley, review of *Chesapeake Blue,* p. 146; September 1, 2003, Margaret Hanes, review of *Remember When,* p. 210; October 1, 2003, Jodi L. Israel, audio book review of *Birthright,* p. 132.

Locus, May, 2001, review of *Betrayal in Death,* p. 29.

Los Angeles Times Book Review, July 15, 1990, p. 14; July 24, 1994, p. 10.

New York Times, March 26, 2001, review of *The Villa,* p. E7.

New York Times Book Review, February 17, 1985; February 14, 1993, p. 23.

Off Our Backs, December, 2001, Mary E. Atkins, review of *Dance upon the Air,* p. 35.

People, July 1, 1996, Kristin McMurran, "Page Churner," p. 31; March 31, 1997, p. 41; May 4, 1998, p. 97; March 26, 2001, review of *The Villa,* p. 48.

Publishers Weekly, November 15, 1991, p. 69; May 18, 1992, review of *Honest Illusions,* p. 57; May 9, 1994, review of *Hidden Riches,* p. 62; December 4, 1995, review of *Born in Shame,* p. 58; January 22, 1996, review of *Montana Sky,* p. 59; February 3, 1997, p. 95; February 23, 1998, Judy Quinn, "Nora Roberts: A Celebration of Emotions," p. 46; July 6, 1998, pp. 29, 57; September 29, 1998, pp. 73, 99; January 11, 1999, review of *River's End,* p. 52; March 22, 1999, review of *Conspiracy in Death,* p. 89; April 12, 1999, Alec Foege, "Close to Home," p. 139; October 11, 1999, review of *Jewels of the Sun,* p. 73; November 1, 1999, p. 24; December 6, 1999, p. 24; January 31, 2000, review of *Carolina Moon,* p. 79; June 19, 2000, review of *Tears of the Moon,* p. 64; October 30, 2000, review of *Once upon a Dream,* p. 53; February 19, 2001, review of *Betrayal in Death,* p. 75; May 14, 2001, review of *Dance upon the Air,* p. 59; July 9, 2001, review of *Out of This World,* p. 53; August 6, 2001, review of *Seduction in Death,* p. 66;

September 3, 2001, review of *Midnight Bayou,* p. 55; September 10, 2001, review of *Once upon a Rose,* p. 68; November 26, 2001, review of *Heaven and Earth,* p. 45; February 18, 2002, review of *Reunion in Death,* p. 81; April 1, 2002, audio book review of *Three Fates,* p. 30, and review of *Three Fates,* p. 52; May 6, 2002, review of *Face the Fire,* p. 41; February 24, 2003, review of *Portrait in Death,* p. 58; March 24, 2003, review of *Birthright,* p. 59; August 25, 2003, review of *Remember When,* p. 39, and review of *Imitation in Death,* p. 45; September 8, 2003, Dick Donahue, "Roberts Rules Redux," p. 18; September 29, 2003, review of *Once upon a Midnight,* p. 49.

School Library Journal, June, 1995, review of *Born in Fire,* p. 146; March, 1996, pp. 234-235; September, 1999, review of *River's End,* p. 244.

Science Fiction Chronicle, June, 2001, review of *Betrayal in Death,* p. 40; March, 2002, audio book review of *Rapture in Death,* p. 39.

Times (London, England), August 11, 1997, p. 84.

Tribune Books (Chicago, IL), June 28, 1992, p. 6; March 24, 1996, p. 4; May 11, 1997, p. 11.

Voice of Youth Advocates, February, 1999, review of *Sea Swept,* p. 418.

Wall Street Journal, February 17, 1984.

Washington Post Book World, February 7, 1999, review of *River's End,* p. 7.

Writer, September, 2003, "What Makes Readers Love Nora Roberts's Romances?," p. 10.

ONLINE

All about Romance, http://www.likesbooks.com/ (June 2, 2003), Blythe Barnhill, review of *The Perfect Neighbor* and *Carnal Innocence;* Jennifer L. Schendel, review of *Once upon a Kiss;* Marianne Stillings, review of *Once upon a Rose* and *Carolina Moon;* Colleen McMahon, review of *Carolina Moon;* Candy Tan, review of *Once upon a Star;* Jane Jorgenson, review of *Brazen Virtue;* Linda Mowery, review of "MacGregor" series; interview with Roberts; Andrea Pool, review of *Dance upon the Air.*

Best Reviews, http://thebestreviews.com/ (June 2, 2003), Harriet Klausner, review of *Birthright* and *Heaven and Earth;* review of *Once upon a Star;* Janice Bennett, review of *Heaven and Earth;* Kelly Hartsell, review of *Heart of the Sea.*

BookReporter, http://www.bookreporter.com/ (June 2, 2003), Sonia Chopra, review of *Three Fates;* Debbie Ann Weiner, review of *The Villa;* Jeanny V. House, review of *River's End.*

Books I Loved, http://booksiloved.com/ (June 2, 2003), Jennifer Santiago, review of *Midnight Bayou.*

Crescent Blues, http://www.crescentblues.com/ (June 2, 2003), "Nora Roberts: The Joy of Make Believer."

MyShelf, http://www.myshelf.com/ (June 2, 2003), Brenda Weeaks, review of *Once upon a Star.*

MysteryReader, http://www.mysteryreader.com/ (April 24, 2001), review of *The Villa.*

Nora Roberts Web site, http://www.noraroberts.com/ (November 20, 2003).

Paranormal Romance Reviews, http://pnr.thebestreviews.com/ (June 2, 2003), Harriet Klausner, review of *Chesapeake Blue, Three Fates, Once upon a Kiss, Once upon a Rose, Dance upon the Air,* and *Heart of the Sea;* Leslie Tramposch, review of *Dance upon the Air* and *Enchanted;* Marilyn Heyman, review of *Once upon a Rose.*

Readers Read, http://www.readersread.com/ (June 2, 2003), review of *Midnight Bayou.*

Road to Romance, http://www.roadtoromance.ca/ (June 2, 2003), Traci Bell, review of *Dance upon the Air.*

RomanceReader, http://www.romancereader.com/ (January 19, 1998) review of *The MacGregors: Alan-Grant;* (February 3, 1999) review of *The Perfect Neighbor;* (February 22, 1999) review of *River's End;* (March 23, 1999) review of *Conspiracy in Death;* (October 13, 1999) review of *Jewels of the Sun;* (October 15, 1999) review of *Enchanted;* (October 25, 1999) review of *Loyalty in Death;* (March 7, 2001) review of *The Villa;* (March 26, 2001) review of *Betrayal in Death;* (August 3, 2001) review of *Seduction in Death* and *Out of This World;* (November 27, 2001) review of *Midnight Bayou;* (January 14, 2002) review of *Dance upon the Air;* (February 19, 2002) review of *Cordina's Crown Jewel;* (March 15, 2002) review of *Reunion in Death;* (March 26, 2002) review of *Three Fates;* Jean Mason, review of *Carolina Moon,* review of *Irish Rebel;* Susan Scribner, review of *Inner Harbor;* Cathy Sova, review of *The MacGregor Brides;* Diane Grayson, review of *The Perfect Neighbor.*

RomanceReview, http://www.aromancereview.com/ (June 2, 2003), review of *Carnal Innocence.**

ROLLINS, Henry 1961-

Henry Rollins

PERSONAL: Born Henry Garfield, February 13, 1961, in Washington, DC; son of Iris Garfield. *Education:* Attended American University, c. 1979.

ADDRESSES: *Office*—2.13.61, P.O. Box 1910, Los Angeles, CA 90078. *Agent*—Imago Recording Co., 152 West 57th Street, New York, NY 10019-3301.

CAREER: Musician, lyricist, and writer. Worked as a pet shop manager and ice cream shop manager, 1979-81; lead singer with State of Alert, until 1981, Black Flag, c. 1981-86, and Rollins Band, c. 1987—; 2.13.61 (publishing company), founder and publisher, 1984—; cofounder, One Records and Infinite Zero. Actor in motion pictures, including *The Chase,* 1994, *Johnny Mnemonic,* 1995, and *Lost Highway,* 1996. Host of Learning Channel's *Full Metal Challenge,* 2002.

AWARDS, HONORS: Man of the Year, *Details,* 1994. Grammy Award nomination for best metal performance, 1995, for "Liar"; Grammy Award for best spoken word album, 1995, for *Get in the Van.*

WRITINGS:

20, 2.13.61 (Los Angeles, CA), 1984.

2.13.61, 2.13.61, (Los Angeles, CA), 1985.

End to End, 2.13.61, (Los Angeles, CA), 1985.

Polio Flesh, 2.13.61, (Los Angeles, CA), 1985.

Hallucination of Grandeur, 2.13.61, (Los Angeles, CA), 1986.

You Can't Run from God, 2.13.61, (Los Angeles, CA), 1986.

Pissing in the Gene Pool, 2.13.61, (Los Angeles, CA), 1987.

Works, 2.13.61, (Los Angeles, CA), 1988.

One Thousand Ways to Die, 2.13.61, (Los Angeles, CA), 1989.

Art to Choke Hearts, 2.13.61, (Los Angeles, CA), 1989.

Knife Street, 2.13.61, (Los Angeles, CA), 1989.

High Adventure in the Great Outdoors (includes *2.13. 61, End to End,* and *Polio Flesh*), 2.13.61, (Los Angeles, CA), 1990.

Bang! (includes *One Thousand Ways to Die* and *Knife Street*), 2.13.61, (Los Angeles, CA), 1990.

One from None, 2.13.61, (Los Angeles, CA), 1991.

Black Coffee Blues, 2.13.61, (Los Angeles, CA), 1992.

Make a Grown Man Cry, 2.13.61, (Los Angeles, CA), 1992.

Now Watch Him Die, 2.13.61, (Los Angeles, CA), 1993.

Get in the Van: On the Road with Black Flag, 2.13.61 (Los Angeles, CA), 1994.

Do I Come Here Often, 2.13.61, (Los Angeles, CA), 1996.

Eye Scream, 2.13.61, (Los Angeles, CA), 1996.

The Portable Henry Rollins, Villard Books (New York, NY), 1997.

Solipsist, 2.13.61 (Los Angeles, CA), 1998.

Smile, You're Traveling: Black Coffee Blues, Pt. 3, 2.13.61 (Los Angeles, CA), 2000.

Contributor to periodicals, including *Details, Face, Interview, Melody Maker, Sounds, Spin,* and *Village Voice.*

LYRICIST; RECORDINGS WITH BLACK FLAG

My War, SST Records, (Long Beach, CA), 1983.
Family Man, SST Records, (Long Beach, CA), 1984.
Live '84, SST Records, (Long Beach, CA), 1984.
Slip It In, SST Records, (Long Beach, CA), 1984.
Loose Nut, SST Records, (Long Beach, CA), 1985.
The Process of Weeding Out, SST Records, (Long Beach, CA), 1985.
In My Head, SST Records, (Long Beach, CA), 1985.
Who's Got the Ten, SST Records, (Long Beach, CA), 1986.

LYRICIST: RECORDINGS WITH ROLLINS BAND

Hot Animal Machine, Texas Hotel, 1987.
Drive-By Shooting, Texas Hotel, 1987.
Life Time, Texas Hotel, 1988.
Do It, Texas Hotel, 1989.
Hard Volume, Texas Hotel, 1989.
Turned On, QuarterStick, 1990.
The End of Silence, Imago, 1992.
Electro Convulsive Therapy, Imago, 1993.
The Weight, Imago, 1994.
Come in and Burn, DreamWorks, 1997.

SPOKEN-WORD RECORDINGS

Short Walk on a Long Pier, Texas Hotel/2.13.61, 1987.
Big Ugly Mouth, Texas Hotel, 1987.
Sweatbox, Texas Hotel, 1989.
Live at McCabe's, QuarterStick, 1992.
Human Butt, QuarterStick/2.13.61, 1992.
Deep Throat, QuarterStick/2.13.61, 1992.
The Boxed Life, Imago, 1993.
Get in the Van, 1995.

ADAPTATIONS: The film *Ten Monologues from the Lives of Serial Killers* was based on writings by Rollins.

SIDELIGHTS: Henry Rollins is a musician and writer who has drawn particular attention as the lead singer in such bands as Black Flag and the Rollins Band. Rollins was born Henry Garfield in 1961 in Washington, DC. After his parents divorced, Rollins lived with his music-loving mother. They moved regularly, and music, notably jazz and popular soul, remained one of the few constants in his early life.

His unsettled home life scarcely proved stabilizing to the scrawny but nonetheless aggressive Rollins. "I was very loud and obnoxious and hyperactive," Rollins later recalled for Alan Prendergast in the *Los Angeles Times.* As a consequence of his radical behavior, Rollins was eventually enrolled at a military academy. There he was branded a failure by his teachers and was the subject of torment from cruel classmates. "I was there," Rollins later confessed to Pat Blashill in an interview in *Details,* "to be antagonized."

Rollins eventually tired of being physically intimidated and took to lifting weights to gain strength. The strict regimen he adhered to made him muscular, which spiked his self-esteem. Rollins recounted how the added muscle made him feel in *Details:* "I felt strong. It was the first time I can remember having a sense of myself." He also indulged his enthusiasm for music by becoming an active figure in Washington, DC's punk-rock subculture. The increasingly muscular Rollins took to slamming, a particularly violent form of dancing in which dancers pound into one another. "I lived for the shows," he explained to Prendergast, "Violence was my girl."

As a further means of self-expression, Rollins established his own punk band, State of Alert. But he continued to patronize other bands, notably Black Flag. Rollins was a staunch supporter of Black Flag, and he eventually met the band members. A few months later, he attended a Black Flag concert in New York City and was invited onstage to sing briefly. Following that appearance, Rollins was asked to join the band and replace its lead singer, who had decided to instead play guitar. Rollins readily accepted Black Flag's offer, and for the next few years he toured and recorded regularly with the band.

Black Flag was hardly among the more widely known bands of the early 1980s, and recordings such as *Family Man, My War, Loose Nut,* and *The Process of Weeding Out* could scarcely be regarded as commercial product. "I know I'm not going to sell millions of records," Rollins told Prendergast. "I don't write for the Everyman. I write for one man—me. If other people dig it, that's cool." The band's followers, however, were intensely loyal, and they sustained the group through an often exhausting multi-year stint of touring and recording. In one two-year period, for instance, Black Flag produced the recordings *Family Man, Live '84, Slip It In, Loose Nut, The Process of Weeding Out,* and *In My Head.* During this period, the band's music evolved from simple punk tunes to aggressive but more complex songs incorporating the extended instrumental interludes prominent in jazz. Rollins's lyrics, meanwhile, expressed his outrage at social conventions and revealed his interest in the work of writers such as Henry Miller and Charles Bukowski. Blashill explained, Rollins "doesn't intend his music or his words to be a catharsis or a kind of sonic obliteration. When Henry talks about his life—that is, when he performs—he says it's all about choices. You choose your path, then you steam down it. . . . And that's inspirational stuff for [Rollins's] audience."

With Black Flag, Rollins developed a reputation as a poet who employed music as one means of expressing himself. Indeed, by the time that Black Flag broke up in 1986, Rollins had established himself independently as a writer. He continued to remain active as a musician after Black Flag and in 1987 established the Rollins Band, another group that produced loud, aggressive music. The band provided adequate musical support for Rollins, who proved an imposing spectacle with his hardened physique, severe hairstyle, colorful tattoos, and screaming delivery. Among the Rollins Band's recordings are *Hot Animal Machine, Drive-By Shooting, Life Time, Do It, Turned On, The End of Silence, Electro Convulsive Therapy,* and *The Weight.* As the band's popularity grew, Rollins used his recognition to open other doors. He appeared on numerous talk shows and performed stand-up comedy.

In 1987, the same year that he founded the Rollins Band, Rollins began making spoken-word recordings. His recordings include *Short Walk on a Long Pier, Big Ugly Mouth, Sweatbox, Human Butt,* and *The Boxed Life.* He has also remained active as a writer of volatile prose works such as *Black Coffee Blues, Make a Grown Man Cry,* and *Now Watch Him Die.* Rollins also gave spoken-word performances in Australia, New Zealand, Sweden, Denmark, Scotland, England, Germany, Belgium, and Holland. In 1995, he won a Grammy Award for best spoken word album for his recording *Get in the Van.* Rollins commented to Blashill in *Details* that his written work has changed slightly. "These days I can use less words and say what I need to quicker. Like a smart bomb."

Through his own publishing company, 2.13.61, Rollins published such works as *20, End to End,* and *Polio Flesh.* The name of the company comes from Rollins's birth date. "In his self-published books, he is obsessed with spilling his guts," commented Blashill. "But writing like this isn't a hostile conversation that [Rollins is] having with himself. . . . It's [Rollins] getting straight with himself, securing his own perimeters," noted Blashill. Rollins explained his writing to Prendergast: "There's no method to the madness; I don't even know if there's madness. It's just expression—random and real. . . . I just want to get to it better, to get more concise, to pinpoint things in my head."

The book *Get in the Van: On the Road with Black Flag,* published in 1994, chronicles the band's touring experiences from 1981 to 1986 through journal entries kept by Rollins. Blashill described Black Flag as "an incendiary monster truck of a band that defined American hardcore punk rock. Black Flag was ugly: They fought with each other, lived in a filthy tour van, and more than occasionally took it all out on people who thought they understood punk." Rollins's diary excerpts in *Get in the Van* reveal exactly how rough this lifestyle was and how it influenced him. *Times Literary Supplement* contributor Alex Truscott commented on Rollins's "intensity," and noted that "Rollins is painfully honest about his insecurities."

Now Watch Him Die is Rollins's tribute to his best friend whom he saw shot to death. Louis Collonge, a reviewer for *Whole Earth Review,* was so impressed with the book that he told readers to "bum your entire pop psychology library and leap into the work of Henry Rollins." A reviewer for *Publishers Weekly* found that the "simple, staccato prose and verse" in *The Portable Henry Rollins* "suit the voice in which he writes," and remarked that "his gifts of honesty and observation shine through in accounts of life on the road." In *Booklist,* Mike Tribby observed that "for those on his wavelength, this intense collection, full of tough-minded attitude and imagery, will be a trusty companion."

Not all of Rollins's writing has been well received by critics. Frank Diller of the *Baltimore City Paper* criticized *The Portable Henry Rollins,* because "the selections demonstrate how little Rollins has matured as both a writer and a human being." Diller also remarked, "Rollins's rants might be tolerable if they were presented in a fresh perspective or stylistic innovation, but his constant barrage of one simple sentence after another is unbearable." Rollins released his next book, *Solipsist,* without sending any copies to the press. In an interview with Stephen Thompson for the *Onion AV Club,* an online news organization, Rollins stated, "I'm tired of critics and their opinions of me." He defined *Solipsist* as "a three-year struggle with these very strange essays and these characters, some of whom are very tragic."

Rollins has also promoted the music of other artists. With prominent record producer Rich Rubin, Rollins established Infinite Zero, a recording label for re-releasing work from artists such as Tom Verlaine, Devo, and Gang of Four. "The goal of this label is basically to seduce a bunch of people who have thirsty ears," Rollins told a reviewer in the *Boston Globe.* He wants listeners to hear "good things besides the good things they're listening to now." A man of many talents, Rollins is a musician, lyricist, poet, publisher, and actor. Despite his success and large number of fans, Rollins does not understand his own appeal or staying power.

BIOGRAPHICAL AND CRITICAL SOURCES:

BOOKS

Hochman, Steve, editor, *Popular Musicians,* Salem Press (Pasadena, CA), 1999, pp. 98-100.

PERIODICALS

Advocate, May 13, 1997, p. 62.
Booklist, September 15, 1997, Mike Tribby, review of *The Portable Henry Rollins,* p. 199.
Boston Globe, February 10, 1995.
Creem, May, 1992.
Details, January, 1993; January, 1994, pp. 64-69, 127.
Detroit Free Press, April 17, 1992.
Detroit News, May 1, 1993.
Down Beat, December, 1994.
Entertainment Weekly, March 12, 1993; February 18, 1994, p. 72.
Library Journal, September 15, 1997, David P. Szatmary, review of *The Portable Henry Rollins,* pp. 76-77.
Los Angeles Daily News, May 31, 1993.
Los Angeles Times, June 14, 1987.
Melody Maker, February 13, 1993.
Musician, April 13, 1993.
New York Times Magazine, November 6, 1994, p. 38.
Publishers Weekly, October 3, 1994, p. 63; November 7, 1994, review of *Get in the Van: On the Road with Black Flag,* p. 32; September 15, 1997, review of *The Portable Henry Rollins,* p. 65.
Pulse!, April 3, 1992.
Rolling Stone, April 16, 1992; March 18, 1993; December 23, 1993, p. 111.
Spin, May, 1992.
Times Literary Supplement, May 19, 1995, p. 18.
TV Guide, September 26, 1992.
Whole Earth Review, spring, 1995, Louis Collonge, review of *Now Watch Him Die,* p. 90.

ONLINE

All Music Guide, http://www.allmusic.com/ (June 2, 2003), "Henry Rollins."
Baltimore City Paper Online, http://www.citypaper.com/ (June 2,2003), "Henry Rollins."
Henry Rollins Official Web site, http://21361.com/ (June 2, 2003).
NYRock, http://www.nyrock.com/ (June 2, 2003), "Have Shorts Will Travel" (interview); "Henry Rollins: A Heavy Weight with Heavy Thoughts" (interview).
Onion AV Club, http://theavclub.com/ (June 2, 2003), "Interview with Henry Rollins."
Pixie Inc, http://www.pixie-inc.demon.co.uk/ (November 18, 2003), Simon Collins, review of *The Portable Henry Rollins.*
Rolling Stone Online, http://www.rollingstone.com/ (November 18, 2003), "Henry Rollins."
Seattlepi, http://www.seattlepi.nwsource.com/ (June 2, 2003), "Henry Rollins."*

* * *

ROSENBERG, Philip 1942-

PERSONAL: Born March 30, 1942, in Worcester, MA; son of Oscar (a manufacturer) and Eva (Weiner) Rosenberg; married Charlotte Schmidt, December 27, 1979; children: Mark Elijah, Matthew Isaiah. *Educa-*

tion: Boston University, B.A., 1963; Columbia University, M.A., 1965, Ph.D., 1972.

ADDRESSES: Home—685 West End Ave., New York, NY 10025. *Agent*—Robert Datilla, 150 East 74th St., New York, NY 10017.

CAREER: Prentice-Hall, Inc., Englewood Cliffs, NJ, editor, 1965; freelance editor, 1965-74; writer, 1974—.

WRITINGS:

The Seventh Hero: Thomas Carlyle and the Theory of Radical Activism, Harvard University Press (Cambridge, MA), 1974.
Contract on Cherry Street (novel; also see below), Crowell (New York, NY), 1975.
(With Sonny Grosso) *Point Blank,* Grosset & Dunlap (New York, NY), 1978.
(With Robert Tanenbaum) *Badge of the Assassin* (nonfiction), Dutton (New York, NY), 1979.
The Spivey Assignment: A Double Agent's Infiltration of the Drug Smuggling Conspiracy (nonfiction), Holt (New York, NY), 1979.
Tygers of Wrath (novel), St. Martin's Press (New York, NY), 1991.
House of Lords (novel), HarperCollins (New York, NY), 2002.

Also author of television screenplays, including *Contract on Cherry Street,* (adapted from his novel), first broadcast in 1977, and *To Sir with Love II.* Contributor of articles to magazines, including *Esquire.*

SIDELIGHTS: In his first book, *The Seventh Hero,* Philip Rosenberg argues that the Victorian social critic Thomas Carlyle was a major precursor of modern activism. It might have marked the beginning of Rosenberg's academic career but for the serious reservations he had about working as both scholar and teacher. After leaving Columbia University with his Ph.D., Rosenberg hoped to make his living as a full-time writer. He has since written both novels and nonfiction books, all joined to the theme of crime and punishment.

Contract on Cherry Street was Rosenberg's first attempt at fiction. The main character of the story, Frank Hovannes, is a detective in the New York City Police Department. When his partner is gunned down by the mob, to the apparent unconcern of the department, Hovannes sets out to avenge the killing. He forms his own undercover unit and launches a private "war against crime," carrying out a series of executions that spreads panic throughout the underworld. Unable to identify its real enemies, the mob strikes out at false targets and turns violently against itself. Hovannes's strike force, however, in its effort to remain undiscovered, must commit another round of murders. Internal dissent and violence eventually overtake Hovannes's men as well.

Critics were impressed by this debut. Gene Lyons of the *New York Times Book Review* commented: "[Rosenberg] has written an admirably crafted entertainment that engages one's attention from beginning to end and gives one something to think about in between. To have done all that without violating one's sense of probability and proportion, while dealing with a subject and theme which do, is no small thing." Another reviewer, Michael Irwin of the *Times Literary Supplement,* observed that the author "has done plenty of homework and written a good, jolting, professional thriller. His narrative is a little over-populated for anything much in the way of character definition, especially as cops and crooks alike converse in gangland Esperanto; but the action is fast and clever."

Rosenberg followed up *Contract on Cherry Street* with another look at crime and police work. Although presented in the form of a novel, *Point Blank* is a work of nonfiction based on the story of police detective Joe Nunziata, named Joe Longo in the book. The source for the story is one that other authors, notably Peter Maas (*Serpico*) and William Phillips (*Rogue Cop*), have found especially rich for books, articles, and films: the revelation of widespread police corruption in New York City during the late sixties and early seventies. In collaboration with Sonny Grosso, the detective who broke the "French Connection" case, Rosenberg dramatizes the events that ended with Nunziata's suicide.

The authors portray Joe Longo as "a devoted father and dedicated cop who was driven to his death by callous manipulators." In the course of a drug investigation, Longo accepts a bribe from a drug dealer and informant working as a double agent of the Bureau of Narcotics and Dangerous Drugs (B.N.D.D.). "When Joe is finally trapped," explained *New York Times Book*

Review writer Evan Hunter, "we are asked to believe he accepted a bribe from the bad guy only to tighten his grip on the man. Why he *really* took the money remains one of the book's mysteries." Officials of the B.N.D.D. confront Longo with three choices: "You can work with us, you can go to jail, or you can blow your brains out." Longo's suicide note makes it clear that he blamed agents of the B.N.D.D. for his death.

Point Blank "reads more like a complicated spy story than a straightforward police narrative, with more double agents and double-crosses than can be found this side of le Carre country," Hunter said. "Joe's eventual death is predicted throughout in flash-forwards . . . creating a foregone-conclusion suspense that does not detract from the cat-and-mouse gam Joe and the drug dealer-informant-double agent are playing. . . . [It is] a story told with insight, indignation and—yes—at times inspiration."

In *Badge of the Assassin,* Rosenberg teamed with prosecuting attorney Robert Tanenbaum for a detailed examination of the criminal justice system, starting with the murder of two New York City policemen in 1971. Officers Joseph Piagentini and Waverly Jones were among the first policemen killed by members of the self-proclaimed Black Liberation Army, which construed the slayings as political acts in the cause of racial war. *Badge of the Assassin* is about the difficult and often frustrating manhunt that went on for four years, the eventual capture of the murderers, and the two courtroom trials needed for a successful prosecution.

According to some reviewers, *Badge of the Assassin* is a suspenseful, well-written book that provides some insight into the fragile traditions of American justice. *New York Times Book Review* contributor Dan Greenberg remarked: "The accounts of the two murder trials in New York, at which coauthor Robert Tanenbaum served as prosecutor, and an intervening chase down to a remote farm in Mississippi where one of the murder weapons (the 'badge of the assassin') is believed to be buried, are almost as suspenseful as the stalking and capture of the killers. . . . The book is nicely researched and documented. The story is complex but easy to follow. The characterizations are brief but ring true, and the scenes build well. The writing is generally as spare and clean as a news story."

New York Times reviewer Christopher Lehmann-Haupt wondered at first if the story reflected the "true legacy of black militancy" in the early seventies: "Does it all come down to this—a story of shots in the back in the dark of night, by vicious punks mouthing incoherent revolutionary slogans?" But the authors make a distinction between being militant and being evil, and "in the long run," Lehmann-Haupt wrote, "Mr. Tanenbaum and Mr. Rosenberg win you over. . . . I was fully caught up in the building drama of the book and turning pages without any awareness of time at all. And if you had interrupted me here and asked me then about its larger meaning, I guess I would have snapped that it signified nothing but right and wrong and justice. And hurriedly gone back to finish an exciting story."

In *The Spivey Assignment,* another nonfiction thriller, Rosenberg delivers a portrait of "the narc as hero." The book purports to be a tribute to narcotics agents who, the author attests, "are roundly damned on the one hand for interfering with the rights of citizens to smoke, snort or ingest the chemicals of their choice, while on the other hand, they are mocked for their failure to win the war against drugs." The hero of *The Spivey Assignment* is Larry Spivey himself, a Georgian who had made and lost a small fortune in the construction business and, finding himself at loose ends, joins the Georgia Bureau of Investigation. During his six months as an undercover agent, Spivey infiltrates a number of drug-smuggling operations, travels to Mexico, Guatemala, and Jamaica, kills two men, and encounters eighteen other homicides.

New York Times Book Review writer Donald Goddard called *The Spivey Assignment,* "a Central American macho trip, full of gun law and gun lore, high-speed chases by land, sea and air, virile adventurers, dashing entrepreneurs, treacherous Latins, [and] beautiful women. . . . The action is fast and frantic; the expertise crisp and convincing, the characters stock, but sufficient for an exercise in the New Romanticism, which sets as much store on jungle country and automatic weapons as it does on psychological insight." In the end, Goddard observed, "Spivey had to be as ruthless, as unprincipled and . . . as brutal as the dopers he tried to catch."

Publishers Weekly contributor Sybil Steinberg compared Rosenberg's 1991 novel, *Tygers of Wrath,* to the school-noir classic *Blackboard Jungle,* with Rosenberg's writing being "denser and the canvas larger." When Timothy Warren, a Bronx junior-high-school student, takes as hostage thirteen-year-old Ophelia James, it is up to teacher Steven Hillyer to try to talk the boy out of violence. When the negotiations break down, both students die—Ophelia by asphyxiation, Timothy by a police bullet. The resulting clamor over the deaths brings inner-city racial politics into the fray as the Board of Education clashes with the police department while a local black leader "uses the incident to his own advantage," as Steinberg related. Steinberg found this novel a worthy entry overall.

In Rosenberg's next novel, *House of Lords,* Wall Street financier Jeffrey Blaine is the host of a party where an underage girl is intoxicated and raped. The scandal could wreck Blaine's life except for a mysterious stranger, Chet Fiore, who steps in and handles the crisis. In short order, Fiore informs Blaine that a gossip columnist who had threatened to break the story "has been taken care of." It becomes apparent that Fiore is involved in organized crime, and now wishes to extract a price from Blaine in return for his protection. Now drawn into the shadowy world of the Mafia, Blaine finds himself becoming an increasingly willing participant in a money-laundering scheme. A *Kirkus Reviews* critic cited "overcooked prose" and "an unsettling denouement" in *House of Lords.* But to Michael Phillips of *Book,* Rosenberg exhibits "crisp style and irreverence" in this thriller.

BIOGRAPHICAL AND CRITICAL SOURCES:

PERIODICALS

Best Sellers, June, 1974; July, 1979.

Book, July-August, 2002, Michael Phillips, review of *House of Lords,* p. 81.

Booklist, December 15, 1990, review of *Tygers of Wrath,* p. 786.

Books, September, 1991, review of *Tygers of Wrath,* p. 22.

Choice, November, 1974.

Commentary, September, 1974.

Kirkus Reviews, December 15, 1990, review of *Tygers of Wrath,* p. 1703; April 15, 2002, review of *House of Lords,* p. 521.

Kliatt Young Adult Paperback Book Guide, November, 1992, review of *Tygers of Wrath,* p. 11.

Library Journal, January, 1991, review of *Tygers of Wrath,* p. 155; June 1, 2002, Craig L. Shufelt, review of *House of Lords,* p. 197.

Nation, December 21, 1974.

New York Review of Books, June 27, 1974.

New York Times, July 12, 1979, Christopher Lehmann-Haupt, review of *Badge of the Assassin.*

New York Times Book Review, July 21, 1974; May 11, 1975, Gene Lyons, review of *Contract on Cherry Street;* July 2, 1978, Evan Hunter, review of *Point Blank;* July 8, 1979, Dan Greenberg, review of *Badge of the Assassin;* December 2, 1979, Donald Goddard, review of *The Spivey Assignment.*

Publishers Weekly, January 4, 1991, Sybil Steinberg, review of *Tygers of Wrath,* p. 58; May 27, 2002, review of *House of Lords,* p. 39.

Times Literary Supplement, February 27, 1976.

Washington Post Book World, January 21, 1979; March 3, 1991, review of *Tygers of Wrath,* p. 8.*

S

SALINGER, J(erome) D(avid) 1919-

PERSONAL: Born January 1, 1919, in New York, New York; son of Sol (an importer) and Miriam (Jillich) Salinger; allegedly married September, 1945; wife's name Sylvia (a physician; divorced, 1947); married Claire Douglas, February 17, 1955 (divorced, October, 1967); children: (second marriage) Margaret Ann, Matthew. *Education:* Graduated from Valley Forge Military Academy, 1936; attended New York University, Ursinus College, and Columbia University.

ADDRESSES: *Home*—Cornish, NH. *Agent*—Harold Ober Associates, Inc., 425 Madison Ave., New York, NY 10017.

CAREER: Writer. Worked as an entertainer on Swedish liner M.S. *Kungsholm* in the Caribbean, 1941. *Military service:* U.S. Army, 1942-46; served in Europe; became staff sergeant; received five battle stars.

WRITINGS:

J. D. Salinger

The Catcher in the Rye (novel), Little, Brown (Boston, MA), 1951.

Nine Stories, Little, Brown (Boston, MA), 1953, published as *For Esme—With Love and Squalor, and Other Stories,* Hamish Hamilton (London, England), 1953.

Franny and Zooey (two stories; "Franny" first published in *New Yorker,* January 29, 1955, and "Zooey," *New Yorker,* May 4, 1957), Little, Brown (Boston, MA), 1961.

Raise High the Roof Beam, Carpenters; and Seymour: An Introduction ("Raise High the Roof Beam, Carpenters" first published in *New Yorker,* November 19, 1955, and "Seymour," *New Yorker,* June 6, 1959), Little, Brown (Boston, MA), 1963.

The Complete Uncollected Short Stories of J. D. Salinger, two volumes, [California], 1974.

Hapworth 16, 1924 (novella), Orchises (Washington, DC), 1997.

Contributor to periodicals, including *Harper's, Story, Collier's, Saturday Evening Post, Cosmopolitan,* and *Esquire.*

Collections of Salinger's correspondence are housed at the Harry Ransom Humanities Research Center, University of Texas at Austin, and at the Firestone Library, Princeton University.

ADAPTATIONS: The story "Uncle Wiggily in Connecticut" was adapted as the motion picture *My Foolish Heart,* 1950.

SIDELIGHTS: J. D. Salinger first rose to prominence with the publication of *The Catcher in the Rye* in 1951. Prior to this, Salinger had written only a handful of short stories published in popular magazines. While Salinger's novel is more complex than many first-time readers perceive, its appeal to both adolescents and adults remains strong, conferring upon it the status of a classic novel. Salinger's work following the phenomenal success of *The Catcher in the Rye* has been modest considering the promise demonstrated by that first book. Salinger collected a number of short pieces in *Nine Stories,* each of which demonstrate his command of middle-class American colloquial speech, mastery of eccentric characterization, and deft irony.

Salinger's *Franny and Zooey* consists of two long short stories, previously published in the *New Yorker,* and featuring the fictional Glass family. Salinger later published another Glass family story sequence, *Raise High the Roof Beam, Carpenters;* and *Seymour: An Introduction,* again from two previously published *New Yorker* pieces. Another part of the Glass family chronicle, *Hapworth 16, 1924,* a novella-length story told in the form of a letter, originally published in the *New Yorker* in 1965, has since been published.

Salinger has been criticized by reviewers for focusing so much of his attention on the Glass family. He has also annoyed critics with his outright refusal to participate in a debate of his works. While Salinger's fictional characters have been endlessly analyzed and discussed, the author himself has remained a mystery. Since the publication of *The Catcher in the Rye,* he has avoided all contact with the public. Because of this, the record of his life remains incomplete.

Salinger published his first short story, "The Young Folks," in 1940 in *Story* magazine, founded and edited by one of Salinger's former teachers. Encouraged by the story's success, Salinger continued to write even while serving in the army during World War II. Back home many of his stories were being published in magazines including *Collier's,* the *Saturday Evening Post, Esquire,* and *Cosmopolitan.*

After the war Salinger continued to write stories for magazine publication. His story "Slight Rebellion off Madison," was published in the *New Yorker* in December, 1946. It was at this time that Salinger began his career as a writer of serious fiction. Between 1946 and 1951 he published seven stories in the *New Yorker.*

Among the stories Salinger published during the late 1940s was "A Perfect Day for Bananafish," the first story featuring the mysterious, brooding, and tragic Seymour Glass, a character who haunts much of Salinger's later work. Initiating the long, complex saga of the Glass family, the story examines Seymour's life, spiritual quest, and unhappy end around which all of the Glass stories are organized. It also contains themes and concerns central to Salinger's work: the conflict between the spiritual questor and the crass materialist, the loss of childhood innocence in a perverse world, and the search for genuine love amidst often adulterated human relationships.

Although this story ends with the shocking scene of Seymour committing suicide, it does not depend on sensationalism to achieve its impact. Rather, the ending builds naturally from the ambivalence created in the reader's mind toward the troubled character of Seymour, who seems simultaneously innocent and threatening, spiritual and vaguely perverse. This depth of characterization is a trademark of Salinger's fiction. In *J. D. Salinger, Revisited,* Warren French, considered "A Perfect Day for Bananafish" among the "best-known" stories written since the end of World War II and declared that its complexities and significance make it more than simply a "springboard" to the later Glass cycle.

Most of the stories Salinger wrote and collected in *Nine Stories* demonstrate the seemingly insoluble dilemmas people face in their lives. In many of these stories, frequent victims of the sinister nature of the modern world are children groping with the mysterious problems of the adult world. Such is the case in the stories "Teddy," "Down at the Dinghy," and "The Laughing Man." Other stories focus upon the problems of adults, portraying them as hapless figures unable to deal with the complex emotional entanglements of their lives or as active exploiters of other people. In the story "Pretty Mouth and Green My Eyes," a man tries to comfort a late-night caller who suspects his absent wife of infidelity. While the man calmly and rationally explains away the caller's fears, he is lying in bed next to his friend's wife. Such lapses in personal morality are also a common feature of Salinger's work, making this story typical of what French called "the pit of the modern urban hell," and one of the writer's most "bitter, cynical stories."

Salinger demonstrates in his fiction what Dan Wakefield described in an article in *Salinger: A Critical and Personal Portrait* as the search for love. Wakefield argued that the search for unadulterated emotional contact is central to Salinger's work, which, he concluded, can be seen as "the history of human trouble and the poetry of love." The power of unqualified love as a restorative agent against the evils of life is perhaps best illustrated in "For Esme—With Love and Squalor." Some critics consider this story Salinger's finest piece of short fiction.

In the story a young English girl, Esme, redeems an American soldier suffering from combat fatigue. Struck by her innocent beauty, precocity, and native charm, the narrator promises to write a story for Esme about "squalor." Almost a year later while the soldier is recovering from a nervous reaction to combat, he receives a battered package from Esme in which he finds, enclosed with a letter, the gift of her dead father's watch. In the letter she reminds him of his promise to write a story for her about "squalor," wishes him well, and remarks that she hopes he comes through the war with all of his "faculties intact." Reading her letter and contemplating its unselfish expression of affection, the narrator finds himself able to sleep (a restorative agent in Salinger's fiction). His recovery allows him to write this story and fulfill his promise six years later, which he does after receiving an invitation to Esme's wedding.

This gesture of Esme's—what Ihab Hassan, in *Salinger: A Critical and Personal Portrait,* called "The Rare Quixotic Gesture"—represents Salinger's most eloquent answer to the dilemma of modern life. It also lies close to the center, as Hassan noted, of *The Catcher in the Rye.* While *Catcher's* Holden Caulfield rebels against his society, he does not attempt to overturn the established values system. Holden instead insists that those values be restored from the perversion they have suffered under the world of "phonies."

As the novel stands today, it represents perhaps the most sensitive portrait of coming-of-age in America in the years following World War II. Few other books have had as great an impact on a generation—so much so that Holden Caulfield has entered the popular mythology of American culture alongside such figures Jay Gatsby and Huck Finn. As Edgar Branch pointed out in *Salinger: A Critical and Personal Portrait,*the pattern of similarity between Huck and Holden is striking, making *The Catcher in the Rye* "a kind of *Huckleberry Finn* in modern dress."

Holden, like Huck, flees from the world of conventionality. Holden's flight from Pencey Prep a few days before the beginning of Christmas vacation is partly a reaction to his inability to cope with his schoolmates, but also a vain attempt to forestall his flunking out of school. During the course of the story readers learn that this is his third failure at school and part of a pattern of neurotic behavior, much of which, one suspects, is Holden's reaction to the death of a younger brother. Although Holden is well aware of his own limitations, he fails to identify or understand his inability to come to terms with the conditions of the adult world; he instead directs his complaints against the world of "phoniness," which includes most adults.

Taking flight from this world, Holden plans to head west, but begins his journey by traveling to New York to say goodbye to his sister. On the way he participates in a series of humorous adventures. Such confusion in direction is characteristic of Holden, who often behaves impulsively. In fact, one of Salinger's more subtle devices is to undercut his main character by placing him in situations wherein his own phoniness is exposed, and yet making his character all the more engaging through what readers perceive as his sensitivity and intelligence. Throughout the story Holden adopts many roles to deceive other people. His motivation, however, is not to exploit others, but rather to establish contact with them. In this respect, much of Holden's sympathetic appeal lies in his loneliness and difficulty in trying to sort out the confusing impulses of the adult world.

Another source of the novel's success lies in its elaborate structure that on the surface seems rambling and inconclusive. However, as Carl F. Strauch demonstrated in *Wisconsin Studies in Contemporary Literature,* a close scrutiny of the novel reveals "complex patterns" of "symbolic structure of language, motif, episode, and character," all of which contribute to its affirmative quality. Strauch took issue with critics who discounted the novel's significance, calling it instead a "masterpiece that moves effortlessly on the colloquial surface and at the same time uncovers, with hypnotic compulsion, a psychological drama of unrelenting terror and final beauty."

Despite his confusion and ignorance, Holden is able to communicate and even express his experience in metaphoric terms. In the most crucial scene in the novel Holden, misquoting a line from Robert Burns, describes his mission in life as a "catcher in the rye," a figure who wishes to keep all of the children in the world from falling off "some crazy cliff." This, then, is Holden's "quixotic gesture," his reaching out to others in an act of selfless love, even from the depths of his own confusion and grief. The ultimate irony is that Holden's gesture is doomed to failure. He cannot prevent his own fall into the adulterated world of experience, much less the fall of others. This irony does not diminish the quality of Holden's gesture, making it instead all the more profound.

It is little wonder that *The Catcher in the Rye* became a favorite among young people. It skillfully validates adolescent experience with its spirit of rebellion. However, it was not until after the publication of *Nine Stories* that Salinger began to attract serious critical attention. Through the later 1950s his notoriety was further enhanced by the gradual unfolding of the Glass saga in the pages of the *New Yorker.*

Perhaps the best way to grasp the long and complex story of the Glass family is to consider its separately published parts as a complete unit. The Glass saga consists of six short stories that have been published as "A Perfect Day for Bananafish" (in *Nine Stories*), *Franny and Zooey, Raise High the Roof Beam, Carpenters; and Seymour: An Introduction,* and *Hapworth 16, 1924.* Eberhard Alsen, in his study *Salinger's Glass Stories As a Composite Novel,* identified three major themes in the Glass cycle: the concern for the lack of spiritual values in contemporary America, the development of Buddy as a writer, and Seymour's quest for enlightenment.

Although Seymour Glass is at the core of the Glass cycle, he actually appears only in "A Perfect Day for Bananafish," in which he commits suicide. Whether or not Seymour's final act confirms his role as a true visionary or a "failed guru" is the subject of considerable critical debate; however, the issue is moot since Seymour's success or failure in resolving his own spiritual conflicts is far less important than the effect his teaching has in helping to resolve the conflicts of his younger siblings. It is the latter influence that makes Seymour the crucial figure in the series.

In "Franny," the youngest of the Glass daughters suffers physical and nervous collapse as she tries to reconcile her desire for a pure spiritual experience with her involvement in a sexual relationship with her crude, insensitive boyfriend. Franny's crisis continues into the companion story, "Zooey," in which her elder brother, a successful television actor, is able to mediate her concerns by reminding her of the example of Seymour, who once helped Zooey understand the importance of accepting the worldly nature of religious experience.

In "Raise High the Roof Beam, Carpenters," Buddy Glass retrospectively narrates his attendance at Seymour's wedding in 1942, an event the groom chose not to attend, eloping instead with his fiancee Muriel. Again, in this story Seymour is physically absent, but his peculiar character generates discussion about him by the indignant wedding guests. Buddy overhears and records their negative comments, which reinforce his own understanding of his brother's special sensibility. Buddy recognizes that Seymour will not allow what he actually is to be compromised by the world's perceptions of him.

In another case, the problem of accurately perceiving his brother prompts Buddy years later to write "Seymour: An Introduction," which he intends to serve as a guide for the "general reader" to the saintly nature of his dead brother. In the narrative, Buddy often reveals more about himself and his own opinions of life and literature than he does about Seymour. In this respect the "Introduction" is never quite complete; Seymour remains a mysterious presence not fully comprehensible to the reader. Buddy's "Introduction" is described by French as a fascinating, "even if not a convincing work."

The final segment of the Glass cycle, "Hapworth 16, 1924," consists of a long letter written by Seymour, aged seven, to his family describing his and five-year-old Buddy's experiences at summer camp. The masterful prose and flashy displays of erudition seem entirely implausible for a young child, even one with Seymour's special gifts; however, as French suggested, the disparity between what is plausible and what appears on the page only underscores the "heart-rending evocations of an exquisitely sensitive young person trapped in a situation for which he can find no physical or metaphysical justification."

While Salinger is generally applauded for *The Catcher in the Rye,* his subsequent work raised questions as to the degree of his overall talent. Norman Mailer remarked in his *Advertisements for Myself* that Salinger was "the greatest mind to ever stay in prep school." Mailer complained that Salinger avoids the discomforting subjects demanded of serious writers. These comments were reinforced by Alfred Kazin who, in a review of *Franny and Zooey* collected in *Salinger: A Critical and Personal Portrait,* accused Salinger of appealing to a "vast public" of readers "released by our society to think of themselves as endlessly sensitive, spiritually alone, gifted, and whose suffering lies in the narrowing of their consciousness to themselves."

Despite the generally negative reaction to *Franny and Zooey,* the novel became a popular success, and for a time through the 1960s Salinger's fiction attracted considerable attention. However, interest in his later work evaporated after the appearance of the final Glass stories. *The Catcher in the Rye* remains a widely read, critical success. There is little doubt that with this novel alone Salinger has made an enduring contribution.

BIOGRAPHICAL AND CRITICAL SOURCES:

BOOKS

Alscn, Eberhard, *Salinger's Glass Stories As a Composite Novel,*Whitson (Troy, NY), 1983.

Authors and Artists for Young Adults, Volume 2, Gale (Detroit, MI), 1989, pp. 201-210, Volume 36, 2000.

Belcher, W. F., and J. W. Lee, editors, *J. D. Salinger and the Critics,*Wadsworth (Belmont, CA), 1962.

Bloom Harold, *The Catcher in the Rye,* Chelsea House (New York, NY), 1995.

Bloom, Harold, editor, *J. D. Salinger: Modern Critical Views,* Chelsea House (New York, NY), 1987.

Cambridge Dictionary of American Biography, Cambridge University Press (New York, NY), 1995.

Carpenter, Humphrey, *Secret Gardens: A Study of the Golden Age of Children's Literature,* Houghton Mifflin (Boston, MA), 1985.

Children's Literature Review, Volume 18, Gale (Detroit, MI), 1989, pp. 171-194.

Concise Dictionary of American Literary Biography: The New Consciousness, 1941-1968, Gale (Detroit, MI), 1987, pp. 448-458.

Contemporary Literary Criticism, Gale (Detroit, MI), Volume 1, 1973, Volume 3, 1975, Volume 8, 1978, Volume 12, 1980, Volume 55, 1989, Volume 56, 1989.

Contemporary Novelists, 7th edition, St. James Press (Detroit, MI), 2001.

Contemporary Popular Writers, St. James Press (Detroit, MI), 1997.

Dictionary of Literary Biography, Gale (Detroit, MI), Volume 2: *American Novelists since World War II,* 1978, pp. 434-444, Volume 102: *American Short-Story Writers, 1910-1945,* 1991, pp. 258-265.

Donelson, Kenneth L., and Alleen Pace Nilsen, *Literature for Today's Young Adults,* Scott, Foresman (Glenview, IL), 1980.

Encyclopedia of American Biography, HarperCollins (New York, NY), 1996.

Encyclopedia of World Biography, 2nd edition, Gale (Detroit, MI), 1998.

Engel, Steven, *Readings on The Catcher in the Rye,* Greenhaven Press (San Diego, CA), 1998.

Filler, Louis, editor, *Seasoned "Authors" for a New Season: The Search for Standards in Popular Writing,* Bowling Green University Popular Press (Bowling Green, OH), 1980.

French, Warren, editor, *The Fifties: Fiction, Poetry, Drama,* Everett/Edwards (De Land, FL), 1970, pp. 1-39.

French, Warren, *J. D. Salinger,* Twayne (New York, NY), 1963, revised edition, G. K. Hall (Boston, MA), 1976.

French, Warren, *J. D. Salinger, Revisited,* Twayne (New York, NY), 1988.

Geismar, Maxwell, *American Moderns: From Rebellion to Conformity,* Hill & Wang (New York, NY), 1958.

Grunwald, Anatole, editor, *Salinger: A Critical and Personal Portrait,* Harper (New York, NY), 1962.

Gwynn, Frederick L., and Joseph L. Blotner, *The Fiction of J. D. Salinger,* Pittsburgh University Press (Pittsburgh, PA), 1958.

Hamilton, Ian, *In Search of J. D. Salinger,* Random House (New York, NY), 1988.

Hamilton, Kenneth, *J. D. Salinger: A Critical Essay,* Eerdmans (Grand Rapids, MI), 1967.

Hassan, Ihab, *Radical Innocence: Studies in the Contemporary American Novel,* Princeton University Press (Princeton, NJ), 1961.

Holzman, Robert S., and Gary L. Perkins, *J. D. Salinger's "The Catcher in the Rye,"* Research & Education Association (Piscataway, NJ), 1995.

Kazin, Alfred, *Contemporaries,* Atlantic Monthly Press (Boston, MA), 1962.

Kotzen, Kip, editor, *With Love and Squalor: Fourteen Writers Respond to the Work of J. D. Salinger,* Broadway Books (New York, NY), 2001.

Laser, Marvin, and Norman Fruman, editors, *Studies in J. D. Salinger,* Odyssey (New York, NY), 1963.

Lundquist, James, *J. D. Salinger,* Ungar (New York, NY), 1979.

Madinaveitia, Catherine, *Brodie's Notes on J. D. Salinger's "The Catcher in the Rye,"* Pan (London, England), 1987.

Mailer, Norman, *Advertisements for Myself,* Putnam (New York, NY), 1959, pp. 467-468.

Marsden, Malcolm M., editor, *"If You Really Want to Know": A Catcher Casebook,* Scott, Foresman (Glenview, IL), 1963.

Maynard, Joyce, *At Home in the World: A Memoir,* Picador USA (New York, NY), 1998.

Miller, James E., Jr., *J. D. Salinger,* Minnesota University Press (Minneapolis, MN), 1965.

Pinsker, Sanford, *The Catcher in the Rye: Innocence under Pressure,* Twayne (New York, NY), 1993.

Rosen, Gerald, *Zen in the Art of J. D. Salinger,* Creative Arts (Berkeley, CA), 1977.

St. James Guide to Young Adult Writers, 2nd edition, St. James Press (Detroit, MI), 1999.

Salinger, Margaret A., *Dream Catcher: A Memoir,* Washington Square Press (New York, NY), 2000.

Salzberg, Joel, editor, *Critical Essays on Salinger's "The Catcher in the Rye,"* Hall (Boston, MA), 1990.

Salzman, Jack, editor, *New Essays on "The Catcher in the Rye,"* Cambridge University Press (New York, NY), 1992.

Schulz, Max F., *Radical Sophistication: Studies in Contemporary Jewish-American Novelists,* Ohio University Press (Athens, OH), 1969, pp. 198-217.

Short Story Criticism, Gale (Detroit, MI), Volume 2, 1989.

Simonson, Harold P., and E. P. Hager, editors, *"Catcher in the Rye": Clamor vs. Criticism,* Heath (Boston, MA), 1963.

Sublette, Jack R., *J. D. Salinger: An Annotated Bibliography, 1938-1981,* Garland (New York, NY), 1984.

Weinberg, Helen, *The New Novel in America: The Kafkan Mode in Contemporary American Fiction,* Cornell University Press (Ithaca, NY), 1970.

Wenke, John, *J. D. Salinger: A Study of the Short Fiction,* Twayne (Boston, MA), 1991.

PERIODICALS

America, January 26, 1963.

American Imago, spring-summer, 1965, pp. 57-76; summer, 1968, pp. 140-162.

American Literature, November, 1968, pp. 352-369.

American Quarterly, winter, 1977, pp. 547-562.

American Scholar, summer, 1999, review of *Franny and Zooey,* p. 128.

American Speech, October, 1959, pp. 172-181.

Atlantic, August, 1961, pp. 27-31.

Booklist, February 15, 1992, review of *The Catcher in the Rye,* p. 1101; June 1, 1995, review of *The Catcher in the Rye,* p. 1761; November 15, 1999, review of *Catcher in the Rye,* p. 601.

Book Week, September 26, 1965.

Chicago Review, winter, 1958, pp. 3-19.

Chicago Tribune, June 17, 1987.

College English, March, 1954, pp. 315-325; November, 1956, pp. 76-80; January, 1961, pp. 262-264; December, 1961, pp. 226-229; December, 1965, pp. 248-251.

College Language Association Journal, March, 1963, pp. 170-183.

Commentary, September, 1987, pp. 61-64.

Commonweal, February 23, 1973, pp. 465-469.

Comparative Literature Studies, March, 1997, review of *The Catcher in the Rye,* p. 260.

Crawdaddy, March, 1975.

Critical Inquiry, autumn, 1976, pp. 15-38.

Criticism, summer, 1967, pp. 275-288.

Critique, spring-summer, 1965.

Daily Eagle (Claremont, NH), November 13, 1953, p. 1.

Dalhousie Review, autumn, 1967, pp. 394-399.

English Journal, March, 1964; April, 1992, review of *The Catcher in the Rye,* p. 87; April, 1993, review of *The Catcher in the Rye,* p. 88.

Entertainment Weekly, July 15, 1994, review of *The Catcher in the Rye,* p. 80.

Globe and Mail, December 1, 2001, review of *The Catcher in the Rye,* p. D34.

Guardian Weekly, September 11, 1994, review of *The Catcher in the Rye,* p. 28.

Harper's, February, 1959, pp. 83-90; October, 1962, pp. 46-48; December, 1962.

Horizon, May, 1962.

Hungry Mind Review, fall, 1995, review of *Nine Stories,* p. 54; summer, 1999, review of *Nine Stories,* p. 45.

Life, November 3, 1961, pp. 129-130, 132, 135, 137-138, 141-142, 144.

London Review, winter, 1969-1970, pp. 34-54.

Los Angeles Times, November 7, 1986.

Mademoiselle, August, 1961.

Mainstream, February, 1959, pp. 2-13.

Modern Fiction Studies, autumn, 1966.

Modern Language Quarterly, December, 1964, pp. 461-472.

Mosaic, fall, 1968, pp. 3-17.

Nation, November 14, 1959, pp. 360-363.

New England Quarterly, December, 1997, review of *The Catcher in the Rye,* p. 567.

New Republic, October 19, 1959, pp. 19-22; April 28, 1973, pp. 30-32.

Newsweek, May 30, 1961; January 28, 1963; July 30, 1979.

New York Herald Tribune Book Review, July 15, 1951.

New York Post Weekend Magazine, April 30, 1961, p. 5.

New York Times, November 3, 1974, pp. 1, 69; April 12, 1977, section 1, p. 3; November 8, 1986; August 4, 1987; October 6, 1987; September 3, 1989; February 20, 1997, review of *Hapworth 16, 1924,* p. C15; September 13, 1998.

New York Times Book Review, September 17, 1961; June 3, 1979.

Observer (London), July 31, 1994, review of *The Catcher in the Rye,* p. 21, review of *The Catcher in the Rye,* p. 2; August 28, 1994, review of *For Esme—With Love and Squalor,* p. 21.

Partisan Review, fall, 1962, pp. 594-598.

People, October 31, 1983.

Publications of the Modern Language Association of America (PMLA), October, 1974, pp. 1065-1074.

Raleigh News and Observer, January 1, 2000, p. A2.

Ramparts, May, 1962, pp. 47-66.

Renascence, summer, 1970, pp. 171-182; spring, 1971, pp. 115-128; spring, 1972, pp. 159-167.

San Francisco Review, May, 1996, review of *Raise High the Roof Beams, Carpenters; and, Seymour: An Introduction,* p. 48.

Saturday Review, September 16, 1961; November 4, 1961.

Studies in Short Fiction, spring, 1967, pp. 217-224; spring, 1970, pp. 248-256; winter, 1973, pp. 27-33; summer, 1981, pp. 251-259; winter, 1981, pp. 1-15.

Time, September 15, 1961, pp. 84-90.

Times Educational Supplement, September 30, 1994, review of *The Catcher in the Rye,* p. 18.

Tricycle, summer, 1996, review of *Franny and Zooey,* p. 107.

Twentieth Century Literature, October, 1958, pp. 92-99.

University Review, autumn, 1966, pp. 19-24.

Village Voice, August 22, 1974.

Washington Post, November 6, 1986; November 8, 1986; November 19, 1986; December 4, 1986; December 12, 1986; January 30, 1987; February 4, 1987; February 9, 1987; February 13, 1987; May 5, 1987; October 7, 1987; December 6, 1989.

Washington Post Book World, December 10, 1995, review of *The Catcher in the Rye,* p. 4; February 7, 1999, review of *For Esme—With Love and Squalor,* p. 4.

Western Humanities Review, spring, 1956, pp. 129-137; summer, 1963, pp. 271-277.

Western Review, summer, 1957, pp. 261-280.

Wisconsin Studies in Contemporary Literature, winter, 1961, pp. 5-30; winter, 1963, pp. 109-149.

ONLINE

Art and Culture Network, http://www.artandculture.com/ (June 2, 2003), biography of J. D. Salinger.

Canoe Web site, http://cgi.canoe.ca/ (November 18, 2003).

Salinger Web site, http://www.salinger.org/ (November 18, 2003).

Today in Literature, http://www.todayinliterature.com/ (June 2, 2003), "J. D. Salinger."*

SANDERS, Richard (Kinard) 1940-

PERSONAL: Born August 23, 1940, in Harrisburg, PA; son of Henry Irvine and Thelma Sanders. *Ethnicity:* "Caucasian." *Education:* Carnegie Institute of Technology (now Carnegie-Mellon University), B.F. A., 1962; trained for the stage at London Academy of Music and Dramatic Art, 1962-63.

ADDRESSES: Office—Blood Star, Inc., P.O. Box 1644, Woodinville, WA 98072-1644. *Agent*—Arlene Thornton and Associates, 12711 Ventura Blvd., Suite 490, Studio City, CA 91604.

CAREER: Actor and writer. Blood Star, Inc., Woodinville, WA, president. U.S. Peace Corps, volunteer in Brazil, 1966-69, director of acting and stage movement for State Theater of Paraiba, 1966-68. Pacific Northwest Writers Conference, keynote speaker, 1996.

Actor in television series, including the roles of Les Nessman, *WKRP in Cincinnati,* Columbia Broadcasting System (CBS), 1978-82; Benjamin Beanley, *Spencer* (also known as *Under One Roof*), National Broadcasting Co. (NBC), 1984-85; Frank Chapman, *Berrenger's,* NBC, 1984-85; voice, *The Inhumanoids* (animated), 1986-87; Paul Sycamore, *You Can't Take It with You,* syndicated, 1987-88; and Les Nessman, *The New WKRP in Cincinnati,* syndicated, 1991-93.

Actor in television movies, including *Alexander: The Other Side of Dawn,* NBC, 1977; *Good against Evil,* American Broadcasting Companies (ABC), 1977; *Bud and Lou,* NBC, 1978; *Keefer* (also known as *Behind the Lines*), ABC, 1978; *Ruby and Oswald* (also known as *Four Days in Dallas*), CBS, 1978; *Diary of a Teenage Hitchhiker,* ABC, 1979; *Trouble in High Timber Country* (also known as *The Yeagers*), ABC, 1980; *Found Money* (also known as *My Secret Angel*), NBC, 1983; *Portrait of an Invisible Woman* (also known as *The Invisible Woman*), NBC, 1983; *Perry Mason: The Case of the Avenging Ace* (also known as *The Case of the Avenging Ace*), NBC, 1988; *Absent Minded Professor,* The Disney Channel, 1989; and *Simon and Simon: In Trouble Again,* CBS, 1995.

Actor in television specials, including *Stop, Thief!,* 1976; *Solid Gold '79,* 1980; *The Joke's on Mr. Little,* 1982; *Ike,* ABC; and *They've Killed President Lincoln;* appeared in the television miniseries *Roots II* and Stephen King's *Rose Red.*

Richard Sanders

Guest actor in television series, including episodes of *Newhart; Who's the Boss?; Married . . . with Children; Coach; Unhappily Ever After; Alice; Barnaby Jones; Gloria; Goodnight, Beantown; Lou Grant; McCloud; Simon and Simon; The Rockford Files; Designing Women; Murder, She Wrote; Night Court; It Takes Two; Charles in Charge; Riptide; Growing Pains; Blacke's Magic; Knots Landing; Days of Our Lives; Alf; Nothing in Common; Kojak; James at Sixteen; Easy Street; Sidekicks; Rafferty;* and *The Fugitive.*

Actor in feature films, including *Billy Jack Goes to Washington,* Warner Bros., 1976; *Midway,* Universal, 1976; *The Gypsy Warriors,* Universal, 1978; *Nude Bomb* (also known as *Maxwell Smart and the Nude Bomb* and *The Return of Maxwell Smart*), Universal, 1980; *Valley Girl,* Atlantic, 1983; *Neon City,* Vidmark, 1992; *The Beans of Egypt, Maine* (also known as *Forbidden Choices*), IRS Releasing, 1994; *Black Circle Boys,* FSI, 1996; *Nowheresville,* Trout Films, 1998; *Anoosh of the Airways,* Sugar Shack Pictures, 1998; *Lovers Lane,* Lovers Lane LLC, 1999; and *Men of Honor,* Twentieth Century-Fox, 2000.

Actor in stage productions, including *Raisin,* produced in New York, NY, at 46th Street Theater, 1974-75; *Travesties,* Los Angeles, CA, Mark Taper Forum, 1976; and *Sunshine Boys,* Toronto, Ontario, Canada, Stage West Theater, 1998; also appeared in *Same Time, Next Year,* in Kansas City, MO, at Tiffany's Attic; *The Boss,* New York, NY, at Chelsea Theater Center; appeared in productions at the Arena Stage, Washington, DC; Barter Stage, Abingdon, VA; Center Stage, Baltimore, MD; Front Street Theater, Memphis, TN; Champlain Shakespeare Festival, Burlington, VT; New York Shakespeare Festival, Lincoln Center, New York, NY; Los Angeles Actors Theater, Los Angeles, CA; Pasadena Playhouse, Pasadena, CA; and Seattle Repertory Theater, Seattle, WA.

MEMBER: Actors' Equity Association, Screen Actors Guild, American Federation of Television and Radio Artists, Writers Guild of America.

AWARDS, HONORS: Fulbright grant for England, 1962-63.

WRITINGS:

(With Michael Fairman) *Found Money* (television movie; also known as *My Secret Angel*), NBC, 1983.

Author of episodes of the television series *WKRP in Cincinnati,* CBS, including "A Date with Jennifer," 1979; "A Commercial Break," 1979; "Most Improved Station," 1980; "The Airplane Show," 1980; and "The Impossible Dream," 1980. Also author (with Marilynn Marko-Sanders) of episodes of the syndicated series *The New WKRP in Cincinnati,* including "Long Live the King," 1991; and "Fever in the Morning: Parts 1 and 2," 1992; and an episode of *The Famous Teddy Z,* CBS, "Teddy Meets His Hero," 1989.

SIDELIGHTS: Richard Sanders is best known for his role as the timid, fact-collecting news reporter Les Nessman on the television series *WKRP in Cincinnati.* In this popular and critically acclaimed prime-time situation comedy, the people who work at an unsuccessful radio station try a variety of schemes to make the station more popular. Ben Fong-Torres, a contributor to *Rolling Stone,* reviewed the series in its troubled first season, when the show was put on hiatus for two months then brought back on a new day and time slot: "*WKRP* deserves to stay alive. Besides being one of the few literate comedy shows left, with good ensemble acting (all in the tradition of the *Mary Tyler Moore Show*), *WKRP* offers comic but on-the-mark glimpses of the radio and record businesses." Sanders's character was often made the butt of jokes for his expert knowledge in trivial matters and his sexual naivete. In addition to writing several episodes for *WKRP in Cincinnati,* Sanders is the coauthor, with Michael Fairman, of *Found Money,* also known as *My Secret Angel,* a made-for-television movie in which two friends attempt to reward the few good acts they encounter in a world they find increasingly callous. In pursuit of this goal they invent an agency called The Invisible Friend, Inc., but soon run into trouble.

BIOGRAPHICAL AND CRITICAL SOURCES:

BOOKS

Contemporary Theatre, Film and Television, Gale (Detroit, MI), 1998.

PERIODICALS

People, November 12, 1979, p. 112.
Rolling Stone, March 8, 1979, Ben Fong-Torres, review of *WKRP in Cincinnati,* p. 17.

* * *

SAUER, Elizabeth M. 1964-

PERSONAL: Born July 4, 1964, in Kitchener, Ontario, Canada; daughter of Albert (a factory worker) and Anneliese (a homemaker; maiden name, Sander) Sauer. *Ethnicity:* "German." *Education:* Wilfrid Laurier University, H.B.A. (magna cum laude), 1986; University of Western Ontario, M.A., 1987, Ph.D., 1991. *Politics:* "New Democrat Party supporter." *Religion:* Roman Catholic.

ADDRESSES: *Home*—15 Valerie Dr., St. Catharines, Ontario, Canada L2T 3G3. *Office*—Department of English, Brock University, St. Catharines, Ontario L2S 3A1, Canada; fax: 905-688-5550, extension 4492. *E-mail*—emsauer@spartan.ac.Brocku.ca.

CAREER: Brock University, St. Catharines, Ontario, Canada, assistant professor, 1991-95, associate professor, 1995-99, professor of English, 1999—. Newberry Library, member of Center for Renaissance Studies; Centre for Reformation and Renaissance Studies, member. Worldwise International Awareness Centre, volunteer, 1995-96.

MEMBER: Canadian Society for Renaissance Studies, Association of Canadian College and University Teachers of English, Milton Society of America (member of executive committee), Shakespeare Society of America, Renaissance Society of America, Society for the Study of Early Modern Women.

AWARDS, HONORS: Fellow of Dartmouth College and University of Western Ontario, 1991; grants from Social Science and Humanities Research Council of Canada, 1992-95, 1995-99, 2000, and Canadian Federation for the Humanities, 1994-97; Irene Samuel Memorial Award, Milton Society of America, 2000, for *Milton and the Imperial Vision;* award of Chancellor's Chair for Research Excellence, Brock University, 2001.

WRITINGS:

Barbarous Dissonance and Images of Voice in Milton's Epics (monograph), McGill-Queen's University Press (Montreal, Quebec, Canada), 1996.

(Editor, with Janet Lungstrum, and contributor) *Agonistics: Arenas of Creative Contest,* State University of New York Press (Albany, NY), 1997.

(Editor, with Balachandra Rajan, and contributor) *Milton and the Imperial Vision,* Duquesne University Press (Pittsburgh, PA), 1999.

(Editor, with Jennifer Andersen, and contributor) *Books and Readers in Early Modern England: Material Studies,* University of Pennsylvania Press (Philadelphia, PA), 2002.

(Editor, with Helen Ostovich, and contributor) *Reading Early Modern Women: An Anthology of Texts in Manuscript and Print, 1500-1700,* Routledge (New York, NY), 2003.

(Editor, with Balachandra Rajan, and contributor) *Imperialisms: Historical and Literary Investigations, 1500-1900,* Palgrave Macmillan (New York, NY), 2004.

Contributor to books, including *Milton and Heresy,* edited by John Rumrich and Stephen Dobranski, Cambridge University Press (New York, NY), 1998; *Sensible Flesh: On Touch in Early Modern Culture,* edited by Elizabeth D. Harvey, University of Pennsylvania Press (Philadelphia, PA), 2002; *Fault Lines and Controversies in the Study of Seventeenth-Century English Literature,* edited by Claude J. Summers and Ted-Larry Pebworth, University of Missouri Press (Columbia, MO), 2002; *Prose Fiction and Early Modern Sexualities,* edited by Constance Relihan and Goran Stanivukovic, Kent State University Press (Kent, OH), 2003; and *Reading Milton Writing Gender: The Place of the Feminine in the Major Poems and Prose,* edited by Catherine Gimelli Martin, Cambridge University Press (New York, NY), 2003. Contributor of articles and reviews to periodicals, including *Explorations in Renaissance Culture, English Studies in Canada,* and *Ben Jonson Journal: Literary Contexts in the Age of Elizabeth, James, and Charles. Renaissance and Reformation,* book review editor, 1997—, coeditor of special issue, 2004; member of editorial board, *Harpweaver,* 1996-97.

WORK IN PROGRESS: "Paper-Protestations" and Textual Communities in England, 1640-1675; editing *Osiris and Urania: Milton and Climates of Reading,* for Duquesne University Press (Pittsburgh, PA); *Toleration and Milton's "Peculiar" Nation.*

BIOGRAPHICAL AND CRITICAL SOURCES:

PERIODICALS

Albion, summer, 2003, Marjorie Swann, review of *Books and Readers in Early Modern England: Material Studies,* p. 275.

History: Review of New Books, summer, 2002, Jeremy Black, review of *Books and Readers in Early Modern England,* p. 154.

International Fiction Review, January, 2003, Andrea Gogrof-Voorhees, review of *Agonistics: Arenas of Creative Contest,* p. 93.

Libraries and Culture, spring, 2003, John Overholt, review of *Books and Readers in Early Modern England,* p. 191.

* * *

SCHOONOVER, Jason 1946-

PERSONAL: Surname is pronounced *Skoon*-o-ver; born September 14, 1946, in Melfort, Saskatchewan, Canada; son of Vernon (in business) and Linda (a teacher; maiden name, Novak) Schoonover; married

Donna Jantzen, December 23, 1967 (divorced, 1973); companion of Su Hattori (a nurse and medical researcher). *Education:* Simon Fraser University, B.A., 1969. *Politics:* "Free enterprise." *Religion:* "I believe in a greater intelligence, not religion." *Hobbies and other interests:* The outdoors, canoeing, hunting, fishing.

ADDRESSES: Home—720 University Dr., Saskatoon, Saskatchewan S7N 0J4, Canada. *Agent*—Mike Hamilburg, Michael J. Hamilburg Agency, 11718 Barrington Ct., Suite 732, Los Angeles, CA. *E-mail*—jason.schoonover@shaw.ca.

CAREER: CKOM-Radio, Saskatoon, Saskatchewan, Canada, announcer, 1970-71; CFQC-Radio, Saskatoon, announcer, music director, promotion manager, and producer, 1971-77; freelance writer, director, and producer for radio, the stage, newspapers, and magazines, 1977-87; novelist, screenwriter, and film producer, 2003. Rolling Thunder Sound, owner, 1972-77; Schoonover Properties (real estate investment company), owner, beginning 1975; Windjammer Trading, owner, 1978-82; Jewelers Gallery, co-owner, 1979-82; anthropological collector in the East Asia for museums worldwide, 1978-87. Member of Saskatoon media committees of foundations for cancer, heart disease, multiple sclerosis, and cystic fibrosis research; also worked as chair of Saskatoon Block Parent Plan.

MEMBER: Explorers Club (New York; fellow), Foreign Correspondents Club of Thailand, Bangkok Obliterati.

AWARDS, HONORS: Human Rights Award, B'nai B'rith, 1976, for work as chair of the Saskatoon Block Parent Plan.

WRITINGS:

The Bangkok Collection (novel), Seal-Bantam (Toronto, Ontario, Canada), 1988, published as *Thai Gold,* Bantam (New York, NY), 1989, revised edition, Asia Books (Bangkok, Thailand), 2003.

Opium Dream (novel), Asia Books (Bangkok, Thailand), 2002.

Thai Gold (screenplay), 2003.

Also author of "The Cariboo," a one-act play, as yet neither published nor produced. Columnist for *Westworld.* Contributor to magazines and newspapers.

WORK IN PROGRESS: The Manila Galleon, a novel.

SIDELIGHTS: Jason Schoonover once told *CA:* "I'm a traveler. I was born with a suitcase in one hand and a typewriter in the other. I stumbled across the Far East in the midst of an around-the-world trip in 1978 and was delightfully stunned by the experience—the most exotic chunk of real estate on the planet. The tremendous variety of cultural and sensory experiences made it impossible to be bored there. Since one has only one life to live, I decided to live it in paradise and moved to Bangkok, the hub, in the most exotic country of them all, Thailand, in 1982. Basically, since 1989 I've split my year between there and Canada, where I'm also in love with the outdoors, canoeing, hunting, and fishing.

"With my strong interest in anthropology, I had been immediately drawn to the jungles and so-called 'primitive' groups of the region—the devil dancers of Sri Lanka, the Sherpa of the Himalayas, the hill tribes of the Golden Triangle, and others—on that first trip and launched on collecting rampages, piecing together comprehensive ethnological collections (complete with sound, film, and full documentation to provide museums with all-encompassing display experiences). Soon I was contracting for museums around the world, including the Smithsonian, the National Museums of Canada and Finland, the Museum of Anthropology in Vancouver, British Columbia, and the Sankoken of Tenri, Nara, Japan, to name a few. At the same time, I freelanced widely for newspapers and magazines around the United States and Canada, usually on more adventurous themes, including trekking to Mount Everest, white-water rafting, jungle expeditions, and so on.

"When I was twelve years old I made two vows to myself: to live the most adventurous life I could and to become a novelist. Everything I had done previously had been targeted to achieve these goals: avoiding journalism and studying literature so as not to channel what creativity I have, a broad media background and an equally broad business background (as much as I hate it), to experience as much as I could. The years after 1978 largely fulfilled the two original goals and the adventures have been many—too many to describe: being charged by a bull elephant in a Thai jungle, having a scuba regulator pack in suddenly at ninety feet off Zamboanga, going on expeditions to explore underground rivers and neolithic caves, and drinking homemade rice wine with loinclothed happily drunken Igorot ex-headhunters who were sacrificing chickens to check the gallbladders during their annual 'canaos.'

"This lifestyle forms the background to my adventure/thrillers. I aim to write fast-paced, complex, highly entertaining novels—but written against an authentic anthropological, archaeological, historical, and cultural background to give the reader a rewarding experience as well. This is very important to me, providing a window to this incredible world, where the unbelievable is regularly believable. Background accuracy is also very important to me; for example, in *The Manila Galleon,* a treasure diving story based on the historical Acapulco-Manila galleons, I was fortunate to have Mel Fisher of Key West agree to vet my copy for state-of-the-art accuracy.

"As in the days of Rudyard Kipling and William Somerset Maugham, the Far East attracts a certain type of rugged individualist—deep-sea divers, retired spooks, mercenaries, correspondents, mountaineers, 'jungologists,' and treasure seekers of all ilk—and they all find their way to the bars of Bangkok, the capital, and from there into my books.

"Writing is an adventure as well, exploring the peaks of one's imagination, delighting in the discoveries that appear in the form of the twists and turns of the plot, the development of unusual and interesting characters, the overall complexity that mysteriously bubbles up from the depths. In fact, the creative one is the greatest challenge and expedition of them all."

* * *

SCHWARTZ, Richard Alan 1951-

PERSONAL: Born February 3, 1951, in Miami, FL; son of Robert I. (a self-employed advertiser) and Evelyn (a teacher) Schwartz; divorced. *Ethnicity:* "American." *Education:* Attended Colby College, 1969-70; University of South Florida, B.A., 1972; University of Chicago, M.A., 1974, Ph.D., 1977. *Hobbies and other interests:* Tennis, drawing, painting, yard work.

ADDRESSES: Home—Miami, FL. *Office*—Department of English, Florida International University, Miami, FL 33199. *E-mail*—schwartz@fiu.edu.

CAREER: Indiana University—Northwest, Gary, adjunct professor, 1975-77; University of Miami, Coral Gables, FL, adjunct professor, 1977-78; New England Telephone Co., Boston, MA, computer programmer, 1978-79; Florida International University, Miami, began as assistant professor, became professor of English, 1979—, associate director of Institute for Public Policy, 1989-90. Lecturer at University of Palermo, University of Catania, and Bogazici University, between 1985 and 1986; guest on radio programs.

MEMBER: American Humor Studies Association, Institute for Evolutionary Psychology.

AWARDS, HONORS: Grants from National Endowment for the Humanities, 1980, 1983, 1988; Outstanding Academic Book citation, *Choice,* 1997, for *The Cold War Reference Guide: A General History and Annotated Chronology, with Selected Biographies.*

WRITINGS:

The Cold War Reference Guide: A General History and Annotated Chronology, with Selected Biographies, McFarland (Jefferson, NC), 1997.

Cold War Culture, Facts on File (New York, NY), 1997.

Encyclopedia of the Persian Gulf War, McFarland (Jefferson, NC), 1998.

Woody, from Antz to Zelig: A Reference Guide to Woody Allen's Creative work, 1964-1998, Greenwood Press (Westport, CT), 2000.

(With Nicholas J. Mason) *Following Your Treasure Map,* XLibris (Philadelphia, PA), 2000.

The Films of Ridley Scott, Praeger (Westport, CT), 2001.

The 1950s, Facts on File (New York, NY), 2003.

Contributor of articles and reviews to periodicals, including *Nation, Journal of Evolutionary Psychology, Mathematical Connections, Literature/Film Quarterly, Journal of Aesthetic Education, Isis,* and *Modern Fiction Studies.* Founding editor, *Journal for the Art of Teaching,* 1992-96.

WORK IN PROGRESS: Pie-Thrower.com, a novel.

SIDELIGHTS: Richard Alan Schwartz once told *CA:* "For me, the dominating question of twentieth-century studies asks how a person can live an authentic, fulfilling, moral, self-actualized life centered around some notion of proper action in a secular, relativistic, machine-dominated, uncertain, and incompletely knowable world, where most social and political relationships center around power and wealth instead of virtue or truth. I see this dilemma as an overriding issue in modern arts and letters, as well as in the conduct of everyday life and international politics.

"The Cold War fostered, though it did not originate, the morally indeterminate environment described above, and I am a Cold War kid. A child when Sputnik inaugurated the space age, Eisenhower was 'getting a bigger bank for the buck' by developing a nuclear arsenal, and Khrushchev was promising to bury us, I am also of the generation that fought and protested the Vietnam war and went on to become yuppies. American Cold War-related literature and film have dominated my research and teaching, and from my courses on the arts and letters of the Cold War grew *Cold War Reference Guide: A General History and Annotated Chronology, with Selected Biographies, Cold War Culture,* an encyclopedia of Cold War-related literature, film, television, performing arts, fine arts, and popular culture, and *The 1950s,* which provides an overview of social, political, scientific, business, literary, artistic, cultural, and pop-cultural developments for each year of the decade.

"Having exorcized some of my Cold War demons, I decided to advance into the 'new world order.' Anticipating offering courses relating to the Persian Gulf War, I wrote *Encyclopedia of the Persian Gulf War* in order to educate myself about it. The book covers both political and military developments." Later, Schwartz added: "I then returned to my academic roots by studying the craft of storytelling in my studies of the creative work of Woody Allen and the films of Ridley Scott. Allen, especially, shares my interest in exploring how we can negotiate our ways through murky, imperfectly knowable reality."

In his original essay Schwartz continued: "Aspects of the modernist world view also appear in my other scholarship and in my creative writing. My articles on *Absalom, Absalom!* and *Thelma and Louise* consider how these stories construct classical tragedies in indeterminate, morally ambiguous settings. Other scholarship shows conceptual affinities between modern science and modern arts. For instance, relativity theory and cubism share an interest in multiple frames of reference, and 'complementarity' theory, Escher drawings, and sophisticated punning all allow for the coexistence of mutually exclusive opposites."

Recently Schwartz commented: "Although wisdom stands at the peak of the hierarchy of facts, knowledge, and sagacity, it often receives scant attention. In the fifteen years I have known Nicholas Mason, I have found him to be a great source of wisdom and inspiration. A practicing psychologist and hypnotherapist, Dr. Mason has synthesized what he has learned into a coherent philosophy of life, which he calls a 'treasure map.' He has found that, by maintaining heightened awareness, respecting our bodies and spirits, and invoking the powers of our subconscious, we can reach our optimum levels of fulfillment. The book *Following Your Treasure Map* develops his philosophy at length and explains how to put it into practice.

"My fiction often skirts the line between the real and the surreal, and the current practices of absurdist political protest and unfettered personal expression on the Internet enable me to walk that line in my recent novel *Pie-Thrower.com.* Among other matters, the book addresses the dangers of terrorism and some of the moral and philosophical issues faced by those who must confront it."

* * *

SMITH, Rosamond
See OATES, Joyce Carol

* * *

SPITZ, Ellen Handler

PERSONAL: Born in New York, NY. *Education:* Barnard College, A.B.; Harvard University, M.A.T.; Columbia University, Ph.D., 1983.

ADDRESSES: Office—UMBC Honors College, University of Maryland, Baltimore County, 1000 Hilltop Circle, Baltimore, MD 21250.

CAREER: Columbia College, co-instructor in psychology and psychoanalysis, 1984, 1985; Barnard College, visiting lecturer in philosophy, 1985; Columbia University Center for Psychoanalytical Training and Research, electives for advanced candidates, 1986, 1990, 1993, lecturer, 1995-96; Graduate Center of the City University of New York, adjunct assistant professor of art history, 1986; New York University, adjunct assistant professor of educational psychology, 1984-87; Hebrew University of Jerusalem, Ayala and Sam Zacks visiting professor of art history, 1987; Cornell University Medical College, lecturer of aesthetics in psychiatry, 1987—; Rutgers University, Livingston College honors program, visiting faculty, 1993; Stanford University, visiting lecturer, department of art and art history, 1997-2000; University of California, Santa Cruz, visiting professor of art history, spring, 2000; University of Maryland, Baltimore County, honors college professor of visual arts, 2001—. Member of advisory board of Oxford University Press and the Lucy Daniels Foundation.

MEMBER: American Society for Aesthetics (member of board of trustees), American Philosophical Association, College Art Association, Association for Psychoanalytic Medicine (special member), American Psychoanalytic Association (academic associate member), Gardiner Seminar on Psychoanalysis and the Humanities, Kappa Delta Pi.

AWARDS, HONORS: American Psychoanalytic Association, grants from Liddle Fund, 1983, and Fund for Psychoanalytic Research, 1988; Fritz Schmidl Prize, Seattle Psychoanalytic Society, 1983; fellow, National Endowment for the Humanities, and NEH Summer Institute on Image and Text, Johns Hopkins University, both 1988; research grant, Fund for Psychoanalytical Training and Research of the American Psychoanalytical Association, 1988; Getty/Kress travel grant, 1989; Getty scholar, Getty Center for the History of Art and the Humanities, 1989-90; Robert S. Liebert Award in Applied Psychoanalysis of the Columbia University Center for Psychoanalytical Training and Research, 1991; scholar-in-residence, Center for Psychoanalysis and the Humanities, University of Tennessee, Knoxville, 1991; fellowships at the Center for Advanced Study at Radcliffe College (formerly The Bunting Institute), Harvard University, 1995-96, Center for Advanced Study in the Behavioral Sciences, Stanford University, 1996-97, and Camargo Foundation, Cassis, France, 1999; senior fellow, Center for Children and Childhood Studies, Rutgers University, 2003-04.

WRITINGS:

Art and Psyche: A Study in Psychoanalysis and Aesthetics, Yale University Press (New Haven, CT), 1985.

Image and Insight: Essays in Psychoanalysis and the Arts, Columbia University Press (New York, NY), 1991.

(Editor, with Peter L. Rudnytsky) *Freud and Forbidden Knowledge,* New York University Press (New York, NY), 1993.

Museums of the Mind: Magritte's Labyrinth and Other Essays in the Arts, Yale University Press (New Haven, CT), 1994.

(Editor, with others) *Bertolucci's "Last Emperor": Multiple Takes,* Wayne State University Press (Detroit, MI), 1998.

Inside Picture Books, Yale University Press (New Haven CT), 1999.

Some of Spitz's books have been translated into Italian, Japanese, and Korean.

Work represented in anthologies, including *Psychoanalytic Perspectives on Art,* edited by Mary M. Gedo, Analytic Press (Hillsdale, NJ), 1985; *The Persistence of Myth,* edited by P. L. Rudnytsky, Guilford Press (New York, NY), 1988; *Postmodern Perspectives: Issues in Contemporary Art,* edited by H. Risatti, Prentice-Hall (Englewood Cliffs, NJ), 1989; *Freud and Art: His Personal Collection of Antiquities,* edited by Lynn Gamwell and Richard Wells, Harry N. Abrams (New York, NY), 1989; *Pleasure beyond the Pleasure Principle,* edited by R. A. Glick and S. Bone, Yale University Press (New Haven, CT), 1990; *Perversions and Near-Perversions in Clinical Practice: New Psychoanalytic Perspectives,* edited by G. I. Fogel and W. A. Meyers, Yale University Press (New Haven, CT), 1991; *Essential Papers on Literature and Psychoanalysis,* edited by E. Berman, New York University Press (New York, NY), 1993; *Transitional Objects and Potential Spaces: Literary Uses of D. W. Winnicott,* edited by P. L. Rudnytsky, Columbia University Press (New York, NY), 1993; *Feminism and Tradition in Aesthetics,* edited by P. Z. Brand and C. Karsmeyer, Pennsylvania State University Press (University Park, PA), 1995; and *Mirroring Evil: Nazi Images/Recent Art,* edited by Norman L. Kleeblatt, Rutgers University Press (New Brunswick, NJ), 2001.

Contributor of articles and reviews to *Baltimore Sun, New Republic,* and *New York Times.* Contributor of more than seventy-five articles, chapters and reviews to academic journals, including *Psychoanalytic Inquiry, Textbook of Psychoanalysis, Chronicle of Higher Education, Lilith, American Imago, Art Bulletin, Journal of Aesthetic Education, Arts in Psychotherapy, Art Criticism, Psychoanalytic Study of the Child, Current Musicology, International Journal of Psychoanalysis,* and *Art Bulletin.* Member of editorial board, *American Imago* and *Gender and Psychoanalysis.*

SIDELIGHTS: Professor and author, Ellen Handler Spitz told *CA:* "From my earliest years, drawing has always been a part of my life (once, to my parents' horror, exuberant childish scribbles appeared all over my freshly wallpapered bedroom)." Spitz examines the relationships between people and the art they come to love. In *Museums of the Mind: Magritte's Labyrinth and Other Essays in the Arts,* she takes "takes an in-depth look at the surrealistic paintings of Rene Magritte," wrote a reviewer for *Booknews,* and then turns to exploring the interrelationship between various genres of art: plastic arts, drama, movies, opera, cartoons, poetry, and others. "Interdisciplinary consideration of art is nothing new," declared Julie C. Van Kamp in the *Journal of Aesthetic Education,* "but rarely has it been accomplished with the stunning breadth of this volume. Spitz's writing and insights dazzle the imagination. If one learns to write in part by reading, this volume is a teacher to be treasured."

Spitz examines another aspect of the relationship between humans and artwork in *Inside Picture Books.* The volume tries to establish an understanding of why some children's picture books continue to enchant children decades after their composition—far longer than most contemporary works for adults. "Read in the security of a parent's arms or in a caregiver's company," Marina Warner wrote in the *New York Times Book Review,* "picture books also act as bridges to the world of outer experience. . . . Shared, repeated, slow reading of such material also defends against the competing claims of television, movies, computer games and comics and their fast-paced, jumbled, raucous and often violent imagery, where 'children encounter . . . unmourned deaths—brutal, frightening and incomprehensible.'"

Works like Maurice Sendak's *Where the Wild Things Are,* published in 1963, and Margaret Wise Brown's *Goodnight Moon,* published in 1947, have won their own literary immortality, and *Inside Picture Books* tries to understand why. "Through the lens of psychology," wrote a *Publishers Weekly* contributor, picture books offer children their first exposure to messages about aesthetics, culture, and morality. "Spitz's text makes a compelling case for the power of art and literature," the contributor concluded, "and the responsibility that accompanies such power, particularly when it relates to children."

Critics largely celebrated Spitz's accomplishment in *Inside Picture Books.* "Without jargon or pretension," stated Hazel Rochman in a review of the volume appearing in *Booklist,* "Spitz celebrates the story and art" of picture books. "Readers—and lovers—of the books she analyzes will differ in their memories and their judgments," Warner concluded, "but Spitz communicates vividly her pleasure in her material and speaks up vibrantly for the importance, complexity and place of shared reading and picture books in young lives and their future." As an example of Spitz's insight, she opens Chapter 4, titled "Behave Yourself," as follows: "With varying overtones of irritation, pride, and chagrin, we adults sometimes use the terms mischievous and disobedient to describe children's behavior. . . . As far as the children are concerned, [these terms] leave out wish and impulse, playfulness, and, above all, curiosity." J. Lane Tanner, writing for the *Journal of Development and Behavioral Pediatrics,* commented: "With this preamble, the author leads us into a re-examination of such classics as *Where the Wild Things Are, The Story of Peter Rabbit,* and *The Story about Ping,* all of which involve various aspects of the preschooler's position, wavering between egocentric fantasy and self-control/compliance. These and other books explore different facets of this dialect. All join the child by taking misbehavior as a given, and moving their characters toward greater knowledge or mastery over the self—a journey that picture books are uniquely suited to describe."

Wendy Lukehart, reviewing the book for *School Library Journal,* noted that "Spitz's psychoanalytical background, her passion for the role of art as a transmitter of culture, her observations of children's experiences with books, her knowledge of Jewish ritual and writings, and her own vivid childhood memories all inform and influence this work," which she called a "fascinating, highly personal treatment of a popular genre." Quentin Blake in the *Times* commended *Inside Picture Books,* for "it's mixture of perception, warmth and commitment." He regarded the book as "a valuable contribution to a subject which asks for serious consideration: what children's books are, and what they do, and what important and curious introductions to life are taking place as we turn the pages together."

BIOGRAPHICAL AND CRITICAL SOURCES:

PERIODICALS

Booklist, May 15, 1999, Hazel Rochman, review of *Inside Picture Books,* p. 1644.

Booknews, September 1, 1995, review of *Museums of the Mind: Magritte's Labyrinth and Other Essays in the Arts.*

Chronicle of Higher Education, May 14, 1999, Jennifer K. Ruark, "Scary and Soothing: How Picture Books Shape the Mind of a Child," review of *Inside Picture Books,* p. A18.

Journal of Aesthetic Education, spring, 1997, Julie C. Van Kamp, review of *Museums of the Mind,* pp. 117-120.

Journal of Developmental and Behavioral Pediatrics, December, 2000, J. Lane Tanner, review of *Inside Picture Books,* p. 452.

Library Journal, January, 1995, Mary Hamel-Schwulst, review of *Museums of the Mind,* p. 99.

New York Times, June 26, 1999, Edward Rothstein, "Stories That Reverberate in Mother's Voice: Good Night Childhood," p. B11.

New York Times Book Review, August 15, 1999, Marina Warner, "Gods and Monsters: An Art Historian Seeks to Identify the Enduring Appeal of Classic Children's Picture Books," review of *Inside Picture Books,* p. 10.

Publishers Weekly, April 12, 1999, review of *Inside Picture Books,* p. 66.

School Library Journal, March, 2000, Wendy Lukehart, review of *Inside Picture Books,* p. 269.

Times (London, England), September 23, 1999, Quentin Blake, review of *Inside Picture Books,* p. 43.

* * *

STEIN, Ben

See STEIN, Benjamin (Jeremy)

STEIN, Benjamin (Jeremy) 1944-
(Ben Stein)

PERSONAL: Born November 25, 1944, in Washington, DC; son of Herbert (an economist, presidential advisor, and writer) and Mildred (a homemaker; maiden name, Fishman) Stein; married Alexandra Denman (an entertainment lawyer), June 22, 1968 (divorced, 1974; remarried, September 7, 1977); children: Tommy (adopted). *Education:* Columbia University, B.A., 1966; Yale University, LL.B., 1970. *Religion:* Jewish.

ADDRESSES: *Home*—Los Angeles, CA. *Agent*—Lois Wallace, Wallace & Sheil Agency, Inc., 177 East 70th St., New York, NY 10021.

CAREER: Writer, lawyer, teacher, and actor. Federal Trade Commission (FTC), Washington, DC, trial lawyer, 1970-73; speech writer for President Richard M. Nixon, 1973-74, and President Gerald Ford, 1974; *Wall Street Journal,* New York, NY, member of editorial page staff and author of a column about popular culture, 1974-76; creative consultant and scriptwriter for Norman Lear, 1976-77; writer, beginning 1977. Practiced as a poverty lawyer in New Haven, CT, and Washington, DC; testified before U.S. Congress. Consultant to LAACO, Inc. Columnist for *Los Angeles Herald Examiner, Los Angeles* Magazine, *New York, E! Online, American Spectator,* and King Features Syndicate. Instructor at University of California—Santa Cruz, 1973; member of adjunct faculty at American University and Pepperdine University. Committee on the Present Danger, member, beginning 1982. Television actor, appearing in the movies *Mastergate,* 1992; *The Day My Parents Ran Away,* 1993; (voice performer) *Santa vs. the Snowman,* 1997; (voice performer) *Breakfast with Einstein,* 1998; *Men in White,* 1998; and *Casper Meets Wendy,* 1998. Cohost of the game show series *Win Ben Stein's Money,* Comedy Central, 1997-2002; and *Turn Ben Stein On,* beginning 1999; also appeared in the series *The Wonder Years,* 1989-91; *Salute Your Shorts,* 1991; (voice performer) *Bruno the Kid,* 1996; *Match Game,* 1998. Guest actor in episodes of *Charles in Charge,* 1987-90; *MacGyver,* 1991; (voice performer) *Animaniacs,* 1993; *Full House,* 1993; *Earthworm Jim,* 1995; *Tales from the Crypt,* 1995; *Lois and Clark: The New Adventures of Superman,* 1995; *Married . . . with Children,* 1995; *Freakazoid!,* 1995; *The Marshal,* 1995; (voice performer) *Duckman,* 1996-97; *Murphy*

Brown, 1997; *Total Security,* 1997; *Hercules,* 1998; (voice performer) *Rugrats,* 1998; *The Hughleys,* 1998; and *Shasta McNasty,* 1999. Also appeared in commercials, including advertisements for Clear Eyes, Oldsmobile, the board game "Sorry!," and Office Max. Film appearances include *The Wild Life,* 1984; *Ferris Bueller's Day Off,* 1986; *Planes, Trains and Automobiles,* 1987; *Frankenstein General Hospital,* 1988; *Ghostbusters II,* 1989; *Easy Wheels,* 1989; *Soapdish,* 1991; *Honeymoon in Vegas,* 1992; *Me and the Kid,* 1993; *Dave,* 1993; *Dennis the Menace,* 1993; *The Mask,* 1994; *Richie Rich,* 1994; *North,* 1994; *My Girl 2,* 1994; *Mr. Write,* 1994; *Miami Rhapsody,* 1995; *Casper,* 1995; *House Arrest,* 1996; and *A Smile Like Yours,* 1997.

AWARDS, HONORS: Gold medal, Freedoms Foundation, 1979, for a column on work in the *Los Angeles Herald-Examiner;* Daytime Emmy Award, outstanding game show host (with Jimmy Kimmel), 1999, for *Win Ben Stein's Money.*

WRITINGS:

(With father, Herbert Stein) *On the Brink* (novel), Simon & Schuster (New York, NY), 1977.

Fernwood U.S.A.: An Illustrated Guide from the Folks Who Brought You Mary Hartman, Mary Hartman, Simon & Schuster (New York, NY), 1977.

The Croesus Conspiracy (novel), Simon & Schuster (New York, NY), 1978.

Dreemz (nonfiction), Harper (New York, NY), 1978.

(Under name Ben Stein) *The View from Sunset Boulevard: America As Brought to You by the People Who Make Television* (nonfiction), Basic Books (New York, NY), 1979.

(Under name Ben Stein, with Herbert Stein) *Moneypower: How to Make Inflation Make You Rich,* Harper (New York, NY), 1980.

Bunkhouse Logic: How to Bet on Yourself and Win, Avon (New York, NY), 1981.

'Ludes: A Ballad of the Drug and the Dreamer (nonfiction), St. Martin's Press (New York, NY), 1982.

The Manhattan Gambit, Doubleday (Garden City, NY), 1983.

Her Only Sin, St. Martin's Press (New York, NY), 1985.

Financial Passages, Doubleday (Garden City, NY), 1985.

Hollywood Days, Hollywood Nights: The Diary of a Mad Screenwriter, Bantam Books (New York, NY), 1988.

Will You Still Love Me Tomorrow?, St. Martin's Press (New York, NY), 1991.

A License to Steal: The Untold Story of Michael Milken and the Conspiracy to Bilk the Nation, Simon & Schuster (New York, NY), 1992.

Tommy and Me: The Making of a Dad, Free Press (New York, NY), 1998.

How to Ruin Your Life, Hay House (Carlsbad, CA), 2002.

(With Phil DeMuth) *Yes, You Can Time the Market!,* Wiley (New York, NY), 2003.

Also author of television scripts, including *Diary of a Stewardess.*

SIDELIGHTS: Stein wrote his first novel, *On the Brink,* in 1977, with technical assistance from his father, Herbert Stein, a former chair of the President's Council of Economic Advisors. Drawing on recent historical facts and events, the novel combines economics and suspense in a story about the disastrous effects of runaway inflation. The year is 1981, and the head of the Federal Reserve Board, who admits, "I am no economist," nevertheless convinces the president that economic prosperity lies in increasing the money supply to keep up with the rising cost of living. At the same time the Organization of Petroleum Exporting Countries (OPEC) raises the price of oil from $20.00 a barrel to $38.00, and inflation skyrockets. Wonder Bread is $2.99 a loaf, bacon sells for $22.00 a pound, the stock market crashes, and anarchy seems imminent. When it becomes necessary for the government to issue "megabucks" in million-dollar denominations the scene is set for a demagogue to take over America. "Impending Disaster novels with crazy Presidents can grip us because extrapolation of recent reality is all too easy," observed Adam Smith in the *New York Times.* "So I can say honestly: I could not put down *On the Brink.* I wanted to see where those wild characters, the prices, would go. . . . As plotters and pamphleteers the Steins are brilliant. Their Disaster is truly frightening."

Stein published two books in 1978. *The Croesus Conspiracy,* his second Washington novel, is a political story about a scheme to reestablish the Third Reich. The novel's fictional characters, including a short, stocky, German-born secretary of state, a power-hungry presidential candidate, and their billionaire patron, bear resemblance to certain real-life personages. In the same year *Dreemz* was published. A memoir-diary of Stein's first year of living and working in Los Angeles, the book is, according to the author, his favorite work. In *Dreemz* Stein recounts his escape from the eastern establishment to life in the western sun. *New York Times* critic Christopher Lehmann-Haupt called the book "a stunning little portrait of what life must be like in the city of angels." At the end of his first year in Los Angeles, Stein lived in a Spanish-style house complete with palm tree and drove a Mercedes Benz 450 SLC with a personalized license plate that read "DREEMZ." Nevertheless, he points out, "The cars and the girls and the Spanish house are only the outward appearances of the dreams that have come true in L.A. For me, L.A. means doing and being free."

Among the opportunities that life in Los Angeles provided for Stein was a job as creative consultant to television producer Norman Lear. It was from this occupational vantage point that Stein developed the thesis that forms the basis of his book *The View from Sunset Boulevard: America As Brought to You by the People Who Make Television.* Exposing the myth that popular culture as represented by television is a mirror of national dreams and nightmares, Stein maintains: "The super-medium of television is spewing out the messages of a few writers and producers (literally in the low hundreds), almost all of whom live in Los Angeles. Television is not necessarily a mirror of anything besides what those few people think."

After conducting long and candid interviews with forty of television's most important writers and producers, Stein concluded: "The fit between the message of the TV shows and the opinions of the people who make the TV shows was excellent. Moreover, the views of these TV people were so highly idiosyncratic and unique that they could not possibly be the dreams of a nation. It was like thinking that a taste for snuff movies or Beluga caviar was the general taste of a nation." Additionally, "In Mr. Stein's view," noted a *New York Times Book Review* critic, "the Hollywood-formed ideas aired on the nation's screens run counter to our traditional folk culture, in which Americans are said to revere small towns, successful businessmen and soldiers, and to have no sympathy for criminals and the poor. The new television culture violates the old-fashioned virtues."

Presenting an "alternate world" juxtaposed to reality, primetime television, observes Stein, broadcasts daily that businessmen and other high-level people are bad, while workers and rebel cops are "the salt of the earth and smart, too." Also, on television, small towns hide evil beneath their superficial veneer, while big cities are portrayed as basically cheerful, friendly places to raise children. Supporting his contention that television posits an alternate reality, Stein writes: "In the thousands of hours I have spent watching adventure shows, I have never seen a major crime committed by a poor, teenage, black, Mexican, or Puerto Rican youth, even though they account for a high percentage of all violent crime." Some critics reviewed the book favorably. *Washington Post* critic James Lardner commended Stein for asking "fresh questions about commercial TV and its treatment of crime, wealth, religion, and daily life."

Following *The View from Sunset Boulevard,* Stein returned to the subject of inflation in a second collaboration with his father. The result was *Moneypower: How to Make Inflation Make You Rich.* A nonfiction self-help book, *Moneypower* offers advice on investments and financial strategies for use in hyperinflationary periods. According to Lehmann-Haupt of the *New York Times,* the book advises "in ways that seem entirely practical, and which ought to be clear even to someone who has trouble balancing a checkbook."

Stein once told *CA:* "I advise all prospective writers to try medicine instead or else try the shoe business. The same qualities that make a writer—sensitivity and awareness—make him vulnerable to torture by publishers and producers."

BIOGRAPHICAL AND CRITICAL SOURCES:

BOOKS

Stein, Benjamin, *Dreemz,* Harper (New York, NY), 1978.

Stein, Benjamin, *The View from Sunset Boulevard: America As Brought to You by the People Who Make Television,* Basic Books (New York, NY), 1979.

PERIODICALS

America, April 7, 1979.

Library Journal, May 1, 2003, Patrick J. Brunet, review of *Yes, You Can Time the Market!,* p. 132.

Los Angeles Times Book Review, February 18, 1979.
Nation, March 10, 1979.
National Review, September 2, 1977; February 16, 1979; July 6, 1979.
Newsmakers, Issue 1, 2001.
New Yorker, December 19, 1977.
New York Times, May 17, 1978, Adam Smith, review of *On the Brink;* January 23, 1979, Christopher Lehmann-Haupt, review of *Dreemz;* January 8, 1980, Christopher Lehmann-Haupt, review of *Moneypower: How to Make Inflation Make You Rich.*
New York Times Book Review, July 3, 1977; February 18, 1979, review of *The View from Sunset Boulevard.*
Saturday Review, May 26, 1979.
Washington Post, February 25, 1979, James Lardner, review of *The View from Sunset Boulevard.*
West Coast Review of Books, May, 1978; November, 1978.*

* * *

STRAUB, Gerard Thomas 1947-

PERSONAL: Born March 31, 1947, in Brooklyn, NY; son of William V. (a business executive) and Frances (Croake) Straub; married second wife, Kathleen Grosso (a television and film production assistant), July 11, 1986; children: Adrienne Frances.

ADDRESSES: Home and office—P.O. Box 1342, Carmel-by-the-Sea, CA 93921. *Agent*—Jay Garon, Jay Garon-Brooke Associates, Inc., 415 Central Park W, New York, NY 10025.

CAREER: Columbia Broadcasting System, Inc., New York, NY, executive, 1964-78; Christian Broadcasting Network, Virginia Beach, VA, producer of *The 700 Club* and creator of the soap opera *Another Life,* 1978-80; American Broadcasting Companies, Inc., Hollywood, CA, associate producer of *General Hospital,* 1980-81; National Broadcasting Company, Inc., New York, NY, executive producer of *The Doctors,* 1982; Dick Clark Productions, Burbank, CA, producer of *You Are the Jury,* 1983; independent television director and freelance writer, San Francisco, CA, and New York City, 1983-86; John Conboy Productions, Hollywood, supervising producer of *Capitol,* 1986-87; freelance writer, beginning 1987. Secular Franciscan brother.

WRITINGS:

Salvation for Sale: An Insider's View of Pat Robertson's Ministry, Prometheus Books (Buffalo, NY), 1986, revised edition, 1988.
Dear Kate, Prometheus Books (Buffalo, NY), 1992.
The Sun and Moon over Assisi: A Personal Encounter with Francis and Clare, St. Anthony Messenger Press (Cincinnati, OH), 2000.
When Did I See You Hungry?, Bright Sky Press (Albany, TX), 2001.

Also author of *God Said What?*

SIDELIGHTS: Gerard Thomas Straub once told *CA:* "My writing mirrors my life's two main interests: show biz and spirituality. As a young teenager, I dreamed of becoming a missionary priest, yet, in an ironic twist of fate, I wound up producing soap operas for all three television networks. However, my two interests merged for two-and-a-half years during the late seventies, when I abandoned my network television career in order to join forces with television evangelist Pat Robertson. During my time at Christian Broadcasting System, I produced *The 700 Club,* created *Another Life*—the first internationally syndicated Christian soap opera—and wrote and produced many variety and dramatic specials.

"*Salvation for Sale: An Insider's View of Pat Robertson's Ministry* is the story of my own spiritual odyssey, played against the fascinating backdrop of fundamentalist Christian television. *God Said What?* is a less personal and more hard-hitting book that examines, not only the emotionalism of faith and the nature of religious beliefs, but also the power and dangers of the fundamentalist dark side of Christianity as it is reflected in the presidential campaign of preacher-turned-politician Pat Robertson.

"With these two serious books under my belt, my goal is to move into more fictional and entertaining writing, especially in the field of films. I want to write work that will be funny and dramatic, yet still touch upon the important philosophical issues that confront our changing society. In that vein, I have just completed a treatment for a television situation comedy, titled 'You Gotta Be Kidding,' that portrays the inner conflict of a television talk show host with lofty ideals who toils in the bottom-line business of ratings, where quality has no value and success is guaranteed with sleaze. On the literary horizon is a book that takes a behind-the-scenes look at the wacky world of soap operas."

BIOGRAPHICAL AND CRITICAL SOURCES:

PERIODICALS

Library Journal, July, 2003, Joyce Smothers, review of *When Did I See You Hungry?,* p. 90.

Los Angeles Times, August 23, 1986; June 12, 1987; June 15, 1987.

Los Angeles Times Book Review, May 3, 1987.

New York Review of Books, August 13, 1987.

New York Times, December 27, 1987.

Toronto Star, May 2, 1987.

USA Today, March 5, 1987.*

* * *

SUZANNE, Jamie

See ZACH, Cheryl (Byrd)

T

TAMARO, Susanna 1958-

PERSONAL: Born 1958, in Trieste, Italy. *Hobbies and other interests:* Gardening.

ADDRESSES: *Home*—Rome, Italy. *Agent*—c/o Author Mail, Doubleday, 1540 Broadway, New York, NY 10036.

CAREER: Screenwriter and novelist.

WRITINGS:

Per voce sola, Marsilio (Venice, Italy), 1991, translation by Sharon Wood published as *For Solo Voice,* Carcanet (Manchester, England), 1995.

Va dove ti porta il cuore, Baldini & Castoldi (Milan, Italy), 1994, translation by John Cullen published as *Follow Your Heart,* Doubleday (New York, NY), 1995.

Il Cerchio magico, illustrated by Tony Ross, A. Mondadori (Milan, Italy), 1995.

Anima Mundi, Baldini & Castoldi (Milan, Italy), 1997.

Cara Mathilda: Non vedo l'ora che l'uomo cammini (originally published in *Famiglia cristiana,* 1996-97), Cinisello Balsamo (Milan, Italy), 1997.

Tobia e l'angelo, Mondadori (Milan, Italy), 1998.

Verso casa, Ares (Milan, Italy), 1999, translation published as *Turning Home: A Memoir,* Crossroad (New York, NY), 2000.

La Testa fra le nuvole, con La Dormeuse electronique: Elogio della grazia (title means "Head in the Clouds"), Marsilio (Venice, Italy), 1999.

Rispondimi (title means "Answer Me"), Rizzoli (Milan, Italy), 2001, translation by John Cullen published as *Rispondimi* Doubleday (New York, NY), 2001.

Piu fuoco, piu vento, Rizzoli (Milan, Italy), 2002.

Fuori, Rizzoli (Milan, Italy), 2003.

Contributor to *The Quality of Light: Modern Italian Short Stories,* edited by Ann and Michael Caesar, Serpent's Tail (New York, NY), 1993.

SIDELIGHTS: Italian writer Susanna Tamaro wrote children's fiction and did some screenwriting before gaining international attention with her adult novel *Follow Your Heart* in 1995. By 1996 the novel had been reprinted eighteen times and translated into English. Other novels from the controversial author have been described by *Observer* critic Kate Kellaway as "funny, fantastical, gruelling, dark." With her controversial *Anima Mundi,* Tamaro looks at Italian prisoners held in communist prisons in Yugoslavia following World War II, and in the 2001 *Rispondimi,* she presents a trio of novellas that once again reached the top of international best-seller charts.

Olga, the narrator in *Follow Your Heart,* is an elderly woman whose own words summarize the book's theme: "It is not the absence of the dead that weighs on us," she tells her estranged granddaughter who is living in the United States, "but the words left unspoken between them and us." Lilian Pizzichini, a reviewer for the *Times Literary Supplement,* commented on Tamaro's portrayal of Olga's revelation of her unhappiness after her silence leads to the death of her illegitimate daughter: "Childlike simplicity is valued as a refuge from the world of politics, religion and adult relationships; the intellectual suppression of the emotions is a tyranny to be resisted." Olga's secrecy, blame, and shame, besides her joyless marriage, have choked the life from her. Now in her eighties, lonely, and dying, she wants to change that through her diary to her granddaughter.

New Statesman and Society critic Boyd Tonkin noted of the English translation, "You may import the words in pristine condition, but their cultural effects stick stubbornly at home." Tonkin added, "Still, if you seek a spot of homespun comfort, far rather this hard-won serenity than the cliches of [*The Bridges of*] *Madison County.*"

In the *Observer,* Kellaway related that *Follow Your Heart* has surprisingly been read by both intellectuals and those who hardly read at all. One reader bought forty copies, which Tamaro explained by saying that in Italy the novel "is used by families as therapy: they read it aloud to each other." According to Kellaway, Tamaro, unmarried and brought up by her mother and grandparents, feels the book speaks to people because, "In Italy . . . people talk easily about sex, uneasily about emotion. This is a book about emotion. There is also, she thinks, a nostalgia for family relationships, even a tattered one like the one she describes." In an Italian interview, Tamaro asserted that all her books are about "failure and death."

After an earthquake in 1976, Tamaro, a survivor when many of her friends and neighbors had died, realized how much she wanted to live. *Follow Your Heart* was the result of that realization. In an Italian magazine interview quoted by the online journal *Canoe,* Tamaro described her 1997 novel, *Anima Mundi,* as "a book against the blindness of all fanaticism—of right and left—that have afflicted this century." In the book, Walter, who detests his communist father, strolls about the countryside pondering good and evil. According to Tamaro, reported a reviewer in *Canoe,* growing up in the port city of Trieste, near Italy's border with the former Yugoslavia, where atrocities were committed by both left and right groups in World War II, explains why she continues to write as she does—about failure and death.

Tamaro again made headlines with her 2001 collection *Rispondimi,* which presents a trio of "cruel, unsettling histories," according to James Urquhart, writing in the *Times Literary Supplement.* Scandal broke out soon after publication when a fellow author and friend accused Tamaro of plagiarism. Sued for almost three million dollars in damages, Tamaro responded with her own countersuit and denied any wrongdoing.

In the title novella, an au pair named Rosa tries to make it on her own in rural Italy, only to be sexually abused by her employer and then fired for supposed theft. In "No Such Thing as Hell," a widow regrets that she did not have the courage to resist her dead husband's sadistic ways, and in "The Burning Wood," the wife of a forester forms a new friendship that frees her of her dependence on her husband. Reviewing the collection in *Booklist,* Carol Haggas found it a "spare yet intricate tapestry" that plumbs the "depths of despair and destruction." Writing in *World Literature Today,* Martha King similarly described the novellas as "stories of unremittingly grim lives." Urquhart thought that the major theme of all three tales is "the power of evil over unassuming lives." However, for Urquhart, "the stories do not get to the heart of the moral dilemmas they propose." Jeff Zaleski of *Publishers Weekly,* on the other hand, called *Rispondimi* a "provocative collection" that "skillfully explores themes of religion, depression, jealousy, violence and isolation." Zaleski further praised Tamaro for the "clear and resonant moral vision" she invested in her narrative.

BIOGRAPHICAL AND CRITICAL SOURCES:

BOOKS

Tamaro, Susanna, *Follow Your Heart,* Secker & Warburg (London, England), 1995.

PERIODICALS

Booklist, March 1, 2002, Carol Haggas, review of *Rispondimi,* p. 1094.

Economist, May 17, 1997, review of *Anima Mundi,* pp. S13-14.

Europe, April, 1995, Niccolo d'Aquino, "Susanna Tamaro," pp. 38-39.

Guardian (Manchester, England), April 2, 2001, Rory Carroll, "Answer Me with Damages," p. 14.

Library Journal, July, 1995, Shannon Dekle, review of *Follow Your Heart,* p. 124.
New Statesman and Society, June 30, 1995, Boyd Tonkin, review of *Follow Your Heart,* p. 40.
Observer, June 25, 1995, Kate Kellaway, review of *Follow Your Heart,* p. 13.
Publishers Weekly, July 3, 1995, review of *Follow Your Heart,* p. 47; February 4, 2002, Jeff Zaleski, review of *Rispondimi,* p. 50.
Times Literary Supplement, October 6, 1995, Lilian Pizzichini, review of *Follow Your Heart,* p. 31; March 1, 2002, James Urquhart, review of *Rispondimi,* p. 24.
World Literature Today, spring, 2002, Martha King, review of *Rispondimi,* p. 218.
World Press Review, June, 1997, Doja Hacker and Maria Gazzetti, "Against the Grain," p. 39.

ONLINE

Canoe, http://www.canoe.ca (April 4, 1997).
HamptonClick, http://www.hamptonclick.com/ (1998).
Publishing Trends, http://www.publishingtrends.com/ (November 3, 2003), "International Fiction Bestsellers."
Share International, http://www.shareintl.org/ (January-February, 1998).*

* * *

TANNER, Karen Holliday (Olson) 1940-

PERSONAL: Born March 30, 1940, in Chicago, IL; daughter of Carl Birger (a developer) and Mary Adele (a homemaker; maiden name, Holliday) Olson; married Charles R. D. Selinger, September 27, 1958 (divorced, 1965); married David C. Mielke, December 21, 1967 (divorced, 1986); married John D. Tanner, Jr. (a professor of history), April 16, 1988; children: (second marriage) Richard A., Scott D., Blair C. *Ethnicity:* "Caucasian." *Education:* Attended Northwestern University, 1957-58; University of Maryland—College Park, B.S., 2001. *Politics:* Republican. *Hobbies and other interests:* Travel, duplicate bridge, gourmet cooking, tennis.

ADDRESSES: *Home*—2308 Willow Glen Rd., Fallbrook, CA 92028. *Agent*—Jon Tuska, Golden West Literary Agency, 2327 Southeast Salmon St., Portland, OR. *E-mail*—khtanner@aol.com.

CAREER: Owner and manager of two restaurants in Fallbrook, CA, 1981-86; self-employed tax accountant, Fallbrook, 1986—; writer.

MEMBER: Toastmasters International, National Outlaw-Lawman Association, Daughters of the American Revolution, Western Writers of America, Western Outlaw-Lawman Association (member of board of directors), Daughters of the Republic of Texas.

WRITINGS:

Doc Holliday: A Family Portrait, University of Oklahoma Press (Norman, OK), 1998.
(With John D. Tanner) *Last of the Old-time Outlaws: The George West Musgrave Story,* University of Oklahoma Press (Norman, OK), 2002.

Contributor to western history magazines.

BIOGRAPHICAL AND CRITICAL SOURCES:

PERIODICALS

Virginia Quarterly Review, spring, 2003, review of *Last of the Old-time Outlaws: The George West Musgrave Story,* p. 55.

* * *

THEROUX, Phyllis 1939-

PERSONAL: Born February 22, 1939, in San Francisco, CA; daughter of John deLafayette (in business) and Phyllis (in business; maiden name Hollins) Grissim; divorced; children: three. *Education:* Manhattanville College, B.A., 1961.

ADDRESSES: *Home*—3210 Northampton St. NW, Washington, DC 20015. *Agent*—Aaron Priest Agency, 150 East 35th St., New York, NY 10016.

CAREER: Writer. Has worked as a secretary, journalist, community activist, school teacher, and legal researcher. Washington, DC, elementary school teacher, 1989-93; *NewsHour with Jim Lehrer,* contributing essayist, 1992-96.

Founder of the nonprofit organization "Winners in Grade School," 1989, the Woodstock Project on Forgiveness consortium (with others), 1993, "Bridge Builders" study circles, 1994, "The Great American Portraits Program," 1997, Ashland Hanover Citizens for Responsible Growth (with others; and president), 1999, and the *Nightwriters* writers' workshop. Has been a guest lecturer and professor at several universities, colleges, and forums.

MEMBER: Authors Guild.

WRITINGS:

California and Other States of Grace: A Memoir, Morrow (New York, NY), 1980.

Peripheral Visions (autobiographical essays), Morrow (New York, NY), 1982.

Night Lights: Bedtime Stories for Parents in the Dark, Penguin Books (New York, NY), 1987.

(Editor and contributor) *The Book of Eulogies: A Collection of Memorial Tributes, Poetry, Essays, and Letters of Condolence,* Scribner (New York, NY), 1997.

Serefina under the Circumstances (for children), illustrated by Marjorie Priceman, Greenwillow Books (New York, NY), 1999.

Giovanni's Light: The Story of a Town Where Time Stopped for Christmas (for children), Scribner (New York, NY), 2002.

Frequent "*Hers*" columnist for the *New York Times.* Past contributing editor to magazines, including *Ladies' Home Journal, Family Health,* and *Washingtonian.* Contributor to periodicals, including *Reader's Digest, Washington Post, Christian Science Monitor, International Herald Tribune,* and *McCall's.* Contributor to anthologies.

WORK IN PROGRESS: A book about her mother's life.

SIDELIGHTS: Phyllis Theroux is a versatile writer, publishing her work as a journalist, a columnist, a humorist, an advocate, and a children's book author. In her first book, *California and Other States of Grace,* Theroux writes about growing up in San Francisco in the years following World War II. Focusing particularly on the members of her family, the author presents a cast of characters that she describes as "emotional, high-powered, egocentric and full of style." She begins her recollections with the gathering of grown siblings at the bedside of their father following his heart attack. "It is a fascinating gathering point for launching a memoir," Wayne Warga observed in the *Los Angeles Times,* "a sharp and detailed contrast between what is and what was." In the *New York Times Book Review,* Ellen Goodman perceived Theroux's book as an attempt to preserve a family that, like many in our fragmented times, has since disintegrated. "The undercurrent of her work is a deep longing both for her own family and, perhaps more importantly, for the very idea of family," noted the critic. "[My family] was brilliant while it existed as a unit," the author allowed in *California and Other States of Grace,* "and instructive to me when it ultimately fell apart."

According to some reviewers, *California and Other States of Grace* is light on social and self-analyses. "Theroux seems to have escaped with her sense of humor intact," noted *Washington Post Book World* critic Susan Cheever. "What she lacks in critical analysis, she more than makes up for in wit, charm, and her perfect little summations of complex experience." Goodman, however, found the author's cursory presentation of events in the memories less than satisfying. "Somehow or other, [Theroux's] memories just don't add up," the reviewer wrote. "Each person in her life is brought out for a quick look, awarded little more than a caption, and then put back . . . . It is unsettling to have her rush through her crises as if she were afraid to linger, to read equal amounts about her terror of suicide . . . and her amusing college weekend at a funeral home. . . . In the end her family album is like a tour of countries in seventeen days. We never get to know anyone quite well enough. Not even the tour guide."

But several critics deemed Theroux a noteworthy writer. "Who is Theroux and why should we read a book about her?" charged Elizabeth Wheeler in the *Los Angeles Times Book Review.* The critic answered, "Theroux is a good writer with an extraordinary memory of an ordinary life. Her memoir is interesting, enjoyable . . . [and] shared in a clear yet intimate way." "You'll like her," Cheever concluded. "Theroux has a self-effacing sense of mischief and a sunny disposition that make her storytelling fun to read . . . . Whether she's describing a weekend she spent as a house guest in a Naugatuck, Connecticut, funeral home in order to get to the Harvard-Yale game, or the fluttering of her mother's hands, or some cockleweeds she used to see transformed by the early morning light at her Aunt Marion Collins' ranch, Pasatiempo, in the summer, she is a sprightly and amusing guide."

Peripheral Visions is a collection of twenty-six of Theroux's previously published essays published in a continuation of the autobiographical *California and Other States of Grace.* In the new volume, Theroux writes of her divorce, aging, and her move to the East Coast. Lisa Mitchell, writing in the *Los Angeles Times Book Review,* suggested that Theroux "stokes a communal fire around which we can all warm our hands" and added that reading of Theroux's life "leads to epiphanies . . . for our own."

In *The Book of Eulogies: A Collection of Memorable Tributes, Poetry, Essays, and Letters of Condolence,* Theroux anthologized an amalgam of tributes to the dead, predominantly from the nineteenth and twentieth centuries, with a few dating much earlier. These tributes were written or spoken by famous people such as Thomas Jefferson, Helen Keller, and Robert Kennedy in celebration of famous figures such as George Washington, Mark Twain, and Martin Luther King, Jr. The book also highlights moving eulogies, letters, and other writings from previously unknown, ordinary people to their lost loved ones. Mary Carroll, in a review of *The Book of Eulogies* for *Booklist,* called the work "a superb source of inspiration—and citations—for readers writing eulogies or coping with their own losses." At a program in celebration of the book, which included readings by several celebrities, Theroux told reporter John Martin why she had chosen the book's eulogies. "When these people died," she said, "somebody wrote about them uncommonly well."

Theroux next lightened her subject matter with *Serefina under the Circumstances,* her first children's book. Written for children ages five to eight, *Serefina under the Circumstances* presents an imaginative young heroine whose grandmother entrusts her with the secret of her brother's surprise birthday party. Throughout the story, Theroux shows the tender and humorous relationship between Serefina and her grandmother as they exchange silly sayings to communicate with one another. "Children and adults alike will have their own examples of verbal and visual puns and ridiculous associations they just can't get out of their heads," wrote *Booklist*'s Hazel Rochman on this aspect of the book. When Serefina lets the secret slip, she finds herself making up stories—something she does quite well—to cover her blunder. "Theroux's quirky, compelling text invites young readers to explore the fine line between being creative and actually lying," wrote one *Publishers Weekly* reviewer.

Giovanni's Light: The Story of a Town Where Time Stopped for Christmas was Theroux's next venture into children's fiction. The story of *Giovanni's Light* takes place in the small town of Ryland Falls, whose residents are hard-pressed to muster Christmas spirit at this particular holiday time, for a number of different reasons. Giovanni is an older man who lives on a mountain with his dog, Max, harvesting Christmas trees and trying to forget the pain of having been left behind by his deceased wife and son. Will Campbell is an art teacher, new to Ryland Falls and frustrated with life's circumstances. Miranda Bridgeman is an eleven-year-old student who wants to be a poet. These characters, and the other residents of Ryland Falls, are taken by surprise when a blizzard hits the small town, knocking out all power. The townspeople must come together to stay warm and help one another through the storm and end up finding the true spirit of Christmas in their compassion for one another. One *Kirkus Reviews* contributor stated that *Giovanni's Light* is "likely to warm hearts, especially if read within sight of a nicely trimmed tree," and Carol Fitzgerald on the *BookReporter* Web site called the book a "wonderfully sentimental story."

BIOGRAPHICAL AND CRITICAL SOURCES:

PERIODICALS

Booklist, January 15, 1987, review of *Night Lights: Bedtime Stories for Parents in the Dark,* p. 738; December 15, 1987, review of *Night Lights,* p. 717; April 15, 1997, Mary Carroll, review of *The Book of Eulogies: A Collection of Memorial Tributes, Poetry, Essays, and Letters of Condolence,* p. 1376; September 1, 1999, Hazel Rochman, review of *Serefina under the Circumstances,* p. 144; November 15, 2002, Margaret Flanagan, review of *Giovanni's Light: The Story of a Town Where Time Stopped for Christmas,* p. 570.

Book World, January 10, 1988, review of *Night Lights,* p. 12.

Bulletin of the Center for Children's Books October, 1999, review of *Serefina under the Circumstances,* p. 71.

Kirkus Reviews, January 1, 1987, review of *Night Lights,* p. 50; September 1, 1999, review of *Serefina under the Circumstances,* p. 1422; September 15, 2002, review of *Giovanni's Light,* p. 1346.

Library Journal, February 1, 1987, review of *Night Lights,* p. 83; July, 1997, review of *The Book of Eulogies,* p. 91.

Los Angeles Times, July 11, 1980.

Los Angeles Times Book Review, July 6, 1980; February 7, 1982; April 12, 1987, review of *Night Lights,* p. 2.

Newsweek, June 23, 1980.

New York Times Book Review, July 20, 1980; March 15, 1987, review of *Night Lights,* p. 13.

Parents, February, 1987, review of *Night Lights,* p. 20.

Publishers Weekly, December 19, 1986, review of *Night Lights,* p. 39; November 20, 1987, review of *Night Lights,* p. 67; March 17, 1997, review of *The Book of Eulogies,* p. 72; July 5, 1999, review of *Serefina under the Circumstances,* p. 70.

School Library Journal, September, 1999, review of *Serefina under the Circumstances,* p. 207.

USA Today, February 13, 1987, review of *Night Lights,* p. 4D.

Virginia Quarterly Review, autumn, 1997, review of *The Book of Eulogies,* p. 139.

Wall Street Journal, July 23, 1997, review of *The Book of Eulogies,* p. A16.

Washington Post Book World, June 22, 1980; January 10, 1982.

ONLINE

BookReporter, http://bookreporter.com/ (January 16, 2003), Carol Fitzgerald, review of *Giovanni's Light.*

Library of Congress Information Bulletin, http://www.loc.gov/ (June 23, 1997), John Martin, "Eloquence for the Departed: Notables Read from *The Book of Eulogies* at Library."

National Public Radio, http://www.npr.org/ (March 22, 2004), "The End of Life: Exploring Death in America," readings from *The Book of Eulogies.*

New York Times Books, http://www.nytimes.com/ (April 16, 2000), Jeanne B. Pinder, review of *Serefina under the Circumstances.*

Nightwriters, http://www.nightwriters.com/ (March 22, 2004), "Phyllis Theroux."

PBS, http://www.pbs.org/newshour/ (December 29, 1995) Phyllis Theroux, "Going Home"; (February 21, 1996), Phyllis Theroux, "Family Secrets."*

* * *

TORRES, Laura 1967-

PERSONAL: Born March 21, 1967, in Yakima, WA; daughter of James R. (a data technician) and Shirley (a loan officer; maiden name, Gray) Hofmann; married John C. Torres (an assistant professor of sociology), December 19, 1987; children: Brennyn, John Andrew. *Education:* Brigham Young University, A.A., 1987. *Religion:* Church of Jesus Christ of Latter-day Saints (Mormon).

ADDRESSES: Home—1643 North 1100 W., Mapleton, UT 84664.

CAREER: Freelance writer, 1990—; creative consultant, 1995—; workshop presenter. Former editor, *American Girl* magazine; Klutz Press, Palo Alto, CA, senior editor.

MEMBER: International Society of Altered Book Artists.

AWARDS, HONORS: National Parenting Publications Award (NAPPA) and Cuffie Award, both 1994, both for *The Incredible Clay Book: How to Make and Bake a Million-and-One Clay Creations;* NAPPA Award, 1999, for *Create Anything with Clay* (with Sherri Haab), and 2001, for *Paper Punch Art.*

WRITINGS:

NONFICTION

Beads, Glorious Beads, Klutz Press (Palo Alto, CA), 1994.

(With Sherri Haab) *The Incredible Clay Book: How to Make and Bake a Million-and-One Clay Creations,* Klutz Press (Palo Alto, CA), 1994.

Laura Torres

Beads: A Book of Ideas and Instructions, Klutz Press (Palo Alto, CA), 1996.

Friendship Bracelets, Klutz Press (Palo Alto, CA), 1996.

The Sticker Book, Klutz Press (Palo Alto, CA), 1996.

Pipe Cleaners Gone Crazy: A Complete Guide to Bending Fuzzy Sticks, Klutz Press (Palo Alto, CA), 1997.

The Fantastic Foam Book, Klutz Press (Palo Alto, CA), 1998.

Clay Modeling with Pooh, illustrated by Francese Rigoli, Mouse Works (New York, NY), 1999.

(With Sherri Haab) *Create Anything with Clay,* Klutz Press (Palo Alto, CA), 1999.

Pompoms Gone Crazy: How to Make Any Pompom Project in Three Easy Steps, Klutz Press (Palo Alto, CA), 1999.

Disney's Ten-Minute Crafts for Preschoolers, Disney Press (New York, NY), 2000.

(With Sherri Haab) *Wire-o-Mania,* Klutz Press (Palo Alto, CA), 2000.

Don't Eat Pete, Klutz Press (Palo Alto, CA), 2000.

Salt Dough!, illustrated by Wendy Wallin Malinow, Pleasant Company (Middleton, WI), 2001.

Paper Punch Art, Pleasant Company (Middleton, WI), 2001.

Disney Princess Crafts, photographs by Sherri Haab, Disney Press (New York, NY), 2001.

YOUNG ADULT NOVELS

November Ever After, Holiday House (New York, NY), 1999.

Crossing Montana, Holiday House (New York, NY), 2002.

Contributor to periodicals, including *Children's Digest* and *Jack and Jill.*

WORK IN PROGRESS: A third novel; a line of books for girls.

SIDELIGHTS: Laura Torres has taken a talent for making all manner of things and fashioned a career as an author of children's how-to books. A senior editor at the California-based publisher Klutz Press, Torres is the brainchild behind such works as *Pompoms Gone Crazy: How to Make Any Pompom Project in Three Easy Steps, Wire-o-Mania, The Fantastic Foam Book,* and *Salt Dough!,* the last a 2001 book that helps students concoct the stiff, dyeable bread dough that has been a classic for creating topographical maps for school geography projects for years. In the late 1990s, Torres expanded her own craft as a writer and has garnered praise for several works of young-adult fiction.

Torres had aspirations to be a writer even as a child; quiet and shy, she came into her own writing stories others could enjoy. While working in a publishing company for several years, she submitted stories to children's periodicals and sold several. However, it was not until she persuaded the publisher she worked for—Klutz Press—to let her develop a book on polymer clay projects for kids that she began writing nonfiction. Talented at explaining techniques in simple terms that children can understand, Torres has since gone on to produce over a dozen books that celebrate the virtues of crafts from the mid-twentieth century, many of which use materials such as pipe cleaners, Styrofoam, and pompoms. In a *Threads* review of Torres's craft manual *The Incredible Clay Book: How to Make and Bake a Million-and-One Clay Creations,* David Page Coffin praised Torres and frequent collaborator Sherri Haab for doing "a witty, imaginative, and attractive job of presenting clay projects," and noted that the book—geared toward younger readers—makes "the whole idea of clay molding seem fun and approachable."

In 1999, Torres made the break into young-adult fiction with her first novel, *November Ever After.* The book introduces sixteen-year-old Amy, whose pastor father is too busy dealing with his parishioners to help Amy cope with the grief over her mother's recent death in a car accident. Turning not only from her father but from her faith as well, Amy clings to her friend Sara for support. More confusion comes when Sara is found in a secret homosexual relationship with another young woman, leaving Amy with feelings of abandonment that a young man named Peter ultimately helps her deal with. A *Kirkus Reviews* critic noted that in response to the questions she raises regarding organized religion's views on homosexuality, Torres "timidly suggest[s] that . . . , in real life, personal bonds may be more powerful than belief systems." Praising the novel's protagonist as "a refreshingly wholesome yet completely realistic teen," *Booklist* contributor Debbie Carton added that the many "lighthearted" turns the plot takes help balance the book's serious focus. In *Publishers Weekly,* a reviewer concluded of *November Ever After* that Torres's "promising prose and credible characterizations make this writer one to watch."

Another young teen figures in Torres's second novel, *Crossing Montana,* which appeared in 2002. At age fifteen, coping with the death of her father and now living with her grandfather and a mother who cannot cope with life, Callie had proved herself a survivor. When her grandfather disappears, Callie decides to go in search of him herself, stealing the family car and a credit card and heading out on the highway. Grandpa, an alcoholic, is ultimately found fishing and brought home, but his condition and her self-reflection while driving cause Callie to realize that her family harbors demons of alcoholism and depression. A fighter, she vows to find a way to make her life better in a novel *Booklist* contributor Hazel Rochman called "stark and beautiful," adding that "Callie's brave, desperate . . . narrative tells the truth and doesn't let you go."

BIOGRAPHICAL AND CRITICAL SOURCES:

PERIODICALS

Booklist, December 1, 1999, Debbie Carton, review of *November Ever After,* p. 697; August, 2002, Hazel Rochman, review of *Crossing Montana,* p. 1963.

Kirkus Reviews, November 15, 1999, review of *November Ever After,* p. 1816.

Lambda Book Report, April, 2000, Nancy Garden, review of *November Ever After,* p. 27.

Publishers Weekly, October 7, 1996, review of *Friendship Bracelets,* p. 78; April 7, 1997, review of *Pipe Cleaners Gone Crazy: A Complete Guide to Bending Fuzzy Sticks,* p. 94; June 15, 1998, review of *The Fantastic Foam Book,* p. 61; January 3, 2000, review of *November Ever After,* p. 77.

School Library Journal, January, 2000, Connie Tyrell Burns, review of *November Ever After,* p. 136; July, 2002, Diane P. Tuccillo, review of *Crossing Montana,* p. 126.

Threads, June-July, 1996, David Page Coffin, review of *The Incredible Clay Book: How to Make and Bake a Million-and-One Clay Creations,* p. 82.*

* * *

TOY, Maggie 1964-

PERSONAL: Born December 29, 1964, in Rugby, England; daughter of Mark (a lecturer in physics) and Pat (a radiographer) Toy; partner of Tim Forster (a criminal barrister); children: Hector Cavanagh. *Ethnicity:* "White." *Education:* Portsmouth Polytechnic, B.A. (with honors), 1986, postgraduate diploma, 1989. *Hobbies and other interests:* Designing and sewing wedding, bridesmaid, and ball dresses; opera, music, theater, cinema, aerobics, cycling, swimming, squash.

ADDRESSES: Home and office—60 Torbay Rd., London NW6 7DZ, England. *E-mail*—maggietoy@tiscali.co.uk.

CAREER: Moxham Clark Partnership (chartered architects), Manchester, England, architectural assistant, 1982; Derek Arend Associates (chartered architects), London, England, architectural assistant, 1986-87; Academy Group Ltd., London, assistant, 1988, deputy editor, 1989-92, commissioning editor and managing editor, 1993-97, senior publishing editor, 1997-2002; freelance writer, 2002—.

WRITINGS:

(With Andreas Papadakis) *Deconstruction: A Pocket Guide,* 1990.

(Editor) *The Periphery,* Architectural Design (London, England), 1991.

(Editor, with Andreas Papadakis and Geoffrey Broadbent) *Free Spirit in Architecture,* 1992.

Maggie Toy

Los Angeles, 1994.

(Editor) *Architecture and Film,* Academy Editions (London, England), 1994.

(Editor) *New Towns,* Academy Editions (London, England), 1994.

(Editor, with Ruth Rosenthal) *Building Sights,* Academy Editions (London, England), 1995.

(Editor) *Architecture and Water,* Academy Editions (London, England), 1995.

(Editor, with Iona Spens and Stephen Watt) *British Architects in Exile,* Academy Editions (London, England), 1995.

(Editor, with Martin Pearce) *Educating Architects,* 1995.

(Editor) *Beyond the Revolution: The Architecture of Eastern Europe,* Academy Editions (London, England), 1996.

Practically Minimal: Simply Beautiful Solutions for Modern Living, Thames & Hudson (New York, NY), 2000.

The Female Architect, Watson-Guptill (New York, NY), 2000.

(Editor) *The Architect: Women in Contemporary Architecture,* Watson-Guptill (New York, NY), 2001.

Contributor of articles and reviews to architecture journals. *Architectural Design,* house editor, 1989-92, editor, 1993—.

SIDELIGHTS: Maggie Toy once told *CA:* "I was trained as an architect. After working as one for a little time, I moved into publishing architectural books. After some years as the commissioning editor for Academy Group and editor of *Architectural Design,* I began to see many opportunities for writing and publishing books of my own.

"My primary motivation is to bring my architectural understanding and fascination to a broader audience and to provide information about the best way to educate architects. I have always felt this is an area of desperate need!"

* * *

TREMBATH, Don 1963-

PERSONAL: Born May 22, 1963, in Winnipeg, Manitoba, Canada; married Lisa Murray (a social worker) August 25, 1984; children: Riley, Walker. *Education:* Northern Alberta Institute of Technology, Diploma in Civil Engineering Technology, 1983; University of Alberta, B.A., 1988.

ADDRESSES: *Home*—10011-104 St., Morinville, Alberta T84 1A5, Canada.

CAREER: Writer. Prospects Literacy Association, Edmonton, Alberta, Canada, special projects coordinator, 1988—. *Morinville Mirror,* Morinville, Alberta, Canada, reporter, photographer, editor, 1988-90. Worked variously as a tutor and writing instructor.

AWARDS, HONORS: R. Ross Annett Juvenile Fiction Award, 1997.

WRITINGS:

"HARPER WINSLOW" SERIES

The Tuesday Cafe, Orca (Custer, WA), 1996.

A Fly Named Alfred, Orca (Custer, WA), 1997.

A Beautiful Place on Yonge Street, Orca (Custer, WA), 1998.

The Popsicle Journal, Orca (Custer, WA), 2001.

"BLACK BELT" SERIES

Frog Face and the Three Boys, Orca (Custer, WA), 2001.

One Missing Finger, Orca (Custer, WA), 2001.

The Bachelors, Orca (Custer, WA), 2002.

The Big Show, Orca (Custer, WA), 2003.

OTHER

Lefty Carmichael Has a Fit, Orca (Custer, WA), 1999.

Author of biweekly column, "To Be a Dad," *Edmonton Journal,* 1993-96.

SIDELIGHTS: Canadian author Don Trembath's first novel, *The Tuesday Cafe,* is about a fifteen-year-old boy who seems to be the ideal child, until he commits an act of rebellion. Harper Winslow shocks his upper-middle-class community by setting a trash can on fire and ending up in juvenile court. After Harper is sentenced to writing an essay for arson charges, his mother signs him up for a writing workshop, not realizing the class is for students with learning disabilities. It is there, however, that Harper finally encounters peers with whom he is comfortable and to whom he can relate.

Kliatt contributor Jacqueline C. Rose commented that Trembath possesses a "fresh, humorous writing style" and applauded "the depth of his characters." Gerry Larson noted in *School Library Journal* that Trembath's style, ending, and inspirational message "combine to create an appealing package." Janet McNaughton of *Quill & Quire* added that the new author is a "welcome" talent who has the ability to "create a character who tells us more about himself than he realizes."

Trembath continued Harper Winslow's story in *A Fly Named Alfred.* In the sequel, Harper continues to improve his writing and even writes a gossip column for the school newspaper, which he secretly submits under the name Alfred. After one of Alfred's columns takes aim at a popular girl in the class, the girl's football-player boyfriend asks Harper to investigate and reveal Alfred's identity. Harper turns to his writing friends for help. "Harper . . . is so quick-witted and engagingly honest about his life that it's hard to put down this latest misadventure," wrote *Booklist* reviewer Anne O'Malley, who concluded that the book provides "a searingly honest look at life through adolescent eyes."

Harper Winslow appears again in *A Beautiful Place on Yonge Street,* and *The Popsicle Journal.* In *A Beautiful Place on Yonge Street,* Harper attends a camp for aspiring writers, where he meets and falls in love with a girl named Sunny Taylor. In the novel, Trembath explores the insecurities and complications of young love. *Booklist*'s O'Malley commented, "We experience [Harper's] angst and inner-voice soul-searching as we are treated to his nonstop, intense wit and commentary."

Harper Winslow becomes a student writer for the local newspaper in *The Popsicle Journal.* When the editor of the paper is busy covering the upcoming election of the town's mayor, Harper is allowed to write his own column, a bittersweet invitation since Harper's father is running for mayor and Harper's sister has been arrested for drunk driving. Harper must write about his own family. While Trembath tackles the ethics of journalism and the impact of drunk driving in this young-adult novel, the book received mixed reviews from critics. Lynn Bryant of *School Library Journal* observed, "Trembath's characterization of the teen excels when he shares samples of his writing," but felt that there was "not enough substance for those who want to invest themselves in a good story." *Kliatt* critic Sarah Applegate wrote, "Too often the book seems to be written for adults," but allowed that "it is easy to follow, the characters are likeable, and the situations are, at times, believable."

Trembath's "Black Belt" series depicts the adventures of three twelve-year-old boys: Charlie, Jeffrey, and Sidney. In *Frog Face and the Three Boys,* the principal, fed up with the boys' behavior, decides to enroll them in a karate class taught by his son, Sensei Duncan. The boys soon realize that their usual antics won't fly with their new teacher and begin to learn new ways to handle themselves in different situations. Betsy Fraser of *School Library Journal* termed the book "a satisfying and humorous tale," and noted, "the characters have definite and entertaining personalities." In the second book in the series, *One Missing Finger,* Charlie develops a crush on a girl he met on the street when his dog tore one finger from her glove. Linda Irvine noted in *Resource Links,* "There are few love novels with young males as protagonists, so this novel should please both boys and girls."

Also part of the "Black Belt" series, *The Bachelors* describes the antics of Jeffrey, Charlie, and Sidney when they are left in charge of caring for Jeffrey's grandfather for a week. In seven short days, the boys manage to get into a heap of trouble, including skipping school and getting caught and attempting to watch "hot" videos (which actually turn out to be old black-and-white movies). Debbie Stewart of *School Library Journal* called the tale "fast-paced and humorous." *Resource Links*' Joan Marshall noted, "This short novel will satisfy fans of the series and provide laughter, especially from younger boys." The boys' fourth adventure, *The Big Show,* is their chance to debut their karate talents and prove themselves to any doubters. The book, according to *Resource Links* writer Carroll Atkins, demonstrates how the boys "can use their martial arts skills to achieve control of their minds, bodies, and emotions."

Trembath also authored the novel *Lefty Carmichael Has a Fit,* which is about a boy named Lefty who suffers from epileptic seizures. The book tracks Lefty's family from their initial concern over Lefty's condition to their annoyance with his overly cautious lifestyle. With the urging of his friend, Penny, Lefty tries to resume a "normal" life and enjoy himself again. A *Publishers Weekly* reviewer noted that Trembath is "deftly balancing humor with grim realism" in this novel. The reviewer continued, "The strength of the author's writing lies in his precise, entertaining depiction of characters and their chorus of lively dialogue."

Don Trembath once commented: "I started writing stories when I was about ten or eleven. I would leave them on the dining room table and my mom and dad and all my brothers would pick them up and read them. Then they would tell me what they thought and ask if I was doing anymore. That kind of support and encouragement is crucial to a writer. I believe it went a long way in convincing me that writing would be a career path worth pursuing, that writing was something I was actually pretty good at. I think all young people should have the opportunity and encouragement to write."

BIOGRAPHICAL AND CRITICAL SOURCES:

BOOKS

St. James Guide to Young Adult Writers, 2nd edition, St. James Press (Detroit, MI), 1999.

PERIODICALS

Booklist, August, 1997, Anne O'Malley, review of *A Fly Named Alfred,* p. 1891; June 1, 1998, review of *The Tuesday Cafe,* p. 1741; March 1, 1999, Anne O'Malley, review of *A Beautiful Place on Yonge Street,* p. 1208; January 1, 2000, Debbie Carton, review of *Lefty Carmichael Has a Fit,* p. 908; March 1, 2001, review of *Frog Face and the Three Boys,* p. 1283.

Bulletin of the Center for Children's Books, May, 1999, review of *A Beautiful Place on Yonge Street,* p. 331.

Canadian Book Review Annual, 1998, review of *A Beautiful Place on Yonge Street,* p. 524; 1999, review of *Lefty Carmichael Has a Fit,* p. 523; 2000, review of *Frog Face and the Three Boys,* p. 508.

Canadian Children's Literature, winter, 1999, review of *A Beautiful Place on Yonge Street,* p. 70, review of *A Fly Named Alfred,* p. 70.

Canadian Literature, summer, 1998, Alexandra and Gernot Wieland, review of *A Fly Named Alfred,* p. 165.

CM: Canadian Review of Materials, February 26, 1999, Mary Thomas, review of *A Beautiful Place on Yonge Street;* April 23, 1999, review of *A Beautiful Place on Yonge Street;* January 21, 2000, Betsy Fraser, review of *Left Carmichael Has a Fit;* March 30, 2001, Liz Greenaway, review of *Frog Face and the Three Boys.*

Globe and Mail (Toronto, Ontario, Canada), July 28, 2001, review of *One Missing Finger,* p. D13.

Kirkus Reviews, January 15, 1999, review of *A Beautiful Place on Yonge Street,* p. 152.

Kliatt, November, 1996, p. 11; July, 1999, review of *A Beautiful Place on Yonge Street,* p. 20; July, 2002, Sarah Applegate, review of *The Popsicle Journal,* p. 25; September, 2003, Stacey Conrad, review of *The Big Show,* p. 22.

Publishers Weekly, June 9, 1997, review of *A Fly Named Alfred,* p. 46; January 3, 2000, review of *Lefty Carmichael Has a Fit,* p. 77.

Quill & Quire, May, 1996, pp. 33-34; November, 1998, review of *A Beautiful Place on Yonge Street,* p. 48; November, 1999, review of *Lefty Carmichael Has a Fit,* p. 47; July, 2001, review of *One Missing Finger* p. 50.

Resource Links, October, 1997, review of *A Fly Named Alfred,* p. 36; February, 1999, review of *A Beautiful Place on Yonge Street,* p. 29; October, 2001, Linda Irvine, review of *One Missing Finger,* p. 20; February, 2002, Margaret Mackey, review of *The Popsicle Journal,* p. 35; October, 2002, Joan Marshall, review of *The Bachelors,* p. 15; June, 2003, Carroll Atkins, review of *The Big Show,* p. 47.

School Library Journal, September, 1996, pp. 228-230; July, 1999, review of *A Beautiful Place on Yonge Street,* p. 101; September, 2001, Betsy Fraser, review of *Frog Face and the Three Boys,* p. 234; July, 2002, Lynn Bryant, review of *The Popsicle Journal,* p. 126; February, 2003, Debbie Stewart, review of *The Bachelors,* p. 148.

Voice of Youth Advocates, October, 1997, p. 248; April, 1998, review of *The Tuesday Cafe,* p. 42; June, 1999, review of *A Beautiful Place on Yonge Street,* p. 118.

ONLINE

Young Alberta Book Society, http://www.yabs.ab.ca/ (November 25, 2002), "Don Trembath."*

V

VERREAULT, Sabine
See VONARBURG, Élisabeth

* * *

VONARBURG, Élisabeth 1947-
(Sabine Verreault)

PERSONAL: Born August 5, 1947, in Paris, France; daughter of Rene (a military officer) and Jeanne (a pharmacist; maiden name, Morchë) Ferron-Wehrlin; married Jean-Joel Vonarburg, December 15, 1969 (divorced, January, 1990). *Education:* University of Dijon, B.A., 1969, M.A. (with honors), 1969, Agregation des Lettres Modernes, 1972; Université Laval, Ph. D., 1987.

ADDRESSES: Home and office—Chicoutimi, Quebec, Canada. *Agent*—Martha Millard Agency, 204 Park Ave., Madison, NJ 07940. *E-mail*—evarburg@saglac.qc.ca.

Élisabeth Vonarburg

CAREER: High school teacher in Chalon-sur-Saone, France, 1972-73; Université du Quebec à Chicoutimi, assistant lecturer in literature, 1973-81; Université du Quebec à Rimouski, assistant lecturer in literature and creative writing, 1983-86; Université Laval, Quebec (City), Quebec, teacher of creative writing in science fiction, 1990. Worked as a singer and songwriter, 1974-82; Aluminum Co. of Canada (ALCAN), technical translator from English to French, 1976-77; organizer and chairman, Boréal I (Quebec Conference on Science Fiction and the Fantastic), 1979; Radio-Canada, weekly science-fiction columnist, 1993-95. Frequent featured speaker at fantasy and science-fiction conventions in Canada, United States, and Europe.

MEMBER: International Association for the Fantastic in the Arts, Science Fiction Canada, Science Fiction Research Association, Science Fiction and Fantasy

Writers of America, Infini (France), Association Professionnelle des Écrivains de la Sagamie (president, 1996-2000).

AWARDS, HONORS: Prix Dagon, 1978, for best science-fiction story of the year, for "L'Oeil de la nuit"; Prix de la Centrale des Bibliothèques de prêt du Saguenay-Lac-St-Jean, 1981, for *L'Oeil de la nuit;* Brix Boréal, 1980 and 1981; France's Grand Prix de la SF française and Prix Rosny Aîné, Prix Boreal, all 1982, for *Le Silence de la cité;* Casper Awards, best science fiction story in French, 1987, for "La Carte du tendre," and 1990, for "Cogito"; Canadian Aurora Awards, 1991, for "Ici, des Tigres" and *Histoire de la princesse et du dragon,* 1992, for *Ailleurs et au Japon,* 1993, for *Chroniques du Pays des Mères,* and 1996, for *Les Voyageurs malgré eux;* Grand Prix de la SF quebecoise, Prix Création du Gala du Salon du Livre du Saguenay/Lac-St-Jean, and Prix Boreal, all 1993, for *Chroniques du Pays des Mères;* Prix Boréal, 1995, for best nonfiction; Prix Boréal for *Tyranaël 1,* Grand Prix de la SF et du Fantastique québécois for *Tyranaël 1 and 2,* Prix Gala du Livre du Saguenay/Lac-St-Jean for *Tyranaël 1, 2, and 3,* and Babet d'or from Saint-Étienne's Book Fair for *Tyranaël 1, 2, and 3,* all 1997; Prix "Femme et littérature" from Conseil Québécois du Statut de la Femme, 1998, for body of work.

WRITINGS:

L'Oeil de la nuit (stories), Editions du Préambule (Longueuil, Quebec, Canada), 1980.

Le Silence de la cité (novel), Denoel (Paris, France), 1981, translation by Jane Brierley published as *The Silent City,* Press Porcepic (Toronto, Ontario, Canada), 1990, Bantam (New York, NY), 1992.

Janus (stories), Denoel (Paris, France), 1984.

Comment écrire des histoires: Guide de l'explorateur (title means "How to Write Stories: An Explorer's Guide"), Editions La Lignée (Beloeil, Quebec, Canada), 1986, 2nd edition, 1992.

Histoire de la princesse et du dragon (children's novella), Quebec/Amerique (Montreal, Quebec, Canada), 1990.

Ailleurs et au Japon (stories), Quebec/Amerique (Montreal, Quebec, Canada), 1991.

Chroniques du Pays des Mères (novel), Quebec/Amerique (Montreal, Quebec, Canada), 1992, translation by Jane Brierley published as *In the Mothers' Land,* Bantam (New York, NY), 1992, also published as *The Maerlande Chronicles,* Beach Holme (Victoria, British Columbia, Canada), 1992.

Les Voyageurs malgre eux, Quebec/Amerique (Montreal, Quebec, Canada), 1992, translation by Jane Brierley published as *Reluctant Voyagers,* Bantam (New York, NY), 1995.

Les Contes de la Chatte Rouge (young-adult novel), Quebec/Amerique (Montreal, Quebec, Canada), 1993.

Contes et legendes de Tyranaël (young-adult novel), Quebec/Amerique (Montreal, Quebec, Canada), 1994.

(With Yves Meynard) *Chanson pour une sirène,* Vents d'Ouest (Hull, Quebec, Canada), 1995.

(With Paul Roux) *Images d'ailleurs,* Éditions Mille Iles, 1996.

Le Lever du récit: Poesie, Les Herbes Rouges (Montreal, Quebec, Canada), 1999.

La Maison au bord de la mer, Alire (Beauport, Quebec, Canada), 2000.

The Slow Engines of Time (short stories), translation by Vonarburg and others, Tesseract Books (Edmonton, Alberta, Canada), 2000.

Dreams of the Sea, Fitzhenry & Whiteside, 2003.

Ailleurs ici (poetry collection), Les Herbes Rouges (Montreal, Quebec, Canada), 2003 .

Le Jeu des coquilles de nautilus (short-story collection), Alire (Beauport, Quebec, Canada), 2003.

"TYRANAËL CYCLE"

Les Rêves de la mer: Tyranaël 1, Alire (Beauport, Quebec, Canada), 1996, translation by Vonarburg and Howard Scott published as *Dreams of the Sea,* Tesseract Books (Edmonton, Alberta, Canada), 2003.

Le Jeu de la perfection: Tyranaël 2, Alire (Beauport, Quebec, Canada), 1996.

Mon frère l'ombre: Tyranaël 3, Alire (Beauport, Quebec, Canada), 1997.

L'Autre rivage: Tyranaël 4, Alire (Beauport, Quebec, Canada), 1997.

La Mer allée avec le soleil: Tyranaël 5, Alire (Beauport, Quebec, Canada), 1997.

TRANSLATOR

Tanith Lee, *La Tombe de naissance* (novel; title means "The Birthgrave"), Marabout (Verviers, France), 1976.

James Tiptree, Jr., *Par-Delà les murs du monde* (novel; title means "Up the Walls of the World"), Denoel (Paris, France), 1979.

Chelsea Quinn Yarbro, *Fausse Aurore* (novel; title means "False Dawn"), Denoel (Paris, France), 1979.

Ian Watson, *Chronomachine lente* (stories; title means "A Very Slow Time Machine"), Lattes (Paris, France), 1981.

Jayge Carr, *L'Abîme de Léviathan* (novel; title means "Leviathan's Abyss"), Albin-Michel (Paris, France), 1982.

Tanith Lee, *Le Jour, la nuit* (novel; title means "Day by Night"), Albin-Michel (Paris, France), 1982.

Jack L. Chalker, *Le Diable vous emportera* (novel; title means "And the Devil Will Drag You Under"), Albin-Michel (Paris, France), 1983.

R. A. Lafferty, *Le Livre d'or de Lafferty* (stories), Presses Pocket (Paris, France), 1984.

Jack Williamson, *Le Livre d'or de Jack Williamson* (stories), Presses Pocket (Paris, France), 1988.

(And editor) Marion Zimmer Bradley, *Le Livre d'or de Marion Zimmer Bradley* (stories), Presses Pocket (Paris, France), 1992.

(And editor) Anne McCaffrey, *La Dame de la tour: Le Livre d'or de Anne McCaffrey* (stories), Presses Pocket (Paris, France), 1992.

Gerald Nicosia, *Memory Babe: Une Biographie critique de Jack Kerouac* (title means "Jack Kerouac: A Critical Biography"), Quebec/Amerique (Montreal, Quebec, Canada), 1994.

Guy Gavriel Kay, *La Tapisserie de Fionavar* (title means "The Fionavar Tapestry"), Quebec/Amerique, Volume I: *L'Arbre de l'Ete* (title means "The Summer Tree"), 1994, Volume II: *Le Feu vagabond* (title means "The Wandering Fire"), 1995, Volume III: *La Route obscure* (title means "The Darkest Road"), 1995.

Marion Zimmer Bradley, *La Chute d'Atlantis* (title means "The Fall of Atlantis"), Presses Pocket (Paris, France), 1996.

Marion Zimmer Bradley and Holly Isle, *En Glenravenne,* Lefrancq (Brussels, Belgium), 1998.

Guy Gavriel Kay, *Les Lions d'Al-Rassan,* Alire (Beauport, Quebec, Canada), 1999.

Guy Gavriel Kay, *La Mosaïque de Sarance,* Buchet/Chastel (Paris, France), 2001.

Also author of the screenplay *Le Silence de la cité.* Contributor of critical essays and short stories to numerous anthologies, including *Invisible Fiction: Contemporary Stories from Quebec,* Anansi (Toronto, Ontario, Canada), 1987; (under pseudonym Sabine Verreault) *Sous des soleils étrangers,* Éditions Ianus (Laval, Quebec, Canada), 1989; *State of the Fantastic: Selected Essays from the Eleventh Conference on the Fantastic in the Arts,* Greenwood Press (Westport, CT), 1992; *Northern Stars,* edited by David G. Hartwell and Glenn Grant, Tor (New York, NY), 1994; *Un Lac, un fjord,* Éditions JCL (Chicoutimi, Quebec, Canada), 1994; *Out of This World: Canadian Science Fiction and Fantasy,* edited by Andrea Paradis, Quarry Press (Kingston, Ontario, Canada), 1995; and (under pseudonym Sabine Verreault) *The Sleeper in the Crystal: Tesseracts VI,* Tesseract Books (Edmonton, Alberta, Canada), 1997. Founding editor, *Solaris,* 1974. Contributor of numerous short stories and essays to periodicals, including *Solaris, Requiem, Tomorrow Speculative Fiction,* and *Protée.*

SIDELIGHTS: Élisabeth Vonarburg is one of the best-known Canadian science-fiction writers working in French. A resident of Quebec since 1973, Vonarburg has produced "significant contributions to the body of feminist sf, making equal partners of politics, style, and storytelling," wrote Joan Gordon in the *New York Review of Science Fiction.* The author's speculative novels and stories approach science fiction from a biological and anthropological perspective, creating future or distant planetary communities "that could serve as a pointer for the renewal of our contemporary society," according to a contributor to the *St. James Guide to Science Fiction Writers.* That same contributor praised Vonarburg for her "fully Canadian-inspired context while retaining a universal appeal," concluding that her work "demonstrates that SF can be independent of context and, as mainstream literature, related to a national identity."

Vonarburg was born Élisabeth Ferron-Wehrlin-Morchë in 1947 in Paris. She was an early and avid reader who grew up in the French countryside with a particular interest in science fiction. Her master's degree thesis was one of the first in French academe to have speculative fiction as its topic, and although she trained as a teacher she knew she wanted to be a writer. In 1973 her husband was assigned a French army position in Chicoutimi, Quebec, and she moved to Canada permanently, obtaining Canadian citizenship in 1976.

While working part time as a professor at various universities in Quebec, Vonarburg began to pursue fiction writing seriously. She was a founding editor of the respected magazine *Solaris* and became a frequent contributor to its pages. Her earliest work was completed in collaboration with her husband, Jean-Joel Vonarburg, but at the beginning of 1978 she published her first solo story, "Marée haute," in *Requiem* magazine. Since then she has earned a living from her fiction, her essays, translations into French of other authors' works, and occasional teaching or lecturing duties. *Dictionary of Literary Biography* contributor Sylvie Bérard noted that, with the release of her first story collection, *L'Oeil de la nuit,* Vonarburg "imprinted her mark on a burgeoning contemporary science-fiction movement in Quebec and set the tone for her whole fictional world."

Vonarburg's translated novels include *The Silent City, In the Mothers' Land,* and *Reluctant Voyagers,* all published by mainstream American presses. *The Silent City* follows the adventures of a mutant named Elisa who lives in a post-apocalypse bunker the size of a city. *In the Mothers' Land* presents an almost all-female futuristic utopia as seen though the eyes of Lisbeï, a young woman coming to terms with her personal identity and her civilization's ancient past. *Reluctant Voyagers* is seen as Vonarburg's most personal work. Its heroine, Catherine Rhymer, is a young teacher/writer who explores alternate realities through excerpts from her short stories and a mystical voyage through the *Pays des Sags* ("Land of the Sags"). Bérard felt that the novel "remains a prime example of the author's creative skills and her global literary project. It shows her mastery of various subgenres and her ability to propose a unified novel based on such diverse styles."

Vonarburg's award-winning "Tyranaël Cycle" is a five-novel saga set on the planet Tyranaël. The first novel of the cycle, *Les Rêves de la mer,* was published in English translation as *Dreams of the Sea* in 2003. Various aspects of the story include a populace with commonplace extrasensory perceptions, a sentient sea, and characters who appear in successive volumes by the process of resurrection. As in her earlier novels, Vonarburg speculates on the tension between free will and a domineering civilization. "The whole saga is rich and complex," observed Bérard. "Even though every volume can be read independently, all five novels have complex ramifications within the entire cycle. . . . [The] perspective can be associated not only with the author's own emigrant status . . . but also within the identifying framework she has been developing in her fiction as well as her essays for more than twenty-five years."

Élisabeth Vonarburg once told *CA:* "I write to make sense of my life, to tell myself my own story, which is also the story of the world I live in and the people I share it with, in order to understand it, them, and myself. I found out that only science fiction allows me to do that in a totally satisfying way.

"I am inspired by curiosity, the need to understand, or at least to make up explanations for, the universe, my being in it, and the relationship between the two. I need to understand what a woman is, what I am as a woman, what it means in the world I live in here and now. I have a taste for and a fear of metamorphosis and change. I feel a sometimes crushing sense of the relationship between past, present, and future. I have a deep belief in and suspicion of the power of stories."

BIOGRAPHICAL AND CRITICAL SOURCES:

BOOKS

Boivin, Aurélien, Maurice Emond, and Michel Lord, *Bibliographie analytique de la science-fiction et du fantastique québécois,* Nuit Blanche (Quebec, Canada), 1992, pp. 539-547.

Dictionary of Literary Biography, Volume 251: *Canadian Fantasy and Science-Fiction Writers,* Gale (Detroit, MI), 2001, pp. 294-308.

St. James Guide to Science Fiction Writers, 4th edition, St. James (Detroit, MI), 1996.

Van Belkom, Edo, *Northern Dreamers: Interviews with Famous Science Fiction, Fantasy, and Horror Writers,* Quarry Press (Kingston, Ontario, Canada), 1998, pp. 211-234.

Weiss, Allan, editor, *Proceedings of the Academic Conference on Canadian Science Fiction & Fantasy,* (Toronto, Ontario, Canada), 1998, pp. 35-49.

PERIODICALS

Amazing Stories, November, 1992, Pamela Sargent, "New Threads in the Tapestry," pp. 52-56.

New York Review of Science Fiction, January, 1994, Joan Gordon, reviews of *The Silent City* and *In the Mothers' Land;* February, 1996, Kathleen Ann Goonan, review of *Reluctant Voyagers.*

Solaris, September-October, 1987, Luc Pomerleau, "Entrevue Élisabeth Vonarburg," pp. 42-48; fall, 1993, Alain Joël Champetier and Daniel Sernine, "Élisabeth Vonarburg," pp. 39-50.

ONLINE

Élisabeth Vonarburg Home Page, http://www.sfwa.org/ (November 14, 2002).*

W

WEISS, Nicki 1954-

PERSONAL: Born January 25, 1954, in New York, NY; daughter of Harry (a textile importer) and Lyla (a sculptress; maiden name, Gutman) Weiss. *Education:* Union College, B.A., 1976.

ADDRESSES: *Home*—New York, NY. *Office*—c/o Author Mail, HarperCollins Publishers, 10 East 53rd St., 7th Floor, New York, NY 10022.

CAREER: Scheck-Rosenblum Textiles, Inc., New York, NY, textile designer, 1977-79; freelance textile designer, 1979-81; freelance author/illustrator, 1981—. Preschool teacher at Walden School in New York, NY, 1983-84; kindergarten teacher in New York City Public Schools, 1993—. Visiting author in schools and libraries, 1983—.

WRITINGS:

FOR CHILDREN; SELF-ILLUSTRATED

Menj!, Greenwillow (New York, NY), 1981.
Waiting, Greenwillow (New York, NY), 1981.
Chuckie, Greenwillow (New York, NY), 1982.
Hawk and Oogie, Greenwillow (New York, NY), 1982.
Maude and Sally, Greenwillow (New York, NY), 1983.
Weekend at Muskrat Lake, Greenwillow (New York, NY), 1984.
Battle Day at Camp Delmont, Greenwillow (New York, NY), 1985.
Princess Pearl, Greenwillow (New York, NY), 1986.
A Family Story, Greenwillow (New York, NY), 1987.
If You're Happy and You Know It, Greenwillow (New York, NY), 1987.
Barney Is Big, Greenwillow (New York, NY), 1988.
Where Does the Brown Bear Go?, Greenwillow (New York, NY), 1988.
Sun Sand Sea Sail, Greenwillow (New York, NY), 1989.
Dog Boy Cap Skate, Greenwillow (New York, NY), 1989.
Surprise Box, Putnam (New York, NY), 1991.
On a Hot, Hot Day, Putnam (New York, NY), 1992.
The First Night of Hanukkah, Grosset & Dunlap (New York, NY), 1992.
Stone Men, Greenwillow (New York, NY), 1993.
The World Turns Round and Round, Greenwillow (New York, NY), 2000.

FOR CHILDREN

Scoop!: Fishbowl Fun, Simple Addition, illustrated by Rose Mary Berlin, Troll Associates (Mahwah, NJ), 1992.
Shopping Spree: Identifying Shapes, illustrated by Rose Mary Berlin, Troll Associates (Mahwah, NJ), 1992.
Snap! Charlie Gets the Whole Picture, illustrated by Rose Mary Berlin, Troll Associates (Mahwah, NJ), 1992.
How Many?, How Much?, Measuring, illustrated by Rosemary Berlin, Troll Associates (Mahwah, NJ), 1992.
Mmmm—Cookies!: Simple Subtraction, illustrated by Rose Mary Berlin, Troll Associates (Mahwah, NJ), 1992.

Pop!: ABC Letters and Sounds: Learning the Alphabet, illustrated by Rose Mary Berlin, Troll Associates (Mahwah, NJ), 1992.

The Biggest Pest: Comparisons, illustrated by Rose Mary Berlin, Troll Associates (Mahwah, NJ), 1992.

Birthday Cake Candles: Counting, illustrated by Rose Mary Berlin, Troll Associates (Mahwah, NJ), 1992.

Guess What!: Drawing Conclusions, illustrated by Rose Mary Berlin, Troll Associates (Mahwah, NJ), 1992.

SIDELIGHTS: It is through the combination of words, illustrations, and overall design that Nicki Weiss creates her picture books, which range from lively, fun read-alouds to sensitive, warm stories. Weiss began publishing her self-illustrated titles while still in her twenties and has continued to release new books even while working as an elementary school teacher. One of her favorite themes is coping with change. The young heroes of such books as *Hank and Oogie, Maude and Sally,* and *Barney Is Big* bravely face such situations as the first day of school and making new friends. In other Weiss picture books, family relationships are examined and celebrated, as in *The World Turns Round and Round,* in which school children receive gifts from grandparents all over the globe.

Among Weiss's first books is the picture book *Waiting.* A youngster named Annalee waits in the yard for her mother's return from the store and is so eager for the reunion that she mistakes certain events for her mother's return. A *Kirkus Reviews* critic wrote that the "still, boundless setting is . . . a metaphor for the stop-time endlessness of Annalee's wait. One small idea, wholly realized." In *Hank and Oogie,* the title character must face that fact that his favorite stuffed animal, Oogie, is not necessarily welcome in kindergarten. A *Publishers Weekly* reviewer felt that Weiss "treats with sensitivity and humor the need for children to adjust to changes wrought by the years."

Best friends Maude and Sally inhabit two Weiss books, *Maude and Sally* and *Battle Day at Camp Delmont.* In the first title, Maude must cope with Sally's absence through a long summer, and in the second Maude and Sally—both at camp this time—have to compete against each other in a field day competition. Peggy Forehand, writing in *School Library Journal,* noted that in *Maude and Sally* Weiss "sensitively portrays the warmth and fun of friendships with all the insecurities that youngsters experience in relationships."

Sibling and intergenerational relationships animate some of Weiss's books, including *Weekend at Muskrat Lake, Princess Pearl,* and *A Family Story.* In the first two stories, Pearl comes to terms with her place in the family and learns that love exists between herself and her sister. *A Family Story* follows a pair of sisters, Rachel and Annie, as they grow up and start families of their own.*A Family Story* "is a warm, loving look at the rare and wonderful relationships between big girls and little girls," observed *School Library Journal* contributor Lucy Young Clem. A *Publishers Weekly* reviewer likewise felt that the book "celebrates love in this softspoken and endearing telling." The 1993 story *Stone Men* explores the bond between Arnie and his grandmother as she tells him a folktale passed from one generation to the next. A *Publishers Weekly* critic concluded: "Economy in prose and art produces a picture book with . . . power and pungency."

Weiss has also produced several well-received picture books meant to be read aloud to very young children. These combine pastel pictures with rhymes and repetitions that youngsters can quickly pick up themselves. *Where Does the Brown Bear Go?* asks where a variety of woodland creatures sleep. *Horn Book* correspondent Elizabeth S. Watson described the title as "an exquisite book to end a young one's day." *On a Hot, Hot Day* celebrates the changing seasons in an inner city neighborhood; Ellen Fader in *Horn Book* praised the work as an "unassuming and reassuring domestic slice of life." In *The World Turns Round and Round,* a class of school children compares the gifts sent to them by their grandparents, some of whom live in foreign lands. The book introduces foreign words for "grandmother" as well as the traditional clothing and hats of such places as Mexico, Egypt, and Vietnam. Bina Williams in *School Library Journal* called the book a "fine introduction to world cultures," and *Reading Today* correspondent Lynne T. Burke commended it as a "simple celebration of geography."

BIOGRAPHICAL AND CRITICAL SOURCES:

PERIODICALS

Horn Book, September-October, 1986, Ann A. Flowers, review of *Princess Pearl,* p. 584; May-June,

1989, Elizabeth S. Watson, review of *Where Does the Brown Bear Go?,* p. 366; May-June, 1992, Ellen Fader, review of *On a Hot, Hot Day,* p. 335.

Kirkus Reviews, August 15, 1981, review of *Waiting,* p. 1008.

New York Times Book Review, April 25, 1982.

Publishers Weekly, July 2, 1982, review of *Hank and Oogie,* p. 55; March 20, 1987, review of *A Family Story,* p. 78; July 28, 1989, reviews of *Dog Boy Cap Skate* and *Sun Sand Sea Sail,* p. 218; February 24, 1992, review of *On a Hot, Hot Day,* p. 53; February 1, 1993, review of *Stone Men,* p. 94; October 16, 2000, review of *The World Turns Round and Round,* p. 76.

Reading Today, October, 2000, Lynne T. Burke, review of *The World Turns Round and Round,* p. 32.

School Library Journal, September, 1981, Carolyn Noah, review of *Waiting,* p. 116; May, 1983, Peggy Forehand, review of *Maude and Sally,* pp. 67-68; December, 1984, Robin Fenn Elbot, review of *Weekend at Muskrat Lake,* p. 78; June-July, 1987, Lucy Young Clem, review of *A Family Story,* p. 91; July, 1992, Liza Bliss, review of *On a Hot, Hot Day,* pp. 65-66; July, 1993, Joy Fleishhacker, review of *Stone Men,* pp. 73-74; October, 2000, Bina Williams, review of *The World Turns Round and Round,* p. 141.*

* * *

WHITE, Randy Wayne 1950-

PERSONAL: Born June 9, 1950, in Ashland, OH; married, February, 1972; wife's name Debra Jane; children: Lee, Rogan. *Hobbies and other interests:* Roy Hobbs Men's Baseball, surfing.

ADDRESSES: Home—P.O. Box 486, Pineland, FL 33945. *E-mail*—rwwhite1@aol.com.

CAREER: Boat captain and fishing guide, Sanibel, FL, 1977-90; writer, 1989—.

WRITINGS:

"DOC FORD" ECO-ADVENTURE MYSTERIES

Sanibel Flats, St. Martin's Press (New York, NY), 1990.

The Heat Islands, St. Martin's Press (New York, NY), 1992.

The Man Who Invented Florida, St. Martin's Press (New York, NY), 1993.

Captiva, Putnam (New York, NY), 1996.

North of Havana, Putnam (New York, NY), 1997.

The Mangrove Coast, Putnam (New York, NY), 1998.

Ten Thousand Islands, Putnam (New York, NY), 2000.

Shark River, Putnam (New York, NY), 2001.

Twelve Mile Limit, Putnam (New York, NY), 2002.

Everglades, Putnam (New York, NY), 2003.

Tampa Burn, 2004.

NONFICTION

Bat Fishing in the Rainforest, Lyons Press (New York, NY), 1991.

The Sharks of Lake Nicaragua: True Tales of Adventure, Travel, and Fishing, Lyons Press (New York, NY), 1999.

Last Flight Out: True Tales of Adventure, Travel, and Fishing, Lyons Press (Guilford, CT), 2002.

Columnist for *Outside,* 1989-94, and *Men's Health.* Contributor to *Condé Nast Traveler, Premier, New York Times, Playboy, National Wildlife,* and *Reader's Digest.*

SIDELIGHTS: Randy Wayne White is a fiction writer and journalist based in Southwest Florida, and his concerns in novels and nonfiction alike are ecology, adventure, and the pursuit of unconventional activities. As a writer for *Outside* magazine he has gone shark-hunting in a landlocked lake and gone to flight school for fighter planes, covered the America's Cup races in Australia and reported from Sumatra, Singapore, Central America, and Vietnam, to name a few locales. As a fiction writer he has created a series sleuth named Doc Ford, an ex-CIA spook turned wildlife biologist who cannot seem to keep clear of trouble. A *Publishers Weekly* reviewer wrote: "Tense action scenes, skillful character development and an unerring eye for local flora and fauna make White a match for any Florida storyteller."

Doc Ford made his debut in White's first novel, *Sanibel Flats.* In that story, Doc finds his idyllic life on a secluded island disrupted by abduction and revolution in Central America. The well-received novel set the tone for subsequent Ford series titles: generally Ford is approached by an old friend who needs detective help, or a grieving parent, or he becomes incensed by an act of violence or eco-terrorism and seeks revenge. According to Bill Ott in *Booklist,* White's novels feature "straight-ahead, leather-tough realism" akin to John D. MacDonald's "Travis McGee" series. The books also take issue with the exploitation of the environment, a theme common to Florida writers of all types. One *Publishers Weekly* reviewer felt that the "real star" of White's novels "is the seascape of Florida, something Ford—and White—know intimately." Ott, in a *Booklist* piece on *Shark River,* concluded that White's novels "mix action and introspection in just the right proportions."

White's nonfiction books include his best writing from *Outside* magazine, for which he completed many bizarre assignments. Some of them—participation in an antiterrorist driving school and a wrestling academy—are written with tongue-in-cheek humor. Others have a more serious purpose and scope. In any case, William O. Scheeren in *Library Journal* found White's nonfiction writing style "pleasing and engaging" and called *The Sharks of Lake Nicaragua: True Tales of Adventure, Travel, and Fishing* a "fine book." In a *Publishers Weekly* review of the same title, a critic declared: "It's hard to imagine a better guide than White. . . . [He] proves his mettle as an incisive humorist and a first-rate travel journalist."

On his Web site, White noted: "The thing I love most to write about is Doc Ford and his friends at Dinkin's Bay. I was a light-tackle fishing guide at Tarpon Bay Marina on Sanibel Island, Florida, for thirteen years, and the Ford novels afford me the opportunity to revisit a time, and people, about which I care deeply."

BIOGRAPHICAL AND CRITICAL SOURCES:

PERIODICALS

Booklist, April 1, 1996, Wes Lukowsky, review of *Captiva,* p. 1346; April 15, 1997, Bill Ott, review of *North of Havana,* p. 1414; August, 1998, Bill Ott, review of *The Mangrove Coast,* p. 1977; May 1, 2001, Bill Ott, review of *Captiva,* p. 1603, review of *Shark River,* p. 1643.

Library Journal, April 15, 1997, Charles Michaud, review of *North of Havana,* p. 121; September 1, 1998, Thomas L. Kilpatrick, review of *The Mangrove Coast,* p. 218; June 15, 1999, William O. Scheeren, review of *The Sharks of Lake Nicaragua: True Tales of Adventure, Travel, and Fishing,* p. 98; February 15, 2002, John McCormick, review of *Last Flight Out: True Tales of Adventure, Travel, and Fishing,* p. 169.

New York Times Book Review, December 26, 1993, Marilyn Stasio, review of *The Man Who Invented Florida,* p. 22.

People, Michelle Green, review of *North of Havana,* p. 36.

Publishers Weekly, March 9, 1990, Sybil Steinberg, review of *Sanibel Flats,* p. 54; September 27, 1991, review of *Batfishing in the Rainforest: Strange Tales of Travel and Fishing,* p. 52; January 1, 1992, review of *The Heat Islands,* p. 50; October 25, 1993, review of *The Man Who Invented Florida,* p. 46; February 12, 1996, review of *Captiva,* p. 62; March 17, 1997, review of *North of Havana,* p. 77; August 10, 1998, review of *The Mangrove Coast,* p. 372; May 24, 1999, review of *The Sharks of Lake Nicaragua,* p. 54; May 8, 2000, review of *Ten Thousand Islands,* p. 1625; May 7, 2001, review of *Shark River,* p. 222.

ONLINE

Randy Wayne White Home Page, http://rwwhite.com/ (September 26, 2003).*

* * *

WISE, Joe 1939-

PERSONAL: Born July 11, 1939, in Fort Worth, TX. *Ethnicity:* "White." *Education:* Texas Christian University, B.S., 1961; University of Texas—Southwestern Medical School, M.D., 1964. *Hobbies and other interests:* Travel, gardening, fly fishing, photography.

ADDRESSES: Home—29 Calle Pagosa, Santa Fe, NM 87501. *E-mail*—pagosa@rt66.com.

CAREER: Cardiologist in Maine and New Mexico. *Military service:* U.S. Air Force, 1965-67; became captain.

MEMBER: International PEN, Western Writers of America, Southwest Writers Workshop.

AWARDS, HONORS: Award for best historical novel, Southwest Writers Workshop, 1995; award for fiction, Colorado Independent Publishers Association, 2000.

WRITINGS:

Cannibal Plateau (novel), Sunstone Press (Santa Fe, NM), 1997.
In the Moro (novel), Western Reflections (Ouray, CO), 1999.
A Primer on Heart Disease, Western Reflections (Montrose, CA), 2000.
The Fish (novel), Western Reflections (Ouray, CO), 2002.
A Sense of Place: A Century in the San Juans, Western Reflections (Montrose, CO), 2003.
If You Go, Western Reflections (Montrose, CO), 2003.

Contributor to magazines and newspapers, including *Journal of the West* and *New York Times.*

SIDELIGHTS: Joe Wise once told *CA:* "I have a lifelong love of words and the Rocky Mountain Southwest. My desire to write 'history-based' fiction was unsatisfied for years, due to the demands of medical practice. My work was first published in 1993, in *Journal of the West,* after ten years of research on John Fremont's fourth expedition. My first real break came with the publication of a travel article in the *New York Times.* The best advice I ever got about writing was from Tony Hillerman: 'Just write the first chapter. You're going to rewrite it five times anyway.' He helped me finally get started on the novel I had been thinking about for years."

* * *

WOLFF, Ruth (Rehrer) 1932-

PERSONAL: Born December 17, 1932, in Malden, MA; daughter of Louis K. (in business) and Etta B. (in business) Wolff; married Martin Bloom (an architect), August 7, 1955; children: Evan Todd. *Education:* Smith College, B.A., 1953; attended Yale University, 1954-55. *Politics:* Democrat.

Ruth Wolff

ADDRESSES: *Agent*—Robert Lantz, Lantz Office, 200 West 57th St., Suite 503, New York, NY 10019.

CAREER: Playwright and screenwriter.

MEMBER: Dramatists Guild, League of Professional Theater Women, Writers Guild of America West.

AWARDS, HONORS: Rockefeller Foundation playwrighting fellowship from Wesleyan University; award from Kennedy Center Bicentennial Commission; MacDowell Colony fellowship.

WRITINGS:

PLAYS

The Golem, first produced Off-Broadway, 1959.
Eleanor of Aquitane, 1965.
The Fall of Athens, 1966.
Folly Cove, first produced in Waterford, CT, at O'Neill Theater Center, 1967.
Still Life with Apples, first produced in Waterford, CT, at O'Neill Theater Center, 1968.

Arabic Two, first produced in New York, NY, at New Theater Workshop, 1969.

The Abdication (first produced in England, at Bristol Old Vic Theater, 1971, then in productions throughout the world), published in *The New Women's Theater,* Random House (New York, NY), 1976, published as *The Abdication: Definitive Acting Edition,* Dramatic Publishing (New York, NY), 2002.

Eden Again, produced by Kennedy Center Bicentennial Commission (Washington, DC), 1975.

Sarah in America, first produced in Washington, DC, at John F. Kennedy Center for the Performing Arts, 1981, then in repertory; later broadcast as a television special in the series *Kennedy Center Tonight,* Public Broadcasting System (PBS).

George and Frederic, first produced in Salt Lake City, UT, at University of Utah Theater, 1982, later in staged reading, New Haven, CT, at Yale University Club, 2001.

Empress of China (first produced in New York, NY, at Pan Asian Repertory Theater, 1984, revived there, 2003), Broadway Play Publishing (New York, NY), 1985.

The Perfect Marriage, performed in workshop, Santa Barbara, CA, 1987, later performed in staged readings in East Hampton, NY, at East Hampton Playwrights Theater, and by Roundabout Theater Company, New York, NY, both 1996.

Joshua Slocum: Sailing Alone around the World, first produced in Newport, RI, at Rhode Island Shakespeare Theater, 1992.

The Second Mrs. Wilson, performed in staged readings in Williamstown, MA, at Williamstown Theater Festival, in East Hampton, NY, at East Hampton Playwrights Theater, in New York, NY, at Intar Hispanic American Theater and at Lincoln Center Theater, between 1988 and 1996, produced in Abington, VA, at Barter Theater, 2001.

Hallie, performed in staged readings in Northampton, MA, at Smith College, in Poughkeepsie, NY, at Vassar College, and in New York, NY, at Writers Theater, 1989.

Buffaloes, performed in staged readings in Newport, RI, Los Angeles, CA, and New York, NY, 1992-93.

Back to Bald Pate, 1997.

The Waltz, performed in staged reading in New York, NY, at Juilliard School Theater, 1998.

Aviators, performed in staged reading in Sag Harbor, NY, at Bay Street Theater, 2003.

OTHER

The Abdication (screenplay), Warner Bros., 1974.

The Incredible Sarah (screenplay), Reader's Digest Films, 1976.

Contributor of articles to periodicals, including *Ms., New York Times Magazine,* and *Dramatist.*

WORK IN PROGRESS: Screenplays titled *Wild Nights, Home Games,* and *Island Fling.*

SIDELIGHTS: Ruth Wolff has been a successful playwright since the late 1950s. Her first produced play, *The Golem,* was an adaptation from Jewish mythology, but she eventually became known for her historical and biographical plays about famous women. *Eleanor of Aquitane,* Wolff's second effort for the stage, featured the famous medieval queen of France and England. *The Abdication,* first produced in 1971, told the story of Sweden's Queen Christina, who left her throne and converted to Catholicism for the love of Cardinal Azzolino. *Sarah in America* depicted the famed nineteenth- and early-twentieth-century actress Sarah Bernhardt, during her various performance tours in the United States. Wolff has also penned plays featuring women writers Mary Shelley and George Sand and the Victorian-era Chinese Empress Tzu-hsi. Renowned actresses such as Lilli Palmer, Glenda Jackson, Anne Wil Blankers, Liv Ullmann, and Katherine Helmond have starred in Wolff's plays and in movies produced from her screenplays. As the book jacket for the published version of Wolff's *Empress of China* proclaimed, "To the question, 'Where are the roles for women?,' Ruth Wolff provides the answer." The play's published introduction added that, although the playwright's characters lived in the past, "Wolff's theatricality is blazingly modern and her themes are sharply contemporary—from the nature of woman, to the consequences of sexual and intellectual freedom, to the use and misuse of power in all its forms."

The Abdication has had a long and distinguished performance record. Premiering at the Bristol Old Vic Theater, it has been presented throughout the United States and in many foreign countries, including acclaimed productions in the Hague in Dutch at De Haagse Comedie, in Montreal in French at the Théâtre de Quat'Sous, and in Italian, in a production which toured all of Italy, presented by Il Gruppo Arte Drammatica. Wolff wrote an article about this Italian tour of her play for the *New York Times Magazine.* She also wrote the script for the film version of *The Abdication,* which starred Liv Ullmann and Peter Finch.

Sarah in America was described in the introduction to *Empress of China* as "a tour de force for one actress." The play, about Sarah Bernhardt's tours of the United States, takes the actress from age thirty-six to age seventy-two, portraying the impetuous actress from her naive first encounters with North America, through the immense success of her middle years, through failure, loss of love, and illness, to great triumph in her old age. The play's premiere at the John F. Kennedy Center for the Performing Arts in Washington, DC, in 1981, starred Lilli Palmer and was directed by Sir Robert Helpmann. The play was produced at the Pasadena Playhouse starring Katherine Helmond and at Hofstra University starring Tovah Feldshuh. Wolff also wrote a screenplay about Bernhardt, *The Incredible Sarah,* which starred British actress Glenda Jackson. The film covers Bernhardt's early career in France through her tenure at the Comédie Française, the beginnings of her career as an independent actress-manager, and her tumultuous marriage.

Empress of China had its premiere production with the Pan Asian Repertory Theater in 1984 and in the same year was produced at the Cincinnati Playhouse. It was also produced by several west coast theater companies and had a notable production, in Italian, at the Todi Fetsival in Italy. As the introduction to the published version notes, the play tells the story of a dowager empress who held power in China at the time of the Boxer Rebellion, the Chinese people's uprising against imperial rule and foreign influence at the beginning of the twentieth century. The book jacket describes the play as "a searing yet sympathetic portrait" of its subject and quotes a *New York Times* review which called Dowager Empress Tzu-hsi "a villainess of epic proportions." In 2003, the Pan Asian Repertory Theater presented an entirely new production of the play.

The play *The Second Mrs. Wilson* is about the events which took place upstairs in the White House in the last year of the Woodrow Wilson administration, when the seriousness of his illness was kept from the people as the president, with the help of his wife, was working to the limits of his energies to insure a future without wars. The play premiered shortly after the World Trade Center bombings of September 11, 2001.

Wolff once told *CA:* "I write Broadway-type plays in a time when, for straight plays, Broadway almost doesn't exist, historical plays in a time when, for many, history doesn't exist, and am an American playwright often writing about Europe and Asia when for Americans these places don't exist. On top of this, I'm a woman.

"Aside from this, I'm sanguine about the work. This is what I want to write this time 'round. From my point of view, I'm not writing about other times and places, but about themes which are timeless. For a long time I found myself writing about subjects which could be classified generally around the theme of 'Love.' Later I wrote about 'Cruelty'—only to discover that in my hands it automatically seemed the other side of the love theme.

"I've written about woman's need to understand her own sexual nature (*The Abdication*), about power and powerlessness (*Empress of China*), about familial complexity when a love triangle involves a woman *after* the revolution (Chopin, Sand, and Sand's daughter Solange in *George and Frederic*), and the ironies and complexities in male-female relationships (Mary and Percy Shelley in *The Perfect Marriage*). But throughout, my overriding theme has always been the urge and necessity for the individual to strive, in spite of any circumstance, to live out his or her best existence. I don't care whether they won or lost as long as they had some vision of a better life and tried to live it. (In the plays, Sarah Bernhardt in *Sarah in America* most singularly embodies this, as do Edith and Woodrow Wilson in *The Second Mrs. Wilson.*) It's a tougher and more complex concept than I can summarize here, but it's the way I've tried to live, too.

"Since I decided on this career, the profession has changed mightily. For most of us, our writing careers have been divided. Film is an exuberant, spacious and sensual medium, and dramatists are lucky to live in a time when they can write for it. Shakespeare would have. He knew that an idea can be conveyed as succinctly by an image as by words.

"On the other hand, some ideas can only be conveyed by precisely expressed language—and this is when it is a glory to be able to write for the stage. In spite of my anger and sorrow that so many of my colleagues must spend so much of their time *not* writing plays, in spite of the fact that in these last two decades so many of their and my plays are *not being written* (or not being produced), I still have faith in the theater as a great and special communicator.

"The theater may be, in the future, one of the last places where people may come together to experience ideas and emotions. In times of increasing isolation, this shared experience will continue to be a precious one—no matter how threatened and how rare."

Wolff also told *CA* that she wanted to offer special thanks "to Audrey Wood, my literary representative from the beginning of my career until the end of hers, and . . . to Roger Stevens, who was the original producer of my plays (including *The Abdication* and *Sarah in America*) for many years. Their faith and encouragement—and that of my husband and son—have been central to my creative existence."

BIOGRAPHICAL AND CRITICAL SOURCES:

BOOKS

The New Women's Theatre, Random House (New York, NY), 1976.

Wolff, Ruth, *Empress of China,* Broadway Play Publishing (New York, NY), 1985.

PERIODICALS

Dramatist, May-June, 2000.

Equity News, March, 2003, "Is Anyone Writing Plays for Women? Ruth Wolff Is!"

New York Times Magazine, December, 1977, article by Ruth Wolff.

* * *

WOODSON, Jacqueline 1964-

PERSONAL: Born February 12, 1964, in Columbus, OH; daughter of Jack and Mary Ann Woodson; children: Toshi. *Education:* Adelphi University, B.A., 1985; also attended New School for Social Research.

Jacqueline Woodson

ADDRESSES: Home—Brooklyn, NY. *Agent*—c/o Charlotte Sheedy Literary Agency, 65 Bleecker St., 12th floor, New York, NY 10012. *E-mail*—letters@jacquelinewoodson.com.

CAREER: Freelance writer, 1997—. Goddard College, Plainfield, VT, M.F.A. Writing Program, associate faculty member, 1993-95; New School University, Eugene Lang College, New York, NY, associate faculty member, 1994; Vermont College, Montpelier, VT, M.F.A. program, associate faculty member, 1996. Writer in residence, National Book Foundation, 1995, 1996. Has also worked as an editorial assistant, and as a drama therapist for runaway children in East Harlem, New York, NY.

MEMBER: Alpha Kappa Alpha.

AWARDS, HONORS: MacDowell Colony fellowship, 1990 and 1994; Fine Arts Work Center, Provincetown, MA, fellow, 1991-92; *Kenyon Review* Award for literary excellence in fiction, 1992 and 1995; Best Books for Young Adults citation, American Library Association (ALA), 1993, for *Maizon at Blue Hill; Publishers Weekly* Best Book citation, 1994; Jane Addams Children's Book Award, 1995 and 1996; Coretta Scott King Honor Book, ALA, 1995, for *I Hadn't Meant to Tell You This,* and 1996, for *From the Notebooks of Melanin Sun; Granta* Fifty Best American Authors under 40 Award, 1996; Lambda Literary Award for best fiction and best children's fiction, 1996; Lambda Literary Award, children/young adult, 1998, for *The House You Pass on the Way; Booklist* Editor's Choice citation; American Library Association Best Books citation; American Film Institute award; Best Books for Young Readers citation, ALA, 2000, for *If You Come Softly; Los Angeles Times* Book Award for young adult fiction and Coretta Scott King Book Award, 2001, for *Miracle's Boys;* nominee for National Book Award in young people's literature category, 2002, for *Hush; Boston Globe-Horn Book* Award nominee in fiction and poetry category, 2003, for *Locomotion.*

WRITINGS:

FOR CHILDREN

Martin Luther King, Jr. and His Birthday (nonfiction), illustrated by Floyd Cooper, Silver Burdett (Parsippany, NJ), 1990.

We Had a Picnic This Sunday Past, illustrated by Diane Greenseid, Hyperion (New York, NY), 1997.

The Other Side, illustrated by Earl B. Lewis, Putnam (New York, NY), 2001.

Our Gracie Aunt, illustrated by Jon J. Muth, Hyperion (New York, NY), 2002.

Coming on Home Soon, illustrated by E. B. Lewis, Putnam (New York, NY), 2004.

FICTION; FOR YOUNG ADULTS

Last Summer with Maizon (first book in trilogy), Delacorte (New York, NY), 1990.

The Dear One, Delacorte (New York, NY), 1991, Putnam (New York, NY), 2004.

Maizon at Blue Hill (second book in trilogy), Delacorte (New York, NY), 1992.

Between Madison and Palmetto (third book in trilogy), Delacorte (New York, NY), 1993.

Book Chase ("Ghostwriter" series), illustrated by Steve Cieslawski, Bantam (New York, NY), 1994.

I Hadn't Meant to Tell You This, Delacorte (New York, NY), 1994.

From the Notebooks of Melanin Sun, Scholastic, Inc. (New York, NY), 1995.

The House You Pass on the Way, Delacorte (New York, NY), 1997.

If You Come Softly, Putnam (New York, NY), 1998.

Lena, Delacorte (New York, NY), 1998.

Miracle's Boys, edited by Nancy Paulsen, Putnam (New York, NY), 2000.

Sweet, Sweet Memory, illustrated by Floyd Cooper, Hyperion (New York, NY), 2000.

Visiting Day, illustrated by James Ransome, Scholastic (New York, NY), 2002.

Hush, Putnam (New York, NY), 2002.

Locomotion, Putnam (New York, NY), 2003.

Behind You, Putnam (New York, NY), 2004.

OTHER

(With Catherine Saalfield) *Among Good Christian Peoples* (video), A Cold Hard Dis', 1991.

Autobiography of a Family Photo (novel), New American Library/Dutton (New York, NY), 1994.

(Editor) *A Way out of No Way: Writing about Growing Up Black in America* (short stories), Holt (New York, NY), 1996.

(Editor, with Norma Fox Mazer) *Just a Writer's Thing: A Collection of Prose and Poetry from the National Book Foundation's 1995 Summer Writing Camp,* National Book Foundation (New York, NY), 1996.

Contributor to short-story collection *Am I Blue?,* edited by Marion Dane Bauer, HarperTrophy, 1994; contributor to *Just a Writer's Thing: A Collection of Prose & Poetry from the National Book Foundation's 1995 Summer Writing Camp,* edited by Norma F. Mazer, National Book Foundation, 1996. Also contributor to periodicals, including *American Voice, American Identities: Contemporary Multi-Cultural Voices, Common Lives Quarterly, Conditions, Essence, Horn Book, Kenyon Review* and *Out/Look.* Member of editorial board, Portable Lower East Side/*Queer City.*

SIDELIGHTS: Award-winning author Jacqueline Woodson is equally proficient in the novel format, verse, and picture books. She writes about "invisible" people: young girls, minorities, homosexuals, the poor, all the individuals who are ignored or forgotten in mainstream America. They are the people, as the author wrote in a *Horn Book* article, "who exist on the margins." An African American and lesbian herself, Woodson knows first-hand what it is like to be labeled, classified, stereotyped, and pushed aside. Nevertheless, her stories are not intended to champion the rights of minorities and the oppressed. Rather, they celebrate people's differences. Her characters are not so much striving to have their rights acknowledged as they are struggling to find their own individuality, their own value as people. "I feel compelled to write against stereotypes," Woodson further remarked, "hoping people will see that some issues know no color, class, sexuality. No—I don't feel as though I have a commitment to one community—I don't want to be shackled this way. I write from the very depths of who I am, and in this place there are all of my identities."

Woodson's sense of not really belonging to one community might be grounded in her childhood. During her adolescent years, she moved back and forth between South Carolina and New York City, and "never quite felt a part of either place," according to a *Ms.* article by Diane R. Paylor. But Woodson began to feel "outside of the world," as she explained in *Horn Book,* even before her teen years. The turning point for her came when Richard Nixon resigned the presidency in 1974 and Gerald Ford took his place instead of George McGovern. "McGovern was my first 'American Dream.' Everyone in my neighborhood had been pulling for him." When Ford stepped into the Oval Office, Woodson felt that she and all of black America had been abandoned. "The word *democracy* no longer existed for me. I began to challenge teachers, and when they couldn't give me the answers I wanted, I became sullen, a loner. I would spend hours sitting underneath the porch, writing poetry and anti-American songs."

Writing soon became Woodson's passion. In the fifth grade, she was the literary editor of her school's magazine. "I used to write on everything," she commented for a Bantam Doubleday Dell Web site. "It was the thing I liked to do the most. I never thought I could have a career as a writer—I always thought it was something I would have to do on the side." Her seventh-grade English teacher encouraged Woodson to write and convinced her that she should pursue whatever career she felt would make her happiest. Deciding that writing was, indeed, what she wanted to do, Woodson endeavored "to write about communities that were familiar to me and people that were familiar to me. I wanted to write about communities of color. I wanted to write about girls. I wanted to write about friendship and all of these things that I felt like were missing in a lot of the books that I read as a child."

Woodson has always had a deep empathy for young girls, who often suffer from low self-esteem in their preteen and adolescent years. "I write about black girls because this world would like to keep us invisible," she wrote in *Horn Book.* "I write about *all* girls because I know what happens to self-esteem when we turn twelve, and I hope to show readers the number of ways in which we are strong." Woodson's first published book, *Last Summer with Maizon,* begins a trilogy about friends Margaret and Maizon. Set in the author's hometown of Brooklyn, the story tells of two eleven-year-olds who are the closest of friends. Their friendship is strained, however, when Margaret's father dies of a heart attack and Maizon goes to boarding school on a scholarship. While her friend is away, Margaret, who is the quieter of the two, discovers that she has a talent for writing. She also finds comfort in her family, who support her in her attempt to deal with her father's death. Maizon, meanwhile, finds that she does not like the almost all-white Connecticut boarding school and returns home after only three months. Glad to be with her loved ones again, Maizon, along with Margaret, goes to a gifted school in her own neighborhood.

Critics praised *Last Summer with Maizon* for its touching portrayal of two close friends and for its convincing sense of place. Julie Blaisdale, writing in *School Librarian,* also lauded the work for its "positive female characters . . . who provide the enduring sense of place and spiritual belonging" in the tale. Roger Sutton of the *Bulletin of the Center for Children's Books,* while generally commending the book, found fault with the way Margaret eases her sadness by writing poetry. "Although underdeveloped," Sutton concluded, "this story will appeal to readers who want a 'book about friends.'" Similarly, *Horn Book* writer Rudine Sims Bishop commented on the story's "blurred focus," but asserted that "the novel is appealing in its vivid portrayal of the characters and the small community they create."

Woodson continues Margaret and Maizon's stories with *Maizon at Blue Hill* and *Between Madison and Palmetto.* The former is not really a sequel but, rather, an "equal" to the first book in the trilogy. *Maizon at Blue Hill* focuses on what happens to Maizon while she is at the Connecticut boarding school. Maizon, who is a very bright girl, likes the academic side of Blue Hill, but she is worried about fitting in socially. Most of the other girls are white and are either snobbish or, at least, not eager to be her friend. Although she is welcomed by a small clique of other black students, Maizon sees this group as rather elitist, too. She decides to return to Brooklyn, where she can comfortably just be herself. An American Library Association Best Book for young adults, *Maizon at Blue Hill* has been acclaimed for its strong and appealing characters. "More sharply written than its predecessor, this novel contains some acute characterization," remarked Roger Sutton in the *Bulletin of the Center for Children's Books.* Noting that the issues about self-esteem and identity that are addressed in the story spring appropriately from the characters rather than vice versa, *Voice of Youth Advocates* contributor Alice F. Stern asserted: "We are in the hands of a skilled writer here. . . . Woodson is a real find."

The last book in the trilogy, *Between Madison and Palmetto,* picks up where the first book left off, with Maizon and Margaret entering eighth grade at the academy. Again, Woodson covers a lot of ground in just over one hundred pages, including Margaret's bout with bulimia, issues of integration as the two girls' neighborhood begins to change and white families move in, and the testing of Margaret and Maizon's friendship as Maizon spends more time with another girl, named Carolyn. A *Publishers Weekly* reviewer applauded Woodson's gift with characterization, but noted that the effect is "somewhat diluted by the movie-of-the-week problems." In another *Voice of Youth Advocates* review, Alice F. Stern acknowledged that Woodson has "a lot of ground to cover," but noted that "she manages admirably." A *Kirkus Reviews* critic described *Between Madison and Palmetto* as a fine portrayal of a "close-knit community . . . [that] comes nicely to life."

In her *Horn Book* article, Woodson grouped her books into two categories: her "good" books, which deal with relationships between family members and friends, and her more controversial books, which address issues of alcoholism, teenage pregnancy, homosexuality, and other issues that skirt the delicate problem of what is "appropriate" for children to read. She reflected on how, after writing her second book, *The Dear One,* the speaking invitations she had formerly received suddenly stopped coming. "Even after *Maizon at Blue Hill,* another relatively 'nice book,' school visits were few and far between. Yet I often wonder, If every book had been like *Last Summer with Maizon,* and I was a young woman with a wedding band on my hand, would I get to visit schools more often?"

The central character of *The Dear One* is twelve-year-old Feni, a name meaning "The Dear One" in Swahili. Feni lives in an upper-class African-American home and basks in her family's attention. This all changes, however, when fifteen-year-old Rebecca is invited by Feni's mother to stay with them. Rebecca, the daughter of an old college friend, is a troubled, pregnant teenager from Harlem. Feni becomes jealous because she is no longer the center of attention. "But gradually and believably, with the patient support of Feni's mother and a lesbian couple who are longstanding family friends, the two girls begin to develop mutual trust and, finally, a redemptive friendship," related *Twentieth-Century Children's Writers* contributor Michael Cart.

The Dear One is a unique book in that it deals with tensions not between blacks and whites but between poor and wealthy blacks. Woodson gives a sympathetic portrayal of Rebecca, who is uncomfortable living in what she considers to be a mansion, and who is also reluctant to change her lifestyle. She misses her boyfriend and her family back in Harlem; she envies Feni and resents the privileges Feni has been given. The novel also offers a fresh perspective on adult relationships. As Hazel S. Moore noted in *Voice of Youth Advocates,* "The lesbian couple seems to be intact, while the straight couples have divorced and suffered." Marion and Bernadette, the lesbian couple, provide Feni with wise advice to add to the support she receives from her mother.

Taking things a step further than *The Dear One, I Hadn't Meant to Tell You This* explores a relationship that spans both race and class when Marie, a girl from a well-to-do black family, befriends Lena, whom Marie's father considers to be "white trash." Both girls have problems: Marie's mother has abandoned her family, and Lena is the victim of her father's sexual molestations. Told from Marie's point of view, the book details the twelve-year-old's internal conflicts as she tries to think of how she can help Lena. In the end, Lena, who has been able to find no other viable solutions to her problem, runs away from home, and Marie must accept the fact that there is nothing she can do about her friend's tragedy. Woodson has been praised by critics for not resolving her story with a pat conclusion. Cart commented: "Woodson's refusal to impose a facile resolution on this heartbreaking dilemma is one of her singular strengths as a writer." "Woodson's novel is wrenchingly honest and, despite its sad themes, full of hope and inspiration," concluded a *Publishers Weekly* reviewer.

In *Lena,* Woodson picks up Lena's own story after she leaves Marie. Lena plans to hitchhike with her little sister Dion to Pine Mountain, Kentucky—their mother's birthplace—in an effort to escape their father's abuse. "In the first novel, the girls' friendship sustained them across racial barriers in a desolate world," declared Hazel Rochman in *Booklist,* "but here everything has a glowingly happy ending." "The great appeal here," the reviewer concluded, "is the survival story. After cold and danger, we feel the elemental luxury of shelter: warmth, cleanliness, breakfast, privacy." "Writing in Lena's voice, striking for its balance of tough-mindedness and tenderness," stated a critic in *Publishers Weekly,* "Woodson conveys the love that the protective heroine feels for her sister as well as the compassion of strangers."

Another Woodson novel, *If You Come Softly,* also explores the issue of race. The book tells of the budding relationship between two fifteen-year-olds: a black boy named Jeremiah, and Ellie, a Jewish girl. "The intensity of their emotions will make hearts flutter, then ache," stated a *Publishers Weekly* reviewer, "as evidence mounts that Ellie's and Jeremiah's 'perfect' love exists in a deeply flawed society." "This, like every story I've written, from *Last Summer with Maizon* to *I Hadn't Meant to Tell You This* to *From the Notebooks of Melanin Sun,* is my story," Woodson wrote in a *Horn Book* essay on writing outside one's own cultural group. "While I have never been Jewish, I have always been a girl. While I have never lived on the Upper West Side, I have lived for a long time in New York. While I have never been a black male, I've always been black. But most of all, like the characters in my story, I have felt a sense of powerlessness in my lifetime. And this is the room into which I can walk and join them."

The issue of homosexuality, which had been peripheral in Woodson's earlier books, comes to the forefront in *From the Notebooks of Melanin Sun* and *The House You Pass on the Way.* Thirteen-year-old Melanin Sun, the central character in the former novel, has a close relationship with his mother, whom he admires as a single working mother who is also putting herself through law school. Their bond is strained, however, when Melanin's mother tells him that she is a lesbian and that she is in love with a white woman. This development makes Melanin question his relationship with his mother, as well as making him wonder about his own sexuality. Torn between his emotional need for his mother and his fear about what her lesbianism implies, Melanin goes through a tough time as his friends also begin to abandon him. Gossip in the neighborhood that Melanin's mother is "unfit" also spreads, making matters even worse. Again, Woodson offers no clear-cut resolution to the story, but by the novel's end Melanin has begun to grow and understand his mother. Critics praised Woodson's portrayal of Melanin's inner conflicts as being right on the money. As Lois Metzger wrote in the *New York Times Book Review,* "Ms. Woodson, in this moving, lovely book, shows you Melanin's strength and the sun shining through." "Woodson has addressed with care and skill the sensitive issue of homosexuality within the family . . . [without] becoming an advocate of any particular attitude," asserted *Voice of Youth Advocates* critic Hazel S. Moore. In *The House You Pass on the Way,* fourteen-year-old Evangeline, the middle child in a mixed-race family, struggles with feelings of guilt and dismay over her awakening sexual orientation. "A provocative topic," noted a *Kirkus Reviews* critic, "treated with wisdom and sensitivity, with a strong secondary thread exploring some of the inner and outer effects of biracialism."

The plight of three orphaned brothers in New York is presented in Woodson's Coretta Scott King Award-winning novel, *Miracle's Boys.* Lafayette, the youngest of the three, tells the story in a "voice that's funny, smart, and troubled," according to *Booklist*'s Rochman. Ty'ree, the oldest brother, has given up his educational possibilities to raise his younger brothers, but faces conflict at every turn from the middle brother, Charlie, who has just returned from a correctional institution for robbing a candy story and now is in gang trouble once again. The boys also carry the sad memory of their dead mother, Milagro; Charlie blames Lafayette, or Laff as he is called, for her death. But through it all the brothers try to stay together, healing their grief as best as they can. A contributor for *Horn Book* praised Lafayette's narrative voice, noting that it "maintains a tone of sweet melancholy that is likely to hold the attention of thoughtful young teens." Likewise, a reviewer for *Publishers Weekly* called the novel an "intelligently wrought, thought-provoking story," and Edward Sullivan, writing in *School Library Journal,* found this "story of tough, self-sufficient young men to be powerful and engaging."

In her 2002 novel *Hush,* Woodson explores the loss of a child's identity when a young girl and her family are forced into the witness protection program. Toswiah Green's father is a black policeman in Denver. Her life is perfect: a wonderful home, caring parents, and cool friends. But when her father chooses to testify against fellow policemen—white—whom he witnessed shooting and killing an unarmed black teen, the lives of the entire family are turned upside down. The white community and his fellow cops turn against Green, and the family must enter the witness protection program, move to another state, and assume new identities. "Woodson's taut, somber novel examines complex themes," wrote Lynda Jones in *Black Issues Book Review.* Such themes as racism, self-identity, the class system, and ethical imperatives are dealt with in the journal that Toswiah—who takes the assumed name of Evie Thomas—keeps. "Woodson shows that while Evie's situation is extreme, everyone has to leave home and come to terms with many shifting identities," commented Rochman in a *Booklist* review. Jennifer M. Brabander, reviewing *Hush* in *Horn Book,* also lauded the story, concluding that Woodson's "poetic, low-key, yet vivid writing style perfectly conveys the story's atmosphere of quiet intensity." Reviewing the same novel in *School Library Journal,* Sharon Grover called it a "complex coming-of-age story," and Claire Rosser, writing in *Kliatt,* declared Woodson to be "one of the best novelists we have in the Y[oung] A[dult] field." Rosser further asserted that Woodson "brings poetry to her prose and always a deep understanding of emotional upheaval."

Woodson brings much the same sensibility to her picture books for younger readers, presenting subjects not usually examined in books for children. These include titles such as *The Other Side,* a "story of friendship across race," according to *Booklist*'s Rochman; *Sweet, Sweet Memory* is the tale of a little girl whose grandmother has died, and one that "will resonate with those who have lost someone dear," as Ilene Cooper observed in *Booklist; Our Gracie Aunt* is the story of two children whose mother is in the hospital and who must go into foster care; and *Visiting Day* is a "poignant picture book," according to a *Publishers Weekly* reviewer, that tells an intergenerational tale about a young girl and her grandmother who go to visit the father in jail. As Rochman noted in *Booklist,* "Woodson brings children close to those whose stories are seldom told." Woodson turns to poetry for her "sad but hopeful" story *Locomotion,* as a critic for *Publishers Weekly* called the book. Young Lonnie tells his story of loss and redemption in sixty poems in various styles from sonnet to haiku. *Horn Book*'s Brabander concluded that "Woodson's finely crafted story of heartbreak and hope won't let [readers] go."

Although most of her works have been aimed at preteen and teenage audiences, Woodson has also written a novel for adults, *Autobiography of a Family Photo,* which addresses issues of sexuality and sexual behavior for a more mature audience. However, its short length and central coming-of-age theme put *Autobiography of a Family Photo* within the reach of young adult audiences. Told in a series of vignettes spanning the 1960s and 1970s, the novel is a reminiscence related by an unnamed narrator. Her family has many problems, including her parents' troubled marriage, her brother Carlos's inclination to be sexually abusive, her brother Troy's struggles with homosexuality that compel him to go to Vietnam, and other difficulties. Despite all of this, the narrator survives adolescence, undergoing a "compelling transformation," according to Margot Mifflin in an *Entertainment Weekly* review. However, some critics have contended that the vignettes fail to form a unified whole. A *Kirkus Reviews* contributor, for example, commented: "Chapters build on each other, but the information provided is too scanty to really create any depth." Catherine Bush, writing in the *New York Times Book Review,* complained that the novel focuses too much on the narrator's growing sexual awareness. "I found myself wishing that the narrator's self-awareness and longing could be defined less exclusively in sexual terms," Bush remarked. Bush concluded, however, that "even in these restrictive terms, the novel is the best kind of survival guide: clear-eyed, gut true."

Woodson has never backed away from portraying truths about life in modern American society. She has written her "good" books about friendship and family that deal with safe, acceptable topics, but she clearly does not shy away from controversial subjects like homosexuality and sexual abuse. Woodson has asserted that she is not trying to force any kind of ideology on her readers, but rather is interested in all kinds of people, especially the socially rejected. "One of the most important ideas I want to get across to my readers," Woodson emphasizes, "is the idea of feeling like you're okay with who you are." "Death happens," Woodson told Samiya A. Bashir in *Black Issues Book Review.* "Sexual abuse happens. Parents leave. These things happen every day and people think that if they don't talk about it, then it will just go away. But that's what makes it spread like the plague it is. People say that they're censoring in the guise of protecting children, but if they'd open their eyes they'd see that kids are exposed to this stuff every day, and we need a venue by which to talk to them about it and start a dialogue. My writing comes from this place, of wanting to change the world. I feel like young people are the most open."

BIOGRAPHICAL AND CRITICAL SOURCES:

BOOKS

Authors and Artists for Young Adults, Volume 21, Gale (Detroit, MI), 1997.

Children's Literature Review, Volume 49, Gale (Detroit, MI), 1998.

Gay and Lesbian Literature, Volume 2, St. James Press (Detroit, MI), 1998.

St. James Guide to Young Adult Writers, 2nd edition, St. James Press (Detroit, MI), 1999.

Twentieth-Century Children's Writers, 4th edition, St. James Press (Detroit, MI), 1995.

Writers for Young Adults, Scribner (New York, NY), 2000.

PERIODICALS

Black Issues Book Review, May, 2001, Samiya A. Bashir, "Tough Issues, Tender Minds," p. 78; March-April, 2002, Lynda Jones, review of *Hush,* p. 67; July-August, 2002, Lynda Jones, review of *Our Gracie Aunt,* p. 75.

Book, March-April, 2003, Kathleen Odean, review of *Hush,* p. 37.

Booklist, February 1, 1999, Hazel Rochman, review of *Lena,* p. 970; February 15, 2000, Hazel Rochman, review of *Miracle's Boys,* p. 1102; February 15, 2001, Hazel Rochman, review of *Miracle's Boys,* p. 1149; February 15, 2001, Hazel Rochman, review of *The Other Side,* p. 1154; February 15, 2001, Ilene Cooper, review of *Sweet, Sweet Memory,* p. 1158; January 1, 2002, Hazel Rochman, review of *Hush,* p. 851; January 1, 2002, review of *The Other Side,* p. 769; February 15, 2002, Stephanie Zvirin, reviews of *Hush* and *The Other Side,* p 1034; September 1, 2002, Hazel Rochman, review of *Our Gracie Aunt,* p. 137; January 1, 2003, review of *Hush,* p. 798.

Bulletin of the Center for Children's Books, October, 1990, Roger Sutton, review of *Last Summer with Maizon,* pp. 49-50; December, 1992, Roger Sutton, review of *Maizon at Blue Hill,* p. 128; September, 1998, Janice M. DelNegro, review of *We Had a Picnic This Sunday Past,* p. 40; April, 1999, Deborah Stevenson, review of *Lena,* p. 298; February, 2001, Janice M. DelNegro, review of *The Other Side,* p. 211; May, 2001, Janice M. DelNegro, review of *Sweet, Sweet Memory,* p. 357.

Childhood Education, summer, 2003, Sharon White-Williams, review of *Visiting Day,* p. 247.

Entertainment Weekly, April 21, 1995, Margot Mifflin, review of *Autobiography of a Family Photo,* pp. 50-51.

Horn Book, September, 1992, Rudine Sims Bishop, "Books from Parallel Cultures: New African-American Voices," pp. 616-620; November-December, 1995, Jacqueline Woodson, "A Sign of Having Been Here," pp. 711-715; May-June, 1999, Kristi Beavin, review of *I Hadn't Meant to Tell You This* (audio version), p. 358; March-April, 2000, review of *Miracle's Boys,* p. 203; January-February, 2002, Jennifer M. Brabander, review of *Hush,* p. 87; November-December, 2002, Roger Sutton, review of *Visiting Day,* p. 743; March-April, 2003, Jennifer M. Brabander, review of *Locomotion,* pp. 219-220.

Kirkus Reviews, December 1, 1993, review of *Between Madison and Palmetto,* p. 1532; October 1, 1994, review of *Autobiography of a Family Photo,* pp. 1307-1308; July 1, 1997, review of *The House You Pass on the Way,* p. 1038; September 15, 2002, review of *Visiting Day,* p. 1403; November 15, 2002, review of *Locomotion,* p. 1704.

Kliatt, January, 1999, Paula Rohrlick, review of *Lena,* pp. 10-11; January, 2002, Claire Rosser, review of *Hush,* p. 8; March, 2002, Claire Rosser, review of *Miracle's Boys,* p. 20.

Ms., November-December, 1994, Diane R. Paylor, "Bold Type: Jacqueline Woodson's 'Girl Stories,'" p. 77; July, 1995, p. 75.

New York Times Book Review, February 26, 1995, Catherine Bush, "A World without Childhood," p. 14; July 16, 1995, Lois Metzger, review of *From the Notebooks of Melanin Sun,* p. 27.

Publishers Weekly, November 8, 1993, review of *Between Madison and Palmetto,* p. 78; April 18, 1994, review of *I Hadn't Mean to Tell You This,* p. 64; June 22, 1998, review of *If You Come Softly,* p. 92; December 14, 1998, review of *Lena,* p. 77; April 17, 2000, review of *Miracle's Boys,* p. 81; December 4, 2000, review of *The Other Side,* p. 73; March 4, 2002, review of *Our Gracie Aunt,* p. 79; September 16, 2002, review of *Visiting Day,* p. 68; November 25, 2002, review of *Locomotion,* pp. 68-69.

Reading Teacher, November, 2002, review of *The Other Side,* pp. 257-258.

School Librarian, November, 1991, Julie Blaisdale, review of *Last Summer with Maizon,* p. 154.

School Library Journal, May, 2000, Edward Sullivan, review of *Miracle's Boys,* p. 178; January, 2001, Catherine T. Quattlebaum, review of *The Other Side,* p. 112; April, 2001, Marianne Saccardi, review of *Sweet, Sweet Memory,* p. 126; August, 2001, Jacqueline Woodson, "Miracles," p. 57; August, 2001, Julie Cummins, "Offstage or Upstaged?," p. 9; February, 2002, Sharon Grover, review of *Hush,* p. 138; September, 2002, Susan Pine, review of *Visiting Day,* pp. 208-209; December, 2002, Anna DeWind, review of *Our Gracie Aunt,* p. 114; September, 2003, Grace Oliff, review of *Visiting Day,* p. 86.

Voice of Youth Advocates, October, 1991, Hazel S. Moore, review of *The Dear One,* p. 236; October, 1992, Alice F. Stern, review of *Maizon at Blue Hill,* p. 235; June, 1994, Alice F. Stern, review of *Between Madison and Palmetto,* p. 95; October, 1995, Hazel S. Moore, review of *From the Notebooks of Melanin Sun,* p. 227; February, 2001, review of *Miracle's Boys,* p. 400.

ONLINE

Bantam Doubleday Dell, http://www.bdd.com/ (April 8, 1997), "Jacqueline Woodson."

BookPage, http://www.bookpage.com/ (February, 2003), Heidi Henneman, "Poetry in Motion."

Official Jacqueline Woodson Web site, http://www.jacquelinewoodson.com/ (November 11, 2003).*

WREDE, Patricia C(ollins) 1953-

PERSONAL: Surname is pronounced "Reedy"; born March 27, 1953, in Chicago, IL; daughter of David Merrill (a mechanical engineer) and Monica Marie (an executive; maiden name, Buerglar) Collins; married James M. Wrede (a financial consultant), July 24, 1976 (divorced, 1992). *Education:* Carleton College, A.B., 1974; University of Minnesota, M.B.A., 1977. *Politics:* Independent. *Religion:* Roman Catholic. *Hobbies and other interests:* Sewing, embroidery, gardening, reading.

ADDRESSES: *Home*—Edina, MN. *Agent*—Valerie Smith, Route 44-55, R.R. Box 160, Modena, NY 12548. *E-mail*—Pwrede6492@aol.com.

CAREER: Novelist. Minnesota Hospital Association, Minneapolis, rate review analyst, 1977-78; B. Dalton Bookseller, Minneapolis, financial analyst, 1978-80; Dayton-Hudson Corp., Minneapolis, financial analyst, 1980-81, senior financial analyst, 1981-83, senior accountant, 1983-85; full-time writer, 1985—. Laubach reading tutor.

MEMBER: Science Fiction Writers of America, Novelists, Inc.

AWARDS, HONORS: Books for Young Adults Recommended Reading List citation, 1984, for *Daughter of Witches,* and 1985, for *The Seven Towers;* Minnesota Book Award for Fantasy and Science Fiction, 1991, and Best Books for Young Adults citation, American Library Association (ALA), both for *Dealing with Dragons;* ALA Notable Book designation, and Best Books for Young Adults designation, both for *Searching for Dragons.*

WRITINGS:

The Seven Towers, Ace Books (New York, NY), 1984.

(With Caroline Stevermer) *Sorcery and Cecelia,* Ace Books (New York, NY), 1988, published as *Sorcery and Cecelia; or, The Enchanted Chocolate Pot: Being the Correspondence of Two Young Ladies of Quality regarding Various Magical Scandals in London and the Country,* Harcourt (Orlando, FL), 2003.

Patricia C. Wrede

Snow White and Rose Red, Tor Books (New York, NY), 1989.
Mairelon the Magician, Tor Books (New York, NY), 1991.
Book of Enchantments (short stories), Harcourt (San Diego, CA), 1996.
The Magician's Ward (sequel to *Mairelon the Magician*), Tor Books (New York, NY), 1997.
Star Wars: Episode I: The Phantom Menace (novelization; based on the screenplay and story by George Lucas), Scholastic (New York, NY), 1999.
Star Wars: Episode II: Attack of the Clones (novelization; based on the screenplay and story by George Lucas), Scholastic (New York, NY), 2002.

"LYRA" FANTASY SERIES

Shadow Magic (also see below), Ace Books (New York, NY), 1982.
Daughter of Witches (also see below), Ace Books (New York, NY), 1983.
The Harp of Imach Thyssel (also see below), Ace Books (New York, NY), 1985.
Caught in Crystal, Ace Books (New York, NY), 1987.
The Raven Ring, Tor Books (New York, NY), 1994.
Shadows over Lyra (includes *Shadow Magic, Daughter of Witches,* and *The Harp of Imach Thyssel*), Tor Books (New York, NY), 1997.

"CHRONICLES OF THE ENCHANTED FOREST" FANTASY SERIES

Dealing with Dragons (Volume 1), Harcourt (San Diego, CA), 1990, published as *Dragons Bane,* Scholastic (New York, NY), 1993.
Searching for Dragons (Volume 2), Harcourt (San Diego, CA), 1991, published as *Dragon Search,* Scholastic (New York, NY), 1994.
Calling on Dragons (Volume 3), Harcourt (San Diego, CA), 1993.
Talking to Dragons (Volume 4), Harcourt (San Diego, CA), 1993, previous edition, Tempo/MagicQuest Books (New York, NY), 1985.
Enchanted Forest Chronicles (contains *Dealing with Dragons, Searching for Dragons, Calling on Dragons,* and *Talking to Dragons*), Harcourt (San Diego, CA), 2003.

Contributor of short stories to anthologies, including *Liavek,* Ace Books (New York, NY), 1985; *Liavek: The Players of Luck,* Ace Books (New York, NY), 1986; *Spaceships and Spells,* Harper (New York, NY), 1987; *The Unicorn Treasury,* Doubleday (New York, NY), 1988; *Liavek: Spells of Binding,* Ace Books (New York, NY), 1988; *Liavek: Festival Week,* Ace Books (New York, NY), 1990; *Tales of the Witch World Three,* Tor Books (New York, NY), 1990; *A Wizard's Dozen,* Harcourt (San Diego, CA), 1993; and *Blackthorn, White Rose,* Morrow (New York, NY), 1994.

ADAPTATIONS: Books in Wrede's "Chronicles of the Enchanted Forest" series have been adapted as audiobooks by Listening Library (New York, NY), 1997-2002.

SIDELIGHTS: The author of almost a score of novels and as many short stories, Patricia C. Wrede is a popular writer of fantasy. Her novels and stories, ranging from modern versions of traditional fairy tales to comic fantasy, break new ground in the genre. According to an essayist in *St. James Guide to Young Adult Writers,* the "two trademarks" of her work "are humor and light romance, two elements sure to appeal to the young adult audience." While much fantasy uses a pseudo-medieval, vaguely Celtic setting, Wrede expands these boundaries to include Renaissance and Regency-era England in *Snow White and Rose Red, Sorcery and Cecelia, Mairelon the Magician,* and *The Magician's Ward.* She has also helped to establish the strong-minded female protagonist as a mainstay in the modern fantasy genre. Among her other novels are the "Lyra" tales, which take place in Wrede's own created world, and the "Enchanted Forest" books, which present comic variations on fairy-tale motifs.

"I was an omnivorous reader as a child," Wrede once commented to *CA*. "I don't think I ever read anything only once. I read the 'Oz' books, and I still treasure a set of those that I collected over the years. *Mrs. Piggle Wiggle* and *The Borrowers,* the Walter Farley horse books, Robert Lawson animal stories, the 'Narnia Chronicles'—practically everything I could get my hands on. They knew me very well down at the library. I also told stories to my younger siblings (I am the eldest of five) and to any of my friends who would listen."

Wrede started writing, in the seventh grade, a "wildly improbable" novel. As she recalled, "I worked on it during class when I was supposed to be studying and brought it home every day. My mother aided and abetted me by typing out the pages and my father read them and told me they were great (he still thinks I should try to publish the book)."

After graduating from high school, Wrede attended Carleton College, where she majored in biology and graduated in 1974. "Of the sciences, I liked biology the best because it dealt on a personal level with living things, as opposed to physics and chemistry, which deal with things in the abstract—little molecules you can't even see. With biology you can pick up a plant and look at the roots and know what you've got."

After working as a secretary for several months, Wrede returned to school and obtained her M.B.A. in 1977. After graduating, she started work on her first novel, *Shadow Magic,* which would take five years to complete. Published by Ace Books in 1982, the novel tells the story of Alethia, daughter of a noble house of the nation of Alkyra. Alethia is of mixed blood—her mother is one of the magic-using Shee, and magic runs in her blood. She is kidnapped from her home in the city of Brenn by the Lithmern, agents of a rival nation. To carry out their plan, the Lithmern have unbound the evil Shadowborn, spirits who inhabit men's bodies and slowly destroy their minds. Alethia escapes the Lithmern with the aid of the Wyrds, a forest-dwelling, cat-like race of people, and meets her mother's folk, who train her in the use of magic. Alethia unites the four races of Alkyra—the Wyrds, the Shee, the sea-living Neira, and the humans—against the threat of the aroused Shadowborn. Finally, she discovers the lost magic treasures of the kings of Alkyra, uses them to defeat the Shadowborn, and is proclaimed queen of the land by the four reunited races.

Shadow Magic introduces the world of Lyra, an alternate earth that many of Wrede's novels share. Lyra is a land literally shaped by magic and by the threat of the Shadowborn. Its history dates from the end of the Wars of Binding, the conflict in which the Shadowborn were finally restrained by the power of the gifts of Alkyra. The land itself was broken, however, and many of its original inhabitants left homeless, forced to wander across the oceans in ships or over the lands in caravans. The ultimate result is a kaleidoscope of different cultures, from the warrior Cilhar nation to the older and more cultured society of Kith Alunel. The Kulseth sailors were left homeless when their island sank in the Wars of Binding; Varna, the island of wizards, was destroyed in a later conflict, and survivors from both places mingled with other peoples, adding to the variety and occasionally causing friction. The events of *Shadow Magic* take place more than three thousand years after the Wars of Binding, and other "Lyra" novels examine other eras in the world's history.

"For me the process of turning the story into a novel is a process of asking questions," Wrede explained to *CA*. "The two most useful tend to be: 'All right, what are the characters doing now?' and 'Why on earth are they doing *that?*' 'What are they doing now' applies not so much to the people who are 'onstage' as to the people who are 'offstage.' For instance, if I've written a scene in which the characters are all sitting around playing cards, I ask myself, 'What are the bad guys doing? That guy who was running away from the

Indians—what's he doing? Did he get away, and if so, how did he do it? Where did he go? Did he have any help? Has he run into anybody interesting? Is he going to show up any minute? If so, why did he decide to break up this particular card game?' It's a whole process of asking questions—starting with the basic idea and asking, 'What does this mean?'"

In 1980, Wrede joined a writing group that later became known as the Scribblies. The group's members, which included Pamela Dean, Emma Bull, Will Shetterly, Steven Brust, and Nate Bucklin, all benefited from the experience because all seven sold at least one piece of writing after the group began and four went on to become professional writers.

In part because of the encouragement of her fellow Scribblies, Wrede followed *Shadow Magic* in 1983 with *Daughter of Witches,* another "Lyra" book, which tells of the sentencing of bond-servant Ranira to death on suspicion of sorcery and her escape from the prison city of Drinn. *The Seven Towers,* published in 1984, while not part of the "Lyra" cycle, nevertheless introduces several of Wrede's most memorable characters. One of these is Amberglas, a powerful sorceress who speaks in a sort of stream-of-consciousness pattern. Another is Carachel, the wizard-king of Tar-Alem, whose struggle against the magic-devouring Matholych has led him to practice black magic. The 1985 addition to the "Lyra" cycle, *The Harp of Imach Thyssel,* is "one of the darker stories in the series," according to a reviewer for the *St. James Guide to Fantasy Writers.* It is also one of the rare Wrede novels with a male protagonist and tells a tale somewhat similar to *The Seven Towers,* about a magical harp and the man destined to play it. Wrede brought out the fourth volume of the "Lyra" series in 1987 with *Caught in Crystal,* a tale of "witches who have renounced their powers, only to be called back to right a wrong committed long ago," according to the *St. James Guide to Fantasy Writers* essayist.

After a seven-year hiatus, Wrede returned readers to Lyra with *The Raven Ring,* published in 1994. Her twenty-year-old heroine, Eleret Salven, has journeyed to the city of Ciaron to claim the property of her late mother, who has been killed in battle. Eleret's efforts are interrupted, however, by villains intent on stealing those personal effects—especially the raven ring, which has great power against the Shadowborn. According to *Booklist* contributor Roland Green, Eleret is "dragged more forcibly than not into a classic tale of mayhem and magic" that he found to be up to Wrede's "usual standard." A *Publishers Weekly* reviewer characterized Eleret as "a lively, spunky heroine" who, in this "refreshingly charming story," is allowed "to find less obvious solutions to the rather typical dilemmas presented."

Talking to Dragons, Wrede's fourth book, although first published in 1985, eventually became the fourth and final volume in her "Chronicles of the Enchanted Forest" series. Mixing elements of traditional fairy tales with modern wit, it tells the story of Daystar, a young man of sixteen who has lived the whole of his life on the outskirts of the Enchanted Forest with his mother, Cimorene. One day a wizard appears at his home, and the consequences of that wizard's arrival send Daystar into the Enchanted Forest, alone and armed only with a magic sword, with no idea what he is supposed to be doing. In the forest, he meets several memorable characters, including Shiara, a young fire witch who cannot quite control her magic; Morwen, a witch who lives with her umpteen cats in a cottage that is bigger on the inside than it is on the outside; and Kazul, the female King of the Dragons. The story reaches its climax as Daystar and Shiara confront the Society of Wizards at the castle of the rulers of the Enchanted Forest. Reviewing the audiobook version of that novel, *Booklist* contributor Anna Rich called it a "complex and fantastic story."

"The 'Enchanted Forest' books did not start off as a series," Wrede once explained to *CA.* "Just after I finished *Daughter of Witches,* we were having trouble with the title: the publisher didn't like the title I had originally come up with. . . . My friend said to me, 'What are some of the good titles with no books?' I listed out a few for him, and the last one I mentioned was *Talking to Dragons.* He said, 'That sounds good. *Talking to Dragons* sounds like a good book; you should write that book some day.' I said, 'That's the whole problem. I've got the title; I don't have any book.'"

The book that begins the "Enchanted Forest" series chronologically is *Dealing with Dragons,* which tells how Cimorene, having been refused the right to pursue her own interests—fencing, Latin lessons, and the like—and forced into a marriage not to her liking, flees to the lair of the dragon Kazul and becomes Kazul's princess. Eventually Cimorene becomes instrumental in securing Kazul's succession as King of the Dragons and helps defeat the Society of Wizards. In *Searching for Dragons,* the second volume of the "Chronicles of the Enchanted Forest," Mendanbar and his queen go in search of Kazul after problems develop in the kingdom. In *School Librarian,* Maureen Porter noted that this "entertaining and charming novel" falls within the tradition of J. R. R. Tolkien's classic trilogy *The Lord of the Rings* while still "making the reader think of this kingdom in a different way." Kristi Beavin, writing in *Horn Book,* likewise praised the "magical landscape" Wrede creates, while *School Library Journal*'s Celeste Steward called the audiobook version a "lighthearted tale of dragon-napping and magic gone awry," and a "charming tale."

Volume three of the series, *Calling on Dragons,* is told from Morwen's perspective. Two of Morwen's highly opinionated cats accompany Queen Cimorene, Morwen, Telemain the magician, Kazul, and Killer, a sort of rabbit-like blue donkey, on a very important quest: the evil wizards have stolen the Enchanted Sword that protects the Forest and a royal family member must retrieve it. Like the two preceding "Enchanted Forest" books, *Calling on Dragons* is a "madcap romp" with the same "bright, witty dialogue [and] clever, fairy-tale spoofs; in short, a treat from start to finish," in the opinion of Bonnie Kunzel in *Voice of Youth Advocates.* "The focus is on the comical repartee and the magic itself," noted a *Kirkus Reviews* critic, adding that several episodes are "laugh-aloud funny." Reviewing the audiobook version of the same title for *School Library Journal,* Brian E. Wilson called the tale a "lighthearted look at a group of misfits," and further commented that this "fluffy romp goes down easy, pleasing fans of the fractured fairytale genre." In fact, "humor predominates" in the entire "Chronicles of the Enchanted Forest" series, according to the critic for the *St. James Guide to Young Adult Writers.* This same contributor further noted, "Wrede plays with fairy-tale convention, turning the familiar motifs upside down and inside out."

Wrede embarked on a very different type of fantasy writing with *Sorcery and Cecelia,* her seventh book. Written with friend Caroline Stevermer, *Sorcery and Cecelia* is set in an alternate early-nineteenth-century England wherein magic is systematized and taught in the public schools following the Napoleonic Wars. The book consists of a series of letters written between two cousins, one of whom has gone down to London to be introduced to the social life there. The two become entangled in a power struggle between wizards but overcome their adversaries and, in true Regency fashion, marry their respective beaus. Reprinted by Harcourt in 2003 as *Sorcery and Cecelia; or, The Enchanted Chocolate Pot: Being the Correspondence of Two Young Ladies of Quality regarding Various Magical Scandals in London and the Country,* the novel was welcomed back by a critic for *Kirkus Reviews* as a "cult epistolary fantasy." The same reviewer went on to note that this "clever romp will appeal to fans of Regency romance and light fantasy."

Wrede's *Snow White and Rose Red* is also set in an alternate England, in this case during Tudor times. It is a retelling of an ancient Grimms' fairy tale but mixes in historical characters such as Dr. John Dee, mathematician and astrologer to the court of Queen Elizabeth. Blanche and Rosamund, the title characters, are daughters of the widow Arden. They live on the edges of a forest near the river Thames that marks the boundary of the magical realm of Faerie. Because of their isolation and occasional odd behavior, the widow and her daughters are suspected of using magic, a serious crime in Elizabethan England that is punishable by death. Through the machinations of the villagers, the Faerie Queen's court, and the magical experiments of Dr. Dee, the girls become involved with the half-human sons of the queen of Faerie.

"*Mairelon the Magician* is more like *Sorcery and Cecelia* or *Snow White and Rose Red,* which are set in an alternate England," Wrede explained of her 1991 novel. "*Mairelon the Magician* is set in this England in about 1816-17, shortly after the Napoleonic Wars ended. The main character, Kim, a street waif who has grown up in the slums, is hired to burgle the wagon of a performing magician. He turns out to be a real magician, however, and she gets caught. Since he is a rather eccentric magician, instead of turning her over to the constable, he decides to take her under his wing. He had, it turns out, five years before been framed for theft and has come back trying to find all of the various things that were stolen so he can clear his name. It turns into very much a lunatic romp. You've got a lot of character types that people who read Regency romances will recognize, although it's not a romance." Sybil Steinberg, writing in *Publishers Weekly,* was sufficiently cast under Wrede's spell to call the book "delightful," and further commented that the author's "confection will charm readers of both Regency romances and fantasies."

In 1997's *The Magician's Ward,* Wrede creates a sequel to *Mairelon the Magician* and leads readers once again into her alternate Regency universe. In this novel, Kim falls in love with her magician/mentor Richard Merrill, although Kim's aunt pushes the young woman to work on honing her feminine wiles in polite society. In *Publishers Weekly,* a reviewer praised *The Magician's Ward* as featuring Wrede's characteristic "charm, humor and intelligence," and maintained that the novel will "enthrall Regency fans and fantasy buffs looking for a new twist." According to *Booklist* reviewer Roland Green in his appraisal of *The Magician's Ward,* "The pacing, the wit, the world-building skill, and the general intelligence" found in the author's other novels are all present here.

Wrede has also written a number of short stories, published both in anthologies as well as in her own 1996 collection, *Book of Enchantments.* Most of the tales in this collection are high fantasy, although some do have a modern setting. Based on fairy tales, ballads, biblical tales, and even humorous send-ups of fantasy traditions, the collected stories offer a "surprisingly varied" and "well-crafted" selection, according to *Booklist* reviewer Carolyn Phelan. Additionally, Wrede has turned her hand to novelizations with two "Star Wars" adaptations: 1999's *Star Wars: Episode I: The Phantom Menace* and *Star Wars: Episode II: Attack of the Clones.* Based on the movies of the same titles, the books closely follow the plot lines of the popular films. *School Library Journal* contributor Wilson praised Wrede's "faithful novelization" of *Attack of the Clones,* noting that the author "does an excellent job" of "conveying [the] confusion and frustration" of Padme and Anakin when they fall in love. For Wilson, in fact, such scenes "work better in the novelization than they do onscreen because Wrede embraces the opportunity to explain what goes on in their heads."

"When you're writing fantasy you're writing about magic," Wrede explained of the genre that has occupied much of her writing life, "and magic is not something that exists in the real world, like rocks. Essentially magic is a metaphor for something else. . . . It varies from writer to writer and frequently from book to book." For Wrede, magic is a metaphor for power: "the essence of the ability to make things happen, to get things done. When you're the CEO of a corporation you can say, 'I want this to happen,' and people will go out and make it happen. You have the power to make it happen. And in my books the fundamental question is, if you can do anything, what do you do? If you've got the power to make stuff happen, good stuff or bad stuff, what do you do with it?"

BIOGRAPHICAL AND CRITICAL SOURCES:

BOOKS

Authors and Artists for Young Adults, Volume 8, Gale (Detroit, MI), 1992.

St. James Guide to Fantasy Writers, St. James Press (Detroit, MI), 1996.

St. James Guide to Young Adult Writers, St. James Press (Detroit, MI), 1999.

PERIODICALS

Booklist, May 1, 1993, Sally Estes, review of *Calling on Dragons,* p. 1582; August, 1993, Sally Estes, review of *Talking to Dragons,* p. 2051; October 15, 1994, Roland Green, review of *The Raven Ring,* p. 405; May 15, 1996, Carolyn Phelan, review of *Book of Enchantments,* p. 1588; November 1, 1997, Roland Green, review of *The Magician's Ward,* p. 457; April 15, 2002, Sally Estes, review of *The Magician's Ward,* pp. 357-358; June 1, 2002, p. 1753; November 1, 2002, Anna Rich, review of *Talking to Dragons* (audiobook), p. 518.

Bulletin of the Center for Children's Books, May, 1996, p. 319.

English Journal, December, 1981, review of *Daughter of Witches,* p. 67.

Horn Book, January-February, 1992, Ann A. Flowers, review of *Searching for Dragons,* p. 76; November-December, 1993, Ann A. Flowers, review of *Talking to Dragons,* p. 760; May-June, 2002, Kristi Beavin, review of *Searching for Dragons* (audiobook), pp. 357-358.

Kirkus Reviews, March 15, 1993, review of *Calling on Dragons,* p. 382; April 15, 1996, p. 609; April 15, 2003, review of *Sorcery and Cecelia; or, The*

Enchanted Chocolate Pot: Being the Correspondence of Two Young Ladies of Quality regarding Various Magical Scandals in London and the Country, pp. 613-614.

Library Journal, November 15, 1994, Jackie Cassada, review of *The Raven Ring,* p. 90.

Publishers Weekly, April 19, 1991, Sybil Steinberg, review of *Mairelon the Magician,* p. 60; October 10, 1994, review of *The Raven Ring,* p. 66; November 24, 1997, review of *The Magician's Ward,* p. 57.

School Librarian, November, 1994, Maureen Porter, review of *Dragon Search,* p. 168.

School Library Journal, February, 1992, Cathy Chauvette, review of *Mairelon the Magician,* p. 122; June, 1993, Lisa Dennis, review of *Calling on Dragons,* p. 112; June, 1996, p. 130; June, 2002, Celeste Steward, review of *Searching for Dragons* (audiobook), p. 72; August, 2002, Brian E. Wilson, review of *Calling on Dragons* and *Star Wars: Episode II: Attack of the Clones* (audiobook), pp. 76, 77-78.

Voice of Youth Advocates, August, 1993, Bonnie Kunzel, review of *Calling on Dragons,* pp. 171-172.

ONLINE

Enchanted Chocolate Pot, http://www.tc.umn.edu/ (May 8, 2003), "Caroline Stevermer and Patricia C. Wrede Page."

Patrica C. Wrede Info Page, http://www.dendarii.co.uk/ (May 8, 2003).

Science Fiction and Fantasy Writers of America, http://www.sfwa.org/ (May 8, 2003), Patricia C. Wrede, "Fantasy Worldbuilding Questions."*

Y-Z

YAMASHITA, Karen Tei 1951-

PERSONAL: Born January 8, 1951, in Oakland, CA; married; husband's name Ronaldo; children: Jane, Jon.

ADDRESSES: *Office*—Department of Literature, Kresge College, University of California—Santa Cruz, Santa Cruz, CA 95064.

CAREER: Novelist, short-story writer, and playwright. University of California—Santa Cruz, assistant professor, 1997—. Japanese-American Internment Fellowship Award, panelist, 1994; National Endowment for the Arts, panelist, 1995.

MEMBER: PEN Center West.

AWARDS, HONORS: Thomas J. Watson fellowship, 1975, to study Japanese immigration in Brazil; first place awards from several short-story contests, including awards from *Amerasia Journal,* 1975, for "The Bath," and "Rafu Shimpo," 1975, for "Tucano;" Rockefeller playwright in residence fellowship, East West Players, Los Angeles, CA, 1977-78; award from James Clavell American-Japanese Short-Story Contest, 1979, for "Asaka-no-Miya;" American Book Award, 1991, and Janet Heidinger Kafka Award, 1992, both for *Through the Arc of the Rain Forest;* cultural grant, City of Los Angeles, 1992-93; Japan Foundation artist fellowship, 1997, to research Japanese-Brazilian labor in Japan.

WRITINGS:

Omen: An American Kabuki (play), produced in Los Angeles, CA, 1978.

Hiroshima Tropical (play), produced in Los Angeles, CA, 1984.

(With Karen Mayeda) *Kusei: An Endangered Species* (screenplay), Visual Communications (Los Angeles, CA), 1986.

Hannah Kusoh: An American Butoh (performance; produced in Los Angeles, CA, 1989), published in *Premonitions,* Kaya Productions (New York, NY), 1995.

Tokyo Carmen vs. L.A. Carmen (performance; produced in Los Angeles, CA, 1990), published in part in *Multicultural Theatre: Scenes and Monologs from New Hispanic, Asian, and African-American Plays,* Meriwither Publishing (Colorado Springs, CO), 1996.

Through the Arc of the Rain Forest (novel), Coffee House Press (Minneapolis, MN), 1990.

GiLAwrecks (musical), produced in Seattle, WA, 1992.

Brazil-Maru (novel), Coffee House Press (Minneapolis, MN), 1992.

Noh Bozos (performance), produced in Los Angeles, CA, 1993.

Tropic of Orange (novel), Coffee House Press (Minneapolis, MN), 1997.

Circle K Cycles, Coffee House Press (Minneapolis, MN), 2001.

Work represented in anthologies, including *A Japanese-American Anthology,* 1975. Author of *Circle K,* a monthly journal series, and *CafeCreole,* an Internet Web site. Contributor of essays and short stories to periodicals, including *Contact II Poetry Review, Chicago Review,* and *Rafu-Shimpo* (Japanese-American newspaper). Member of editorial board, *Amerasia Journal,* 1994—.

ADAPTATIONS: Through the Arc of the Rain Forest has been recorded on audio cassette.

SIDELIGHTS: Karen Tei Yamashita, an American of Japanese descent, is a novelist, short-story writer, and playwright. In 1975 she traveled to Brazil on a fellowship to study Japanese immigration and ended up staying nine years. This long sojourn reveals itself strongly in her first two novels, *Through the Arc of the Rain Forest*—which received an American Book Award in 1991—and *Brazil-Maru.*

Taking place in the Brazilian jungle of the twenty-first century, *Through the Arc of the Rain Forest* involves such improbable characters as an Indian guru with magic feathers, a three-handed businessman from New York, and a Japanese man who, ever since he was hit by a meteor, has had a permanent sphere twirling in front of his face. In the words of *Choice* reviewer M. Ditsky, *Through the Arc of the Rain Forest* is "an elaborate parable about the effects of Western culture on the Brazilian rain forest." Donna Seaman noted in *Booklist,* "Incisive and funny, this book yanks our chains and makes us see the absurdity that rules our world."

Brazil-Maru, begun while Yamashita was living in Brazil, is a more down-to-earth history set in the early twentieth century. It is based upon her encounters with a group of Japanese Christian immigrants who came to Brazil in the 1920s wanting to establish a new communal society inspired by the teachings of Rousseau. Yamashita explained her own inspiration for the novel in an interview for *Amerasia Journal* by pointing out that the immigrants she met were guided by spiritual rather than commercial concerns: "The people on these communes were actually questioning. They were trying to create a philosophy, a civilization. . . . And because of that, there was an intellectual involvement in the reason for being there, and that's what I wanted for the book. . . . And then, at the same time, within this project, there were stories about great love. There were stories about travel and meeting the forest for the first time."

In *Brazil-Maru,* Yamashita chronicles the settlers' lives through the voices of four characters—young Ichiro (Emile), the leader Kantaro, the compliant wife Haru, and artist Genji—taking them through such activities as clearing land, educating children, experiencing love, hardship, and loss, and dealing with the divisive effects of Japan's involvement in World War II. *Library Journal* reviewer Faye A. Chadwell found that the characters in *Brazil-Maru* "deftly reveal" the problems the community faces as "the Japanese strive to make Brazil their home." A *Kirkus Reviews* critic observed, "Though often seeming more a work of reportage than a novel, Yamashita's characters are vital, full-bodied creations offering sufficient balance, as well as answers to the questions raised." In *Booklist,* Seaman praised Yamashita's "engrossing multigenerational immigrant saga" for its "energy, affection, and humor," also commending the author's "heightened sense of passion and absurdity."

Yamashita's third novel, *Tropic of Orange,* takes place in Los Angeles—more specifically, on a freeway that the homeless have turned into a thriving, festive neighborhood after a fuel truck overturns, causing drivers to abandon their cars. The novel—apocalyptic and satirical, with characters named Arcangel and Buzzworm—explores the relationships between north and south, rich and poor, delving into the spaces behind the illusions of everyday life in Los Angeles. Janet Ingraham of *Library Journal* called *Tropic of Orange* a "dense, hip, multifaceted story" and a "stunner." A *Publishers Weekly* contributor praised Yamashita's "panache" in handling her "eccentric" characters and settings.

BIOGRAPHICAL AND CRITICAL SOURCES:

PERIODICALS

Amerasia Journal, Volume 20, number 3, 1994, interview with Yamashita, pp. 49-59.

Booklist, August, 1990, Donna Seaman, review of *Through the Arc of the Rain Forest,* p. 2157; August, 1992, Donna Seaman, review of *Brazil-Maru,* p. 1997.

Choice, March, 1991, M. Ditsky, review of *Through the Arc of the Rain Forest,* pp. 1139-1140.

Contemporary Literature, winter, 2000, Caroline Rody, review of *Through the Arc of the Rain Forest,* p. 618.

Kirkus Reviews, July 1, 1992, review of *Brazil-Maru,* pp. 813-814.
Library Journal, September 1, 1990, p. 259; August, 1992, Faye A. Chadwell, review of *Brazil-Maru,* p. 153; August, 1997, Janet Ingraham, review of *Tropic of Orange,* p. 136.
Publishers Weekly, August 4, 1997, review of *Tropic of Orange,* p. 66.
Review of Contemporary Fiction, spring, 2002, Jason Picone, review of *Circle K Cycles,* p. 135.

* * *

YORKE, Malcolm 1938-

PERSONAL: Born September 2, 1938, in England; son of Kenneth (an engineer) and Iris (a homemaker; maiden name, Kelsey) Yorke; married Mavis (a lecturer), 1966; children: Rachel, Jonathan. *Ethnicity:* "English." *Education:* University of Durham, B.A., 1960; University of London, postgraduate certificate in education, 1961, M.Phil., 1968; University of Sheffield, Ph.D., 1977. *Hobbies and other interests:* Tennis, painting, sculpturing, travel.

ADDRESSES: *Home*—Newcastle-on-Tyne, England. *Agent*—David Higham Associates Ltd., 5-8 Lower John St., Golden Sq., London W1R 4HA, England.

CAREER: Worked as primary and secondary schoolmaster; University of Jyvaskyla, Jyvaskyla, Finland, lecturer, 1965-67; Northumbria University, Newcastle-on-Tyne, England, senior lecturer, 1968-96. Artist, with solo exhibitions of sculpture, oil painting, and portraiture.

MEMBER: Royal Society of Arts (fellow).

WRITINGS:

NONFICTION

Eric Gill: Man of Flesh and Spirit, Universe (New York, NY), 1982.
The Spirit of Place: Nine Neo-Romantic Artists and Their Times, Constable (London, England), 1988, St. Martin's Press (New York, NY), 1989.
Keith Vaughan: His Life and Work, Constable (London, England), 1990.
Matthew Smith: His Life and Reputation, Faber & Faber (London, England), 1997.
Barry Burman, Goldmark (London, England), 1997.
David Blackburn: A Landscape Vision, Hart Gallery (London, England), 1997.
Mervyn Peake: My Eyes Mint Gold: A Life, Overlook Press (Woodstock, NY), 2002.

FOR CHILDREN

Ritchie F. Dweebly Thunders On!, illustrated by Margaret Chamberlain, Dorling Kindersley (New York, NY), 1994.
Molly the Mad Basher, Dorling Kindersley (New York, NY), 1994.
Miss Butterpat Goes Wild!, illustrated by Margaret Chamberlain, Dorling Kindersley (New York, NY), 1994.
Scarem's House, Scholastic (New York, NY), 1994.
The Wishing Horse, Scholastic (New York, NY), 1995.
Class Four's Wild Week, Scholastic (New York, NY), 1995.
Beastly Tales: Yeti, Bigfoot, and the Loch Ness Monster, DK Publishers (New York, NY), 1998.
The Wishing Horse Rides Again, Scholastic (New York, NY), 1999.

WORK IN PROGRESS: *Edward Bawden and His Circle,* a biography of the English artist.

SIDELIGHTS: Artist and retired university lecturer Malcolm Yorke is the author of books for children, as well as a variety of critical works for adults. In *Mervyn Peake: My Eyes Mint Gold,* Yorke discusses the life and works of British fantasy writer and illustrator Mervyn Peake. Although Peake is not as well known as J. R. R. Tolkien, author of *The Lord of the Rings,* or C. S. Lewis, who wrote the "Narnia" books, he was, like these authors, an important figure in twentieth-century fantasy literature. Yorke describes Peake's childhood in China, as the son of a medical missionary, and its influence on his later life; although Peake moved back to England when he was eleven, he never felt at home in England.

A *Publishers Weekly,* reviewer commented that the book is "entertaining, touching, and often amusing," but that Yorke's psychological analysis of Peake is "on shakier ground." In the *New York Times,* Claudia La Rocco praised the book, noting that Peake is well-depicted "in all his eccentric glory."

BIOGRAPHICAL AND CRITICAL SOURCES:

PERIODICALS

Booklist, June 1, 2002, Ray Olson, review of *Mervyn Peake: My Eyes Mint Gold: A Life,* p. 1669.
Burlington, August, 1992, review of *Keith Vaughan: His Life and Work,* p. 537.
Children's Book Review Service, spring, 1994, review of *Ritchie F. Dweebly Thunders On!* and *Molly the Mad Basher,* p. 141.
Children's Playmate, July-August, 1994, Susan Todd, review of *Miss Butterpat Goes Wild!,* p. 8.
Horn Book Guide, spring, 1994, review of *Miss Butterpat Goes Wild!,* p. 59; fall, 1994, review of *Ritchie F. Dweebly Thunders On!* and *Molly the Mad Basher,* p. 295.
Kirkus Reviews, December 15, 1993, review of *Miss Butterpat Goes Wild!,* p. 1598; April 15, 2002, review of *Mervyn Peake,* p. 555.
Library Journal, May 15, 2002, Denise J. Stankovics, review of *Mervyn Peake,* p. 99.
London Review of Books, June 27, 1991, review of *Keith Vaughan,* p. 5.
New York Times Book Review, July 21, 2002, Claudia La Rocco, review of *Mervyn Peake,* p. 21.
Observer (London, England), February 16, 1992, review of *Keith Vaughan,* p. 59.
Publishers Weekly, November 15, 1993, review of *Miss Butterpat Goes Wild!,* p. 79; May 27, 2002, review of *Mervyn Peake,* p. 48.
School Library Journal, March, 1994, p. 210.
Spectator, September 27, 2997, review of *Matthew Smith: His Life and Reputation,* p. 40.
Times (London, England), December 3, 1981.
Times Literary Supplement, September 5, 1997, review of *Matthew Smith,* p. 20; February 23, 2001, review of *Mervyn Peake,* p. 24.

* * *

ZACH, Cheryl (Byrd) 1947-
(Jennifer Cole, Jamie Suzanne; Nicole Byrd, a joint pseudonym)

Cheryl Zach

PERSONAL: Surname is pronounced "Zack"; born June 9, 1947, in Clarksville, TN; daughter of Smith Henry (a military officer) and Nancy (a sales manager) Byrd; married Q. J. Wasden, June 2, 1967 (divorced, September, 1979); married Charles O. Zach, Jr. (president of a die casting company), June 20, 1982 (died, 1990); children: (first marriage) Quinton John, Michelle Nicole. *Education:* Austin Peay State University, B.A., 1968, M.A., 1977. *Religion:* Episcopalian.

ADDRESSES: Home—Franklin, TN. *Agent*—Axelrod Agency, 55 Main St., P.O. Box 357, Chatham, NY 12037.

CAREER: High school English teacher in Harrison County, MS, 1970-71; freelance journalist, 1976-77; high school English teacher in Dyersburg, TN, 1978-82; writer, 1982—.

MEMBER: Romance Writers of America, Society of Children's Book Writers and Illustrators (regional advisor chair), Novelists Inc., Phi Kappa Phi.

AWARDS, HONORS: Romance Writers of America, Golden Medallion Awards, best young adult novel, 1984, for *The Frog Princess,* and 1985, for *Waiting for Amanda,* RITA Award, for *Runaway,* inducted into Hall of Fame, 1996; cited for children's choice book, International Reading Association and Children's Book Council, 1989-90, for *The Class Trip;* Holt Medallion, Virginia Romance Writers, 1996, for *Hearts Divided;* Desert Rose Golden Quill Award, Arizona Romance Writers of America, 2003, for *Lady in Waiting.*

WRITINGS:

HISTORICAL ROMANCE NOVELS; WITH DAUGHTER, MICHELLE PLACE, UNDER JOINT PSEUDONYM NICOLE BYRD

Robert's Lady, Jove Books (New York, NY), 2000.
Dear Imposter, Jove Books (New York, NY), 2001.
Lady in Waiting, Jove Books (New York, NY), 2002.
Widow in Scarlet, Jove Books (New York, NY), 2003.
Beauty in Black, Jove Books (New York, NY), 2004.

YOUNG ADULT ROMANCE NOVELS

The Frog Princess, Silhouette (Buffalo, NY), 1984.
Waiting for Amanda, Silhouette (Buffalo, NY), 1985.
Fortune's Child, Silhouette (Buffalo, NY), 1985.
Looking Out for Lacey, Fawcett (New York, NY), 1989.
Paradise, HarperCollins (New York, NY), 1994.
Dear Diary: Runaway, Berkley Publishing (New York, NY), 1995.
Dear Diary: Family Secrets, Berkley Publishing (New York, NY), 1996.
Kissing Caroline, Bantam (New York, NY), 1996.
Carrie's Gold, Avon (New York, NY), 1997.
Silent Tears, Berkley Publishing (New York, NY), 1999.
Secret Admirer, Berkley Publishing (New York, NY), 1999.
Shadow Self, Berkley Publishing (New York, NY), 2000.

YOUNG ADULT ROMANCE NOVELS; UNDER PSEUDONYM JENNIFER COLE

Three's a Crowd, Fawcett (New York, NY), 1986.
Star Quality, Fawcett (New York, NY), 1987.
Too Many Cooks, Fawcett (New York, NY), 1987.
Mollie in Love, Fawcett (New York, NY), 1987.

"SWEET VALLEY TWINS" SERIES; UNDER PSEUDONYM JAMIE SUZANNE

Second Best, Bantam (New York, NY), 1988.
The Class Trip, Bantam (New York, NY), 1988.
Left Behind, Bantam (New York, NY), 1988.
Jessica, the Rock Star, Bantam (New York, NY), 1989.
The Christmas Ghost, Bantam (New York, NY), 1989.

"SMYTH VS. SMITH" SERIES; FOR YOUNG ADULTS

Oh, Brother, Lynx Books (New York, NY), 1988.
Stealing the Scene, Lynx Books (New York, NY), 1988.
Tug of War, Lynx Books (New York, NY), 1988.
More Than Friends, Lynx Books (New York, NY), 1989.
Surprise, Surprise, Lynx Books (New York, NY), 1989.

"SOUTHERN ANGELS" SERIES; FOR YOUNG ADULTS

Hearts Divided, Bantam (New York, NY), 1995.
Winds of Betrayal, Bantam (New York, NY), 1995.
A Dream of Freedom, Bantam (New York, NY), 1995.

"MIND OVER MATTER" SERIES; FOR CHILDREN

The Mummy's Footsteps, Avon (New York, NY), 1997.
Phantom of the Roxy, Avon (New York, NY), 1997.
Curse of the Idol's Eye, Avon (New York, NY), 1997.
The Gypsy's Warning, Avon (New York, NY), 1997.

OTHER

Twice a Fool (romance novel), Harlequin Enterprises (Buffalo, NY), 1984.
Los Angeles (juvenile nonfiction), Dillon (Minneapolis, MN), 1989.
Benny and the Crazy Contest (juvenile fiction), Bradbury (Scarsdale, NY), 1991.
Benny and the No-Good Teacher (juvenile fiction), Bradbury (Scarsdale, NY), 1992.
Here Comes the Martian Mushroom (juvenile fiction), Willowisp (Pinellas Park, FL), 1994.

Contributor of articles, poetry, and short stories to magazines and newspapers.

WORK IN PROGRESS: (Under pseudonym Nicole Byrd) *Vision in Blue,* 2005.

SIDELIGHTS: Cheryl Zach writes for both adults and juvenile readers. Her novels for young adults have won several awards and attracted a loyal readership. Zach once reminisced to *CA* about the roots of her writing career: "Because my father was a career army man, I led a gypsy's life as a child, changing schools ten times in twelve years. I was born in Tennessee and have also lived in Georgia, Mississippi (the Gulf coast), Texas, California, Germany, and Scotland. I read early and well, and a deep love for books perhaps made it inevitable that my oldest and greatest ambition would be to create my own. I wrote poems, stories, and plays during childhood and won writing awards in college, but commercial success eluded me. I married, had children, taught school, and continued to write when I could.

"At my first writing conference, at Vanderbilt University in the late 1970s, I discovered that writing was not just an art form but also a business. After the first shock, I decided that I wanted my writing to be read, so I began to pay attention to marketing as well as craftsmanship. After years of trying to write 'on the side,' while going to school, teaching, and raising my two kids, I remarried, moved to California, and took a year to pursue my lifelong ambition. Thirteen months later, I sold my first novel. My books have been published in more than a dozen countries outside the United States.

"I came into writing for young people almost by accident, but I do have strong convictions about its importance. I believe young readers deserve the best, and writers for young people have even more responsibility as far as truth and excellence than writers in general."

Zach's books have covered many subjects, from contemporary romance to family relationships to American and English history. The author noted that some of her stories include a young person who is abandoned or fears abandonment. She traces this motif, seen in books like *Runaway* and *Looking Out for Lacey,* to her own childhood, when her father was often away on assignment and her mother spent some time isolated from her children due to tuberculosis.

Recently, Zach told *CA:* "After years of writing mainly for children and teens, I found my writing revitalized when I took a new—or an old—direction. I've been a history buff and an Anglophile from very early on. According to family lore, I have English ancestors, though my cousin, Dr. Suzanne Byrd, has so far traced our roots only as far back as the American Revolution. But whatever the reason, I have always felt a strong connection to England. (I felt entranced—and at home—when I discovered the "Dr. Doolittle" series at the age of six and have sought out English writers ever since, and I wrote my master's thesis on Jane Austen's works.) My original goal was to write historical novels for adults.

"After years of successfully publishing for younger readers, I finally returned to my first love and started a novel set in early-nineteenth-century England. (Jane Austen's era!) I enlisted my daughter, who was also an Anglophile, also widely read in the historical field, and just beginning to write on her own, to critique the first chapters. Her comments were so good that I suggested she try writing a scene, and a writing partnership was born. Our first novel, *Robert's Lady,* was published in 2000 under the pen name Nicole Byrd (her middle and my maiden name), and our most recent work got strong reviews in *Publishers Weekly* and *Booklist,* so we're pleased with their reception. The Nicole Byrd historical romance novels contain mystery-adventure subplots, allowing me to incorporate another favorite genre, along with accurate historical backgrounds, touches of humor, fast-paced plots and gutsy characters. I'm having enormous fun with them!"

BIOGRAPHICAL AND CRITICAL SOURCES:

BOOKS

Authors and Artists for Young Adults, Volume 21, Gale (Detroit, MI), 1997.

Something about the Author Autobiography Series, Volume 24, Gale (Detroit, MI), 1997.

PERIODICALS

Booklist, December 1, 1984, pp. 528-529; January 1, 1996, p. 822.
Children's Writer, December, 1999.
Kliatt, November, 1994, p. 17.
Publishers Weekly, September 9, 1988, p. 138; April 15, 2002, p. 47.
Romance Writers Report, October, 2003.
School Library Journal, January, 1985, p. 89; January, 1986, p. 81; October, 1995, p. 161.
Voice of Youth Advocates, October, 1984, p. 202; June, 1985, p. 124; February, 1986, p. 389; April, 1995, p. 30; April, 1996, pp. 33-34.
Writer, November, 1988; December, 1990; August, 1998.

ONLINE

Nicole Byrd Web site, http://www.nicolebyrd.com/ (February 5, 2004).